940
S

CHELMER L FLYNN
1st Lt   Inf

MODERN AND
CONTEMPORARY
EUROPEAN HISTORY
(1815–1941)

BY

J. SALWYN SCHAPIRO, Ph.D.

Professor of History in The City College of The College of the City of New York

UNDER THE EDITORSHIP OF

JAMES T. SHOTWELL, LL.D.

Professor of History in Columbia University

New Edition

HOUGHTON MIFFLIN COMPANY

BOSTON · NEW YORK · CHICAGO · DALLAS
ATLANTA · SAN FRANCISCO
The Riverside Press Cambridge

The Riverside Press

CAMBRIDGE · MASSACHUSETTS

PRINTED IN THE U.S.A.

TO THE MEMORY OF
WILLIAM G. McGUCKIN
INSPIRING TEACHER AND DEAR FRIEND WHO
AWAKENED IN ME THE LOVE FOR THE
STUDY OF HISTORY

NOTE TO THE 1940 EDITION

THE outbreak of the Second World War in 1939 has created a new task for the writer of history. Merely to narrate the events that led to the great catastrophe would be inadequate. During the period between the two world wars new forces came to the front, new conflicts arose, and new ideologies were propagated. In order that the reader may grasp the fundamental issues at stake in the Second World War, this volume has emphasized events and political and social trends that at the time of publication of the last edition did not seem significant, but which have subsequently proved to be the determining factors in bringing on the new world conflict. Such topics as Communism, Fascism, Nazism, the collapse of the peace movement, the new militarization of Europe, the struggle for power in the Mediterranean are treated with fullness. It is more important now than ever before to know and to understand the great questions that divide Europeans — questions that find repercussions throughout the world.

J. SALWYN SCHAPIRO

THE CITY COLLEGE OF
THE COLLEGE OF THE CITY OF NEW YORK

PREFACE

THE World War changed the perspective of the history of Europe during the nineteenth and twentieth centuries. The fundamental causes of that great struggle, the issues that arose during its progress, and the great changes that followed made the period after 1870 vastly more important. It was during this period that the political, social, and economic issues in European life were developing that prepared the way for the World War. The new edition of *Modern and Contemporary European History* has, therefore, been considerably enlarged in order to give more space to the period after 1870. New chapters have been added and old chapters have been enlarged; special attention has been given to the new Industrial Revolution and to colonial imperialism.

A totally new feature of the book is the chapter "Progress of Science," contributed by Professor Frederick Barry, of Columbia University. It is not only a résumé of the scientific advance during the nineteenth century, but a philosophic exposition of the scientific attitude of mind.

I wish to acknowledge my indebtedness to my colleagues, Professor Nelson P. Mead who read the chapters on the Conference of Paris, International Conditions after the World War, and Europe and Asia after the World War, Professor William H. Steiner who read the chapter on the New Industrial and Agricultural Revolutions, Dr. Jesse D. Clarkson who read the chapters on Russia, and Professor John Whyte who wrote most of the section on German literature after 1870; to Professor Robert L. Schuyler, of Columbia University, who read the chapter on the British Empire; and, above all, to Professor William L. Langer, of Harvard University, who read the entire manuscript which was greatly improved by his many excellent suggestions. Finally, I wish to acknowledge my indebtedness to Professor James T. Shotwell, of Columbia University, my former teacher and editor of this volume, whose wide range of scholarship has been at my disposal in revising the book.

J. S. S.

THE CITY COLLEGE OF
THE COLLEGE OF THE CITY OF NEW YORK

CONTENTS

CONTENTS

CONTENTS

PART III

PART IV

PART V

CONTENTS

LIST OF ILLUSTRATIONS

LIST OF MAPS

MODERN AND CONTEMPORARY EUROPEAN HISTORY

．．

INTRODUCTION

EUROPE AT THE END OF THE EIGHTEENTH CENTURY

MODERN history is of comparatively recent origin. The present system of society, with its industrial organization, democratic government, and scientific outlook, is a product of conditions that came into existence hardly a century ago; for in spite of Columbus, Luther, Copernicus, and Newton, the life and thought of the average person in Europe at the end of the eighteenth century differed very little from those of his ancestors in the later Middle Ages. The Renaissance had broken up the educational monopoly of the Catholic clergy by giving education to the laity and by giving the classics a prominent place in the curriculum, but ecclesiastical influence continued because the new schools were under Church control and the new teachers were chiefly clergymen. Through the inventions of printing and of paper and through the use of the vernacular the popularization of knowledge had made its first beginnings. Nevertheless, the great mass of people in the eighteenth century were illiterate, as there were no national systems of education, free, compulsory, and secular. The pioneers of modern science during the sixteenth century had begun to make those discoveries in physics and astronomy which were destined to reconstruct the intellectual horizon of Europe, but these discoveries had little influence on the masses, who continued to adhere to ancient superstitions.

The Commercial Revolution following the voyages and discoveries of the sixteenth century produced important changes in the economic life of Europe. No longer did trading vessels confine themselves to inland waterways nor did they creep timorously along the Atlantic coast; they now sailed boldly on all oceans. Trade

was no longer intertown, but international. The docks of London,
Limitations of the Commercial Revolution Amsterdam, Antwerp, and Lisbon were crowded with shipping from the Americas, Asia, and Africa. But the new trade was chiefly in the raw products of the New World and in the luxuries of the East. Articles were still made by hand and were transported by animals on land and by sailing vessels on sea. The Commercial Revolution, therefore, produced little change in the life of the average man. By occupation the overwhelming majority were still peasants and artisans.

The Protestant Revolution had broken up the religious monopoly of the Catholic Church, but it had by no means established re-
Limitations of the Protestant Revolution ligious equality, or even toleration. Indeed, Protestant theologians such as Luther, Calvin, Knox, and Cranmer were as insistent on conformity to the established religion as their Catholic opponents. The fundamental principle of the Protestant Revolution was religious independence rather than religious freedom, the idea that every nation had the right to establish its own type of Christianity. "One World, one Faith," was the ideal of Catholicism. During the warfare of creeds in the seventeenth century, the futility of this ideal became apparent, and a new principle, "one Nation, one Faith," took its place. But as the nation had not yet attained any adequate means of self-expression, the monarch and the governing class were generally able to force upon it their own form of religion. Hence it came about that the religion of the king became, by law, the religion of the people, and official churches were organized to preach it. Toleration was the one thing that both Catholics and Protestants rejected, yet they were forced to grant it, at least partially, to the most powerful of the religious minorities. By the Edict of Nantes (1598) Catholic France granted toleration to the Huguenots; and by the Toleration Act (1689) Anglican England granted toleration to the Dissenters. By toleration was meant that any religious groups that refused adherence to the official Church were permitted to worship unmolested. Those who were tolerated did not have full civil rights; they could not hold public office and could not follow certain occupations; moreover, they were taxed for the support of the established Church. It was far indeed from the idea of religious liberty which favored equal rights for all sects and special privileges to none.

The government of nearly every European country, at the end of the eighteenth century, was monarchical. And everywhere the monarch was absolute, except in England, where parliament was supreme. Absolutism was upheld on the principle of divine right, a principle subscribed to by Catholic Spain as heartily as by Lutheran Prussia. *Limitations of monarchical nationalism*
As the king's power extended, the scope of government increased, which necessitated the establishment of a bureaucracy, a body of royal officials appointed by and responsible to the king. However, the modern nation, with uniform laws, a common language and culture, and a common administration, had not yet come into existence. The people owed their king allegiance, by which was meant that they paid him taxes and obeyed his officials; but they continued to observe their provincial laws and customs and to speak their local dialects. Moreover, socially and economically, feudalism flourished on the Continent, in united France no less than in divided Germany. In the country the peasants gave dues and services to the lord as in the Middle Ages. In the city the guilds maintained their monopoly of commerce and industry. The Middle Ages had ended, but Modern Times had not yet come into existence.

CHAPTER I

THE HERITAGE OF THE FRENCH REVOLUTION

AT the end of the eighteenth century there took place three great revolutions which transformed every aspect of European society and created the world of to-day. These movements were the intellectual revolution which gave a new outlook upon social, economic, and political problems, and new points of view on religion, philosophy, literature, and science; the economic revolution which established machine industry and transformed the economic life of the world; and the French Revolution which proclaimed political liberty and inaugurated democratic government. If conditions and ideals at the end of the eighteenth century were still largely medieval, the advanced thought of the day was distinctively modern, not only in tendency, but even in substance. It has seldom happened that great thinkers were so completely out of joint with their time as was the case with the eighteenth-century philosophers and scientists; and they began an attack on the Old Régime which was unparalleled for audacity, virulence, and uncompromising radicalism. Never had the Catholic Church encountered a more bitter enemy than Voltaire, who mocked her most sacred beliefs, who questioned her every right and privilege, and who would be satisfied with nothing less than her complete destruction. Rousseau proclaimed doctrines that threatened to undermine the very foundations of the old political system by questioning every reason for its existence. Adam Smith founded the science of political economy which repudiated the policies of the Mercantilist System according to which commerce and industry were hindered by unwise regulations and unfair taxation. Bentham denounced the system of civil and criminal law as irrational in its principles, unfair in its methods, and brutal and stupid in its judgments. A new science and a new philosophy came to the fore. Lavoisier laid the basis of modern chemistry by proving the indestructibility of matter and by his analysis of combustion. Lamarck's theory of the evolution of bodily organs gave a new turn to the study of biology. Kant's philosophy enthroned moral law as the supreme governor of mankind, thereby substituting an ethical for a religious view of human life. Although aristocratic by temperament and moderate in his opinions, Goethe was nevertheless a great revolutionary. According to his view of life self-culture should be the chief aim of all human striving, and, therefore, he repudiated all traditions that hampered the individual in his development.

The ideas of the philosophers and scientists of the eighteenth century prepared the way for the French Revolution. That mo-

The French Revolution mentous event left a memory which could never be effaced, the stirring tale of a successful uprising against kings, classes, and conditions. But it was not merely a political reconstruction in which despotisms were overthrown and nations liberated. This tremendous event set loose ideas, systems, parties and principles that created a new world in old Europe. The French Revolution was the first definitely *social* revolution in history in that it made far-reaching changes in the economic, religious, legal, educational, administrative, and even in the moral institutions of society. By its uncompromising hostility to all existing systems and to all accepted traditions it broke the spell that held men fast to the evils from which they were suffering. Mankind was at last on the road to freedom.

Although it was followed by reaction, the French Revolution had done its work so thoroughly that the Old Régime was never fully

Principles of the French Revolution restored. Nevertheless, there was a reaction which modified the changes that had been introduced. The Revolution therefore was a promise for the future as well as an achievement of the past; in a broad general way it indicated the line of progress along which Europe was to march for a century. Its principles became the battle-cry of all who sought to free mankind from the shackles of the past. These principles may be summarized as follows:

(1) *Democracy.* In a general way democracy may be defined as a system of political organization wherein the mass of people, through universal suffrage, exercise supreme power in the State. It was England that contributed the mechanism of democracy, parliament, by which laws were enacted in conformity with the will of the electors. America contributed a written constitution which established democratic government and guaranteed the liberties of the people. The French Revolution proclaimed the doctrine of popular sovereignty based upon universal manhood suffrage. It

was the leading idea at the point of the Revolutionary bayonets that overturned autocratic monarchies and established self-governing commonwealths throughout western Europe.

(2) *Nationalism.*   A nation may be defined as a people that possesses its own territory, language, traditions, and culture and enough self-consciousness to preserve them.   Since the sixteenth century much of modern European history is the story of the political development of nations into statehood.   Before that time Europe had been divided into a large number of independent and semi-independent regions, the inhabitants of which were strangers to one another in laws, in customs, and in language.   From the ruins of feudalism arose powerful, united nations, held together by the absolute power of the king.   The feudal nobles lost their political independence and became his courtiers.   As a result of the Protestant Revolution the Church was shorn of most of her secular authority and reduced to a position of subservience to the king. There was now only one supreme authority in the land, that of the king, who was the symbol of national unity.   "To die for the king" was then a form of patriotic devotion.   This early patriotism was, however, confined mainly to the upper classes; the mass of the people were still animated by the old, provincial spirit; nationalism had not yet entered into the common consciousness.   By establishing democratic institutions and uniform laws the French Revolution roused among all classes and all localities a common national feeling.

(3) *Intellectual freedom.*   "The free communication of ideas and opinions is one of the most precious of the rights of man," said the Declaration of the Rights of Man.   For ages the human mind had been restrained by censorships, and, as a consequence, progress had been slow and uncertain.   The French Revolution taught that the liberation of humanity would come only when the human mind was liberated from the fetters of tradition and superstition; it was therefore opposed to all censorships, both civil and religious.

(4) *Religious freedom.*   The essential meaning of religious freedom is that religion is a private matter with which the government has no concern.   Any one is, therefore, free to worship or not to worship any faith whatsoever, without suffering any disabilities. The French Revolution was the first movement to proclaim clearly and boldly the principle of religious freedom.   For the first time in Europe, Catholics, Protestants, and Jews were put by law on an

equal footing.   The State was to be "lay," or secular, in all its activities; furthermore, it was to have control of marriage and education, long recognized as matters pertaining to the Church.

(5) *Economic freedom.*   The principles later known as *laissez faire* and "freedom of contract" were advocated by the French Revolution.   When it abolished feudalism in the country and the guilds in the city, the Revolution destroyed a semi-caste system that had grown up in Europe during the Middle Ages.   Any one was now permitted to engage in any lawful occupation, business, profession, or labor, and on any terms agreed upon.   The individual, not the economic group, was now the new unit of society.

The heritage that the French Revolution gave to the world was of incalculable importance for the progress of mankind.   It intro-

Heritage of the French Revolution
duced a dynamic element into society by showing that it was possible to accelerate the rate of progress, and, by so doing, to hasten the ripening of history.   Its violent period, the Reign of Terror, when control passed from the middle to the lower classes, inspired the revolutionary movements of the working class during the nineteenth century; and, as a consequence, the word "revolution" acquired a sinister meaning. Once universal suffrage was established, peaceful revolutions, by way of elections, took place periodically in almost every country. Violent methods were, therefore, discountenanced by all who favored orderly progress; for only by peaceful means were necessary changes made permanent in democratic communities.

CHAPTER II

THE AGRICULTURAL REVOLUTION

IT requires a great effort to imagine our present world, with its factories, railways, steamboats, telephones, airplanes, and radio, to have been, at any other time, different from what it is to-day. Yet these wonderful mechanisms are but a century old, and the product of a great change in human affairs known as the "Industrial Revolution." Until its advent the economic life of the world for countless ages had been much the same. A Greek of the time of Pericles coming to France in the reign of Louis XIV would have seen little to astonish him in the methods of farming, manufacturing, trading, building, and transportation. Should he, however, come to America of the twentieth century, he would literally believe himself to be in an enchanted world. He would see things made with lightning-like rapidity by machines, wheat cut and the sheaves bound without human labor, vehicles speeding along without horses, ships moving through water without sails, houses brilliantly lighted without lamps, birdlike contrivances flying in the air, and hear and see some one speaking thousands of miles away!

Industrial Revolution of very recent origin

The term "revolution" is generally applied to a popular uprising that is characterized by violence of speech and action. During the economic revolution no speeches were made, no conventions were held, no battles were fought! Nevertheless, this silent change, by altering radically the conditions of life for millions of human beings, may be truly regarded as the greatest of all revolutions in history, and as marking the end of the civilization of the past and the beginning of the civilization of the present and of the future. "It was a revolution," a modern writer says, "which has completely changed the face of modern Europe and of the New World, for it introduced a new race of men — the men who work with machinery instead of with their hands, who cluster together in cities instead of spreading over the land in villages and hamlets; the men who trade with those of other nations as readily as with those of their own town;

Modern industry marks advent of new civilization

the men whose workshops are moved by the great forces of nature instead of the human hand, and whose market is no longer the city or the country, but the world itself."

The economic revolution had two aspects, agricultural and industrial. Although the former was far less important than the latter, it will be treated first because the Agricultural Revolution preceded the Industrial Revolution and greatly accelerated its progress.

Until very recently the overwhelming majority of the people in every country in the world were engaged, either directly or in-Lords and directly, in tilling the soil. Tradition and custom landlords ruled even more firmly among the peasants in isolated hamlets than among the artisans in the towns; hence, progress in the methods of farming was very slow. At the end of the eighteenth century the medieval manor still flourished on the Continent, where the lord collected dues and services from a servile peasantry. England was the one country in which the manorial system had been considerably modified. The lord had become the "landlord" who owned his estate outright. Serfdom had entirely disappeared, and the land was worked by peasant proprietors, by tenant farmers, and by agricultural laborers.

Methods of farming in England did not, however, differ from those on the Continent, and they were much the same as in the The "open- Middle Ages. The farms lay beyond the village, and field" consisted of cultivated fields and common lands. The system former were worked according to the "open-field" system, under which each peasant had strips of land scattered in the various fields, not compact, fenced-off areas as is the case to-day. The evils of the "open-field" system were many and serious. All had to plant similar crops at the same time, and to take equally good care of their land. If the lazy or inefficient farmer allowed weeds to grow on his strip, that of his diligent neighbor suffered. Moreover, the system involved a twofold economic waste: of much cultivable land given over to numerous footpaths; and of time spent in going from one to another of the strips. As there were no fences, dishonest farmers were tempted to increase their holding by removing the landmarks of their neighbors. There was still in vogue the centuries-old "three-field" method of cultivation that required one field to lie fallow every three years in order to preserve its fertility. Root crops, such as carrots and turnips, were virtually unknown. Progress in agricultural methods was difficult, as the entire village community had to take the initiative, which was seldom possible among conservative, old-fashioned country folk. To introduce new machinery required an outlay of capital far beyond the means of the husbandman, who was considered well off when he made a living. Consequently he still used the spade, hoe, sickle, scythe, harrow, and wooden plow, implements as ancient as those used in Egypt and Babylonia.

The common lands consisted of meadows and "waste." By the latter was meant unimproved land such as woods, swamps, and sandy wastes. Every villager had the right to send The common cattle to graze in the meadow, in numbers proportional mon lands to the size of his holding. He also had the right to cut firewood and to send his pigs and sheep to roam in the woods. Squatters would sometimes settle on "waste" land, where they eked out an existence by herding and gardening. Promiscuous herding of cattle in the commons tended to promote disease among them; hence, the livestock of those days was ill-fed and ill-kept, consequently small and lean. The manure from the livestock, so valuable as a fertilizer, was wasted on the common meadow, which was not cultivated.

During the eighteenth century England, in some regions, presented the appearance of a pioneer country. Thousands of acres were given over to moorland, heath, marsh, sandy Poor trans-wastes, and forests. Population was sparse, less than portation 9,000,000 inhabitants, scattered chiefly in small villages. Here and there quaint towns dotted the landscape or magnificent manor houses were outlined against the sky. Transportation was difficult, as the highways had hardly undergone repair since Roman times. Often they were merely muddy paths through brush and thicket wherein lurked highwaymen. During some months the roads were entirely impassable, and goods were transported by means of pack-horses. The lack of good roads was due largely to the fact that water transportation was easy because of the many streams and because of the indented coast of England.

For all their inefficiency the peasants managed to get a comfortable livelihood from their strips. Whether proprietors or tenants they felt secure in their holding. They The sturdy worked hard, and produced enough to feed themselves yeomanry plentifully and to dispose of their surplus for the goods that they needed. Sturdy and independent, the "yeomanry" have been much praised in English literature and history as the virile element in the nation that had upheld England's honor on many a battle-field.

NEW METHODS

Toward the end of the eighteenth century the pressure of a growing population, mainly urban in character, was directly the cause of an agricultural revolution which, if not so profound in its influence as its industrial counterpart, nevertheless deeply affected the history of the English people. In order to supply the rapidly increasing demand for food, it became necessary to convert the self-sufficing village farms into factories of bread and meat. The Agricultural Revolution had two important aspects: (1) a reform in methods, and (2) the establishment of a new system of land tenure.

Pressure of population

One of the most distinguished of modern agricultural reformers was Jethro Tull, who became the English pioneer in what is now termed scientific agriculture. About the middle of the eighteenth century he invented a "drill" which deposited the seeds in straight furrows with sufficient space between to permit growth. It displaced the immemorial custom of sowing seeds broadcast, a wasteful method, as some seeds did not take root at all, and some were sown too closely together for healthy growth. Another of Tull's discoveries was the importance of pulverizing the soil, which he did by frequent hoeing. Of him it was said that he made two blades of grass grow where one had grown before.

Invention of the "drill"

Viscount Townshend was a contemporary and an enthusiastic follower of Tull. He had inherited an estate which was in a very poor condition, sand wastes alternating with marshes where "two rabbits fought for every blade of grass." Townshend turned his lands into an agricultural laboratory. By planting root crops and artificial grasses alternately with grain upon the same land in successive seasons, he demonstrated the value of the new system which was coming into vogue, called the "rotation of crops." Careful rotation conserves the mineral contents of the soil; hence the selection of a crop to follow another is based upon its special mineral needs. A further advantage of this method was that all the land was cultivated all the time.

Rotation of crops

Townshend devised a regular system of four-year rotation, wheat, turnips, barley, and clover, which did not exhaust the soil as quickly as the same crop planted year after year. He was an enthusiastic grower of turnips, then a new vegetable, and for that reason was called "Turnip" Townshend. As a result of his experiments, Townshend's estate doubled in value during the decade, 1730–40, which gave a great impetus to scientific agriculture. Rotation of crops was the chief outcome of the early phase of the Agricultural Revolution. It dealt a deathblow to the wasteful three-field system that had existed for countless ages.

Another great step of progress was the discovery of new methods of fertilization. Plants, like animals, require food and drink. Their important foods, nitrogen, potash, and phos- *Artificial* phorus are found generally as ingredients in good soil. *fertilizers* As these ingredients become exhausted through successive plantings, it becomes necessary to replace them. Long ago it was discovered that manure, which contains most of the ingredients, restored the fertility of exhausted soil, and it was almost universally used as a fertilizer. In the forties of the nineteenth century the German chemist, Justus von Liebig, proved that the fertility of the soil could be almost constantly maintained by means of artificial fertilizers containing the necessary ingredients. His researches laid the foundation of scientific agriculture, and extensive farming gave way to intensive farming. Formerly, when more food was needed, more land was brought into cultivation which, owing to the limited supply, was bound, in time, to create a serious food problem. By the application of science, however, larger crops could be raised on the same land. Artificial fertilizers are as important in the history of agriculture as the rotation of crops; poor soils were made fertile, and, together with irrigation, even arid wastes could be transformed into arable land.

The pioneer in scientific cattle breeding was Robert Bakewell, who discovered that cattle could be improved as well as plants. Hitherto, cows had been bred chiefly for milk; oxen, *Cattle* for draught purposes; and sheep, for wool. The meat *breeding* used was chiefly pork and fowl, not beef and mutton. Cattle and sheep were generally scrawny, large-boned animals with long legs and long horns. Bakewell's idea was to breed these animals chiefly for food; hence he sought to increase their weight, especially in those parts that made the most desirable meat. About 1750 he began a number of experiments through artificial selection. His method was to mate the finest specimens within a certain breed, and then mate their offspring. By this system of in-breeding, he succeeded in producing a new type of sheep, the famous "Leicester," small of bone, that matured much sooner than the prevailing type and was double its weight. Bakewell's farm became widely known as a breeding laboratory, and his methods were widely copied. Other breeders, notably Charles and Robert Colling, were successful in experimenting with cattle. They succeeded in producing a famous breed of short-horned cattle called "Durhams" that weighed twice as much as the others. There was now a large supply of beef and mutton which quickly became the most important element in the Englishman's diet.

An agitation in favor of new methods in agriculture was carried on by Arthur Young whose book *Travels in France* has made his Arthur name famous to students of the French Revolution. Young Young was a practical farmer as well as a student of agriculture. He traveled in Britain and on the Continent to study the various methods of farming; and his observations show a keen insight into agricultural problems. He wrote several volumes and published an agricultural journal advocating the new methods. Through his influence the English government, in 1793, established a Board of Agriculture to encourage and assist English farmers to adopt progressive farming. Young was convinced that no progress could be made as long as the "open-field" system existed, and he, therefore, favored large farms composed of fenced-off fields worked by men with capital for the purpose of profit. In the past, farming "had been the pastime of the town, the inspiration of the poets, the relaxation of statesmen, the pursuit of individual owners"; it was now to be an industry like any other, based upon capital and science.

Agricultural machinery began to appear, due largely to the progress of metallurgy. At the end of the eighteenth century, Farming iron plows, drawn by horses, began to displace wooden machinery ones drawn by oxen. A threshing machine was invented which displaced the flail. The most important agricultural machine came from America. It was the famous "reaper," patented in 1834, by Cyrus Hall McCormick, which in time was to revolutionize the process of harvesting. Invention in the field of agriculture did not keep pace, however, with that in the field of industry, as small farms could not use expensive machinery as easily and as profitably as large factories.

ENCLOSURES

Along with changes in agricultural methods there came changes in land tenure that radically transformed the system of landholding in England. In many districts the land was divided The land into large and small properties; the great proprietor, system with his estate, existed alongside the peasants with their strips and common lands. The peasants, generally called the "yeomanry," held their lands either as "freeholders," who owned their farms outright; or as "leaseholders," who leased their farms from the lord for a definite period or for life; or as "copyholders," so called because they possessed a copy of the roll of the manor which stated their rights and obligations without, however, giving them a definite tenure. The advantages of the new methods of cultivation could not be fully realized until a system of land tenure was established that permitted greater freedom of experiment and more efficient management than the conservative, easy-going, and wasteful system of strip cultivation by the peasants.

Enclosure, or the enclosing of the commons and the consolidation of strips into unified, fenced-off fields, was the only solution. But how was this to be brought about? The easiest way Acts of was the one that appealed to the selfish interests of enclosure the great landed proprietors who then dominated the politics of the country. In order to enclose land legally, it was necessary to obtain the unanimous consent of its holders. As this method was seldom possible, an act of Parliament would be passed, ordering enclosure on the petition of the large proprietors in the district. The act provided for a valuation of each villager's strips and of his interest in the commons; and, in return for surrendering them, he was to receive solid fields.

The carrying-out of an act of enclosure was entrusted to commissioners, who were to examine the claims of the villagers; to a surveyor, who was to make the necessary changes; and Methods of to a lawyer, who was to conduct the legal processes. enclosure All of these officials, though appointed by Parliament, were actually named by the large proprietors, who therefore controlled them. The villagers were then asked to present the legal evidence of their claims. Many had none. Some had lost their title deeds; others had, through custom, cultivated their fields for generations. In such instances their claims were declared invalid, and the lands given to the lord. Those who did have legal title were ruined by expensive lawsuits, and forced to sell their claims at a nominal price. The few that managed to get solid fields could not compete with the lord, who had capital with which to introduce new machinery and scientific methods. They, too, in time were forced to sell. The commons, to which no legal title had ever existed, fell an easy prey to the rapacity of the great landowners. The squatters were driven off these lands which were enclosed and given to the lord.[1] Enclosure had taken place earlier in English history, especially in the sixteenth century, but it had been sporadic. Between 1750 and 1810 no fewer than 2921 acts of enclosure were passed, which added millions of acres to the estates of the lords.

There was a great outcry at what was virtually the confiscation of the property of the poor for the benefit of the rich. Young, The deserted though favoring enclosure, was opposed to such village methods. He declared that "the poor look to facts, not to meanings; and the fact is, that by nineteen enclosure bills in twenty they are injured, in some grossly injured." The poor man "may say, and with truth, Parliament may be tender of property; all I know is I had a cow, and an act of Parliament has taken it from me." A petition against enclosure, drawn up by the yeomen of a district, declared that it would result in "the almost depopulation of their town, now filled with bold and hardy husbandmen, from among whom, ... the nation has hitherto derived its greatest strength and glory," and who would be driven into the factory town, where they would "waste their strength, and consequently debilitate their posterity." As a result of the enclosures thousands of yeomen, ruined and rendered homeless, flocked to the towns, where they constituted a supply of cheap labor for the manufacturers. "The peasant with rights and a status," declare J. L. and B. Hammond in their book, *The Village Labourer*, "with a share in the fortunes and government of his village, standing in rags, but standing on his feet, makes way for the laborer with no corporate rights to defend, no corporate power to invoke, no property to cherish, no ambition to pursue, bent beneath the fear of his masters, and the weight of a future without hope." Those

[1] In 1760 about 2,500,000 acres of common lands and about 750,000 acres of waste land were enclosed.

who remained on the land became tenants and laborers on the estates. Many others went to the colonies or joined the army to fight in the war against Napoleon or became tramps along the highways. In many districts the countryside was almost depopulated. Goldsmith's *The Deserted Village* gives a vivid description of the effects of enclosures.

> "Ill fares the land, to hastening ills a prey,
> Where wealth accumulates, and men decay!
> Princes and lords may flourish, or may fade;
> A breath can make them, as a breath has made;
> But a bold peasantry, their country's pride,
> When once destroyed, can never be supplied."

Unquestionably the change from strip to field cultivation, and the extinguishing of the old village community was a great step of progress. It made possible modern agriculture with its scientific methods and labor-saving machinery. But the change was made at the expense of the many for the benefit of the few. The enclosures were responsible for modern rural England with its huge estates, tenant farmers, and landless agricultural laborers

REFERENCES

GENERAL:

R. E. Prothero (Lord Ernle), *English Farming, Past and Present* (ed. 1927), a recognized authority on the subject; W. H. R. Curtler, *Short History of English Agriculture* (1909); N. S. B. Gras, *A History of Agriculture in Europe and America* (1925); M. E. Seebohm, *The Evolution of the English Farm* (1927).

ON THE ENCLOSURE MOVEMENT:

J. L. and B. Hammond, *The Village Labourer, 1760–1832* (ed. 1927), a scholarly, well-written study describing the ruin of the yeomanry; G. Slater, *The English Peasantry and the Enclosure of the Common Fields* (1907); E. C. K. Gonner, *Common Land and Enclosure* (1912); A. Johnson, *The Disappearance of the Small Landowner* (1909); H. Levy, *Large and Small Holdings* (1911); W. Hasbach, *A History of the Agricultural Labourer*, translated from the German (1908); W. H. R. Curtler, *The Enclosure and Distribution of Our Land* (1920); P. Mantoux, *The Industrial Revolution in the Eighteenth Century*, translated from the French (1927), chap. III.

CHAPTER III

THE INDUSTRIAL REVOLUTION

LIKE all other great events in history, the Industrial Revolution did not come suddenly. Long before its advent, important changes

The Commercial Revolution increases supply

were taking place in commerce and industry which prepared the way for the notable transformation of economic life at the end of the eighteenth century. Chief among the antecedents of the Industrial Revolution was the Commercial Revolution of the seventeenth century which marked the first break in the old economy. Through the

(1) of raw materials

discovery of America and the rediscovery of China and India, a vast storehouse of raw materials became available, but the then existing methods of manufacture were too inadequate to convert this superabundance into commodities. Great rewards awaited those who could devise quick methods of turning raw material into manufactured articles.

From America came also precious metals. Few persons realize that the universal use of money is fairly recent, and came as a

(2) of money

result of the discovery of America. Previously, barter economy was the rule; money was used only by merchants. The importation of gold and silver from America had the effect of introducing a money economy. Fluid capital became possible, as money could easily be transported from one place to another. Even more important was the rise of modern banks with their gold and silver reserves, which made possible an extensive credit system, so necessary to large business enterprises.

The modern corporation, with its large investments, had its origin in the joint-stock companies that appeared in the seven-

(3) of capital

teenth century, notably the East India Companies. Large-scale investments could now be made because of the large aggregations of capital, which made possible the exploitation of the natural resources of a country; such undertakings require far more capital than an individual commercial venture.

In a sense the discovery of America was also a discovery of the

Atlantic and Pacific Oceans. Formerly, trading vessels sailed on
navigable rivers or along the seacoast. The Medi- (4) and of
terranean, an inland sea, was the only highway of world
commerce
international commerce. Now, trading vessels sailed
on all seas to all lands; and, for the first time, world commerce in
the modern sense began.

England, more than any of the other nations, was in a position
to take full advantage of the economic opportunities opened up by
the Commercial Revolution. That is chiefly the reason England,
why the Industrial Revolution had its origin in that mother of
country. It is, therefore, necessary to study the modern
industry
movement in relation to England, just as it is necessary to study the Renaissance in relation to Italy, the Protestant
Revolution in relation to Germany, and the French Revolution in
relation to France. To develop industrially, three elements are
necessary: capital, labor, and natural resources, such as coal and
iron. England, at the end of the eighteenth century, had all three
elements in abundance. She had conquered her chief competitors,
Holland and France, in the great struggle for colonies and trade.
Wealth poured into England, and her merchants accumulated a
large amount of surplus capital ready for investment. A plentiful
supply of cheap labor came to the factory towns as a result of the
Enclosure Acts, which ousted many peasants from their holdings.
In the north were large deposits of coal and iron, close together,
ready to set in motion a new industrial system based upon steam
and steel. The guild system, which existed on the Continent in
all its medieval rigidity, had been considerably loosened in England
as a result of the Commercial Revolution. Joint-stock companies
had replaced the merchant guilds, and the Domestic System of production had replaced the craft guilds. England had colonies from
which to draw raw materials for her factories and customers for
her manufactures. She had a splendid merchant marine to carry
her wares to all parts of the world. All that England needed to be
transformed into a great industrial nation was the magic touch of
invention.

THE DOMESTIC SYSTEM

Food, shelter, and clothing constitute the basic material needs
of mankind. A change in the system of producing any of these
needs is bound to have a profound influence upon human affairs.

Machinery was first applied in the making of clothes, which gave
rise to machine production, the basis of the Industrial
Revolution. The prevalent use of cotton cloth in
the manufacture of clothes is of comparatively recent date. Prior to the eighteenth century, wool
or linen, especially the former, was the material most widely used
in the making of cloth. For many centuries the woolen industry
had been one of the chief factors in the economic life of England.
Before the advent of machinery, the process of converting raw
wool into cloth was quite simple. In the first place, it was cleansed
and "carded," or combed, in order to convert the knotted mass
into straightened fibers for easy manipulation. The fibers were
then fastened to a stick which was attached to a simple machine
called a spinning wheel, consisting of a wheel and spindle worked
by a treadle. As the wheel revolved, it drew out from the mass a
fine, strong thread attached to the distaff.

How thread was made by the spinning wheel

The weaving of thread into cloth was done by means of another
simple contrivance, the hand loom, which consisted of a frame
made of wooden rollers. Horizontal threads, called
the "warp," were attached to the frame, and vertical
threads, called the "woof," were then inserted by
means of the "shuttle" pushed back and forth by two
weavers. The interlacing of the warp and the woof resulted in
cloth, closely or loosely woven as one desired, ready to be made
into garments by the tailor's art.

How cloth was made by the hand loom

The system of production was known as the Domestic or Cottage
System because the work was done mainly at home. Under the
guild system, prevalent in the Middle Ages, the master
craftsman had bought the raw material, had worked
it up into the finished product in his shop with the
aid of assistants, and had sold it directly to his neighbors or at the
fairs. Under the Domestic System there appeared a middleman,
who distributed raw material to the artisans to be manufactured
on the basis of "piece work," so much wages for so much work.
Sometimes he rented the tools to the artisans. But the work was
performed by the latter at home, which was generally in the
country or in the city suburbs, under conditions determined by
the workers. All the members of the household were employed,
young children no less than the wife and domestics. The women
did the spinning. So universal was the Domestic System and so

Appearance of the middleman

closely were the women associated with spinning, that a woman at the spinning wheel was the symbol of home life. The term "spinster," applied to an unmarried woman, originated in the fact that, having no family, she gained her living by spinning all her life.

Conditions under this system were simple in comparison with those in our modern industrial life. There was no overproduction, no great fluctuation of price, no panics, and no great unemployment because the goods made were staple articles for a limited and definitely known market. Such luxuries as were in demand were importations from the East for the use of the wealthy few. What was manufactured was produced neither at random nor for speculation, but to supply the needs of the locality, and consequently trade was fairly regular. "Economic activities in the pre-capitalist period," writes Sombart, the German economist, "were regulated solely in accordance with the principle of a sufficiency for existence: the peasant and craftsman looked to their economic activities to provide them with their livelihood and nothing more." With their simple tools they could produce very little. Furthermore, the artisan did not depend solely on his trade for a living; he supplemented it by farming on a small scale. He generally owned a plot of ground, a half-dozen acres at most, to which he and his assistants turned in times of diminished demand. If the Domestic System rarely made for wealth, it as rarely brought destitution. By working hard and regularly one could gain a comfortable livelihood, and no more. Unemployment for any length of time was rare, there being a constant and steady demand for yarn and for cloth, the supply of which was limited by the slow process of hand labor. Conditions of life for the laborers, although not at all like the happy state often pictured by old-fashioned admirers of the Domestic System, were yet far better than those under the Factory System in the early days of the Industrial Revolution. The laborer under the Domestic System "worked long hours, but they were his own hours; his wife and children worked, but they worked beside him, and there was no alien power over their lives; his house was stifling, but he could step into his garden; he had spells of unemployment, but he could use them sometimes for cultivating his cabbages."

Capital under the Domestic System was as yet too closely inter-

twined with labor to play the distinctive rôle that it does to-day,
Introduction but a change was coming with the growing use of
of cotton cotton goods. Originally, cotton had been introduced
goods into Europe by the East India Companies from India,
where it was finely woven and beautifully dyed, hence expensive.
It became quite the fashion to wear "calico" (from Calicut, in
India) which actually competed with wool and even silk. Two
circumstances popularized the use of cotton: it was grown in
America, where, after the invention of the cotton gin, it became
plentiful and cheap; and the moist climate of England was ideally
suited for the production of cotton goods, as the fiber requires
humidity in order to be spun into a firm and strong thread. Cotton
began to displace wool, and marked a revolution in the history of
clothes. Being an imported article, it was free from craft regulation, and in this freedom the capitalistic middleman, who had
already made his appearance in the Domestic System, found his
great opportunity. He became the importer of raw cotton which
he gave to the artisans to be spun into thread, and to be woven
into cloth. But the spinning wheel and hand loom were unable
to turn out enough goods to supply the rapidly growing demand
for cotton clothes. The Domestic System as applied to cotton
broke down, and this situation stimulated many to try more rapid
methods of manufacture. Necessity was to prove the mother of
invention.

MECHANICAL INVENTIONS

Conditions favorable to an industrial change, as has already
been explained, had been created by the Commercial Revolution.
True nature Important experiments and inventions had taken
of the place a century before its coming. Nevertheless, there
machine was a culmination at the end of the eighteenth century, when an outburst of inventive genius occurred in England
which far exceeded all previous efforts. A large number of mechanical inventions appeared which completely revolutionized the
process of manufacture and introduced machine industry. To
understand the true nature and function of a machine, it is essential
to realize that it is not merely a more dexterous tool to aid man in
the production of goods; a machine is, more accurately speaking, a
kind of non-human slave, tireless and nerveless, that is itself the
producer, a "device designed to transfer energy and to apply

power to the production of utilities or goods." Man's part is perfunctory: to pull a lever, to push a button, or to turn a crank; the more automatic the machine becomes, the less the need of man's labor. The complicated machine is now the maker of goods, and man has become its simple assistant. Its motive power is generally non-human — wind, tide, waterfall, steam, or electricity — and marks man's supreme success in harnessing Nature to the service of humanity. Space and time are annihilated by the locomotive, the steamship, the telegraph, the airplane, and the radio. Articles are made in immense quantities and with incredible speed by nimble fingers of steel.

The creators of the machine, and therefore the fathers of modern industry, were practical scientists known as inventors. They were generally skilled artisans or scientific experimenters whose work was in no sense entirely new. The heroic theory of invention — that a new idea springs fully developed from the brain of a "wizard" — is, like other heroic theories, a myth. An inventor is always one who has perfected a process which others, as well as himself, have been experimenting with, studying, and investigating. Prospects of great riches awaiting a successful inventor set ingenious men to experiment with machinery. Many of those who made important contributions to invention are unknown because they had no money with which to put their machines on the market. Their work was utilized by others who had the means and the ability to commercialize it, and it was they, rather than the inventors, who became immensely wealthy.

Invention the product of many minds

The first of the inventions in the textile trade was the "flying shuttle," an improved hand loom invented by John Kay in 1733. It enabled one weaver to jerk the shuttle back and forth by means of a handle, thus increasing the speed of operation. More rapid weaving stimulated a demand for more thread, and led to the invention, in 1765, by James Hargreaves, of a spinning machine known as the "jenny." It consisted of a simple, wooden frame on which eight spindles revolved by the turning of a wheel, producing eight threads at one time. The jenny was rapidly improved, and a child, by turning the wheel, could do the work of a hundred spinners. Both the flying shuttle and the jenny were tools rather than machines; the former being an enlargement of the hand loom, and the latter, of the spinning wheel.

The "jenny"

The first machine was the famous "water frame" (1769), an invention credited to Richard Arkwright. It was run by water power, not by hand or foot; and consisted of a series of revolving rollers, rotating at various speeds, which spun cotton thread so firmly that all-cotton cloth could now be made. Arkwright was a shrewd business man, not an inventor. He perfected the inventions of others whose work he made a practical success through his ability to get money to put the machines on the market. The water frame marked the establishment of the Factory System. In 1771, Arkwright set up the first cotton factory run by water power. Now, for the first time, machinery was applied to work hitherto done by hand.

The "water frame"

Another important machine was the "mule," invented by Samuel Crompton in 1779. It was a combination of the jenny and the water frame which spun more rapidly than either, and produced a thread even finer than the finest Indian muslins. It made muslin cheaper than that produced by the cheap labor of India, and finer than that produced by the skilled craftsmen of that land. Crompton's "mule" gave tremendous impetus to the cotton industry by making cheap a cloth once as exclusive as silk. The inventor, however, got nothing out of his invention, which was used as a model by others who refused to pay anything for it.

The "mule"

There was now a disproportion between spinning and weaving. Increased production of thread called for more rapid methods of weaving. This demand was met by the "power loom," invented in 1785 by Edward Cartwright. Weaving was done with great rapidity in a factory operated by water power. The hand loom of the "Domestic System" was doomed.

The "power loom"

There were now rapid methods of spinning and weaving cotton, and a demand arose for a greater supply of this raw material. It was answered by another famous invention, the "cotton gin," invented in 1793 by the American, Eli Whitney. The cotton gin made possible the rapid removal of seeds from the cotton fibers by a mechanical device instead of by slow human fingers. It stimulated enormously the production of cotton, which was henceforth universally used for making cheap clothing. Cotton manufacturing became the greatest factor in England's industrial development and the main source of her

The "cotton gin"

prosperity. In 1785, cylinder printing was invented, whereby a roller, with a design engraved upon it, was run over the cloth. Previously, patterns had been cut on wooden blocks, and then stamped on the cloth. Finally, in 1800, a quick method of bleaching by the use of chemicals was discovered, and thereafter it was no longer necessary to expose cloth to the sun in order to accomplish this result.

THE STEAM ENGINE

The use of water power led to the building of factories called "mills," like those which ground wheat into flour. But the disadvantage of a mill was that its location was deter- Limitations mined by geographic conditions: it must perforce be of water placed near a rapid stream or waterfall, irrespective of power the distance from the source of the raw material or of centers of distribution. This limitation was a serious drawback to a full and free development of machinery, a limitation imposed by Nature itself.

It is very doubtful whether the Industrial Revolution would have advanced very far had it not been for the invention of the steam engine, the giant that operates machinery in factories, Importance propels ships through seas, and hauls trains across of engineer-continents. With the steam engine a revolution in ing engineering was inaugurated, even more important than that in spinning and weaving. Engineering, in its numerous applications, made possible the utilization of machinery and the sources of power on a large scale.

Though complicated in structure, the steam engine is based upon a simple principle; namely, that water, when heated, expands in the form of steam. This principle had been known Origin of for a long time, but its practical application is com- the steam paratively recent. The first experimenter with steam engine was Denis Papin, a French physicist who, in 1688, invented a steam engine equipped with a cylinder and piston. The cylinder was heated from the outside causing the water in it to become steam, which forced up the piston; when the fire was removed, the steam cooled and the piston fell. The next important step took place in 1704, when Thomas Newcomen invented a simple engine in which a piston was pushed up and down by alternately filling a cylinder with steam, and then condensing it. The piston was connected with a rod, and the rod in turn with a pump, and the result was a steam pump. Newcomen's engine was a crude affair; it had to be alternately heated and cooled, thereby losing much of the power it generated.   In 1769, James Watt made a capital improvement by adding a condenser separate from the cylinder. He devised a system of valves through which steam escaped to a separate condensing chamber which was always cool. The cylinder no longer had to be constantly reheated; hence, most of the heat was saved.   Watt's signal contribution to the Industrial Revolution was the application of steam power to drive machinery. By attaching a wheel to a steam engine, and connecting it by means of a belt with spinning or weaving machines, the process of manufacture was greatly accelerated.   The steam engine made the factory independent of stream and waterfall. It could now be established in places where coal and raw materials were plentiful and cheap. Through the steam engine man won his first great victory in his efforts to gain mastery over the forces of Nature. Here was a tremendous power that he exerted at will, independently of geography, of climate, of wind, of tide, of current.

STEEL

Fundamental in the changes that were taking place in engineering was the transformation of the metal industries through the use

Early method in steel making
of coal and coke as a fuel to reduce iron ore. For centuries the smelting of iron ore, or the burning-out of the impurities that it contains, had been done by means of a charcoal furnace with the aid of hand bellows; a large quantity of wood was required to smelt a small quantity of iron. Highly skilled labor then transformed the product into a much harder metal, steel. So expensive was the process that steel was used chiefly in the making of weapons.

The demand for the new machinery in turn created a demand for steel from which it was constructed. Coal was plentiful and

The use of coal in smelting
cheap, and had been successfully used by Abraham Darby early in the eighteenth century as a fuel for the smelting of iron. The invention, in 1760, of the "steam blast" by John Smeaton marked the real beginning of modern smelting. By this method, coal was burned into coke with which the iron was smelted by the aid of a "blast," an air pump driven by steam which kept the flame constantly burning. Another great step in the process was the invention, in 1783, of

"puddling" by Henry Cort. "Pig" iron, which contains much carbon, was reduced to a semi-liquid form in a furnace and then stirred until most of the carbon was burned out, thus becoming steel. The metal was then rolled out into bars or plates. Cort's process led to the establishment of rolling mills.

Coal was now married to iron. They became inseparable in the development of industry based upon power-driven machinery. Sir Humphry Davy's invention of the safety lamp, in 1815, was an important factor in the development of mining upon which industry was now dependent. With coal as fuel, steel could be made cheaply and in large quantities, but not quickly. Another revolution occurred in steel-making with the famous Bessemer process, invented by Henry Bessemer in 1856. By this method the ore was put into a blast furnace from which it emerged molten pig iron; the latter was then poured into a "converter"; a hot current of air was blown through the mass which had the effect of removing the carbon; a definitely measured amount of carbon was then restored to the molten mass, which was then poured into molds; and when it cooled the product was the best steel yet known. By the Bessemer process steel could be made very quickly, and very cheaply, as little fuel was used to maintain a high temperature in smelting. The Age of Steel had now succeeded the Age of Wood and Stone. So various and manifold have been the uses of steel that it is hard to imagine how our present industrial system could go on long without it. Machinery, tools, cutlery, rails, bridges, locomotives, the framework of buildings, cars, ships, and armor, innumerable and indispensable articles to be seen on every side in factory, office, and home, from immense building girders to fine watch springs, are made from steel. As coal was the food, and iron the bone and sinew, of the machine, an enormous stimulus was given to the production of these two basic commodities which have become the mainstay of modern industry.

The Bessemer and open-hearth processes

REVOLUTION IN TRANSPORTATION

The ever-increasing quantity of goods produced by the new machinery soon went far beyond the requirements of the locality, and even of the nation. How could the surplus be transported from the factory, cheaply and quickly, to distant places? How could raw materials and coal be transported

The turnpikes

to the factory when needed? The sailing vessel and horse-drawn wagon, both small and slow, were moreover uncertain, being dependent upon weather conditions. During the latter half of the eighteenth century new methods of road-building were introduced which facilitated transportation. "Turnpike" companies, chartered by Parliament, built roads of a new type, known as "turnpikes," throughout England. At certain points on the turnpike were "toll" gates that collected toll from those who used the road. Famous in the annals of English road-building are Thomas Telford and John Macadam. The latter, from whose name comes the term "macadamized," was the first to use broken stone in road construction. But even the turnpikes were unable to cope with the situation. Necessity again proved to be the mother of invention; and there appeared the steamboat and railway, the most efficient means of transportation the world had ever known.

Like other inventions the steamboat was the work of many men experimenting in the same direction. As long ago as 1690, Papin applied the steam engine to navigation, and built a steamboat which proved successful on its first trial. It was destroyed by workingmen who feared that the invention would put them out of employment. Toward the end of the eighteenth century a number of steamboats appeared, one built by a Frenchman, James Perier, and another by an American, John Fitch. A Scotsman, William Syminton, built a steamboat, the Charlotte Dundas, which, in 1802, appeared on the Forth and Clyde Canal towing two loaded vessels against a strong wind. Like the boat of Papin, the one of Symington was destroyed by riotous laborers.

Pioneers of the steamboat

The most famous of all experiments in steam navigation was that of the American, Robert Fulton, who had been on board the Charlotte Dundas. In 1807, he launched the steamboat Clermont, on the Hudson River, which made the trip from New York to Albany, a distance of one hundred and fifty-four miles, in thirty-two hours. This epoch-making voyage on a mighty stream against wind and tide proved the feasibility of steam navigation, which, however, was slowly introduced. In 1819, the steamer Savannah crossed the Atlantic in twenty-nine days, but she had to use sail for part of the voyage. The first ship to cross the Atlantic using steam for the entire trip was the Great Western, which, in 1838. made the voyage

The Clermont and the Great Western

in fifteen days. At first steamships were built of wood, but it was found that iron ships were actually more buoyant than wooden ones and, moreover, they were stronger and more rigid. By the middle of the nineteenth century the building of iron ships became general.

While some inventors were experimenting with steam navigation, others were experimenting with steam locomotion on land. Among the pioneers of the railway was Richard Trevithick, who, in 1801, built the first locomotive, which, however, proved incapable of continuous hauling. The most famous name associated with the invention of the "iron horse" is that of George Stephenson. He was a practical engineer who was engaged by capitalists to design a locomotive which was to be used on the first railway, the "Stockton and Darlington," near Durham. There was great excitement, in 1825, when this railway trip was to be made. With Stephenson as engineer the locomotive hauled a train of thirty-four cars for twenty-five miles in three hours, with a stop of an hour. It was a great triumph, and marked an epoch in the history of transportation. However, many were averse to this new method of transportation by a "traveling steam pot." It was considered too dangerous to travel at the rate of twelve miles an hour! The turnpike and canal companies, fearing competition, vigorously opposed the building of railways. Stephenson, however, continued his experiments, and, in 1830, he produced a famous locomotive, the Rocket, which drew a train of cars on the Liverpool and Manchester Railway at the rate of twenty-nine miles an hour. This demonstration put an end to all doubts as to the future of the railway. A fervor of railway-building followed, which resulted in spanning England with a network of steel rails connecting all important towns.

Pioneers of the locomotive

REVOLUTION IN COMMUNICATION

In the past, communication was almost entirely a part of transportation. If one wished to send a message to a distant place, the only means was by wagon, post-rider, or boat. Perhaps the most marvelous of all inventions have been in methods of communication. In the middle of the nineteenth century the electric telegraph was produced, the work chiefly of an Englishman, Charles Wheatstone, and of two Americans, Samuel F. B. Morse and Alfred Vail. The

The telegraph, cable, and telephone

principle of telegraphy is based on a code of signals which are sent from one end of a wire and are reproduced at the other end by the action of an electro-magnet. An American, Cyrus W. Field, and an Englishman, Sir Charles Bright, established telegraphic communication across water, in 1866, by laying the famous Atlantic cable. The principle of the telephone was first discovered in 1860 by a German, Philip Reis, but the practical application of the idea was made, in 1876, by an American, Alexander Graham Bell. The telephone is based on a system of changing sound waves into an electric current which travels along a wire and is reproduced into sounds at the other end.

The new means of transportation and communication marked man's conquest of time and space. They profoundly affected human relations throughout the world by bringing distant places within easy reach. Distances were now measured by time, not by miles. Once, man had lived in isolation, whether in hamlet or in large city; to travel meant a large outlay of time and money. Now he strode over the earth in seven-league boots. By means of the telegraph and telephone, and later the radio, he could be instantly in communication with his fellow beings in all parts of the world. A statesman delivers a speech in London; the wheat crop in the Argentine is blighted by a frost; an explorer in an airship passes over the North Pole; a riot breaks out in Cairo; a visiting queen is entertained in Chicago — instantly news of the event is sent to the press, and almost as instantly printed. The world has become a whispering gallery.

The world, a whispering gallery

After the Napoleonic wars the Industrial Revolution spread from England to western Europe. At first, England tried to maintain a monopoly of her inventions by forbidding the export of machinery and the emigration of her skilled workmen. But all attempts to enforce such regulations proved unsuccessful, and England began to aid in the industrial development of her sister nations. British labor and British capital came to the Continent, where factories were started. During the first half of the nineteenth century the Industrial Revolution made slow progress in western Europe, but later in the century, when coal and iron mines were opened, it advanced very rapidly, especially in Germany. Eastern Europe, Russia, Austria-Hungary, and the Balkans did not establish factories and railways until the latter part of the nineteenth century. In America the Industrial Revolution began early in the nineteenth century, but its great progress came after the Civil War. After transforming Europe and America, the Industrial Revolution invaded Asia and Africa, where it rapidly effected changes in the lives of the inhabitants as no other influence had done in centuries.

THE FACTORY SYSTEM

The Industrial Revolution caused England to break with her past even more thoroughly than did the French Revolution in the case of France. Within half a century, the face of England changed startlingly. Instead of farms, hamlets, and an occasional town, there appeared immense cities, with teeming populations huddled around gigantic factories. Lancashire and the West Riding, the great cotton manufacturing centers, seemed like a forest of factories, with their thousands of tall chimneys belching clouds of smoke and their "hundreds of windows blazing forth a lurid light in the darkness and rattling with the whir and din of ceaseless machinery by day and night." England had become the "workshop of the world," by utilizing the forces of Nature in the manufacture of goods. "Nowhere does man exercise such dominion over matter," said Macaulay.

England, workshop of the world

To the Industrial Revolution was due a radical change in the distribution, character, and increase of population. The effect upon distribution was twofold: on the one hand, there was a general growth of the north of England at the expense of the south; and, on the other hand, a constant movement of population from the rural to the industrial centers. In the north, where there were large deposits of coal and iron, the textile, cutlery, and pottery industries made their homes. In one generation this section of the country, which had been sparsely inhabited, became the most densely populated part of Great Britain. Instead of migrating to the New World, many now preferred to seek their fortunes in the new cities which beckoned all those who sought to improve their conditions. Manchester, Leeds, Sheffield, and Birmingham, at one time little towns, became crowded industrial cities almost overnight. Manchester, in 1774, had about 40,000 people; in 1831, about 271,000. In the south, where agriculture continued to be the main occupation, population was at a standstill or had actually decreased. The entire natural increase was absorbed into industrial life, and the countryside was being emptied

Growth of cities

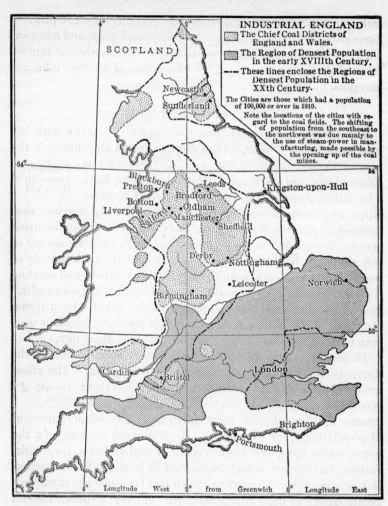

INDUSTRIAL ENGLAND

The Chief Coal Districts of England and Wales.

The Region of Densest Population in the early XVIIIth Century.

These lines enclose the Regions of Densest Population in the XXth Century.

The Cities are those which had a population of 100,000 or over in 1910.

Note the locations of the cities with regard to the coal fields. The shifting of population from the southeast to the northwest was due mainly to the use of steam-power in manufacturing, made possible by the opening up of the coal mines.

for the benefit of the town. This is the first instance in history of a rapid shift of a large population from the country to the city. Moreover, the rate of increase in population more than doubled. It is estimated that, before the Industrial Revolution, every decade saw an increase in population of about six per cent; during the decade 1801–11, the increase was twenty-one per cent.[1]

The factory town was as typical of the new order as the hamlet

[1] England and Wales had a population of about 9,000,000 in 1801 when the first census was taken.

had been of the old. An outward and visible sign of the Industrial Revolution, the factory appeared on the landscape to announce the coming of machine industry. A factory has been defined as "a compact and closely organized mass of labor composed of hundreds or thousands of individuals coöperating with large quantities of expensive and intricate machinery through which passes a continuous and mighty volume of raw material on its way to the consuming public." As the machine displaced the tool, so did the factory displace the shop. With the establishment of the factory as the new unit of production, division of labor became possible. Every part of the article was made separately by workers who specialized in the making of one part and in nothing else. So minute was the subdivision of labor that recently there were about ninety processes in the making of a shoe: some machines punched holes in leather; others cut heels; others fitted soles; others sewed on buttons; others polished the leather. The parts were then assembled, assorted, and packed according to sizes. Those who tended the machines were not shoemakers, but unskilled laborers who merely turned wheels, pressed springs, pulled levers, and pushed buttons. Labor of this kind required, not trained skill, but manual dexterity, easily acquired through the constant repetition of the same process. A machine needed but slight guidance to turn out unerringly thousands of articles; recent improvements have made it almost human in its automatic intelligence, while man has become machine-like in his monotonous labor. He spends his life "in making the twenty-fourth part of a pin."

So many laborers were employed in the factory that regimentation became necessary to insure the smooth running of the system. A hierarchy of factory officials appeared, foremen, superintendents, managers, and owners who commanded the "soldiers of industry," the laborers. The latter were divided into "gangs," and assigned to a particular task which they did daily. Factory discipline was rigid. At the sound of a whistle or bell, all began and ceased working. The number of hours, the time allowed for meals, the part of the working day or night, the holidays, all were strictly regulated. Wages were standardized. The same rate was paid to all engaged in the same kind of work, but as the work varied little, so did the rate of wages. Especially rigid were the rules regarding slackness. Should the worker stop to rest or slow up his pace, he was liable to fine or dismissal. The throbbing machines relentlessly demanded the constant attention of those who tended them.

Another aspect of the Factory System is the standardization of production. Articles of a given kind which are made by machinery Machine are exactly alike in texture, quality, color, and size. versus hand The machine merely duplicates many times over any production given pattern. In this respect machine industry differs markedly from the handicrafts. No two articles made by hand are alike; there is bound to be variation, depending upon the mood and imagination of the worker, and in the possibility of variation lies the opportunity for artistic production. Variation produced by the machine means a spoiled product which is thrown away. Consequently machine-made goods were at first generally ugly, coarse, and cheap. However, so great has been the progress of invention that machinery now makes articles so beautiful in design and color and so fine in texture that they compare favorably with the workmanship of the artist-craftsmen of former times.

The increase in output due to the introduction of machinery has been so great that it is impossible to estimate it in definite figures. Increase in By delivering humanity from its dependence upon the production forces of Nature, the machine has been able to produce any number of articles, provided it has power and raw material. A surplus of articles has now become possible, and no one need be without food, shelter, and clothing. Large-scale production for the world market has become the order of the day, and a great commercial expansion followed in the wake of the Industrial Revolution. As the railway and steamship have made possible rapid transportation to all parts of the world, every effort has been made to stimulate old markets and to open new ones. Rapid means of communication by cable, telegraph, telephone, and later by "wireless," have tended to unify the world market. Prices are quoted instantly the world over; hence buyer and seller are quickly brought together. Safety devices, a widespread system of insurance, and good policing have abated most of the dangers from accidents and robbery that had formerly attended commerce.

To the Industrial Revolution was directly due the appearance of The cap- two new elements in society, the capitalists and the italist class working class. The capitalist was the new rich man who appeared side by side with the landed aristocrat in the country and the wealthy merchant in the city. By a capitalist is meant a person who invests his money in industrial enterprises from which he derives profits. It is important to note the difference between the old-fashioned merchant and the new industrial capitalist. The former was a trader or a money-lender who dealt with various intermediaries, farmers, stock-raisers, artisans, to whom he sometimes advanced money. But the industrial capitalist controlled entirely the whole process of production: he employed the labor, owned the raw material, the factory, the machinery, the finished product. The opportunity for making money was greatly increased by the new inventions, as the resources of the world could now for the first time be fully exploited. Profits were large; and enormous fortunes were made by shrewd and enterprising "captains of industry," who quickly outstripped in wealth both aristocrats and merchants. Most of the industrial capitalists came from the wealthier townsmen; many members of the old trading companies and sometimes even craftsmen found opportunities to apply their money or ingenuity in the new industrial order. In the early days of the Industrial Revolution, little capital was required to start a business which, if successful, would grow rapidly because of the great demand for the cheap products of the factory. If one man did not have enough money, he would form a partnership, generally with members of his own family. Later, as the business grew, more capital was required, and the joint-stock company appeared which was an enlarged partnership. It was able to utilize the savings of many by selling shares of stock to those who had some money, but not enough to start an enterprise. The great power of the capitalists lay not only in their wealth but even more in their ownership or control of the new machinery of production. In the factory towns almost the entire population depended for its livelihood upon the factory owners. Directly they employed the largest element, the workingmen, and, in addition, a considerable number of clerks and factory officials. The others, tradesmen and professionals, lived by catering to the needs of the factory employees. Let a factory shut its doors and the population would flee the town as if it were visited by a plague. The influence of the old landed aristocracy began to wane before that of the new moneyed aristocracy, the nobility of industrial society. The middle classes, likewise, greatly increased in numbers and influence. As tradesmen and professionals, they found in the rapidly growing cities greater opportunities for money-making than they had ever before known.

Equally important was the appearance in society of the new poor man, the workingman. By the "working class" is specifically meant those laborers who are employed in modern industry, factory workers, miners, builders, railwaymen. Unlike slaves, serfs, and journeymen they were free from masters and lords, and from restrictions of all kinds. The coming of free labor has been well described as a change "from status to contract." A workingman had the right to work at whatever he pleased, for whom he pleased, and on what terms he pleased, provided he could find some one to employ him. Between him and his employer there was only the "cash nexus," wages. By wages are meant the payment of a definite sum to the workingmen in return for a definite number of hours of labor. Complete separation of labor and capital was characteristic of the new industrial order. The workingman, having no capital, could not participate in the enterprise; the capitalist, unlike the guild master, could add little to his business by working in the factory.

The working class

How did the working class arise? When the factory came, thousands of peasants flocked to the city to find work, some because they were rather glad of an opportunity to leave the dull, monotonous life of the farm; others, because they were ousted from their agricultural holdings by the enclosures. Large numbers of Irish, forced out of their own country by poverty, emigrated to the factory towns of England, especially to Manchester. The craftsmen could not stand the competition of the factory, as the machine made things much cheaper, though not better, than their handiwork; consequently, many artisans were ruined by the labor of the "iron men," as the machines were called. It was no comfort to them to be told that the world would benefit in the long run from the use of the new inventions which tended more to increase the profits of the capitalists than to better the condition of the laborers. Riots broke out against the "iron men," many of which were destroyed by infuriated mobs of workingmen, who depended for their living on old-time ways. But it was all in vain. The artisans were soon forced to give up their hopeless struggle against machinery and to find places in the factory.

Origin of the working class

The coming of the machine made the laborers equal; all were

"hands" whose function was merely to guide in dull monotony the new slave of steel. As the factory became a social group, often a very large one, it was impossible to maintain anything like the personal relations that had existed between employer and employee in the days of the Domestic System. The individual worker was lost in the great mass, and the owner of the factory was often not a person at all, but a corporation that employed managers to conduct the business. This situation tended to weaken the sense of responsibility; and evil conditions were often tolerated in the factories because the owners did not know of their existence. The greed for large profits caused some capitalists to exploit their laborers mercilessly and blinded them to the evils that they were creating in society.

Separation of employers and employed

In spite of the fact that the factory worker was outwardly more free than the peasant or artisan, he was in reality more dependent than either. The peasant, although he might be a serf, had land from which he could eke out an existence no matter how meager; the artisan had his tools by means of which he could gain a livelihood; but the landless and toolless "hand" was at the mercy of the man to whom he came seeking for a "job," for he was obliged to accept whatever terms were offered. Free labor was a benefit to the employers, who had all the advantages of a master without any of his responsibilities; they were not compelled to support their employees when there was no work. Hiring men was cheaper than buying them. Wages were low, hours of labor varied from twelve to fourteen, and the factories were unsanitary and even dangerous. During working hours the factories were locked to prevent any of the laborers from deserting their posts. The laborers were housed in "industrial barracks" — badly ventilated, dingy, and crowded living quarters. Great numbers were constantly on the edge of starvation, the result of low wages and unemployment. Work itself sometimes became a luxury. Women and children were employed on a large scale because the part of human labor in machine production was so simple that unskilled women and little children could supply it without great difficulty. The wages that they received were pitifully low. "It is questionable," wrote John Stuart Mill, "if all the mechanical inventions yet made have lightened the day's toil of any human being. They have enabled a greater population to

Evil conditions in the factory

live the same life of drudgery and imprisonment, and an increased number of manufacturers and others to make large fortunes. They have increased the comforts of the middle classes. But they have not yet begun to effect those great changes in human destiny which it is in their nature and in their futurity to accomplish."

If the introduction of machinery separated capital and labor, it also resulted in consolidating labor. Massed together under one roof, doing the same or similar work, and getting the same wages, the factory workers came to feel a sense of solidarity and of common interest. Low wages and long hours caused the workingmen to realize that they would sink into a condition of abject slavery unless they found some means of alleviating their conditions. In theory the employer and employee were on an equal footing in bargaining for terms; both were legally free to accept or reject. In practice, however, the latter was generally compelled to accept the terms of the former or starve. A refusal of one or several workers to accept the conditions offered by the manufacturers would not seriously disconcert the latter, as they could easily get others to fill the vacant places.

Inequality between employer and employee

Out of these conditions a new institution arose, the "trade" or "labor union," which has been defined as a "continuous association of wage-earners in the same trade for the purpose of improving the conditions of their employment through common action." The union asserted the principle of "collective bargaining," or the negotiation for terms of employment by the union for all of its members. It claimed also the right to "strike," whereby all the members ceased working in order to compel the acceptance of their terms. As it was difficult to replace a large group of workingmen, a strike might result in the shutting down of the factory; and, if prolonged, in the financial ruin of the manufacturer.

Rise of trade-unionism

Trade unions spread rapidly from factory to factory. A number of violent strikes took place which greatly alarmed employers and the well-to-do generally. In 1799 and 1800 Parliament passed a series of acts, known as the Combination Laws. Trade unions were declared illegal on the ground that they were in restraint of trade; all contracts by unions for better wages and hours were declared null and void; workingmen were forbidden to combine to improve their wages and hours, to persuade or to prevent any worker from hiring himself to an

The Combination Laws

employer, or to attend any meeting for the purpose of making collective agreements. Strikes were classed with conspiracies, and those who participated in them were severely punished. The Combination Laws forbade combinations of employers as well as of employees, but they were enforced against the latter, not against the former.

The trade unions were under the ban of both law and public opinion. Employers opposed them because they were continually demanding better wages; aristocrats feared them as expressions of that radical democracy which had brought on the French Revolution; the clergy denounced them as breeders of discontent among the working classes, whose lot in life had been fixed by Providence; and many people, otherwise sympathetic with the poor, feared that, if trade unions got control, British industry would be driven from the markets of the world by foreign competition.

Trade unions arouse hostility of upper classes

As long as society was based on agriculture and commerce was merely local, there was a high degree of security for all classes of the population. Prices varied but little, employment was regular, and panics were almost unknown. Only when a bad harvest occurred there was what might be termed an "agricultural panic." But the change to an industrial society, although it brought great prosperity, at the same time brought with it instability and uncertainty. Trade based upon a world market is bound to be irregular and fluctuating; the supply of raw material varies every year; capital is sometimes unwisely invested; new machinery constantly displaces labor, and changes the character of the industry; often, too, there is overproduction. Such conditions sometimes produce a general dislocation of trade, known as a "panic," which reduces or destroys the profits of capital, throws thousands of laborers out of work, bringing misery and ruin to many. Insecurity of employment, even more than low wages, was the haunting fear of millions of workingmen, who seldom earned enough to tide them over periods of enforced idleness.

Insecurity

In spite of its many evils the Industrial Revolution yet marked the greatest step of progress in the history of the lower classes. Who was the common man before its advent? — a peasant who was a serf or semi-serf on a landed estate, dwelling in a hovel amid conditions that were almost primitive, clad in sheepskin, and living on food that was coarse if

Progress of the working class

plentiful. To many peasants the factory spelled opportunity to be free, to work for regular wages, and to gain the social and educational advantages offered by the town. Although legal freedom was, at that time, a mockery of the workingman's actual condition, yet it was the necessary first step in his emancipation. Starvation was not always the alternative of leaving his job. He might, and often did find a better one. He might emigrate to America, and begin life anew. He might combine with his fellows in a union that would exact better conditions. Rooted to the soil and tied to a lord, the serf had made almost no progress in centuries; he was in about the same condition in the time of Louis XIV as he had been in the time of Charlemagne. What a different story is that of the workingman after a century of the Industrial Revolution!

So great a change in human relations as that produced by the Industrial Revolution was bound to find expression in a new Individual- philosophy. "Individualism" was the ideal preached ism by the defenders of the new order. They declared that the individual was to be allowed to work out his own salvation, particularly in economic affairs, unhampered by governmental restrictions. It was believed that the rivalry between individuals would develop strength of character and would stimulate originality by offering the rewards of wealth and fame; society would thereby be the gainer, for it would lead to an increased production of wealth. "Competition is the life of trade" was one of the aphorisms of the new school. Those individuals who survived the struggle were considered the "fit," and those who did not survive, the "unfit." The Individualists were also believers in the doctrines of liberty and equality, which they desired to see applied to political, religious, and intellectual affairs on the principle of equal rights to all and special privileges to none. They became stanch advocates of freedom of speech, equality of all classes before the law, religious toleration, and extension of the suffrage.

A group of brilliant writers appeared as defenders of the new industrial order. Chief among them were Thomas Robert Malthus, The Man- David Ricardo, and John Stuart Mill, who are known chester as "the classical economists." Their views were pop-School ularized by John Bright and Richard Cobden, leaders of the Manchester School. All of them were inspired by Adam Smith, who was the chief founder of the science of political economy. His great treatise, *Inquiry into the Nature and Causes of the Wealth of Nations*, first published in 1776, was the bible of the Manchester School to whom it was an almost infallible guide to right principles and wise policies in the realm of economics. Smith's fundamental thesis was that economic institutions were of natural origin and were subject to natural laws; hence, there was no human responsibility for the manner in which they worked. On the whole they worked beneficently, like other natural things; therefore, they should not be interfered with by human laws.

At the very base of the system of thought erected by the economists was the principle of *laissez faire* (French, leave things alone). According to its advocates, intervention by the State *Laissez faire* or by any combination, whether of capitalists or of workingmen, in the relations between buyer and seller, between employer and employee, was both mischievous and futile. The law of supply and demand fixed the price both of wages and of commodities. Freedom of contract should be stringently maintained in the "obvious and simple system of natural liberty." Every individual was to be free to buy in the cheapest market and sell in the dearest; to accept the best terms that he could get for his labor; to enter any occupation or business; and to trade with any one in his own or in a foreign country. Therefore the economists were opposed to tariffs, navigation laws, colonies, labor unions, and monopolies. "Hands off business enterprise!" was the injunction that they laid upon government, whose activities were to be limited to the protection of life and property. The government was to conform to conditions created by economic laws, not try to mould them artificially through legislation. Freed from government interference the activities of the "economic man," inspired by "enlightened self-interest," would stimulate business enterprise. The interests of labor and capital, argued the economists, were identical; hence, capital would treat labor well in order to stimulate its best efforts. Any attempt to regulate conditions of labor by legislation or by labor unions would result in the flight of capital and in the consequent impoverishment of the country. The ideas of the classical economists harmonized well with the interests of the manufacturers who dreaded state intervention in economic matters lest it be in favor of their rivals, the landed aristocracy, or of their subordinates, the working class.

Especially significant was the interpretation given by the economists of the position of labor in modern industry. In his famous *Essay on the Principle of Population*, Malthus declared
Malthus's theory of population that "it is the constant tendency in all animated life to increase beyond the nourishment prepared for it." Population increases much more rapidly than the food supply. The yield of the land diminishes its rate of production in proportion as its rate of cultivation is increased. To double the amount of labor on a given piece of land would not double its yield. As population grows there is not sufficient food for all; hence, poverty is unavoidable; the poor are the cause of their own poverty. War, disease, famine are therefore natural, even beneficial, as they act as checks upon a too great increase of population.

Ricardo's theory of wages was based upon Malthus's theory of population. "The natural price of labor," he declared, "is the
Ricardo's theory of wages price which is necessary to enable the laborers, one with another, to subsist and to perpetuate their race, without either increase or diminution." When, in time of prosperity, wages rise, more marriages take place, which increases the population; there is now a greater supply of labor, and, as a consequence, the rise of wages is halted. The cost of living advances, and real wages, or the purchasing power of money falls until it reaches its "natural level" which is just enough to procure the necessities and conveniences to which the laborer and his family are accustomed according to the standard of living prevalent in the country. The workingman was in the grip of the "iron law of wages" which held him fast and from which he could never escape. Wages and profits were in direct opposition; hence, one could be increased only at the expense of the other. Capital and labor were then in natural conflict with each other. Ricardo favored capital because he regarded labor merely as a commodity to be exploited for the interest of mankind.

For fully a century did the theories of the classical economists profoundly influence public opinion. Progressive statesmen, like
Labor regarded as a commodity Gladstone, Bright, and Cobden; leading thinkers, like Macaulay and Herbert Spencer, accepted them wholeheartedly. At the very time when the Industrial and Agricultural Revolutions were producing the necessities of life in greater abundance than ever before, the masses of mankind were condemned to eternal poverty. This paradox may be explained

by the attitude of society toward the working class. Labor, like raw material and machinery, was regarded as a commodity to be bought and sold. Being an important item in the cost of production, the employer wished to pay as little as possible for it. True, labor was human, but the ancient tradition of slavery still clung to the free workingman. In the time of the Industrial Revolution few realized that machine production was inaugurating a new system of society; it was regarded merely as a method for getting rich quickly. National prosperity was identified with profits of capital, not with wages of labor, and society "accepted the standing misery of the poor as a recognized and indispensable condition of national welfare."

AGE OF PROGRESS

Once a momentum was given to invention, one improvement succeeded another in rapid succession, with the result that much of the labor in the factory, on the farm, and even in the home is now performed by machinery. Buildings are constructed, bread is baked, land is plowed, clothes are sewn, and floors are swept by machinery. It is not too much to hope that the time will come when human labor of the roughest kind will be entirely done away with. In the past, when labor was performed by slaves or serfs, leisure was enjoyed only by the few. But when machinery superseded human labor, leisure became possible for the many. The work-day was gradually shortened; holidays were more frequent; and vacations more general. Opportunities for recreation and culture were now possible to many who, in the past, were sunk in misery and ignorance. Nature, before which man once crouched in terror and helplessness, was now his willing slave, performing the most gigantic tasks at his bidding. By harnessing Nature great engineering enterprises became possible. Lofty mountains like the Alps were tunneled; suspension bridges spanned wide rivers; oceans were connected by great canals like the Suez and Panama; the continents of Europe and Asia were united by the trans-Siberian railway; ancient rivers like the Nile were made entirely navigable. Nothing seemed to bar the progress of man, who removed with the utmost ease obstacles on land and water that once appeared insuperable.

Widespread leisure gave new opportunities for recreation. Modern athletics is indirectly an outcome of the Industrial Revolution.

Before its advent, outdoor sports, baseball, cricket, golf, and
tennis, were virtually non-existent. The average man
got his exercise through labor on the farm and in the
workshop; his chief recreation was dancing in the open air on
holidays. With the coming of the machine the masses were cooped
up for long hours in factory, mine, and office, engaged in tasks
which were enervating, and even stupefying. By doing one thing
only the laborer exercised only one set of muscles, not his whole
body. Athletic sports were introduced and popularized first, naturally enough, in England, whence they spread to other industrialized nations. Under conditions which compelled men to work in
offices and factories and to live in crowded cities, outdoor exercise
became essential to health.

Popular recreation

The Industrial Revolution was a revolution in consumption as
well as in production. Machine-made goods were very cheap,
which stimulated the demand for them. Larger production necessitated larger consumption, and even a
poor man was now able to buy articles which, at one
time, only the rich could afford, such as a muslin shirt, a steel
pocketknife, a book, or a carpet. Luxuries became necessities. A
new system of selling appeared with the establishment of "stores."
Hitherto, goods had been sold at bazaars on market days, in the
workshops of artisans, or by wandering peddlers. The store was a
convenient method of distributing large quantities of goods of all
sorts easily and quickly. A higher standard of living for the masses
was the outcome of these changes.

Rise in the standard of living

The effects of the Industrial Revolution upon politics were far-
reaching. It brought into the political arena the capitalists and
workingmen, who immediately began to clamor for
political power, which up to this time had been enjoyed almost exclusively by the landed aristocracy. Democracy,
hitherto an idea advocated by philosophers, became the rallying
cry of the new classes who gave it the powerful support of wealth
and numbers. The nineteenth century witnessed an almost continuous struggle to break down the power of aristocracy and absolute monarchy, which in many countries finally terminated in
the triumph of democracy. Nationalism, too, received a great impetus as a result of the Industrial Revolution. The railways,
steamboats, telegraphs, and telephones were like a network of
veins and arteries that carried the blood of the nation pulsating

Advance of democracy

to the farthest part of the body. The economic interests of the nation, hitherto scattered in different districts, were now concentrated by means of the factory; and this concentration gave a powerful momentum to greater nationalism. The loosely knit agricultural nation, with its special privileges to localities, classes, and religions, controlled by a landed aristocracy and headed by an absolute monarch, gave place to a firmly knit industrial nation, with uniform laws for all citizens, controlled by the industrial classes and governed by parliaments. Old nations like France and England lost their provincial differences in customs, habits, laws, and speech. Common economic interests at last gave a solid foundation to the national aspirations of both Germans and Italians, divided for so many centuries, and led them to unite, each into a common fatherland.

Advance of nationalism

If nationalism was intensified, so was internationalism. The new means of transportation carried not only goods, but also people and ideas. A "migratory society" was a novel feature of modern industrialism. Large numbers were constantly changing their place of abode, from country to country, from the rural districts to the city, from city to city, even from neighborhood to neighborhood, always in search of better opportunities to make a living. Foreign travel increased at an astonishing rate, and many were enabled to visit foreign lands who formerly had never set foot outside of their own region. An inevitable result was a better understanding among the nations of the world of one another's ideals and institutions. The vast international trade that grew up as a result of the Industrial Revolution tended more and more to bind the various nations into a common economic life, each dependent for its very existence upon the other. No nation could now be self-sufficient.

Advance of internationalism

The rate of human progress was greatly accelerated by the Industrial Revolution. Formerly changes took place so slowly that many people were not aware that they had taken place at all. The only noticeable changes were those produced by invasions of hostile armies, by pestilential diseases, or by natural calamities like earthquakes and fires. Hence, conservatism was the accepted principle; it meant the conservation of civilization. Moreover, an agricultural society is static; communication is slow and arduous; and it is consequently difficult to spread new ideas. As long as the basis of a people's social

Increase in rate of progress

life remains unchanged, their ideas remain likewise unchanged. But an industrial society is dynamic. A factory appears in an isolated hamlet, and immediately a bustling city comes into being, with railways, telegraphs, telephones, and newspapers connecting it with the rest of the world. As a result, old habits are broken up; new relations are established; and sometimes a new population appears in the place of the old. The "good old times" pass quickly, and new traditions take root; progress becomes the law of life, and backward communities soon decay and die.

In the Age of Machinery there has appeared a new politics, a new history, and even new subjects of study such as economics, political New sub-   science, and sociology. History, particularly, is being jects of   explained from new points of view. Instead of de-study   scribing battles, sieges, treaties, dynasties, constitutions, and political parties almost exclusively, it concerns itself also with explaining how social and economic conditions influence the life and character of a people. These forces, although they have always been influential in moulding the destinies of nations, were lost sight of in the study of the more sensational happenings of war and politics. But the Industrial Revolution has made these forces visible. We see more clearly to-day how economic changes affect political development; how weak, divided, agricultural Germany became strong, united, industrial Germany; how the British system of government has been modified as a result of social and economic changes; how semi-agricultural, semi-industrial France has oscillated between revolution and reaction; and how the American railway, more than the Federal Constitution, has made of the United States a "more perfect Union."[1]

REFERENCES

GENERAL:

J. B. Williams, *Guide to the Printed Materials for English Social and Economic History, 1750–1850*, 2 vols. (1926), a bibliography for advanced students; A. E. Bland, P. A. Brown, and R. H. Tawney (eds.), *English Economic History, Select Documents* (1914), source book for period 1660–1846; W. Bowden, *Industrial Society in England Towards the End of the Eighteenth Century* (1925), describes eve of the Industrial Revolution, view that the change benefited the working classes; L. W. Moffit, *England on the Eve of the Industrial Revolution* (1925), descriptive survey of agri-

[1] For a description of the Industrial Revolution in Germany, see pp. 107–08; in France, pp. 82–84; in Russia, pp. 451–53; and of the new Industrial Revolution, see Chapter XXVII.

cultural and industrial methods; P. Mantoux, *The Industrial Revolution in the Eighteenth Century*, trans. from the French (1927), the best book on the subject, scholarly and well written; A. Toynbee, *Lectures on the Industrial Revolution* (ed. 1919), a pioneer work on the subject, first published in 1884 and still good; F. Salomon, *William Pitt*, 2 vols. (1901–06), a German biography which contains excellent chapters on the industrial changes; L. C. A. Knowles, *The Industrial and Commercial Revolutions in Great Britain during the Nineteenth Century* (ed. 1926), well organized, emphasizes the importance of transportation; J. L. and B. Hammond, *The Skilled Labourer 1760–1832* (ed. 1926), *The Town Labourer, 1760–1832* (ed. 1925), and *The Rise of Modern Industry* (1925), scholarly, brilliantly written, humanitarian in viewpoint; H. de B. Gibbins, *Industry in England* (ed. 1910), a popular account; A. P. Usher, *An Introduction to the Industrial History of England* (1920) emphasizes engineering aspects, contains excellent bibliography; and H. Sée, *Modern Capitalism, Its Origin and Evolution*, translated from the French (1928) describes Commercial Revolution and old Colonial system.

INVENTIONS AND INDUSTRIES:

E. W. Byrn, *The Progress of Invention in the Nineteenth Century* (1900); R. H. Thurston, *History of the Growth of the Steam Engine* (ed. 1902); B. A. Fiske, *Invention, the Master-Key to Progress* (1921); S. Smiles, *Lives of the Engineers*, 5 vols. (ed. 1874), contains good popular biographies of Watt and Stephenson; E. A. Pratt, *A History of Inland Transportation and Communication in England* (1909); A. W. Kirkaldy and A. D. Evans, *The History and Economics of Transport* (1915); C. Jones, *British Merchant Shipping* (1925); L. S. Wood and A. Wilmore, *The Romance of the Cotton Industry in England* (1927); G. W. Morris and L. S. Wood, *The Golden Fleece* (1922); T. S. Ashton, *Iron and Steel in the Industrial Revolution* (1924).

RESULTS:

J. A. Hobson, *The Evolution of Modern Capitalism: a Study of Machine Production* (ed. 1926), a comprehensive study of the effects of modern industrialism; W. Sombart, *Der moderne Kapitalismus*, 3 vols. (ed. 1928), a synthetic treatment of the origin and methods of capitalistic production; by the same author, *The Quintessence of Capitalism*, trans. from the German (1915), a social psychological study of business and of the middle classes; L. Stephen, *The English Utilitarians* (1900), contains fine descriptions of Bentham and Mill; C. Gide and C. Rist, *A History of Economic Doctrines from the Time of the Physiocrats*, trans. from the French (1915), an excellent study of social and economic theories; L. C. Marshall (ed.), *Industrial Society*, 3 vols. (ed. 1930). Informing articles on every phase of modern industrialism may be found in R. H. I. Palgrave (editor), *Dictionary of Political Economy* (1910–13), and in L. Elster and others (editors), *Handwörterbuch der Staatswissenschaft* (ed. 1923–28).

ADDITIONAL REFERENCES

I. Pinchbeck, *Women Workers and the Industrial Revolution* (1930); W. J. Warner, *The Wesleyan Movement in the Industrial Revolution* (1930); A. P. Usher, *A History of Mechanical Inventions* (1929); J. Lord, *Capitalism and Steam Power (1750–1800)* (1923); N. S. B. Gras, *Industrial Evolution* (1930); W. Bowden, *The Industrial Revolution* (1928); E Lipson, *Europe in the Nineteenth and Twentieth Centuries, 1815–1939* (1941); C. Day, *Economic Development in Europe* (1942); E. L. Bogart, *Economic History of Europe, 1760–1939* (1942).

For additional titles consult the bibliography at the end of Chapter IX.

PART 1
NATIONALISM AND DEMOCRACY
1815–1870

PART I

NATIONALISM AND DEMOCRACY
1815-1870

THE vast changes introduced by the French and Industrial Revolutions were the prelude to the history of Europe in the nineteenth century. During the period 1815-48, known as the Restoration, an epic struggle took place between the "reactionaries" and the "liberals" for the control of society and government. The reactionaries, chiefly aristocrats and clergy, supported the monarchs restored by the Congress of Vienna, who returned full of hatred for the French Revolution. However, those in power realized that they could not restore the Old Régime and contented themselves in maintaining the system established by the Congress and in fostering aristocratic ideals and manners. Indirectly they were aided by the Romantic movement in literature which glorified ancient loyalties, and by the religious revival which, once more, cast the spell of the altar upon the throne.

Opposed to the reactionaries were the liberals, who championed the principles of the French Revolution. The liberals came almost exclusively from the bourgeois class whose ranks were now augmented by the industrial capitalists. After 1815 the Industrial Revolution spread from England to the Continent, and there appeared a powerful group of wealthy capitalists who were hostile to the pretensions of divine-right kings and privileged aristocrats. Liberalism was the rising hope of those who wished to free their country from tyranny, foreign or domestic, from religious intolerance, from censorship, and from economic restrictions. It inspired the popular movements for nationalism that swept over western Europe. Divided peoples, such as the Germans and the Italians, longed to be united; and subject peoples, such as those in Austria, Russia, and Turkey, longed to be free and independent. Democracy was then closely identified with nationalism; both ideas were inspired by the movement for political freedom.

Although liberalism was a creed of progress, its votaries, the bourgeois, were progressive only when confronted by their enemy from above, the aristocrats. When confronted by their enemy from below, the working class, the bourgeois often made common cause with the aristocrats.   In their struggle for political democracy and social reform the working class generally found the bourgeois strongly opposed to " reform " which they so vehemently espoused when it suited their interests.

CHAPTER IV

RESTORATION AND REACTION

THE CONGRESS OF VIENNA
(*September*, 1814 — *June*, 1815)

AFTER the abdication of Napoleon a great international congress
was called at Vienna to settle the conflicting claims of dynasties
and nations to the parts of the Napoleonic Empire. Europe
The Congress of Vienna was a truly European assem- assembles
bly, as it contained representatives from every nation at Vienna
in Europe except Turkey. It was not a deliberative body, as was
the Conference of Paris in 1919, with power to make decisions binding upon the members. Vienna was really a convenient meeting-
place for the diplomats of Europe to which they came to make
arrangements with one another and to agree upon general policies.
It was a meeting of Europe "without distances," as Metternich said.

The Big Five, Russia, England, Austria, Prussia, and France,
dominated the conferences. The leading delegates were Tsar
Alexander I, liberal-minded but confused; Lord Castle- Delegates
reagh, calm and practical, the very embodiment of reaction-
traditional English statesmanship; Metternich, the naries
master mind of the old dynastic diplomacy; Talleyrand, astute and
unscrupulous, yet passionately seeking the welfare of France. All
regarded the French Revolution as a "bad dream" and aimed to
bring about a "restoration" of the king to his divine-right throne,
the lord to his privileges, the priest to his dominance over the
minds of men, and the people to their burdens.

In partitioning the Napoleonic Empire the Congress paid more
regard to dynastic than to national claims. It recognized the
principle of "legitimacy," the prior right of the old Regard for
dynasties to govern their former subjects, irrespective "legiti-
of the wishes of the latter or of the claims of the mon- macy"
archs set up by Napoleon. Wherever possible the old dynasties
were restored,[1] and the old rulers came back as absolute monarchs by divine right.

---

[1] Only one Napoleonic king, Bernadotte of Sweden, was allowed to keep his
throne because he had helped the Allies against Napoleon.

It was also the intention of the Congress to restore the map of Europe as it was in 1789. But so many changes had taken place Disregard of that it was impossible to do so. Nationalism had been nationalism the potent cause of the defeat of Napoleon; nevertheless, the Congress disregarded it in making the new boundaries of Europe. Territories were assigned to princes without consulting the inhabitants, quite in the eighteenth-century manner.

Each of the great powers demanded a share of the spoils and a recognition of what they had acquired during the Napoleonic Wars. Gains of Russia received most of the Grand Duchy of Warsaw, Russia thereby enlarging her Polish possessions; [1] now her western frontier was thrust almost into central Europe. She had acquired Finland from Sweden, and Bessarabia from Turkey; and these acquisitions were recognized by the Congress.

Austria made great gains in territory. She received the lands bordering on the eastern coast of the Adriatic and Lombardy-Gains of Venetia, the latter as a compensation for giving up Austria Belgium, which she no longer desired. She shared in the redivision of Poland. Austria's population was now more heterogeneous than ever; Italians were added to the many nationalities already within her borders.

Prussia, who had all but disappeared as a result of her crushing defeat by Napoleon, was now considerably strengthened. She re-Gains of covered her former territory; in addition, she received Prussia about half of Saxony, Pomerania from Sweden, and lands in the Rhine region. Prussia emerged from the Congress strong enough to be a rival of Austria for the control of Germany.

England, following her traditional policy, asked for colonies and strategic islands. She received Cape Colony and Ceylon from Gains of Holland; the island of Helgoland from Denmark; England Malta and the Ionian islands in the Mediterranean; and Trinidad and Tobago near the mouth of the Orinoco River. During the Napoleonic Wars England had financed the campaigns of the Allies through subsidies and loans. When peace came, she was the creditor of the Allied nations. However, the debts were not paid in full; Austria, England's chief debtor, liquidated her debt in 1824 by paying about one eighth of the amount due.

The small nations were seriously affected by the arrangements

[1] The part that Russia received was later called "Congress" Poland; it was taken in part from the Polish territories of Prussia and Austria.

of the Congress. Denmark had sided with Napoleon and Sweden with the Allies. To punish the one and reward the other, Norway, contrary to her wishes, was taken from Denmark and given to Sweden; to the latter the addition of Norway was a compensation for the loss of Finland to Russia. The Austrian Netherlands (Belgium), much against their will, were incorporated with Holland in order to form a strong bulwark against possible French aggression. *Norway given to Sweden, Belgium to Holland*

France escaped with her national life at the cost of her empire. She was deprived of all the territory that she had gained since 1791; she was required to pay an indemnity of $140,000,000, and to support an army of occupation. The treatment of France by the Allies was generous, considering the fact that she had been the disturber of the peace of Europe for a quarter of a century. It was partly due to Talleyrand's clever diplomacy in distracting the attention of the Allies from France by pitting one power against the other in their quarrels about territory. However, the terms were deliberately made moderate. In the opinion of Castlereagh "no arrangement could be wise that carried ruin to one of the countries between which it was concluded." Tsar Alexander favored generous treatment of France on the ground that the Allies had warred against Napoleon, not against the French people. *Losses of France*

Two "geographic expressions," Germany and Italy, issued from the Congress. A crowd of exiled German princelings came to Vienna demanding to be restored on the ground of "legitimacy." But the larger states, like Prussia, Bavaria, and Württemberg, which had profited by the suppression of their small neighbors, successfully opposed them; therefore, the great consolidation effected in Germany by Napoleon was allowed to remain virtually undisturbed. Instead of the Holy Roman Empire, with its hundreds of tiny states, there was now organized the German Confederation consisting of only thirty-eight states. *The German Confederation*

The other "geographical expression," Italy, fared badly at the hands of the Congress. The country was once more broken up into petty states, and the exiled rulers were restored to their thrones. In the south was erected the Kingdom of the Two Sicilies, which included the island of Sicily and the mainland called Naples; the States of the Church were once more *Italy redivided* put under the rule of the Pope; the duchies of Parma and Modena and the Grand Duchy of Tuscany were reëstablished. In the north, the Kingdom of Sardinia, consisting of the island of Sardinia and the mainland called Piedmont, was restored and enlarged by the addition of Genoa. Lombardy-Venetia was given to Austria, thereby adding a foreign complication to the problem of unifying Italy.

Besides restoring "legitimate" kings and rearranging boundaries the Congress gave some attention to matters of international well-being. The slave trade was condemned as being contrary to the principles of civilization and of humanity; and it was abolished by some of the powers. Freedom of navigation of international rivers, such as the Danube and the Rhine, was advocated. Switzerland was neutralized, and her independence guaranteed.

Progressive measures of the Congress

At best, the Europe of the Restoration was but a phantom of its former self. Many of the changes inaugurated by the French Revolution and by Napoleon could not be abolished without a violent wrench of the entire social system, and so were allowed to remain. The Holy Roman Empire was gone, the feudal spirit was gone, and gone was the old authority of the Church. Divine right of kings was fervently preached, but the generation that had seen so many kings hurled from their thrones during the Revolutionary and Napoleonic periods found it difficult to believe in a divine sanction of governments that could be so easily overturned. Absolute monarchy, feared for ages as all-powerful, had but to show its weakness to become ridiculous. Although Napoleon had preached divine right, he did more to discredit the doctrine than even the French Revolution. For the first time, mankind saw in the bright light of the nineteenth century how kings were made and unmade by force of arms. And now that its moral authority was gone, absolutism could maintain itself only by resorting to brute force. Sullen obedience had succeeded loyal devotion among the masses of Europe.

Failure of the Restoration

THE HOLY ALLIANCE

A spirit of religious conservatism characterized the Restoration period. The rationalistic philosophy of the eighteenth century, with its disbelief in revealed religion, was now relegated to the background by a revival of religious enthusiasm which found expression both in literature and in politics. Chateaubriand's great work, *The Genius of Christianity*, is an eloquent tribute to the ideals of the Christian faith and to its influence on character and civilization. In Joseph de Maistre's *The Pope* the ideal of the supremacy of the Church in all matters, temporal as well as spiritual, is advocated with great ability and learning.

Religious revival

But the most remarkable expression of the religious revival was the formation of the Holy Alliance. It was initiated by the deeply religious Tsar Alexander I, who saw in the French Revolution and Napoleon the hand of God that had smitten the kings because they had not ruled in the spirit of Christianity. In 1815 the monarchs of Russia, Austria, and Prussia issued a manifesto to an astonished world in which they declared their belief in the "solemn truths taught by the religion of God, our Saviour," and pledged themselves "to take for their sole guide the precepts of that Holy Religion, namely, the precepts of Justice, Christian Charity, and Peace" which could remedy all human imperfections. It was their intention, they solemnly averred, to be fathers to their subjects, who were urged "to strengthen themselves every day more and more in the principles and exercise of the duties which the Divine Saviour taught to Mankind." The manifesto was signed by nearly every ruler in Europe, and constitutes a strange document in diplomatic history. A chorus of criticism and ridicule greeted its publication. It was variously described as a "sonorous nothing" and as a "sublime piece of mysticism and nonsense." To many liberals, the Holy Alliance signified a combination of despots who were plotting to make the world safe for autocracy by suppressing democratic movements under cover of religion. The Holy Alliance may be regarded, not as a treaty, but rather as an expression of the state of mind of the restored monarchs regarding the great problems raised by the French Revolution. Once more benevolent despotism prepared to make democracy undesirable by making it needless.

Tsar Alexander initiates the Holy Alliance

The great problem that confronted the statesmen of the Restoration was how to prevent the order established by the Congress of Vienna from being destroyed by revolutionary outbreaks or by the return of the Bonapartes. France, especially, as the home of revolution needed careful watching. A coalition of great powers, known as the Quadruple

The Quadruple Alliance

Alliance, composed of Russia, Austria, Prussia, and England, was organized, in 1815, for the purpose of preserving the "tranquillity of Europe" against a revival of revolution or Napoleonic militarism. Its representatives were to meet periodically to hold a sort of political inquest on the state of Europe and to proceed "to the examination of the measures which, at any of these periods, shall be judged most salutary for the repose and prosperity of the peoples." The Allies were convinced that the only way to fight revolutionary movements which, owing to the French Revolution, had become international, was by a compact of the despots pledged to support one another in case of an uprising. If revolution was to be international, so would be repression.

The treaty of the Quadruple Alliance marked a great change in diplomatic methods. There was now to be diplomacy by conference through the periodic congresses. As their chief aim was the prevention of revolution, the Allies favored the doctrine of "intervention." Europe, they declared, was a social and political unit with a uniform system of government and society; hence, an attack on any part of it would be fatal to the whole, therefore the Allies should intervene in the domestic affairs of a nation to defend the existing order. The Alliance had another and more worthy purpose; namely, the maintenance of peace. As the "Concert of Europe" it undertook to settle international disputes and to formulate international policies, and for over a generation peace reigned in Europe. The system of international government in the interest of autocracy became popularly known as the Holy Alliance because the leading members of the latter were also members of the Quadruple Alliance.

For a generation the chief figure on the political stage was the Austrian statesman, Prince Metternich. He became the master spirit of the Restoration period, which was so dominated by his views that it has been called the "Age of Metternich." His advice was eagerly sought by the restored rulers, to whom he became a guide, philosopher, and friend. Metternich was the consistent foe of democracy in any and every form; the system established by the Congress of Vienna was to him almost the last word in political wisdom. He set his face like flint against suggestions of change of any sort. Reformers should be reduced to silence, as "concession will not satisfy but only embolden them in their pretensions to power," he declared. The sum of all evil was

Diplomacy by conference

Metternich (1773–1859)

revolution, "a hydra with open jaws to swallow the social order." Liberty was a malady of which the people must be cured if social health was to continue. Parliamentary government was a "perpetual somersault," which led to a lack of responsibility in both rulers and ruled. Metternich was quite sincerely convinced that an orderly civilization could not exist without a system of absolute monarchy dominated by religious motives. He advised the princes to "maintain religious principles in all their purity, and not to allow the faith to be attacked and morality to be interpreted according to the social contract or according to the visions of foolish sectarians." Like many others of his day, he had been frightened by the violence of the Reign of Terror, and so had confused democracy with terrorism, and even with anarchy. He did not and could not see the great good which the French Revolution had accomplished because he was, above all, a statesman of things as they are. "Let the governments govern, let them maintain the foundations of their institutions both ancient and modern," he declared. This mirror of diplomacy was fully conscious of his importance. "My position is notable in that all attention is centered on that point where I happen to be," he proudly said. Metternich was a devoted servant of the despots, a master of subtle and secret intrigue, and an adroit manipulator of government in the interest of the aristocratic class to which he belonged. However, his place in history is also determined by the fact that he constantly sought to maintain the peace of Europe. Until 1848 his restraining hand prevented wars as well as revolutions and enabled Europe to recover from the Napoleonic Wars.

INTERNATIONAL REPRESSION

No sooner were the restored monarchs on the throne than they faced a determined opposition led by the liberals. As the severe censorship made open agitation impossible the liberals were forced to have recourse to secret methods. Suppression was answered by conspiracy. A remarkable secret organization appeared in southern Italy, called the Carbonari (Italian, charcoal burners), composed of revolutionaries sworn to establish constitutional government. It was organized into sections of twenty members, called *Ventes*, and directed by a central committee. The members were armed and drilled in secret places. So effective were the Carbonari that the organization spread

The Carbonari

throughout Italy and became the model for similar organizations in Spain, Portugal, and France. For a generation the Carbonari terrorized the governments by fomenting uprisings and by assassinating public officials. Its record of violence brought disgrace to the society, and it was superseded by the republican and socialist movements that relied more upon propaganda than upon conspiracy and terrorism.

In 1820, uprisings, organized by the Carbonari, took place in Spain, Portugal, Naples, and Piedmont. The kings were compelled to flee or to grant constitutions. This situation aroused the Holy Alliance. A congress of the great powers met in Troppau, in 1820, to consider the situation in Naples where the Carbonari were in control. Russia and Austria urged that the powers should intervene to restore the King of Naples. England, however, opposed intervention, and virtually withdrew from the Quadruple Alliance. Castlereagh, who directed English foreign affairs, issued a famous statement of England's foreign policy. He declared that she had entered the Alliance in order to maintain the boundaries established by the treaty of Vienna, not to intervene in domestic affairs of the nations; and that England herself, having a representative system of government, could not consistently act according to the principle of intervention. England's "liberalism" in this matter was really a return to her historic policy of isolation, now that the Continent was no longer in danger of being dominated by an aggressive power. She wished, above all else, to develop her industry which was beginning to recover from the effects of the Napoleonic Wars. "Be yours the glory of a victory followed by disaster and ruin, be ours the inglorious traffic of industry and an ever increasing prosperity," said Canning, the successor of Castlereagh, to the French ambassador who urged him to intervene in Spain.

England leaves the Quadruple Alliance

Another congress of the powers was held in Laibach, in 1821, which decided on intervention. One Austrian army marched into Naples and restored Ferdinand. Another Austrian army helped to overthrow the revolutionists in Piedmont. A congress, held in Verona, in 1822, decided upon intervention in Spain. A French army invaded Spain and suppressed the constitution.[1] Behind each tyrant now loomed the

Intervention in Naples and Spain

---

[1] The details of the revolutionary movements of 1820 are given in following chapters.

Holy Alliance ready to set in motion international armies to maintain him on the throne.

During the rebellion in Spain the South American colonies had declared their independence. It was feared that the Holy Alliance would extend its activities to the New World by suppressing the new republics. In order to forestall possible intervention the United States, with the encouragement of England, came to the side of the South American republics. In 1823, President Monroe issued a paper which became famous as the Monroe Doctrine. He declared that the "political system of the allied powers is essentially different in this respect from that of America . . . that we should consider any attempt on their part to extend their system to any portion of this hemisphere as dangerous to our peace and safety. With the existing colonies and dependencies of any European power we have not interfered and shall not interfere. But with the governments who have declared their independence and maintained it and whose independence we have on great consideration and on just principles acknowledged, we could not view any interposition for the purpose of oppressing them or controlling in any other manner their destiny by any European power in any other light than as the manifestation of an unfriendly disposition towards the United States." America's bold pronouncement might not have gone unchallenged had not England, who had commercial interests in South America, come to the side of America by recognizing the independence of several of the revolting colonies. The British Foreign Minister, Canning, proudly boasted that he had "called in the New World to redress the balance of the Old."

The Monroe Doctrine

During the revolutionary movement of 1820 an uprising took place in Greece which attracted considerable attention.[1] The desperate struggle of the Greeks against the Turks was watched with great sympathy throughout Europe. The Holy Alliance dared not intervene in favor of the Mohammedan Sultan against the Christian Greeks. On the contrary, a growing sentiment in Europe favored intervention in *behalf* of the rebels. Russia saw an opportunity in the Greek uprising to attack Turkey and made ready to intervene. England also decided to intervene, at the same time keeping an eye on Russia to see that she did not seize Constantinople. In 1827, Russia, England, and

Greek independence

[1] See page 161.

France compelled the Sultan to recognize the independence of Greece (1829).

The outcome of the revolutionary movement of 1820 was a distinct triumph for the Holy Alliance. The first effort of liberalism to establish constitutional government failed chiefly because of intervention. Nevertheless, the despots were uneasy. For the first time they were confronted by an international, liberal movement that was well organized and was supported by many from the well-to-do classes. Suppression merely raised up more enemies of the Metternich System.

THE UPRISINGS IN 1830

A decade later, there took place another general uprising against the Metternich System. It began in July, 1830, in Paris, where the Bourbon dynasty was overturned, and the liberal Louis Philippe was made king.[1] The success of the revolt in Paris inspired a revolutionary movement in Europe that had far more important results than that of 1820. Uprisings took place in central Italy, but they were quickly suppressed by Austrian armies. The movement was more successful in Germany where several of the smaller states succeeded in gaining constitutions. Discontent in England gained a great momentum, and the outcome was the Reform Bill of 1832 which will be described later. Revolution raged with especial violence in two small, but significant, countries, Belgium and Poland. In 1815, "Congress" Poland had been organized as a kingdom with the Tsar of Russia as king. The Poles enjoyed a considerable degree of self-government, but they longed for complete independence. In 1831 the Poles rose against Tsar Nicholas I, but they were ruthlessly suppressed.[2]

At the other end of Europe, in Belgium, another uprising was taking place. Like the other unions arranged by the diplomats of **Differences between the Belgians and the Dutch** the Congress of Vienna, the union between Holland and Belgium proved unhappy. There were sharp differences between them which were all the more exasperating to the Belgians because they occupied an inferior position in the union. Chief among these differences was religion. In the main, the Dutch were Protestant, belonging to the rigid Calvinist sect, while the Belgians were intensely Catholic.

[1] See page 76.

[2] For details of the Polish rebellion see page 171.

Economically the Dutch were chiefly seafaring and trading people, whereas the Belgians were agricultural and industrial. Although of similar racial origin their traditions and culture were different. The Belgians, many of whom were French-speaking, looked to France for cultural inspiration. The Dutch, however, were influenced by German culture.

King William I was determined to subordinate his Belgian to his Dutch subjects. He imposed upon them Dutch officials, Dutch laws, and Dutch as the official language. There was *The Belgian* intense feeling in Belgium, and when news came that *Revolution* barricades had gone up in the streets of Paris, barricades went up in the streets of Brussels. The city was soon in the hands of the revolutionists who proclaimed the independence of Belgium.

King William appealed to the powers on the ground that the Belgian Revolution violated the Treaty of Vienna in two ways: it flouted the "legitimate" rights of the House of *Russia and* Orange and it undid the territorial arrangements of *Austria not* the treaty. But the international situation favored *in a position* the Belgians. Russia was engaged in suppressing the *to intervene* uprising in Poland. Austria was likewise engaged in Italy. France was only too eager to undo the Treaty of Vienna; moreover, Louis Philippe, who was eager for popularity, openly sided with the Belgians. England was not opposed to the independence of Belgium, provided the latter could be turned into a bulwark against France.

In 1831 a national assembly met in Brussels and chose Prince Leopold of Saxe-Coburg as Leopold I, King of the Belgians. This choice was the outcome of a treaty with the powers, *France and* but King William refused to accept it. A French army *England aid* and an English fleet now joined the Belgians, and the *the Belgians* Dutch were forced to acknowledge the independence of Belgium.

A new question arose, however: what was to be the status of the new state whose strategic position was all-important? *Belgium* was a "pistol pointing at the heart of England," a *Neutraliza-* road into France from Germany, and a road into Ger- *tion of* many from France. England was particularly inter- *Belguim* ested in the question because she wanted a bulwark against an aggressive France. An important treaty was signed in 1839 by England, Austria, Prussia, Russia, France and Belgium which declared that Belgium was to be a "perpetually neutral state" whose territory was guaranteed in that the powers agreed to defend her against aggression. Belgium also agreed not to ally herself with any other nation and to defend her neutrality against invasion.

For centuries Belgium had been the battle-ground of Europe. This choice morsel, with its fine harbors and extensive manufac-

Favorable position of Belgians

tures, had been coveted by the nations of Europe. At various times Spain, Austria, France, and Holland had possessed it. Now, in the interest of European peace, it was decided that Belgium should belong to herself; and for the first time in all her history she became an independent nation. The new kingdom was given a peculiarly advantageous position in the state system of Europe; not only was her existence recognized like that of any other nation, but her frontiers were protected by the powers. The former battle-ground was to be forever at peace and she therefore need not enter into alliances in order to protect herself against aggression. Europe was to be her protector.

The Metternich System emerged seriously damaged from the uprisings of 1830. The independence of Belgium was the first

Partial dis- ruption of Metternich System

violation of the Treaty of Vienna. The principle of legitimacy was repudiated by the choice of Louis Philippe and of Leopold I. Revolution had triumphed in spite of the Holy Alliance. Democracy had made great strides in France, in Belgium, and in England. Rifts appeared in the Holy Alliance which seriously interfered with the policy of repression. England and France refused to coöperate with the reactionary powers. But the citadels of reaction, Austria and Prussia, were as yet undisturbed by revolutionary storms. Therefore the Metternich System, though badly shaken, was still intact.

REFERENCES

GENERAL:

   Although the number of books treating of special countries, of special periods, and of special aspects is large, the number of general histories of modern Europe is small. Chief among these are two large, coöperative histories, one, English, the *Cambridge Modern History*, edited by Lord Acton; and the other, French, *Histoire générale du IVe siècle à nos jours*, edited by E. Lavisse and A. Rambaud. Both are informing, accurate, and thorough. The various chapters are written by different historians, some of them distinguished scholars in their special fields. But the quality of the work throughout is uneven; and there is a lack of unity almost inescapable from a scholarly enterprise of this character. Of the two, the *Cambridge Modern History* is more narrowly political than the *Histoire générale;* the latter contains many excellent chapters on social and cultural matters. The volumes in the *Cambridge Modern History* that deal with the nineteenth century are vol. x, "The Restoration" (1814–48), vol. xi, "The Growth of Nationalities" (1848–70), and vol. xii, "The Latest Age" (1870–1900). The volumes in the *Histoire générale* covering the same period are vol. x, *Les monarchies constitutionnelles* (1814–48), vol. xi, *Révolution et Guerres nationales* (1848–70), and vol. xii, *Le Monde contemporain* (1870–1900). A. Stern, *Geschichte Europas seit den Verträgen von 1815 bis zum Frankfurter Frieden von 1871*, 10 vols. (1894–1924), is the best general history of the period, scholarly and impartial, chiefly political and diplomatic; C. Seignobos, *A Political History of Europe Since 1814*, translated from the French (1900), a political history, valuable chiefly for chapters on religious and radical movements; on diplomacy; A. Debidour, *Histoire diplomatique de l'Europe, 1814–1914*, 4 vols. (1891–1917); F. M. Anderson and A. S. Hershey, *Handbook for the Diplomatic History of Europe, Asia and Africa, 1870–1914* (1918), a "case book"; J. H. Rose, *The Development of the European Nations, 1870–1900*, 2 vols. (1916); W. A. Phillips, *Modern Europe, 1815–1899* (ed. 1902), valuable for diplomacy up to 1878; G. P. Gooch, *History of Modern Europe, 1878–1919* (1923), best diplomatic history of the period; Sir E. Hertslet, *The Map of Europe by Treaty since 1814*, 4 vols. (1875–91), indispensable source book of important treaties; and P. Albin, *Les grands traités politiques* (1932), texts of important treaties from 1815 to 1912; constitutional, F. A. Ogg, *The Governments of Europe* (ed. 1913); W. F. Dodd (ed.), *Modern Constitutions*, 2 vols. (1909), texts of constitutions before the World War; social and economic; F. A. Ogg, *Social Progress in Contemporary Europe* (1912) and *Economic Development of Modern Europe* (1917), reliable and informative; M. M. Knight, H. E. Barnes, and F. Flugel, *Economic History of Europe in Modern Times* (1928), good survey; L. K. Frankel and M. M. Dawson, *Workingmen's Insurance in Europe* (1910); P. Sandiford (ed.), *Comparative Education* (1919), articles on popular education in the United States, Canada, England, Germany, France, and Denmark.

THE RESTORATION:

For the best general account consult A. Stern, *Geschichte Europas*, vol. ii, chaps. v, vi, ix, xi, and xii. On the Congress of Vienna: C. K. Webster, *The Congress of Vienna* (1919), and C. D. Hazen, *Europe Since 1815* (ed. 1910), chap. i. On the Holy Alliance: W. A. Phillips, *The Confederation of Europe* (1914), study of Alliance from point of view of internationalism, best on the subject; R. Muir, *Nationalism and Internationalism* (1917); G. B. Malleson, *Life of Prince Metternich* (1895); *Memoirs of the Prince de Talleyrand*, translated from the French (1891–92); H. Temperley, *The Foreign Policy of Canning* (1925); C. K. Webster, *The Foreign Policy of Castlereagh, 1815–1822* (1925), a defense of the English diplomat; W. P. Cresson, *Diplomatic Portraits* (1923), a study of the Monroe Doctrine, contains excellent pen pictures of the diplomats of the Restoration;

D. Perkins, *The Monroe Doctrine* (1928), the latest and best study of the subject; E. C. Corti, *The Rise of the House of Rothschild,* translated from the German (1928), history of the famous banking family, describes the financial side of the Restoration; A. Sorel, *Essais d'histoire et de critique* (1884), estimates of Metternich and Talleyrand by a famous historian of European diplomacy.

ADDITIONAL REFERENCES

GENERAL:

J. F. Scott and A. Baltzly, *Readings in European History, 1815–1928* (1930), excellent selection; B. Birnie, *An Economic History of Modern Europe, 1760–1930* (1930); L. C. A. Knowles, *Economic Development in the Nineteenth Century* (1932); H. von Srbik, *Metternich der Staatsmann und der Mensch* (1925); A. Cecil, *Metternich* (1933); B. Croce, *History of Europe in the Nineteenth Century* (1933); G. Weill, *L'Éveil des Nationalités et le mouvement libéral (1815–1848)* (1930); L. Cahen, *Les Débuts du Monde Contemporain, 1789–1848* (1932); F. B. Artz, *Reaction and Revolution: 1814–1832* (1934); R. C. Binkley, *Realism and Nationalism: 1852–1871* (1935); F. A. Ogg, *European Governments and Politics* (1934); E. L. Woodward, *War and Peace in Europe, 1815–1870* (1931); H. E. Barnes, *An Economic History of the Western World* (1937); W. Bowden, M. Karpovich, and A. P. Usher, *An Economic History of Europe Since 1750* (1937); C P. Jones and A. L. Poole, *A Hundred Years of Economic Development* (1939).

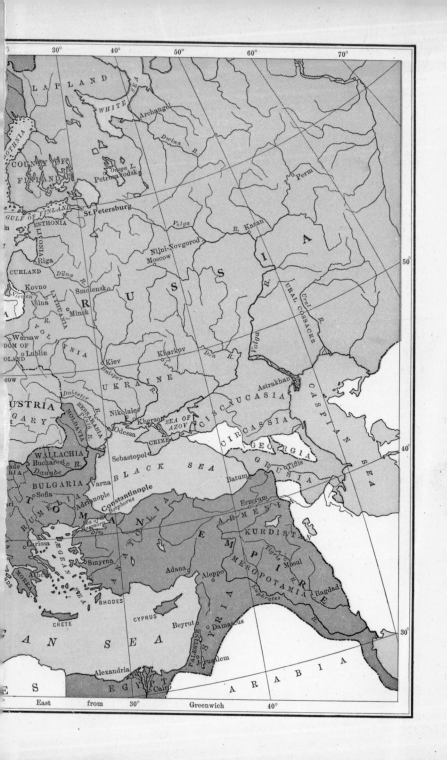

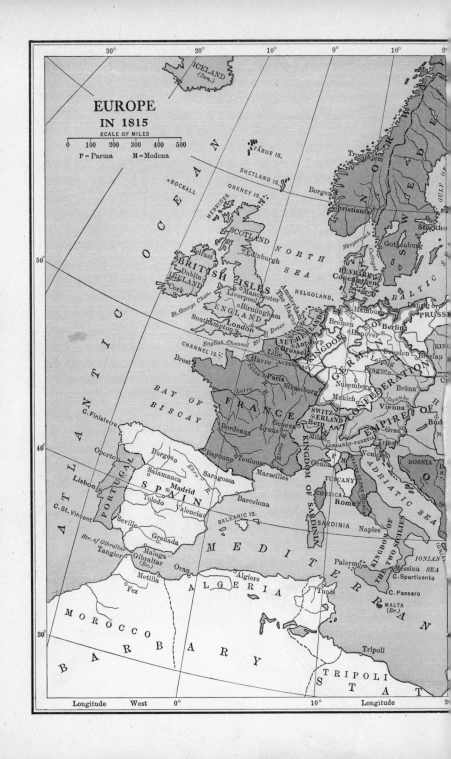

EUROPE
IN 1815

SCALE OF MILES

0   100   200   300   400   500

P = Parma   M = Modena

among many diverse forms of government and the civil institutions of Christian states." But to the French Catholics monarchy meant protection and republic persecution; hence, they rallied to the former.

To combat the spirit of innovation engendered by the French Revolution there existed the tradition of military glory associated with the name of Napoleon. Frenchmen could not *The military* easily forget the time when the tricolor had waved *tradition* triumphantly on the great battle-fields of modern times. It needed but a phrase, a book, a "legend" to rekindle in France the desire for military conquest. "The man on horseback" remained an appealing figure to the imagination of Frenchmen despite his having frequently trod on principles very dear to them.

REIGN OF LOUIS XVIII

After the battle of Waterloo the Allies once more triumphantly entered Paris, "carrying the Bourbons in their baggage." Louis XVIII [1] was reseated on the throne, and, in order to *The Charte* win the people to the new order, he granted a *charte*, or charter establishing constitutional government. According to its provisions full executive authority was lodged in the king; he could appoint and dismiss all public officials including the cabinet, direct foreign policies, propose laws, and dissolve parliament. There was also established a legislature of two houses. Birth, age, and property were to insure conservatism in the new parliament. The upper house consisted of aristocrats, most of whom were appointed by the King; and the Chamber was elected by wealthy citizens at least thirty years old. Suffrage restrictions were so great that only one man in seventy had the privilege of voting. An aristocratic parliament, hardened by the spirit of Bourbon despotism, was the government instituted by the returned monarch.

Louis XVIII made more substantial concessions in the domain of civil liberty. The *charte* established equality of *Bourbons ac-* all before the law irrespective of rank, the right of *cept changes* all citizens to enter the public service in any capac- *made by the* ity, freedom of speech and of the press, religious free- *Revolution* dom, and protection against arbitrary arrest. These *Napoleon* Revolutionary principles, maintained by the restored Bourbons, did

[1] In order to maintain the continuity of the Bourbon dynasty, the son of Louis XVI, who had died during the Revolution, was declared to be Louis XVII.

much to reconcile many to their return. Even more important was the attitude of Louis XVIII toward the political and social changes made by the Revolution and by Napoleon. He accepted nearly all of them: the abolition of feudalism, the confiscation of Church and noble property, the Concordat, and the Napoleonic Code. Especially did he maintain Napoleon's administrative systems, both local and national. "When the Bourbons return they would do well to sleep in my bed; it is very well made," the ex-Emperor had remarked. Louis realized that all attempts to restore the Old Régime would prove futile; it would have resulted in a dislocation of French society which had now become firmly knit by the life of a generation born and reared under the new régime.

The Bourbons had been restored by the armies of the Allies, not by the will of the French people, and there was sullen resentment against their pretensions among all classes, even among the wealthy. Therefore, in spite of the restricted suffrage, a Chamber hostile to the government might be chosen. Fear of this prompted the government to institute a system of "official" candidates. Stanch royalists were nominated, and every effort was made to elect them by the coercion of voters, patronage, and bribery, which assured a majority in the Chamber on the side of the government.

Control of parliament by king

The spirit of the Old Régime now and then flashed forth. The exiled nobles, the *émigrés*, returned cherishing an undying hatred of democratic principles. They formed an ultra-royalist party, known as the "Ultras," which demanded nothing less than a return to the "good old times." At the head of these reactionaries was a brother of the King, the Count of Artois, a true Bourbon, "who never learned anything and never forgot anything." Thirsting to avenge their sufferings during the Revolution, the *émigrés* organized a "White Terror," so-called because the *fleur-de-lys* [1] of the Bourbons was restored as the national flag. Outrages were committed by bands of royalists against the "Reds" — those who had been prominent in Revolutionary and Napoleonic times. Spies were put on the track of men suspected of disloyalty to the Bourbons. Marshal Ney, who had deserted Louis XVIII for Napoleon during the Hundred Days, was executed.

The "Whites" and "Reds"

Louis, however, did not sympathize with the Ultras. He had

---

[1] This flag consisted of a white field with golden lilies.

been in exile almost a quarter of a century, and, like the English King Charles II, he did not wish "to go on his travels" once more.   Moreover, he was both sick and lazy, and wished to remain quietly on his throne, "the softest of chairs."   France, he knew, was tired of revolutionary "liberty" associated with bloodshed and disorder, and of Napoleonic "glory" associated with exhausting wars; she would, therefore, prefer the quiet of the Restoration, provided it did not arouse too much hostility.

Moderation of Louis XVIII

REIGN OF CHARLES X

Louis died in 1824, and was succeeded by the Count of Artois as Charles X.   The new king was a child of the Old Régime to whom the French Revolution brought bitterness without en- lightenment.   He had returned from exile a sadder but not a wiser man; hence, he was fully determined to restore both the spirit and the institutions of former days.   To Charles a divine-right monarchy was the only legitimate form of govern- ment, an intolerant Church the only true Christianity, and a privi- leged aristocracy the only class worthy of high regard.   His mind was a curious blend of mediocrity and fanaticism, a most detesta- ble combination in the eyes of the French which was bound to arouse bitter opposition and to lead to his eventual overthrow.

Character of Charles X

Charles forthwith proceeded to take steps to restore the Old Régime.   Under his influence a law was passed which aimed to indemnify the nobles whose estates had been confis- cated by the Revolution.   It was inadvisable to raise the large sum necessary by levying additional taxes; therefore, the government proposed a scheme of funding the public debt at a lower rate of interest, and giving the amount saved to the émigrés in the form of annuities.   This "act of justice," as Charles called it, cut into the income of the bondholders, chiefly bourgeois, who thenceforth became more hostile than ever to the régime.

Attempt to indemnify the émigrés

Another step in the attempted Restoration was in the interest of the Catholic Church.   In order "to purify the morals of the age by a system of education based upon Christianity and monarchism," a priest was made head of the state university with its monopolistic control of all public education in France.   Teachers and courses of instruction suspected of "un- soundness" in regard to religion were not tolerated.   The historian,

Influence of the Church

Guizot, and the philosopher, Cousin, were compelled to resign their professorships in the Sorbonne.   Divorce, instituted by Napoleon, was abolished.   Public charities were put under the control of the clergy.   Severe laws were passed against those who attacked the Catholic faith; one law prescribed the death penalty, under certain circumstances, for the profanation of sacred vessels in a church. Charles firmly believed that only an alliance between throne and altar could maintain his régime against revolutionary onslaughts.

The influence of the "priest party" in politics brought forth sharply the issue of clericalism *versus* anti-clericalism.   By clerical-
Clericalism   ism was meant the political activity of the Church in order to influence the State to uphold Catholic prin-
ciples.   The clericals favored the recognition of Catholicism as the State religion, public support of the Church, the forbidding of divorce, religious control of public education and charity, and a religious censorship of books and journals.   As the monarchy favored the Church, the Catholics supported the royalist party so whole-heartedly that "Catholic" and "royalist" became synonymous terms in France.

If clericalism was royalist, anti-clericalism was republican. Ardent champions of the French Revolution, the anti-clericals
Anti-   were inspired by the first French Republic that had
clericalism   warred so ruthlessly against Catholicism and royalism.
They favored separation of Church and State, civil marriage and divorce, secular education, and complete religious equality.   Most of the anti-clericals were Voltaireans, or free-thinkers, and they consequently sought to undermine all religious influences in the country.

However, the French Revolution cast its spell over many devout members of the Church.   Was it possible to reconcile its principles
The Liberal   with Catholic ideals?   A priest, Abbé Lamennais,
Catholics   wrote a number of books that attracted wide atten-
tion.   He pleaded eloquently for the regeneration of Christianity through the separation of Church and State in order to permit the former freely to pursue her divine mission.   Lamennais ardently proclaimed his belief in democracy which, he declared, it was his mission to Christianize.   He gathered about him a group of brilliant Catholics, among them the scholar, Montalembert, and the preacher, Lacordaire, who later became known as "Liberal Cath-
olics."   They championed democratic government, freedom of

speech, and "liberty of teaching," or the equality of Church and State in all educational matters. Lamennais's views aroused great opposition within the Church, and his agitation was condemned by the Pope. He refused to submit, and denounced the existing order as a conspiracy of kings and priests against the people. As he became more and more radical in his politics, he became more and more heretical in his theology. Lamennais finally left the Church and became a popular preacher of Christian socialism.

Charles's reactionary policies antagonized influential elements in France, the bourgeois bondholders, the intellectuals, the workingmen. But due to the limited suffrage and "official" candidates, the opposition party in parliament was The Doctrinaires very small. It consisted of a group, called the "Doctrinaires," led by Royer-Collard and François Guizot. The Doctrinaires were not revolutionists, but liberal monarchists who sought to find a compromise between the French Revolution and the Restoration. They were firm believers in the doctrine of political progress, and conceded that the Revolution had been a step of progress, but that it had gone too far; hence, there must be a reaction, but not too far. The Doctrinaires championed constitutional government, freedom of speech, and religious freedom, and they denounced the government as blindly reactionary. They represented not the masses but the upper bourgeois who wished to wrest the government from the control of the aristocrats.

A more formidable opposition to Bourbon rule showed itself in the activity of secret political societies. The most important was the *Charbonnerie* modeled on the Carbonari of Italy. The *Charbonnerie* It was composed of republicans, who prepared to overthrow the régime by organizing popular uprisings and by inspiring mutiny in the army.

THE JULY REVOLUTION

Like Louis XVI, Charles marched to disaster "with the crown over his eyes." As his reign progressed, it became evident that The July Ordinances he intended to disregard the *charte* altogether and establish naked absolutism. In July, 1830, he issued a series of decrees known as the "July Ordinances" which suspended the liberty of the press; dissolved a newly elected Chamber even before it met; and modified the suffrage law in such a manner as to disfranchise the wealthy bourgeois who were generally liberals.

When the July Ordinances were published, there was a stir in Paris. Mobs began to assemble ominously as in the days of the
Downfall of great Revolution. Cries were heard, "Up with the
the Bour- Charter!" "Down with the Government!" On July
bons 28, Paris awoke and found the streets a network of
barricades made of paving-stones, old furniture, scrap iron, wagons, boxes, and similar objects. On the top of the barricades flew the tricolor, the symbol of revolution; behind them were armed revolutionaries singing the *Marseillaise*. This was the first time that barricades had been used on an extensive scale in revolutionary warfare. The army was called out to suppress the uprising, but the soldiers fought half-heartedly because they sympathized with those behind the barricades. Moreover, it was difficult for the soldiers to advance through the narrow and crooked streets, which made artillery fire and cavalry charges almost impossible. After three days Paris was in the hands of the revolutionaries. "There was nothing to destroy but the dynasty," declared Thiers. Charles, realizing that his rule was over, abdicated and fled to England.

What new government would arise from the July Revolution? This question faced parliament, which now took charge of the
Louis situation. A sharp division arose between the work-
Philippe ingmen, who desired a democratic republic, and the
chosen king bourgeois, who desired merely a constitutional mon-
archy. The former had done the fighting but the latter, better organized and more influential, soon got control of the situation. Their choice for the throne was Louis Philippe, Duke of Orléans, a member of the younger branch of the Bourbon dynasty, who was not only willing, but even satisfied to be a strictly constitutional king. "He will respect our rights because he will hold his from us," was the announcement made on his behalf. The aspirant for the throne became popular by showing his sympathy with the revolutionaries. Seizing the moment of his popularity, parliament proclaimed Louis Philippe "King of the French" by the "grace of God and the will of the nation." The tricolor was restored as the national flag, and the people were declared to be "citizens, not subjects." The Revolution of 1830, like that of 1789, was the work of Paris, and the country accepted the decision of its capital.

THE BOURGEOIS MONARCHY

The new régime made important changes in the constitution. The July Ordinances were repealed, and freedom of the press and of assembly assured. The cabinet was made respon- Suffrage sible to parliament, not to the King. Universal suf- denied to frage was not established, but the property qualifica- the working tions for voting were lowered sufficiently to include class most of the bourgeois, though high enough to exclude the working-men. Although the electorate was doubled by these provisions, it numbered only about 200,000 out of a population of about 30,000,-000. It soon became evident that the center of political gravity had shifted from the landed aristocracy to the upper bourgeois.

The new king had had a checkered career. Exiled during the French Revolution, he had traveled in Europe, and even in America. He returned to his native land during the The bour-Restoration, after an exile of twenty-one years. Un- geois king like his Bourbon predecessors, he was shrewd enough to see that a new class, the capitalists, was rising to power and influence and that it would displace the old nobility in the government of the country. He, therefore, did everything in his power to ingratiate himself with these newly rich, greatly to the disgust of his aristocratic friends, who regarded bankers, stock-brokers, and manufacturers with haughty contempt. It was his custom to walk the streets unattended, dressed in a frock coat and top hat and carrying an umbrella, the symbols of the new régime, as wig, knee-breeches, and sword had been of the old. He also delighted to parade ostentatiously his liberal views, and was fond of calling himself the "Citizen King." In the opinion of many, this man, who in his youth had fought in the armies of the Revolution and was now so democratic in his manners and sentiments, would be the ideal constitutional monarch dreamed of by liberals in all lands.

Louis Philippe's policy was to favor the bourgeois in order to win their support for his throne. As Napoleon had created a nobility from his soldier supporters, Louis Philippe created a The cap-capitalist nobility, the "July nobles," as they were italist nobles derisively called. Bankers, speculators, and manufacturers received patents of nobility, and the old aristocrats, greatly to their astonishment, found themselves unwelcome at court. France was entering the era of the Industrial Revolution, and the capitalists were displacing the landed aristocrats as the dominant class in society.

But the working class fared badly under the new régime, and deep was their disappointment with the outcome of the July

Discontent of the workingmen

Revolution. They had ardently fought behind the barricades to establish a democratic republic, and the result of their efforts was a bourgeois monarchy. In one sense, they were worse off under the new régime than they had been under the old, because their employers, who were now in control, had a direct interest in keeping them in subjection. The laws against trade unions, already in existence, were severely enforced. The hours of labor were long; the factories were unsanitary; and women and children were employed under outrageous conditions. Strike after strike broke out in the industrial centers, but all were ruthlessly suppressed. The silk weavers of Lyons, exasperated by a reduction of their already low wages, rose in revolt, declaring that they would either "live by working or die fighting." Many died fighting.

Bitter antagonism arose between the lower and the middle classes which was to have tragic consequences in 1848 and again in 1871.

Socialism

The workingmen now organized on a new basis, hostility to capitalism. One revolution, they argued, that of 1789, had benefited the peasants and middle classes; another, that of 1830, the capitalists; the next was to be a revolution for the benefit of the working classes. "We have in view," they declared in a manifesto, "not so much a political as a social change. The extension of political rights, electoral reform, universal suffrage, may all be excellent things, but simply as a means to an end. Our object is to divide the burdens and benefits of society equally and to establish the complete reign of equality." This new working-class movement came to be known as "socialism." Its

Louis Blanc and the "national workshops"

leading figure was Louis Blanc, whose book, *The Organization of Labor*, was widely influential in its day. His plan was to establish an industrial republic by organizing "national workshops," factories to be financed by the State, "the banker of the poor" and to be managed by the workers, who were to be employees of the State. The product of the national workshops was to be divided among the workers on the principle of "from each according to his capacity and to each according to his need"; in this way the workers were to be liberated from economic dependence upon the capitalists.

Republican sentiment, even among the middle classes, finally became strong enough to frighten the July Monarchy. Incipient insurrections and violent demonstrations were continually breaking out, and several attempts were made on the life of the King. As in the reign of Charles X, secret revolutionary societies were preparing to overthrow the government. As successor to the *Charbonnerie* there arose the Society of the Rights of Man composed of middle-class republicans. Even more radical was the Society of the Seasons organized by Louis Auguste Blanqui. The latter was a revolutionary conspirator who played an important rôle in underground France for a generation. He had fought behind the barricades in 1830 and emerged a deadly enemy of the bourgeois. "To disarm the bourgeois and to arm the proletariat" was his method of social revolution. By profession Blanqui was, as he said, "a proletarian." Cool, daring, eloquent, and with an amazing gift for secret organization, he greatly attracted the disaffected elements in Paris. His society was organized on a remarkable plan, and its members were a picked corps of revolutionary workingmen who were secretly drilled in barricade fighting. "Forty-eight hours are enough to make a revolution," Blanqui once declared.

Opposition to the Bourgeois Monarchy arose from another and unexpected quarter, the champions of the Bonapartes. In the rather commonplace reign of Louis Philippe, France revived her glorious memory of the Revolutionary and Napoleonic periods. Lamartine's eloquent *History of the Girondins*, portraying the struggles of those idealistic republicans, was a "best-seller." In 1840 the remains of Napoleon I were brought from Saint Helena and deposited with elaborate ceremonies in a magnificent tomb. Adolphe Thiers, who was an historian as well as a politician, wrote his *History of the Consulate* glorifying Napoleon's life and deeds. The Napoleonic "legend" was seizing upon the imagination of the French at a time when their country occupied a humiliating position in international affairs. After Waterloo, France suddenly sank from the position of dictator of Europe to that of a second-rate power. A crisis in 1840 in the Near East revealed her impotence. When the Viceroy

Secret revolutionary societies

The Napoleonic "legend"

of Egypt, Mehemet Ali, rebelled against the Sultan of Turkey, he received the support of France.   But the other powers supported the Sultan.[1]   The international situation became tense and a war party appeared in France.   But Louis Philippe favored a peace policy and France suffered a diplomatic defeat.   The King was determined that his reign should be distinguished for peace and good business, not for splendor and glory.

There appeared an heir and claimant to the rights of the Napoleonic dynasty in the person of Prince Louis Napoleon Bonaparte.   He was a son of Louis Bonaparte, brother of Napoleon I, and of Hortense Beauharnais, the daughter of Empress Josephine by her first husband; hence, he was related to the Emperor by ties of blood and marriage.   After the downfall of the Empire, Louis Napoleon had led a life of exciting exile in many lands.   In Italy, he became a member of the Carbonari; in England, he became a special constable to suppress the Chartist rioters.   Throughout his life he was obsessed with the idea that France had still another imperial life to lead, and that he, the sole inheritor of the Napoleonic tradition, was destined to revive the glories of the Empire.   He pleaded for a "reconstruction of French society, shattered by fifty years of revolution, and the reconciliation of order with liberty, of popular rights with the principle of authority."   He contended that the Emperor had been a faithful servant of the French Revolution, but that the tyrant kings had combined to thwart his aim to establish its principles.   Hence Napoleon's work still remained to be done.   In 1836 and again in 1840, Louis Napoleon made attempts to provoke an uprising in the French army, but each time he failed miserably and was imprisoned.   When, after his second attempt, he was brought to trial, he took the opportunity of presenting his claims to public notice.   "I represent before you," he declared eloquently, "a principle, a cause, a defeat.   The principle is the sovereignty of the people; the cause is that of the Empire; the defeat is Waterloo."   However, he was regarded as an adventurer, and was not taken seriously.   Some considered him commonplace; others, crafty; others, dreamy and fantastic; all considered him insignificant and ridiculous.   But the revival of a great emotion was to give this singular man his opportunity.

The rise of an imperialist party increased popular disaffection

Louis Napoleon Bonaparte (1808–73)

[1] See page 163.

with the Orléanist régime. Fearful of the rising tide of opposition, Louis Philippe, like the Bourbons, determined on a policy of suppression. Laws were enacted requiring all socie- The Septem- ties to submit their constitutions for approval by the ber Laws government. In spite of the guarantees of freedom of the press, republican journals were suppressed and their editors jailed, fined, or deported. The most famous of the repressive measures were the "September Laws" (1835), which prohibited, by severe penalties, criticism of the King in any form. Caricatures of Louis Philippe were especially forbidden, as the comic journals of Paris were fond of picturing him with a pear-shaped head. The famous cartoons of Daumier, "the Michelangelo of caricature," mercilessly satirized the bourgeois régime, its morals and its manners. It was, likewise, made unlawful to question the institution of property or to defend any but the monarchical system of government. The monarch whose throne was "perched on the barricades" now used the same methods as did the reactionary Charles X.

By these methods Louis Philippe managed to get rid of opposi- tion, for a time. But the more liberal-minded men of all classes were now convinced that liberty would not be safe Guizot's under any monarch, no matter how democratic his methods of professions. More and more did the King assert his controlling prerogative to govern, for he firmly believed that the parliament throne was not an "empty armchair." He began a policy of per- sonal government by choosing the cabinet, irrespective of the wishes of parliament. Thiers, who had been his sponsor and stoutest supporter, was compelled to resign his position as Prime Minister because he believed in the English theory that the king should reign, but not rule. In Guizot, the King finally found a minister in harmony with his ideas. According to Guizot the essence of free government was that of a king and parliament, the latter to be chosen by the propertied classes; the cabinet was to be appointed by the king and receive the support of parliament. In order to insure this support, Guizot organized a system of political corruption to grind out majorities for the government. Those entitled to vote were known as the *pays légal*, or the legiti- mate source of political power. Both local and national patronage, as well as special favors to localities, were used by Guizot to gain supporters. There were actually more office-holders than voters; hence, patronage played a decisive part in the election of "official" candidates. Deputies were permitted to hold office under the government. Sometimes they were bribed by being made stockholders in industrial corporations or by being given government contracts. Although Guizot was personally honest, and a man of high principle, he turned parliament into a "bargain-counter" where votes were exchanged for offices, contracts, and favors of all kinds. By these methods he succeeded in making parliament a willing tool in the hands of the King; the system was not unlike that which existed in England under George III and Lord North. To Guizot, whose mind was of the rigid, pedantic type, adherence to parliamentary forms constituted political liberty; consequently he was exceedingly careful to observe the constitution in regard to parliament and its powers.

Naturally enough this system encountered great opposition. Sharp demands were made for universal, manhood suffrage to which the government replied, "Get rich and you will have a vote"; or, "Go into business, make money, and leave politics alone." When he entered the ministry, Guizot determined, as it was said, "to put an absolute veto upon all innovations in public life." The tyranny of the July Monarchy was all the more resented because it had come in on the wave of revolution; moreover, unlike the Bourbons or the Bonapartes, it could point to no great traditions or achievements that aroused enthusiasm. Hypocrisy was the stamp of its birth, as mediocrity was of its life. The commonplace King and his stilted, pedantic Minister were beginning to bore France, always a fatal thing in that vivacious land.

"France is bored"

THE INDUSTRIAL REVOLUTION

Louis Philippe's reign was notable in the economic history of France because it was the period of the Industrial Revolution. The abolition of the guilds during the French Revolution had prepared the way for the new economy by making possible freedom of enterprise and of labor. After the Napoleonic Wars machinery was imported from England which facilitated the introduction of the factory system.

As in England machine production and steam power was first applied to cotton manufactures which centered in Mulhouse. This city became the Manchester of France, containing, in the middle of the century, about one third of all the

Textiles

spindles in the country.[1] France produced a great invention, the famous Jacquard loom (1804), which wove rapidly complex patterns in silk. Although it was operated by hand, the Jacquard loom did for the silk industry what Cartwright's loom did for the cotton industry, and France became the greatest silk manufacturing country in the world with Lyons as the center. In the textiles France specialized in silk and linen, as England did in cotton and wool.

Lack of sufficient coal and the poor quality of the iron ore seriously delayed French metallurgical development. Moreover, coal was mined in the northeast, and iron at a distance away, in Lorraine; hence, the additional cost of transportation discouraged smelting. As late as the sixties most of the smelting was done by means of charcoal, near the forests, where wood was plentiful. Because of these hindrances, steel production was low, and the deficiency for industrial purposes was met by imports from England.

Coal and iron

France was slow in introducing the railway. During the seventeenth and eighteenth centuries she had developed a fine system of roads and canals, and the railway therefore had keen competition which it did not have in England. So slowly did railways develop that, in 1841, the railway mileage in all France was only three hundred and sixty. However, a comprehensive scheme was adopted by the government of Louis Philippe for building a national system of railways radiating from Paris, to be undertaken by chartered companies aided by government subsidies. This encouragement to private enterprise resulted in the building of several lines which added considerably to the railway mileage.

Railways

Although the Industrial Revolution made marked progress in France, it did not develop as rapidly as in England. Its slow advance may be judged by the size of the industrial population; in the middle of the nineteenth century only about twenty-five per cent of the population of France was urban in comparison with about fifty per cent in England. The lack of coal was a serious handicap, and many of the factories had to be built near streams in order to get water power. A plentiful supply of cheap labor was also lacking. The

Slow progress of industry

[1] In 1834, France had about 5000 mechanical looms; in 1846, the number had increased to about 31,000.

widely prevalent system of peasant proprietorship induced the country folk to remain on the land and not to migrate to the industrial centers. The spread of machinery was retarded by the importance of the luxury industries. France was famous for the exquisite workmanship of expensive articles, such as jewelry, porcelains, women's clothes, laces, and tapestries which were not adapted to machine production. They were produced by skilled craftsmen in shops or in small factories.

Although industrially backward as compared with England, France was a wealthy nation because of her naturally rich soil, her

Prosperity of France

splendid wine districts, and her luxury industries. The manufacture of wines, liquors, brandies, and beet sugar constituted an important element in the national economy; in 1846 more than half of the exports consisted of silks and wine. During the first half of the nineteenth century, England and France were economically the most important nations in Europe; the former because of her cheap machine-made goods, and the latter because of her luxury industries.

THE ROMANTIC MOVEMENT

French literature during the first half of the nineteenth century saw the rise and decline of the Romantic movement. The Restora-

Classicism and Romanticism

tion brought in its train a hatred for the writings of the eighteenth-century philosophers, who were regarded as responsible for the French Revolution. In contradistinction to the latter, who wrote in a clear, faultlessly "classic" style about "reason," the writers of the new period, influenced by Rousseau and Chateaubriand, threw "reason" to the wind, and wrote in a style and on subjects in which emotion and imagination had free play. The Romanticists, as they were called, preached vehemently against the cold rationalism of their predecessors, and turned for inspiration to the fantastic tales and marvelous deeds of the Middle Ages. The movement has been well described as the "renaissance of wonder"; anything that was wonderful, strange, curious, and imaginative made a powerful appeal to the writers of the new school.

The Romantic movement in France began with a small group in Paris calling itself the *Cénacle*, of which Victor Hugo was the leading spirit. It was the production, in 1830, of his play, *Hernani*, a grandiloquent melodrama of an heroic brigand that started a storm of applause and condemnation. So strong was the feeling that almost every performance was followed by lively scrimmages between "Romanticists" and "Classicists." The battle of the schools raged for almost a generation; books, pamphlets, and manifestoes were issued, defending or attacking Romanticism.

Victor Hugo, the chief protagonist of Romanticism, became a sort of literary dictator to the rising generation of French writers. Gifted with an extraordinary imagination, he wove a magic web over everything that he wrote, whether poem, drama, novel, history, or essay. "He can conjure up the strangest vision of fancy; he can evoke the glamour and the mystery of the past; he can sing with exquisite lightness of the fugitive beauties of Nature; he can pour out, in tenderness or in passion, the melodies of love; he can fill his lines with the fire, the stress, the culminating fury, of prophetic denunciation; he can utter the sad and secret questionings of the human spirit and give voice to the solemnity of Fate." Half-prophet, half-journalist, Hugo had both a wide and a deep influence on his generation, whose spokesman he regarded himself. His verbal facility was amazing. Words poured from his pen in a swift and steady stream, and he almost exhausted the resources of the French language of whose treasures he was master. Like many other French writers, Hugo was keenly interested in public affairs, and he became an eloquent champion of democratic principles. For denouncing the *coup d'état* of Louis Napoleon he was driven into exile, where he wrote bitter invectives against the Emperor whom he called "*Napoléon le petit.*"

> Victor Hugo (1802–85)

His most famous novel is *Les Misérables*, a prose epic of modern society, which is an eloquent indictment of inhumane social conditions. The characters that appear in this book constitute a wonderful portrait gallery of saints and sinners, whose characters and ideals are depicted in a style suffused with emotion and in a spirit of fervent humanitarianism.

Hugo's chief title to fame is, however, as a poet. The lyrical quality and vivid imagery of his verse is unexcelled in French poetry. The collection of poems called *Châtiments* is a lyrical outburst of love of humanity and hatred for tyranny. In his *Contemplations* other qualities are shown, symbolic and even mystic brooding over religion, love, and destiny.[1]

[1] For further account of Hugo, see page 218.

The chief followers of Hugo were the poets, Alfred de Vigny (1797–1863) and Alfred de Musset (1810–57); and the novelists,

The Romantic poets and novelists   Théophile Gautier (1811–72) and Alexandre Dumas (1803–70).   De Vigny's poetry is at times idealistic and full of delicate imagery; at other times, it is melancholy to the point of pessimism.   It was said of him that he was like a beautiful angel who had drunk of vinegar.   Brilliant, vivacious, and sentimental was Alfred de Musset, the "poet of love," whose poems and plays have a high place in French literature.   His most famous work is *Les Nuits*, a series of philosophic poems in the form of dialogues.   Théophile Gautier, novelist, essayist, and poet, was an ardent Romanticist, whose sensational appearance at the first performance of *Hernani*, with his long hair disheveled and his person adorned with a flaming red waistcoat, aroused much hilarity.   Master of a style which was almost flawless in its perfection, his themes are often trivial.   His most famous novel is *Mlle. de Maupin*, a highly sensational romance.   The best-known Romantic novelist of the day, next to Victor Hugo, was Alexandre Dumas, whose tales have been described as "cloak-and-sword" romances because they deal with daring adventures, wicked conspiracies, and romantic loves.   Dumas is the great favorite among boys, few of whom have not read his famous novels, the *Three Musketeers* and the *Count of Monte Cristo*.

The chief contribution of the Romantic movement to French literature was a revival of lyric poetry, particularly in the work

Romanticists become radicals   of Hugo.   It also created a new type of prose which profoundly influenced later French literature.   Unlike the German Romanticists who became reactionaries, the French Romanticists became democrats, "contemners of kings and laws," despite their love for the Middle Ages.   They were too close to the great Revolution, and too much inspired by its ideals, to welcome the return of medievalism; what they did was to fuse the themes of the Middle Ages with the spirit of the French Revolution.

Alphonse Prat de Lamartine is the unique example of a poet turned statesman.   His volume of *Méditations* consists of philo-

Lamartine (1790–1869)   sophic elegies written in a beautiful, melodious style on such themes as religion, love, and nature.   His famous *History of the Girondins* is less a history than an eloquent tribute to the ideas of the Girondins, whom he greatly admired.

Lamartine was a sincere lover of freedom, and he threw himself into the revolutionary movement of 1848 with ardor, hoping to establish true democracy on the ruins of the bourgeois monarchy. He proved himself a remarkable orator, and was elected a member of the provisional government. But his popularity was short-lived, as both socialists and monarchists opposed him and he was compelled to retire from politics.

Aurore Dupin, better known by her pseudonym, "George Sand," was the representative of the Idealist school in French literature. Her novels of country life, written in a clear, flowing George Sand style, have an idyllic charm which has endeared her (1804–76) to thousands of readers. She effected something like a revolution in literature by introducing peasants and common laborers as heroes. Later in life she became a warm advocate of the rights of women and of workingmen, and an ardent adherent of Utopian socialism.

In the novels of Honoré Balzac the problems of the middle classes, for the first time, become the leading themes in literature. His famous *Comédie Humaine*, in which about five Balzac thousand characters pass and repass through a series (1799–1850) of one hundred novels, constitutes a veritable storehouse of "human documents" illustrating the social life of France during the first half of the nineteenth century. The virtues and vices of the middle classes are analyzed and portrayed with wonderful power and insight in this bourgeois epic, in which money, not love or war, is the theme, the moral, and the tale. Balzac's attitude toward human beings is almost that of a naturalist toward animals; he analyzes them as objectively, classifies them as emotionlessly, and judges them as dispassionately. He loves to ferret out the hidden motives for human action, and to expose mercilessly the secret springs and hidden trapdoors of society. In the opinion of many literary critics Balzac is the greatest of all the French novelists.

REFERENCES

GENERAL:

E. Bourgeois, *History of Modern France*, 2 vols. (1919), vol. I, good for political matters, poor in social matters, has excellent bibliography; F. M. Anderson, *Constitutions and Other Select Documents Illustrative of the History of France* (ed. 1909), source book; G. Weill, *La France sous la monarchie constitutionnelle 1814–1848* (ed. 1912), excellent for social matters;

by the same author, *Histoire du parti républicain en France de 1814 à 1870* (ed. 1929). On the Restoration: R. Viviani, *La restauration, 1814–1830* (1906), from socialist standpoint; H. Houssaye, *1815*, 3 vols. (1896–1905), a detailed work, authoritative. On the July Monarchy: Louis Blanc, *History of Ten Years, 1830–1840*, translated from the French, 2 vols. (1844–45), a vivid account of the period by the famous radical; S. Charléty, *La Monarchie de Juillet* (1921); H. R. Whitehouse, *Life of Lamartine*, 2 vols. (1918), gives fine idea of Lamartine and of his period; J. E. Fournière, *Le règne de Louis Philippe* (1906), from socialist viewpoint; J. M. S. Allison, *Thiers and the French Monarchy* (1926).

SOCIAL AND ECONOMIC:

E. Levasseur, *Histoire des classes ouvrières et l'industrie en France de 1789 à 1870*, 2 vols. (1903–04), a masterly treatment of the social and economic development of France; by the same author, *Histoire du commerce de la France*, 2 vols. (1911–12), vol. II covers the period 1789–1910, and *La population française*, 3 vols. (1889–92).

LITERATURE:

L. Petit de Julleville, *Histoire de la Langue et de la Littérature française*, 8 vols. (1896–99), vols. VII–VIII deal with the nineteenth century; G. Lanson, *Histoire de la littérature française* (ed. 1916); C. H. C. Wright, *A History of French Literature* (1912); G. Pellissier, *Le mouvement littéraire au XIXe siècle* (ed. 1912); I. Babbitt, *The Masters of Modern French Criticism* (1912).

ADDITIONAL REFERENCES

G. Lacour-Gayet, *Talleyrand*, 2 vols. (1928–30); C. S. Phillips, *The Church in France, 1789–1848* (1929); H. Sée, *La vie économique de la France sous la Monarchie censitaire (1815–1848)* (1927); P. F. G. de la Gorce, *Louis Philippe* (1931); R. Soltau, *French Political Thought in the Nineteenth Century* (1931); F. B. Artz, *France under the Bourbon Restoration* (1931); A. Viallate, *L'activité économique en France* (1937); J. B. Wolf, *France: 1815 to the Present* (1940); F. A. Haight, *A History of French Commercial Policies* (1941).

CHAPTER VI

THE RESTORATION IN ITALY AND IN SPAIN

CAUSES OF DISUNION IN ITALY

ITALY, proudly acclaimed the "eldest daughter of civilization" by her children, had to wait till the latter part of the nineteenth century before she became a nation. For centuries she was divided into small, weak states, and was consequently an easy prey for the strong nations of Europe who frequently invaded the peninsula to satisfy their territorial ambitions. Spain, France, and Austria had, each in turn, seized portions of Italy where they set up puppet princes. At one time nearly all the Italian rulers were foreigners, generally Spaniards and Austrians.

Foreign domination

During the nation-forming period in the fifteenth and sixteenth centuries, Italy did not produce a prince powerful enough to conquer the whole peninsula and to unite all Italians under one rule. The great political thinker, Machiavelli, had dreamed of a united Italy, and had hoped to see it realized under a powerful monarch. But the various states, notably the Republics of Venice and Florence and the Kingdom of Naples, were too powerful to be absorbed in this way. An intense local patriotism developed which led to bitter rivalries, to internecine quarrels, and to frequent wars. Union was then regarded merely as something that would benefit one state at the expense of all the others; as a consequence, the national ideal faded from the Italian mind.

Internal rivalries

One element in the situation, the Papacy, had no parallel in any other country. Ever since the days of Pepin and Charlemagne, the Popes had been the rulers of the region known as the Papal States, and therefore princes in their own right. The Popes well knew that the unification of Italy would spell the extinction of the Papal States and the disappearance of their temporal power. They claimed that, in order to maintain the international character of the Catholic Church, they must be independent rulers. The "Babylonian Captivity of the Church" [1] had never been forgotten by the Popes, who deter-

Papacy opposed to unification

[1] This term is used to describe the period in Church history (1309–77) when the Popes lived in Avignon, in France, where their policies were dominated by the French kings.

mined that under no circumstances would they become "captives" in Italy. They therefore consistently opposed and, for a time, effectively prevented the unification of Italy.

In spite of division and misrule, Italy of the fifteenth and sixteenth centuries reached the very heights of civilization and prosperity. Decay of   perity. The whole world flocked to Venice, Florence, Italy   Genoa, and Rome that they might sit at the feet of the great masters of art, scholarship, and science, who were the glory of the Italian Renaissance. But a great change was wrought in the destiny of Italy by the discovery of America and of the Cape route to India. During the seventeenth century the Atlantic displaced the Mediterranean as the world's highway of commerce, and trade shifted from southern to northern Europe. Slowly but surely the prosperity of Italy declined and, by the eighteenth century, Venice, Genoa, Florence, and Milan, once great commercial centers, were stricken with economic death. Their once busy marts, where the merchants of Europe and of Asia used to congregate, were now silent and empty; their influence in international affairs disappeared; their culture decayed and became degenerate. What remained were political division, tyranny of the petty despots, and a great and glorious memory. The history of Italy during the eighteenth century is almost a blank. During this period the great mass of the population was sunk in poverty, ignorance, and superstition. The educated classes contented themselves with contemplating the grandeur of the past and with imitating its language and manners. Italy seemed to have fallen into a deathlike sleep from which she would never waken.

She was, however, rudely awakened by the resounding trumpet call of the French Revolution. The revolutionary armies of France Revival dur-   poured over the Alps, and the Italian princes fled in ing the   terror, greatly to the astonishment of their subjects French   who, in their ignorance, had always regarded them as Revolution   great and powerful monarchs. Liberty, Equality, and Fraternity were proclaimed, and the French set energetically to work abolishing the old order and inaugurating the new. The various states were organized as republics. The remnants of medievalism, semi-serfdom, inequality before the law, and religious intolerance were abolished, and enlightened legal and administrative systems were established. Far-reaching social, political, and economic reforms were also introduced; in one decade of

UNIFICATION OF ITALY

SCALE OF MILES
0   50   100   150

The dates are those of annexation to the Kingdom of Sardinia, and after 1861 to the Kingdom of Italy.

French rule Italy made centuries of progress. The Italians were dazed; liberty instead of tyranny had now suddenly descended upon them from beyond the Alps.

During the Napoleonic régime, the country was practically unified under the French Emperor and his relatives whom he set up as princes. A uniform system of administration and law was established throughout the peninsula. Union under Napoleon Italy was now under the control of a foreign despot, but it was united for the first time since the days of ancient Rome. Liberty and union were the two miracles performed by the French for the Italians.

THE RESTORATION

As already described,[1] the Congress of Vienna redivided the country into seven principal states. The restored monarchs returned full of hatred for the changes introduced by the French, and they determined to revive the old tyrannies, inequalities, and intolerances. Freedom of speech Reaction during the Restoration and of association were banned, and the slightest manifestation of political liberty was mercilessly suppressed. The Church was restored to its former power, and non-Catholics were again denied religious freedom. Education was placed almost entirely in the hands of the clergy. In the Papal States the Inquisition was reëstablished to suppress intellectual freedom which was regarded as a dangerous disease. The "class called thinkers" was especially watched and harassed, for their influence was looked upon as dangerous to the Restoration. Everything of French origin was suspected as revolutionary. A botanical garden was destroyed because it had been built by the French; vaccination and street lighting were suppressed as revolutionary innovations of the French; excavations at Pompeii, begun by French scientists, were discontinued. In Naples, hunting liberals became an art and a pastime. Not only were the governments reactionary, they were also corrupt and inefficient. Brigands roamed over the south, committing outrages and openly defying the authorities; finances were mismanaged; taxes were high and bore most heavily on the poor; and the public service was disorganized by favoritism and corruption.

By far the most powerful influence in the peninsula was Austria. Lombardy-Venetia were directly under her rule, and the princes of

[1] See page 57.

Modena, Parma, and Tuscany were related to the Hapsburg dy-
Influence of   nasty.   King Ferdinand of Naples, though a Span-
Austria   ish Bourbon, was in close alliance with Austria,
pledged to direct his foreign and domestic policies in accordance
with her wishes.   Although the administration of Lombardy-
Venetia was far more efficient and honest than that of the other
states, it was nevertheless more bitterly detested, for Austria represented to the Italians everything that they wanted to be rid of —
foreign domination, absolutism, invasion, and division.   Though
divided into many states and factions, the Italians were nevertheless united in a common hate for the Austrians.

There was another difficulty in the Italian situation.   The differences between the north and south were so great that these sec-
Differences   tions constituted two different civilizations.   Almost
between   every Mediterranean strain was present in the racial
north and   composition of the south, including even the Arabic.
south   In the north the racial origins were largely Celtic and
Teutonic.   A Neapolitan and a Venetian did not appear to be of
the same nationality.   Each region had its own peculiar dialect
that was unintelligible elsewhere.   The dialects in the south were
strange mixtures of all sorts of words, Italian, Spanish, Greek, and
Arabic.   Italian was a common language only in the sense that it
was used by people from the different regions when they wanted
to communicate with one another.   In the north there was a fairly
large middle class that had been deeply influenced by the French
Revolution.   The south was inhabited chiefly by a poor, illiterate
peasantry in a serf-like relation to large proprietors.

THE UPRISINGS OF 1820

The political history of Italy from 1815 to 1870 flows in two
main currents, liberty and union, or the establishment of constitu-
Obstacles to   tional government in the various states and the union
union   of all into a common nationality.   In the attainment
of these objects the Italians encountered the opposition of Austria;
in addition, they had to face the bitter opposition of the papacy,
whose great power in Italy and enormous influence in the world
would be marshaled against any movement looking toward unification.   Nearly all the Italians are Catholics, and they are very
proud of the Papacy, which they regard as an Italian institution
that influences the whole world.   To favor unity meant to many

devout Catholics a possible break with their Church, something which they viewed with dismay; and it was a cruel dilemma for sincere men and women who were obliged to choose between their country and their Church. Curious as it may seem the Papacy actually constituted a bond of disunion.

Although the petty monarchs restored much of the old order, there was one thing that they could not restore, the old spirit of subserviency and fear. French rule had given the Italians a taste of liberty and union, and the tyranny of the despots soon met with vigorous opposition. The first phase of the unification movement is associated with the Carbonari, a far-reaching secret society that aimed to establish a constitutional government and to unite Italy. As peaceful agitation was made impossible by a severe censorship, the Carbonari resorted to conspiracy, assassination, and insurrection. They had no carefully thought-out plan of unification, and their violence was inspired by the belief that the removal of the obstacles to union would result in bringing forth such a plan.

The Carbonari

Inspired by the success of the Spanish uprising of 1820, the people of Naples, led by the Carbonari, rose in revolt during the same year. King Ferdinand I, frightened by the support which the uprising received from the army, readily promised to grant concessions. A democratic constitution was drawn up, which Ferdinand accepted and solemnly swore to observe. But he had no intention of keeping his word, and he therefore appealed to the Holy Alliance to intervene in the affairs of his kingdom in order to overthrow the constitution which he himself had just granted. His appeal was answered. An Austrian army was sent into Naples which ousted the recently established democratic government and reseated Ferdinand as absolute monarch. A terrible repression followed. To satisfy the vengeance of the faithless monarch, thousands were imprisoned, exiled, or executed.

The uprising in Naples

But no sooner was one rebellion suppressed than another was begun. In 1821 an uprising took place in Piedmont, where the revolutionists demanded not only a constitution, but also war with Austria as the enemy of the Italian people. Fearful of a civil war in case he refused these demands, and unwilling to seek foreign intervention, King Victor Emmanuel I abdicated his throne in favor of his brother,

Austria suppresses Italian uprisings

Charles Felix, who obtained Austria's aid in suppressing the up-rising.   In 1831, uprisings in Modena, Parma, and the Papal States were likewise put down through the aid of Austrian armies. The hatred of Austria rose to a white heat of fury.   Italian patriots bitterly denounced this "fire department of Italy," that was always rushing in to quench the flames of revolution.   The idea took firm root that Austria must be defeated and driven from Italy, otherwise all strivings for freedom would be in vain.

YOUNG ITALY

Far from being discouraged by the failure of the attempts to win political freedom, the Italians set to work more energetically than ever before.   The chief cause for the failures lay in the fact that the revolutionary movement was rooted in conspiracy and therefore lacked a broad popular basis. The uprisings in the several states were local and had received little support among Italians generally.   What was easily gained through a sudden insurrection of small groups was as easily lost through the Austrian bayonets that were ever at the beck and call of the Italian despots.   Heroic work had been done by the Car-bonari in keeping alive the revolutionary spirit, but its propaganda had never touched the people who seemed apathetic to the agitation for liberty and union.

Failure of the Carbonari

In the thirties there appeared a new movement which goes by the general name of the *Risorgimento* (the Resurrection) and which was destined to realize the dream of an Italian father-land.   This movement was largely the work of highly educated young men whose intense earnestness, glowing enthusi-asm, and self-sacrificing devotion to their country aroused the ad-miration of the world.

The Risorgi-mento

Foremost among these young patriots was Joseph Mazzini.   He came of a well-to-do family of Genoa, and studied law at the uni-versity of his native city.   But he had a bent for litera-ture, and for a time was a contributor to a literary journal in which he wrote articles on Dante, of whom he was a devoted admirer.   Dante exercised a deep influence on the rising generation of Italians, who beheld in him their spiritual father. "They talk Dante, write Dante, and think and dream Dante to an extent that would be ridiculous but that he deserves it," declared Byron.

Mazzini (1805-72)

While a student Mazzini had become interested in the condition of his country. He had read much of her history, and he was greatly saddened at the fate that had befallen the once great Italy, now mutilated, insignificant, and under the heel of foreigners. So deeply did he grieve for his native land that he was wont to dress himself in black, as if in mourning for her. Young Mazzini was convinced that he had no moral right to follow his profession as a lawyer or his inclination as a literary man so long as his country was divided and enslaved. At the age of twenty-five he joined the Carbonari, and was arrested for participating in an uprising. While in prison, where he had plenty of time to think, he evolved the plan for resurrecting Italy.

Soon after his release he left the Carbonari, and founded a new society called Young Italy. It was composed of young intellectuals who dedicated themselves to the task of liberating their country from foreign and domestic tyrants and to the establishment of a unified Italian republic on a democratic basis. "God and the People" was the motto of Young Italy, for Mazzini was as ardent a democrat and moralist as he was a nationalist. Democracy, he defined, as "the progress of all through all under the leadership of the wisest and best." The plan of the new society was to conduct an incessant campaign of agitation among the people who were to rise under its leadership, expel the tyrants, and call a national convention to inaugurate the Italian Republic. "Place the youth of the nation at the head of the insurgent masses," Mazzini declared; "you do not realize the strength that is latent in these young men or what magic influence the voice of youth has on crowds. You will find in them a host of apostles for the new religion." Mazzini dedicated himself to his "apostolate," as he called his patriotic activity. He had a religious, almost a mystic, enthusiasm for his work, for he loved Italy "above all earthly things." In spite of his country's degradation, he believed that "a nation which has been enslaved for centuries can regenerate itself through virtue and through self-sacrifice." Italy had a third life to lead. Once she had ruled the world through Rome; then through the Papacy; and now the Third Italy, the "Rome of the People," "radiant, purified by suffering, would move as an angel of light among the nations that thought her dead."

Although an intense nationalist, Mazzini was not at all a chauvinist. His conception of nationalism was to love one's country

Mazzini's nationalism

most devotedly and, at the same time, to admire and respect every
His inter-   other nation because each had something precious
nationalism   to give to civilization.   He believed that if every
nation were permitted to exist undisturbed, the chief cause for war
would disappear.   Italy's mission was to teach mankind to love
and to cherish the ideal of the brotherhood of nations.   He became an active champion of oppressed nationalities, Hungarians,
Poles, and Irish, and organized an international society called
Young Europe, whose object was to form a Holy Alliance of the
peoples as a counterweight to the Holy Alliance of the despots.

Mazzini's magic voice aroused the Italian youth as nothing else
had ever done before.   A new spirit, that of moral enthusiasm for
His con-   a holy cause, was breathed into a political movement
tribution   by the fervent eloquence of this prophet of Italian
freedom, who asserted that the Italians had not only Austrians to
fight but also "the dissension, the vices, the impotence, and the
hopelessness that come of servitude."   Although gentle and pure-
hearted, Mazzini sometimes resorted to conspiracies as desperate
as those of the Carbonari.   He lived most of his life in exile, mainly
in England and in France, where he was incessantly organizing insurrections.   Mazzini was neither a statesman nor an organizer,
having little if any practical ability.   His real contribution was to
awaken the Italian people to patriotic enthusiasm, without which
the great plans of unification could not have succeeded.

The movement for unification appealed so deeply to Italians
that even the Papacy was affected by it.   In 1846, a new Pope was
Pius IX   chosen, Pius IX, who for a time became very popular
because of his liberal policies.   He showed himself
hostile to Austrian influences, greatly to the delight of the Italian
patriots, who hailed Pius as the coming redeemer of Italy.   "They
want to make a Napoleon of me who am only a poor country
parson," the Pope declared.

There was a *Risorgimento* in the literary as well as in the political
history of Italy in the course of the nineteenth century.   A con-
Literary   suming nationalism characterized the Italian writers
influences   of that period.   It was present in poem, novel, and
drama, all of which found their chief inspiration in patriotism.
The description of no scene, the delineament of no character or
emotion was complete without the suggestion that behind it all was
Italy, past, present, and future.   Italian authors studied the

records of the past of their country with zealous care in order to gain inspiration for their work.

Classicism was another marked characteristic of Italian writers of the period. Like those of the Renaissance they regarded classic antiquity as the prime source of their culture; to them classicism was an integral part of their intellectual life, not merely an æsthetic theory. This passion for antiquity may be ascribed to a desire to seek refuge from the misery of their present in the glories of their past. The literature of this period abounds in allusions to the struggles for liberty among the ancients; it was an expression of the nation's mood, and was designed as a subtle form of propaganda against Austrian and Bourbon tyranny.

The passion for antiquity

The most important figure in Italian literature during the early nineteenth century was Alessandro Manzoni, the greatest of Italian novelists. His famous work, *I Promessi Sposi* (*The Betrothed*), is a historical romance, the importance of which lies, not in the plot or incidents, but in the penetrating study of a host of characters that have since become household names in Italy. Manzoni was a poet as well as a novelist, and his ode on the death of Napoleon, *Cinque Maggio* (*May Fifth*), met with universal admiration when it appeared.

Manzoni (1785–1873)

A common type among Italian writers was the scholar-poet, among whom Giacomo Leopardi is an example. Leopardi was greatly interested in the classics, many of which he edited and translated; but his real significance lies in his poetry. A spirit of deep and gloomy pessimism pervades nearly all of his work. He sees eternal warfare everywhere. The great enemy of man is nature, to whose ravages everything sooner or later succumbs. In his odes to Italy and to Dante, Leopardi rises to a noble height of patriotic fervor; in melodious verse he pictures his beloved Italy awakened from her sleep of centuries only to find herself weak and despised.

Leopardi (1798–1837)

THE RESTORATION IN SPAIN

Since the days of the Catholic Reformation in the sixteenth century, Spain has made little contribution to the social, political, or cultural life of Europe. Spaniards lived far from the main currents of European life, proud of their isolation and of their splendid past, and seeming to care little

Isolation of Spain

whether their country made any progress or not. The liberal movement which took place in Spain during the nineteenth century was merely a faint or dying echo of revolutionary movements in France.

During the Napoleonic invasion a group of liberals had taken advantage of the situation to call together a parliament which, in 1812, adopted a democratic constitution that decreed the sovereignty of the people, equality before the law, and religious freedom. The constitution of 1812 became the Magna Charta of Spanish liberalism; its principles were constantly appealed to in the struggle for democracy which followed during the nineteenth century.

The constitution of 1812

In 1814 the Spanish Bourbon, Ferdinand VII, was restored amid popular acclaim. Like most Bourbons, Ferdinand had neither learned nor forgotten anything; he was, moreover, cruel, stupid, treacherous, and unscrupulous, "having the heart of a tiger and the head of a mule." Upon his restoration he immediately set to work to abolish the reforms that had been adopted. The constitution of 1812 was suppressed; the privileges of the nobles and clergy were restored; the Jesuits were given control of education; and the Inquisition was reëstablished. As Ferdinand's rule was scandalously corrupt as well as incompetent, Spain was continually on the brink of bankruptcy. The King gathered about him a group of favorites known as the *camarilla*, or "kitchen cabinet," who conducted the government merely to suit their personal interests and whims. Freedom of speech and of association were completely suppressed, and thousands of Liberals were driven out of the country or sent to prison.

Rule of Ferdinand

As in Italy the Carbonari appeared, and carried on a vigorous agitation against Bourbon despotism. In the towns, revolutionary committees, called *juntas*, were active in directing an agitation among the workingmen. More important was the growing disaffection in the army. During the Napoleonic invasion the popular uprising against the French had been led by army officers who became infected with the spirit of revolution. During the Restoration the army was neglected; soldiers and officers did not get sufficient food and clothing and their pay was irregular, which greatly irritated them. Ferdinand relied more upon the priests than upon the soldiers to keep the masses loyal to the dynasty, and he therefore showered favors upon the Church.

The *juntas*

In 1820, mutinies occurred in the army which was the signal for a popular uprising.   A demand arose for the restoration of the constitution of 1812, which Ferdinand was forced to   The upris-
grant.   "Let us advance frankly," he declared, "my-   ing of 1820
self leading the way, along the constitutional path."   A parliament was convened, which was composed almost entirely of Liberals. It suppressed the Inquisition and many of the religious orders, decreed freedom of speech and of association, and restored the constitution of 1812.   The King was obliged to assent to these laws because he was practically a prisoner in the hands of parliament. He was, however, secretly sending appeals for help to the other despots of Europe.   The clergy on their part were actively organizing a counter-revolution among the peasantry, who were exhorted to rescue the "captive King" from the hands of the free-thinking Liberals.

Although Ferdinand's rule had been condemned by Europe, it was generally felt that the evil example of a successful uprising must be avoided at all costs.   The new government   French
was not recognized by the Holy Alliance which was   armies sup-
preparing to intervene.   Tsar Alexander I enthusiasti-   press the
cally volunteered to lead a Russian army across   uprising
Europe to suppress the Spanish revolutionists, but France was entrusted with the undertaking.   In 1823, a French army crossed the Pyrenees.   The Spaniards, who in the days of Napoleon had fought French armies that came to liberate them, now welcomed French armies that came to enslave them.   The Liberals, being a small minority, could offer little resistance and Ferdinand was restored to absolute power.   The revenge that he took shocked all Europe.   Thousands were summarily executed or imprisoned. The constitution was suppressed, and the acts of parliament were declared null and void.   Political and religious inquisitions, called "juntas of purification," were organized to ferret out Liberals, and many were exiled or hounded to death.   Not even in Italy did reaction triumph so completely as in Spain.

REFERENCES

ITALY:
    The Italian national movement attracted considerable attention and sympathy in England and America and led to the publication of excellent histories of the movement in English.   By far the best general account is

Bolton King, *A History of Italian Unity, 1814–1871*, 2 vols. (1899); for a good narrative of the early history of the movement see W. R. Thayer, *The Dawn of Italian Independence*, 2 vols (1893); Evelyn (Countess) Martinengo-Cesaresco, *The Liberation of Italy, 1815–1870* (1894), a sympathetic narrative. For additional titles see bibliography at the end of Chapter XIV.

SPAIN:

M. A. S. Hume, *Modern Spain* (ed. 1923); H. D. Sedgwick, *Spain: A Short History* (1925); and F. L. Paxson, *The Independence of the South American Republics* (1903).

ADDITIONAL REFERENCES

G. O. Griffith, *Mazzini* (1932); S. Barr, *Mazzini* (1935); K. R. Greenfield, *Economics and Liberalism in the Risorgimento* (1934); G. F.-H. Berkeley, *Italy in the Making, 1815–1846* (1933); G. F.-H. and J. Berkeley, *Italy in the Making: 1846–1848* (1935).

CHAPTER VII

THE RESTORATION IN GERMANY

THE political development of Germany was in striking contrast to that of France and England. As early as the seventeenth century, France and England became unified nations; and their national spirit grew stronger as the people became more homogeneous, the laws more uniform, and the language and culture more common. It was quite otherwise in Germany. By a curious irony of circumstances those forces which made for nationalism in France and England produced the opposite effect in Germany. During the Middle Ages the King was the efficient cause in the process of national consolidation in France and in England. In Germany, however, the Holy Roman Emperor retarded the growth of nationalism by his fruitless efforts to reëstablish the Empire of Otto the Great. His defeat in Italy and his humiliation by the Pope so weakened his authority that the feudal lords were able to maintain their political privileges. The Emperor's power was still further weakened by the Protestant Revolution. In the wars between Catholics and Protestants, the Emperor sided with the former, but many of the German princes sided with the latter. The outcome of the struggle was a victory for the Protestants, and the Emperor lost what little power and prestige he had enjoyed. Germany was now more disrupted than ever. The Holy Roman Empire was but a political shadow without any substance, "neither holy, nor Roman, nor yet an empire," in Voltaire's witty phrase.

A map of Germany during the eighteenth century had the appearance of a crazy-quilt. There were over 300 independent states, the "Germanies" as they were then called by the French, varying in size from a large kingdom like Prussia to a tiny territory of a knight of the Empire, each with its own flag, system of government, tariff, and army. More confusing still was the fact that some states lay wholly or partly within the boundaries of other states like scattered strips on a medieval farm. Among the Germans of that day love for the Fatherland did not exist; there was none to love. Those who emigrated to other lands readily became assimilated with other nationalities, and quickly forgot their native language and customs. At home the Germans were apt to be narrow and provincial, cherishing a strongly developed spirit of "particularism," or love of their state and especially of their princes. This sentiment is wittily described by Heine in the following manner:

"Our Elector was a fine gentleman, a great lover of the arts, and himself very clever with his fingers. He founded the picture gallery at Düsseldorf, and in the Observatory in that city they still show a very artistic set of wooden boxes, one inside the other, made by himself in his leisure hours, of which he had twenty-four every day.

"In those days the princes were not overworked mortals as they are to-day. Their crowns sat very firmly on their heads, and at night they just drew their nightcaps over them, and slept in peace, while peacefully at their feet slept their peoples; and when these woke up in the morning they said, 'Good-morning, Father,' and the princes replied, 'Good-morning, dear children.'"

The problem of democracy, like that of nationalism, was also solved, at least partially by England and France. At the beginning of the nineteenth century, England had the machinery of a democratic state; all that she needed in order to become a complete democracy was to reform and to broaden her electoral system. Although France had remained an autocracy down to the end of the eighteenth century, she accomplished during the decade of the French Revolution what it had taken England a century to achieve. The Bourbon Restoration was not, as has already been described, a restoration of absolutism.

Problem of democracy solved by England and France

Germany, possessing neither the English tradition of liberty "broadening down from precedent to precedent," nor the revolutionary impulses of France, entered the nineteenth century a naked absolutism, unchecked by representative institutions and unquestioned by the mass of the people. It has been the history of almost every country in Europe that the solidarity of the people always preceded the sovereignty of the people; modern democracy cannot take root except in the soil of nationalism. A people divided in their allegiance, as were the Germans, meant a people divided in their energies. They exhausted themselves in fratricidal strife and petty quarrels, and consequently they had no energy left to struggle for democracy

Not solved by Germany

The narrow atmosphere of the little "Germanies" cramped their souls and starved their national spirit.   In despair they took to philosophy.   For in the wide realm of metaphysics the German spirit could soar freely and majestically, knowing neither the constraint of boundaries nor the repression of despots.   It was then a common jest that whereas France ruled the land and England the sea, Germany ruled the clouds.   Many Germans affected to despise the nationalism to which they could not attain, and they became cosmopolitans, calling themselves "citizens of the world."   "The love of country," declared the dramatist, Lessing, "is a sentiment which I do not understand.   It is, as it seems to me, at best a heroic infirmity which I am most happy in not sharing."

THE GERMAN CONFEDERATION

The Liberation movement against Napoleon had roused the German people to a sense of their common nationality.   Much was expected by ardent patriots, but all that was granted by the Congress of Vienna was the German Confederation pledged to the "maintenance of external and internal security and the independence and integrity of the individual states."   The Confederation was an exceedingly loose union of sovereign states, not unlike that established in America by the Articles of Confederation.   It possessed no common executive and no common judiciary, but only a common legislature, the Diet, which met at Frankfort under the presidency of Austria. The Diet was really a congress of ambassadors, as the members were appointed by the local sovereigns and were subject to their instructions on matters before that body; hence, its powers were limited by the wishes of the princes.   Moreover, no important measure could pass that body without a two-thirds vote, and it was therefore almost impossible to get anything done.   The Diet was ridiculed as a "center of inertia"; the delegates spent most of their time debating inconsequential matters or quarreling over their relative dignity.   "Bound together by a spider's web," Germany was not united by the Confederation.

The Confederation, a loose union

Nearly every state of the Confederation was an absolute monarchy.   In some of the southern states, Bavaria, Baden, and Württemberg, the monarchs granted moderate constitutions establishing parliaments elected on a property basis and having limited powers.   In general, con-

Absolutism in government

stitutions and parliaments were regarded as revolutionary innovations to be resisted at all cost.

The Confederation became the field for a sort of internal diplomacy. The "great powers" were Austria and Prussia; in the
Internal
diplomacy
second rank were Bavaria, Saxony, and Württemberg;
the rest were the "minor powers." The Germans
exhausted their diplomatic genius on themselves; the various
states formed alliances and counter-alliances with one another and
against one another. Nothing delighted the German princes so
much as this game of internal diplomatic intrigue which they
practiced to their hearts' content.

With the establishment of peace there was revived the old
rivalry between Prussia and Austria for the leadership of the
Prussia, a
German
state
German people. In the struggle, Prussia had the advantage of condition; Austria, of prestige. The population of the former was almost entirely German; her
efficient bureaucracy, her strong army, and her leadership of the
German people in the struggle against Napoleon convinced all
those who were dreaming of unity that Prussia alone could become
the effective leader of a united German people. All that was
necessary was to persuade the Hohenzollerns to pursue a German
rather than a Prussian policy.

Austria was not a nation, but a "monarchical machine." Around
the Hapsburg dynasty were grouped a conglomeration of nations
Austria, a
polyglot
state
and surviving remnants of former nations who regarded German nationalism with indifference if not
with distrust. Only about one fifth of the population
in the Hapsburg dominions were of German origin and speech.
In spite of the great prestige of Austria, whose supremacy in Germany had been recognized for centuries, it was felt that she was too
non-German and too inefficient to become the leader in the movement for unity.

The Austrian policy was bent on maintaining the *status quo* at
all costs. Even its apologists declared that the country was like
Repression
in Austria
a rickety old building which would fall to pieces the
moment attempts were made to repair it. The
French Revolution, which had directly modernized western Germany and which had indirectly led to the regeneration of Prussia, exerted little influence in Austria, where the Old Régime was
still intact. There Metternich's ideas reigned supreme. Em-

peror Francis I, even more than his famous minister, was responsible for a system of repression that lay like a dead weight on the people of Austria. Journals, books, plays, and schools were subject to a censorship so severe that intellectual life became stagnant. Books expressing liberal views, even of the most moderate kind, were forbidden. Spies were in the class room, in the library, in the printing shop, to report the utterance of a liberal thought or the reading of a liberal book.

YOUNG GERMANY

After 1815 the political life of Germany was drawn into two powerful currents: one, toward democracy, or the establishment of constitutional government in each of the states; and the other, toward nationalism, or the more perfect union of the various states in a German nation. Some- *Nationalism and democracy* times these currents flowed parallel with each other; sometimes, in opposite directions; generally, they united to form one mighty stream. A united German people, passionately devoted to the Fatherland and not to the various princes, would inevitably mean a lessening of their power; hence, the rulers were as opposed to union as they were to liberty.

At no time did the dream of a united country seem harder of realization than at the beginning of the nineteenth century. The French Revolution was now over, and the restored despots, full of hatred for its principles, determined to crush any attempt to lessen their power. However, *Opposition of the princes* the popular uprising against Napoleon had left a memory of the might of an aroused people which boded ill for the princes who were now determined to suppress that popular sentiment that had been so useful to them when their thrones were in danger.

Opposition to the princes arose from an unexpected quarter, from the youth of the nation. There began a "youth movement" that spread rapidly among all classes, especially among the students. The rising generation repudiated the *The youth movement* ideas of their elders which they identified with political stagnation and with intellectual timidity. Young Germany was swayed less by ancient memories than by the events of the immediate past; the French Revolution and the Liberation movement. They felt their souls cramped and their minds warped in the petty, autocratic

"Germanies" and they longed for a free and united country "in which a free spirit might find room to soar."

Student societies were organized in the universities, which became known as the "Burschenschaft," or brotherhood of young men. Their motto was "Honor, Liberty, Fatherland!" This youth movement was animated by high personal ideals, and its members pledged themselves to lead noble lives in order to deserve well of their country. "By moral elevation and patriotic inspiration they hoped to lead the state of the future to the great goal of nationality." Any German student of whatever state was permitted to join the Burschenschaft, which was founded on a national basis in opposition to those student societies that were organized on a state basis. The students adopted a flag of black, red, and gold, and began an agitation for a united and free Fatherland. A new war of liberation was begun, this time against the tyrant princes at home.

The Bur-schenschaft

The Burschenschaft determined to arouse the German people by holding a patriotic national festival. Accordingly, on October 18, 1817, the jubilee year of the Protestant Revolution and the fourth anniversary of the battle of Leipzig, a great student celebration took place at the Castle of Wartburg, famous in the history of early Protestantism. Patriotic addresses were made, and the students partook of the Lord's Supper to solemnize their holy resolve to strive for their country. The closing of the festival was marked by a hilarious meeting around a bonfire where, in imitation of Luther's burning of the Papal Bull, the young patriots consigned to the flames certain reactionary books, a corporal's baton, and an officer's wig and corset, the symbols of tyranny.

The Wartburg Festival

The Wartburg Festival was followed by an assassination. Kotzebue, a reactionary journalist known to be a spy in the secret pay of the Tsar of Russia, was murdered by a student patriot. The Festival and the assassination caused consternation among the princes who feared that a revolution was in process. They denounced the universities as breeding-places of discontent that were educating the rising generation to hate authority and to commit deeds of violence. Metternich, as usual, took upon himself the guardianship of the established order. He called a conference of the princes at Carlsbad where, in 1819, they drew up the Carlsbad Decrees, which fettered the intellectual life of Germany for an entire generation.

These decrees, later adopted by the Diet of the Confederation, provided that special officials should be appointed in all the universities to supervise the conduct of students and teachers. These officials were to report any departure from conservative principles, and to give a "salutary direction" to instruction. Any teacher who was known to "propagate harmful doctrines hostile to public order, or subversive of existing governmental institutions," was to be dismissed from his position. The Burschenschaft was ordered dissolved. The display of the black, red, and gold flag was forbidden, and persons were prosecuted for even wearing a combination of these colors in their clothes, such as a yellow hat, black coat, and red waistcoat. A press censorship was established so rigid that free expression of opinion on political matters became impossible. Even the heroes of the Liberation movement were now persecuted as demagogues. "Father" Jahn, whose patriotic gymnastic societies had once roused the youth of Prussia against the French invaders, was imprisoned. Arndt, whose patriotic poems were on every one's lips, was removed from his position in the university. Fichte's famous *Address to the German Nation*, which had stirred all Germany against Napoleon, was forbidden republication.

The Carls-bad Decrees

THE ZOLLVEREIN

The Industrial Revolution came to Germany after the Napoleonic Wars. Its progress, however, was seriously hampered by the lack of unity; the barriers between the German states were economic as well as political. Each member of the Confederation had a tariff against the goods of every other member; furthermore, nearly every one of the states had internal, or provincial tariffs; Prussia had no fewer than sixty-seven provincial tariffs. The transit of goods from one part of Prussia to another, and from one German state to another, was enmeshed in a network of duties which hindered the development of German commerce and industry. The economist, Friedrich List, declared that the many tariffs had "much the same result as binding up the various members of the human body in order to prevent the blood from circulating from one to the other." So slowly did German industry develop that, as late as 1850, the twelve largest cities had a combined population of only 1,340,000. Many of German towns were still "the quiet places of the fairy books, with huddled

Tariff barriers

roofs and spires," and with ploughlands and orchards in the background.

Prussia early realized that tariff impediments had to be removed in order to allow the free growth of modern industry.   In 1818 she swept away all her provincial tariffs, and initiated a policy which finally led to the formation, in 1834, of the famous customs union known as the "Zollverein."

Prussia forms the Zollverein

With her territory scattered throughout Germany, Prussia lay athwart most of the trade routes.   She used this advantage to compel the other states to join the Zollverein by heavily taxing their goods in transit.   She even built roads to divert the trade of the states opposed to her policy.   By 1842 nearly all the states were members of the Zollverein.   Austria, however, was deliberately kept out through the influence of Prussia.

There was now a large free trade area in Germany, which greatly encouraged business enterprise.   The Zollverein established uniformity in fiscal matters.   It adopted free trade for its members and a common tariff on foreign goods; introduced the metric system of weights and measures;

Reforms of the Zollverein

reduced the many currency systems to only two; and negotiated commercial treaties.   At first the tendencies of the Zollverein favored low tariffs, even free trade.   Its chief supporter, List, was a strong protectionist.   He enthusiastically advocated what he called a "national system of political economy," according to which there was to be free trade within Germany, but high protective duties on foreign products.   Protection, in his view, would make Germany an economic unit, which would inevitably lead to a closer political union.   "On the development of the protection system," he declared, "depends the existence, the independence, and the future of German nationality."   List's ideas on protection and national unity were inspired by the experience of the United States, where he lived in exile for a number of years.

The Zollverein was an important step in the direction of unification.   Being stronger than the Confederation, it became an example as well as an inspiration to those favoring national unity.   As industry developed under its enlightened policies, the rising middle class were converted to German unity more by the solid benefits of business prosperity than by the speeches of patriotic orators.

The Zollverein and unification

INTELLECTUAL DEVELOPMENT

Although the history of Germany during the first half of the nineteenth century was sterile politically, it was yet most fruitful intellectually. As the German people were prevented from expressing themselves in public life, their genius turned to philosophy, scholarship, and science, to which they made notable contributions. Philosophy, particularly, had always claimed Germany's attention. "History shows us," declared Hegel, "that when all but the name of philosophy was lost in other lands, it had maintained itself as the peculiar possession of the German nation, who have received from nature the high calling to be the guardians of this sacred fire."

Intellectual progress of Germany

Next to Immanuel Kant, the greatest figure in German philosophy is Georg Wilhelm Friedrich Hegel, the philosophic dictator of his day. To students of history, Hegel is especially interesting for the reason that he was one of the first to work out a systematic philosophy of history. In his book, *The Philosophy of History*, he propounds the idea that each period is characterized by the predominance of a "world people," who are possessed of a "universal idea" which must be given to mankind. Once this has been accomplished, the "world people" has fulfilled its mission; it then sinks into decadence and yields the scepter to its successor. In another work, *The Philosophy of Law*, Hegel glorifies the State as the very essence of freedom and reason. Its laws are the "footsteps of God upon earth"; through the State alone can the individual attain his highest development, and social organization its supreme expression. As the organic expression of the people, its primary function is to embody the public weal of all classes and in all ways. He became so ardent a champion of the Prussian monarchy and so bitter an opponent of revolution that he was regarded as the "official philosopher." The spirit of the people, he declared, does not speak through parliaments, but through the continuous life of the State as represented by the king. In his opinion aristocracy and democracy were primitive forms of government, both of which were superseded by monarchy, the highest form yet devised.

Hegel (1770–1831)

The national revival which took place in Prussia after the Battle of Jena found expression in a renewed study of German history. A great historical enterprise was planned by a group of historians, who proposed to reprint and edit all the sources relating to

German history. The first volume of this series, which is known
as the *Monumenta Germaniae Historica*, was issued
in 1826. Many volumes of the *Monumenta* have
since appeared, and this documentary history of the German people
has made for itself an enduring place in the world of scholarship.

The Monumenta

The first of the modern scientific historians was Leopold von
Ranke, through whose influence German historical scholarship
became supreme in Europe. Ranke emphasized,
above all things, the value of studying original sources
which, to him, were the very wells of historical truth. He ransacked the libraries and archives of Europe and discovered many
historical documents long unknown or forgotten. He was one of
the first to institute the seminar method of training students to
become professional historians by organizing small groups of
scholars to make a systematic study of original documents. Ranke's
great aim was to rewrite the history of the world according to this
rigorous, scientific method. He never completed the task, although
his collected works number many volumes. Ranke's ideal of historical composition was a dispassionate presentation of facts "as
they really were," unbiased by party, opinion, or nationality. The
views and acts of important monarchs and statesmen, rather than
the condition of the mass of the people, were for him the essence
of history; hence, his books are cold and dry recitals of facts based
largely on diplomatic correspondence and on the state papers of
kings and ministers.

Ranke (1795–1886)

German historical writing has produced no greater master than
Theodor Mommsen whose famous *History of Rome* continues to
be a standard work on the subject. Although as
great and as thorough a scholar as Ranke, Mommsen
possessed, in addition, a brilliant historical imagination which
enabled him to reproduce the past in a vivid and fascinating way.
He was not only a narrator of facts, carefully gathered and scientifically classified, but also an interpreter of original power. Mommsen's *History* is a luminous résumé of the political history of the
Roman Republic based on all the knowledge of the subject
available.

Mommsen (1817–1903)

German literature at the end of the eighteenth century reached
its apex of creative power. Goethe and Schiller had succeeded in
raising the German language from a more or less despised dia-

THEODOR MOMMSEN

lect to the very front rank of the tongues of Europe. Their successors were inspired by the ideals of Young Germany, Heine
and aimed to enlist literature in the service of politi- (1797–1856)
cal reform. A new literary species was created, half-journalism,
half-literature, which proved to be exceedingly effective in fighting
the entrenched forces of reaction. A leading figure of the new
Germany in literature was Heinrich Heine, who was of Jewish
origin. As poet, critic, and essayist, he spent almost his entire life
waging relentless war against despotic government and intellectual repression. He could with truth declare, "Lay on my coffin
a sword, for I was a brave soldier in the Liberation War of humanity."

It is easier to read Heine's works than to describe them. Brimful
of airy wit, poetic imagination, delicate sentiment, acid irony, and
blasphemous scoffing; by turns, grave and gay; over- Character of
flowing with pathos and stabbing with cruel irony — Heine's
that is Heine. His comments on political and philo- work
sophic ideas have a piquancy seldom to be found in the discussion
of such serious subjects. Such, for example, is his explanation of
how liberty is loved by the various nations. "An Englishman
loves liberty like his lawfully wedded wife. She is a possession.
He may not treat her with much tenderness, but he knows how to
defend her. A Frenchman loves liberty like his sweetheart, and
he will do a thousand follies for her sake. A German loves liberty
like his old grandmother. And yet, after all, no one can tell how
things will turn out. The grumpy Englishman, in an ill-temper
with his wife, is capable of dragging her by a rope to Smithfield.
The inconstant Frenchman may become unfaithful to his adored
and be off flirting around the Palais Royal with another. But the
German will never quite desert his old grandmother; he will always
keep for her a nook near the chimney-corner, where she can tell
fairy tales to the listening children."

Under Heine's magic touch German prose became simple, easy,
fluent, and plastic, almost like that of the great masters of French
prose. His widely read *Reisebilder* (*Pictures of Travel*) Heine's
is a unique work containing descriptions of places and prose
scenes, criticism of current ideas, confessions, satirical comments on
his contemporaries, and poetical outbursts. This "German Aris-
tophanes," as Heine called himself, was especially fond of directing
the shafts of his brilliant wit against contemporary men, manners,
and morals, which made him many bitter enemies.

If Heine's pen was satirical, it was also lyrical; no man was more truly the poet born than this scoffer.　His poems, collected in the

Heine's poetry

famous *Buch der Lieder* (*Book of Songs*), have a lyric beauty unsurpassed in German literature.　Their haunting charm and delicate, strange imagery, their simplicity and artlessness, their melody and sweetness, have made them known wherever the German tongue is spoken.　"A nightingale nesting in the wig of a Voltaire" was Heine, the lyric poet and satirical reformer.

REFERENCES

GENERAL:

Many volumes have been written on various aspects of the history of Germany during the nineteenth century.　But most of them are disfigured by violent partisanship, the reflection of the passions aroused by the bitter struggles of Germany to achieve her unity.　The most famous work is Heinrich von Treitschke, *History of Germany in the Nineteenth Century*, translated from the German, 7 vols. (1915–19), covers period of the Restoration, very nationalist (see page 232); H. von Sybel, *The Founding of the German Empire by William I*, 7 vols., translated from the German (1890–98), another famous national history, scholarly in method, but marked by a decided Prussian bias; the best treatment is in A. Stern, *Geschichte Europas*, vol. I, chaps. IV and VIII, vol. IV, chap. VI, vol. V, chap. III, vol. VI, chaps. IV, VI, and VIII; brief account, E. F. Henderson, *A Short History of Germany* (ed. 1916), vol. II; W. O. Henderson, *The Zollverein* (1939).

SOCIAL AND ECONOMIC:

T. von der Goltz, *Geschichte der deutschen Landwirtschaft*, 2 vols. (1902–03), vol II; W. Sombart, *Die deutsche Volkswirtschaft in neunzehnten Jahrhundert* (ed. 1919); W. H. Dawson, *Protection in Germany: a History of German Fiscal Policy during the Nineteenth Century* (1904).

CULTURAL:

T. Ziegler, *Die Geistigen und Sozialen Stromungen Deutschlands in neunzehnten Jahrhundert* (ed. 1911).　On the German historians: A. Guilland, *Modern Germany and her Historians*, translated from the French (1915), and G. P. Gooch, *History and Historians in the Nineteenth Century* (1913), chaps. I–VIII; F. Kummer, *Deutsche Literaturgeschichte des neunzehnten Jahrhunderts* (1909); K. Francke, *A History of German Literature as determined by Social Forces* (ed. 1901); J. F. Coar, *Studies in German Literature in the Nineteenth Century* (1903); F. Schnabel, *Deutsche Geschichte im neunzehnten Jahrhundert*, 3 vols. (1929–34).

CHAPTER VIII

OLD ENGLAND

BEFORE the French Revolution, England was universally admired
as the land of freedom. She was the first modern nation that
had repudiated absolute monarchy, flouted divine
right, beheaded one king and deposed another, and
had actually succeeded in establishing a system of
government in which Parliament ruled the country.
From the Revolution of 1689 flowed many liberties. Civil liberty
was protected by the Bill of Rights which guaranteed the persons
and property of Englishmen against arbitrary action of officials.
Religious liberty to a large degree was established by the Toleration
Act which granted toleration to the Dissenters, the most numerous
and the most powerful opponents of the established Anglican
Church. Freedom of the press was decreed by the abolition of an
official censorship. By the end of the eighteenth century feudalism
had disappeared from English life. Serfdom and peasant dues
were not even memories. The guilds were in a state of decay, and
capital and labor were free to engage in any enterprise. Noble
and commoner were equal before the law; a title was more a badge
of social prestige than a claim to political privilege. The contrast
between England and the other nations was striking. Absolute
monarchy by divine right, arbitrary imprisonment, religious persecution, oppressive censorships, serfdom, guild monopolies, and
aristocratic privileges, all flourished on the Continent.

Because of England's primacy in parliamentary government she
was regarded by progressively minded persons as the home of
political freedom and liberty. The great French
writers, Montesquieu and Voltaire, had written ful-
some praise of the English system, which they had
recommended as a model to the oppressed peoples of Europe. In
the opinion of the jurist, Blackstone, the English government was
the perfection of human wisdom. England, too, was the only
country which had passed safely through the terrific upheaval
caused by the French Revolution that had transformed every
other nation in western Europe. Freedom combined with stability seemed to be the happy condition of the inhabitants of

(margin notes) England, pioneer of civil and religious liberty

England, model of Europe

Great Britain.   As Euripides boasted of Athens, so might an
Englishman boast of his country:

> "Thou hast seen
> Our ordered life, and justice,
>   and the long
> Still grasp of law not changing
>   with the strong
> Man's pleasure."

POLITICAL CONDITIONS

In truth, however, England was far indeed from being a political
paradise.   Behind the veil of Parliament an oligarchy held sway

Unfair representation in Parliament

through a system of unfair representation and shame-
less corruption.   Representative government in those
days was based on the theory that members of Parliament represented the nation as a whole; of necessity
they were elected in certain localities and by certain persons.
Which localities should elect them and who should be the electors
had little to do with population and with citizenship.   Certain
places were designated as constituencies because they had had
that privilege from time immemorial or because they had been so
designated by the King.   There was no periodic reapportionment.
Whether a constituency gained or lost population, or even became
totally uninhabited, it continued to send the same number of representatives to Parliament.   The great changes in the size and distribution of population due to the Industrial Revolution resulted
in discrepancies so glaring that Parliament became a mockery of
representative government.   In the industrial regions of the north,
small villages had grown into large cities; in the agricultural south
population remained stationary or had actually declined.   Towns
such as Buckingham, with thirteen voters; Gatton with five;
Orford with twenty; Middlehurst with thirteen; Old Sarum with
none; and Dunwich, sunk under the waters of the North Sea, all
duly elected members to Parliament; whereas, great cities such as
Manchester, Birmingham, and Leeds had no representation.   Scotland was given forty-five seats, and the county of Cornwall, with
only one eighth of her population, forty-four seats.   Lord John
Russell, who led in the attack upon these conditions, declared that
if a stranger coming to England full of admiration for the land of
political freedom, were taken "to a green mound, and told that

this green mound sent two members to Parliament; or to a green wall with three niches in it and told that these three niches sent two members to Parliament; or, if he were shown a green park, with many signs of flourishing vegetable life but none of human habitation, and told that this green park sent two members to Parliament," he would be greatly surprised. "But his surprise would increase to astonishment if he were carried into the north of England, where he would see large flourishing towns, full of trade and activity, containing vast magazines of wealth and manufactures, and were told that these places had no representation in the assembly which was said to represent the people."

Parliamentary representation before 1832 was generally known as the "Rotten Borough System." A "rotten borough" was a decayed constituency whose representatives were virtually appointed by the local landlords, who had little difficulty in coercing the few electors, usually their tenants. Many seats were uncontested because of the certainty of the election of the lords' candidates. In some of the constituencies known as "pocket" boroughs the lord had an absolute right to "nominate"; namely, to appoint outright its representatives. So widespread was the Rotten Borough System that a large majority of the members of Parliament were nominated by "noblemen and gentlemen." A system of "borough-mongering" had grown up whereby rich men, desirous of the social distinction of being in public life, would purchase nominations for seats in Parliament.

The Rotten Borough System

The right to vote, too, was limited to comparatively a very few. According to the prevailing theory, suffrage was not a human *right* of every citizen, but a *privilege* attached to property, particularly to landed property, to certain offices, to the payment of certain taxes, and even to birth. In some towns the mayor and council, in others the wealthy merchants chose the members of Parliament. In the counties, or country districts, only the "forty-shilling freeholders," or those who owned land yielding forty shillings a year income could vote in the parliamentary elections. Hence, only about five per cent of all the adult males in Great Britain and Ireland had the right to vote. In Scotland, there were only about three thousand voters, in a population of about two million. The county of Bute with a population of fourteen thousand contained only twenty-one voters. In some

Suffrage restrictions

constituencies only one voter appeared, the candidate himself. "He of course took the lead," it was reported, "constituted the meeting, called over the roll of freeholders, answered to his own name. . . . He then moved and seconded his own nomination, put the question to a vote, and was unanimously returned." Moreover, bribery was open and prevalent, no shame being attached to such practices; candidates openly advertised their prices for votes. As the method of voting was a public declaration of one's choice, coercion of voters was resorted to by those who had power over them, such as landlords, employers, and officials.

The system of government was in outline what it is to-day, King, Lords, and Commons. After George III the King became System of government a figurehead; the government was conducted in his name by a cabinet responsible to the Commons. The Lords consisted chiefly of hereditary peers, and the Commons was elected for a term of seven years, unless sooner dissolved by the King. The two parties, Tories and Whigs, were not organized on a popular basis as political parties are to-day. They were manipulated by two groups of aristocratic families that succeeded each other in office whenever it suited their purposes.[1]

During the days of the "unreformed" House of Commons the government of England was in the hands of the aristocrats. Directly they controlled the House of Lords, where their leading Government by the aristocracy members, the peers, had hereditary seats; indirectly, through the Rotten Borough System, they controlled the Commons. The monarchy had become their puppet. The magistracy, the universities, the army, the navy, the higher administrative offices, the Established Church, all were the perquisites of the aristocracy. Before 1832 the English political system might be described as a government of the people, by the aristocrats, for the aristocrats.

RELIGIOUS CONDITIONS

Privilege was as dominant in the Church as in the State. Until Toleration, but no equality the Revolution of 1689, English law presumed every subject to be a member of the national Established Church. The Toleration Act of that year granted freedom of worship to Dissenters; later, it was extended, with restrictions, to Catholics and Jews. At the beginning of the nineteenth

[1] For a detailed description of the British system of government, see page 257.

century, there was toleration of every faith in England, but there was no religious equality. According to law the inhabitants were classified as (1) Anglicans, or members of the Established Church; (2) Nonconformists, formerly known as Dissenters, such as Baptists, Congregationalists, and Presbyterians,[1] who refused to conform to the Anglican faith; and (3) Catholics and Jews.

The Anglican was the privileged Church. Its head was the King; and its bishops, appointed by the government, had seats in the House of Lords. It was supported by incomes from endowments and from properties given to the Church in times past by the kings; by special taxes, *Privileges of the Anglicans* such as the tithe and Church rate, levied on citizens irrespective of their belief; and by direct subsidies from the national treasury. All public officials had to be Anglicans. None but Anglicans could receive degrees from Oxford and Cambridge, then the only important universities in Great Britain. As the Anglican was the Church of the upper classes, it was considered unfashionable to belong to any other, and those who did consequently suffered social ostracism.

Non-Anglicans were barred from public office by Test Acts passed during the religious struggles of the seventeenth century. To-day the only "test" that is required of a public official is that he take an oath of loyalty to the government which he serves. In those days he had to *Disabilities of the non-Anglicans* recognize the King as the head of the Anglican Church, to subscribe to its doctrines, and especially to disavow the Catholic doctrine of transubstantiation. These laws, in effect, barred from public office all conscientious Nonconformists, Catholics, and Jews. In proportion as these faiths varied from the Anglican so did the disabilities. Being Protestants, the Nonconformists were not very harshly treated, and the Test Acts were not enforced against them. They were permitted to be members of Parliament and to hold public office; their acts were legalized by Parliament which, annually, passed an act of indemnity for that purpose.

Against Catholics the Test Acts were strictly enforced because of the great fear that, otherwise, the Catholics would seize political power. They were popularly regarded as the bitter enemies of the Protestant government as *Position of the Catholics* established by the Revolution of 1689. In 1793, a concession had

---

[1] In Scotland the Presbyterian, not the Anglican, was the Established Church.

been made to the Catholics, who were given the right to vote, but not to be members of Parliament.

Catholics were regarded with fear as enemies, but Jews were regarded with contempt as aliens. In theory Jews were not citizens, Position of and lived in England only by sufferance. Foreign the Jews Jews could not be naturalized. Religious tests barred Jews from public office, from Parliament, from voting, from the universities, and from the legal profession. Popular prejudice against Jews was great, despite the fact that they were few in number and very influential in the business world.

SOCIAL AND ECONOMIC CONDITIONS

England entered the nineteenth century a modern industrial nation. But her economic development was greatly hampered by Restrictions the restrictions of the Mercantilist System which was of the Mer- still largely intact. Commerce was shackled by tariffs cantilist and prohibitions on imports and by export duties on System raw materials with the object of having a favorable balance of trade, or an excess of exports over imports. The most onerous of the restrictions were those on "corn," or breadstuffs, such as wheat, barley, rye, and oats. When peace came in 1815 the landowners, who controlled Parliament, succeeded in putting through a famous Corn Law which prohibited the importation of food except when the price of the home product rose to a figure which insured British farmers sufficient security; later a sliding scale was adopted which provided for lowering the duties when prices rose and for raising them when prices fell. Equally onerous were the Navigation Laws, a relic of the old colonial policy. Foreign vessels were excluded from the colonial trade and from the coasting trade; and certain foreign articles could be imported only in native ships. As long as these Mercantilist restrictions remained, England could not take full advantage of the marvelous inventions that came with her Industrial Revolution.

There were evils new as well as old. In the newly established factory system, the working classes suffered great abuses, especially Child labor the most helpless of them, the women and children. Large numbers of workers, men, women, and children, were gathered in huge buildings with little or no provision for the safeguarding of health or for the preservation of decency; and, as a consequence, factories became hot-beds of disease, misery, and vice. The hours of labor were from twelve to sixteen, even for children; wages were down to the starvation level, and frequently the entire family, father, mother, and children, were compelled to work in the factory in order to eke out an existence. In some places women were employed in the mines, where they were harnessed to coal carts which they dragged around creeping on hands and feet through narrow and dangerous passages. Boys and girls, naked to the waist, worked in the coal mines thirteen hours a day pulling loads of coal. At first only pauper children were "apprenticed" to the factory owners by the overseers of the poor who wanted to get rid of the burden of supporting them; as the need for labor increased, non-pauper children were employed, their only wages being food and clothes of the coarsest kind. These children, some only five or six years old, were obliged to live in dormitories near the factory, where they were treated like slaves. Early every morning they were awakened and taken to the factory where, "in stench, in heated rooms, amid the constant whirling of a thousand wheels, idle fingers and little feet were kept in ceaseless action, forced into unnatural activity by blows from the heavy hands and feet of the merciless overlooker, and the infliction of bodily pain by instruments invented by the sharpened ingenuity of insatiable selfishness." If any were suspected of a desire to run away in order to escape from their unbearable misery, they were regarded as criminals and mercilessly chained to the machines which they operated. To the claims of humanity, many employers had become entirely deaf through their desire for large profits. But thoughtful and patriotic Englishmen realized that the rising generation of the working class was growing up under conditions which produced physical degeneracy, abject ignorance, and shocking immorality.

During the early part of the nineteenth century the cost of living was continually rising, whereas wages either remained stationary or rose very slowly. The employment of women and children had the effect of throwing many men out of   Pauperism
work. Thousands were unable to support their families, and appealed to the public authorities for help. In 1795 a method of poor relief had been adopted, known as the "Speenhamland System," according to which insufficient wages were to be supplemented from the rates, or local taxes. Instead of being sent to the poorhouse, the poor were to be given "outdoor relief," in their homes.

It was an evil system as it encouraged employers to pay low wages and encouraged the workingman to depend upon public charity. At one time the number of "assisted" poor rose to about a quarter of the total population.

Popular education being in a very low state, the overwhelming majority of the lower classes could neither read nor write.   Private
Illiteracy   religious and philanthropic societies conducted schools
               in which the rudiments of knowledge were crudely imparted by ill-paid teachers assisted by "monitors," or pupil teachers.   The advance of popular education was greatly retarded by the powerful opposition of aristocratic influences.   It was feared that if the common man were educated he would become discontented; hence, ignorance was a safeguard against revolutionary ideas.   When, in 1807, Samuel Whitbread proposed in Parliament that the government should establish a system of popular education he was opposed on the ground that education would teach the lower classes "to despise their lot in life instead of making them good servants in agriculture and other laborious employment to which their rank has destined them; instead of teaching them subordination it would render them fractious and refractory as was evident in the manufacturing counties; it would enable them to read seditious pamphlets, vicious books, and publications against Christianity; it would render them insolent to their superiors."

Although freedom of the press was theoretically established in 1695, when Parliament abolished official censorship, a system of
"Taxes on   "taxing knowledge" made a mockery of this principle.
knowledge"   Special taxes on paper and stamp taxes on pamphlets, newspapers, and advertisements so increased the cost of publication that the average price of a newspaper was fourteen cents a copy. A cheap press, it was feared, would curry favor with its readers by advocating democratic ideas and undermine the authority of the upper classes.   It was often possible to evade the law by resorting to irregular publication or by secret circulation.   "Private papers" appeared, poorly printed, badly written, and ill-informed.   Presaging better days, the London *Times* installed its first steam press in 1814; its circulation rose to five thousand, but the price of a copy was eighteen cents!

Restriction and suppression were the watchwords of the Old Régime in its normal functions.   But when its laws were violated,

punishment was cruel and inhuman.   The attitude toward the
criminal was clearly shown by the barbarous crimi- Harsh treat-
nal code and by conditions in the prisons. Death ment of
was the penalty prescribed for about two hundred offenders
and fifty offenses, some of them as trivial as stealing five shillings'
worth of goods from a shop, stealing linen from bleaching-grounds,
wounding a cow, maliciously cutting a piece of serge, and going
about in disguise.   The humanity of the juries, however, softened
the application of the code, as they frequently refused to send men
to the gallows for committing petty crimes.   Injured persons often
preferred to suffer losses rather than be the cause of visiting terrible
punishment upon offenders.   The prisons, maintained by keepers
subsidized by the government, were generally filthy places; men,
women, and children were indiscriminately herded together, the
hardened criminals with the first offenders.   As a consequence,
prisons became schools for crime, young criminals learning to
become more expert in their dishonest calling.

In the rising power and growing influence of the middle classes
lay the hope of a new and happier England.   Opposed to oligarchic
rule in politics, to religious discriminations, to general illiteracy,
and to barbarous and archaic systems of law, the middle classes
became the champions of progress throughout the nineteenth century.   From their ranks came political reformers such as Gladstone
and Bright, leaders of thought such as John Stuart Mill, Darwin,
and Carlyle, and, in many cases, even the champions of the working
classes.   To organize society on an industrial basis was the prime
function of the middle class.   In the process much needless suffering was inflicted, serious problems were created, and many vicious
practices were condoned.   Nevertheless, the task once accomplished, it marked the greatest advance mankind had yet made.

REFERENCES

GENERAL:
E. Halévy, *A History of the English People*, translated from the
French, 3 vols. (1924–27), vol. I, 1815, vol. II, 1815–30, and vol. III, 1830–
41, a great work by a French scholar, a comprehensive synthesis of politics,
economics, religion, and culture, based entirely on original sources; Halévy's
work deals with nineteenth-century England, but he has continued it in
Epilogue, Vol. I, 1895–1905.   Good one-volume histories: G. M. Trevelyan,
British History in the Nineteenth Century and After, 1782–1919 (1938);
A. L. Cross. *Shorter History of England and Greater Britain* (new ed., 1929);

J. A. R. Marriott, *England Since Waterloo* (1913); S. Low and L. C. Sanders, *Political History of England*, 1837–1901 (1907); and J. H. Rose, *The Rise and Growth of Democracy in Great Britain* (1898); H. W. Paul, *A History of Modern England*, 5 vols. (1904–06), covers period 1845–95, largely parliamentary, liberal in viewpoint; O. F. Christie, *The Transition to Democracy: 1867–1914* (1934); J. F. Bright, *History of England*, 5 vols. (1884–1904), vols. iv–v, and S. Walpole, *History of England since 1815*, 6 vols. (ed. 1902–05), continued in another work, *History of Twenty-Five Years, 1856–1880*, 4 vols. (1904–08), are old-fashioned political histories, scholarly, but out of date in viewpoint; A. D. Innes, *History of England and the British Empire*, 4 vols. (1913–15), vol. iv, very detailed, reliable but uninteresting; E. C. Wingfield-Stratford, *The History of British Civilization*, 2 vols. (1928), vol. ii covers period from the Restoration to the World War, an interpretative history, very interesting.

ENGLAND IN 1832:

W. L. Mathieson, *England in Transition, 1789–1832* (1920), good study of social and political conditions of the period; the standard works on the Reform Bill of 1832 are E. and A. G. Porritt, *The Unreformed House of Commons*, 2 vols. (1903), and J. R. M. Butler, *The Passing of the Great Reform Bill* (1914); B. Guttmann, *England im Zeitalter der Bürgerlichen Reform* (1923), a valuable social study, good description of the reforms before 1832; F. J. Klingberg, *The Anti-Slavery Movement in England* (1926), a contribution to an important but neglected field; O. F. Christie, *The Transition from Aristocracy* (1927), describes influence of Reform Bill of 1832 on the political and social institutions of England.

CHAPTER IX

THE MAKING OF MODERN ENGLAND

REFORMS AND REFORMERS

THE history of England during the nineteenth century was largely a history of reforms. Long-established institutions, political, religious, social, and economic were swept away or were radically modified by the liberal tide which rose at the close of the Napoleonic Wars.

As Rousseau was the intellectual father of revolution in France, the great scholar-reformer, Jeremy Bentham, was the intellectual father of reform in England. To every law, tradition, Bentham custom, and institution Bentham applied the simple (1748–1832) but devastating question, What is its use? If it was of no use, it should be abolished, he asserted. In his *Principles of Morals and Legislation* he developed his philosophy, which became known as "Utilitarianism." In Bentham's view the foundation of morals and legislation is the "greatest happiness of the greatest number"; hence, government should concern itself primarily with the promotion of human welfare through legislative measures. Bentham's special interest was law reform. He had a profound knowledge of English law and custom, which he severely criticized as being irrational in procedure and barbarous in methods of punishment, and he advocated the adoption of a new civil and criminal code based upon enlightened principles and rational methods.

Bentham's teaching was the inspiration of a group of political reformers, known as the Radicals. They were uncompromising champions of democracy, and demanded "root" reforms such as universal, manhood suffrage, secret ballot, and equal electoral districts in order to make Parliament the true representative of the people. Chief among the Radicals were William William Cobbett and Francis Place. The former was the first Cobbett influential popular editor in England. Cobbett pub- (1762–1835) lished and edited a radical newspaper, *The Weekly Political Register*, the price of which he reduced from one shilling to twopence a copy. It was brilliantly and forcefully written, and was widely read by the working classes who came to regard Cobbett as their leader and spokesman.   Cobbett vigorously denounced the abuses of the day, social and economic as well as political, as a consequence of which his paper was regarded by the authorities as libelous and seditious.   He threw himself with ardor into the movement for parliamentary reform which he regarded as all important.   "Let us have this reform [universal suffrage] first, and all other good things will be given unto us," he once declared.   Cobbett was a typical English agitator, virulently eloquent and shrewdly humorous, who was ready to attack the existing order by tongue and pen, but who was opposed to revolutionary violence.

Quite a different personality was Place, who was neither a writer nor a speaker, but a very able organizer.   Place was a master tailor who, after making a fortune, devoted himself tirelessly to the cause of reform.   He was a self-educated man, widely read in political and social matters, and his shop, which contained an excellent library, was a rendezvous for Radical thinkers and politicians, such as James Mill and Joseph Hume.   Place schooled them with arguments and directed their movements with great skill and shrewdness.   His influence spread even to Parliament, where an influential Radical group looked to him for guidance.   At times this tailor-reformer actually dictated parliamentary decisions.

Francis Place (1771–1854)

After Waterloo the Tories continued to control the government. They had saved England from the French Revolution and from Napoleon; and now the upper classes looked to them to save the Old Régime from the reformers.   The defeat of Napoleon brought peace, but not prosperity. Thousands of discharged soldiers and sailors were now without employment.   Merchants were ruined by the reëntrance of foreign competition which came with peace; and many laborers were therefore thrown out of work.   Discontent of all kinds was skillfully directed by the Radicals into the channel of parliamentary reform.   Political societies were founded, monster demonstrations were organized, and petitions demanding reform were drawn up. Riots broke out in almost every part of the kingdom.   The government became frightened and, in 1817, suspended the Habeas Corpus Act.   Two years later an event occurred which aroused the greatest indignation.   A popular mass meeting was to be held at Saint Peter's Field, in Manchester, for the purpose of demanding

Economic dislocation brings discontent

reform. As the meeting had been prohibited by the authorities, the military were ordered to break it up; they charged the crowd, killing some and injuring many, amid the wildest confusion. This "Massacre of Peterloo," as it was called, was followed by the passage of the famous Six Acts [1] which greatly limited the freedom of speech, of the press, and of assembly. Disraeli well describes the attitude of the Tory ministers toward the problems that confronted England after the Napoleonic Wars. "The peace came; the stimulating influences suddenly ceased; the people, in a novel and painful position, found themselves without guides. They went to the ministry; they asked to be guided. . . . What did the ministry do?

"They fell into a panic. Having fulfilled during their lives the duties of administration, they were frightened because they were called upon, for the first time, to perform the functions of government. Like all weak men, they had recourse to what they called strong measures. . . . In the language of this defunct school of statesmen, a practical man is a man who practices the blunders of his predecessors."

However, the reactionary spirit of the Restoration on the Continent was not the spirit of Tory rule in England. A number of reforms were put through that prepared the way for the great reforms which began in 1832. Inspired by Tory reform Bentham's ideas, an agitation arose for a modification of the criminal code, led by Sir Samuel Romilly, who was a tireless advocate of humane treatment of criminals. The harshness of the code in holding life cheap and property dear, far from discouraging crime, actually incited it. One might just as well be hanged for murder as for stealing a fish. Opposition to reform came especially from lawyers and judges who feared that a modification of the code would lead to the spread of crime. In 1823, Sir Robert Peel became a champion of law reform, and put through a bill abolishing the death penalty in about a hundred cases. This was the first breach in the Draconian code which was, later, to be entirely revised.

A breach was also made in the Mercantilist System, largely

---

[1] These Acts were: (1) the prohibition of military exercises by persons not authorized to perform them; (2) quick trials for offenders; (3) issuing of search warrants for arms; (4) suppression of seditious literature and the banishment of the authors; (5) restriction of the right of public meeting; and (6) heavy stamp duties on newspapers.

through the efforts of William Huskisson.   He was a disciple of
Huskisson's   Adam Smith and therefore favored the abolition of
measures   artificial restrictions and encouragements to trade.   In
1823, he induced Parliament to modify the Navigation Laws by
permitting reciprocity arrangements with foreign nations concerning the equal treatment of ships.   Although not a free-trader, he
favored a simplification of the tariff system in the interest of freer
trade.   Through Huskisson's efforts the tariff on raw materials
was scaled down considerably, and the restrictions on exports were
abolished.

An attempt was also made to repeal the Combination Laws.[1]
Because of the rapid development of English industry, the trade
Repeal of   unions grew despite the restrictive laws and the
the Combin-   poverty and ignorance of the workingmen.   As
ation Laws   champions of freedom of association the Radicals took
up the cause of the trade unions, and Place became the leader in a
movement to repeal the Combination Laws.   In a quiet but effective way he brought pressure to bear upon Parliament, and, in
1824, the Combination Laws were repealed.   But an outbreak of
strikes brought a demand from the manufacturers to restrict the
activities of trade unions.   In 1825, a new law was passed which
virtually restored the Combination Laws; it permitted workingmen
to organize but, in effect, forbade them to strike.

More substantial progress was made in the field of religious
liberty.   Outside of Ireland the religious question concerned
Repeal of   mainly the Nonconformists whose numbers were in-
the Test and creasing rapidly due to the growth of Methodism.   In
Corpora-   1828, Parliament repealed the Test and Corporations
tions Acts   Acts, thereby removing in theory, as well as in fact,
the civil restrictions imposed on Nonconformists.   The law of 1828
was the first step toward religious equality in England.

To emancipate the Catholics was a much more difficult undertaking, partly because of the inherited opposition to Catholicism
Catholic   of the English people, but chiefly because the over-
emancipa-   whelming majority of the Catholics were the Irish, a
tion   subject nationality.   Religious emancipation of the
Irish might lead to their political and economic emancipation, a
state of affairs then not desired by the dominant English.   A
widespread agitation for the removal of Catholic disabilities was

[1] See page 40.

started in Ireland under the leadership of Daniel O'Connell, a remarkable orator and efficient organizer. Almost the entire Catholic population of Ireland was enrolled in the Catholic Association which, under O'Connell's leadership, conducted an orderly yet menacing agitation. Parliament dissolved the Association, but it immediately reappeared under another name. As it was not illegal for a Catholic to be a candidate for Parliament, O'Connell was nominated, in 1828, and was triumphantly elected. But, as a devout Catholic, he would not take the anti-Catholic oath prescribed for members. The issue was now joined. The Wellington Ministry adopted a plan of Peel in favor of Catholic emancipation. There were two elements in the situation favorable to this plan: fear of a possible uprising of the Irish and admiration of the Catholic Church for the part it had played in France as the foe of revolution. It was no longer the Jesuits but the Jacobins who were now regarded with terror by the English. In 1829, Parliament abolished the disabilities of the Catholics, who were made eligible to nearly all offices in the United Kingdom. However, a new electoral law in Ireland raised the property qualifications for voting which, in effect, disfranchised many Catholics.

THE REFORM BILL OF 1832

All these reforms were put through by the Tories who controlled both houses of Parliament. They were persuaded by moderate leaders like Peel and Huskisson who wished to avoid catastrophic changes through moderate concessions. But when parliamentary reform became the issue, all Tories consolidated against it. They feared, and quite rightly, that democratic government would mean the end of their rule and of the privileges of the aristocracy whose interests they represented. *Tories consolidate against parliamentary reform*

Who, then, were to take up the cause of reform? The traditions of 1689 pointed to the Whigs. But the Whigs were aristocrats and were not at all favorable to radical changes. However, as they had been out of power for a generation they were inclined to favor a popular cause, particularly if it was to be under aristocratic direction. The uncompromising champions of reform were the Radicals, who were few but influential. The real force for reform, however, was the "street," the masses of industrial laborers concentrated in the factory towns *Elements favorable to reform* who were encouraged, and even aided, by their employers who wished to overthrow aristocratic rule in order to get control of the government.

England seethed with discontent, which grew in volume from year to year, but the Ministry, headed by Wellington, turned a
Wellington opposed to reform   deaf ear to all demands for reform.   The Duke had neither the views of a statesman nor the tact of a politician; he was a soldier accustomed to sharp commands and prompt obedience.   The government of which he was head was attacked, and he, therefore, came to its defense.   He declared that he had "never read or heard of any measure up to the present moment which could in any degree satisfy his mind that the state of representation could be improved," and that it would be difficult to reproduce a political system like the present one, "for the nature of man was incapable of reaching such excellence at once."   A wave of popular indignation swept over the country as a result of this speech, and Wellington was driven from office by a combination of Whigs and of those Tories who opposed him because he had put through Catholic emancipation.

A Whig Ministry came into power in 1831 headed by Earl Grey. A reform bill was introduced by his associate, Lord John Rus-
Tory and Whig arguments   sell, who had become known as an enthusiastic Whig reformer.   It was the occasion of a great debate in which the fundamental principles of politics as well as the political situation in England were freely discussed.   Russell's speech laid bare the electoral anomalies of the unreformed House of Commons.[1]   The Tories defended the existing system on the ground that it had secured the rights and liberties of the people far more than any other system in history; that it had made possible the careers of great statesmen, the Pitts, Burke, Fox, who sat as representatives of rotten boroughs.   They denounced the Reform Bill as revolutionary, "destructive of all property, of all right, of all privilege."   Macaulay, then a young Whig member of Parliament, argued that the Bill, far from being revolutionary, would safeguard the country from revolution by consolidating the propertied classes.   The object of the Bill was, he declared, "to admit the middle class to a larger and direct share in the representation,

[1] See page 114.

without any violent shock to the institutions of our country." On another occasion he said that "at present we oppose the schemes of the revolutionists with only one half, with only one quarter of our proper force. . . . We exclude from all share in the government great masses of property and intelligence, great numbers of those who are most interested in preserving tranquillity, and who know best how to preserve it. We do more. We drive over to the side of revolution those whom we shut out from power. Is this a time when the cause of law and order can spare one of its natural allies?"

The Bill was defeated. Parliament was dissolved, and the elections that followed were the most memorable in English history. Each side was determined to win, by fair means or by foul; and intimidation, bribery, violence were openly practiced. "The Bill, the whole Bill, and nothing but the Bill," was the cry of the reformers. Many voters, who had been corrupt and subservient electors, now defied their lords, and voted against the Tory candidates. The outcome of the elections was a great victory for the Whigs. Again, Lord John Russell brought forward the Reform Bill. In 1832 it passed the Commons, but was thrown out by the Lords. The hostile attitude of the Lords to reform aroused the liveliest indignation throughout the country. Great mass meetings were held at which they were denounced as a corrupt and selfish oligarchy. Enormous processions were organized that paraded in favor of the Bill; and riots broke out in many cities. England seemed to be on the verge of revolution. The problem was how to pass the Bill in a constitutional manner, despite the opposition of the Lords. To King William IV came Prime Minister Grey with a suggestion that he create a sufficient number of peers pledged to vote for the Bill. After some hesitation the King consented to the plan of swamping the House of Lords. Realizing that further opposition was useless the Lords passed the Bill.

Lords forced to pass Reform Bill

The provisions of the new law concerned (1) the redistribution of seats and (2) the qualifications for suffrage. Important changes were made in the system of representation: fifty-six boroughs were disfranchised, and thirty-two lost one seat each; twenty-two towns got two seats each; twenty others got one each; and the larger counties got additional seats. Equal electoral districts were not, however, created; neither were any pro-

Provisions of the Bill

visions made for a periodic redistribution of seats. The changes made in the suffrage were not very great. In the counties the vote extended to include chiefly tenants of land, known as "copyholders" and as "leaseholders," whose holdings paid an annual rent of at least £10. Lodgers remained unenfranchised. In the boroughs the anomalous franchises were abolished, and a uniform franchise was adopted which gave the vote to those men who owned or rented a building of the annual rental value of at least £10. The increase in the number of voters was small, from about 435,000 to about 656,000, nearly all from the well-to-do middle class. It is estimated that only fifteen per cent of the adult males now had the vote. The farm and industrial laborers, as well as many of the lower middle class, still remained unenfranchised.

In spite of its moderation the Reform Bill of 1832 effected as great a change in the politics and government of England as did Importance the Revolution of 1689. The House of Lords, though of Bill it remained under the control of the aristocracy, came out of the struggle with shattered prestige and partial loss of power. It was now established as a precedent that, in case of a disagreement between the two houses, the Lords must yield if, in elections following a dissolution of the Commons to test popular sentiment regarding the issue, the country upheld the latter. The Crown grew in popularity because it had aided in the passage of the Reform Bill; whatever republican sentiment existed now disappeared. That the aristocracy yielded to the demands of the people without any other than a contest at the polls was a great gain to orderly progress. The idea that great reforms could be brought about without revolution, if only sufficient popular pressure were exerted on the ruling classes, took deep root in English political life. It was to the great credit of the English aristocrats that they never sought to undo a change once made: unlike the French aristocrats, they were conservative, not reactionary. Although the Reform Bill was far from being a democratic measure, nevertheless it made a breach in the aristocratic wall, large enough only for the middle classes to enter, but destined to be widened later to admit all classes to the suffrage.

ERA OF REFORM

After the Reform Bill of 1832 the middle classes succeeded the aristocrats as the dominant influence in public life. The remarkable growth of industry, due to the Industrial Revolution, increased the numbers and augmented the wealth of the Middle-middle class. Money, not family, was now all-power- class ful. The "men of property" excited the envy of the England "men of family," who now condescended to invest their money in " crade" which they had always affected to despise. A new aristocracy appeared, manufacturers, bankers, merchants, stockbrokers, who were raised to the peerage because of their great wealth. England was now ruled by a consolidation of propertied classes, the landed gentry and the industrial capitalists.

Middle-class England was greatly concerned with "trade" and with "reform," and the parties who represented the middle classes were in power, almost continuously, for a generation after 1832. Business prosperity became the touchstone of political success, and all policies, domestic and foreign, were directed chiefly with the object of increasing trade. The middle classes strongly favored reform, and the progress of England during the nineteenth century was largely due to them. It should be noted, however, that the reforms that they favored coincided with their interests: franchise reform which gave them control of Parliament; free trade which gave them control of the world markets; and religious reform which, being Nonconformists, gave them equality with Anglicans. The reforms demanded by the workingmen, on the other hand, excited their lively hostility. They opposed democracy because it gave the vote to the workingmen; trade unions because they strengthened the power of their employees; and social reform because it meant higher taxes for them.

The Reform Bill of 1832 opened the floodgates to many other reforms. For a generation, Parliament busied itself in abolishing old abuses and in instituting far-reaching changes in Abolition of almost every field of public life. Negro slavery existed slavery under the British flag, chiefly on the plantations in the British West Indies and on the farms of South Africa. As a consequence of an anti-slavery agitation, led by William Wilberforce, Parliament passed a law, in 1833, abolishing slavery throughout the Empire. The slave-owners were mollified by the payment of $100,000,000 voted by Parliament as a compensation.

A parliamentary report on the Poor Law recommended a radical revision of the laws regarding pauperism. In 1834 a new system was inaugurated which limited outdoor relief to sick and aged

paupers, and established workhouses where able-bodied paupers
were put to work. It ended the vicious system of
giving charity to laborers to make up for low wages.
A new system of administration was established by dividing the
country into districts, which elected boards of "guardians" to
administer the Poor Law.

Poor Law reforms

Municipal reform followed parliamentary reform. The cities
were then governed by "corporations" that were either self-
perpetuating or chosen by a limited number of privileged persons, known as "freemen." These municipal
oligarchies, "close corporations," were notoriously inefficient and
corrupt. In 1835, Parliament passed the Municipal Corporations
Act which established a new system of local government. City
councils were instituted, elected by those who paid "rates," or
local taxes.

Municipal reform

Judicial reform made notable progress. A law passed in 1837
abolished the death penalty for a large number of offenses. By
1861 only three offenses, murder, piracy, and treason
remained capital crimes. Criminals were now treated
in a spirit of compassion, not in a spirit of vengeance. Contrary
to general expectations crime, instead of increasing, actually
diminished.

Judicial reform

The introduction of cheap postage was another achievement of
the reformers. The charge for transmitting a letter depended upon
its size, shape, weight, and the distance that it was
carried. In 1840, Rowland Hill, an ardent advocate
of cheap postage, prevailed upon Parliament to pass a law charging
a uniform rate of one penny to any part of the United Kingdom.
The penny post proved a success because the increase in the use
of the mails more than made up for the lower charge.

Penny post

The remarkable spread of general education has almost abolished
illiteracy, at one time nearly universal. Until well along in the
nineteenth century, the mass of English people could
neither read nor write; only the upper and middle
classes had any degree of education. The first attempt to abolish
illiteracy was through the Factory Act of 1802 which required that
apprentices should be sent to school for part of the time; but the
law was generally evaded by the employers who wanted their employees in the factory, not in the school. In 1833, Parliament
voted an annual grant of $100,000 to be distributed among the vol-

Educational reform

untary schools, most of which were managed by religious societies. Appropriations for education increased every year, but the increases were small, and popular education consequently lagged. In 1839, Parliament appropriated $150,000 for the schools, and, as it was satirically pointed out by the educational reformers, voted $350,000 for the care of the Queen's horses. Every attempt to establish a national system of popular education met the determined opposition of the Anglican Church, which was bitterly hostile to any system of secular education.

A great agitation for factory reform was started by philanthropic people who were shocked at the cruelty of industrial life, particularly as it affected women and children. Chief of these factory reformers was a prominent aristocrat, Lord Shaftesbury, whose unselfish and tireless devotion to the cause of the wretched factory workers entitles him to a great place among modern humanitarians. "Avarice and cruelty will be found," he declared, "among any class where the means of profit are combined with great and, virtually, irresponsible power."

Lord Shaftesbury champions factory reform

The strongest opposition to factory reform came from the manufacturers, most of whom were Liberals in politics. John Bright, the famous Liberal orator, declared that such legislation would be "most injurious and destructive to the best interests of the country," and that it was "a delusion practiced on the working classes which would lead to retaliation on the part of the employers." A staunch believer in the doctrines of the Manchester School, he denounced the proposed reforms as a violation of "the liberty of the subject" and of "the freedom of contract." Fear was expressed by the manufacturers that factory reform would prove so expensive to them that they would be unable to compete with their foreign rivals, who then had no such burdens.

Bright opposes factory reform

Aristocrats took up the cause of factory reform, partly, because they were desirous of improving the lot of the workers, and partly, because the burden of the reforms would fall on the manufacturers whom they cordially disliked. In 1833, largely through the efforts of Shaftesbury, Parliament passed the first important factory law. It prohibited the employment, in the textile factories, of children under nine; and restricted the labor of those between nine and thirteen to forty-eight hours a week, and

Factory laws

of those between thirteen and eighteen to sixty-eight hours; night work was forbidden to those under eighteen. An important innovation was the provision for factory inspectors to aid in the administration of the law. Famous in the annals of factory reform is the report of a parliamentary commission on labor in the mines (1842).[1] The country was horrified to learn of the fearful conditions under which women and children labored underground. A law, passed in 1842, forbade the employment in the mines of women and girls, and of boys under ten. In 1847, Parliament took a step which was then regarded as revolutionary. It passed the Ten-Hour Law limiting the labor of women and children in the textile factories to ten hours a day. Further legislation widely extended the scope of factory reform to the great benefit of the working classes who, otherwise, might have sunk to a condition of degeneracy.

The movement for religious reform abated with Catholic emancipation. Jews and atheists continued to suffer political discrimina-

Jews and atheists emancipated

tion. Jews were virtually debarred from Parliament by an oath required of each member which contained the words "on the true faith of a Christian." A member of the Rothschild family was elected, but he was not permitted to take his seat because he refused to take this oath. In 1858, Parliament passed the Jewish Relief Act which prescribed an oath that Jews could conscientiously take. The disabilities of atheists were removed in 1888. But there was no religious equality as the Anglican Church continued to enjoy her special privileges as the Established Church of England.

POLITICAL HISTORY (1832–67)

The Reform Bill of 1832 completely transformed the two historic political parties. Both took new names, advocated new principles,

Conservatives and Liberals

and found new leaders. The Tories became the Conservatives, in theory still committed to the aristocratic ideals of society and of government, but in practice ready to accommodate themselves to the new conditions in political life. Peel, who was now their leader, declared that the Reform Bill was a "final and irrevocable settlement of a great constitutional question," and pledged his party to a loyal acceptance of the new political order. The Whigs and Radicals joined forces and became known, first, as the Reformers, later, as the Liberals; they cham-

[1] See page 119.

pioned reform and progress, but with due regard to the traditional English way of making substantial changes without undermining the cherished institutions of the land.   During the first half of the nineteenth century, the dominant political figures were, among the Liberals, Lords Melbourne, Russell, and Palmerston; and among the Conservatives, Peel and the Earl of Derby, all of whom recognized the necessity of broadening the institutions of England in response to the new spirit which had arisen.   They were, however, strongly opposed to universal suffrage which was then regarded as revolutionary; they considered the lower classes unfit to exercise political power.   Macaulay, who was a typical Liberal, declared that universal suffrage was "incompatible, not with this or that form of government, but with all forms of government," with property, and with civilization.   Lord John Russell regarded the Reform Bill as a "finality," and he was consequently averse to any change that would undermine the political structure erected in 1832.   It was not till Gladstone and Disraeli appeared that the Liberals and Conservatives were willing to take further steps toward democracy.

In 1837, King William IV died, and he was succeeded by his niece, Victoria, then a young girl of eighteen.   During the years of her long reign Victoria occupied a unique place in the life of England.   She was careful not to overstep the constitutional limits of an English monarch; yet, indirectly, she exerted a powerful influence on the conduct of affairs. Her marriage to Prince Albert, of Saxe-Coburg, was one of affection, and the happy royal pair became the models of domestic virtue to millions of English men and women.

Queen Victoria (1819–1901)

The most distinguished man in public life during the early-Victorian period was Sir Robert Peel.   Cautiously progressive in the best traditions of English statesmanship, "a complete Briton" as he was admiringly called, he exercised a liberalizing influence on his own party and a moderating one on the radical reformers who opposed him.   Peel's abilities lay in his masterly grasp of financial and administrative problems.   On these matters he spoke with authority, and was listened to with "unutterable anxiety" by his colleagues in Parliament.

Peel (1788–1850)

REPEAL OF THE CORN LAWS

Of the many reforms that followed the Reform Bill the most important was the establishment of free trade. As modern industry *Arguments of tue free-traders* developed, England chafed under the restrictions of the Mercantilist System. A movement for free trade began which rapidly gained headway, especially in the industrial centers. Its supporters argued that free trade would stimulate the native producer to greater enterprise and ingenuity in order to compete successfully with the foreigner; and that it would encourage the various nations to produce only those things for which they were best fitted: England, for example, would specialize in cotton goods, woolens, and hardware; France, in silks, wines, and laces; Russia, in agriculture, lumber, and furs. The world would therefore benefit by getting the best products at the lowest cost. If foreigners were to buy manufactured articles from England, declared the free traders, they must have the freedom to sell her their products; namely, food and raw materials. Moreover, if English ships carrying cargoes of manufactures to foreign countries had no return cargoes it would mean serious losses to the shipping interests.

The heaviest protective duties were those on breadstuffs. In defense of the Corn Laws, as they were called, it was argued that *Arguments of the pro-tectionists* every encouragement should be given to the nation to produce its own food; that agriculture gave employment to many; and that rural life produced a healthy population which was the stamina of a nation.

In 1839, Richard Cobden and John Bright founded the famous Anti-Corn Law League, which began an energetic propaganda in *The Anti-Corn Law League* favor of free trade. Cobden was a brilliant writer and organizer who gave his fortune and services freely to the cause which became his life's passion. Bright was one of the greatest orators of the nineteenth century and a devoted champion of all Liberal causes. Both men toured the country together and succeeded in rousing the greatest enthusiasm for their cause. At meetings of the League, Cobden would first present the arguments so clearly and logically that it was impossible to refute him. Bright would follow, and drive home Cobden's arguments with matchless eloquence. England was flooded with Anti-Corn Law pamphlets which denounced protection as an economic evil because it artificially raised the cost of food, and as a moral evil because it incited nations to needless and fruitless rivalries, thereby causing wars. Free trade, it was claimed, would promote international peace by removing national barriers. Great mass meetings were held to protest against the "dear bread" maintained by a selfish landed aristocracy. The League received the powerful support of the manufacturers who favored free trade in both agricultural and industrial products for the following reasons. Cheap food from abroad would lower the cost of living; hence, wages might be lowered, or at least might not be advanced. Raw material, of which England had little, would come in freely. There was then little fear of foreign competition, England being so much further advanced industrially. The champions of free trade were able "to combine comparatively selfish class interests with other motives springing from philanthropy and patriotism, a combination which tended to give them that combination of moral fervor, efficient organization, and shrewd political tactics, which made the Anti-Corn Law League one of the most effective organizations which has ever taken part in British political history. Neither money nor ability was wanting."

In 1845, the potato crop in Ireland was ruined by the "blight," or potato disease. Starvation faced thousands of Irish peasants, to whom the potato was the chief article of food. At the same time the English grain crop proved to be unexpectedly bad. The cost of living rose, which gave

Repeal of the Corn Laws

the free traders the opportunity to demand effectively the immediate repeal of the Corn Laws in order to facilitate the importation of cheap food. The Conservative Ministry, headed by Peel, was committed to protection, but the seriousness of the situation caused some of the Conservatives in Parliament to waver. Peel himself changed front. In 1846, he carried through Parliament the repeal of the Corn Laws, which gave a body blow to the protective system. Peel's action infuriated his party, which repudiated his leadership and cast him out of its ranks. He proudly replied that he would be remembered with gratitude by those who earned their living by the sweat of their brow, "when they shall recruit their strength with abundant and untaxed food, the sweeter because it is no longer leavened by a sense of injustice." Free trade was not entirely established until 1867 when the last of the protective duties were removed. A tariff on tobacco, tea, sugar, and spirits was, however, maintained, but for purposes of revenue only.

With the Corn Laws went the Navigation Laws.   In 1849, they were repealed, and foreign ships were put on the same basis as
Repeal of the Naviga- tion Laws   English in the carrying trade of the British Empire. The liberal navigation policy of England resulted in an increase of her commerce, as foreigners could now send their goods to England more easily and more cheaply.

CHARTISM

While the Anti-Corn Law League was agitating for free trade, a movement for political and social reform, known as Chartism, made
Agitation for political reform   great headway.   The Reform Bill had proved a bitter disappointment to the working classes, who had hoped to see universal suffrage established.   Instead it had put into power the middle classes, who now opposed the working-men as bitterly as they once had opposed the aristocrats.   The workingmen felt that they had been cheated out of the fruits of the victory that their efforts had largely won, and they smarted with disappointment.   As both Liberals and Conservatives were opposed to a further extension of the suffrage, the working classes determined upon another reform agitation.   Great popular meetings were held, and in 1838 the People's Charter was drawn up which demanded the famous Six Points: (1) universal manhood suffrage; (2) vote by secret ballot; (3) abolition of property qualifications for members of Parliament; (4) salaries for members of Parliament; (5) annual elections; and (6) a division of the country into equal electoral districts.

Although Chartism was chiefly political in character, it also had vague social aspirations, being allied with trade unionism and
Chartism   inspired by the Utopian ideals of Robert Owen.[1]   Its Six Points, all of which have now been virtually adopted, then excited the greatest apprehension among the governing classes who were determined to suppress the movement.   A bitter class conflict now arose that threatened to plunge England into revolution.   At first the "moral force" element among the Chartists, those who believed in peaceful agitation, was in the ascendant.   Radical clubs were organized to conduct a democratic propaganda; monster processions and mass meetings were held and impassioned speeches were delivered.   A gigantic petition, embodying the demands of the People's Charter, was presented to Parlia-

[1] See page 567.

ment, first in 1839 and again in 1842, but each time it was summarily rejected. The revolutionary movement of 1848 on the Continent gave great encouragement to the "physical force" element who, under the leadership of Feargus O'Connor, got control of the movement. A petition, demanding the Charter, was drawn up to which about six million signatures were affixed. It was feared that if the petition were rejected, an uprising would follow. The government prepared to meet the situation by organizing a force of special constables who were put under the command of Wellington. The petition was rejected, and the street demonstrations which followed were quickly suppressed.

THE REFORM BILL OF 1867

Although Chartism was suppressed, its principles made an ever-deepening impression upon English political life. Within each party there was an element that favored the extension of the franchise. In the Liberal party Gladstone and Bright urged that the party of reform should not stop with the Reform Bill of 1832. Disraeli appealed to the Conservatives to champion the rights of the people as against the middle classes who now governed the country. In the sixties electoral reform again came to the fore; but, unlike the situation in 1832, it was not an issue between the two parties, but between its opponents and supporters in each party.

Element in each party favors electoral reform

In 1866, a Liberal Ministry was in power with Lord Russell as Premier, but with Gladstone as its most influential member. As the champion of reform, Gladstone introduced a franchise bill drawn along moderate lines. It was defeated by the Conservatives with the aid of those Liberals who feared that even this moderate measure would herald the coming of democracy. The Russell Ministry fell, and was succeeded by a Conservative Ministry under Lord Derby, of which the most influential member was Disraeli. It was naturally assumed that the Conservatives would be less likely to extend the suffrage than the Liberals. Mass meetings were held throughout the country demanding universal, manhood suffrage, and the scenes of 1832 were repeated. In defiance of the authorities a great throng of workingmen assembled in Hyde Park, London, where they denounced the government. Disraeli came to the conclusion that the extension of the ballot was now inevitable. He, therefore, determined "to

Reform Bill of 1867

dish the Whigs" by making concessions to the demands for reform. In 1867, he introduced a franchise bill that went far beyond that of Gladstone by giving the ballot to the working classes in the towns. The opponents of the measure implored the "gentlemen of England," with "their ancestry behind them and their posterity before them," to save the Constitution "from the hands of a multitude struggling with want and discontent." Disraeli's tactics succeeded, and the bill became law. It gave the vote, in the boroughs, to all householders, and to lodgers who paid not less than $50 (£10) a year rent for unfurnished rooms. The property qualification in the counties was reduced in order to enfranchise the tenant farmers. Again there was a redistribution of seats, though not so drastic as the redistribution in 1832. In regard to the franchise the second Reform Bill was a sweeping measure, as it doubled the number of voters. It was now realized that England was on the highroad to democracy, and those who feared the new order characterized the law as a "leap in the dark" and as "shooting Niagara."

The Reform Bill of 1867 was the second installment of democracy. As in 1832 the suffrage was expanded by contracting, not by abolishing, the property qualifications; and the chief beneficiaries were the better paid workingmen in the towns who now shared the vote with the upper and middle classes. To have accomplished this reform without revolution was another testimony to the political sagacity of the English propertied classes. After the violence of the Chartists had been vigorously suppressed, a substantial concession was made to their demands. How different was the attitude of the propertied classes in France!

FOREIGN AFFAIRS

After 1815 England enjoyed a long period of peace. Her redoubtable enemy, France, was now a second rate power, more intent on recovering from the results of the Napoleonic Wars than upon recovering her lost empire. However, the Holy Alliance caused England much uneasiness. Here was an allied group of powers whose interests might, under certain circumstances, be opposed to hers. This uneasiness was responsible for the policies of Castlereagh and Canning in taking England out of the orbit of the Holy Alliance.

Their most famous successor was Lord Palmerston. who directed

England's foreign policy almost continuously for over a generation. Palmerston was a Liberal, but he had very little inter- Lord Palm-est in domestic affairs; his Liberalism consisted chiefly erston in being a member of every Liberal Cabinet during his (1784–1865) political lifetime. The chief aim of Palmerston's policy was to create a group of constitutional states on the Continent to balance the Holy Alliance. Therefore he gave encouragement and support to the revolutionary movements in Italy, Spain, Germany, and Hungary; patriots and liberators, such as Cavour and Kossuth, found in him a stanch friend and admirer. So, while England was suppressing the Chartists at home, she was encouraging revolution abroad. Palmerston was a vigorous upholder of the rights of British subjects and British interests in foreign countries, and, on several occasions, he gave utterance to "jingo" sentiments that won him great popularity. "England," he declared, "is strong enough to brave consequences." Temperamentally irrepressible and indiscreet, "Old Pam," as he was popularly known, frequently shocked and delighted his contemporaries by blurting out his true sentiments regarding foreign affairs.

Palmerston's influence was felt in many great crises. When the Belgians declared their independence of Holland, it was he who was chiefly responsible for the settlement that resulted Palmerston's in the neutralization of Belgium. He scored notable diplomatic diplomatic triumphs in the Near East where he vigor- triumphs ously upheld England's traditional policy of supporting the Sultan of Turkey.[1] During the crisis of 1854 he opposed Russia's plan to dismember Turkey, and the outcome was the Crimean War.[2] Palmerston was Premier during the American Civil War, and strongly supported the South. When the South was blockaded, a cotton "famine" took place in England where many of the cotton factories closed down bringing ruin to their proprietors and throwing many out of work. The British government aided the Southern vessels, notably the Alabama, that were preying upon the American merchant marine.

INDUSTRIAL PROGRESS

To both nature and man was due the extraordinary development of British commerce and industry. An abundance of coal and iron, fine harbors, a long coast line, a large merchant marine,

[1] See page 161.   [2] See page 164.

plenty of capital, and, above all, priority of invention, gave the
England's   English people overwhelming advantages over all
economic   other nations in the race for economic supremacy.
advantages   France was seriously handicapped by a lack of coal;
Russia was rich in natural resources but, owing to a lack of capital, they were undeveloped; America had both resources and capital, but she was devoting her energies to her enormous home
market; and Germany was not yet in existence either as an economic or as a political factor.

An era of railway building began with the construction, in 1830,
of the Liverpool-Manchester Railway, the first line planned for
Railway   the purpose of transporting passengers. It proved to
progress   be so successful that there was no longer any doubt
about the superior accommodations and cheapness of this new
method of transportation. "A railway mania" began, and Britain
was, in a short time, covered with a network of railways that established a fine system of internal communication. There was no
need to stimulate traffic, as there was an urgent necessity to connect
the rapidly growing industrial centers. Owing to the widespread
belief in the efficacy of competition, private, not state ownership,
was favored; and Parliament freely granted charters to private
companies permitting them to build railways.

Unlike an ordinary road a railroad is by nature a monopoly; the
owners have exclusive right of transport. It became evident that
Railway   the rights of the public needed protection against the
regulation   railway companies. In 1845, Parliament passed the
first important railway law, which established the principle of
government supervision over schedules, safety devices, rates, and
profits. However, the law gave so much discretion to the companies that they were virtually uncontrolled. It was not until
1873 that a permanent railway commission was appointed to supervise the railways.

A new era in navigation began in 1839–40 with the establishment
of two famous ocean steamship lines, the "P. and O." (Peninsular
Progress of   and Oriental), running steamers to Asia and Africa,
steam navi-   and the Cunard Line, running steamers to America.
gation   In time, these companies and other lines extended
their traffic to all parts of the world. However, the steamboat did
not displace the sailboat as quickly as the railway displaced the
wagon. The sailing vessels were plentiful and cheap, and offered

keen competition to the steamship companies, although the latter were subsidized by the government.

The establishment of free trade, the repeal of the Navigation Laws, and the improvement of the means of transportation made England an international trading concern organized on the basis of world economy. There began an extraordinary expansion of commerce and industry. The period, 1850–80, was England's economic Golden Age, when profits from every sort of enterprise, from every part of the world, poured into her coffers. She was the *workshop* of the world. Her textile factories produced enormous quantities of cotton, woolen, and linen goods that were exported everywhere. At that time England had a minimum of foreign competition; if one bought a machine-made shirt in Lisbon or Moscow it was likely to have the label "Manchester," the cotton capital of the world. Her cotton manufactures were especially prosperous, due to the new machinery and to the increased production of raw cotton in America.[1] She was the *forge* of the world. Next to textiles the iron and steel industry was most important, and England produced all sorts of hardware, from iron nails to steel rails. The Bessemer process made her the sole producer of steel, which was exported in large quantities. If one bought a pocket knife anywhere in the world, it was likely to have on it the label "Sheffield," the iron and steel capital of the world. Coal production went hand-in-hand with iron. From Newcastle, the coal capital of the world, came the source of the new power to the many factories in England and to the rising factories on the Continent. Foreign trade, chiefly in textiles, hardware, and coal, became the backbone of England's prosperity.[2] She was the *carrier* of the world. Shipbuilding became virtually a British monopoly, and the world not only bought English goods, but had them transported in English vessels. Shipping was second in importance to foreign trade in the economic life of England.[3] She was the *entrepôt*, or *emporium* of the world. Ideally situated to receive goods from overseas and to distribute them on the Continent, England developed a great re-export business by importing

England's economic Golden Age

[1] The value of the exports of cotton manufactures rose from $27,000,000 in 1800 to $364,000,000 in 1871.

[2] At the beginning of the nineteenth century, England's foreign trade, excluding precious metals, was valued at about $200,000,000, which rose, in 1872, to about $3,000,000,000.

[3] It is estimated that between 1821 and 1849 shipping increased over 2500 per cent.

foreign and colonial products for export purposes. If a Berlin merchant wished to buy tea from India or rubber from Brazil he bought them in London; the price included a handsome commission to the English dealer. She was the *broker and banker* of the world. Insurance of all sorts was centered in England where insurance companies did business throughout the world either directly or through agencies. In finance particularly was England dominant. To London came not only business men, but also governments to float loans. Branches of English banks were to be found in almost every large Continental city. The London Stock Exchange was the chief scene of investment, and therefore the business barometer of the world. "The extension of British trade to all countries, the growth of British shipping, the rise of British banking and insurance in a world in which British capitalists found themselves in a position of commercial dominance with the very minimum of foreign competition, all coöperated to produce a golden stream of almost boundless profits, taking the form of constantly swelling incomes for the capitalist class, a heaping up of all the accompaniments of luxurious living, and a perpetual investment of the surplus in additional instruments of wealth production."

One outcome of England's prosperity was the migration of capital, a phenomenon new in economic history. Profits were so great that there was heaped up a surplus of capital. Some of it was used to enlarge and to improve the industrial system at home; much of it, however, was "exported," used to fructify foreign industry, which brought handsome returns to the English investors. The Continent became the scene of concession hunting. English contracting companies, financed from London, and including all grades of labor, from engineers to common workmen, wandered over the Continent, building railways and telegraphs, installing machinery in factories and mines, and building bridges and tunnels. Before 1875 nearly all the foreign capital invested in Russia was English. The early railways of France and Germany were financed largely by English capital. Without it the Industrial Revolution in many countries would have been seriously retarded.

In 1851, the Universal Exposition was opened at the Crystal Palace, London. The products of commerce, industry, and agriculture were shown to visitors who came from all parts of the world to admire and possibly to emulate British industrial genius.

RELIGIOUS MOVEMENTS

No contrast is more interesting than that of religious conditions on the Continent and in England during the nineteenth century. On the Continent all the radical movements were anti- *English radicalism religious* religious in tendency, and as bitterly hostile to the Church as to the State. It was quite otherwise in England, where the reform movements were often inspired by religious ideals and led by deeply religious men. Gambetta was a militant free-thinker, but Gladstone was a devout Christian.

The early nineteenth century witnessed the rise of the Evangelical movement in the Anglican Church. Like the Methodists by whom they were inspired, the Evangelicals preached *The Evangelical movement* what was called "Bible" Christianity. They exhorted the people to read the Bible diligently and to follow its teaching, rather than to repeat dogmas and perform ceremonies. Although they fully accepted the doctrines of the Anglican Church, they were not inclined to emphasize them. In one sense, the Evangelical movement was a reaction against the worldly bishops and "sporting parsons" in the Church who scandalized people by their lack of devotion.

Social reform was the great secular passion of the Evangelicals. Anti-slavery, prison reform, factory reform, temperance, moral reform, and law reform found enthusiastic champions among them. Wilberforce, prominent in the anti-slavery movement, and Lord Shaftesbury, father of factory reform, were enthusiastic supporters of the Evangelical movement, the ideals of which inspired their life work.

Quite opposite in tendency was the Oxford movement, so called because it was initiated by a group of scholars in Oxford University. It proclaimed the medieval ideals of the Church as the *The Oxford movement* center of all activity, of the supremacy of ecclesiastical ideals over all others, and of the importance of ritual in service and of holiness in life. A group of writers, among them John Keble, the author of *The Christian Year*, John Henry Newman, the famous preacher and writer, and Dr. Pusey, the most eminent ecclesiastical scholar in England, advocated their ideas in a series of pamphlets called *Tracts for the Times*. The Tractarians, as they were called, asserted the continuity of the Anglican Church from the days of Christ; hence, the separation from the Church of Rome, effected in the sixteenth century, did not make it any the less Catholic.

Before long a trend toward Roman Catholicism became noticeable among the Tractarians, whose leader, Newman, finally embraced the Catholic faith. Those who remained within the Anglican fold initiated a movement, known as High Church, that favored the adoption of Catholic ritual and ceremony in Anglican services.

More radical than the Evangelicals, though inspired by the same ideals, were the Christian Socialists. Their chief spokesman was

The Christian Socialists

Charles Kingsley, novelist and Anglican minister, whose books and sermons deeply influenced public opinion. The Christian Socialists believed that if the world were ordered according to the teachings of Christ, poverty and its attendant evils would disappear; hence, they became fervent preachers of social reform. Kingsley was a strong defender of the labor unions, and sympathized with the Chartists in their demand for better conditions. His novel, *Alton Locke*, is a moving description of the conditions of the London tailors, whom grinding poverty had reduced to a state of misery and hopelessness. The Christian Socialists busied themselves among the working class, founding trade unions, workingmen's colleges, and social settlements; they were influential in laying the foundations of the social reform movement that swept over England at the end of the nineteenth century.

ROMANTIC AND VICTORIAN LITERATURE

The first quarter of the nineteenth century witnessed the high tide of the Romantic school in English literature. The period was

Characteristics of English Romanticism: (1) revolutionary fervor

especially rich in poetry, and the works of Shelley, Byron, Keats, Coleridge, and Wordsworth left an imperishable influence on English literature and life. Like those in France, the English Romanticists were deeply stirred by revolutionary feeling of which the lyrical outbursts of Shelley and Byron were typical expressions. Even the calm and retiring Wordsworth wrote of the French Revolution:

"Bliss was it in that dawn to be alive,
But to be young was very heaven!"

During the period of reaction that followed Waterloo, revolutionary sentiments were frowned upon in England as elsewhere; both Byron and Shelley found their native land unresponsive to their message, and they lived in exile during the latter part of their lives.

Another characteristic of the English Romanticists was their love of nature. It might almost be said that they discovered nature, as the writers before them had rarely appre- (2) love of ciated either the charms or the terrors of field, stream, nature sea, and mountain. It was the aim of the Romanticists not merely to describe nature, but to interpret her moods and to show her various aspects in order that man might find himself in greater sympathy with the universe. Byron expressed his temperament by vividly describing the picturesque and the grand, such as the sea and mountain; Wordsworth, by pensive musings on the more quiet aspects, the shady nook and the gentle hill.

Percy Bysshe Shelley was aflame with the spirit of revolt. His greatest poem, *Prometheus Unbound,* is an apotheosis of revolution, in which he describes how the god Prometheus, the Shelley "friend of man," was chained to a mountain by Jove (1792–1822) who personifies conservatism, and how he is finally released by the spirit of revolution. In grace, melody, and sheer loveliness, Shelley's lyrics are unsurpassed. So refined and delicate are his sentiments, so insatiate is his craving for the "Spirit of Beauty," and so generous is his sympathy for the unfortunate, that Shelley has come to embody the ideal in its revolt against the gross, the stupid, and the reactionary forces of the world. Although he died at the age of thirty, he is regarded as the supreme genius of English lyric poetry.

The poetry of Lord Byron is characterized by great virility, intense passion, and hostility to accepted ideas and institutions. He excels in magnificent descriptions of scenery and in Byron oratorical declamation which are, however, frequently (1788–1824) marred by tawdry bombast. Byron's life, like his poetry, was stormy. Having roused the hostility of his countrymen by flouting their social conventions, he was perforce exiled for the remainder of his life, and died aiding the Greeks in their revolution against Turkey. Byron's popularity as a poet was so great on the Continent that a Byronic cult grew up which glorified romantic revolt against narrow conventions.

John Keats, like Shelley, was a seeker after the beautiful, and not even the latter was more devoted to the ideals of beauty, pure and undefiled. For Keats, poetry existed for its own sake, and he

held himself aloof from the world of men, things, and "problems"
Keats   in order to devote himself to his muse.   His poems
(1795–1821) are perfect models of grace and exquisite loveliness.
His death at the age of twenty-five cut short a most promising
poetic genius.

Quite different in temperament from his contemporaries was
Samuel Taylor Coleridge.   Although he wrote very few poems,
Coleridge   these have been considered masterpieces because of
(1772–1834) their almost flawless mechanism and enchanting melody.   His themes are romantic, mysterious, weird.   His best-
known poem, *Rime of the Ancient Mariner*, contains wonderful
passages, the product of a rich imagination and a strange mysticism.   Coleridge is famous also as a literary critic and philosopher.
But it is as a poet of regions beyond the earth and of dreams beyond
the heavens that he is best remembered.   No English writer succeeded as he did in making the supernatural seem natural.

William Wordsworth is universally regarded as the greatest
Wordsworth   English poet of nature.   To Wordsworth nature has
(1770–1850) a conscious soul expressing herself in the daisy, the
cloud, or the skylark's song, and profoundly influencing the moods
of men.   His great aim was to reveal the significance hidden in
the commonplace.   He believed that the supreme function of the
imagination was to dignify simple people, places, and incidents;
hence, his poems contain no striking themes or personalities, and
are entirely free from embellishments.   There is another note in
Wordsworth, Duty, "Stern Daughter of the Voice of God," rather
a strange one for a Romanticist; he apostrophizes common virtues as he does common things.   Although unsurpassed at his
best, Wordsworth is often dull and tedious.

Sir Walter Scott stands out as the leading prose writer among
the British Romanticists.   He was to a considerable degree the
Scott   creator of the historical novel, and was a master in the
(1771–1832) art of invoking bygone ages.   Romanticism came to
Scott "whispering the last enchantment of the Middle Ages,"
a period which he delighted to describe.   Scott excels in the
power of vividly portraying romantic characters and stirring incidents, and he quickly became the most popular novelist in the
English language.   He was also a fervent lover of his country,
Scotland, whose history and legends are the themes of many of
his novels and poems.

The period from about 1840 to the end of the nineteenth century is designated in English literature as the Victorian Age, in honor of Queen Victoria, whose long reign was so notable in English history. For many centuries social ideals had been largely fashioned by the upper classes; now that the middle classes were in power, there came with them new ideals of personal and social conduct which quickly found expression in the literature of the day. Moral purpose dominates much if not all of the writing of the Victorian Age. Art was practiced for morality's sake. The new writers produced novels, poems, dramas, histories, and essays, primarily as aids to better thinking and better living, and incidentally as works of art. Dickens, Thackeray, and George Eliot wrote novels not only to "adorn a tale," but especially "to point a moral." Browning wrote poems to edify and instruct his readers. Macaulay wrote history with a "purpose," to show why the Whigs were right and the Tories wrong. Carlyle wrote biographies of heroes as the embodiment of the "eternal verities." To Ruskin painting itself was a form of moral expression.

The Victorian Age

The progress of popular education and the establishment of cheap magazines and newspapers created a new and large reading public. Writers were forced to cater to a wider and more varied demand, and as a result literature became more democratic. It began to concern itself with the problems of humble people; it searched for comedy or tragedy in the daily routine of the masses; and it became a passionate advocate of social and political reform.

Democracy

Another striking characteristic of the Victorian Age was the great rôle that science played in the affairs of mankind. The wonderful discoveries of the inventors and the writings of the great scientists, such as Darwin and Huxley, exercised a profound influence, directly and indirectly, upon imaginative literature. The idea of evolution was constantly made use of by the novelists; and the theme of some of the greatest poems was the origin and destiny of man in the light of evolution.

Science

A truly great and representative Victorian was Lord Macaulay, historian and essayist. He had a wonderful faculty of investing history with dramatic power, and his *History of England* remains to this day one of the most popular books in the English language. Macaulay is a panoramic rather

Macaulay (1800–59)

than a philosophic historian; he gives graphic pictures of the exterior of human society, but seldom sees the underlying causes of human affairs.   Brilliance of style, vividness of narrative, and a luxuriant imagination combine to make him one of the great writers of English prose.

Thomas Carlyle was the great censor of the Victorian Age.   It was a thrilling message that this Scottish philosopher, historian, Carlyle   and biographer preached to his generation.   A man's (1795–1881)   prime duty was to recognize the hero qualities, to tear away shams, and to pierce the only reality, the inner spirit.   He denounced in prophet-like language the materialism and selfishness of his time, and attempted to demonstrate that the new industrialism had made a "swine's trough" of the world by establishing only a "cash nexus" between man and man.   Carlyle, however, had no faith in democracy, for his ideal government was one by an aristocracy of talent.   His influence upon his own and succeeding generations was profound, and he may be justly regarded as one of the spiritual makers of modern England.

The three great novelists of the Victorian Age were Dickens, Thackeray, and George Eliot.   Of these, Charles Dickens was Dickens   the most popular and the most typical representative (1812–70)   of the spirit of the times.   Few authors combine humor and pathos so effectively as does Dickens; generations of English-speaking people have laughed and cried over his pages. He is above all a social-reform novelist, and his attacks on charity schools, law courts, and workhouses led to beneficent reforms in those institutions.   Dickens was the first to introduce the poor and the degraded of industrial England into literature, and he succeeded in arousing the widest sympathies for the unfortunate classes of society.

Quite different from Dickens was William Makepeace Thackeray, novelist of the elegant world.   His smooth style, delicate wit, Thackeray   and urbanity contrast sharply with the rollicking (1811–63)   humor and grotesqueness of Dickens.   Thackeray was essentially a satirist who delighted to expose the foibles of the great, and for that reason his work has sometimes been called "a whispering-gallery of scandal."   But he was a satirist touched with sentiment; it is his habit to take his readers aside in order to preach little private sermons on the evils of mankind.

Mary Ann Evans, known to the world by the pseudonym of

George Eliot, is the novelist of the middle classes as Dickens is of the lower, and Thackeray of the upper classes. An ethical atmosphere pervades all her books which, were it not for the author's art, would be mere moral tracts. George Eliot took particular delight in analyzing her characters psychologically in order to discover the hidden spring of good and evil. Although not so popular as Dickens or Thackeray, she continues to hold an important place in English literature.

George Eliot
(1819–80)

REFERENCES

GENERAL:
Consult bibliography at the end of Chapter VIII.

BIOGRAPHIES:
There exist a number of notable biographies of prominent British statesmen. Chief among them are William Henry Lytton, *Life of Sir H. J. Temple Viscount Palmerston*, 2 vols. (1871), continued by Evelyn Ashley in vol. III (1874); P. Guedalla, *Palmerston* (1926), a brilliant literary and historical study; S. Walpole, *Life of Lord John Russell*, 2 vols. (1879); John (Viscount) Morley, *Life of Richard Cobden* (1881); J. A. Hobson, *Richard Cobden* (1919); E. Hodder, *Life and Work of the Seventh Earl of Shaftesbury*, 3 vols. (1888); J. L. and B. Hammond, *Lord Shaftesbury* (1923); J. W. Bready, *Lord Shaftesbury and Social and Industrial Progress* (1927); G. Wallas, *Life of Francis Place* (ed. 1918); Earl of Rosebery, *Sir Robert Peel* (1899); A. A. W. Ramsan, *Sir Robert Peel* (1928), an effort to rehabilitate Peel; H. de B. Gibbins, *English Social Reformers* (1902), contains sketches of Wesley, Wilberforce, Kingsley, and the factory reformers; E. I. Carlyle, *William Cobbett; A Study of his Life as Shown in his Writings* (1904); G. D. H. Cole, *The Life of William Cobbett* (1924), an interpretation of an old radical by a modern one; F. Podmore, *Life of Robert Owen*, 2 vols. (1906); G. D. H. Cole, *Robert Owen* (1925); Sir G. O. Trevelyan, *The Life and Letters of Lord Macaulay*, 2 vols. (1876); and G. M. Trevelyan, *Lord Grey of the Reform Bill* (1920).

SOCIAL CONDITIONS:
E. L. Woodward, *The Age of Reform, 1815–1870* (1938); S. Maccoby, *English Radicalism, 1832–1852* (1937); H. D. Traill, *Social England* (1909), vol. VI, contains articles by different writers on various aspects of nineteenth-century England; G. Slater, *The Growth of Modern England* (ed. 1933), a series of essays chiefly on social conditions, good bibliography; E. Jenks, *A Short History of the English Law* (1912), a brief reliable account describing the reforms in the criminal code; Sir G. Nicholls, *A History of the English Poor Law in Connection with the State of the Country and the Condition of the People*, 2 vols. (ed. 1898), is the best work on the subject, goes down to 1834, and is continued to 1899 by T. Mackay in a third volume. On factory legislation, the best work is B. I. Hutchins and A. Harrison, *A*

History of Factory Legislation (ed. 1926). On conditions of factory life: F. Engels, *The Condition of the Working-Class in England in 1844*, and the two novels, B. Disraeli, *Sybil, or the Two Nations*, and C. Kingsley, *Alton Locke*. On education: A. E. Dobbs, *Education and Social Movements, 1700–1850* (1919) and G. Balfour, *The Educational System of Great Britain and Ireland* (ed. 1903).

ECONOMIC CONDITIONS:

J. H. Clapham, *An Economic History of Modern Britain: The Early Railway Age, 1820–1850* (1926), a scholarly work describing the reorganization of economic life, full of valuable information; L. C. A. Knowles, *Industrial and Commercial Revolutions in Great Britain during the Nineteenth Century* (1921), reliable, clear, and well organized; W. Smart, *Economic Annals of the Nineteenth Century*, 2 vols. (ed. 1910–17), full of information on all economic matters during the period 1801–30; for statistical information see G. R. Porter, *Progress of the Nation in its Various Social and Industrial Relations*, edited by F. W. Hirst (1912) and A. L. Bowley, *A Short Account of England's Foreign Trade in the Nineteenth Century* (1905); C. Wright and C. E. Fayle, *A History of Lloyd's* (1928), history of the world-famous insurance house; B. H. Holland, *The Fall of Protection, 1840–50* (1913), best study of the free-trade movement; L. H. Jenks, *The Migration of British Capital* (1927), a pioneer study of the export of capital from England, goes to 1875; J. R. Taylor, *Industrial History of Modern Britain* (1920) and E. P. Cheyney, *Industrial and Social History of England* (ed. 1920), contain good descriptions of economic changes; C. R. Fay, *Great Britain from Adam Smith to the Present Day* (1928), social and economic history chiefly of first half of nineteenth century.

LABOR CONDITIONS:

The foremost authorities on English labor history are Sidney and Beatrice Webb, Socialists, and G. D. H. Cole, Guild Socialist. S. and B. Webb, *History of Trade-Unionism* (ed. 1920); G. D. H. Cole, *A Short History of the British Working-Class Movement, 1789–1937*, 3 vols. (1938), i, 1789–1848, ii, 1849–1900, iii, 1900–37; G. Wallas, *Life of Francis Place* (ed. 1918), and G. D. H. Cole, *Robert Owen* (1925), contain excellent description of conditions of the working class. On Chartism: J. West, *History of the Chartist Movement* (1920); M. Hovell, *The Chartist Movement* (1918); E. Dolléans, *Le Chartisme*, 2 vols. (1912); F. F. Rosenblatt, *The Chartist Movement in its Social and Economic Aspects* (1917); and P. W. Slosson, *The Decline of the Chartist Movement* (1917).

RELIGIOUS REFORMS:

B. Ward, *The Eve of Catholic Emancipation, 1803–1829*, 3 vols. (1912), and *The Sequel to Catholic Emancipation, 1830–1850*, 2 vols. (1915), describe the removal of Catholic disabilities; D. Gwynn, *The Struggle for Catholic Emancipation* (1928); H. W. Clark, *History of English Nonconformity* (1913), vol. ii, describes removal of the disabilities of the Nonconformists; F. W. Cornish, *A History of the Church of England in the Nineteenth Century*

(1910); R. W. Church, *The Oxford Movement: Twelve Years, 1833–1845* (1900) and W. Ward, *The Life of John Henry, Cardinal Newman, based on his private journals and correspondence*, 2 vols. (1912), describe the Oxford movement.   On Christian Socialism: C. W. Stubbs, *Charles Kingsley and the Christian Social Movement* (1900); A. V. Woodworth, *Christian Socialism in England* (1903); and H. de B. Gibbins, *English Social Reformers* (1902).

CULTURAL:

A. V. Dicey, *Lectures on the Relation between Law and Public Opinion in England during the Nineteenth Century* (ed. 1914), a brilliant study by a philosophic conservative, good interpretation of Bentham; O. Elton, *A Survey of English Literature, 1780–1880*, 4 vols. (1912–20), excellent studies of great writers and of literary movements; A. W. Benn, *Modern England: A Record of Opinion and Action from the Time of the French Revolution to the Present Day*, 2 vols. (1908); and L. Stephen, *The English Utilitarians* (1900).

ADDITIONAL REFERENCES

B. Newman, *Lord Melbourne* (1930); G. C. Clark, *Peel and the Conservative Party* (1929); J. L. and B. Hammond, *The Age of the Chartists, 1832–1854* (1930); S. and B. Webb, *The English Poor Law*, 2 vols. (1929); R. L. Hill, *Toryism and the People, 1832–1846* (1929); H. W. C. Davis, *The Age of Grey and Peel* (1929); D. O. Wagner, *The Church of England and Social Reform Since 1854* (1930); N. S. Bushnell, *Historical Background of English Literature* (1930); G. M. Young (ed.), *Early Victorian England*, 2 vols. (1934); J. H. Clapham, *Economic History of Modern Britain, 1850–1886* (1932); P. Flavigny, *Le Régime agraire en Angleterre au XIXe siècle* (1932); H. C. F. Bell, *Lord Palmerston* (1936); S. Maccoby, *English Radicalism, 1853–1886* (1938).

CHAPTER X

THE NEAR EASTERN QUESTION

RACES IN THE EMPIRE

In 1453, the Ottoman Turks, who had already gained a foothold in Europe, captured Constantinople. They soon overran the Balkan Turks invade Europe Peninsula, and, for several centuries, Christian Europe was threatened by Mohammedan invasions which swept all before them. In 1683, Turkish armies laid siege to Vienna; but, fortunately for western Europe, they were driven away. From that time on, the Turkish flood began to recede.

The Ottoman Empire was at its height at the end of the seventeenth century. In Europe it included the Balkan Peninsula, The Ottoman Empire Hungary, and the lands bordering on the Black Sea; in Asia, the region that lay between the Mediterranean and the frontier of Persia; and in Africa, all of the northern coast except Morocco. The Mediterranean had become almost a Turkish lake. Great difficulties were naturally experienced in holding so vast a region under one régime, and fissures appeared in the imposing imperial structure. Tripoli, Tunis, and Algeria became semi-independent under local rulers who, however, acknowledged the suzerainty of the Sultan of Turkey. During the eighteenth century the Turks were driven from Hungary by the Austrians, and from the northern shore of the Black Sea by the Russians.

In 1815, the Balkan Peninsula, Asia Minor as far as Persia, Syria, Egypt, Tripoli, Tunis, and Algeria were still under the rule Diversity of races and faiths of the "Sublime Porte," as the Turkish government was called. Situated at the meeting-place of three continents, the Ottoman Empire consisted of a conglomeration of races professing different faiths, speaking different languages, and strongly attached to their various national ideals and customs. In Asiatic Turkey the majority of the inhabitants, Turks, Arabs, and Kurds, were Mohammedan in religion; the minority were composed of Armenian and Greek Christians. In European Turkey the Turks were a small minority; the overwhelming majority were Slavic in race and Christian in faith. The Near Eastern Question concerned itself mainly with the in-

habitants of the Balkan Peninsula.   For centuries this region was
the "danger zone of Europe," and many wars were fought to
determine the fate of its inhabitants.

In no other part of Europe are there so many different races
within so small a compass as in the Balkans.   A succession of
barbaric hordes from northern Europe and western   The Serbs
Asia had invaded the Peninsula, and had become per-   and Bul-
manent settlers, mixing with the native inhabitants   garians
and, in some cases, adopting their customs and language.   The
most important groups were the Serbs and the Bulgarians.   The
Serbs were of Slavic origin and speech and dwelt in Serbia, Montenegro, Bosnia, and Herzegovina.   The Bulgarians, or Bulgars,
were also Slavic in speech and supposedly in blood as well, although
the original Bulgars were a Turanian tribe from Asia who had

conquered what is now Bulgaria, but who were assimilated by the native Slavic inhabitants.

The people of Rumania are of mixed origin. They proudly believe themselves to be the descendants of the Roman settlers in the ancient province of Dacia, as their language belongs to the Latin family. But the majority of the inhabitants are, in all likelihood, the descendants of the Slavic tribes who had invaded the region centuries ago. The Rumanians occupied the districts formerly known as Moldavia and Wallachia.

The Greeks boast of their descent from the people of ancient Hellas; hence, they consider themselves the leading nation of the Balkans. These "Hellenes" are of mixed origin. Although speaking a language founded on ancient Greek, they are descendants mainly of Slavic tribes who had invaded the country and intermarried with the native Hellenes and their slaves. Of all the Balkan peoples the Greeks were the most Western in their ideals and customs. Until the Greek Revolution they were much favored by the Sultan, who frequently appointed them to high office, and used them as agents to oppress the Slavs and the Rumanians.

The Albanians were a nomadic, warlike people who spoke a jargon made up of the various languages of the Peninsula. Although a wild mountain country Albania has a fine geographic location, being the outlet of the Peninsula to the Adriatic.

Scattered all over the Balkans were Armenians and Jews. The former are a remnant of an ancient race, Christian by faith, who have tenaciously clung to their religion, traditions, and ideals. The Jews were few in number, and lived chiefly in Saloniki and Constantinople. They were of Spanish origin, descendants of those who had fled to Turkey to escape the Inquisition; their language was a Spanish dialect known as "Ladino."

To a considerable degree, racial groups corresponded to economic groups. The Rumanians and Bulgarians were peasants, in a condition of virtual serfdom on the estates of the Mohammedan conquerors. The Serbs were known as a race of swineherds, as hog raising was the chief industry of their region. Like the ancient Hellenes, the Greeks were a seafaring people, and their ships and sailors were seen in every Mediterranean port. Commerce was in the hands of Armenians, Greeks, and Jews who constituted the middle class of the Peninsula. The upper class were the Turks most of whom were landed aristocrats and government officials.

Each of the Christian nations formed a compact group living in a definite territory; in addition, each had communities of its members scattered throughout the Peninsula. There were Greek "enclaves," or racial islands in Serbia; Albanian enclaves in Greece; Rumanian enclaves in Bulgaria. Macedonia was a veritable "ethnographic museum," with communities of all the Balkan races. Naturally each state wanted to annex its enclaves which led to bitter quarrels and wars. Another complicating element in the situation was that Austria-Hungary and Russia contained inhabitants of the same races as their Balkan neighbors. There were Serbs in Austria, and there were Rumanians in Hungary and in Russia, a situation which bred hostility between these Balkan states and their powerful neighbors.

Religion, even more than race, influenced affairs in the Peninsula. The great majority of the inhabitants were Christians, members of the Greek Church which, in doctrine, ritual, and organization, was almost identical with the Orthodox Church in Russia. At its head was the Patriarch in Constantinople, whose power was in no way comparable to that of the Pope in Rome. The fact that the Patriarch was always a Greek, and that he was an appointee of the Sultan, the head of the Mohammedan faith and the oppressor of the Christians, aroused jealousies and fears. Generally, the Patriarch was hostile to the nationalist aims of his adherents. As soon as they gained some degree of national independence, the Rumanians, Bulgarians, Serbs, and Greeks established independent national churches, free from the control of the Patriarch.

THE TURKS

The Turks were the ruling race. From their ranks came most of the higher officials, the great landowners, and the upper classes generally. Like the other races in the Balkans, the Turks had become very much mixed as a result of intermarriage; hence, religion, not race, was their distinctive characteristic. They were Moslems, and regarded the Christians with contempt as "rayahs," or "cattle." An impassable gulf separated

Christians and Moslems; religious differences deepened the hatred between conquered and conqueror into a fanatical bitterness that often resulted in bloodshed.

In the courts of law the word of a Mohammedan outweighed that of a Christian, the two faiths not being equal before the law. Chris-

Cruel treat-
ment of
Christians

tians were not admitted into the army in any capacity, for their loyalty was suspected; besides, as war to the Mohammedan was generally a crusade against the infidel, it could, therefore, be undertaken by the faithful only. The Christians were more heavily taxed than the Moslems; the former paid a head tax in addition to the regular taxes. Christians had .to give, formerly, a tribute of children who were torn from their families and brought up as Moslems. Some were trained as Janissaries, a body of picked troops that formed a sort of Prætorian Guard in the palace of the Sultan. Strange as it may seem, the Turks did grant religious toleration to the non-Moslems. Each religious group constituted a *millet*, to which was given a considerable degree of local autonomy; and the religious head of the group was officially recognized as the leader of his community.

As the Turks were a small minority in the Balkans, they relied on the principle of *divide et impera* to maintain their rule. The

Mutual
hatred of
the Balkan
races

rivalries and jealousies of the subject nationalities were so bitter that they would not unite against their common enemy. Bulgarians and Serbs hated each other; so did Serbs and Greeks; likewise, Rumanians and Bulgarians. These hatreds were stimulated by the Turks who favored now one, now another. Attempts at revolt were suppressed by the Turkish soldiery whose ferocity inspired unbounded terror. In Asiatic Turkey lived the Kurds, fanatical Mohammedan tribesmen, who were used in the massacres of the Christians. To kill a Christian was, to a Kurd, an act of piety.

The government of Turkey was an absolute monarchy, all power being lodged in the Sultan. In addition to his temporal power, he

System of
government

was the spiritual leader of all Mohammedans by virtue of being the Caliph, or Lord of Islam, as the Mohammedan world was called. His two chief assistants were the Grand Vizier, who corresponded to a Prime Minister, and the Sheik-ul-Islam, who took charge of religious affairs. In each *vilayet*, or province was a governor appointed by the Sultan. Local affairs among the non-Moslems were administered by the religious head of each *millet*. Turkey was not a nation with uniform laws and a common administration, but a heterogeneous empire held together by the authority of the Sultan.

In theory an independent state, Turkey was in fact a protectorate of Europe. There were limitations on her sovereignty imposed by the powers through special treaty arrangements. The most important of these limitations were known as the Capitulations, which gave special privileges to foreign residents in Turkey. Foreigners were exempted from the jurisdiction of the Turkish courts whose laws were based upon the Koran, and therefore repugnant to Christians; they were subject to the jurisdiction of the consular courts of their nation. Foreigners were exempted from paying most of the taxes. Foreign business enterprises were given special concessions, and were not subject to Turkish laws. Tariff duties were fixed by special treaties with the powers. In 1881, the Ottoman Public Debt Commission was founded by the powers to protect the interests of the foreign creditors of the Turkish government. The commission supervised the financial policies of the government. Another limitation on Turkish sovereignty was the right secured by France to protect all Roman Catholics, and the right claimed by Russia to protect those of the Greek Church. "Protection" was a vague right, and it was usually exercised when either power desired to intervene in Turkish affairs. Until the Congress of Paris in 1856, Turkey was not recognized by the powers as a member of the European family of nations; hence, she was outside of the pale of international law.

Turkish rule in Europe was a long story of despotism, incompetence, and corruption unrelieved by any notable contributions to civilization, a striking contrast to Mohammedan rule in Spain. All that the Turks desired of their subjects was tribute and obedience; and they did not succeed in organizing the former into a regular system of taxation and the latter into a stable and orderly administration. Spasmodic fleecing was the practice, and when the money was not forthcoming, cruel punishment was the lot of the miserable "rayahs." The corruption of the Turkish government became a byword in Europe. Money appropriated for public improvements went into the pockets of officials. Bribery (*baksheesh*) was almost universal. As the officials were neither well nor regularly paid, they sought to recompense themselves by corrupt methods. In some regions disorder prevailed continually; bands of brigands terrorized the inhabitants and put their lives and property in continual jeopardy. As in western Europe some of the Sultans endeavored to play the part of benevolent despots, notably Mahmoud II, who reigned during 1808–39. He made vigorous efforts to reform the administration and to introduce Western customs and institutions, but his efforts were largely nullified by the conservatism of the ruling classes who feared that reform would weaken the military and religious spirit of old Turkey.

Until the twentieth century the Turks made few attempts to adopt European civilization. They were, in reality, an army of Turks, a garrison in Europe occupation encamped on European soil, interested only in exploiting their subjects. Turkey was "an alien, incompatible entity, . . . attached to obsolete conceptions of theocratic feudalism, ignorant of the first principles of judicial administration, and addicted to making spasmodic efforts for welding together heterogeneous elements by means of brute force and massacre."

The Near Eastern question had three aspects: (1) the relation of the Sultan to his Christian subjects; (2) the ambitions of the various nationalities in the Peninsula who sometimes hated one another even more than they hated the Turks; and (3) the intervention of the powers in the affairs of Turkey. The last was perhaps the most important aspect, as the rivalries of the powers resulted in many wars, and was not least among the causes of the World War. Economically the Peninsula was of little value; it contained few natural resources, and its commerce was negligible. Geographically, however, it was one of the most important regions of the world, being the bridge connecting Europe and Asia, and the route of eastern Europe to the Mediterranean. The control of the Peninsula was, therefore, vastly important to those European powers that had interests to protect or ambitions to satisfy in regions that lay beyond.

Constantinople had been the goal of Russian foreign policy since the days of Peter the Great. That famous city was Russia's key Russia, enemy of Turkey to the Mediterranean because of its command of the Bosphorus and the Dardanelles; once in her hands, Russia would no longer fear being bottled up in time of war. She, therefore, became Turkey's uncompromising enemy, bent upon ousting her from Europe. The ambition to acquire Constantinople was not the only cause of Russia's hostility to Turkey. Her racial and religious affinities with the Slavic subjects of the Sultan inspired her with the idealistic motive of liberating the "little Slav brothers" from the rule of the hated Turk. Moreover, to supplant the crescent with the cross on the dome of the great mosque of Saint Sophia, once a Christian church, greatly appealed to the religious imagination of the Russian people, to whom a war with Turkey partook of the nature of a crusade.

The chief opponent of Russian ambitions in the Balkans was England, whose fixed policy was to maintain the integrity of Turkey. More than once was Turkey saved from the destroying hand of Russia by the timely intervention of England. That a nation as liberal as England should give whole-hearted support to a government as reactionary as that of the Sultan was indeed surprising. England's support of Turkey was due to her desire to safeguard the route to India. Russia in Constantinople might be preliminary to a Russian advance upon India, long the dread of English statesmen. Hence the safety of the British Empire depended upon the integrity of the Ottoman Empire. *England, friend of Turkey*

INDEPENDENCE OF GREECE

During the nineteenth century the history of Turkey was almost a continuous story of insurrections of the subject races, revolts of vassal states, and interventions of the powers. Turkey was in the process of dissolution. After centuries of oppression, national movements began among the subject races who were inspired by the ideals of nationalism and democracy proclaimed by the French Revolution. Especially strong were these sentiments among the Greeks, who found it intolerable that the "descendants of the wise and noble people of Hellas," should bow beneath the Turkish yoke. A powerful secret society was formed, the *Hetairia Philike* (Association of Friends), which conducted a vigorous and widespread agitation for Greek independence. In 1821 an uprising took place in Morea in southern Greece, and Turkish officials were brutally massacred. "The Turk shall live no more, neither in Morea nor in the whole world!" was the war-cry of the Greeks. In revenge the Sultan ordered a massacre of Greeks living in Constantinople. Terrible scenes were enacted in which *Uprising of the Greeks* religious and racial hatreds were given free rein.   On Easter Sunday the Patriarch of the Greek Church was hanged in his full pontifical vestments.   War followed between Greeks and Turks, which was waged with savage fury by both sides for eight years.   The encounters which took place were more in the nature of massacres than battles.   Captured towns would be given over to pillage and slaughter; neither age, condition, nor sex was respected.

The uprising of the Greeks awakened general enthusiasm throughout Europe.   Many ardent lovers of ancient Hellas, among them the English poet Byron, volunteered to help in the Greek struggle for independence.   In spite of many valorous deeds, the Greeks would have succumbed to the superior forces of Turkey had not Russia, England, and France intervened in their behalf.   The powers were induced to champion the cause of Greece chiefly through the influence of thousands of their citizens in whom the memory of the ancient land of philosophy, literature, and art had roused an intense desire to see it freed from Turkish misrule.   A conference of the powers met in 1827 and demanded that an armistice be declared.   Before final arrangements were made, a Turkish squadron was destroyed by the fleets of the Allies at the battle of Navarino.   The Sultan was furious, and he determined to resist at all costs.   A new war now began, this time between Turkey on one side, and Russia and France on the other.   The Russians invaded the Balkans and were marching rapidly toward Constantinople.   French armies drove the Turks out of Morea.   These reverses compelled the Sultan to yield, and, in 1829, he signed the treaty of Adrianople, which granted autonomy to Serbia, Moldavia, and Wallachia, and independence to Greece.

The chief outcome of the struggle was the independence of Greece, which was acknowledged by the Sultan in 1829.   Later, in 1833, Greece was organized as a kingdom, and a Bavarian prince, Otto, was chosen as ruler with the title "King of the Hellenes."   The territory of the new nation was limited; it did not include the Greek-speaking district of Thessaly and the Greek islands of the Ægean.   Greece was the first fully independent nation that emerged from the Turkish flood that had overwhelmed the Balkans.

Revolt against the Sultan's authority next took place in an unexpected quarter, Egypt.   Mehemet Ali, the Governor of Egypt, was ambitious to become an independent ruler, and possibly even to establish a rival Mohammedan empire. At the head of an Egyptian army he invaded Asia Minor and conquered Syria (1832). The Sultan was alarmed, and appealed to the Christian powers for help. To every one's surprise, Russia alone came to his aid, but for a consideration. In 1833, Russia and Turkey signed the Treaty of Unkiar Skelessi, which made them allies and which gave Russia the privilege of stationing warships in the Straits, a privilege that Turkey denied to every other foreign power. England and France were furious, and a European war was threatening. The real crisis, however, came later, in 1840, when the Sultan prepared to reconquer Syria. Russia, fearing England and France, refused to intervene independently. A curious confusion arose. Russia and England agreed to come to the aid of the Sultan, but France sided with Mehemet Ali. England, Russia, Austria, and Prussia made an agreement with the Sultan pledging their support against Mehemet Ali. France was isolated and ignored. The French war spirit was aroused. "If France throws down the gauntlet," declared the bellicose Lord Palmerston, "we shall not refuse to pick it up," and Mehemet Ali would be "chucked into the Nile." The pacific Louis Philippe backed down, and the crisis passed. Mehemet Ali was forced to give up his conquests, but he gained the right of being the hereditary Governor of Egypt which, though nominally a fief of the Sultan, became virtually an independent country. In 1841, a new Straits Convention was signed by Turkey, the Allies, and France, which closed the Straits to all warships except those of Turkey.

THE CRIMEAN WAR (1853-56)

Russia emerged from the war of 1828-29 with great prestige among the peoples of the Balkans. She was now the "big Slav brother" who was to liberate them from Turkish oppression. To Turkey, Russia was the enemy to be feared above all others; she well knew that the Tsar's ambition to gain "a window on the Mediterranean" would lead to renewed attempts to capture Constantinople. Tsar Nicholas I was convinced that the Ottoman Empire was on the point of dissolution. He constantly referred to Turkey as the "sick man of Europe," whose death was imminent and whose estate ought, therefore, to be partitioned among the powers. He suggested that England and Russia agree upon a plan for the dismemberment of

Turkey. England, however, refused to fall in with the scheme, and the Tsar determined to take the matter into his own hands.

An excuse for war was found in a quarrel that arose over the holy places in Palestine. For centuries Christian pilgrims had been visiting the places in the Holy Land that were considered especially sacred because of their connection with the life of Christ. In 1850, a quarrel arose between the monks of the Roman Catholic and those of the Greek Church living in Palestine over the control of the holy places. Russia came forward as the champion of the Greek monks, and made a peremptory demand that the Sultan grant her a protectorate over the Greek Christians in Turkey. The Sultan refused on the ground that such a concession would give Russia the right to interfere in the internal affairs of his dominions. In 1853, Russian armies invaded the Turkish provinces of Moldavia and Wallachia, and once again Turkey and Russia were engaged in mortal combat.

Outbreak of Crimean War

The Crimean War, as it was called, was not, however, limited to these two nations; it became almost a general European war. In 1854, Turkey was joined by England and France; in 1855, by Sardinia. England's motive in joining Turkey was fear of Russia in Constantinople; the motives of the other allies are explained elsewhere.[1] To the amazement and anger of Tsar Nicholas, Austria maintained an attitude of friendly neutrality toward the allies. He had fully expected Austria's help in return for the services that he had rendered to the Hapsburgs in the trying days of 1848,[2] and he bitterly resented what he regarded as ungrateful conduct. The estrangement between Russia and Austria, begun as a result of the Crimean War, continued with increasing bitterness; it was to influence international relations for many years to come. Prussia alone maintained an attitude of benevolent neutrality toward Russia, which was now faced by a coalition of practically all the great powers of Europe.

The allies

It was now decided to punish Russian aggression by invading the Tsar's territory. Accordingly, large Allied armies invaded Crimea and laid siege to Sebastopol, which had been magnificently fortified by Russia with the object of dominating the Black Sea. Many bloody battles were fought during the siege, the most famous of which were Alma, Balaklava, and

The conduct of the war

[1] See pages 223, 224.   [2] See page 197.

Inkermann. No great general appeared during the Crimean War, which was characterized by amazing incompetence and fearful recklessness. A notable instance was the charge of the Light Brigade, a troop of six hundred British soldiers, against a large Russian army. The bravery of the doomed men roused the greatest admiration and was immortalized in a poem by Tennyson. Owing to the breakdown of the English commissariat and medical service, there was a heavy toll of lives through disease, negligence, hunger, and cold. In eloquent words, John Bright depicted the tragic situation: "The Angel of Death has been abroad throughout the land; you may almost hear the beating of his wings." Only one famous name is associated with the conduct of the Crimean War. It is that of Florence Nightingale, an English nurse, whose tenderness and bravery while nursing the sick and wounded soldiers won her the greatest admiration. She organized a nursing corps which greatly aided the army in battling with death and disease. The activities of Florence Nightingale resulted in creating a new profession for women, that of nursing; later, it inspired the establishment of the Red Cross.

The crucial event of the war was the siege of Sebastopol. The fortress was gallantly and ably defended, but it fell after a siege of eleven months. The war was now virtually at an end. Fall of In 1856, peace delegates assembled in Paris, represent- Sebastopol ing all the belligerents; and, in addition, Austria and Prussia.

The Congress of Paris was the first great European assembly since the Congress of Vienna. It gave an opportunity to discuss the state of Europe as well as peace terms to Russia. Treaty of Among the prominent delegates was Cavour, who de- Paris livered a famous address in favor of Italian unity.[1] The Treaty of Paris provided: (1) that the Black Sea should be neutralized — that is, that no nation was to build arsenals on its coast or to station warships in its waters; (2) that the Danube should be free to all nations, and that a commission be appointed representing the nations bordering upon its shores to regulate traffic; and (3) that Moldavia and Wallachia should be given local autonomy under Turkish suzerainty. The Congress also adopted a famous "Declaration" in reference to neutral trade in time of war. The Declaration of Paris established the following rules: (1) privateering was abolished; (2) a neutral flag covered enemy goods except contra-

[1] See page 224.

band of war; (3) neutral goods, except contraband of war, were not liable to capture under the enemy flag; and (4) a blockade, to be binding, must be maintained by a force sufficient to prevent access to the enemy's coast.

Although it engaged the attention of all Europe, the Crimean War accomplished nothing toward solving the Near Eastern Ques-
Futility of   tion.   Turkey came out unscathed, and even respect-
the Crimean   able; her territorial integrity was guaranteed, and she
War
was recognized, for the first time, as a member of the European family of nations by being invited to the Congress of Paris.   During the treaty negotiations the Sultan had issued a proclamation, the *Hatti Humayun*, promising equality before the law of all his subjects.   But this proclamation was not carried into effect, and the Sultan continued to oppress his Christian subjects.   Russia openly violated the clauses of the treaty relating to the neutrality of the Black Sea.   England was more determined than ever to bolster up Turkish power in Europe.

REFERENCES

GENERAL:
    Excellent one-volume studies are: E. Driault, *La Question d'Orient depuis ses origines jusqu'à la Paix de Sèvres* (ed. 1921); F. Schevill, *The History of the Balkan Peninsula* (1933); W. Miller, *The Balkans* (ed. 1923); W. S. Davis, *A Short History of the Near East from the Founding of Constantinople* (1922); N. D. Harris, *Europe and the East* (ed. 1926); N. Forbes and others, *The Balkans* (1915); and J. A. R. Marriott, *The Eastern Question in European Diplomacy* (ed. 1926).

THE CHRISTIAN NATIONS:
    N. Jorga, *History of Rumania*, translated from the French (1926), brief study by an authority on Rumanian history; O. Brilliant, *Rumania* (ed. 1915); H. W. V. Temperley, *History of Serbia* (1917); E. Denis, *La Grande Sérbie* (ed. 1915), by the leading authority on Serbia; A. H. E. Taylor, *The Future of the Southern Slavs* (1917); W. Miller, *History of the Greek People, 1821–1921* (1922), by the leading authority of modern Greece; G. Songeon, *Histoire de la Bulgarie depuis les origines jusqu'à nos jours, 485–1913* (1913); F. S. Stevenson, *A History of Montenegro* (1912); J. Swire, *Albania* (1930).

TURKEY:
    S. Lane-Poole, *The Story of Turkey* (1897), a reliable summary; Sir E. Pears, *Turkey and its People* (ed. 1912), an intimate study by an Englishman long resident in Turkey, and N. Jorga, *Geschichte des osmanischen Reiches*, vol. v (1913), a standard work.

CHAPTER XI

REACTION AND REFORM IN RUSSIA

BACKWARDNESS OF RUSSIA

FOR many centuries Russia had stood almost apart from the general current of European history. Her size was so great, and her development was so different from that of her sister nations that it might have been said, with some degree of truth, that she constituted a separate continent wedged in between Europe and Asia. Russia had lagged far behind the other European nations in political development. During the thirteenth century, when western Europe had succeeded in establishing a degree of stable civilization under feudalism and had taken the first steps toward national monarchy, Russia was in part semi-barbaric, in part, feudal; during the sixteenth and seventeenth centuries, when western Europe had passed from feudalism to national monarchy, Russia was in part feudal, in part monarchical; during the eighteenth and nineteenth centuries, when western Europe was shaping constitutional governments, Russia was a thoroughly absolute state. For a generation preceding the World War, when western Europe was rapidly putting government on a democratic basis, Russia was desperately trying to establish a constitutional régime.

Russia behind western Europe

The explanation for this backwardness must not be sought in the character of the Russian people, for it was no more the nature of the Russian to be conservative than it was the nature of the Frenchman to be progressive. In the highest forms of human endeavor, art, literature, and science, Russia gave striking evidence of a high degree of culture and originality. Tolstoy, Turgeniev, and Dostoievsky in literature; Tschaikovsky and Stravinsky in music; Antokolsky and Verestchagin in art; Mendeleiev and Metchnikov in science are names of which the most civilized nations could be proud. The answer or answers must be sought elsewhere. In the first place, Russia had never been a part of the ancient Roman Empire; hence, it did not receive the advantages of the classical civilization, the inestimable

Reasons for her backwardness

heritage of the nations of western Europe. Secondly, Russia was outside of the pale of the Catholic civilization of the Middle Ages, for the Slavic barbarians were Christianized by missionaries from Constantinople, who did not spread Greek civilization as effectively as the missionaries from Rome had spread Latin civilization. Thirdly, the Russians, unfortunately, were conquered early in the thirteenth century by semi-barbarous Tartars who ruled the country for almost three centuries, and did their part in keeping it backward. In her early history Russia consisted of an inland region of which Moscow was the center. Having no seacoast, she could not get into close communication with the Mediterranean civilization of the south or with the Atlantic civilization of the west. Russia was a vast, landlocked, undulating plain over which barbarians roamed, a land so wild that it was hard to tell where "man left off and nature began." Cut off as she was from western Europe, Russia missed the enlightenment and stimulus of the Renaissance and the vigorous shock of the Protestant Revolution. Even the waves of the French Revolution, which rolled over and flooded the lands of the Western nations, dashed in vain against the granite breakwater of Russian conservatism.

REIGN OF ALEXANDER I (1801–25)

Russian history during the nineteenth century was concerned chiefly with two problems, expansion and democracy. At first sight it seems strange that the Empire of the Tsars, covering about one sixth of the land surface of the globe, stretching from the Baltic to the Pacific, with its southern regions near the Mediterranean and its northern regions towering above the Arctic Circle, should have sought to expand. In truth, it was more water rather than more land that Russia wanted, as she had the smallest coast-line in proportion to her size of any of the great nations. In Europe her only free outlet to the open sea was Archangel, whose harbor was frozen half of the year. The other ports were no more advantageously situated. Odessa was at the mercy of Turkey, who could close the Straits in time of war. The harbors of Riga and Cronstadt were frozen during the winter months; moreover, these two ports were at the mercy of whatever power controlled the Baltic during war. Russia, therefore, was in a highly disadvantageous position in case of war. The other problem, democracy, hardly existed until the second half

Problems of Russia

of the nineteenth century. The Russian people were not yet infected with the virus of revolution, therefore the Romanovs sat more firmly on their throne than did the Hapsburgs and the Hohenzollerns.

During the first quarter of the nineteenth century, Russia was ruled by Alexander I. A curious man was this "Tsar of all the Russias": extravagantly liberal at one time and harshly reactionary at another, with a mystical turn of mind and given to morbid musings, having "all the gifts of Heaven except common sense." Alexander was a weak-minded dreamer, easily influenced by charlatans who imposed upon him and by reactionaries who used him for their purposes. *Character of Alexander*

For about five years after Waterloo, Alexander's course was very liberal. He suppressed flagrant abuses in the government, and treated the serfs on the crown lands with consideration. Toward the subject races in the Empire, the Tsar was very tolerant. Russian Poland was granted complete autonomy, being united with Russia only through the Tsar, who was also King of Poland. The Polish constitution provided for a Diet, having full power over legislation. Polish officials administered the affairs of the kingdom, and a Polish army was organized. Curiously enough, conquered Poland became a limited monarchy, while the predominant partner, Russia, remained an autocracy, greatly to the anger of the Russians, who disliked the Poles as their hereditary enemies. *Liberal treatment of the Poles*

Alexander's attitude toward Finland was likewise generous. As a result of the Napoleonic Wars, Sweden had ceded Finland to Russia. Finland was not, however, annexed as a conquered province; she was joined to Russia through a personal union with the Tsar, who was given the title of Grand Duke of Finland. Alexander swore to uphold the Finnish constitution, which gave to the Grand Duchy the right to have her own parliament, administration, code of laws, coinage, army, and official language, which was Swedish. *Liberal treatment of Finland*

At the beginning of his reign, Alexander was inclined to be liberal, but a number of events aroused his fears and dampened his none too ardent liberalism. His agent, Kotzebue, was assassinated in Germany; secret societies multiplied; the Poles manifested a desire for complete independence. These events inclined him to turn an attentive ear to the *Alexander becomes reactionary* arch-enemy of democracy, Metternich, who convinced him that the path of liberalism would lead to revolution and anarchy. Reaction followed, and once more Russia felt the heavy hand of oppression. The censorship of the press became more severe; university teaching was hampered; restraints were placed on the Polish Diet; and the government became harsh and oppressive. Alexander ardently seconded Metternich's efforts to stamp out the revolutionary movement in western Europe.

REIGN OF NICHOLAS I (1825–55)

Alexander left no son, and his successor was to be his brother, Constantine. But the latter had married a woman, not of royal blood, and had renounced his right to the throne, which was to go to a younger brother, Nicholas. When the death of Alexander was announced, a group of liberal-minded nobles, influenced by the ideas of the French Revolution and inspired by the activities of the Carbonari, formed a conspiracy to overthrow the autocracy by declaring in favor of Constantine as a constitutional monarch. Strangely enough, the birth-cry of Russian freedom was heard in a dynastic quarrel because Nicholas insisted that he was the rightful heir. The conspirators managed to win over some of the troops who, in December, 1825, revolted, shouting, "Long live Constantine and the Constitution!" So deeply ignorant were the soldiers of the forms of free government that they actually believed that "Constitution" was Constantine's wife. The uprising of the Decembrists, as the conspirators were called, ended in a fiasco. It was ruthlessly and speedily crushed by Nicholas, and the leaders were executed, imprisoned, or exiled to Siberia.

The Decembrist uprising

Nicholas I was a typical Russian tsar. A man of magnificent physique, a soldier by temperament and training, loving nothing so much as the battle-field and parade-ground, he naturally regarded government as military discipline in another form. Criticism of policies was insubordination; a desire for self-government was, like mutiny, not to be tolerated for a moment. Deeply influenced by the fact that he had mounted the throne in the shadow of a revolutionary conspiracy, he had a morbid fear of any kind of opposition. In a letter of advice to his son and heir, Nicholas told him that when his time came to rule to "command the council to be summoned to you and declare that

Character of Nicholas

you absolutely require the preservation of everything in the existing state of affairs, without the slightest infringement."

During his reign there was established what was called the Nicholas System." It had for its object the eradication of all liberal ideas and the suppression of all liberal-minded The Nicholas System people in order to seal Russia hermetically from the pestilential air of western Europe. Foreign books and foreign visitors entering Russia were carefully examined at the frontiers to prevent the smuggling in of contraband ideas. So severe was the censorship that the utterance of an unguarded word or the reading of a forbidden book brought swift and terrible punishment. Even musical compositions were censored, as it was feared that the notes might be used as a cipher code by revolutionists. Teaching, especially, was under strict surveillance, because the universities were regarded as hotbeds of revolution. The declared object of the educational system was the "multiplication of mental dikes for the struggle with destructive notions." Official textbooks were introduced that glorified the autocratic system and condemned liberal ideas and movements. Police spies were sent into classrooms to watch teachers and students. Lest foreign ideas corrupt good Russians students were forbidden to study in foreign universities. Russia was "frozen."

Nicholas was a loyal adherent of the established Orthodox Church, which he regarded merely as another phase of the Russian State; in his eyes Church and State were one and indivisible. An attempt to convert an Orthodox believer to any other faith was made punishable by imprisonment; and if the attempt were repeated, by exile to Siberia. Roman Catholics, Jews, and dissenters were harried by hostile laws and persecuting officials. Proselytizing among non-Orthodox, however, was greatly encouraged by rewards and special privileges. "Autocracy, Orthodoxy, and Nationalism" was the formula of militant tsarism.

Opposition to Nicholas arose, not among the Russians, but among the Poles. In spite of the considerable degree of autonomy guaranteed to them by the Constitution, the Poles The Polish were discontented and desired to be independent of Rebellion of Russia. Oddly enough, the Poles developed a strong national spirit after they ceased being a nationality. Divided politically among three powers, they were yet united in their sent-ments as they had never been before. The national movement was especially strong among the Russian Poles, the most numerous and the most militant group. Inspired by the revolutionary movement in France and Belgium, the Poles rose against the Tsar. In 1831, the Diet deposed the Romanov dynasty and proclaimed the independence of Poland. Tsar Nicholas was aroused to fury. A Russian army swept into Poland and ruthlessly suppressed the rebellion, and "Peace reigned in Warsaw." Nicholas revoked the Polish constitution and suppressed the Diet.

Severe punishment was now visited upon the Poles. Poland was annexed outright to Russia and governed by Russian officials.

Russia suppresses Polish nationalism
Russian displaced Polish as the official language of the conquered land. Polish families were forcibly transplanted and scattered all over Russia. In almost every capital of western Europe, especially in Paris, forlorn Polish refugees excited the deepest sympathy. Crushed to earth, they, nevertheless, continued to dream of a restored fatherland. "Poland is not yet lost" was the watchword of the Polish patriots.

Nicholas was as hostile to revolutionists in foreign countries as he was to those at home. His foreign policy had two important
Foreign policy of Nicholas I
objects, the suppression of the revolutionary movement on the Continent and the extinction of the Ottoman Empire in Europe. The Revolution of 1848 left Russia unshaken. Nicholas, the sole monarch at peace with his subjects, planted himself in the midst of a revolutionary continent, and became the efficient cause of reaction by assuming the rôle of an international policeman.[1] "Saddle your horses, gentlemen, the French have declared a republic," announced the Tsar to his courtiers when news came of the February Revolution. Against Turkey he waged two wars, described in the previous chapter. Greatly to the chagrin of Nicholas, who regarded western Europeans with dislike and even with contempt, England, France, and Sardinia came to the aid of Turkey and succeeded in defeating the redoubtable Russian armies. Disappointed and broken-hearted, the Tsar died, in 1855, during the siege of Sebastopol, and was succeeded by his son, Alexander II. The "Nicholas System" was doomed when Sebastopol fell, as the Era of Great Reforms which followed was indirectly due to the defeat of

[1] See page 204.

Russia in the Crimean War.   Even the most conservative Russians were now convinced that their institutions must be reformed; otherwise their country would lose her place among the great nations of the world.

REIGN OF ALEXANDER II (1855–81)

Alexander II was quite different temperamentally from his father. Impressionable, yet gifted with prudence and common sense, he generally tried to steer a middle course between revolu-   Character of tion and reaction.   He determined to rule in the spirit   Alexander II of his age, not in the spirit of his father.   Although he was not himself a great statesman, he wisely followed the counsels of enlightened advisors, and his reign is therefore distinguished in Russian history as an era of reform and progress.

It is as the emancipator of the serfs that Alexander won fame as a liberal ruler.   Serfdom had been widespread in Europe during the Middle Ages; it had begun to disappear in England   Serfdom in and France by the fourteenth century, and was en-   Russia tirely abolished in western Europe by the French Revolution and by Napoleon.   Serfdom in Russia resembled that in western Europe during the Middle Ages, but certain features of the system were peculiar to Russia.   Most of the 23,000,000 serfs, the number estimated in 1859, were on the estates of the "proprietors"; the rest were on the lands of the Orthodox Church, of the state, and of the imperial family.   As in western Europe a Russian estate consisted of two parts, the private fields of the proprietor and the fields of the serfs.   Generally the serf was bound to the soil which he cultivated.   He could not leave the estate without his master's permission, and usually he was not sold away from the estate; like the trees he was rooted to the soil, and he changed masters only when the estate changed hands.   For the right to cultivate his holding, the serf had to give dues and services to the proprietor.   Having no civil rights, he could own no property, real or personal; all his personal belongings and the farm that he worked were legally the property of his master.   In addition to dues and services, the serf had to pay a poll tax to the government, the amount being fixed by the proprietor.   He could not marry of his own free will.   It was the custom, at certain times, for the proprietor to draw up a list of his peasants of marriageable age and arbitrarily select mates for them.   To have permitted the peasant freedom of marriage might have resulted in his marrying out of the estate, and the proprietor would consequently have lost a "soul," as the serf was called in Russia. The wealth of an aristocrat was often measured by the number of male "souls" on his estate. Female "souls" were not counted.

In respect to dues and services the serfs were divided into three groups, the *bartschina*, the *obrók*, and the *dvorovie*. A *bartschina* peasant owed the proprietor labor on the latter's private fields; the number of days was regulated by local custom, the maximum being three, as fixed by imperial law. An *obrók* serf had to pay the proprietor a definite amount of money, fixed by the proprietor. In order to earn this money, the serf frequently hired himself out as a laborer in town and gave part of his wages to his master. *Obrók* tended to displace *bartschina*, as it was favored by both master and serf; by the former, because he could get money when he did not need labor, and by the latter, because it gave him a certain degree of freedom. The *dvorovie* were household domestics, slaves in all but name, being subject to the caprice of the proprietor and his family. The *dvorovie* had no counterpart in the serfdom of western Europe; they were like the domestic slaves in ancient Greece and Rome.

Classes of serfs

Although the law tried to protect the serf from extreme tyranny, its enforcement was difficult in a country so poorly organized as Russia and so completely under the influence of the landed aristocracy. The proprietor could transfer a serf from one group to another, inflict upon him corporal punishment short of death, or have him drafted into the army. The power to draft into the army was a terrible weapon in the hands of a tyrannical master, who could, by this means, summarily remove a refractory peasant from his farm, home, and family. It was not unusual to sell a serf away from the estate in spite of widespread custom which forbade such practices. Corporal punishment was a common form of chastisement in Russia for all sorts of offenses. The peasant was unmercifully beaten by the proprietor when he was behind in dues, by the government officials when he was behind in taxes, by the judge when he was disorderly. As in the case of the American slave-owners in the South before the Civil War, there were many kind-hearted and generous masters; but the absolute control of human beings, made possible by the institution of serfdom, inevitably led to outrageous abuses. The

Power of the proprietor over the serf

only barrier to the rapacity of a tyrannical master was the wonderful spirit of passive resistance developed by the peasants, who would be beaten almost to death without revealing the hiding-place of the little money that they might have saved.   The peasants often resorted to robbery, murder, house-burning, and even to rebellion to revenge themselves on the proprietors.   Many ran away to become tramps on the highways or pilgrims wandering to the numerous holy places in Russia.

Serfdom was universally regarded as a great evil, and even the upper classes were in favor of emancipation provided they did not suffer thereby.   Unlike the Negro in America, the serf *Opposition* in Russia was of the same race as his master; hence, *to serfdom* ardent patriots as well as liberal humanitarians were in favor of his emancipation.   It was felt by thoughtful Russians that the institution of serfdom was a blot on their country, and a powerful movement was started early in the nineteenth century to abolish it.   There was also an economic motive for emancipation.   A large number of the estates were heavily mortgaged, and peasant emancipation, if done by the government on terms favorable to the proprietors, would save many of them from bankruptcy. Alexander II determined on a policy of immediate emancipation because he believed that it was "better to abolish serfdom from above than to wait until it will be abolished by a movement from below."   A circular was sent by the government to leading officials in which emancipation was openly broached.   The Tsar also appointed a committee to investigate the problem of bondage and to recommend reforms.   These efforts of Alexander were received with great enthusiasm among liberals, and found favor even among many landed proprietors.   To those who opposed emancipation, Alexander frankly stated that "serfdom was instituted by absolute power.   Only absolute power can destroy it; and to do so is my will."   Acting under the inspiration of the Tsar, a committee, composed of officials and nobles, drew up the Emancipation Law, which was then issued as an *ukáse*, or imperial decree on March 17, 1861.   This Magna Charta of the Russian peasants freed the serfs on the landed estates only; two years later, those in domestic service were freed; and in 1866, the work of emancipation was completed by the freeing of the crown serfs.

The main provisions of this famous law were: (1) that the serfs should at once receive full rights of citizenship, and be subject to the authority of the government, not to that of the proprietor; Provisions of (2) that the cottages, farm buildings, domestic ani- the Emanci- mals, and implements which they had been using pation Law should be legally their property; and (3) that allot- ments of land should be given to the freedmen in order to guarantee them the means of a livelihood. To have given the serfs freedom without land would have brought into existence an agricultural proletariat working for wages and therefore economically depend- ent upon their former owners. "Liberation without land," de- clared the Tsar, "has always ended in an increase of the pro- prietor's power." Moreover, the peasants themselves would have strenuously objected to a landless freedom, because, through generations of cultivating the soil, they had come to believe that they were actually its owners. "We are yours, but the land is ours," they would say to the proprietors.

How to apportion the land and on what terms were problems very difficult to solve justly. The government was less concerned Division of with the interests of the peasants than with those of the land the proprietors, who were considered the bulwark of the State. For the lands that they ceded to the peasants, the pro- prietors received liberal compensation from the government. But the peasants had to pay the government for the farms that they received. As they had little ready money, they were required to pay a special annual tax, known as the "redemption dues," for a period of forty-nine years.[1] The peasants were freed at their own cost, having to pay the price of emancipation. To become in a sense the "serfs of the State" was not what they had bargained for; they had fondly imagined that emancipation would give them land free of all charges. They also complained that the allotments came from the poorest portions of the estate, that the prices charged were too high, and that the farms given to them were too small. The lords had kept the forests, the good pasturages, and the most fertile fields; to the peasants they gave meager patches of their worst lands. The peasant was now a free citizen, and, as it was said, had the "right to die on his own property." The govern- ment had indeed dealt rather generously with the proprietors and rather niggardly with the peasants. There was great disappoint- ment at the outcome, and rumors spread that a second emancipa-

---

[1] The domestic serfs were given no land; hence, they did not have to pay the special tax. Many remained in their old positions on wages.

tion was coming. Uprisings occurred which greatly disturbed the government. To quiet the peasants, Alexander, who was greatly beloved, went among them to explain the Emancipation Law, and to tell them that no more land was to be distributed. But it was widely believed that he was not really the Tsar, but a "general" who was impersonating him in order to deceive the peasants, who could not believe that the Little Father would uphold a law that was so unfair to his "dear people."

It must not be supposed that emancipation created a large number of peasant proprietors in Russia. Ownership of the allotments was vested in the *mir*, as a whole, which was responsible for the payments to the government and which divided the land among the various families. The mir was not an institution peculiar to Russia alone, but a belated form of the village community which had once flourished in western Europe. Its membership was composed of the heads of families in the village, who elected elders to represent the village in relation to the government, particularly in the matter of taxes. The mir decided when to plow, when to sow, and when to reap; no one could leave the village without its consent on pain of having his holding confiscated.

The *mir*

Undoubtedly the emancipation of the serfs was the most important event in the history of Russia during the nineteenth century. By this change in legal status a slave-like peasantry became the people of Russia. A higher standard for the masses was bound to influence the entire country for the better and to become the starting-point for other reforms. There was now a large supply of free labor, as many peasants, not having sufficient land, came to the cities, where they found work in the factories that were being established. Emancipation paved the way for the revolutionary movement which finally culminated in the destruction of tsarism.

Importance of emancipation

The Tsar-Liberator was also willing to play the part of Tsar-Reformer. In 1864, Alexander made important changes in the judicial and administrative systems of the Empire. The administration of justice had been arbitrary, backward, and corrupt. Emancipation had brought new lawsuits as well as new citizens, which necessitated the reorganization of the courts. A new code of laws was issued, based largely on the judicial practices of England and France, which decreed equality of all

Judicial reform

classes before the law and introduced trial by jury in criminal cases.

The growth of city life, due to the advance of commerce and industry, and the growth of communal life, due to emancipation, Local gov- made necessary the introduction of some kind of local ernment self-government. For the cities Alexander established municipal councils, which were partly elected. For the country he established *zemstvos*, made up of representatives of the various classes in the community. The zemstvos had charge of the schools, roads, asylums, hospitals, and agricultural improvements of the locality.

Alexander was also liberal in educational matters. The restrictions placed by Nicholas I on teaching were removed, and the Tolerant universities were given large powers of self-govern- policy of ment. Secondary education was reorganized on the Alexander German model. The censorship of the press was greatly relaxed, and Russia began to breathe freely. The laws against the Jews were not strictly enforced. The constitution of Finland was respected. Alexander was inclined to treat the Poles kindly, but he refused unconditionally to restore the constitution demanded by the Polish patriots.

There was a rising discontent among the Poles, who were inspired by the nationalist movements in Germany and Italy. In 1863, Polish upris- Russia again faced a Polish uprising organized by a ing of 1863 secret committee in Warsaw. Encouraged by a few successes, the insurgents prepared to seize Lithuania, where the Polish landed aristocracy was in sympathy with the uprising. Nationalist sentiment in Russia was now aroused, Russian armies invaded Poland and speedily crushed the uprising.

Alexander's policy toward the conquered Poles was as harsh as that of Nicholas in 1831. The leaders were executed, and thou- Persecution sands were transported to Siberia. The use of the of the Poles Polish language was forbidden; all schools were com- pelled to teach in Russian. The heaviest blows fell upon the clergy and nobility, who had been the leaders in the rebellion. Many monasteries were suppressed and their property confiscated. A commission was appointed in St. Petersburg to administer the affairs of the Catholic Church in Poland. A radical land reform was put through by the government according to which the ten- ants became the proprietors of the lands that they cultivated.

Slight compensation was given to the landowners many of whom were ruined. The uprising resulted, not in freeing Poland from Russia, but in freeing the Polish peasant from the *Slachta*, the Polish landed aristocracy.

The Polish uprising and the spread of revolutionary ideas had the effect of frightening Alexander into a policy of reaction. He became convinced that liberalism, instead of quieting rebellion, was encouraging it. The revolutionary movement in Russia was growing and becoming more and more violent. An attempt on his life produced a deep impression on Alexander's mind, and caused him to give ear to the reactionaries that advised him to rule in the spirit of Nicholas. Moreover, the Russo-Turkish War [1] turned Alexander to the old dream of acquiring Constantinople and to forsake the new dream of an enlightened Russia. Reaction gained full swing. A strict censorship of the press was again established; the universities were once more put under surveillance; and the liberals were again persecuted. The "Nicholas System" was thus partially restored.

Alexander becomes reactionary

THE INTELLIGENTSIA

During the period of the Restoration in western Europe there had existed a sharp divergence between restored absolutism and the new system of society that had come into being as a result of the French and the Industrial Revolutions. The political system based upon absolute monarchy was of the Old Régime, but the social changes made by the French Revolution and the economic changes made by the Industrial Revolution were modern. Absolute monarchy was, therefore, an anachronism which could be maintained only by military force and which was bound to go as soon as the new elements in society, the capitalists and the workingmen, made their power felt, which they did in the Revolution of 1848. But no such divergence existed in Russia during the early part of the nineteenth century; hence, there was no revolutionary movement of any consequence. Russian absolutism then harmonized perfectly with an agricultural society, general ignorance, legal inequality, and religious persecution. In other words, Russia still had to go through her period of enlightenment as well as through her

Harmony of political and social conditions

[1] See page 470.

political and industrial revolutions before she could become a truly modern nation.

Many Russians had traveled and studied abroad, and so had imbibed the ideas of the radical thinkers of western Europe.

Opposition
to the gov-
ernment by
the educated

When they contemplated their own country, with its autocratic government and medieval society, they recoiled in indignation, horror, and disgust. Nothing that was modern, nothing that was good, seemed to be present in Russia; on the contrary, everything was old and bad. Educated and enlightened Russians formed a group by themselves known as the "intelligentsia," or the intellectuals, who came from all classes of society, even from the nobility. The intelligentsia had no counterpart in any other country in that it was recognized as the spokesman of the illiterate masses in the struggle for freedom. It furnished the leadership of the revolutionary movement in all its phases, from the most moderate to the most radical. In Russia alone could it be said that in almost every liberal-minded person the government had an opponent.

The nucleus of the intelligentsia were students and writers of both sexes. They would foregather in secret meeting-places, where

Intelligentsia
repudiates
all traditions

they sat far into the night, drinking hot tea, smoking cigarettes, and discussing philosophic ideals. From that to hatching plots against the government was but an easy and quick transition. Many if not most of the terrorists came from this class, to whom the assassination of tyrants was the moral duty of a freedom-loving individual. The traditions and conventions of their country, and for that matter of the world, counted for naught among them. As an outward and visible sign of their spirit of revolt, the men wore their hair long, and the women wore theirs short. "An intellectual Russian," wrote Herzen, "is the most independent being in the world. . . . We are independent because we have no possessions — nothing to lose. All our memories are full of gall and bitterness. . . . We have no traditions; therefore, far from being inferior on that account to countries who possess them, we are superior to them."

At first the intelligentsia were influenced by the ideas of the French philosophers of the eighteenth century. Later, in the

Nihilism

forties and fifties, the writings of the German metaphysicians, Fichte and Hegel, greatly attracted them. In abstract metaphysics and argumentative dialectics the intelligentsia found a mask for revolutionary thinking. A philosophical attitude known as "nihilism" was popular in the sixties. It was a crudely materialistic view of life which ridiculed all idealism and which exalted science. "Life was a workshop," declared the nihilists, "and to the rubbish heap with art, poetry, and music." They renounced all cherished traditions and conventions, and professed to believe in "nothing"; hence, the name (Latin *nihil*, nothing). "A nihilist," says one of the characters in Turgeniev's novel, *Fathers and Sons*, "is a man who does not bow before any authority whatsoever, does not accept a single principle on faith, with whatever respect that principle be endowed." A novel appeared in 1863, *What is to be Done?* written by Nicholas Chernyshevski, which had a tremendous vogue among young Russians. It discussed personal problems in relation to social institutions and accepted traditions, especially those of love and marriage. A spirit of nihilist disillusionment pervaded the book, for the author believed that poetry and romance could be found "only in the truth of life." Fundamentally, nihilism was a repudiation of the principles underlying the political and social structure of Russia. "Nihilism," declared Herzen, "does not reduce something to nothing, but discerns that nothing was taken for something under the influence of an optical illusion." It was not concerned with matters political, yet the term "nihilist" was later applied to those who favored terroristic methods against the government.

The intelligentsia may be said to have received its inspiration from two remarkable men, Alexander Herzen, the father of Russian liberalism, and Michael Bakunin, the father of Russian radicalism, who profoundly influenced the course of the revolutionary movement in Russia. From his earliest youth, Herzen devoted his life to waging war against all forms of oppression. In 1847, he was obliged to leave Russia, and thereafter lived as an exile in various countries of western Europe. He finally settled in London, where he founded and edited a weekly journal, called the *Kolokol* (*The Bell*) which became the organ of liberalism. It was smuggled into Russia, where it was widely read; even Tsar Alexander read it, as copies of the *Kolokol* were regularly laid on his table by an unknown hand. Herzen attacked the existing régime in Russia with bitter satire, sparkling wit, and glowing eloquence. His program demanded, as he expressed it, the freeing of speech

Herzen
(1812–70)

from the censor, the peasant from the landowner, and the taxpayer from the knout.[1] He was convinced that progress even in Russia could come only through general enlightenment and not through violence. In one sense, he was a typical nineteenth-century liberal, yet he criticized liberalism for relying too much upon the bourgeois in society and upon parliament in government. There were tinges of Utopian socialism in Herzen's political philosophy, and he became the inspirer of a revolutionary movement among the Russian youth.

A man of quite different temperament was Bakunin. He was of aristocratic parentage, and, for a time, served as an officer Bakunin   in the Imperial Guard. Bakunin became a pas-
(1814–76)   sionate student of philosophy, which led him, as it did other young Russians, into the revolutionary movement. He was convinced that the goal of all human striving was freedom, which could only be reached through anarchy. Visionary and uncompromising, Bakunin became a fanatical anarchist and an advocate of the "propaganda of deed," violence of all sorts, assassination, riots, mutinies, and popular uprisings. What is necessary, he declared, is a "world that is lawless, and consequently free," and, to be free, mankind must repudiate God, the family, and the State. The last, he considered, as the most complete negation of humanity, as it guaranteed "to the rich their wealth, and to the poor their poverty." Bakunin was an international terrorist, an "apostle of universal destruction," wandering from land to land. Where revolution was brewing, there was Bakunin: in Germany, in Austria, in Italy, in France, in Spain. A prisoner in many lands, an exile in Siberia, he yet managed to escape and to continue his activities. The revolutionist, according to Bakunin, was a "consecrated person" who ought to have "no personal interests, no sentiments, no business, no property.... For him everything is moral that favors the triumph of revolution." A man of savage energy and unbalanced imagination, "eternal movement hidden in the very depths of his soul," Bakunin was ready at any moment to embark on a desperate revolutionary enterprise. Strangely enough, he combined with his demoniac violence a childlike simplicity and a gentle kindliness that made him appear like a character in one of Dostoievsky's novels.

[1] A knout was a Russian whip.

THE REVOLUTIONARY MOVEMENT

In its early phases the revolutionary movement in Russia was inspired by the ideals of Western liberalism. It aimed to reorganize Russia according to the principles of the   The liberals
French Revolution, which would enable her to reenter Europe as a modern nation, as, in the seventeenth century, she had entered Europe as an autocracy. But how? The liberals believed that despotism was maintained by the Tsar and the upper classes because they were not "enlightened." Hence, it was necessary to enlighten them through discussion and literary propaganda. The intelligentsia formed "circles" to study history, economics, and sociology in order to find a peaceful solution of their country's problems. Among the liberals were many "penitent noblemen," wealthy aristocrats who were conscience-stricken at the evil state of affairs from which they profited.

But the Tsar and the upper classes refused to become "enlightened" when it meant a surrender of their privileges. Many ardent spirits, who longed to be doing things instead of talking   The Narod
about them, advocated a movement to intimidate the government into concessions by a threat of revolution from below. They declared that Russia would not progress very far unless the bulk of her people, the peasants, realized their own and their country's condition. Emancipation had freed the peasants, but they were still steeped in moral serfdom, as centuries of bondage had left their evil impress on their minds and characters. During the decade following 1870 there began the *Narod*, or "Go-to-the-People" movement,[1] which aimed to leaven the mass by a revolutionary propaganda among the peasants by demanding "Land and Freedom." Nothing could exceed the self-sacrifice and daring of these enthusiasts, generally students, who longed to "melt into one" with the people. They became village doctors, school teachers, and even laborers, in order to spread the gospel of freedom.

[1] It is vividly described by Stepniak in the following way: "With the spring of 1874 all discussion abruptly ceased among the circles of the revolutionary youth. The time for talking was over: actual 'work' was in contemplation. The working-people's gear — boots, shirts, etc. — were hurriedly being prepared. Short greetings and laconic answers were heard: 'Whither?' 'To the Urals,' 'To the Volga,' 'To the South,' 'To the river of Don,' and so on. . . . There were warm wishes for success and robust squeezings of hands . . . 'The spring is ending; it is high time.' . . . And so like an electric spark, the cry 'To the people,' ran through the youth. Sure of themselves, daring and wide-awake, though unarmed and unorganized, they dashed in full sight of the enemy into the storm."

The government, fearful of the new activities of Young Russia, determined to spare no one and to stop at nothing in order to destroy the movement. Hundreds of men and women of the finest type languished in prison or spent a lonely exile in the wilds of Siberia. Many fled to Switzerland which became a haven for Russian refugees. The conduct of the peasants toward their would-be liberators was anything but friendly. These simple people were shocked and angered by the denunciation of the Tsar, whom they loved and revered as the "Little Father," and would often themselves hand the propagandists over to the police.

Suppression of the Narod movement

Disappointed with the attitude of the peasants and exasperated by police persecution, Young Russia resolved upon a short cut to its hopes by a "propaganda of deed." The revolutionary movement entered on a new phase, terrorism, when, in 1879, the "People's Will" movement was organized. It issued a stirring manifesto, demanding complete democracy in government and full freedom of speech and of association. As no concessions were made, the terrorists declared war to the death against the government, and all officials, high and low, civil and military, stood in danger of bomb, pistol, and dagger. The situation in Russia was unlike that of any other country in history. The great mass of people were simple, almost primitive peasants whose lives were spent in constant toil and whose interests ranged little beyond those of the farm and village. They were ruled by an oligarchy of landlords and officials, who, though refined in manners, were corrupt, incompetent, brutal, and callous to an incredible degree. Vowed to destroy the oligarchy were groups of revolutionists who, with the utmost coolness and daring, gambled with their own lives in order to destroy those of their enemies. Secret revolutionary societies hatched conspiracies, circulated books and pamphlets, and organized demonstrations. A new type appeared in Russia, the professional revolutionist, who dedicated his life to the crusade against tsarism. The professional revolutionists were "illegal" men and women who assumed aliases and lived in "Underground Russia," where they plotted against the government, wrote for "illegal" journals, made bombs, forged passports, smuggled arms, and organized revolutionary societies. Those who had no means of livelihood were supported by contributions from sympathizers in all ranks of life. Secret government agents entered

The terrorists

the ranks of revolutionists to spy upon them; and secret revolutionists entered the ranks of the officials for the same purpose. Prison doors would sometimes be mysteriously unlocked for the benefit of an imprisoned comrade. In the war against tsarism all methods were considered legitimate by the revolutionaries, who would not hesitate to "execute" a spy or a traitor. To observe the ordinary rules of morality would, they believed, play into the hands of a government that was without mercy as it was without scruple.

Alexander became the shining mark of the terrorists because, in their opinion, he had betrayed the cause of political freedom by not going far enough in his reform measures. Three unsuccessful attempts were made upon his life. In one of these, a terrorist disguised as a carpenter blew up a part of the Winter Palace, killing several persons; the Tsar escaped only because he came late to dinner. In 1881, he was assassinated by terrorists who threw bombs at his carriage as he was driving through the streets of the capital. All Russia was shocked by the tragedy that laid low the Tsar-Liberator, who paid with his life for the sins of his father.

Assassination of Alexander

THE RUSSIAN NOVEL

It was not until the nineteenth century that great writers appeared in Russia, which, until then, had made little or no contribution to the world's literature. Like unknown planets suddenly flashing forth their brilliance in the heavens, a group of Russian novelists appeared who astounded the world by their striking originality, moral depth, and literary art. "Russian literature is the voice of a giant, waking from a long sleep, and becoming articulate. It is as though the world had watched this giant's deep slumber for a long time, wondering what he would say when he awakened. And what he has said has been well worth the thousand years of waiting."

Russian authors excel chiefly in the domain of fiction, and the novels of Turgeniev, Dostoievsky, and Tolstoy almost immediately took first rank as works of literature. Fiction is the best medium for analyzing human motives and for describing social conditions; and the Russian writers displayed such freedom and largeness in portraying man as an individual and as a social being that they have been given an undisputed place as

Russian fiction

the masters of realism.   No motive is so hidden that they cannot reveal it to the pitying gaze of humanity; no society is so complex that they cannot unravel its strands of good and evil.   They rise to the loftiest heights of moral grandeur and sublime idealism, and they shrink at nothing in stripping bare the human soul in its deepest degradation.

Ivan Turgeniev lived most of his life in France and Germany and was greatly influenced by the culture of western Europe. Turgeniev   His work is characterized by an exquisite art, and (1818–83)   few writers in any language have equaled Turgeniev's power of evoking a whole society by a delicate touch or suggestion, so that the moral is brought home with striking effect.   This is notably true in *The Diary of a Sportsman*, which consists of sketches of peasant life before the Emancipation.   Instead of denouncing the evils of serfdom, the author merely portrays the serfs in their ordinary routine life; but so real and true are the portraits that the book was a powerful influence in the freeing of the serfs.   In *Rudin* the Russian national type finds its classical expression.   Keen in thought, eloquent in word, the hero, Rudin, yet remains incapable of sustained effort, for he can be roused to action only by sudden passion.   An atmosphere of "tender gloom" pervades Turgeniev's masterpiece, *Fathers and Sons*, in which is described the struggle between the older and the younger generations.   The hero, Bazarov, is a brilliant nihilist at war with the ideals of the older generation, but who has no plans or even constructive ideas for a new society.

Feodor Dostoievsky, the painter of saints, outcasts, criminals, and madmen, was pursued by poverty and ill-health all his life. Dostoievsky   At the age of twenty-eight he was condemned to death (1821–81)   on the charge of rebellion, but just as he was about to be executed the sentence was reprieved to four years' exile in Siberia.   Dostoievsky is the creator and supreme master of the psychologic novel, which aims to diagnose the mind as a physician does the body.   His most famous book, *Crime and Punishment*, tells the story of a poor student, Raskólnikov, who deliberately murders an old woman because he feels that he is able to put her money to better use than she can.   The planning and execution of the crime and the attempts of the murderer to escape detection are described with a minuteness and a piercing analysis of motives that border on the morbid.   Raskólnikov feels no remorse, but only regret for his crime, which he considers a misfortune deserving of sympathy, not condemnation. In *Crime and Punishment* and in his other famous novels, *The Brothers Karamazov* and *The Idiot* Dostoievsky exhibits extraordinary mastery over the emotions of terror and pity. His most frequent theme is the sublimity of human suffering, which to his "mystic Slavic soul" means the redemption of mankind.

Count Leo Tolstoy was the literary colossus of Russia during the latter half of the nineteenth century. His extraordinary art, his views on life and religion, and his character as a man made a profound impression on the whole world, and he was the most widely read of all the Russian authors. A novel by this author-preacher consists of a series of incidents rather than of a continuous narrative, with a great theme instead of a plot as the connecting link. Tolstoy is at his best in describing critical moments in the life of a nation or of an individual. His historical novel, *War and Peace*, is a colossal prose epic, a modern Iliad, which treats of Russian conditions in the time of the Napoleonic invasion. Like that of a Greek tragedy, the leading theme of this book is that, when elemental forces are let loose, individuals are only the playthings of fate. Circumstances, not leaders, determine the outcome of great combats; therefore a true leader is one who, like the Russian general, Kutusov, does not attempt to hinder the inexorable laws of destiny, but allows them free play. Another Tolstoy masterpiece is *Anna Karenina*, the theme of which is that happiness comes only to those who are engaged in doing good to others. The novel tells the story of two couples: in one case, the lovers, passionately devoted to each other and seeking their own happiness only, find their fate in misery and death; in the other, the lovers, devoting themselves to the welfare of the community in which they live, find that happiness which they sought to bring to others. With amazing art the author reveals the souls of men and women as they drift onward to their destiny, himself moved by compassion almost as great as that found in the Gospels.

Tolstoy
(1828–1910)

A profound change gradually came into the life of Tolstoy. The novelist turned preacher and reformer. He came to the conclusion that modern civilization is a failure, that religion has been corrupted by the church, law by government, teaching by schools, and love by marriage. Not love of art, but love of mankind was the greatest thing in the world; and only those artists who loved their fellow men could hope to do anything worth while. "Everything that unites mankind is good and beautiful; everything that divides mankind is wicked and hateful." Simplification of life became Tolstoy's first aim, but his solution of the problem was not a return to nature as preached by Rousseau, but a return to the Christianity that Christ preached. He then became a "seeker after God," and sought salvation in poverty, humility, and peace. Tolstoy was a thorough believer in the doctrine of non-resistance and in the theory that bloodshed, whether of man or of animal, is wicked under any and all circumstances. He strongly opposed war, capital punishment, and the slaughter of animals for food. The common peasant alone, according to this Russian seer, had achieved true happiness and understanding; therefore he determined to live the life of a common peasant. He deeded all of his property to his wife but continued to live in his old home. He dressed in the rough blouse of a peasant, worked daily in the fields or in the shop, and ate the simple fare of the common man. His home became a place of pilgrimage for people from all over the world.

REFERENCES

GENERAL:

A. Kornilov, *Modern Russian History*, translated from the Russian, 2 vols. (ed. 1924), a standard work, contains good bibliography; Sir B. Pares, *History of Russia* (revised ed. 1937), a standard work, about half of the volume devoted to the nineteenth century; R. Beazley and others, *Russia from the Varangians to the Bolsheviks* (1918); A. N. Rambaud, *Histoire de la Russie depuis les origines jusqu'à nos jours*, a standard work, revised and completed to 1913 (1914), most of it translated into English; A. Leroy-Beaulieu, *The Empire of the Tsars and the Russians*, translated from French, 3 vols. (1893–96), good description of religious conditions; M. Kovalevsky, *Russian Political Institutions* (1902), brief study by Russian scholar; M. Baring, *The Russian People* (ed. 1911) and Sir D. M. Wallace, *Russia* (ed. 1908), good popular descriptions; G. Vernadsky, *History of Russia* (1929), mainly of modern times, fine bibliography.

SPECIAL TOPICS:

J. Mavor, *An Economic History of Russia* (ed. 1925), best in English, especially good on condition of the peasants; M. Kovalevsky, *Le Régime économique de la Russie* (1898), describes the beginnings of the Industrial Revolution; G. Drage, *Russian Affairs* (1904), on economic conditions and on expansion; Peter (Prince) Kropotkin, *Russian Literature, Ideals, and Realities* (1915), by the famous scholar-revolutionist; K. P. Pobiedonostsev, *Reflections of a Russian Statesman*, translated from the French (1898), see page 446; T. K. Masaryk, *The Spirit of Russia*, translated from the German, 2 vols. (1919), a scholarly study of revolutionary, literary, and social matters by the Czech scholar-statesman; A. Brückner, *A Literary History of Russia*, translated from the German, (1908); on expansion: F. H. Skrine, *The Expansion of Russia* (ed. 1913), the best brief treatment; C. F. Wright, *Asiatic Russia*, 2 vols. (1902), an authoritative survey of conditions, political, economic, and racial; A. Vámbéry, *Western Culture in Eastern Lands: a Comparison of the Methods adopted by England and Russia in the Middle East* (1906), by a famous traveler and Orientalist, favorable to England.

Subject Races:

V. Bérard, *The Russian Empire and Czarism*, translated from the French (1905). On the Poles: N. Hill, *Poland and the Polish Question* (1915); R. Dmowski, *La Question Polonaise* (1909), by a Polish nationalist brings out international aspect of question. On the Jews: S. M. Dubnov, *History of the Jews in Russia and Poland*, translated from the Russian, 3 vols. (1916–20), standard work on the subject; I. Friedlaender, *The Jews of Russia and Poland* (1915); L. Wolf, *The Legal Suffering of the Jews in Russia* (1912), description of the Anti-Jewish laws; S. Joseph, *Jewish Immigration to the United States* (1914), explains the economic causes of Jewish emigration from Russia; A. Reade, *Finland and the Finns* (1914).

ADDITIONAL REFERENCE

S. R. Tompkins, *Russia Through the Ages* (1940).

CHAPTER XII

THE REVOLUTION OF 1848

DURING the middle of the nineteenth century, the Metternich System was attacked by a revolutionary movement that spread to nearly every country in western Europe. It began in Paris in February, 1848, and throne after throne was overturned as the revolutionary tide rolled on from Paris to Vienna. For a time the movement seemed to realize the republican dreams of the Jacobins of '93: then the tide receded, but not without leaving the Metternich System a mass of wreckage. Both the successes and failures of the Revolution of 1848 had a profound influence on the subsequent history of Europe down to the World War.

FRANCE

The government of Louis Philippe became increasingly unpopular in France. Opposition showed itself in street demonstrations and in "reform banquets" that demanded universal suffrage. A great meeting was arranged on Washington's Birthday, February 22, 1848, but the government forbade it. Nevertheless, a crowd gathered at the meeting-place, a typical Parisian crowd of workingmen, students, artists, agitators, and loafers. Rioting began on the following day and the National Guard was sent to maintain order, but the soldiers joined the insurgents. Louis Philippe, realizing that he was now without power, promised reforms. Guizot resigned. But the march of events was swifter than tardy concessions. Barricades were erected in the streets of Paris, and the city was in the hands of the revolutionists, who proclaimed a republic. Louis Philippe abdicated and fled to England.

The success of the February Revolution was as much a surprise to the victors as to the vanquished. A confluence of turbulent political streams from many directions had suddenly and swiftly overwhelmed the Bourgeois Monarchy. Idealistic republicans inspired by the principles of the French Revolution, chauvinistic imperialists plotting to restore the empire of the Bonapartes, revolutionary socialists aiming to establish a labor commonwealth, visionary Utopians dreaming of a perfect society, all had united to overthrow a régime that was more despised than feared. The leaders of the uprising were of a new type: journalists, students, and actors, and their followers were the workingmen of Paris. For the first time a revolution in Paris was the work of the proletariat led by intellectuals.

Two rival governments now appeared, one republican and the other socialist. After much negotiation a provisional government was established representative of both elements. Its leading members were Lamartine, poet and orator, who was the spokesman of the idealistic bourgeois; and Blanc, journalist and agitator, who was inspired by the ideas of early socialism. The chief concession made to the socialists was the recognition of the principle of the "right to work." Decrees were issued providing for the establishment of "national workshops" [1] demanded by Blanc and his socialist followers. But it was not at all the intention of the government to promote socialistic experiments. What was established was a caricature of Blanc's plan. Men of all trades were given the "right to work" for forty cents a day building fortifications. Yet so widespread was unemployment that thousands of workingmen were enrolled in these "national workshops." *Establishment of "national workshops"*

A Constitutional Assembly was elected by universal manhood suffrage that assumed charge of the government. The workingmen soon realized that socialism was as little favored by republicans as by monarchists. Almost the first act of the Assembly was to abolish the "national workshops" and to discharge the laborers, who were denounced as a "reserve army of insurrection, a perpetual strike supported by public money." Many were now unemployed, a mass of misery in the streets of Paris, embittered by poverty and disappointed with the republic. *Suppression of the "national workshops"*

With the cry, "Bread or Lead," the Paris workingmen rose in insurrection. Once more the barricades went up, this time against those who had recently been behind them. It was not the tricolor, but the red flag of socialism that now floated from the barricades. Street fighting took place during the "June Days" (June 23–26, 1848), such as had not been seen since the Reign of Terror. The government was so alarmed that it gave *The June Days*

[1] See page 78.

General Cavaignac full power to establish order. After bitter fighting between the military and the workingmen, the uprising was finally suppressed. The terrible "June Days" was the first war between bourgeois and proletariat, and it left a legacy of bitter antagonism between them which was to have important consequences on future events in France.

A constitution was now adopted by the Assembly for the Second French Republic. It provided for a parliament of one house and Election of for a president, both to be elected by universal man-Louis Napo- hood suffrage. Among the candidates for President leon Bona- was Prince Louis Napoleon Bonaparte, who suddenly parte appeared upon the political scene. As the representative of the Bonaparte dynasty, he had the advantage of a great name and a great tradition which aroused much enthusiasm. He was elected by an overwhelming majority over his republican and socialist opponents. "Why should I not vote for him," said a Napoleonic veteran, "I whose nose was frozen at Moscow"? When he took office, the Prince-President declared that he would regard as enemies of the country "all those who endeavor to change by illegal means that which France has established."

The result of the elections for the Legislative Assembly, as parliament was called, was also a surprise, as the overwhelming The Mon- majority were monarchists. There was now a "re-archist As- public without republicans." The President and sembly Assembly vied with each other in suppressing republican journals and in jailing republicans. In order to "purify" universal suffrage, the Assembly passed a new electoral law which, in effect, disfranchised the working class.

Having disposed of their common enemy, the President and Assembly fell to quarreling with each other, as their ambitions Rivalry of clashed. The aim of the former was to become Em-the Presi- peror, and that of the latter was to restore the mon-dent and archy. Louis Napoleon sought the favor of various Assembly elements in the nation. To win the support of the Catholics he sent an army to Rome which suppressed the Roman Republic and restored the Pope.[1] To win the masses he denounced the new electoral law, and demanded the restoration of universal suffrage. But the army was the vital factor in his ambitions.

[1] See page 202.

He did all in his power to win the favor of the soldiers who were enthusiastic in having a Bonaparte at their head.

Everything was prepared for a *coup d'état*, or the overthrow of the Republic by a military conspiracy. The day chosen was December 2, 1851, the anniversary of the battle of Austerlitz. One morning Paris awoke to find the *The coup d'état of 1851* whole city placarded with announcements by the President that he had dissolved the Assembly and had ordered the reëstablishment of universal suffrage in order to "save the country and the Republic from harm." The soldiers forcibly ejected the members of the Assembly, arresting all who opposed them. Republicans in all parts of France were suddenly seized and cast into prison. What the conspirators feared most were the barricades. The army was prepared, and when the Paris mob rose it was swiftly and mercilessly suppressed. Louis Napoleon was now virtual master of France. A plebiscite was then ordered, in which all citizens were asked whether they approved or disapproved of the President's acts and of the new constitution which he proposed. By a vote of 7,481,000 to 647,000 France gave her seal of approval to the *coup d'état*.

The constitution provided that Louis Napoleon should serve as President for a new term of ten years, with full power to appoint and dismiss the cabinet. There was also to be a *Napoleon proclaimed Emperor* parliament elected by universal manhood suffrage. Shortly afterward (1852) Louis Napoleon was proclaimed Napoleon III, Emperor of the French. This action, too, was ratified by a plebiscite. There was now a second Restoration, this time of the Napoleonic dynasty in the person of the fantastic adventurer and poverty-stricken exile on whom had been poured so much ridicule and contempt.

It would be only too easy to ascribe the startling change from the Republic of 1848 to the Empire of 1852 to the instability or "frivolousness" of the French. There are more *Why France accepted Napoleon III* worthy explanations. In the first place, the propertied classes had become badly frightened at the growth of revolutionary socialism among the workingmen. The "June Days" had inspired fear that private property was in danger. and there took place a consolidation of conservative sentiment among property-owners who saw in the insurrection a menace to their prosperity, even to their very existence. "The agitation set

on foot by the liberals," declared Jules Simon, "resulted in the
Republic which they dreaded, and at the last moment universal
suffrage, set on foot by certain republicans, resulted in promoting
the cause of socialism which they abhorred." Napoleon appeared
to many substantial citizens as the "savior of society," the strong
man who would suppress the socialists as his great uncle had suppressed the Jacobins, with a "whiff of grapeshot." In the second
place, the workingmen had come to regard a bourgeois republic
with the same hatred as a bourgeois monarchy. And was not
Napoleon in favor of restoring universal suffrage, abolished by the
Assembly? In the third place, the French people were not in a
position to prevent the change to autocracy, even had they been
willing to do so, because the plebiscite was a tricky form of referendum. Instead of asking the people whether they wished to
make a change, Napoleon first made the change and then asked
for approval. It was, then, a choice between accepting the new
government or nothing; hence, there was no alternative but to vote
approval. Many electors stayed away from the polls rather than
take part in this farcical referendum. The new Emperor combined
with a dreamy and impulsively generous disposition a cunning
that was almost unfathomable and an unscrupulousness that was
almost unbelievable. Finally, Napoleon with his romantic history
and great tradition made a powerful appeal to the highly imaginative French. They believed that under his rule France would
again assume a dominant position in European affairs; and, as
events proved, they were not mistaken.

AUSTRIA

The February Revolution in Paris gave the signal for revolt
throughout Germany. Uprisings took place in nearly all the
states, and constitutions were granted by the frightened princes,
who thereby hoped to save their thrones if not their prerogatives.
The Diet was in a panic, and made haste to repeal the Carlsbad
Decrees. From all sides came demands that Germany be united
and free.

The movement for nationalism and democracy made its most
furious assaults in the Hapsburg empire. *There* was the citadel
of the Metternich System. *There* were the many peoples whose
national sentiments were flouted by the government. The Hungarians, especially, proud and militant, were restive under Austrian

rule. A nationalist movement swept through Austria that affected Hungarians, Slavs, and Italians which was strengthened by the democratic movement among all the nationalities in the Empire.

The leading figure among the revolutionists was the Hungarian patriot, Louis Kossuth, a typical radical of the era of 1848. Humanitarian in his sympathies and outlook, and a stanch believer in intellectual, political, and religious Kossuth (1802–94) freedom, he was, nevertheless, an uncompromising nationalist. Kossuth first became known as the editor of a radical journal, and was imprisoned because of his views. While in prison he employed his time studying the English language; later, when visiting England and the United States on a speaking tour, he astonished his audiences by his extraordinary command of English. Kossuth was one of the great orators of the nineteenth century; his fine voice, dignified presence, and superb eloquence aroused his countrymen to the highest pitch of enthusiasm.

Hungary was then a feudal state under the control of powerful landed aristocrats. The Emperor in Vienna was the absolute monarch, but the government of the country was Conditions carried on by a Diet dominated by the aristocracy. in Hungary Many of the inhabitants were peasants of Slavic and Rumanian stock who were in a semi-feudal relation to their lords who were of the dominant race of Magyars, or Hungarians.

Kossuth advocated the abolition of the dues and services of the peasants, the equality before the law of noble and commoner, the establishment of a popularly elected parliament to Uprising in govern the country, and complete autonomy. On Vienna March 3, 1848, he delivered a stirring speech before the Hungarian Diet which electrified the entire Hapsburg dominions. He denounced the Austrian government as a political charnel house whence came stifling odors and pestilential winds which deadened freedom and the national spirit. This speech was the immediate cause of an uprising in Vienna. As in Paris, revolutionary workingmen, led by students, erected barricades in the streets. A mob surrounded the imperial palace, crying, "Down with Metternich!" The once powerful statesman was compelled to flee in disguise to England. With the flight of Metternich, the whole system of repression, so laboriously constructed since the Congress of Vienna, went crashing to destruction. Emperor Ferdinand was compelled to grant a liberal constitution establishing a democratic parliament, to abolish the dues and services of the peasants, and to guarantee freedom of speech and of the press.

In Hungary the march of revolution was even swifter. Under the influence of Kossuth, the Diet passed the famous "March Laws" which transformed Hungary from a feudal to a modern state. A constitution was adopted which established a system of popular self-government. The privileges of the nobility and the dues and services of the peasants were abolished. Freedom of speech, of the press, and of religion was guaranteed. Radical changes were made in the relations between Hungary and Austria. Henceforth, the former was to have her own army, her own national flag, her own system of taxes, and even the control of her foreign relations. Hungary was now united to Austria only by the slender tie of a personal union through the Emperor. Pressed by the revolution in Vienna, Ferdinand was forced to consent to these revolutionary changes.

The "March Laws" in Hungary

Bohemia, too, raised the flag of revolt, and was likewise granted liberal concessions. A movement was also begun to unite all the Slavic peoples against the hated domination of the Germanic Austrians. A Pan-Slavic Congress was convened in Prague, to which came representatives from nearly all the Slavic nations in Europe. As no one Slavic tongue was understood by all the delegates, they were forced to have recourse to the hated German language in conducting the Congress.

Uprising in Bohemia

The ancient House of Hapsburg was now on the brink of ruin. Ferdinand fled from Vienna, and the capital fell into the hands of his rebellious subjects. The Hapsburg dominions were rapidly disintegrating and, for a time, it seemed as though the Empire would dissolve into many nations and possibly into anarchy and chaos. Yet there were several elements in the situation, serious as it was, favorable to the dynasty. When it came to dividing the fruits of victory, the heterogeneous character of the population was bound to produce discord. To play off one race against the other and thereby divide the victors into hostile factions was the astute policy of the government.

Hapsburg policy of divide et impera

In Bohemia a bitter race feud arose between the Czechs and the Germans. The government quickly took advantage of the situation, and sent an army under an able general, Windischgraetz, who captured Prague. Bohemia was now conquered and once more reduced to a Hapsburg province. Windischgraetz marched on Vienna, which surrendered after a fierce bombard- Suppression ment. The government determined to put a stop of the upris- to the "parliamentary game." Parliament was dis- ing in Vienna solved and the constitution withdrawn. Many of the revolutionists were imprisoned, exiled, or executed.

Meanwhile the situation in Hungary was critical for the Hapsburgs But here again division among the revolutionists proved their undoing. When the Slavs and Rumanians re- Abrogation quested the Diet to recognize their national rights, of the they received a haughty refusal. Hungarian freedom, "March it was now seen, meant the freedom of the Hungarians Laws" to oppress the other races. A fierce race war now broke out between the Hungarians and Slavs, the latter receiving the aid of Austria, who was eager to drive a wedge of discord into the ranks of her enemies. A Croat, named Jellachich, who was a bitter opponent of the Hungarians, was made "Ban," or Governor of Croatia, in Hungary. Austria determined on a plan to nullify the liberties gained by Hungary. Emperor Ferdinand was forced to abdicate, and was succeeded by his nephew, Francis Joseph. The March Laws were abrogated on the theory that the oath of Ferdinand to uphold them was not binding upon his successor. The Diet in Budapest was dissolved, and Hungarian liberties were no more.

All Hungary rose under the enthusiastic leadership of Kossuth, who denounced the Hapsburgs as false and perjured. In 1849, Hungary declared her independence of Austria. A Suppression struggle followed in which the Hungarians had to con- of Hungary tend against the Slavs under Jellachich as well as against Austrian armies Whatever doubt there was as to the outcome of the struggle was settled by the entrance of Russia on the side of Austria. Tsar Nicholas I regarded the uprising of the Hungarians with great misgiving; he feared lest an independent Hungary would be an incentive to rebellion among the subject nationalities of Russia. Moreover, that fervent believer in absolutism was eager to come to the rescue of a fellow autocrat in distress. Russian armies poured over the Carpathians, and the Hungarian revolt was soon quelled. The concessions granted to Hungary were abrogated, and she was reduced to the position of a province in the Empire.

Reaction was now in full swing in Austria. The leaders of the uprising were severely dealt with, but Kossuth managed to escape. Fate of Kos- He went to England and to the United States, where suth   he aroused tremendous enthusiasm by his eloquent speeches. For many years, he lived in exile in various countries in Europe refusing a grant of amnesty extended to him by Austria. Kossuth's noble character and his unselfish devotion to his country, whether on the battle-field or in exile, enshrined him in the hearts of the Hungarian people by whom he has since been regarded as their national hero.

PRUSSIA

The news of the revolt in Vienna and the flight of Metternich let loose a revolutionary storm in Germany. King Frederick William Uprising in of Prussia tried to avert revolution by calling together Berlin   a United Diet composed of delegates from the local assemblies; but this body refused to grant the loan demanded by the King, and it was summarily dismissed. Matters became serious when a great mob appeared in the courtyard of the royal castle, shouting for a constitution and threatening open rebellion in case it was not granted. The King appeared on the balcony and promised a constitution and the summoning of a parliament. Inadvertently a fight broke out between the mob and the military in which several people were killed by the soldiers. Almost immediately Berlin was in a state of insurrection. Barricades went up and the streets became impassable; for several days street fighting raged between the citizens and the troops. The King endeavored in vain to appease "his dear Berliners" by assuring them of his good intentions, but the only thing which would satisfy the rioters was a withdrawal of the military, which was accordingly ordered; whereupon the tumultuous "March days" came to an end.

A funeral service for those who had fallen in the barricade war was arranged in the courtyard of the royal castle. The bodies of Humiliation   the dead were wreathed in laurel, and their gaping of Frederick wounds exposed. Cries went up from the crowd William   below that the King come out and see his handiwork. As he appeared, the mob shouted, "Take off your hat!" The proud Hohenzollern obeyed and bowed low before the bodies of the dead citizens. He ordered the black, red, and gold flag flown from the castle, and fervently declared that his only wish was for German freedom and unity.

But there was one power yet to be reckoned with; namely, the army which remained loyal to the King. Frederick William recovered his courage as it became evident that most of the Prussian people, particularly the peasants, had no sympathy with revolution. Berlin was declared in a state of siege, and the army took charge of the situation. Many of the leaders of the revolution were arrested, and thousands fled to America to escape the vengeance of the Hohenzollerns. Some of these "Men of '48," like Carl Schurz and Franz Sigel, became prominent citizens in their adopted country. Reaction took full swing, and all popular manifestations were sternly suppressed. In 1850, the King promulgated a constitution which provided for a parliament elected by a three-class system of suffrage that insured the predominance of the propertied elements. To the King was given full executive power and an absolute veto on all bills. He was no longer absolute, but his power was not appreciably diminished.

Suppression of the uprising

The democratic movement in Germany was accompanied by a movement for national unity. In 1848, a self-constituted body of liberals drew up a plan for a national assembly to be elected by universal manhood suffrage throughout the Confederation with the object of framing a constitution to unite the German people. The Assembly met in Frankfort, amid great enthusiasm, for it was generally believed that the outcome of its deliberations would be a united Fatherland.

The national movement

The two most important questions before the Frankfort Assembly were the inclusion or exclusion of Austria and the form of government of the proposed union. On the first, the Assembly was sharply divided into two parties, the *Grossdeutschen*, who wished to include Austria, and the *Kleindeutschen*, who favored the exclusion of Austria on the ground that her population was largely non-German. This division of opinion soon developed into a rivalry between Austria and Prussia for the leadership of Germany. It was finally decided to admit only the German-speaking provinces of the Hapsburg dominions. On no condition would Austria consent to this plan, which she declared was an attempt to destroy her national unity. "Austria will know how to maintain her position in the projected German body politic," was the Hapsburg threat.

The Frankfort Assembly

On the question of the form of government there was a violent debate, a considerable number desiring a republic or, at least, a constitutional monarchy.   Finally, it was agreed that

King Frederick William spurns offer of Assembly

the union should be a federal empire, presided over by an hereditary monarch; and the Assembly voted to offer the position of Emperor to the King of Prussia. A constitution was adopted for the proposed union based upon the best features of the English and American systems of government. Would King Frederick William consent to become the constitutional head of a democratic Germany?   His consent was vitally necessary to the success of the movement.   But that monarch had a horror of revolution, and regarded the deliberations of constitutional assemblies as an infringement of his favorite doctrine of divine right.   "Do not forget that there are still princes in Germany, and that I am one of them!" he had once admonished a popular audience.   It was against his principles, against his temperament, to "pick up a crown from the gutter," as he termed the offer of the Frankfort Assembly.   A deputation from the Assembly was coolly, even insultingly, received by the King, who informed them that he would not accept their offer without the consent of his fellow princes.

The refusal of the King of Prussia to be the leader of a unified democratic Germany meant that the work of the Assembly was

Suppression of the Assembly

fruitless, and many of the states now withdrew their delegations.   Those who were left decided on a radical step; namely, to disregard the princes altogether and to call upon the German people to rise.   But this rump Assembly was soon dispersed by soldiers with drawn swords.

Deep was the disappointment in Germany when the democratic attempt to unite the country failed so miserably.   During its

Democratic methods discredited

sessions the Assembly had aroused much ridicule owing to the wordiness of the delegates who engaged in lengthy discussions of abstract political principles. The Assembly was more like a symposium of philosophers than a convention of politicians, and, as a consequence, political assemblies in Germany became synonymous with incapacity and futility. Ardent patriots now looked to sources other than conventions and to methods other than peaceful agitation to realize their dream of a united Fatherland.

ITALY

During the movement for Italian unification three plans gradually emerged for its realization. The most discussed was the plan advocated by Mazzini of establishing in Italy a highly centralized republic based upon the principles of the French Revolution. The second plan was to unite Italy into a federal union leaving to the princes considerable power in local affairs. The third plan, which came into prominence in 1848, was a centralized monarchy under the Savoy dynasty. Any one of these plans, if carried out, meant war with Austria whose position in Italy barred unification. *Plans of unification*

The year 1848 in Italy, as in Germany, saw the confluence of the two political movements, nationalism and democracy. Rebellions broke out throughout the Peninsula, and constitutions were granted in many states. A sensational uprising took place in Rome. Pope Pius IX was forced to flee, and the city was organized as the Roman Republic with Mazzini and Garibaldi as the leading spirits. In Sardinia the liberal King Charles Albert, of his own accord, granted a constitution. This document, known as the *Statuto*, later became the constitution of united Italy and lasted until the Fascist *coup d'état* in 1922, when it was revised. *Uprisings in Italy*

Uprisings against princes inspired nationalist uprisings against Austria in Lombardy-Venetia. Milan rose and expelled the Austrian troops. Venice, under the heroic leadership of Daniel Manin, declared herself an independent republic. The nationalist movement received a great impetus when Charles Albert declared war against Austria in order to free Italy from foreign rule. "*Italia farà da sè*" (Italy will do it herself), he proudly declared. Austria, hard pressed by the uprising in Vienna, began a retreat from Italy. Everything seemed propitious for realizing liberty and union, long awaited and now at hand.

But disappointment was in store for the Italian patriots. Sardinia's bold challenge received no organized support from the other states, who were more intent on overthrowing their local tyrants. An Austrian army under Radetzky invaded Italy and inflicted a great defeat on the Sardinians at the battle of Novara (1849). King Charles Albert was so despondent over the outcome that he deliberately sought death on the battle-field; but even death had cast him off, he bitterly complained. In disgust he abdicated the throne in favor *Austria defeats Sardinia* of his son, Victor Emmanuel II, and went into voluntary exile. Milan and Venice were recaptured, and Lombardy-Venetia was again under Austrian domination.

Austria offered advantageous terms of peace to the new King, provided he would revoke the constitution granted by his father.

Victor Emmanuel maintains the constitution But Victor Emmanuel's proud reply to Austria was: "What my father has sworn to, I will maintain. If you wish a war to death, so be it. . . . If I must fall, it will be without shame; my House knows the road to exile, but not to dishonor." The Sardinian King's loyalty to the constitution won for him the admiration of the Italian patriots who hailed him as *Il Re galantuomo* (the honest King).

A wave of reaction swept over Italy. The revolutionary governments, set up in the various parts of the Peninsula, were all overthrown.

Suppression of revolutionary movement In Naples the suppression was particularly severe, as no mercy was shown by King Ferdinand, whose ferocity excited great indignation in Europe. Gladstone denounced the Neapolitan government as the very "negation of God created into a system." Thousands of liberals were executed or tortured in prison with inhuman cruelty. The Roman Republic was overthrown, and Pius IX was restored through the aid of a French army sent by Louis Napoleon.

The results of the uprising of 1848 were most depressing to those who had consecrated their lives to the liberation of Italy.

Rise of Italian anti-clericalism Reaction was triumphant everywhere, and there was now another foreign army, the French, encamped on Italian soil. The Pope repented of his liberalism and became an unflinching opponent of Italian nationalism and democracy; as a consequence, the movement for unification became strongly tinged with anti-clericalism.

There was one crumb of comfort for the revolutionists. Sardinia had emerged defeated but morally victorious. Henceforth, Italian *Sardinia hope of Italy* hopes centered in the House of Savoy that had fought the common enemy, Austria, and had remained faithful to the principle of popular government.

UPRISINGS IN OTHER LANDS

No country in Europe, except Russia and Turkey, was untouched by the Revolution of 1848. The Young Ireland movement in Ireland and the Chartist movement in England are described elsewhere.[1]   Although there was no uprising in Denmark, the King granted a constitution (1849) in response to a widespread and growing liberalism.   It was a very moderate concession, as parliament was elected by a propertied suffrage, and the King continued to exercise full executive power.   In the Netherlands the liberal movement was led by Johan Rudolf Thorbecke, a distinguished jurist and statesman.   In 1848, King William II granted a new constitution which introduced a democratic feature in the long-established States-General by widening the suffrage for the lower house to which the cabinet was made responsible.   In Belgium, too, there was an important extension of democracy, which doubled the number of electors.   In Switzerland the problem was nationalism rather than democracy.   The Catholic cantons seceded from the Confederation, and organized a separate union called the *Sonderbund*.   Civil war followed, which resulted in the defeat of the secessionists.   In 1848, Switzerland adopted a new constitution which established a union modeled on that of the United States.[2]

RESULTS OF THE REVOLUTION OF 1848

The revolutionary movement, although everywhere suppressed, resulted in notable gains to democracy and nationalism.   Feudalism was abolished in the Hapsburg dominions.   The March Laws became the inspiration of Hungary, and were later to be the model for Hungarian autonomy.   There was now a parliament in almost every state in Germany; if the governments were not fully democratic, neither were the rulers fully autocratic.   Although it failed of its purpose, the Frankfort Assembly was the first attempt to unite Germany, an attempt which sank deep into the popular consciousness.   In France popular suffrage triumphed, and Napoleon III was compelled to rule under constitutional forms.   The most important gain of the Revolution of 1848 was the severe check given to the Metternich System.   Shortly afterwards it collapsed, and with it went the international system of repression which had foiled nearly all attempts for political freedom since 1815.

Gains of the Revolution

But why did the Revolution fail to complete its work begun so auspiciously?   For a time there was hardly a throne in western Europe that was not vacant.   One explanation is economic.   The Industrial Revolution had not advanced

Its failure

[1] See pages 138, 313.   [2] See page 439.

very far on the Continent, and there was not as yet a numerous
working class and a powerful group of capitalists which, together,
would have been able to cope successfully with the system represented by absolute monarchy.   Another explanation is social.   The
year 1848 marked the début of the revolutionary proletariat.   The
"June Days" in France, the rioting of the Chartists in England,
the appearance of the Communist Manifesto[1] frightened the
bourgeois who feared the loss of their property.   They now realized with dismay that their efforts to establish democracy had
called forth the "red specter" of socialism; and, therefore, they
made haste to come to terms with the monarchs.   Without the
support of the bourgeois any uprising was hopeless.   Still another
explanation is political.   Even in its dying moments the Metternich System was, nevertheless, strong enough to turn the tide in
favor of reaction.   Russian armies in Hungary and Austrian and
French armies in Italy were able to roll back the revolutionary
waves.   Russia, especially, paralyzed many a revolutionary arm.
During the middle of the nineteenth century the other autocracies
looked to her as the "policeman of Europe," ever ready to use her
great military power to suppress popular uprisings.   Tsarism was
now the standing menace to European democracy.

REFERENCES

GENERAL:

   C. M. Andrews, *The Historical Development of Modern Europe, 1815–
1897*, 2 vols. (1896–98), vol. I, chaps. VIII–X, contains a good summary of
the Revolution of 1848; C. E. Maurice, *The Revolutionary Movement of
1848–1849 in Italy, Austria-Hungary, and Germany* (1887), very detailed;
H. A. L. Fisher, *The Republican Tradition in Europe* (1911), chaps.
VIII–X; and Count Egon Caesar Corti, *The Rise of the House of Rothschild*
and *The Reign of the House of Rothschild*, translated from the German
(1928), describe the interrelations between politics and finance.

FRANCE:

   C. Seignobos, *La Révolution de 1848: Le Second Empire* (1921), scholarly,
unbiased; J. Tchernoff, *Associations et sociétés secrètes sous la deuxième
république* (1905), an interesting study, based upon original documents,
of the secret societies that carried on the republican propaganda; E.
Renard, *Louis Blanc* (1921); G. Weill, *Histoire du parti républicain en
France de 1814 à 1870* (1900), an impartial, scholarly work on French republicanism; J. A. R. Marriott (ed.), *The French Revolution in 1848 in
its Economic Aspects*, 2 vols. (1913), contains reprints of important social

[1] See page 569.

documents of the period; H. R. Whitehouse, *Life of Lamartine*, 2 vols. (1918), a well-written scholarly biography, deals chiefly with the uprising in 1848; D. C. McKay, *The National Workshops* (1933).

GERMANY:

E. F. Henderson, *A Short History of Germany* (ed. 1916), 2 vols., vol. II; P. Matter, *La Prusse et la Révolution de 1848* (1903); H. Blum, *Die deutsche Revolution, 1848–1849* (1897), interesting and scholarly, well illustrated. On the uprising in the Hapsburg dominions: L. Léger, *Histoire de l'Autriche-Hongrie depuis les origines jusqu'en 1919* (1920), and C. M. Knatchbull-Hugessen, *The Political Evolution of the Hungarian Nation*, 2 vols. (1908).

ITALY:

Consult bibliography at the end of Chapter VI.

ADDITIONAL REFERENCES

J. Legge, *Rhyme and Revolution in Germany, 1813–1850* (1918); V. Valentin, *Geschichte der Deutschen Revolution von 1848–49*, 2 vols (1930–33); *1848. Chapters of German History* (1941).

CHAPTER XIII

THE SECOND FRENCH EMPIRE

PERIOD OF ABSOLUTE RULE

FROM the Revolution of 1848 in France there had unexpectedly emerged a Napoleonic empire. But Napoleon III was far too clever a man to establish a naked absolutism in France on the model of the Old Régime, or even on that of his great uncle. Parliamentary government, although it had not yet become an integral element in the political life of the French people, was nevertheless connected with the undying traditions of the great Revolution; hence, some concessions had to be made to it. The Emperor resolved to inaugurate a system which would give the shadow but not the substance of self-government; the people, he believed, would be satisfied with such an arrangement, provided their attention was distracted by other activities.

The Imperial constitution provided for a popularly elected parliament having considerable legislative authority. Napoleon realized that in order to maintain his personal government this body must be made innocuous. A system of nominating candidates was instituted with the object of electing members favorable to the Emperor. In every constituency a strong political machine was organized, backed by the power and prestige of the government, which nominated candidates. Every form of pressure was brought to bear on the electors to vote for the " official" candidates. Patronage was distributed to their supporters, and public money was used to further their election. The country was gerrymandered to such a degree that the opposition found itself a minority in almost every district. Republican candidates were hampered in every way: they were frequently forbidden to hold meetings and to form associations; threats of government persecution drove many of their followers from the polls; moreover, the election machinery was in the hands of Imperial officials, who often cheated in favor of the "official" candidates. The powerful and highly centralized bureaucracy, always obedient and faithful to those in power, became the willing tool of the "Emperor-boss" whose hand was felt in all stages of political life, from the nomination of a candidate for parliament to the passing of laws, from the appointment of a petty local official to that of a prime minister. Although universal suffrage was maintained, very few of the opponents of the Emperor were elected to parliament.

Napoleon was bound to make sure of the loyal support of even this "official" parliament by controlling its internal organization. Its chairman was appointed by the Emperor; no pub- Control of lication of its debates was permitted; and all important parliament committees were appointed through the Emperor's influence. Bills were drawn up by the Council of State, appointees of the Emperor, and then submitted to parliament. In theory the Second Empire was a parliamentary monarchy; in practice it was an autocracy.

No more important organ of public opinion exists in France than the press. There obtains among the people a passion for ideas and for discussion unequaled anywhere else in the The Paris world; freedom of thought is, therefore, prized above press all other liberties handed down by the Revolution. Often scurrilous and sensational, the Paris journals are brilliantly edited and generally independent in their views. To establish a newspaper then cost comparatively little, as it usually consisted of a few pages, badly printed on paper of poor quality. Any one with ideas and a gift for writing could easily establish a daily, which was read, not for its news, but for its leading articles. Many journals were born in Paris every year, some to live but for a short time; they served to give expression to a rich and varied intellectual life, ever buoyant and fruitful. Caricature was another powerful weapon of the Paris journalist; and cartoons were apt to be sharp, cruel, and biting, and drawn with unusual skill.

As a rule the press was critical of every régime in power, but it generally remained faithful to the spirit of the Revolution and was the sworn enemy of all absolutism, naked or masked. Muzzling Napoleon knew well its great power, and he deter- the press mined to suppress it, but in his usual roundabout way. He fervently espoused the principle of freedom of thought, and then proceeded to make regulations to strangle it. New journals could be established only with government permission, which was refused to those suspected of being republican. Newspapers had to deposit a large sum with the government as security for good behavior, which was forfeited in case they became hostile to the Emperor.

Napoleon next laid a heavy hand on the universities, where there was great opposition to the "crowned conspirator." The Intellectuals day after the *coup d'état*, Jules Simon, Professor of oppose the Philosophy, when meeting his class at the Sorbonne, Emperor made the following statement which rang throughout France: "Gentlemen, it is my duty here to teach you philosophy. To-day, I owe you not a lesson, but an example. France is to be convoked to-morrow to approve or disapprove of what has just taken place. If there is going to be recorded one vote of disapproval, I wish to say to you now, openly, that it will be mine." He was immediately dismissed from his position. The historians, Michelet and Quinet, were likewise ousted from their academic chairs for opposing the Empire. Victor Hugo was driven into exile. History and philosophy were regarded with suspicion by the government, which discouraged teaching in these fields. Courses in modern history were entirely suppressed.

Like Napoleon I, Napoleon III regarded the Catholic Church as the bulwark of social and political conservatism. After the Church sup- terrible "June Days" the bourgeois, although free ports Em- thinkers generally, sought the aid of the Church to pire combat the spirit of revolutionary socialism that had spread among the workingmen. "Let us throw ourselves at the feet of the bishops; they alone can save us," was the cry. As President, Napoleon had won the support of the Catholics by sending the Roman expedition and by favoring the Falloux law.[1] During the first part of his reign, Napoleon was assiduous in showing deference to the clergy, by having religious exercises associated with public ceremonies and by encouraging Catholic societies, schools, and charities. In return the Church supported the Empire, not as ardently, however, as it had supported the Bourbons.

Napoleon was desirous of founding a dynasty. He sought to marry into the royal families of Europe, but no dynasty had sufficient confidence in his future to give him a consort. The Imperial court He therefore married a Spanish lady, Eugénie de Montijo, for love and not for her antecedents. Under the Second

---

[1] This was an education act, passed in 1850, which gave to the Catholic Church the control of education. The schools conducted by the Church were to receive public support. Ministers of the recognized faiths, Catholic, Protestant, and Jewish, were eligible, without examination, for appointment as teachers in the public schools; lay teachers were required to have a certificate from the state. To the clergy was given the power to supervise the instruction given in the elementary schools. The Falloux law was a triumph of clericalism in education.

Empire the court became a center of fashion and of gayety which attracted many people from all parts of the world. Innumerable banquets and fancy-dress balls were organized to which almost any one having money could gain entrance, as the Emperor wished to encourage the idea of a democratic court. Thither came all sorts of people, penniless adventurers, newly rich bankers, stock-jobbers, political schemers, gamblers, bohemians as well as men of letters and of science. A conspirator by temperament, Napoleon naturally surrounded himself with a group of advisers better known for their crafty, unscrupulous methods than for their solid statesmanship. Chief of these was his illegitimate half-brother, the Duke de Morny, a cool, elegant, cynical man of fashion, who was master of the undercurrents of politics, business, and society.

At no time did this government by adventurers receive the enthusiastic support of the people. The royalists regarded the Second Empire with contempt and the Emperor as a charlatan, and many scrupulously kept away from his gaudy, democratic court. The republicans were banished from public life; their leaders were in prison, in hiding, or in self-imposed exile. Napoleon was not so much upheld as he was tolerated by the property-owners, peasants and bourgeois, who regarded him as the "savior of society" because he suppressed without mercy all revolutionary activity. Under the great Napoleon these two elements, the peasants and the bourgeois, had combined against the old nobility; under his nephew they combined against the working class.

Napoleon the "savior of society"

SOCIAL AND ECONOMIC PROGRESS

In spite of many serious defects of character, the Emperor had a kindly sympathy for the unfortunate classes and for the unfortunate nations. He criticized the royalists for being champions of the aristocrats, and the parliamentarians for being the champions of the bourgeois; the Empire, he declared, would advance the interests of all classes, including the hitherto neglected proletariat. Marked activity was shown by the government in favor of the poor. Many charitable foundations, such as hospitals, asylums, and public pawnshops, were established. Sanitary dwellings for workingmen were built at public expense. Arbitration of disputes between employer and employee was greatly encouraged by the establishment of industrial councils. A begin-

Social reforms

ning was also made in establishing systems of old-age pensions and of sickness and accident insurance by the grant of subsidies to societies having these objects in view. "Saint-Simon [1] on horseback," his admirers called the Emperor.

Napoleon had a wholesome fear of the unemployed Paris laborer. He encouraged building of public works, which gave employment to many, and gave renown to his reign. His greatest achievement in this field was the rebuilding of Paris. Under the direction of the famous civic architect, Baron Haussmann, the capital was completely remodeled. From a semi-medieval town, with narrow, crooked streets, paved, if at all, with cobblestones, there appeared the most beautiful city in the world, the present Paris, with its magnificent boulevards, smoothly paved streets, and superb squares. Street revolutions were now impossible. Barricades could not be easily improvised, and a mob charging along a broad avenue would be exposed to artillery fire and to cavalry charges. Thousands of visitors came to see the beautiful city, which became known as the pleasure capital of the world. Places of amusement of all types, from the highest to the lowest, were encouraged by the authorities, and Paris began to acquire an unenviable reputation as the modern Babylon. The shopkeepers reaped a golden harvest from the visitors who spent their money freely in order to enjoy "Parisian life."

The Second Empire was the great period of the expansion of French industry. France was now in a fever of business enterprise, and able men forsook politics for commerce. Napoleon, desiring the support of a wealthy class that would owe its prosperity to his policies, did everything in his power to encourage business undertakings. He asserted that all means of ruling were good and legitimate provided material prosperity was assured. Factories were built and machine production made rapid headway.[2] Foreign commerce increased five-fold during the period of the Second Empire. There was also a marked development in the metallurgical industries through the introduction of the Bessemer process and through the consolidation of many small steel plants. The famous steel works of Le Creusot became one of the great steel centers of the world.

Rebuilding of Paris

Industrial development

---

[1] Saint-Simon was a famous Utopian socialist; see page 565.

[2] The total horse-power of machines used in industry in 1855 was 66,642; in 1869 it had risen to 320,447.

Most notable progress of all was in the improvement of the means of transportation.   In 1850, there were in all France about 1800 miles of railway, operated by many small companies.   Rates were high, service bad, and management wasteful.   A law was passed in that year which completely transformed the railway system.   The railways were given ninety-nine year leases in order to assure them stability; the government guaranteed interest on capital invested in new lines; and all the railways were consolidated into six trunk lines under the management of as many companies.   By 1869 the railway mileage had increased to about 9500.   Marine transportation was also improved through the substitution of large iron ships for small wooden ones, and of steam for sail.   Trans-Atlantic steamship lines were established, aided by subsidies.   The improvement in the means of transportation greatly advanced internal commerce, particularly in agricultural products, which could now find a profitable market in the growing cities.

Progress of railway and steamboat transportation

A spirit of speculation seized the French.   There came a period of rising prices, rising profits, and rising wages, and many became rich quickly, though many others were ruined through over-speculation.   Financial institutions were founded through government aid, the most notable being the Crédit Mobilier which financed big enterprises such as railways and mines; and the Crédit Foncier which financed landholders.   Paris began to rival London as a banking center.

Financial progress

An important change in the tariff policy of France took place under the Second Empire.   The French economist, Michel Chevalier, who was a friend of Richard Cobden, and, like him, an ardent free-trader, persuaded Napoleon to abandon protection in favor of tariff reform.   During 1853–55, the tariff on oil, iron, steel, and wool was considerably lowered.   In 1859, the Emperor secretly negotiated a reciprocity agreement with England in a treaty agreed upon by Chevalier and Cobden.   According to the Cobden Treaty, as it was called, France reduced her tariff on English iron and steel goods, and on manufactures of all sorts; and England abolished all tariffs on French manufactures and reduced the duties on wines and brandies.   The restrictions on foreign-built ships were removed.   Napoleon's low-tariff policies aroused opposition among the protectionists, who denounced the Cobden Treaty as an "economic *coup d'état*."

The Cobden tariff treaty

In 1855, there took place the first Paris Exposition.   Thousands
from all over the world came to see the products of French industry
The Paris   and art, and to admire the beautiful capital.   The
Exposition   Emperor's renown spread far and wide.   He was now
universally admired as a great statesman who had brought order,
peace, and prosperity to his country.   Even the royal families of
Europe, whose attitude toward him had hitherto been disdainful,
now began to cultivate friendly relations with the "adventurer."

THE LIBERAL EMPIRE

France was prosperous, but not contented.   The shadow of
Cæsarism lay over the land, which caused many to acquiesce for a
Concessions   time, sullenly and silently, to a régime that they hated.
to liberalism   After a decade of rule, Napoleon found himself openly
opposed by many influential elements.   His strongest supporters
hitherto, the Catholics, were alienated by his support of the Italians
in the Austro-Sardinian War which they believed would lead to
the unification of Italy and to consequent loss of the Pope's temporal power.   The Liberals, who had hailed the Emperor's alliance
with the Italians as an augury for liberalism at home, denounced
him for deserting Cavour in the midst of the war for Italian unity.
The manufacturing interests were incensed at his low-tariff policies.   Nothing that he would do could, of course, satisfy the republicans.   Napoleon now felt that liberalism might bring new
strength to the dynasty, so he resolved on a policy of concessions.
In 1859, a general amnesty was granted to those who had been
driven out of France because of their political views.   During the
following year parliament was allowed more freedom; it was
permitted to frame an address criticizing the government, and
its debates were allowed to be published.   The press laws were
also generally relaxed.   These concessions, however, resulted
in increasing instead of decreasing the attacks of the opposition.

Napoleon's rising unpopularity was enhanced by his ill-starred
Mexican expedition.   In 1861, taking advantage of the Civil War
Napoleon's   in America, England, France, and Spain decided to
motives for   intervene in Mexico on the ground that their nationals
intervening   in that country were not sufficiently protected.   An
in Mexico
expeditionary force landed in Mexico, but it soon became evident that Napoleon was using intervention as a pretext to

overthrow the Mexican Republic. His motives in this matter were an illustration of his tendency to grandiose scheming. Napoleon believed in a vague Pan-Latinism according to which all the Latin nations would form a fraternity under the inspiration of France. He had another motive. As the destroyer of a republic in France, he was hostile to republics anywhere; and to overthrow the Mexican Republic would reëstablish monarchy in the New World. Moreover, a Mexican Empire, under the protection of France, would put a bar to a possible advance southward of the Republic of the United States.

England and Spain withdrew their forces from Mexico and left France alone in the field. Fighting began between the Mexicans and the French, in which the latter were triumphant. The Mexican expedition In 1862, the Republic was overthrown, and an empire was proclaimed by a Mexican Assembly dominated by the French. Archduke Maximilian, brother of Emperor Francis Joseph of Austria, was chosen Emperor. The intervention of France aroused great opposition among the Mexican people, who rose in rebellion against Maximilian and his French backers. At the close of the Civil War, the American government demanded the immediate withdrawal of the French army, and Napoleon now deserted Maximilian as he had once deserted Cavour. Without the French army, Maximilian was unable to maintain his government. In 1867, he was seized by the Mexicans and executed. The Mexican Republic was then reëstablished.

The disastrous outcome of the Mexican expedition reacted seriously on the fortunes of Napoleon; it had been expensive, humiliating, and utterly useless. The opposition became More concessions to liberalism bolder and sharper than ever before. Thiers, who was the leader of the moderate liberals, made a great speech demanding the "necessary liberties." A group was formed, calling itself the Third Party, composed of liberals who desired a régime that would steer a middle course between an autocratic empire and a democratic republic. They demanded freedom of elections, freedom of speech and of association, and ministerial responsibility. Their leader was Émile Ollivier, a former republican, who desired to play the rôle of reconciler of the Empire with democracy. During 1867–69, the way was being prepared for the new political edifice, "the Empire crowned with liberty . . . equally removed from reaction and from revolutionary theories." Napoleon gave parliament more legislative power, relaxed the censorship of the press, and freely permitted public meetings.

These concessions satisfied many, but they merely strengthened the opposition of the irreconcilable republicans who demanded

Rochefort attacks the Emperor
nothing less than the abolition of the Empire. During its last days there emerged two remarkable men, Léon Gambetta and Henri Rochefort, who declared war *à outrance* against the Empire and all its works, good and bad. Rochefort was a brilliant journalist who wielded a rapier-like pen; his paper, *La Lanterne* (*The Lamp Post*), fiercely attacked the Emperor. It was suppressed many times and its editor driven into exile; but, as often as the journal was suppressed, it reappeared under a different name and in a different place.

In 1868, a trial took place which attracted considerable attention. It was that of a journalist who was being prosecuted for starting a

Emergence of Gambetta
subscription to raise a monument to one of the victims of the *coup d'état* of 1851. A young lawyer, hitherto unknown, named Léon Gambetta, was chosen to defend him. Instead of confining himself to the defense of his client, Gambetta delivered a powerful indictment of the Second Empire, denouncing its origin as criminal, its conduct as tyrannical, and prophesying its speedy downfall. "On December 2," he declared, "there grouped themselves around a pretender men whom France had never before known, men without talent, without honor, without rank, without position; men of the type who in all times have been the organizers of conspiracies. . . . And these men had the audacity to pretend that they were the saviors of France." He went on to denounce the character of the government founded by them, and ended with a peroration which resounded throughout the country: "Listen! You, who for seventeen years have been the absolute masters of France! . . . The proof of your remorse is that you have never dared to say: 'Let us consecrate December 2 as a solemn national holiday, as the men of 1789, 1830, and 1848 celebrated the days of their triumph.' . . . This anniversary which you have refused to signalize, we will take for ourselves. We shall celebrate each year, regularly and without fail, the memory of those who fell on that day, until the time will come when France, having regained her freedom, shall impose upon you a great national expiation in the name of Liberty, Equality, and Fraternity."

Never had the Empire been denounced with such invective and

NAPOLEON III

LÉON GAMBETTA

with such thrilling eloquence; the speech sounded like the coming
doom of the Napoleonic régime. It made Gambetta Gambetta, leader of the republicans
famous. He immediately sprang to the forefront of
the opposition and became the rising hope of the irreconcilable republicans, who hailed him as their leader. "The
dominant idea in my political activity," he declared, "is the sovereignty of the people, completely and thoroughly organized. I am
a radical democrat, passionately devoted to the principles of liberty
and fraternity, and I shall tirelessly aim to show that Cæsarean
democracy is incompatible with the ideals and methods of true
democracy."

In the face of the advance of republicanism, which was daily
becoming more threatening and defiant, the Emperor turned to the
counsels of moderation offered by the Third Party. A Triumph of the liberals
series of decrees deprived the Senate of its power to
amend the constitution, and gave parliament full control over all
legislation. The Empire was now fully a constitutional monarchy,
and Ollivier was appointed Prime Minister, with a cabinet composed of men of all parties except the republican. Napoleon was
eager for popular approval of the Liberal Empire, as he was half
sincere in his constant assertion that the Empire was based on a
democratic ideal. He determined, therefore, to submit his reforms
to a plebiscite which would give him the popular backing that he
needed to face the bitter attacks of the republicans, who denounced
the Ollivier Ministry as "sentinels who mounted guard" over
despotism. On May 8, 1870, the electors were asked to vote on
the following proposal: "The French nation approves the liberal
reforms made in the Constitution since 1860, and ratifies the decrees of 1870." The result was an overwhelming popular endorse-
ment. To all appearances the régime was now firmly established,
and Napoleon was congratulated by his Ministers, who assured
him of "a happy old age" as Emperor and of the undisputed succession of his son, the Prince Imperial.

FOREIGN POLICIES

When Napoleon ascended the throne there was a feeling of
anxiety throughout Europe. Would he, like his uncle, launch
France into a career of conquest? In order to reassure the nations Napoleon declared that he preferred "moral and material
conquests" to those on the battle-field. "The Empire means

peace," he said, "because France desires it, and when France is
satisfied, the world is at peace." But he well knew
that his name had aroused the imagination of the
French people, and that he owed his success to the
popular belief that a Napoleonic régime would establish France once more as *la grande nation* of Europe. Napoleon,
therefore, resolved to launch France on a career of aggression.
His reign was filled with wars, the Crimean, the Austro-Sardinian,
the Mexican, and finally the Franco-Prussian, which are described
elsewhere. Conditions on the Continent favored Napoleon III as
they had favored Napoleon I. Prussia and Austria were deadly
enemies, each desiring to dominate Germany. Russia and Austria
were estranged because the latter had refused to aid the Tsar during the Crimean War. Germany was disorganized and divided.
So was Italy. Napoleon was a diplomat of great ability, and he
took advantage of the situation to make France the arbiter of
European quarrels. In the tortuous maze of the Emperor's constantly shifting policy, often carried on behind the backs of his
own Ministers, there stands out a dominant purpose; namely, to
uphold the principle of nationalism. How could France make
war on her neighbors without causing them to combine against
her, as in the days of Louis XIV and Napoleon I? The Holy Alliance had followed a policy of intervention in favor of absolutism,
which made that policy odious. The rising tide of nationalism
convinced Napoleon that, if France intervened in its favor, she
would gain prestige, power, and perhaps territory. "When France
draws her sword," declared the Emperor, "it is not to dominate,
but to liberate." However, nationalism was often a liberal cloak
to hide Napoleon's desire for conquest and glory.

Unlike his uncle, Napoleon was no soldier, although he carefully
cultivated the appearance of being one. It was his custom to ride
in resplendent uniform on a dashing charger; his de-
tractors insinuated that he rouged his cheeks and wore
a corset in order to make a fine appearance on parade.
Napoleon's war policy was to associate himself with allies; in case
of victory, he could claim the credit, and in case of defeat, he could
put the blame on his allies. What he dreaded most of all was an
unsuccessful war; a Napoleon that could not win would be ridiculous, and would be quickly driven from power. The successful
outcome of the Crimean and Austro-Sardinian Wars put France

Napoleon champions cause of nationalism

France dominates the Continent

once more at the pinnacle of international power. For a time Napoleon played the rôle of dictator in Europe; no treaty could be entered into, no territorial cnanges could be made, and no diplomatic policy inaugurated without his being consulted. This greatly inflated the pride of *la grande nation*, and added to the popularity of the Emperor, who was beginning to feel that he, too, had a "star." But it was a pinchbeck imperialism that Napoleon gave to the French people. Behind the resplendent court, subservient bureaucracy, and magnificently attired army, there was incompetence, corruption, discontent, and short-sightedness which, in case of a real trial of strength with a powerful foe, would send France headlong to disaster.

Napoleon's misunderstanding of Prussia's ambition, his total lack of appreciation of the strength of the national sentiment in Germany, and his fatal inconsistency in opposing   Downfall of German unity were to end in his undoing. The story   the Empire of the Franco-Prussian War is described elsewhere. At the battle of Sedan the French were badly defeated, and Napoleon was taken prisoner. The news of the disaster sounded the doom of the Second Empire. A mob broke into the parliament building, shouting, "Down with the Empire!" "Long live the Republic!" The members were dispersed, and the mob, led by Gambetta, proclaimed a republic. Empress Eugénie fled. After his release, Napoleon escaped to England, where he died in 1873.

A Government of National Defense was organized with Gambetta as its leading spirit. It continued the war with great energy, but without success, and was forced to agree to an   The National armistice. Elections were then held for a National   tional Assembly, which convened at Bordeaux in 1871, and   sembly assumed full authority over France. It chose Thiers as head of the government with power to negotiate a treaty of peace with Germany. After peace was concluded, the National Assembly almost unanimously voted the abolition of the Empire, which it declared was "responsible for the ruin, the invasion, and the dismemberment of France." Once more did a Napoleon prove to be an "architect of ruin."

LITERATURE DURING THE EMPIRE

By the middle of the nineteenth century Romanticism was a spent force in French literature. Alone of the Romanticists, Victor

Hugo, who bestrode the century like a literary Colossus, continued
in unabated strength.   He reached a poetic height
Hugo
unattained by any other French poet in his *La
Légende des Siècles* (*Legend of the Ages*), a lyrical history of man, in
which he sings the pæan of human progress in a series of epical
and philosophical poems.

Modern literary criticism can boast of no greater name than that
of Charles Augustin Sainte-Beuve, who became the European
Sainte-Beuve arbiter of literary good taste.   According to Sainte-
(1804–69)   Beuve the main function of the critic is to reveal "the
natural history of the human intellect"; therefore, he should have
no set formula and no philosophic system.   His method should be
that of "universal curiosity": to inquire into the antecedents, life,
character, and temperament of the author, and to show how these
were reflected in his work.   Above all, the critic was not to obtrude
his own views on the reader; his function was "to be and to remain
outside everything," and to exhibit the author as he would a picture
or a statue, indicating both good and bad points; the reader would
then be able to pass judgment for himself more intelligently.   Few
critics were so well endowed as Sainte-Beuve, who possessed a wide
knowledge, not only of literature, but also of history, philosophy,
art, and religion.   He was, above all else, an intense admirer of the
classic French style and, for that reason, he failed to appreciate
fully so great a novelist as Balzac, who lacked it.   Sainte-Beuve's
greatest work, *Histoire de Port-Royal*, is a description of the Jan-
senist mystics of the seventeenth century; in addition, it is an historical and philosophical study of the entire period.   His most
famous work of criticism is *Causeries du lundi* (*Monday Chats*),
which consists of short but pregnant estimates of writers and other
famous persons.

Quite the opposite of Sainte-Beuve in ideals and methods was
Hippolyte Taine, the philosophic critic and historian.   He was
Taine   an excellent example of the dogmatic thinker who has
(1828–93)   a passion for classifying all human phenomena into
formulas and systems.   In Taine's opinion, race, epoch, and
environment determine all human development; the individual is
merely the product of these forces which fashion his ideals and
character.   It is important to study, therefore, not this great man
or that, but the social, political, and physical conditions which
produced him.   He applied this formula even to literature and to

art.   Taine's most important work is a series of histories entitled *Origines de la France contemporaine*, a highly original philosophic study of the Revolutionary and Napoleonic periods.   It is, however, defective in scholarship and colored by partisanship, as he was strongly opposed to the ideas and methods of the Jacobins.

By far the most perfect type of French *savant* was Ernest Renan, whose great learning was combined with a literary style of the highest order.   Although educated for the priesthood,   Renan he became the master skeptic of the age, and as such   (1823–92) he exercised a profound influence on his contemporaries.   The one unpardonable sin, according to Renanism, which became a cult among the intellectual *élite* of France, is dogmatism; the greatest virtue is a refined sympathy for all ideas, even for those which one believes to be false, so long as they are of value to mankind; the true saint is the skeptic who gives up the good of this world without expecting anything in return.   Renan was criticized by his opponents as a dilettante, a man who deliciously fingered great ideas for sensuous enjoyment, and whose interest in art was greater than his interest in anything else.   His exquisite style, elegant, suave, and fluid, and his romantic imagination gave fascination to his scholarly work, which was mainly in the field of religious history. Renan's most important book, *Histoire du peuple d'Israël*, is an attempt to rationalize the Old Testament and to explain its origin by the environment and race characteristics of the ancient Jews. His *Vie de Jésus* caused a sensation in Europe, and he was denounced by his opponents as a blasphemer because he pictured Christ as a lovable human being, not as a divinity.

In fiction a new school, Realism, displaced Romanticism.   Unlike the latter, Realism found its themes and scenes in the present and not in the Middle Ages; it dealt with the actual and   Realism the probable in human life, and avoided what smacked of the fantastic and of the extravagant.   According to the Realists the writer must be objective, merely a medium through which nature and society find expression; he must efface his own personality completely from his work in order to reproduce life truthfully.   "An artist ought no more appear in his work, than God does in nature," was the dictum of the greatest master of the school, Gustave Flaubert.

The best example of a Realistic novel is Flaubert's *Madame Bovary*, which is considered by many to be the greatest novel in

French literature. It tells the tragic story of a simple woman, the

Flaubert   unhappy wife of a country surgeon, whose romantic
(1821–80)   temperament leads her to degradation and finally to
suicide. The evolution of the character of the heroine, Emma
Bovary, as she falls lower and lower in the moral scale, is described
with such penetrating insight into human weakness and such cold
aloofness that he makes the tragic end seem the natural outcome
of the commonplace beginning. Flaubert was an artist, first, last,
and all the time. He hated the mediocre, "the bourgeois," and
loved "art for art's sake." His is the perfect French style; every
sentence which he wrote was polished with the greatest care. To
this "patient gold-beater of words and phrases" the correct expression was an eternal search, and he never rested till he found it.

The most important dramatist of the Second Empire was
Alexandre Dumas *fils*, the son of the famous novelist. He was the

Dumas *fils*   originator of the type of drama known as the "problem
(1824–95)   play," in which the moral difficulties arising out of the
marriage tie are the main theme. Dumas's plays, the most famous
of which is *La Dame aux Camélias* (*Camille*), frequently deal with
a type of woman who lives in what he called the *demi-monde*, or the
outskirts of respectable society. He criticizes severely the system
of laws and customs which sacrifices the welfare of children to the
vices of parents.

REFERENCES

P. Guedalla, *The Second Empire* (1922), an impressionistic study largely
of Napoleon III; A. Thomas, *Le second empire* (1907), from socialist viewpoint; E. Ollivier, *L'Empire Libéral*, 17 vols. (1895–1914), a greatly detailed defense of the Empire by the Minister of Napoleon III; H. A. L.
Fisher, *Bonapartism* (1908), on the two Napoleons, suggestive and interesting; G. Weill, *Histoire du mouvement social en France, 1852–1924* (ed.
1924), excellent study of social problems and social theories of the period;
A. L. Guérard, *French Prophets of Yesterday: A Study of Religious Thought
under the Second Empire* (1913), fine essays on Renan, Sainte-Beuve, and
Taine; L. F. Mott, *Ernest Renan* (1921) and *Sainte-Beuve* (1924), standard
English works on these writers; F. A. Simpson, *The Rise of Louis Napoleon*
(1909), to 1848, and *Louis Napoleon and the Recovery of France* (1848–
1856) (1923); A. L. Dunham, *The Anglo-French Treaty of Commerce of 1860
and the Progress of the Industrial Revolution in France* (1930); E. B.
D'Auvergne, *Napoleon III* (1929).

For additional titles consult bibliography at the end of Chapter V.

CHAPTER XIV

THE UNIFICATION OF ITALY

CAVOUR'S PLAN

SINCE 1815 every effort to unite Italy had failed miserably. The Carbonari with its conspiracies, Young Italy with its sporadic uprisings, Sardinia with its little war against Austria, all had proved to be unequal to the task. "What method could now succeed?" many patriots asked in despair.

A new phase of the *Risorgimento* came with the appearance on the scene of Camillo Benso, Count di Cavour, who was to prove himself to be one of the master statesmen of an age Cavour that could boast of Bismarck, Gladstone, Disraeli, (1810–61) Webster, and Thiers. Cavour was descended from an old noble family of Piedmont. He traveled extensively, especially in France and in England, where he was often thrown in contact with the well-known liberals of the time, and he became an enthusiastic admirer of the parliamentary system of government. "Parliamentary government, like other governments," he once declared, "has its inconveniences; yet, with its inconveniences, it is better than all the others. I may get impatient at certain oppositions, and repel them vigorously; and then, on thinking it over, I congratulate myself on these oppositions because they force me to explain my ideas better and to redouble my efforts to win over public opinion. . . . Believe me, the worst of Chambers is still preferable to the most brilliant of antechambers." The use of military force to suppress opposition was as abhorrent to Cavour as was absolutism. Under martial law any fool can govern, he once declared. Early in life he became a strong nationalist, and was instrumental in founding the *Risorgimento*, a newspaper devoted to the cause of Italian unity. Cavour read and wrote much on economic subjects, in which he was greatly interested. He proposed plans for an extensive railway system which would facilitate commerce and unite Italy economically. He favored policies which would develop his country industrially and so enlarge the numbers and influence of the middle class. From the nobility, tied by their interests to the old system, and from the peasantry, dulled by poverty and ignorance, little was to be expected; only an intelligent and independent middle class would be willing and able to take the leadership in the movement to unite the country.

Cavour, unlike Mazzini, had no gift for poetic flights of oratory. His mind was clear, cool, and practical, with an unerring "tact to

His ability as a diplomat

discern the possible," that could foresee, plan, and direct the enthusiasm and energies of others. "I cannot make a speech, but I can make Italy," he is said to have remarked. There was hardly a diplomat in all Europe who was a match for this Sardinian, whose "fine Italian hand" could weave a diplomatic web so finely and skillfully that his enemies would be entangled in it unawares. Like his contemporary diplomats, and for that matter like the diplomats of all ages and of all nations, he was usually unscrupulous as to the means that he employed to accomplish his ends. "If we did for ourselves what we do for our country, what rascals we should be," he once said.

Cavour was convinced that there was only one practical plan to unite Italy: Sardinia [1] must stand forth as the unswerving

His liberalism

champion of unity, and she must call upon the Italian people to support her in the struggle against despotism, whether domestic or foreign. "Piedmont, gathering to herself all the living forces of Italy," he declared, "will be soon in a position to lead our mother country to the high destinies to which she is called." A believer in the doctrine that no government is legitimate without the consent of the governed, Cavour was determined that Sardinia should not conquer and annex the rest of Italy, but should drive out Austria and the petty monarchs, and then ask the people themselves to determine their political destiny by a plebiscite. "Italy must make herself through liberty or we must give up trying to make her," was his policy.

Cavour became Prime Minister in 1852, a position which he filled almost continuously till the end of his life. The relations be-

His reforms

tween Victor Emmanuel II and Cavour were not unlike those of William I and Bismarck: both monarchs relied absolutely on their extraordinary ministers, who really ruled while the former reigned. Cavour was active in encouraging the economic development of Sardinia. Railways were built; commerce and industry were stimulated by enlightened laws and by

[1] The terms "Sardinia," "Piedmont," and "Savoy" are used synonymously for the territory ruled by the House of Savoy.

CAMILLO DI CAVOUR

favorable commercial treaties; and the finances were put on a sound basis. Like many liberals of that day, Cavour was hostile to the Catholic Church, which he regarded as the most powerful prop of the old system. Largely through his influence, parliament passed the Siccardi Laws (1850), which abolished the civil jurisdiction of the ecclesiastical courts, and forbade the acceptance of property by any corporation, civil as well as religious, without the consent of the State. Five years later he made war on the religious orders, and, in spite of stormy opposition, more than half of the monasteries in the Kingdom were suppressed.

Every effort of Cavour was directed ultimately to one end, unification. He was the one Italian patriot who realized that it could not be brought about by the Italians alone. He had little faith in popular uprisings, so often badly organized and poorly led and consequently doomed to failure. *His plan of an alliance with France* Mazzini he regarded as a fanatic who would ruin any cause by his lack of moderation and practical ability. The defeat of Sardinia in 1848 was, in his opinion, the natural result of her quixotic attempt to war against Austria, whose military power was far greater than her own. A new and bold plan was born in Cavour's mind; namely, that *Europe* should unite Italy! For many centuries the nations had intervened in Italian affairs for their own good; why should they not now intervene for Italy's good? In other words, Cavour's project was to form an alliance between Sardinia and some great power for the purpose of driving out the Austrians. But which power? His choice, for several reasons, fell upon France. In the first place, Napoleon was himself partly of Italian origin; and, in the days of his exile, he had wandered into Italy where he had joined the Carbonari. He was, moreover, a champion of the principle of nationalism, and the Italians could appeal to him on that basis. In the second place, a war with their old enemy, Austria, would be very popular among the French, and all the more so if it were waged in the interest of a people of Latin civilization. Finally, Sardinia had something substantial to offer to France in return for her assistance; namely, the French-speaking districts of Savoy and Nice.

ANNEXATION OF LOMBARDY

It now behooved Sardinia to show that she was worth fighting with as well as for. Cavour, to every one's amazement, made war,

not on Austria, but on Russia; under his influence Sardinia joined
Cavour and the allies in the Crimean War. So remote was Sar-
the Crimean dinia's interest in the Near Eastern question that the
War expedition was universally condemned as foolhardy,
chimerical, and financially ruinous to a small and poor state. But
Cavour, of whom it was said that he had a "sure instinct for the
necessity of the moment," saw in the Crimean War an opportunity
for Sardinia to show her fighting qualities, and, above all, to gain
representation at the peace conference. At the Congress of Paris,
in 1856, Cavour made a short but incisive address, on the question
of Italian unity. He declared that the situation in Italy was a
menace to the peace of Europe; and that Austria, the arch-enemy
of Italian freedom and independence, was the disturbing factor in
the situation. The address created a favorable impression on the
delegates.

Napoleon III had been moving in the direction of an alliance
with Sardinia. What probably hastened it was an attack upon
Napoleon his life by an Italian patriot named Orsini, who threw
decides on a bomb at him as he was driving through the streets
an alliance
with Sar- of Paris. Napoleon escaped unharmed, but many
dinia bystanders were killed. Orsini, before his execution,
wrote a pathetic letter to the Emperor, claiming that he had committed the crime in order to call the attention of the world to his
country's woes, and begging the Emperor to come to Italy's rescue.
Napoleon, deeply moved by this appeal and perhaps also by fear
of another attempt on his life, decided to intervene in Italian
affairs.

On July 21, 1858, Cavour and Napoleon met "by accident" at
Plombières, a town in France, where they held a momentous
Alliance of interview. They agreed upon an alliance between
France and France and Sardinia, the chief object of which was to
Sardinia
against drive Austria out of Italy; France was to get Nice and
Austria Savoy as part of the bargain. In order to make
Austria appear as the aggressor in the coming conflict, disturbances
were instigated by Sardinia in the parts of Italy under Austrian
control. Austria was infuriated and threatened war against Sardinia. England intervened and proposed a conference to settle
the quarrel, but Austria refused to accept this proposal. Instead,
she sent an ultimatum to Sardinia demanding that she disarm
within three days. "The die is cast and history is made," ex-

claimed Cavour. He promptly rejected the ultimatum; whereupon Austria declared war against Sardinia. Public opinion in Europe severely arraigned Austria for what was regarded as an act of brutal aggression by a big nation against a little one. French armies poured over the Alps to help the little nation, and at their head was the Emperor himself, who promised to free Italy "from the Alps to the Adriatic." Italians from all over the Peninsula flocked to join the armies of Sardinia. Cavour's deep-laid plans proved startlingly successful.

The Austro-Sardinian War took place in 1859, and lasted about two months. The chief object of the allies was to drive the Austrians from a line of strongly fortified places in Lombardy-Venetia, called the Quadrilateral. Two great battles were fought, Magenta and Solferino, in both of which the French and Sardinian armies were victorious; the Austrians were compelled to abandon Lombardy. Preparations were being made to invade Venetia when news came that Napoleon, without consulting Sardinia, had made a separate peace with Austria at Villafranca. This act of faithlessness so astounded and infuriated Cavour that his condition at times bordered upon madness. He lost his habitual coolness, and in a fit of rage at the Emperor he counseled Victor Emmanuel to continue the war alone. But the latter saw the folly of such a course, and declined to follow his Minister's advice.

Why had Napoleon deserted his ally? The Emperor was a man who was willing to help a friend, but not to help him too much lest he become a troublesome rival. His original intention was merely to enlarge Sardinia into a North Italian kingdom. The defeat of Austria, however, set Italian hearts beating fast, for they now saw an opportunity to unite the entire country. While the war was in progress, revolutions were taking place in Modena, Parma, Tuscany, and in that part of the Papal States known as Romagna; the rulers were driven out and popular assemblies voted for annexation to Sardinia. These uprisings were the work of the National Society, a patriotic organization fathered by Cavour. A united Italy was not to the liking of Napoleon, for he feared that France might be confronted with a too powerful rival on the Mediterranean. Another cause for his withdrawal was that the Catholics in France were clamoring against the Emperor's alliance with the Italian nationalists, the sworn enemies of the Pope's temporal power; Napoleon decided to appease them by retiring from the contest.

According to the terms of the Treaty of Zurich, which officially terminated the war, Lombardy was annexed to Sardinia. Napoleon's intervention had given such a momentum to Italian unity as no other event in all Italian history had given it. Austria, the arch-enemy, had been beaten, and the petty tyrants could no longer rely upon her support. On the contrary, should uprisings take place, the insurgents could now count on the active support of Sardinia. All Italian parties, republican, federalist, and monarchist, now rallied to the side of Sardinia as the state that was destined to accomplish the unification of the country. Enthusiastic republicans like Garibaldi openly and freely offered their services to Cavour. Mazzini, however, remained irreconcilable. "I bow my head sorrowfully to the national will," he declared, "but monarchy will never number me among its servants or followers."

The use of foreign armies to restore unpopular rulers was now universally condemned. In England Lord Palmerston vigorously asserted that every people had the right to dispose of itself politically in whatever manner that it wished. During 1860, plebiscites were held in Modena, Parma, Tuscany, and Romagna, and the result was an almost unanimous vote in favor of joining Sardinia. Annexations promptly followed. To carry out the agreement of Plombières plebiscites were also held in Savoy and Nice, which voted to join France. These districts were ceded to France, though not without protest as Sardinia was in a mood to gain, not to lose, territory.

ANNEXATION OF THE SOUTH

Joseph Garibaldi, whose romantic character and extraordinary exploits made him the leading hero of the *Risorgimento*, now appeared most prominently on the scene of his country's history. Garibaldi was one of the young men whose patriotism was awakened by the eloquence of Mazzini; and, at the age of twenty-four, he joined Young Italy. Condemned to death for participating in an insurrection, he managed to escape to South America, where he took a prominent part in several revolutionary wars, earning a reputation as a daring and resourceful guerrilla chieftain. He returned to Italy during the uprisings in 1848, and organized a volunteer army of dare-devil patriots who were ready to follow him anywhere. His gallant defense of the Roman Republic won him the love and admiration of his fellow republicans who hailed him as the military leader of their party. After the capture of Rome, he and his little band were driven all over Italy by French, Austrian, and Neapolitan armies. He showed remarkable skill in dodging his pursuers, and finally managed to reach the coast and escape to America. For several years he again lived in exile, sometimes as a candle-maker on Staten Island, sometimes as captain of a sailing vessel trading with South America. In 1854, he returned to Italy, where he settled down as a farmer.

Garibaldi's name had become one to conjure with, and his exploits were on every one's lips. The Risorgimento had produced many men who were ready to sacrifice themselves unreservedly for their country, but none more unselfish, more chivalrous, or more heroic than Garibaldi. He seemed a half-legendary hero, like Bayard or Joan of Arc, sent by Providence to lead his fellow countrymen to victory. In many respects Garibaldi resembled the American, Andrew Jackson; like him, he was hot-headed, stubborn, and foolhardy, but generous, brave, and patriotic to a fault. He disliked Cavour as a cold, calculating schemer; yet he realized half regretfully that unity could be obtained only through the House of Savoy. Although he loved the republic, he loved Italy more, and therefore decided to rally to the monarchy. In the war of 1859 he rendered notable service as the head of a volunteer corps.

But Garibaldi's most famous exploit was the "Expedition of the Thousand." He had formed the daring design of making war on his own account against the King of Naples. In 1860, about a thousand poorly equipped, badly armed men, wearing red shirts and slouch hats, set sail from Genoa with the purpose of invading the Kingdom of Naples. The story of the expedition of the "Red Shirts" reads like an heroic epic. Garibaldi and his Thousand landed at Marsala, at the extreme western tip of Sicily. Through extraordinary marching and fighting against tremendous odds, he finally entered Palermo in triumph, having conquered all Sicily, of which he was proclaimed Dictator in the name of Victor Emmanuel. Italy was thrilled. There had been only too many instances of foolhardy attempts by small bands of patriots to overthrow the despots that had failed; this one, equally foolhardy, succeeded, and gave to Garibaldi and his Thousand immortal fame.

Expedition of the Thousand

Garibaldi, at the head of an army of 4000, set sail for the mainland. The moment he landed, the people of Naples and many of
Conquest of   the soldiers in the Neapolitan army became his en-
Naples   thusiastic followers. His ranks soon swelled to 50,000.
The march to Naples was a triumphal procession. Whole armies,
sometimes without striking a blow, surrendered to him. Many of
the Neapolitan troops mutinied, murdered their officers, and joined
the Garibaldians. One desperate battle took place, that of Volturno, in which Garibaldi defeated an army twice the size of his
own. King Francis fled, and Garibaldi assumed the dictatorship
of his kingdom.

The question now was, "What was to be the fate of the conquered regions?" Cavour, who had half countenanced the expedi-
The King-   tion, feared that Garibaldi might lose all that had been
dom of Italy gained by an imprudent step which he was now meditating; namely, a march on Rome. It would lead to a conflict
with the French army stationed there, quite a different matter
from attacking a demoralized kingdom like Naples. Sardinia must
now take charge of the situation. Victor Emmanuel, at the head
of his army, crossed into the Papal States, occupying Umbria and
The Marches, though carefully avoiding Rome, and entered Naples.
The Sardinian parliament then voted for the annexation of the recently conquered territory, provided the inhabitants agreed to it.
A plebiscite was held in the Kingdom of the Two Sicilies, The
Marches, and Umbria, and the result was an overwhelming vote
in favor of joining Sardinia. Victor Emmanuel and Garibaldi
drove together through the streets of Naples amid the wild applause of the people. Garibaldi magnanimously resigned his dictatorship. In 1861, Victor Emmanuel was proclaimed "King of
Italy" by the first Italian parliament which met in Turin. Sardinia was now merged in Italy, and the work of Mazzini, Cavour,
and Garibaldi was crowned with success. Garibaldi refused all
honors, titles, offices, and pensions, and retired to his farm.

THE ANNEXATION OF ROME

Unfortunately for his country, Cavour died soon after the proclamation of her unity, leaving to his successors the solution of the
The Roman   knotty Venetian and Roman problems. The Aus-
Question   trians were still in Venetia, and the Pope was still in
Rome. Cavour had firmly believed that, without Rome as the

capital, Italy's unification would be sadly incomplete. The historic position of the Eternal City, with its immortal memories, was such that Italians could not allow another power to possess it. "To go to Rome," said his successor, Ricasoli, "is not merely a right; it is an inexorable necessity." In regard to the future relations between Church and State, Cavour's famous dictum was, "A free Church in a free State," by which he meant that the former should be entirely free to exercise her spiritual powers and leave politics entirely to the latter.

Pope Pius IX refused to recognize the new kingdom, which he condemned as the creation of revolution. He denounced the King of Italy as a usurper "forgetful of every religious prin- Rome opposes Italy ciple, despising every right, trampling upon every law." In spite of the popular desire to seize Rome, the government was loath to take such a step. It well knew that to attack the Pope would be to invite war with France, where the Catholics were clamoring for intervention on behalf of the Papacy. There was also the danger of offending the entire Catholic world, and possibly of bringing about armed intervention by the Catholic powers. The government, therefore, decided to bide its time and to pursue a policy of watchful waiting, hoping that a favorable opportunity would arrive for decisive action. Rome was defended by the French army, sent over in 1849, and by a Catholic army of Irish, Belgians, and Austrians, who had volunteered to defend the Pope against Italian aggression.

Garibaldi became impatient at the delay of the government, and he decided to attack Rome independently. In 1862, against the earnest advice of the authorities, he led an army of Garibaldi moves against Rome volunteers against Rome. Italian troops were sent to stop him; and there actually took place a battle between the Garibaldians and the Italian army. Garibaldi was wounded "by an Italian bullet," as he put it, and he retired in disgust from public life.

During the Seven Weeks' War between Austria and Prussia, in 1866, Italy joined forces with the latter. Although Austria defeated Italy in several battles, Prussia's overwhelming Annexation of Venetia success compelled Austria to cede Venetia to Italy, which was annexed after a favorable plebiscite.

When the Franco-Prussian War broke out, Napoleon withdrew the French garrison from Rome. The Italians took immediate

advantage of the situation.   On September 20, 1870, an Italian
Annexation   army entered Rome in triumph. A plebiscite was then
of Rome   held, and by a vote of 134,000 to 1500 the Romans
declared their desire to join Italy.   Parliament voted the annexation of Rome which was then proclaimed the capital of the Kingdom.   Italy was no longer a "geographical expression."   The
weak petty states were now consolidated into a united nation,
which immediately took rank as one of the great powers in Europe.

REFERENCES

For the general works on the history of Italy see bibliography at the
end of Chapter VI.

CAVOUR:

W. R. Thayer, *The Life and Times of Cavour*, 2 vols. (1911), a famous
biography by an American historian, a model of scholarship; M. Palé-
ologue, *Cavour*, translated from the French (1927), chiefly diplomatic,
written by a French diplomat; P. Matter, *Cavour et l'Unité Italienne*,
3 vols. (1922–27); Evelyn (Countess) Matinengo-Cesaresco, *Cavour*
(1898), a brief but brilliant study; see essay on Cavour in A. D. White,
Seven Great Statesmen (ed. 1919), by the American educator; F. X. Kraus,
Cavour, die Erhebung Italiens im neunzehten Jahrhundert (1902), from
Catholic viewpoint; P. Orsi, *Cavour and the Making of Modern Italy, 1810–
1861* (1914); A. J. Whyte, *Political Life and Letters of Cavour* (1930).

GARIBALDI:

The standard books on Garibaldi are those by an English scholar, G. M.
Trevelyan, whose work is characterized by fine scholarship and literary
style, *Garibaldi's Defence of the Roman Republic* (1907), *Garibaldi and the
Thousand* (1909), and *Garibaldi and the Making of Italy* (1911).

MAZZINI:

Unfortunately there exists no biography of Mazzini as good as those of
Cavour and Garibaldi.   Bolton King, *Joseph Mazzini* (1902) is the best;
Mazzini's *Duties of Man* and *Essays* give an excellent idea of his ideals and
temperament.

MISCELLANEOUS:

R. S. Holland, *Builders of United Italy* (1908), short sketches of heroes
of the Risorgimento; G. M. Trevelyan, *Manin and the Venetian Revolution of 1848* (1923); C. S. Forester, *Victor Emmanuel II and the Union of
Italy* (1927).

CHAPTER XV

THE UNIFICATION OF GERMANY

PRUSSIA AND GERMAN UNITY

AFTER the Revolution of 1848, the political situation in Germany underwent a remarkable change. The movement for unity had been suppressed, but it took on a new life in a new *Steps toward* form. It is necessary to review the situation in order to *unity* see what steps had already been taken to unify the German people.

(1) *Napoleon's Reorganization of Germany.* The suppression of the Holy Roman Empire and the great consolidation of German states effected by Napoleon I in 1806 was the first step. Napoleon was, in a sense, the grandfather of united Germany.

(2) *The German Confederation.* Although the union of German states established by the Congress of Vienna was a loose one, it nevertheless clarified the problem. To many patriots the German Confederation was an incentive to a "more perfect union."

(3) *The Zollverein.* The tariff reform established by the Zollverein was one of the causes of the rising prosperity of Germany. It clearly showed the economic advantages of a united country and therefore enlisted the support of the industrial classes who were convinced that political unity would make Germany a great industrial nation.

(4) *The Frankfort Assembly.* Ridiculed as an "assembly of professors" and suppressed as a revolutionary body, the Frankfort Assembly yet produced a profound effect on the German people. It was the first truly representative body in Germany, and its sessions were followed with breathless interest. As a consequence the unification movement awakened popular enthusiasm which it had previously lacked.

German unity lay in the logic of history. The German people were bound to become a nation because, under modern conditions, national unity is essential to the political progress of *The Hohen-* every people. But how? A new answer came with *zollerns* the decision of Prussia to become the Sardinia of *champion unification* Germany. She was the largest of the states; she had the best army; she was German in speech and sentiment; and she was superbly organized politically.

In the new and Prussian phase of the unification movement the writings of historians played a prominent part. Ink as well as "blood and iron" was to be a factor in the making of the German Empire. During the nineteenth century there arose a Prussian school of historians who believed that it was Prussia's historic mission to unite Germany, chiefly because she had been the leader in the liberation movement against Napoleon, which they regarded as the true beginning of modern Germany. These historians asserted the doctrine of "historic necessity," by which they meant that the evolution of states compels them to adopt a course of action demanded by political needs, irrespective of kings, parliaments, laws, or traditions. In the hands of the Prussian historians, who combined great learning with fervent patriotism, history became a form of political propaganda, and the historian, a learned partisan of a political movement. These historians were popular professors in the various German universities where they deeply influenced the minds of the rising generation. Among the best known were Ludwig Häusser, Gustav Droysen, Heinrich von Sybel, and, especially, the famous Heinrich von Treitschke.

The patriotic historians

Almost all his life Treitschke was a professor of history in various German universities, where his lectures attracted wide attention because of their eloquence, learning, and intense patriotism. "We have no German Fatherland; the Hohenzollerns alone can give us one," was Treitschke's constant refrain before 1870. Great crowds were thrilled by this patriotic professor, whose lectures on history were in the nature of passionate declamations. The Germans, according to him, were the best of all peoples, and the Prussians, the best of all Germans; Prussia had performed every great deed in German history since the Treaty of Westphalia; she alone had realized the true ideal of national greatness, for the nation was an army, and the army, a nation. So great was Treitschke's influence that he was universally acclaimed as the "national historian."

Treitschke (1834–96)

When Prussia decided to unite Germany, she realized that there were two serious obstacles in the way. One was from the inside, Austria, who neither desired unification, nor did the German people desire to be united under her leadership because her population was largely non-German. In 1850, the King of Prussia attempted to unify Germany by

The "humiliation of Olmütz"

OTTO VON BISMARCK

negotiating with the other princes. He was peremptorily ordered by Austria to abandon his plans, which he meekly did in the Austrian town of Olmütz. This "humiliation of Olmütz," as it was called, infuriated all Prussia against Austria.

The other obstacle was from the outside, France. For long the leading position of France on the Continent was due largely to the fact that her neighbors were either weak, as were Opposition of France Belgium, Switzerland, and Spain, or divided, as were Germany and Italy. Time and again had divided Germany served as an outlet for the ambitions of France and as a convenient battle-ground for her wars, notably in the days of Louis XIV and of Napoleon. A united, therefore a powerful, nation on the other side of the Rhine might prove a thorn in the side of France, and eventually lessen the prestige of *la grande nation*.

STRUGGLE BETWEEN KING AND PARLIAMENT

On the death of Frederick William IV, in 1861, his brother ascended the throne as William I. The new King had been unpopular during the uprising of 1848 because of his King William favors conscription opposition to parliamentary government. But he now accepted the constitution of 1850 under which, he believed, he could rule as well as reign. William was brought up in the military traditions of his dynasty, and was a soldier to the core. He was especially interested in army reform, and determined to reorganize the entire military establishment in Prussia. Conscription had been established in Prussia during the Liberation movement, but after 1815 it had not been strictly applied. Many recruits were permitted to serve for a short period only, and many others were excused altogether. William and his Minister of War, Albrecht von Roon, determined to change the law so as to establish universal conscription, which would double the military forces of the nation. What could be the object of the government in desiring so large an army in time of peace? "To stifle democracy," said the Liberals, and they determined to oppose the plan of the King with might and main.

In spite of the efforts of the government to have candidates elected favorable to its policies, the elections of 1862 Parliament opposes conscription resulted in an overwhelming victory for the liberals. Parliament promptly defeated the army budget, to the deep chagrin of the King. If he was not to be supreme in military matters, William was no longer willing to be king, and he actually wrote out his abdication. His ardent supporters advised the King to suppress parliament altogether, but he remained loyal to his oath to maintain the constitution.

At this juncture "the man of the hour" arrived on the scene in the person of Otto Eduard Leopold von Bismarck, who was ap-

Bismarck (1815–98) pointed Prime Minister of Prussia. Henceforth, for a generation, the history of Germany and of Europe was largely the biography of this extraordinary man. Bismarck came of a noble family which had dwelt for centuries in Brandenburg, where he was born on the family estate of Schönhausen. Brought up in the narrow but intensely German environment of a Prussian landowner, he was early imbued with the aristocratic feelings of his class. He was sent to the university, where he acquired the reputation of being a roistering student, more devoted to beer-drinking and dueling than to law, which he was supposed to be studying. After leaving the university he entered the government service, but the plodding atmosphere of bureaucracy ill suited his lively and boisterous temperament. He resigned his position, and returned to his estate. Bismarck greatly enjoyed the life of a country gentleman, and he was very popular among his neighbors, in spite of the wild pranks which he often played upon them. He was also at home in fashionable Berlin society, where his wit and good-nature won him many friends.

Bismarck entered political life in 1847, when he was chosen a member of the United Diet, an assembly of estates called by the

Opposes democracy King. He became notorious in this body by his bitter opposition to parliamentary government, which he contemptuously denounced as "government by phrases," leading inevitably to chaos, corruption, and incompetency. A constitution, "a sheet of paper," should not be permitted to intervene between the royal will and state action. Liberals were unpractical people who mistook doctrines for realities, and whose schemes would surely bring the country to ruin. Parliamentary government, he declared, was all right for Englishmen who were practiced in the art, but would never suit Prussians who had no aptitude for such methods.

Bismarck was a typical Teuton in appearance. He was a powerfully built man over six feet, with fair hair, blue eyes, and a rough, jovial face. He possessed but few of the natural gifts of an orator, as his voice was somewhat shrill and his gestures awk- ward. But this blond giant had a sharp tongue and a cool insolence which infuriated his opponents. Once, while he was speaking, the assembly broke into an uproar at his denunciation of democratic principles. Bismarck coolly turned his back to the assembly, and began reading a newspaper. The tumult subsided. During the Revolution of 1848 he raised a company of peasants on his estate with the object of marching on Berlin to rescue the King from the mob. More royalist than the King, he was one of a minority of two who voted against a resolution of thanks to the King for granting a constitution.

Characteristics of Bismarck

To Bismarck, German nationalism was as abhorrent as democracy. He poured withering scorn on the efforts of the Frankfort Assembly to unite Germany. At that time he greatly admired Austria as the foe of revolution and as the "inheritor of ancient German might which has so often gloriously wielded the German sword." He even rejoiced at the humiliation of Prussia at Olmütz because she had risked a war for the sake of Germany. "Prussians we are and Prussians we shall remain," was then his verdict.

His opposition to German unity

During the reaction which followed the Revolution of 1848, Bismarck was continually advising the authorities to deal harshly with the revolutionists. His rabid speeches against democracy angered the Liberals who regarded him as a "political rowdy." Greatly to their chagrin the King appointed him, in 1851, to the important position of Prussian delegate to the Diet of the German Confederation.

Appointed delegate to the Diet of the Confederation

It was in the Diet that Bismarck first got a clear view and thorough understanding of the problems which confronted Germany. *There* he realized the deep-seated hatred of Austria for Prussia. *There* he saw the persistent efforts of Austria to block the union of Germany, to which he was now becoming a convert. He also clearly foresaw the inevitable conflict between these two powerful states. Lively altercations continually took place between the cool and insolent Bismarck and the Austrian envoys, whose "cautious dishonesty" exasperated him and whose domineering control of the Diet he resented. It was as a result of his experiences in this body that Bismarck became a convert to the cause of German

His conversion to German nationalism

nationalism; he now ceased to be merely a Prussian and became a German.

In 1859, he was appointed minister to Russia, where he became exceedingly popular on account of his desire to establish good relations between Prussia and Russia. Bismarck's mission to Russia was of prime importance in the diplomatic history of Europe. He keenly realized the value of Russian friendship to Prussia, and later, to Germany, as an offset to France; an alliance or, at least, a friendly understanding with Russia became the corner-stone of his foreign policies. Later, he was sent to France, where he saw much of Napoleon, whose shallow character he quickly divined. "A great unrecognized incapacity," was his judgment of the French Emperor. The Prussian's exuberant frankness and his blunt discussion of great questions convinced Napoleon that he was "not a person to be taken seriously."

Minister to Russia and to France

As a result of these experiences Bismarck changed greatly. His mental horizon had widened, and his character had deepened. He developed an extraordinary keenness in his judgment of men and an unerring insight into the real nature of the politics of Europe. When it was a question of advancing the interests of his country and king, Bismarck was utterly unscrupulous, using cunning, deceit, or brute force as best suited the occasion at hand. What was most deceptive in him was a kind of adroit frankness that completely confounded the master diplomats of the day. As lying and deception were the very soul of diplomacy, Bismarck sometimes told the truth in order better to deceive his opponents. Combined with his acquired diplomatic abilities were his old daring, boldness, and iron will. The moment Bismarck appeared on the European scene he was master, and master he remained till the day of his retirement.

Bismarck's character and methods

Bismarck's appointment as Prime Minister aroused the greatest indignation in Prussia; it was an open challenge to Liberal opinion which he had so often derisively flouted. He advised the King to tear up his letter of abdication and to govern in defiance of parliament. It was Bismarck's determination to make the appropriations for the army without the consent of the people's representatives; in short, to violate the constitution. Parliament was not to be suppressed but defied; the constitution was not to be abrogated but flouted. "As to what is

Determines to defy parliament

the law, when no budget is voted," he declared, "many theories are advanced, the justification of which I will not consider here. The necessity for the State to exist is enough for me; necessity alone is authoritative."

It was a bold and daring move, as widespread indignation was aroused by his open violation of the constitution, which might have led to his impeachment and execution. Bis- *Widespread* marck was often threatened with the fate of Strafford, *indignation* who had performed a similar service for Charles I. *at his action* Petitions from public bodies demanded the removal of "the rude and insolent Minister."   Demonstrations against the government took place throughout the country.   Even at court, Bismarck had to face the opposition of the Queen, the Crown Prince, and the English wife of the latter, all of whom felt that he was endangering the throne by inviting a revolution.   Sometimes the King himself wavered, but Bismarck heartened him with the words, "Death on the scaffold under certain circumstances is as honorable as death on the field of battle."

From 1862 to 1866, parliament was annually summoned to vote the budget, but each time it refused to do so.   "If you do not vote the money we shall take it where we can get it," *Governs* was Bismarck's defiant rejoinder.   Taxes were there- *without* upon levied, collected, and spent by the government *parliament* without presenting a budget or an accounting.   A system of terrorism was instituted against the Liberals; their meetings were forbidden and their papers gagged by censors.   The worst days of the Carlsbad Decrees had now returned.

Bismarck's defense was that parliament stood in the way of the country's destiny.   "Prussia's kingship has not yet fulfilled its mission," he declared.   "It is not yet ripe enough to *Bismarck's* form a purely ornamental trimming for your constitu- *defense* tional structure, not yet ready to be inserted as a dead piece of machinery in the mechanism of parliamentary rule."   By this time Bismarck clearly had in view the unification of Germany and how it was to be accomplished.   On a memorable occasion he gave utterance to a sentiment which rang throughout the world.   "Germany," he declared, "does not look to Prussia's liberalism, but to her power. . . . The great questions of the day are not to be decided by speeches and majority resolutions — therein lay the weakness of 1848 and 1849 — but by blood and iron!"   Bismarck's very boldness carried the day, as all opposition to him proved vain.

All Germany watched with intense concern the grave constitutional crisis in Prussia. The defeat of parliament was as great a blow to democracy as the defeat of the Frankfort Assembly had been to nationalism. Popular opinion in Germany became skeptical as to the value of a constitution, hitherto the goal of all democratic striving. Though Bismarck had in view a patriotic end, his arbitrary methods started an evil tradition in Germany, where a constitution was now regarded as a "sheet of paper" to be respected or flouted by the rulers as suited their purposes. Against a determined autocrat who "did things" the people felt that they were helpless, despite constitutions and parliaments.

Arbitrary government, an evil tradition

THE SEVEN WEEKS' WAR

The weapon was now forged with which to strike those who stood in the way of German unity. An army appeared which was to give a great account of itself on the battle-fields of Europe. At its head was the greatest soldier since Napoleon, General Helmuth von Moltke, the first of modern scientific warriors. There was nothing dashing or heroic in the manner of this "battle thinker." He was a calm, rather dry person, with a wonderful capacity for scientifically planning the road to victory. Three wars were to be fought before German unity was accomplished: with Denmark in 1864; with Austria in 1866; and with France in 1870.

The new army

The Danish war grew out of the question of disposing of the two duchies, Schleswig-Holstein. The population of the former was partly Danish and partly German; that of the latter, entirely German. For centuries the duchies had been united with Denmark through a personal union with her King. Since the rise of the nationalist movement in Germany, patriotic Germans were much concerned over the duchies because Holstein was a member of the German Confederation, and especially because of the German population in both duchies. In 1863, Denmark incorporated Schleswig, which roused German nationalists to fury. Had Denmark a right to do so? Germany and all Europe debated the Schleswig-Holstein Question, which bristled with so many complications that Lord Palmerston

The Schleswig-Holstein Question

once declared that only two men besides himself had ever under-stood it; one was dead, the second was crazy, and he had forgotten it. Bismarck became intensely interested in the controversy be-cause he saw in it, on the one hand, a possibility of annexing the entire region with its fine harbor at Kiel; and, on the other hand, an excellent opportunity for a reckoning with Austria. "Our re-lations with Austria," he declared, "must be better or worse. We desire the first, but we must prepare for the second."

Prussia and Austria were determined to prevent the incorpora-tion of the duchies, and, in 1864, they declared war against Den-mark. A line of Danish fortresses, which it was be- Defeat of lieved could hold an army at bay for two years, was Denmark carried in five days by the Allies. Denmark was compelled to sign a treaty renouncing all rights to Schleswig-Holstein and also to the Duchy of Lauenburg, a little neighbor of the latter. The Danish difficulty was now over, but another one arose about the division of the spoils. According to the Treaty of Gastein, signed in 1865, Holstein was to be administered by Austria, and Schleswig by Prussia. Prussia obtained also the right to construct a canal which would join the North Sea, at Kiel, with the Baltic.

This treaty, however, was by no means the final settlement of the perplexing Schleswig-Holstein Question. A claimant for both duchies appeared in the person of Prince Frederick of Claims of Augustenburg, who wished to organize them into a the Prince of new German state with himself as ruler. This plan Augusten-appealed to German popular sentiment; moreover, burg Austria championed his cause and encouraged a propaganda in his favor. But Bismarck was totally averse to the plan. Increasing the number of German states, of which there were already too many, and giving another supporter to Austria would complicate still more the problem of unification. He was determined to annex the duchies outright, which would arouse Austria to a fighting mood. War between Prussia and Austria suited his plans exactly.

Bismarck was bold but he was also prudent. In the diplomatic moves that now began, he displayed a masterly, if unscrupulous handling of the situation which ended in the total Isolation of discomfiture of Austria. His main object was to iso- Austria late Prussia's rival. With this end in view he entered into a treaty of alliance with the newly formed Kingdom of Italy, promising her Venetia for assistance to Prussia in a war against Austria. At a

famous meeting in Biarritz, Bismarck lulled Napoleon III into in-
activity by vague promises to permit France to annex Belgium.
On Russian friendship Bismarck could securely count because, in
1863, he had signed a convention with the Tsar promising Prussia's
help in suppressing the Polish uprising.

Bismarck then began leading Austria on, now feigning a willingness to yield, now urging arbitration, now goading her to fury, till
Rift in the   all was prepared for a blow.   First, careful planning,
Confedera-   then audacious execution, was the Bismarckian
tion   method.   When everything was ready, he suddenly
proposed a new plan for reorganizing the German Confederation,
which included a provision for universal suffrage in elections for the
Diet.   Great was the astonishment at the sudden conversion to
democracy of the "parliament-tamer," and many doubted his sin-
cerity.   His object was undoubtedly to win the German Liberals to
the side of Prussia in the coming conflict.   Austria, confident of
the support of the Confederation, brought the Schleswig-Holstein
matter before the Diet with the object of once more humiliating
Prussia, as at Olmütz.   Prussia denounced Austria's move as a
violation of their agreement to decide on the status of the duchies
by mutual consent; and she refused to be bound by any action of
the Diet in the matter.   In 1866, on a motion of Austria, the Diet
ordered the mobilization against Prussia of the armies of the
Confederation.   In so doing the Diet decreed its own death.
Prussia immediately declared the Treaty of Gastein null and
void, and the German Confederation dissolved.

Civil war followed in Germany, most of the states siding with
Austria; a few in the north supported Prussia.   The conflict was
Prussia's su-   known as the Seven Weeks' War, being one of the
periority   shortest on record.   The careful and minute prepara-
over Austria   tions that Prussia had made now stood her in good
stead.   Her soldiers were armed with the new "needle gun," which
could fire three shots to one by the old-fashioned "muzzle loaders"
used by the Austrians.   Commanding the Prussian army was
General von Moltke whose success in this conflict was to result in
revolutionizing methods of warfare.   He was the first to make military use on a large scale of the modern means of communication,
the railway and the telegraph.   The Austrians, on the contrary,
were disorganized, poorly led, and badly armed.

Prussian armies were dispatched against the states on the side of Austria, which were quickly overrun and conquered. Other armies invaded Austria through Bohemia. At König- Sadowa gratz, or Sadowa, a great battle took place between the Prussians and Austrians, as about half a million men were engaged. The Austrians were defeated, and compelled to retreat.

At last the "humiliation of Olmütz" was avenged. It was the intention of King William to make Austria pay dearly for her arrogance in the past by marching into Vienna and Bismarck dictating severe terms of peace. But it was no part favors moderate terms of Bismarck's plan so to humiliate Austria as to drive erate terms her into permanent opposition to Prussia. "The ques- to Austria tion at issue is now decided; what remains is to regain the old friendship of Austria," was his opinion. He wanted to gain her good will in case of a future conflict with another power. Almost with prophetic eyes he saw that the future Germany had nothing to gain from a weakened Austria, which might break up into Slavic and Hungarian nationalities permanently hostile to everything German. In Bismarck's mind the idea had already arisen of an alliance between Germany and Austria, and he was willing to make peace at this time on Austria's terms in order to mollify her wounded pride.

A bitter controversy arose between Bismarck and William over the question of the treatment of Austria. Bismarck threatened to resign; and he went so far as to contemplate suicide, so The Treaty keenly did he feel the situation. Finally, the King of Prague yielded and consented "to bite the sour apple," as he called it, of a moderate peace. The terms of the Treaty of Prague, signed in 1866, were: (1) that the Confederation should be dissolved, and a new union formed of which Austria was not to be a member; (2) that Schleswig-Holstein should be incorporated with Prussia; [1] and (3) that Venetia should be annexed to Italy who had supported Prussia during the war. Austria was not forced to cede any of her territory to Prussia, and she paid only a small indemnity.

The results of the Seven Weeks' War amply justified the years of toil and preparation. By putting an end to the century-old domination of Germany by the Hapsburgs, it cleared the way of the chief obstruction to the union of the German people. Hanover,

---

[1] A provision declared that the inhabitants of North Schleswig shall be reunited with Denmark, should they express such a desire by a plebiscite. Prussia refused to carry out this agreement.

Nassau, Hesse-Cassel, and the free city of Frankfort were annexed

The North German Confederation

to Prussia as a punishment for taking Austria's side in the war. The Frankfort Diet was abolished, and a new union was formed, the North German Confederation, consisting of the twenty-two states north of the river Main. The four southern states, Bavaria, Württemberg, Baden, and Hesse-Darmstadt, were not forced into the Confederation by Bismarck; it was his policy to persuade these states to follow Prussia's lead, and he, therefore, entered into a secret alliance with them. The constitution of the North German Confederation was written, for the most part, by Bismarck, and accepted by the princes. In 1867, a convention, elected by universal manhood suffrage, accepted the constitution which was then ratified by the individual states. The constitution of the North German Confederation was identical with the one adopted by the German Empire in 1871.[1]

Prussia was now at the head of a powerful federal state that could put a million men in the field. Bismarck, once the most

Triumph of Bismarck

unpopular, now found himself the most popular man in Germany. The triumphant Prime Minister was, nevertheless, eager to mollify the Liberals who had opposed him. At his request the Prussian parliament passed an act of indemnity legalizing his actions in governing without a budget. Might was made right.

THE FRANCO-PRUSSIAN WAR

If the road to German unity was cleared of Austria, another obstruction, and a far more serious one, appeared in the hostile atti-

Napoleon's vacillating diplomacy

tude of France. To the latter a divided Germany, and therefore a weak Germany, was a far more desirable neighbor than the united nation which was now emerging from the chaos of former days. Napoleon III prepared to do his utmost to hinder the completion of German unity by diplomatic intrigues and threats of war. Now he would intrigue with Austria against Prussia; now with Prussia against Austria. On the eve of the Seven Weeks' War he had an agreement with Austria concerning a rearrangement of Germany in case of an Austrian victory. During the war, France was, however, neutral, a fatal error committed by Napoleon who had no idea of the real

[1] See page 382.

strength of Prussia. He believed that she would be defeated; or that the combatants would exhaust themselves in a long-drawn-out war, which would give him the opportunity of interfering to gain something for France. When Prussia was victorious, he came forward with an irritating demand that the southern states be left out of the German union. Prussia yielded, but she resolved that France should pay dearly for trying to block the road to German unity. Napoleon's blindness, his fatal fatuity, his vacillation may, in part, be attributed to a racking illness from which he was then suffering, and which may have dulled his otherwise acute mind.

"Revenge for Sadowa" was now the cry in France. The drift of events beyond the Rhine made it evident that all Germany would soon unite in a powerful single state. The feeling between the French and the Germans was constantly growing more bitter; and the newspapers of both nations frequently fanned the flames of national hatred through the publication of articles abounding in taunts, insults, and recriminations. *Hostility between the French and the Germans*

In the trial of strength between France and Prussia which was about to ensue, the advantage was really with the latter, though appearances favored the former. Prussia had the best army in the world, the best general, Moltke, the best diplomat, Bismarck, and the better cause, nationality. France, on the contrary, was to be badly served by a poorly organized though valiant army, by incompetent generals, by a weak and vacillating statesman, Napoleon III, and worst of all, by a bad cause; namely, insolent interference in the internal affairs of a neighboring people. When, in 1870, the French tried to prevent their neighbors from becoming a nation, they were untrue to the very principle which they themselves had so passionately proclaimed during the French Revolution, and for which they had so often bravely and generously fought, namely, nationalism. Unfortunately, it was the policy of the older nations to regard newcomers as intruders, and to try to prevent their entrance into the European family. Had a wiser and more generous policy been followed, the conflict which humiliated and mutilated a proud nation, France, and which compelled the German people to stand guard over their newly born Fatherland with drawn sword, would not have taken place. If ever there was a useless, senseless war it was that between France and Prussia in 1870. France entered *Absence of real issues in the struggle between France and Prussia* the conflict in order to maintain her "prestige" over Germany; there were neither economic nor territorial issues between the two nations. However, "France" meant Napoleon III whose chief aim was to secure the safety of his dynasty.

The attempts of France to foil Prussia's plan to unite Germany convinced Bismarck that war between France and Prussia was

Bismarck
desires war inevitable, that "it lay in the logic of history." He even deemed such a conflict desirable, for the effect of rousing the patriotism of all the Germans against a common enemy would be to strengthen the newly formed bonds of union. Particularism, that age-old German characteristic, would vanish on the battle-field when Prussians, Saxons, Hanoverians, Hessians, and Württembergers fought side by side for their common Fatherland. There would then be generated a common heroic memory which would do more to unite Germany than constitutions and zollvereins.

The problem was how to manage the situation so that France would appear in the light of aggressor. From 1866 to 1870 a diplo-

Bismarck's
masterful
diplomacy matic web was craftily being woven by that master-weaver of diplomacy, Bismarck, with the object of sheltering Prussia and entangling her enemies. Bismarck's finesse, his unscrupulous methods, his daring boldness were most effectively used during those momentous years. He knew just the arguments that would persuade his opponents, and showed himself remarkably apt in subtly suggesting favorable terms, yet never committing himself definitely to anything. Bismarck was one of the first to make extensive use of the press for purposes of diplomatic intrigue. A number of journalists, both German and foreign, were in his secret pay; a special fund, popularly known as "the reptile fund," had been created for this purpose. "Inspired" articles, sometimes written in Bismarck's own office, would appear in prominent European newspapers attacking certain men, suggesting certain plans, or threatening certain acts. In this way he was able to hide his own plans and, at the same time, cause his opponents to reveal theirs.

Bismarck's main object was to complete the unification of Germany. The appearance of a new great power would, he knew,

Isolation of
France upset the balance of power in Europe; therefore, he had to tread warily lest he give offense by flouting the practices and prejudices of the other nations. To sting France to action at the right moment, and yet to make her appear as the disturber of the peace of Europe, was Bismarck's aim. He began the process of isolating France, so that all the nations would look on calmly while Prussia was delivering her master-stroke. Italy was still an ally; besides, in case of a war between Prussia and France, Italy would distract attention by attacking Rome. The friendship with Russia could be counted upon. Austria, if not friendly, was at least not hostile as a consequence of the policy of mollification after Sadowa; besides, Austria's fear of Russia would keep her from intervening. England would intervene only if Prussia violated the neutrality of Belgium, and Bismarck, therefore, determined to respect this agreement at all costs. The southern German states, presumably under the influence of France, had signed a secret treaty with Prussia, promising to put their troops at her disposal in case of war. Napoleon also made diplomatic preparations for the coming conflict by trying to form an alliance with Austria and with Italy, but his efforts proved fruitless, owing to Bismarck's superior diplomacy.

In the meantime, Moltke set himself the task of preparing the German armies for war with France. There began a systematic preparation which was almost uncanny in its perfec- Moltke's tion. Every possible difficulty was foreseen and pro- preparedness vided for. France was carefully mapped, and the Prussian officers came to know the topography of the land of their enemy far better than did the French themselves. Strategic railways were built for the purpose of transporting troops quickly to important points on the frontier. The equipment of the army was of the latest and best pattern; everything was prepared for the comfort and welfare of the soldiers, from the rifles on their shoulders to the handkerchiefs in their pockets. Preparedness for war had never before been so thorough and so comprehensive; all that was now necessary was to give the word of command, and the great military machine would be immediately launched in all its completeness against the unwary enemy.

The leading figures in the drama of 1870 were all old men. King William was seventy-three; Moltke was seventy; Roon, sixty-seven; the youngest was Bismarck, and he was fifty-five. Yet age had neither impaired their mental powers nor softened their iron will, and the new and mighty Germany that was soon to arise was largely of their making.

It was in an unexpected quarter, in Spain, that an incident arose that was to draw France and Prussia into mortal combat. In 1868,

The Hohen-
zollern can-
didacy

a revolution occurred in Spain, and Queen Isabella II was exiled. The throne being vacant, a search began for a new ruler, and the choice at one time fell upon Prince Leopold of Hohenzollern-Sigmaringen, a Catholic relative of the King of Prussia. France regarded the candidacy of a Hohenzollern for the Spanish throne in an unfavorable light, fearing that a possible "family compact" might result to her disadvantage. Napoleon informed William that, if a Hohenzollern ascended the throne of Spain, it would be sufficient ground for war between them. Prince Leopold, thereupon, of his own accord, withdrew his candidacy. Here the crisis would have ended had it not been for the reckless attitude of the French chauvinists. Denunciatory articles against Prussia appeared in the Paris journals, and a war party was formed headed by the reckless and incompetent Duke de Gramont and the Empress Eugénie. They prevailed upon the Emperor to make a new demand upon King William; namely, that he should promise not to permit, at any future time, a Hohenzollern to occupy the throne of Spain. This new demand was presented by the French Ambassador, Count Benedetti, to William at the town of Ems, where he was sojourning. Although he was astonished at the insolence of Napoleon, William received Benedetti courteously, but refused the demand. He then sent a dispatch to Bismarck describing the circumstances of the interview.

Bismarck was in Berlin at a private conference with Moltke and Roon when the Ems dispatch came. On being assured by his

The Ems
dispatch

associates that all was in readiness, and that they were confident of victory, he proceeded to "edit" the dispatch with the object of converting it into "a red flag for the Gallic bull." Bismarck so changed the wording that it read as though there had been a heated interview between the King and Benedetti, that the former had refused the demand sharply, and had dismissed the French Ambassador without ceremony. "Now it has a different ring," said Moltke. "In its original form it sounded like a parley; now it is like a flourish of trumpets in answer to a challenge."

On July 14, 1870, the famous "Ems dispatch" was published. It was timed on the French national holiday, and the effect was exactly what Bismarck had intended. Frenzied crowds paraded up

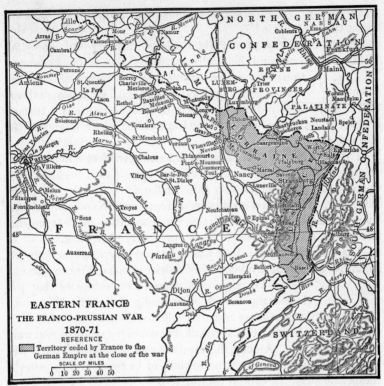

EASTERN FRANCE
THE FRANCO-PRUSSIAN WAR
1870-71
REFERENCE
////// Territory ceded by France to the
German Empire at the close of the war
SCALE OF MILES
0 10 20 30 40 50

and down the boulevards of Paris demanding war with Prussia and shouting, "*À Berlin!*" "*À Berlin!*" The French Minister of War assured the Emperor that all was in readiness "down to the last button on the last gaiter of the last soldier." France declared war against Prussia, and entered the momentous conflict, as Premier Ollivier said, "with a light heart."

France declares war

If the Ems dispatch roused the French, it also profoundly stirred the Germans. A wave of indignation swept over all Germany at what was believed to be the insolent conduct of the French Ambassador. The southern Germans enthusiastically joined their northern brethren, to the disappointment of the French. Men fell into their places promptly and were transported with amazing rapidity to the frontier. What the French Minister had said of the readiness of the French armies was, in reality, true only of the German, as about a million men were mobilized in two weeks without the slight-

Rapid mobilization of German army

est disorder. This period of mobilization, Moltke said, was the most tranquil of his life.

On the other side of the Rhine all was disorder and confusion; soldiers could not find their officers; cannon were without ammuni-

Chaos in French army

tion; horses were without harness; means of transport were lacking; the food supply was insufficient; officers were not provided with the necessary maps. Instead of everything being ready "to the last button," chaos reigned in the French armies.

To the amazement and chagrin of France, she found herself completely isolated, as all the other nations immediately declared their

Isolation of France

neutrality. To gain England's sympathy Bismarck published an unsigned treaty with Napoleon showing how the latter was contemplating the annexation of Belgium, the neutrality of which Prussia was scrupulously respecting.

The Franco-Prussian War was short and sharp, lasting only ten months. German armies under Moltke invaded France through

Sedan

Alsace-Lorraine. In nearly all the battles that followed the French were badly defeated. The most famous battle was that of Sedan, at which a French army of 120,000 was routed; about 17,000 were killed or wounded, and the rest were taken prisoners. Among the captives was Napoleon. Paris was then surrounded by an "iron girdle" of German armies; after a desperate siege the capital capitulated.

The fall of Paris was followed by an armistice and peace negotiations. Thiers and Jules Favre, the chief negotiators for France,

Treaty of Frankfort

came to bargain with the triumphant Bismarck. The latter, however, virtually dictated the terms of the treaty, which was signed at Frankfort, on May 10, 1871. The chief terms were: (1) that France cede to Germany, Alsace and the part of Lorraine containing Metz; and (2) that France pay an indemnity of $1,000,000,000 and support a German army of occupation until the entire amount was paid. Never was a victory so complete as that of Germany, and never a defeat so humiliating as that of France.

While the siege of Paris was in progress an historic ceremony took place in the Hall of Mirrors, in the great palace at Versailles, once the residence of French kings. On January 18, 1871, King William, surrounded by the princes, generals, and statesmen of Germany was acclaimed German Emperor, as William I. The North German

SIGNING THE TREATY OF FRANKFORT

Bismarck and the French delegates, Favre and Thiers

Confederation was abolished, and a new union, including both
northern and southern states, was organized, called   Proclama-
the German Empire.   At last the unification of Ger-   tion of the
many was accomplished, and by the Bismarckian   German
method of "blood and iron."   Empire

During the war the sympathy of the world was on the side of
Germany as the nation that was defending herself against the
aggressive militarism of France.   But the harsh terms   Harshness of
of the Treaty of Frankfort turned world sympathy   the terms
to the side of France as the victim of German ruth-   of peace
lessness.   The indemnity was the largest, up to that time, in the
history of modern Europe.   It was evidently Germany's intention
to crush France, "to bleed her white," and to reduce her to the
status of a second-rate power.   The French were stunned.   Hurled
from the pinnacle of power by a nation that they had long despised, they now faced economic ruin and the dismemberment of
their territory.

What was most resented was the disposition of Alsace-Lorraine.
Germany annexed the region on the ground that it had formerly
been German territory, and that the inhabitants were   Protest of
of German stock.   Both the French and the Alsatians   Alsace-
demanded that a plebiscite be held to determine the   Lorraine
wishes of the inhabitants.   This demand was refused   against an-
                                                        nexation
by Bismarck; he believed that a plebiscite would result in favor of
France.   Alsace-Lorraine had once formed part of the Holy Roman
Empire, and had been conquered by Louis XIV and annexed to
France.   The inhabitants, though of German stock speaking a
German dialect, had become greatly attached to France during
the French Revolution, when every benefit gained by that movement was freely extended to them.   A protest, issued by the Alsa-
tian representatives in the French National Assembly, denounced
annexation without a plebiscite as moral slavery.   "We call our
fellow citizens to witness," it declared, "that we consider null and
void, in advance all treaties and acts that agree to give Alsace-
Lorraine to a foreign country.   We proclaim the inviolable right
of Alsace-Lorraine to remain part of the French nation, and we
swear in behalf of our constituents and their descendants to vindicate it eternally, and by all manner of means, in the face of all
usurpers."

Why did Bismarck dictate such severe terms?   Had he not

g,iven evidence at Sadowa of great foresight in refusing to trample
Reasons for on a fallen foe? He must have realized that the
the annexa- annexation of Alsace-Lorraine would arouse in France
tion an unconquerable desire for revenge, and he was not
the man to store up trouble for his country. There is some ground
for believing that Bismarck favored milder terms, but that he was
finally persuaded by Moltke that Germany's safety demanded the
possession of Metz and Strasbourg, "the Gates," in order to shut
out invading French armies. These two cities were later magnificently fortified and garrisoned. There was an economic as well
as a military motive. Bismarck was informed that Lorraine contained vast iron deposits, which, though not of good quality, might
prove of value in case new processes were discovered for making
steel. The annexation of Alsace-Lorraine created an unbridgeable
chasm between France and Germany, and was not least among the
causes of the World War.

REFERENCES

BISMARCK:

The best biography of Bismarck in English is C. G. Robertson, *Bismarck* (1919); M. Smith, *Bismarck and German Unity* (ed. 1910), an excellent sketch; H. Hofmann, *Fürst Bismarck, 1890–1908*, 2 vols. (1913),
important for his relations to William II; E. Marcks, *Bismarck, eine Bi-
ographie*, authoritative biography by one who had access to both official
and family sources, vol. I (1919), covers period 1815–48; P. Matter, *Bismarck et son temps*, 3 vols. (ed. 1914), the best biography in French, and
very fair to the German statesman; M. Lenz, *Geschichte Bismarcks* (1902),
study of Bismarck before 1870; Bismarck's memoirs were translated into
English as *Reflections and Reminiscences*, 2 vols. (1899), and the third volume, long suppressed, finally appeared under the title, *The Kaiser vs. Bismarck* (1921); M. Busch, *Bismarck: Some Secret Pages of His History*,
translated from the German, 2 vols. (1898), diary of one of Bismarck's
political intimates; H. Kohl, *Die Politischen Reden des Fürsten Bismarck*,
14 vols. (1892–94); H. Schoenfeld, *Bismarck's Letters and Speeches* (1905), a
selection; see essay on Bismarck in A. D. White, *Seven Great Statesmen* (ed.
1919).

THE UNIFICATION MOVEMENT:

E. F. Henderson, *A Short History of Germany* (ed. 1916), vol. II, chaps.
IX–X; F. Schevill, *The Making of Modern Germany* (1916), chap. V; H. von
Sybel, *The Founding of the German Empire by William I*, translated from
the German, 7 vols. (1890–1898), from Prussian viewpoint: H. Friedjung,
The Struggle for Supremacy in Germany, 1859–1866, translated from the
German (1935), from German national viewpoints, by an Austrian. E.

Denis, *La fondation de l'empire allemand, 1852–1871* (1906), by a French authority, and on the whole the best book on the subject.

The Franco-Prussian War:

R. H. Lord, *The Origins of the War of 1870* (1924), best in English, based on the most recent knowledge of the diplomacy of 1870; H. Oncken, *Napoleon III and the Rhine*, translated from the German (1928), reveals Napoleon's persistent efforts to thwart German unity, strongly anti-French; A. Chuquet, *La Guerre de 1870–71* (1895), a brief narrative.

For additional titles see bibliography at the end of Chapter VII.

ADDITIONAL REFERENCES

W. Sombart, *Die deutsche Volkswirtschaft im neunzehnten Jahrhundert* (1927); P. Benaerts, *Les origines de la grande industrie allemande* (1933); L. D. Steefel, *The Schleswig-Holstein Question* (1932).

PART II
POLITICAL AND SOCIAL REFORM
1870–1914

PART II

POLITICAL AND SOCIAL REFORM
1870–1914

THE period of 1870 is famous in the annals of nationalism and democracy. Nationalism witnessed a signal triumph in the emergence of United Germany and United Italy after centuries of division. The establishment of the Dual Monarchy recognized Hungarian nationalism though not Hungarian independence. The partial dismemberment of Turkey resulted in the emergence of Rumania, Serbia, Montenegro, and Bulgaria. In the New World the United States was now "an indestructible union of indestructible states," the outcome of the victory of the North over the South in the American Civil War. A new type of nationalism appeared, colonial nationalism, with the establishment of the Dominion of Canada.

Democracy kept pace with nationalism. France was now a democratic republic. England enfranchised her working classes. In granting universal suffrage for the Reichstag, Germany made an important concession to democracy. Italy was a parliamentary monarchy. The new Balkan nations and the new Japan established parliaments. The abolition of serfdom in Russia and of slavery in the United States was inspired by democratic ideals.

But the problems solved by political democracy were chiefly those that affected the middle classes. By establishing a new environment for the working classes the Industrial Revolution had created more problems than political democracy was able to solve. The period 1870–1914 witnessed the rise of a new type of reform, social reform, which aimed to ameliorate the economic condition of the working class. As a consequence the political state, restricted in its activities to the protection of life and property, gave place to the social state that intervened in the affairs of capital and labor by regulating wages, hours, and conditions of employment, and by establishing systems of social insurance. Germany was the pioneer social state, and her success encouraged the other nations to follow her example. The establishment of the social

state came as a result of a new agitation, not of a new revolution. The newly enfranchised workingmen used their ballots with
the purpose of ameliorating their lot in life. Nothing was more
characteristic of the political life of Europe during the period,
1870–1914, than the prominence of social reform.

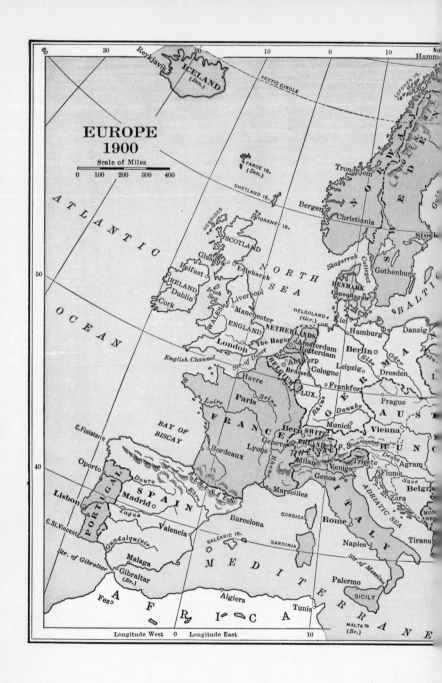

EUROPE
1900

Scale of Miles

0   100   200   300   400

ATLANTIC

OCEAN

ARCTIC CIRCLE

Reykjavik

ICELAND
(Den.)

Hamm

No

FAROE IS.
(Den.)

SHETLAND IS.

Bergen

Trondhjem

Christiania

NORWAY

SWEDEN

LOFODEN IS.

Stock

HEBRIDES

ORKNEY IS.

SCOTLAND

Glasgow

Belfast

Edinburgh

NORTH

SEA

Skagerrak

Cattegat

Gothenburg

DENMARK

Copenhagen

BALTIC

IRELAND

Dublin

Cork

Irish Sea

Liverpool

WALES

Manchester

ENGLAND

HELGOLAND
(Ger.)

Kiel

Hamburg

Danzig

London

NETHERLANDS

The Hague

Amsterdam

Rotterdam

Berlin

Oder

Elbe

Leipzig

Dresden

Prague

English Channel

Str. of Dover

Havre

BELGIUM

Antwerp

Brussels

Cologne

Frankfort

LUX.

Rhine

GERMANY

Danube

Seine

Paris

Loire

FRANCE

BAY OF
BISCAY

C.Finisterre

Oporto

Bordeaux

Bern

Geneva

SWITZ.

Munich

Vienna

AUST

HUN

Lyons

Rhone

THE ALPS

Milan

Drave

Agram

Fiume

Save

Belgr

Genoa

Po

Venice

Trieste

Zara

MON
NES

Tirana

ADRIATIC SEA

Lisbon

PORTUGAL

Madrid

SPAIN

Douro

Tagus

Ebro

PYRENEES

C.St.Vincent

Guadalquivir

Valencia

Barcelona

BALEARIC IS.

CORSICA

SARDINIA

Rome

ITALY

Naples

Str.of Messina

Malaga

Gibraltar
(Br.)

Str. of Gibraltar

Fez

AFRICA

Algiers

MEDITERRANE

Palermo

SICILY

Tunis

MALTA
(Br.)

Longitude West   0   Longitude East   10

30   20   10   0   10

50

40

CHAPTER XVI

POLITICAL AND SOCIAL PROGRESS IN GREAT BRITAIN

(1867–1914)

SYSTEM OF GOVERNMENT

As a middle-class England emerged from the Reform Bill of 1832, a working-class England began to emerge from the Reform Bill of 1867. New issues arose that shifted the struggle from political and religious reform to that of ameliorating the social and economic condition of the masses. But the "Victorian Compromise," or steering between revolution and reaction, continued to be England's method of progress.

In spite of the many changes effected by the Reform Bills, the English political system maintained its ancient framework, King, Lords, and Commons. Every time a change took place there was a shift of power within the framework; in this way the absolutism of the Tudors was, in time, superseded by the supremacy of a democratic Commons. But royal and aristocratic institutions persisted, more as relics to preserve the spirit of continuity than as working parts of the political system.

England's framework of government

The government of England is by King and Parliament. "The King reigns, but does not rule." In theory he is an absolute monarch by the "grace of God," but in practice he never interferes with, and seldom influences, the conduct of the government. He no longer vetoes bills; and appointments to office are made by the cabinet in his name. The king is a figurehead in the English political system; his sole prerogative being "the right to encourage and the right to warn." Nevertheless, he still performs a useful political function in being the symbol of the unity and continuity of the Empire. There is a dramatic appeal in the institution of monarchy which helps to promote a spirit of loyalty among the many races under the British flag. At home, monarchy is greatly respected by all classes of the English people, who regard it as the only non-partisan element in their government and therefore a truly patriotic institution.

The King

The leading feature of the British system is the cabinet. It originated in England, where it was developed to the highest point of efficiency. The cabinet is a committee of members of Parliament whose head, the Prime Minister, is always the man who commands a majority in the Commons. Technically, he is appointed by the King. Cabinet government is strictly party government. The ministers are all members of the same party, and its leader, the Prime Minister, is the one who determines the appointment of his associates and formulates the policies of the cabinet. The "efficient secret" of the British cabinet system is the union of powers, in contrast to the American system of separation of powers. The cabinet exercises executive power by appointing officials and by supervising the administration; and it exercises legislative power by introducing all the important bills. Should any bill introduced by a cabinet member fail to pass the Commons, or should the Commons pass a resolution of "no confidence," the cabinet as a whole must immediately resign; it is not appointed for a definite term of office, but on the principle of "ministerial responsibility," according to which the Commons may at any time terminate its political life. Upon an adverse vote the King may either request the leader of the opposition to form a new ministry; [1] or he may dissolve the Commons and order new elections, which is now the general practice. If the newly elected house contains a majority in favor of the cabinet, it continues in office; otherwise, the opposition takes office. A new ministry, composed of entirely different men having entirely different policies, now controls the government. In England the defeat of a ministry is an historic event, not, as in France, merely a shuffle. It is of the greatest importance that harmony should exist in the government, and the elastic method of dissolving Parliament is used to bring about harmony in case it has ceased to exist. Strict party discipline has, in recent years, seriously affected the principle of ministerial responsibility. The party leaders in the cabinet now control more firmly their followers in the Commons; as a consequence the latter seldom asserts its power to overthrow ministries.

Parliament consists of two houses, the Lords and the Commons, though the term "Parliament" generally refers to the latter. The

[1] The cabinet is the core of a larger group of officials, called the ministry, which consists of all the important administrative officials; but the terms "cabinet" and "ministry" are used synonymously.

SYSTEM OF GOVERNMENT 259

House of Lords is composed mainly of hereditary peers, known
by the titles of duke, marquis, earl, viscount, and   The Lords
baron; a small minority consists of the bishops of
the Anglican Church and some of the Scottish and Irish peers.
This most ancient governing body, from which grew nearly all the
other organs of the government, has now become almost as "decora-
tive" as the monarchy.   As a legislature it can pass laws, but since
the Parliament Act of 1911[1] its powers have been so curtailed that,
at the utmost, it can now only delay legislation for two years.

The rise of the Commons from a humble adviser to the King
to supreme power in the government is the salient fact in the
history of English democracy.   By exercising the   The Com-
"power of the purse," once its only function, it could   mons
bring the entire machinery of government to a standstill by refusing to vote supplies.   It crushed the absolutism of the Stuarts.
It absorbed the executive power of their successors by controlling
the cabinet.   It reduced almost to nought the legislative power of
the Lords.   The prerogatives of the King and the privileges of the
aristocracy were transformed by the Commons into the liberties
of the people.   Elected by universal suffrage [2] for five years, it
may be dissolved by the government, in the name of the King, at
any time before its term has expired, and for any or no reason.   The
power of dissolution is exercised by the government in power in
order to test public opinion on its policies.   Bills passed by the
Commons are not defeated by the Lords, are not vetoed by the
King, and are not declared unconstitutional by the courts; hence,
the Commons are supreme in the government of the country.
However great its powers the Commons does not exercise them
directly.   They are focused in the cabinet which acts in the name
of Parliament and which must conform to its wishes or go out of
existence.   "To say that at present the cabinet legislates with the
advice and consent of Parliament would hardly be an exaggeration," writes A. Lawrence Lowell in his authoritative book, *The
Government of England*.

Britain, unlike every other nation, has no written constitution;
namely, a single document which establishes the gov-   The "un-
ernment and lays down its fundamental principles.   written"
Everything that Parliament does is constitutional,   constitution
and all its acts are by a majority vote.   And yet there is an "un-

[1] See page 281.   [2] See Chapter XXXIX.

written" constitution which, though invisible and intangible, is
often more faithfully adhered to than the written constitutions in
other countries. Great documents, such as the Magna Charta
and the Bill of Rights, which proclaim the fundamental rights of
Englishmen; precedents and customs, such as ministerial responsibility and the disuse of the royal veto; famous laws, such as
the Reform Bills, profoundly influence Parliament against actions
which would be against the political traditions of the English
people.

If the English government is democratic, English society is
aristocratic. In no other country in Europe are there such sharp
class divisions based upon family and property. The
masses feel great respect for the aristocrats, "their
betters" whom they have traditionally regarded as
their rulers, and this feeling engenders a spirit of conservatism in public life. The popularity of the English aristocracy
is largely due to the fact that it has been conservative, not reactionary. To progressive measures it has generally been hostile,
but once a reform was established it did not attempt to overthrow
it. The aristocrats could, therefore, be trusted to maintain the
status quo, whatever that was. This attitude satisfied both the
liberal and conservative elements of the nation: the former because
sufficient pressure would bring concessions, and the latter because
revolutionary changes would be impossible. And so the English
aristocracy has been able to survive in the hostile environment of
modern democracy.

*English
aristocracy
conservative,
not reac-
tionary*

England is the original home of party government. The two
political parties are so intimately related to the governmental
system that they are considered a necessary part of it.
"His Majesty's Government," or the party in power,
is always faced by "His Majesty's Opposition," or the party out
of power; the former has complete control of all legislation, and the
latter limits itself merely to criticism. Historically, the two great
parties were the Conservative and Liberal which, between them,
divided the suffrages of the nation. As the issues changed so did
the parties; nevertheless each maintained a characteristic attitude
toward public questions. All that was traditional and established;
all that was privileged, the peerage, the landed estates, the Established Church, the Empire found their champion in the Conservative Party. Yet it has not always been opposed to progress. The

*The Con-
servatives*

Conservatives have loyally accepted the changes made, and sometimes have put through important reforms, such as Catholic Emancipation, factory legislation, the Reform Bill of 1867, and Irish land acts. Macaulay aptly compared the Conservatives to the hind legs of a stag whose fore legs are the Liberals. When in office the Conservatives were concerned mainly with Imperial and foreign affairs. They exhorted their fellow countrymen "to think imperially" and to take pride in England's great position in the world. For long it was dominated oy the aristocracy; nearly all its leaders were of that class or were promoted into it. But a change came at the end of the nineteenth century when a capitalistic element entered into the Conservative ranks, and succeeded in capturing the leadership and dictating the policies of the party. It now had behind it the powerful forces of both land and capital.

The Liberals appealed to another section of the people and to another tradition. It was the middle classes and the spirit of reform that gave vitality to the Liberal Party of the nineteenth century. The Reform Bill of 1832 may be said to have been its inspiration. Progress was to be made through political means; above all it was to be moderate and cautious. The "Condition of England" question chiefly interested the Liberals, who cared little for foreign affairs and neglected the Empire. A Liberal victory at the polls was generally due to the solid support of Scotland and Wales, the "Celtic fringe." England herself was Conservative. A new source of strength came to the Liberals with the enfranchisement of the working classes who, for a time, flocked to their standard. At the beginning of the twentieth century the inspiration of 1832 was exhausted, and the Liberal Party found itself without a program. It was saved from possible political extinction by Lloyd George, under whose influence it became the party of social reform.[1]

Although the two-party system was dominant, there existed two other parties, the Irish Nationalists and the Laborites. The former, however, were interested only in Home Rule, and they used all other issues to further their cause. The Laborites were at first few in numbers and cooperated with the Liberals; but the new situation created by the enfranchisement of the working class was fraught with danger to the Liberals. Should the Laborites succeed in detach-

The Liberals

The Irish Nationalists and the Laborites

[1] See page 271.

ing the workingmen from them, they would lose the support of
an immense number of voters. This proved to be the case. After
the World War the Labor Party grew so rapidly that it superseded
the Liberals as one of the two governing parties.[1]

GLADSTONE AND DISRAELI

During the latter half of the nineteenth century two great personalities, Gladstone and Disraeli, dominated English public life
Gladstone   to a degree almost unparalleled in its history. Their
(1809-98)   ideals and characters made a lasting impression upon
their own generation, and greatly influenced the generation that
followed them. William Ewart Gladstone came of a wealthy
middle-class family, and he received the best education possible
in the England of that day. Soon after his graduation from Oxford, where he greatly distinguished himself both as student and
debater, he entered politics and was elected a member of Parliament, in 1833, as a Tory. His eloquence and ability gained him
immediate recognition, and he was acclaimed by Macaulay as the
"brightest hope of the stern, unbending Tories." For some years
he was the faithful follower of Peel, from whom he learned the art
of adapting himself to changing political conditions. An earnest
study of English political institutions, a slowly dawning conviction
that a democratic England was inevitable, and a natural desire to
be the leader in the new time drew the rising young statesman to
the Liberal Party. He became its leader, and the chief spokesman
of progressive liberalism. Although frequently accused of being
a demagogue because of his eloquent defense of democratic principles, he was far indeed from being a radical. No statesman so
completely exemplified mid-Victorian Liberalism in all its strength
and weakness as did Gladstone. He was an earnest advocate of
reform, political, religious, educational, economic, but with full
consideration for the interests affected. To advance slowly and
hold fast to what was gained, liberty "broadening down from
precedent to precedent," as Tennyson expressed it, was the sum
and substance of Gladstone's political philosophy. His mind was
not speculative; he did not become interested in a question until
it was "ripe for settlement." Once convinced that a reform was
urgently demanded he would become its ardent champion and endeavor to put it through against the bitterest opposition. His

[1] See Chapter XXXIX.

BENJAMIN DISRAELI

WILLIAM EWART GLADSTONE

chief interest lay in domestic affairs, and there was hardly an important reform enacted during his career that was not directly or indirectly due to him.

Gladstone had but little interest in the Empire as a whole; like other Liberals of his day he regarded colonies largely as a source of expense and a burden to the mother country. In foreign affairs he followed pacific policies; whenever war threatened, his great anxiety was how to avoid it. "My name," he proudly declared, "stands in Europe for a symbol of the policy of peace, moderation, and non-aggression." Gladstone was a man of many abilities. As an orator he was unsurpassed, and received the homage of a generation that knew Bright, Disraeli, and Macaulay. He was also a master of national finance, and he could make the intricacies of a budget as interesting as an exposition of human rights. He once held the rapt attention of Parliament for five hours while he was expounding the budget for the year. Gladstone's political activity was, to a large extent, inspired by religious ideals, as he was a devout member of the Anglican Church. Political questions, in his view, were fundamentally moral questions; hence, party issues were struggles between what was eternally right and eternally wrong.

However, the Grand Old Man, as he was popularly called, had serious limitations. He was strongly opposed to social reform, partly because he believed in the doctrine of *laissez* His limita-*faire*, but mainly because he lacked both knowledge tions and understanding of the problems of the working class. "I reserve my worst billingsgate for socialism," he once declared; in his ignorance of social problems he confused socialism with social reform. He blundered badly in foreign affairs, having little understanding of the vast significance of Great Britain as a world power. As an orator Gladstone was very wordy, and often diffuse; his speeches are difficult reading. Disraeli once described him as a sophisticated rhetorician "intoxicated with the exuberance of his own verbosity."

It is hard to imagine a man more different from Gladstone than his great rival, Benjamin Disraeli. He was born of Jewish parents, but received Christian baptism at the age of thirteen. Disraeli Although he was not sent to any of the great English (1804–81) colleges, Disraeli was carefully educated by his father, Isaac Disraeli, who was a literary man of some talent. From his earliest youth, Disraeli was consumed with the ambition to play a prominent rôle in politics. In 1837, he was elected to Parliament where he created a sensation. When he rose to make his maiden speech, the House beheld a tall, thin, dark-faced young man with hair falling on his shoulders in ringlets, and dressed in a multi-colored costume. The members, solid, conventional Englishmen, were amazed. As Disraeli began speaking, his florid oratory produced such an uproar that he sat down, shouting defiantly that the day would come when Parliament would be glad to hear him. He continued to attract attention as a writer of political novels, which were remarkable not so much as works of fiction, but for their analysis of English political and social conditions. So profound and keen is the analysis, and so witty and eloquent the style, that all England was amazed. Disraeli leaped into fame as a political philosopher, second only to Burke.

Encouraged by his literary success, he determined to try his fortunes once more in the field of politics. He was elected to Parliament as a member of the Conservative Party. Peel, its leader, did not take kindly to Disraeli, whom he regarded as fantastic and unpractical. A deep personal antagonism arose between leader and follower, and when Peel yielded to the demand for the repeal of the Corn Laws, Disraeli came forward as the champion of protection. One day he rose in Parliament and delivered a philippic against Peel that vibrated with scorn and sarcasm; every sentence was a poisoned arrow that went straight to the mark. He characterized England's leading statesman as a "watcher of the atmosphere ready to trim his sails to the passing wind," whose Conservatism was "organized hypocrisy"; a man devoid of originality, a "sublime mediocrity" who, in order to rise in politics, became the "burglar of other men's minds." The effect of this speech was tremendous, and Peel was ousted from the leadership of his party.

Split into factions on account of the tariff issue, and discredited because of their opposition to reform, the Conservatives were in a bad way when Disraeli became their leader. He resolved "to educate his own party" to confront the problems of the day. In speeches and in novels, especially in *Coningsby* and *Sybil*, he pleaded with the Conservatives that they should cease being a "clique of nobles," as were the Tories, and become a national party representing all classes and advocating

Becomes leader of the Conservatives

Disraeli's principles

new principles in harmony with the new conditions. According to Disraeli control of government through privilege was no longer possible; hence, an aristocracy could maintain its ascendancy only through popular leadership by becoming the champions of reforms in harmony with the manners, the customs, the laws, and the traditions of the English people. The Conservatives should favor the extension of the franchise, a policy opposed by the Liberals, which would win for them the support of the working classes. Furthermore, they should favor social reform. "The time has arrived," Disraeli declared, "when social and not political improvement is the object which they ought to pursue." Unlike his contemporaries in politics, he fully realized the seriousness of modern social problems. "Two nations," he wrote, "between whom there is no intercourse and no sympathy, who are as ignorant of each other's habits, thoughts, and feelings as if they were dwellers in different zones or inhabitants of different planets, who are formed by a different breeding and fed by a different food, are ordered by different manners, and are not governed by the same laws — the Rich and the Poor." To Disraeli "the rights of labor were as sacred as the rights of property"; hence, he was opposed to the policy of *laissez faire*. The Liberals, he declared, represented the interests of the middle classes only, and were led by "a combination of oligarchs and philosophers who practice on the sectarian prejudices of a portion of the people." Startling as it may seem, Disraeli advocated an alliance between the aristocrats and the working class against the bourgeois, the two extremes as against the middle. The crown, too, must experience a new birth. Freed from the control of an oligarchy by the Reform Bill of 1832, it now had the opportunity to be a popular institution by becoming the nonpartisan voice of all England. Ancient reverences coupled with "Tory democracy" would make an irresistible appeal to all classes. Imperialism was another policy advocated by Disraeli. In a remarkable speech, delivered in 1872, he declared that the Liberals regarded a colony merely as a financial burden, and that they would destroy the Empire were it not for the loyalty of the colonies; and that colonial self-government should have been given as "part of a great policy of Imperial consolidation" accompanied by new and closer ties with the mother country, such as the establishment of an Imperial policy of defense and an Imperial representative council. Along with imperialism Disraeli advocated a vigorous foreign policy. England, he declared, should assert herself in international affairs; being a world power, it was her right to play a leading rôle in world politics. The highly imaginative Disraeli made a vivid appeal to the "sublime instinct of an ancient people," and he was acclaimed as the prophet of a new imperial England.

Personally, Disraeli was a good deal of a *poseur*. He cultivated a sphinx-like attitude which made him appear wiser than he really His limita-   was. In debate he was often specious, and his tions   speeches sometimes had a tinsel glitter that led many to suspect that he was more eager to attract attention than to pronounce a policy. In truth Disraeli was an actor on the political stage, but an actor who played in a drama of which he himself was the author.

THE GLADSTONIAN REFORMS

Although the workingmen had been enfranchised by the Conservatives they flocked to the Liberals who, under Gladstone's leadership, became more progressive than they had been since 1832. Gladstone became Premier for the first time in 1868, and he set himself earnestly to the task of creating a newer and better England through "Peace, Retrenchment, and Reform." During his four ministries he put through a number of reforms as notable as those that followed the Reform Bill of 1832.

The working classes were now triumphant. They demanded legal recognition of trade unions, which was granted by Parliament Establish-   in 1871.[1] Even more important was the passage of ment of   the Forster Education Act (1870) establishing a napopular   tional system of popular education. "We must education   educate our masters," was the sentiment of the new generation of statesmen, who were convinced that popular education was an essential condition of modern democracy. The declared aim of the Forster Act was to establish schools only where they were needed, "to complete the voluntary system and fill up the gaps." Great Britain was divided into school districts, and new schools were built, known as "Board schools," which were supported mainly by local taxation, and controlled by elected boards of education. As in France the national schools encountered the bitter opposition of the Church, in this case, the Anglican, which

[1] See page 286.

maintained many schools under its auspices. A controversy arose over religious instruction in the Board schools. It was finally decided to permit instruction in the Bible only, and to forbid the teaching of any "catechism or religious formulary which is distinctive of any denomination." As a result of the Forster Act popular education made great progress. Illiteracy decreased until it became practically non-existent.

A number of political reforms were passed, notably the establishment of the Australian, or secret ballot (1872), and a Corrupt Practices Act (1883) which forbade, under severe penalties, the bribery of voters, directly or indirectly. Reform Bill of 1884 But the most important of all the political measures of this period was the Reform Bill of 1884 which was the work of Gladstone ably seconded by Bright. The new reform gave the vote to the agricultural laborers by putting the county franchise on the same footing as that of the borough; henceforth, all householders who paid at least fifty dollars (£10) a year for lodgings had the privilege of voting. It is estimated that this third installment of democracy increased the electorate from three to five million. Universal, manhood suffrage was now virtually established in Great Britain; those still excluded from voting, chiefly sons living with their parents, and servants living with their employers, were comparatively few. Again England expanded the suffrage by contracting the property qualification. Parliament followed up the reform by a redistribution act which reapportioned the country into constituencies more or less equal in size.

Religious reform also enlisted the hearty support of Gladstone. The new voters, mainly Nonconformists, objected vigorously to an established church in whose doctrines they did not believe. An important step in the direction of religious equality was taken in disestablishing the Anglican Church in Ireland.[1] The requirement that only Anglicans should be granted degrees at Oxford and Cambridge was repealed in 1871 by an act of Parliament. The right to be a member of Parliament had been granted to Christians and Jews. Could it be withheld from atheists? Charles Bradlaugh, a well-known atheist agitator, was elected to Parliament in 1880. Instead of taking the customary oath, in which the words "so help me God" occurred, he wished to make merely an affirmation of loyalty. His request was

[1] See page 309.

denied, and he then offered to take the oath; but he was told that an oath could have no meaning for an atheist, and his election was declared null and void. A heated controversy arose over the question whether belief in God ought to be a test for membership in Parliament. Bradlaugh was reëlected but was again refused admission. But he persisted in his cause with the "zeal of a Christian martyr," and was finally admitted. The matter was definitely settled in 1888 by an act which legalized an affirmation of loyalty as a substitute for the customary oath. Now that an atheist was permitted to sit in Parliament, the last religious test for holding public office disappeared.

The problem that loomed up most threateningly during the Gladstone régime was Ireland. The Premier's sympathies had been enlisted on the side of the Irish, and when he assumed office he declared that his mission was to pacify Ireland. He zealously tried to carry out his mission through laws establishing religious equality, land reform, and Home Rule, all of which will be described in the chapter on Ireland. Disappointed with the defeat of the second Home Rule Bill and weakened by advancing age, the veteran statesman retired from public life in 1894. His last great speech was an attack on the House of Lords for its opposition to Irish Home Rule.

Gladstone's Irish measures

Gladstone's record in foreign affairs is short; he always sought peace. When the Boers defeated a British army, he promptly made peace and recognized their independence. In spite of earnest entreaties, he delayed sending a British army to relieve General Gordon who was besieged in Khartum, for which he was driven from office. In 1871, he amicably settled a controversy between Great Britain and the United States, known as the "Alabama Claims," which grew out of the claims of the United States against Great Britain for aiding the Alabama and other Southern privateers during the American Civil War. The matter was settled by a board of arbitrators who awarded the sum of $15,500,000 to the United States.

His foreign policy

THE DISRAELI MINISTRY

In 1874, Disraeli became Prime Minister of England. He was raised to the peerage as the Earl of Beaconsfield by Queen Victoria who greatly admired the statesman-novelist. His ministry, lasting six years, was as notable in foreign affairs as Gladstone's had been in domestic affairs. Not since Lord Chatham's day was England's foreign policy as vigorous as it became under Beaconsfield. Yet, for all his vigor, he closely followed England's traditional policy in international Disraeli's foreign policy affairs; namely, aloofness from Continental entanglements and the maintenance of the integrity of Turkey against Russian designs. He scored a great triumph in acquiring control of the Suez Canal (1875) which led to the British occupation of Egypt.[1] He also annexed the Transvaal and Baluchistan.[2] To dramatize his Imperial policy, Beaconsfield persuaded Parliament to confer a new title on the Queen. In 1877, Victoria was proclaimed Empress of India amidst great ceremonies; in India she was now the successor of the Mogul emperors. When the Russo-Turkish War broke out in 1877, England was greatly aroused. The advance of the Russian army was regarded as a threat to the existence of Turkey, to whose support England was pledged. The war spirit was fanned into a flame by Beaconsfield who compelled Russia to submit the Near Eastern Question to a European conference which met at Berlin.[3] At the Congress of Berlin, "Dizzy," as the Premier was popularly known, played a leading part in Europe's effort to solve the baffling problems in the Near East. For England he acquired the island of Cyprus which safeguarded still more the route to India. He returned home in triumph, bringing, as he said, "peace with honor."

In domestic affairs the Ministry had a more modest record. Its most important social reforms were the Trade Union Act of 1875, and the act of 1878 which codified and extended the factory laws. Beaconsfield's vision of social recon- His domestic policy struction faded when his aggressive imperialism brought him prestige and popularity. At one time, when the reforming zeal of the Liberals had somewhat abated, he had referred to them as "a range of exhausted volcanoes." Now his own zeal for reform abated. There was great discontent with the Ministry for its neglect of domestic affairs, and the outcome of the elections of 1880 was an overwhelming triumph for the Liberals.

THE CONSERVATIVE ERA (1895–1906)

When Beaconsfield died, in 1881, he left behind him a powerful Conservative Party which was largely his creation. His successor, as leader, was the Marquis of Salisbury, a member of the Cecil

[1] See page 650.   [2] See pages 632 and 642.   [3] See page 471.

family, famous since the days of Queen Elizabeth. He was a disciple

Salisbury   of Disraeli, and, like his master, was noted for caustic
wit, "a master of flouts and jibes"; but, unlike him,
he was a man of narrow, aristocratic outlook and therefore
lacking in sympathy with progressive ideas. Salisbury's chief
interest was foreign affairs, and he conducted England's foreign
policy very ably from the point of view of an aristocrat and an
imperialist.

Salisbury's chief associates were his nephew, Arthur James Balfour (later Lord Balfour), and Joseph Chamberlain. Although an

Balfour   aristocrat and a Conservative, Balfour's fine personal
character and tolerant open-mindedness brought him
respect even from the extreme radicals. He was an excellent example of the scholar in politics, his speeches being distinguished
by literary and philosophic qualities of a high order. In 1902, he
succeeded his uncle as leader of the Conservatives, but as he was
more interested in philosophy than in politics he was not much of
a success as a party leader.

By far the ablest of the new Conservative leaders was Joseph
Chamberlain. He began his political career as a Liberal, and

Chamberlain   attracted attention by reforming the government of
Birmingham, his home city, whose politics he dominated for many years. When Gladstone introduced the first Home
Rule Bill, Chamberlain was so strongly opposed to it that he led a
secession from the Liberal Party that went over to the Conservative
side where they formed a group called the "Unionists." Chamberlain was a typical business man in politics. Aggressive, decisive,
shrewd, and efficient, he was not much beholden to the aloof Salisbury and to the refined Balfour, yet his importance in British
politics was greater than either, for his name is identified with
the movement for tariff reform and with the reorganization of the
British Empire, which will be described later.

The rising tide of imperialism swept the Conservatives into
office again and again. In 1895, they won an overwhelming victory,

Imperial and   and stayed in office for a decade. During this period
foreign   the Boer War took place, the most important event
affairs   in the history of the British Empire since the American
Revolution.[1] The government was equally aggressive in foreign
affairs. Strained relations with France reached a crisis in the

[1] See page 667.

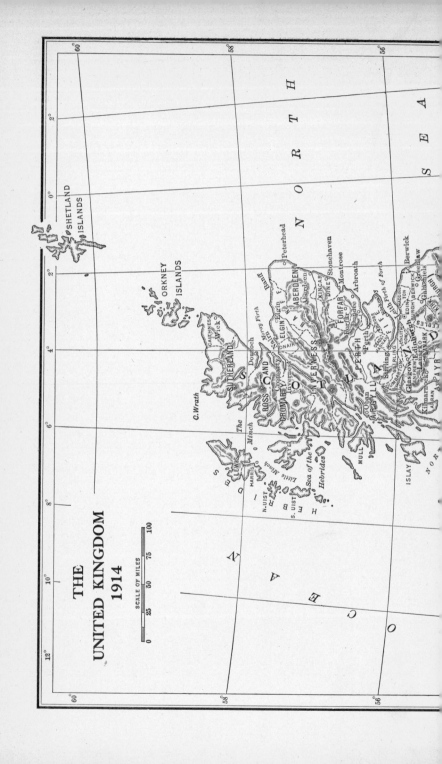

Fashoda Affair,[1] but the question was amicably settled. A dispute with Venezuela, in 1895, over the boundary line between that country and British Guiana almost led to a war with the United States on account of the Monroe Doctrine; but, in this instance also, the question was amicably settled.

In domestic affairs the Irish question chiefly occupied public attention. The Conservatives were opposed to Home Rule, yet they clearly realized the necessity of doing something for Ireland in order to quiet the agitation. In 1898, they established popularly elected local councils in Ireland; in 1891 and again in 1903 they passed drastic land reforms.[2] For England, however, the Conservatives did little during their long lease of power. Their most important reform was the County Councils Act (1888) which established popularly elected councils in the rural districts. A general reaction was setting in against the Conservatives, who had neglected what Carlyle called the "Condition of England" question. The elections of 1905 resulted in a great triumph for the Liberals, who won a large majority of the seats. A notable feature of these elections was the appearance of a new party, the Labor Party, which won twenty-nine seats.

Neglect of domestic matters

THE LIBERAL ERA (1906-16)

(a) THE NEW LEADERS

There now came into power a Liberal ministry whose work was epoch-making. The laws that it passed made revolutionary changes in the social and political structure of the nation. The liberal England of Gladstone, with her concern for political freedom, religious toleration, and individual liberty, was transformed into a radical England that was deeply concerned with the social and economic welfare of the lower classes. Radical and even revolutionary forces, socialism and syndicalism, that had long been active among the lower classes, now rose to the surface of English society, and challenged the existing middle-class order just as, a century before, the forces of democracy had challenged those of aristocracy. As a consequence, the historic English policy of *laissez faire* was completely abandoned, and the state became actively interested in the problem of labor, bringing the weight of its authority to bear on the solution

Liberals repudiate laissez faire

[1] See page 652.   [2] See page 312.

of this problem in the interest of all classes in general and in that of the working classes in particular. In this work the Liberal Ministry had the coöperation of the Labor Party which made its first appearance in the elections of 1905. The circumstances of its origin and the causes of its rapid growth will be described presently.

A remarkable group of statesmen now came to the front. The leading members of the Ministry were Sir Henry Campbell-

The new Liberal leaders
Bannerman, who was Prime Minister until 1908, when he was succeeded by Herbert Henry Asquith, who remained at the head of the government till 1916; John Morley (later Lord Morley), the eminent historian and philosopher; John Burns, the famous labor leader; Winston Churchill, a Conservative who had become a Liberal; Sir Edward Grey (later Lord Grey), a Foreign Minister who was destined to play a part in the drama of 1914; and David Lloyd George. Asquith (later, Lord Oxford) had been for many years a faithful follower of Gladstone. A man of moderate views, a logical and forceful orator, and with large experience in public life, the Premier had considerable influence with the British public. His abilities, however, lay in harmonizing the moderate and radical elements in his party, rather than in initiating new policies.

Chief among the architects of social England was Lloyd George, whose rise to power in British politics was phenomenal. The son

Lloyd George (1863-)
of a poor Welsh schoolmaster, he had none of the advantages of wealth, education, or social position which were then so essential to any aspirant for a political career in Britain. Early in life he studied law, and became a lawyer in his home town. He soon became active in politics, and was elected to Parliament as a Liberal. During the Boer War, Lloyd George was prominent as a pacifist, and assailed the government for waging war against a simple, peaceful people in the interest of the capitalist exploiters of South Africa. He exhibited such extraordinary powers both as a popular orator and as a politician that, in spite of his brief experience, he was made a member of the cabinet when his party took office in 1906. Thereafter, he was the leading figure in British politics, as nearly all the great laws passed during the Asquith Ministry were inspired or fashioned by him. Few men in English politics were so enthusiastically acclaimed and so bitterly denounced as this "little Welsh attorney," as Lloyd George was contemptuously called by his Conservative

opponents. He became the voice and the arm of the new radical England that was bent upon a reconstruction of the social system in favor of the poor and the unfortunate. Gifted with a keen intelligence, a winning personality, burning eloquence, and, above all, with a social imagination, Lloyd George became the popular idol of his countrymen, who turned to him, as they had once turned to Gladstone, to lead them in the battle for reform.

(b) SOCIAL REFORM

England, the eldest daughter of the Industrial Revolution, had forged ahead of all other nations. Her manufacturers, merchants, capitalists, and shipbuilders reaped immense wealth, but the great mass of her workingmen shared only slightly in this prosperity. On the other hand, they suffered in full measure from all the evils of the new system: unemployment, low wages, long hours, child labor, industrial accidents, and industrial diseases. Seldom were wages sufficiently high to enable a workingman to save for a "rainy day." Unemployment and sickness brought hardships to millions who were forced to have recourse to charity. Old age stared tragically in the face of the workingman who could rarely find employment when he grew old and feeble. Great wealth and dire poverty were strikingly evident in England. In the beginning of the twentieth century, according to the most authoritative writers, three per cent of the population of the United Kingdom was classified as rich, nine per cent as comfortable, and eighty-eight per cent as poor. About one half of the entire income of the nation was enjoyed by twelve per cent of the population; and one third, by three per cent. As the English rich inherited wealth so did the English poor inherit poverty. Millions lived on the verge of starvation, and the physical condition of many of the workers in the large cities bordered on degeneracy.

There was deep interest in the condition of the masses. Many feared that the stamina of the English race would be undermined, which might possibly lead to national ruin in case of a conflict with a powerful enemy. During the Boer War the physical requirements for the army had to be reduced considerably in order to get sufficient soldiers. It was clearly realized that charity, whether private or public, could do but little to solve the problem of poverty. There was only one power, the State, reaching into every corner of the land and con-

trolling every individual in the nation, that was sufficiently powerful to cope with the situation.   A new school of writers appeared,
notably Sidney and Beatrice Webb, Charles Booth, George Bernard
Shaw, and L. G. Chiozza-Money, who repudiated the ideas of the
Manchester School, and forcefully advocated that the State should
become active in bettering social conditions in order to help those
who were handicapped in the struggle for existence.

During the early part of the twentieth century, England, inspired
by the social reforms of Germany, passed a number of social laws
Factory re-   which had far-reaching effects on the life and character
form   of her people.   The factory laws were unified in a single
code, issued in 1902, which embodied the chief factory reforms
gained during the nineteenth century; new provisions were added
in order to remedy some of the worst evils of the industrial system.
The employment of children under twelve, in a factory, was forbidden; the labor of those between the ages of twelve and eighteen
was strictly regulated as to hours, holidays, overtime, and meals;
and factory sanitation was carefully supervised.   In 1906, Parliament adopted a mine code: employment of women and children
was forbidden; conditions in the mines were minutely regulated;
and severe penalties were provided for infractions of the rules.
Two years later (1908) a law established an eight-hour day for all
labor in the mines.

To better the conditions of employment in factory and mine
was to go but a slight distance toward the solution of the social
Problem of   problem.   Poverty due to low wages was a great evil,
insecurity   but a still greater evil was the insecurity felt by
millions of workingmen, who might, at any time, find themselves
utterly destitute, not because of their fault or of that of their
employers, but because of accidents, illness, unemployment, and
old age.   "The root trouble of our social system is the precarious-
ness of living," declared Lloyd George.   Something had to be
done by the community as represented by the State "to fill up the
gaps in the life of the industrial classes," by giving a sense of
security to the millions who were at the mercy of modern industrialism.

In 1906, a comprehensive Workmen's Compensation Act was
passed applying to industrial and agricultural workers, clerks,
servants, and sailors.   Employers had to compensate their employees for injury or disease sustained in the course of employ-

ment without appeal by the latter to the courts of law. Compensation was graded according to the seriousness of the injury; in case of death the dependents of the employee were to receive a benefit. This law recognized *Workmen's compensation* the principle that a workingman is a part of the industrial machine; hence, the responsibility for his well-being is placed on the employer.

To remedy the evil of poverty in old age, the Old Age Pensions Act was passed in 1908. It provided for pensions to laborers after the age of seventy;[1] the funds were to come entirely from the public treasury. Those who favored *Old Age Pensions* the law argued that it was the duty of the State to care for the veterans of industry, and that the pension, although not large enough to support a man, might save him from going to the poorhouse. The law was opposed by the Conservatives on the ground that it was non-contributory. They argued that it would tend to weaken the spirit of self-reliance of the laborer, and that it would prove a great burden on the taxpayers.

A parliamentary report, issued in 1890, on conditions in the needle trades, revealed a very bad state of affairs. Hours were long, and wages below the poverty line. Most of the workers in these trades were women who were un- *Minimum wage* skilled and unorganized. In 1909, a minimum wage law was passed to apply only in the "sweated" trades; the rate of wages was to be determined by boards composed of representatives of the employers, of the employees, and of the government. This act, though moderate, was an innovation, and was greatly favored by the trade unions. In 1912, minimum wage legislation was extended to the coal industry.

By far the most important social reform was the National Insurance Act of 1911, fathered by Lloyd George. It provided for insurance against sickness and unemployment for workingmen, which was to be contributory and com- *Social insurance* pulsory. When the plan for national insurance was introduced in Parliament, it encountered the opposition of the Conservatives. They declared that, by making insurance compulsory, the act violated the English ideal of individual freedom and established a principle foreign to Englishmen; namely, the control of the individual by the State. In reply the Liberals asserted that sufficient provision had been made for voluntary insurance for the better-

[1] Important changes were made in this law after the World War. See Chapter XXXIX.

to-do workingmen, but for the very poor, who were either unable
or unwilling to insure themselves, compulsion coupled with State
aid was necessary.

The law consisted of two parts: (1) insurance against sickness
and invalidity,[1] and (2) insurance against unemployment.   All
Insurance   employed men and women, between sixteen and sixty-
against sick-   five whose wages were below a certain amount, had to
ness   insure against sickness and invalidity. The employers,
workers, and the government all contributed to the fund on the
theory that it was to the interest of all.   Various kinds of benefits
were to be given: money for a definite period, free medicines, free
treatment in a sanatorium, and free medical attention by physicians
selected by the government.

Unemployment insurance was an innovation in social legislation.
Hitherto noticeable only in times of industrial depression, unem-
Insurance   ployment in England became a chronic condition at the
against un-   end of the nineteenth century. Population increased at
employment   a faster rate than industry, and only few workingmen
emigrated.   The situation at times became alarming, and remedies
were sought for this industrial illness.   In 1909, Parliament passed
a law establishing a national system of labor exchanges to function as unemployment bureaus.   More important was insurance
against unemployment provided for in the National Insurance Act.
Workers in specified trades, where unemployment was prevalent,
were compelled to insure against unemployment. The fund was
to be made up of contributions from the employers, the employees,
and the government; the insured, when out of work, were to
receive money benefits for a limited period.

The social reforms of the Asquith Ministry constituted its chief
title to fame.   These reforms did not abolish poverty, but they did
much to ameliorate the lot of the working classes.   They gave a
sense of security to millions who had no surplus to fall back upon
in case misfortune or old age deprived them of their earning
capacity.

(c) RELIGIOUS, EDUCATIONAL, AND POLITICAL REFORMS

Social reforms were not advanced by the Liberals to the neglect
of other matters.   True to their traditions they gave earnest atten-

---

[1] By "invalidity" is meant total or partial disablement such as the loss of sight
or of limbs.

tion to religious, educational, and political reforms. In spite of many changes in the religious life of the nation, the Anglican Church still remained the official church as by law established. However, the movement for separation was gaining headway. Although neither party was committed to any religious belief, the Conservatives were generally favored by the Anglicans, and the Liberals, by the Nonconformists; hence, it was to the Liberals that the country looked for changes in the religious system.

When George V ascended the throne, Parliament repealed the coronation oath which contained a denunciation of the Catholic religion as "superstitious and idolatrous." It substituted a royal declaration according to which
the King promised to maintain the laws governing
the Protestant succession. An important step taken
toward religious equality was the disestablishment of the Anglican Church in Wales. For many years it had been the national grievance of the Welsh people, most of whom are Nonconformists, that they were compelled to support an "alien" church. The Liberals came out in favor of disestablishing the Anglican Church in Wales, a policy which was opposed by the Conservatives, who feared that such a step would be a precedent for a similar policy in England. In 1912, a bill was passed by the Commons separating Church and State in Wales. The Anglican bishops in Wales lost their seats in the House of Lords; and the Church was "disendowed" of much of its property.[1]

Disestablishment of the Welsh Church

After the Forster Act an educational problem arose which caused much controversy. There were now two systems of education, the national Board schools and the private voluntary
schools, chiefly Anglican, where sectarian instruction
was obligatory. Both received subsidies from Parliament; the former, however, got most of its support from local taxes, and the latter from voluntary contributions. In 1902, a Conservative government put through a new education law which abolished the local school boards, and put both the Board and the voluntary schools under the control of the county and borough councils. But the voluntary schools retained their sectarian teaching, though provision was made for "undenominational" religious teaching.

The school question

---

[1] The Lords refused to pass the bill which, according to the Parliament Act, became law in 1914. Owing to the World War the law was suspended until after the war when it became operative.

Provision was also made for the support of both systems from local taxation. This law encountered strong opposition from the Non-conformists and from those who favored secular education.

The Asquith Ministry had embarked on an ambitious program of social reform which required a large outlay of money.   In order
The Budget   to raise the necessary funds the government decided
of 1909   to lay new taxes.   In 1909, Lloyd George, as Chancellor of the Exchequer, introduced the now famous budget.   It proposed to "lay the heaviest burden on the broadest back," or to raise money by taxing the rich landlords.   Its chief provisions were: (1) an "unearned increment" duty of twenty per cent on the increase in the value of land when due to site and not to improvement by the owner, on the ground that the public should get some return for the values which it creates; "luck sharing," the Chancellor called this provision; (2) a "reversion" duty of ten per cent on the increase in the value of land leased for over twenty-one years, to be paid by the lessor on the expiration of the lease; (3) an undeveloped land duty of two per cent on idle land, and particularly on game preserves; and (4) a mineral rights duty of five per cent on mining royalties received by the owners of mines from the companies that operated them.   Land used for agricultural purposes was exempted from the new taxes.   The budget introduced a new principle in taxation; namely, that those who acquired property without laboring for it were to pay a special tax. The tax collector, in future, would ask not only, "How much have you?" but also, "How did you get it?"   This was a "war budget," said the Chancellor, the object of which was to wage war against poverty which, he hoped, would some day be "as remote to the people of this country as the wolves which once infested its forests."

The budget was assailed by the Conservatives as a social and political revolution without a mandate from the people, as a
Lloyd   subversion of the constitution, and as a demagogic
George de-   attempt to confiscate private property in land.   Feel-
nounces the   ing ran high on both sides.   Lloyd George, as the
landlords   chief protagonist of the "People's Budget," delivered
eloquent speeches, both inside and outside of Parliament, which roused the greatest enthusiasm among the middle and lower classes, who hailed him as their champion against the aristocrats.   In one of his speeches the Chancellor threateningly asked these questions: "Who ordained that a few should have the land of Britain as a

perquisite? Who made ten thousand people owners of the soil and the rest of us trespassers in the land of our birth? . . . Where did the table of the law come from? Whose finger inscribed it?" The budget passed the Commons by an overwhelming majority, but it was thrown out by the Lords. In defeating the measure the Lords had violated the historic precedent that required the enactment of money bills passed by the lower house. Immediately a resolution was passed by the Commons which denounced the action of the Lords as a breach of the constitution and a usurpation of the privileges of the Commons. Premier Asquith declared that the "power of the purse," once used against the crown, would now be used against the Lords. Parliament was then dissolved, and elections followed in January, 1910, with the budget as the issue between the parties.

The result was a disappointment to both Liberals and Conservatives; neither had a majority of the seats. In order to stay in office, the Asquith Ministry accepted the support of Problem of the Irish Nationalists and the Laborites, who now held the Lords the balance of power in the Commons. But this support was given for a price, the promise of an Irish Home Rule Bill and of labor legislation. The budget was again passed in the Commons, and true to the precedent of 1832,[1] the Lords now also passed it. Unfortunately for the latter, however, the Liberal Ministry was dependent for its existence on the Irish and Laborites, two uncompromising enemies of the aristocracy, who were determined to undermine its influence, the Irish because the Lords would oppose a Home Rule bill, and the Laborites because the Lords would oppose their radical program. The question of the relation between the two houses now came prominently before the public. Before 1832 the power of both Lords and Commons over legislation had, in theory, been equal; in fact the former were supreme because, owing to the rotten-borough system, they controlled most of the representatives. In spite of the precedent established by the Reform Bill of 1832, the Lords continued to exercise almost as much legislative power as the Commons. Should the Ministry insist on having its way, it would have to appeal to the country by a dissolution of Parliament in the hope of receiving a new majority which would convince the Lords that the people supported the Commons. But elections are proverbially uncertain. Though not

[1] See page 130.

responsible to the Lords, the Ministry would yield to them rather than risk defeat by appealing to the country. Theoretically the representatives of the people in its more sober mood, "the nation's second thought," the Lords in reality represented the economic interests of the landed aristocracy and the political interests of the Conservative Party, as at all times an overwhelming majority of the upper house was of this class and party. Liberals were often created peers when a Liberal government was in power. But these peers did not long remain Liberal. To be a member of the upper house is a great social distinction; its leaders, coming from old Conservative families, would bring social pressure to bear on the new peers, which often had the effect of "converting" them from Liberalism to Conservatism. When a Liberal ministry was in power, the Lords bristled with opposition to its measures, sometimes drastically amending them and sometimes defeating them altogether. In this way the Conservative Party, when out of power, always relied on the Lords to obstruct the legislation of its opponents, which so exasperated the Liberals that they often threatened "to mend or end" the Lords.

When the Liberals returned to power in 1906, the Commons promptly passed a number of reforms to which the Liberals were
Liberal threat to the Lords
pledged, but they were as promptly defeated by the Lords on the ground that the people were also opposed to them. The anger of the Liberals now rose to a high pitch. In 1907, the Commons passed a resolution which declared that in order "to give effect to the will of the people as expressed by elected representatives, it is necessary that the power of the other house to alter or reject bills passed by this house shall be so restricted by law as to secure that, within the limit of a single parliament, the final decision of the Commons shall prevail."

When the budget of 1909 came before the Lords, Lord Rosebery, although strongly opposed to the measure, advised its passage on
The Parliament Act of 1911
the ground that its rejection would be followed by a determined effort to reduce the powers of the upper house. "The menaces," he said, "which were addressed to this house in the old days were addressed by statesmen who had at heart the balance of the constitutional forces in this country. The menaces addressed to you now come from a wholly different school of opinion, who wish for a single chamber and who set no value on the controlling and revising forces of a second

chamber — a school of opinion which, if you like it and do not dread the word, is eminently revolutionary in essence, if not in fact." After the elections following the rejection of the budget, the Liberals were infuriated at having lost their great majority in the Commons. They now determined to come to grips with the Lords. In December, 1910, the Commons was again dissolved, but the outcome of the new elections was about the same as that in January, 1910. The Asquith Ministry continued in office, backed by the Liberal-Irish-Labor combination. A bill was introduced in 1911, later known as the Parliament Act, which provided (1) that any bill, specified by the Speaker of the Commons as a money bill, which passes the lower house must also pass the upper house within one month; otherwise, it becomes law without its consent; (2) that all other bills, if passed in three successive sessions of the Commons, whether by the same house or not, and defeated by the Lords, become law without their consent, provided two years have elapsed between the first consideration of the bill and its final enactment; and (3) that the duration of a Parliament shall be limited to five instead of to seven years. Parliament was in the throes of heated debates on the subject. Asquith declared that a second chamber dominated always by the same party was a "system of false balance and loaded dice" which the Liberals would no longer tolerate. Balfour pleaded for a strong second chamber because Britain "alone among the great countries of the world had no written constitution and no safeguards against violent changes." The Commons passed the measure, but it was thrown out by the Lords. As in 1832, the problem arose of passing a bill in the face of the opposition of the Lords, and once more it was solved in a similar manner. Asquith appealed to King George V and received guarantees that peers, pledged in support of the bill, would be created in sufficient numbers to insure its passage. The Lords, confronted with the prospect of being "swamped," yielded, and the bill became law.

As great a change in the British system of government was wrought by the Parliament Act of 1911 as by the Reform Bill of 1832. It fixed anew the relation between the two Single-houses by giving almost unchecked power to the Com- chamber mons and merely a suspensive veto to the Lords; in government effect, it established a single-chamber government for England. Instead of following the French policy of abolishing institutions opposed to democratic ideas, the English have endeavored to preserve the continuity of their national life by keeping ancient institutions intact, but depriving them of all real power. The Lords, like the crown, was now an honored appendage, not an integral part of the British system of government.

THE LAND QUESTION

The political problem of the House of Lords brought to the public mind the economic problem of landlordism. A land monopoly
Land monopoly existed in England which had no counterpart in any other country of Europe. At the beginning of the twentieth century it was estimated that two thirds of all the land in England and Wales was owned by about 10,000 persons, and nine tenths of all Scotland by about 1700 persons. Fully one tenth of all Great Britain was the property of twenty-seven lords. Many of the large estates were "entailed," and could not be legally sold, mortgaged, or divided. Agriculture was based upon what was called the "three-interest system," the lords who owned the land; the tenant farmers who rented their farms for a definite period; and the agricultural laborers who were employed by the farmers. In England the peasant proprietor of the Continent had no counterpart.

Land had attractions for certain classes of Englishmen because it brought social, political, and economic privileges to the owner.
Privileges of landowners The highest social rank was accorded to the owner of an estate, who was generally the local justice of the peace, controlled the "living," or the appointment of the Anglican minister of the parish church, and took precedence in all matters of consequence in his vicinity. If the "squire" desired to enter political life, he found a ready-made constituency in his tenants, who were expected to vote for him. Social and political advantages of land ownership were so great in England that the cultivation of the soil was of secondary importance. Large tracts of land were kept as game preserves. On the land rented to farmers there were also "sporting tenants," generally rich men from the city who paid the lord for the privilege of hunting during certain times of the year. Hunting was a social entertainment indulged in by the upper classes, and often the lord spent more on improving the game preserves than on improving the arable land.

The tenant farmers held their land on short leases. Whatever improvements they made belonged to the lord at the expiration of the lease; hence, they were slow to introduce new methods of cultivation. Compensation for improvements made by the tenant and for damages done to the crops by game was allowed, but the difficulty of computing such compensation threw the burden on the farmer, not on the lord. Insecurity of tenure, due to short leases, was a serious evil, and farmers were forced to pay increases in rent in order to continue in their holding upon which they had expended labor and money. Landlordism was frequently softened by the paternal attitude of the lord to the tenant. Unlike the case in Ireland, the English landlords and tenants were of the same race, of the same faith, and of the same political party.

Condition of the tenant farmers

Far worse was the lot of the agricultural laborers. They worked long hours, received low wages, and lived in "tied" cottages belonging to the estate. A laborer was paid partly in money wages and partly in being allowed the use of a cottage. Strange as it may seem, there was a serious problem of congestion in the English countryside. The cottages, although picturesque in appearance, were often overcrowded and unsanitary, as the owners refused to improve them or to build new ones because they were not rented on a commercial basis. Attempts of the agricultural laborers to form unions were frustrated by the lords and farmers, who were able to inflict a double punishment upon the recalcitrants, loss of employment and eviction from their homes. In despair, thousands of rural laborers went to the cities or emigrated to the colonies.

The agricultural laborers

Conditions in the world as a whole, as well as land monopoly, helped to create the rural problem in England. The railway and steamboat brought large quantities of cheap food from abroad. With the introduction of cold storage in transit, the importation of meats and of dairy products became feasible. The farmers on the Continent, sheltered by high tariff walls, managed to survive — at least to a considerable degree. But those in free-trade Britain could not stand the severe competition, and many were forced to the wall. In 1914, Great Britain produced only twenty per cent of her food supply. Her cereals and beef came from the Americas; her mutton, from Australia; her dairy products, from Denmark and Holland; and her vegetables, from France.

Decline of agriculture

The decline of agriculture led to the decline of the rural population. In 1914, it was only twenty-two per cent of the total population of Great Britain. Certain parts of England presented the strange phenomenon of "part slum, part desert," teeming cities surrounded by an almost deserted countryside. "We wish to develop our undeveloped estates," declared Sir Henry Campbell-Bannerman, "and to colonize our own country. The health and stamina of the nation are bound up with the maintenance of a large class of workers on the soil. The town population redundant, the country population decimated is a subversion of healthy national life."

Decline of the rural population

So deeply was England absorbed in developing her commerce and industry that she paid scant attention to her agriculture. When her rivalry with Germany became acute she first realized that her dependence upon foreign food might put her in a dangerous position in case of war. Were England's supremacy at sea destroyed and her shores effectively blockaded she would be brought to the point of starvation in a very short time. A movement began for the rehabilitation of agriculture. It was realized from the start that the existing land monopoly would have to be modified or destroyed in order to encourage the growth of an agricultural population. A parliamentary commission was appointed to investigate the land situation, and its reports, issued in 1913–14, made the following recommendations. Parliament was to enact a minimum wage law for agricultural laborers; the government was to finance a scheme of rural housing; the landlords were to be deprived of the right to let land for sporting purposes; full compensation was to be paid to the tenant for all improvements made by him; the government was to regulate leases of farms and encourage "small holdings," or the leasing of farms by local county councils; and, finally, a land commission was to be established to regulate the relations between landlord and tenant, and to encourage the development of agriculture.

Movement for land reform

PROGRESS OF TRADE UNIONISM

At the beginning of the twentieth century, the trade unions assumed a position of great importance both to their members and to the nation at large. How they came into existence has already been described; it now remains to tell of their remarkable progress.

The Combination Laws,[1] for all their severity, did not succeed in stamping out combinations of workingmen who or- Revolu-ganized under assumed forms. Being deprived of the tionary unionism right to strike, the workingmen readily gave ear to revolutionary agitation which, in the first half of the nineteenth century, developed into Chartism. Among those who interested themselves in the working-class movement was the Utopian social-ist, Robert Owen.[2] Under his inspiration there was organized, in 1834, the Grand Consolidated Trades Union, consisting of about half a million men in various trades. All labor was to join one big union whose primary object was to usher in a new social system by means of a general strike. The scheme failed, and the Grand Consolidated soon broke up into small craft unions.

In the middle of the nineteenth century there appeared the Amalgamated Society of Engineers, consisting of workingmen in the engineering trades. It was exceedingly moderate Moderate in its policies, avoiding agitation and even strikes. It unionism had a large treasury which was used chiefly as a benefit fund for those members who were sick or unemployed, an innovation in those days, which attracted a large following. Many unions were formed on the model of the Amalgamated, which caused public opinion to view organized labor more favorably. In 1859, a law permitted a laborer peaceably "to persuade others to cease or abstain from work, in order to obtain the rate of wages or the altered hours of labor agreed to by him and others." The unions were now in an anomalous position: they were permitted to strike, but if they did so they were liable to be prosecuted on the charge of conspiracy, as unions were still held by the law to be "in re-straint of trade," and strikes were still regarded as criminal con-spiracies.

The Reform Bill of 1867, which enfranchised the working classes, was bound to result in laws favorable to trade unionism, as both Liberals and Conservatives competed for the support Repeal of of the new voters. During the years 1867–69 there the Combi-nation laws was widespread labor unrest; strikes, accompanied by violence, were matters of everyday occurrence. In order fully to understand the questions in dispute between capital and labor, a royal commission was appointed to investigate all aspects of the differences between them. The report of this commission was a

[1] See page 40.   [2] See page 567.

notable one; its recommendations were embodied in the law of 1871 passed by the Liberals, and in that of 1875, passed by the Conservatives, which constitute the "charter of liberties" of English trade unionism.   The Combination Laws were repealed, and workingmen were henceforth permitted to perform those acts in combination that they could legally do as individuals.   The unions were put on a legal basis, and the old theory of "restraint of trade," under which they had been prosecuted, was abrogated; hence, a unionist could no longer be charged with conspiracy.   Strikes were made legal; peaceful picketing, or the right of strikers to persuade other workingmen not to take their places, was permitted; and the principle of "collective bargaining" was allowed.   These laws were passed against the opposition of the manufacturers who contended that they alone had the right to determine the conditions of industry, and that any attempt to limit this right, either by the trade unions or by the government, was a violation of the fundamental rights of liberty and property.   Once social stigma and legal barriers were removed from the trade unions, their membership grew rapidly.   A national Trade Union Congress was organized, representing organized labor, which met annually to decide on common policies.   The English labor unions became models for workingmen throughout the world; their discipline was excellent, their treasuries well filled, and their morale admirable.   They showed such moderation that even the conservative classes became finally convinced of the utility of labor unions under modern conditions.

Those workers who had won the fight for recognition were mainly the skilled who were organized.   Among the unskilled, there was much discontent; but the difficulties in the way of organizing poorly paid and overworked workingmen were very great.   The first strike of unskilled laborers was that of the dockers, who were organized by John Burns, the most famous labor leader of his day.   It was a remarkable demonstration by many thousands of laborers, whose wages were low, hours long, and employment uncertain.   The strike was free from violence, and it aroused the greatest sympathy among prominent men in all walks of life, who warmly supported the dockers in their demand for better conditions.   The strikers won, and the victory helped to spread the idea of unionism among the unskilled.

After their enfranchisement the English workingmen were di-

vided as to what course to pursue politically. Some followed the
example of the workingmen on the Continent and The Taff
organized socialist parties.   But the overwhelming Vale deci-
majority affiliated themselves with the Liberal Party sion
as the party of reform and progress.   But a movement began for
a third party to represent labor, which received a great impetus
as a result of the Taff Vale decision of 1901.   During a strike of the
railway men against the Taff Vale Railway, in Wales, efforts were
made by the strikers to prevent the company from bringing in
strike-breakers by picketing the railway stations.   The union was
sued by the railway company, and the case came before the House
of Lords, acting as the supreme court of England.   It rendered a
decision according to which a union was held responsible for illegal
acts of its members acting by its authority; to station pickets in
order to force others to strike and to boycott an enterprise were
declared illegal proceedings; and the court therefore ordered the
union to pay damages to the company.   The strike was broken as
a result of the heavy damages that the union was forced to pay.

The Taff Vale decision alarmed the trade unions.   It was denounced by them as a nullification of the laws of 1871 and 1875
by making strikes virtually impossible through the The Trades
liability of the union for damages in a trade dispute. Disputes Act
Any union that posted pickets during a strike now put its funds
in jeopardy. A conference met, consisting of representatives of
the trade unions and of several socialist organizations, which determined to form a new party to represent the interests of organized labor and of the lower classes generally.   In this way was
born the Labor Party which, at its first venture in the elections of
1905, succeeded in winning twenty-nine seats.   When the Laborites
appeared in Parliament there was a sensation.   What was to be
the attitude of the older parties?   Would they ignore them?   In
the small Labor group the English statesmen saw a great historic force which could not be ignored; they represented the
largest and best organized working class in the world, now politically conscious as a class and determined to be a factor in the
affairs of state.   Both Liberals and Conservatives welcomed the
Laborites because they now wished to coöperate with them in
solving the social problems that troubled the country.   To conciliate the aroused workingmen, Parliament passed the Trades
Disputes Act (1906), which (1) nullified the Taff Vale decision by

legalizing peaceful picketing; and which (2) put the trade unions in the privileged position of associations against which no damage suits could be brought because of alleged "tortious acts" of its members in respect to trade disputes. "An act done by a combination of persons in furtherance of a trade dispute," declared the law, "shall not be actionable if it would not have been actionable if done by one person."

Organized labor now had two weapons, the trade union and a political party, and it was not slow to use either or both, as the Character of occasion arose, to advance its interests. At all the the Labor succeeding elections the Laborites consolidated and Party increased their forces until they formed, in 1914, a compact group of about forty members. The chief leaders were Keir Hardie, a labor leader of unusual ability; and J. Ramsay MacDonald and Philip Snowden, intellectuals, who had espoused the cause of the working class. Although the leaders were socialists, the great body of their followers held views not very different from those of the Liberals. The party at first refused to commit itself to socialist doctrines; it was content to leaven Parliament with men having a knowledge of the wants of the masses.[1]

In order to pay the campaign expenses of its candidates and the salaries of its representatives, the Laborites drew upon trade-union The Os- funds. But the House of Lords, in 1909, rendered a borne decision, known as the "Osborne Judgment," which Judgment prohibited the use of trade-union funds for political purposes. This decision was a severe blow to the party, which had no other financial resources. A new law (1913), however, defined a trade union so as to include the right of political action; but money to finance political activity had to come from a special fund, and any member of a union who was opposed to its political activity was exempted from contributing to this fund. As a result of the Osborne Judgment, payment of members of Parliament was established in 1911, thus realizing one of the "points" of the Chartists.

Unrest among the laboring classes was rapidly increasing. At first socialism, and then syndicalism, made headway among the Fall of hitherto stolid and conservative English laborers. "real" wages Perhaps a more potent cause for discontent than radical agitation was the rapid rise in the cost of living, which took place during the first decade of the twentieth century. Wages

[1] For further description of the Labor Party, see pages 591, 798–803.

also rose, but not as rapidly as prices; hence, "real wages," or the purchasing power of money, actually fell in some years.

During 1911–14 a series of great strikes took place that alarmed both government and public. A strike of the seamen and firemen belonging to the Transport Workers' Union won an increase in wages. It was followed by a strike of the railway employees, who succeeded in tying up the transportation of the whole country; but only a partial victory was won by the union because of the vigorous action taken by the government. A strike of the miners proved so serious a menace that Parliament enacted a minimum wage law to be applied to the industry. The strike fever infected even the agricultural laborers, who formed unions and demanded better conditions.

Era of great strikes

A marked transformation was taking place in British trade-unionism. The craft unions, composed of small groups of laborers engaged in special occupations, were giving place more and more to large industrial unions, composed of all the workers of a particular industry. In 1914, the Miners' Federation, the National Union of Railwaymen, and the Transport Workers' Federation formed a triple industrial alliance which, in case of a general strike in these industries, would be able to paralyze the industrial life of the country.

Industrial unionism

ECONOMIC PROGRESS

After 1870, England grew in wealth and prosperity, but not so rapidly as in the period preceding it. Some industries advanced slowly; others remained stationary; and a few actually declined. This condition was chiefly due to the fact that England no longer had a monopoly of modern industry; other nations, especially Germany, were now in the field as her competitors.

Relative decline of industry

Cotton manufacturing was one of the pillars of England's economic structure. It was concentrated in Lancashire, and especially in Manchester which, in 1913, had one third of the cotton spindles of the world. From America came most of the raw materials; large quantities also came from Egypt and India. Cotton goods and cotton yarn were exported in large quantities, constituting about one quarter of all the exports. The chief markets for cotton goods were India and China, where the handicrafts were disappearing and where fac-

The cotton and woolen industry

tories were few.   To the Continent England exported large quantities of cotton yarn which were made up into piece goods.   High tariffs on the Continent kept out cheap cotton goods, and England specialized in the better grades in which she was able to defy competition.   England's woolens ranked next to her cottons in the textile market.   Much of the raw material came from Australia, and it was worked up into woolen goods of the finest quality, most of it for export.   The best market for English woolens was the United States.

Coal production was one of the chief elements in England's prosperity.   She mined enough to supply her own great needs and

Coal   to export a third of her output.   Coal was an important item in England's trade with the Mediterranean countries, which produced little or none of this commodity. A ship would leave an English port loaded with coal, practically as ballast, and proceed to Marseilles or Genoa, where it could sell its cargo at low prices; then it would take on a cargo of wines or oil for Odessa; finally it would return to England laden with Russian wheat.   Without cheap coal these profitable transactions would have been difficult.

Although England's output of coal kept on increasing, she was outdistanced by the United States and closely followed by Germany.   In 1880, she produced 46 per cent of the world's output which, in 1910, sank to 24 per cent.   Some of the coal mines were exhausted, others were operated at a loss, due to bad management and to antiquated methods of mining.   The mines were owned by aristocratic landlords and leased to mining companies, who gave to the former a royalty on every ton mined.   Low wages resulted in much discontent among the miners, who struck frequently.   The coal industry, so vital to the prosperity of the country, was approaching a state of demoralization.

The iron and steel industries, centering in Birmingham and Sheffield, had long been famous.   During the middle of the nineteenth

Iron and   century, England had been the unchallenged leader in
steel   the metallurgical industries.   But a serious decline took place, due to the growing exhaustion of her iron mines, which put England far behind the United States and Germany.[1]   From 1870 to 1913 England's production of steel sank from 50 to 10

[1] In 1913, the United States produced 42 per cent; Germany, 25 per cent; and England 10 per cent of the world's steel.

per cent of the world's output.   The new steel that was made available by new processes in Germany and in America outdistanced even the famous Bessemer steel of England.

British shipping maintained its proud eminence in spite of rising competition.   In the days of wooden ships America had challenged the British merchant marine.   But the former ceased   Shipping to be a rival, due partly to the depredations of the Southern privateers during the Civil War and partly to the fact that America devoted her energies to railway building in order to develop a home market.   When iron and steel displaced wood in shipbuilding, England was ideally situated to take advantage of the change.   She had coal and iron close together, and both close to the sea.   Glasgow on the Clyde, Newcastle on the Tyne, and Belfast Harbor became the great shipbuilding centers of the world. England was far in the lead as a maritime nation.[1]   More and better ships of the latest pattern were constantly being built; and old vessels were sold to foreigners.   English ships carried foreign as well as domestic cargoes; in 1913 they carried about half of the sea-borne trade of the world.   Most of the merchantmen were "tramps" that went from port to port without a regular schedule.

Germany's challenge to the British merchant marine was chiefly in the ocean liners.   There began a race for the "Admiralty of the Atlantic" in which the British were hard pressed.   In   Rivalry of order to maintain the lead, the British government   England and heavily subsidized the Cunard Line, on condition that   Germany it build passenger vessels capable of maintaining a high rate of speed in moderate weather.   Under modern conditions of rapid transportation by water, seas are no longer a barrier; on the contrary, they are a favorable means of communication.   Shipping plays as important a part in binding together the scattered lands in the British Empire as do the railways in binding together the continental area of the United States.   Therefore England felt that she must maintain her maritime supremacy in peace as well as in war.

[1] The following table shows the share of the nations, in 1914, of the steam tonnage in the world.

	Net tons	Per cent of total
England	11,538,000	44.4
Germany	3,106,000	11.9
United States (exclusive of Great Lakes)	1,195,000	4.6
Norway	1,153,000	4.4
France	1,098,000	4.2
Japan	1,048,000	4.0

England was the leading exporter of capital in the world. Her surplus wealth found employment in foreign lands and in the Brit-

Export of capital

ish Empire where capital was in demand,[1] and from these investments came a golden stream of wealth that poured into England from all over the world. Free trade was essential to England as a creditor nation. She permitted her debtors to sell their goods to her, which insured their prosperity.

"England lives on foreign trade and every Englishman knows it" was a well-known saying in England. She imported food and

Unfavorable balance of trade

raw material; and exported manufactured articles, such as cotton and woolen goods, iron and steel goods, glassware, pottery, and coal. To maintain the continued prosperity of her export trade was a vital necessity. England had an unfavorable balance of trade, which was more than made up by large invisible earnings, chiefly the income from foreign investments and the earnings of English ships in carrying foreign goods. The continued excess of imports over exports was disturbing, inasmuch as it was noticed that the proportion of manufactured imports, to the total imports was rising, and the proportion of the manufactured exports to the total exports was falling. Was England ceasing to be the "workshop of the world"?

After 1870, England's foreign trade advanced more slowly than hitherto. She had a serious competitor in Germany, who made

Germany, her economic rival

inroads into English markets, both domestic and foreign. A notable report of the situation (1886) caused much concern among business men. "In every quarter of the world," it declared, "the perseverance and enterprise of the Germans are making themselves felt. In actual production of commodities we have now few, if any, advantages over them, and in knowledge of the markets of the world, a desire to accommodate themselves to local tastes or idiosyncrasies, a determination to

---

[1] The following table gives an idea of the marked tendency of British capital to shift from domestic to foreign investments.

DESTINATION OF NEW CAPITAL

DATE	TOTAL	UNITED KINGDOM	BRITISH POSSESSIONS	FOREIGN COUNTRIES
1909	£182,356,800	£18,681,400 (10%)	£74,758,200 (40%)	£ 88,917,200 (50%)
1910	267,439,100	60,296,500 (22%)	92,378,100 (34%)	114,764,500 (44%)
1911	191,759,400	26,145,900 (14%)	64,994,800 (34%)	100,618,700 (52%)
1912	210,850,000	45,335,300 (21%)	72,642,400 (34%)	92,872,300 (45%)
1913	196,537,000	35,951,200 (19%)	76,137,200 (39%)	84,448,600 (42%)

(Commercial History of 1927, p. 76, in *Economist* (London), vol. 106, 1928.)

obtain a footing wherever they can, and a tenacity in maintaining it, they appear to be gaining ground upon us." Although Germany and England were each other's best customers, many believed that industrial supremacy was passing to the former.[1]

The relative decline of England's foreign trade was largely due to the fact that she found difficulty in adjusting her industrial system to the demands of modern methods. Her business men had held the field so long that they relied more upon prestige than upon initiative. They hesitated to scrap old machinery and to depart from time- Conservatism of English business men honored methods, therefore they were slow in introducing mass production, automatic machinery, and the results of scientific research.

At the beginning of the twentieth century a movement, known as "tariff reform," appeared in England which aimed to reestablish protection. It was initiated by Joseph Chamberlain in a widely quoted speech delivered by Tariff reform him in 1903. Chamberlain "viewed with alarm" the growing excess of imports over exports; in his opinion the size of the latter was the test of the prosperity of the country. He saw "cracks and crevices in the walls of the great structure" built up by free trade; and he advocated an economic union of Great Britain with her dominions, on the basis of free trade among themselves and a tariff on foreign goods, which, in his opinion, would insure to the British a market for their manufactures and to the colonies a market for their raw material. In the meanwhile a system of reciprocity was to be established called Imperial Preference, whereby England and her Dominions would give one another preferential tariff rates. Chamberlain furthermore stated that Imperial Preference would have the effect of drawing the colonies and the mother country into a closer union; otherwise, they would inevitably drift apart.

A Tariff Reform League was organized for the purpose of conducting an agitation to convert the British people to protection.

---

[1] The total foreign trade of England in 1872 was about $3,000,000,000, which, in 1913, rose to about $6,500,000,000, an increase of 120 per cent; that of Germany in 1872 was about $1,500,000,000 which, in 1913, rose to about $5,100,000,000, an increase of 340 per cent. In the matter of exports the rivalry between England and Germany was very keen. During the decade 1903–13 the exports of England rose from about $1,450,000,000 to about $2,630,000,000; those of Germany from about $1,232,000,000 to $2,520,000,000. Germany's exports more than doubled, while those of England less than doubled; moreover, the addition to Germany's exports during this decade was actually larger than that of England.

The tariff reformers declared that the policy of free trade was
Tariff re-   adopted by England with the idea that the other na-
form divides   tions would follow her example; instead, they adopted
the parties   the system of high protective tariffs. The British manufacturer was, therefore, doubly at the mercy of his foreign competitor, who kept out British goods by hostile tariffs and "dumped"
his surplus goods into England unhindered. High tariffs on both
industrial and agricultural products to protect the British manufacturers and farmers was the plan advocated by the tariff reformers, who finally succeeded in committing the Conservative
Party to this policy. The Liberals opposed protection on the
ground that it would destroy the great foreign trade on which
England's prosperity depended and increase the cost of living by
keeping out cheap foreign food.

At the beginning of the twentieth century England found that
her economic grip upon the world was relaxing. One competitor,
Germany, was pressing her hard, and another and greater one, the
United States, was looming up in the distance. A European
island, as large as Minnesota, had, in the eighteenth century, conquered a world empire; and in the nineteenth century had supplied
the world with manufactures. She had destroyed rivals and had
outdistanced competitors. And she faced the new challenge un-
dismayed.

LITERATURE

The second half of the nineteenth century saw the Victorian Age
at its very highest. Although lacking a supreme master like
Tennyson   Shakespeare, it surpassed all other periods of Eng-
(1809–92)   lish literature in the number of writers of the first
rank that it produced. Alfred, Lord Tennyson, was the poetic
voice of Victorian England; no other writer of this period expressed its moods and ideals as faithfully as he. The spirit of
Tennyson's work is a calm acceptance of the order established in
state, church, and society; he nowhere exhibits either the revolutionary outbursts of Byron and Shelley or the mild humanitarianism of Wordsworth. Tennyson is, above all, a great artist, a
master of color, form, and music, who "jeweled and polished" his
verse into haunting meters that won him extraordinary popularity
throughout the English-speaking world. His almost flawless
poetic art enables him to invest conventional ideals with an en-

chanting atmosphere which transforms them into very models of purity and goodness. In his elegy, *In Memoriam*, Tennyson becomes philosophical and discourses upon human destiny and the immortality of human love with the hopeful assurance that there is

> "One God, one law, one element,
> And one far-off divine event,
> To which the whole creation moves."

Robert Browning, with whom Tennyson has often been contrasted, is the supreme philosophic poet of English literature. Browning's verse, unlike that of Tennyson, is not musical and flowing; frequently his meters are ragged and his meaning obscure. But what he lacks in melody he makes up in vigor, originality, and depth. Browning's chief interest is to stress "the incidents in the development of a soul"; little else he considers worthy of study. To seek the individual soul, to analyze its reactions upon the problems of life, and to find the moral sources of action is his favorite method. He excels in subtle, sometimes too subtle, analysis of ethical problems and in the portrayal of characters faced by moral crises. Browning was a true Victorian in that he believed that man was essentially a moral being living in a universe governed by moral laws. He, therefore, had a robust faith in the eventual triumph of the good and the true over the evil and the false. He describes himself as

(Browning (1812–89))

> "One who never turned his back but marched breast forward,
> Never doubted clouds would break,
> Never dreamed, tho' right were worsted, wrong would triumph,
> Held we fall to rise, are baffled to fight better,
> Sleep to wake."

Browning was a prophet, and like all prophets he had a tendency to be obscure which, for a long time, prejudiced the reading public against him. But some of his poems, especially the shorter ones, give evidence of simplicity and melody worthy of comparison with the best of Tennyson. His masterpiece is *The Ring and the Book*, a long poem in which a murder is described by different characters, each telling the same tale from his own viewpoint and in doing so revealing unconsciously his own character. The poem is a remarkable study of the moral psychology of different temperaments.

Matthew Arnold, essayist, critic, and poet, was one of the great intellectual influences of his generation. There could be no greater

contrast than that between Carlyle and Arnold as to temperament,
Arnold   method, and aim, although both were censors of the
(1822–88)   men and morals of their age.   Carlyle thundered
against vices and shams and stridently preached his gospel of the
"Everlasting Yea" and the "Everlasting Nay."   But the "elegant
Jeremiah," Arnold, in a spirit of "sweet reasonableness" and in a
manner refined and urbane, reproached his fellow countrymen for
their bad taste, provincialism, and lack of interest in ideas.   The
"Philistines," as he called the narrow-minded, self-satisfied people
of the middle classes, the "strong, dogged, unenlightened opponents of the chosen people, of the children of the light," were his
especial abhorrence.   The supreme aim in life, in his view, ought
to be "culture," or intellectual and moral perfection.   This
"apostle of culture," as Arnold was called, was temperamentally
opposed to all partisanships and dogmatisms, and was tolerant
toward all ideas, especially to those that were new or foreign.   Like
Erasmus he firmly believed that true and lasting progress can
only be made by allowing the intellect to play freely on the problems of life; "sweetness and light" would then be the outcome,
and mankind would become mellow, kindly, and tolerant.

As a critic Arnold resembled the Frenchman, Sainte-Beuve.
Like him he believed that the chief duty of a critic was to
"exhibit" the author in every possible way in order to stimulate
the readers to think for themselves.   Literature, Arnold defined as
"the best which has been thought and said in the world"; and the
first requisite of a critic was "disinterestedness," or detachment
from schools, dogmas, and systems.   Influenced by the scientific
thought of his day, Arnold came to doubt the truths of revealed
religion, though he never entirely broke away from Christianity;
he sought rather to give it new interpretations and new values.
Religion he defined as "morality touched with emotion"; God, as
a "stream of tendency not ourselves making for righteousness."
He regarded the Bible as a great work of "literature," describing
the history and experiences of the ancient Hebrew people.

An inspiring figure during the latter part of the nineteenth century was John Ruskin, art critic, social reformer, and ethical
Ruskin   teacher.   Having a vivid sense for natural beauty and
(1819–1900)   masterly descriptive power, Ruskin created a sensation
in England with his books on art.   In his opinion art, being the
highest form of truth, has of necessity a moral basis, and is the

exponent of the strength and weakness of those who produce it. His overflowing enthusiasm for art led him to become the "apostle of beauty" to his countrymen; and he began a propaganda to spread a love of art among all classes.

Ruskin's generous nature was shocked at the degradation and poverty of the lower classes. He saw nothing but ugliness and misery in the modern industrial system, and he therefore became an ardent social reformer. The political economy of the Manchester School, with its emphasis on the "economic man" bent on profits, he regarded as false and mischievous. "There is no wealth but life. . . . That country is the richest which nourishes the greatest number of noble and happy human beings," he declared. The laborer, according to Ruskin, was only incidentally a profit producer, but essentially a soldier of industry, working for the welfare of the whole community; he should, therefore, be trained, honored, and pensioned. Believing that culture should be diffused among all the people, he went among the London poor, lecturing to them on art and life, and founding educational societies to spread his ideals. Ruskin's influence was widespread, and he may be considered as the spiritual forerunner of the great social reform movement that took place in England at the beginning of the twentieth century.

The Victorian Age ended gloriously with a galaxy of brilliant and original writers. George Meredith might fitly be described as a novelist's novelist, as his books are admired mainly Meredith by those initiated in the craft. Meredith's extraordi- (1828–1909) nary gift for analyzing human character and motives suggests Browning; but, unlike him, he possessed a subtle irony and a sharp wit that he used like fine instruments with which to probe human problems. The Comic Spirit, with its "silvery laughter of the mind" hovers over his pages, darting here and there to expose egoism, hypocrisy, and selfishness.

Another master of fiction was Thomas Hardy, the greatest realist among the Victorians. Hardy's descriptions of nature are so extraordinary that sometimes his characters sink Hardy into the landscape, which itself then becomes the (1840–1928) hero of the book. He took Dorsetshire, which he made known as Wessex, and its rural inhabitants for his literary province and succeeded in making that region famous in English literature. Hardy generally depicts the individual pitted in an uneven struggle with nature and society, with a sardonic god looking on pitilessly. Failure or death is frequently the outcome of the struggles of his heroes and heroines. According to Hardy, man is a feeble creature whose background is nature, beautiful but sinister, therefore he cannot be saved either through God's grace or through his own works. Hardy is pagan rather than Christian in spirit, and therefore not a true Victorian.

During the last decade of the nineteenth century a new era began in English literature which was in marked contrast to the Imperialism Victorian Age. England was outgrowing the liberal-in literature ism of the middle classes who, for two generations, had fashioned her ideals. New forces came to the fore, imperialism and socialism, which, though utterly dissimilar in spirit and aim, were nevertheless united in protest against the narrowness and contentment of Victorian England. Imperialism was, in one sense, a challenge to the insularity of the English people who then cared little for affairs beyond their island shores, even for those of their Empire. Kipling's voice, speaking for the Greater Britain beyond the seas, stimulated the imagination of the English and made them conscious of their vast influence in the world.

Victorian England exhibited its narrowness in the lack of interest shown by the triumphant middle classes in the fate of the sub-merged masses. This spirit of class insularity is re-Social reform flected in the writings of the Victorian novelists who seldom, if ever, treated of the problems of the working class. In the works of the writers of the new era, the gentleman of leisure, long the undisputed hero in the play or novel, is retired to the background or even shown as the villain of the piece; into his place steps the toiler by brain or by hand, the man from statecraft, from the professions, from business, from the plow, from the machine. Social reform, socialism, efficient government, feminism, and trade unionism, are the absorbing themes of the writings of the new time. One must go back to the days of Milton to find a similar identification of literature with life. Conviction of original sin and the need for grace did not determine the law and the prophets of old more imperiously than did the conviction of preventable human waste and the need for social readjustment determine the laws and prophets of twentieth-century Britain. These newer writers are not mere social revivalists in the manner of Carlyle and Ruskin; they are active publicists and propagandists as well as artists, and their writings might be described as sociology clothed, sometimes thinly, in the garb of fiction.

No modern English writer enjoyed such prodigious popularity as Rudyard Kipling, story-writer and poet. The revival of imperialism which began in England at the end of the   Kipling nineteenth century found in Kipling its supreme lit-   (1865–1936) erary spokesman. Born in India, widely traveled, and knowing every part of the British dominions, he was well qualified to be the "Poet Laureate of the Empire." Moreover, Kipling intensely believed that the "Sons of the Blood," as he called the Anglo-Saxons, are the best fitted of all Europeans to rule the "lesser breeds," and he constantly exhorted his fellow countrymen to take up "the white man's burden" and bring Western civilization to the colored peoples of Asia and Africa.

Kipling's literary power lies in his mastery of a racy, colloquial style which is vigorous to the point of audacity; as a writer of short stories of adventure he is unsurpassed. His favorite characters are soldiers and adventurers, and he has immortalized "Tommy Atkins," whose praises he sings in prose and verse. Violent action, vividly felt and vividly described, is Kipling's forte. Seldom does he show the power of subtle analysis of problems, or of unraveling the tangled skein of human motives; his characters merely live but do not grow. Of the social problems which dominated the writings of his contemporaries, Kipling betrays neither knowledge nor interest in the slightest degree.

The drama as a vehicle of radical agitation reached unusual influence and power in the hands of the Irishman, George Bernard Shaw. The essential fact about Shaw is that he is a   Shaw socialist. Even before he became famous as a writer   (1856–   ) of plays, he had become well known as a trenchant writer and expounder of socialistic ideas. Shaw, therefore, entirely repudiates the present social and economic system; there is hardly a modern social problem which has not engaged his busy pen. As he himself once declared, "I am up to the chin in the life of my times." Shaw is even more revolutionary in the sphere of morals; and he has criticized severely the established standards of conduct in the earnest desire to effect a radical change in the moral code in order to give people a justification for their newly born desires. His method is satire, which he employs with such daring, brilliance, and wit that cherished institutions and ideals emerge from his hands ragged and ridiculous. His plays are a mirthful exposition of a mournful world. Family, church, state, property, and educational systems are judged as being founded on class interests and prejudices compounded with stupidity. Philistine morality, according to Shaw, has for its chief virtue Duty, which is not "the Stern Daughter of the Voice of God," but a means of enslaving the souls of the people that they may accept willingly an outrageous system of society. Hence, the first step of those who would be free is to emancipate themselves from "duties": the workingman from those to his employer, the citizen from those to the state, the communicant from those to the church, and the married from those to the family. The highest duty is to one's self. Shaw also inveighs against sentimental romanticism. He believes firmly in a cool, common sense view of all relations in life, and considers romanticism as very harmful because it creates illusions by covering reality with a golden haze.

A Shaw play is not a drama in the ordinary sense, with a plot involving the fate of the leading characters. There is no plot, hero, heroine, or villain; instead, there is brilliant and witty conversation concerning a grave social problem, which the various characters discuss according to their temperament and ideals. The problem itself is the center of interest. Shaw has performed a remarkable feat in the dramatic field by holding the attention of his audiences through sheer intellectual power.

Herbert George Wells shared with Shaw the literary hegemony of the new age. Although a socialist like Shaw, Wells's views are
Wells
(1866–   )
the expression of a temperament quite different from that of his brilliant contemporary. Shaw is clear, cool, unemotional, and unromantic in his expositions, but quite dogmatic in his solutions. Wells, on the contrary, is temperamentally a "dweller in the innermost." He analyzes social problems in quite a spiritual-romantic manner, sometimes wondering at the stupidity of mankind in not solving them, sometimes wondering whether they can be solved at all. He is essentially a sociologist touched with emotion. Although a superb story-writer, his best work has been done in a field partly created by himself, the sociological novel, in which the heroes and heroines struggle to escape from the evil effects of bad education, outworn ideals, and cramping institutions instead of the evil machinations of their enemies.

Wells calls himself a socialist, but he would not be classified as such by the strict adherents of socialism. In his view present society is in a sad state of "muddle"; inefficiency, planlessness, and stupidity have done their very worst to make life unbearable for the major portion of humanity. He, therefore, desires to see an educational process generated, which he calls "love and fine thinking," that will set people to reorganize their institutions on a more humane and intelligent plan. This must be done without class hatred and without rancor of any kind; those who profit from the present evil system must be made to see that they could lead a larger and richer life in a world from which poverty and its attendant evils are banished. Few writers of the day are as suggestive as Wells. His novels and essays are likely to set the reader to thinking of social problems in a new way and, what is more, to make him see his own relation to these problems. Wells is also endowed with abundant humor, not the sparkling wit of Shaw's repartee, but the humor that is woven into the construction of a character or a situation that exposes incongruities and absurdities.

Wells's great search is the future. His test of a moral act is its consequences for individual and social welfare, not its relation to a code of morals; of an idea, its bearing upon a new view of life, not of its truth or falsehood; of an institution, its value to a new society, not to an old one. He never tires of reiterating the sentiment that the chief business of mankind ought to be to prepare itself, its ideals, and its institutions for the great future that is soon to dawn upon us.

REFERENCES

GENERAL:
Consult the bibliographies at the end of Chapters VIII–IX.

GOVERNMENT AND PARTIES:
A. L. Lowell, *The Government of England*, 2 vols. (ed. 1912), the standard work on the subject, treats fully all aspects of the British system, local, national, and imperial; Sir Thomas E. May, *Constitutional History of England since the Accession of George III*, edited and continued by F. Holland, 3 vols. (1912), an old but important treatise; E. M. Violette (ed.), *English Constitutional Documents Since 1832* (1936), a work of reference; Walter Bagehot, *The English Constitution*, with an Introduction by the Earl of Balfour (ed. 1928), a brilliant interpretation of English political institutions and customs, old but still worth reading; good studies are A. V. Dicey, *Introduction to the Study of the Constitution* (ed.

1915), H. R. G. Greaves, *The British Constitution* (1938), S. Low, *The Governance of England* (ed. 1914), and L. Courtney, *The Working Constitution of the United Kingdom* (1901); brief descriptions: T. F. Moran, *The Theory and Practice of the English Government* (1903) and D. D. Wallace, *The Government of England, National, Local, Imperial* (ed. 1925); Sir J. A. R. Marriott, *Mechanism of the Modern State* (1927), especially good for English administrative system; Sir C. Ilbert, *Parliament — Its History, Constitution, and Practice* (1911), excellent handbook by an authority on Parliamentary procedure; on political parties: Lord Hugh Cecil, *Conservatism* (1912), L. T. Hobhouse, *Liberalism* (1911), C. F. Brand, *British Labour's Rise to Power* (1941), and H. Tracey (ed.), *The Book of the Labour Party*, 3 vols. (1925); M. Ostrogorski, *Democracy and the Organization of Political Parties*, trans. from the French, 2 vols. (1902), Vol. I, England, Vol. II, America, a famous work by a Russian scholar, considers that parties are inadequate to express democratic ideas and methods; I. Jennings, *Cabinet Government* (1936), new interpretation; and K. B. Smellie, *A Hundred Years of English Government* (1937).

BIOGRAPHIES:

John (Viscount) Morley, *The Life of William Ewart Gladstone*, 3 vols. (ed. 1911), the standard biography of the Liberal leader by his distinguished disciple; O. Burdett, *W. E. Gladstone* (1928); W. F. Monypenny (continued by G. E. Buckle), *The Life of Benjamin Disraeli, Earl of Beaconsfield*, 6 vols. (ed. 1929), the standard biography of the Conservative leader; Sir E. Clarke, *Benjamin Disraeli — The Romance of a Great Career* (1926), based on Monypenny and Buckle; A. Maurois, *Disraeli*, translated from the French (1927), sentimental and clever; L. Strachey, *Eminent Victorians* (1918) and *Queen Victoria* (1921), subtle and ironic literary portraits of famous English men and women; Sir S. Lee, *Queen Victoria, a Biography* (1903), an "official" biography; G. M. Trevelyan, *The Life of John Bright* (1913), distinguished for scholarship and high literary merit; C. W. Boyd (ed.), *Speeches of Joseph Chamberlain*, 2 vols. (1914); J. L. Garvin, *The Life of Joseph Chamberlain*, 2 vols. (1933).

SOCIAL CONDITIONS:

C. Booth (ed.), *Life and Labour of the People in London*, 17 vols. (1892–1903), an "encyclopedia of poverty," consisting of detailed studies of the social and economic conditions of the London poor; B. S. Rowntree, *Poverty: A Study of Town Life* (ed. 1902), a similar study though on a smaller scale for the city of York; L. G. Chiozza-Money, *Riches and Poverty* (1911), a popular but reliable study of the distribution of wealth in the United Kingdom; C. W. Pipkin, *The Idea of Social Justice* (1928), on social legislation in England and France; B. G. de Montgomery, *British and Continental Labour Policy* (1922) contains information on social reform, trade unions, and industrial conditions; W. B. Catlin, *The Labor Problem in the United States and Great Britain* (1926), a good text on labor problems; Sir W. H. Beveridge, *Unemployment, a Problem of Industry* (ed.

1930), the most reliable study of the problem in England; J. A. Hobson, *The Economics of Unemployment* (1924), views of a Liberal economist; P. Alden, *Democratic England* (1912), essays on England's social problems by a Liberal; F. Tillyard, *The Worker and the State* (1936), an analysis of the laws relating to wages, health, accidents, and conditions of employment; E. Guyot, *Le socialisme et l'évolution de l'Angleterre contemporaine, 1880–1911* (1913), a study of British social politics; B. L. Hutchins and A. Harrison, *A History of Factory Legislation* (ed. 1926); on social insurance: L. G. Chiozza-Money, *Insurance against Poverty* (1912); A. S. C. Carr and others, *National Insurance* (ed. 1913); C. J. H. Hayes, *British Social Politics* (1913), a well-selected collection of extracts from speeches delivered in Parliament on social legislation, contains a reprint of the social reform laws; Georgiana P. McEntee, *The Social Catholic Movement in Great Britain* (1927), an interesting little book on the attitude of Catholic leaders toward social reform; John Galsworthy, *The Forsyte Saga* (1928), a novel dealing with late Victorian England, fine analysis of the property spirit of the middle classes.

TRADE-UNIONISM:

The best studies of British trade-unionism are S. and B. Webb, *The History of Trade Unionism* (ed. 1920), and G. D. H. Cole, *A Short History of the British Working Classes*, 3 vols. (1925–27), scholarly, sympathetic with labor; C. M. Lloyd, *Trade Unionism* (ed. 1928), good handbook, contains reprint of the Trade-Union Law of 1927; H. B. Lees-Smith (ed.), *The Encyclopedia of the Labour Movement*, 3 vols. (1928); A. Henderson, *Trade Unions and the Law* (1927), history of laws and decisions in reference to labor; R. H. Tawney, *The British Labor Movement* (1925); M. F. Robinson, *The Spirit of Association, being some account of the Gilds, Friendly Societies, Coöperative Movement, and Trade Unions of Great Britain* (1913); S. & B. Webb, *Industrial Democracy* (ed. 1920), scholarly study.

INDUSTRIAL CONDITIONS:

A. Shadwell, *Industrial Efficiency — A Comparative Study of Industrial Life in England, Germany, and America* (1913); W. J. Ashley, (ed.) *British Industries* (ed. 1907); Lord Aberconway, *The Basic Industries of Great Britain* (1927); Sir R. Giffen, *Statistics* (ed. 1913), and *Economic Inquiries and Studies*, 2 vols. (1904), by an expert statistician of industrial matters; on tariff reform: F. Benham, *Great Britain Under Protection* (1941); E. E. Todd, *The Case against Tariff Reform* (1911); R. J. S. Hoffman, *Great Britain and the German Trade Rivalry* (1933), authoritative study.

THE LAND QUESTION:

The best study of the land question in Great Britain is a Parliamentary Report entitled *The Land: the Report of the Land Enquiry Committee*, vol. I, Rural (1913), vol. II, Urban (1914); R. E. Prothero (Lord Ernle), *English Farming Past and Present* (ed. 1922), by a recognized authority on the subject, conservative in tendency; C. S. Orwin and W. R. Peel, *The Tenure of Agricultural Land* (1925); J. Collings, *Land Reform* (1906), a plea for peasant proprietorship by a pioneer of land reform; by the same author, *The Colonization of Rural Britain: a Complete Scheme for the Regeneration of British Rural Life*, 2 vols. (1914); H. Harben, *The Rural Problem* (1914), a short study; B. S. Rowntree, *How the Labourer Lives: A Study of the Rural Labour Problem* (1913); H. Rider Haggard, *Rural England*, 2 vols. (1906); C. Turnor, *Land Problems and National Welfare* (1911); G. Cadbury and T. Bryan, *The Land and the Landless* (1908); F. E. Green, *History of the English Agricultural Laborer, 1870–1920* (1920); M. E. Seebohm, *The Evolution of the English Farm* (1927); O. J. Dunlop, *The Farm Labourer, the History of a Modern Problem* (1913); C. Dampier-Whetham, *Politics and the Land* (1927), proposed solutions of the land question.

ADDITIONAL REFERENCES

E. Halévy, *A History of the English People, Epilogue Vol. I, 1895–1905, Vol. II, 1905–1915* (1934); R. H. Gretton, *A Modern History of the English People (1880–1922)*, 3 vols. (1913–29); W. Dibelius, *England*, trans. from the German (1930); J. M. Gaus, *Great Britain* (1929); P. Guedalla, *Gladstone and Palmerston* (1928); J. H. Edwards, *David Lloyd George*, 2 vols. (1929); F. A. Ogg, *English Government and Politics* (1929); R. Muir, *How Britain is Governed* (1930); E. Wertheimer, *Portrait of the Labour Party* (ed. 1930); T. Rothstein, *From Chartism to Labourism* (1929); G. D. H. Cole, *The World of Labour* (ed. 1915); W. M. Bailey (ed.), *Trade Union Documents* (1930); G. Slater, *Poverty and the State* (1930); G. Drage (ed.), *Public Assistance* (1930); L. Brentano, *Eine Geschichte der Wirtschaftlichen Entwicklung Englands*, 3 vols. (1927–28), vol. III; J. W. Adamson, *English Education, 1789–1902* (1930); R. C. K. Ensor, *England, 1870–1914* (1935).

For additional titles consult bibliographies at the end of Chapters VIII–IX; for bibliography on England's foreign policy consult bibliography at the end of Chapter XXXIII.

CHAPTER XVII

THE IRISH QUESTION

THE determining factor in the history of Ireland was her conquest by England. An antagonism between the two countries resulted, which persisted for many generations, in spite of the fact that their relations were closely intertwined. The hatred that naturally arises between conquered and conqueror was aggravated by racial and religious differences: the Irish are largely Celtic and Catholic, and the English, largely Teutonic and Protestant. An economic factor intensified the antagonism still more. The land of Ireland was appropriated by the English invaders who reduced the inhabitants to a condition bordering upon serfdom. Political, racial, religious, and economic differences combined to make the Irish Question so difficult of solution that, for many centuries, it baffled the best efforts of English statesmanship.

Complicated nature of the question

During the Middle Ages, Ireland was, in theory, ruled by the King of England and by a Parliament established in Dublin; in fact it was ruled by native chieftains who owed allegiance to the King. Little attempt was made to strengthen English rule until the coming of the Tudors whose rule over the Irish became as thorough and as despotic as that over the English. Uprisings of the Irish occurred constantly, and in the reign of the Stuarts a new policy was adopted which riveted English rule upon Ireland. Protestant emigrants from Scotland were settled in Ulster on the lands of the natives who were ousted from their holdings. This policy was followed by Cromwell and by William III until virtually all the land of Ireland was in the hands of the British. The Irish became tenants and laborers on land which had once belonged to them.

English plantations in Ireland

A system of legislation was then devised by the English government which had for its object to keep the Irish people in permanent subjection. No Irish Catholic could inherit or buy land from a Protestant or lease it for a period longer than thirty-one years. If the eldest son of a Catholic became a Protestant, he could oust his father from his property; if a relative of a deceased Catholic landowner turned Protestant, he inherited

The Penal laws

all the property to the exclusion of the rightful heirs. A special tax was laid on all Catholics engaged in industry; they were also forbidden to employ more than two workingmen. As no Catholic could vote or hold office, the Dublin Parliament was entirely in the hands of the Protestant minority. All education had to be under Protestant auspices, and Catholics were not permitted to enter any liberal profession except that of medicine. The Catholic faith was permitted, but under severe restrictions. Monks and the higher clergy were banished on pain of death; secular priests had to be registered, and their number was limited by law. In the words of Edmund Burke, these laws constituted "a complete system . . . as well fitted for the oppression, impoverishment, and degradation of a people, and for the debasement in them of human nature itself, as ever proceeded from the perverted ingenuity of man." The Irish suffered economic as well as political and religious tyranny. When cattle-raising became a prosperous industry, the English government put a high export duty on cattle and so destroyed that industry. The Irish then turned to wool-raising, but the English put a high export duty on wool, and this industry, too, was ruined. "The law does not suppose any such person to exist as an Irish Roman Catholic," once declared an English Lord Chancellor.

Curious as it may seem, Ireland had "home rule" during the period of her greatest misery. There was a Parliament in Dublin with large powers over Irish affairs. But, as only Protestants could vote and hold office, it represented their interests only. Political corruption was so flagrant that the Irish government, according to Lecky, was "reduced to a system of jobbery, where the most momentous material and moral interests were deliberately crushed by a tyranny at once blind, brutal and mean."

Protestant rule

Cowed and disheartened the Irish remained quiet until they were aroused by the American Revolution. A vigorous agitation against English rule began, which spread so rapidly that the government was alarmed. A striking phase of the movement was the union of the Protestants of Ulster with the Catholics of the south in a common cause against England. The commercial restrictions on Irish commerce were as ruinous to Protestants as to Catholics. The United Irishmen, a society organized in 1791 by the Protestant Wolfe Tone, carried on a revolutionary agitation throughout the island. Attacked both in

Repeal of Penal laws

America and in Ireland the government was compelled to grant important concessions to the Irish. In 1782, the Poynings Act[1] was repealed, and the Irish Parliament was now free to legislate. Ten years later, those Catholics who possessed the required property qualifications were given the right to vote, but not to hold office. Under the leadership of Henry Grattan, the Irish Parliament repealed most of the Penal laws and the restrictions on Irish trade.

The French Revolution stimulated Irish discontent to a furious pace. When war broke out between England and France, the Irish raised the cry, "England's difficulties are Ireland's opportunities." A movement for independence was on foot, which sought the aid of French armies. In 1798, there took place a great rebellion which, however, did not get the support of Ulster. Religious animosities had dissolved the union between Catholics and Protestants. The rebellion was suppressed by the English, who now determined to bring Ireland once more under firm control. Prime Minister William Pitt, by resorting to flagrant corruption, succeeded in having the Act of Union (1800) adopted by the Irish Parliament. It provided for the abolition of the Irish Parliament and for Irish representation in the British Parliament, where the Irish constituted a small minority. Unlike the union of England with Scotland the union with Ireland was one of governments only, not of peoples. The Irish were a conquered people oppressed by England; hence, they did not wish to be "united" with their oppressors.

Act of Union

Following the Act of Union, Ireland made many attempts to free herself from the evils inherited from past ages. She faced three general problems: religious, to establish equality between Catholics and Protestants; economic, to restore the land to the original owners; and political, to create a system of self-government.

Two parties appeared that proposed to solve these problems in entirely different ways. One was constitutional, favoring peaceful agitation to induce the British government to repeal the anti-Catholic laws; to expropriate, or buy out the landlords in favor of the tenants; and to establish home rule under the British crown. There was also a revolutionary party, which was convinced that only by terrorism and revolt could England be compelled to do justice to

The constitutional and revolutionary solutions of the Irish problems

[1] An act, passed in 1494, declared that no law could be submitted to the Dublin Parliament without the consent of the King and Privy Council of England.

Ireland; hence, they were not averse to the use of violence of all sorts, from assassination to a popular uprising. The revolutionaries favored an independent Irish republic which, once established, would decree political and religious equality, and give the land to the peasants by confiscating the estates of the English landlords.

Although the various racial elements in Ireland had lived together for centuries, they did not fuse into a completely homogeneous nation. The Celtic Irish were numerically the most important, about seventy-five per cent of the total population. They belonged, almost entirely, to the Catholic faith. Most of them were peasants or industrial laborers. The second group were the Anglo-Irish, known as the "Ascendancy," who constituted the aristocracy of the island. They were of English origin, and professed the Anglican religion. To this element belonged landlords, high civil and military officials, professionals, and wealthy business men. In Ulster there existed another element, commonly called the Scotch-Irish. They were largely the descendants of the Scottish settlers of the seventeenth century, and were Presbyterian in religion. Most of the Scotch-Irish were small farmers and business men. Ulster, especially Belfast, was a thriving industrial center famous for its linen and shipbuilding. The various elements divided on the Irish Question according to their interests. On one side were Catholic Irish who favored reform in the entire system; and on the other were the Anglo-Irish and the Scotch-Irish who opposed any change in the established order. Ireland was the only country in western Europe, where class corresponded to race and religion, a condition common in eastern Europe.

Racial elements

RELIGIOUS REFORM

The religious problem was the first to be solved. It has already been described how the "Liberator," Daniel O'Connell, succeeded in bringing about Catholic Emancipation. Nevertheless, religious inequality continued because the Anglican Church was still established, and therefore entitled to public support. It was generously endowed, having large revenues and giving princely incomes to its bishops. The law required that every one, irrespective of his religion, who held land either as tenant or as a proprietor, was to pay a tithe for the support of the Established Church. In many places in Ireland only

The Anglican Church in Ireland

a tiny minority were Anglicans, which greatly aggravated the situation. "On an Irish Sabbath morning," wrote Sydney Smith, the English humorist, "the bell of a neat parish church often summons to worship only the parson and an occasional conforming clerk, while two hundred yards off a thousand Catholics are huddled together in a hovel, and pelted by the storms of Heaven."

The poor Irish peasant, already burdened by his voluntary support of the Catholic Church, often refused to pay the tithe to a church which he regarded as heretic and hated as The tithe alien. Often the Anglican clergyman, accompanied by "wars" the police, attempted to take away the peasant's cow or pig for non-payment of this tax. In 1831, a "tithe war" occurred throughout Ireland, which caused considerable disturbance. It became so difficult to collect the tithe that, in 1838, it was converted into a land tax to be paid by the landlord, but he dodged the burden by increasing the rents of his tenants.

The opposition to the Established Church in Ireland won the sympathy of the Liberals, many of whom were opposed to the Establishment in England. In 1869, Gladstone in- Disestab-duced Parliament to pass a law separating Church and lishment of State in Ireland. All taxes for the support of the the Irish church Church were abolished, and its landed property was taken by the government; partial compensation, however, was made by the creation of a special fund for the support of some of the Anglican clergy in Ireland. There was now religious equality in Ireland.

LAND REFORM

Ireland was overwhelmingly an agricultural country. To secure prosperity and contentment among an agricultural people, it is essential that the system of landholding be liberal and Ireland, an the methods of farming progressive; otherwise the agricultural people, having no industries to fall back upon, must country sink into hopeless poverty. Until recent times Irish farming was very backward, and the system of landholding so vicious that it had no redeeming qualities whatever.

The ownership of the soil was vested, not in those who tilled it, but in those whose ancestors had profited from the confiscations of former years. These Irish landlords, mainly of Landlordism English origin, regarded their estates merely as sources of revenue, and cared little about the condition of the tenants, whom they greatly despised.   Many were absentee landlords living in England; their properties were managed by agents who, in order to please their employers, would raise the rents of the tenants on every possible pretext.

Improvements on the farm had to be made by the tenant.   If he drained a marsh, built a fence, or improved his cottage, his rent "Rack-   was raised by the landlord; and if he refused to pay it, renting"   he was evicted, being generally a "tenant-at-will" without the security of a lease.   In such instances the improvements, as well as the farm, became the landlord's property without compensation to the tenant.   Competition for land was very keen, and an evicted peasant was therefore replaced without difficulty. Often the fear of losing the money invested in improvements compelled the peasant to suffer the greatest privations in order to satisfy the greed of the landlord.   In this way the latter used as a means of coercion the very values created by the peasant. The owners of the estates refused to improve their properties, and the tenants were naturally slow to invest labor and money for the benefit of the landlords; hence, the land was wretchedly cultivated. This system of exploiting the Irish tenants became known as "rack-renting."   As there was little industry in Ireland, the peasant had to accept the harsh conditions or starve, or flee the country as an emigrant.   Thousands of Irishmen came to America as to a Promised Land in order to escape starvation in the land of their birth.

The condition of the Irish peasants became notorious the world over, and excited the greatest sympathy for them.   "As poor as an The "Hun-   Irishman" became a proverb.   Living almost exclu- gry Forties" sively on potatoes and in wretched huts which sheltered alike human beings and animals, the peasants were in a state of poverty and misery.   The failure of the potato crop in 1845–47 resulted in a great famine that brought the climax of suffering to a people already half starved.   The landlords aggravated the tragic situation by turning agricultural into grazing lands.   Many farmers were evicted in order to create "clearances" for cattle-grazing. "Cows ate men," was the common saying.   As a consequence of these calamities, thousands died of starvation during the "Hungry Forties," and, in five years, over a million Irishmen emigrated to America.

The hatred of the Irish peasants for their landlords knew no

LAND REFORM

LAND REFORM

LAND REFORM   311

bounds, and it found expression in acts of terrorism.   Landlords
and their agents were murdered, their cattle were   *The Boycott*
killed or maimed, and their houses burned.   Severe
Crimes Acts were passed which established what was virtually
martial law in the disturbed districts.   To apprehend the terrorists
appeared the Royal Irish Constabulary which was directed from
London.   This body of half-policemen, half-soldiers proved to be
very effective in suppressing rural crime.   A milder form of hostility
to landlords was "boycotting," a method invented by the Irish.
An English land agent, named Boycott, roused the anger of his
Irish neighbors, who thereupon decided to have no dealings with
him.   No one would buy from him or sell to him; no one would
work for him; no one would recognize him on the streets.   As a
consequence he was compelled to leave town.   Boycotting proved
so effective that it spread rapidly.

In 1879, Michael Davitt, the son of an evicted tenant, organized
the famous Land League with the object of uniting the Irish on
the one issue that affected them most, land reform.   *The Land
League*
He was joined by Parnell who, though chiefly interested in political reform, was convinced that his cause would progress more rapidly if the people were in better economic circumstances.   "A starving man is not a good nationalist," was his
dictum.   The League was constitutional in its methods, and the
far-reaching agitation that it set on foot succeeded in enlisting
almost the entire peasantry in Ireland.   It demanded the three
"F's," "free sale, fixity of tenure, and fair rent": a tenant who
desired to leave his holding should have the right to sell to his
successor the improvements which he had made; that eviction
should not be at the will of the landlord solely; and that rents
should be regulated by public authority.   The return of the soil
to its original owners was the ultimate solution advocated by the
League.

Ireland was in a state of turmoil.   The agitation of the Land
League and the violent acts of the revolutionaries presented a
serious problem to the government.   As in the crises   *Gladstone's
land reforms*
that led to Catholic Emancipation, there was fear that,
if reforms were denied, rebellion would be the outcome.   Gladstone's interest in Ireland began, about this time, to dominate his
political thought.   Already, in 1870, he had been instrumental in
the enactment of a law that established throughout Ireland the

land system of Ulster which recognized the principle of "tenant right" by giving compensation for improvements to tenants who were evicted for causes other than the non-payment of rent. In 1881, Gladstone put through a land law which marked the beginning of the solution of the land problem. The chief feature of this law was the public regulation of land through the appointment of a Land Commission with powers to adjust relations between landlord and tenant. Evictions were to be made on reasonable grounds only; rents were to be regulated by the Commission; a tenant was to be free to sell his holding to another; and full compensation for improvements was to be given to an outgoing tenant. Although it was denounced by its opponents as a combination of "force, fraud, and folly," the law had the effect of quieting the land agitation. The growing contentment of the Irish peasantry was a tribute to Gladstone's constructive statesmanship.

The most radical step in land reform was taken, however, by the Conservatives. In 1903, the Balfour Ministry put through the celebrated Wyndham Act, whose object was to bring about gradually the transfer of the soil of Ireland from the landlords to the tenants. It was based upon the theory that the Irish would cease to be revolutionary when they became property-owners. Large sums of money were put at the disposal of the Land Commission by the British government to aid the tenants in buying out the landlords. In order to induce the former to buy, the government loaned them money on easy terms: by paying three and one fourth per cent interest on money that he borrowed, the tenant could extinguish his debt, both principal and interest, at the end of sixty-eight and one half years. In order to induce the landlords to sell, they were given a bonus by the government of twelve per cent of the purchase price. Many peasants were enabled, in this way, to become proprietors. In the opinion of John Redmond, the Irish Nationalist leader, the land purchase acts were "the most substantial victory gained by the Irish race in the reconquest of the soil of Ireland." A contented, hardworking peasantry, struggling for improvement, took the place of the wretched, rebellious tenants of former days. Emigration decreased, and dire poverty became the exception instead of the rule in Ireland. The land problem was now virtually solved.

HOME RULE

One more Irish problem, self-government, still remained. Throughout the nineteenth century the revolutionaries were inspired by the rebellion of 1798; and the constitutionalists were inspired by Catholic Emancipation. "The vast majority," declared Sir Horace Plunkett, "regarded the Government as alien, disputed the validity of its laws, and felt no responsibility for administration, no respect for the legislature, or for those who executed its decrees." The revolutionary currents of the middle of the nineteenth century brought forth the Young Ireland movement of 1848. A group of idealistic young Irishmen, headed by Charles Gavan Duffy and William Smith O'Brien, conducted an agitation for national independence. They founded a paper, *The Nation*, which expressed their views with great force and eloquence, and aimed to stir the Irish people into revolt against England. A small uprising did occur in 1848, but it was quickly suppressed, and the leaders, exiled or imprisoned.

Young Ireland

The Irish emigrants in America brought with them a deep hatred of England and a keen interest in the Irish Question. It was among them that a new revolutionary movement appeared in the seventies, known as Fenianism (Gaelic, *national militia*). The Fenians were a secret, revolutionary brotherhood who aimed to establish an independent Irish republic. In America they formed the Clan-na-Gael society, and in Ireland, the Irish Republican Brotherhood. They resolved to achieve the independence of their country by a policy of terrorism. Riots broke out, prisons were blown up, officials were murdered, and an attempt was made by the Irish in America to invade Canada. The Fenian outrages culminated, in 1882, in the Phœnix Park murders. Lord Frederick Cavendish, the Chief Secretary for Ireland, and his associate were assassinated in Dublin, a deed which shocked all England. The government determined to suppress Fenianism at all costs. Trial by jury was suspended, and many of the Irish terrorists were executed or imprisoned.

The Fenians

Fenianism was the greatest effort of the revolutionaries, and it failed. A constitutional movement began in the seventies, known as Home Rule, which aimed to establish the autonomy of Ireland within the British Empire. It is associated with the name of Charles Stewart Parnell, one of the most remarkable political leaders of his day. Parnell came of an Anglo-Irish

Parnell (1846–91)

landholding family.   He was a Protestant, and was educated in England.   Personally he was a man of cool temper, grim, haughty, and domineering.   Yet he became the idol of the Irish people who followed him as enthusiastically as they had once followed O'Connell.   Intensely nationalist in his views, Parnell hated English rule in Ireland, and he devoted his life to the cause of Irish freedom. "Ireland," he declared, "is not a geographical fragment [of Great Britain]; she is a nation."   Though not a revolutionist and opposed to terrorism, he won the sympathy of the Fenians who admired his uncompromising nationalism.   Parnell succeeded in welding together Home Rule, Fenianism, and the Land League, which made the Irish Question so prominent that it became the leading issue in British politics for a generation.

The Irish representatives in Parliament were not effective politically, being few in number, and, in addition, torn by factional quarrels.   In 1870, the representatives from southern Ireland were organized into the Irish Nationalist Party; and shortly afterwards, Parnell succeeded to its leadership.   Through his efforts the Nationalists became a united, harmonious party that followed him unquestioningly.   How could they, a small minority in the Commons, have a powerful influence in that body?   Parnell answered the question by adopting a policy of obstructing legislation, "filibustering," a method of which he was largely the originator.   He openly declared his intention to stop the working of the British government unless the claims of Ireland were given consideration.   By taking advantage of the rules of the house, which then permitted unlimited debate, Parnell and his followers would make long speeches on irrelevant matters.   At one time the Commons sat for twenty-two consecutive hours bombarded by Irish speeches.   The house was compelled to adopt a method of limiting debate by a vote, called "closure."   Parnell showed remarkable ingenuity in filibustering: he demanded roll calls on all bills, introduced numerous resolutions, took advantage of the rules of debate, and, in other ways, clogged the wheels of legislation.   When neither the Conservatives nor the Liberals had a majority, Parnell was in a strategic position of which he took full advantage.   In 1885, he joined the Conservatives, and the Gladstone Ministry fell; in the following year, he joined the Liberals, and the Salisbury Ministry fell.

Parnell's tactics drew the attention of many Englishmen to the

Irish Question. Most important of all was the conversion of Gladstone to Home Rule. Gladstone had given ample Gladstone favors Home Rule evidence of his sympathy with Ireland in his church and land laws. The Fenian outrages had given him a vivid impression of the bitterness of Irish feeling toward England. These outrages, he declared, "produced among Englishmen an attitude of attention and preparedness which qualified them to embrace, in a manner foreign to their habits in other times, the vast importance of the Irish controversy." The widespread agitation of the Land League and the filibustering of Parnell finally convinced him that the Irish Question was "ripe for settlement." In 1886, having need of the votes of the Irish Nationalists to remain in office, Gladstone agreed to support Home Rule. He denounced England's traditional attitude to Ireland as a "broad and black blot" on the pages of her history. "What we want to do," he asserted, "is to stand by the traditions of which we are the heirs in all matters except our relations with Ireland. . . . We hail the demand of Ireland for what I call a blessed oblivion of the past."

There was a great outcry throughout Britain when, in 1886, the first Home Rule Bill was introduced. "An intolerable, an imbecile, an accursed bill," was the opinion of the Con- Defeat of the first Home Rule Bill servatives. Gladstone was denounced as an enemy of his country for yielding to the Irish who, it was asserted, would use Home Rule as a step toward independence. In an independent Ireland, England would have a deadly enemy on her flank, who could block the exit of her fleet, and who could be used as a base of operations by an enemy on the Continent. Ulster proclaimed her opposition to Home Rule, asserting that *Home* Rule would mean *Rome* Rule; namely, that an Irish Parliament, having a Catholic majority, would pass laws hostile to the Protestant minority. Deep religious prejudices were aroused by the appeal of the Protestants in Ireland to the Protestants in England to save them from Catholic persecution. Although religious antagonism was a powerful factor in keeping Ireland divided there was another cause for Ulster's antagonism to Home Rule. Being the wealthiest part of Ireland, it feared that an Irish Parliament, the majority of which would come from the poorer sections, would lay the burden of taxation upon its shoulders. Disorders in Ireland had hardened many otherwise liberal Englishmen against Irish self-government. What Ireland needed, declared Salisbury, was "twenty years of resolute government," not Home Rule. "The ebbing tide is with you, and the flowing tide is with us," replied Gladstone. So deep-rooted was the distrust and dislike of the Irish that the Liberal Party split on the issue. Led by Chamberlain, a group of Liberals, calling themselves "Unionists," joined the Conservatives to defeat the bill. Parliament was dissolved, and, in the elections that followed, the Conservatives were successful. The new ministry, headed by Salisbury, announced its policy of consistent and pitiless repression of disorders in Ireland, a policy which he carried out vigorously.

A wave of disappointment swept over Ireland. The prospects for Home Rule had been so favorable, yet the outcome had proved Ousting of   to be so disappointing. Shortly afterwards a grave Parnell from   scandal came to light concerning Parnell, which had leadership   the effect of discrediting his cause. He was named as a co-respondent in a divorce case. Despite the fact that he married the divorcée, he was compelled to resign his leadership of the Nationalist Party. Defeated in his efforts for Irish freedom, repudiated by the party which he had made so powerful, Parnell was now a tragic figure. He died, in 1891, a disappointed and brokenhearted man.

Gladstone made another attempt to establish Home Rule. In 1893, the Liberals were again a minority in Parliament, and therefore had need of the Nationalists to stay in power. A Defeat of   second Home Rule Bill was introduced, which was the second   denounced with as much vehemence as the first. After Home Rule   ter long and heated debates, the measure was finally Bill passed by the Commons, but was thrown out by the Lords. Gladstone thereupon retired from the premiership, and was succeeded by Lord Rosebery. The latter refused to press the Home Rule question because, in his opinion, the "predominant partner," England, must first be convinced of its rightfulness. Elections for Parliament were held, in 1895, with Home Rule as the issue, and the result was an overwhelming Conservative victory. A Conservative government came into power which ruled the country for a decade. "To kill Home Rule with kindness," the government put through a number of radical land reforms, the most important being the Wyndham Act, already described.

Following the defeat of the second Home Rule Bill there was a lull in Irish political activity. Land reform did have the effect of quieting, for a time, Irish discontent; moreover, so strongly intrenched were the Conservatives that the outlook for Home Rule was almost hopeless. Could Ireland become a nation in a sense other than political? A movement for cultural nationalism began which aimed to express, in literary and artistic forms, the spirit of Ireland. In 1893, the Gaelic League was founded with the object of preserving Gaelic as the national language of Ireland. Under the leadership of Douglas Hyde it fostered energetically the almost vanished language and customs of the Gael. An Irish renaissance was in progress; economic and fiscal history were investigated; the ancient dances, music, and crafts were revived; plays, lyrics, and novels — in English — were poured forth in a variety of moods. Ireland became a "nest of singing birds." William B. Yeats, John Synge, and George Russell set forth the ideals of the Irish by means of plays, poetry, and essays. *Revival of cultural nationalism*

Another movement, economic in character, engaged Ireland's attention. Following the land reforms the peasants were in a better way to improve their condition, provided they made better use of their land. At best the Irish peasant with his small holding, lack of capital, and backward methods, was bound to suffer in competition with the cheap food from the New World. He had no tariff wall to protect him. Under the leadership of Sir Horace Plunkett a coöperative movement was launched, in 1894, known as the Irish Agricultural Organization Society. It was non-political and non-sectarian. Inside of a decade it succeeded in enrolling almost the entire peasantry. The coöperative societies bought expensive machinery for the common use of their members; established creameries and cheese factories; banished usury by organizing credit banks; acted as middlemen for the sale of their products; and, in many other ways, aided the peasants by directing and utilizing their common efforts. *The coöperative movement*

Meanwhile the political atmosphere was changing. The constitutional movement for Home Rule had failed, as had the revolutionary movement for independence. What plan could now succeed? A new answer was given by the rising generation who began a more ardent and more ambitious form of nationalist propaganda. In 1905, there appeared a new political society, called Sinn Fein (Gaelic, *ourselves*), which was *Ideas of the Sinn Fein*

founded by a journalist, Arthur Griffith. According to the Sinn
Feiners the great error of the Home Rulers was in looking to England for a solution of the political problem; whatever the solution,
it should be decided by the Irish, and by them only. A popular
uprising was impractical because England was too powerful to be
overthrown. The Sinn Feiners believed that the English government in Ireland would collapse if it did not receive the coöperation
of the Irish people. Alongside the existing government the Irish
should, therefore, establish a government of their own which they
should support and obey. The existing revenue system was to be
attacked by a boycott of taxed articles; and the existing political
system, by a boycott of the courts and the administration. Irishmen should refuse employment in the public service in any capacity. Especially should they refuse to recognize the British
government by refusing membership in Parliament. Members
elected from Ireland should form a national assembly to legislate
on Irish affairs. The agitation of the Sinn Fein was directed not
only against the British, but also against the Nationalists, because
the latter desired to maintain the British connection.

During the decade of Conservative government, Home Rule
languished in Parliament. John Redmond, leader of the Nation-

Redmond's
efforts to
mollify the
English
alists, believed that the "predominant partner"
needed to be convinced of the desirability of Home
Rule. He stated that Ireland wished to remain in
the British Empire, and assured the English that, like
Canada and Australia, she would be all the more loyal if she enjoyed self-government. He also declared that the Catholics had
no intention of persecuting the Protestants; on the contrary, they
wanted to live in harmony with them in order to form a united
Irish nation.

When the Liberals swept into office, in 1906, Irish hopes rose
once more. But the Ministry refused to consider Home Rule

The third
Home Rule
Bill
which had proved so disastrous to their party. But
the elections of 1910 resulted in giving the Nationalists
the advantage of holding the balance of power.[1]
Premier Asquith, thereupon, came to an agreement with Redmond
in which he promised Home Rule in return for Irish support. In
1912, the third Home Rule Bill was passed in the Commons by the
Liberal-Irish-Labor combination; it was thrown out by the Lords,

[1] See page 279.

but, according to the Parliament Act of 1911, the bill was expected to become law two years later.

Opposition to Home Rule was, if anything, more bitter than formerly. A wave of "Ulsteria" swept Ulster, which determined to resist Home Rule even to the point of rebellion. Sir Edward Carson, a Conservative leader, formed a military organization, the Ulster Volunteers, which drilled with the proclaimed purpose of resisting, by armed force, the jurisdiction of the proposed Irish parliament. Ulster was greatly encouraged in its opposition by an open declaration of the British army officers, stationed in Ireland, that they would refuse to lead their troops to "coerce" the rebellious province.

Opposition of Ulster to Home Rule

During July, 1914, the situation in Ireland became critical. The war-like preparations of Ulster and the "mutiny" of the British officers encouraged a military movement in southern Ireland. Nationalist Volunteers were enrolled who drilled in expectation of a conflict with Ulster. The moment the Home Rule Bill became law would be a signal for civil war in Ireland. When Parliament met to discuss the critical situation in Ireland, it was confronted by a situation that was far more serious, the World War, in which England was soon involved. Carson and Redmond immediately declared the loyalty of their followers to the British flag. In the interest of domestic peace, Parliament passed a resolution postponing Home Rule until the end of the World War.

Ireland and the World War

There was great disappointment in Ireland. The last phase of the Irish Question, self-government, still remained. Ulster's recalcitrant attitude and the weakness of the Liberal government in the face of Carson's threats created a bitter mood in Ireland. The appeal of Redmond to the Irish to show their loyalty to Great Britain in the World War found little response. A resentful Ireland confronted England now engaged in a life-and-death struggle with Germany.

REFERENCES

GENERAL:

Sir J. O'Connor, *History of Ireland 1798-1924*, 2 vols. (1926), favors connection with Britain, good chapters on financial aspects of the Irish Question; S. L. Gwynn, *Ireland* (ed. 1925), a social survey; M. Hayden and C. A. Moonan, *A Short History of the Irish People* (1922), and C. Johnston and C. Spencer, *Ireland's Story* (1905), brief accounts; Alice S.

Green, *Irish Nationality* (1911), sympathetic with Nationalist movement; L. Paul-Dubois, *Contemporary Ireland*, translated from the French (1908), good study of the Irish Question, emphasizes social and cultural matters.

SPECIAL TOPICS:

E. R. Turner, *Ireland and England* (1919), a good brief study of the relations between them, fair to both sides; F. Hackett, *Ireland: A Study in Nationalism* (1918), an impressionistic study of Irish character and history; M. Davitt, *The Fall of Feudalism in Ireland* (1904), describes activities of the Land League by one of its founders; on Home Rule: Lord Eversley, *Gladstone and Ireland* (1912); St. John Ervine, *Parnell* (1925); J. H. Parnell, *Charles Stewart Parnell* (1914); E. Childers, *The Frame-Work of Home Rule* (1911); S. Rosenbaum (ed.), *Against Home Rule* (1912), articles by prominent Unionists, Balfour, Chamberlain, Carson, and others; on social and economic aspects: Sir H. Plunkett, *Ireland in the New Century* (1904), chiefly about the coöperative movement by its founder; E. Barker, *Ireland in the Last Fifty Years 1866–1916* (1917), good for peasant problems; J. D. Clarkson, *Labour and Nationalism in Ireland* (1925), a scholarly study of the Irish labor movement, sympathetic; L. Smith-Gordon and L. C. Staples, *Rural Reconstruction in Ireland* (1919), describes situation arising from the Land Acts.

ADDITIONAL REFERENCES

M. MacDonagh, *Daniel O'Connell and the Story of Catholic Emancipation* (1929); J. E. Pomfret, *The Struggle for the Land in Ireland, 1800–1923* (1930); R. H. Murray and H. Law, *Ireland* (1924); D. Gwynn, *The Life of John Redmond* (1932); E. Curtis, *A History of Ireland* (1936).

CHAPTER XVIII

THE THIRD FRENCH REPUBLIC

THE NATIONAL ASSEMBLY

REPUBLICANISM in France was born during the French Revolution. It became the supreme ideal of the partisans of the Revolution who regarded the establishment of a republic as the complete repudiation of everything upheld by the Old Régime. The First French Republic, associated with the heroic days of the Revolution, lasted only about a decade. The Second French Republic, proclaimed amidst the wildest enthusiasm during the Revolution of 1848, had an even shorter life, only four years. The Third French Republic was the child of defeat, not of revolution, having come into existence as a result of the defeat of France by Prussia in 1871. Nevertheless it has proved to be the most stable government that France has had since 1789, outlasting kingdoms, empires, and revolutionary republics.

Stability of the Third Republic

The decade following the Franco-Prussian War may be described as the critical period in the history of the Third French Republic. Although a republic had been proclaimed, the National Assembly, elected to make peace with Germany, was overwhelmingly royalist, the republicans constituting only one third of its membership. Fortunately for the Republic the royalists were divided into factions that favored rival candidates for the throne. Some were partisans of the Bourbon dynasty, represented by the Count de Chambord, grandson of Charles X; and others, of the Orleans dynasty, represented by the Count de Paris, grandson of Louis Philippe.

Triumph of the royalists

The Assembly chose Thiers as the "Chief Executive," with full authority to conduct the government. He was now an old man of seventy-three, and throughout his long political career he had been known as a shrewd politician whose tactics might be shifty, but whose consistent support of the interests of the middle classes was never in doubt. He was opposed to absolute monarchy, but he greatly feared the "vile mob," whose outbreak during the June Days of 1848 had convinced him that only men of property should have the right to vote. Thiers was, therefore, a royalist of the school of Guizot; hence, a partisan of the

Thiers (1797–1877)

Orleans dynasty. In appearance he was a little old man with a smooth-shaven face, wearing "the eternal frock coat" of the bourgeois. His speeches were logical and convincing as well as eloquent. During the period following the Franco-Prussian War, Thiers was a tower of strength to his distracted countrymen. He eschewed all party politics and devoted himself whole-heartedly to the welfare of France, coöperating with any faction and with any man who was willing to join him in the patriotic work. The Assembly, inspired by Thiers's patriotism, adopted what came to be known as the *union sacrée*, whereby it was agreed that political differences should be put aside in order to carry through the work of reconstruction.

The first problem that confronted the Assembly was peace with Germany; and it ratified, though unwillingly, the Treaty of Frankfurt. How was the indemnity of a billion dollars to be paid? It was due to the efforts of Thiers that the loans floated by France for this purpose were readily subscribed to, both at home and abroad, and the indemnity was quickly paid. By 1873, the German army of occupation was out of France, and Thiers was gratefully hailed as the "Liberator of the territory." The payment of so large a sum in so short a time was evidence of the great confidence in their country's future felt by millions of Frenchmen, who freely gave their savings to a government that was not yet firmly established. For Germany, however, the quick payment of the indemnity was no boon. It resulted first in speculation, and later in financial disorganization which ruined many business firms. "Next time that we defeat France," Bismarck is said to have remarked, "I shall insist that Germany pay an indemnity."

Payment of the indemnity

THE PARIS COMMUNE

Misfortunes followed one after the other during *l'année terrible*, as the French call the year following the outbreak of the Franco-Prussian War. On the heels of a disastrous defeat there came a bloody uprising known as the Paris Commune, which far surpassed anything of its kind in the revolutionary history of France. The merciless suppression during the June Days had never faded from the memory of the French workingman, whose unshaken conviction was that, no matter what form of government existed, his enemy was the bourgeois. A generation of

Hatred of the bourgeois

suppression under the Second Empire had resulted in the growth of secret revolutionary societies, whose propaganda was all the more violent because secret. And when the Empire fell, the revolutionists suddenly appeared from "underground," ready to take advantage of the disorganized state of the country.

However, the revolutionists would have gained little headway had it not been for the general discontent felt among all classes of Parisians. Ardently republican, the Parisians did not wish to be governed by the royalist "clodhoppers," as they termed the Assembly because it contained a large number of peasants. Fear of mob violence, as in the time of the great Revolution, caused the Assembly to make Versailles the seat of government, which infuriated the Parisians still more. *Discontent of Paris*

During the war, business had suffered as a result of disorganization, and to relieve the situation the payment of rents, debts, and notes had been temporarily suspended. But when fighting ceased, the Assembly refused to grant any further dispensation, and ordered the immediate payment of all indebtedness legally due. This order brought great hardship to the Parisians, especially to those whose business had been almost ruined by the siege. Many were evicted from their homes because of non-payment of rent, and small shopkeepers were compelled to close their doors. *Economic distress*

There was widespread unemployment due to the disorganization of business. During the siege all able-bodied men in Paris had been provided with arms and enrolled in the National Guard. When peace was declared, the Assembly abolished the National Guard, and ordered the militiamen to surrender their arms. Destitution now stared them in the face, as they depended for their livelihood on the pay that they received from the government. This demobilization threw on the labor market a large number of men who could not find employment. Thousands of destitute men trod the streets of Paris, which created a dangerous situation, as many of them were secretly armed; they had refused to surrender their guns when the National Guard was abolished. *Unemployment*

The election of a royalist Assembly and the choice of the bourgeois Thiers as the head of the government infuriated the masses of Paris. Revolutionary agitators organized committees of former Guardsmen to defend the Republic against the royalist Assembly at Versailles. The Assembly, fear- *The Commune* ing trouble, sent troops to seize the cannon in Paris, but the soldiers were surrounded by mobs and disarmed. War now began between Paris and the rest of France. The committee of "communards," as the revolutionists were called, ordered elections to be held in Paris for a General Council. Conservative electors, out of fear, kept away from the polls, so that only extreme radicals were chosen. The General Council then proclaimed Paris a "Commune," adopted the red flag, and declared all acts of the Versailles government null and void. Paris virtually seceded from France.

The communards were a heterogeneous group of revolutionaries: socialists, anarchists, utopians, and radical republicans who, though The communards differing in their schemes for reorganizing society and government, united in opposing the Assembly. In their plans the Jacobin ideals of '93 were fused with the socialist ideals of '48; they revived the old Revolutionary calendar and attempted to establish national workshops. More significant, however, were certain aspects new in the revolutionary history of France which, in the twentieth century, inspired the Bolshevists. In the first place, the uprising was chiefly the work of men who had been soldiers and who fought in military fashion not only with ordinary arms but with artillery. They were not the mobs of 1793 nor the barricaded workingmen of 1830 and 1848. In the second place, the communards had a new idea of political organization. They denounced parliaments and the existing administrative system, and favored a political organization in which all power, executive, legislative, and judicial, would be lodged in one body controlled absolutely by revolutionists representing the proletariat. The Commune, in their view, inaugurated "a new political era, positive and scientific. It marks the end of the old political and clerical world, of militarism, bureaucracy, exploitation, stock-jobbery, and special privileges to which the proletariat owe their servitude and the Fatherland its misfortunes."

The revolutionaries of '71 evidently came to the conclusion that the establishment of socialism in France as a whole was impossible; Communards favor decentralization in case of an uprising the peasants always came to the aid of the bourgeois in the cities and undid the work of the revolutionary element. The communards turned to the idea of decentralizing France by giving each unit, or commune, great powers of local self-government. If this were accomplished, the industrial centers might be able to establish the socialist commonwealth; deprived of peasant help the bourgeois would easily succumb to the attacks of the working classes. To the charge of the Assembly that they were destroying the unity of France, the communards replied that that unity, "imposed upon us to this day by the Empire, by the monarchy, and by parliamentarism, is merely despotic, unintelligent, arbitrary, and onerous centralization," and that the true unity of France would consist in the free and spontaneous coöperation of the communes.

When the captive French armies were released by Germany, the Assembly determined to put down the Commune without mercy. A new siege of Paris was begun in April, 1871, this time by the French army with the Germans looking on. The city was taken after six weeks. Then followed a gigantic street struggle between the troops and the communards, each side desperate and merciless. Seeing themselves overcome by superior force, the communards resorted to frightful methods. They executed prominent persons whom they held as "hostages," one of them being the Archbishop of Paris; and began the destruction of the city by setting fire to famous buildings, such as the Hôtel de Ville, the Palais de Justice, and the Tuileries. The Vendôme Column was pulled down. Several streets were masses of flame. Nothing so frightful had ever taken place in Paris, not even during the Reign of Terror.

Outrages committed by the communards

The final stand of the communards was at the cemetery of Père Lachaise, where a desperate encounter took place. The troops managed to get the upper hand, and order was restored. The vengeance taken by the Versailles government equaled in ferocity that displayed by the communards. Those captured with arms in their hands were stood up against a wall and summarily shot. Thousands were arrested and, after a brief trial by court-martial, were sentenced to imprisonment, exile, or death. Thousands more fled to foreign countries to escape the fury of the Assembly. It is impossible to state accurately how many were killed during the uprising, but it is estimated that about 17,000 communards perished.

Suppression of the Commune

TRIUMPH OF REPUBLICANISM

Once the Commune was suppressed, the Assembly turned its attention to the problem of giving France a permanent govern-

ment.   That body had been elected chiefly for the purpose of
The Rivet   making peace, but the royalist majority determined
law   to continue its existence after peace had been made.
By the Rivet law the Assembly conferred upon Thiers the new
title of "President"; it also gave power to the Assembly to draw
up a constitution.   In spite of these concessions to republicanism,
there was an understanding that a monarchy would be established
as soon as the royalist factions had composed their differences.

What attitude Thiers would adopt became a matter of vital
concern.   Not only did he enjoy the confidence of the people, but
Thiers be-   he was also the leader of an important group in the
comes a re-   Assembly, the Left Center, that sometimes held the
publican   balance of power between the various factions.   All his
life he had been a royalist, but he was now willing, on patriotic
grounds, to accept the Republic, "that form of government which
divides us least," as he called it in criticism of the royalist factions.
But he let it be clearly understood that if the government was to
be republican in form, it must be conservative in policy.   "The
Republic will be conservative or it will not be," he warned his colleagues.   His change of view greatly incensed the royalists, who
denounced the Republic as a breeder of "radicalism, anarchy, and
moral chaos."   In 1873, the Assembly passed a vote of censure
against the President, who thereupon resigned.   As his successor
it chose Marshal MacMahon, a staunch royalist, with the understanding that he would make way for a king as soon as one was
chosen.

The action of the Assembly in forcing the resignation of the
"Liberator of the territory" disgusted the country.   To voice
Gambetta   this change of sentiment came Gambetta, who now
(1838–82)   entered the lists as the republican champion against
the royalists.   Gambetta's heroic part during the Franco-Prussian
War had endeared him to masses of Frenchmen who had but little
sympathy with his radical opinions.   It now remained for him to
begin the "republican education" of France; namely, to convert
these masses to the idea of a republic.   With this object in view he
toured the country several times, addressing huge audiences and
rousing his countrymen to a high pitch of enthusiasm.   "The
traveling salesman of the Republic" his opponents called Gambetta, an appellation which he adopted with pride.

As Thiers was in appearance the typical bourgeois, Gambetta was the typical bohemian. His dark, curly hair and flowing beard, his flashing eyes and careless, joyous manner, his deep resonant voice rolling like musical thunder over great audiences, his flowing eloquence and exuberant imagination fascinated all those who came to hear him. Gambetta's very presence was an oration. He appealed to all sorts of people in France, from solid bourgeois who admired his shrewd common sense to artists of the Latin Quarter in Paris who applauded his unconventional ways and thrilling eloquence. Gambetta believed firmly in the principles of the French Revolution; in addition, he had a warm sympathy for the "new social strata," the working classes, to whom he believed political power was destined to pass. But mindful of the Commune, he warned his fellow republicans not to disturb the social order till democratic principles triumphed, and to endeavor to solve social problems in a spirit of moderation. "There is no Social Question," he once declared; "there are only social questions which have to be dealt with, one by one, as they come up." Gambetta was essentially an opportunist, asking for much and taking what he could get, and he was willing to work with a conservative like Thiers in order to realize at least some of his political ideals. "I belong to a school that refuses to dogmatize," he declared, "that believes in analyzing things, in observation, in the study of facts, to a school that takes account of environment, of tendencies, of prejudices, even of hostilities, for one must take account of everything." Once a democratic republic was established in France it would result, he enthusiastically believed, in the "efflorescence of the élite of the nation" who, as in ancient Greece, would make their country glorious. The policies of the Third French Republic for a whole generation were deeply influenced by Gambetta's ideas, which were espoused by his disciples, Ferry, Waldeck-Rousseau, and Clemenceau.

The rising tide of republicanism convinced the royalists that they must come to a decision without delay. They agreed to offer the throne to the Count de Chambord, with the understanding that he, being childless, would be suc- The flag question ceeded by the head of the House of Orleans. The views of the Count bore out the characteristic of the Bourbons that they never learned anything and never forgot anything. He believed that France had at last repudiated democracy, whether republican or imperial, and was now returning to the ideals of the Old Régime.

"The issue at stake," he declared, "is none other than that of reconstructing society, now deeply disturbed, on its natural base . . . and not to fear to employ force in the service of order and justice." The Count agreed to accept the crown, and, as a sign that France had fully recanted her democratic past, he demanded of the Assembly that it abolish the tricolor flag, the "symbol of revolution," and to restore the *fleur-de-lys* of the Bourbons, "received as a sacred trust from the old King, my grandfather, dying in exile." But the Assembly hesitated to restore the white flag of the Bourbons which, they feared, would rouse the old hatred for that dynasty. They endeavored to persuade the Count to accept the tricolor with the crown, but without avail.

This curious situation was fortunate for the Republic; it postponed the establishment of a monarchy, and made the country realize the true nature of the proposed restoration. In order to continue the royalist control of the government through MacMahon, the Assembly passed the Septennate Act, extending the presidential term to seven years. The Count de Chambord, being old, would probably die within this period, and the Count de Paris, who was willing to accept the tricolor, would then be chosen king. A number of organic laws, passed by the Assembly in 1875, provided for a Chamber of Deputies elected by universal, manhood suffrage, and for a Senate chosen by local bodies. On the last day of 1875 the National Assembly went out of existence.

The government, nominally a republic, then proceeded to make war upon the republicans. They were dismissed from office; their journals were harassed and frequently suppressed; and their associations and meetings were put under strict surveillance. During the elections for parliament the government exerted its influence in favor of the royalist candidates. In spite of official pressure, however, the first Chamber was overwhelmingly republican; the Senate was royalist only because one quarter of its membership had been appointed for life by the Assembly before it had dissolved. Political conditions in 1876 were anomalous: the lower house was republican, but the upper house, the President, and the administration were royalist. This situation was bound to lead to a renewal of the struggle between the two forces to obtain a more decisive result.

President MacMahon met the situation by a compromise. He

appointed a republican ministry headed by Jules Simon; but he maintained that it was responsible to him, not to the   Social forces Chamber.   The republicans, on the contrary, held to   on each side the principle of the responsibility of ministers to parliament.   All political, social, and religious forces made ready for a trial of strength to decide whether France was to be a republic or a monarchy.   Behind the royalists were the aristocrats, many of the peasants, the bureaucracy, the upper middle class, and the Church, all of whom feared that the Republic would encourage the revolutionary elements.   They pointed to the Commune as a warning to conservative citizens to beware of giving power to the lower classes. Behind the republicans were the lower middle class, the intellectuals, and the workingmen who, swayed by the eloquence of Gambetta, were determined that no king, whether reactionary or liberal, should ever again reign in France.

The Catholic Church was especially active on the side of the royalists. The French Catholics believed that a monarchy, whether royal or imperial, would be a friendly protector, and   Church fa- that a republic would be a bitter enemy.[1] In Gam-   vors the betta and the republicans the Catholics beheld the   royalists successors of Danton and the Jacobins; and they feared that a republic based upon the principles of the French Revolution would wage war against Catholicism.   Many priests preached political sermons in favor of royalism, which infuriated the republicans, who denounced the political activity of the Church.   "Le cléricalisme, voilà l'ennemi!" exclaimed Gambetta, and his phrase became the rallying cry of the republicans.

On May 16, 1877, the famous Seize Mai, President MacMahon dismissed the Simon Ministry, although it had the confidence of the Chamber. He then appointed a royalist ministry   Seize Mai which had his confidence though not that of parliament.   This action was denounced by the republicans as a coup d'état, an attempt by the President to inaugurate a system of personal government.   The reply of MacMahon was to dissolve the Chamber with the consent of the Senate.   In the elections that followed, royalists and republicans once more entered the political arena, determined to fight with every weapon at their command.

To preserve the "moral order," as the royalists called conserva-

[1] See page 70

tism, the government used every influence at its command to elect
Triumph of the republicans a royalist Chamber. It resorted to "official" candidates, gerrymandering, and coercion of all sorts.
Again, Gambetta went on one of his famous speaking tours, and he succeeded in arousing the country against the royalists and their methods. In one of his speeches he gave utterance to another famous phrase, which became the electoral cry of 1877. "When France has spoken in her sovereign voice," he told Mac-Mahon, "you will be forced to give in or give up." The elections resulted in a notable triumph for the republicans, who controlled the new Chamber by a large majority. MacMahon "gave in." He dismissed the royalist ministry, and appointed a republican ministry that had the confidence of the Chamber. In 1878, the Senate, too, fell under the control of the republicans, who now determined to force MacMahon out of office. A demand was made by the Chamber that he dismiss certain royalist officials. Rather than to comply with the demand, he "gave up." In 1879, MacMahon resigned, and he was succeeded by Jules Grévy, a lifelong republican, who declared that he would always recognize the Chamber as the supreme power in the government.

France was now definitely a republic, safe from royalist plottings and from revolutionary uprisings. July 14 was made a national holiday. The government moved from Versailles to Paris, which again became the capital. Unlike the First and Second Republics, which were established as a result of revolutionary enthusiasm, the Third Republic owes its existence largely to the mistaken tactics of the royalists whose factional differences and reactionary ideas disgusted the country; the republicans, united and well led, took advantage of the situation and triumphed over their opponents.

SYSTEM OF GOVERNMENT

Although France is a republic, her system of government is modeled upon that of England with a popularly elected parliament
France a centralized republic and a responsible ministry. Unlike the American Republic, which is a federal union, the French Republic is highly centralized. The country is divided into *départements*, administrative divisions presided over by prefects appointed by the central government. In each *département* there are popularly elected councils, but their powers are largely advisory. A measure of local self-government was given to the

municipalities by the law of 1884, which permitted them to elect
their mayors and councils.

The head of the government is the President, who is elected for
a term of seven years by the National Assembly, the name given
to a joint session of both houses.   Mindful of Louis   The Presi-
Napoleon's rise to power through popular election, the   dent
French constitution proscribes this method of choosing a President,
and prohibits a member of a French royal or imperial family from
being a candidate.   The powers of the President are limited: all his
acts must be countersigned by a cabinet minister; he has no real
veto power over laws passed by parliament; appointments to office
are made in his name by the cabinet; he may, with the consent of
the Senate, dissolve the Chamber before its term has expired, but
since President MacMahon's famous dissolution in 1877 no French
President has exercised this power.   The position of the President
has been well described thus: the King of England reigns but does
not rule; the President of the United States rules but does not
reign; the President of France neither reigns nor rules.

Parliament is bicameral, consisting of a Senate and a Chamber
of Deputies.   The Senators are chosen by electoral colleges in the
départements, composed of delegates from the various   The Senate
local bodies and the Deputies from the *département*,
for nine years.   In theory, the Senate has equal legislative authority with the Chamber; in practice its main function is to act
as a check on the Chamber by revising, amending, and sometimes
defeating bills.   Its powers are not so great as those of the
American Senate nor yet so small as those of the British House
of Lords.

The Chamber of Deputies is elected by universal, male suffrage
for a term of four years, and is the "sovereign voice" of the French
people.   Its powers are like those of the British House   The Cham-
of Commons after which it was modeled.[1]   As a legisla-   ber
ture the Chamber has power over all bills; and as a parliament it
controls the cabinet, which it may overthrow by a vote of "no
confidence" or by defeating an important bill introduced by a
cabinet member.

The cabinet is officially appointed by the President; actually he
appoints those men whose names are submitted to him by the
parliamentary chiefs who dictate the appointments.   Although

[1] See page 259.

the French cabinet system is modeled on that of the British, its
The cab- working has been quite different because of the multi-
inet plicity of political parties, no one of which ever has had
a majority in the Chamber. A cabinet is, therefore, composed of
men belonging to various groups, not to a majority party, and is
supported in the Chamber by a coalition of these groups known as
a *bloc*. Parliamentary coalitions are hard to keep together, particularly in France, where party ties are very loose; cabinet crises are,
therefore, of frequent occurrence. As much energy is frequently
expended in keeping the cabinet together as in promoting legislation. A favorite method of upsetting a ministry is through an
interpellation, by which any deputy may direct questions and demand answers of a cabinet minister on the conduct of his office.
An interpellation is, however, more often a challenge than a request for information; a sharp debate ensues, frequently resulting
in the fall of the cabinet.

It must not, however, be supposed that the instability of cabinets
means the instability of the government. Below the play of
Administra- factional politics flow steady political currents that
tive stability continue in the same direction no matter who is Prime
Minister. When a cabinet falls, the Chamber is not dissolved, as
in England under similar circumstances; a new shuffle is made, and
the new cabinet, as often as not, continues the policies of its
predecessor. A great, though silent, part in steadying the wheels
of government is played by the bureaucracy. Since its reorganization by Napoleon, the highly centralized administrative system of
France has continued the practical work of administration in the
spirit of its conservative traditions, irrespective of what government rules in Paris. It has given continuity to the political life of
France by absorbing the shocks of revolutions and *coups d'état*, and
by remaining independent of cabinet changes.

The French constitution, adopted in 1875, still remains essentially an outline. It contains no statement of general principles,
The consti- like the documents adopted during the French Revolu-
tution, an tion, and no definite articles protecting liberty, persons,
outline and property like the Bill of Rights in the American
constitution. Its only prohibition is in the article which declares that
"the republican form of government shall not be made the subject
of a proposed revision." Amendments can be made very easily; a
proposal for an amendment may be made by the President or by a

majority in both houses; to pass, it must be ratified by a majority of the National Assembly. In other words, an ordinary statute and a constitutional amendment are adopted by the same persons.

There is no party government in France like that in England and the United States. Instead of two compact, well-organized groups of electors with candidates, conventions, and plat- Party versus forms striving for the control of the government, there faction government are many loosely organized groups with certain political tendencies, royalist, moderate, radical, or socialist. Each candidate for public office is practically his own party; he writes his own platform, conducts his own campaign, and pays his own expenses, aided sometimes by hastily organized societies. After his election he seeks out other members of the Chamber who profess the same or similar views, and these constitute a "party." A party may be born at the opening of the parliamentary session and die before its close; often a Deputy belongs to more than one group, or he passes serenely from one to another. In the Chamber the Deputies sit from left to right of the President of that body according to their opinions, the "left" being radical, the "center" moderate, and the "right," conservative. Political leaders, rather than political organizations, are the important factors in French parliamentary life; nearly every group is dominated by a prominent politician whom it follows as long as he can lead. Only the socialists are well organized as a political party, with platforms, candidates, party workers, and party journals. Their success at the polls stimulated their opponents to organize more efficiently and the various groups tended to combine at the polls into "coalitions." [1] Newspapers, edited by political leaders, are a powerful factor in directing political opinion. A bold editorial, a brilliant speech, a penetrating book often does the work that party platforms and party organizations do in England and America.

RECONSTRUCTION

In spite of the great losses suffered during the Franco-Prussian War in life, property, and through business disturbance, in spite of humiliating defeat, in spite of bitter political and Recovery of religious dissensions, France rapidly recovered her old- France time vigor. Indeed, the national resurrection of France after 1870

---

[1] After the World War the French political group showed a marked tendency to organize on party lines.

was one of the amazing chapters in the history of the nineteenth century. Europe, and particularly Germany, was astonished to see the nation that but yesterday was so humiliatingly defeated, rise to her feet, bind up her wounds, and spring again to the fore. A comprehensive plan of reconstruction was adopted, and carried through with vigor and thoroughness.

Military reform was urgent, the war having shown the woeful disorganization of the army.   As Prussia learned from France
Conscription   after Jena, so France learned from Prussia after Sedan.
A new military law, passed in 1872, reorganized the French army on the Prussian model.   Conscription was introduced, and men were obliged to give five years of active service, which, in 1889, was reduced to three, and, in 1905, to two years.   Powerful fortresses were erected along the German frontier, notably at Verdun and at Belfort.

The Third Republic created a colonial empire second only to the British.   It completed the conquest of Algeria, which was an-
Colonial   nexed to France and given representation in parlia-
expansion   ment.   In 1881, it acquired Tunis; in 1885, Anam and Tonkin; in 1895, Madagascar; and in 1912, Morocco.[1]   French imperialism was encouraged, and even aided, by Bismarck, who was opposed to the acquisition of colonies by Germany.   He believed that France would forget the *revanche* if she found compensation in colonies.

"It was the schoolmaster who triumphed at Sedan" was the common view in France in explanation of the defeat of 1870.   The
The Ferry   superiority of the Prussians was explained on the
Laws   ground that their national system of popular education had abolished illiteracy, and so gave the mass of people a conscious and intelligent interest in the welfare of their country.   Popular education was then in a bad way in France; schools were few and poorly equipped, hence illiteracy was common, especially in the rural districts.[2]   If democracy was to succeed, argued the republicans, all Frenchmen must be educated to appreciate it, and universal suffrage, "the master of us all," would favor progressive ideas, and not become the means of reaction as under the Second Empire. The republicans also realized that a national system of popular

[1] See page 654.

[2] An education law, put through by Guizot in 1833, required the localities to establish schools, but education was not made compulsory; hence, many children were not sent to school.

education would be the best means of educating the rising generation to be loyal to the Republic. Educational reform in France was chiefly the work of Jules Ferry, a strong anti-clerical who, as Minister of Education and as Prime Minister, was an ardent advocate of secular education. He was ably seconded by Ferdinand Buisson, a prominent French educator. During 1881–86 the Ferry Laws were passed, which established, for the first time, a national system of free, popular education supported by the localities and by the national government. Elementary education was made compulsory, either in public or private schools, and the government voted large sums for the establishment of schools. Religious instruction in the public schools was forbidden; only civic and moral instruction by laymen was permitted. Normal schools for the training of teachers were established, and only lay persons, who held teachers' diplomas from the government, were appointed as teachers. The religious schools were denied public support; and members of religious orders were prohibited from teaching in the public schools. Higher education for women, long neglected, was now greatly encouraged, and women were given equal opportunities with men in nearly all the educational institutions of France. The creation of a national system of popular education was a great and enduring achievement of the Third Republic.

Another anti-clerical law was the establishment of divorce in 1884. The Restoration, inspired by Catholic influences, recognized the indissolubility of marriage by abolishing, in Divorce 1816, divorce instituted by the Napoleonic Code. But the anti-clerical republicans recognized marriage as a civil contract, not as a sacrament, which could be dissolved by law.

Business revived rapidly after the Franco-Prussian War. The amount of damage done by the invading armies was comparatively small, and France energetically turned her attention Economic to business enterprise. Her credit was excellent, due revival to the prompt and rapid payment of the indemnity to Germany. Railways were built, harbors were deepened, new machinery was installed, and new iron mines were opened. Expositions were held in 1878 and 1889, and a surprised world beheld the new France that emerged from the disasters of 1870.

THE BOULANGER AFFAIR

The rapid recovery of France was mainly due to the vigorous reconstruction policy of the government. But several political The Panama scandals took place, which cast discredit on the Republic and on the parliamentary system generally. In scandal 1887, it was discovered that a son-in-law of President Grévy was using his influence for the purpose of trafficking in the bestowal of decorations, especially in the greatly sought-for Legion of Honor. Although himself innocent, the President was forced to resign. Far more serious was the Panama scandal. A company had been organized by Ferdinand de Lesseps to pierce the Isthmus of Panama, in which many Frenchmen had invested their hard-earned savings. In 1888, the company went bankrupt, and a judicial investigation disclosed doubtful financial transactions in which officials high in the public service were implicated. Members of parliament had been subsidized through presents of shares of stock and through payment of campaign expenses in return for government favors. Even ministers were implicated in the "Republican scandal," as it was termed by the royalists, who charged that the Republic was in control of "panamaists," or "grafters." The exposure drove several prominent politicians into private life, and some even to suicide.

Discontent was also aroused by the peaceful policies of the Third Republic. In foreign affairs it pursued a cautious and defensive The *Re-* policy, sometimes at the price of national humiliation, *vanche* for it feared a victory almost as much as a defeat. A disastrous war would surely bring to an end the Third Republic as it had brought to an end the Second Empire; a victorious war might bring to the fore another "man on horseback" to plot against its existence. Because of this peaceful policy the royalists denounced the republicans as a cowardly party that feared to take vengeance on Germany. The *revanche* idea became a cult among some elements; and patriotic societies were organized to keep alive the bitter memories of the Franco-Prussian War, and to spread a propaganda of hostility to Germany. On every possible occasion great demonstrations would take place around the statue erected to the city of Strasbourg in the Place de la Concorde, the famous public square in Paris.

Before long a man appeared who became the leading exponent of discontent with the Republic. He was General Boulanger, a handsome, dashing soldier who made a brilliant figure as he rode on a black charger along the boulevards of Paris. Boulanger entered politics, and soon rose to be Minister of War. At every opportunity he would make speeches appealing to chauvinistic sentiments which brought him great popularity. Every time he ran for office he was elected by immense majorities. Whenever he appeared in the streets of Paris, crowds would follow him about cheering enthusiastically and demanding that *le brave général* be put at the head of affairs. Many saw in him another Napoleon who would lead French armies across the Rhine to fulfill the *revanche*. "Remember that they are waiting for us in Alsace-Lorraine," Boulanger reminded his fellow-countrymen.

Boulanger

It soon became evident that the General was merely a tool in the hands of those that were hostile to the Republic. He was the long-sought-for "man on horseback" who would over-throw the Republic by a *coup d'état*; consequently royalists and clericals flocked to his standard. A Boulanger party was organized which was liberally financed and ably managed; popular journalists, among them Rochefort, became his champions. In the face of this new danger there took place once more, as in the days of MacMahon, a "republican concentration"; the various factions ceased their quarrels and united to defend the Republic against its enemies. In 1889, Boulanger was suddenly summoned for trial before the Senate, charged with conspiring against the state. The issue was now joined, but the General showed himself to be a vain and empty show. His audacity vanished quickly, and he fled the country ingloriously and committed suicide. At one time a serious danger, the Boulanger movement suddenly and completely collapsed, and the Republic was safe once more.

Collapse of the Boulanger movement

THE DREYFUS AFFAIR

No event in the history of the Third Republic was so dramatic as the famous Dreyfus Affair which, for ten years, convulsed France and attracted the liveliest attention the world over. In 1894, Alfred Dreyfus, a captain of artillery attached to the general staff, was arrested on the charge of having betrayed his country by selling important military secrets. He was tried secretly by a court martial, which found him guilty and sentenced him to expulsion from the army and to

Condemnation of Dreyfus

imprisonment for life. Dreyfus was sent to Devil's Island, a penal settlement near French Guiana, where he was to serve his sentence in the fearful heat of the tropics.

Dreyfus was a Jew, a matter of significance in the situation. An anti-Semitic movement had developed in France since the Franco-Prussian War, which was encouraged by the extreme nationalists. There was a widespread belief that Jewish financiers were secretly working in the interests of Germany, and against the interests of France. A vigorous anti-Semitic propaganda was launched by a journalist, named Edouard Drumont, who secured a popular following through his paper, *La Libre Parole* (*Free Speech*). Drumont constantly repeated the charge that the Republic was dominated by Jewish bankers who dictated the policies of France through their corrupt control of the politicians. Prejudice against Dreyfus because he was a Jew helped materially to confirm the opinion that he had been justly condemned.

Anti-Semitism

The trial and condemnation of Dreyfus had almost been forgotten when the case was unexpectedly and dramatically reopened. In 1896, Colonel Georges Picquart was appointed chief of the Intelligence Bureau, the department of the army in which military secrets were guarded. There he found the *bordereau*, a document containing the list of military secrets sold to the enemy which, it was charged, was in Dreyfus's handwriting. This document, though it bore no date, address, or signature, constituted the most important evidence against the condemned Captain. On examining the *bordereau*, Picquart came to the conclusion that it was not in the handwriting of Dreyfus, but in that of Major Esterhazy, an officer well known in the army as a dissolute spendthrift. He imparted this discovery to his superiors, whom he tried to convince that Dreyfus was the victim of a judicial error and that Esterhazy was the real culprit. But his superiors gave him no encouragement. Their attitude convinced Picquart that Dreyfus was the victim, not of a judicial error, but of a military conspiracy. He began an agitation for a revision of the case, as a consequence of which he was ousted from the army.

Picquart

By this time great interest in the case was aroused in France. The element of mystery, the possible innocence of one condemned to so cruel a punishment, the fear of foreign complications, all led the sensitive French to take sides either

The anti-Dreyfusards

for or against the prisoner on Devil's Island.   The overwhelming majority of the people were anti-Dreyfusard because they accepted the judgment of those in authority.   To question the verdict of the army "for the sake of a Jew accused of treason," seemed to many Frenchmen the height of anti-patriotism.   An anti-Dreyfusard party appeared, the Nationalists, which attracted the support of royalists, clericals, former followers of Boulanger, and other reactionaries.   The Church, too, took an active part on the side of the anti-Dreyfusards.   A daily paper, *La Croix* (*The Cross*), published by an order of monks, led in the attack on Dreyfus and on the Jews generally.   The familiar combination of royalism, clericalism, and militarism disquieted many thoughtful Frenchmen. Was there another conspiracy against the Republic?

On the side of Dreyfus was a small minority consisting mainly of intellectuals, who denounced his conviction as a stain on the honor of the country.   They demanded a revision of The Drey-
the case by a civil tribunal in order to give Dreyfus fusards
an opportunity to prove his innocence.   Among his champions were the famous novelists, Anatole France and Émile Zola, the journalist-politician, Georges Clemenceau, and the scholar, Joseph Reinach.   To the side of the intellectuals came the socialists who, at first, regarded the Affair merely as "a squabble among the bourgeois."   But their eloquent leader, Jaurès, convinced them that a bourgeois unjustly condemned ceases to be a member of a class and becomes a representative of humanity, and the socialists rallied to the side of Dreyfus.   By far the leading figure among the Dreyfusards was Colonel Picquart, whose burning zeal for justice, daring courage, and knowledge of the situation made a profound impression on his fellow countrymen, and caused many seriously to doubt the guilt of Dreyfus.

One of the sensational incidents in the Dreyfus Affair was an open letter, entitled *J'accuse*, written by Zola to the President of the Republic.   Zola boldly charged that members of Zola's open
the general staff and their tools in the army were in letter
league with forgers and conspirators, and he denounced the verdict of the court-martial as "a crime of high treason against humanity." This letter was a bombshell thrown into the ranks of the anti-Dreyfusards.   He was prosecuted for defamation, but fled from France to avoid the sentence of imprisonment.

The government now proposed to settle the Dreyfus matter

once for all.   Minister of War Cavaignac, in a carefully prepared
Cavaignac's address, announced that he had examined all the docu-
report ments relating to the case, and that, even omitting the
much-discussed *bordereau*, Dreyfus had been justly condemned because his guilt rested on three other documents which he named.
The Dreyfus Affair was once more "closed."

But the more it was closed, the more it was opened.   Immediately Picquart came forward and caused another commotion by
Confessions declaring that two of the three documents cited by
of Henry Cavaignac bore no relation to the case, and that the
and flight of third was a forgery.   He offered to prove his statement
Esterhazy
and was promptly arrested.   Shortly afterwards the
public was greatly disturbed by the suicide of Colonel Henry, who
had left a confession saying that he had forged the document referred to by Picquart.   The country was again startled by the news
that Esterhazy had confessed to being the author of the *bordereau*,
and had fled to England.   The anti-Dreyfusards defended themselves by saying that the guilt of Henry and Esterhazy did not
prove the innocence of Dreyfus.

But suspicion was growing among the people that they were
being duped in order to shield forgers and conspirators.   The
The Repub- activity of the royalists alarmed the republicans, who
lican Bloc now feared that the "honor of the army" was being
used as a cloak to hide a conspiracy against the Republic.   When
this situation became evident, there took place once more a "republican concentration" against royalism.   A coalition, known as
the Bloc, was formed in the Chamber, composed of all the republican
groups, from the most moderate to the most radical, including the
socialists, which pledged itself to support the "Cabinet of Republican Defense," organized in 1899 by Premier Waldeck-Rousseau.
This ministry contained General de Galliffet who had mercilessly
suppressed the Commune, and the socialist, Alexandre Millerand,
who was the first socialist to become a cabinet minister.   The
government declared its readiness "to defend energetically republican institutions," and "to put an end to all agitations the object of
which, it is easily seen, is against the system of government consecrated by universal suffrage."   A noteworthy group of new statesmen arose to face the situation, Waldeck-Rousseau, Briand,
Clemenceau, Jaurès, Viviani, and Combes.   The policies of the
Bloc, which may be summed up as anti-clericalism and social re-

form, were energetically pursued by the government down to the outbreak of the World War.

A new trial was ordered for Dreyfus, who was brought back to France. In the town of Rennes far from the madding crowds of Paris he again faced a court martial. This time the trial was public, and it became evident that the judges were hostile to the accused. They admitted all evidence against him, and excluded evidence favorable to him. Dreyfus was again found guilty of treason, this time under "extenuating circumstances"; his life sentence was reduced to ten years' imprisonment. But the sentence was not executed, as President Loubet pardoned the prisoner. *Second trial of Dreyfus*

This decision, however, satisfied neither side. The Dreyfusards demanded the complete exoneration of the Captain and rejected a pardon carrying with it the stigma of guilt. The anti-Dreyfusards were in a rage. Street riots between the two factions were of common occurrence, but quiet was restored by a grant of amnesty to all implicated in the Affair, whether on one side or on the other. In 1906, when the situation had become normal, the supreme court of France itself undertook to revise the case. It rendered a decision which completely exonerated Dreyfus, who was declared wholly innocent of any act of treason, the evidence against him consisting of forgeries and lies. Esterhazy was found guilty of being the author of the *bordereau*. As in popular novels, all the heroes were rewarded and all the villains were punished. Dreyfus was restored to the army and promoted in rank. Picquart was made a general and, later, Minister of War. Zola died before the Affair was completely closed; his remains were buried with great pomp in the Panthéon, the Westminster Abbey of France. The honor of the French army was vindicated by the degradation or dismissal of the officers concerned in the conspiracy against Dreyfus. *Vindication of Dreyfus*

Superficially the Dreyfus Affair was a detective story on a national scale, but it really marked an important epoch in the history of the Third Republic. Although the Republic owed its existence mainly to the efforts of the radical Gambetta, it had been governed in the spirit of the conservative Thiers. Only when attacked, as in the Boulanger Affair, did it defend itself; unlike the First Republic, it made no aggressive move against the royalists. However, royalism was so discredited by *Suppression of militarism* the defeat of MacMahon and by the Boulanger fiasco that its influence in the public life of the nation rapidly declined. But the army, sworn to defend the Republic, was officered by royalists, a situation that arose from the fact that most of the officers came from the upper classes who were royalist by tradition and sympathy. In the army, therefore, lay the one hope of the enemies of the Republic who, at a propitious moment, were prepared to execute a *coup d'état* in order to restore the monarchy. The revision of the Dreyfus case by the civil courts and the quashing of the verdicts of two military courts, vigorously asserted the supremacy of the civil power. The army was compelled humbly to acknowledge its subordinate position in the Republic. Officers suspected of being royalists were forced to retire, and republicans were put in their place. Once the army was republicanized, all hope of restoring the monarchy disappeared.

ANTI-CLERICAL LEGISLATION

The Dreyfus Affair resulted in reviving the old feud between Church and State. Since the establishment of the Republic the relations between them had often been strained to the breaking point. The republicans, inspired by Gambetta's warning cry, watched the Church with an unfriendly eye. Although the Concordat of 1801 was maintained, it was often violated in spirit by both sides. The annual appropriation was too small for the needs of the Church, and it was always voted grudgingly. The Ministry of Public Worship, generally occupied by an anti-clerical, administered the affairs of the Church in a manner quite unfriendly to her. Nevertheless, both parties favored the maintenance of the Concordat: the Church, because of the great prestige which it gave her in being recognized as the established religion and because of the assured, if small, income that she received; the anti-clericals, because they feared "an armed Church in an unarmed State," by which they meant to imply that the Church would be far more dangerous to the Republic if freed from its supervision and control.

The Concordat maintained by the Republic

The strained relations between the Church and the Republic were the subject of an encyclical, issued by Pope Leo XIII in 1892. He reminded the French Catholics that the Church was not committed to any particular form of government, and that "when a new government is founded,

The Pope recognizes the Republic

acceptance thereof is not only permissible but a duty." He advised them to accept the Republic which was now firmly established; by doing so they could exert a mollifying influence on the anti-clericalism of the government. Some of the French Catholics followed the Pope's advice and "rallied" to the Republic, forming a group in the Chamber known as the Ralliés; but most of them remained royalists, and criticized the Pope for interfering in their political affairs.

It was the Dreyfus Affair which brought about a critical situation in the relations between the Catholic Church and the Republic because the Catholics were active in opposing a revision of the case. When the Waldeck-Rousseau Ministry assumed power, it determined on an aggressive anti-clerical policy. The first attack was made on the Congregations, or orders of monks and nuns, who had been especially active against Dreyfus. Most of the Congregations were engaged in the work of education and charity. Alongside of the public schools, established by the Ferry Laws, there had grown up a rival school system conducted by monks and nuns, which greatly disturbed the republicans who charged that the religious schools were permeated with royalist ideals. Waldeck-Rousseau delivered an address, in 1900, which profoundly influenced public opinion. He declared that the moral unity of the French people was being undermined by rival systems of education which artificially perpetuated the divisions caused by the French Revolution: one system, that of the public schools, was inspired by the democratic and republican ideals of the Revolution, and the other, that of the Church, was inspired by those of the Old Régime. This situation, he declared, was intolerable.

In 1901, an Associations Law was passed which required all Congregations to be "authorized," or incorporated; those who did not receive authorization would be dissolved, and their property, confiscated. The enforcement of the law was entrusted to Émile Combes who, in 1902, succeeded Waldeck-Rousseau as Premier. Combes was an extreme anti-clerical, and he determined to apply the law in the most drastic manner possible. Those orders that refused to seek authorization were immediately suppressed; nearly all of those that did apply were refused authorization on the ground that they were not socially necessary, and were also suppressed. Comparatively few were permitted to continue their corporate existence. Thousands of monks and nuns found themselves homeless and destitute, the government having seized their convents and their property. The Ministry was especially severe on the teaching orders. In 1904, a new law forbade all teaching of whatever grade by Congregations, whether authorized or not. Thousands of schools conducted by the orders were closed by the government or put under lay control.

The stringent laws directed against the orders were only preliminary to the far more important law separating Church and

L'état laïc

State. Many republicans had become converted to the doctrine of *l'état laïc*, or the absolute independence of the State of all religious dogmas, and its supremacy over every religious denomination; hence, separation was the leading feature of the platform of nearly every republican group. The elections of 1902 resulted in a large anti-clerical majority, and the government determined to settle the question once for all. A bill was introduced separating Church and State, largely the work of Aristide Briand, then a young socialist Deputy. It was the occasion of a series of debates in which the general principles of religious polity, as well as the bill itself, were discussed, as befitted the seriousness of a procedure which proposed to terminate a system that had flourished in France for so many centuries.

Briand was the leading protagonist of the bill. He declared himself opposed to extreme anti-clericalism which sought to frame

Protagonists of separation of Church and State

a measure calculated to disrupt the Church. In his opinion the "State must remain neutral in respect to all religions. It is not anti-religious, for it has not the right to be so; it is merely non-religious"; therefore, it should neither persecute nor favor any religion. "There is only one way of establishing religious peace in France," declared Jean Jaurès, the socialist leader, "and that is by completely destroying all ecclesiastical pretensions, by fully secularizing the State, and by taking from the Church the public powers conferred upon it by the Concordat."

The Catholic opposition was led by Count de Mun, who declared that he was opposed to separation in general and especially in

Opposition of the Catholics

France, where the history, customs, and temperament of the people favored the ideal of a union between civil and religious life; that the proposed law was inspired by a hatred of Christianity and of religion, and constituted a revolution in the moral order which would inevitably lead to the destruction of Christianity in France; that the only change needed was a revision of the Concordat by France and the Papacy; and that, by ignoring the Pope, the government had acted in the spirit of reprisal and not in that of amity. He denounced the proposed law as an act of spoliation and persecution.

In 1905, the bill passed parliament by a large majority. The now famous Separation Law abrogated the Concordat; in future the State would neither recognize nor subsidize any faith, and would no longer nominate bishops for appointment by the Pope. Henceforth, the Catholic Church, as well as the Protestant and Jewish churches, which also received subsidies, were to be entirely self-supporting and self-governing. In order not to break the bonds too abruptly, life pensions were given to those of the clergy who had been long in the service, and allowances for a limited period to the others; newly ordained ministers had to be entirely supported by their parishioners. An inventory was to be made by the State of all Church property, and then turned over to "associations for public worship," or boards of trustees to be formed by the Church in accordance with her principles. Church buildings were declared to be the property of the nation, but were to be held in trust by the "associations." The law abolished the privileges enjoyed by the Church, yet fully guaranteed liberty of worship.

The government had ignored the Pope in abrogating the Concordat; and the Separation Law ignored the hierarchy in giving the Church in France a new legal status. There was bitter opposition among the Catholics. Pius X declared the law null and void, and enjoined upon French Catholics not to obey it. Separation of Church and State he characterized as a pernicious error. He denounced the proposed "associations for public worship" which, he said, could not be formed "without violating sacred rights upon which the very life of the Church depended" because associations of laymen would intrude upon the duties of a divinely ordained hierarchy, and he forbade the French Catholics to form these associations.

The Pope denounces the law

In 1906, Clemenceau became Premier. A former follower of Gambetta, he was a strong anti-clerical. He vigorously enforced the Separation Law, especially in the matter of taking inventories of Church property. Crowds of faithful Catholics came to the churches in order to prevent the officials

Enforcement of the law

from entering them; and, in several instances, troops had to be called out to disperse the rioters. When the time allotted for the formation of the associations expired, it was feared that a religious war would break out. But nothing happened. The government did not carry out the threat of closing the churches, for it desired to avoid anything which looked like persecution. Briand, now Minister of Public Worship, found a way out of the difficulty by ruling that religious services could be held under the general law providing for liberty of assembly. In 1907, an amendment to the law was passed which provided that churches could be kept open for public worship by contracts between priests and the local authorities.

In spite of the great difficulties involved in the question and the bitter controversies aroused by it, the separation of Church and State became an accomplished fact. Both parties gradually accommodated themselves to the new situation, which gave freedom in religion to the Church and freedom in politics to the State. Many Catholics now turned away from the royalists whom they blamed for making the Church the object of hostile legislation. They organized the Popular Liberal Party which openly accepted the Republic. By losing Catholic support, the royalists became an insignificant element in French politics, "four nuts rattling in a bag," as it was called in derision by the republicans. The question as to the formation of the associations was not solved, and the status of Church property was left in abeyance.

SOCIAL LEGISLATION

Until the Dreyfus Affair the Third Republic had no definite policy toward social reform. The republicans had been too busy fighting royalists and their clerical allies to concern

Republicans take up cause of social reform

themselves much with the problems of the working class. Moreover, France was not highly industrialized; hence, the social problem was not as acute as in Germany and England. The crisis in the life of the Republic, revealed by the Dreyfus Affair, brought home to the republicans the necessity of allying themselves with the socialists who had helped materially in bringing about a revision of the celebrated case. When the Waldeck-Rousseau Ministry assumed office, it promised "not to limit itself to mere political reforms, but to embark on the new path of social reform." The French middle classes were now no longer obsessed by the fear of a social revolution which had haunted their imagination all through the nineteenth century. The suppression of the Commune, having shown the futility of uprising under modern conditions, the workingman was now welcomed as an ally because he was no longer feared as a foe.

Factory legislation in France was initiated by the law of 1892, which limited the labor of minors in factories to ten hours a day, of women to eleven hours, and of men to twelve. A law of 1900 reduced the number of hours for all operatives to eleven; in 1906, as a result of an agitation for an eight-hour day, the number was still further reduced to ten; and, in 1907, the eight-hour law was established for minors. In 1906, a Sunday rest law was passed, entitling every employee to one day's rest during the week, either on Sunday or on some other day. *Factory laws*

The first workman's compensation law was passed in 1898. It provided for a regular scale of compensation for injuries received by workingmen in the course of their employment, the amount paid being in proportion to the seriousness of the injury. *Workman's compensation*

Following the French Revolution, many attempts were made to establish a system of old-age pensions. No serious step, however, was taken in that direction by any government save by that of the Third Republic. In 1893, parliament appointed a commission to study the subject and to recommend legislation. A heated controversy arose over the question whether the pensioning system should be compulsory or voluntary. The Senate defeated bills sent up by the Chamber because they contained compulsory clauses. A law of 1905 granted pensions to indigent men over seventy years of age; the fund was to be raised by local taxation supplemented by government subsidies. This system resembled the old-fashioned outdoor relief, and it was for that reason considered unsatisfactory. However, it prepared the way for the Pensions Law of 1910 which, for the first time, was both compulsory and contributory for all wage-earners, including servants and farm laborers; it excluded miners, railway workers, and sailors for whom special provision had already been made. Most of the fund was made up of contribution by the State, though employees and employers also had to contribute. At the age of sixty-five, the employee was entitled to a small pension; in case of death before sixty, his dependents were given a death benefit.[1] *Old-age pensions*

[1] For the extension of social legislation see Chapter XXXIX.

THE LABOR MOVEMENT

In no other country was the labor movement so closely identified with the political and philosophic tendencies of the day as in France. In the checkered history of French trade unionism may be read the story of political progress and reaction, of bold theories and revolutionary violence which characterized the France of the nineteenth century.

The Law of Coalitions, passed in 1791, abolished all guilds and corporations, and established freedom of contract for individuals The Law of only. It forbade even the gathering of men of the Coalitions same trade to discuss their common affairs lest they should organize as a group; the "general good" alone was considered a legitimate object for organized effort. Trade unions were considered illegal, and to strike was criminal. The law forbade combinations of employers as well as of workers, but it rested heavily on the workingmen and lightly on the employers. The Industrial Revolution, however, made trade unions inevitable; and, as they could not be organized openly, they were organized secretly or in the guise of benevolent societies. The unions sometimes fomented violent strikes, and were often closely allied with the secret political societies that were instrumental in bringing about the Revolutions of 1830 and 1848.

The Revolution of 1848 greatly promoted the labor movement, of which it was partly the outcome. Influenced by the socialist Influence of theories of Blanc, the Parisian workingmen organized the June trade unions, which were largely responsible for the Days uprising during the "June Days." Although the uprising was mercilessly suppressed, it gave a vivid idea to the revolutionary workingmen of Paris of a general revolt of the proletariat against the bourgeois, directed by trade unions.

During the early days of the Second Empire, trade unions were not permitted save under exceptional conditions. Workingmen Labor under were carefully watched through the *livret*, first insti- the Empire tuted by Napoleon I, whereby each laborer was obliged to have a booklet, analogous to a passport, in which his comings and goings were noted by his employer. In 1864, an important concession was made to the workingmen by a law permitting strikes; later, unions were legally recognized. These concessions were made with many restrictions, as the law of 1791 was not repealed; what was granted was toleration, not freedom. But the uprising in 1871 discredited all working-class activity, whether moderate or revolutionary, and nearly all the trade unions were suppressed.

After 1870 the French labor movement took an entirely new start. At first, it showed moderate tendencies; it discouraged strikes and sought to better the condition of the workers by coöperating with the employers. In 1884, came the law which was hailed as the "charter of liberties" of organized labor in France. This law gave to workingmen full freedom to organize and to strike, thereby, for the first time, nullifying the law of 1791. It was largely the work of the radical republicans, fervid disciples of Gambetta, who recognized the importance of the new "social strata." Trade-unionism spread rapidly, and the various socialist groups began an agitation among the unions with the object of converting them to their particular views. This agitation almost disrupted the labor movement, and generated among the workingmen a feeling of distrust for politics and politicians. In 1895, nearly all the French unions organized a federation, known as the "General Confederation of Labor" (*Confédération Générale du Travail*), which declared itself independent "of all political schools." The chief object of the Confederation was "to unite the workingmen in the economic field with the bonds of class solidarity to struggle for their integral emancipation."

Repeal of the Law of Coalitions; the "C.G.T."

Another development of the labor movement appeared in the formation of the *Bourses du Travail*, or Chambers of Labor. The first Bourse was organized in Paris, in 1887, with the object of providing a central meeting-place for workingmen, where they could come together to discuss their affairs. Similar establishments were founded in other French cities, often with the aid of subsidies from the municipalities. Under the energetic direction of Fernand Pelloutier, the Bourses became centers of agitation, from which strikes were organized and directed. A national federation was organized which, in 1902, united with the General Confederation of Labor.

The Bourses

The union of the two federations resulted in the adoption of syndicalism, the most revolutionary policy in the history of trade unions. Syndicalism pushed to the extreme the socialist theory of the class struggle, and the Confederation (the "C.G.T.") was to direct a truceless war against

Syndicalism

capital by means of general strikes. All gains in wages and hours were to strengthen the proletariat in the final struggle to overthrow the capitalist system by means of a general revolt of all labor directed by the Confederation. The syndicalists were opposed to "political action," or political agitation for reforms; they favored "direct action," or the winning of reforms by direct attacks on capital through strikes.[1]

The Confederation began an agitation for an eight-hour day for all labor. May 1, 1906, was the day agreed upon for beginning of The General a general strike, when all labor was to cease in order to Strikes compel the government to pass such a law. When the day arrived there was almost a panic throughout France, and the troops were called out to preserve order. Many stopped work on that day, but the strike was not sufficiently general to prove successful. A strike of the employees in the public postal and telegraph offices took place, which failed mainly because volunteers took the places of the strikers. To prevent a similar occurrence the Chamber passed a resolution denying the right of public employees to strike, and forbidding them to join the Confederation.

Syndicalism's greatest effort was the railway strike of 1910, one of the most remarkable labor demonstrations in recent times. A The railway demand made by the railwaymen for an increase in strike of wages was refused; and a strike took place which tied 1910 up the entire railway system. Food supplies for the cities were not delivered, inflicting great privation. Rioting followed, and much railway property was destroyed. The strikers had expected that Premier Briand, who in his radical days had himself advocated the general strike, would sympathize with them. But they were soon disillusioned. Briand discovered a new way of breaking a strike. The government issued mobilization orders to the strikers, calling them "to the colors," that is, to perform military duty as reservists. When they answered the call they were ordered to operate the railways which, as soldiers, they could not refuse to do; in other words, the strikers became their own strike-breakers. The railway strike immediately collapsed. Briand was bitterly denounced by the workingmen as a tyrant and dictator. He defended himself by saying that the government was faced by what was virtually rebellion, and therefore it had the right to use all means to protect itself from being overthrown.

[1] For a detailed description of syndicalism see pages 577–80.

After the failure of the railway strike the influence of syndicalism began to wane in France. The workingmen now realized the decisive influence of the State in the struggle between capital and labor, and once more they flocked to the standard of the socialists in the hope of winning control of parliament.

ECONOMIC PROGRESS

Unlike England and Germany, France was not a highly industrialized nation during the period preceding the World War. The majority of the French people, about fifty-five per cent, were engaged in agriculture; the towns were small and inhabited mainly by shopkeepers and artisans. There was neither a large working class nor a powerful group of industrial capitalists, except in the coal and iron regions of the northeast, where there were fairly large industrial centers.

France was a large producer of iron chiefly in the region of Briey and Longwy, the continuation of the rich iron basin of Lorraine. Having insufficient coal she exported much of her iron ore to Germany where it was converted into steel. The Ruhr in Germany was France's smelting furnace.

Iron and steel

Silk and wine continued to be important elements in French industrial life. The silk industry was as distinctively French as cotton was English. For long Lyons was the silk capital of the world, and derived handsome profits from the export of this expensive commodity. At that time, only the rich could afford a silk dress, which often lasted a lifetime. But the industry underwent great changes. When the Suez Canal was opened, large quantities of silk from China and Japan were brought to Europe, which competed with the French product. Italy became a manufacturer of silk, and Milan soon rivaled Lyons. This competition made silk cheaper, and consequently its use was more widespread. Finally, the invention of "fiber silk," or rayon, made from wood pulp, threw on the market a new textile, which was a serious competitor of silk.

Silk

The vine, formerly cultivated over the greater part of France, was now almost entirely confined to the south, where large areas were given over to its cultivation. During the latter part of the nineteenth century, this highly lucrative industry was almost ruined by the spread of a vine disease which caused the production of wine to sink to one third of what it had

Wine

been in previous years.[1] Strong efforts were made by the wine-growers to combat this evil. American vine stock was grafted upon the native French; and scientific cures, discovered by the scientist, Pasteur, were applied. Through these efforts the industry began slowly to improve, but it did not recover its former prosperity. Another attack on the wine industry came in the form of competition of adulterated wines, which were sold at low prices.

Transport facilities under the Republic were greatly improved and extended.[2] The railway system was well organized and well

Transportation   developed. It was built on a comprehensive plan; the lines all radiated from Paris, and to each was given a monopoly of all rail transportation in a certain region in order to avoid ruinous competition. Some of the lines were owned by the government; others, by private companies. French shipping was slow in developing in spite of government subsidies, largely because the ships had no bulky cargoes such as coal, iron, and cotton goods for export overseas. France bought as many ships as she built. The Atlantic and Mediterranean ports were too far from the coal and iron regions; and the Channel ports were unfit for shipbuilding. The merchant marine of France was, therefore, small as compared with that of England or Germany, and was largely engaged in the coast trade. The only marked increase was in the tonnage of steam vessels, which rose from twelve to sixty per cent of the total tonnage during the period from 1872 to 1912.

France is the most important tourist country in the world. Her pleasant climate, her historic places, her famous pleasure resorts, her

The tourist trade   excellent cuisine, her courteous people, and, especially, Paris, attract enormous numbers of foreign visitors. In summer, tourists go to the north where it is cool; in winter, they go to the south, where it is warm. A not inconsiderable part of the national income is derived from tourists who, being on a holiday, generally spend freely. Thousands depend upon them for their prosperity, and even for their livelihood.

The Third Republic abandoned the free trade policy inaugurated

Foreign trade   by the Second Empire. The tariff law of 1892 established high protective duties on industrial and agricultural products. It gave the government freedom to follow any

---

[1] In 1875, the wine product of France amounted to 2,214,000,000 gallons; in 1895, it had sunk to about 737,000,000 gallons.

[2] In 1911, there were 31,056 miles of railway, which was more than three times as much as in 1870.

tariff policy that it chose toward any country by providing for maximum and minimum duties to be applied at its discretion. The foreign trade of France steadily increased,[1] and imports rose in excess of exports. France sold expensive wares to foreign nations, and in return bought cheap commodities, raw materials, and coal. The unfavorable balance of trade was made up chiefly by the returns from foreign investments and from the money spent by tourists.

Of prime importance for the welfare of the country were the banking institutions. The savings of millions of thrifty Frenchmen were invested by the banks in industrial enterprises *Finance* and governmental loans, abroad as well as at home.

French finance was the handmaiden of French diplomacy. More than once did the "woolen stocking" of the French peasant play a great rôle in international affairs; it was largely responsible for the quick payment of the indemnity to Germany and for the enormous loans to Russia. Investments were made generally in business enterprises that were soundly organized and amply protected. The savings of a frugal people and the large returns from the luxury industries resulted in the piling up of a surplus, not all of which could be profitably invested at home; hence, French capital sought foreign fields of investment, generally in foreign government bonds. A favorite form of French investment at home was in government bonds; many a peasant, small shopkeeper, or laborer possessed a *rente* of which he was very proud. This form of popular finance was encouraged by the Republic because it gave millions of citizens an economic interest in the stability of the existing government, and so helped to discourage both revolution and reaction. Kings, emperors, and even republics had suffered swift destruction when they had antagonized the interests of this numerous class of small investors.

France was the home of the small peasant proprietor in contrast to Great Britain, the home of the great proprietor.[2] But she was not quite the agricultural paradise that has been so *Peasant pro-* often painted by enthusiastic foreigners. While the *prietorship* majority of the holdings were small and worked by peasant pro-

---

[1] In 1912, the total foreign trade, exclusive of precious metals, was valued at about $3,723,000,000, which was three times as much as that in 1870.

[2] The system of peasant proprietorship, though it existed in part before 1789, was established fully and firmly by the French Revolution. In order to prevent the consolidation of the farms into great estates, the Law of Partition compelled a testator to divide his land equally among his heirs.

prietors, the greater portion of the arable land was in the hands of those who, in France, were considered large proprietors. Some of the large estates were cultivated by tenants; others, by a system, called *métayage*, according to which the owner of the land provided the buildings, animals, and the machinery, and the peasant, the labor, both sharing in the product.

France was almost entirely self-supporting. She raised a variety of crops: cereals, especially wheat, vegetables, dairy products, fruits, beet sugar, and wine. There was a luxury agriculture that was as remunerative as the luxury industries. The wines, brandies, olive oil, and fancy vegetables were sold at high prices all over the world. However, in spite of hard labor, rigid economy, and the natural fertility of the soil, many peasants found it difficult to make a living from their little farms. As elsewhere there was a marked trend toward the city. Many of the landless laborers migrated to the industrial centers; their places were taken, in part, by immigrants from Italy, Spain, and Belgium.

French agriculture

Agricultural machinery was introduced but slowly into France, largely because it could not be used to advantage on small farms which, in many cases, consisted of "strips" as in medieval times. The ox and horse, not the tractor, did the plowing. Every effort was made to protect the interests of the peasant proprietor who was regarded as the backbone of the nation's economic life. High tariffs protected his product from foreign competition. Farmers' coöperative societies were formed to promote the welfare of their members. Provision was made by the laws of 1908 and 1910 for government loans to small landowners, at low interest rates, to encourage them to enlarge and to improve their holdings. To protect the peasant a law was passed, in 1909, which limited the right of seizure and of public sale of small farms by those who had financial claims upon them.

Protection of the peasants

France was a prosperous country, and prosperity was more wide-spread than in any other country in Europe. Neither abject poverty nor great riches was common among Frenchmen, many of whom were proprietors, either of a farm in the country or of a shop in the city.[1] The people worked hard,

Prosperity of France

---

[1] In 1911, it was reckoned that there were, in France, about 8,500,000 employers and about 10,200,000 employees.

lived well though economically, and saved all they possibly could. Although the average earnings were small compared with those in America, there was a fairly high standard of living, due, partly, to small families, and partly to the thrifty habits of the people. If France played a comparatively minor rôle in the world of modern industry, she fully shared in the world's prosperity

POLITICAL HISTORY (1906–14)

The political parties underwent marked changes as a result of the Dreyfus Affair. There took place a notable shift to the Left when the republican groups emerged triumphant from the crisis. The Right was discredited by militaristic plottings on account of which it lost many supporters, even among the conservative peasants.

On the extreme right, in the Chamber sat the Nationalists, royalists who favored the establishment of monarchy "by all and every means." With the death of the Count de Chambord, the Bourbon dynasty in France became extinct; The Right the only claimant now is the head of the Orleans dynasty. Next to the royalists sat the Popular Liberal Party composed of Catholic republicans. It was founded by Count de Mun with the object of bringing about friendly relations between the Church and the Republic. It favored social reform, Proportional Representation, public support of the Church schools, and protection of property rights. The supporters of the Right came chiefly from the aristocracy, from the clergy, and from the peasantry.

In the center were the moderate republicans, who represented the interests of the upper middle class, especially manufacturers and bankers. They were strong upholders of the rights of The Center property and of the liberty of the individual "to work, to acquire, to possess, and to bequeath." Like Thiers they believed that the Republic, to exist, must pursue conservative policies; hence, they were opposed to social reform, to trade-unionism, and to income and inheritance taxes.

On the left were the radical and socialist groups. The Radicals were uncompromising republicans who owned Gambetta as their intellectual father. They had stood guard over the The Left Republic since its birth, and more than once had they been engaged in deadly combat with its enemies, the royalists and the clericals. To the Radicals were due the establishment of secular education and the separation of Church and State. Their supporters came chiefly from the lower middle class and from those engaged in the professions. An offshoot of the Radicals were the Radical Socialists, "the bourgeois party with a popular soul." They favored state regulation of industry, the public ownership of railways and mines, social insurance, and the protection of women and children in industry. On the extreme left sat the socialists, elected chiefly by the working class. Like all other socialists they favored the establishment of the coöperative commonwealth,[1] but they were divided into many factions, the most important being the Unified Socialist Party.

Among the new leaders that appeared in French politics the most prominent was Aristide Briand. He had entered politics as a socialist but he soon became more interested in prac-

Briand (1862–1932)

tical political problems than in socialist theories. After his notable work on the Separation Law, Briand rose rapidly and became *ministrable*; he was made Prime Minister many times. His eloquence as an orator and his shrewdness as a politician, whether in or out of office, made him one of the master minds of French parliamentary life. He deserted the socialists as he rose to power, and was consequently hated by them as a "careerist" who cared more for his political advancement than for the welfare of the working class. Briand's policies were those of the Radical Socialists, though he was not clearly identified with any group in the Chamber.

The career of the socialist leader, Jean Jaurès, attracted world-wide attention. As an orator, his eloquence recalled Gambetta; he thrilled his audiences, even those who were opposed to

Jaurès (1859–1914)

his socialist views. But Jaurès was more than eloquent. His speeches showed the knowledge of the scholar who had studied deeply the problems that he was trying to solve, and the attitude of the philosopher who ever sought reasonable and humane methods. His socialist views were reformist, not dogmatic, and his political tactics were, therefore, conciliatory.[2] Militarism and war aroused Jaurès's uncompromising opposition. During the Dreyfus Affair his was the most powerful influence behind the Bloc that put through the anti-militarist and anti-clerical legislation. He was opposed to a war of *revanche* against Germany, and, during the crisis of 1914, his eloquent voice was raised for peace. Jaurès

[1] For a more detailed description of socialism in France, see pages 588–89.
[2] For a description of Jaurès's attitude toward socialism, see page 589.

paid with his life for his anti-militarist activity. When the World War broke out he was assassinated by a fanatical nationalist.

The career of Georges Clemenceau was that of a journalist-politician who is as typical of France as the lawyer-politician is of America. Clemenceau was a brilliant editor whose articles were lively, witty, pungent, and cynical. As a young man he became a follower of Gambetta, and all his political life he was a doughty foe of royalism and clericalism. Clemenceau's parliamentary career was more sensational than notable. His biting tongue and intimate knowledge of political undercurrents made him a dangerous opponent of any ministry, and he became known as a "wrecker of ministries." Although a cynic, having faith neither in God nor in man, Clemenceau's militant nature drove him to espouse unpopular causes. He was a strong champion of Dreyfus, and did much to bring about his rehabilitation. In office Clemenceau proved to be as determined and decisive as, in opposition, he had been truculent and irreconcilable. Clemenceau (1841–1929)

Raymond Poincaré was as representative of the Center as Clemenceau, Briand, and Jaurès were of the Left. A moderate republican, Poincaré championed policies favored by the wealthy middle class, *la haute bourgeoisie*, to which he belonged. He came into prominence because of his knowledge of national finance, and, as Minister of Finance, he showed great ability as a master of the problems of the budget. Apart from finance, Poincaré's interests were in the field of foreign affairs. An intense nationalist and a bitter enemy of Germany, he did all in his power, as Premier and as President, to strengthen the alliance with Russia and the entente with England. Poincaré (1860–1934)

The leading political issue after the Separation Law was electoral reform. In France, as elsewhere, parliamentary representation, based on the single-member district system, often made a mockery of democracy. According to this system, a candidate having a majority or plurality of the votes in his district was declared elected. From this method followed serious evils, declared the advocates of electoral reform. In the first place, the minority in a district, no matter how large, was unrepresented, and the majority or plurality, no matter how small, was often over-represented; hence, the size of the parties in the legislature was generally out of all proportion to the votes cast for them. When a candidate was elected by a Criticism of district system of representation plurality, as was frequently the case in the United States and Eng land, the injustice was even more glaring. More than once was the party in control of parliament elected by a minority of the voters in the country. A representative assembly, under this system, was a "broken mirror" in which the nation's political image was distorted. In order to get the small number of votes necessary to make the majority or plurality in a district, all kinds of corrupt devices were resorted to, gerrymandering, bribery, and coercion. The evils of district representation were intensified in a highly centralized country like France, where the influence of the national government was used in favor of candidates supporting its policies. Once elected, the Deputy became the dispenser of governmental favors, such as appointments, promotions, licenses to sell matches and tobacco which were government monopolies, decorations, furloughs from the army, and the like. Only too frequently was the country forgotten by the representatives in their desire to please their districts which, in the expressive phrase of Briand, became "stagnant pools," infesting with moral disease the political life of the people.

There was only one remedy, according to the electoral reformers, and that was Proportional Representation. There are various Proportional schemes of Proportional Representation, but all of Representa- them agree in substituting a multiple member for a sin- tion gle member constituency. The unit of representation would be a fairly large region in which voting would be, according to one method, for party lists; to each party would be assigned a number of seats in proportion to its popular vote. Another method is preferential voting, which requires the voter to indi- cate his choice, in order of preference, from a list of all the can- didates; those candidates are elected who receive the number of votes required.[1] By enlarging the unit of representation, argued the advocates of Proportional Representation, the political vision of the voters would also be enlarged. And they would conse- quently be influenced more by national policies than by district politics in voting for members of parliament. The advocates of Proportional Representation in France were chiefly the socialists and the Popular Liberal Party who suffered most from district representation.

[1] For full descriptions of the various schemes of Proportional Representation con- sult C. G. Hoag and G. H. Hallett, *Proportional Representation.*

Domestic politics during the decade preceding the World War were greatly influenced by foreign affairs.   The year 1913 was a critical one, and Europe was trembling on the brink of war as a result of the Moroccan and Balkan crises.   To face the situation, Poincaré was chosen President, and Briand, Premier.   Poincaré had been a strong partisan of the alliance with Russia and of the entente with England which, as Premier, he had done much to strengthen.   Bitterly hostile to Germany, he determined to make every preparation for a possible conflict.   But how was France to get large armies in case of a war with Germany whose increase in population during two months equaled that of France for five years?   "Every year we win a battle against France," once remarked General von Moltke.   There was only one possible way; namely, to increase the term of military service. The Three Years' Military Law   Largely through the influence of Poincaré, a bill was introduced, raising the term of active service from two to three years.   It encountered strong opposition from the socialist parties, and from many of the Radical Socialists. Jaurès delivered eloquent speeches against the measure which, he declared, would put an intolerable burden on the people.   He denounced the system of conscription generally, and proposed the substitution of a popular militia for a standing army.   Enormous mass meetings were organized by socialists and syndicalists to protest against three years' service; and several times troops had to be called out to disperse the mobs.   The bill became law in 1913 when the situation in Europe demanded that France be fully prepared.

The elections of 1914 were fought over the issue of the three years' military law, and the results showed a large gain for the socialists.   But the European storm clouds were The World War   gathering.   As the World War drew near, the socialists organized great peace demonstrations and made preparations for a general strike.   When war broke out and the German armies invaded France, all elements, including the socialists and syndicalists, rallied to the support of the government.   A united nation now faced the invaders.

LITERATURE UNDER THE REPUBLIC

French literature after 1870 displayed neither the joyous buoyancy of the Romanticists nor the calm strength of the Realists.   A spirit of pessimism took possession of the new generation, on whose minds the national disaster of 1870 produced a profound impression. To the world at that time, the defeat of France by Germany was a sign of the decadence of the former, and so widespread was this idea that even many Frenchmen believed it. They became skeptical about the destiny of their country and of humanity in general, and there developed what was called the *fin-de-siècle* spirit, a nonchalant attitude of mind characteristic of France at the end of the nineteenth century.

Pessimistic tone of literature after 1870

The last of the great Realists was Guy de Maupassant, universally regarded as the greatest of short-story writers. Like his master, Flaubert, Maupassant strove to describe life with impersonal objectiveness; he, too, believed that the true function of the author is to stand passively by and allow his characters to play their part. His stories depict human vices and virtues, as seen in all classes of people and under all circumstances. Whether frightful or idyllic, the story is told in a detached, almost anonymous way, so that an impression of absolute truthfulness is made on the reader. Each story is its own comment. Although Maupassant seems to have no point of view about life, there runs through his work a hidden vein of melancholy which might be interpreted to mean that, though life is really not worth living, it is interesting: so let us live.

Maupassant (1850–93)

Toward the end of the nineteenth century, Realism passed to its logical conclusion, Naturalism. To get "slices of life" the novelists of the new school worked among miners and fishermen, became patients in hospitals, and had themselves incarcerated in prisons in order to reproduce in literature these experiences which they considered "human documents." The most distinguished writer of the Naturalist school was Émile Zola, whose novels created a world-wide sensation. In imitation of Balzac, Zola set himself the task of writing a *comédie humaine* of the middle nineteenth century. In the Rougon-Macquart series of twenty novels he describes "the natural and social history of a family living under the Second Empire." Zola regarded man as a "human beast" who could be moved only through his appetites. Yet, for all his pessimism, he showed himself a hero during the Dreyfus Affair when, at great personal risk, he jumped into the fray in order to right the wrong done to an innocent man. Zola,

Zola (1840–1902)

unlike Flaubert, had no talent for analyzing the individual soul, but he greatly excelled in describing masses of men in action, mobs, street crowds, and tumultuous assemblies.

The charming and pathetic tales of Alphonse Daudet have endeared him to millions of readers. Daudet combined pathos with humor to a degree attained only by Charles Dickens, Daudet with whom he has been frequently compared. He (1840–97) was "ever trembling into tears or flashing into laughter." His most famous work is *Les Aventures prodigieuses de Tartarin de Tarascon* (*The Extraordinary Adventures of Tartarin of Tarascon*). Tartarin is a typical southern Frenchman, whose exuberant imagination gives the neighborhood the general impression that he is a mighty hunter. Forced at last by public opinion to give proof of his prowess, Tartarin leaves for Algiers on a lion-hunting expedition. There, he shoots a tame old lion and returns home in triumph with his trophy. The story is told with great charm and humor, and the character of the hero is described in inimitable style.

A unique figure in French literature is Paul Verlaine whose poems have a quality quite original in French poetry. Verlaine excels in what he calls *nuance*, delicate suggestion Verlaine in tuneful words. He plays upon words as upon a (1844–96) musical instrument, and his verse has been well described as "disembodied song," so lute-like is its quality and so haunting its charm. Verlaine had no message to give to mankind nor did he care to have any; he merely wished to express the mood of exquisite melancholy that frequently seized him. Curiously enough, this great artist lived much of his life as a Parisian vagabond, now in the café, now in the gutter, now in the hospital. He was a child that fell into evil ways, and remained a child.

No writer more truly expressed the mood of the generation that grew up under the Third Republic than Jacques Anatole Thibault, better known by his pseudonym, Anatole Anatole France. After the death of Renan, his master, he was France the leading spirit among the intellectual *élite* of France. (1844–1924) A true French man-of-letters, France is learned, witty, and wise; and the style of his disquisitions, generally in the form of loosely constructed novels, is almost perfect in charm and lucidity. A satirical spirit pervades nearly all his writing, but the satire of France is not bitter invective, but a delicate irony which makes the reader smile at the follies of mankind.

France has chosen to aim the shafts of his wit at two subjects, early Christianity and modern society. His attacks on Christian ideals take the form of stories of the early martyrs of the faith, in which this twentieth-century Voltaire satirizes their motives and their practices. "Bibles of modern unbelief," a critic has called his books. His attacks upon the modern social system are most biting. The following excerpt is characteristic of his manner: "The State, with its majestic sense of justice and equality, forbids the rich man as well as the poor man to sleep under bridges, to beg in the streets, and to steal bread." In a description of primitive life which pretends to explain the origin of cherished institutions, we read: "See how this furious man is biting the nose of his fallen adversary; and how the other one is pounding the head of a woman with a big stone!" cries one character to another. "I see them well enough. Do not interfere! They are creating law; they are founding property; they are establishing the principles of civilization, the basis of society and the foundation of the State," is the reply. Yet this master of irony is full of pity for the very persons and things that he so mercilessly satirizes; he believes that it is the spirit of folly, not of evil, which is responsible for our incongruous world. "Irony and Pity are goddesses," he writes, "the former with her smile makes life agreeable; the latter sanctifies it with her tears. The irony that I invoke is no cruel deity. She mocks neither love nor beauty. She is gentle and kindly. Her mirth disarms and she teaches us to laugh at rogues and fools whom, but for her, we might be so weak as to despise and hate."

One of France's most famous books is *Ile des Pengouins* (*Penguin Island*), a satirical history of his country, in which religion, morals, art, and politics are dissected with an elegant dagger held in the delicate but firm fingers of this aristocrat of letters. The story has a pessimistic conclusion; the world is plunged into a universal cataclysm of revolution and the wearisome process of rebuilding civilization has to begin anew. His *Histoire Contemporaine*, a series of four novels, is a penetrating study of French political and ecclesiastical life. The hero, Bergeret, is a professor at a provincial university who loves his books, his daughter, and his dog. He is "irreligious, but with decency and good taste." It is M. Bergeret's wont to go among his neighbors, like Socrates, and start discussions; and, like the latter, he is regarded as a nuisance and suffers in consequence.

Anatole France lived for many years in "an ivory tower," a literary recluse interested only in art and literature; but the Dreyfus Affair aroused him to action, and he became an ardent champion of the condemned Captain. In some of his stories he mercilessly satirizes the Affair. That tragedy is made into a screaming farce in which is shown how a great and intelligent nation is deluded into doing absurd things by appeals to its prejudices and its fears. As a result of the Affair, France emerged a socialist, convinced that modern society was full of evil and injustice. He was ever ready to use his powerful pen in defense of unpopular causes. When he died, his funeral was made the occasion of a national demonstration; both government and people paid homage to the great writer who is one of the glories of French literature.

REFERENCES

GENERAL:
J. C. Bracq, *France under the Republic* (ed. 1916), a good popular account of the problems of the Republic by an ardent republican and anti-clerical; D. W. Brogan, *The Development of Modern France* (1939), from 1879 to 1939, social and political; J. E. C. Bodley, *France* (ed. 1899), a well-known but over-estimated work by an Englishman, hostile to the parliamentary system in France; Gabriel Hanotaux, *Contemporary France*, 4 vols., translated from the French, brilliant narrative of the years 1870–82 by a distinguished French statesman, contains splendid descriptions of Gambetta and Thiers, translation poor; J. Labusquière, *La troisième république, 1871–1900* (1909), from socialist standpoint; E. Bourgeois, *History of Modern France*, 2 vols. (1919), Vol. II good for political matters, poor for social matters, has excellent bibliography; A. Zévaès, *Histoire de la Troisième République* (1926); Ch. Seignobos, *L'Évolution de la Troisième République, 1875–1914* (1921).

GOVERNMENT AND PARTIES:
Excellent handbooks are E. M. Sait, *Government and Politics of France* (1920), W. R. Sharp, *The Government of the French Republic* (1938), and R. Poincaré, *How France is Governed*, translated from the French (1914); L. Jacques, *Les partis politiques sous la troisième république* (1913), a detailed description of the various parties; A. Siegfried, *Tableau politique de la France de l'Ouest* (1913), a social study of political opinion in relation to region and class.

THE COMMUNE:
E. Lepelletier, *Histoire de la commune de 1871*, 2 vols. (1911–12), a good treatment of a much-disputed subject; M. du Camp, *Les convulsions de Paris*, 4 vols. (ed. 1881), hostile to the Commune; sympathetic are

L. Dubreuilh, *La commune, 1871* (1908), and P. O. Lissagaray, *History of the Commune of 1871*, translated from the French (ed. 1898); R. W. Postgate, *Out of the Past* (1926), tells life of Blanqui; and G. Laronze, *Histoire de la commune de 1871* (1928), a detailed study based on new documents, impartial.

CHURCH AND STATE:

A. Debidour, *L'Église catholique et l'État sous la troisième République*, 2 vols. (1909), Vol. II devotes considerable space to the movement for separation, contains texts of Ferry Laws, Association Law, and Separation Law; G. Weill, *Histoire de l'idée laïque en France au XIXe siècle* (1925), interesting volume largely cultural, anti-clerical; E. Faguet, *Anticlericalisme* (1906), critical of anti-clericalism; A. Galton, *Church and State in France, 1300–1907* (1907), anti-clerical viewpoint; P. Sabatier, *Disestablishment in France* (1906), by non-Catholic, moderate and fair; A. Briand, *La séparation des églises et de l'état* (1905), official report of the law by its author; A. Briand, *La séparation* (1908) and Comte A. de Mun, *Contra la Séparation* (1906), contain best discussion of the problem, the former favoring separation and the latter opposing it; article "Concordat" in the Catholic Encyclopædia.

CULTURAL:

A. L. Guérard, *French Civilization in the Nineteenth Century* (1914), excellent essays on education, religion, labor, and literature; W. C. Brownell, *French Traits* (ed. 1902), a penetrating study of French life and manners by an American literary critic; B. Wendell, *The France of To-Day* (1907), on French culture and education by the well-known American teacher.

COLONIAL EXPANSION:

E. Levasseur, *La France et ses colonies, géographie et statistique*, 3 vols. (1890-˜3); V. Piquet, *La Colonisation française dans l'Afrique du nord* (1912); A. Girault, *The Colonial Tariff Policy of France* (1916), excellent analysis, contains good historical introduction.

SOCIAL AND ECONOMIC:

The monumental works of Levasseur have already been referred to under Chapter V; see also his *Questions ouvrières et industrielles en France sous la troisième république* (1907); J. H. Clapham, *Economic Development of France and Germany, 1815–1914* (1921); M. Augé-Laribe, *L'Évolution de la France agricole* (1912), by the authority on French agrarian history; H. O. Meredith, *Protection in France* (1904); E. Théry, *Les Progrès économiques de la France* (1909); A. de Lavergne and L. Paul Henry, *La Richesse de la France* (1908); P. Pic, *Traité élémentaire de législation industrielle; les lois ouvrières* (ed. 1912), description of the labor laws; C. W. Pipkin, *The Idea of Social Justice* (1928), on social legislation in England and France; B. G. de Montgomery, *British and Continental Labour Policy* (1922), contains information on social and economic matters; G. Weill, *Histoire du Mouve-*

ment Social en France, 1852–1924 (1924), excellent study of social problems and social theories of the period; L. Lorwin, *Syndicalism in France* (1914), best brief study of the revolutionary labor movement; P. T. Moon, *The Labor Problem and the Social Catholic Movement in France* (1921), excellent study of social Catholicism in French politics.

MISCELLANEOUS:

On the Dreyfus Affair: J. Reinach, *Histoire de l'Affaire Dreyfus*, 7 vols. (1898–1911), a detailed work by a Dreyfusard; T. Reinach, *Histoire sommaire de l'affaire Dreyfus* (1924); and article "Dreyfus" in the Jewish Encyclopædia; biographies: A. Rambaud, *Jules Ferry* (1903); H. Stannard, *Gambetta and the Foundation of the Third Republic* (1921); and H. M. Hyndman, *Clemenceau* (1919); on Proportional Representation: J. H. Humphreys, *Proportional Representation* (ed. 1911) and C. G. Hoag and G. H. Hallett, *Proportional Representation* (1926); on foreign policy see bibliography at the end of Chapter XXXIII.

ADDITIONAL REFERENCES

H. Lagardelle, *L'Evolution des Syndicats ouvrier en France* (1901); E. S. Mason, *The Paris Commune* (1930); W. B. Worsfold, *France in Tunis and Algeria* (1930); S. H. Roberts, *A History of French Colonial Policy (1870–1925)*, 2 vols. (1928); C. Ballot, *L'introduction du machinisme dans l'industrie française* (1923); A. Siegfried, *Tableau des Partis en France* (1930); J. Kayser, *The Dreyfus Affair*, trans. from the French (1931); F. Jellinek, *The Paris Commune of 1871* (1937); J. M. S. Allison, *Monsieur Thiers* (1932); H. I. Priestley, *France Overseas* (1938); D. W. Brogan, *France Under the Republic* (1940); R. W. Hale, Jr., *Democratic France* (1941); H. F. Armstrong, *Chronology of Failure. The Last Days of the French Republic* (1940).

CHAPTER XIX

ITALY, SPAIN, AND PORTUGAL

ITALY

(a) GOVERNMENT AND PARTIES

"ITALY is made. Let us now make Italians," was the dictum of the patriots after unification. The system of government that was

Centralization

established and the policies that were followed were largely inspired by this dictum. Centralization was to counteract the age-old spirit of localism, therefore the country was divided into provinces, which were ruled by prefects appointed by the central government. The prefects were assisted by popularly elected councils. Historic units, such as Lombardy, Tuscany, and Naples, were deliberately ignored in the process of centralizing the administration in order to weaken separatism that had kept Italy divided for so many centuries.

The constitution of United Italy was based on that of Sardinia, granted in 1848 by Charles Albert. It established a "representa-

The king

tive monarchical government" in which powers were shared by king and parliament. The position of the king in Italy was not unlike that of the king in England; he, too, reigned but did not rule. Owing to the patriotic services rendered by the House of Savoy during unification there was great loyalty to the dynasty.

Parliament was composed of a Senate and a Chamber of Deputies. The former was a body of great dignity, but of little legisla-

Parliament

tive authority; its members were appointed for life, generally for distinguished services in various fields. It was the Chamber that had control of legislation. Elected at first by a suffrage highly restricted by property and educational qualifications, it represented only the middle and upper classes. In 1882, a new suffrage law gave the vote to all literate male citizens, and reduced the property qualifications. Universal, manhood suffrage was not established until 1912.

Executive power was exercised by a ministry appointed by the king and responsible to parliament. As in France the premier was

Cabinet

the spokesman, not of a compact majority party, but of a number of factions who were as ready to oust as to support a ministry.

Political parties hardly existed. Excepting the socialists, they were loosely organized factions without any definite body of principles, and largely the personal followings of political leaders. Generally speaking, the political groups in The parties the Chamber could be classified as Constitutionalists, or Liberals who inherited the traditions and ideals of Cavour; Radicals, mainly from the South, who favored advanced legislation in a vague sort of way; Republicans, who upheld the traditions and ideals of Mazzini; Catholics who represented the influence of the Vatican; and Socialists who stood for the same things as their comrades the world over.

(b) PROBLEMS AFTER UNIFICATION

The unification of 1870 brought to a close an era of revolutionary violence, and established internal peace as well as unity. But the new nation inherited many of the grave problems of The North and South the past, which it bravely tried to solve. Italy was described as a "country in which two stages of civilization exist in the same state," so markedly different were conditions in various parts of the peninsula. The North was highly developed industrially, with many large cities inhabited by a progressive and prosperous middle class and by a spirited working class. In the rural districts the land was cultivated largely by peasant proprietors who managed to live well, though frugally. South of Tuscany the scene changed. Few large cities were to be found, and one beheld dreary, desolate regions that were uncultivated and only partially inhabited. Centuries of bad government under the Bourbons had produced contempt for the orderly administration of justice, and many became accustomed to substitute private vengeance for public justice. Secret criminal societies, such as the *Mafia* of Sicily and the *Camorra* of Naples, gained a demoralizing influence over the inhabitants. Illiteracy was so common in the region that, in 1870, fully 90 per cent of its inhabitants were said to be unable to read and write.

The government began energetically to remove some of the most flagrant evils. Brigandage was entirely suppressed, and a systematic effort was made to uproot the secret criminal Problem of societies. A compulsory education law was passed, illiteracy but no adequate provision was made to enforce this law. Schools were few and badly equipped, teachers were poorly paid, and the school year was short. Italy was poor; and the cost of maintaining the army and navy consumed so much of the public revenues that economy was practiced on education. The middle classes, who came into power after 1870, were rather averse to spending money on the common schools lest the lower classes become more dangerous through being better educated. But the vast areas of ignorance in Italy were becoming a matter of common reproach. A new law was, therefore, passed in 1904, which required every commune to provide for public schools to be supported by local taxation. Provision was also made for educating the recruits in the army. A marked decrease in illiteracy took place; in 1914, it had fallen to about twenty-five per cent.

Italy's foreign policy, which is described elsewhere,[1] had a special domestic significance. Though an ally in the Triple Alliance Austria was Italy's national enemy. She still *Italia Irre-* held Italian districts, the Trentino, and the cities of *denta* Trieste and Fiume. A movement known as *Italia Irredenta* (Unredeemed Italy) aimed to "redeem" these places from Austria. Irredentism aroused almost as much emotion in Italy as did the "lost provinces," Alsace-Lorraine, in France.

Conscription was established in Italy after 1870. The support of a large standing army bore heavily on a poor country like Italy High taxes   who, in her eagerness to appear as a great power, had to tax herself very heavily. In spite of high taxes the management of the finances was so bad that Italy was always on the verge of bankruptcy. A great reform in the finances was inaugurated in 1905–06 by Luigi Luzzatti, and the national treasury began to show a surplus instead of a deficit.

Italy had a very high birth rate, and many, due to the existence of widespread poverty, were forced to seek homes in other lands. Emigration   Entire districts became depopulated through emigration.[2]   Large numbers went to the United States and to South America, and even to France and Germany, where cheap labor was needed. The Italian became the common laborer of the industrial world. Emigration was beneficial to Italy, as it drained off some of the surplus population; besides, the money sent from abroad to relatives and friends at home was the means of bettering conditions for thousands of families. Many emigrants returned

[1] See Chapter XXXIII.
[2] In 1878, about 96,000 Italians emigrated; in 1906, the number rose to 788,000

to Italy bringing with them higher standards of comfort and of education, which stimulated a demand for better conditions at home.

For a time the most serious question that confronted the country after 1870 was the hostility between Church and State. The famous Law of Papal Guarantees, passed in 1871, proposed to solve the question on Cavour's principle of a free Church in a free State. The Pope was permitted to receive and to send ambassadors, and to conduct diplomatic affairs without any interference from the Italian government. A district in Rome, in which the Vatican is situated, was assigned to him, and into which no Italian officer could enter without permission from the papal authorities. As indemnity for the loss of his domains the Pope was voted, in perpetuity, an annual sum of $645,000; in addition, the palaces, churches, museums, offices, villas, and gardens in the Vatican were to be exempt from taxation, and the papal government was to have the use of the Italian railway, postal, and telegraph systems. The Church was guaranteed full freedom of self-government, and the old interference by the State in Church affairs was declared terminated. Church and State were, in effect, separated, though Catholicism was recognized as the national religion.

> Law of Papal Guarantees

Pius IX, however, indignantly refused to accept the terms of the "sub-Alpine" Government, as he contemptuously called the House of Savoy. Parliament regularly voted the annuity, but it was as regularly refused; to accept it would have meant to recognize the Kingdom of Italy as a legitimate government. Pius IX shut himself up in the Vatican, and refused to leave it under any circumstances, regarding himself as the "Prisoner of the Vatican"; his successors followed this policy until 1929, when the difficulty was settled. A Papal encyclical known as the *Non expedit*, forbade Italian Catholics to vote at elections for parliament or to hold office under the crown. At first the situation was embarrassing, and even dangerous, to Italy, who feared that France might champion the cause of the Pope. During the early period of the Third French Republic clerical sentiment was so strong in favor of intervention that it was one of the reasons for Italy becoming a member of the Triple Alliance. As time went on, there began a *rapprochement* between the Vatican and the Italian government though, in theory,

> The "Prisoner of the Vatican"

the successors of Pius IX continued to advocate the restoration of their temporal power.[1]

An anti-clerical spirit arose in Italy which was distinctively nationalist in character. The Church was regarded as the invet-
Carducci erate enemy of United Italy, ready to promote division
(1835-1907) within and to encourage her enemies without. As in France many of the bourgeois and workingmen were alienated from the Church, the former being free-thinking liberals, and the latter, free-thinking socialists. The greatest Italian writer since unification, Giosuè Carducci, was anti-Catholic in spirit. He found his highest ideals in ancient paganism, and he continually attacked Christianity as the enemy of liberty and happiness. His *Ode to Satan* created a sensation. He pictured Satan, not as the traditional devil at war with all that is good, but as the spirit of liberty and progress continually in revolt against the chains of dogma; Satan is reason defying authority as represented by the Church. Carducci believed that the Church had corrupted Italy whose true spirit was pagan; and that, after 1870, Italy became her ancient self once more. He was above all else a poet of United Italy, whose aspirations he sang in enthusiastic verse and whose heroes, Garibaldi and Mazzini, he rapturously glorified.

(c) POLITICAL HISTORY (1870-1914)

Once unity was achieved, the vibrant idealism so characteristic of the Italians during the *Risorgimento* began to abate. Italian
Rule of the political life after 1870 was a sorry tale of parlia-
Right mentary intrigue, office-seeking, and corruption. Up to 1876 the government was in the hands of the Right, who reorganized and centralized the administration, nationalized the railways, and established universal, military service. But there was great dissatisfaction with the rule of the Right because of the high taxes that were imposed on foodstuffs.

The elections of 1876 were a triumph for the Left, which came into power as a result of the general demand for universal suffrage,
Rule of the for the lowering of taxes, and for compulsory educa-
Left tion. New political leaders now came to the front, Depretis and Crispi, who controlled Italian politics for almost a generation. Once in power, the Left failed to perform as much as it had promised. Those in office devoted most of their energies to

[1] For the solution of the Papal Question, see Chapter XL.

keeping themselves in power through corrupt bargains with the factions in parliament and through debauching the electorate. The South was now in the saddle, and it was "solid" for whatever group was at the head of the government. Politics became scandalously corrupt. Elections were manipulated by ministers who used patronage, coercion, and bribery to elect supporters. Party lines in the Chamber broke down completely in the general scramble for office, and, for a time, there was practically no opposition except by socialists and republicans. Nevertheless, the Left did make some effort to redeem its promises, for it enacted the education and suffrage laws already described.

The most famous Premier was Francesco Crispi, a fiery Sicilian, brilliant but erratic, who directed political affairs during the decade following 1887. Crispi proved himself a master at the game of managing elections, and Italian politics became largely a matter of personal and factional intrigue. In 1893, Italy had its "Panama" in the Bank of Rome scandal. An investigation of this institution revealed peculation on an immense scale, involving many prominent men in public life, among them Crispi. A feeling of disgust swept over the country; many began to abstain from voting altogether, while others turned to socialism as a protest against political corruption.

Serious labor troubles continually broke out during the Crispi régime which, at times, threatened the very existence of the social order. Poverty and heavy taxes led to the rapid growth of a revolutionary movement, and socialism and anarchism found many adherents among the working classes. Unions of agricultural laborers appeared in Sicily that began a widespread agitation for better conditions. During 1893–94 serious labor riots took place on the island, which were suppressed with a fury that recalled the days of Bourbon rule. Hundreds were arrested and given heavy prison sentences.

Crispi tried to distract attention from domestic problems by engaging in colonial adventures. He secured a region in eastern Africa, known as Eritrea, and prepared to advance into Abyssinia. But the Abyssinians were determined to defend themselves against Italian aggression, and, in 1896, they almost annihilated an Italian army at the battle of Adowa. This defeat led to the fall of Crispi, and checked, for a time, Italian ambitions in Africa.

Social discontent increased as a result of the disastrous war with Abyssinia. Bread riots were of frequent occurrence in the in-

Riots in Milan

dustrial centers, and the middle classes became frightened at what seemed to be an approaching social revolution. An insurrection of the workingmen broke out in Milan, in 1898, which threatened to grow to the proportions of a revolution. Barricades were erected in the streets, and fighting took place between the proletariat and the military as in the Paris Commune. When order was restored, the government meted out severe punishment to the insurgents and to those who had encouraged them. Men were sentenced to long terms of imprisonment for "exaggerating the sufferings of the poor" and for "attacking the monarchy with subtle irony."

Giovanni Giolitti became Premier in 1903, succeeding Crispi as the leading figure in Italian politics. His attitude toward the

Giolitti

workingmen was conciliatory, and he issued a statement saying that, henceforth, the government would remain neutral in the struggle between capital and labor. Giolitti favored the extension of the franchise and the enactment of social legislation as a means of quieting discontent. Nevertheless, an epidemic of strikes took place which greatly disturbed the economic life of the nation. Socialism was making rapid strides, and the socialist delegation in the Chamber was constantly growing larger. Syndicalism, too, was making headway, and the Italian workingmen were organizing revolutionary trade unions on the model of those in France.

In 1904, a general strike spread rapidly throughout the North, and paralyzed the economic life of that region. At times Italy

Truce between Church and State

seemed to be living on the edge of a social volcano, so widespread and so energetic was the radical agitation. The conservative forces in the nation, realizing their peril, began to harmonize their differences in order to present a solid front to the revolutionists. A truce was called in the war between Church and State; and the *Non expedit* was partially removed, in 1905, by Pope Pius X. Catholics were permitted to vote, but only by special permission and under the guidance of the hierarchy. A Catholic party, called the Popular Party, appeared which favored social reform and the coöperation of labor and capital in economic life.

A nationalist revival took place during the second decade of the twentieth century which had the effect of counteracting the socialist agitation. Italy asserted her "sacred egoism," her determination to maintain her prestige as a great nation and to extend her power in the Mediterranean by "redeeming" Italian territory from Austria and, especially, by seizing territory in North Africa. A colonial adventure in Africa would, if successful, silence the recalcitrant elements in the nation. Taking advantage of the revolution in Turkey, Italy suddenly declared war against that country, giving scarcely a pretext for her action. An Italian army invaded Tripoli, then under Turkish sovereignty, and succeeded in conquering the region. The treaty that closed the Turco-Italian War (1911–12) gave Tripoli and Cyrenaica to Italy, which were organized as an Italian colony under the name of Libya; in addition, Italy was allowed to occupy temporarily the Dodecanesos Islands in the Ægean. *The Turco-Italian War*

Even a successful war failed to allay discontent at home. The year 1914 witnessed a remarkable demonstration by the Italian workingmen. The labor unions, having organized a General Confederation of Labor, voted a general strike of all labor in Italy as a protest against the shooting of a workingman by the police during a local strike. Industrial life was virtually suspended: factories, shops, mines, railways, and stores were at a standstill. The authorities hesitated to take energetic measures lest the general strike, which had been called as a protest, might develop into a social revolution. At the end of two days the men quietly returned to work. *General strike*

The situation in Italy was fraught with dangers to the existing order. As in France, the workingmen had become alienated from what they regarded as a bourgeois régime. The rapid growth of the socialist parties and the violent strikes conducted by the radical trade unions were a menacing challenge to the existing order. The outbreak of the World War found Italy on the brink of revolution.

(d) ECONOMIC AND SOCIAL PROGRESS

Italy was not the land of smiling plenty, overflowing with corn and wine, as she had so often been pictured. Large areas consisted of barren rocks and unhealthy swamps; in the center was the Apennine ridge, bleak and deforested; only in the north was agriculture fairly prosperous. Although industrious, the peasants were too poor and too conservative to apply modern *Agriculture* scientific methods to farming; hence, the yield per acre was small compared with that in Germany, England, or France. Agricultural coöperative societies, organized by socialists and by Catholics, endeavored to remedy conditions by establishing rural banks which loaned money at low interest, and by introducing better methods of tilling and marketing. Great attention was paid to wine culture, and "vine-clad hills" were a common sight in many parts of Italy. Peasant proprietorship was the rule in the north; in the south, however, land was held in large estates, the "latifundia," and worked by tenants and laborers.

Although Italy lacked the two essentials of a modern industrial nation, coal and iron,[1] she made marked industrial progress through extensive utilization of "white coal," or the rapid streams which were harnessed and used to produce electrical power. However, hydro-electric power was not sufficient, and Italy had to import large quantities of coal, chiefly from England. The revival of Mediterranean trade at the end of the nineteenth century gave her an opportunity to expand commercially. Her merchant marine grew rapidly. Foreign capital, mainly German and French, came into the country, attracted by the possibilities of Italian economic development. The chief industry was silk, and Milan became a great silk-producing center. Cotton manufacturing, too, made surprising progress, and numerous cotton factories were established in the north.

Industry

A protective tariff, adopted in 1888, led to a tariff war with France, with disastrous results for Italy; the south, which lost a valuable market for its agricultural products, was almost ruined. But good relations were later reestablished through new commercial treaties. A growing trade developed with the Balkans and with South America, but most of Italy's commerce was with the other European countries and with the United States. Germany was the leading nation in Italy's foreign commerce.[2] Italian exports were mainly wheat, silk and cotton goods, wines, olive oil, fruits, and artistic products in marble and alabaster; her imports were coal, iron, machinery, raw cotton, and raw material generally.

Foreign trade

Although chiefly agricultural Italy did not produce sufficient

[1] Italy's output of coal was insignificant. Her iron production was small; in 1913 she produced about 663,000 tons.

[2] In 1913, the total foreign trade of Italy was valued at about $1,200,000,000, which was almost three times that in 1870.

food for her population; hence, she was obliged to import food-stuffs. Having limited natural resources and no raw *Poverty of Italy* materials, her manufactures were seriously handi-capped; every year showed an unfavorable balance of trade, and with little invisible earnings to make up the difference. She had no surplus capital for foreign investments. Her merchant marine was large, but not large enough to do a great carrying trade. There were two sources of invisible earnings that kept Italy from being constantly on the brink of bankruptcy: remittances from Italian emigrants abroad and the expenditures of the many tourists who came from all over the world to see the classic land. Emigration was a vastly important factor in Italy's economic life; she did not have to support those who emigrated, and, in addition, the re-mittances from the emigrants helped her to support those who remained in the country.

The position of the industrial worker in Italy was worse than that in any other Western nation except Spain. Factory laws were passed regulating the labor of women and children *Backward-* in industry, but these laws were inadequate and little *ness of fac-* effort was made to enforce them. In 1908, a law was *tory laws* passed providing for a weekly day of rest for industrial laborers.

With regard to social insurance Italy made some progress. An accident insurance law was passed in 1898 (amended in 1903), compelling employers to insure their workingmen *Social insu-* against industrial accidents. Compensation to in- *ance* jured workingmen was to be given in proportion to the seriousness of the injury; the funds were to be provided by the employers. A law of 1898 (amended in 1906) established an old-age and invalidity pension fund for workingmen, membership in which was voluntary. It was made up of contributions by members, supplemented by government subsidies. In 1910, a law was passed establishing maternity insurance for workingwomen, who were to receive a benefit, in case of childbirth, from a fund made up of contribu-tions from themselves, their employers, and the State.

SPAIN

(a) DYNASTIC STRUGGLES

During the first half of the nineteenth century, Spain was in the throes of a constitutional struggle. The despotic régime of

Ferdinand VII [1] roused every liberal element in the country, who

Carlists and resorted to secret societies and conspiracies. After
Christinos the death of the King, in 1833, the struggle continued in the form of a dynastic conflict between the Carlists who
supported Don Carlos, a pretender to the throne, and the Christinos who supported the queen-mother, Christina, who was Regent
during the infancy of Isabella, the Queen. The cause of Don
Carlos was espoused by reactionaries and clericals, and the cause
of the Regent by liberals because she granted a constitution establishing a Cortes, or parliament. Carlist uprisings constantly occurred, which kept the country in a tumult.

Isabella became of age in 1843, and her reign was disgraced by
scandal, incompetency, and corruption. An uprising took place in
Political in- 1868, and Isabella was forced to flee. For seven years
stability no regular government existed, and Spain was on the
verge of anarchy. The provisional government gave way to a
military dictatorship, which sought to reëstablish order by seeking
a new dynasty. The Carlists seized the opportunity to rise. Many
candidates for the throne appeared, among them a Catholic Hohenzollern. The choice, for a time, fell on Amadeo, the younger son
of Victor Emmanuel of Italy. But the clergy were opposed to
Amadeo because he was the son of a king who had despoiled the
Pope. So great was the opposition to him that Amadeo abdicated,
after reigning two years. In 1873, a republic was proclaimed which
roused still greater opposition. The country seethed with revolt,
and a number of presidential dictators followed one another in
rapid succession. The most famous President of the short-lived
Republic of Spain was Emilio Castelar, a remarkable orator whose
speeches attracted world-wide attention. In 1875, the Republic
was overthrown, and the Bourbon monarchy restored in the person
of Alphonso XII, son of Isabella.

Alphonso called to his side two able men who guided and advised him throughout his reign. One was Marshal Campos who
Reign of Al- completely suppressed the Carlist insurgents, and a
phonso XII rebellion in Cuba which had been going on for ten
years. The other was Canovas del Castillo who, as Prime Minister, virtually ruled the country for a decade. Canovas reorganized the finances and the administration, and suppressed disaffection with a stern hand. A new constitution was proclaimed in

[1] See page 99.

1876, which established a popularly elected parliament and a responsible ministry.

(b) POLITICAL HISTORY (1885–1914)

Alphonso died in 1885, leaving an infant son who succeeded him, in 1902, as Alphonso XIII. The uncertainties arising from the succession to the throne had been responsible for many "Rotativism" troubles in the past. To avoid a repetition of these evils, Canovas, the leader of the Conservatives, struck hands with Sagasta, the leader of the Liberals, and reached an understanding according to which both parties rotated in office by managing the elections through coercion and corruption. Canovas graciously permitted Sagasta to become Prime Minister several times, thus giving the Liberals a chance at the spoils of office. This system of "rotativism" produced mimic political strife, and popular government, though complete in its mechanism, became farcical. In 1897, Canovas was assassinated by an anarchist as a protest against this régime.

Discontent spread to the colonies where the rule of Spain was despotic and corrupt. Uprisings took place in Cuba and in the Philippines. After ten years of rebellion the Cubans The Spanish-had submitted, in 1878, on promises of reform; but American these promises were not kept, and the Cubans rose once War more, in 1895. General Weyler's savage methods in suppressing the rebellion roused great indignation in the United States. War followed between Spain and America (1898), in which the former was badly defeated. Spain was compelled to cede the Philippine Islands and Puerto Rico to the United States, and to acknowledge the independence of Cuba. She was now almost entirely shorn of her once world-wide colonial empire.

Alphonso XIII restored the popularity of the Bourbon dynasty by his genial personality and democratic manners. A question arose in the course of his reign concerning the relations Anti-between Church and State. Although almost unani-clericalism mously Catholic, the Spanish people began to show signs of hostility to the Church to which they had given such unswerving devotion for so many centuries. This change of attitude was due to several causes. The radical elements, republicans, socialists, and anarchists, blamed the Church for the evils that afflicted Spain, and conducted an anti-clerical propaganda among the workingmen.

The increasing number of religious orders, whose wealth escaped taxation, roused the hostility of the business elements who regarded the orders as detrimental to the economic life of the country. Anticlericalism in Spain was really a protest against the government with whom the Church was allied.

In 1909, the government was confronted by a serious uprising of the Riff tribesmen in Morocco. It endeavored to recruit armies
The Ferrer case to fight the Riffs which resulted in great demonstrations by the workingmen of Barcelona. After many encounters between the military and the workingmen, peace was finally restored. Francisco Ferrer, well known as an anti-clerical educator and founder of the libertarian Modern School, was accused of being the chief instigator of the rebellion. He was seized and shot after a brief trial by a court-martial. The execution of Ferrer led to world-wide demonstrations, not only against the Spanish government, but also against the Catholic Church in Spain which was regarded as the instigator of his execution.

In 1910, an advanced Liberal, Canalejas, became Prime Minister, pledged to an anti-clerical program. An act, known as the
The Padlock Law "Padlock Law," was passed forbidding the establishment of any more religious houses without the consent of the government. Taxes were laid on industrial enterprises conducted by the orders. Premier Canalejas also declared himself in favor of secular education and of separation of Church and State; but Catholicism in Spain proved strong enough to prevent the adoption of these measures.

Anti-clericalism in Spain, as elsewhere on the Continent, was confined to the bourgeois and working classes. These elements
Economic conditions were not numerous, as Spain continued to be chiefly an agricultural country. However, an important industrial development was taking place in the region of Barcelona, which became a thriving industrial center. Commerce and shipping advanced rapidly, due to Spain's excellent location, as she has ports both on the Atlantic and on the Mediterranean. Having little coal, Spain's industrial progress was seriously hampered. The productivity of the land was not very great, as large sections are barren mountain regions. Consequently large numbers migrated annually, chiefly to Latin America.

Although a great empire had been lost to her, Spain did not lose her spirit of imperialism. Being close to Africa she looked to that continent for colonies. She got little, only a few settlements and islands. As a result of an agreement with France she got a small part of Morocco. The warlike tribes- Morocco men, the Riffs, in her Moroccan colony rose again and again, and Spain had to send armies to suppress them. Although very costly she clung to her strip of Morocco with tenacity, the pathetic tenacity of a small nation that had once been a great empire.

PORTUGAL

During the first half of the nineteenth century the political history of Portugal was concerned chiefly with dynastic quarrels and factional strife. Now and then a dictator would Dynastic seize power and rule until ousted by a popular upris- strife ing or by another dictator. In 1852, a parliamentary system was established, which ushered in an era of political stability.

Peace meant that the various factions had composed their differences and were now agreed on dividing the spoils. They adopted the Spanish practice of "rotativism"; one "Rotativ- party would succeed the other in office, and elections ism" were "made" to suit the prearranged game of "ins" and "outs" by coercing and bribing the voters. This farcical parliamentary rule led to the growth of an active republican propaganda, particularly among the working classes.

King Carlos, who ascended the throne in 1889, gained unenviable notoriety as a corrupt man both in his public and private life. Discontent grew, especially in the cities, where uprisings, Dictator- strikes, and conspiracies were frequent. Especially ship of active were the intellectuals who were the leaders in Franco the republican movement. Fearful of a revolution Carlos, in 1906, appointed Joao Franco as Premier with dictatorial power. Franco governed in defiance of parliament, and meted out severe punishment to the opponents of his régime. The system of administrative terror was answered by a conspiracy against the life of the king. In 1908, Carlos and his eldest son were shot dead in the streets of Lisbon.

The younger son of the late King ascended the throne as Manuel II. Franco's régime came to an end, and he was forced to flee the country. But neither the King nor the politicians Manuel II had learned much from the recent tragedy. Manuel followed closely in his father's footsteps, and the factions resumed their practice of "rotativism."

The opposition now determined to change the government as well as the governors. Definite plans were made to overthrow the monarchy by secret political societies. Suddenly, in 1910, an uprising took place in Lisbon. The fleet in the harbor raised the republican colors, and began shelling the royal palace. The troops mutinied, and, aided by mobs, took possession of the city. Manuel, seeing the hopelessness of his position, fled the country. A provisional government was established which proclaimed Portugal a republic and proscribed the Braganza dynasty. A thoroughly democratic constitution was adopted which established a system of government modeled on that of France, with a parliament elected by universal, manhood suffrage, a president, chosen by parliament, and a cabinet respon sible to the lower house.

The Portuguese Revolution

Almost the first act of the Republic was to make war on the Catholic Church which was regarded as sympathetic with the royalists. The religious orders were suppressed, and their property confiscated. A law was passed separating Church and State, the principles of which were inspired by the French Separation Law of 1905. A new education law provided for the establishment of a national system of popular education that was to be free and secular.

Anti-clerical laws

The coming of the Republic did not allay all discontent. The workingmen had expected that the new government would decree their economic emancipation, and they were grievously disappointed when it vigorously protected property rights. Great strikes took place which were suppressed by the army. The Revolution of 1910 in Portugal was a belated echo of the Revolution of 1848 in France.

Discontent of the working classes

Like Holland, Portugal has considerable colonial possessions, Angola and Portuguese East Africa, and islands and ports in various parts of the world. The colonial trade is the most important element in Portugal's economy, as her agriculture and industry are very backward.

REFERENCES

ITALY:

B. King and T. Okey, *Italy To-Day* (ed. 1909), discusses the social and political problems of Italy after unification, needs revision; F. M. Underwood, *United Italy* (1912); W. K. Wallace, *Greater Italy* (1917); B. Croce, *A History of Italy, 1871–1915*, trans. from the Italian (1929).

SPAIN:

M. A. S. Hume, *Modern Spain* (ed. 1923), a good sketch; G. Hubbard, *Histoire contemporaine de l'Espagne*, 6 vols. (1869–1883), an authoritative work covering the first half of the nineteenth century; J. L. M. Curry, *Constitutional Government in Spain* (1889); E. H. Strobel, *The Spanish Revolution, 1868–1875* (1898); A. Marvaud, *La Question sociale en Espagne* (1910) and *L'Espagne au XXᵉ siècle* (1913); H. D. Sedgwick, *Spain: A Short History* (1925); Salvador de Madariaga, *Spain* (1930), an interpretation.

PORTUGAL:

A. Marvaud, *Le Portugal et ses colonies* (1912); G. Diercks, *Das Moderne Portugal* (1913); G. Young, *Portugal, Old and Young* (1917).

ADDITIONAL REFERENCES

R. Altamira, *A History of Spanish Civilization* (1930); L. Bertrand and Sir C. Petrie, *The History of Spain, 711–1931* (1934).

CHAPTER XX

THE GERMAN EMPIRE

(1871–1914)

GOVERNMENT

By far the most important event in the history of Europe during the nineteenth century was the advent of the German Empire. Germany's The amazing victories that led to its formation, its rise to power still more amazing rise to wealth and power, and finally its dramatic collapse as a result of the World War constitute a tale of unequaled interest. During the forty-seven years of its life, the German Empire was the center of world attention. First admired, then feared and hated, it finally roused so much hostility that the nations of the world combined against it. The outcome was the most terrible war in history.

The political system established in Germany was primarily designed to unify the country without destroying the power of the reigning princes. It consisted of a federal union of Nature of the federal twenty-five states enjoying large powers of local au- union tonomy, and united for common purposes under a central government in Berlin. Matters like the regulation of corporations, social insurance, industrial relations, and civil and criminal law which, in America, were left largely to the states, were, in Germany, subjects of Imperial legislation. But the federal laws were administered by state officials, appointed by the local rulers. The central government was monarchical in form, the head being known as the *Deutscher Kaiser*, or German Emperor. Each state, except the three city republics and Alsace-Lorraine, was likewise a monarchy, the local ruler being known as king, grand duke, duke. or prince, generally according to the size of his domain.[1] Unlike the American federal union, where equal rights were guaranteed to the states, the German federal union gave special privileges to

---

[1] There were four kingdoms: Prussia, Bavaria, Saxony, and Württemberg; six grand duchies: Baden, Hesse, Mecklenburg-Schwerin, Saxe-Weimar-Eisenach, Mecklenburg-Strelitz, and Oldenburg; five duchies: Brunswick, Saxe-Meiningen, Saxe-Altenburg, Saxe-Coburg-Gotha, and Anhalt; seven principalities: Schwarzburg-Sondershausen, Schwarzburg-Rudolstadt, Waldeck, Reuss Elder Line, Reuss Younger Line, Schaumburg-Lippe, and Lippe; three city-states: Lübeck, Bremen, and Hamburg; and the Imperial territory, Alsace-Lorraine.

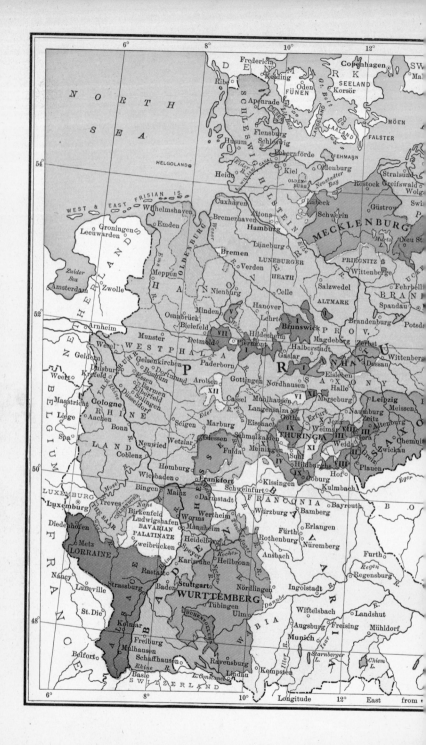

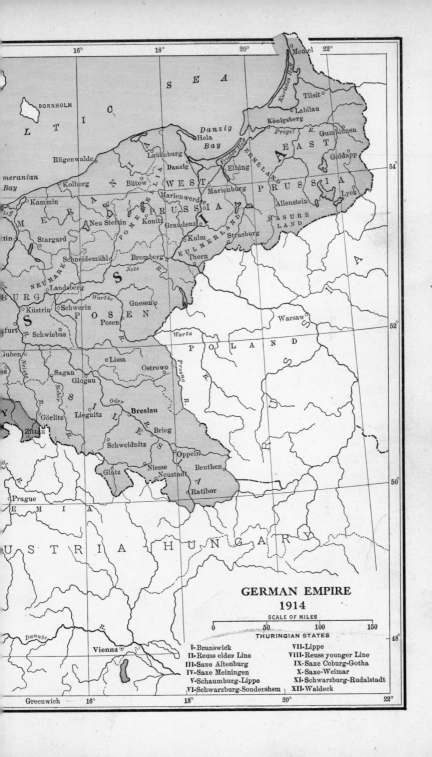

GERMAN EMPIRE
1914

SCALE OF MILES

0   50   100   150

THURINGIAN STATES

I - Brunswick
II - Reuss elder Line
III - Saxe Altenburg
IV - Saxe Meiningen
V - Schaumburg-Lippe
VI - Schwarzburg-Sondershsm
VII - Lippe
VIII - Reuss younger Line
IX - Saxe Coburg-Gotha
X - Saxe-Weimar
XI - Schwarzburg-Rudalstadt
XII - Waldeck

some of the states. Bavaria had her own postal and telegraph system; Bavaria, Baden, and Württemberg were not subject to the federal taxes on brandy and beer; Bremen and Hamburg were, for a time, not included in the federal tariff; Bavaria was given the chairmanship of the committee on foreign affairs in the Bundesrat; and Prussia had so many special privileges that she dominated the union.

The federal government consisted of the Kaiser, as president of the union, the Bundesrat representing the states, and the Reichstag representing the people. The position of Kaiser was vested in the Hohenzollern dynasty; therefore, the
The Kaiser
King of Prussia was at the same time German Emperor. His powers in domestic affairs were greatly circumscribed: he had no veto power over bills passed by parliament; he had little executive power, there being few federal officials to appoint; virtually, his chief function was that of commander-in-chief of the army and navy. However, the real power of the Kaiser came from the fact that he was King of Prussia which will be described presently. In foreign affairs, however, the Kaiser had great authority. The constitution declared that the "Kaiser shall represent the Empire in international matters, and in the name of the Empire, shall declare war and make peace, shall enter into alliances and treaties with foreign states, and shall send and receive ambassadors."

The Bundesrat was composed of sixty-one members, distributed among the states roughly according to size. Prussia had seventeen; Bavaria, six; Saxony and Württemberg, four
The Bundesrat
each; Alsace-Lorraine, Baden, and Hesse, three each; Mecklenburg-Schwerin and Brunswick, two each; and the rest, one each. A delegation to the Bundesrat voted as a unit and under instructions from the monarch by whom they were appointed. As a legislature the consent of the Bundesrat was necessary to all laws. Its consent was likewise necessary for the acceptance of treaties, for the dissolution of the Reichstag by the Kaiser, and for the appointment of some of the federal officials. It acted as judge in quarrels between the states, and had the power to coerce any refractory state that refused to obey its decisions. It could prevent changes in the Imperial constitution; an amendment first had to pass the Reichstag by a majority vote; then it was submitted to the Bundesrat, where fourteen votes sufficed to defeat it. This powerful element in the government of the Empire was entirely

subject to the will of the reigning princes who, by the unification of Germany, had lost their independence but not their power.

The distinctively democratic feature of the German government was the Reichstag, which was elected by universal, manhood suf-
The Reichs-   frage.   It was a legislature, and therefore it had the
tag   power to pass or defeat bills.   But the Reichstag did not initiate laws though it could do so; that was left to the Bundesrat.   Unlike the British House of Commons, it could not overthrow the cabinet which was responsible to the Kaiser.   The power of the Reichstag was negative; it could stop things from being done by the government, which it sometimes did, to the great embarrassment of those in power.   The part that the Reichstag played in German politics was chiefly that of a forum for political discussion, and was the best means that the government had of gauging public opinion.   It was said of the members of the Reichstag that they did not feel "as if they were actors who perform in the play, but as if they were the critics who looked on."

There was no cabinet system in the English sense of the phrase. The Chancellor was the whole cabinet; he was assisted by ad-
The Chan-   ministrative functionaries appointed by him who per-
cellor   formed the duties generally assigned to cabinet min-
isters.   Generally he was the Prussian Prime Minister.   As chairman of the Bundesrat he directed the policies of the Empire, subject to the approval of the Kaiser by whom he was appointed and dismissed.   As the principle of ministerial responsibility was not admitted, the Chancellor did not resign on an adverse vote of the Reichstag, but only when he displeased his master, the Kaiser. A Chancellor independent of the Reichstag was deliberately the plan of Bismarck in order to have a counterpoise to universal suffrage.   As the mouthpiece of the Kaiser and as the head of the Imperial administration, the Chancellor had great influence in shaping the policies of the government.

The political system of Germany was unlike that of any other country.   The Kaiser was not a president; the Bundesrat was not
Dominance   a senate; the Reichstag was not a parliament; and
of Prussia the Chancellor was not a prime minister.   Its federal system was even more unusual, in that its chief characteristic was the dominance of Prussia over the other states in the union. Prussia's king was Emperor; her Prime Minister was Chancellor; all proposed changes in the army, navy, or taxes had to have

WILHELM II

Prussia's consent; the chairman of every standing committee in the Bundesrat, except the one on foreign affairs, had to be a Prussian; moreover, her seventeen votes in the Bundesrat were sufficient to prevent changes in the Imperial constitution. The Fatherland was not formed by the absorption of Prussia into Germany, but by the absorption of Germany into Prussia; the part swallowed the whole.

In the political structure of Prussia lay the "efficient secret" of the government of the Empire. Prussia had been a constitutional state since 1850, but the limited power enjoyed by the Landtag, or parliament, made that body merely a veil for autocratic rule. The Landtag consisted of a house of lords and a house of representatives. The former was an aristocratic body, its members being chiefly landed aristocrats. The latter was elected by a three-class system of voting which divided the electors of a district into three groups: first, the wealthy who paid one third of the direct taxes of the district; then, the moderately well-to-do who paid the second third; and, finally, the mass of poor who paid the remaining third. Each class elected, by public ballot, one third of the members of an electoral college which, in turn, elected the representatives for the district. As votes were not counted but weighed in the scale of property to determine their value, the electoral colleges were naturally controlled by the property-owners. The conservative parties, though possessing a minority of the suffrage, were assured by this system of a perpetual majority in the popular chamber.

The actual government of Prussia was in the hands of the King. He appointed and dismissed all officials including the cabinet; and he had an absolute veto over all legislation passed by the Landtag. He appointed Prussia's delegation to the Bundesrat, and directed its vote in that body. The voice of the people was heard but faintly in the councils of those who governed Prussia which was essentially a "state of soldiers and officials." Although the other states of the Empire had fairly democratic constitutions, the influence of Prussia was the determining force in the government of the German people. The King, as Kaiser, wielded all the power that Prussia had in Germany. As Kaiser he could not veto bills passed by the Reichstag and Bundesrat; but as King he fashioned bills to his liking through the Prussian members of the Bundesrat whom he appointed. As

Kaiser he had little executive power; but as King he appointed the officials who enforced the federal laws in Prussia which, in size, was about two thirds of Germany. As Kaiser he had no power over federal amendments; but as King he could defeat an amendment through his control of seventeen votes in the Bundesrat. As Kaiser-King he appointed and dismissed the Chancellor. Germany was then, in reality, a semi-autocratic state.

It is rather astonishing that the Germans, who had made such wonderful progress in almost every field of human endeavor, should Reasons for have maintained in the twentieth century a political autocracy in system which had become archaic in the nineteenth. Germany: (1) strength It must not be supposed that the Germans were con- of the army tent to be the "political kindergarten of Europe." Far from it. Time and again public opinion showed a decided preference for democratic rule. Why, then, was the semi-autocratic system tolerated? Germany had been made by "blood and iron," and the system had been riveted on her by a conservative military class. To change it peaceably was impossible without the consent of Prussia, that is, of her King; to rise in revolt would have been a quixotic proceeding because an armed uprising, no matter how widespread, would have been easily suppressed by the military machine which had proved its prowess at Sadowa and Sedan. Neither Charles I nor Louis XVI had an army of the size and efficiency that the Kaiser possessed.

The German people were, moreover, loath to rise in revolution for fear of losing what they gained in 1870, their Fatherland. It (2) Fear of was widely believed that Germany was surrounded by foreign en- deadly enemies who would take advantage of a popular emies uprising to make war against the Fatherland. A united people must, therefore, stand behind a strong army, and the government, no matter how distasteful, must be supported on patriotic grounds.

The Germans were very proud of their government, and with good reason. It was progressive, enlightened, economical, and (3) Effi- marvelously efficient. Laws were the result of thor- ciency of the ough study, and were enacted with an eye to the government welfare of every class in the community. Administration was in the hands of a body of highly trained officials who regarded public service as a profession. Far-reaching social reforms were enacted for the benefit of the common man who, for the first time, received government help in his struggle for existence. "So, why revolt?" he reasoned.

Finally, there existed a condition which effectively barred the way to the establishment of democracy. It will be recalled that the Revolution of 1830 in France had been brought about by a combination of the middle and working classes; and that the Reform Bill of 1832 in England was brought to pass by a similar combination. (4) Division among the opponents History has proved that it takes two classes out of power to cope successfully with one class in power which has the advantage of controlling the military forces of the State. In Germany the working classes continually refused to combine with the middle classes against the intrenched aristocracy on the ground that the middle classes would reap the benefit, as in France and England. "Why should the German workingmen have their heads cracked in order to put the bourgeois in power," said the socialist Bebel. Curiously enough, the bourgeois refused to combine with the workingmen to overthrow the autocratic régime because they feared that the workingmen, being socialists, would use democracy as a stepping-stone to socialism. In spite of their liberalism the German bourgeois consistently supported the semi-autocratic régime because it encouraged business enterprise from which they profited, and because it kept down the socialists whom they feared. Its opponents being divided, the government, strongly supported by the landed aristocracy, was able to maintain itself without serious difficulty.

The Prussian military system of "a nation in arms" was incorporated in the constitution of the Empire, which required military service of every citizen capable of bearing arms. A recruit was "called to the colors" generally at the Conscription age of twenty to serve for two years; those who gave evidence of superior education served only one year. After active service, military duties continued in various reserves until the age of forty-five. Reservists were drilled for short periods during the year in order to keep them ready and prepared to answer the call to arms. Strictly speaking there was no "German" army; each state organized and officered its own military force. But all the armies were subject to the supreme command of the Kaiser who appointed the Great General Staff, a body of military experts that guided the military machine and planned campaigns in the event of war. The officers of the army were practically a military caste. They came mainly from the landowning, or Junker class, and were soldiers by tradition, temperament, and training almost from childhood. The recruits underwent severe training: tests of endurance, discipline, and courage were devised in order to bring them to the highest pitch of military efficiency. During his term of service the young German was imbued with a spirit of "corpse-like obedience," and when he returned to civil life he generally became a faithful employee and a loyal supporter of the autocratic régime.

POLITICAL PARTIES

As elsewhere on the Continent parliamentary elections were contested by loosely organized, political groups, "fractions," as they were called in Germany. In the Reichstag they consolidated into five main divisions, Conservatives, Center, National Liberals, Radicals, and Social Democrats. To pass laws various groups would from time to time form a block, or *blok*.

The Conservatives favored a high protective tariff, especially on agricultural products, colonial expansion, an aggressive foreign policy, and an ever stronger army and navy. They presented an unflinching opposition to all efforts to reform the political system in the interest of democracy.

The Center was a Catholic party, its stronghold being the Catholic regions of Germany: Bavaria and the Rhenish provinces. The political principles of the Center were not definitely formulated, but its attitude toward public questions was moderate; hence, it sat between the Right and the Left.

The National Liberals were "national" in that they favored colonial expansion and an aggressive foreign policy; and "liberal" in that they favored a low tariff on agricultural products and moderate political reforms. At first they united with the Conservatives against the Catholics and socialists; later, when they were weak, they became an opposition party. More advanced were the Radicals. Formerly allied with the National Liberals they broke away from them because the National Liberals had become timorous in their liberalism. The Radicals demanded the establishment of a complete parliamentary system as in England, individual liberty, secular education, the elimination of military and clerical influences in the government, heavy income and inheritance taxes, and free trade.

On the extreme left sat the Socialists, or Social Democrats. In Germany they stood alone as an organized, political party with central and local organizations that nominated candi- The Social dates and adopted platforms; and with an enthusiastic Democrats corps of party workers that conducted a ceaseless propaganda in favor of their principles. The Social Democrats advocated socialism as their ultimate goal; their immediate demands were similar to the platform of the Radicals.[1]

All the German parties frankly represented the interests of special economic groups. The Conservatives were the party of the great landowners in Prussia; the Center, of the Economic peasant proprietors of Bavaria; the National Liberals, and religious of the great industrialists; the Radicals, of the pro- character of the parties fessionals; and the Social Democrats, of the working- men. Moreover, they had marked religious or anti-religious tendencies. The Conservatives were chiefly Lutherans, and favored the strengthening of the principles of Christianity among the people; the Center was entirely Catholic; the National Liberals were free thinkers and mildly anti-clerical; and the Radicals and Social Democrats were free thinkers and strongly anti-clerical.

German political life was sterile in leadership. No great party leader appeared, no Gladstone, no Gambetta, who succeeded in winning the confidence of the people. This situation Lack of po- was partly due to the impotence of the Reichstag, litical lead- which discouraged political talent; and partly to the ership fact that parties appealed to narrow class or religious interest; seldom did they attempt to win the people by broad national appeals. As a consequence, debates in the Reichstag often became bitter wrangling or challenges of defiance. In that "Hall of Echoes" the speeches were heard by the members within, but not by the nation without.

BISMARCK AS CHANCELLOR

The history of the German Empire may be divided into two periods, each dominated by a striking personality. The first was the period of Bismarck; the second, that of William II. Bismarck, Unlike his great contemporary, Cavour, Bismarck the realist lived to direct the fortunes of the political structure of which he had been the master-builder. He became the first Chancellor of

[1] For further description of German socialism, see pages 586–88.

the German Empire, which he ruled as long as William I reigned. Problems as momentous as those of unification now faced the veteran statesman, who set about solving them with his old daring and insight. Bismarck's intellectual mobility was amazing; he "grew visibly." He frequently boasted of being entirely free from "doctrinairism," by which he meant that he had no fixed ideas or principles, but suited his theories to the needs of every problem. "No theory!" was his constant rejoinder to those who wished to solve Germany's new problems according to set formulas. Bismarck was a lone realist in a land of theorists. A striking illustration was his change of attitude toward universal suffrage which he had bitterly opposed all his life. When he was convinced by the socialist, Ferdinand Lassalle, that to inject a popular element into the government would mean the "moral conquest of Germany," he adopted universal suffrage for the Reichstag.

In foreign affairs Bismarck's object was to make secure what had been gained in 1870. He declared that Germany was now Foreign "satiated," having accomplished her unity and having policy taken a leading position among the nations of the world. But she had earned the bitter enmity of France whose quick recovery astonished and dismayed Bismarck. Germany had emerged from the Franco-Prussian war triumphant but insecure. And she knew it. Therefore, Bismarck sought to isolate France who was not strong enough to attack Germany single-handed. His remarkable diplomacy succeeded in combining Germany, Austria, and Italy in the famous Triple Alliance.[1]

Bismarck and his associates had an ever-present fear that local loyalties, or "particularism," so deeply embedded in the consciousness of the German people, might loosen the foundations of the new Germany. In order to make the Germans sink their localisms in the common consciousness of national unity, the Imperial Centraliza- government constantly enlarged its functions. An tion Imperial bank was created to harmonize the financial operations of the various state governments; a civil and criminal code was issued establishing a common private law for the Empire; all the state railways were put under the supervision of an Imperial railway board; new coins were issued, bearing on one side the effigy of the Kaiser and on the other, the arms of the Empire, to be missionaries "preaching the glad tidings of unity."

[1] See Chapter XXXIII.

During Bismarck's chancellorship Germany's policy was purely Continental. She then had no colonial ambitions, and was content to play the part of a great Continental power. "I am no colonial man," Bismarck would repeatedly say. "I do not want any colonies at all," he once declared, "their only use is to provide sinecures. For us Germans, colonies would be exactly like the silks and sables of the Polish nobleman who had no shirt to wear under them." When the Partition of Africa took place Bismarck agreed to take colonies for Germany, only on the most urgent insistence of the business interests who hoped to find, in Africa, sources of raw materials. Bismarck was also opposed to naval armament; and, as long as he was Chancellor, Germany was not a naval power.

Bismarck's opposition to colonies and to a navy

THE KULTURKAMPF

During the decade following unification, a bitter conflict raged between the Catholic Church and the State. Unlike the case in France, where the Catholics were avowed enemies of the Republic, the Catholics in Germany were loyal supporters of the Empire. During the Franco-Prussian War they had rallied to the side of Protestant Prussia as against Catholic France. And yet their whole-hearted devotion to the Fatherland was questioned. A spirit of intolerant nationalism took possession of many Germans who prided themselves on being *echt Deutsch*, or fully and truly German, and they denounced as "internationalists" those of their fellow-countrymen who had connections outside of Germany such as Catholics, socialists, and Jews. Especially bitter was the feeling against the Catholics, and the Pope was accused of being an enemy of the new German Empire as his predecessors had been of the Hohenstaufen Empire during the Middle Ages.

"True" Germanism

The nationalists were joined by many free-thinking liberals who denounced Catholicism as the irreconcilable foe of human freedom. Since the French Revolution, secularism had displaced Protestantism as the uncompromising enemy of Catholicism. In 1864, Pope Pius IX issued a noted encyclical, *Quanta Cura*, which was followed by the *Syllabus of Modern Errors*, both of which defended most vigorously the religious conception of society and of government. Pius denounced, as "modern errors," liberty of conscience, civil marriage, divorce, and secular education. During 1869–70 there was convened in

The Syllabus and the Vatican Council

Rome a great Catholic assembly, known as the Vatican Council, the first general assembly of the Church since the Council of Trent in the sixteenth century. It adopted the dogma known as "papal infallibility," by which is meant that the Pope is infallible when he "speaks *ex cathedra,* that is when, in discharge of the office of pastor and teacher of all Christians, by virtue of his supreme apostolic authority, he defines a doctrine regarding faith or morals to be held by the universal Church." These pronouncements were received by liberals throughout the world as a declaration of war against modern tendencies.

In Germany the anti-Catholic movement became political. A demand arose that a war for modern civilization be waged against the Church as the upholder of medievalism; hence, the expression *Kulturkampf* (Battle for Civilization). Bismarck became the leader of a bitter anti-clerical movement, and for political motives. Although a Protestant, his politics was little influenced by religion, and still less by theology. In Bismarck's view the Catholics in Germany were the representatives of localisms and separatisms: Bavarians who had sympathized with Austria, Alsatians who sympathized with France, and Poles who wished to maintain their own nationality. A blow at the Catholics would, in his view, strengthen the unifying influences in the new Empire. In 1872, he began the war against the Church by inducing the Reichstag to pass a law expelling the Jesuits from Germany. Then followed the "May Laws" (1873–75), enacted by the Landtag in Prussia, which put under state control the education and the appointment of the Catholic clergy; a candidate for the priesthood was obliged to attend government schools and universities and to pass government examinations. Civil marriage was made compulsory. A strict supervision was also instituted over Catholic institutions, and the government asserted its authority in the appointment and dismissal of priests. Many religious orders were suppressed.

The "May Laws"

The answer of Pope Pius IX was to declare these laws null and void, and to enjoin the faithful in Germany not to obey them. The intervention of the Pope aroused Bismarck's ire, and he determined to crush all opposition of the Church. "We shall not go to Canossa,[1] either in the flesh or in the spirit,"

Persecution of Catholics

[1] The Italian town where, in the eleventh century, the Emperor Henry IV humiliated himself before Pope Gregory VII.

was his famous challenge. Priests who refused obedience to the "May Laws" were fined and jailed; Church property was confiscated, and many churches were closed. In order to divide the Catholics, Bismarck encouraged a schism, formed by a group calling itself the "Old Catholics," who refused to accept the doctrine of papal infallibility. But they failed to attract many supporters, as the overwhelming majority of the German Catholics remained loyal to the Pope.

The "Diocletian persecution," as it was called by the Catholics, resulted in rousing them to stubborn resistance. They flocked to the support of the Center Party which, under the able leadership of Ludwig Windthorst, gained many seats. The Social Democrats were also gaining rapidly. But the National Liberals and Radicals, who supported the government, were losing heavily. This situation caused much anxiety to Bismarck, who did not wish to repeat his exploit of 1863 by governing without parliament. One such performance was enough, even for Bismarck. He, therefore, decided to "go to Canossa." In 1878, a new Pope, Leo XIII, was elected, who was more moderate in his views than his predecessor, Pius IX. Bismarck offered terms of peace to the Church, which were accepted. Between 1878 and 1887 nearly all the anti-Catholic legislation was repealed, and the Church was restored virtually to its former status in Germany.

Repeal of the May Laws

An indirect outcome of the *Kulturkampf* was a protective tariff law. As Germany advanced industrially she felt the need of a tariff to protect her home market; moreover, she feared that her agriculture could not stand the competition of the immense food supplies coming from the Americas. Bismarck was converted to protection, a policy especially favored by the Conservatives, the party of the great landed interests. The Radicals were free-traders, and the National Liberals were divided. The Center favored protection because its supporters were chiefly peasants. A farmers' Blok was formed of the Conservative and Center parties that, in 1879, succeeded in putting through a high tariff law on both agricultural and industrial products. The government now had the support of the Center, the largest party in the Reichstag.

Protection

THE ATTACK ON THE SOCIALISTS

If the "black international," as Catholicism was called, was considered a danger to German unity, the "red international," or

The "red international" socialism, was looked upon as its open and avowed enemy. The Social Democrats uncompromisingly opposed the Bismarckian order, and openly favored the establishment of a democratic republic. It was their internationalism, even more than their democracy, that infuriated Bismarck. He denounced the socialists as men "without a country" and as "enemies of the Empire," and prepared to suppress them without mercy.

The sought-for opportunity came in 1878, when two attempts were made on the life of the aged and beloved Emperor William by

The "Exceptional Laws" men who were known to be socialists. The Reichstag passed a series of "Exceptional Laws" against the "publicly dangerous endeavors of Social Democracy," prohibiting the formation or existence of all associations, meetings, or publications which sought to subvert the existing system of society and government. Large powers were given to the police who, under certain circumstances, had the right to send a socialist out of the country. Socialist meetings were rigorously censored, and their leaders arrested on the slightest pretexts, often on the charge of *lèse majesté*. Socialist publications were constantly suppressed, their funds confiscated, and their editors fined or jailed. A state of minor siege might be proclaimed in any town where socialists were numerous and influential, and those arrested were tried by martial law.

Socialist agitation, however, continued; it was merely driven "underground." Secret associations were formed that carried on

Futility of these laws a far more vigorous propaganda than heretofore. Socialist papers developed an art of communicating their ideas "between the lines" in order not to give sufficient cause for court proceedings. When a paper was suppressed, it reappeared under a different name. Some of the socialist papers had a "sitting editor" who, in case of prosecution, would appear as the defendant, and if convicted, would sit in jail in place of the real editor whose name was kept secret. Branches of the Social Democratic Party organized as bowling and singing clubs in order to avoid police interference. Conventions of the party met in Switzerland, where they used the freedom of speech, permitted in that country, to denounce the reactionary policy of Bismarck. In spite of persecution, or because of it, the Social Democratic Party grew.[1] At no time did the Reichstag exclude Social Democrats who were duly elected, a proceeding which would have been unconstitutional. Under the able leadership of August Bebel and William Liebknecht the socialists desisted from violence, which would have encouraged the government to suppress them entirely. After ten years of strife the government saw the futility of the repressive measures; and, in 1890, the year of Bismarck's retirement, the "Exceptional Laws" were not renewed. Once more Bismarck was beaten.

SOCIAL REFORM

To Bismarck's alert mind the struggle with the socialists was a revelation of the new social forces in a Germany that was being rapidly industrialized. He realized that the State would have an irreconcilable enemy in the great masses of industrial laborers unless something was done to mollify them. Through his influence Germany became the pioneer of social reform; she was the first nation to repudiate the doctrine of *laissez faire* by intervening in the affairs of capital and labor. Unlike Gladstone, Bismarck regarded the policy of *laissez faire* as fraught with great danger to society and to the State because it produced an unbridled capitalism intent upon its own interests only, and a sullen working class alienated from the State which it regarded as an enemy. The Chancellor determined to avoid such an outcome in Germany at all costs; a healthy, contented working class was, in his view, the surest guarantee of social peace and national power.

Bismarck opposed to laissez faire

Bismarck, however, originated neither the idea nor the system of social insurance. The idea was advocated by influential German economists, notably Adolf Wagner and Gustav Schmoller, who refused to accept the ideas of the Manchester School, which they regarded as obsolete. Workingmen's insurance systems had existed in Germany even before 1870, but they were local and voluntary. What Bismarck did was to combine them into a great national system and introduce the compulsory feature.

Influence of the economists

Three great measures were passed by parliament, the Sickness Insurance Law of 1883, the Accident Insurance Law of 1884, and

the Old-Age and Invalidity Law of 1889.   Later, in 1911, these
The insur-   acts were unified in a great social insurance code, which
ance laws   constituted the most comprehensive effort yet made by
any modern state for the amelioration of the lot of the working
classes.   It constitutes Bismarck's surest title to fame.

Sickness insurance was made compulsory for all employed persons whose wages were less than a fixed minimum.   It was so
Sickness in-   high that it included virtually the whole working
surance   class.   The fund from which benefits were drawn was
made up of contributions by employers and workingmen, in the
proportion of one third from the former and two thirds from the
latter.   In case of sickness, the insured man or woman received
half of his or her wages for a period of twenty-six weeks and free
medical attendance, including medicines.   In case of death, the
expense of the funeral was paid from the same source.   The funds
were administered by a commission composed of representatives of
employers and employees.

Accident insurance, or Workmen's Compensation, was made
compulsory for nearly all workers employed in industry.   The
Accident   funds were made up entirely by the employers, who
insurance   contributed according to the number of their employees
and according to the degree of risk in their trade.   The administration of the funds was in the hands of the employers; but the scale
of compensation to injured workingmen was determined by law
according to the degree of injury sustained by the latter in the
course of their employment.   In case of death the dependents of
the insured received an annual pension of twenty per cent of the
wages paid to the deceased.

Workingmen were also compelled to insure against old age and
invalidity.   The pension fund was made up of contributions by
Old Age   the employers, the workingmen, and the State; and
Pensions   it was administered by public officials.   At the age
of seventy, later reduced to sixty-five, the insured received a pension, the amount of which varied according to the contributions
which he had made.[1]

In parliament the social insurance laws were supported by the
Conservatives, aided sometimes by the National Liberals and sometimes by the Center.   They were opposed by the Radicals, the

[1] After the World War the social insurance laws were radically revised.   See
Chapters XXXIX, XL, XLI.

only party that upheld *laissez faire* doctrines, and by the Social
Democrats who "feared Greeks bearing gifts" to the working
class. The socialists denounced the laws as "bribes" given by the
capitalists to the workingmen to cease their agitation.

During the debates the motives for social insurance were freely
and frankly discussed. It was the duty of the State, urged Bismarck, to look after its unprotected members, "that
they may not be run over and trampled under foot
on the highway of life." He was not at any time,
however, opposed to the interests of the employers.
"I am not antagonistic to the rightful claims of
capital," he declared; "I am far from wanting to
flaunt a hostile flag; but I am of the opinion that the masses, too,
have rights which should be considered." What was necessary
was "to add a few drops of social oil" in the recipe which was to
restore the State to health; it was desirable that the working classes
should regard the State as a friend, not as an enemy. This idea
is forcefully enunciated in the following statement made by the
government. "It should be our aim to spread the idea, particularly among the non-propertied classes who form at once the
most numerous and the least instructed part of the population, that
the State is not merely a necessary but a beneficent institution.
If direct benefits are secured to these classes by legislation, they
will not regard it as a contrivance for the benefit only of the
better classes but as an institution serving their own needs and
interests." The workingman was a soldier of industry who, Bismarck urged, should "receive a pension just as the soldier in the
army who has been disabled or the civil servant who has grown
old in the service."

Reasons for social reform: (1) the State as benefactor of the lower classes

As has already been told, the rapid growth of socialism frightened
Bismarck. He was convinced that social legislation would result
in making the workingmen more contented, and therefore less inclined to support revolutionary parties.
"Give the workingman the right to employment as
long as he has health," he once told the Reichstag,
"assure him care when he is sick, and maintenance when he is
old, ... then these gentlemen [the socialists] will sound their bird
call in vain. Thronging to them will cease as soon as the workingmen realize that the government is earnestly concerned with
their welfare." The objection, raised by the Radicals, that laws

(2) to dis-suade work-ingmen from socialism

for the benefit of the working classes were socialistic did not disturb Bismarck. "If you believe that you can frighten any one or call up specters with the word 'socialism,' you take an attitude which I have abandoned long ago," he once told an opponent.

The reforms of Stein and Hardenberg which emancipated the peasantry by royal edict constituted a great Prussian tradition, (3) Paternal- and the Hohenzollerns were proud of their "pater-
ism   nalism," or interest in the condition of the lower classes. "In Prussia," declared Bismarck, "it is the kings, not the people, who make revolutions." Why, then, should not the government improve the condition of the new poor man, the factory laborer, as it once had improved that of the other poor man, the peasant? Moreover, the ideal of an efficient nation would be greatly advanced by social legislation; a healthy working class would make better soldiers, better citizens, and even better work-ingmen; social legislation would, in the end, advance the interests of the employers as well as those of the State. A workingman who looks forward to an old-age pension "is far more contented and much easier to manage. . . . A great price is not too much to pay if the disinherited can be made satisfied with their lot," said Bismarck.

Germany's bold experiments in social reform attracted world-wide attention. At first they were denounced as "socialistic" and as a charge upon industry; later, they were imitated, and even improved upon, by nearly all the nations of Europe. Social reform became as much of a sign of progress in the twentieth century as political reform had been in the nineteenth.

ECONOMIC PROGRESS

The rise of Germany in the economic world was as phenomenal as her rise in the political world. During the first half of the
Backward-   nineteenth century, Germany was a poor country,
ness of Ger- inhabited by a frugal, hardworking people engaged
many before   in agriculture and in the handicrafts. Few countries
1870   then presented a less inviting field for economic de-velopment than Germany. Her soil was generally poor, her rivers shallow, her harbors few, and her coal and iron so inferior in quality that little mining was done. In order to engage in manufacturing, the raw materials had to be assembled from widely separated dis-tricts; moreover, the long distance to the seaboard from the manu-

facturing regions was a serious handicap to overseas trade. There was, however, an excellent railway system, constructed for military purposes during the wars for unification.

Until 1850 the Industrial Revolution had made very slow progress. After that year German industry began to develop very rapidly, and still more rapidly after unification. The "nation of poets and thinkers," whose empire was "in the clouds," became one of business men whose enterprise astonished the world. The period 1870–75 is known in Germany as the *Grundjahre*, "foundation years"; so rapidly were factories built during these years that, as it was said, "tall chimneys grew like mushrooms." Once the impetus was given, there seemed to be no limit to Germany's mounting prosperity. The products of her factories and workshops invaded the markets of the world, and the legend "Made in Germany" became the symbol of commercial success.

Rapid industrialization

The industrial centers were chiefly in the west where large deposits of coal and iron were found. The Ruhr and the Saar regions produced most of the coal; and Lorraine produced about eighty-five per cent of all the iron ore mined in Germany. Coal mining was developed so rapidly that, by 1912, Germany ranked after the United States and England as a producer of coal. For long the Lorraine iron was considered useless, as it contained a large amount of phosphorus; but the "Gilchrist-Thomas process" made these deposits of great value. This process also produced a by-product, a "slag," which was found useful as a soil fertilizer. Germany immediately advanced as a producer of iron; by 1903 she passed England and became the second iron-producing country in the world, ranking after the United States. In the production of steel there was a similar rise. From 1890 to 1910 the German steel industry grew seven times as fast as that of England in point of production; in 1912, Germany's product was double that of England. Germany's export of machinery in 1908 was about half that of England; five years later she completely outdistanced her rival.

Coal and iron

The creation of a merchant marine second only to that of England was one of the signal accomplishments of industrial Germany. In spite of handicaps her merchant marine grew so fast that, in 1913, she had a net tonnage of over 3,000,000, nearly all new vessels using steam. The government

Shipping

did much to encourage shipping by exemption from taxation, by
rebates on railway shipments of the parts for ship construction, by
government orders, by reimbursement of port and canal dues, and
by direct subventions.   Germany specialized in passenger traffic,
and produced famous liners which were unsurpassed in size, speed,
luxurious equipment, and service.   German ships captured most
of the immigrant traffic from Europe to America, and much of
the tourist traffic from America to Europe.

Two typical German industries were the electrical and the
chemical, the extraordinary growth of which was largely due to
The chem-   excellent technical education.   Most of the electrified
ical indus-   railways in Europe were built with German apparatus.
tries   Germany led the world in the chemical industries,
especially in pharmaceutical products and synthetic dyes.   The
dye industry was developed by German chemists aided by government subsidies.   Years of research and experiment resulted in
producing good and fast colors from coal tar, and at prices so cheap
that Germany virtually had a monopoly of the dye industry.
Potash, a mineral salt, used extensively in the manufacture of
fertilizers, was found chiefly in Germany which exported large
quantities of this mineral to all parts of the world.   German chemists, in a sense, abolished the tropics; they discovered processes for
making artificial indigo, musk, vanilla, and camphor.

The annexation of Alsace-Lorraine gave an impetus to the
German textile industries, Alsace being a large cotton-manufactur-
Cotton   ing center.   But the cotton industry was not suffi-
             ciently developed to make Germany a great textile-
producing nation; her annual production being only a fifth of that
of England.

Although the industrial development was remarkable, it was not,
as in the case of England, at the expense of agriculture.   Germany's
Scientific   economic ideal was a harmonious development of all
agriculture   her resources, and she was as careful to protect and
develop her agriculture as to protect and develop her industries.
In 1914, although her rural population was only thirty-five per
cent, Germany was largely self-supporting.   How did she manage
to perform this almost impossible feat?   Largely through the application of science to agriculture.   Careful soil preparation and nursing, scientific fertilizers, and agricultural machinery resulted in
giving ever-increasing crops despite a constantly decreasing agri-

cultural population. Germany was the greatest grower of potatoes in the world, producing many times more than Russia, the leading agricultural nation of Europe. The cultivation of sugar beets was highly developed. By careful planting and selection the beet was made to increase its yield of sugar. The chief farming regions were eastern Prussia, where land was divided in large estates and cultivated by farm laborers, and Bavaria, where peasant proprietorship was the rule.

From a land of emigration, Germany became one of immigration. Before the industrial era, Germans emigrated at the rate of 200,000 a year;[1] since then, in spite of a large increase of population, German industry was able to provide work for so many that emigration sank to about 20,000 a year. Thousands of foreign workingmen, mainly from Italy, Austria, and Russia, came into Germany to help harvest the crops and to work in the mines. These immigrant laborers were permitted to remain in the country under special conditions, and only for a specified time, in order to prevent them from competing with the native laborers.

Immigration

As in the case of England the economic life of Germany depended largely upon foreign trade. Her success in this field was astounding. In 1870, her total foreign trade was about a billion dollars; in 1913, it rose to over five billions, of which nearly all the imports were raw material and food, and nearly all the exports, manufactured articles. During the nineties Germany began showing an "unfavorable" balance of trade; like England, she was now an international trading concern with invisible earnings from her merchant marine and from her foreign investments.

Unfavorable balance of trade

The principal center of German industry was the Ruhr. A region no larger than Rhode Island, this ant-hill of industrialism was literally covered with mines, factories, and railways. Its chief city was Essen, which was the seat of the famous Krupp works, the greatest steel plant in the world. In 1913, the Ruhr produced over half of the coal and over half of the steel output of Germany. It has been observed that iron will go where coal is mined because coke is needed to make steel. Therefore, the coal mines of the Ruhr "drew" the iron of Lorraine,

The Ruhr

[1] During the period 1851 to 1895 about 4,500,000 Germans emigrated, most of them to America.

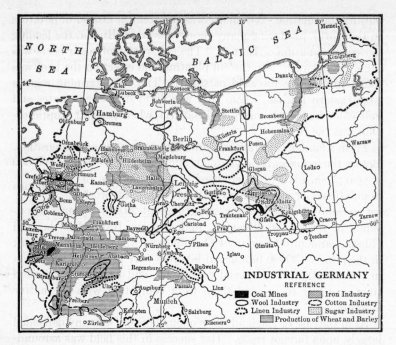

INDUSTRIAL GERMANY

REFERENCE

Coal Mines   Iron Industry
Wool Industry   Cotton Industry
Linen Industry   Sugar Industry
Production of Wheat and Barley

of Luxemburg, of France, and of Belgium. A lace-work of railways, intricate yet perfectly organized, covered the region, which distributed the products of its mines and factories to all parts of the Continent.

There were many causes for Germany's astounding industrial development. First and foremost was the unification of the country which united the energies of a highly capable people and gave them unbounded confidence in their powers. Germany was now able to develop the home market of a large and rapidly growing population, and to use her powerful influence in international matters to negotiate favorable commercial treaties.

Causes for industrial progress: (1) unification

The Germans were pioneers in the application of science to industry. Many chemical laboratories were established, wherein an army of highly trained scientists were constantly at work inventing new processes and devising new methods, with the result that many articles produced in Germany were cheaper than those produced elsewhere. This union of laboratory and workshop was an efficient

(2) application of science to industry

cause of Germany's prosperity; it enlisted trained intelligence to solve the problems of industry. German business men spared no expense in providing for scientific experiments, well knowing that, in time, they would be amply rewarded. German laborers, even those doing simple work, were trained by the numerous and excellent technical schools that prepared men and women for their vocations in life.

The Germans developed an extraordinary genius for efficient organization, or the art of putting every man in his place and of getting the most out of him. Business was a career (3) efficiency for which men prepared themselves as carefully as those who prepared themselves for a profession. German commercial representatives in foreign lands learned the language of their prospective customers, their likes, and their dislikes; and they endeavored to please them in every possible way. Time and again did the Germans capture the trade in certain articles by paying special attention to little things, such as the color of a garment, the shape of an egg cup, or the method of packing needles.

Germany's late entrance into the field of modern industry proved to be, not a handicap, but a positive advantage in her struggle for economic supremacy. Instead of going by rule of (4) adopts thumb along an unknown path, she carefully planned the latest and directed her economic development. Profiting by machinery the experience of other nations, especially by that of England, Germany avoided their mistakes and improved on their successes, so that many problems arising from the Industrial Revolution were solved before they had become serious enough to become obstacles to social betterment and to business enterprise. It was easier for Germany to adopt the most improved machinery and the most modern methods; she had no old plants to dismantle and no cherished business traditions to hamper her progress.

Although Germany's geographic position was bad strategically, it was excellent commercially. Being in central Europe and having ports on the North Sea she became a distribu- (5) Germany, an tor of foreign goods to the other nations on the Con- entrepôt for tinent. Her two greatest ports, Hamburg and the Continent Bremen, were rebuilt; no expense was spared in enlarging and improving their harbors. They were organized as "free ports" with the right of importing, free of duty, goods that were to be made up for the export trade or were to be reëxported.

The two cities grew amazingly as they became the entrance and exit of vast quantities of goods that were destined for foreign as well as for German markets. For long England had been the entrepôt by sea; now Germany, with its excellent railway system, was performing that function by land.

However, Germany did not neglect her large and growing home market. When the Empire was founded, low tariff, and even free trade was most favored. As industry was developing

Protection

Bismarck was convinced that it needed protection against foreign competition. Free trade, he declared, was the "weapon of the strongest," a good policy for England, "the mighty industrial athlete" who could compete successfully against less developed nations. A high protective tariff on both industrial and agricultural products was adopted and applied with great intelligence. Germany's tariff was "flexible"; the rates could be increased or decreased on the recommendation of a tariff commission, which changed the schedules in response to the needs of German business.

Government regulation was an important cause of Germany's prosperity. There was hardly a business enterprise which did not

Government regulation and ownership

feel the regulating hand of the government. Regulation had for its object, not the hampering, but the promoting of business. Soon after the establishment of the Empire the railways were nationalized. Each system was owned and operated by the individual states, but was supervised by an Imperial Railway Board which established uniform regulations for the Empire. State ownership of railways proved a brilliant success; the management was economical and efficient, fares were low, equipment good, and the service excellent. The state governments made large profits from their railways, which enabled them to embark on many undertakings without resorting to additional taxes. The German railways were primarily regarded as a transport institution for the welfare of the nation, not as a profit-making industry. Especially low rates were allowed on export goods in order to enable the German manufacturer better to compete in foreign markets. Foreign competition was prevented by high rates on foreign goods. If a new industry was to be started, the rates on the raw material coming from distant parts were lowered in order to encourage the enterprise. The evil effects of bad harvests were minimized, and many farmers saved from ruin by the lowering of freight rates on agricultural products. Rebating in Germany was open and legal, and it was permitted for the purpose of helping, not of destroying, business enterprises. The government built a system of canals connecting the various rivers which made possible a means of transportation that was cheap and easy. Large sums were spent in deepening the shallow German rivers in order to make them more navigable.

One of the remarkable facts in the history of German industry was the quick transition from small enterprise to large consolida- tion. In order to compete successfully with the well- The Cartels established English firms, German business had to be well organized and consolidated. The consolidations, known as Cartels, were pools, or business agreements among firms rather than amalgamations; they regulated output, fixed prices, and as- signed sales territory. The individual plants, in many cases, had separate management. Cartels existed chiefly in the heavy in- dustries such as coal, iron, steel, and chemicals. There was little anti-trust sentiment in the country, and there were no anti-trust laws as in the United States. Public opinion in Germany regarded consolidation as a normal development, and even the socialists favored the cartels as steps toward socialism.

Germany's industrial transformation was so extraordinary that, economically, it might be said she never lived in the nineteenth century. In 1870, her economic situation was not Transition unlike that of England in the early days of the In- from small dustrial Revolution. Within several decades she to big busi-ness made a flying leap into the era of big business. She, therefore, largely missed the first stage of industrial society with competition and *laissez faire*; instead, there was consolidation and State regulation.

As an industrial nation, Germany succeeded in becoming a close second to England and challenged that long-established "workshop of the world" for economic leadership. However, Economic Germany's industrial structure, so imposing in appear- rivalry of ance, was not as solidly built as that of England. It Germany and England was based upon a huge system of credit which de- pended for its maintenance upon the export of manufactured goods in ever-increasing quantities. Imports were outstripping exports, and, like England, Germany had "invisible" earnings to make up for the "unfavorable" balance of trade. But these earnings were far smaller than those of England. A great fear often haunted the mind of the German industrialists that they would be denied free access to the sources of raw material, and that their foreign markets would be closed by high tariffs. Having little raw material and depending more and more upon foreign trade, Germany would be in a serious situation in case her industrial progress was hampered. It was this condition that caused her to favor so energetically a policy of colonial expansion.

ERA OF THE KAISER

Germany's emergence as a great economic and political power had a marked effect upon popular sentiment, and especially upon the ruling classes. It inspired the Germans with an unbounded confidence in their prowess, and led them to believe that they were indeed a superior race. A Teutonic cult arose which had for its votaries influential writers, statesmen, and soldiers who fervently believed that the day of the Teuton had at last arrived, and that Germany was now to be the new model for the peoples of the world. Other races, they contended, had already accomplished their destiny, and were now therefore decadent; the trial by battle had proved it conclusively for them in the case of France; the seeming absence of a definite purpose and efficient system in the loosely hung British Empire convinced them that the English were fast losing their grip upon the world. In their view the Russians were a barbaric horde without European traditions or culture and a constant danger to Western civilization, which it was now Germany's special mission to protect. In a wonderful way Germany proceeded to organize herself as the New Model. The development of almost every phase of human activity, political, economic, and cultural was planned beforehand. Difficulties were foreseen and provided for, and waste was eliminated by a marvelously efficient system of organization. System, Efficiency, Discipline were enthusiastically proclaimed by the Germans as watchwords in human affairs as, at one time, the French had proclaimed Liberty, Equality, and Fraternity. Such was *Deutsche Kultur* which, according to its votaries, was destined to spread throughout the world. The term *Kultur* is well explained by the philosopher, Santayana. "Every nation," he writes, "has certain characteristic institutions, certain representative writers and statesmen, past and present, certain forms of art

Deutsche Kultur [marginal note]

and industry, a certain type of policy and moral inspiration. These are its Kultur. . . . It is not, like culture, a matter of miscellaneous private attainments and refined tastes, but, rather, participation in a national purpose and in the means of executing it."

The new mood of Germany found expression in a new monarch, Emperor William II, who succeeded his father, Frederick, in 1888.[1] No monarch of his day was more widely known than "the Kaiser." A man of striking personality and gifted with unusual ability as an orator, he succeeded in winning great popularity. Eager to appear in the public eye, the Kaiser made speeches on any and every occasion, and on any and every subject. He lectured learned bodies on archæology, disputed points in theology with theologians, advised artists how to paint, and recommended courses in the teaching of history. He frequently took occasion to discuss his political views boldly and freely, and his resounding phrases and emphatic declarations often caused world-wide sensations. The army and religion were the two subjects that constantly engaged his attention. When he ascended the throne he made the following declaration: "I solemnly pledge myself always to keep in mind that the eyes of my ancestors look down upon me from the other world, and that I shall have to render account to them of the glory and honor of the army." To a body of recruits he once declared: "You are now my soldiers; you have given yourselves to me body and soul. There is now but one enemy for you, and that is my enemy." Not even in the twentieth century did he relinquish the outworn theory of divine right to rule as King of Prussia. In 1910, he declared that his "grandfather in his own right placed the crown upon his head, insisting once again that it was bestowed upon him by the grace of God alone, and not by parliaments or by the will of the people. . . . I too consider myself a chosen instrument of Heaven, and I shall go my way without regard to the views and opinions of the day."

William II (1859–)

Bismarck soon came into conflict with his young master who was only twenty-nine when he ascended the throne. The Kaiser resented the overshadowing importance and complete dominance of German politics by the veteran statesman and he was too self-confident to follow his grandfather's course of allowing Bismarck to rule while he reigned. Germany

"Dropping the pilot"

[1] William I died in 1888, and was succeeded by his son Frederick, who, however, lived only a few months.

was too small to hold two such self-willed autocrats. Moreover, it was felt by the rising generation that Bismarck's work was now over; he would therefore be an obstacle in the path of the new Germany that was about to be launched. Accordingly, the Kaiser determined to "drop the pilot." In 1890, the Iron Chancellor "resigned," and he retired to private life full of humiliation and bitterness. He spent his remaining days writing his memoirs and inspiring malicious articles against the Kaiser, whom he secretly distrusted as hot-headed and flighty.

(a) THE NEW POLICIES

It became evident that William would be his own Chancellor; hence, any one that he chose for that office would merely be his mouthpiece. As successor to Bismarck he appointed Count von Caprivi, a soldier by profession, who had only one rule: to obey his master. It was during Caprivi's chancellorship that demands were made to lower the tariff on foodstuffs in order that cheaper food might be imported. Germany, it was argued, was

Agrarian policies dominant

no longer an agricultural but an industrial state;[1] hence, industrial interests should be paramount. Caprivi signed reciprocity treaties with Russia, Austria, and Italy, which materially reduced the tariff on foodstuffs coming from these countries. These treaties were inspired by a movement in Europe to establish an agricultural Continental system against the importation of foodstuffs from America which was seriously threatening European agriculture. But Caprivi's reduction of tariffs on foodstuffs roused the landed interests in Germany, who organized an association called the *Bund der Landwirte* (League of Landlords) that began an agitation against the renewal of these treaties. By a revision of the tariff in 1902 the landed interests succeeded in restoring the high duties on agricultural products.

A decided change took place in Germany's foreign policy almost from the beginning of the new reign. Bismarck's policy of "satiation" no longer satisfied the ambitious, exuberant Germany that was now striving to be a world power and to play a leading rôle in *Weltpolitik.* "The waves beat power-

The new foreign policy

---

[1] In 1870, the population was about 40,000,000, sixty-five per cent of which was agricultural; in 1914, it rose to about 69,000,000, sixty-five per cent of which was industrial.

fully at our national gates, and call us as a great nation to maintain our place in the world, in other words, to follow world policy," declared the Kaiser in a widely quoted address. Germany's expanding trade, rapid increase in population, and exuberant energy were seeking an outlet, and a great desire arose for "a place in the sun," or a colonial empire. Imperialism was strongly favored by the Junkers and the industrialists; by the former because it meant opportunity for military activity and for positions as governors over subject peoples; and by the latter because it meant opening up new sources of raw material for their factories and new fields of investment for their surplus capital. Germany's colonial ambitions turned to Morocco, the only desirable part of Africa not yet acquired by a European power; but she encountered the opposition of France, who also desired that country.[1] The only territory that the Kaiser acquired was the port of Kiao-chau in China and some islands in the southern Pacific.

To the Kaiser's initiative was due the creation of a German navy. He was convinced that Germany's rapidly growing merchant marine and world-wide economic interests needed a The Navy fleet for their protection in case of war. Moreover, a powerful navy was the best means of gaining and holding overseas possessions, which Germany was now eager to acquire. In a series of eloquent speeches the Kaiser emphasized Germany's need of a navy in order to maintain her position as a world power. "World power and sea power are complementary; the one cannot exist without the other." "Our future lies on the water," and "The trident must pass into our hands," were his oft-quoted sayings. Navy leagues were founded that carried on a successful propaganda. In 1898, and again in 1900, the Reichstag passed laws appropriating large sums for the establishment of a great navy. "Germany must possess a fleet of such strength that a war against the mightiest naval power would endanger the supremacy of that power," was the open challenge of the government to England's control of the seas. The building of war vessels went on at a rapid rate, and, in a short time, Germany had the second largest navy in the world, ranking after England. Under the administration of Admiral von Tirpitz, the new navy was splendidly organized on the English model. In 1890, the little island of Helgoland, near the entrance to the Kiel Canal, was acquired by Germany from

[1] See page 653.

England in exchange for African territory. This transaction, made by Lord Salisbury, was regarded in England as a good trade, an "exchange of a button for a suit of clothes." Helgoland was strongly fortified, and became the Gibraltar of the North Sea, protecting the Kiel Canal.

Closely connected with the movement for naval armament was the colonial question. Germany's African colonies were a heavy liability. Hot and malarious, and inhabited by warlike natives they were not attractive to German emigrants. It was charged that the colonial officials were cruel to the natives who often rose in rebellion, and that the administration was corrupt and incompetent. Nearly every year the government was obliged to make up large deficits. In 1907, Bernhard Dernburg was appointed to the newly created office of Colonial Minister. Dernburg visited Africa, and made drastic reforms in the administration. He recommended that the government appropriate large sums to exploit the colonies economically; scientific experts had declared that cotton and rubber could be grown which would make the colonies an asset instead of a liability to the mother country.

The Colonies

Colonial reform received the hearty support of the Kaiser and of Chancellor Bernhard von Bülow. The latter, who was appointed in 1900, was the best-known and the ablest of the successors of Bismarck. An adroit parliamentarian he generally managed to arrange combinations in the Reichstag to support the policies of the Kaiser. But the heavy colonial budget aroused so much opposition against "colonial adventures" that the Center refused to support it. The budget was defeated by a combination of the two largest parties, the Center and the Social Democrats. Popular sentiment was aroused against the "black and red internationals," who were denounced as being opposed to German national interests. The Reichstag was dissolved, and the new elections resulted in a victory for the parties that favored the budget. The Social Democrats lost many seats, and the Center barely managed to hold its own. A new blok was formed by the Chancellor, "the Bülow Blok," consisting of Conservatives and Liberals who put the colonial budget through the Reichstag.

The Colonial budget

(b) PROBLEM OF THE NON-GERMANS

Although homogeneous to a considerable degree, Germany, nevertheless, contained non-German elements. There were Danes in Schleswig; Poles in the territory acquired by Prussia as a result of the Partition of Poland; and Alsatians and Problem of French in Alsace-Lorraine. The Germans desired assimilation to assimilate them, but the non-Germans, being conquered people, not immigrants, stubbornly refused to give up their nationality. The government inaugurated a policy of uncompromising "Germanism" by suppressing all manifestations of national sentiment by the non-Germans, especially the use of their language. There is an almost magical quality in the power of language to maintain the spirit of nationalism. The surest way to destroy a nation, therefore, is to destroy its language; hence, an oppressed people will cling desperately to its language in order to maintain itself. Another method pursued by the government was to settle Germans among the non-Germans. Induced by special favors, such as appointment to office and aid in the purchase of land, many Germans migrated to non-German districts where they upheld German language and culture.

The Danes were few; hence, they were not a serious problem. But the Poles numbered about 4,000,000, and they held tenaciously to their language, traditions, and sentiments. Fear- The Polish ful that this alien and hostile element living on the problem Russian frontier might prove a danger in time of war, the government made special efforts to Germanize the Poles. In 1886, the Prussian Landtag established a Settlement Commission with power to purchase land in the Polish districts with the object of establishing German colonies. In addition, drastic laws were passed prohibiting the public use of the Polish language; Polish historic names were abolished, and German names substituted for them; and the right of public meeting was indirectly curtailed by the requirement that all addresses had to be in German. The German settlements grew, and the Poles, fearful of being driven from their historic home, formed coöperative societies and land banks to tide them over in times of financial difficulty. In many instances the Germans were compelled, through systematic boycotting by the Poles, to resell their land to the latter at low prices. But a new law was passed, in 1908, which empowered the Settlement Commission to expropriate Polish landowners. The laws against the use of the Polish language were made more severe. All teaching, even that of religion, had to be in German. Polish school children would refuse to answer their teachers in German, and school strikes were

THE GERMAN EMPIRE

a Polish child saying, "If I say my prayers in German, my father
beats me; if I say them in Polish, my teacher beats me; if I don't
say them at all, my priest beats me."

Even more serious was the struggle against Germanization in
Alsace-Lorraine. Here the problem was complicated by the fact
that the cause of the inhabitants received the moral
support of France. After the Franco-Prussian War
thousands of families left Alsace-Lorraine for France rather than
live under the German flag. In spite of the fact that Alsace-
Lorraine was well governed and enjoyed great prosperity, the
inhabitants resented being under German rule. Their representatives in the Reichstag openly protested against the annexation
of the provinces. The government made every effort to stamp
out French influences and sentiments among the Alsatians, but
without avail. Germans were encouraged to settle in Alsace-
Lorraine in order to have a loyal population in the disaffected
provinces. Germany was determined to hold them at all costs, for
economic as well as for military reasons. The iron of Lorraine
and the textiles and potash of Alsace were important elements in
the economic life of Germany. Until 1911, Alsace-Lorraine was
an Imperial territory, ruled by a governor appointed by the Kaiser.
In that year the region was deemed sufficiently safe to be entrusted
with home rule. A constitution was, therefore, granted to Alsace-
Lorraine, which provided for a legislature to be elected by universal,
manhood suffrage, and for a delegation of three members to the
Bundesrat to be chosen by the governor who, as hitherto, was to
be an appointee of the Kaiser.

(c) MOVEMENT FOR POPULAR CONTROL

From the very beginning of the establishment of the Empire a
movement was begun to democratize its government. Supported
at first only by Social Democrats and Radicals, it attracted other
adherents during the decade before 1914. It was generally agreed
that ministerial responsibility would be the first necessary step
toward a democratic Germany. "Our constitutional system is, in
many respects, a sham," said a Radical member of the Reichstag,
"because it does not fulfill the aims of a modern constitutional
state. . . . Complete responsibility of the cabinet to parliament is
the very cornerstone of constitutional government." Although

this reform was never realized in the German Empire, a number of incidents took place which clearly showed a marked tendency in its favor.

The first incident was the *Telegraph* interview. In 1908, a great sensation took place. The London journal, *The Daily Telegraph*, gave out an interview with the Kaiser in which he freely discussed Anglo-German relations. The Kaiser declared that he was friendly to England, *The Telegraph inter-view* and, as proof, he asserted that, during the Boer War, he had foiled a plan of the powers to intervene in favor of the Boers, and that he himself had drawn up a plan of campaign against the Boers, which he had submitted to the British army. The interview caused great indignation throughout Germany, and the Reichstag, by an overwhelming vote, passed a resolution condemning the irresponsible action of the Kaiser. "When was there an opportunity more favorable than the present one to extort parliamentary government?" declared a Social Democrat. ". . . Who does not grasp the means at hand . . . that man is recreant to his civic duties." But the National Liberals feared to make a decisive move, and the opportunity passed by.

What was regarded as a precedent for ministerial responsibility came with the resignation of Chancellor von Bülow, which followed the defeat of a budget sponsored by him. The *Resignation of Bülow* Block of conservatives and National Liberals split over the question of taxation. In order to pay for the mounting expenditures of the army and navy, Bülow included an inheritance tax in the budget of 1909. The Conservatives refused to support it and joined the Center in opposition, with the result that the budget was defeated. Shortly afterwards the Chancellor resigned, not because his budget was defeated, but because his relations with the Kaiser had become strained.

The new Chancellor, Dr. Theobald von Bethmann-Hollweg, made it perfectly plain that he was not responsible to the Reichstag. "Put me in a minority if it pleases you," he declared *The "Blue-Black Block"* defiantly; "I shall remain at my post just the same, as long as I retain the confidence of my sovereign." Nevertheless, he had to have a majority to pass laws, and this majority was formed by a combination of the Conservatives and Center which became known as the "Blue-Black Block," or aristocratic-clerical combination. The Block laid heavy taxes on articles of general consumption, such as tobacco, beer, tea, and sugar in order to shift the burden of taxation to the shoulders of the consumers. The high tariff on foodstuffs was vigorously maintained and the cost of living rose rapidly.

In the movement for popular control, the most important incident was the elections of 1912 which resulted in an anti-government
Elections of 1912   majority.   Discontent was rife all over Germany. Demonstrations took place against the government which was denounced as favoring the agrarian interests as against the common welfare. The middle class parties were now almost as bitterly opposed to agrarian rule as were the socialists. To oppose the activities of the agrarians, business men organized the *Hansabund* which conducted a campaign against high tariffs on food and high taxes. The elections of 1912 resulted in a crushing defeat for the Block. The Conservatives lost almost half their seats; the Social Democrats more than doubled theirs; [1] and even the Center lost a number of seats. The parties of the Left had a majority in the Reichstag, and the Social Democrats were now the largest single party, displacing the Center from that position. For the first time in the history of the Empire, the elections had gone against the government, and very emphatically, as the popular vote of the parties of the Left was more than double that of the Right.

The government now faced a hostile Reichstag. Was there to be a repetition of the Bismarckian defiance of parliament?
Reichstag votes "no confidence" in the government   Bethmann-Hollweg, however, was not a Bismarck; and 1912 was not 1862. On January 30, 1913, the Reichstag, for the first time in its history, passed a vote of "no confidence" in the government. This action was due to the disapproval of Prussia's harsh treatment of the Poles. The Zabern Affair was another instance of the hostility between the Reichstag and the government. Zabern was a little garrison town in Alsace where a clash took place between the inhabitants and the military. The government sustained the military, which caused great indignation throughout the country because the army officers had acted in a very arbitrary manner. On December 4, 1913, the Reichstag again passed a resolution of

---

[1] Representation in the Reichstag closely approached a "rotten-borough" system. No reapportionment had taken place since 1871, despite great changes of population. There were "giant" constituencies of 300,000 and over, and "dwarf" constituencies of 15,000 and less. In the elections of 1912, 74 Conservatives were elected by about 2,000,000 voters and 110 Social Democrats by about 4,250,000.

"no confidence" in the government.   The Chancellor did not resign, but the government promised constitutional reforms.

The movement for democratizing Germany, however, came to naught.   The Balkan Wars of 1912–13 produced several great crises in international relations, and the issue in Germany quickly changed from domestic reform to national defense.   In 1913, the government presented a military budget appropriating large sums for increasing the army; the money was to be raised by heavy income taxes.   It passed the Reichstag by an almost unanimous vote; even the Social Democrats voted for the measure.   Reforms were set aside, and the nation prepared to face the next international crisis.   When the World War broke out, the German Empire plunged into a conflict from which it never emerged.

LITERATURE

The founding of the German Empire had little effect on German literature in the seventies and eighties.   The traditional forms in which the lyric, the novel, and the drama had been cast continued to serve for the creative expression of German literary artists.   In these forms they produced works of a high degree of excellence, but nothing that was distinctive and new.

The most famous literary figure in Germany was Friedrich Nietzsche, philosopher and moralist, who became the most discussed writer of his day.   Nietzsche's revolutionary ideas on Nietzsche life and morals caused an intellectual storm in Europe (1844–1900) that has not yet subsided.   With the zeal of a prophet and the imagination of a poet Nietzsche attacked traditional morality as bitterly as the French philosophers of the eighteenth century had attacked traditional religion.   The fundamental principle of life, according to Nietzsche, is "will to power" which has been the distinguishing characteristic of all great men at all times.   Their urge to conquer and to rule is similar to the driving force in the whole scheme of cosmic evolution which has brought about the supremacy of man over plants and animals and the supremacy of the strong races and classes over the weak ones.   Nietzsche proceeds to revaluate all moral values according to the principle of the "will to power."   In his best-known books, *Thus Spake Zarathustra* and *Beyond Good and Evil*, he makes a sharp distinction between what he calls "master morality" and "slave morality."   The former is the morality of masterful individuals who possess power, beauty, intellect, strength, and pride. The latter is the morality of the masses who have idealized their evil condition; their weakness has become "gentleness"; their baseness, "humility"; their cowardice, "patience"; their poverty, "honesty." Christianity, according to Nietzsche, was a "slave revolt in morals." By extolling the virtues of weakness and suffering, it created a weak and suffering race, and was, therefore, the greatest obstacle to the development of the "superman." Man is in time to be surpassed, as he is "no more than a bridge" over which to pass to a higher race of beings, the "superman," who would be free from all trammels of "slave morality."

As Christianity debased man morally, Nietzsche declares, so did democracy debase him politically. Democracy marked a decline in the history of government in that the slave became the master and imposed his slavish ideals on every one. No one poured such withering scorn on the "herd" as did Nietzsche. "The masses," he writes, "are worth notice in three aspects only: first as bad copies of great men; next as a contrast to great men; and lastly as their tools — for the rest, let them go to the devil and to statistics." Nietzsche favors aristocratic government, but not by an aristocracy based on family or wealth, but by an aristocracy of masterful men who are self-selected. Napoleon is his hero. Nietzsche's dislike of "herds" caused him to denounce nationalism as well as democracy. He has often been described as an extreme German nationalist, which is a great error. He severely criticized nationalism, including German nationalism, and boasted that he was a "good European."

As a writer Nietzsche occupies a great position in German literature. His colorful symbolic language and his marvelous handling of words and rhythms has given distinction to modern German prose of which he was a supreme master.

The closing years of the eighties witnessed a violent literary revolution, a new "storm and stress" period which, in the early nineties, yielded a rich harvest. Influenced on the one hand by Zola and by Scandinavian and Russian writers, and on the other, by the political and economic struggles in Germany, the literary revolutionists turned to naturalism and enriched German literature by many striking achievements.

The outstanding figure in the new movement was Gerhart Hauptmann. He was a social dramatist who chose his themes from the lives of the working classes and dramatized them in their vernacular. His play, *The Weavers*, marked a new era in German drama. Based upon the uprising of the Silesian weavers in 1844, he wrote the play as a prose drama with no protagonist, unless it be the mob or starvation. The overpowering effect of this grim tragedy opened the way for many other plays dealing with similar themes, and exerted an influence on German political and social life. The socialists, especially, encouraged such plays as excellent propaganda for their cause. Political panaceas, however, were not Hauptmann's chief concern. He was impelled by an all-embracing social pity which, in the words of a critic, "chose broken and imperfect members of the family of man, and wrung rare spiritual energies from their confused and frustrated souls."

Hauptmann (1862–)

Hauptmann is an unusually versatile artist. His comedy *Biberpelz* (The Beaver Coat), satirizing German bureaucracy, ranks with the best German comedies. His romantic dramas, *Die Versunkene Glocke* (The Sunken Bell) and *Der Arme Heinrich*, reveal him as a mystic poet of great power.

Famous for her poets and philosophers, Germany, until very recently, produced few novelists of note. With Thomas Mann the German novel came of age. His most famous work, *Buddenbrooks*, tells the story of the rise and fall of a great merchant family during the nineteenth century. It is a social study depicting the inevitable ruin of the old-fashioned trader in the modern era of industrial capitalism. Mann's other famous work is *Der Zauberberg* (The Magic Mountain) describing a colony of consumptives isolated from their fellow beings. The personalities of the characters and their tragic situation are depicted with rare psychological insight. In most of his novels Mann describes characters in conflict with themselves and with the world about them. Generally they are wounded by society or by nature in their efforts to adjust their lives. "I gaze into an unborn, unregulated world that demands to be ordered, shaped: I behold the formless shadows of human figures beckoning to me to evoke, to free them: tragic figures, ridiculous figures, and some that are both at once — and for these last I care most of all."

Mann (1875–)

REFERENCES

GENERAL:

W. H. Dawson, *The German Empire, 1867–1914*, 2 vols. (1919), by a great authority on German history, especially good for foreign affairs; Sir A. W. Ward and S. Wilkinson, *Germany, 1815–1890*, 3 vols. (1917), detailed and rather dry political narrative; R. H. Fife, *The German Empire Between Two Wars* (1916), a brief readable volume, topical in treatment; B. von Bülow, *Imperial Germany*, translated from the German (1914), a defense of Germany's domestic and foreign policies by the former Chancellor; J. Ellis Barker, *Modern Germany, her Political and Economic Problems, her Foreign and Domestic Policy, her Ambitions, and the Causes of her Success* (ed. 1915), title sufficiently describes the book, whose object is to persuade England to adopt a protective tariff against Germany; H. Lichtenberger, *Germany and its Evolution in Modern Times*, translated from the French (1913), emphasizes the religious and educational aspects; Karl Lamprecht, *Deutsche Geschichte der jüngsten Vergangenheit und Gegenwart*, 2 vols. (1912–13), by a distinguished German historian especially interested in social and economic history; *Memoirs of Prince von Buelow*, trans. from the German, 3 vols. (1931–32); C. Gauss, *The German Emperor as Shown in his Public Utterances* (1915).

GOVERNMENT AND PARTIES:

The authority on the German constitution is P. Laband, whose books, *Das Staatsrecht des deutschen Reiches*, 4 vols. (ed. 1901), and *Deutsches Reichsstaatsrecht* (ed. 1912), are the standard works on the subject; Fritz-Konrad Krüger, *Government and Politics of the German Empire* (1915), an excellent handbook; B. E. Howard, *The German Empire* (1906), a detailed study of the Imperial structure; a similar work for Prussia is H. G. James, *Principles of Prussian Administration* (1913); F. Salomon, *Die deutschen Partei Programme*, 2 vols. (ed. 1912), contains the platforms of the German parties from 1845 to 1912; O. Stillich, *Die politschen Parteien in Deutschland*, a series of studies of German political parties of which only two volumes have so far appeared, Vol. I, *Die Konservativen* (1908), and Vol. II, *Der Liberalismus* (1911).

SOCIAL AND ECONOMIC:

The great authority on social and economic conditions in the German Empire is W. H. Dawson, whose books are *Bismarck and State Socialism* (1891), *Protection in Germany: A History of German Fiscal Policy during the Nineteenth Century* (1904), *The German Workman: A Study in National Efficiency* (1906), *The Evolution of Modern Germany* (ed. 1919), *Social Insurance in Germany, 1883–1911; its History, Operation, Results, and a Comparison with the (British) National Insurance Act, 1911* (1912), and *Municipal Life and Government in Germany* (1914); F. C. Howe, *Socialized Germany* (1915), a popular account of the many reforms; U.S. Bureau of Labor Bulletin, vol. XXIII, contains a translation of the social insurance code issued in 1911; A. Ashley, *The Social Policy of Bismarck*

(1912); Ch. Andler, *Les Origines du Socialisme d'état en Allemagne* (ed. 1911), a study of the theoretical bases of social reform; W. J. Ashley, *Progress of the German Working Classes in the last quarter of a century* (1904); on industrial development: K. Helfferich, *Germany's Economic Progress and National Wealth, 1888–1913* (1913); E. D. Howard, *The Cause and Extent of the Recent Industrial Progress of Germany* (1907); A. Shadwell, *Industrial Efficiency: a Comparative Study of Industrial Life in England, Germany, and America* (1913); T. Veblen, *Imperial Germany and the Industrial Revolution* (1915), a penetrating study of the union in Germany of the military state with modern industrialism; A. S. von Waltershausen, *Deutsche Wirtschaftsgeschichte, 1815–1914* (1920); and J. H. Clapham, *Economic Development of France and Germany, 1815–1914* (1921); L. Pohle, *Die Entwicklung des deutschen Wirtschaftslebens im letzten Jahrhundert* (ed. 1908); M. Hermont, *Les paradoxes économiques de l'Allemagne moderne* (1931).

SPECIAL TOPICS:
On the Kulturkampf: G. Goyau, *Bismarck et l'église: le Culturkampf 1870–1887*, 4 vols. (1911–13), for the clerical side; and L. Hahn, *Geschichte des Kulturkampfes in Preussen* (1881), for the anti-clerical side; on Alsace-Lorraine: C. D. Hazen, *Alsace-Lorraine under German Rule* (1917), from the French viewpoint; B. Weill, *Elsass-Lothringen und der Krieg* (1914), from the German viewpoint; and C. Phillipson, *Alsace-Lorraine, Past, Present, Future* (1918), neutral; on colonial expansion: G. Schmoller (ed.), *Handels-und Machtpolitik* (1900), essays by German economists in favor of expansion; A. Zimmermann, *Geschichte der deutschen Kolonialpolitik* (1914), by an authority on colonial history; K. Hassert, *Deutschlands Kolonien* (ed. 1910); Mary E. Townsend, *The Rise and Fall of Germany's Colonial Empire, 1884–1918* (1930); on foreign policy, see bibliography at the end of Chapter XXXIII.

ADDITIONAL REFERENCES

J. Ziekursch, *Politische Geschichte des neuen deutschen Kaiserreiches*, 3 vols. (1925–30); R. J. S. Hoffman, *Great Britain and the German Trade Rivalry, 1875–1914* (1933); J. F. Rees, *Social and Economic History of Germany from William II to Hitler* (1940); G. Stolper, *German Economy, 1870–1940* (1940).

For additional titles see bibliographies at the end of Chapter VII and XV.

CHAPTER XXI

AUSTRIA–HUNGARY

ESTABLISHMENT OF THE DUAL MONARCHY

FOR many centuries Austria was a dynasty rather than a nation. There was hardly a people in central Europe that was not at one Hapsburg time or another under the sway of the Hapsburgs, autocracy whose antiquity and renown filled the courts of Europe. By means of marriage and conquest they had succeeded in establishing a polyglot empire which was ruled autocratically from Vienna. As in many other countries containing a heterogeneous population, absolute monarchy was considered to be the best means of maintaining harmony, order, and stability among the various races. Absolutism was a passion, almost a propaganda, among the Austrians, just as democracy was among the French. During the Restoration, Vienna was the citadel of reaction in Europe; whenever a blow at democracy was to be struck, Austria could be depended upon to strike it.

Austria's leadership in Germany was unquestioned for centuries. The element of romance in the Holy Roman Empire greatly appealed to German sentiment, even though the Empire Influence of was but a tradition and the Emperor but a shadow. Austria in When the Hapsburgs became Emperors of Austria Germany after Napoleon had abolished the Holy Roman Empire (1806), their influence among the German people sensibly diminished; and it vanished almost completely when Prussia came forward as the doughty wielder of the German sword.

The defeat of Austria in the Austro-Sardinian and in the Seven Weeks' Wars was responsible for important concessions both to democracy and to nationalism. In 1861, Emperor Francis Joseph granted a constitution, called the February Patent, which established a moderate parliamentary system for the Empire. The constitution, however, was opposed by the Hungarians because it did not recognize what they claimed were the "historic national rights of Hungary." Francis Deák, formerly an associate of Kossuth, became the leader of a new nationalist movement in Hungary. What Deák advocated was, not independence, but complete autonomy which would allow Hungary to live her own national life and yet permit her to coöperate with Austria in matters which directly concerned them both. After the Seven Austria's Weeks' War the Austrians realized acutely their isolation dangerous situation. Cut off from Germany they now had to depend entirely upon themselves to control the many nationalities, whose aspirations were fired by the unification movement in Germany and in Italy. As they were a small minority in the midst of a hostile majority, the Austrians felt that they must have the aid of a strong race in the Empire. They, therefore, determined to ally themselves with the Hungarians, the most numerous and most militant element in the Hapsburg dominions. "What does Hungary want?" asked the Emperor of Deák. "Only what she wanted before Sadowa," was the reply.

Negotiations began between the government and the Hungarians. A new constitution was drawn up, largely by Deák and Count von Beust, the representative of the Emperor. It was The Aus- adopted by an assembly especially elected for that gleich purpose, to which, however, Hungary sent no delegates; later, it was also adopted by the Hungarian Diet. The February Patent was abrogated, and the constitution, known as the *Ausgleich*, or Compromise, was promulgated in 1867. It established a unique political system, the Dual Monarchy, consisting of the Empire of Austria and the Kingdom of Hungary. The two countries were separate states under one flag; each had its own constitution, parliament, ministry, courts, administration, and language, but were united in a personal union through a common sovereign, who was known as "emperor" in Austria and as "king" in Hungary. Interests common to both, such as foreign affairs, war, and finance, were conducted by a common ministry, and supervised by a body known as the "Delegations." It consisted of one delegation from the Austrian parliament and another from the Hungarian parliament; they sat separately and met alternately at Vienna and Budapest. The Ausgleich also provided for an agreement on tariffs, currency, and trade, to be renewed every ten years by the Delegations, which also voted the budget for foreign affairs and for the army.

The "dualism" established in 1867 was really an alliance between two dominant races, the Germans in Austria and the Magyars in Hungary, against the other races in the Empire. Count von

Beust is quoted as having said to the Hungarians: "You take
Alliance of   care of your barbarians [Slavs] and we will take care
Austrians   of ours." Hungary's gain was considerable; the Aus-
and Hun-
garians   gleich gave her even more than had the March Laws
against the   of 1848.[1] When the Ausgleich was proposed the Czechs
Slavs
                  demanded that they, too, be given autonomy, and the
Empire be reorganized on the basis of "trialism," or a triple union
of Austrians, Hungarians, and Slavs. No attention was paid to
this demand, and, as a consequence, the Ausgleich was bitterly
opposed by the Slavs to whom it appeared as a conspiracy of the
two dominant races to keep them in permanent subjection.

THE RACE PROBLEM

Austria-Hungary was once described as a "Slav house with a
German façade"; the Germans, known as Austrians, constituted
The Aus-   only about one quarter of the population of the Em-
trians   pire.[2] They were a majority in the region around
Vienna and in the Tyrol, and an important minority in Bohemia
and Moravia. The Austrians were generally of the middle and upper classes, the prosperous and educated elements who, for long,
had dominated the country. The Hapsburgs were Austrian; so
were nearly all of the important officials. The government, the
Church, the schools, the courts, the army, all were chiefly under
Austrian control.

Second in importance to the Austrians were the Magyars, or
Hungarians. They formed a solid mass in the very center of the
The Hun-   Empire with minorities in Slovakia and in Transyl-
garians   vania. Originally, the Hungarians were an Asiatic
tribe who had invaded the region later called Hungary, mixing
with the native inhabitants. Their language is totally unrelated
to the European language families, Latin, Germanic, and Slavonic.
The mass of Hungarians were poor peasants who labored on the
estates of great landed magnates. There were no prouder aristo-

[1] See page 196.

[2] According to the census of 1910 the population of Austria was about 28,500,000.
Of these 10,000,000 were German; 16,250,000 were Slav; and 800,000 were Italian.
Of the Slavs there were 6,500,000 Czechs and Slovaks, 5,000,000 Poles, 3,500,000
Ruthenians, 1,250,000 Slovenes, and 800,000 Croats and Serbs (those in Bosnia and
Herzegovina not included). The population of Hungary was about 20,500,000, of
which 10,000,000 were Magyars; 5,500,000, Slavs (Slovaks, Croats, and Ruthenians);
3,000,000, Rumanians; and 2,000,000, Germans. There were many Jews who were
reckoned as Magyars in Hungary and as Austrians in Austria.

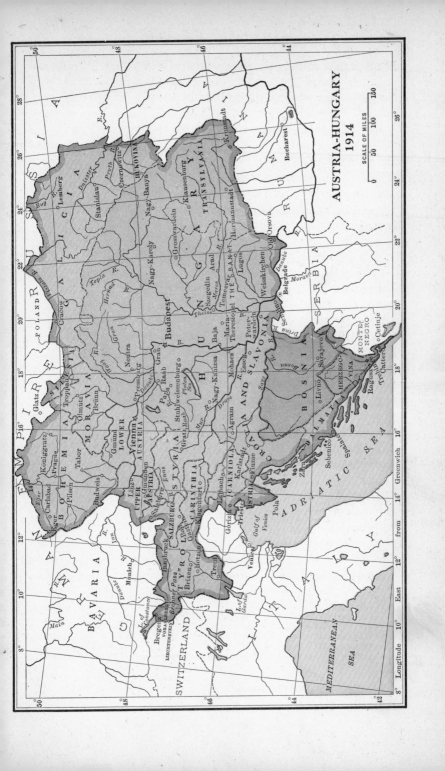

crats in Europe than those of Hungary, who held vast tracts of land and controlled all political power. Commerce was carried on chiefly by Jews, who had become so thoroughly assimilated that they were regarded as Hungarians.

Of the Slavs the most important were the Czechs who were the majority in Bohemia and in Moravia. Long under the rule of the Germans, by whom they had been conquered, the Czechs developed a higher degree of civilization than any of the other Slavic groups. Bohemia, having coal and iron, became the industrial part of the Empire. As a consequence the Czechs developed a prosperous middle class that challenged the control of their country by the German minority. Compact, nationally self-conscious, literate, and politically well organized, they maintained that Bohemia, like Hungary, was an historic unity; hence, they were entitled to the same degree of independence as the Hungarians. The Germans in Bohemia, being the wealthy and ruling element, were opposed to Czech control which, they feared, would result in the suppression of the German language and influence. There was bitter feeling between Czechs and Germans which frequently resulted in riots. The Czechs boycotted the German language, and insisted on speaking their own tongue under any and all circumstances. Closely related to the Czechs were the Slovaks in Slovakia, who were under the rule of Hungarians. Unlike the Czechs the Slovaks were chiefly poor and illiterate peasants.

In Galicia, once part of the kingdom of Poland, lived two Slavic groups, Poles and Ruthenians. Unlike the other partitioners of Poland, Austria was generous in her treatment of the Poles, who were granted autonomy and the right to use their language in the schools. In gratitude the Poles were loyal supporters of the Hapsburgs, without, however, giving up hope of a restored Poland. A large minority of the population in Galicia consisted of Ruthenians, closely related in race and language to the Ukrainians of Russia. They were poor peasants, who worked on the estates of the Polish landowners. Commerce, as in other parts of eastern Europe, was carried on chiefly by Jews. Both Ruthenians and Jews were discriminated against and oppressed by the Poles who controlled the government of Galicia.

The Southern Slavs, called Yugo-Slavs, were separated from

their northern kinsmen by a wedge of Hungarians and Austrians.

The Yugo-Slavs   They formed several groups, closely related to one another, Croats, Serbs, and Slovenes, who were of the same race and speech as the people of Serbia and Montenegro. The Yugo-Slavs occupied almost the entire territory south of the Drave River; it was a backward region inhabited by peasants and herdsmen.

Transylvania and the Banat contained a mixed population. The mass of people were closely related in blood and speech to the

The Rumanians   Rumanians across the border. They were chiefly peasants on the estates of Hungarian aristocrats. The upper and middle classes in these regions were largely Hungarian.

The cities along the shores of the eastern Adriatic were predominantly Italian, especially Trieste and Fiume, the chief seaports

The Italians   of Austria-Hungary. Another Italian region was the Trentino in the Alps. The Irredentists in Italy agitated for a "redemption" of these places, which they claimed should be part of Italy. Austria held on tenaciously to Trieste and Fiume, as the loss of these ports would ruin her as a maritime nation. The government therefore encouraged the settlement of Yugo-Slavs in Italian districts in order to weaken Italy's claim to them.

What were the bonds which united this many-nation Empire, which seemed ever on the point of dissolution, and yet managed to

Bonds of union (1) the dynasty   survive for so many centuries? First and foremost was the Hapsburg dynasty itself, which was the pivot and center of all the unifying forces. As there was no common nationality, the Dual Monarchy developed a dynastic patriotism, which found expression in loyalty to the Emperor-King, Francis Joseph. He was a kindly person who greatly endeared himself to all of his subjects.

The bureaucracy was another powerful bond of union. It was an established policy of the government to appoint, as officials, repre-

(2) bureaucracy   sentatives of the various races; Germans, Hungarians, and Slavs were to be found in Austrian officialdom in numbers proportionate to their influence. This policy softened the antagonism to the monarchy among influential elements in the Empire.

A unifying force was the Catholic Church, which united in one religious society millions of Austrians, Hungarians, Italians, and

RACES IN
CENTRAL AND EASTERN EUROPE
1914

Legend	
▨ TEUTONIC	▨ Russians
☐ Italians	☰ Poles
▨ Rumanians	▨ Ukrainians or Ruthenians
▨ Turks	⫼ Czechs & Slovaks
▨ Magyars	▨ Slovenes
☰ GREEKS	▨ Croats & Serbs
▨ ALBANIANS	⫼ Bulgars

Longitude   East   from   25°   Greenwich

Slavs.[1] The Church was favored by the government in many ways; the Hapsburgs had been ardent champions of the Catholic faith ever since the Protestant Revolution. (3) Catholicism

Church influences were powerful in the politics and government of the Dual Monarchy, and emphasized the unity of the Catholic empire as against the separatism of the various races. This separatism was not as striking as it appeared in the political arena. A process of inter-marriage had gone on for centuries, and many if not most of the nations were of mixed origin.

The Empire constituted a large free trade area which greatly facilitated domestic commerce. Each region was, moreover, the economic complement of the other. Hungary was agricultural and produced a large wheat supply; (4) economic

Bohemia had mines and factories; Vienna was the financial and commercial center; Trieste and Fiume supplied the shipping; Croatia and Slavonia produced cattle, horses, and swine; and Galicia produced oil. To break up the Empire meant to break up an economic unit which would be disastrous to all the nationalities. Although there was no love for Austria there was no marked separatist movement; what the nationalities desired was autonomy, not independence. Many felt that Austria fulfilled an important function in uniting a heterogeneous population that could be united in no other way. "If Austria did not exist, it would have been necessary to invent her," was the opinion of a Czech historian.

Strange to say, the very struggles between the nationalities contributed to the stability of the Hapsburg Monarchy. There was a bond of disunion. Emperor Francis II was said to have explained the situation to the French ambassador (5) *Divide et impera*

in the following manner: "My people are strangers to one another, and yet it is for the best. They never have the same ills at the same time. In France, when there is an epidemic of fever, you all have it on the same day. I have Hungarians in Italy, and Italians in Hungary. Each suspects his neighbor; they never understand one another, and, in fact, detest one another. Their mutual antipathies, however, conduce to order and to general peace." The Hapsburgs were exceedingly clever in following the policy of *Divide et impera* (Divide and rule), and they were aided

[1] The large majority of the people of Austria-Hungary were Roman Catholics. There were Protestant minorities in Hungary and in Austria proper. Among the Slavs, the Poles, Czechs, Slovaks, Slovenes, and Croats were Catholics. The Ruthenians, Serbs, and Rumanians were members of the Greek Church.

by the circumstance that each region was inhabited by a dominant and by a subordinate race. In Bohemia there were Germans and Czechs; in Hungary, Hungarians and Slavs; in Galicia, Poles and Ruthenians; on the Adriatic coast, Italians and Yugo-Slavs. Intraracial struggles were often encouraged by the government to distract the nationalities from an anti-Austrian propaganda. Sometimes, it placated them by timely concessions, conducting a species of internal foreign policy by making alliances with some races as against others. If the dominant race in a region became too arrogant and threatened to secede, the government favored the subordinate race. More than once were the haughty Hungarians brought to terms by a threat from Vienna to rouse the Slavs against them. In this way the Dual Monarchy was able to lead a charmed life.

AUSTRIA (1878–1914)

The constitution of Austria, adopted after the Ausgleich, was based on the Patent of 1861. Parliament, known as the Reichsrat,
The constitution was composed of an aristocratic upper house of nobles and officials, and of a lower house, elected indirectly according to a class system of voting similar to that in Prussia. The cabinet was nominally responsible to the Reichsrat, but factional and racial struggles within this body so weakened it that the Emperor really controlled the cabinet. An extraordinary power was given by the constitution to the Emperor, who could issue decrees having the force of laws when the Reichsrat was not in session. Political parties were based upon race, such as the German Liberals, the Polish party, the Young Czechs, and the Croatio-Slavonian club, and they struggled largely over racial questions.

Shortly after the Ausgleich went into effect a mild *Kulturkampf* took place in Austria. The party of "German Liberals," who con-
Anti-clerical trolled the government, was anti-clerical, and suc-
legislation ceeded in putting through a series of secularization laws. Civil marriage was permitted under certain circumstances; the public elementary schools were taken away from the control of the Church; and civil equality was decreed between Catholics and non-Catholics. These laws were denounced by Pope Pius IX, but a conflict was avoided because of the well-known loyalty of the Hapsburgs to the Church.

Over and above all other problems was that of the racial minorities.   The first half of the nineteenth century witnessed the revival of German and Italian nationalism; and the latter half, of Slav nationalism, especially in the Dual Monarchy.   The submerged nationalities continually denounced the régime established by the Ausgleich, and demanded equal rights of all in "school, in office, and in public life."   The recognition of the non-German languages was regarded as the first step toward equality; and each nationality demanded that its language be made official in the region where it was prevalent, and that the government establish a university where its language and history would be taught.   The Germans were strongly opposed to the recognition of the Slavic languages which they despised as barbarous dialects, without a literature or history, and unknown to the world of letters and science.   In derision of their claims for recognition a German once entered a local Slovene assembly carrying the whole of Slovenian literature under his arm.

The language question

After the Seven Weeks' War a great change took place in the political attitude of the Hapsburgs.   They no longer presented, as in the days of Metternich, an unflinching opposition to popular demands; they were now conciliatory and inclined to grant concessions to nationalism and democracy.   In 1879, a new ministry, headed by Count Taaffe, came into power and remained in office fourteen years.   During this period there was a marked tendency to shift the Empire from a German to a Slavic basis.   Concessions were granted to the Czechs, the advance guard of militant Slavism, by dividing the German University of Prague into two institutions, one, German, and the other, Czech.   The Czech language was made partially official and the other Slavic languages were recognized more or less.   The Germans were greatly incensed, and threatened to leave the Empire and join Germany.   When, in 1897, it was proposed to grant full equality to the Czech and German languages in Bohemia pandemonium broke loose in the Reichsrat.   German and Czech members hurled epithets and inkstands at each other.   The street took the cue from parliament, and riots broke out between the racial factions.

Concessions to the Czechs rouse the Germans

It was the opinion of the government that democracy would tend to weaken the intense racialism of the contending nationalities by giving them a wider horizon, and by bringing to the front new voters and new issues.   In 1907, a new electoral law established

direct, equal, universal manhood suffrage for the Reichsrat. In
the elections that followed, two inter-racial parties
made large gains, the Socialists who appealed to the
workingmen of all the races, and the Christian Socialists, an anti-Semitic party, that opposed the influence of the Jews
in economic and political life.

Universal
manhood
suffrage

But democracy did not prove a solvent of Austria's political
problems. Before long the new electors divided along racial lines;
racial fissures appeared even among the Socialists who
split into factions, such as the German Socialists,
Czech Socialists, Polish Socialists. The racial struggles also had an international aspect that threatened
the peace of the world as well as the stability of the Dual Monarchy. Though an ally, Italy was looking for an opportunity to
"redeem" the Italian regions. Rumania cast longing eyes toward
Transylvania and the Banat. Far more serious was the propaganda of Serbia, backed by Russia, which aimed to detach the
Yugo-Slavs from their allegiance to the Hapsburgs.[1]

Interna-
tional aspect
of the racial
question

Austria determined to take the offensive in the Balkans. She
believed that she would not be able to hold her Yugo-Slav subjects
if Serbia became too powerful. And Serbia had emerged from the
Balkan Wars of 1912–13 with increased territory and prestige. Her
ambition for a Greater Serbia menaced the existence of the Dual
Monarchy. After the Balkan wars Austria decided that, at the
next crisis, she would have a final reckoning with Serbia by making war upon her. And the next crisis came in July, 1914.

HUNGARY (1867–1914)

The Ausgleich gave Hungary the status of a quasi-independent
State, and reconciled her 'historic rights' with Imperial control.
The Emperor was crowned separately, in Budapest, as
King of Hungary. A constitution was adopted in
1867 which established a parliament of an aristocratic
upper house, largely hereditary, and a lower house elected according to a complicated franchise law which insured the ascendancy
both of the Hungarian race and of the upper classes. There were
so many qualifications for voting, property, educational, and occupational, that only about one third of the men had the franchise.

The aristo-
cratic con-
stitution

Two great problems faced Hungary, Hungarian ascendancy and

[1] See page 704.

relations with Austria. The Hungarians were intensely nationalistic, and were determined to root out all other nation- Dominance
istic influences in the country. Hungarian was made of the Hun-
the only language of instruction in the public schools. garians
The public use of other languages was ruthlessly suppressed. To
prevent the non-Hungarians from electing the few representatives
to parliament to which they were entitled, Hungarian officials resorted to gerrymandering, coercion, ballot-box stuffing, and physical violence. The question of maintaining Hungarian ascendancy
consolidated all political opinion on matters of internal policy;
hence, there were no political parties, even in the loose Continental
meaning of that term. Political strife was, therefore, largely along
personal lines. Aristocratic families, such as the Tiszas, the An-
drássys, the Károlyis, and the Hedérvárys, had their personal
followings, a situation not unlike that of the political families in
eighteenth-century England. There was only one party, the Socialist, which championed the cause of the lower classes, Hungarian and
non-Hungarian, who were unenfranchised. Demonstrations and riots
took place in favor of universal, manhood suffrage, but the government opposed the extension of democracy on the ground that it
would "compromise the Magyar character of the Hungarian State."

Relations with Austria was a problem that divided the Hungarians into two factions: those who wished to maintain the
Ausgleich on the ground that Hungary had all the Nationalism
self-government that she wished, and, in addition, the *versus* dual-
military aid of Austria in case of war; and those who ism
wanted to loosen, if not actually to sever, the few ties that bound
the two countries. The Independence Party, led by Francis Kossuth, son of the great revolutionist, boldly declared in favor of
"nationalism" as against "dualism." Its opposition was strongly
felt at those times when the decennial economic agreement was
to be renewed. Whenever the situation became critical, Austria
threatened to use her influence in favor of the non-Magyar races,
which had the effect of quieting the Hungarians.

As the war clouds were gathering over the European skies, there
began a *rapprochement* between Hungary and Austria. Even the
recalcitrant Independence Party realized that a war Hungary's
which involved Russia might be disastrous to Hungary, fear of
which lay open to direct invasion by Russian armies. Russia
The bird call of Pan-Slavism, sounded by Russia, was heard by the

Slavs of Hungary as well as by those in Austria and in the Balkans. Out of fear of Russia, Hungarians and Austrians buried their differences in order to present a solid front "to the dread power of the North."

REFERENCES

GENERAL:

L. Léger, *Histoire de l'Autriche-Hongrie depuis les origines jusqu'en 1919* (1920), the best general history óf Austria; H. W. Steed, *The Hapsburg Monarchy* (ed. 1914), discussion of its problems favorable to the Hapsburgs; G. Drage, *Austria-Hungary* (1909), general survey; E. S. Bagger, *Francis Joseph* (1927), a popular biography, impressionistic; J. Redlich, *Francis Joseph of Austria* (1928), by an authority on political conditions in Austria; R. J. Kerner, *Slavic Europe: A Selected Bibliography in the Western European Languages* (1918), valuable for advanced students of subject; H. Friedjung, *Das Zeitalter des Imperialismus, 1884–1914*, 3 vols. (1919–22), by the authority on Austria, valuable for policy in Balkans, pro-Austrian.

MISCELLANEOUS:

On the Ausgleich: L. Eisenmann, *Le Compromis austro-hongrois de 1867* (1904), by the outstanding authority on the Ausgleich; and R. Sieghart, *Zolltrennung und Zolleinheit* (1915), an economic study of the relations between Austria and Hungary; on Hungary: C. M. Knatchbull-Hugessen, *The Political Evolution of the Hungarian Nation*, vol. II (1908); A. de Bertha, *La Hongrie Moderne de 1849 à 1901* (1901); and R. W. Seton-Watson, *Corruption and Reform in Hungary* (1911); on racial problems: R. W. Seton-Watson is the authority on this subject, and his volumes, *Racial Problems in Hungary* (1908), *The Southern Slav Question and the Hapsburg Monarchy* (1911), *German, Slav and Magyar* (1916), and *Sarajevo* (1926), are sympathetic with the Yugo-Slavs; B. Auerbach, *Les races et les nationalités en Autriche-Hongrie* (1898), a study of the racial composition of the Empire; E. Denis, *La Bohême depuis la Montagne-Blanche*, 2 vols. (1903), a standard work on Bohemia.

ADDITIONAL REFERENCES

O. Jaszi, *Dissolution of the Hapsburg Monarchy* (1929); P. Teleki, *Evolution of Hungary* (1923); K. Tschuppik, *Frances Joseph I* (1930).

CHAPTER XXII

THE SMALL NATIONS

In the eighteenth century, Europe was a continent chiefly of small states; in the nineteenth it had become one chiefly of large states. However, a number of small states persisted, but their continued existence was due more to the sufferance of the great powers than to their own strength. The rôle of the small states was an important one in spite of their military insignificance. Wedged in here and there, often in strategic positions, they were vitally essential in maintaining the balance of power. An attack by a big nation, of Belgium by France, Holland by England, Denmark by Germany, Switzerland by Italy, Serbia by Austria, and Sweden by Russia would have upset the balance of power and led to serious conflicts. The little nations had another, an intangible influence, on the political life of Europe. To the subject races in the great empires, their freedom and independence was an ever-inspiring example. Especially was this true after the emergence of the Balkan nations, whose independence of Turkey gave an impetus to the nationalist movements among the subject nationalities in Russia and Austria.

SCANDINAVIA

Denmark's defeat in 1864 by Prussia and Austria was followed by an important extension of democracy. In 1866, the property qualification for voting was lowered considerably so that the working classes were given the franchise. Later, ministerial responsibility was established. In 1914, Danish democracy reached its apex when universal suffrage, including woman suffrage, was adopted.

As Denmark had no coal and iron, it had little industry; hence, agriculture was the pursuit of a large majority of the population. The Danish farmers specialized in dairy products which were exported to the neighboring nations, chiefly to England and Germany. The peasants and dairymen organized extensive coöperative societies that lent money to their members, marketed their produce, and purchased expensive machinery for common use. Economically speaking the Danish nation was a great coöperative dairy.

The union of Norway and Sweden [1] was not a happy one, despite the fact that each country had its own parliament and administra-

Contrast between Norway and Sweden
tion. Although of the same race, different conditions among the Norwegians and Swedes made for different ideals. Norway was inhabited by fishermen, sailors, merchants, and peasant proprietors, an independent, hardy folk. Sweden, on the contrary, was an aristocratic country, a land of large estates and tenant farmers. Their common sovereign had little power in Norway where a popularly elected parliament controlled affairs. In Sweden, however, he was virtually an autocrat until 1866, when a parliament was established chosen by a propertied suffrage.

After 1870 the nationalist movement in Europe found an echo in Norway. Quarrels arose between Norway and Sweden, some

Norway secedes from Sweden
petty, some serious, which soon developed in a movement for Norwegian independence. In 1905, the Norwegian parliament took a decisive step by passing a resolution which declared the union with Sweden dissolved. The question now was whether the latter would permit secession. For a time civil war threatened, but better counsel prevailed; and it was agreed to allow the Norwegian people to settle their national destiny by means of a plebiscite.

The result of the plebiscite was an overwhelming vote in favor of independence. Sweden was chagrined, but she loyally accepted

Independent Norway
the popular verdict. Norway, thereupon, became an independent nation, and chose a Danish prince as her king. In 1906, he was crowned Haakon VII, successor to Haakon VI, the last independent king of Norway before she was united with Denmark during the Middle Ages. A treaty between Norway and Sweden provided that all disputes between them should be decided by arbitration, and that no fortifications should be erected on their common frontier. Since their separation the two nations have lived amicably as neighbors.

The secession of Norway was an important influence in the move-

Extension of Democracy
ment to democratize Sweden. In 1909, universal, manhood suffrage was adopted and the cabinet was made responsible to parliament. Norway, too, made strides toward

[1] See page 57.

democracy. In 1913, the franchise was granted to all women citizens, and Norway had the distinction of being the first independent nation to establish woman suffrage.

SCANDINAVIAN LITERATURE

The Scandinavian nations exercised comparatively little influence on the political and economic history of Europe. Culturally, however, they were great powers, as their literary contributions placed them in the very forefront of the nations of Europe. A race of literary vikings arose, who boldly set sail for unknown seas of thought, daring to face the storms of criticism and the shafts of ridicule. A veritable literary invasion of Europe by Scandinavian writers took place during the latter part of the nineteenth century, and the bold literary adventurers succeeded in conquering and holding a great place in the cultural life of the Continent.

Influence of Scandinavian literature

A unique personality was the Dane, Hans Christian Andersen, the greatest of all children's story-tellers. His immortal fairy tales transformed the nonsense of the nursery into stories which have charmed and delighted millions of children. Andersen had the soul of a child, and life to him was a fairy tale; he, therefore, wrote with that naïve seriousness and simplicity that only children can appreciate. One can almost see, hear, and touch the characters in his tales; even the animals speak as animals would if they could. Andersen may be said to have discovered the soul of the child; and so universally beloved is he that there is hardly a person in Europe or America who has not heard or read his tales.

Andersen (1805–75)

Few modern writers have exercised so wide and so deep an influence as the Norwegian, Henrik Ibsen, whose dramas were the literary sensation of Europe and America for many years. Ibsen was a stern social moralist. His chief aim was to expose the shams and illusions of middle-class society, whose respectability he regarded as a mask for cowards and as a pitfall for the good and the simple. He despised democracy as a vulgar invention intended to deceive the masses into the belief that they ruled because they voted, whereas they were really the tools of the philistine bourgeois who used them to crush those that were the true champions of freedom and progress. "The most dangerous foe to truth and freedom in our midst is the compact majority," declares one of his characters. Ibsen was firmly con-

Ibsen (1828–1906)

vinced that the majority was always wrong, and that the true
benefactors of the race were those individuals who proclaimed their
independence of the conventions of the day and dared to live their
own lives in their own way. The more a man finds himself in a
minority the more apt is he to be right; "the strongest man in the
world is he who stands most alone." The right of the individual
to assert himself as over against society, family, State, Church, is
the fundamental principle of Ibsen's philosophy of life.

His drama, *An Enemy of the People*, is an exposure of political
and commercial dishonesty masquerading as democracy. Dr.
Stockmann, the hero, finds that the baths of his town, which is a
famous health resort, are contaminated by sewage; and instead of
being a cure for the sick they are really pest-holes. He so informs
the authorities who, fearing that the town would be ruined financially if this were generally known, determine to hush up the
matter. Instead of being regarded as a benefactor, Dr. Stockmann
suddenly finds that he is being hounded by all classes in the community. The town is in an uproar over his determination to
expose the evil, and mass meetings are held denouncing him "as
an enemy of the people." He bravely holds his own, fully expecting that the liberal elements, "the friends of the people," will come
to his aid. To his amazement, "a compact liberal majority" is
organized, which incites the mob to attack him so that he barely
escapes with his life.

Another exposure of social hypocrisy is contained in *The Pillars
of Society*. Consul Bernick is a respectable merchant with a fine
reputation among his neighbors as a good citizen, loving father,
and faithful husband. He is particularly desirous that the "moral
tone" of the community be rigorously upheld, and he is consequently active in all civic duties. But this pillar of society is
hollow and rotten within; he secretly profits from his public
activity, oppresses his workingmen, browbeats his wife, and enters
into shady commercial transactions, all the while maintaining an
appearance of great respectability. He always has a glib mouthful
of platitudes about "the moral foundations of society," "good citizenship," and "one's duty to one's neighbors." His reprehensible
dealings are finally discovered, but he manages to throw the blame
on an innocent man who is sailing for America, and so "the moral
tone of the community" is saved.

In *The Doll's House* Ibsen created a new type in literature, the emancipated woman. This drama caused a great sensation throughout the world, for it was a bitter attack on the conventions of family life. It also brought the subject of the rights of women prominently before the public. Torvald Helmer is a model husband and father, loving his wife, Nora, and his children most devotedly. Nora becomes anxious about her husband's health; and, in order to get money to enable him to go to a health resort, she forges her father's name to a note. She secretly works to pay off the debt, but the forgery is discovered. Helmer is roused to a high pitch of moral indignation at his wife; he denounces her for putting in jeopardy his future and his honor, forgetting that she had forged the note for his sake. Nora now realizes that all these years she had been regarded by her husband, not as an individual with a soul of her own, but as a petted child living in "a doll's house"; that her sole function had been to serve as wife and mother in return for support and shelter. She comes to loathe such a life as degrading and dishonorable. "I believe that before all else I am a human being, just as much as you are, or at least that I should try to become one," she tells her husband. She believes herself unfit to be a true wife and mother until she is able to share in the burdens and responsibilities of the world outside the home, and proposes to leave her husband. Helmer is outraged, and remonstrates with her on her duty to him, to her children, and to God. But Nora's reply is that her supreme duty is toward herself, and she resolutely leaves him.

August Strindberg, the Swedish writer, was the leading iconoclast in European drama. Strindberg's work is characterized by a fanatic hatred of what he conceived to be the vices Strindberg of women bred in them by their subordinate position. (1849–1912) Fear of women became almost an obsession with him, and he passionately insisted that they are the inveterate enemies of men of genius whom they try either to ruin or to cheat. Women, he believed, care only for their children and are interested in men only as fathers and as bread-winners.

Strindberg was a master of the one-act play, a type of literary composition of which he was to a considerable extent the originator. His characters are generally brutal, selfish, gross, and constantly quarreling. Although a seeker after the ideal, he was so much at odds with every one and with everything that he finally arrived at being a hopeless pessimist. As he himself once declared, "To search for God and find the Devil! — that is what happened to me." He was a master of biting irony, and his characterizations of persons leave a burning sensation in the reader. He speaks of one man as "an intellectual cannibal" who devours the reputations of his rivals; and of another as "a wandering shame whose face was known to all and who was branded with his own name."

Georg Brandes, a Danish Jew, was the greatest literary critic since Sainte-Beuve. Brandes's conception of criticism was to blend literature, philosophy, history, and sociology in order to give a true and complete idea of the evolution of the human spirit. In the great work, *Main Currents of Nineteenth Century Literature*, he takes all of Europe for his province and writes profoundly and convincingly on the writers and movements of the period. Unlike Sainte-Beuve, whose knowledge was mainly of the Romance nations, Brandes was equally at home in English, Russian, German, Polish, French, and Italian, as well as in Scandinavian literature; moreover, his sympathies were decidedly with the new men and the new ideals. He was the first to discover Nietzsche and to give that highly original German philosopher his place in the world of letters.

> Brandes (1842–1927)

HOLLAND AND BELGIUM

Although ranking as small nations, Holland, Belgium, and Switzerland occupied an important place in the European political system because of their geographic location. Holland is a landing place on the North Sea through which invading English or German armies might pass. Belgium is a buffer state between France and Germany, and a "pistol pointing at the heart of England." Switzerland is wedged in among four great nations, Germany, France, Italy, and Austria, and serves the purpose of preventing them from being too near neighbors.

> Strategic positions of these nations

After 1848 the Liberals controlled Holland for over a generation. They reorganized the administration, promoted popular education, and encouraged the development of modern industry. As elsewhere the bourgeois, who controlled the government, were opposed to the extension of the suffrage. Socialist agitation led to an important electoral reform in 1896, which virtually established universal, manhood suffrage.

> Liberalism in Holland

Holland occupied a position in the economic life of the world far out of proportion to her political importance. To her ports came Continental goods, especially German, on their way Holland, an overseas, and goods from overseas on their way to entrepôt the Continent. The Dutch colonial empire was considerable: Java, Sumatra, the Celebes, part of Borneo, and part of New Guinea in the East Indies; and Dutch Guiana in South America. Java and Sumatra produced large quantities of tea, coffee, sugar, tobacco, and spices which were exported to all parts of the world.

The people of Belgium are divided into two races, the Flemings who are closely related to the Dutch and speak Flemish, a language resembling Dutch; and the Walloons who are closely Flemings related to the French and speak French. In 1830, the and Wal- two elements had combined to overthrow Dutch loons domination; but once it was accomplished, a sharp division arose between them. Two parties appeared, the Catholics representing the Flemings, and the Liberals representing the Walloons, who fought over popular education, the suffrage, and the official language. The Catholic Party favored the control of the schools by the Church, high property qualifications for voting, and the equality of Flemish with French as an official language. On the other hand, the Liberals favored popular education on a secular basis, the broadening of the suffrage, and the maintenance of French as the only official language.

The Liberals were in control during most of the latter half of the nineteenth century. In 1879, they established a secular, public school system which was strongly opposed by the The educa- Catholics, who now demanded public support of their tion problem schools. The Catholic Party triumphed in the elections of 1884, and immediately reversed Belgium's educational policy. A new education law provided that any locality could choose to support either a "neutral" or a "free" school.[1] The government favored the "free" schools in every way possible at the expense of the "neutral" schools, which roused a strong opposition, especially among the Walloons who were influenced by the anti-clerical movement in France.

A new political force appeared with the birth of the Labor Party in 1885, which was both socialist and anti-clerical. It began an

[1] The public schools were called "neutral" because they were neutral in religion; the Catholic schools were called "free" because they were free from government control.

agitation in favor of universal, manhood suffrage that culminated
in a great general strike in 1893.   The government
made a concession by establishing universal, manhood suffrage but with plural votes for those having
property and higher education.   There was great objection to
plural voting, which insured the supremacy of the well-to-do
classes; and, in 1899, another concession was made by the adoption
of Proportional Representation.   The scheme established in Belgium provided for the presentation of a list of candidates by each
of the parties; the voter cast his ballot for the party list of his
choice; and seats were assigned to the parties in proportion to their
electoral strength.

Proportional Representation

However, plural voting was maintained.   The agitation for "one
man, one vote," was conducted by the Liberal and Labor Parties.
In 1913, there took place an extraordinary demonstration, a political general strike.   Men of all trades
stopped working and demanded, not better wages or shorter hours,
but equal, manhood suffrage.   Many business and professional
men closed their doors to show their sympathy with the movement.   After ten days the strike came to an end, on the promise
of the government to revise the electoral laws.

General strike of 1913

Through the activities of King Leopold II, Belgium acquired an
enormous region in Africa, the Congo Free State,[1] rich in rubber.
At first it was under the direct government of the
King, but mismanagement and cruelty to the natives
brought about a change of government.   In 1908, the region was
annexed outright to Belgium, and renamed Belgian Congo.

Belgian Congo

In spite of the guaranty of neutrality [2] Belgium feared that, in a
conflict between Germany and France, her frontiers
would be violated.   She prepared to defend herself
by establishing conscription (1913) and by strengthening her fortifications.   When, in 1914, Germany
violated her neutrality, Belgium promptly and loyally joined the
Allies.

Belgium prepares to defend herself

SWITZERLAND

The revolt of the Sonderbund in Switzerland [3] resulted in a
radical change in the system of government.   A new constitution
was adopted in 1848, which organized Switzerland into a federal

[1] See page 645.   [2] See page 65.   [3] See page 203.

union, modeled on that of the United States. Local government of the cantons was maintained, and a strong central government was established with ample power to enforce its supremacy. The Swiss political system presented unique and interesting features. Executive authority was lodged in a board, called the Federal Council chosen by parliament; its chairman was designated as the President of the Swiss Confederation. Another unique feature was the Initiative and Referendum, operative in both cantonal and federal affairs. By the Initiative is meant that a measure could be proposed by a specified number of voters and presented to the legislature for adoption. By the Referendum is meant that, if a specified number of voters so petitioned, a bill passed by the legislature had to be submitted to a popular vote for final decision. *The new constitution*

The people of Switzerland are of three nationalities, German, French, and Italian.[1] In spite of these differences they have managed to get along very well, as none of them is favored by the government. All three languages are official, and a member of parliament may address his colleagues in any one of them. Having learned to be tolerant of national differences in their own country, the Swiss, more than any other modern people, have shown great sympathy for foreigners. During the nineteenth century Switzerland was a house of refuge for political refugees from many lands: Italian nationalists of the Risorgimento, Hungarian patriots of 1848, French communards, German socialists, and Russian revolutionists. Switzerland also became a great center for all sorts of international meetings and humanitarian associations. When the League of Nations was established, Switzerland was greatly honored by the choice of Geneva as the capital of the League. *Switzerland, an international center*

REFERENCES

SCANDINAVIA:

R. N. Bain, *Scandinavia, a Political History of Denmark, Norway and Sweden, from 1513 to 1900* (1905); P. Drachman, *The Industrial Development and Commercial Policies of the three Scandinavian Countries* (1915); J. Carlsen and others, *Le Danemark, état actuale de sa civilisation et de son organisation sociale* (1900); F. C. Howe, *Denmark: A Coöperative Commonwealth* (1921), describes coöperative farming; K. Gjerset, *History of the*

[1] In 1914, the German Swiss numbered 65 per cent of the inhabitants; the French Swiss, 23 per cent; and the Italian Swiss, 12 per cent.

Norwegian People, 2 vols. (1915); G. G. Hardy, *Norway* (1925); G. Sund-
bärg (ed.), *Sweden, its People and Industries* (1904), a government report;
F. Nansen, *Norway and the Union with Sweden* (1905).

HOLLAND AND BELGIUM:

P. J. Blok, *History of the People of the Netherlands*, vol. v, *Eighteenth
and Nineteenth Centuries*, translated from the Dutch (1912), the work of
a distinguished Dutch historian; C. Day, *The Policy and Administration
of the Dutch in Java* (1904), an excellent study of Dutch colonial methods;
A. J. Barnouw, *Holland under Queen Wilhelmina* (1923); H. vander Linden,
Belgium (1920), goes to 1914; R. C. K. Ensor, *Belgium* (1900), a brief
study; J. Barthélemy. *L'Organisation du suffrage et l'expérience belge* (1912),
good study of political life; F. van Kalken, *La Belgique contemporaire* (1930),
general survey.

SWITZERLAND:

P. Seippel (ed.), *La Suisse au dixneuvième siècle*, 3 vols. (1899–1901),
an authoritative work by a group of Swiss writers; W. Oechsli, *History of
Switzerland, 1499–1914*, translated from the German (1922), the best
single volume history of Switzerland; W. D. McCrackan, *Rise of the Swiss
Republic* (ed. 1901), a historical outline, mainly political; on government: J. M. Vincent, *Government in Switzerland* (1900) and R. C. Brooks,
Government and Politics of Switzerland (ed. 1920); E. Fueter, *Die Schweiz
soit 1848* (1928); W. E. Rappard, *The Government of Switzerland* (1937);
A. Rothery, *Denmark* (1937).

ADDITIONAL REFERENCES

A. A. Stomberg, *A History of Sweden* (1931); W. W. Childs, *Sweden:
The Middle Way* (1936); F. van Kalken, *La Belgique contemporaine (1780–
1930)* (1930); M. Cole and C. Smith (eds.), *Democratic Sweden* (1939).

CHAPTER XXIII

OLD RUSSIA

RUSSIA, the "adopted child" of Europe, was the enigma of modern civilization. The intensely religious atmosphere, the fine simplicity of the masses, and the idealism and originality of the intellectuals made Russia a land of mystery and wonder. An English traveler well described the country in the following words: "Russia possesses the variety of the ages. Men and women, with the thoughts of the fourth century, the fifteenth or the eighteenth in their hearts, jostle others who are eager to cure the ills of mankind with the latest political and social nostrums of the twentieth. People of all periods rub shoulders, like the dancers in a masquerade. If one wants to know what an Anglo-Saxon villein was, it is more to the point to talk to a Russian peasant than to rummage in the libraries. The pilgrims, dressed like Tannhäuser in the third act, with staves in their hands and wallets at their sides, who wander through Russia on their way to pray at the Holy Sepulchre, belong to the age of the Crusades. The ascetic who spends his life in prayer and fasting and wears chains about his body seems to have found his way into modern Russia from the Egyptian Thebaïd of the fourth century."

Contrasts in Russia

As a result of the reforms of Alexander II Russia again came prominently before the view of western Europe. She was now admitted into the circle of modern nations, despite the fact that her government continued to be despotic. But the westernization of Russia encountered the opposition of a small but influential group known as Slavophiles. As has already been explained, Russia, because of adverse circumstances, had lagged behind the other nations of Europe in the march of civilization. What was a misfortune became a philosophy. To the Slavophiles the peculiar history of their country meant that she was destined to develop a civilization wholly different from that of western Europe; therefore, she, too, had a "mission" in the world. Early in the nineteenth century discussion raged over the question, "What is Russia?" The nihilists declared that she was "virgin soil," a land fortunate in having no history; hence, a *tabula*

"What is Russia?"

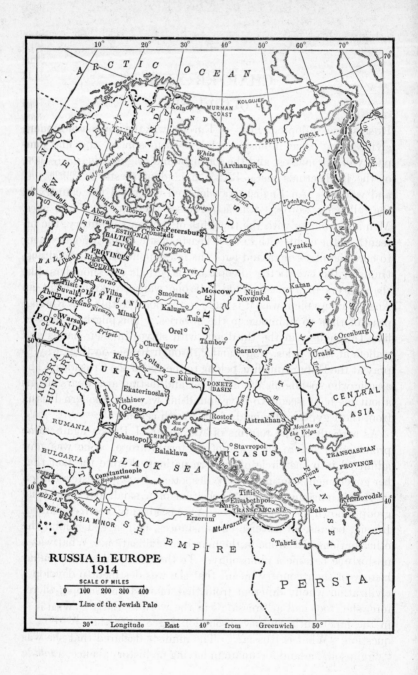

RUSSIA in EUROPE
1914

SCALE OF MILES

0   100   200   300   400

———— Line of the Jewish Pale

rasa upon which the future was free to write. "Not at all," replied the Slavophiles, "we are an old nation with a distinctive type of government, benevolent autocracy, with a distinctive type of religion, the Orthodox Church, and with a distinctive type of communal life, the mir. Western Europe is decadent, rotting from rationalism in religion, revolution in politics, and class hatred in society; hence, Russia can borrow nothing from other nations except their vices." "You are both wrong," replied the champions of Western culture, "Russia is merely backward in her development; those institutions which she thinks original and peculiar to her are like those which had existed in the rest of Europe in times past, and the more she progresses the more like western Europe she will become." By their opponents the Slavophiles were ridiculed as a small group of "Old Believers" in politics who tried to cover up an evil system of government and society by romantic appeals to an imaginary past.

RACES IN THE EMPIRE

Russia was not a homogeneous nation, but an empire inhabited by a conglomeration of many nations, varying from Mongolian tribes on the Pacific coast to Germans on the Baltic coast, all bound together by a highly centralized government. The majority of the inhabitants were Slavic Russians who, according to the census of 1897, numbered about 84,000,000 out of a total population of about 129,000,000. The Slavic Russians were divided into (1) Great Russians, who inhabited the central plain known as Great Russia, of which Moscow was the center; (2) Little Russians, or Ukrainians who inhabited the southwestern plain, of which Kiev was the center; and (3) the White Russians, a small group, who lived chiefly in Lithuania. From Great Russia came the Russian language and literature; the languages of the Ukrainians and White Russians were closely related to Russian. Most of the Russians were members of the Orthodox Church, an offshoot of the Greek Church of ancient times, from which it derived its doctrines and ritual. Its head was the tsar whose powers were exercised by a commission of ecclesiastics, appointed by him, known as the Holy Synod, whose chief was a civil official, called the Procurator. There were many dissenters from the official faith. The leading group of dissenters was known as the "Old Believers," who accepted the doctrines of the Orthodox

Church, but differed very sharply on slight matters of ritual. They arose as a result of a revision of the holy books during the seventeenth century. The "Old Believers" stood by the old editions on the ground that the alteration of certain words meant the alteration of the original pure faith. Some of the Russians belonged to what was called the Uniate Church, which acknowledged the headship of the Pope in Rome, yet maintained the liturgy of the Orthodox Church and permitted their priests to marry.

Racially akin to the Russians were the Poles, who inhabited Russian Poland and certain districts in Lithuania and the Ukraine. The Poles   Their language bears about the same relation to Russian as Dutch does to German. However, their culture and traditions are very different from those of the Russians. The Poles are Roman Catholic by faith; hence, Latin by tradition and Western in culture. Between the Russians and the Poles there existed a deep hostility, dating from the wars of the sixteenth century, which was greatly aggravated by the Partition of Poland.

In the Baltic Provinces, Esthonia, Livonia, and Courland, the inhabitants, known as Esths and Letts, were dominated by Germans, known as the Balts, whose ancestors had conquered the region during the Middle Ages. The Balts were great landlords and wealthy bourgeois who succeeded in making the German language and culture predominant in the region. The Letts were chiefly peasants who worked on the estates of the Balts under conditions that were almost feudal. They stoutly maintained their own traditions and language, desiring neither "to drown in clear German water" nor "sink into the Russian morass."

In Finland there were likewise two races: the Finns, a race supposedly non-European in origin, and the Swedes who had once conquered the region. There was friction between the two races, but not as bitter as in the Baltic Provinces where the Esths and the Letts hated the Balts much as the medieval serfs hated their lords.

Lithuania had formerly been part of the Kingdom of Poland. The majority of the inhabitants were Lithuanians, generally poor peasants who were dominated by a Polish aristocracy. Most of the Lithuanians were Catholics in religion. The cities were inhabited chiefly by Jews, who constituted the middle class in the region.

In Bessarabia lived a racial group known as Moldavians, closely allied to the Rumanians. In the Caucasus were Georgians and Armenians. Many Tartars, Mohammedan by faith, Other races were to be found in Crimea and in the southeastern provinces. Siberia was sparsely inhabited, chiefly by native Mongolian tribes and by Russian colonists.

Of all the non-Slavic races in the Empire the most important were the Jews. About half of the entire Jewish race lived under the Russian flag, which created a situation that at- The Jews tracted world-wide attention. Russia acquired most of her Jewish population as a result of the Partition of Poland; the parts which fell to her had been a Jewish settlement for centuries. The largest Jewish settlements were in Poland and Lithuania, where the Jews constituted the bulk of the urban population. As in western Europe during the Middle Ages the Jews lived in communities of their own, where they preserved their traditional customs and manners. Their language was Yiddish, a jargon based upon a German dialect, which had been introduced during the Middle Ages by Jews from Germany. However, there were many Jews, especially in southern Russia, who had been assimilated, and were Russian in sentiment and culture.

REACTION UNDER ALEXANDER III

The assassination of Alexander II shocked the liberals no less than it did the conservatives. In spite of the reaction during the latter part of his reign, Alexander II had done almost as much as Peter the Great to make Russia a true member of the European family. When Alexander III ascended the throne the revolutionists issued a warning manifesto, which declared that imprisonment, exile and death would not stop them from prosecuting their aim of establishing democratic government in Russia; that autocracy was an evil, whether the autocrat was good or bad; that there were only two ways of establishing democracy: one, through a bloody revolution which would result in needless waste of blood and energy that could be better used for the welfare of Russia; the other, through the voluntary action of the Tsar in granting a general amnesty for all political crimes, and, especially, by summoning a representative assembly. The revolutionists promised to submit unconditionally to the will of a constitutional government. In reply, Tsar Alexander issued a statement which indicated plainly enough what his future course would be. "The voice of God," he declared, "orders us to stand firm at the helm of government . . .

Reactionary
attitude
of Alex-
ander III
with faith in the strength and truth of the autocratic power, which we are called upon to strengthen and preserve for the good of the people." Shortly afterwards, he called upon his faithful subjects "to strive for the extirpation of the heinous agitation which had disgraced the land." "Gentlemen, rise! A *government* is now coming in!" exclaimed the reactionary, Katkov.

Alexander III was a soldier both by training and by temperament. He was moderately educated, rather dull, narrow-minded,
Pobie-
donostsev
stubborn, and intensely nationalistic in his sympathies and prejudices. The power behind the throne for a quarter of a century, and the most influential man in the government, was Constantine Pobiedonostsev, Procurator of the Holy Synod. Pobiedonostsev, called the "evil genius" of Russia, hated democracy in any and all forms, thoroughly and consistently. In his view the institutions of western Europe and of America were a warning, not a model for Russia. Democracy, he declared, was a sham employed by the wealthy to hide their control of the government; a free press meant the free dissemination of lies and calumnies; religious toleration meant division in the Church and rebellion in the State. Russia alone was unspoiled; under the protecting care of her benevolent autocracy and of the Orthodox Church reigned peace, love, and true religion. Pobiedonostsev was the real author of many important declarations issued by the Tsar.

War to the death was declared against the revolutionists by Alexander. The "Nicholas System" was fully restored, and opponents
Restoration
of the
"Nicholas
System"
of the government were sentenced to imprisonment, exile, or death by "administrative process," a form of court-martial which superseded regular court trials. Thousands found in Siberian[1] wilds their eternal abiding-place; thousands more fled to Switzerland, France, and America. Education in particular felt the heavy hand of reaction. The universities were deprived of the self-government granted to them by Alexander II. A severe press law practically prohibited the existence of any but conservative journals. By these methods the revolutionary agitation was entirely suppressed, and Russia was once more "frozen."

[1] Siberia was then a penal colony, where political prisoners as well as criminals were sent.

Next to the revolutionaries the non-Russians in the Empire provoked Alexander's resentment. "One Russia, one Creed, one Tsar," was to him a living motto, and there began a ruthless Russification of the subject races. Russian was made the official language in Finland. In Poland, the use of the native language was prohibited in all educational institutions. Even the favored Balts were compelled to accept Russian as the official language of the Provinces.

Russification

Alexander's heaviest blows fell upon the Jews. There began a systematic persecution of the Jews which had for its declared object, ascribed to Pobiedonostsev, to force one third to emigrate, to convert another third to the Orthodox Church, and to harry the remaining third to destruction. It was inspired by the idea that the Jews, because of their race, religion, and traditions would ever be aliens. The Jewish persecution in Russia recalled the Middle Ages, with segregation, exceptional laws, and even massacre. Alexander's anti-Jewish policy was, in part, the outcome of conditions in Russia. As in western Europe during the Middle Ages, the Jews were the money lenders in the rural districts. They loaned money to the peasants, often at usurious rates of interest, which made them very unpopular. Moreover, the government feared that under a system of equal rights the Jews would quickly rise to power and influence because of their commercial abilities. And the landed aristocracy in control of the government had no desire to see its power challenged by Jewish capitalists.

Persecution of the Jews

A number of anti-Jewish laws were passed in the eighties, which contained many restrictions on Jews in respect to residence, occupation, and education. Already in the early nineteenth century a Pale of Settlement had been created consisting of Poland, Lithuania, and the Ukraine, where Jews were segregated by law. The regulations regarding the Pale were now made more severe, and were more strictly enforced. Many Jews were torn from their homes in all parts of the country and driven into the Pale. Residence within the Pale itself was not altogether unrestricted. Jews were forbidden to move from the cities to the villages; they were compelled to live in cities, where they congregated in large numbers. The special privilege of living outside of the Pale was granted to those Jews who were graduates of higher institutions of learning, to professional men, to wealthy merchants,

The "Jewish Pale"

and to artisans. This privilege did not extend to the children, who were obliged to leave their homes as soon as they came of age, unless they could qualify on their own part. Foreign Jews were forbidden to travel in Russia regardless of passports obtained from the government of which they were citizens.

Jews were denied the opportunity for higher education. Their numbers in the secondary schools and in the universities were Educational limited to a definite proportion of the student body. restrictions Within the Pale it was ten per cent; outside it was five per cent, except in St. Petersburg and Moscow, where it was three per cent. Those who had means went to Germany or to France for their higher education; the others entered into fierce competition for the few coveted places available in Russian institutions of learning.

All public employment of whatever nature was closed to the Jews. Exception was made in the case of army doctors, many of Occupa- whom were Jews. Even in those cities where they tional re- constituted a majority, they did not have the right to strictions vote for members of the town council; the governor of the district usually appointed a number of Jews to these bodies to represent the Jewish community. No Jew could become a lawyer unless he got special permission from the Minister of Justice, and very few received this permission.

Jews were not permitted to buy or lease land in the rural dis- Economic tricts anywhere in Russia. Hindrances to their in- restrictions dustrial progress were also created by laws limiting the number of Jewish stockholders in industrial corporations.

In the matter of rights, the Jews were regarded as aliens, but in the matter of duties, they were full citizens. They were required Special to serve in the army although they were not permitted burdens to become officers. In addition to the ordinary taxes, they were required to pay special taxes.

Not only did the laws weigh heavily on the Jews, but they were capriciously enforced. In fact, it was well-nigh impossible to Capricious enforce them because of their complexity; hence, enforcement they were frequently evaded, and became a prolific of the anti- source of corruption. Outside of the Pale there were Jewish code many "unlicensed" Jews, who lived in constant fear of being driven out. His status being that of semi-outlaw, the Jew led a precarious existence under the watchful eye of the police.

When anti-Jewish feeling was particularly acute, raids would be organized against "unlicensed" Jews who were driven out of town. Some were later allowed to return on payment of a bribe. Sometimes a town within the Pale would be declared a "village," and a wholesale expulsion of Jews would follow.

To this persecution the Jews opposed a policy of passive resistance. "Infirm of body, but firm of mind," they resolved to weather this storm as they had weathered so many Resistance other storms by clinging all the more firmly to their of the Jews religion and traditions, relying upon their solidarity to break the force of the laws meant for their destruction. Thousands fled to foreign lands, particularly to America, cherishing undying hatred for the Russian government. Those who remained lived in wretched poverty, earning a meager livelihood as small shopkeepers, peddlers, tailors, and cobblers in congested cities where the government hoped that they would be "miserably crushed together until the fruitless struggle for life should have done its work."

The persecution of the Jews in Russia and the growth of anti-Semitism in France, revealed by the Dreyfus Affair, led to a national revival among Jews everywhere, known as Zionism Zionism. Its aim was the restoration of Palestine to the Jews as their national homeland, where they would be free from persecution. The father of political Zionism was the Austrian writer, Theodor Herzl, a prophet-like personality who succeeded in focusing the attention of the Jews of the world to this new solution of their age-old problem. Palestine was then under the sovereignty of the Sultan, who was naturally opposed to the Zionist movement. However, Jewish agricultural colonies were established in Palestine which laid the foundation of a new Jewish life in that ancient land.

SYSTEM OF GOVERNMENT

The Russian Empire, comprising half of Europe and a vast stretch of Asia, was governed by a highly centralized administrasion located at St. Petersburg. All power and au- The Tsar thority radiated from the Tsar, the "Autocrat of all the Russias," who ruled by divine right. Laws had to have his sanction, and officials held their positions through his grace. He was assisted by various bodies, the most important being the

Council of the Empire, a sort of cabinet which was the center of Imperial administration.

Because of great distances and variety of population, Russia was well adapted to a federal system, but little local government was Centraliza-   permitted lest it should disrupt the unity of the Em-
tion   pire.   Russia was divided into "governments," which were ruled by a governor and an administrative council appointed by the Tsar.   In some instances, there was also a governor-general who had supreme military authority over a historic entity, such as Poland or Finland.   The sparsely settled regions of Asia were divided into provinces, each under the rule of a military governor. Very little power was given to the zemstvos in the country and to the city councils because, to some extent, they were elected, and the government did not wish to encourage self-government.

As in all other autocracies the government was really carried on by a bureaucracy.   Its members were recruited from the ranks of The bureau- the aristocracy and the middle class.   Many of the
cracy   highest positions were filled by the Balts who, though Germans, were yet welcomed by the Tsar because of their efficiency. The Balts gave to the autocracy unflinching loyalty; they even preferred Russia to Germany, considering the latter too "demo- cratic."   In Russia they were favored at court, in the army, in the diplomatic service, and in the civil administration.   Russian officialdom was notoriously corrupt, a "despotism tempered by corruption."   Bribery was almost universal, reaching from cabinet ministers to the lowest clerks.   "The administration's inertia or duplicity, duly paid for," writes Anatole Leroy-Beaulieu in *The Empire of the Tsars and the Russians*, "paralyzed bad laws as well as good ones.   The functionary sold liberty to one, tolerance to another; he sold immunity to both innocent and guilty.   The Russian dissenters (*Raskolniki*) could not have weathered two cen- turies of persecution but for the willingness of the police and the clergy to ignore them — for a consideration.   The Russian spirit could never have withstood the pressure put on it under Nicholas but for the connivance of the officials who secretly suffered the forbidden books and the revolutionary papers of Herzen and the other revolutionaries to be circulated — for a consideration."

Very important in the administration were the police who formed the Prætorian Guard of tsarism.   There were several kinds of police of which the secret service, known as the Third Section, exerted great power and influence. Organized by Nicholas I, it was suppressed by Alexander II; later, it was reorgan- *The Police* ized under another name, but continued to be known as the Third Section. It was made independent of the other police, and almost of the government itself, by being given extralegal powers to arrest without warrant and to punish without trial. This political inquisition became so powerful that it inspired fear even among the high officials. Its agents were found wherever Russian revolutionists congregated, in Paris, in London, in New York as well as in St. Petersburg and in Moscow. Between the two "undergrounds," the political police and the revolutionists, there was a duel to the death; neither side asked nor gave quarter. Spies entered the ranks of the revolutionists by pretending to be violent enemies of the government; they succeeded, in some instances, in becoming the most trusted men in the secret societies. Frequently, the inciters to deeds of terrorism and the organizers of conspiracies were *agents provocateurs*, who would then betray their "comrades."

THE INDUSTRIAL REVOLUTION

As long as serfdom existed, modern industry made little progress in Russia. Labor, being tied to the soil, could not be easily used in the factory where free labor was essential. It was, *Russia's* therefore, not until the latter part of the nineteenth *natural re-* *sources* century that the Industrial Revolution really began. Russia was rich in natural resources, coal in the Donetz Basin, iron in the Urals and in the south, and oil in Baku. After Emancipation there was a great supply of cheap labor; those peasants who could not make a living on their small farms migrated to the factory towns. What Russia lacked, however, was capital.

From France and Germany, chiefly, came large importations of capital which found a profitable field of investment. Foreign capital was greatly encouraged by Sergius Witte, a *Witte* famous Minister of Finance under Alexander III and Nicholas II. Witte was a new type of Russian, a keen business man conversant with the problems of modern finance and industry, and an energetic organizer of business enterprises. He offered special inducements to capitalists who desired to establish factories: they were given large government orders; high tariffs protected them against foreign competition; and their goods were transported in Russia at low rates on the public railways. Witte put the public finances on a sound basis by establishing the gold standard in Russia's monetary system.

As a result of these policies Russia underwent a marked industrial development. Many factories were established. The mines
Industrial development were rapidly exploited; in the production of iron and steel, Russia soon outstripped France, Austria, and Belgium. From 1870 to 1900 coal production tripled. Railways developed rapidly under state ownership. In 1860, there were less than a thousand miles of railway in the Empire; in 1895, there were over 40,000 miles. During the last decade of the nineteenth century the government constructed and operated the greatest railway in the world, the Trans-Siberian, which traversed the entire Empire from the Baltic to the Pacific. It was financed largely by French loans to the government. The Trans-Siberian helped to develop Siberia as a home for emigrants and as a market for Russian manufactures.

French investments were in government loans, but German investments were in private industrial enterprises. There began an
Influence of German capital intimate economic relation between Germany and Russia that benefited both countries. Russia was a great market for German goods; in 1913, over forty per cent of Russian imports came from Germany. Russian exports to Germany consisted chiefly of foodstuffs. German firms established branches, and German capitalists established factories in Russia. German technicians and administrators came to Russia to introduce modern economic methods, as in the days of Peter the Great. Russia benefited greatly by having a highly developed nation at her door.

Poland was the chief industrial center of the Empire, partly because of her geographical position which made her a convenient
Poland, the industrial center trade route between western Europe and Russia; partly because of her coal and iron deposits; and partly because of the commercial activities of the large Jewish population settled within her borders. During the first decade of the twentieth century, Poland produced one seventh of the entire industrial output of the Empire; Russia proper constituting the chief market for Polish manufactures. Lodz became a cotton center, rivaling in importance some of the textile cities of England. The engineering works and textile factories of Warsaw made that historic city an industrial beehive.

In spite of the advance of the Industrial Revolution, Russia, in 1914, was still overwhelmingly agricultural. She imported manufactured articles as well as raw materials because she produced far too few manufactures to supply her needs. She had to pay foreign shipowners who carried her goods. She had to pay dividends to foreign capitalists. The export of foodstuffs, which she raised in abundance, was the only means that Russia had of balancing her imports and of meeting her obligations to foreign capital. But even this huge export was not sufficient to balance her trade, and Russia, therefore, had to have recourse to borrowing on a large scale. She became the great debtor nation of Europe.

Russia, a debtor nation

The results of the Industrial Revolution were the same in Russia as elsewhere. A prosperous middle class and a numerous working class made their appearance. Both were opposed to the autocracy because it represented the interests of the landed proprietors and because it was despotic and corrupt. Large numbers of peasants surged toward the cities looking for employment in the newly built factories, and a working class arose which began to organize unions and to strike for better conditions, activities hitherto quite unknown in Russia. The government, fearing that any organized discontent would soon become political, declared unions illegal; strikes were suppressed by the police in the belief that they were organized rebellions.

Appearance of middle and working classes

Both the middle and the working classes were excellent soil for the seeds of revolution. Grouped in large cities, it was easier to form societies, to distribute pamphlets, and to organize demonstrations among them than among the widely scattered peasants. The factory, with its many laborers meeting daily, became the nucleus of a revolutionary society. Hitherto, the movement against tsarism had been the work of small groups of militant idealists who had waged a desperate war against an autocracy intrenched by the loyalty of a helpless and ignorant peasantry. Were a new revolutionary movement to arise it would command the powerful support of the industrial classes. Strange as it might have seemed, it was during the iron régime of Alexander III that conditions were ripening for the Revolutions of 1905 and of 1917.

REFERENCES

Consult bibliographies at the end of Chapters XI and XXIV.

CHAPTER XXIV

THE RUSSIAN REVOLUTION OF 1905

THE NEW REVOLUTIONARY MOVEMENT

OLD RUSSIA was passing away with the introduction of the Industrial Revolution. But the Old Régime showed no signs of being influenced by the new conditions; on the contrary, tsarism was more than ever determined to maintain its privileges. In 1894, Nicholas II, a young man of twenty-six, ascended the throne, and many hoped that a new era would now dawn in the nation. But at the outset of his reign, Nicholas made it plain that he had no intention of granting concessions. He told a delegation from the zemstvos that they were indulging in "senseless dreams" in hoping that he would coöperate with these elective bodies in governing the country. He was firmly resolved to uphold the principle of autocracy as firmly and as unswervingly as his father, Alexander III. It was soon evident that Nicholas resembled neither his father in strength of will nor his grandfather in liberality of spirit. He was a weak man without ability of any sort, but stubbornly insistent on maintaining his autocratic powers.

A new revolutionary movement now made its appearance. It took the form of popular agitation in the cities, particularly among the workingmen, who frequently went on strike for better wages, shorter hours — and a constitution. Great mass meetings and parades took place in favor of reform. In spite of the censorship, a radical press appeared. Revolutionary societies multiplied rapidly. Private association, such as engineering societies, academies of science, lawyers' clubs, trade unions, chambers of commerce, and even public bodies, like the zemstvos and city councils, became identified with some form of agitation for political freedom. At first the government was puzzled by the movement; and not until it assumed alarming proportions did the authorities realize that they were face to face with a social upheaval, supported by the industrial elements that had come into existence with the factory system.

In the new revolutionary movement there were three distinct elements that differed widely in aims and methods. The most moderate might be described as liberals, who represented the progressive elements among the bourgeois and the no- The liberals bility, and who were led by Paul Miliukóv, a well-known historian and sociologist. The liberals aimed to establish in Russia a constitutional monarchy on the model of England; hence, they favored a parliament elected by universal, manhood suffrage, a cabinet responsible to parliament, and complete freedom of speech and of association. On the land question which, next to free government was the most important problem, the liberals favored giving more land to the peasants by expropriating the larger estates at prices fixed by public commissions, and by selling the state lands.

During the eighties, after the failure of terrorism, the exiled revolutionaries continued to ask the question, "What is to be done?" They now learned of a new revolutionary The Social movement that was agitating western Europe, social- Democrats ism. They studied the writings of Karl Marx, and many became enthusiastic converts to socialism. To the rigid Marxian doctrines they brought a revolutionary fervor that made Russian socialism far more vivid than its counterpart in western Europe. How tsarism would be overthrown seemed plain to the socialists: the Industrial Revolution was bringing into existence a liberal bourgeois and a revolutionary proletariat, who together would overthrow the autocracy and establish a democratic government in Russia. But democracy would be merely a "rest house" in the march toward socialism, therefore the workingmen, not the bourgeois, were to lead in the revolutionary movement which, unlike that in western Europe, would fight both autocracy and capitalism. "The Russian Revolution will triumph as a revolution of the working class, otherwise it will not triumph at all," declared Plékhanov, the father of Russian socialism. The socialists had little hope of revolutionary aid from the peasants, and they were consequently not greatly concerned with them. They believed that the ultimate solution of the land question was nationalization, with the peasant as the tenant of the state. In the meantime, however, they advocated the confiscation of the estates in favor of the peasants, who would then become proprietors of larger farms. Both the liberals and the Social Democrats favored the abolition of the mir as an outworn institution. The Social Democratic Party, or the "S—D," appeared, and it quickly won the support

of large numbers of the working class. Early in the twentieth
century a sharp division arose in the "S—D," as to the tactics to
be adopted in the revolutionary movement. A majority faction,
called the Bolshevists (Russian, *majority*), led by Nicholas Lenin,
favored an armed insurrection of the working class which, if successful, was to be followed by the "dictatorship of the proletariat" in order to establish socialism. A minority-faction, called
the Menshevists (Russian, *minority*), favored coöperation with the
liberals for the purpose of establishing a constitutional government
based upon democratic principles.[1]

The third element in the revolutionary movement was the Social
Revolutionists, or the "S—R." Inspired by the Narod move-

The Social
Revolution-
aries
ment [2] they believed that the peasant, not the workingman, was to play the chief rôle in the revolution.
No revolution, they contended, could succeed in Russia
unless the peasant participated, and he would do so only when
moved by the hope of "land and freedom." The Narod movement had failed because it had preached Liberty, Equality, and
Fraternity, vague ideals, of which the peasant had not the slightest
understanding; but the magic words "More land" would make him
receptive to revolutionary propaganda. The "S—R" adopted the
slogan, "the whole land to the whole people," according to which
the state lands and the estates were to be given free to the peasants.
Every family was to have as much land as it could cultivate without hired labor. Ownership of the land was to be vested in the
mir, not in the state or in the peasant. The "S—R" were opposed
both to capitalism and to Marxian socialism; they did not believe
that Russia " had to be boiled in the cauldron of capitalism before
she could attain socialism." Unlike the other parties the "S—R"
enthusiastically championed the mir as a communistic institution
of the Russian peasantry which, in future, would be the nucleus
of a great national commonwealth of self-governing communes.
The mir was, therefore, to be preserved, but transformed into a
coöperative society on a modern basis. In the movement to overthrow tsarism the "S—R" favored united action on the part of
peasants, workingmen, and intelligentsia. Many of its members
favored terrorism as a means of promoting revolutionary ardor and
of bringing the situation to a head. The "S—D," on the contrary,

[1] For further description of the Bolshevists and Menshevists see pages 581–84.
[2] See pages 183–84.

favored "mass action," strikes, demonstrations, and uprisings; but acts of individual terrorism they considered futile because they resulted in exasperating not in terrifying the government. There was now an organized effort to rouse against tsarism all the elements of the nation, the bourgeois by the liberals, the working class by the "S—D," and the peasants by the "S—R." Tsarism would have only the great landlords and the officials as its supporters.

THE COUNTER-REVOLUTIONARY MOVEMENT

At the beginning of the twentieth century the revolutionary movement was in full swing in all its phases. Strikes, demonstrations, petitions, and mass meetings were of almost daily occurrence. "Terror squads," organized by the "S—R," assassinated officials. The spirit of revolt spread even to the peasants, who attacked the estates and threatened the lives of the proprietors. *Spread of terrorism*

The government determined to meet the situation with every resource at its command. Nicholas found in his Minister of Interior, Plehve, a determined and resourceful supporter of the autocracy. Plehve resolved on a policy of "Thorough" in the struggle against revolution. A net of secret police was cast over the entire country. Spies were everywhere, in classrooms, in business houses, in workshops, in public offices, in clubs, even in private families. It was estimated that, in 1903, there were as many as 12,000 political cases; many were imprisoned, exiled to Siberia, or executed by "administrative process." When a peasant uprising occurred, the Cossacks would be sent to restore order; and when these savage warriors were turned loose on a village, the horrors which they perpetrated were beyond description. Shootings, whippings, and the burning of homes were the order of the day, and neither sex nor age was spared. *Plehve's policy of "Thorough"*

It was part of Plehve's policy to excite racial and religious animosities in order to distract the people from revolutionary activity. Societies, called "Leagues of True Russians," were organized by government officials for the purpose of convincing the people that all truly patriotic Russians supported the Tsar, and that his opponents were enemies of the Fatherland. In order to fight terror with terror, bands of roughs called "Black Hundreds" were encouraged to attack Jews and revolutionists. Proclamations were spread broadcast denouncing the Jews as in- *The Pogroms* stigators of revolution and as enemies of the Russian government because it was so truly Christian and patriotic.   A series of attacks on the Jews, called "pogroms," took place with the connivance of the authorities that culminated in the massacre of Kishinev in 1903.   Hundreds of houses and stores belonging to Jews were pillaged and burned, and many were killed and wounded.   Little effort was made by the authorities to stop the rioting.

The massacre of Kishinev horrified the world.   Plehve had breathed a spirit of savagery into the bureaucracy such as had not been known even in the days of the "Nicholas System."   The revolutionists determined to "execute" him; in 1904, he was blown to pieces by a bomb. In explanation of this deed the revolutionists issued a proclamation, declaring that it was justified because peaceful means of agitation did not exist as a check upon irresponsible power; therefore, the only means left was to meet the "violence of tyranny with the force of revolutionary right."

Assassination of Plehve

A liberal aristocrat, Prince Mirski, now became the chief adviser of Nicholas.   Through Mirski's efforts the censorship of the press was relaxed, and, for a brief period, Russia enjoyed comparative freedom of speech.   Mirski encouraged the moderate reformers to present their plans in the hope of establishing a cordial understanding between Tsar and people.   A convention of delegates from the zemstvos drew up a petition to the Tsar, which frankly declared that the conduct of the bureaucracy had alienated the people from the dynasty; that, in order to restore good feeling between the people and the government, it was essential to establish full civil, political, and religious liberty; and that a representative assembly should be immediately summoned. Similar petitions poured in from civic bodies, learned societies, and commercial organizations.   Mirski, finding that his efforts to introduce liberal measures were being thwarted by Nicholas, resigned in disgust.

Mirski

COLLAPSE OF THE AUTOCRACY

War has sometimes been the safety valve of despots hard pressed by their subjects.   When, in the beginning of the twentieth century, Russia advanced to the Pacific and threatened Korea, the Far Eastern situation became critical.[1]   The relations between Russia and Japan were very

The Russo-Japanese War

[1] See page 630.

strained, and, in 1904, war broke out between the two nations. To Nicholas the Russo-Japanese War was a great opportunity of rallying the country behind the government. He issued a stirring appeal to his subjects to save their country from foes at home and abroad for the sake of "the Faith, the Tsar, and the Fatherland." There was, however, little enthusiasm for the war, the conduct of which was characterized by mismanagement and corruption. The terrible defeats of the Russian armies in the battles with the Japanese, the capture of Port Arthur, and the destruction of the Russian fleet in the Straits of Tsushima shattered the almost universal belief in the military impregnability of Russia. She was shown to be a giant with feet of clay. The outcome of the war served to swell the ranks of the opponents of the government, as many moderates were incensed against the Tsar because of the humiliating defeat of their country.

The revolutionary movement now assumed immense proportions. In the vanguard were the socialist workingmen, led by the intelligentsia who now had organizations and public opinion behind them. The autocracy keenly realized the danger from a working-class uprising. It endeavored, therefore, to circumvent the agitation in two ways: first, by bringing pressure to bear on the employers to provide good conditions in their factories; and, secondly, by fostering labor unions under its protection. "No politics!" was the motto of the government unions, who chose, as their chief, a priest known as Father Gapon. *The government trade unions*

During 1905 a strike fever seemed to seize upon the Russian masses; even the government unions were swept into the current of agitation, which soon became political in character. It was Father Gapon's idea to organize a procession of working people who were to present a petition to the "Little Father" in person, asking him to show his confidence in his people by convoking a popular assembly. On Sunday, January 22, 1905, an enormous crowd, led by Father Gapon in priestly attire and carrying a crucifix, began to move through the streets of St. Petersburg. *"Red Sunday"* When they arrived at the Winter Palace, instead of finding the Tsar, they found a body of Cossacks, waiting to receive them. The order was given to fire; and, at each volley, men and women fell on all sides. "Red Sunday," as the day of the massacre was called, horrified the world, and implanted a grim determination among all classes of Russians to destroy a government which knew no other way of communicating with its people than through rifle and saber.

Revolutionary fury raged throughout the country. Barricades were erected in the capital, and strikes involving thousands of workingmen took place in almost every industry. The subject peoples in the Empire took advantage of the situation to add to the general turmoil in the hope of getting concessions for their nationality as well as for democracy. They reasoned that a fallen autocracy might mean the breaking or the loosening of the chains which bound them so tightly. Warsaw was a hotbed of insurrection, and mobs paraded carrying Polish flags and demanding autonomy for Poland. In Finland a general strike took place which brought that country to the verge of anarchy. In the Baltic provinces the Lettish peasants rose and pillaged the estates of the German landlords. In the Caucasus the Armenians and Georgians rebelled. In the "Pale" the Jewish Bund, a socialist organization of Jewish workingmen, battled against the "Black Hundreds."

Uprising of subject nationalities

The rising tide of discontent culminated in one of the most extraordinary popular demonstrations in modern history. During 1905 a general strike was declared throughout the Empire. It began with the railway men and telegraphers, and all communication was cut off when they ceased working. It then spread rapidly to the shipyards, factories, mines, and shops, and there appeared a new organization, the *Soviet*, or Council of Workers' Delegates, which led in the demonstration. It consisted chiefly of delegates from the trade unions of St. Petersburg, and one of its leaders was a young revolutionist, later known as Leon Trotsky. A veritable strike epidemic began. Gas and electric companies refused to operate their plants, and many cities were in darkness; merchants closed their stores; teachers dismissed their classes; domestic servants refused to cook, to clean house, or to wait on table; druggists refused to prepare prescriptions, and doctors closed their offices; lawyers refused to plead in court, and judges and juries refused to render verdicts; city councils and zemstvos adjourned their meetings; and even the ballet dancers refused to dance. Life in Russia came virtually to a standstill.

The General Strike

The government was now face to face with a situation such as had never confronted it or any other government, and there was nothing else to do but to yield. On October 30, 1905, Nicholas issued a famous manifesto which yielded to the de- The October mands of the more moderate of the revolutionists. It Manifesto contained the following provisions: a guarantee of the "immutable foundations of civil liberty, based on inviolability of person, freedom of conscience, of speech, of meeting, and of association"; an extension of the franchise for the election of a Duma, or parliament which the Tsar had already promised; and a promise "to establish as an immutable rule that no law can ever come into force without the approval of the Duma." Later decrees granted universal, manhood suffrage, but on a class basis; and established an upper house, partly appointed by the Tsar, and partly elected by various bodies of notables. The cabinet was to be appointed by the Tsar and be responsible to him. These Fundamental Laws established what was virtually a constitution. As a further sign of his liberal intentions, Nicholas dismissed the hated officials, General Trepov and Pobiedonostsev, and appointed as his Prime Minister, Count Witte, who was regarded as a moderate liberal.

But these concessions did not satisfy the extreme revolutionists to whom the capitulation of the government was a sign of weakness. Now was the opportunity, reasoned they, of destroy- The Moscow ing tsarism, root and branch. Moscow was the scene uprising of a new demonstration. An uprising of socialist workingmen took place in that city during December, 1905, that recalled the June Days of 1848. For a week there was desperate barricade fighting between the insurgents and the military. The government finally succeeded in quelling the uprising.

THE DUMAS

There was now a lull in revolutionary activity, and preparations were made for elections to the Duma. Great enthusiasm was shown by the people who, for the first time, were to parti- Parties in cipate in the government of their country. Nearly the Duma every candidate elected was opposed to the autocracy. A number of political groups were organized on the model of those in the other Continental countries. The most moderate were the Octobrists, whose demands were limited to the concessions of the October Manifesto. Its supporters were nobles and capitalists who wished to see established in Russia a system of government similar to that in Prussia. More progressive were the Constitutional

Democrats, popularly known as the "Cadets," who championed the ideas of the liberals. The "S—D" represented the working-men, most of whom had become converts to socialism. The "S—R" boycotted the elections because they disdained to sit as representatives in a body created by the Tsar. A group representing the peasants, called the Labor Party, appeared which proposed a radical solution of the land question.

On May 10, 1906, the Duma began its sessions in the Taurida Palace, St. Petersburg. It was an historic day for Russia, and the meeting was opened with impressive ceremony by Nicholas in person. He exhorted the representatives "to work for the rejuvenation of Russia's moral outlook and for the reincarnation of her best powers." The most important group in the Duma were the Cadets, who together with the Labor Party, controlled that body. Though not a member of the Duma, Miliukóv, as leader of the Cadets, was recognized as the chief spokesman of the parliamentary opposition to the government. Almost from the start the Duma became the scene of forensic battles. A demand was made that amnesty be immediately granted to all political prisoners. Committees were appointed to investigate the charges of corruption in the conduct of the Russo-Japanese War. Bills granting autonomy to Poland and Finland were favored by overwhelming majorities. To all of these demands the government gave flat refusals or evasive replies. The Duma soon found itself impotent to accomplish any vital reforms, as the Tsar had no inclination to allow a representative body to assume the reins of power. Never before in the history of Russia were the shortcomings of the autocracy so freely discussed. Scathing denunciations of the government were delivered by impassioned orators who demanded an accounting for the brutal and illegal acts of the officials.

Conflicts between Tsar and Duma

A conflict over the question of land reform arose between the Duma and the government. The former demanded more land for the peasants through sales of the state lands and of some of the large estates. On July 21 a manifesto was issued by Nicholas which declared that the Duma was meddling with affairs which were not its concern, and that its refusal to "coöperate" with the government was "a cruel disappointment to him." He then ordered its dissolution and the election of another Duma.

Dissolution of the Duma

A critical moment had now arrived. Would the Russian people rise in case the Duma defied the Tsar? About half of the members retired to Viborg, in Finland, where they drew up a The Viborg manifesto to the people, exhorting them to refuse taxes Manifesto and military service to the government which was flouting parliament. But there was no organized response on the part of the people. The signers of the Viborg Manifesto were prosecuted for conspiracy.

A well-known reactionary, Stolypin, was appointed Premier. He was determined to restore the lost power of the autocracy by rendering the Duma innocuous. What surprised and frightened the government was the revolutionary attitude of the peasants who, for centuries, had been so docile and so obedient. Something must be done to placate them. Accordingly, half of the redemption dues for 1906 were remitted; in the following year they were entirely abolished. The peasant was no longer the Agrarian re- "serf of the State." In 1906, a notable agrarian law form was decreed by the Tsar, which instituted a fundamental change in the relations of the peasants to the mir. It provided for the right of a peasant to withdraw from the mir at pleasure, and thereupon to receive his allotment of land, which must be given to him, not in strips, but in solid fields. Many peasants became proprietors in the full sense of the term, but they continued to observe the customs and traditions of the mir under which they had lived for many generations. The land law was the work of Stolypin whose aim was to establish a large number of peasant proprietors who, as in France, would be inclined toward conservatism because of their property interests. As no more land was given to the peasants, those who could not make a living from their farms now had the opportunity of selling them to their neighbors. The agrarian reform had the effect of introducing class divisions in the villages. A number of well-to-do peasants appeared, who had bought the land of those who wished to leave the mir, often very cheaply. The *kulak* (Russian, *fist*), as the rich peasant was called, was disliked by the poor peasant, who regarded him as a hard man who took advantage of the misfortunes of his neighbors.

In the elections for the second Duma, Stolypin exerted govern- ment influence in favor of "official" candidates. But The second it was even more anti-government than its predecessor. Duma Many "S—D" and "S—R" candidates were elected; this time

the latter had participated in the elections.   The second Duma
met in 1907; after a stormy life of 104 days, it was dissolved on the
ground that its composition was unsatisfactory.   A government
manifesto declared that the two Dumas did not truly represent
the Russian people because of the "imperfections of the electoral
law which enabled men who were not representatives of the needs
and desires of the people to be elected to membership."   The Tsar
made an open declaration that he had the right to make and un-
make laws, "as it was God who bestowed upon us our power of
autocrat, and before His altar that we shall answer for the destinies
of the Russian state."

A new electoral law was promulgated by the Tsar which established an electoral system on the model of that in Prussia.   The
The third   population was divided into four classes, landowners,
Duma   merchants, peasants, and workingmen; to each was
allotted a certain number of members in electoral colleges that
chose the representatives to the Duma.   The landowners got 60
per cent of the electors; the peasants, 22 per cent; the merchants,
15 per cent; and the workingmen, only 3 per cent.   As was expected, the third Duma, which met in 1907, contained an overwhelming majority of reactionaries and Octobrists with a sprinkling
of "Cadets."   In this "landowners' Duma," the Tsar finally got
an assembly which did not "cruelly disappoint" him.

The autocracy was again in the saddle, and a counter-revolution
was begun under Stolypin.   He grimly determined to snuff out the
Reaction   flickering flames of revolution.   Thousands were sum-
under   marily executed.   Processions of exiles to Siberia were
Stolypin   once more resumed.   An old revolutionist, Nicholas
Tchaikovsky, was arrested on charges based upon acts committed
thirty years before.   A remarkable old woman, Katherine Breshkov-
sky, known as "the little grandmother of the Revolution," was sent
to Siberia at the age of seventy.   The terrorists of reaction, the
"Black Hundreds," once more organized pogroms.   Stolypin was
hated, much as Plehve had been, and many attempts were made
on his life.   In 1911, he was assassinated, but his successors continued the same policies.

In 1912, elections took place for the fourth Duma.   As in the case
of its predecessor the reactionaries were successful.   Stolypin's ruthless policy had stamped out all opposition.   At last the voice of revolution was stilled, and, for a time at least, peace reigned in Russia.

REASONS FOR THE FAILURE OF THE REVOLUTION

The Russian Revolution of 1905 failed in its main object of establishing a thoroughly constitutional régime. There was not only universal disappointment, but also astonishment at the outcome. The autocracy, discredited by the humiliating defeat inflicted by Japan, by corruption and incompetence at home, by weakness in the face of revolution, nevertheless did manage to cope successfully with the greatest popular uprising since the French Revolution. Several explanations may here be offered tentatively, as the event is as yet too near to be comprehended fully.

In the first place, the loyalty of the army was a matter of vital importance to the government. Under the system of huge standing armies, based upon conscription, it is well-nigh (1) Loyalty impossible for a rebellion to succeed unless it has the of the army support of the military. Louis XVI had but a small army to defend his throne, but Nicholas II had the support of a vast military machine which, in spite of mutinies here and there, rallied loyally to his side. Most faithful of all were the Cossacks, who formed a special "rough rider" contingent in the Russian army. Although Russians they lived apart from their fellow countrymen in a semi-tribal state. Hence, they were not bound by social, cultural, and economic ties to the rest of the Russian people; their chief interest was to fight for the Tsar by whom they were favored. These savage warriors were always used when the government resolved upon severe measures, as their well-known cruelty excited terror and dismay.

As Russia was a vast domain with poor means of communication and inhabited by a heterogeneous population, it was difficult for the opponents of the autocracy to organize their forces (2) Lack of effectively. There was no central revolutionary organ- efficient ization to direct the movement, to plan attacks when organization most propitious, and to confront the government at every turn with a well-thought-out plan of opposition. What really occurred was a series of sporadic uprisings without effective leadership and without sufficient direction, desperate and dangerous, it is true, but not difficult to suppress by a determined autocracy having a large army and the savage Cossacks at its command.

Foreign peoples hailed with enthusiasm the uprising against tsarism, but not so foreign governments. Austria was fearful lest

the uprising would spread across her border.   The Kaiser, as a
(3) Support   fellow autocrat, was naturally sympathetic with the
of foreign   Tsar, and stood ready to give him military aid if
governments   necessary.   At this time Germany was eager to form an
alliance with Russia, therefore she showed every possible friendli-
ness to Nicholas.   The German authorities were active in seizing
escaping revolutionaries whom they turned over to the Russian
officials.   It was republican France, however, that rendered the
greatest aid to the tottering autocracy.   Russia was financially
exhausted as a result of the war with Japan and of the revolutionary
movement.   Without money for the army the autocracy was
doomed.   In 1906, the Tsar sent Witte to Paris to negotiate a large
loan with the French government.   France was fearful lest an overturn in Russia would lead to the disruption of the Dual Alliance,[1]
and she, therefore, agreed to float a Russian loan.   Witte bribed the
Paris newspapers, who began a propaganda in favor of a popular
subscription.   The Russian revolutionists warned all foreign governments and foreign bankers not to loan money to the Tsar.   The
Viborg Manifesto declared that all loans "contracted without the
consent of the people's representatives will not be considered valid
by the Russian people who will never acknowledge them and
never pay them."   But the Tsar got the money.

There was another, and more important cause for the failure of
the Russian Revolution.   In the beginning of the movement, all
(4) Division   the opponents of the autocracy, from the most mod-
among the   erate liberal to the most violent terrorist, united to
revolution-   present a solid front to the government.   The tempo-
ists   rary collapse of tsarism as a result of the general strike
and its complete surrender, as shown by the October Manifesto,
encouraged the extreme element among the revolutionists to believe
that the time had now come for a redistribution of property as
well as of political power.   Many violent strikes occurred in which
factories were burned, and their owners maltreated.   The capitalists replied with a series of lockouts, and thousands of men were
thrown out of work.   On the heels of a half-accomplished Revolution, a serious struggle was going on between capital and labor.
The middle classes, hitherto opposed to the government, were
frightened at this turn of affairs.   They hated the autocracy, but
they hated still more to lose their property; hence, many now rallied

[1] See page 691.

to the side of the Tsar. The government took advantage of the division in the ranks of its opponents, and quickly recovered its courage and energy. It is, therefore, not surprising that the proletariat, weak in numbers and still weaker in organization, being now left alone to fight the battle with the autocracy, went down to swift destruction.

Not all of the gains made during the Revolution were lost during the reaction. Russia was now a constitutional state, even though the constitution was a poor protection against acts of despotism. There was now a parliament, even though Revolution it was unfairly chosen and limited in power. The results of the Revolution of 1905 in Russia were somewhat similar to those of the Revolution of 1848 in western Europe. By far the greatest outcome of the Revolution was the moral downfall of the autocracy. The masses were now less inclined than formerly to regard the Tsar reverently as the "Little Father" who had been commissioned by God to rule over them. The Revolution of 1905 was the first great step in their political education. It taught them in a highly dramatic manner that the autocracy, which they had long regarded as the special gift of God to his beloved Russia, was essentially brutal and selfish. Sullenly, the masses waited for the next opportunity to settle accounts with tsarism.

REFERENCES

REVOLUTIONARY MOVEMENT:

The most comprehensive study of the Russian revolutionary movement is that of L. Kulczycki, *Geschichte der russischen Revolution*, translated from the Polish, 3 vols. (1910–14), covers the period 1825–1900, the entire third volume being devoted to the socialist phase; the best brief account is in J. Mavor, *An Economic History of Russia* (ed. 1925), vol. II; Peter (Prince) Kropotkin, *Memoirs of a Revolutionist*, by the famous scholar-revolutionist, describes his early life as a landowner in Russia under Alexander II; S. Stepniak, pseudonym of a terrorist, gives vivid pictures of the revolutionary movement in the eighties and nineties in *Underground Russia* (1883), *Career of a Nihilist* (1901), and *King Stork and King Log* (1895); G. Kennan, *Siberia and the Exile System*, 2 vols. (1897), an account by an American journalist, a severe indictment of the exile system; Vera Figner, *Memoirs of a Revolutionist*, translated from the Russian (1927), describes terrorist activities in the eighties; A. S. Rappoport, *Pioneers of the Russian Revolution* (1919), from the Decembrists to the socialists; J. Martov, *Geschichte der russischen Sozial demokratie*, translated from the Russian (1926), by well-known Russian socialist; M. J. Olgin, *The Soul of the Russian Revolution* (1918), impressionistic interpretation of the

movements in 1905 and 1917; on the Russian Revolution of 1905: P.
Miliukóv: *Russia and its Crisis* (1905), an interpretation by the famous
Russian liberal; M. Kovalevsky, *La crise russe* (1906); Sir B. Pares,
Russia and Reform (1907), a good survey of Russia at the beginning of the
twentieth century; G. Alexinsky, *Modern Russia* (1913), by a socialist,
good for socialist parties; M. G. Hindus, *The Russian Peasant and the
Revolution* (1920), good for the attitude of the parties to the land question;
and *The Memoirs of Count Witte*, translated from the Russian (1921), the
recollections and impressions of the famous minister of Nicholas II.

For additional titles consult bibliographies at the end of Chapter XI.

ADDITIONAL REFERENCES

V. O. Kluchevsky, *A History of Russia*, Vol. V, trans. from the Russian
(1931); P. Miliukóv and others, *Histoire de Russie*, 3 vols. (1932–33);
G. T. Robinson, *Rural Russia under the Old Régime* (1932); R. Labry,
Alexandre Ivanovic Herzen (1928); J. Wuorinen, *Nationalism in Modern
Finland* (1931).

CHAPTER XXV

THE DISMEMBERMENT OF THE OTTOMAN EMPIRE

THE RUSSO-TURKISH WAR (1877–78)

THERE could be no permanent peace in the Balkans as long as the Christian nationalities remained subject to the Sultan. As the Greeks had been inspired to revolt by the French Revolution the Serbs, Bulgarians, and Rumanians were inspired by the unification movements in Italy and in Germany. After 1876 a wave of intense nationalism swept the Balkans, and the Near Eastern Question once more came to the front.

In 1876, a new sultan ascended the throne, Abdul Hamid II, who proved to be as cruel and despotic as he was cunning and resourceful, "a creature half fox, half rat." His reign was a story of uprisings, massacres, conspiracies, interventions, which became so intolerable that even the Turks finally revolted and deposed him. *Abdul Hamid II*

At the outset of his reign, Abdul Hamid faced an insurrection of the Bulgarians. Russia was active in fomenting discontent among them with a view of bringing about the disruption of Turkey. In 1876, the Bulgarians rose and killed many Turkish officials. Abdul Hamid realized *The Bulgarian atrocities* that unless the Bulgarians were severely punished his empire would disintegrate by a general uprising of the subject races, secretly aided by Russia. In desperation he resorted to fearful methods. Savage warriors, called Bashi-Bazouks, were turned loose on the Bulgarians who were slaughtered without mercy. These "Bulgarian atrocities" roused all Europe against Abdul Hamid. Gladstone came forward as the champion of the Christians, and denounced the "unspeakable Turk" in unqualified language. He demanded that England cease to support a power that was an "affront to the laws of God," and that the Turks "one and all, bag and baggage" should be forced to "clear out of the province that they have desolated and profaned."

The uprising of the Bulgarians spread throughout the Peninsula, especially among the Slavic elements. Many Russians, out of sympathy with their "little Slav brothers," joined the insurgents.

Public sentiment in Russia demanded war against Turkey as the enemy of the Slavic race and of the Christian faith. Tsar Alexander II declared that the situation in the Balkans was intolerable, and that, unless Europe intervened promptly and firmly, Russia would act alone. Knowing well England's sensitiveness regarding Constantinople, Alexander positively stated that he did not have "the smallest wish or intention to possess Constantinople."

Russia champions the Bulgarians

But Europe acted neither promptly nor firmly; therefore, in 1877, Russia declared war against Turkey. Russian armies moved swiftly forward into Bulgaria, and laid siege to Plevna, a great fortress which commanded the passes of the Balkans. After a stubborn siege lasting five months, Plevna surrendered. Russian armies now poured through the Balkans, captured Adrianople, and prepared to march on Constantinople. But the Sultan decided to sue for peace.

The Russo-Turkish War

The Treaty of San Stefano (1878), signed by Russia and Turkey, recognized the independence of Serbia, Montenegro, and Rumania; and established a new state, "Greater Bulgaria," consisting of Bulgaria, Rumelia, and Macedonia. Of all his European territory the Sultan was allowed to keep only Constantinople and its vicinity and Albania. Had this treaty been carried out, the Near Eastern Question might have then been solved, as Turkish rule would virtually have ceased in Europe. But great objections were raised to this settlement by the Greeks and Serbians, who opposed the creation of a "Greater Bulgaria" because they wanted parts of Macedonia for themselves. Far more serious was the opposition that came from England and Austria. The former did not propose to sit tamely by and see Turkey dismembered to the advantage of Russia, who would, in all likelihood, dominate the new states which her arms had brought into existence. Austria, on her part, was ambitious to get a port on the Ægean, perhaps Saloniki, which the Treaty of San Stefano put out of her reach. "Greater Bulgaria" was a violation of an agreement that she had made with Russia to prevent the establishment of a large state in the Balkans. The powers decided to save vanquished Turkey from triumphant Russia by refusing to accept the treaty. Tsar Alexander was plainly told that the Balkan situation was a matter that affected all of Europe; hence, it could be settled only by a congress of the powers, who would

Intervention of the powers

declare war against Russia unless she submitted the whole matter to the judgment of an international convention. Russia felt obliged to yield.

A congress of the powers met in Berlin in 1878. Once more, as at Vienna and at Paris, assembled Europe sat in judgment over questions affecting the Continent. To the Congress of Berlin came the most famous statesmen of the day; Bismarck, who was its president; Disraeli, who scored diplomatic triumphs as England's envoy; and Prince Gortchakov, who came as the champion of Russia. The Treaty of San Stefano was totally disregarded by the Congress, which proceeded to make quite another settlement of the Near Eastern Question.

The Congress of Berlin

Like the Congress of Vienna, the Congress of Berlin was concerned chiefly with "strategical rectification of frontiers" rather than with legitimate national aspiration. In the assignment of territory little regard was paid to national claims when these claims conflicted with the interests of the powers. Even before the Congress met, secret arrangements had been made: one between England and Turkey promised Cyprus to the former; another between Austria and England promised Bosnia-Herzegovina to Austria; France was assured that her status in Egypt and Syria would not be subject to debate. The Congress was also the scene of an important realignment of the powers.[1]

The main provisions of the Treaty of Berlin were as follows: Montenegro, Serbia, and Rumania were declared entirely independent of Turkey. "Greater Bulgaria" was split into three parts: Bulgaria proper was made an autonomous principality with the Sultan as her suzerain; Eastern Rumelia was given "administrative autonomy" under a Christian governor; and Macedonia was allowed to remain a part of Turkey. To Austria-Hungary was given the right to occupy and to administer Bosnia-Herzegovina, which continued to be legally part of Turkey. England was given the right to occupy the island of Cyprus. Russia was allowed to retain the towns of Batum, Ardahan, and Kars in the Caucasus which she had conquered, and to take a strip of Bessarabia[2] from Rumania in exchange for

The Treaty of Berlin (1878)

---

[1] See page 687.

[2] During the eighteenth century Bessarabia, inhabited chiefly by Rumanians and Russians, was the object of a struggle between Russia and Turkey; in 1812, it became definitely Russian. During the nineteenth century the region was a subject of dispute between Russia and Rumania. In 1856, the Congress of Paris gave a strip of Bessarabia to Moldavia, then under Turkish suzerainty.

Dobrudja taken from Turkey. The Congress recommended that Turkey give Thessaly and part of Epirus to Greece, which Turkey did later, in 1881. To the Sultan was still left considerable territory in Europe: Albania, Macedonia, and Thrace. After taking away about half of her European territory, the powers again solemnly guaranteed the "integrity of Turkey."

The Treaty of Berlin did not at all solve the Near Eastern Question. The states that were freed from the rule of the Sultan

Discontent with the Berlin settlement were embittered because they were not given the frontiers that they had demanded. Irridentist movements began, known as Greater Bulgaria, Greater Serbia, Greater Rumania, and Greater Greece, which aimed to redeem the lands under foreign rule. Bulgaria, especially, was disappointed, and began preparing for the recovery of the "Greater Bulgaria" of San Stefano. England, in the words of Disraeli, achieved "peace with honor" in settling the affairs of Turkey; but time was to prove that she "put her money on the wrong horse." Austria now entered prominently into Balkan affairs. It was through her influence that Serbia was separated from her sister state, Montenegro, by a tongue of Turkish land, Novi Bazaar. Serbia was infuriated with the disposition of Bosnia-Herzegovina, inhabited by people of her race. A hatred arose between Serbia and Austria which was fraught with ominous consequences for the history of Europe. Germany, as yet, took no interest in Turkey. In the opinion of Bismarck the whole Near Eastern Question was not worth "the bones of a Pomeranian grenadier." As president of the Congress he contented himself with playing the part of "an honest broker" among the powers by acting as intermediary between the various claimants.

In spite of its shortcomings the Congress of Berlin did accomplish, to a considerable degree, the dismemberment of Turkey in Europe. There were now five Christian states in the Balkans who were ready to aid their kinsmen that were still subjects of the Sultan. The "sick man of Europe" was surrounded by expectant heirs.

BULGARIA (1878-1912)

Bulgaria owed her existence to Russia, who regarded the newly created Balkan state as her special protégé. On the suggestion of the Tsar, Alexander of Battenberg was made Prince of Bulgaria in

1879. A liberal constitution was adopted, establishing a parliament elected by universal, manhood suffrage. Most of the Russians, who directed Bulgarian policies to suit the Tsar, which greatly irritated patriotic Bulgarians, who did not wish to be dominated even by their deliverers. A nationalist party was formed that demanded freedom of Bulgaria from Russian influence. The political history of the country for a generation was largely concerned with the struggles of the Russian and the nationalist parties for the control of the government.

Dominance of Russia

In 1885, Eastern Rumelia flouted the Treaty of Berlin, and joined Bulgaria. The union displeased Russia, who did not wish to see her protégé become so strong that she would be able to manage without her protection. Tsar Alexander III, thereupon, withdrew the Russian officers from the Bulgarian army, which seriously crippled it. Serbia, ever the watchful foe of Bulgaria, immediately declared war, but the Bulgarians defeated the Serbs and compelled them to sue for peace.

War between Bulgaria and Serbia

Prince Alexander had aroused the enmity of the Russian party which, in 1886, succeeded in forcing him to abdicate. A dynastic crisis arose that distracted the country. The Nationalist Party raised the cry of "Bulgaria for Bulgarians." Its candidate for the throne, a German Prince, Ferdinand of Saxe-Coburg, was chosen Prince of Bulgaria by parliament (1887). Ferdinand greatly relied upon the leader of the Nationalists, Stambulov, who was the uncompromising foe of Russian interference. Stambulov became known as the "Bulgarian Bismarck" because of the thoroughness with which he reorganized the government, and because of his ruthless suppression of opposition to his rule. The many enemies that he made conspired to destroy him, and, in 1895, they succeeded in having him assassinated.

Stambulov

Bulgaria was ambitious, above all else, to be an independent nation, free from the Tsar's interference and from the Sultan's suzerainty. In 1908, she declared her complete independence of Turkey. As a sign of her new dignity, Bulgaria proclaimed herself a "kingdom," and Ferdinand took the title of king.

RUMANIA (1878-1912)

From the time of their conquest by the Turks, the Rumanians in Moldavia and Wallachia were directly ruled by native princes,

who were vassals of the Sultan.   Both provinces wished to be
Cuza   united and free of Turkey; in 1859, each province
             elected Alexander Cuza as its prince.   Three years later,
both provinces were completely united under one government
with Cuza as "Prince of Rumania," and the problem of unity
was solved.   Cuza proved to be a radical reformer.   He freed the
peasants from feudal dues, and confiscated the property of the
monasteries.   His reforms incurred the hostility of the nobility
and clergy who, in 1866, forced him to abdicate.   As his successor
they chose a member of the Roman Catholic branch of the House
of Hohenzollern who became Charles I, Prince of Rumania.

When the Russo-Turkish War broke out, Rumania promptly
joined Russia.   She was rewarded by the Congress of Berlin in
Independ-   being recognized as an independent nation.   The
ence   problem of freedom was now solved.   In 1881, Rumania declared herself a "kingdom."

Although a foreigner Charles was popular with his subjects.   He
was given large powers under the constitution which provided for
King Charles a parliament, organized on the Prussian model with a
              class system of voting.   Charles was an able and con-
scientious ruler, and he succeeded in introducing a high degree of
efficiency in the administration and the army.

One of the serious problems confronting Rumania was that concerning the Jews.   She was the only Balkan state that had a
The Jewish   considerable number of Jews, who constituted virtu-
problem   ally the middle class of the country.   In recognizing
the independence of Rumania, the Congress of Berlin stipulated
that equality be granted to all citizens irrespective of their religious
beliefs, a provision adopted to protect the interests of the Jews.
But Rumania ignored it, and adopted a law which classed Jews
as aliens, and therefore not entitled to the privileges of citizenship.
The persecution of the Jews which followed caused many of them
to emigrate to the United States.

Another serious problem was that concerning the land.   Most
of the land was in the hands of large proprietors, called "boyars,"
The Agra-   which caused great discontent among the peasantry.
rian problem In 1907, a peasant uprising took place against the
boyars and their agents, which was so widespread that the government became alarmed.   A large army was required to restore
order.   The government put through agrarian reforms which, for
a time, allayed discontent.

GREECE (1832-1912)

At the beginning of her national life Greece was a devastated, poverty-stricken land with less than a million inhabitants. Two great problems faced the Greek people: to reorganize their country on a sound economic and political basis and to acquire the parts of Turkey inhabited by Greeks. Problems of Greece

King Otto was hailed with enthusiasm on his accession to the throne. But his popularity did not last long, due to the fact that he, being a Bavarian, filled the highest offices with his fellow countrymen. Had the Greeks overthrown the rule of the Turks in order to come under the rule of Bavarians? In order to avoid an uprising, Otto granted a liberal constitution (1844), which won him a new lease of power. Great disappointment was felt at the outcome of the Crimean War; the Congress of Paris gave no territory to Greece who had hoped to acquire Thessaly. King Otto became very unpopular, and, in 1862, he was forced to abdicate. In the following year a Danish prince was chosen king under the name of George I. The constitution was then radically revised, and the government was put under the control of a parliament of one house, elected by universal, manhood suffrage. King Otto

The territory of Greece was enlarged, in 1864, by the acquisition of the Ionian Islands, ceded to her by England; and, in 1881, by the acquisition of Thessaly from Turkey. Nevertheless, fully one half of the Greek people were still under Turkish rule, distributed through Macedonia, Epirus, the islands of the Ægean Sea, and Asia Minor. A pan-Hellenic movement, known as the "Great Idea," was organized with the purpose of wresting these lands from the Sultan. Some of the more enthusiastic patriots dreamed of taking Constantinople itself and of reëstablishing the old Byzantine Empire under Greek auspices. Crete, inhabited almost entirely by Greeks, made many attempts to throw off Turkish rule. In order to aid the Cretans, Greece, in 1897, declared war against the Sultan, but she was badly defeated. The "Great Idea"

A remarkable figure, Eleutherios Venizelos, appeared as the leader of the Pan-Hellenic movement. Venizelos was a Cretan who had taken an active part in arousing the island against the Turk. In 1910, he became Prime Minister of Greece, and was soon recognized as the leading statesman in the Balkans. Venizelos

SERBIA AND MONTENEGRO (1878-1912)

Even before the revolt of the Greeks, the Serbs had risen against the Turks. In 1804, an uprising took place under a popular hero, Kara George and Milosh Obrenovitch named Kara George. At first the Serbs won their independence; but they were later reconquered by the Turks. In 1815, another nationalist movement took place under another popular hero, Milosh Obrenovitch, who was an enemy of Kara George. Milosh induced the Sultan to grant concessions to the Serbs who, in 1830, were given local autonomy with Milosh as their hereditary prince.

But the Obrenovitch dynasty found bitter opponents in the descendants of Kara George who claimed the throne. The political Dynastic feuds history of Serbia during the nineteenth century was largely a narrative of dynastic feuds that raged violently between the Karageorgevitches and the Obrenovitches, Plots, assassinations, and uprisings were common occurrences in Serbian affairs, and the possession of the crown oscillated between the two dynasties.

Prince Milan, an Obrenovitch, assumed the more dignified title of king in 1882. He ruled as an absolute monarch, supported Rule of Obrenovitch dynasty by the aristocratic party and by Austrian influences. The unsuccessful war with Bulgaria, in 1885, made the King very unpopular, and he sought to conciliate his disaffected subjects by granting a liberal constitution. But dissatisfaction was not allayed by this concession, and he was forced to abdicate in favor of his son, who succeeded to the throne as Alexander I (1889).

The new king was even more autocratic than his father. He disregarded the constitution, and inaugurated a period of personal Assassination of Alexander rule. He was strongly supported by Austrian influences which now dominated Serbian policies. A pro-Russian party organized a conspiracy against Alexander in which the leading spirits were army officers. Domestic policy was chiefly concerned with the problem whether Russia or Austria would control the affairs of Serbia. In 1903, the world was shocked to learn of a tragedy in Belgrade; King Alexander and his wife were suddenly assassinated. A Karageorgevitch, named Peter, was proclaimed King.

The assassination had important diplomatic consequences. Austrian influences in Serbia waned because Peter's policies were

pro-Russian. Serbia now succeeded Bulgaria as the protégé of
the Tsar. A vigorous anti-Austrian policy was in- Serbia's
augurated with the object of annexing Bosnia-Herze- anti-
govina. Patriotic Serb societies carried on an active Austrian policies
propaganda in these provinces to the great anxiety of
the Austrian authorities. In retaliation Austria began a tariff war
on Serbia by excluding her exports, mainly swine and farm products. As Serbian trade was mainly with Austria, the "pig war"
of 1905 brought great hardship to the Serbs and still further embittered them against Austria. When, in 1908, Austria announced
the formal annexation of Bosnia-Herzegovina, the Serbs were infuriated to the point of war; it required the restraining hand of
Russia to prevent an instant outbreak of hostilities.[1]

The other Serb nation, Montenegro, was for many years an
autonomous state in the Ottoman Empire. After her independence was recognized by the Congress of Berlin, Monte- Montenegro
negro was ruled autocratically by Prince Nicholas; it
was not until 1905 that he granted a constitution establishing a
parliamentary régime. In 1910, Nicholas, although the ruler of
the smallest state in the Balkans, assumed the title of king.

TURKEY (1878–1912)

Turkey came out of the Congress of Berlin greatly reduced in
size, but she was still a European power, and one to be reckoned
with. In spite of solemn promises to reform, Abdul Turkey un-
Hamid's régime continued to be corrupt, incompetent, repentant
and tyrannical. Turkey was beaten but unrepentant. For a
generation the wily Sultan managed to avoid foreign intervention
by playing off one Christian power against another, knowing full
well that the nations of Europe were far more interested in advancing their own interests than in the fate of his Christian subjects,
about whom they pretended to be so solicitous.

Disorder was rife in Macedonia, where rival bands of Bulgarians,
Serbs, Rumanians, and Greeks, aided by their compatriots from
without, made war on the Turks and upon each other. The Ar-
Innocent travelers were frequently sufferers from these menian
brigand-patriots, who infested the mountains and who massacres
were not averse to robbing any one who came their way. In
Albania the warlike mountaineers were ever ready to rise in re-

[1] See page 702.

bellion at the approach of the Turkish tax collectors.   In Constantinople plots were being continually hatched against Abdul Hamid and his régime.   In 1894, the world was shocked by wholesale massacres of the Armenians, who were suspected of being implicated in these plots.   Thousands of men, women, and children were cruelly slaughtered by the fanatical Kurds whose religious zeal was fanned into a flame by the Turkish authorities.   Once more the world, and especially England, gave vent to moral indignation at the slaughter of these Christians who had no country of their own to defend them.

During the period following the Congress of Berlin a great change was taking place in the attitude of the European powers toward Turkey.   Russia, disappointed with the outcome of the Russo-Turkish War, shifted her chief interest from the Near to the Far East, hoping to find a "window on the Pacific."   However, she kept an eye on the Near East in order to maintain her prestige with the "little Slav brothers."   England, the traditional upholder of Turkish integrity, began to abate her interest in the Near Eastern Question because the acquisition of Cyprus, Egypt, and the Suez Canal safeguarded her route to India.

Russia and England lose interest in the Balkans

A new power, Germany, now came prominently on the Balkan scene and quickly assumed the leading rôle in Ottoman affairs.   On the retirement of Bismarck, the German attitude toward the Balkans was reversed; the former indifference gave place to an intense interest in the fate of Turkey.   The goal of Germany's ambitions lay, not in European, but in Asiatic Turkey, where she planned to secure economic control of Anatolia and Mesopotamia, which offered a rich field for the investment of German capital.   To get concessions to exploit this region, studied efforts were made by the Germans to cultivate the friendship of the Turks.   In 1883, General von der Goltz, a German, was appointed by the Sultan to reorganize the Turkish army.   The Kaiser paid several visits to Abdul Hamid, and fervently proclaimed himself the friend of the Mohammedans. An able diplomat, Marschall von Bieberstein, was the German ambassador to Turkey for over a decade.   He achieved great success in establishing German influence in the conduct of the Sultan's policies.   The first important gain made by Germany was a concession to her capitalists to build the Bagdad Railway.[1]

Germany, interested in the Near East

[1] See page 635.

Abdul Hamid's régime was arousing great discontent, and uprisings were constantly taking place. The finances were in such a bad condition that the government was always verging The Young on bankruptcy. Promises of reform were often made Turks and as often disregarded. Many patriotic Turks began to realize that any day might witness the spontaneous dissolution of their country, so great was the disorder, incompetence, and corruption. At last a movement to reform the government appeared among the Turks themselves. A group, known as the "Young Turks," advocated radical reforms in the hope of rejuvenating their country by introducing Western ideas, methods, and institutions. Many of the younger generation had been educated in the schools of western Europe, particularly in those of France, where they had imbibed modern ideas.

Secret societies were organized, the most famous of which was the Committee of Union and Progress, that conducted an active revolutionary movement. The Young Turks, realiz- The Turkish ing that it was necessary to win over the army, con- Revolution ducted their propaganda among the officers, and induced many of them to join the movement. With a swiftness and sureness that astonished the world, the Committee of Union and Progress, backed by the army, overthrew the autocracy in 1908. The constitution of 1876 [1] was proclaimed and the Sultan was compelled to issue a call for the election of a parliament, on the basis of universal, manhood suffrage, irrespective of religion and of race. When the first Turkish parliament assembled, many felt that a new era had dawned in the Empire. It contained representatives of the various races and faiths who met in concord and proceeded to inaugurate new policies. But this situation did not at all suit Abdul Hamid who plotted to overthrow parliament. He was promptly deposed, and his brother proclaimed Sultan.

Great was the joy felt over the fall of Abdul Hamid. The terror which, for so many years, had hung over the inhabitants of the Empire vanished with the fall of the dread Sultan. Freedom of speech, of the press, and of assembly was granted; Mohammedans, Jews, and Christians were declared equal before the law; Christians were now admitted into the army, hitherto restricted to the Mohammedans. A new era had indeed opened for Turkey, with lib-

---

[1] On his accession, in 1876, Abdul Hamid had proclaimed a constitution, which he abrogated two years later.

erty, equality, and fraternity for all the races and religions under the Ottoman flag.

The Young Turks were intense believers in nationalism. They centralized the administration, established a system of national schools, and removed the privileges as well as the disabilities of the various races. By these reforms they hoped to generate a spirit of patriotism among the diverse elements so that the government would no longer have to appeal to the religious sentiment of the Mohammedans. The Young Turks also wished to free their country from the interference of foreign nations in its internal affairs. They chafed under the Capitulations,[1] and began to abrogate them, which aroused the hostility of the powers. The new régime looked with friendly eyes toward England because she was considered the chief supporter of liberal government. Germany, being regarded as the supporter of the old régime, lost her ascendancy for a time.

Nationalism of the Young Turks

But the era of good feeling was destined to last only a short time. The various races did not wish to be Ottomanized, and they vigorously resisted the nationalistic tendencies of the Young Turks. For centuries they had lived a life apart, with their own customs, language, and laws, protected by special laws. To give them up in return for "equality" might make matters much worse. They had hailed the downfall of Abdul Hamid with delight, expecting still more privileges from the new régime; now they feared the liberty of the Young Turks far more than they had the tyranny of the old Sultan. What they really wanted was to join their kinsmen across the borders, to which the Young Turks objected just as vigorously as had Abdul Hamid.

Opposition to Turkish nationalism

The powers were not over-eager to see Turkey reformed; evil conditions furnished them with pretexts to intervene. Taking advantage of the confusion caused by the Turkish Revolution, Bulgaria repudiated Turkish suzerainty, and Austria annexed Bosnia-Herzegovina. In 1911, Italy declared war against Turkey, and seized Tripoli. The Young Turks were alarmed lest Turkey be dismembered in spite of her rejuvenation. They repented of their liberalism, and revived the methods and policies of Abdul Hamid. Germany now came forward as the champion of Turkish integrity; and, once more, her influence gained ascendance at Constantinople.

Reaction in Turkey

[1] See page 159.

THE BALKAN WARS (1912–13)

The Balkan nations, long divided by jealousies and rival ambitions, saw their opportunity in the distracted state of Turkey. In 1912, Greece, Bulgaria, Serbia, and Montenegro, with The Balkan the secret support of Russia, formed an alliance with alliance the object of making war upon their ancient enemy. The powers, who had just been on the brink of war on account of Morocco, were consequently in no mood for another international crisis; they, therefore, warned the Allies that no territorial changes would be permitted in European Turkey. But the Allies flouted the warning, and sent an ultimatum to the Sultan demanding local autonomy for Macedonia. The ultimatum was refused, and war followed.

Turkey was attacked on four sides at the same time, as the movements of the Allies were well coördinated. The Montenegrins invaded Albania; the Serbians, northern Macedonia; the The first Bulgarians, Thrace; and the Greeks, southern Mace- Balkan War donia. By far the best army of the Allies was that of the Bulgarians who won a great victory over the Turks at the battle of Lule Burgas. The Serbs defeated the Turks in several engagements, and entered the seaport of Durazzo, in Albania. No less successful were the Greeks, who captured Saloniki. There was great astonishment in Europe at the successes of the Allies, whose soldiers were generally considered far inferior in fighting power to the Turks. The year 1913 brought more notable victories to the Allies. An army of Bulgarians and Serbs captured Adrianople: and an army of Montenegrins captured Scutari, a great fortress in Albania. Turkey was overcome by defeat, and sued for peace.

A conference met in London, and adopted a treaty which practically ousted Turkey from Europe. She was com- Turkey sues pelled to cede to the Allies all her European territory, for peace except Constantinople and the adjacent region, which lay between the Sea of Marmora and the line connecting Midia on the Black Sea with Enos on the Ægean. Crete was given to Greece. The status of the islands in the Ægean and that of Albania were left for a later decision.

Far more difficulty was experienced by the Allies in partitioning the estate of the "sick man of Europe" than in con- Division quering him. A bitter quarrel arose as to the share of among the each. What aggravated the situation was the inter- Allies vention of the powers whose ambitions in the Balkans confronted those of the Allies. Russia supported Serbia's demand for Albania. But Austria opposed it because she feared that a "Greater" Serbia would menace her existence. Bulgaria demanded all of Macedonia as her prize. But her demand was opposed by Greece, by Rumania, and by Serbia, all of whom desired to share in this booty.

A second Balkan War broke out, this time between Bulgaria and her erstwhile allies. Hostile armies began to converge on Bulgaria The second from three directions, Serbs and Montenegrins from Balkan War the west, Greeks from the south, and Rumanians from the north. Several battles were fought in which the Bulgarians were defeated. The Turks, taking advantage of the dissensions, reopened hostilities, and recaptured Adrianople. Bulgaria was overwhelmed, and signed the Treaty of Bucharest which deprived her of nearly all the territory that she had won from Turkey. The new arrangements provided for the following territorial changes: Greece got the largest share, southern Macedonia, including the rich prize of Saloniki, and Crete; Serbia, part of Macedonia and half of Novi Bazaar; Montenegro got the other half of Novi Bazaar; Bulgaria got part of Macedonia and western Thrace, which was considerably less than the gain of Greece or that of Serbia; Rumania got a strip on the Black Sea, ceded to her by Bulgaria. By the Treaty of Constantinople between Turkey and Bulgaria, the former doubled the European territory left to her by the Treaty of London; Adrianople and eastern Thrace were given back to the Sultan.

A thorny problem in the new Balkan settlement was Albania. Both Serbia and Greece were ambitious to divide the province Problem of between them, but strenuous objections were raised by Albania Austria who feared that the expansion of Serbia would permanently block her march to the Ægean; and by Italy, who was ambitious to control the lands bordering on the Adriatic. Both Austria and Italy favored "autonomy" for Albania, each hoping to draw the region under her influence in order to control the Adriatic. Austria demanded that the Serbs evacuate the places that they had conquered in Albania. A European crisis was almost precipitated by the Albanian question, but the Serbs were induced to accede to the demands of Austria. Albania was organized as an independent principality with a German prince as ruler.

The Balkan Wars solved the Near Eastern Question so far as Turkey was concerned; her territory in Europe was virtually dis-

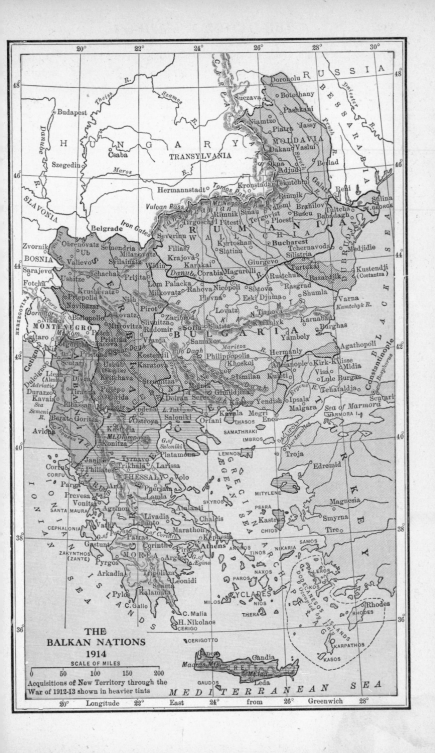

THE
BALKAN NATIONS
1914

SCALE OF MILES

0   50   100   150   200

Acquisitions of New Territory through the
War of 1912-13 shown in heavier tints

20°   Longitude   22°   East   24°   from   26°   Greenwich   28°

membered. But they left behind a legacy of hatred and distrust which was to have momentous consequences. Bulgaria cherished deep resentment against her neighbors for taking away the fruits of her victory. Serbia saw her dream of a Greater Serbia vanish because of Austria's interference. She hated Austria as the power that blocked the union of the Yugo-Slavs as she had once blocked the union of the Germans and of the Italians. Backed by Russia she began a propaganda among the Yugo-Slavs in the Dual Monarchy to detach them from their allegiance to the Hapsburgs. The dismemberment of Turkey brought out vividly the conditions in the Dual Monarchy where, as in the Sultan's former domains, diverse nationalities were striving for independence. Austria, therefore, clung all the more tightly to Germany to protect her from disruption.

Discontent with the peace settlement

The Balkan Wars produced several crises which threatened the peace of Europe.[1] During these crises Russia and England reappeared on the Balkan scene. Driven away from the Pacific by Japan, and halted on the way to the Persian Gulf by England, Russia returned to her old dream of getting Constantinople. England was now her friend,[2] and no longer barred the way. Turkey, however, found a powerful protector in Germany whose interests in Asia Minor bound her to defend the Sultan's domains. As champion of the Slav race, Russia now faced Austria who had succeeded Turkey as the oppressor of the Balkan Slavs. England's revived interest in the Near East was due to a new threat to India. The German plan to extend the Bagdad Railway to the Persian Gulf caused uneasiness in England. Might not German armies pour into Mesopotamia aided by a friendly Turkey? Might not a German fleet be stationed in the Gulf? If England was to safeguard the route to India she must wrest Turkey from the grip of Germany. Russia and England, who for long had battled against each other in the Balkans, now joined hands against Turkey, backed by Germany and Austria.

Reappearance of Russia and England

REFERENCES

On the Turkish Revolution: C. R. Buxton, *Turkey in Revolution* (1909); and R. Pinon, *L'Europe et la jeune Turquie* (1911); S. P. Duggan, *The*

Eastern Question (1902), excellent for diplomatic aspect; M. I. Newbigin, *Geographical Aspects of the Balkan Problems* (1915); H. N. Brailsford, *Macedonia: Its Races and Their Future* (1906); C. Phillipson and N. Buxton, *The Question of the Bosphorus and Dardanelles* (1917), advocate internationalization of the Straits; on Austria and the Balkans: T. von Sosnosky, *Die Balkanpolitik Oesterreich-Ungarns seit 1866*, 2 vols. (1913–14); G. M. Trevelyan, *The Servians and Austria* (1914); R. W. Seton-Watson, *The Southern Slav Question and the Habsburg Monarchy* (1911), *The Rise of Nationality in the Balkans* (1917), and *Sarajevo* (1916), sympathetic with the Yugo-Slavs; Sir Thomas Barclay, *The Turco-Italian War and its Problems* (1912), by a noted English diplomat; J. G. Schurman, *The Balkan Wars, 1912–1913* (1914); C. U. Clark, *United Roumania* (1922); R. W. Seton-Watson, *A History of the Roumanians from Roman Times to the Completion of Unity* (1934).

For additional titles consult bibliography at end of Chapter X; for advanced students, R. J. Kerner, *Slavic Europe: a selected bibliography in the Western European Languages* (1918).

PART III
SCIENTIFIC, SOCIAL, AND ECONOMIC MOVEMENTS

PART III

SCIENTIFIC, SOCIAL, AND ECONOMIC MOVEMENTS

THE progress of Europe during the nineteenth and twentieth centuries was often in disregard of national boundaries. Having more or less a common civilization because of the classical heritage and the Christian faith, Europe has been profoundly influenced by international ideas and movements. Science, especially, knew no barriers of race, nationality, religion, or region; the laboratory was the common meeting-place of all scientists whatever their origin. A discovery once made immediately became the common possession of mankind. With the spread of modern industry, social and economic movements became international in aim and even in organization. It now remains to describe those movements that emphasized the common life of the peoples of Europe.

CHAPTER XXVI

PROGRESS OF SCIENCE [1]

THE SCIENTIFIC REVOLUTION

THE nineteenth century, of all past centuries, was preëminently notable as the period in which man's scientific knowledge expanded and developed most remarkably. The evidence which is usually adduced to demonstrate this fact is familiar to everybody: it is that of the unprecedented achievements of modern technology. The nineteenth century saw, not only the successful development of the first steam engines, but also the invention and perfection of the dependent but uniquely adaptable electric dynamo, which magically extended the range of its usefulness to include the production and control of every type of physical energy, and that of the specially serviceable internal combustion engine, which made possible the generation of concentrated power in any location at will. At the same time there were discovered methods and devices for the economic production of fuels, steel and other material, which were necessary for the construction and maintenance of these engines, and for the building of those magnificent structures and intricate mechanisms which had been made possible by their employment: fleets and railroads, bridges and tunnels, great dams and canals, architectural constructions — all on an unprecedented scale; extensive systems of heating and lighting; agricultural, mining, textile, and other industrial machinery, and special tools both gross and delicate in bewildering variety — designed for the mass production of staple and experimental material continually improved or cheapened, or for the multiplication of novel instruments of convenience for individual use everywhere, to serve efficiency, security, economy, comfort, and pleasure. There were simultaneously established widespread systems of communication which depended, first, upon the accelerated service of railway and steamship, and later, upon the employment of instantaneous telegraphic and telephonic instruments. These facilities encouraged the development of a world-

Influence of mechanical inventions

---

[1] This chapter is contributed by Frederick Barry, Associate Professor of the History of Science, Columbia University.

embracing journalism, which cheap mechanical printing made universally available. At the beginning of the century, the vicarious experience of the untraveled man was slight and laboriously acquired: at its close, nothing but his native limitations stood in the way of his becoming a citizen of the world.

By such means, in the last decades of the century, the common needs of men were supplied in unlooked-for abundance with unanticipated ease. Hours of labor were shortened, and a new leisure secured; so that, in the degree that external conditions could determine it, the general well-being was greatly improved, not only by widespread alleviation of want and the attainment of an increased security against mischance and calamity, but by the establishment of better conditions of living for ordinary men, and by the provision of new interests and enjoyments, and new opportunities for general education, which a restimulated development of personal aptitude and resource encouraged, and novel conditions of life in some degree compelled.

The effects of the technical control of physical energies, however, by no means summarize the cultural advantages which the science Science and of the nineteenth century secured. The technology of medicine the physicist and chemist was matched by that of the biologist. The productivity of the fields was multiplied, not by systems of irrigation and chemical fertilization and agricultural machinery alone, but by the improvement of food-supplying plants through artificial breeding, by the understanding control of their growth, and by the protection of crops against the depredations of parasites. Wherever it was necessary, a similar control was then extended to the forests. A corresponding protection, based upon similarly acquired knowledge, was afforded man himself, by the extensive protection and purification of water supplies, by the hygienic improvement and systematic inspection of foodstuffs, and by the harmless disposition of sewage and waste. And, finally, this same knowledge not only thus and otherwise prevented the inception of many of those epidemic diseases which had been a scourge of all preceding ages, but afforded the means for a medicinal control of their ravages whenever they accidentally appeared; made possible a bold and seemingly miraculous surgery; established, in short, for the first time in the history of the world, the basis of a rational and dependable medicine, and stimulated also renewed and more promising efforts to extend its range toward the similar control of normal but erratic physiological and psychological processes.

Even such fragmentary recollection is sufficient to make it clearly evident that the instruments of power and advantage and the methods of biological control which the technical genius of the century invented and developed, made possible, and almost inevitable, a veritable cultural mutation. The full extent of this far-reaching change is never fully realized until its most obvious manifestations, those that have been thus far dwelt upon, are closely examined and their consequences traced; and its deeper significance is not apparent until their underlying causes are revealed. It is then perceived that the external — that is to say, the physical and physiological — transformation of the modern world, which daily stimulates our ingenuous wonder and simple pride, is only one aspect of a change which strikes far deeper and modifies profoundly, not physical and economical life alone, but throughout its individual and social range the life of imagination and intelligence, of morals and aspiration.

Science and culture

In perspective, the extensive control and utilization of natural energies which the science of the nineteenth century made possible provided, undoubtedly, the greatest advantage that man had yet secured in his age-long struggle for existence. Wherever the new Western culture extended and became a dominant influence, the ceaseless battle for survival, which throughout the ages had kept man bound to earth, provoked his ruthless warfare, and perpetuated the savage predispositions which kept him enslaved alike by brutish passion and superstitious dread, was so far mitigated that a released intelligence quite confidently promised to free him from its bondage. Inevitable death awaited each individual, but his average term of life was already greatly lengthened. The new and unfamiliar dangers which now beset him were more than offset by those which his altered habits of life eliminated. His adaptation to this new life was not yet wholly successful, for earlier habits, customs, and mental attitudes are not easily altered or controlled; and it was not the material condition of his civilization alone which had been changed: the whole internal complex of its social equilibrium had been overturned, and, from an historical point of view, rather suddenly.

The mere physical superiority of Western culture, moreover, insured its ultimate domination of the world. Under its rapidly ex-

panding influence, this world, with every improvement in transport
and communication, was more closely knit together—
in common metaphor, grew smaller. Its civilization
embraced an increasing number of diverse cultures
which were reconcilable with difficulty, and not at all excepting by
the profound modification of customs which had persisted for ages.
Practical intelligence, however, had been quickened by new knowledge, and the social barriers of arrogance and prejudice and fear
were already giving way to the unsentimental toleration which accompanies a mutually advantageous coöperative effort. The further implications of such facts as these need not be elaborated. It
is clear enough that the technology of the nineteenth century, which
effected this economic and social revolution, is the most important
single factor among all which together have determined the basic
conditions of present cultural tendencies throughout the world.

The deeper significance of this revolution is less commonly appreciated: quite naturally, since in common thought science and
technology are seldom clearly distinguished. A tech-
nologist, probably, would have no popular credentials
if he called himself such: our "wizards" of science, in fact, are all
inventors. A scientist, that is to say, is commonly conceived as one
who devotes his talents to the acquisition of special knowledge
which shall be useful in the practical arts. This excusable but
erroneous conception restricts the humanistic and historical understanding in two significant ways: first, by assigning to scientific
labors a field of interest and activity far narrower than the actual;
second, by misinterpreting the motive of scientific investigation and
thus undervaluing its past and future influence in productive
thought.

CULTURAL SIGNIFICANCE OF THE SCIENTIFIC ENLIGHTENMENT

Scientific knowledge is the product, not of specifically purposive
intelligence, but of naïve and wholly unrestricted curiosity concerning, as the ancients were fond of saying, "the nature of things."
Its primary motive is no more definite than exactly this: to find out
the nature of things; to discover by observation and study alone the
hidden relations between phenomena, occurrences, events, of any or
every sort; causes and effects, meanings and significances. In the
past this motive has placed the thought and will of the scientist in

opposition, not only to the authoritarianism of religious and moral, philosophical and æsthetic idealists, whose fixed conceptions of the sacred, the good, the ultimately real or the ineffable, would restrict his curiosity to the harmless realm of material things, but also to that of the utilitarian who would confine it more narrowly still to the investigation of the immediately useful.

The history of science, more vividly than any argument, substantiates this characterization of scientific research. If this history be recalled, the inference is inevitable that the background of nineteenth century science, so far from being technological, was philosophical and critical; and this is a very significant thing. The source of modern science was experience, surely; but it was experience derived from systematic investigations which had been stimulated and coördinated by theoretical speculations, and controlled and safeguarded by procedures critically developed in a philosophical manner; the results of which were verified by experiments carefully designed, whose relevance and significance had been determined, with logical rigor, in advance. Its method, which suggested these procedures, was that of common sense, but not of an instinctive and ingenuous common sense. It was the product *Science, organized common sense* of a critical philosophy which had discovered in experience alone the source of dependable knowledge, and in the processes of the thought which accompanies action — the adaptative thought of humanity, which is the product of the instinct of self-preservation — the most thoroughly tested procedures for the attainment of such knowledge. The erratic character of common thought, however, had long been notorious. The scientific thought derived from it, therefore, had been carefully expurgated; it was a common sense from which emotional fantasies and impulsive generalizations, together with the common errors of primitive conception which were derived from them had been, so far as possible, eliminated. And finally, unlike ordinary common sense, that of science had been logically organized and elaborated into a self-consistent scheme of representation, the ultimate terms of which were sharply definite concepts, which represented the simple, unanalyzable elements of primitive apperception.

It was this careful organization which gave to modern scientific thought its unique fertility and power; without it, the vast complexity of natural phenomena would have been unintelligible, and natural processes, therefore, excepting within very narrow limits, unpredictable and uncontrollable. All this means that the vital force of science has lain, not in the accumulation of facts alone by industrious observation and trial experimentation, but in the continuous theoretical organization of successive increments of knowledge, by which their interrelation has been discovered and its further necessary consequences revealed. It is thus that scientific knowledge has grown: not by accretion, but by organization; and consequently, in modern times, not so much by fortuitous discoveries as by fulfilled predictions. Its method has insured its truth; its theory has made it fruitful.

The general import of these observations is clear enough. The science of the nineteenth century was the sum total of its theoretically organized knowledge, which in this period reached at last the critical stage at which this organization made possible an understanding of natural phenomena sufficiently extensive and profound to permit, for the first time, an effective human control of physical energies and vital processes. By the genial irony of fate this control, which the consummate craftsmanship of ages could never grasp, yielded itself at last to the unrestricted curiosity of the natural philosopher, and by this surrender effected a cultural revolution. The full significance of this revolution is now quite clearly apparent. It means the growing domination of the human mind by a habit of thought which heretofore had governed the prosecution of practical affairs alone: a naturalistic habit of thought. Man shares with every other living being the primary impulse of self-preservation; and in the partial security of civilized life, he dares to expect the further amelioration of his condition — and even, unreasoningly, to demand an imaginary right to happiness. This impulse, obviously, expresses the primary motive of all conscious life and thought. In the remote and helpless past, completely baffled through ignorance in all attempts to command the resistless processes of nature, he had desperately appealed by magic and propitiation to supernatural powers which were the figments of his terrified imagination — and in vain. In modern times, a chastened intelligence has shown the hopelessness of such attempts; but he has found consolation in religions and philosophies, born likewise of his need, which have discovered in hours of plenty and peace and joy the evidence of an ultimately compelling good in nature; the usual failure of which to protect him from disaster and suffering, and above all from cruel wrong, he has ascribed, not without reason, to his sins and weaknesses. This theory of the world, though inconsistent with experience, has served his need by taming his crude passions and inculcating unselfish purposes derived from the sympathy of common suffering and hope; and it has made his social world at least tolerable. It has, however, but slightly mitigated the effects of natural calamity, and has neither shown a way to their avoidance nor effected their control. This service has at last been rendered by scientific knowledge. With the continuous growth of this knowledge, it is becoming more and more clearly evident that the hopes which have been built upon religious and philosophical conceptions of this type have overreached all possibility; and the conviction is already established, even in common thought, that the first prerequisite of actual salvation is neither instinctive morals, nor metaphysical enlightenment, nor faith itself, but practical intelligence. There is no answer to the argument of achievement. We are witnessing, therefore, as the final and most impressive phase of the scientific enlightenment of the nineteenth century, a radical revision, both of moral codes and of traditional beliefs; that is to say, not merely an economic, but an ethical, philosophical, and religious revolution. The readjustment of social life to novel physical conditions is paralleled by a readjustment of conceptions and ideals. This readjustment, like the other, is incomplete. Our social turmoil is accompanied by a ferment of new thought, the effect of which cannot fail to be even more far-reaching; but there is little doubt that, in the end, an inevitable accommodation of aspiration to positive knowledge will have equal, or even greater salutary consequences.

ASTRONOMY AND GENERAL MECHANICS

At the beginning of the nineteenth century, the science of astronomy was very nearly completely summarized by the systematic celestial mechanics which had been elaborated by the French mathematicians of the immediately preceding period. This science represented the consummation of a purpose which had continually guided the efforts of astronomers during more than a thousand years of active labor; and it embodied the conceptions, methods, and generalizations of fact which determined the essential character and trend of all subsequent progress in physical science. The history of its gradual development, therefore, yields knowledge which is indispensable to a clear understanding of the science of the nineteenth century.

The very earliest observation of the heavens, which was devoted primarily to the practical purposes of agriculture, and derivatively Early to the determination of the proper seasons for religious astronomy festivals and to the development of a more inclusive astrological magic, had yielded the conception of uniformly flowing time and the chronology from which our own is directly derived, together with the sense of temporal perspectives which has made a science of history possible. The early Greeks, who were the first naturalistic philosophers, rejected the mythical cosmogonies and the astrology of their predecessors, and sought at first to explain by physical images the nature of the celestial world. In imaginative grandeur, their representations have never been surpassed; but none of them was by any possibility verifiable. The later Greek astronomers, therefore, with admirable scientific insight, restricted their inquiries to those aspects of the phenomena which alone, at that time, could be made intelligible, and, incidentally, useful; that is, to the study of celestial movements and related phenomena. The science of geometry, which they had invented, and which they concurrently developed — essentially to perfection — made this possible. Astronomy henceforth became a mathematical science exclusively, a kinematic elaboration of applied geometry. Geometrical schemes of representation were invented which, successively modified to make them consistent with the results of increasingly precise observations, aimed to picture the apparently irregular movements of sun, moon, and planets, with reference to the apparently uniform motions of the stars, as compounded or superimposed revolutions; and, probably for the sake of avoiding the difficult analysis of changing velocities, these revolutions were all represented as exactly circular.

Thus ultimately, in the second century of our era, the Ptolemaic theory arose. This represented a spherical earth — consistently with The Ptole- appearances — as the center of the universe, around maic theory which the distant stars revolved uniformly together — again consistently with appearances — as if they were fixed in a crystal sphere. Within this sphere the sun revolved in a circle eccentric to the earth, and the moon and planets in individually peculiar and more complicated ways: typically in circular orbits called epicycles, the centers of which in turn revolved in larger circles whose centers, outside the earth, were in similar motion. This scheme of representation, the complication of which was an unavoidable necessity and the least possible to their thought, was very nearly consistent with the results of observation; or, as the Greeks would have said, saved the phenomena very well.   Its very character showed it to be, in the modern sense, scientific; that is, not an attempt to describe motion indubitably actual, but a scheme of representation only, at most a geometrical hypothesis, designed to render observed motions understandable and predictable. As a consequence of Aristotle's materialization of the prior system of Eudoxus, which had represented the planets as carried round the earth by transparent concentric spheres, the Ptolemaic representation was confused in common thought, especially during the Middle Ages when clerical authority supported as the final expression of eternal truth an agreeably modified Aristotelian philosophy; and even in scientific thought its constructions lost through familiarity something of their original hypothetical character.

These influences, however, did not affect in the least the methodical procedures of the astronomers.   Copernicus, who in his famous *De Revolutionibus Orbium Coelestium* (1543), replaced the geocentric scheme of Ptolemy by a simpler and better heliocentric system which had been suggested by an earlier Greek conception, might well, so far as the Copernicus, Tycho Brahe, and Kepler character of his work is concerned, have been an immediate successor to the famous Alexandrian; for with him the postulate of circular motion had become a dogma, and the ancient epicyclic constructions were still retained, which made the centers of all revolutions mere points in empty space.   The subsequent labors of Tycho Brahe (*ca.* 1580), however, led to wholly novel developments which finally resulted in the complete transformation of astronomy from a kinematic into a mechanical science.   His thousands of observations, which were of quite unprecedented accuracy, betrayed such defects in the Copernican system that its revision became imperative; and this revision his illustrious successor, Kepler, after the most arduous and devoted labor, at length effected.   In his *De Motibus Stellae Martis* (1609), and later, Kepler showed that the phenomena would be almost exactly accounted for if the planetary orbits were assumed to be ellipses of which the common focus was within the sun.   This construction, which broke completely with the dogma of circular motion, for the first time placed a material body at a common center of revolution, and at once provoked attempts to explain the planetary movements mechanically; but, at the time, such explanation was impossible for lack of knowledge.

Contemporaneously, however, the searching experiments of Galileo, which were summarized in his epoch-making *Discorsi e dimonstrazioni matematiche* (1638), provided the basis of a new science, the science of dynamics, primarily the mechanics of motion. The mechanics of the Greeks had never been successfully extended beyond the analysis and correlation of the phenomena of balanced forces. The work of Archimedes (*ca.* B.C. 240) had, therefore, provided all necessary conceptions for the development of a mathematical science of statics; but the ancient studies of mechanical movements were limited by a superficial knowledge derived from commonplace observations, and yielded nothing more valuable than plausible conjectures, the inferences from which were inconsistent with experience. It remained for Galileo to discover by methodical experimentation that constant forces are proportional to the uniform accelerations they produce in bodies that are free to move; and thus to realize that terrestrial objects in motion do not tend of themselves to come to rest, as the ancients had supposed, but on the contrary continue indefinitely to move with uniform velocity in straight lines unless they are compelled by force to move otherwise. The far-reaching implications of these discoveries were fully clarified and developed within the next half-century, and led to the sharp definition of those fundamental conceptions of modern mechanics which have remained until the present day the ultimate terms of all its intricate formulations, and consequently — as the history of later scientific developments makes fully clear — the elements of all physico-chemical theory: the concepts, namely, of inertia, momentum, force, work, potential, and derived ideas, expressed in terms of the primary intuitions of distance, time, and mass.

All these ideas, together with the principal generalizations which resulted from their formal development, were explicitly and unambiguously defined by Newton in 1687. Meanwhile, the analysis of complicated mechanical effects which they made possible found application in astronomy. In 1673, the physicist Huygens showed that circular motion, considered heretofore to be unanalyzable, was in reality the resultant of uniform tangential velocity and centripetal acceleration. The laws of planetary

Galileo (marginal note beside paragraph 2)

Newton (marginal note beside final paragraph)

motion, discovered by Kepler, permitted him then to determine the variability of such acceleration, and consequently that of centripetal force, with distance.   These inferences were generalized by Newton and shown to apply to elliptical motions.   The final result of this searching investigation, thereafter systematically extended and thoroughly developed by Newton, was the theory of universal gravitation, enunciated in his great treatise, the *Philosophiae Naturalis Principia Mathematica* (1687).   According to this theory, the planetary movements were explained in mechanical terms: the ancient kinematic astronomy became celestial mechanics.

The principal efforts of the astronomers of the eighteenth century were directed toward a general verification of Newtonian theory. The surpassingly difficult problem presented itself of analyzing the mutual gravitative influence of several bodies, a problem which permitted no complete solution, and presented such obstacles to adequate approximate solution that it engaged the absorbed attention of the greatest mathematical geniuses of Europe for a hundred years.   The astronomers of this period, however, enjoyed two great advantages over their predecessors.   The first effectively practicable telescope had been designed and utilized with excellent educational effect by Galileo, in 1609; and thanks to the labors of his successors — especially to those of Kepler, Huygens, Newton, and the technicians of the observatories of Paris and Greenwich — fine instruments of high power and precision, refractors and reflectors both, were available.   Their second invaluable possession was the infinitesimal calculus.   Without this mathematics, which had been developed as a general method by Newton and Leibnitz on the basis of a century of prior research, their task might well have been hopeless. This calculus had to be methodically developed with the utmost ingenuity to serve their purpose; and while their work progressed, its application involved increasingly elaborate formulations as observation became more and more nearly exact, and new variabilities (not all of which were confirmatory) were discovered.   At length, however, their task was satisfactorily accomplished; so that, excepting in the cases of a few perturbations, it was proved within a gratifyingly narrow margin of error that the gravitational formula was accurately descriptive of all planetary movements, and defined, therefore, a law of nature applicable to the entire solar system, or, assuming the uniformity of nature, universally.   These were the

Astronomy in the eighteenth century

labors which we associate with the names of the great observers Bradley, Lacaille, and Mayer, and of the mathematicians D'Alembert, Clairaut, Euler, Lagrange, and Laplace.   It was completely summarized in the monumental *Mécanique Céleste* of Laplace, the first and the greatest astronomical treatise of the nineteenth century (1799–1825).

Gravitational astronomy was thereafter still further developed and extended.   The continual improvement of both types of telescopes made possible a steadily increasing precision of measurement which yielded data more and more exact; new discrepancies between theoretical inferences and actual observations necessitated still further improvements in mathematical method, which in turn, by new predictions, led to further discovery.   Thus gravitational astronomy in the nineteenth century continued and elaborated that of the eighteenth century; and reduced, though it could not wholly eliminate, its remaining errors of theoretical approximation.   A few of its achievements have compelled more than a professional interest.

In 1806 and 1809, the mathematicians Legendre and Gauss established the method of least squares, which has since been generally employed in scientific work, whenever it has been necessary to determine a probable error of measurement less than the discrepancies between the results of similar observations.   Like procedures of a more elaborate character have been since designed for the general correlation of statistical data of all sorts, and are of the highest utility in both scientific and common practice.   Such methods are based on principles which were first systematically developed by Laplace in his *Théorie analytique des probabilités,* published in 1812.

The first dramatic achievement of the mathematical astronomers of this century was that of Bessel who, in 1838, determined for the first time the distance of a fixed star.   In the sixteenth century, it had been reasonably argued against the Copernican astronomy that if the earth moved around the sun, the stars should be seen in different positions at different times of the year.   The hope of proving such variability had stimulated the continued efforts of observers ever since; its discovery was a notable event.   According to Bessel's calculation, his star was so far away that light, which traversed the earth's orbit in about sixteen minutes, would take more than six years to cover the distance; or

Distance of fixed stars

otherwise, the star was about four hundred thousand times the distance of the sun, or thirty-seven million millions of miles away. Almost at once, other like distances were measured: another star was found to be only four light-years distant. These are the nearest stars. During the century, by more elaborate methods, much greater distances were measured.

Another dramatic event, significant for different reasons, was the discovery of Neptune. In 1781, F. W. Herschel, with an improved reflector, had identified a new planet, Uranus: the first which had been discovered in historic times. *Discovery of Neptune* Later analytic studies of its motion suggested to several astronomers that its perturbations might be due to the gravitative action of a still more distant planet. In 1843, Adams in England calculated the orbit and relative position of this hypothetical body, and in 1846, shortly after Leverrier in France had independently arrived at like results, the planet was discovered close to its predicted position.

The newly improved techniques of observation resulted in the discovery of still other bodies within the planetary system. Prior to the observations of Herschel, four satellites of Jupiter, discovered with the first astronomical telescope by Galileo, and five satellites of Saturn, discovered by Huygens and Cassini, were known: to these were now added one to the system of Jupiter, three to that of Saturn; two were discovered attending Uranus, one attending the new planet Neptune; and two very close to Mars, revolving rapidly. *Discovery of other planetary bodies* More interesting were the discoveries of the small minor planets, which in eccentric and tilted orbits, revolve between Mars and Jupiter. The largest of these, called Ceres, a body only five hundred miles in diameter (not quite a quarter of the diameter of the moon) was discovered on the first day of the century; and in 1807, three others were known. Thereafter more were detected at intervals, until, at the end of the century, over four hundred had been discovered, and their orbits traced. Finally, of the more than two hundred comets whose paths were meanwhile calculated, fifty or more were found to belong to the solar system. The improved precision of measurement which yielded these results afforded, also, a much closer estimation of astronomical distances. In particular, the distance of the sun was determined much more exactly than ever heretofore.

Thus far, the astronomy of the nineteenth century continued and developed the work of preceding years. At the very beginning of the century, however, the extensive and careful observations of Herschel, which were guided by the ambitious purpose of examining anew and as minutely as possible every aspect of the sky, opened up a new realm to scientific research. The ingenious procedures by which he compared and correlated slight similarities and differences between the various objects he examined, and the imaginative yet reasonable conjectures by which he interpreted them, stimulated new departures in both method and theory. Henceforth, the attention of astronomers was directed more and more frequently beyond the confines of the planetary system, to the all-inclusive system of the stars. By studying the distribution of the stars which he could see, with reference to their brightness, Herschel himself first ventured by plausible evidence to validate a current vague conjecture that this system had the configuration, not of a sphere, but of a thick, rounded disk; and he roughly mapped its probable section. He examined and classified thousands of nebulæ, and proved that while many of them were star-clusters, others of quite different appearance might well be tenuous, rotating bodies of gas like that from which Laplace had conjectured the solar system had been formed by condensation, or even "island universes" external to our galaxy. It had been first discovered by Halley, in 1718, that certain stars were moving relatively to each other. Herschel reëxamined a number of such proper motions, so called, and was able ingeniously to show that the solar system was moving as a whole among the stars, about as rapidly as the earth in its orbit, toward the constellation of Hercules. Finally, in the search for stellar parallax, he discovered many pairs of stars, the occurrence of which was beyond probability unless each pair were a mechanical system, and the relative apparent motions of which suggested that they revolved around each other. This conjecture, in the case of several such pairs, he substantiated by direct observations; and similar more searching work has later clearly shown that, in certain cases, the orbital motions of such binaries are elliptical, consistently with the law of gravitation. In this manner, the assumed universality of Newtonian mechanics was first substantiated in the nineteenth century by positive evidence.

These and a multitude of related observations by Herschel and others, which led to theoretical explanations and conjectures concerning the rotations of the planets and their satel- Astrophysics lites, the physical markings of the planets, the structure of the sun, the nature of comets, the periodicity of variable stars, and so on — together with new mechanical problems suggested by gravitational theory, such as possible minor effects of the earth's ellipsoidal configuration (approximately known since Newton) or of its imperfect rigidity, or of the tidal friction of the ocean — brought within the range of astronomical interest a large variety of purely physical problems of a sort which heretofore had lain beyond its scope, with which its method thus far developed was quite incapable of dealing. Before the middle of the century, for instance, the actual movements of the stars in space were quite unknown, since their angular components alone could be measured; their brightness and the quality of light they emitted could be neither accurately measured nor interpreted; and the physical constitution of the sun and planets could be only conjectured, while that of the stars could not even be imagined. Such knowledge was made possible, however, by the development of experimental physics and chemistry: and thus, in the second half of the century, a new science was established, that of astrophysics, a monument of scientific achievement in every respect as impressive as the gravitational astronomy itself. Each of the physical sciences has contributed to the upbuilding of astrophysics, but the new science was actually founded on theoretical optics.

OPTICS

The scientific optics of the ancients was restricted to a knowledge of the phenomena of reflection and refraction and of the laws of reflection. That of the moderns, prior to Snell's dis- Newton's theory of color covery of the law of refraction in 1621, was similarly limited, although a much more considerable body of empirical knowledge had been acquired, sufficient not only for the making of refracting telescopes of various designs but for the stimulation of active studies of more obscure phenomena. Before the beginning of the eighteenth century, the velocity of light had been approximately determined by Roemer from observations on the satellites of Jupiter. The science of geometrical optics then included, besides theoretical explanations of telescopic refractions, Huygens's precise analysis of the newly discovered phenomena of double refraction and polarization exhibited by Iceland spar, and Grimaldi's description of the equally inexplicable bending or inflection of partially intercepted beams of light which we call diffraction; but the phenomena of color remained unanalyzed. In the second half of the seventeenth century, Newton, by a series of exceptionally ingenious and conclusive experiments, fully explained the formation of colors by prisms and lenses, and measured with precision the accompanying dispersions; he examined and measured minutely the not dissimilar phenomena of inflexion; and he correlated his results by the famous "emission theory," which pictured a beam of light as a stream of invisible projectiles or corpuscles which, under different circumstances, were attracted or repelled by the surfaces of adjacent media which they closely approached or penetrated, and were thus in definite ways reflected, refracted and dispersed, inflected and polarized. His work was summarized in his *Opticks*, the first (Latin) edition of which was published in 1704. It stimulated at once a more extensive investigation of all optical effects, which resulted in the accumulation at the beginning of the nineteenth century of a wealth of new knowledge concerning phenomena fascinating alike for their beauty and for their tantalizingly puzzling interrelations; and thus inevitably led to the rapid development of theory.

Before Newton, the accepted theory of light was that of Huygens, according to which the light ray was a longitudinal wave like that of sound; a wave of compression and expansion in the direction of propagation. This theory did not explain satisfactorily the rectilinear path of light, and was otherwise defective: the Newtonian theory, consequently, prevailed throughout the eighteenth century. In 1801, the English physicist Young revived the Huygenian theory by explaining the bands of color (or of brightness and darkness in the case of light of one color) produced by diffraction or otherwise, as caused by the interference of trains of waves in different phase, which would periodically reënforce and impede each other. This hypothesis was at first ignored; but thirteen years later, when it was independently announced by the French physicist Fresnel, and supported by experimental evidence which admitted no other simple explanation, it was established as a rival theory; and when, to explain polarization, it was finally altered by the hypothesis that the waves were transverse to the line of propagation, and was mathematically developed on this basis by Fresnel,

Arago, and others, it met all requirements. The emission theory, meanwhile, had been elaborated, and in the opinion of Biot, Brewster and its other adherents, satisfactorily; but its growing complication by the multiplication of hypotheses, and particularly its own necessary assumption of accessory wave motions, lost it much support. It was not wholly abandoned, however, until its fundamental premises were invalidated by the crucial experiment of Foucault in 1853. According to the emission theory, the velocity of light in water must be greater than its velocity in air; according to the wave theory, the velocity in water must be less. In 1849 Fizeau, who had collaborated with Foucault in previous years, had determined the velocity of light, for the first time by measurement over terrestrial distances, by projecting a beam through the edge of a rapidly revolving toothed wheel and similarly receiving it upon its return after reflection from a mirror some miles distant. Foucault resorted to another method, by which the beam was sent upon its journey (in this case a much shorter one) by reflection from a rapidly revolving mirror which slightly displaced the position of the returning beam from that of the projected beam. By Foucault's method, it was possible to lead one beam for a sufficient distance through water while another traversed the same distance through air; a comparison of their displacements then showed that the velocity of light was greater in air, and this finally settled the controversy.

Thereafter, for the satisfactory development of optical theory, it was felt necessary to give these light undulations a mechanical explanation, to coördinate them with the rest of physical theory, as astronomical motions had been coördinated. To this end the mathematical physicists were already working. Their crucial problem was to define in mechanical terms the structure of that hypothetical æther which, for two centuries or more, had been vaguely imagined as the medium by which all physical effects were transmitted across interplanetary and interstellar space. The propagation of gravitative force had never received such explanation; but this problem had been quietly — and profitably — abandoned, despite the mystery involved in the conception of action at a distance. A light wave, however, was an actual movement of measurable velocity which could be manipulated and transformed. With reference to this movement, therefore, the theory of the æther became a wholly justifiable and a very important scientific concern.   It engaged the attention of nearly all mathematical physicists during the greater part of the century.

A solid foundation for a mechanical theory of light had been already laid.   Following Lagrange, who had perfected the systematization of analytical mechanics, Poinsot, and after him, Poisson and others, had devised new mathematical methods, synthetic rather than analytical, which greatly facilitated the study of complicated effects, and, consequently, there had been developed in a thoroughgoing manner the theory of a large variety of terrestrial mechanical phenomena, among which those which involved the impact, friction, distortion, and vibration of material bodies provided a hitherto neglected field for investigations of both scientific and practical importance — the field now covered in greater part by the modern theory of elasticity.   It is this work which we associate particularly with the names of Poisson, Cauchy, MacCullagh, Green and Stokes, though nearly all of the theoretical physicists of the time participated in it.

The particular study of wave motions had been stimulated by the earlier experimental work of Chladni and Savart, which summarized and developed all previous knowledge of acoustics, for the most part descriptively, and especially by the comprehensive *Wellenlehre* of the brothers Weber, published in 1825, which, with reference to all relevant phenomena, defined with great clearness the whole field of research.   From this starting-point, the two analogous sciences of sound and light were similarly but independently developed.   Acoustics was brought to a fairly approximate completion in the latter part of the century, especially by the work of Helmholtz, whose famous treatise, *Die Lehre von den Tonempfindungen,* appeared in 1863; its theory was practically perfected by Lord Rayleigh in 1894.

Acoustics

The development of a corresponding mechanics of light presented far more difficult problems.   The undulatory theory demanded a mechanical picture of vibrations transverse to the direction of propagation; and this necessitated an æther which, though too tenuous to retard the motion of celestial bodies, possessed, nevertheless, the properties, not of a yielding fluid, but of an elastic solid which did not, apparently, vibrate longitudinally.   This combination of properties was, of course, not characteristic of any known matter; but this did not prove its impossibility, against the evidence provided by the behavior of light.

Mechanics of light

The optical phenomena themselves, however, demanded such modifications of the properties of the æther by the presence of matter
that its mechanical behavior could never be consistently defined.
A profounder knowledge of the nature of light, yet to be referred to,
reduced these inconsistencies, but at the same time rendered a
purely mechanical characterization even more remote.   The theory
of the æther, therefore, remained throughout the century a purely
mathematical representation: the sciences of optics and mechanics
were never united.   Meanwhile, however, the rapid growth of
knowledge concerning optical phenomena, successfully coördinated
by the original kinematic wave theory, led to very important
scientific discoveries and inferences, and incidentally to the invention of instruments and techniques of great practical value.

The methods of Fizeau and Foucault permitted for the first time
determinations of the velocity of light independently of astronomical observation, and therefore provided new   Measure-
means for the measurement of celestial distances.   ment of
Both methods were improved by several experimental- celestial
                                                     distances
ists; and in 1882 and later, this fundamentally important constant of nature was determined with high precision
by Newcomb and Michelson, who had perfected the method of
Foucault.   This work has served astronomy particularly as the
basis of a valuable method for estimating the distance of the sun.

The most productive of the experimental investigations of this
period, however, were studies of spectra.   At the very beginning
of the century, the German technician Fraunhofer was   Spectrum
engaged with experiments designed for the improve-   analysis
ment of lenses.   In Newton's time no lens had been free from the
defect of chromatic aberration: all images were fringed with color,
an inevitable result of dispersion.   It was in consequence of Newton's opinion that this could not be prevented that the reflecting
telescope first came into use.   At a later time, however, the optician
Dollond, by combining lenses made of different materials, produced a practicable achromatic lens; and this achievement, more
than any other, perhaps, contributed to the marked improvement
of all optical instruments, in the nineteenth century.   Fraunhofer,
in seeking for lines of reference in spectra whereby to measure different indices of refraction, discovered and located dark lines in
the spectrum of sunlight and characteristic lines in flame spectra.
Similar phenomena in great number and variety were later de-

scribed by many observers. In 1859, and in the immediately succeeding years, the knowledge thus accumulated and the scattered
inferences which had been based upon it were summarized, extended, and substantiated by Kirchhoff, at first in collaboration with
Bunsen. It was thus made clear that different substances in the
state of a gas or vapor had characteristic spectra which consisted
of lines and bands; that the continuous spectra of glowing liquids
and solids were characteristically modified when viewed through
layers of different gases and liquids; notably, that the dark lines
of the solar spectrum were caused by such absorption. Thus was
founded the science of spectrum analysis. Its techniques were
immediately utilized for the detection of small quantities of substances; the metals cæsium and rubidium had been thus discovered
by Bunsen and Kirchhoff. For the first time it became possible
to learn something of the chemical constitution of the sun and
stars: several terrestrial elements were discovered in the sun; an
unknown line in the solar spectrum revealed an element helium,
long afterward discovered on the earth; by Kirchhoff's interpretation of the dark solar lines, the structure of the sun was revealed;
the spectra of different stars showed that they were bodies of incandescent gases of different compositions. When, at a later time,
the effects of temperature, pressure, and states of chemical combination and dissociation came to be partially understood, the very
variability of spectra, which at first appeared to invalidate many
theoretical inferences, yielded equally important knowledge: led, for
instance, to plausible theories of stellar evolution. And, finally, the
discovery of a Doppler effect in spectra — a shifting of spectral lines
by motion in the line of sight, analogous to the change in pitch of a
musical note the source of which is approaching or receding — made
possible for the first time a measurement of all the components of
stellar motion. Among the most important of the researches here
referred to were those carried out, before Kirchhoff by John Herschel, Brewster and Balfour Stewart, and after him by Roscoe,
Lockyer, Huggins and Ångström.

　All this and a wealth of similar knowledge provided a basis for the
new science of astrophysics. But, in addition, meanwhile, the
Optical and　range of spectroscopy was greatly extended. In 1800,
thermal　　F. W. Herschel had discovered by means of ther-
radiation　　mometers that the heating effects of sunlight were de-
tectable, not only in the visible spectrum, but in a dark region be-

yond the faintest red. It appeared from this that rays of heat could be refracted like those of light, and that many of them were invisible. Subsequent investigations, indeed, established the identical character of optical and thermal radiation. In particular Melloni, who, in 1830 and later, examined the infra-red region with the first thermopile, proved that the invisible rays of heat could be not only refracted and reflected, but also polarized and made to show interference effects. Also, in 1801, Ritter discovered invisible rays beyond the violet end of the spectrum which blackened silver chloride. Both types of radiation were later observed by photography, an art first practiced and scientifically perfected within the century; their absorption by various media was extensively studied; by the use of prisms of rock salt for calorific rays, and of quartz for ultra-violet rays. Later by the use of new instruments — the gratings of Rowland, the bolometer of Langeley, and others — the range of measurable radiation was at length extended to more than ten times that of light; and a multiplicity of interesting effects observed, the further investigation of many of which had very important theoretical consequences.

The delicate techniques of spectroscopy have found extensive applications, either directly or indirectly, in nearly all fields of research. Its own instruments, and many others which have been discovered largely by its aid — specially constructed telescopes, microscopes, spectrometers, diffraction gratings, photometers, interferometers — have yielded in one way or another a very remarkable improvement in nicety of discrimination and precision of measurement in all sorts of research, as also in technology and industry; and, supplemented by the techniques of photography, have made possible more than one type of observation beyond the range of vision, and the collection of whole treasuries of valuable data to be interpreted at leisure: astronomical, chemical, biological. Finally, the further study of spectra themselves has yielded in recent years a great enrichment of our deepest knowledge "concerning the nature of things," through the correlation in the later decades of the century of the sciences of radiation and electricity.

THE SCIENCES OF ELECTRICITY AND MAGNETISM

Before the beginning of the seventeenth century, there was little or no coördinated knowledge of electrical and magnetic phenomena. The "attractive virtues" of amber and the lodestone were known

to the early Greeks, but provoked no serious interest, either in
Early ex-   ancient or modern times, until the peculiar be-
periments   havior of the floating magnetic needle suggested the
possibility of its use in navigation.   A practicable mariner's compass was developed in the Middle Ages, and its behavior had been
minutely described, for the benefit of seamen, before the close of
the sixteenth century.   In 1600, the famous *De Magnete* of Gilbert
appeared, which clearly distinguished, for the first time, magnetic
and electrical phenomena, amplified the knowledge and corrected
the illusions then current concerning them, and expounded the
first experimentally verified theory of terrestrial magnetism.   For
nearly two centuries thereafter, the study of electric and magnetic
effects was intermittent and seemingly casual, the serious attention
of the ablest scientific men being otherwise directed.   In the latter
half of the eighteenth century, however, the common behavior of
magnets was well known, and all the more apparent phenomena of
static electrification were correctly understood.   A final clarifica-
tion of this knowledge was effected by Dufay (*ca.* 1734) and by
Canton (*ca.* 1754).   At the same time, the frictional electric machine had been improved to the point of yielding powerful discharges; the behavior of its condenser, the Leyden jar, was analyzed, and lightning identified as an electric discharge by Benjamin
Franklin (*ca.* 1750); and "electric fluid" theories of simple character were proposed — a two-fluid theory by Dufay, and a one-fluid
theory by Franklin — which permitted easy visual representations
of the facts then known.   Subsequently, the methods of exact
measurement which characterized the later work of the eighteenth
century in other experimental fields were applied to these phenomena.   The famous natural philosopher Cavendish discovered
(*ca.* 1775) that electric attractions varied as the inverse square of
the distance between charges; defined electric capacity, and otherwise anticipated the work of several successors who were ignorant
of his unpublished researches.   In 1785, Coulomb, by measurements with a torsion balance, established the inverse-square law
for both electric and magnetic attractions; and thereupon, in
France, the science was rapidly developed in a mathematical
manner.

At the beginning of the nineteenth century, a true science of
electricity had been established, but with reference to electrostatic
phenomena only; the corresponding science of magnetism was

quite independent.   The modern science which comprises both, dates from the investigation of low-tension currents by Volta.   In 1790, the Italian physiologist Galvani had discovered, upon touching muscle and nerve in the amputated legs of a frog with metallic forceps, a twitching which he ascribed to the production of an electric current; but, misled by his interest in the recently discovered electric discharges produced by living animals, he believed it to be of physiological origin. Volta, however, in 1800, reëxamined these phenomena, and found that they could be produced by bringing together the extremities of dissimilar metal plates elsewhere in contact with salt solution. Though the source of such currents was long in dispute thereafter, their physical origin was thus demonstrated from the start; and it was soon learned that several combinations of chemical material would produce them.   Thus the first primary batteries were made, instruments now represented by our commonly used dry cells and storage batteries.   The currents thus made available, unlike the violent discharges of static machines, were continuous, and consequently more easily studied; and their effects could be intensified and amplified within wide limits by the multiplication of connected cells.   With these batteries new chemical changes were effected: in 1800, water was quantitatively analyzed by Nicholson and Carlile, who used the original voltaic pile; and in 1807, by similar means, Humphry Davy isolated the alkali metals.   The sciences of electricity and chemistry were thus brought into intimate relation for the first time, and were blended in the new science of electro-chemistry, which subsequently became both theoretically and technically productive.   By Davy also, at the same time, the first arc light was made.

Not long afterward, a remarkable discovery made possible the mechanical measurement of electric currents, and consequently the definition of a group of new concepts, in terms of which electrical phenomena have since been commonly described.   In 1819, Oersted discovered that the electric current would deflect a magnetic needle, placed near it, in a definite manner.   His experiments were immediately followed up.   The galvanometer, directly suggested by his observation, was designed and thenceforth used to define the strength of currents.   In 1826, Ohm discovered the relation between this strength, the intensity of the current, and the resistance of the circuit: a relation which gave a first definition to these conceptions. Following him, other instruments of measurement were invented and developed, and two systems of units were established, particularly by the effort of Wilhelm Weber: an electromagnetic system derived directly from the phenomena here referred to, and an absolute system of reference derived from the metric units already adopted in mechanics, analogous to that proposed by Gauss in 1832 for the measurement of terrestrial and other magnetic phenomena which were then being studied in a similarly quantitative manner. Meanwhile, an even more important work had been carried out by the French physicist Ampère. Immediately after Oersted's experiment was made known, Ampère discovered that an electric current had mechanical effect, not only on the magnet, but on other currents; and his thoroughgoing studies of these phenomena, which were developed mathematically with perfect generality and exactitude, established, upon their publication in 1823, the foundation of a completely unified science of electro-magnetism.

Ampère

There followed the extensive and remarkably productive labors of Faraday, whose investigations, begun in 1821, were fully described in his *Experimental Researches in Electricity*, which was published in 1839–55. In 1821, Faraday effected the continuous movement of an electric wire around a stationary magnet. In 1831, he discovered that, just as stationary charges induced other charges in adjacent conductors, so currents induced other currents in adjacent circuits, though momentarily; and he later showed that similar extra currents were generated in a single circuit whenever it was broken: a fact independently discovered by the American physicist Henry two years previously. Faraday's exhaustive studies of these and related phenomena amply confirmed Ampère's conclusions, and laid the foundations of electro-dynamics. In one memorable experiment, Faraday produced an electric current by rotating a copper disk between the poles of a magnet. The first electric dynamo was thus invented: within another twenty-five years, or thereabout, it had been developed into a powerful industrial instrument; reversed in action, it became the electric motor; by its agency, electric lighting was made practicable, and after transformers had been similarly developed from experimental apparatus, large currents suitable for various technological purposes could be transmitted over long distances. From the same productive sources sprang a variety of other im-

Faraday

portant inventions. The electric telegraph was in commercial use in 1844; the second — successful — Atlantic cable in 1866; the telephone in 1876; and shortly afterward, the incandescent lamp appeared. It is with the theoretical and more difficult technical aspects of these and related developments that the name of William Thomson, Lord Kelvin, is commonly associated, though his profound researches actually contributed to the progress of physics in nearly every field.

Faraday's work included, in addition, the study of static charges, and this directly led to equally important developments; for his conception of electric fields as regions of stress, which could be graphically defined by lines and tubes of force, was the basis of the masterly final development of electrical theory in this century. This, primarily, was the work of Maxwell, which was summarized in his classical *Treatise on Electricity and Magnetism* (1881). With extraordinary skill and insight, Maxwell, starting with the physical images of Faraday, gave them precise mathematical definition, and thus elaborated equations which are fundamental in modern theory. With reference to a static æther, they formulate the behavior of electro-magnetic systems in mechanical terms; but, since the phenomena are not clearly describable by visual imagery, they represent an actual transcendence of sensory experience by physical knowledge: a remarkable achievement, though one which the theory of the æther had already foreshadowed.

An important consequence of Maxwell's theory was that oscillating electric discharges should generate waves, in all respects similar to those of light, which moved with the velocity of light. Maxwell conjectured, therefore, that light itself, and inferentially radiant heat and invisible ultra-violet radiation as well, were all electromagnetic phenomena. In 1887, the German physicist Hertz succeeded in proving that such discharges did actually generate electric waves, much longer than any undulations known heretofore, which moved in straight lines, and could be reflected, refracted, and polarized. The theory was thus substantiated; and, henceforth, the science of radiation became a part of electro-dynamics. It was by the technical improvement of Hertz's apparatus, that the wireless telegraph was made possible, and, subsequently — by the use of ingenious inventions, suggested by new knowledge of the nature of electricity — the instruments of radio-telephony and telephotography.

This new knowledge, which was derived in the first instance from concurrent studies of different character upon the electromagnetic behavior of various material systems, has been acquired for the most part in our own time. It has yielded a deeper insight, not only into the nature of electricity, but also into the energetics of radiation and the constitution of matter, and effected a general though imperfect organization of physical science as a whole on the basis of an inclusive doctrine of energy and an elaborate atomic theory. The fundamental conceptions involved in this synthesis were yielded in the nineteenth century by the study of heat and of chemical change.

THE SCIENCE OF HEAT AND OF ENERGY

It is clear that the scientific progress thus far reviewed effected the intimate correlation of many bodies of scientific knowledge which,

Advance of the physical sciences

at the beginning of the century, had been either partially or completely independent. A new mechanics of friction and distortion was applied to gravitational astronomy; the law of gravitation was extended to the stars; there was brought into being a new science of astrophysics, quite generally inclusive; the science of acoustics was systematized as a branch of mechanics; optics was given a secure kinematic, if not a fully developed mechanical, theory, and its range was extended to include the phenomena of radiant heat and invisible actinic radiation; the sciences of electricity and magnetism were unified; new sciences of electro-chemistry and electro-dynamics were founded; and the whole of an extended and generalized science of radiation was brought within the scope of electrical theory. The concomitant study of heat effected a still more extended synthesis — indeed, a perfectly general theoretical correlation of all science — by the development of the universal doctrine of energy.

The ancients had nothing more than commonplace knowledge concerning heat and its effects; and the contemporaries of Copernicus were quite as ignorant as they with respect to

Ancients, ignorant of science of heat

these exceptionally puzzling phenomena, which were looked upon as chemical changes, and appeared no less obscure than any other of those natural mysteries with which the alchemist, in particular, concerned himself. Before the nineteenth century, the closely related processes of thermal and chemical change were hardly distinguished in theory; and chemistry was still "the science of heat and mixture." It was not until the thermometer made possible a consistent comparative measure-ment of temperatures that there was, properly speaking, any science of heat.

The thermometer was invented by Galileo in 1593. His instru-ment, a bulb of air attached to a narrow tube which dipped in water, measured, by the rise and fall of liquid in the   The ther-tube, the contraction and expansion of the enclosed   mometer air, and therefore, simultaneously, the effect of changing tempera-ture and that of atmospheric pressure, then unknown. After Torri-celli, in 1643, had discovered and measured this pressure, it was possible thus to measure temperatures alone on an arbitrary scale. Meanwhile, however, as techniques were improved in nicety, liquids had come into use as thermometric substances — water first, then alcohol and mercury; and, before long, sealed mercury instruments, very similar to our own familiar thermometers, were in common use. By their aid, a large variety of natural thermal effects were thereafter minutely studied, and much valuable knowledge was gained concerning fusion and ebullition and the behavior of gases and liquids with change of temperature and pressure. This knowl-edge, however, remained inexact so long as temperature scales were various and arbitrary. To fix these scales, natural tempera-tures which were measurably constant were sought; several were discovered, among which that of the healthy human body and that of deep cellars held favor for a time; but, at length, the tem-peratures of melting ice and of water boiling under constant pres-sure were found to be more nearly constant, and were generally adopted as standards. The study of the obscure fluctuations of these temperatures yielded further interesting knowledge of the properties of matter; the study of the irregular behavior of ther-mometers of different form and material yielded still more. Finally, the philosophical technician Fahrenheit produced the first com-parable instruments of mercury-in-glass, which he described in 1725. Subject to further refinements of knowledge and technique, the most useful of fixed temperature intervals were thus deter-mined; their division, however, remained arbitrary, for different liquids expanded unequally, and irregularly also, as comparison showed.

Thus, slowly and laboriously, the difficult study of these com-plicated effects was prosecuted. Two centuries elapsed before its importance was fully apparent. Its first significant result was the organization, during the nineteenth century, of a systematic science of the general behavior of matter in its several states of aggregation. For example, it had been discovered by the combined researches of Boyle (1662), Amontons (1702), Gay-Lussac (1802) and their contemporaries, that for all gases the relations of corresponding volumes, pressures, and temperatures were approximately the same. Similar researches were made with greater care and precision in the nineteenth century: much wider ranges of temperature and pressure were brought under measurable control, and thermometry was made at once more extensive and more precise by the marked improvement of the older instruments and by the invention of new ones, electrical and optical. Irregularities were discovered which invalidated the old laws of expansion; these were found in turn to be capable of generalization, and more complicated laws were thus established. Further general regularities of behavior were discovered which covered the whole range of physical change from the liquid to the gaseous condition. Among the most important of these researches were those carried out by Regnault, whose masterly experimental work covered the whole range of thermal phenomena, and by Amagat, van der Waals, de la Tour

Liquefaction of gases

and Andrews in special fields. In these investigations, the heat absorbed in fusion and evaporation (revealed long ago by the study of fixed temperatures) was utilized with great ingenuity. Substances, known heretofore only as gases, were liquefied; at first a few, easily enough, by Faraday in 1823; at last — but not until the beginning of the present century, so great were the experimental difficulties — all gases without exception were condensed. In the later decades of the nineteenth century, this type of work was still further extended. The conditions of the coexistence of different states of aggregation were determined, both for single substances and for mixtures of substances; the physical behavior of mixtures, and particularly that of solutions, was likewise made clear; and by the use of liquefied gases and electric furnaces, high vacuum pumps, and powerful compressors, the field of inquiry was extended to include phenomena at extremely low and very high temperatures and pressures. The practical value of these researches is obvious; their techniques find general application, especially in the production of the raw materials of industry, in chemical manufacture, in metallurgy, and in refrigeration

These techniques, however, involved in their later development the application of a knowledge more inclusive than that derived from thermometry alone: the product of another type of research, which was even more productive.

This type of research was initiated by the Scottish chemist Black, who, in 1761 and later, first measured the heat absorbed in fusion and ebullition, and in the changing to like degree the temperatures of different substances. He thus defined the fundamental concepts of latent and specific heat; and his techniques, which, roughly speaking, measured quantities rather than intensities of heat, were the first of those which we call "calorimetric." His work was epoch-making, and for two reasons, which perhaps are equally important. First, it gave direction to those investigations which culminated in the establishment of the universal science of thermodynamics, and yielded the general concept of energy: second, it stimulated, correlatively, the scientific techniques which perfected the steam engine. Watt, who constructed the first practical steam engine, was Black's assistant and collaborator; his successors were, by necessity, scientists as well as technicians.

Thermodynamics

In the seventeenth and eighteenth centuries, two conceptions of the nature of heat were current. The first was suggested by the mechanical effects of changes in temperature, as shown in flames, draughts, and the expansion and contraction of all matter which is heated and cooled, and by the generation of heat by friction. As early as 1620, Francis Bacon had inferred from such phenomena that heat was an internal motion of the smallest particles of substances, but neither he nor his successors during the following century or more could give scientific definition to the idea. In 1738, Daniel Bernoulli accomplished this, but another group of conceptions concerning the structure and thermal transformation of matter was then established, which were inconsistent with his mechanical representations, and explained the facts then known quite adequately and more plausibly. This was essentially a chemical theory, according to which heat was an imponderable substance, the corpuscles of which (like similarly electrified particles) were mutually repellent, and, by insinuating themselves between corpuscles of matter, caused its dilatation. In solids, their expansive forces were overcome by those of cohesion; in liquids, they began to prevail, causing mobility and evaporation; in gases, which expand without limit, they were obvi-

Mechanical and chemical theories of heat

ously wholly predominant. At particular saturations, also, they entered into chemical combination with matter, changing solids to liquids and liquids to gases; and while thus combining, they were latent, that is, without effect on the thermometer. This ingenious theory was generally accepted at the beginning of the nineteenth century. It was first successfully disputed by Rumford, who, in his famous cannon-boring experiments of 1798, showed that, in the language of the theory, caloric could be squeezed out of metal by friction, in undiminishing and apparently limitless quantities. Following him, Davy, in 1799, produced water, which by the theory was a compound of ice and caloric, by the friction of metal in contact with ice, insulated *in vacuo* at an environmental temperature below that of fusion. This experiment was crucial, and invalidated the theory. The alternative mechanical theory, however, was then too vague to replace it. During the next two decades, therefore, many experimental investigations were undertaken to provide new knowledge which might either render the old conceptions tenable or the new ones scientifically useful. A protracted study of the specific heats of gases suggested, at length, a solution of the difficulty. It had been inferred from a variety of phenomena that less heat was required to raise the temperature of a gas if it were not allowed to expand against pressure. The fact was explicable in terms of either theory; but when, in 1829, the French chemist Dulong showed, by the correlation of his own experimental results with those of his predecessors, that in comparable measurements the difference between the heat absorbed at constant volume and that absorbed during expansion at constant pressure was the same for all gases and proportional to their expansion, the opinion seemed justified that this difference represented a quantity of heat equivalent to the work done in expansion. Assuming this, the German physician Mayer, in 1842, calculated from the data a mechanical equivalent of heat, and brilliantly generalized the far-reaching implications of the new conception, that of the transmutation of heat and work. All such inferences, however, remained hypothetical until the English physicist Joule, in 1843 and later, carried out his classical researches which proved the approximate invariability of a measured quantity of heat produced by the same mechanical work variously performed, and the similar invariability of the interrelations of comparable effects in electrical, electro-magnetic, chemical, and electro-

(margin note) Law of conservation of energy

chemical changes. By this work, it was proved that the vaguely definable processes of thermal, electrical, and chemical change must be conceived as transmutations of an undiminishing universal energy, measurable as mechanical work.

The law of the conservation of energy was thus established: by the quantitative conversion of various types of energy, particularly of mechanical energy, into heat. Meanwhile, the converse problem of the conversion of heat into work naturally engaged the attention of engineers, who were attempting to improve the efficiency of the steam engine. In 1824, the French engineer Carnot, by a masterly analysis of the operation of an ideal engine, was able to define the conditions of maximal efficiency, and thus to prove that this was a function of temperatures alone, of such character that heat could never be converted completely into work, nor at all excepting by the establishment of a difference of temperature. It followed that in the varied processes of nature a steadily increasing quantity of energy was converted irreversibly into heat; so that, within the range of human experience, all physical changes tended toward the slow diminution of every other form of energy. Thus a second general law, that of the degradation of energy, Law of was established. It was not long before the implica- degradation tions of these two principles were extensively elabor- of energy ated mathematically, both in their generality and with reference to their particular applicability to various types of change by Kelvin, Rankine, Clausius, Helmholtz, Gibbs, van t'Hoff, Nernst, and many others almost equally notable. The science of thermodynamics was thus elaborated, in the third quarter of the century, as a general science of energy which, though incomplete in detail, and, on this account presumably inexact, has served ever since as a conceptual scheme of correlation, in terms of which all physical phenomena are, with respect to every type of aggregate effect, still theoretically interpreted.

CHEMISTRY, AND SCIENTIFIC ATOMISM

The modern science of chemistry may be considered to date from the time of Robert Boyle, whose critical work *The Skeptical Chymist* (1661), first defined and defended empirical theory and Contribu- method in this field of research. Before Boyle, the tions of professional alchemists — whose scientific purpose and Boyle superior techniques had set them apart from the class of industrial craftsmen ever since the Alexandrian period — had based their entire theory of chemical change upon the Aristotelian doctrine of matter and form. Their essences and principles were types of forms or qualities which were assumed to have objective existence apart from matter, and to be transferable by chemical processes. With Boyle, the idea of substance took on new meaning, the meaning we now assign it; and the conceptions of chemical elements and compounds were given by him their first clear definition. These new ideas were fertile; and, together with the simple atomistic representation of chemical reaction which he also introduced, greatly stimulated the progress of research. The alchemists, by the continuous labor of centuries, had learned much; the successors of Boyle, in a twentieth of the time, learned much more. The eighteenth century was a period remarkable for chemical discovery: a large number of new substances were isolated and classified by their chemical relationships; qualitative tests were designed for their separation and identification; techniques which took advantage of new physical knowledge were improved and elaborated; and imperfect but valuable investigations were made of relative activities or affinities. It is this work which we associate with the names of Boerhaave, Mayow, Stahl, Bergman, Scheele, and Priestley.

The chemical knowledge of the later eighteenth century was theoretically interpreted by the large majority of chemists in terms of a conception which reëxpressed an old alchemical idea: that of a fire-material, elusive and, as we now know, imaginary, which escaped during combustions and which was transferred in various kinds of process. This was the famous phlogiston theory of Stahl which, though erroneous, well served the primary purpose of hypothesis, that of coördinating extensive bodies of fact, and of thus stimulating productive research. In particular, it led to an accentuation among chemists of the interest in quantitative investigation which characterized the later scientific spirit of the century, inasmuch as it was to this sort of inquiry that appeal was made by those whose work was critical. It was on the basis of this quantitative work that chemistry, hitherto almost wholly descriptive, was raised in the nineteenth century to the status of an exact science, coördinate with physics. The first distinguished research of this character was that of Black on the alkaline earths, in 1754. This was followed by the classical investigations of Lavoisier, who was the first to prove that chemical reactions in isolated systems cause no change in the total mass of reacting material, thereby demonstrating the fundamental law of the con- Contribu-servation of mass; who finally invalidated the phlo- tions of giston theory and showed that combustions and like Lavoisier phenomena were chemical combinations with oxygen; who thus explained the process of respiration, and founded the modern science of chemical physiology; and who, by his thoroughgoing and cautious methods, established as fundamental in chemical research the procedures of quantitative analysis.   It was by similar methods that Cavendish discovered the composition of water, nitric acid, and air; and others afterward the compositions and chemical relations of our most familiar substances.

This study of chemical composition, moreover, had a further consequence still more significant: it led to the establishment of a substantiated theory, and ultimately to an actual demon- The atomic stration of the atomic constitution of matter.   This constitution contribution must be accounted one of the supreme of matter achievements of science, comparable to the establishment of the law of gravitation and to that of the doctrine of energy.   The early Greek philosophers had elaborated, four centuries before our era, an atomic scheme of nature which prophetically anticipated our own scientific conceptions to a remarkable degree; but this atomism, which was consciously designed to meet the necessities of any self-consistent scheme of physical representation, remained an empty form.   The early modern corpuscular theories of light, heat, and chemical change were intuitive and of necessity much simpler, lacking almost completely the clear detail which the ancient conception forevisioned.   With the rise and development of modern atomic theory, however, the old conceptual form has been not only filled in, but elaborated with a wealth of detail which no philosopher could possibly have imagined.

Before 1792, the German chemist Richter discovered that acids and alkalis entered into combination invariably in the ratios of quantities each of which was characteristic of a par- The atomic ticular acid or alkali.   In 1799 and later, the French- theory man Proust, by a series of masterly analyses, proved against the most acute and searching skepticism that unmixed substances were of invariable mass composition.   In 1802, the Englishman Dalton had further shown that, if two such substances combined to form compounds chemically different, the mass compositions of these

were in simple arithmetical ratio.   There was only one hypothesis
that could explain these surprising regularities, and this Dalton had
already conceived: that the smallest particles of matter, or better,
those which were indivisible in chemical change, had characteristic
masses, and must, therefore, combine in the ratio of these masses or
of their multiples.   The combining ratios were easily determined by
chemical analysis; it wâs difficult, however, to discover which of
these represented the relative masses of single atoms.   But, in 1805,
Gay-Lussac discovered that gases, under like conditions, combined
in simple ratios, not only by mass but by volume also; and this
and other independent regularity of behavior enabled the Swedish
chemist Berzelius and his successors to decide the question by
shrewd inductive inferences, the errors of which were gradually
eliminated afterward.   Furthermore, the ratios of combining volumes were such that, to account for them by atomic theory, it was
necessary to assume, as the Italian physicist Avogrado showed in
1811, that the smallest particles of all the free elementary gases then
known were multiple atoms: thus molecules, the smallest particles
of a free substance, and atoms, the particles which were indivisible
in chemical change, were distinguished.

Upon this basis the atomic theory was gradually developed, with
increasing assurance as it was found to remain consistent with a
Organic   very rapidly accumulating mass of new chemical knowl-
chemistry   edge; and this knowledge itself compelled its extensive
and minute elaboration.   In 1828, Wöhler, and later many others,
discovered that substances which, it had always been believed,
were formed only by the agency of life, could be synthesized in the
laboratory.   A new science, organic chemistry, then came into
being, which was quickly developed and systematized by Berzelius,
Liebig, Dumas, Laurent, Gerhardt, Frankland, Kekulé, and a host
of others.   Substances were made which had the same mass composition and the same molecular weight, and could be distinguished,
in accordance with the theory, only by assuming that their molecular structures were different; and later similar evidence compelled
the representation of these structures in three dimensions.   In this
way, the formulæ of the chemist, which were, and are for the most
part, only graphic symbols of chemical relations, became, in certain
instances, rough representations of actual physical forms.   Thus by
an atomic theory, the cumulative evidence in favor of which quickly
became overwhelming, the probable invisible composition of matter

was revealed, and even its structure very vaguely.   Every per-
ceptible particle of matter was henceforth conceived as a vast aggregate of molecules; and these as systems of atoms of definite,
though undetermined configuration.   The disruption, recombina-
tion, or rearrangement of the molecules was chemical change;
their motion, it might now be considered certain, was heat.

The theory of heat, consequently, was henceforth elaborated as a
theory of molecular motions, and thus a new and very important
scientific advance was made; for a still more rapidly   Molecular
accumulating knowledge, made minutely quantitative   mechanics
by measurements of greater and greater precision, permitted now
the establishment, if not of a complete atomistic mechanics, at least
of a molecular mechanics.   The laws of gases were derived from
simple postulates concerning the primary character of this motion,
which were thus substantiated; irregularities of behavior were interpreted by hypotheses of molecular attraction; a general kinetic
theory of matter was outlined; the speeds of molecules, their mean
free paths, their number in a specified volume, their approximate
sizes, were calculated.   Cumulative evidence verified these findings
as matters of fact, and new mathematical methods were designed
to improve and elaborate the new knowledge: the laws of energy,
now definitely characterized as statistical generalizations, were re-
examined from this point of view and correspondingly elaborated.
This was the work of Clausius, Maxwell, Boltzmann, and their
collaborators and successors.

The last phase of the development of atomism is contemporane-
ous.   It is common knowledge that the chemical atom has been
decomposed, not only theoretically but actually, into   "Within the
electric charges; of which one, which we call the   atom"
electron, has a mass of little more than the two-thousandth part
of the lightest atom; the other, which we call the nucleus, being of
atomic mass.   Electric discharges are known to consist of countless
swarms of electrons in free motion; within the atom, these electrons
appear to revolve, insensibly, like planets round the sun.   This
furthest extension of atomistic theory is, in its generality, as fully
substantiated by observation as the atomic and molecular theories
themselves.   The evidence which supports it was yielded by many
different investigations.   As far back as 1833, Faraday had discovered that when salt solutions were decomposed by electric currents
equal charges were conveyed across the solutions by chemically

equivalent weights of salt. This phenomenon suggested that the
currents themselves might be streams of corpuscles
which, in the solution, attached themselves to migrating atoms in numbers proportional to their valences;
but no evidence was then forthcoming which proved
this, since, clearly enough, the current, if continuous in metallic conductors, might have been thus broken up by the solution. Its
production by primary batteries, however, pointed to its generation by chemical decomposition, and thus to an original atomic
character. Conclusive proof that the electric current was in fact
a stream of corpuscles was obtained much later from the study of
electrical discharges through rarefied gases. The experiments of
Crookes in 1870–1874 showed that in such discharges streams from
the negative electrode which produced fluorescence when they fell
on glass — cathode rays, as they were later called — would rotate
a light mica vane in their path, and could be bent aside by a magnetic field as if they consisted of electrically charged particles.
Hertz and Lenard, shortly afterward, showed that the same rays
would penetrate the glass of the tube, or thin sheets of metal, and
produce luminosity or fluorescence in air or glass beyond; and it
was also found that they rendered gases highly conducting.
Furthermore, rays not dissimilar were discovered — the so-called
canal rays — which in these discharges moved in an opposite
direction.

Thereafter further researches on these and related phenomena
multiplied themselves — until it was definitely proved (first by
Perrin in 1895), that both sorts of rays were streams of material
particles. By ingenious means the difficult problem was then attacked of determining their masses and charges; and it was solved,
at length, first by Townsend, and later more accurately by J. J.
Thomson, whose extensive work in this field has proven to be the
most productive and significant. At the beginning of the new
century, it was thus made known that the electrical current was a
stream of atoms of electricity, electrons, the masses of which were
about one two-thousandth that of the lightest chemical atom.

Meanwhile, it was demonstrated that these electrons were actual
constituents of certain chemical atoms. Investigation of the luminosity of salts of uranium led Becquerel to the discovery that it was independent of previous excitation:
was caused, that is to say, by changes which occurred spontane-

Atoms and the nature of the electrical current

Radio-activity

ously within the salt. This very remarkable phenomenon was called radioactivity. It was soon learned that other salts were radioactive — those of thorium, for instance. The new elements, polonium and radium, were discovered by Madame Curie, as a consequence of her observation, in 1898, that certain ores of uranium were more radioactive than the purified salts of this metal. The radiations from all these and similar substances were closely studied, particularly by Rutherford and by Soddy, in 1899 and later; whence it was learned that they were of three types, of which the least penetrating, called by Rutherford alpha rays, were identified with the canal rays of the discharge through gases; and the much more penetrating beta rays were identified with the cathode rays. It was also discovered that radioactive elements gave off material emanations which behaved like radioactive gases of high atomic weight; and in 1903 the alpha radiation from radium was identified as a positively charged atom of helium. It was thus and otherwise made evident that the atoms of radioactive elements were spontaneously disintegrating to yield atoms of lower atomic weight and corpuscles of free electricity. Further investigations, particularly those of Soddy, defined the character of such disintegrations with great completeness and precision, and led to the further discovery that many elements, not all of them radioactive, existed in two or more forms, chemically identical but of different atomic mass, which were called isotopes. Later, the similar disintegration of elements not radioactive was effected artificially by electrical bombardment. A large mass of evidence of this and similar nature has at length made it practically certain that the chemical elements are all compounds of positively charged atoms and electrons. The current atomic model is that of Rutherford, as modified by Bohr and others. It pictures the simplest atom, that of hydrogen, as consisting of a single massive positively charged nucleus or proton around which a single electron revolves; and atoms of greater mass as consisting of very dense nuclei which are aggregates of protons and electrons, around which many electrons similarly revolve, probably in orbits of different sizes and eccentricities in several planes, in systems not dissimilar to that of the planets and comets in the solar system.

The physical researches which have thus revealed the elementary character of electricity and the constitution of matter have simultaneously yielded equally important results in the extension and elaboration of our knowledge of radiation. In 1895, the German physicist Roentgen discovered that the electric discharge through gases generated, upon impact with matter, radiations of a new type, which penetrated many substances that were opaque to light. Unable to determine their character, he called them X-rays. The later analysis of radioactivity revealed radiations not dissimilar but more penetrating which were called gamma rays. Both of these radiations accompanied the discharge of electrons, but were not deflected, like cathode and canal rays (beta and alpha rays) by electric and magnetic fields. For several years their nature was in doubt: but in 1912, a critical experiment, suggested by Laue, was carried out which showed that they could be diffracted by the regularly spaced atoms in crystals; and it was later shown by Bragg that they could be similarly reflected. This behavior proved that the X-rays were undulations similar to visible light; but, the configurations and dimensions of the atomic aggregates which reflected them having been determined, made it also clear that their wave lengths were very short, about one ten-thousandth that of yellow light. Since then, the range of X-ray wave lengths has been much extended, and, those of various other types of radiation having been likewise extended, it now appears that all radiation is homogeneous and of a total range which extends from electro-magnetic waves of meters' length — such as are used in wireless telegraphy — to invisible thermal radiation of millimeters' length, to visible light, to ultra-violet radiation, to X-rays, of which the shorter wave lengths are less than the hundred millionth of a millimeter: and the existence of radiant undulations still more minute has very recently been demonstrated.

From the phenomena it is evident that X-rays are generated by the violent movements of electric corpuscles. It is also known that visible light is similarly generated. This was made evident by the early work of Zeeman, who discovered in 1895 that powerful magnetic fields split the line spectra of metallic vapors in a manner which was explicable only on the assumption that the vibrating bodies which caused the radiation were electrified constituents of the atoms. These are now identified with the orbital electrons within the atoms. In contemporary physics, consequently, studies of atomic constitution and of radiation are inextricably interwoven.

These studies, and those with which they are most closely related, present peculiar difficulties of a type not heretofore encountered.

The motions of electrically charged bodies and of free electric charges, which not infrequently approach the velocity of light, are fundamentally different from those of larger masses.   The laws of such motions cannot be inferred from the principles of classical mechanics, and must be discovered by the analysis of the new phenomena themselves.   The hypotheses which have been thus suggested, even those which appear to be fully substantiated by their remarkable accord with wide reaches of complicated phenomena, involve conceptions which are at variance with scientific principles fully established with reference to the behavior of systems of sensible dimensions.   These latter must now be interpreted as descriptions of aggregate effects.   In the newly discovered world of subatomic electrical motions and their accompanying radiations, the conceptions suggested by sensory experience appear no longer to apply.   Experimental analysis seems to have transcended common sense altogether; so that, not improbably, the adequate description of these fundamental phenomena may finally remain a matter for mathematical analysis alone.   There is at present no escape from this situation.   It is not only the subatomic phenomena which are forcing us to modify our basic physical concepts.   The distribution of energy in isolated radiating systems is inexplicable excepting in terms of an hypothesis concerning the nature of energy — the quantum theory, proposed by Planck in 1900 — which gives it a discontinuous character impossible yet to visualize: the minimal quantum which this theory posits appears as an indivisible unit of energy in the most diverse effects.   Finally, the discovery made by Michelson and Morley, that the velocity of light, and inferentially of electromagnetic waves in general, is unaffected by the motion of its source, has consequences even more farreaching; for, assuming that their conclusions are generally valid, it appears to compel the abandonment of one of our primary scientific postulates, that of the independence of spatial and temporal relations.   Upon this basis has arisen the new scientific doctrine of relativity, which we associate particularly *Relativity* with the names of Lorentz and Einstein.   This theory, in its further development, effects the unification of solar mechanics with electro-dynamics, and concurrently the logical correlation and corresponding simplification of primary physical conceptions — inertia and gravitation, mass and energy — at the cost, however, of a considerable complication of our ideas of physical relations; that is to say, at the cost of a radical revision of our mathematical representations, which makes them quite uninterpretable in the imagery of common sense. Meanwhile, however, the classical physics of the nineteenth century remains unimpaired within the range of its applicability; and the outcome of the present ferment of theoretical conjecture is not yet a matter for historical record.

GEOPHYSICS AND GEOLOGY

The scientific progress thus far considered exhibits a progressive correlation of several bodies of knowledge, each of which in the earlier stages of its development had been independently organized to some extent by characteristic theory. As these bodies of knowledge grew and interpenetrated, their separate theoretical representations were adjusted and blended with an ease which, in retrospect, seems rather remarkable, and which finds explanation only in the conception that the whole aggregate of phenomena which the nineteenth century succeeded in describing by its atomistic mechanism is in reality a single complex of interdependent effects. Assuming this to be a fact, we give to our generalized knowledge of this complex the one name, physical science; and, encouraged and justified by past successes, seek to include within its scope the total range of all natural phenomena.

The development of the descriptive sciences in the nineteenth century was guided by this purpose. Already in its first decades, Physiog- physicists and chemists had successfully applied their raphy   general knowledge to the explanation of a variety of complicated terrestrial phenomena. The gradual organization of astronomy as a physical science has been reviewed: this involved a parallel development of the science of geodesy, which was continuous from the times of Huygens and Picard (*ca.* 1670) and of Clairaut (1743) to those of Bessel, Struve and their successors (1820 and later). Somewhat afterward, the descriptive science of geography was developed in a scientific manner, especially after the time of von Humboldt, whose comprehensive treatise *Kosmos* (published in 1845–47) presented in readable form the extensive observations of a lifetime, which in every field of geographical and meteorological research well represented the knowledge of his day. Since then, the work of physiographers has become of necessity to some extent particularized. The science has been more or less artificially divided into geomorphology, oceanography, and climatology, and thus developed with reference to different foci of interest, though all researches are closely interrelated. Of late studies of general scope, those of Suess on geographical configurations and those of George Darwin on the tides are typical of the highest achievements of the century in this field. In more particular aspects, these same phenomena had been studied for a much longer time. Toward the end of the eighteenth century, the sciences of meteorology and terrestrial magnetism, crystallography and mineralogy, which, before this time had been wholly descriptive, were organized with reference to general knowledge of the phenomena with which they were severally concerned by physicists and chemists whose interests were theoretical. In crystallography, which became the basis of systematic mineralogy and later of petrology, this organization was made complete by Hessel, who, in 1830, deduced from the regularities of crystal structure, revealed by the work of his predecessors, the total number of possible crystal forms. In the other special fields of geographical research, however, it progressed very slowly, and for obvious reasons remained incomplete; though it produced, in the end, an extensively amplified and theoretically coördinated science of geophysics.

The science of physiography may properly be considered a part of the more general science of geology, which comprises the study of the structure and development of the earth, as well as that of its configuration and superficial change. Geology The carefully inductive study of rocks and rock formations dates from the sixteenth century; its background, clearly enough, being the ancient lore of the miner, which in this period was developed and rationalized by the famous Agricola. In Italy, a century later, more systematic studies, particularly of stratified and volcanic rocks and of fossils, were undertaken by Steno, Vallisneri and Moro, whose methods and inferences were perfectly sound. Their labors, however, were not significantly extended for another century, since their successors were lesser and more imaginative men, who sought to reconstruct upon the basis of the meager data then acquired, and consistently with the Biblical legend of the deluge, complete cosmogonies. In 1749, this tendency of thought was diverted by the naturalist Buffon (under the influence of the prior speculations of Descartes and Leibnitz) into more philosophical channels; and from this time onward, rational conceptions of cosmic and terrestrial development persisted in the background of scientific and popular thought alike, though vaguely and imaginatively until Laplace and Lamarck gave them scientific definition at the beginning of the nineteenth century. Among geologists, however, the cosmogonists, still influenced by Old Testament authority, continued to obstruct the development of scientific theory until the time of Darwin.

Meanwhile, nevertheless (in 1750–1760), Guettard and Desmarest, in France, had identified certain rocks as of igneous origin: and their extensive studies of superimposed formations, together with the similar studies of Arduino in Italy and of Lehmann and Fuchsel in Germany, laid the foundations of a rational structural and historical geology. The importance of fossils in determining the relation of separated strata was recognized by them and their successors; and at length was made the basis of systematic stratigraphy by Cuvier and Brongniart in 1808. Thereafter, during the first half of the nineteenth century, all the great rock systems were successively identified: by William Smith down to the coal measures, by Murchison and Sedgwick to the Silurian and Cambrian, and by Logan to the Laurentian. After them, the general scheme of geological succession was verified and amplified in detail by increasingly minute observations guided by methods correspondingly improved. Thanks to the early labors of Hutton (1785) and Playfair (1802) and to the later work of Lyell (1830) and others — and contrary to the catastrophic theory of Cuvier (1821) — these evidences were interpreted as cumulative effects of the continuous operation throughout geological time of familiar natural forces. The discovery of an epoch of widespread glaciation by Agassiz (*ca.* 1840) is a striking illustration of this type of inference, which is the basis of dynamical theory in geology. The observed succession of fossil forms had meanwhile indicated very clearly a progressive development of species in animals and plants. The French biologist Lamarck, whose researches provided (1801–06) the basis for the science of invertebrate paleontology, interpreted this succession as evidence of the evolution of species, one from another. On the other hand, his younger colleague, Cuvier, who in 1812 similarly founded the science of vertebrate paleontology, held fast to the venerated dogma of the fixity of species, and by his unusual powers of persuasion gave new scientific life to all corresponding preconceptions.

BIOLOGY.   THE DOCTRINE OF EVOLUTION

Historical geology was thus united with the science of life: biology. Throughout the course of its long development, this science, until the nineteenth century, had progressed along two separate paths: that which led from the practice of medicine to the study of human anatomy and physiology; and that which arose from the arts of agriculture and horticulture and the lore of the herdsman, the fisherman, and the hunter, and became natural history — of which the two great branches, botany and zoölogy, remained distinct until, quite recently, the theories of comparative morphology, cytology, and physiology and the doctrine of evolution united them with one another, and with human anatomy and physiology.   Of all the sciences, excepting, perhaps, astronomy, that of the human body has shown the most nearly continuous development.   Four centuries before our era, the medical practice of Hippocrates was conducted by a strictly scientific inductive method. A century later, the Alexandrian physicians advanced far in anatomy; and, at the close of the ancient period, the encyclopedic Galen handed down to posterity a veritable treasury of knowledge, and shrewd, though erroneous theory. The sciences of geology and botany had been descriptively organized long before, the first by Aristotle, extensively and even theoretically in terms of an essentially sound though infertile doctrine of vitality; the second, in a fragmentary manner by Theophrastus.   During the Middle Ages this natural history was wholly lost, and was replaced by primitive folk-lore; but ancient medicine, and with it the old knowledge of human anatomy, was kept alive, and even developed, though very slowly.   In the time of Copernicus (1543), Vesalius revived the independent study of human anatomy by original observations which corrected many old errors: and thereafter, continuously until the present time, its rapid progress has been uninterrupted.   In the sixteenth and seventeenth centuries, the anatomy of all the organs of the body, including that of the vascular and nervous systems, was minutely elaborated by Eustachius, Fabricius, Asselli, Willis and others, and the circulation of the blood was demonstrated by Harvey. Later, the microscope, in the hands of Malpighi (*ca.* 1660) and his successors, and the techniques of injection perfected by Ruysch (*ca.* 1665), made possible a minute elaboration of this work and the foundation of the modern sciences of histology and embryology. In the eight-

Early progress of anatomy

eenth century, the great work of Haller summarized and amplified all this knowledge, and thus established a new basis for similar investigation.

Meanwhile, in the seventeenth century, the sciences of zoölogy and botany were being developed anew. Familiar animals and Of botany plants were described and compared with increasing and zoölogy care and accuracy; species were defined, and rough schemes of classification devised. A new world of microscopic organisms was discovered by Leeuwenhoek (*ca.* 1680) and his successors; and their minute dissection of plants and of insects and other animals yielded the first data of comparative morphology. In the eighteenth century, a wealth of new material was made available for such studies by local collectors and by explorers, and the growth and habits of life of various species were extensively studied and described. The results of this labor were summarized in a systematic manner by Linnæus in 1735, 1758, and later; and thenceforth much attention was given to the development and improvement of his artificial but useful classifications.

In the nineteenth century, every type of biological investigation which had been previously undertaken was methodically developed; and the new knowledge thus acquired, of the forms and structures of a rapidly increasing number of known animals and plants, and of their embryonic and later growth, functional activity and habits of life, was extended to many times the compass of all that was known before. It followed, inevitably, that by this enrichment the scope of every sub-science was enlarged until, interpenetrating with every other, it covered the whole field of research and assumed the character, not of a body of knowledge definably limited, but of a fluctuating aspect of one organic science. The study of the forms and grosser structures of animals and plants became, after Cuvier, comparative; and the superficial similarities thus revealed suggested the possibility of defining, if not explaining, the natural relations between species and groups of species. A similar study of tissues, and, later, of their microscopic elements by Bichat (1800) and Treviranus (1806) and their successors remarkably extended the range of this comparison and defined with greater clearness the evidences provided by dissection. In this way the sciences of anatomy, histology, and cytology were bound together as aspects of a general morphology, which, developed further, and with respect to different organisms comparatively, revealed at length the essential likeness of all forms of life. The science of growth, particularly embryology, by exhibiting the actual formation of organs and tissues, contributed similarly to the progress of histology, and by its own comparative development, supplied at the same time a much more certain evidence of close similarities between species, which indicated clearly even if it could not be held to prove, their actual genetic relation. Thus embryology became in one aspect a part of an extended morphology. It pictured also, however, a vital process, that of growth. The particular study of vital processes, which was the older physiology, had always been coördinated with anatomy, since the structures and functions of organs were inseparable. With the growth of morphology, therefore, physiology also became general and comparative; and especially by its experimental development, which, after the rise of organic and physical chemistry was exceptionally rapid, yielded a wealth of new knowledge concerning the physical aspects of vital processes which was fundamental. Finally, the further study of growth by artificial breeding through selection and hybridization, and the investigation of physiological processes as determined by adaptation to environmental conditions and by coöperative habits of life, supplied fresh information of the phenomena of heredity and variation and a proof of the possibility of the evolution of species, which completed the cumulative evidence already provided by comparative morphology, embryology, and paleontology; thus demonstrating as a fact the unity of all life and its differentiation by natural evolution. All of this remarkable progress in the biological sciences — which finally blended them completely, made clear by the development of experimental methods the possibility of an extensive and perhaps a general interpretation of vital phenomena as physico-chemical processes, and established the doctrine of organic evolution — was, in its primary essentials, the work of sixty years. Thereafter, and until the present time, the further progress of biology has been one of elaboration and development. By continued improvement of method, and by the elaboration and correction of theory on the basis of a more minute and greatly amplified knowledge, the earlier science has been much improved — in precise detail with respect to fact, and in cautious circumspection with respect to specific theory; but its findings in general have been amply confirmed.

It was the microscope, somewhat tardily perfected early in the cen-

[margin note:] Study of morphology prepares way for theory of evolution

tury, which made possible the first important advances in morphol-
The cell ogy. Early studies of the cellular structure of plants
theory made by Hooke, Malpighi, and Grew between 1665 and
1682, were then at last developed, especially by the botanists Treviranus and von Mohl in 1806 and 1830 respectively. In 1838, the
botanist Schleiden and the zoölogist Schwann recognized the similar nucleated character of the contents of plant and animal cells;
and Schwann, having observed the development of different tissues out of embryonic animal cells which appeared to be very much
alike, put forth, in 1839, a general theory of structure applicable to
plant and animal life alike, which derived all tissues and organs from
the proliferation and differentiation of similar organic units. Thus
originated the famous cell theory, which thereafter served for the
correlation of all morphological investigations. After Schleiden
and Schwann, studies of the spontaneous movements of the cell
contents in both plants and animals — its internal streaming, contraction and separation from the cell walls, dilatation by vacuoles,
and so on — and the discovery of unicellular organisms in which
an enclosing membrane was absent, made it apparent that the
mobile substance itself was the essential cell. The likeness of its
properties and behavior in all animals and plants led to the inference, expressed and justified by Schultze in 1861, that it was one
substance, to which von Mohl's designation *protoplasm* was applied.
Subsequent observations, particularly the more searching study of
the reproductive phenomena of cell division, confirmed the general
theory while demonstrating the inhomogeneity and complicated
activity, in short, the organization of the simplest cells; and it was
made apparent that, within the range of knowledge, all animals and
plants originated as single cells, which themselves were generated
by parent cells — the life substance, derived by no synthesis from
any other matter, perpetuating itself by processes of assimilation,
excretion, growth, and reproduction, which, however variable and
elaborate, were of one definable general character.

With reference to such phenomena, and in terms of such conceptions, the descriptive sciences of morphology, embryology, and
Physiological physiology were thereafter developed by a host of
chemistry able men, among whom the morphologist Haeckel, the
cytologist Koelliker, the embryologist Balfour, the physiologists
Mueller and Bernard, and the pathologist Virchow represent the
highest achievements of the century. It was especially through

the influence of Bernard that physiology became, in the modern sense, an experimental science. Before him, following Lavoisier, the botanist N. T. de Saussure, the chemist Liebig and others had applied the quantitative methods of chemistry to the study of physiological processes; and E. H. Weber had initiated the study of sensation by physical measurement. From these beginnings arose the modern sciences of physiological chemistry and psychophysics, which seek to describe, so far as possible, all vital activities in physico-chemical terms, and which, by brilliant achievement, have already brought a wide range of biological phenomena within the grasp of physical theory. From a scientific point of view, this aspect of the modern development of biology is more significant than any other, since it presages a final coördination of all scientific knowledge.

From the humanistic point of view, another achievement of the century was of still greater importance. This was the discovery of the causes of infectious diseases, and its immediate consequences, namely, the establishment of an effective preventive medicine and antiseptic surgery. These are commonly held to be the most valuable of all scientific contributions to human welfare. They were made possible by the work of the French chemist Pasteur. His early studies of the forms of tartaric acid led him, in 1855, to an exhaustive investigation of the then obscure phenomena of fermentation, at the conclusion of which he had proved that they were invariably due to the presence of living micro-organisms. The similar phenomena of putrefaction and of certain animal diseases he then ascribed to like causes, and, by original methods which this theory suggested, successfully controlled them. In 1885, with equal success, Pasteur inoculated human beings against hydrophobia. In 1876, Koch had begun those bacteriological researches which resulted in the successive isolation of various pathogenic organisms, and in the establishment of the science of immunology. Meanwhile, Lister had devised and tested and successfully practiced the techniques of antisepsis, which, together with the practice of anesthesia (which was general in 1850), made possible unprecedented advances in surgery. Since Pasteur, the continued progress of biology in many fields of research has made possible the understanding control and treatment, not only of an increasing number of infectious diseases, but also of others due to abnormal physiological processes, the study of which now promises to be equally fertile. In a word, by purely scientific research, the art of medicine has itself now become a science, and its future possibilities have been correspondingly expanded.

If, in this phase of modern scientific progress, the rise of physico-chemical biology seems to the scientist to be most significant, and

Evolution   if, to the humanist, the development of experimental medicine seems most important, to the philosopher — that is to say, to scientist and humanist alike — the crowning scientific achievement of the century was the demonstration of the universal process of evolution. In the middle of the eighteenth century, the ancient and ill-defined conception of a slowly developing natural world — a conception familiar to the early Greek philosophers which became the actual basis of Aristotelian philosophy, and was thereafter adumbrated in various ways by several modern speculative philosophers — assumed in the mind of the naturalist Buffon a quasi-scientific character, and after him became gradually more definite. At the beginning of the nineteenth century, the evidence of specific types of similarity between animal species and groups of species, and the fragmentary but suggestive evidence of their chronological succession which geological observation provided, appeared sufficient to justify the opinion that animal forms were derived from one another. At the middle of the century, the geological evidence alone was sufficiently impressive to compel belief in the absence of fixed preconceptions to the contrary, among all who did not demand the final persuasion of a theory that would show how, by the operation of natural causes, it could have happened. A scientific doctrine of evolution, certainly, demanded such explanation. The geological theories of Hutton and Playfair provided this, in part: the rocks themselves, quite evidently, might have been formed by natural agencies; they were, in fact, being thus formed under men's eyes. A corresponding theory of the origin of species was more difficult to conceive. It was, however, conceived by Lamarck, who, in 1802, advanced the theory that, in adaptation to changing conditions of life, by the use and consequent development of certain organs and the disuse and consequent atrophy of others, each organism was to some extent modified during the course of its life; and that its descendants, inheriting these acquired characters, were thus changed in structural form. The accumulation of such modifications in geological time, he maintained, might well account for all differences in the forms of animal life. As is

LOUIS PASTEUR

CHARLES DARWIN

well known, Lamarck's theory was either ignored or ridiculed by the majority, who still adhered to the venerable Hebraic doctrine of special creation; and the very tendency of his thought was opposed by the influential Cuvier, who gave this old conception a scientific color.   Nevertheless, the work had been done, and supernatural explanations of the phenomena slowly gave way in scientific thought to the suggestions of common sense.   At length, in 1859, Charles Darwin's epoch-making work, *The Origin of Species*, appeared.   For Lamarck's inheritance of acquired characters, Darwin substituted as the more probable or more effective cause of evolution the effects of a universal struggle for life, which permitted the survival, among the slightly different individuals of a species, of those only whose peculiar characters were advantageous in the conflict: these reproduced their kind, whose own variability in successive generations accentuated, under like conditions of life, their differentiating characteristics.   The force of Darwin's arguments lay in the fact that he was able to demonstrate, by reference to the results of artificial breeding, and by an overwhelming mass of correlative evidence, the spontaneous variability of species and their actual transformation by artificial selection.   His justification of the theory of natural selection was therefore conclusive. Since his time, it has been learned that other causes are operative in altering the character of species.   De Vries has demonstrated by experimental breeding that sudden changes, or mutations, may occur, which are persistent.   Weissmann and his followers have denied the possibility of Lamarckian inheritance; but the matter is still disputed.   No present controversy, however, affects the general issue.   Cumulative evidence makes it practically certain that the process of evolution is a fact: its causes are not improbably many.   All theoretical research and discussion of organic evolution now has for its aim nothing more than to discover these, and to evaluate them with respect to their relative importance.

With reference to this great conception, the classification of animals and plants was successively revised, after the early work of Cuvier (1812) and Owen (1855), by several men, among whom Huxley and Haeckel, the great protagonists of evolutionary doctrine, were preëminent, and the scope of the science was greatly enlarged by the rapid development of paleozoölogy and paleobotany. The idea of development guided new geological and geophysical research beyond the range of the biological record; astronomy provided evidence of actual processes of evolution in the solar system and among the stars. The new scientific conception thus pictured a universal process, first completely envisaged by Herbert Spencer, the contemporary of Darwin, and since his time substantiated by a rich diversity of evidence. One stage in the process and one alone remains to be bridged by pure conjecture: the origin of life is still obscure. But even here, the chemist will not admit complete defeat. Though it may always remain impossible to synthesize living matter, it is not impossible that its physico-chemical character may be so far determined that the conditions necessary for its natural genesis, though they be unattainable, may yet be as clearly definable as those which determine the constitution of the stars.

The scientists of the nineteenth century thus organized the positive knowledge of their predecessors; not completely — for its correlating theories are not yet perfected, and leave much work to be done, the results of which may prove to be of profound significance — yet marvelously well. And their three universal doctrines, all substantiated by masses of uncontrovertible evidence, of the atomic constitution of matter, the flux of energy, and evolution, remain, in all probability, the greatest of all the achievements of human intelligence.

REFERENCES

PROGRESS OF SCIENCE:

J. T. Merz, *A History of European Thought in the Nineteenth Century*, Part I, Scientific Thought (1896), both philosophical and critical, and explains admirably the continuity of scientific thought; the *Annual Report for 1900* of the Smithsonian Institution of Washington contains excellent brief surveys of the progress of the several sciences during the nineteenth century; more systematically descriptive are S. Günther, *Geschichte der Anorganischen Naturwissenschaften in Neunzehnten Jahrhundert* (1901) and F. K. Müller, *Geschichte der Organischen Naturwissenschaften in Neunzehnten Jahrhundert* (1902); F. Dannemann, *Die Naturwissenschaften in ihrer Entwickheng und ihrem Zusammenhange*, 4 vols. (ed. 1920–23), best general treatment of the history of science from its beginning, untechnical, well-illustrated, and readable. On astronomy: A. M. Clarke, *A Popular History of Astronomy during the Nineteenth Century* (ed. 1908), best general treatment; A. Berry, *A Short History of Astronomy* (1898), brief general sketch; T. Moreux, *Astronomy Today* (1926), explains recent progress. On physics: F. Rosenberger, *Geschichte der Physik* (1882–90), best general history; H. Buckley, *A Short History of Physics* (1927), treats of recent developments; K. K. Darrow, *Introduction to Contemporary Physics* (1926), excellent exposition of recent advances; M. Planck, *A Survey of Physics* (1925), an historical, synthetic, and profoundly critical essay; V. E. Pullin and W. J. Wiltshire, *X-Rays, Past and Present* (1927), an historical account; F. Soddy, *The Interpretation of Radium* (ed. 1920); L. Bolton, *An Introduction to the Theory of Relativity* (1920?), fundamental conceptions of theory clearly presented; A Einstein, *Relativity* (1920), by the famous scientist, easily understandable and almost uniquely exact logically; and B. Russell, *The Analysis of Matter* (1927), philosophical interpretation. On chemistry: E. von Meyer, *A History of Chemistry* (ed. 1906), general progress most satisfactorily presented; F. P. Armitage, *A History of Chemistry* (1918), another excellent work of similar scope; W. A. Tilden, *Chemical Discovery and Invention in the Twentieth Century* (1916), best on recent progress; Al Ladenburg, *Lectures on the History of the Development of Chemistry since the Time of Lavoisier* (1900), by far the best exposition of the foundation of chemistry, keenly critical. On geology: K. von Zittel, *A History of Geology and Palœontology* (1901), a standard general history, translation somewhat abbreviated; A. Geikie, *The Founders of Geology* (1905), delightfully written biographical sketches; and H. B. Woodward, *History of Geology* (1911), good brief history. On biology: E. Nordenskiold, *The History of Biology* (1928), most satisfactory general treatment in English; E. M. Radl, *Geschichte der biologischen Theorien in der Neuzeit*, 2 vols. (1909–13), excellent; and J. A. Thomson, *The Science of Life* (1900), brief but instructive. On botany, J. von Sachs, *History of Botany, 1530–1860* (ed. 1906) a classical history of the subject; J. R. Green, *History of Botany, 1860–1900* (1909), a continuation; and R. J. Harvey-Gibson, *Outlines of the History of Botany* (1919), brief, readable, corrects Sachs in several particulars. On evolution: Delage and Goldsmith, *The Theories of Evolution* (1913), a comprehensive survey; E. Clodd, *Pioneers of Evolution* (1907), a biographical and critical work, already classic; W. B. Scott, *The Theory of Evolution* (1918), present status of doctrine; and R. C. Punnett, *Mendelism* (ed. 1927), C. Singer, *A Short History of Medicine* (1928), excellent and readable; P. De Kruif, *Microbe Hunters* (1926), exceptionally good popular treatment. On method and philosophy of science: J. A. Thomson, *An Introduction to Science* (1911), an easy introduction; F. Barry, *The Scientific Habit of Thought* (1927), more critical; J. Dewey, *Reconstruction in Philosophy* (1920), influence of scientific way of thinking on modern philosophy; and W. James, *Some Problems of Philosophy* (1911), scientific philosophy vividly and clearly explained.

CHAPTER XXVII

THE NEW INDUSTRIAL AND AGRICULTURAL REVOLUTIONS

TOWARD the end of the nineteenth century there took place a new Industrial Revolution as startling as that at the end of the eighteenth century. New methods of production and new means of transportation and of communication appeared which made Cartwright's power loom, Stephenson's locomotive, and even Morse's telegraph as antiquated as the spinning wheel and the stage coach. Germany and the United States were the pioneers of the new Industrial Revolution. Germany's chief contribution was the application of science, especially chemistry, to industry.[1] The American contribution was "mass production," or the vast output of standardized goods made rapidly by automatic machinery. The United States was indeed well fitted to be the scene of the new industrial era: it was the greatest storehouse in the world of raw materials; it had considerable capital; a large and constant stream of cheap labor in the form of immigration; and it had a magnificent home market in the high standard of living of a large and rapidly growing population. The new Industrial Revolution spread to the rest of the world, even to backward countries such as eastern Europe, Asia, and Africa. It was not difficult to introduce new machinery in countries that had no old machinery to scrap.

Germany and America the pioneers of new industry

Methods of invention underwent great changes. Formerly, discoveries were made by an "inventor," often a lone genius untrained scientifically, who experimented in secret. Success depended sometimes on a "hunch," often on chance; hence, inventions were sporadic. In the new Industrial Revolution the laboratory of industrial research supplanted the garret of the romantic "inventor." The laboratories were furnished with expensive apparatus and staffed by highly trained scientists, who conducted systematic research on a problem set before them. They invented to order.

The new inventors

Germany was a pioneer in establishing industrial laboratories.

[1] See page 402.

There was hardly an industry that did not have its "Institute," where research was carried on. Much material and time were often consumed before definite results were possible, but, in time, the industrial laboratory became a trade machine of great importance. It was supported, partly by trade associations, partly by the government which was eager to advance German industry. In the eighties the Imperial Institute for Physical and Technical Research (Physikalish-Technische Reichsanstalt) was founded for the purpose of scientific investigation into industrial problems. It gave rise to similar institutions throughout the country, and became the inspirer of the industrial laboratories maintained by private concerns. In the twentieth century, industrial research became important in the United States, where business enterprises spent large sums in establishing laboratories and enlisting the services of eminent scientists. America soon outclassed even Germany in this new method of industrial promotion.

The industrial laboratory

In the old Industrial Revolution it was the engineer who was chiefly responsible for its progress; in the new, it was the chemist. At first, the chemist was engaged mainly in analyzing substances; later, he concentrated his attention upon the more creative aspect of his subject, synthetic chemistry. By means of chemical treatment, substances found in nature were so radically altered that they became far more valuable. Even more remarkable was the imitation of natural products by artificial means. What nature took many ages to produce, the laboratory often did in a few minutes. From the laboratory came artificial indigo, nitrates, leather, and even rubber. Sometimes chemistry created wholly new substances, often from by-products that had formerly been thrown away. Wonderful were now the uses of coal tar, a viscous fluid that is a by-product of coking. In 1856, William Henry Perkin, an English chemist, discovered that in this dark, sticky substance were imprisoned all the colors of the rainbow. He proved to his fellow countrymen that dyes could be made from coal tar, but received no encouragement. In Germany, however, the discovery received considerable attention. After many years of research, the German chemists succeeded in making artificial dyes, which rapidly supplanted the natural dyes from plants, used from time immemorial. Furthermore, from coal tar came not only dyes, but perfumes, oils, explosives, and medicines. Processes of

Chemistry and industry

manufacture were revolutionized by chemistry, such as bleaching, tanning, dyeing, glass-making, steel-making. It is impossible to state the many and various ways that chemistry has affected industry; there is hardly an article which has not felt its transforming touch.

THE NEW POWER

The Age of Steam gave place to the Age of Electricity. In the progress of the old Industrial Revolution, the factory, by using Electricity steam, became independent of streams and waterfalls. But steam power had a disadvantage in that there was often a great distance between the coal mine and the factory, and the cost of transporting coal raised the cost of production. Electricity, however, could be generated at its source, the coal mine, the waterfall, and rapid streams, and transmitted by means of wires. The factory, therefore, could be built wherever it was to its advantage because it could receive power from a long distance. The limited supply of coal led to a return to the original source of power, water. Italy, France, and Switzerland, having little coal, were pioneers in the development of hydro-electricity. They found an inexhaustible source of energy in their rapid streams which they harnessed to do the work of their factories. The most recent development in the Age of Electricity is, what is called, in America, "super-power." Gigantic hydro-electric stations were erected, notably at Niagara, Keokuk, Muscle Shoals, and Boulder, that distribute power over large areas, operating factories, lighting cities, driving street cars, churning butter, and many other things. A rival to the steam engine came with the invention of the internal combustion engine, which uses chiefly oil and gasoline. The steam engine is wasteful of power; only one quarter is derived from a given amount of fuel, which is much less than the amount derived by the internal combustion engine. Moreover, oil or gasoline can be used in small or large units, thus eliminating another form of possible waste. The internal combustion engine began to supplant the steam engine in many industries. Its chief use was in operating the automobile and the motor ship which will be described later.

Nevertheless, coal continued to be the chief source of power. Without a plentiful supply the new Industrial Revolution would Coal not have been able to maintain its extraordinary pace. New coal mines were opened up, and more scientific methods of mining were introduced. Before 1870, England was practically the only producer of coal, but after that date coal was extensively mined in the United States and Germany. A new source of supply, but of inferior grade, was the "brown coal," or lignite, mined chiefly in Germany and Belgium. Mining operations underwent a great change. In those mines using modern methods, the miner no longer loosed the coal by means of a pick. It was now blasted by dynamite, cut by power machinery, and thrown into waiting freight cars. The new methods largely eliminated the most exhausting form of human toil known.

Iron is indissolubly wedded to coal because together they produce the most useful metal of modern times, steel. The first great advance in steel-making was the Bessemer process.[1] But the steel produced by that process was not always sufficiently hard and durable to be used in the construction of bridges and of buildings. Moreover, it could be applied only to that sort of iron that was free from phosphorus. Two new methods of steel-making appeared, one in the sixties known as the Siemens-Martin, or open-hearth process, and the other in the seventies known as the Gilchrist-Thomas process which made possible the utilization of low-grade iron ore for making high-grade steel. By the former, a mixture of molten pig iron, steel scrap, and limestone was exposed to a gas flame; at the same time heated air played upon it, keeping up a high and even temperature. The impurities contained in the iron were burned out, but only to the extent desired; other elements were added in order to make the grade of steel desired. The Gilchrist-Thomas process was a method of absorbing the phosphorus from the molten iron so that the poorest grade of iron ore could be converted into excellent steel. This process made possible the development of the extensive iron deposits in Germany and France which, hitherto, had not been mined to a great extent because the ore contained too much phosphorus. The greatest source of supply of iron ore was the Great Lakes region in the United States which rapidly became the leading iron and steel country in the world.[2] The best steel was made by mixing the molten iron with certain "alloys" which gave the steel unusual hardness and toughness. These "ferro alloys," chiefly manganese, nickel, and tungsten, became all-important in

New processes for making steel

[1] See page 29.

[2] In 1913, the United States produced 63, Germany, 34, and England, 16 million tons of iron ore. France produced more iron ore than England, but, because of a lack of coal, far less steel.

the steel industry. As in the case of coal, methods of mining iron underwent great changes. Slabs of ore were now torn from their beds by power machinery and dropped into waiting freight cars. As a result of the new sources of supply and of new methods of mining, iron and steel production increased enormously.

TRANSPORTATION

A new era of transportation began with the building of transcontinental railways and trans-oceanic canals. Instead of the small railway lines connecting points, at no great distance from one another, trunk lines were now built spanning continents, having branches radiating in every direction. In the old Industrial Revolution the railway had been merely a stage in its progress: in the new it often played the chief rôle in opening up a country to modern industry, notably in Russia, India, and China.

Trunk lines

The first trans-continental railway was built across the United States. From 1862 to 1869 several railways were built, beginning at Chicago and going westward toward the Pacific, by private companies aided by government subsidies. Lines had already been built from New York to Chicago; and when the western lines were completed, in 1869, there was railway connection between New York and San Francisco.

The American transcontinental

The American continent was again spanned, this time by the Canadian Pacific (1881–85), with its termini at St. John, New Brunswick and Vancouver. It was built by a private corporation aided by subsidies from the Canadian government. The American and Canadian transcontinental railways opened up the wheat lands of the West, which greatly increased the food supply of the world.

The Canadian transcontinental

A still greater railway enterprise was the Trans-Siberian (1891–1902). It was 5500 miles long, and spanned both Europe and Asia, connecting Leningrad on the Baltic with Vladivostok on the Pacific. The Trans-Siberian was built by the Russian government [1] with the object of developing eastern Siberia and Manchuria; through Manchuria Russia also built the Chinese Eastern Railway. Along the Trans-Siberian the government built cities with streets and houses to accommodate the population that was streaming in from Russia and from China.

The Trans-Siberian

[1] See page 452.

The great railway in western Asia was the famous Bagdad Railway, which is described elsewhere.[1] Beginning at Constantinople, it was to run to the Persian Gulf. As the railways *The Bagdad* of central Europe connected Hamburg with Con- *Railway* stantinople, the Bagdad, like the Trans-Siberian, joined Asia and Europe.

From the imperial imagination of Cecil Rhodes came the project to span Africa with a railway connecting Cape Town with Cairo. Because of great natural difficulties, the Cape-to-Cairo *The Cape-* could not be made a continuous railway; it had to be *to-Cairo* a combination of rail and water transportation; when completed it will be 5700 miles long, of which 2000 will be by steamer on lakes and rivers. The enterprise may be said to have begun in 1897, when the railway from Cape Town to Buluwayo was completed; by 1909, it had been extended to the southern border of Belgian Congo. As a result of the British occupation of Egypt, the northern section was built starting from Cairo; by 1925, it had reached a point three hundred miles south of Khartoum. More than half of the Cape-to-Cairo was now completed.

The trunk line presented a picture quite different from the railways of the early nineteenth century. Gigantic locomotives pulling a mile length of cars and going at a speed of over *The long* fifty miles an hour took the place of the small, slow *trains* trains that looked almost like toys in comparison. The earth was now girded with a network of railways, and the toot of the locomotive was heard in darkest Africa, on the plains of Asia, in the mountains of western America and in the deserts of Australia.

More humble yet as significant as trans-continental railways in the history of transportation was the automobile. The "horseless carriage," as it was first called, appeared in the *The auto-* eighties when a German, Gottlieb Daimler, invented a *mobile* gasoline engine that drove the new vehicle. Little progress was made in the automobile industry until the beginning of the twentieth century, when mass production was introduced into its manufacture in the United States by Henry Ford. The cheap and serviceable car that he produced gave impulse to automobile manufacturing; in a short time the automobile almost entirely supplanted the horse-drawn vehicle in the United States. Motor trucks and 'buses took the place of trolley cars in many sections;

[1] See page 635.

and, in short hauls, they threatened to supplant even the railway.[1] Road-building was revolutionized by the automobile. The old macadamized roads were not fitted for heavy, rubber-tired vehicles that demanded perfectly smooth highways. In answer to this demand roads were built, first of asphalt, and later of concrete.

Inter-oceanic canals, as well as trans-continental railways, joined the farthest corners of the earth. A short all-water route The Suez to India, long the object of search of the sixteenth-Canal century navigators, and never found, was made by the construction of the Suez Canal (1859–69). It was a French enterprise, organized by Ferdinand de Lesseps, who formed a company that received a concession from the Khedive of Egypt through whose territory it was to run. Most of the stock of the company was held by French investors and by the Khedive. Later, the British government got a controlling interest in the enterprise by purchasing the Khedive's shares.[2] The Suez Canal revolutionized water transportation between Europe and Asia, and was the chief cause of the revival of the Mediterranean as a highway of commerce. The old route from London to Bombay, by way of the Cape, was 11,220 miles; the new one, by way of Suez, was 6332 miles. There was consequently a great stimulus to the trade between Europe and India, the Far East, East Africa,[3] and Australasia.

The Suez Canal was controlled by a company consisting chiefly of representatives of the French stockholders and of the British Internation- government, the latter being the largest single stock-alization of holder. By an international agreement, in 1888, equal Suez Canal treatment was guaranteed to all nations. The Canal was to be "free and open, in time of war as in time of peace, to every vessel of commerce or of war without distinction of flag."

Again it was the indefatigable de Lesseps who organized a company to build a canal across the Isthmus of Panama, joining the The Panama Atlantic and the Pacific. The company received a Canal concession from Colombia through whose territory it was to run. In 1881, it began digging, but soon got into financial

[1] In the United States between 1860 and 1920 the railway mileage increased eightfold; between 1916 and 1924 more railway mileage was abandoned than built, chiefly because of the advance of motor transportation.

[2] See page 650.

[3] In 1870, the tonnage that passed through Suez was about 650,000; in 1913, about 20,000,000.

difficulties and went out of existence. Its rights were purchased by another company that planned to finish the work. However, a new situation arose when public opinion in the United States demanded that a canal in that region should be under American auspices. After much negotiation the United States, in 1902, bought out the rights of the French company, but failed to come to terms with Colombia. Suddenly, in 1903, the region of the canal zone revolted, and set itself up as the Republic of Panama. The new nation was promptly recognized by the United States who, in turn, was given sovereign rights over the Canal Zone. The American government now took complete control of the situation. Work began vigorously in 1907, under the direction of Generals George W. Goethals and William C. Gorgas, of the War Department. In spite of great natural obstacles, it proceeded rapidly, largely through the use of the steam shovel, an invention of great use in excavating. The Canal, forty miles in length, was finally completed in 1914. It shortened greatly the all-water route between the eastern coast of North America and the Far East, which hitherto had been by the way of Cape Horn. The Panama Canal is owned and operated by the United States. In 1901, a treaty between England and the United States provided, in effect, that the Canal should be open to all nations on equal terms.

The new era of rapid transportation saw the appearance of new types of ships. In the sixties, iron began to displace wood in shipbuilding; and, in the eighties, steel displaced iron. Steel vessels Ships built of steel were actually lighter than those built of wood; the hull of steel was only half an inch thick, that of wood sometimes as much as two feet. Moreover, steel vessels were safer than wooden ones, inasmuch as they were less likely to catch fire. The steel ship was propelled by means of "screws," driven by a steam "turbine" which was a considerable advance over the steam engine in navigation. In the former, the steam directly produced a revolving motion; in the latter, it did so indirectly. Swift liners, gigantic in size, now plied the oceans on regular schedules. The largest of the ocean greyhounds, in 1914, was the German liner, the Vaterland (taken over by the United States during the World War and renamed the Leviathan). It was 950 feet long, having a gross tonnage of 54,500; it accommodated 5100 persons, passengers and crew; and could cross the Atlantic in less than six days.

Oil began to displace coal as a means of generating steam in the propelling of vessels. The advantages of oil over coal are many:

Oil
(1) its bulk is considerably less, hence the ship can carry more fuel and more cargo; (2) it saves space by eliminating the stokehold and the steam boilers; (3) it saves labor of loading and stoking coal; and (4) it is much cleaner than coal. The demand for oil became so great that an international rivalry began for the control of the oil supply of the world. In 1926, the greatest producers of oil were the United States, which produced seventy per cent of the world's supply, Mexico, Russia, Venezuela, and Persia.

A striking innovation in navigation was the motor ship. This automobile of the sea is operated by an oil-burning internal com-

The motor ship
bustion engine, known as the Diesel engine, perfected, in 1902, by the German, Rudolf Diesel. At first it was not powerful enough to propel large ships, but so many improvements have been made that the motor ship may, in the future, oust the steamship as the latter ousted the sailing vessel.

Man's conquest of the air followed long after his dominion over land and sea. It required all his ingenuity, all his daring, aided by

The balloon
the scientific knowledge of a century to accomplish this result. There are two distinct methods of air transportation: (1) by sailing, as in a balloon which uses a gas lighter than air; and (2) by flying, as in an airplane which is heavier than air and which uses power generated by its own internal combustion engine. The first attempt, in modern times, to sail in the air took place in 1783, when the brothers Montgolfier, Frenchmen, launched a balloon filled with gas. Since then, balloons became fairly familiar, but they were not considered seriously as inventions because their success depended largely on weather conditions.

Many scientists were engaged on the problem of flying, notably the German, Otto Lilienthal and the American, Samuel P. Langley.

The airplane
The latter made many notable experiments in airplane flying which proved the feasibility of the new method. In 1903, Langley attempted a flight in an airplane of his invention. It rose about a hundred feet, but was unable to sustain itself, and slowly sank. On December 17, 1903, at Kitty Hawk, North Carolina, the brothers Orville and Wilbur Wright, Americans, launched an airplane of their invention. The machine rose about 850 feet, *flew* for about a minute, and landed safely. It was the first sus

tained free flight of a heavier-than-air machine, carrying a man, and propelled by its own power. The Wright brothers improved their airplane and repeated their flights, staying longer in the air. Their claim to being the fathers of aviation rests upon the facts that they launched the airplane correctly, stayed in the air, contrived methods of balance and of steering, and landed in safety.

After the Wrights' feat, aviation progressed rapidly. In every country great interest and enthusiasm were aroused, and many lost their lives in this latest adventure in science. To encourage flying large sums were contributed by private persons and by governments. Constant improvements were made: in the construction of the airplane, in the motor, in the methods of flight, and in the study of the atmosphere. Two important inventions were a light, air-cooled engine which made possible long-sustained flights; and an earth inductor compass which is to the aviator what the mariner's compass is to the seaman. The first notable long-distance flight was made by the Frenchman, Louis Blériot, who, in 1909, flew across the English Channel in thirty-seven minutes. Blériot's achievement set at rest all doubts as to the future of the airplane.

> Improvements in aviation

Long-distance flights with frequent stops were many. The great test was a non-stop long-distance flight, and to conquer the Atlantic became the aim of daring aviators. In 1919, an expedition of American naval officers, headed by A. C. Reid, left Rockaway Beach in several airplanes. Only the airplane containing Reid and five companions succeeded in flying to Newfoundland, thence to the Azores, and finally to Lisbon. They covered about 2500 miles in about 27 flying hours. This feat was followed by a greater one in the same year. Two British army officers, John Alcock and Arthur W. Brown, flew from Newfoundland to Ireland, a distance of about 2000 miles, in about 16 hours. It was the first non-stop flight across the Atlantic. Another remarkable Atlantic flight was made, in 1926, by an expedition of Spanish aviators led by Ramon Franco. In imitation of Columbus, they started from Palos, Spain, and flew to Pernambuco in Brazil, stopping at the Canary and Cape Verde Islands; they continued their voyage to Buenos Aires. The Columbus of the air covered a distance of over 6000 miles in about 63 hours of flying time. The most sensational trans-Atlantic flight was made, in 1927, by Charles A. Lindbergh, a young American aviator. Alone, with only one

> The conquest of the Atlantic

engine operating his airplane, without sleep, and with little food, the intrepid young man flew from New York straight to Paris, a distance of 3610 miles in 33 hours, 20 minutes. Lindbergh's feat aroused the greatest enthusiasm in Europe and America. It was followed almost immediately by several other notable flights across the Atlantic.

The conquest of the Atlantic was immediately followed by the conquest of the Pacific. Two American army officers, Lester J. Maitland and Albert F. Hegenberger, flew from Oakland, California, to Honolulu, a distance of 2400 miles, in about 26 hours.

Of the Pacific

Flights across continents were no less daring than those across seas. In 1919, Ross Smith, an English army officer, flew from England through Europe, India, the East Indies and finally to Melbourne; he covered a distance of about 11,500 miles in 27 days. The year 1924 witnessed notable long-distance flights. Russell L. Maughan, an American army officer, flew from New York to San Francisco in about 22 hours, making five stops. Pelletier d'Oisy, a French army officer, flew from Paris across Europe and Asia to Tokio; in spite of delays and accidents, he covered a distance of about 11,000 miles in about 45 days. The most notable flight in 1924 was that around the world. A number of American army airplanes under the command, first of Frederick L. Martin, and later of Lowell H. Smith, left Santa Monica, California, and flew to Seattle, their official starting-place. There began an air argosy that thrilled the world. The aviators flew to Alaska, Japan, China, India, Europe, Greenland, Canada, Boston, Santa Monica, and finally to Seattle. Storms, fogs, accidents, and delays could not stop the dauntless aviators who flew around the world in 175 days. The sensational aviation event in 1926 was the flight over the North Pole by an American naval officer, Richard E. Byrd.

Flights across continents

The airship, too, made notable progress. The balloon underwent great improvement and was transformed into a dirigible airship. During the first decade of the twentieth century two types of dirigibles appeared: one invented by a Brazilian living in Paris, Alberto Santos-Dumont, and the other, by a German, Count Ferdinand von Zeppelin. The latter was more successful, and the "Zeppelin," with its rigid frame, huge gas bag, and hanging cabins, became the model. Like the airplane

The dirigible

the airship began a career of conquering the Atlantic. In 1919, a British airship was the first to cross the Atlantic. In 1924, a Zeppelin built in Germany for the United States (named the Los Angeles) sailed across the Atlantic, covering a distance of 5000 miles in 81 hours. The most famous performance of a dirigible took place in 1928. The Graf Zeppelin, a German dirigible, under Captain Hugo Eckener, left Friedrichshafen carrying about sixty persons. It took a long route, and, in spite of storms, landed safely in Lakehurst, covering 6300 miles in $111\frac{1}{2}$ hours. Its return trip was by another route, which took 69 hours to cover 4400 miles.

During the World War, aviation made rapid progress because both airplane and airship were found to be important in military and naval operations. Flights between London and Paris were very frequent; in 1919, a regular air line was established between the two capitals. It was soon followed by the establishment of air lines connecting most of the capitals of Europe. Regular air mail service was established in the United States. Not so long ago only the most venturesome dared travel by air; now air travel became so common that it was hardly noticed.

Progress of air travel

COMMUNICATION

Equally marvelous were the new methods of communication, known as the "wireless," or radio. The telephone and telegraph seemed almost the limit of human ingenuity in devising methods of rapid communication; but to communicate without wires seemed magical. As in other great inventions the theoretical scientist preceded the practical inventor. James Clerk-Maxwell, the English physicist, came to the conclusion that there were invisible electric "waves" in the æther which permeate all space and matter. This theory was confirmed by a German physicist, Heinrich Hertz, who discovered these "waves," called after him "Hertzian waves."

The "Hertzian waves"

These researches were the basis of experiments conducted by an Italian, Guglielmo Marconi, who, in 1896, devised a mechanism to send and receive messages by means of these "waves" and without wires. After many successful tests over short distances Marconi finally succeeded, in 1901, in sending a wireless message across the Atlantic, which established the future of the new method of communication. Great improvements in

Marconi

the mechanism led to the rapid development of wireless telegraphy which became a rival of the telegraph and cable.

Wireless telegraphy soon led to the radio which broadcasts sounds. Concerts of great orchestras given in large cities are

Radio   heard in lonely farmhouses thousands of miles away.
             An address delivered by means of the radio can be
heard by millions all over the world. The printed word was now outdistanced by the spoken word. In 1926, came the radio telephone, when a conversation, lasting four hours, was held between New York and London. Other remarkable developments followed: radio photography, or the sending of pictures by means of images flashed through the air; and television, or a method of actually seeing the person to whom one is speaking many miles away. A single incident illustrates the extraordinary progress made in transportation and communication. On the day following his flight across the Atlantic, Lindbergh spoke from Paris to his mother in Detroit, and a picture of his reception appeared in the New York newspapers.

The printed word, too, made notable progress. In 1885, came the invention of the "linotype," the work of a German-American,

The linotype   Ottomar Mergenthaler. It is an electrically operated
               mechanism by means of which type is set by manipulating a keyboard resembling a typewriter. The linotype was rapidly introduced in the field of large publication, such as newspapers and books. So great was the demand for paper that new sources of supply had to be found. Wood pulp, subjected to chemical treatment, became the source of much of the cheap paper, especially that used by newspapers.

Almost instantaneous communication and exceedingly rapid transportation by land, water, and air has caused the earth to "shrink" immeasurably. Mankind is now united in a manner undreamed of by the pioneers of the old Industrial Revolution.

PRODUCTION

Production of goods on an increased scale naturally resulted from increased power and more rapid means of transportation. In the

Mass pro-   United States "mass production" became the leading
duction   characteristic of its remarkable industrial development. Two distinctive types of this method appeared: (1) the manipulation of large masses of material, as in the Bethlehem steel

works; and (2) the manipulation of material in a continuous series of operations, as in the Ford automobile works. The latter attracted considerable attention because of its novelty. Briefly the system is as follows: The various parts of the automobile, all standardized and interchangeable, are first manufactured in different factories, and then brought together in the assembling plant. An endless conveyor belt is the means of having operations done in sequence. As it moves between two lines of workers, at a regular pace, each worker does his special part in the construction of the car, which keeps on "growing" until finished. The essential features of mass production are (a) the making of standard interchangeable parts, and (b) the assembling of these parts into the completed unit, with the minimum of handicraft labor. Mass production has been defined as the "focusing upon a manufacturing project the principles of power, accuracy, economy, system, continuity, and speed." It is the most efficient way of producing large quantities cheaply, being economical of time and of labor. Through the use of automatic power machinery and the extreme division of labor, the part of the worker became insignificant. "The men are not running the machines, but the machines are running the men, setting for them an inexorable pace with which they must hurry and struggle to keep up. The machine does so much and man so little. The man who puts in the screw does not screw it down, the man who screws it down does not give it the final tightening." In some industries automatic machinery is so highly developed that human labor is entirely eliminated. Raw material put in at one end starts a series of operations which result in the finished product coming out at the other, wrapped and packed, all without the touch of human hands.

Great changes also took place in the manufacture of textiles through the introduction of automatic machinery. In the new spinning process thousands of threads are drawn through   New textile rollers, and one man tends to hundreds of spindles.   machinery So wonderful is the automatic character of textile machinery that when a thread is broken in spinning, the machine attempts to tie it again; if it fails, it notifies the worker to do so by means of a click. When the amount of yarn in the shuttle is beginning to run low, the worker is notified of that fact by the loom.

New cotton manufacturing centers were established in the twentieth century. Continental Europe, India, Japan, and the South

appeared as rivals of old England and New England, who formerly
New cotton   had almost a monopoly of the cotton industry. The
centers   South, particularly, was in a favorable situation: it
produced most of the raw cotton in the world, had excellent hydro-
electric power, and an abundant supply of cheap labor.

A new material for clothes came with rayon, or artificial silk.
When wood pulp is treated by a chemical process it produces, in
Rayon   appearance, the work of the silkworm. Silk was ex-
               ceedingly expensive and dresses of this material were
handed down as heirlooms. But rayon was cheap, and the aristocrat of textiles found a serious rival in its imitator. The rayon
industry developed rapidly as the wearing of "silk" became
popular.

Another new article, even more important, was rubber. One can
hardly imagine how industry to-day could function without this
Rubber   cheap article which is useful in a variety of ways, from
               elastic bands to automobile tires, from erasers to rain-
coats. Rubber is made from the sap of a tree, found originally in
Brazil. It was not of much use until the thirties of the nineteenth century when a process, called "vulcanization," was discovered by an American, Charles Goodyear. By this process the
crude rubber was treated chemically so that its strength and elasticity were increased. The chief sources of supply at first were
the wild trees of South America and the Congo; later, the Malay
Peninsula and Ceylon, where rubber trees were grown scientifically
on plantations operated by British corporations.

The "plant" of the new Industrial Revolution was in striking
contrast to the factory of the old. A group of enormous buildings,
The plant   some one quarter of a mile square, run by electric
               power, worked by an army of laborers, equipped with
scientific laboratories, and capitalized by millions of dollars supplanted the small "mills" as they were still called.

The production of goods was so great and their distribution so
rapid that new methods had to be devised to dispose of them.
Advertising   Foreign trade increased tremendously, but it was not
               sufficient to dispose of the surplus that a country pro-
duced. In order to create a large domestic market, there began a
development of advertising, especially in the United States which,
until 1914, had a large production and little foreign trade. The
"science of publicity" aimed to stimulate the demand for old

goods and to create a demand for new ones. In turn, production was stimulated by the belief that a large sale could be counted upon through advertising, which lowered costs. Advertising, in this way, became the "handmaiden" of mass production.

The railway and steamboat, bringing goods from all parts of the world, seriously affected the local market. The shopkeepers were unable to compete with mail-order houses and depart- The "chain" ment stores that could use the new facilities to great store advantage. Many were forced out of business, and the locality found a new marketing institution in the "chain" store, which was the local distributor of a large enterprise organized on a nation-wide basis.

THE NEW CAPITALISM

In order to get sufficient capital, the old Industrial Revolution had developed the joint-stock company. But investment was generally limited to certain persons, generally those interested The in the enterprise. The need of large amounts of financier-capital to finance the "plant" produced the "corpora- capitalist tion" whose stock was held by thousands of persons all over the world who knew nothing of the nature of the enterprise, but who invested their money in it in the belief that it would pay dividends. A new type of business man appeared, the financier-capitalist, whose function was to get the capital, not, as in the case of the industrial-capitalist, to manage the industry. The financier, generally a banker, floated the stocks and bonds of the corporation much in the manner of a minister of finance floating a loan for his government; sometimes, the amount of money that he raised was larger than that raised by some governments. Although the stockholders were many, those who controlled the corporation were few; they employed capital to which they paid dividends as they employed labor to which they paid wages.

A tendency toward consolidation began resulting in the "trust" in America and the "cartel" in Germany. The former was generally an amalgamation of many plants under one direc- Consolida-tion, each plant being a branch of a great corporation. tion In the cartel system the various plants maintained their independent management and kept their own profits, but agreed to have a common policy as to prices, output, raw material, and sales territory.[1] There were two types of consolidated industries, the "hori-

[1] See page 405.

zontal" and the "vertical." By the former was meant the amalgamation of competing firms in the same line; by the latter, amalgamation of the firms that dealt in the raw material, semi-finished products, finished products, and even the means of transportation. The trusts were denounced as monopolies, and laws were passed against them. But all in vain, as no law could stop the march of industry toward consolidation.

So vast was the new industrial unit and so complicated its activities that one could no longer "go into business," but had to prepare
The technician
for business as for a profession. Schools of business arose in the universities where the principles and methods of industry were studied just as scientifically as those of medicine and law. Between capital and labor a new element appeared, the technician and the administrator, who really managed the industry, though they did not control its policies. Men were trained in "scientific management," a method elaborated by Frederick W. Taylor, an American, who suggested ingenious ways to avoid waste in labor, time, energy, and material. In every great corporation there was a hierarchy of industrial officials, from the general manager to the foreman of a gang of laborers, each with his special duties. Even more important in some industries were the technicians, generally engineers and chemists, who labored to produce large quantities cheaply and well. Separation of capital and management was as characteristic of the new Industrial Revolution as separation of capital and labor had been of the old.

The worker in the new industry became an almost perfect cog, and a very small one, in the automatic machine. The machine
The laborer
tool robbed him of the little skill left him by the old Industrial Revolution. A few highly skilled men were needed to design the machinery and to direct its process. However, the worker was compensated by higher wages and shorter hours; the eight-hour day became almost universal in highly industrialized countries.

After a century of struggle to establish the trade union, the workers discovered that it was as little able to cope with the trust
The industrial union
as the individual worker had been able to cope with the firm. A strike in one branch of the industry or by one group of workingmen affected the trust but little; the work would be done by those who were not on strike in other branches of the industry. The worker now virtually had no choice of an

employer, and capital was in a position to enforce its terms. In order to redress the balance, a movement toward consolidation began in trade unionism. Industrial unions appeared, composed of men engaged in the whole industry or organized in close federations.[1] When a general strike was called, it involved thousands of workers in the industry in any capacity throughout the country.

The new Industrial Revolution is too recent to give any adequate idea of its results. Nothing in history, not even the old Industrial Revolution, has had so deep, so immediate, and so widespread an influence upon mankind. It has set dreamers dreaming of a new humanity united by indissoluble bonds, living in peace and plenty without harassing toil, and enjoying to the full the gifts of science and of art.

THE NEW AGRICULTURAL REVOLUTION

Agriculture lagged far behind industry in the application of science to production. It was much more difficult to introduce scientific methods, involving large outlays of money, on millions of small farms than in several large factories. Whatever progress was made in Europe took place on the large estates. It was not until the immense lands of the American and Canadian West were opened up that the application of science to agriculture began on a large scale. The American Homestead Act (1862), granting a farm of 160 acres free to any one who agreed to cultivate it, was an event of great importance in the history of agriculture. It led to the rapid cultivation of the largest and finest wheat areas in the world.

Progress of farming

As in the case of industry, the pioneers of the new Agricultural Revolution were Germany and the United States, the former contributing chemistry, and the latter, machinery. The work of Liebig during the first half of the nineteenth century was the beginning of agricultural chemistry.[2] It was followed by many important discoveries which, however, were not utilized until late in the nineteenth century. In the eighties the German chemist, Hellriegel, discovered that legumes, such as beans, peas, and clover, "feed" on the nitrogen contained in the air; hence, it was not necessary to add that ingredient to their soil, which helped solve one of the problems of agriculture. When industrial Germany faced the problem of being self-support-

German agricultural chemistry

[1] See page 579.   [2] See page 15.

ing, she turned to agricultural chemistry as the one means to produce sufficient food from her limited and generally poor soil.[1]

The large farms in the United States and the lack of sufficient
agricultural labor stimulated invention. McCormick's "reaper"
Agricultural   started a series of inventions, especially during the
machinery   latter part of the nineteenth century, which made agricultural machinery as extraordinary as that used in industry.   The
"rotary plow" appeared, worked by power, which automatically
plowed the soil, pulverized it, planted the seeds, and even smoothed
the surface.   The combined harvesting and threshing machine,
worked by power, automatically cut, gathered, threshed, and
cleaned the grain, and even bundled it in sacks ready for the market.

Equally important with machinery was the change in power
from the horse to the tractor.   The latter possessed a great advan-
The tractor   tage in that it could be used twenty-four hours a day
                in all kinds of weather which, in harvest time, often
saved the crop from destruction from bad weather.   Hitched to a
gasoline tractor, a rotary plow could plow as much as fifty acres a
day.

The harvest was no longer stored in barns, often to rot or to be
devoured by animals, but in "elevators," immense granaries built
Grain "ele-   of concrete near marketing or shipping centers.   Elevators"   vators were operated by corporations who stored the
wheat for the farmers of a region and even marketed it for them.

Specialization in agriculture became possible with the use of
machinery.   The old farm produced every variety of food, both
Specializa-   plant and animal, but the farm of to-day generally
tion   produces one article, wheat, corn, fruit, dairy, or
vegetables.   The production of so essential a food as milk was
regulated.   Great herds of cattle were carefully selected, stall-fed
scientifically, and their milk pasteurized and graded.   The invention of cream separating and churning machines did away with
the hard and slow labor of making butter and cheese, and greatly
increased the production of these foods.

Rapid transportation resulted in a world market for agricultural
as well as for industrial products.   The wheat of North Dakota,
Preservation   the mutton of Australia, the butter of Denmark, the
of food   fruit of California were to be found in all the markets
of the world.   Fresh vegetables were procurable all the year round,

[1] See page 400.

as the railway outdistanced climate.   Methods of preserving food by means of canning and refrigeration created a new industry. Canning originated in France during the Napoleonic Wars, when food, preserved fresh in glass bottles, was used by the French armies.   In order to dispose of the immense harvests of modern times, it was necessary to have recourse to canning on a large scale. Refrigeration was used chiefly to preserve meats and fish.   Frozen beef from the Argentine and frozen mutton from Australia were loaded in ships built for refrigerating purposes and sent throughout the world.   Food preservation enriched the diet of mankind by making possible a variety of food from all parts of the world and at all times of the year.

The competition of lands having the best soil and cultivated scientifically had a great effect upon European farming.   In England, agriculture virtually disappeared.[1]   Den-   Flight from mark and Holland specialized in dairy farming for   the land which they are well fitted.   Other countries, like France and Germany, sheltered themselves behind high tariff duties on foodstuffs. But cheap food from abroad overleaped even high tariff walls.   To protect themselves, the peasants formed coöperative associations that bought expensive machinery for common use, founded credit banks, and helped their members in many other ways.   But farming on a small scale became precarious, and there began a flight from the land.   The migration from the country to the city was a universal phenomenon.   Cities grew so fast that housing became one of the great problems of city life.

Agriculture, long chiefly a means of independent livelihood, was now a business enterprise.   Its methods of production were scientific, and its methods of marketing, commercial.   The great transformation of life that began with the old Industrial Revolution finally overtook the oldest, the most conservative pursuit in the history of mankind, the tilling of the soil.

REFERENCES

GENERAL:

On the new Industrial Revolution in America: R. G. Tugwell and others, *American Economic Life* (1925), describes new industrial and agricultural methods in America, emphasizes the social aspects; R. G. Tugwell, *Industry's Coming of Age* (1927), describes consolidations of individual industries

[1] See page 283.

and their great development; W. H. Hamilton (ed.), *Current Economic Problems* (ed. 1919), readings in modern industry, very good selection; F. W. Wile (ed.), *A Century of Industrial Progress* (1928), a series of articles on various industries by experts; P. M. Mazur, *American Prosperity, its Causes and Consequences* (1928); Henry Ford, *My Life and Work* (1922) and *Today and Tomorrow* (1926), the new industrial philosophy expounded by the famous automobile manufacturer; Frederick W. Taylor, *The Principles of Scientific Management* (1911), by the pioneer of the system; H. T. Warshaw (ed.), *Representative Industries in the United States* (1928); M. Keir, *Manufacturing* (1928); on the new Industrial Revolution in Germany: B. Harms (ed.), *Struktur Wandlungen der Deutschen Volkswirtschaft* (1928), essays by experts in industry, agriculture, labor, and finance; W. Sombart, *Das Wistschaftsleben im Zeitalter des Hochkapitalismus*, 2 vols. (1927), a sociological treatment of the Industrial Revolution; and W. Meakin, *The New Industrial Revolution* (1928), chiefly on Germany after the war.

INVENTIONS:

B. A. Fiske, *Invention the Master Key to Progress* (1921); E. Cressy, *Discoveries and Inventions of the Twentieth Century* (1915); W. B. Kaempffert (ed.), *Popular History of American Invention*, 2 vols. (1924); J. A. Fleming, *Fifty Years of Electricity*, (1921); on wireless telegraphy: C. R. Gibson and W. B. Cole, *Wireless of Today* (1924); on aviation: E. C. Vivian, *A History of Aeronautics* (1921); and C. L. M. Brown, *The Conquest of the Air* (1927).

SPECIAL TOPICS:

On consolidation in industry: R. Liefmann, *Kartelle und Trusts* (ed. 1924); O. Lehnich, *Kartelle und Staat* (1927); E. Jones, *The Trust Problem in the United States* (1922); J. W. Jenks and W. E. Clark, *The Trust Problem* (ed. 1917); F. W. Taussig, *Principles of Economics*, vol. I (ed. 1923); and A. H. Stockder, *German Trade Associations: the Coal Kartells* (1924). On the application of chemistry to industry: E. E. Slosson, *Creative Chemistry* (1921); and E. E. Howe (ed.), *Chemistry in Industry* (1924); on mining: C. R. Gibson, *The Romance of Coal* (1923); E. S. Moore, *Coal* (1922); E. C. Jeffrey, *Coal and Civilization* (1925); R. Marsh, *Steam Shovel Mining* (1920); and F. W. Harbord and J. W. Hall, *The Metallurgy of Steel*, 2 vols. (1923), a standard technical work by experts. On the automobile: F. A. Talbot, *Motor Cars and Their Story* (1912); R. C. Epstein, *The Automobile Industry, Its Economic and Commercial Development* (1928); and L. H. Seltzer, *A Financial History of the American Automobile Industry* (1928). On the new sources of power: J. A. Fleming, *Fifty Years of Electricity* (1921); and A. P. M. Fleming and H. J. Bocklehurst, *A History of Engineering* (1925), brief volume, contains select bibliography. H. G. Moulton, *Financial Organization of Society* (1921). On agricultural changes: E. B. Voorhees, *Fertilizers* (ed. 1926); F. N. G. Kranich, *Farm Equipment for Mechanical Power* (1923); J. H. Collins, *The Story of Canned*

Food (1924).   Criticism of the new industry: S. Chase, *The Tragedy of Waste* (1925), an indictment of the existing order as being wasteful of raw material, labor, and in methods of marketing; H. W. Laidler and N. Thomas (eds.), *New Tactics in Social Conflict* (1926), a symposium on the new relations between capital and labor.

ADDITIONAL REFERENCES

P. S. Brown (ed.), "Second Industrial Revolution and its Significance," in *Annals of the American Academy of Political and Social Science* (May, 1930); C. A. Beard (ed.), *Toward Civilization* (1930); W. J. Lauck, *The New Industrial Revolution and Wages* (1929); S. Chase, *Men and Machines* (1929); F. Delaisi, *Political Myths and Economic Realities*, trans. from the French (1927); A. P. Usher, *History of Mechanical Inventions* (1929); *Recent Economic Changes. The Report of President Hoover's Committee on Recent Economic Changes*, 2 vols. (1929); M. Keir, *Manufacturing* (1928); H. Feis, *Europe, the World's Banker, 1870–1914* (1930); W. Z. Ripley, *Main Street and Wall Street* (1927); H. W. Laidler, *Concentration of Control in American Industry* (1931); R. Liefman, *Cartels, Concerns, and Trusts* (1932); A. A. Berle and G. C. Means, *The Modern Corporation and Private Property* (1932); O. M. Kile, *The New Agriculture* (1932); W. N. Polakov, *The Power Age* (1933); C. W. Hallberg, *The Suez Canal* (1932); W. E. Spahr (ed.), *The Economic Foundations of Business*, 2 vols. (1932); T. N. Beckman and H. C. Nolen, *The Chain Store Problem* (1938); G. W. Edwards, *The Evolution of Finance Capitalism* (1938).

For additional titles consult bibliography at the end of Chapter III.

CHAPTER XXVIII

REVOLUTIONARY LABOR MOVEMENTS

SOCIALISM

ONE of the most distinguishing characteristics of the nineteenth century was the advance of freedom. How oppressed and divided

Revolution-
ary charac-
ter of so-
cialism

peoples achieved national independence, how unenfranchised lower classes gained political equality, and how persecuted faiths won toleration has already been told. There still remains to tell the story of the extraordinary advance of a movement which, unlike the others, did not merely seek to liberalize existing institutions, but aimed to change the very constitution of the present system of society and to establish an entirely new one, in which the production and the distribution of wealth would be radically different from what it is at present. This revolutionary movement goes by the general name of "socialism," and it arose as the result of the Industrial Revolution which, for the first time, brought capital and labor into sharp contrast. Socialism has enlisted the enthusiastic devotion of millions of followers throughout the world, and has profoundly influenced the views of many who are not its adherents. It has been fervently defended and bitterly attacked. By many of the working class socialism has been accepted as the gospel which would free them from economic slavery; by many of the property-owning class it has been regarded as a "red specter," threatening to inaugurate a reign of terror, which would destroy organized society and plunge the world into chaos and ruin.

Socialism is the most comprehensive as well as the most widespread of modern social movements. It is at once a bitter indict-

(1) The so-
cialist in-
dictment:
exploitation
of labor

ment against the present social order, a philosophy of life, a program of action, and a promise of a future goal. The existing economic system, which is based on private ownership of capital and on competition in industry, underwent severe criticism at the hands of the socialists. They claimed that, in spite of the extraordinary increase of wealth since the Industrial Revolution, the masses of people lived in a state of dire poverty and misery because, through a faulty and unjust method of distribution, the few reaped the benefits of industrial progress at the expense of the many. Production, asserted the socialists, is "social," as many laborers coöperate to produce an article; but distribution is "individual," as each laborer is paid a certain sum of money as wages by the owner of the machine, the capitalist. The laborer's wages are just sufficient to maintain himself and his family on the barest necessities. Moreover, he may be deprived of his job at any time by his employer, or he may lose it through no fault of his own or that of his employer, but through the uncertain working of the industrial system. Unemployment is an essential feature of this system, for capitalism needs an "industrial reserve army," ready to supply the demand for more labor in case of a sudden expansion of the market or to take the places of those who may be unwilling to work for the wages offered to them. The much-lauded freedom of the workingman, argue the socialists, is an illusion, for, deprived of his tools by the competition of machinery, he must either sell his labor at the price offered him by the capitalist or starve. Economic necessity is the invisible whip that drives him to his daily task; hence, he is in reality a slave with "liberty simply to change masters." The present industrial system is based on the exploitation of labor. As producers, the workingmen are exploited by the capitalists; as consumers, by the middle classes; and as tenants, by the landlords. There can be no solution of the labor problem, conclude the socialists, without a dissolution of the capitalist system.

Capitalist methods, assert the socialists, are wasteful and corrupt. Overproduction one year, and underproduction the next, dislocate market conditions and cause panics which bring ruin and destitution to many. Competition engenders wastefulness in energy, time, money, and product, because competitors maintain separate establishments with their attendant expenses. The various middlemen, from wholesaler to retailer, take toll from the product as it passes from producer to consumer. A centralized industry, argue the socialists, would save in countless ways by regulating the output of the whole of the product itself, and by distributing it directly to the consumers. To be strictly honest in business is to invite disaster; hence, business men who would prefer to deal fairly are forced to adopt the methods of their dishonest competitors. Modern business reeks with corruption, from stock-watering by financiers to

(2) Incompetence and corruption

putting sand in sugar by corner grocers.   Swindling purchasers through dishonest advertisements and through adulteration is widely practiced.   Colossal fortunes are made in stock exchanges by manipulating the market or by sheer gambling, frequently to the ruin of thousands of innocent investors.   Capitalism, declare the socialists, has created a world in which the swindler, the manipulator, and the corruptionist prosper at the expense of millions of toilers who are thus condemned to misery and want.   The much vaunted freedom of enterprise of the capitalist is largely the "freedom of a fox in a free hen-roost."

Conversion to socialism is not an indication of a change of political belief only; it frequently means a change of attitude toward the problems of life, both private and public.   The convert to socialism rejects many cherished traditions and principles that guide the thoughts and actions of his fellows.   He is apt to question institutions of all kinds, religion, property, marriage, nationalism.   In their earlier days, socialists were wont to attack these institutions as "bourgeois prejudices"; later they concentrated their attacks upon capitalist production, and relegated religion and marriage to the position of "private matters."

Socialism: as an attitude toward life

As a program of action, socialism was the advance guard of radical political movements.   It maintained a political party which, unlike all other political parties, was international in scope.   The socialists held international conventions to direct the common aims of socialism throughout the world.   Socialists were everywhere actively fighting reactionary measures, exposing corruption, championing the cause of the labor unions in their struggles with capital, and, above all, maintaining a vigorous propaganda for their cause.

As a program of action

Finally, as a future goal, socialism meant the public ownership and democratic management of all means of production, factories, mines, railways, land, and stores, and the distribution of wealth by public authority.   It did not mean, as popularly believed, the confiscating of private property and dividing it equally among all the people.   Quickly or slowly, as conditions would determine, the public authorities in the central and local governments would take over the ownership and operation of the industries.   The existing state, which, according to Marx, was the "weapon of capital in its war against labor," would "wither

As a future goal

away" as political power shifted to the working class. It would be finally superseded by a socialist state whose main function would be the "administration of things" not the "government of men." Under a socialist régime there would exist a vast civil service; all would be required to work at salaries fixed by the government according to position and ability. People would continue to possess private personal property, such as clothes, houses, books, and furniture, but not industrial property, such as factories, mines, or railways, which were to be state monopolies. By this system, known as the Coöperative Commonwealth, socialists hoped to abolish poverty and misery, and to inaugurate the golden age of a happy humanity.

(a) UTOPIAN SOCIALISM

Early in the nineteenth century a movement appeared, known as Utopian socialism which was a precursor of the socialist movement. It had its origin in France where the French Revolution had given a great impetus to schemes for reconstructing society. During the stirring days of that great upheaval men beheld institutions, hallowed by age, custom, and sentiment, vanish overnight, and new institutions suddenly called into being. It was not surprising, therefore, that many came to believe that social institutions were merely creations of man who, by his own fiat, can easily usher in a new system of society and government provided he has a plan ready. This idea was common during the early part of the nineteenth century, especially in France, where it inspired a group of social reformers, known as Utopians,[1] who desired to emancipate humanity from capitalism as their fathers had emancipated it from feudalism.

Influence of the French Revolution

The first of the Utopian socialists was Claude Henri, Comte de Saint-Simon, a French noble who, when a young man, had fought under Washington during the American Revolution. He became intensely interested in reforming mankind, and spent his life and fortune advocating schemes of social reconstruction, with the result that he became so poor that he was reduced to utter destitution. Saint-Simon's writings, hardly known while he lived, attained influence after his death when a group, calling themselves "Saint-Simonians," advocated his ideas.

Saint-Simon (1760–1825)

[1] The Utopians were so named after the book *Utopia*, by Sir Thomas More, which describes an ideal society.

Some of the members of this group later became famous, such as Auguste Comte, Ferdinand de Lesseps, and Michel Chevalier. Saint-Simon was among the first to recognize that modern industry had effected a revolution in society, and that its real rulers were now scientists and industrialists, not kings and nobles. Exploitation of man by man has been the rule, he argued, but in the society of the future men will associate with one another in the exploitation of nature. The new society was, therefore, to be based on coöperation; and the new state was to concern itself with supervising the production and distribution of goods. The sharing of goods was to be according to the principle of from each according to his capacity and to each according to his services. Inheritance was to be abolished because it was a privilege that industrial society took over from feudalism. The State was to be the sole inheritor, and it was to use the wealth as capital to be loaned to coöperative societies. The new society, declared Saint-Simon, was the new Christianity that would usher in the golden age which was in the future, not in the past. Saint-Simon's views were hazy but very suggestive, and they greatly influenced early socialist thought.

Another famous Utopian socialist was Charles Fourier, whose books present a carefully worked-out ground-plan of the new society. Like Saint-Simon, Fourier believed that the chief evil of the present social system was its spirit of antagonism between persons, classes, religions, and countries. "Harmony" would be the basic principle of the new stage of civilization. He worked out a scheme of communal living to which he gave the name of "phalanstery": it was to comprise farm lands, workshops, and living apartments in which a "phalanx," a group of about eighteen hundred persons, were to live and work coöperatively. A person entering a phalanstery would engage in such work as suited his tastes and desires; and he would be permitted to change his occupation freely until he found one congenial to his temperament. It was Fourier's idea to allow free play to human instincts which, he declared, frequently worked harmfully because the existing system of society gave them no legitimate outlet. Once an environment was created which gave opportunities to all sorts of people to express themselves, harmony would result, and the world would become peaceful and happy. Fourier's ideas were taken up by many ardent reformers of his day. They found an echo even in America in the famous Brook Farm Colony,

Fourier
(1772–1837)

CLAUDE HENRI DE SAINT-SIMON

KARL MARX

which numbered among its members such men as Horace Greeley and Nathaniel Hawthorne.

A far different type of Utopian was the Briton, Robert Owen, practical business man, philanthropist, and reformer. At the age of nineteen, Owen became the manager of a large cotton mill in New Lanark, Scotland, of which he later became the chief proprietor. New Lanark was a wretched factory town inhabited by a laboring class sunk in poverty, squalor, and drunkenness. Owen's heart was touched by this state of affairs, and he energetically set about transforming the place; he believed firmly that a good environment would result in an improved population. Owen gave his employees good wages; he improved factory conditions; he organized schools for the children; and he built wholesome houses for his operatives. New Lanark was transformed into a model town with happy, contented people. In spite of the additional expense, Owen's business continued to prosper, and his factory became a place of pilgrimage for people who were interested in the experiment. Owen, however, was not content to play the part of a philanthropist. He was a man of fine mind as well as of great heart; and he believed that true reform would come as a result of people solving their own problems and not in having them solved for them by "good men." Owen was convinced that men were naturally neither bad nor good, but were always the creatures of their environment; hence, the sole function of government should be the improvement of social conditions. A good environment would make man good and happy. He therefore became deeply interested in schemes of social reform and was converted to socialism,[1] to which he devoted his life and fortune. Owen was active in establishing communistic colonies in many parts of the world. Believing that America, being a new country, would offer a freer field for social experiments, he came to Indiana, in 1825, and founded a colony called New Harmony. For many years Owen was a notable figure in English public life and a leader in the radical movements of his day.

Owen (1771–1858)

Utopian socialism was essentially a humanitarian movement. It made no special appeals to the working classes for support and was, therefore, not revolutionary in its methods. Saint-Simon appealed even to the Pope and to Louis XVIII to establish his ideal society. Fourier was

Failure of Utopian socialism

[1] It is said that the word "socialism" was coined by Owen; it was then synonymous with "utopianism."

regularly at home every day at noon for twelve years, hoping that
philanthropists would come to finance his scheme.   Kings and
other famous persons were welcomed at New Lanark by Owen,
who was eager to convince them of the beneficence of his reforms.
Utopian socialists, however, were generally regarded as unpractical,
fantastic persons.   Their schemes were discredited, partly because
their colonies proved failures, and partly because of their attacks
on religion and the family.   Moreover, Utopian socialism was displaced by a new movement, first called communism and later
socialism, which broke sharply with utopian schemes and founded
its philosophy and methods on an entirely different basis.

(b) MARXIAN SOCIALISM

The father of modern socialism was Karl Marx, who was born
in Trier, Rhenish Prussia.   The family of Marx were well-to-do
Karl Marx   Jews who had been converted to Christianity, in which
(1818–83)   faith young Karl was reared.   He went to the university to study law, but found that his interests lay rather in philosophy and history.   Like many other young Germans of this period
he became an ardent admirer of the philosophy of Hegel, who was
then the guiding star of the rising generation of German intellectuals.   At the age of twenty-four, Marx became the editor of a
radical paper which was suppressed because of its attacks on the
government.   Shortly afterwards he was married to Jenny von
Westphalen who came from a noble family.   But the young couple
were not destined to spend their lives in peace and plenty.   Hearing
of the new social doctrines preached by the French Utopians, Marx
determined to know more of them and their ideas; accordingly, he
and his young bride left their native land and went to live in Paris.
Henceforth, to the day of his death, Marx's life was one of long
exile, sometimes that of a hunted agitator driven from land to land,
at other times a poverty-stricken recluse poring over books in the
British Museum.   Throughout all his vicissitudes, his wife was his
faithful and loving companion, sharing his exile, privation, and
obloquy.

Marx's visit to Paris was the beginning of his new life and of his
new ideas.   There he fell under the influence of the Saint-Simonians,
whose doctrines awoke new trains of thought in his mind.   There
he met Friedrich Engels, who became his lifelong friend and co-
worker.   Like himself, Engels came of well-to-do German parents,

but he nevertheless dedicated his life to the service of the working class. Marx was driven out of Paris in 1845, and fled to Brussels, where he joined an association of radicals calling itself the Communist League. In 1848, this organization issued the famous *Communist Manifesto*, "the birth-cry of modern socialism," which was written by Marx and Engels. When the Revolution of 1848 took place in Germany, Marx returned to his native land where he organized a socialist agitation. He was promptly expelled from Germany; and he fled to London where he lived to the end of his life, devoting himself to study and writing. The result of Marx's labors in London was his famous book, *Das Kapital*. In spite of the fact that it is a serious work on economics, and is, in many parts, quite obscure, no book since Rousseau's *Social Contract* has had such an enormous and far-reaching influence. It was translated into almost every living language, and became a bible for socialists in every part of the civilized world.

Marx was one of the great figures of the nineteenth century, and a world force like Luther and Voltaire. He possessed an unusual combination of qualities, profound learning, striking originality, a keen mind, and, at times, a rare gift for literary expression. This scholar, philosopher, and agitator was a man of stern, unbending uprightness, with indomitable will power and dynamic energy. He was indeed well fitted to be the spokesman of the most revolutionary thought of the nineteenth century.

To this day the recognized principles of socialism, those that inspire fear in its opponents and hope in its adherents, are Marxian, pure and simple. These principles are:

The economic interpretation of history. "In every historic epoch," reads the preface to the *Communist Manifesto*, "the prevailing mode of economic production and exchange, and the social organization necessarily following from it, form the basis upon which is built up, and from which alone can be explained, the political and intellectual history of that epoch." In other words, the entire course of history in all its manifold phases has been determined by economic conditions. Changes in history take place only when changes take place in methods of producing and exchanging goods. Revolution is the conflict that arises between new forms of production and the institutions of society based upon the old forms. "No social order," declares Marx, "ever disappears before all the productive forces for which there is room in it, have been devel-

Marxism

oped." Ideas and emotions centering within race, religion, culture, and fatherland are "ideological veils" obscuring the real motive forces, which are economic. According to the socialists the economic interpretation of history is "the one pass-key which will unlock all the secrets of the past."

The class struggle. "The history of all hitherto existing society," begins the *Manifesto*, "is the history of class struggles. Freeman and slave, patrician and plebeian, lord and serf, guildmaster and journeyman, in a word, oppressor and oppressed, stood in constant opposition to one another, carried on an uninterrupted fight, now hidden, now open, a fight that each time ended, either in a revolutionary reconstitution of society at large, or in the common ruin of the contesting classes." Out of the economic divisions of society arise classes of exploiters and exploited which correspond in the political sphere to the governors and the governed. In a capitalist society founded on wage labor, the exploiters and governors are the bourgeois, and the exploited and the governed are the proletariat.[1] In the past the historic stage was the scene of conflict between landlord and peasant, now it is between capitalist and workingman. The *Manifesto* sings a pæan of praise to the bourgeois as the revolutionary class that has swept away "all fixed, fast-frozen relations with their train of ancient prejudices and opinions" characteristic of the feudal and ancient worlds, and that has inaugurated the modern dynamic world in which constant change is the law of life, and in which all newly formed institutions become "antiquated before they can ossify." The bourgeois, being masters of society, are necessarily masters of the State, which is merely an "executive committee" for the management of their common affairs. Capitalism has simplified the class struggle by abolishing the many grades and ranks characteristic of feudalism. "Society as a whole is splitting up more and more into two great hostile camps, into two great classes facing each other, bourgeois and proletariat," the only bond between them being "cash payment." It is, therefore, of vital importance for the proletariat to become "class conscious"; namely, to recognize that all laborers have common interests which are irreconcilably opposed to those of the capitalists. This common interest must always be first

[1] "By bourgeois is meant the class of modern capitalists, owners of the means of social production and employers of wage labor; by proletariat, the class of modern wage-laborers who, having no means of production of their own, are reduced to selling their labor power in order to live." (Engels.)

and foremost in the minds of the working class, to whom law, morality, and religion are "so many bourgeois prejudices, behind which lurk in ambush so many bourgeois interests." Class consciousness will result in class solidarity, which is essential to the proletariat in their struggle to overthrow the capitalist system.

Surplus value. The fundamental doctrine of Marx's economic system, and the central theme of *Das Kapital*, is known as the theory of "surplus value." In brief, the following is a statement of this theory: Commodities are produced in order to be sold. They vary in size, in physical properties, and in many other ways, but they all have one thing in common; namely, they are produced by human labor. According to Marx the exchange, or market value of a commodity depends upon the amount and degree of labor necessary to produce it. He defines a commodity as a "mass of congealed labor-time." Labor is, therefore, the source of value. It is likewise the measure of value, as "commodities in which the same quantities of labor are embodied or which can be produced in the same time have the same value." By "labor" Marx means, not that of an individual but "socially necessary labor time" that is required to produce a commodity under normal conditions; it includes the labor of highly paid managers as well as that of poorly paid operatives.

What does the laborer receive? Not the full product of his toil, but just enough to maintain himself and reproduce his kind. Marx accepts the theory of wages, formulated by the classical economists,[1] according to which the laborer can get only his mere sustenance under existing conditions. Only part of the work day is devoted to producing what the laborer gets; what he produces during the remainder of the day, "surplus value" is confiscated by the capitalist in the form of profits. Surplus value is, therefore, the difference between what the laborer produces and what he gets. Wages, declares Marx, are the illusion of the free laborer that he is paid for a full day's work; in reality he is paid only for a part of the day. Machinery brings no benefit to the laborer; it merely increases the "surplus value" of the capitalist by making the laborer more productive. As the capitalist contributes nothing to the creation of value, what then is his function? It is to bring about the coöperation of labor by assembling it in large quantities in order to operate modern industry. Under the capitalist system,

[1] See page 44.

asserts Marx, labor is systematically exploited for the benefit of the capitalist, but under a just system of distribution to be created by socialism, the workingmen would receive the full product of their toil; exploitation would cease, as all value created by labor would go to labor.

Inevitability of socialism.   "Capitalism produces above all its own grave-diggers," states the *Manifesto.*   Centralization of industry and of labor is, according to Marx, the inevitable tendency of the modern system of production; more and more will the capitalists combine, and wealth will be consequently in fewer and fewer hands.   As with capital, so with labor.   The factory tends to centralize many laborers of different trades and localities, and to reduce them to a common wage level.   Their lot will steadily grow worse, till finally they are reduced to a state of semi-pauperism. The theory of "increasing misery," advanced by Marx, is based upon his belief that the workingmen, because of their low wages, are unable to buy the enormous quantities of goods produced by machinery.   This condition causes overproduction, resulting in crises, which bring more misery through unemployment.   Sometimes the situation is eased by exporting goods to backward nations; but when these nations are developed, and goods can be sold neither at home nor abroad, a great world crisis would ensue. Into the ranks of the proletariat will sink the middle classes, shopkeepers, small farmers, and professional people, ground out of existence by the upper and nether millstones of capital and labor. In time there will be facing each other only two classes, the propertied few and the propertyless many.   To save themselves from destruction, the working class will be compelled to overthrow capitalism, and to establish the Coöperative Commonwealth, in which class rule will be forever abolished.   This change will be accomplished by force if necessary, but preferably through the peaceful action of parliaments controlled by representatives of the proletariat.   Unlike other revolutions, which were the work of minorities, the socialist revolution will be the first truly democratic one, as the working class constitutes the majority of the population. Marx thus summarizes the inevitability of socialism.   "Centralization of the means of production and socialization of labor at last reach a point where they become incompatible with their capitalist integument.   This integument is burst asunder.   The knell of capitalism is sounded.   The expropriators are expropriated."

Internationalism. "The proletarians have nothing to lose but their chains; they have a whole world to win. Workingmen of all countries, unite!" concludes the *Manifesto.* In their struggle for emancipation the workingmen must not be diverted from their goal by patriotism, for the proletarian has no country, only a "birthplace." All socialists are "comrades," whatever be their nationality. Class interests must, therefore, always take precedence over national interests, even in times of war, as there is more in common between the workingmen of different countries than between workingmen and capitalists of the same country. Modern wars, the socialists assert, are due to the machinations of capitalists, who rouse the masses of the various nations to slaughter one another for the benefit of the capitalists. Internationalism does not mean that socialists advocate the abolition of national frontiers; what they favor is the organization of the world into an international union, which would lead to the establishment of permanent peace and to fraternal relations between peoples.

Marxism, or "scientific socialism," is grounded on the theory of social evolution. Capitalism, according to Marx, is not an evil system inflicted on the world by wicked men, but a stage, and a necessary one, in the development of mankind; and socialism is not an ideal commonwealth to be called into being by enthusiastic reformers, but the logical and inevitable outcome of capitalism. The advent of socialism in a country was to be the result of certain necessary conditions: (1) a highly developed, concentrated industry; (2) the existence of a small but powerful capitalist class; (3) a majority of the population consisting of workingmen, organized and disciplined; and (4) a conscious and active class struggle between capitalists and workingmen. Marx had scant sympathy with readymade schemes to reorganize society, and he sarcastically referred to the Utopian experiments as "duodecimo editions of the New Jerusalem." For the first time in the nineteenth century, a philosophy appeared which gave assurance to millions that the stars in their courses were fighting the battle of the proletariat, whose emancipation might be delayed but not frustrated by the antagonism of the propertied classes. The socialism that emerged from Marx was bristling with the heavy armament of a new philosophy, a new economics, and a new international organization that immediately began an aggressive war on capitalism.

(c) CRITICISM OF SOCIALISM

To the challenge of socialism, its opponents reply that, although society is far from being perfect, the remedy is not socialism, but social reform. Were socialism, with its regimenta-
Socialism, enemy of progress
tion of humanity into an office-holding hierarchy, ever to come, it would destroy initiative and enterprise by eliminating the incentive to gain; and the consequence would be calamitous for the progress of mankind. Socialism would not eliminate the class struggle; it would, in fact, accentuate it. All being office-holders, a struggle would ensue for the best places in the government, and the political faction in control would be able to exercise an intolerable tyranny over their less fortunate fellows who, having no other avenue for a livelihood, would have to submit. Politics would be the one channel for all discontent, and revolutions would be more likely under a socialist régime than under the existing system, in which discontent expresses itself through many channels.

Marxian analyses and prophecies are declared by anti-socialists to be faulty. They maintain that the economic interpretation of history is a gross exaggeration, and that by its crass materialism it holds a low view of human nature. If economic motives played their part in the great epochs of history, so did racial, religious, cultural, and patriotic; it is impossible to say which one of these motives was most influential in any given period of history. Men are not sharply divided into three classes but into many, whose interests and ideals shade into one another so imperceptibly that frequently the interests of one group of laborers harmonize more with those of capitalists than they do with those of another group of laborers. The only true goal is the welfare of all the people, and not that of one class, the laborers. Furthermore, "the increasing misery" prophecy of Marx has not been fulfilled, because
The case against Marxism
the average workingman is better fed, housed and clothed, than at any previous period. Neither are the middle classes disappearing; on the contrary, they are constantly increasing in numbers and in influence. The concentration of industry is admitted by anti-socialists, and they advocate government regulation of great corporations to prevent economic injustice. "Surplus value" is essentially untrue, argue the opponents of Marx, for it leaves out of consideration the leading part played by capital in the creation of value by initiating enterprises

and by directing their development. Without capital, labor is of no value at all; hence, the laborers are not an exploited class but share in the product, though at times to an insufficient degree; higher wages, shorter hours, and better conditions generally would eliminate whatever exploitation existed. Anti-socialists deny that the workingman is a man without a country or even that he thinks that he is. Patriotism, they declare, is the monopoly of no class, but is the common emotion of a community with common ideals and traditions, and they instance the spontaneous loyalty of the working class to the flag in times of national crises.

The term "socialism" is frequently used to designate ideas quite different from and even hostile to the revolutionary working-class movement that goes by that name. By "state State social-socialism" is meant the intervention of the State in ism the affairs of capital and labor through regulation and through social legislation. Capital is regulated as to investments, prices, and rates; and labor, as to hours, wages, and factory conditions. Government control of railway rates, and eight-hour and minimum wage laws are examples of "state socialism." Another important aspect of state socialism was the system of social insurance inaugurated by Bismarck in Germany and by Lloyd George in England. The essential idea of state socialism, or social reform, as advocated by the German economists, Wagner and Schmoller, was to maintain the present economic system, but to give its benefits to labor as well as to capital.

"Christian socialist" is a term used to describe a type of social reformer whose aim is to apply the principles of Christianity to the present economic system, which he condemns as un- Christian christian because of the suffering it entails among the socialism laboring classes. The Christian socialist is as much opposed to the materialism and class hatred of Marxism as he is to the ruthless competition and *laissez faire* of individualism. Some of the Christian socialists accept the ideal of the Coöperative Commonwealth, and agitate for its establishment through moral and religious appeals, but most of them are radical social reformers. The original Christian socialists were Kingsley and his followers who greatly influenced the radical movement in England.[1] In 1891, Pope Leo XIII issued a famous encyclical, *Rerum Novarum*, in which he declared that the hostility between capital and labor was growing

[1] See page 146.

because of the tyranny and the greed of employers, and that the condition of the lower classes must be improved. But the remedy was not socialism, as its principles violated the natural right to property and incited to class hatred, which is unchristian. Harmonious relations between capital and labor, declared the Pope, was the solution of the social problem. He enjoined workingmen to be peaceful and loyal to their employers; and he enjoined the latter to treat their laborers as Christian freemen and not to exploit them as slaves. Christian socialists, both Catholic and Protestant, greatly influenced public opinion in favor of social reform.

ANARCHISM

In its early history socialism encountered an uncompromising foe in another revolutionary movement, anarchism. In principle anarchism is the very opposite of socialism. The latter favors the concentration of all authority in the State; and the former repudiates all authority in whatever form, State, Church, or family. To substitute freedom for authority in all relations of life is the chief object of anarchism. "The liberty of man," declared Bakunin, "consists solely in this, that he obey the laws of nature because he himself has recognized them as such and not because they have been imposed upon him externally by a foreign will, human or divine, collective or individual." According to anarchism, all classes, all privileges are to be completely abolished; and there is to be absolute equality between races, between the sexes, and between nationalities. All of life's activities are to be carried on by free associations that combine and dissolve at will. Coöperative productive associations, in which the product is shared among the laborers, are to supersede the present capitalist system; and mutual protective associations, the State. The latter, being the embodiment of the highest authority, is, according to anarchists, the archenemy of freedom; it must therefore be destroyed, the democratic no less than the autocratic, because "all government of man by man, under whatever name it may disguise itself, is tyranny." Religion is another deadly enemy of man's freedom; hence, atheism forms an essential part of the anarchist creed. Inasmuch as anarchy is the extreme of individualism, and socialism is the extreme of collectivism, these two movements have been constantly at war with each other.

Opposition to all law and to all government

The most famous names in the history of anarchism are those of the Frenchman, Pierre Joseph Proudhon (1809–65) and the Russian, Michæl Bakunin.[1] Proudhon was a self-educated man who developed remarkable gifts as a controversial writer. He wrote many pamphlets, the best known being *What is Property?* To this question *"Communist" versus "individualist" anarchism* Proudhon answers, "Property is theft"; for it reaps without sowing and consumes without producing, thereby enabling its possessor to rob other men of the fruits of their toil. He was an exponent of "communist" anarchism which is primarily interested in establishing a system of coöperative production. Another advocate of this system was the Russian scientist and sociologist, Prince Peter Kropotkin. "Individualist" anarchism was advocated by a German, Max Stirner, whose book, *The Ego and Its Own*, is a passionate denunciation of all social and moral bonds that hamper the egoism of the individual.

Many of the anarchists were philosophers and humanitarians, and were strongly against violence of any sort. They opposed the slaughter of animals, capital punishment, and war. *Methods of anarchism* They firmly believed that their ideas would triumph through the power of persuasion; hence, they favored freedom of speech without any restrictions whatsoever. But there were anarchists who believed in the "propaganda of deed," or violence against constituted authority. The assassination of rulers was the favorite method of these anarchists in their war against the State. King Humbert of Italy, Empress Elizabeth of Austria, President Carnot of France, and President McKinley of the United States were victims of anarchist terrorism. The chief exponent of violent anarchism was Bakunin whose influence was felt among the anarchists of every country.

As a revolutionary movement anarchism did not play an important rôle, for it appealed to few workingmen. But, as an attitude toward life and toward society, it greatly influenced the thought of many writers. Those who felt hampered and restrained by social conventions saw in anarchism the one philosophy of freedom.

SYNDICALISM

At the end of the nineteenth century, a new revolutionary movement appeared, known as "syndicalism," that attracted many

[1] See p. 182.

radical workingmen.   Socialism had appealed to workingmen because it offered them a definite plan of emancipation and clearly
indicated ways of realizing it.   The socialist vote grew apace, and
socialist parties became so strong that their coöperation was sought
by the other parties; their leaders were even made cabinet min-
Growing   isters.   Face to face with practical problems, they
moderation   tended to become moderate in their views and
of the social- methods; their revolutionary fervor abated, and the
ists
great day of emancipation was put off or forgotten.
The success of the socialists attracted to their ranks aspiring young
men of the middle class to whom socialism offered a political career;
almost the entire leadership of the socialist parties was in the
hands of men whose traditions were bourgeois.

This situation led to uneasiness among the workingmen.   They
charged the socialist parties with being more eager to win elections
Discontent   than to win emancipation for the proletariat.   Social-
with social- ist leaders were denounced as parliamentary politi-
ist parties   cians who preferred their own and their party's welfare
to that of the working class.   There was also a growing conviction
that the capitalists would never permit the socialists to get control
of parliament.   Was then the work of Marx all in vain?

As a result of this discontent syndicalism appeared and spread
among the working classes in Europe and in America.   It had its
Direct   roots in both socialism and anarchism, the two contra-
action   dictory philosophies.   Syndicalism subscribed fully to
the socialist indictment of present society and to socialist philosophy; but its practical program and future goal were very different
from those of socialism.   According to the syndicalists the dependence on parliamentary action was the great error of socialists.
Parliaments, they contended, could not be the means of emancipat-
ing the working class; they were essentially bourgeois institutions
created by the bourgeois in their struggle against the landed aristocracy represented by absolute monarchy.   Hence, the political
activity of the working class was a waste of time and energy; moreover, it dulled their revolutionary ardor, as the class struggle was
frittered away in fruitless party strife.   The few reforms passed by
parliaments in the interest of labor were nullified in effect by hostile
or corrupt officials and judges.   Real reforms could be obtained in
one way only, directly by the workingmen from the capitalists, not
indirectly through acts of parliament.   "Direct action" was, there-

fore, the only logical policy for the proletariat; they should eschew politics and give their whole time and energy to the struggle in the economic field, the real battleground of capital and labor. The syndicalists, like the anarchists, completely repudiated the State which they regarded as a mechanism of oppression.

The only pure working-class institution, created by them and for them alone, was the trade union; and the only true working class weapon was the strike, declared the syndicalists. On them only must the workingmen depend for their "integral emancipation." Hitherto, the trade union had been weak and inefficient because its potentialities were not realized. Once its scope was broadened by larger organization and its significance deepened by a revolutionary philosophy, this much-despised working-class institution would become a powerful weapon in the hands of the proletariat. The unions were, therefore, to be reorganized on an industrial basis; small craft unions within an industry were to amalgamate into an *industrial union*, comprising both skilled and unskilled workers. For example, the carpenters, iron-workers, steam-fitters, painters, and others employed in the building trades were to form one union having a common policy and a common direction. A strike was to be *general*, namely, of all the workers in the industry. If the carpenters had a grievance, a strike was to take place, not of the carpenters only, but of all those employed in the building trades. An industrial union would emphasize class solidarity more than the craft union, which is merely a labor corporation; and a general strike would give the workingman a vivid sense of the class war, which was all-important in syndicalist methods. Laborers should make no contracts or agreements with their employers; the war between capital and labor was unceasing and ruthless, and workingmen should strike whenever an opportunity arose. Strikes, whether they achieved their immediate end or not, were never lost; for they kept alive the revolutionary spirit of the working class, and prepared for the day when all labor would rise to take possession of the means of production. Even when at work, the laborers were to fight capitalism by means of "sabotage,"[1] or the impeding of the process of production in all possible ways: by breaking machinery, by spoiling materials, by deliberately

Industrial unionism

---

[1] The term comes from the French word *sabot*, a wooden shoe commonly worn by French workingmen. It is related that at one time, when a strike was declared in a French factory, the laborers threw their *sabots* into the machinery, thereby ruining it.

making errors, and by "conscious withholding of efficiency," or working in a dilatory fashion. "Poor work for poor pay" was the syndicalist alternative to a strike. The syndicalist movement was most active in France where it captured the labor unions.[1]

If the methods of the syndicalists were concrete, their aims were vague. They preached a "social myth," a universal strike of all labor, a "revolution with folded arms," when the capitalists would be rendered powerless, and the laborers would take over the factories, mines, and railways. The industrial union, now "a group of resistance," would in the future be "a group of production and distribution." It was to be the "cell" of future society, and a general federation of industrial unions would supersede the State. Although bitterly opposed to the State the syndicalists preferred to wage war against the capitalists directly, not, as they said, against the capitalist agents in the government. Many of the syndicalists favored violence, but against capitalist property, not against kings and presidents. They ridiculed the idea that "political action" through parliament would ever emancipate the working class. In their view the supreme need was effective and daring leadership by a group of revolutionary workingmen, the class conscious "minority of a minority," to lead the masses in a revolutionary uprising against capitalism.

Aims of syndicalism (margin note)

REVISIONISM

Within the socialist movement itself new tendencies appeared which threatened to disrupt it. In the twentieth century, a prominent German socialist, Eduard Bernstein, proclaimed the doctrine of "revisionism" which roused a great controversy. He declared that not all of Marx's prophecies had been fulfilled because the rich were not growing richer, and the poor, poorer; the middle class was not disappearing, but increasing; the consolidation of industry did not mean the consolidation of wealth because of the larger number of small shareholders; and peasant proprietorship was increasing. Hence, the time had come to "revise" Marxian theories and tactics. Bernstein and his followers, known as "Revisionists," fully accepted socialism as an ultimate goal, but they urged that the Social Democrats work "less for the better future and more for the better

"Revisionist" and "Orthodox" (margin note)

[1] See page 349

present" by coöperating with the progressive forces in German political life. They asserted that the mass of workingmen were unwilling to wait "until some fine day when the roast pigeons of the socialist revolution would fly into their mouths," but desired immediate reforms. Opposed to them were the "Orthodox" socialists, led by Bebel and Kautsky, who stood hard and fast by Marxism. They declared that reforms were "bribes" offered by the government to the workers in order to quiet their demands for fundamental changes; that agitation and criticism were the only legitimate activities of socialists in a capitalistic society; and that the only function of their representatives in parliament was "to speak through its windows" to the masses without. The Social Democratic Party was, therefore, to hold itself aloof from all the bourgeois parties, even from the most radical, for it aimed to bring about a revolutionary reconstruction of society. The differences between "Orthodox" and "Revisionist" did not lead to a split in the Social Democratic Party.

The issue between the moderates and the extremists came to a head, in 1904, at the International Socialist Congress of Amsterdam. A notable debate took place between Bebel, Triumph of who represented the Orthodox viewpoint, and Jaurès, the Orthodox who represented the Revisionist, or "reformist" viewpoint in which the hard logic of the former won over the glowing eloquence of the latter. A resolution was passed by the Congress supporting the Orthodox view, and the Reformists were compelled to submit.

BOLSHEVISM

Far more significant was the division within the ranks of the Russian socialists. As a movement, socialism came to Russia much later than to western Europe; it was not until Split in Russian socialist century that the sian socialist Russian Social Democratic Party was organized, party chiefly through the efforts of a lecturer and writer named George Plekhánov. As they were outlawed by the tsarist government, the Social Democrats were compelled to conduct their agitation in secret or in foreign countries among the Russian exiles. In 1903, in London, there took place a convention of the Russian Social Democratic Party. The proceedings were in Russian; the delegates were political exiles; and the place of meeting was in a small hall in the poor quarter. Therefore, the convention was unnoticed. What took place at that obscure meeting, however, was to have a profound influence upon world history.

A serious question was ardently debated by the delegates. How was socialism to be attained? Sharp differences arose which later,

Menshevism   in 1910, resulted in splitting the party into two factions: the Bolshevists,[1] led by Nicholas Lenin, and the Menshevists, led by Plekhánov. Both factions accepted the principles of Marxism, but they differed widely as to the tactics to be used by socialists. Whether Orthodox or Reformist, the Menshevists believed that the road to socialism lay through democracy, and only through democracy; hence, the party should agitate among the workingmen, educate them in the principles of socialism, and organize them politically. As the socialist movement grew, existing institutions would be modified in the interest of the working class, and socialist institutions would grow "under the shell" of capitalism. A socialist society would be called into existence only when the time was ripe; namely, when the socialist party was in control of the government backed by a majority of the people. The Menshevists were opposed to an uprising of the workingmen; in a democracy the transition from capitalism to socialism was to be through orderly, constitutional methods.

A far different plan was proposed by the Bolshevists. They declared that no truly revolutionary party would ever gain power

Bolshevism   through constitutional methods. Democracy, they as-
(1) opposition serted, was a cunningly devised system for maintaining
to democracy the rule of the bourgeois who control parliaments by controlling the means of influencing public opinion, the press, the school, the Church, the courts, and the administration. The socialists are, therefore, doomed to remain a minority party. Should they, by chance, find themselves a majority they would be compelled to modify their program in order to keep the governmental machine going because the courts, the administration, the army, and the other organs of government would still remain under capitalist control. No parliamentary majority, declared the Bolshevists, can therefore overthrow capitalism, and no parliamentary minority can threaten it politically.

It was chiefly Lenin who developed new revolutionary tactics for the attainment of socialism. He was a close student of the writings of Marx which appealed to him more as a manual of

[1] See page 456.

action than as a system of thought.   According to Lenin, revolutions are accomplished by small, well-organized groups, having a definite goal clearly in view, who lead discontented masses in times of crisis.   Therefore it was essential that the socialists should be of one mind in regard to the transition from capitalism   (2) Uncompromising to socialism.   They must establish an iron discipline   Marxism and ruthlessly eliminate any one who does not freely accept Marxism.   Even though few, the socialists would be effective because, having a clearly defined policy, they would act promptly and daringly when their opportunity came.

Themselves uncontaminated, the socialists should contaminate all other radical elements.   To gain the confidence of the workingmen, they should identify themselves with their daily   (3) "Boring struggles for better living conditions.   Especially   from should they enter the trade unions, even the conserva-   within " tive ones, because the unions are historically destined to unite the entire proletariat.   In these organizations the socialists are to be centers of revolutionary agitation.   Wherever there is discontent among the workingmen, there should be the socialist to intensify the discontent in order to produce a "revolutionary mood."   Socialists should also form nuclei in every working-class political party, and labor ceaselessly to get control of its machinery by "boring from within."   As every government, democratic as well as autocratic, proscribes revolution, socialists should maintain both "legal" and "illegal" political parties; the former should organize in conformity with the laws, but it should be directed by the "illegal," or secret political party.   Unless socialists followed these tactics, declared Lenin, they would remain a small sect of "mere babblers" without any real influence upon the masses.

Being prepared, "shod on all fours," socialists must await their opportunity.   According to Lenin there could be no greater folly than a blind, desperate uprising of the working class,   (4) Uprising which would be drowned in blood.   No revolution is   of proletariat in time possible without a national crisis which vitally affects   riat in time of war both capital and labor.   And a national crisis is inevitable, argued Lenin, because capitalist economy drives the nation to adopt imperialist policies which lead to conflicts with other nations.   When war breaks out, socialists should work for the defeat of their country; defeat would discredit the government and bring ruin to many.   When discontent mounts high, the revolu-

tionary hour will strike. Socialists should then seize this opportunity by rousing the working class to "mass action," or armed
insurrection, in order to overthrow the existing system and to establish the "Dictatorship of the Proletariat," or the military rule of
the working class.

No principle is more fundamental in the Bolshevist "science of
revolution" than the Dictatorship of the Proletariat. It differen-
(5) Dictator-   tiates them sharply from all other socialists who are
ship of the   as much opposed to proletarian dictatorship as to any
Proletariat   other. Once in power, the proletariat will proceed to
destroy every existing institution, political, economic, social, educational, legal, and religious, because, in the Bolshevist view, they
cannot use for their benefit institutions created by their enemy, the
bourgeois. After the ground has been thoroughly cleared, new
institutions should be established in harmony with the new socialist
society. The Dictatorship should give rights only to the workers,
and should suppress mercilessly all other classes, but its rule will be
temporary. "As the opposition of the bourgeois is broken, as it is
expropriated and gradually absorbed into the working class the
proletarian dictatorship disappears, until finally the State dies, and
there are no longer any class distinctions."

Bolshevism was practical, hard, shrewd, and daring. It had
nothing of the spirit of idealism that had characterized former
Character-   revolutionists, the Cromwells, the Jeffersons, the
istic of Bol-   Dantons, the Mazzinis. "To accept the workers'
shevism   Revolution," declared Leon Trotsky, "in the name
of a high ideal means not only to reject it, but to slander it. . . .
The Socialist Revolution tears the mask from illusions, from
elevating as well as from humiliating illusions, and washes in blood
the disguises assumed by reality. The Revolution is strong to
the extent to which it is realistic, rational, strategic, and mathematical."

THE FIRST AND SECOND SOCIALIST INTERNATIONALS

The first political effort of socialism was to found an international
organization of the proletariat. In 1864, a meeting of workingmen
The First   from many countries took place, in London, which
International   formed an association, known later as the First International. Radicals of all sorts were present: English trade-
unionists, Polish nationalists, Italian republicans, German social-

ists, Russian nihilists, and even anarchists. Among its prominent members was Marx, who drew up a constitution committing the organization to socialism. Thereupon the moderate elements seceded. From time to time the International held congresses, which were attended by representatives from trade unions and from radical political societies, and the idea grew of having a rallying center of revolutionary workingmen throughout the world. In its manifestos the International declared that the economic dependence of the workingman upon the capitalist was the "basis of every kind of servitude, of social misery, of spiritual degradation, and political dependence." Within the organization factional quarrels arose between the anarchists, led by Bakunin, and the socialists, led by Marx, which greatly weakened the International. Through the influence of Marx the anarchists were expelled, and the International was now definitely committed to Marxian principles. The movement failed to make much progress, though it attracted considerable attention. In 1873, the First International went out of existence. It left, as a heritage, the idea of an international organization of the working class pledged to relentless war against capitalism the world over.

An important influence in the history of socialism was the failure of the Paris Commune of 1871. It dampened the ardor of the revolutionary workingmen, who were now convinced The Paris that, due to the growth of standing armies, all popular Commune uprisings were doomed to failure. The enfranchisement of the working class in England, the establishment of universal, manhood suffrage in Germany, and of a democratic republic in France inclined the socialists to favor political action. Socialist parties appeared that quickly won large followings, and in almost every European parliament socialists challenged the existing order. The rostrum had displaced the barricade.

Once more a movement began for an international organization. In 1889, a socialist congress was held in Paris, which formed an association later known as the Second International. The Second Unlike its predecessor, it was a federation of national International socialist parties, and it rigidly excluded all those who favored violence as against political action. "In a modern democratic state," it declared, "the conquest of the public power by the proletariat cannot be the result of an uprising; it must be the result of long and assiduous labor of proletarian organization in both political and economic fields, of the physical and moral regeneration of the working class, and of the gradual conquest of municipal and legislative assemblies." Agitate, Educate, Organize, was the method advocated by the Second International. Supreme authority in the International was exercised by a congress that met periodically to decide upon general policies and principles. Representation to the congress was allotted to each "national section" in proportion to its relative importance in the labor and socialist movement. A permanent central bureau was established in Brussels to act as a clearing house for the movement. The Second International grew rapidly. In 1914, it included twenty-seven countries, and had a membership of 12,000,000. The socialist parties were efficiently organized and ably led, with dues-paying members, a well edited press, and an enthusiastic corps of volunteer workers who proclaimed the gospel of socialism in all places and at all times.

Germany was the home of the new movement in all its phases, and the socialists throughout the world took their philosophy from Marx and their methods and policies from the German Social Democratic Party. The founder of this famous organization was Ferdinand Lassalle, the son of a wealthy Jewish merchant. Like Marx, Lassalle was a deep student of philosophy and history and an active propagandist. This intellectual agitator had received all the advantages that wealth and education could bestow. "Every line that I write," he proudly declared, " I do so fortified with the whole culture of my century." Possessing a chivalrous, romantic temperament as well as a brilliant mind, Lassalle became the idol of the German working classes, whose cause he warmly championed.

Lassalle
(1825–64)

In his book, *The Working Class Program*, Lassalle declared that history may be divided into three periods: (1) the period prior to the French Revolution, which was dominated by the landed aristocracy; (2) that between the French Revolution and the Revolution of 1848, dominated by the bourgeois; and (3) that since the Revolution of 1848, in which the aspirations of the working class have been the dominant feature. Lassalle, like the classical economists, believed that the workingmen were subject to the "iron law of wages," but he favored the intervention of the State, which alone could save them from their otherwise hopeless situation. Lassalle denounced the bourgeois conception of the State as that of a "night watchman" whose sole

Ideas of
Lassalle

function was to protect life and property. But the working class viewed the State as the greatest agency for benefiting mankind in every possible way. As long as the workingman was economically dependent, argued Lassalle, he could not be politically or morally free. Socialism was, therefore, the only solution of the problem of human freedom; under a socialist régime, capital would be the servant, not the master, of labor. Unlike Marx, Lassalle was a strong nationalist and an admirer of Prussia as the supreme type of a strongly organized state, able to solve the problems of the working class, provided its direction was in their hands.

In 1863, Lassalle founded the General Workingmen's Association, which adopted his program. It failed, however, to attract many followers. Two years later Lassalle was killed in a duel over a love affair, and the organization was left in a precarious state. In 1869, Wilhelm Liebknecht, a journalist, and August Bebel, a wood-turner, both converts to Marxism, organized the Social Democratic Labor Party, which met at Eisenach and adopted a Marxian program. The "Eisenachers," as they were called, and the Lassalleans were for a time rivals; but they united at Gotha, in 1875, to form what later became known as the Social Democratic Party.

Origin of the German Social Democratic Party

Bismarck became apprehensive of the rapid growth of socialism and he determined to stem the "red flood" by drastic measures. The struggle that followed between the government and the socialists has already been described elsewhere;[1] its outcome was a distinct triumph for the socialists. In 1891, soon after the repeal of the anti-socialist laws, a congress of the Social Democrats was held at Erfurt. It revised the Gotha Program, and adopted a new one which was thoroughly Marxian. This Erfurt Program later became the model for the socialist parties throughout the world. Its maximum demands were the abolition of private capital and the establishment of the Coöperative Commonwealth; but it included *minimum* demands, or immediate reforms, the most important of which were universal suffrage, proportional representation, the substitution of a popular militia for the standing army, freedom of speech and assembly, civil equality of men and women, separation of Church and State, free secular education, heavy income and inheritance taxes, a universal eight-hour workday, and factory reforms.

The Erfurt Program

[1] See page 394.

The growth of German socialism was phenomenal, as nearly every election saw a large increase in its vote.[1] The socialist leader,

Growth of German socialism
Bebel, was a self-educated workingman who developed marked ability as a parliamentary orator and tactician. He was a man of high ideals and inflexible character, and was greatly admired by his opponents as well as by his followers. His best-known associate was Karl Kautsky, the ablest scholar in the socialist movement, whose writings on socialism and on history gave him a high position in the socialist world.

The growth of socialism in France was seriously retarded by the Paris Commune. Its ideas and methods were discredited, and its

Socialism in France
leaders imprisoned and exiled as a result of the bloody uprising of 1871. Soon after the exiled communards were permitted to return, a vigorous socialist agitation was begun among the French working classes. A prominent agitator was Jules Guesde, who had spent several years in Germany, and who came back filled with admiration for the theoretical system of Marx and for the unity and discipline of the German Social Democrats. A number of socialist factions appeared in the early eighties, each with its own views and methods, the Guesdists, the Broussists, and the Allemanists, so called after their leaders, Guesde, Brousse, and Allemane. In 1893, a group calling itself the "Independent Socialists," was organized by Jaurès and Millerand, who believed in the progressive establishment of socialism, one step at a time. In general, the French socialists were of two kinds: Marxists who closely followed the model of the German Social Democrats, and "possibilists," or "reformists" who favored the

[1] The following table shows in round numbers the votes of the Social Democratic Party:

	VOTES	SEATS
1871	124,500	2
1874	352,000	10
1877	493,000	12
1878	437,000	9
1881	312,000	13
1884	550,000	24
1887	763,000	11
1890	1,427,000	35
1893	1,787,000	44
1898	2,107,000	56
1903	3,011,000	81
1907	3,260,000	43
1912	4,250,000	110

more moderate policy of progressive social reform with socialism as the ultimate aim. In spite of these divisions, the socialist parties polled about 500,000 votes in the elections of 1893.

Two dominating personalities came to the fore as leaders of French socialism, Guesde and Jaurès. Guesde was a rigid adherent of the principles and methods of Marx, and was pro- Guesde and foundly convinced that the world was predestined to Jaurès socialism; he, therefore, would not tolerate any modification of its plan of social salvation. No compromise with the bourgeois State and no alliance with bourgeois parties, was his policy. The socialist workingmen must agitate until a socialist national assembly will abolish capitalism as feudalism was abolished in 1789. A different type was Jaurès, who gained world renown as the greatest orator of his day. Unlike Guesde, he was an opportunist; he favored the peaceful penetration of democracy by socialism "until the proletarian and socialist State shall have replaced the oligarchic and bourgeois State." Jaurès, therefore, advised his followers to join the Radicals in the Chamber who were fighting to maintain the French Republic against the royalists and clericals.

The Dreyfus Affair brought further division into the ranks of French socialism. Guesde believed that the socialists should remain neutral; but Jaurès took the side of Dreyfus The Mille-with passionate ardor, and played an important part rand Affair in the celebrated case and in the events that followed. Alexandre Millerand, a follower of Jaurès, joined the Waldeck-Rousseau Ministry.[1] French socialism was seriously divided over the question whether a socialist should join a non-socialist ministry. Guesde denounced Millerand as a "hostage" held by a bourgeois government for the good behavior of the socialists. At his instance the international socialist Congress of Amsterdam (1904) decreed that no *bona fide* socialist should be permitted to hold office in a bourgeois cabinet. Jaurès accepted the decision, and the outcome was a consolidation of the various socialist groups in the Unified Socialist Party which made large gains both in seats and in votes.[2]

In spite of the fact that England is the classic land of capitalism,

[1] See page 340.

[2] The following table shows the growth of the party:

	Votes	Seats
1906	878,000	54
1910	1,125,000	76
1914	1,500,000	102

the growth of socialism in that country was very slow.   English
workingmen generally looked to the Liberals for political reform, and to their trade unions for economic
betterment.   The pioneers of English socialism were
Henry M. Hyndman and the poet William Morris,
who, in 1881, organized the Social Democratic Federation.   This
body, later known as the Social Democratic Party, adopted
Marxian principles.   But it failed to make much headway among
the working classes, and a new organization, called the Independent Labor Party, was formed, in 1893, by Keir Hardie, a popular
trade-unionist, who committed the party to a policy of "reformist"
socialism.

The "S.D.F." and the "I.L.P."

An influential element in the history of British socialism was the
Fabian Society which appeared in the eighties.   It attracted some
of the intellectual *élite* of England, George Bernard
Shaw, H. G. Wells, Sidney Olivier, and Sidney and
Beatrice Webb.   The Fabians were socialists in principle, but they
refused to commit themselves to any party; in their view socialism
was a principle of social action, not a formula or party platform.
They proposed to follow a "Fabian" policy,[1] and sought to influence all parties and all sections of opinion in favor of socialism
This group of brilliant intellectuals carried on a ceaseless agitation,
and succeeded in converting England from *laissez faire* to social
reform.

The Fabian Society

During the early twentieth century another group of intellectuals
organized a movement called "guild socialism."   Its chief advocates were A. R. Orage and G. D. H. Cole, well-known
writers on social subjects.   The "guildsmen" favored
a scheme whereby production would be carried on by "guilds" of
workers who would control the affairs of their industry and share
in its product.   As the guilds were to represent the producers, the
State was to represent the consumers.   It was to function as the
supreme power in the nation by administering such matters as
affected all equally as citizens, such as education, housing, roads,
and international affairs; in addition, it was to regulate prices of
goods produced by the guilds.

Guild so-cialism

The most important event in the history of British socialism was

[1] The name of the society was taken from the famous Roman general Fabius
the Delayer, whose tactics against the Carthaginians was not to engage them in a
decisive battle, but to wear them out by many delays.

the advent of the Labor Party.[1]   It was not a single political organization, but a federation of trade unions, coöperative societies, and socialist groups, such as the Independent Labor Party and the Fabians.   The Social Democratic Party refused to join the Laborites because the latter refused to adopt a Marxian platform.   For a time the Labor Party limited itself to specific de- The Labor mands in the interest of labor because the bulk of its Party supporters were trade-unionists who were not socialists.   However, the leaders, Hardie, Philip Snowden, Sidney Webb, and J. Ramsay MacDonald, were all socialists, and they finally succeeded in committing the party to their principles.[2]

In Italy, socialism found a strong rival in anarchy.   The poverty of the country and the spirit of violence that had been encouraged by the wars for unification influenced many working- Italian men to favor the violent methods of anarchists.   A socialism compromise was effected, in 1885, when socialists and anarchists joined to organize a workingmen's party.   But the former got control of the organization and expelled the anarchists.   The triumph of the socialists attracted to the movement prominent intellectuals, such as Enrico Ferri and Arturo Labriola, who became the leaders of the Socialist Party.   As in other countries there was a struggle between the extreme and the moderate elements.   A congress, held in 1906, decided in favor of the latter; and the two factions, for a time, healed their differences.   But the Turco-Italian War, supported by some members and opposed by others, once more rent the party in twain.   In spite of this division and in spite of the strong rivalry of syndicalism, Italian socialism attracted a considerable following; in the elections of 1913 it polled about 1,000,000 votes.

Though socialists differed radically in their views on many matters, there was one article in their creed upon which they were in complete unanimity, and that was hostility to mili- Opposition tarism.   Everywhere they consistently opposed stand- of socialists ing armies, and regularly voted against military budg- to militarism ets.   In Germany the socialists stubbornly fought against the influence of the army in the government.   In France they went to the length of launching an anti-militaristic crusade which threatened the morale of the French army.   Jaurès flouted the *revanche,* and sought to establish good relations between his country and

[1] See page 287.   [2] See Chapter XXXIX.

Germany.   Nevertheless, socialists believed in defending their country against invasion.   Bebel himself declared that German socialists would fight shoulder to shoulder with the bourgeois if Germany was invaded by Russia, "a barbarian who is the greatest enemy of our [socialist] aspirations."   Jaurès, too, believed that aggression should be fought, and he declared that the nation who refused to submit its case to arbitration was to be considered the aggressor.

What attitude socialists should take in the event of war was frequently discussed at their international congresses.   The Congress of 1907 passed a resolution which declared that, if a crisis arose that threatened war, socialists should vigorously favor peace; and, if war came, socialists should strive for an early peace.   Efforts were made at subsequent congresses to commit the Second International to a more radical plan, but these efforts failed.   A feeling of uneasiness arose in the socialist world when the German Social Democrats voted for the military budget of 1913.   Like other Germans, they were convinced that their country was threatened by the "encirclement" policy of its enemies, and gave their support to a policy of defense.

Resolution against war

During the anxious days preceding the World War, socialists in all countries organized peace demonstrations.   Jaurès made a stirring address at a great mass meeting, in Brussels, in which he warned the governments of Europe against plunging the world into a general conflict.   When Germany declared war, all eyes were turned toward the Reichstag.   To the amazement of the world the Social Democrats supported the government, and voted for the war credits. Their defense was that, as Germany was being invaded by the Russians, it was their duty to defend the Fatherland.   The French socialists, thereupon, also voted for the war credits of their government.   Guesde, a lifelong opponent of compromise with the "bourgeois State," himself went into the cabinet.   Nearly all the socialist parties in the belligerent countries supported their governments.   And so the great socialist international, which, for two generations, had preached the solidarity of the working classes of all countries, went down to ruin in the general conflagration.

Disruption of the Second International

REFERENCES

SOCIALISM — SOURCES:

Karl Marx, *Capital: a Critique of Political Economy*, translated from the German, 3 vols. (ed. 1907–09); G. Deville, *The People's Marx*, translated from the French (1900) and W. H. Emmett, *Marxian Economic Handbook and Glossary* (1925) brief summaries of Marxism; Friedrich Engels, *Socialism: Utopian and Scientific*, translated from the German (ed. 1911), a criticism of Utopianism by the co-worker of Marx; K. Marx and F. Engels, *The Communist Manifesto*, translated from the German in every European language and in many cheap editions; Ferdinand Lassalle, *Reden und Schriften*, 3 vols., a collection of his speeches and writings issued in 1892–95, and edited by E. Bernstein; C. Grünberg (ed.), *Archiv für die Geschichte des Sozialismus und der Arbeiterbewegung*, a collection of socialist writings of which 11 volumes have appeared during 1911–25; R. C. K. Ensor (ed.), *Modern Socialism, as set forth by Socialists in their Speeches, Writings, and Programmes* (ed. 1910); W. E. Walling and others (eds.), *The Socialism of To-Day* (1916).

SOCIALISM — GENERAL:

H. W. Laidler, *History of Socialist Thought* (1927), an indispensable handbook by a scholarly socialist. Good general histories of the movement: J. Rae, *Contemporary Socialism* (ed. 1908); T. Kirkup, *A History of Socialism*, revised and largely rewritten by E. R. Pease (1913); and S. F. Markham, *A History of Socialism* (1930), good narrative, fair. Compère-Morel (ed.), *Encyclopédie socialiste*, 8 vols. (1912–13), covers every phase of the socialist movement, especially good for France; M. Tugan-Baranowsky, *Modern Socialism in its Historical Development*, translated from the Russian (1910); W. Sombart, *Der proletarische Sozialismus*, 2 vols. (1924); B. Földes, *Die Haupströmungen der Sozialistischen Gedankwelt* (1923); O. Warschauer, *Zur Entwicklungs Geschichte des Sozialismus* (1909); E. C. Robbins (ed.), *Socialism* (1915), and D. Bloomfield (ed.), *Selected Articles on Modern Industrial Movements* (1920), collections of essays; G. M. Steklov, *The History of the First International* (1928). On the socialist movement in Germany: F. Mehring, *Geschichte der deutschen Sozialdemokratie* (1904); A. Bebel, *My Life*, translated from the German (1912); and G. Brandes, *Ferdinand Lassalle* (ed. 1925); in England: M. Beer, *A History of British Socialism* (1919) and H. Tracey (ed.), *The Book of the Labour Party*, 3 vols. (1925); in France: A. Zévaès (ed.), *Histoire des partis socialistes en France*, 11 vols. (1911–12); P. Louis, *Histoire du socialisme français* (1901); and vols. II–III of *Encyclopédie socialiste;* in Russia: J. Martow, *Geschichte der russischen Sozialdemokratie*, translated from the German (1926); and L. Kulczycki, *Geschichte der russischen Revolution*, translated from the Polish, 3 vols. (1910–14) vol. III. For extensive bibliographies see J. Stammhammer, *Bibliographie des Sozialismus und Communismus*, 3 vols. (1893–1909) and S. Zimand, *Modern Social Movements* (1921).

SOCIALISM — WORKS BY SOCIALISTS:

K. Kautsky, *The Social Revolution* (1908), *The Class Struggle* (1910), *Ethics and the Materialist Conception of History* (1907), and *The Economic Doctrines of Karl Marx* (1925), the chief works of the leading German socialist scholar, Orthodox in viewpoint; S. and B. Webb, *Socialism and Individualism* (1911), *A Constitution for the Socialist Commonwealth of Great Britain* (1920), and *The Decay of Capitalist Civilization* (1923), the chief works on socialism by the leading English socialist scholars, reformist viewpoint; L. Boudin, *The Theoretical System of Karl Marx in the Light of Recent Criticism* (1907), Orthodox defense of Marxism; J. Spargo, *Socialism: A Summary and an Interpretation of Socialist Principles* (ed. 1910), a clear popular exposition by an American socialist; J. R. MacDonald, *The Socialist Movement* (1911) and *Socialism: Critical and Constructive* (1924), by the leader of the British Labor Party; M. Hillquit, *Socialism in Theory and Practice* (1909), by the leader of the American Socialist Party; J. Jaurès, *Studies in Socialism*, translated from the French (1906), by the leader of the French socialists; E. Bernstein, *Evolutionary Socialism: a Criticism and an Affirmation*, translated from the German (1909), by the leader of the Revisionists in Germany; *Fabian Essays in Socialism* (1909), by famous English writers.

SOCIALISM — WORKS BY ANTI-SOCIALISTS:

O. D. Skelton, *Socialism: A Critical Analysis* (1911), a brief but excellent study, fair and moderate; J. E. Le Rossignol, *What is Socialism?* (1921); Y. Guyot, *Socialistic Fallacies* (1910), by a well-known French economist; P. Leroy-Beaulieu, *Collectivism*, abridged translation from the French (1908); A. E. F. Schaeffle, *The Quintessence of Socialism*, translated from the German (1908); V. Cathrein, *Socialism, its Theoretical Basis and Practical Application*, translated from the German (1904), from Roman Catholic standpoint; A. Fouillée, *Le socialisme et la sociologie réformiste* (1909); B. Croce, *Historical Materialism and the Economics of Karl Marx*, translated from the Italian (1914); L. von Mises, *Socialism*, translated from the German (1937).

ANARCHISM:

P. J. Proudhon, *What is Property?* translated from the French (1902); P. Eltzbacher, *Anarchism* (1908), consists mainly of extracts from the writings of prominent anarchists; E. V. Zenker, *Anarchism: a Criticism and History of the Anarchist Theory*, translated from the German (1898); B. R. Tucker, *Instead of a Book* (1897), an exposition of anarchism by an American anarchist; A. Naquet, *L'Anarchie et le Collectivisme* (1904), a sympathetic description of anarchy as an impractical ideal.

UTOPIAN SOCIALISM:

F. Engels, *Socialism, Utopian and Scientific*, translated from the German (1892), by the famous associate of Marx; C. Gide and C. Rist, *History of Economic Doctrines from the time of the Physiocrats to the Present Day*, translated from the French (1915), contains excellent chapters on the

Utopians; M. Beer, *Social Struggles and Socialist Fore-runners* (1925); J. O. Hertzler, *The History of Utopian Thought* (1923); P. A. R. Janet, *Saint-Simon* (1878); H. Burgin, *Fourier* (1905); G. D. H. Cole, *Robert Owen* (1925).

GUILD SOCIALISM:

A. R. Orage (ed.), *National Guilds: An Inquiry into the Wage System and the Way out* (1914), a series of essays by guild socialists; S. G. Hobson, *National Guilds* (1919), by one of the founders of the school; M. B. Reckitt and C. E. Beckhofer, *Meaning of National Guilds* (1920); G. D. H. Cole, *Self-Government in Industry* (1920); and N. Carpenter, *Guild Socialism* (1921).

SYNDICALISM:

L. L. Lorwin, *Syndicalism in France* (1914), good study of the origin of syndicalism; P. Louis, *Histoire du mouvement Syndical en France* (1911); vol. VII of *Encyclopédie socialiste*; H. Lagardelle, *Le Socialisme Ouvrier* (1911), by a prominent French syndicalist; J. Spargo, *Syndicalism, Industrial Unionism, and Socialism* (1913), a criticism by a socialist; P. F. Brissenden, *The I.W.W., A Study in American Syndicalism* (1919), a pioneer work on the subject, indispensable for understanding the American phase of the movement.

COMMUNISM:

There is not as yet a scientific study of communism; all of the books on the subject are bitterly partisan. H. J. Laski, *Communism* (1927), is very brief, but is the only study on the subject that has a scholarly approach. Nearly all the books on communism are in pamphlet form, written originally in Russian and translated. The chief writings of Lenin are: *The State and Revolution, The Proletarian Revolution in Russia, On the Road to Insurrection,* and *The Bolsheviks and the Peasants*; of Trotsky, *Terrorism and Communism, The Defence of Terrorism,* and *Dictatorship versus Democracy*; R. W. Postgate, *The Bolshevik Theory* (1920), sympathetic; N. Bukharin and E. Preobrazhinsky, *The A. B. C. of Communism* (1922), a communist pamphlet that clearly explains aims of the movement; K. Kautsky, *Terrorism and Communism* (1920), by the ablest socialist opponent of communism; M. Eastman, *Marx and Lenin: the Science of Revolution* (1927), a penetrating study of socialist theories and communist tactics; J. Stalin, *Leninism* (1928), by the successor of Lenin as leader of the Communist Party; F. Borkenan, *World Communism* (1939); B. Souvarine, *Stalin* (1939).

CHAPTER XXIX

THE FEMINIST MOVEMENT

POSITION OF WOMAN IN SOCIETY

THE nineteenth century witnessed the rise of a movement among women that was universally regarded as strange and fantastic. This movement, known as "feminism," aroused not so much hostility as ridicule; and it was a long time before its claims received serious attention. Although having aims distinctively revolutionary, feminism was not feared because women could not, like the workingmen, threaten the existing order by an armed uprising. Nevertheless, in spite of general hostility, contempt, and ridicule, feminism made surprising progress both as a philosophy and as a program of action.

At the beginning of the nineteenth century the position of woman in society was not very different from what it had been for centuries. Women, being universally regarded as the inferior sex, "the weaker vessels," were not given equal rights with men in government or equal opportunities with them in society. Their only function was the bearing and rearing of children, and their only occupation, housekeeping. Women led secluded lives, sheltered in their homes and busied with their household duties. They played no part in the public life of the world, in government, industry, education, or religion, spheres of interests preëmpted by men in a "man's world." A woman's views on general affairs were received with contempt as foolish and childish; her sphere was the home. "Women are only children of a larger growth," said Lord Chesterfield, the first gentleman of his age, "a man of sense only trifles with them, plays with them, humors and flatters them as he does with a sprightly, forward child." In the State women were non-existent even in the days of property suffrage; they were excluded from voting whether they possessed property or not. In the Church they were welcomed as communicants but excluded from the ministry; neither Catholics nor most Protestants permitted them to be ordained. In commerce and industry women had no share, either

Inferior position of women

as capitalists or as workers, their economic activity being entirely in the home.

The most important fact in a woman's life was her relation to man.   Not being engaged in any gainful occupation, she was dependent for her support on her husband, father, or   Woman's brother.   This economic dependence was reflected in   dependence legal dependence.   Before the civil law, woman was   on man treated as a minor: she could make no contracts; could not sue or be sued; her husband or father was liable for civil offenses that she committed.   In criminal matters only was she responsible for her acts.   Marriage meant woman's complete surrender of her person and property to her husband, whom she promised "to love and to obey."   According to the law, husband and wife were "one," but as the husband bore the responsibilities of both, he had the rights of both.   Since a wife could legally hold no property, her possessions passed to her husband on marriage.   The children born to them were legally his, the mother having few rights over them.   It was generally believed that woman was by divine design made for man; hence, it was her highest duty to please him in every way possible.

Woman's mentality was considered inferior to that of man, and she was consequently denied higher education.   An intellectual woman was regarded as a monstrosity, and was socially   Her lack of ostracized.   Women of the higher classes were sent to   education boarding-schools and female seminaries, where much of the time was devoted to "lady-like accomplishments," such as music, dancing, dress, and etiquette.   Woman's sole aim was to be attractive in order to win a husband; sound learning, it was thought, would spoil a girl's "charm" and consequently ruin her prospects for marriage.

This inferior position of woman was veiled by certain deferences that were paid to her by man.   She was regarded as the chosen of God and nature for the welfare of the race; and, there-   Chivalry of fore, entitled to special protection in society.   Her   man physical constitution was more delicate, her nature more refined, and her person more comely than man's; it consequently behooved him to treat her with consideration in all personal relations: to be kind and gentle in speech and in action, and to be ever ready to sacrifice his comfort and even his life for the sake of the "fair sex." This chivalrous attitude cast a halo of romance about women, through whose spiritual influence man was inspired to brave deeds, noble sentiments, and virtuous acts. As they were considered incapable of producing great works of art, literature, or science, their part was to be an "inspiration" to men of genius.

ORIGIN OF FEMINISM

The French Revolution, which set all social institutions rocking on their foundations, caused bold inquiries to be made into the The French status of woman as well as into that of man. Perhaps Revolution the first one to favor the equality of women with men was the Revolutionary philosopher-statesman, Condorcet. When the Constituent Assembly was in session a group of women drew up a Declaration of the Rights of Women, demanding equal rights of women with men, which they sent to that body for adoption. Scant attention was paid to it. The woman's liberal movement was suppressed by Napoleon, whose Code, very liberal and enlightened in many respects, was reactionary in regard to woman; it put the wife completely under the control of her husband.

It was England rather than France that saw the rise and growth of the feminist movement. Its pioneer was Mary Wollstonecraft Mary Woll- whose book, *Vindication of the Rights of Woman*, pubstonecraft lished in 1792, was an eloquent appeal for the full and (1759–97) complete equality of women with men in every sphere of life. Woman, Mary Wollstonecraft declared, was an individual, with her own powers to develop, for which she needed the fullest opportunity. It was to her detriment that so much emphasis had been put on her sex. Her welfare demanded that she be regarded as a human being as well as a wife and mother, because "the desire of always being women is the very consciousness that degrades the sex." Woman's intellectual inferiority, she argued, was not due to her nature, but to her inferior education; she would quickly gain in mental capacity if she had every opportunity for education. Women must be enfranchised, as the vote is as much her natural right as man's; to keep unenfranchised half the human race was to make a mockery of democracy. Above all, women must become economically independent of men; they should, therefore, be permitted to engage in industry and in the professions; too long have they lived by their "charm." Mary Wollstonecraft's bold pronouncements shocked her contemporaries. She was denounced as a "hyena in petticoats," and good women were warned not to fall under her influence.

Far more influential than radical theories in changing the status of woman was the Industrial Revolution. The factory drew women from the home as it did men from the shop. The Industrial Revolution Home industries, like spinning, sewing, baking, and trial Revolu- brewing, largely conducted by women, rapidly became tion obsolete. Women were, therefore, forced to go into the factory, as were the men. Employers preferred women to men wherever possible because they accepted lower wages than men, and were less likely to prove recalcitrant. The factory, for all its evils of low wages, long hours, and unsanitary conditions, yet proved of immeasurable importance in the emancipation of women; for the first time an opportunity was given to them to become wage-earners and thereby gain a degree of economic independence. Soon, many began to rise in the economic field by entering the semi-skilled occupations and even the professions. Driven from the confining influences of the home into the great world and forced to earn their livelihood like men, women began seriously to consider the problem of their political and social status. In large measure it may be said that the rise of modern industry was responsible for the growth of feminism.

WOMAN SUFFRAGE

England, as the home of the Industrial Revolution and of political liberalism, naturally became the center of the woman's movement. Its first demand was for woman suffrage because in England political activity plays a great part in the life of the people; the enfranchisement of women would be universally regarded as a step of prime importance in their emancipation. Woman suffrage found a powerful champion in John Stuart Mill, whose book, *Subjection of Women* (1869), remains to this day the classic exposition of the case for woman suffrage. During the debates on the Reform Bill of 1867, Mill introduced an amendment for the enfranchisement of women, which was received with ridicule and promptly defeated. When the Reform Bill of 1884 came before parliament a woman suffrage amendment was proposed; again it was defeated. Many woman suffrage societies were organized for the purpose of conducting a vigorous agitation to convert England to the new reform. Equal franchise bills were introduced in

parliament which, at first, were treated flippantly, but which later
led to serious debates.   The women claimed the vote
both as a moral right and as a practical desirability.
They declared that as long as they remained unenfranchised they were aliens in their own country, subject to its laws, but having no share in making them.   At best they
were citizens who bore the obligations, but received few of the privileges of citizenship; and they raised the time-honored cry, "No
taxation without representation!"   They also urged that the enfranchisement of women would lead to the improvement of their
condition and to that of society in general, for women would exert
their political power in favor of social and moral reforms.   The opponents of woman suffrage contended that the entrance of women
into politics would lead to the neglect of their home duties with dire
consequences for family life.   Women would become coarsened in
the rough-and-tumble game of politics, which is more to the taste of
men.   In answer to the claim of the suffragists that the ballot was
their right, the anti-suffragists replied that government rests on
force, and since women were not required to fight for their country
they should have no voice in directing its policies.

Pro-suffrage and anti-suffrage requirements

The agitation for woman suffrage proceeded along constitutional
lines for about a generation.   Its progress was slow, and the more
ardent spirits among the suffragists became impatient.
In 1903, the Women's Social and Political Union was
organized by Mrs. Emmeline Pankhurst and her two daughters,
Christabel and Sylvia.   This body resolved to bring the question
of woman suffrage prominently before the English people by adopting "militant" methods.   The "suffragettes," as the militant suffragists were called, began in a mild way by "heckling" prominent
speakers.   Before long they took to breaking up political meetings,
and no public man was safe from their questions or their missiles.
They finally resolved on a policy of committing outrages.   Buildings were set on fire, windows broken, letter-boxes ruined, pictures
and statues in museums destroyed, telegraph wires cut, and the
sessions of Parliament disturbed by riotous demonstrations in the
galleries.   For a decade all England was in a turmoil.   No one
knew what outrage the daring suffragettes would commit next, so
that extra guards had to be stationed in many public places.   The
militants were of the opinion that political rights were not granted
save in response to an irresistible demand; and as the women could

The "suf-fragettes"

not threaten revolution, as did the middle classes in 1832 and the
working classes in 1867, they resolved to coerce the government
through annoyances and outrages.   The outbreak of the militants
did serve to bring the question of woman suffrage prominently
before the English public, though many were repelled from the
movement because of the methods of the "wild women."   Bills
to enfranchise women were frequently introduced in Parliament
and gained considerable support from both Liberals and Conservatives.

When the World War broke out, the suffragists rallied to the
support of the government.   They rendered patriotic service by
working in the munition factories, in the fields, and in   Women and
the hospitals, which caused many Englishmen to view   the World
the suffrage movement more favorably.   The triumph   War
of woman suffrage came with the Reform Bill of 1918.[1]

PROGRESS OF WOMAN

English women have made notable progress in the emancipation
of their sex.   The institutions of higher learning, the colleges, universities, and professional schools, gradually opened   Progress of
their doors to them.   An important change in their   women in
legal status came with the passage of the Married   England
Women's Property Act in 1882 which, for the first time, established
the married woman as a distinct legal personality by giving her the
right to own property in her own name.   Another important law,
passed in 1886, gave the mother equal right with the father in the
control of their children.

The woman's movement was farthest advanced in the Scandinavian countries.   Norway and Denmark became the pioneer nations
in granting the vote to women.[2]   In 1907, Norway ad-   Scandinavia
mitted property-owning women to the suffrage; and in
1913, a new law established universal equal suffrage.   In 1915, the
women of Denmark were enfranchised.   The legal and social status
of woman in all the Scandinavian countries was improved so greatly
that it was almost the same as that of man.

In France the woman's movement did not progress as rapidly as
in England and Scandinavia.   There was little suffrage agitation

[1] See Chapter XXXIX.
[2] Women were enfranchised first in New Zealand in 1893, then in Australia in
1902.

among French women, partly because they were more sensitive to
criticism and ridicule than their English sisters,
France   partly because the vote was not considered all important in France as it was in England.   Educational and professional
opportunities, however, were opened to women, of which many took
advantage.   The Napoleonic Code was modified so as to give
married women the right to their earnings.

In Germany the cause of woman had to contend against the unfavorable atmosphere of autocratic rule and military ideals.   The
only element that sympathized with the movement
Germany   was the least influential, the socialists.   The woman-
suffrage movement was very weak; but many women's organizations existed that agitated for the rights of women in the social and
economic spheres.

Considering the many handicaps women had to face in their
struggle for equality, the progress of their cause was very rapid.[1]
Woman's entrance into the world outside the home had the effect
of stimulating her to do many things of which she was once generally thought incapable.   There was hardly a field of endeavor in
which women were not to be found, so that the "man's world"
became a "man's and woman's world," wherein both were free to
give their best to the progress of the race.

REFERENCES

GENERAL:

W. L. Blease, *The Emancipation of English Women* (1910), a sympathetic
narrative of the struggles for equality by the English women; Kaethe
Schirmacher, *The Modern Woman's Rights Movement* (1912), a description
of the movement in all countries; E. H. Hecker, *Short History of Woman's
Rights* (1910); Lily Braun, *Die Frauenfrage: ihre geschichtliche Entwicklung
und wirtschaftliche Seite* (1910); G. Richard, *La Femme dans l'histoire*
(1909); Rosa Mayreder, *A Survey of the Woman Problem*, translated from
the German (1913); J. Langdon-Davies, *A Short History of Women* (1927);
A. Bebel, *Woman in the Past, Present, and Future*, translated from the
German (1893), socialist viewpoint; B. L. Hutchins, *Women in Modern
Industry* (1915), progress of women in the trades; W. L. George, *The Story
of Woman* (1925), sympathetic; Mary B. Messer, *The Family in the
Making* (1928), a history of woman.

FEMINISM:

Mary Wollstonecraft, *A Vindication of the Rights of Woman* (ed. 1891);
Charlotte P. Gilman, *Women and Economics* (ed. 1910), a plea for co-

[1] For the progress of woman after the World War, see Chapter XXXIX.

operative housekeeping and for the economic independence of woman; Ellen Key, *Love and Marriage*, translated from the Swedish (1912) and *The Woman Movement*, translated from the Swedish (1912), by a pioneer feminist; Olive Schreiner, *Women and Labour* (1911), an eloquent statement of woman's contribution to progress; W. L. George, *Woman and To-morrow* (1913), sympathetic with feminism; L. Abensour, *Histoire générale du Feminisme* (1921); Katherine Anthony, *Feminism in Germany and Scandinavia* (1915); Gina Lombroso, *The Soul of Woman*, translated from the Italian (1923), anti-feminist; Alice B. Parsons, *Woman's Dilemma* (1926), an analysis of the differences between men and women; T. R. Smith (ed.), *Feminism* (1918), collection of essays by Mary Wollstonecraft, Westermarck, Wells, Ellen Key, Havelock Ellis, and others.

THE SUFFRAGE MOVEMENT:

John Stuart Mill, *Subjection of Women* (ed. 1911), famous essay by the great economist in favor of woman suffrage; A. E. Metcalfe, *Woman's Effort: A Chronicle of British Women's Fifty Years' Struggle for Citizenship, 1865–1914* (1917); *Feminism and Woman Suffrage*, in the *Annals of the American Academy of Political and Social Science* (November, 1914); J. Barthélemy, *Le Vote des femmes* (1920), a study of the progress of woman suffrage; Ida H. Harper, *Brief History of Woman Suffrage in the United States* (1919); R. Strachey, *The Cause. A Short History of the Women's Movement in Great Britain* (1928).

PART IV
EXPANSION OF EUROPE

PART IV

EXPANSION OF EUROPE

WITH the discovery and settlement of America, a momentous process began in world history, a new expansion of Europe. For several centuries the European nations were busily en- Colonial imgaged in planting colonies and staking out colonial perialism empires in the New World. At the same time they were getting a foothold in India and China, where they established trading posts. Colonial imperialism, as this form of expansion is called, was a new phenomenon in that the nations sought colonies in order to have access to the raw materials that they lacked. It was the outcome of the Commercial Revolution of the sixteenth century which greatly enlarged the commerce of the world. Ancient imperialism was financial rather than economic. Rome sought colonies in order to exploit the population by laying heavy burdens of taxation. After the discovery of America, colonial imperialism became a dominant passion in Europe, and, for two centuries, wars raged for the possession of the lands of the New World and for the trade of the Orient. All the nations emerged from these imperialist wars more or less defeated. Spain, Holland, and France lost to England. But England lost her best colonies as a result of the American Revolution. Through revolution, Spain and Portugal lost South America.

A great reaction against colonial imperialism followed. During most of the nineteenth century, the passion for colonies was stilled, and Europe turned her attention to domestic Reaction matters. The French Revolution, Napoleon, the na- against coltionalist wars, and the democratic revolutions and agi- onies tations sufficiently engaged the energies of the European peoples. Furthermore, the Industrial Revolution discredited the ideas of the Mercantilist System; and colonies were no longer considered necessary to national prosperity.

Toward the end of the nineteenth century there took place an extraordinary revival of colonial imperialism. Once more the nations entered into a feverish scramble for colonies, which resulted in conflicts far greater than those in the eighteenth century. The causes for the revival were territorial, economic, political, and religious.

Territorial. Central Africa was discovered, an immense territory inhabited by weak, savage peoples, consequently, a new world for the nations to conquer and to divide. China and Japan were opened up which, as in the case of India during the seventeenth century, excited the commercial ambitions of Europe. As a result of the building of the Suez Canal there began a revival of the Mediterranean as a highway of commerce. North Africa, long neglected, now became the object of European ambitions.

Economic. The old Industrial Revolution transformed the economic life of Europe only. But the new Industrial Revolution, (1) Increase at the end of the nineteenth century, caused Europe in produc- to burst her industrial bonds and to encompass the tion entire world in its influences. Production was multiplied enormously, and new markets had to be found. The trunk railways and the large steamboats could transport large quantities of goods very quickly to all parts of the world. As competition in Europe became very keen, the eyes of the captains of industry turned to those regions that were at the same time densely populated and industrially undeveloped. The vast populations of Asia and Africa were so many potential customers. What fabulous profits awaited the manufacturers who got the opportunity of clothing the teeming millions of China and India!

The new Industrial Revolution demanded a great supply of raw materials and of the most varied sorts. In Asia and (2) Raw Africa, the chief scenes of the new imperialism, lay materials untold wealth of undeveloped resources that could be exploited profitably with the cheap labor of the natives. European capitalists were drawn as if by magic to the virgin sources of wealth in backward regions, to the rubber forests of South America, the diamond mines of South Africa, the iron mines of China, and the oil wells of Persia. There took place a revival of the colonial phase of the Mercantilist System, and colonies were again considered as producers of raw material for the mother country and as consumers of her manufactures.

With the tremendous increase in business came an accumulation of capital seeking investment. But home industries had developed to such a degree that additional investment would not greatly increase the rate of profit. Capital, therefore, would have to be satisfied with a moderate return or remain idle. The possibility of large returns for capital invested in backward regions (3) Export resulted in the export, or migration, of capital on a large of capital scale. Railways, docks, dams, factories, and telegraphs of the latest pattern were built by European capitalists in backward Asia and in primitive Africa. The governments of Europe, in order to safeguard the investments of their nationals, began to acquire political control over these regions. The flag followed investments.

Political. The intense nationalism which grew up in Europe during the nineteenth century stimulated the movement for expansion. Germany and Italy, being new nations, wanted colonies to maintain their position as great powers. Moreover, they were no longer content to see their people emigrate to foreign lands; they desired to have colonies where their surplus population could settle and maintain the ideals of their homeland. France sought solace for her defeat in 1871 by acquiring a colonial empire in Africa and Asia in order to balance the loss of Alsace-Lorraine. Russia, foiled in the Balkans, turned to the Far East, where she acquired large regions. The British once again awakened to the fact of their world-wide Empire, and an intense feeling of imperial patriotism arose which was fostered by prominent soldiers, statesmen, and writers.

Religious. Human motives are strangely mixed. Along with the desire for new markets and new territory there was also the desire for new converts to the Christian faith; to many devout Christians the millions of heathen in Asia and Africa were so many souls to be saved. Since the sixteenth century, the Catholic Church had been sending missionaries to all parts of the heathen world; and they had succeeded in converting most of the inhabitants of Latin America and of the Philippine Islands and in gaining many adherents in Japan, China, and India. For a long time the Protestants had neglected the missionary field; but early in the eighteenth century they had founded several societies for spreading the Gospel among the heathen. During the later half of the nineteenth century, both Catholics and Protestants had active and devoted foreign missionaries in almost every part of the heathen world.

The Christian missionaries were the advance guard of European civilization; they established schools, colleges, and hospitals which disseminated the arts and sciences of the West. They brought to savage peoples the rudiments of education, taught them orderly living, healed their sick, and induced them to abandon such inhuman practices as cannibalism and human sacrifice.

As a result of the old and new imperialism, European civilization spread throughout the world. The smallest of the continents, Europe, Europe, succeeded in imposing her systems, her ways, mother of and her ideas upon the rest of mankind. She governs civilization nearly all of Africa, Asia, and the Antipodes, and she has peopled nearly all of the New World. The spread of European civilization is a remarkable fact in world history, even more remarkable than the spread of Hellenic and Roman civilizations in ancient times. A few fundamental causes may be noted.

Political. Europe is organized on a national basis. Being a compact political organization, the nation is capable of utilizing quickly and efficiently all of its resources in men and materials. The European nation was bound to triumph when pitted against a savage tribe in Africa or against the inhabitants of an Asiatic country who were divided by religion, race, and caste.

Military. What Europe lacked in numbers she more than made up in military equipment. African tribes and Asiatic hordes armed with bows and arrows, spears, and old muskets, were no match for the disciplined European armies armed with cannon, repeating rifles, and machine guns. There were no braver men than the followers of the Mahdi, who, at the battle of Omdurman, charged British artillery, armed with spears and muskets. European naval armament played an important part in the march of colonial imperialism. A fleet would enter a native harbor and shell the port without opposition, there being no harbor defenses and no opposing fleet. By means of warships European armies could be poured into Asia and Africa without any hindrance whatsoever.

Economic. After conquest came European methods of control. Machine-made goods poured into the colony and drove out the native handicrafts. Capital also came, and railways and factories were established, all owned and managed by Europeans. The natives were reduced to economic helplessness; they had to export food and raw material in order to get the goods and services of the Europeans; and, as industrial laborers, they were directly under the control of their European employers.

European rule was masked. In some places the native ruler was

kept, but as a puppet controlled by European "advisers." In
others the high officials, civil and military, were Euro-   Rule of Eu-
peans; the lower officials were natives. The common   ropeans
soldier, the postman, the policeman, the tax collector   masked
being natives, the masses were not fully conscious that they were
under alien rule. Moreover, the large body of native officeholders
formed a powerful bureaucracy under the control and direction of
the European rulers.

European governments were very careful to respect the religion
and customs of the colonies. The British in India upheld the
Hindu and Moslem faiths and the caste system; and   Respect for
the French in North Africa upheld the Moslem faith.   native cus-
This attitude was prompted less by tolerance than by   toms
policy. What the Europeans feared most was a united opposition
to their rule which could be aroused only by an attack on the native
faith and customs.

In acquiring colonial possessions the European powers resorted
to all sorts of methods and pretexts. As there were no strong
governments in the backward regions, life and prop-   Methods of
erty were unsafe. If a European was killed or robbed   imperialism
his country would demand satisfaction from the native ruler on
the ground that it was a nation's duty to protect its citizens abroad
if the foreign government was unable or unwilling to do so. Sometimes, Christian missionaries, too zealous in spreading their faith,
violated cherished customs of the natives, which led to their being
killed. The "satisfaction" demanded by their country was in the
form of cessions of territory or in special economic privileges. In
this way the blood of martyrs became the seed of colonial empires.
When civil war was raging in a backward country European powers
would intervene "to restore order"; once there, they generally
remained. Should the officials or flag of a European power be
insulted, the power would intervene "to vindicate its honor,"
generally by occupying the country. Sometimes a corrupt native
ruler fell heavily in debt to European bankers, who would appeal to
their government in case he could not pay. European armies then
occupied the country of the bankrupt ruler.

The processes of colonial imperialism were in ever-tightening
stages of control. If the native government was too strong to be
set aside, as in the case of Turkey, it could be induced by threats,
appeals, and bribery to grant "concessions" to groups of capi-

talists. If the native government was weak, as in the case of
China, the country would be divided into "spheres of influence" in each of which the capitalists of a certain nation had the exclusive right of economic exploitation
By this method of "peaceful penetration" the European nations made invisible though very substantial conquests. The "pro tectorate," as in the cases of Tunis and Morocco, was a stage which definitely showed the tightening of the European grip; the native ruler was maintained, but he was "advised" by officials from the European power which he was forced to recognize as his "protec tor." These officials really governed the country. A variation of the protectorate was the "leasehold" as in the cases of Port Arthur and Kiao-chau, "leased" for a definite number of years by a Euro pean power, but really under its control. Finally, came the "col ony," as in the cases of Algeria and parts of South Africa, the last stage in the imperialist process, whereby the backward country was annexed outright.

With the advent of colonial imperialism a great problem arose as to the relations between the West and the East. The latter
resented the rule of the former, and liberation move ments arose, reaching from China to Morocco, that aimed to overthrow foreign control. For the first time the sentiment of nationalism began to stir the Oriental masses. The example of Japan rising to the position of a great power through adopting Western arts and ideas greatly encouraged the other Eastern peoples. At first they had resented the introduction of Western ways, now they eagerly adopted them as a means of liberating themselves from Western rule.

DISCOVERY AND EXPLORATION

The expansion movement had other besides imperialist causes and consequences; the nineteenth century, like the sixteenth, was
an age of discovery and exploration. At the beginning of the nineteenth century, about half of the globe was still unknown. In the New World, Alaska, all of Canada except the region of the Great Lakes and the St. Lawrence, the Far West of the United States, and
most of South America; in Asia, the vast central region between the Caspian and China proper; all of Africa except the coast; nearly all of Australia; and the Arctic and Antarctic regions were

entirely unknown.   The discoveries and explorations following the discovery of America, great as they were, had merely begun the great process of making known the entire world.

Early in the century (1799–1804) a German, Alexander von Humboldt, explored the regions of the Amazon and Orinoco valleys in South America.   His book *Kosmos* laid the New discov-
basis of the science of physical geography, being the eries and
first to describe scientifically the physical universe and explorations
its influence upon civilization.   About the same time (1804–06), the Lewis and Clark expedition opened up the Far West in North America.   Later, Alaska and western and northern Canada became better known.   How central Africa was discovered and explored will be described later.   Russian explorers made known Turkestan and certain parts of Siberia.   Tibet remained an undiscovered country until the end of the nineteenth century.   During 1899–1908, a Swede, Sven Hedin, made several expeditions to Tibet as a result of which the geography of the country became known.

At the beginning of the twentieth century, the only parts of the globe that still remained undiscovered were the Polar regions.   The renown that would attend the discoverer of the Poles Discovery of
and the immense difficulties that stood in the way the North
attracted the most daring explorers of modern times. Pole
During the nineteenth century many attempts were made to reach the Poles that resulted in extending the world's knowledge of those regions.   One of the most important was an expedition led in 1881–83 by the American, A. W. Greely, which reached 83°44′ north latitude.   Another was that led by the Norwegian, Fridjof Nansen, who in 1893–95 reached 86°14′ north, or within 272 miles of the North Pole.   The honor of discovering the North Pole belongs to an American, Robert E. Peary.   On July 6, 1908, at the head of an exploring party, he sailed from New York and landed at a point in northernmost Greenland.   The rest of the journey was continued in sleds.   For over four hundred miles Peary traveled in the Arctic amidst the greatest dangers, and only he, a colored servant, Matt Henson, and several Eskimos completed the journey.   On April 7, 1909, Peary reached the North Pole.

Antarctic exploration was attended with similar success.   A British expedition under Sir Ernest Henry Shackleton, in 1907–09, reached 88°23′ south latitude, or within ninety-seven miles of the South Pole.   The honor of discovering the only place, still un-

reached, belongs to a Norwegian, Roald Amundsen, who reached
Discovery of the South Pole on December 16, 1911. A British
the South expedition under Captain R. F. Scott started for the
Pole
South Pole about the same time as the Norwegian.
Captain Scott reached the Pole on January 18, 1912, and found that
Amundsen had been there before him. On his way back Captain
Scott and his party perished through exposure. At last, after
many centuries of effort, the entire earth's surface has become
known to mankind.

RESULTS OF IMPERIALISM

Not all the expectations of the enthusiastic advocates of expansion were realized. The colonial trade of Germany was insignifi-
Economic cant, though the expense of maintaining the colonies
results not was very great. France was more successful; but she,
very favor- too, had to make up annually a large colonial deficit.
able
England had more to justify her imperialism than any
other country, for she had a large and growing colonial trade; but
her important customers were Germany, France, and the United
States, and not Canada, Australia, or South Africa.

The colonies did not prove successful in drawing off the surplus
population of the mother countries. Because the German colonies
Little emi- in Africa were not attractive to white settlement, few
gration to Germans emigrated to them. But many emigrated
the colonies to the United States and to the British possessions.
French colonies, although near the mother country, contained few
Frenchmen besides military and civil officials. The immigration of
Italians to Libya was insignificant. Even Great Britain, with a
large surplus population and colonies in every climate, failed to
people the Empire with her children. From 1870 to 1905, a generation which saw the high tide of imperialism, about 6,500,000 emigrated from the United Kingdom; of these, only 2,000,000 settled in
the colonies.

One element in the new imperialism proved eminently successful; namely, the investment of capital. Enormous fortunes were
Views of made by those who invested money in the development
imperialists of backward lands. The success of these ventures was
due mainly to the power of European armies and navies to force
modern economic life on backward races. These methods were
defended on the ground that progress was accelerated among those

races who, otherwise, would have had to go through the slow stages of evolution; and thus the entire world was likely to be brought to the same high level of progress in a comparatively short time. Those who were in favor of economic imperialism argued that capital, not needed at home, found profitable employment abroad. Labor at home also benefited. When an English company, for example, secured a contract to build a railroad in China, it usually stipulated that the equipment be made in England, thus stimulating home industry.

The critics of imperialism replied that foreign investments had the effect of draining a country of its capital, as investors sent their money abroad because of the inducement of greater profit. Furthermore, economic imperialism, which benefited only a small group of investors, threatened grave danger to the entire nation; in the struggle to acquire colonies, the nations were drawn into quarrels which led to war. Frequently, also, the nation had to intervene in the affairs of those countries that had no strongly organized governments to protect the lives and property of its investing nationals. In the view of many, economic imperialism threatened the peace of mankind.

Views of the anti-imperialists

REFERENCES

P. T. Moon, *Imperialism and World Politics* (1926), scholarly, well-written and interesting, anti-imperialistic; C. H. J. Hayes, *A Political and Cultural History of Modern Europe* (1936), vol. II, pp. 695–742, contains an excellent summary; H. F. Fraser, *Foreign Trade and World Politics* (1926), with special reference to America after the war; A. G. Keller, *Colonization: A Study of the Founding of New Societies* (1908), a sociological treatise; on the history of expansion: H. C. Morris, *The History of Colonization*, 2 vols. (1908); A. Zimmermann, *Die europäischen Kolonien*, 5 vols. (1896–1903) and P. Leroy-Beaulieu, *De la Colonisation chez les peuples modernes*, 2 vols. (ed. 1902); on colonial tariffs; J. W. Root, *Colonial Tariffs* (1906); and *Colonial Tariff Policies*, Report of the U.S. Tariff Commission (1922); on government: P. S. Reinsch, *Colonial Government* (1902) and *Colonial Administration* (1904); on missions: J. S. Dennis, *Christian Missions and Social Progress*, 3 vols. (1898–1906); and R. E. Speer, *Missions and Modern History: A Study of the Missionary Aspects of some Great Movements of the Nineteenth Century*, 2 vols. (1904); J. A. Hobson, *Imperialism* (ed. 1938) and L. Woolf, *Empire and Commerce in Africa* (1920), are critical of imperialism; A. Viallate, *Economic Imperialism and International Relations* (1923); Lord Cromer, *Ancient and Modern Imperialism* (1910), an essay in defence of British imperialism.

For additional titles consult bibliographies at the end of Chapters XVIII, XX, XXX, and XXXI.

ADDITIONAL REFERENCES

G. Clark, *A Place in the Sun* (1936); E. Staley, *Raw Materials in Peace and War* (1937); *The Colonial Problem*, Royal Institute of International Affairs, London, 1937; G. Hardy, *La politique coloniale et le partage de la terre aux XIXe et XXe siècles* (1937); *Raw Materials and Colonies*, Royal Institute of International Affairs, London, 1936; M. E. Townsend, *European Colonial Expansion Since 1871* (1941).

CHAPTER XXX

EXPANSION OF EUROPE IN ASIA

FROM the days of the Persian Wars in ancient Greece down to the seventeenth century Europe had been subject to invasion by Asiatic hordes. Persians, Huns, Magyars, Tartars, Arabs, and Turks, had swept into Europe and had conquered considerable sections of it. But conditions have now changed. It is the giant Asia, largest of the continents, that is in the grip of little Europe. Before the nineteenth century the vast northern stretch, Siberia, had been annexed by Russia; and the great peninsula, India, had been conquered by the British. During the nineteenth century the rest of the continent fell more or less under European control. Only one nation remained truly independent, and that was the island-empire of Japan.

Unlike Africa, Asia is the home of highly civilized races who had made great contributions to literature, art, science, religion, and industry. It would hardly be an exaggeration to say that Asia was the mother of civilization, but, for many centuries, its people had made little progress; they remained static while the Europeans ventured into new fields. Modern civilization is European in origin, and it was not till our day that the Asiatics awakened to the need of modernizing themselves.

CHINA

(a) SOCIETY AND GOVERNMENT

From the point of view of size, China is a continent, having an area larger than that of Europe and an estimated population of 300,000,000. China proper lies in the valleys of the Yangtze-kiang and Hwang Ho rivers, where live the bulk of the teeming millions. The outlying districts, Manchuria, Mongolia, Tibet, and Sin-Kiang, are all vast in extent but sparsely inhabited.

Extent of China

Europe's knowledge of the Chinese came chiefly during the thirteenth century as a result of the missionary efforts of the Franciscan friars; and, more especially, from the accounts of the famous Venetian traveler, Marco Polo, who sojourned for a number of

years in China. Early in the sixteenth century, Portuguese mer-
European chants established a trading post at Macao, near
settlements Canton; and in the following century the British
in China established themselves at Canton which, in time, became the chief trading center for Chinese and Europeans. The
European traders were harassed by the Chinese officials, who asserted that their country had no need of "foreign barbarians" or
of their goods. They managed to stay by bribing and cajoling the
officials; but their property, and even their lives, were frequently
in danger. The Chinese had come to believe that their civilization had reached a height unattained by any other people; what
they wished above all, therefore, was to maintain it uncontaminated by the rest of the world, and to remain loyal to their immemorial customs and traditions.

Chinese civilization dominated eastern Asia as Roman civilization had once dominated western Europe. The Japanese, the
Chinese Koreans, the Siamese, and the peoples of Indo-China
civilization were in the sphere of China's cultural influence. Their
literature, rich in profound philosophy and exquisite poetry; their
wonderful painting; their artistic work in lacquer and ceramics;
their marvelously colored silks and brocades; their highly refined
manners, all testified to the greatness of the Chinese. They also
possessed in rudimentary form such modern inventions as printing,
paper, and gunpowder. But the natural resources of the country,
coal, iron, copper, and other metals, remained undeveloped until
the coming of the Europeans. A slow, conservative, pacific people
the Chinese were content to live by agriculture, by fishing, by the
handicrafts, and by merchandising. The merchant class, especially, was greatly respected, and commercial honesty was highly
regarded.

Buddhism was the religion of the lower classes, and Confucianism
of the upper. Confucianism is an ethical code rather than a re-
Confucian- ligion; it is based upon the teachings of the great sage,
ism Confucius (551–479 B.C.), whose writings contain rules
for the conduct of life, both individual and social. Confucius
stresses duty to parents rather than duty to God; hence, filial
piety is regarded by the Chinese as the supreme virtue. It is
the basis of ancestor worship which is practiced by nearly all
classes.

There was no common spoken language in China; instead there

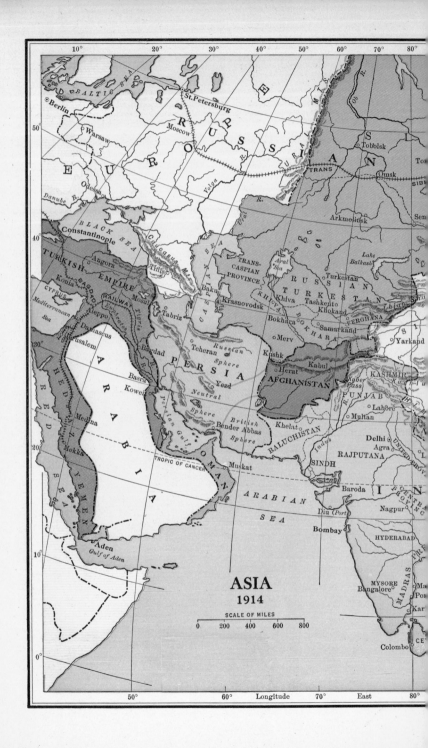

ASIA
1914

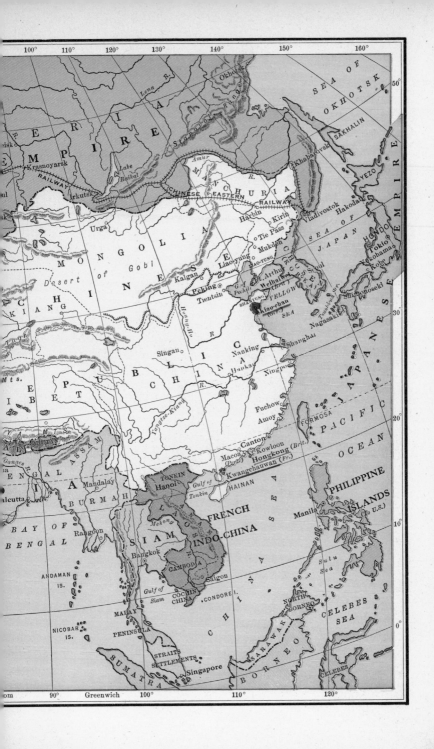

were many dialects. But there was a common written language, the language of the classics that was used by the Chinese language learned, much as Latin was used during the Middle Ages in Europe. Chinese was very difficult to learn because it had no alphabet; different symbols were employed for different words. Until very recently there was no system of public education, and consequently the masses of the people were illiterate.

The government of the Celestial Empire, as China was called, was that of an absolute monarchy under the rule of the "Son of Heaven," the Emperor. During the seventeenth century China had been conquered by a Tartar tribe, the Manchus, who displaced the native dynasty by one of their race. Most of the high officials were Manchus, who were hated by the Chinese as a ruling class not of their race. In the outlying regions the Emperor ruled through viceroys, whose chief function was to collect tribute for their master. Tibet was almost an independent state, being ruled by the Dalai Lama who acknowledged the Emperor as his suzerain. Government officials, called "mandarins" by the Europeans, were recruited in a manner quite extraordinary in an Oriental country. Selection for office was made as a result of examinations in Chinese literature, philosophy, and history, based upon the ancient classics. Scholastic attainment was the test of fitness for public office. The system was democratic inasmuch as any one, irrespective of birth, had the right to enter the civil service examinations.

(b) OPENING UP OF CHINA

No diplomatic relations existed between China and the other nations. Early in the nineteenth century, England sent a diplomatic mission to Peking, which the Emperor declined to receive. He demanded that the British representatives undergo a humiliating ceremony of obeisance, called "kowtow," which they refused to perform. The British determined to use force in order to compel the Emperor to enter into treaty relations, and their The Opium War opportunity came with the Opium War (1839–42). The Chinese had become addicted to the use of opium, a harmful drug made from plants grown chiefly in India. Large profits were made from the sale of opium by the British growers in India and by the British merchants in Canton. So widespread was the havoc among the Chinese caused by the evil habit that the government forbade the importation of opium. But it was smuggled into Canton by the British merchants with the connivance of corrupt officials. In 1839, a special commissioner took charge of the situation, and demanded of the British merchants that they surrender their stocks of opium. When the demand was refused, the British in Canton were besieged and reduced almost to starvation. This situation led to the intervention of Great Britain on the side of her nationals. War followed between England and China, which ended in the humiliating defeat of China. The Treaty of Nanking (1842) provided (1) that, in addition to Canton, the ports of Amoy, Ningpo, Fuchow, and Shanghai be open to foreign trade; (2) that Hongkong be ceded to England; and (3) that China pay an indemnity of $21,000,000.

The next important step in the process of opening up China took place in 1857, when England and France made war on China, and Treaty of   compelled her to sign the Treaty of Tientsin (1858). Tientsin   This treaty opened more ports to foreign commerce; allowed foreigners to trade along the Yangtze-kiang River; gave special protection to Christian missionaries; ceded Kowloon, opposite Hongkong, to England; compelled China to pay an indemnity; and provided for a British diplomatic mission in Peking. The last provision recognized the equality of foreign nations with China, which destroyed a widespread belief among the Chinese that the Emperor was the suzerain of all the other rulers of the world whose lands were subject to China, the "center of the universe." The Treaty of Tientsin was followed by treaties with all the other nations.

(c) THE UNEQUAL TREATIES

China's isolation was now over. Many foreigners came, traders, missionaries, scholars, and travelers, who wrote much of China (1) The con-   and her ways. Through the "treaty" ports China sular courts   did a thriving business, exporting tea, silk, and porcelain, and importing the machine-made products of the West. Foreigners were given special privileges as a result of unequal treaties forced upon China by the powers; these privileges were known as extra-territorial rights. Special districts, called "concessions," were set aside in the treaty ports as residential quarters for foreigners. The government had no jurisdiction over the "concessions," which were entirely self-governing. Foreign governments were given judicial control over their nationals, who came under the jurisdiction of the consular courts, because it was claimed that the native courts were corrupt and incompetent, and that Chinese codes of law were not compatible with Occidental ideas of justice.

China was not permitted to have tariff autonomy. Her tariff was, at the highest, to be five per cent, and could not be changed without the consent of the treaty powers. Moreover, the (2) Tariff inspector-general of the customs had to be a foreigner, fixed by the of the nation that did most business with China. Sir powers Robert Hart, an Englishman, held that post for many years. The low tariff prevented the Chinese government from getting large revenues; therefore, it had to have recourse to foreign loans. But the credit of China was not very good, and she had to pledge certain taxes as security for a loan. These taxes were collected by agents of the creditors until the loan was paid. By these methods China was held in fiscal subjection.

Foreign troops were quartered in the treaty ports to protect the lives and property of the foreign residents. Foreign warships patrolled the coast and the rivers. The Chinese government was too weak to give sufficient protection to (3) Foreign occupation foreigners who were intensely disliked by the natives.

Great discontent spread among the people who blamed the Manchu dynasty for allowing the "foreign devils" to humiliate the Celestial Empire. A popular uprising, known as the The Taiping Taiping Rebellion, broke out in 1853, and raged for uprising over a decade. City after city fell into the hands of the ever victorious army of the rebels, and the throne of the Manchus was in danger. During this crisis the government was controlled by Li Hung Chang, who sought the aid of foreigners to fight the Taipings. The Imperial troops were put under the command of an English officer, Charles Gordon, who proved himself to be a gallant soldier as well as an inspiring personality. Largely through the efforts of Gordon, the rebellion was suppressed.

(d) FOREIGN AGGRESSION

During the second half of the nineteenth century, Europe became increasingly aggressive toward China. Her immense size, her teeming population, her natural resources made Powers seize China a rich prize. And her weak government and territory pacific people made her an easy one. The powers were no longer content to exact privileges; they began to sieze ports and even whole provinces, while solemnly asserting their intention to maintain the integrity of China. By the treaties of 1858 and 1860, Russia was given the coast district of the Amur River, which she annexed to Siberia. The tributary kingdom of Burma was seized by England in 1885, and added to India. By means of "peaceful penetration" and "punitive expeditions," France steadily encroached upon the tributary states of Annam, Tonkin, and Cambodia. In 1883, China demanded of France that she evacuate Tonkin; a Franco-Chinese war followed which resulted in the defeat of China. During 1885–87, France established a protectorate over the region now called French Indo-China.

Japan also took a hand in the game. She felt that if China was to be dismembered, she should assist in the process and so gain Sino-Japanese War her share. Japan was especially eager to get Korea, another tributary kingdom of China; and with this end in view she began to interfere in Korean affairs, greatly to the anger of the Chinese. The outcome was the Sino-Japanese War (1894–95), in which the Chinese, greatly to their surprise, were badly beaten by the Japanese whom they regarded contemptuously as "dwarfs" and "upstarts." The Treaty of Shimonoseki provided (1) that China pay an indemnity of $150,000,000; (2) that Korea be declared independent; (3) that the island of Formosa and the Liao-tung Peninsula be annexed to Japan. The treaty roused the opposition of Russia, who was opposed to Japan's presence on the mainland. A coalition of Russia, France, and Germany "advised" Japan to relinquish her conquest of the peninsula. To refuse meant war with three great powers; therefore, Japan accepted the "advice," and was gratefully permitted by the coalition to take $23,000,000 additional indemnity from China.

The coalition then gathered the fruits of Japan's victory. On the plea of avenging the murder by Chinese of two German missionaries, the Kaiser sent a fleet to shake the "mailed Powers seize more territory fist" in the face of China. In 1898, she was compelled to grant to Germany a "leasehold" of Kiao-chau with its fine harbor. Russia got a "leasehold" of Port Arthur and the Liao-tung Peninsula; France, the port of Kwang-chau-wan; and England, the port of Wei-hai-wei. The powers then proceeded to divide China into "spheres of influence." German capitalists claimed a monopoly of concessions in the province of Shantung;

French capitalists, in the region bordering upon French Indo-China; English capitalists, of the valley of the Yangtze-kiang; and Russian capitalists, of Manchuria. "In China," declared a Russian diplomat, "there is room for us all — for us, for France, and for Germany."

The aggression of the powers in China called forth a protest from the United States. In 1899, John Hay, Secretary of State, issued his famous "Open Door" note to the powers which proposed (1) equality of commercial opportunity among all the nations dealing with China, and (2) the preservation of China's territorial and administrative integrity. This policy of the "Open Door," Hay later declared, would "safeguard for the world the principle of equal and impartial trade with all parts of the Chinese Empire." The powers gave their approval of the Hay note, though in an evasive manner.

(e) AWAKENING OF CHINA

The victory of Japan over China greatly disturbed the equanimity of the Chinese. It was generally ascribed to the fact that Japan had become Westernized, therefore, strong and united. Among the rising generation of Chinese many had studied abroad and in the missionary schools in China. They were filled with enthusiastic admiration for everything Western and disdain for everything Chinese. The "Westerners" succeeded in influencing the young Emperor, Kwangsu, who, in 1898, issued a series of reform edicts, affecting the administration, the civil service examinations, and the system of education. The Emperor favored the introduction of factories and railways. Foreign capitalists came to the "spheres of influence," which offered excellent opportunities for investment. Railways and factories were built; mines were opened; modern steamers began to appear alongside the picturesque "junks"; the telegraph and telephone were installed. Modern scientific progress was, however, not at all to the liking of the conservative Chinese. Railways, especially, were regarded as a desecrating innovation because the lines were sometimes built across graveyards, which aroused popular fury against those who violated the sanctity of ancestral tombs.

At the court in Peking the reforms met with bitter opposition. A queer "palace revolution" took place, led by the dowager

Empress, Tsze-Hsi, a determined and vigorous old woman.
The young Emperor was virtually deposed, and the
dowager Empress ruled as regent. She nullified the reform edicts, discouraged the industrial enterprises, and set a price on
the head of all reformers. The government secretly encouraged a
powerful secret society, popularly known as the "Boxers," who
desired to rid their country of the foreigners who were "lacerating
China like tigers" and who were violating the cherished and immemorial traditions of the land. During 1899–1900, anti-foreign
outbreaks took place, and many foreigners lost their lives. The
Europeans in Peking fled for shelter to their legations, which were
thereupon besieged by mobs. The situation was critical, and the
powers decided to send an expeditionary force to relieve the legations. An international army, composed of European, Japanese,
and American troops, invaded China, captured Peking, and relieved
the legations. In revenge for the uprising the European troops
committed frightful outrages against the Chinese, killing many
people and looting palaces and temples, which cast great discredit
upon the Christian nations. China was forced to pay an indemnity
of $320,000,000 and to suppress all anti-foreign societies.[1]

The Boxer uprising (margin note)

But the reform movement could not be stayed. It received a
great impetus as a result of the Russo-Japanese War, which demonstrated that Westernized Japan was more than a
match for China's persistent aggressor, Russia. Chief
among the reformers was Dr. Sun Yat-sen, an eloquent orator and
writer, who was to China what Mazzini was to Italy. He founded
secret patriotic societies, composed mainly of young students, who
enthusiastically devoted themselves to the regeneration of their
country through the introduction of the arts and sciences of the
West. Young China favored the establishment of a democratic
republic; hence, it was opposed to the Manchu dynasty. It was
also strongly nationalist, and denounced the aggressions of the
powers in China.

Young China (margin note)

At first the dowager Empress resisted the introduction of reforms
and hounded the reformers out of the country. But
she was finally forced to follow the reformers' lead.
At the beginning of the twentieth century, there began an

Awakening of China (margin note)

---

[1] America later renounced part of her share of the indemnity, which was used
by China as a scholarship fund for Chinese students. In 1925, America remitted
to China the balance of her share in the indemnity on condition that it be used
to further scientific education.

"awakening of China" which astonished the world. In 1905, a decree was issued abolishing the ancient system of examinations and establishing a new system based upon modern history, European languages, economics, and political science. In the enthusiasm for the new learning, ancient temples were converted into modern schools and colleges on the Western model. The army was reorganized on European lines. A commission was sent to Europe to study constitutional government.

But European aggression continued, and the dismemberment of China was openly advocated. As a consequence a powerful nationalist movement appeared which saw in the The Chinese Manchu dynasty the chief cause of the country's Revolution woes. In 1911, a revolution broke out, led by Sun Yat-sen and backed by the army, which had been won over to the cause of the nationalists. Events moved swiftly. In 1912, the Manchu dynasty was overthrown, and a republic proclaimed. Yuan Shih-kai, a former general in the Imperial army, was chosen President. A parliament was elected, and a constitution was proclaimed. The Revolution of 1911, however, resulted in a serious division between North and South, and China passed from the turmoil of revolution to the turmoil of civil war.

JAPAN

(a) OPENING UP OF JAPAN

The history of Japan during the nineteenth century filled the world with wonder and admiration. In the period of about one generation an isolated, almost unknown country, Rise of whose inhabitants were regarded by Europeans merely Japan as charming little people, beautifully dressed in colored gowns, with pretty manners and artistic tastes, rose to be a great nation whose friendship was eagerly sought by the European powers.

Japan consists of four large islands and about 3000 small ones, strung along the coast of China for 2000 miles. The islands are volcanic and mountainous, with only about fourteen The island-per cent of the area fit for cultivation. In 1925, the empire population of Japan, exclusive of Formosa and Korea, was 60,000,-000, occupying a territory as large as California. Although closely allied to the Chinese in race and in civilization, the Japanese differ from them in temperament. The Chinese are a rather stolid, phlegmatic people, whereas the Japanese are lively, quick-witted, and possess great powers of adaptation.

The first Europeans to visit Japan were Portuguese navigators who, in 1542, chanced to come to the islands.   A few years later, Saint Francis Xavier, the Jesuit missionary, came to convert the inhabitants.   He and his followers were welcomed by the Japanese, and they succeeded in gaining many converts to Catholicism.   But the anti-foreign feeling became strong, and the Christians were accused of conspiring against the government in the interest of Europeans.   Thousands of converts were put to death; by the end of the sixteenth century, Christianity in Japan had almost entirely disappeared.   The government now determined on a rigid policy of isolation; foreigners and foreign goods were excluded, and the profession of Christianity was made a capital offense.

Coming of the Europeans

Japan remained in a state of seclusion for two centuries longer. She was opened to the world by the famous visits, in 1853 and in 1854, of an American fleet under Commodore Perry, who came to demand of Japan that she give shelter to American sailors wrecked on her coasts and allow American sailors to provision in her ports.   These demands were granted by Japan.   In 1858, Townsend Harris, the first American representative to Japan, negotiated a treaty establishing regular commercial relations between the two countries.   This treaty ended Japan's policy of seclusion.   Shortly afterwards she entered into treaty relations with the European powers.   Treaty ports were designated in which foreigners could trade, and extra-territorial privileges were given to foreign residents in Japan.

The visit of Commodore Perry

Many marveled at what was revealed in Old Japan.   A system of society and government existed that strangely resembled that of western Europe during the Middle Ages.   The mass of people were serfs on the estates of a military aristocracy who ruled their districts and conducted private war in the manner of feudal nobles.   A warrior caste, the *samurai*, fought in armor, engaged in tournaments, and lived according to a code of chivalry like medieval knights.   The ruler of the land, the *Mikado*, lived in seclusion, and was regarded as a kind of deity.   Real power was exercised by an official, the *Shogun*, who was the chief of a powerful clan.

Old Japan

(b) WESTERNIZATION

The Japanese were the first Asiatic people to become fully Westernized. Very early they realized that the strength of the Europeans lay in national organization, and their weakness lay in the divisions caused by feudalism. As a fighting race they beheld in European gunnery a superior force against which all their valor with sword and spear was in vain. During the sixties a group of ardent young reformers began a revolution unparalleled in modern times. In one generation the public and private life of the Japanese people was almost completely transformed. Hundreds of young Japanese became students in the schools and colleges of Europe and America with the purpose of bringing Western knowledge to their native land. Commissions were sent abroad to study the institutions of the West, and to recommend the adoption of the best that the various nations had to offer. Foreigners were welcomed and treated with consideration; and many were employed by the government to instruct the natives in the arts of the West.

Young Japan

As a consequence there began the wholesale introduction of Western institutions in this Eastern land. Young Japan keenly realized that the first step must be the establishment of a strong, central government in order to solidify the people into a nation. In 1867, the Shogun was compelled to resign, and the Mikado Mutsuhito, now called "Emperor," was "restored" to his full powers. His reign (1867–1912) is justly celebrated in Japanese history as the Era of Enlightenment. "We shall extract," declared the Emperor, "all that is best in the whole world in order to increase the prosperity of the Empire." Beginning with 1868, a famous year in Japanese history, a number of remarkable reforms were put through by means of Imperial decrees, in the manner of the Stein-Hardenberg reforms in Prussia, which were carefully studied. Feudalism was abolished in 1871. Most of the lords freely surrendered their privileges; those who rose in rebellion were ruthlessly suppressed. To compensate the lords for the loss of their privileges, the government granted them pensions, gave them European titles such as marquis, count, and baron, and appointed them to positions in the public service. In place of fiefs Japan was divided into administrative areas like those in France. Tokio was declared the capital of the nation, and a national administration was organized. The aboli-

Era of great reforms: (1) abolition of feudalism

tion of feudalism was followed by the suppression of serfdom; the peasants became tenants or proprietors of the lands which they tilled.

To replace the feudal levies conscription was instituted on the German model.   The national army was a deathblow to the

(2) Military and naval reforms

samurai, who thereby lost their military privileges. These proud warriors rose in rebellion, but they fought in vain against gunnery and discipline.   A navy was built on the British model, and Japan rapidly emerged as a great sea power.   Most of the officers in the army and navy came from the *samurai*.

A constitution was promulgated in 1889.   It was chiefly the work of Marquis Ito, a leading reformer, who was the head of a

(3) Constitutional reforms

commission that went to Europe to study systems of government.   The constitution established a parliamentary régime like that of Prussia.   To the Emperor was given full executive power and an absolute veto over legislation.   The government was to be carried on by a ministry responsible to the Emperor.   Legislative power was vested in a Diet consisting of an aristocratic upper house, and a lower house elected by a suffrage based upon property and class.   A bill of rights was adopted, which established equality before the law, civil liberty, religious toleration, and freedom of speech and of assembly.   A new civil and criminal code was promulgated, based upon the best European models.   As a consequence of her judicial reforms, Japan demanded a revision of the treaties which granted extra-territorial privileges to foreigners, a demand to which the treaty powers agreed (1899).   A national system of popular education was adopted, modeled on that of America which, in one generation, abolished illiteracy.   The leaders in the reform movement acquired great prestige as patriotic statesmen, and they exercised great influence in the new government.   Although unofficial, the "elder statesmen," as they were called, virtually controlled the policies of the nation.

Industrial changes were even more potent in the transformation of Japan than enlightened decrees.   Although her natural resources

(4) Industrialization

are not abundant Japan rapidly introduced the factory system.   Machine-made goods displaced the artistic products of her famous handicrafts.   Railways and steamboats made rapid progress.[1]   Foreign commerce made notable advances;

[1] In 1872, Japan had 18 miles of railway; in 1912, over 6000 miles.

Japanese products competed successfully in the markets of America, Europe, and Asia.   During the period 1877–1913 her foreign commerce increased twenty-seven-fold.

The new Japan that emerged as a result of these changes was a nation of alert, ambitious, efficient people, thoroughly familiar with modern progress and animated by a patriotism almost religious in character.   Primarily, Japan assimilated *Imperialism* Western civilization in order to protect herself against Western encroachment; but, once in possession of the new arts and sciences, she became aggressive like the Western nations.   Her large population demanded an outlet; her active capitalists wanted concessions; and her imperially minded statesmen wanted to spread Japanese influence.   China offered a fair field for these ambitions.   The Sino-Japanese War, already described, was the first attempt of Japan to dominate China in order to exploit her resources.

THE RUSSO-JAPANESE WAR (FEBRUARY, 1904– SEPTEMBER, 1905)

As a result of her defeat in the Russo-Turkish War, Russia turned her attention from the Mediterranean to the Pacific.   Her movement toward the East was wide and irresistible, *Russia oc-* like that of a glacier; its object was the control of *cupies Man-* Manchuria, the Liao-tung Peninsula, and Korea in *churia* order to get to the warm waters of the Pacific.   Russian diplomacy became all-powerful at Peking, where Li Hung Chang, who was pro-Russian, controlled foreign policy.   In 1896, through the efforts of Count Witte, a Russo-Chinese bank was established that loaned money to China to pay her indemnity to Japan.   In return, Russia got an important concession to build the Chinese Eastern Railway across Manchuria, making a direct route to the terminus, Vladivostok.   Russian troops were sent into Manchuria, there to remain until "lasting order shall have been established."

The next move of Russia was southward, into a warmer climate and a richer land.   In 1898, she obtained a "lease" from China of the Liao-tung Peninsula, including Port Arthur; and *Russia gets* a concession to build a railway connecting the latter *lease of Port* with the Chinese Eastern.   In Port Arthur, Russia *Arthur* secured an ice-free port and a "window on the Pacific."   Russia also had designs on Korea which lay in her imperialist march to the Pacific.

Japan was greatly alarmed.   Once the mainland opposite fell into the grip of Russia, she would be shut out from her best mar-

Alarm of Japan

ket and from her chief source of raw materials.   Port Arthur was splendidly fortified and became a great naval base.   Japan felt that her very existence was at stake, and she made careful preparations for the coming conflict with Russia.

In order to prevent a European coalition against her, as in the Sino-Japanese War, Japan realized that she must have a Western

Anglo-Japanese alliance

ally.   English and Russian interests in Asia frequently clashed; therefore Japan sought the friendship of England.   In 1902, an alliance was formed by the two island-empires, negotiated by Lord Lansdowne and Count Hayashi, which provided for mutual support in case their interests in the Far East were threatened.   The Anglo-Japanese alliance was the first alliance between a Western and an Asiatic power on equal terms.

The Japanese began to make careful preparations for the coming war with Russia.   The army and navy were enlarged and organized

War preparations of Japan

on an efficient basis.   Munitions of war of the latest and best patterns were assembled in large quantities. Thus prepared, Japan was ready to challenge the great military power of the West, who, though immensely superior to her in men and resources, was yet seriously handicapped by the fact that the scene of conflict was over three thousand miles from her base of supplies.   The Trans-Siberian Railway was Russia's only means of transporting troops and supplies to the Pacific.

Russia refused to give a definite date when she would withdraw from Manchuria, and she also refused to give up her ambitions in

The Russo Japanese War (1904–05)

Korea.   The outcome was the Russo-Japanese War. Japanese armies invaded Manchuria and the Liao-tung Peninsula, defeating the Russians in several battles.   The Japanese, under General Nogi, laid siege to Port Arthur; a desperate conflict ensued lasting ten months, at the end of which the great fortress was compelled to surrender.   Russian armies, under General Kuropatkin, were routed at the battle of Mukden and compelled to beat a demoralizing retreat.   Japan's victories on sea were no less decisive than those on land.   Several naval engagements took place, culminating in the battle of Tsushima in which the Russian fleet was annihilated by the Japanese under Admiral Togo.

Both sides were now tired of war and eager for peace: Russia, because she was defeated and facing revolution; and Japan, because she was victorious and facing bankruptcy, as the war was a great drain on her finances. At the suggestion of President Roosevelt, a peace conference met in Portsmouth, New Hampshire, where a treaty was signed in 1905. It recognized Japan's paramount interests in Korea, and transferred Russia's rights in the Liao-tung Peninsula, including Port Arthur, to Japan; Russia gave to the latter the southern half of the island of Sakhalin; Manchuria was divided between Russia and Japan into "spheres of influence." No indemnity was paid by Russia. *The Treaty of Portsmouth*

England now welcomed her victorious ally into the ranks of the great powers. Her treaty was renewed and strengthened in 1905 and again in 1911; it was now a hard-and-fast alliance to aid each other in case of an attack by any other power on their possessions in eastern Asia and India. It also recognized Japan's paramount interest in Korea, which Japan utilized by annexing that country, in 1910, against the strong protests of the Koreans. *The new Anglo-Japanese alliance*

The overwhelming defeat of Russia, long regarded as a formidable military power, by an Asiatic people just out of Oriental seclusion, astounded the world. Japan leaped forward as one of the great powers and as the dominant influence in the Far East. A wave of discontent with European rule, which had been accepted as inevitable, began to spread throughout the East, where it was now realized that Orientals, armed and trained like Europeans, could fight as effectively as they. The West was disturbed by the dread of what was termed the "Yellow Peril," the fear that the millions of the yellow race, inspired and led by Japan, might start a world war against the whites. *Awakening of the East*

THE MIDDLE EASTERN QUESTION

Central Asia, sometimes called the Middle East, includes Persia, Afghanistan, Baluchistan, and Tibet. Here, as in the Far East, there was also a clash of European imperialism, especially between Russia and England. The region is neither rich nor thickly populated. Tibet is a bleak plateau; Afghanistan and Baluchistan are savage and mountainous; *Rivalry of Russia and England*

and much of Persia is a sandy waste. Russia's object in trying to control these countries was to reach the warm waters of the Persian Gulf and the Indian Ocean. England's object was strategic: to protect the northern frontier of India against Russian advance.

During the latter half of the nineteenth century, Russian expansion in Asia was southward as well as eastward. Very slowly she penetrated the desert fastness of Turkestan, and brought under her sway the marauding tribes of that region. Her continued advance southward greatly disturbed England, who feared for India. In the meanwhile England had not been idle. She advanced her Indian frontier by conquering the Punjab and Baluchistan. A contest then took place between the two powers for the control of Afghanistan. English armies invaded the country and set up a puppet Ameer, or ruler; Russian agents subsidized marauding tribes on the Indian frontier. In 1895, the Russian forces reached the northern boundary of Afghanistan, and the road to India lay open.

Advance of Russia and of England

At the same time another Russian threat appeared from Tibet. For long that land had remained closed to Europeans; its ruler, the Dalai Lama, who was at the same time the high priest of the Buddhist faith, had forbidden Europeans to enter the sacred city of Lhasa. Russian diplomacy broke through the barriers and succeeded in bringing the Dalai Lama under its influence. Lord Curzon, the Viceroy of India, appeared as the militant champion of British imperialism in the Middle East. Through his influence an armed "mission" was sent, in 1904, to Tibet, led by Colonel Younghusband. He entered Lhasa and dictated a treaty to the government of Tibet, which gave England virtual control of its foreign policies.

Tibet

Far more important was the problem that arose in Persia. The home of an ancient but unprogressive civilization, Persia, at the beginning of the twentieth century, was in a situation similar to that of other Oriental countries that had fallen a prey to European imperialism. Her ruler, the Shah, was weak and corrupt; the country was backward and disorderly; and Europeans were hunting for concessions. Russia began the "peaceful penetration" of Persia by extorting concessions to build railways and to open mines. Both English and Russian bankers capitalized the vices of the Shah by loaning him money which he squandered. But the loans were secured by the

"Peaceful penetration" of Persia

customs and revenues, and Persia rapidly fell into the financial coils of the Europeans, which could have but one outcome, the loss of her independence.

Patriotic Persians became alarmed.   A nationalist party arose that organized an uprising against the Shah, who, in 1906, was compelled to grant a constitution and to call a parlia- Uprising ment.   When parliament demanded control of the against the finances, the Shah, backed by Russia, refused to Shah respect the constitution.   A civil war followed which brought the country to the verge of anarchy.

In 1907, a treaty was negotiated by Alexander Isvolsky and Sir Edward Grey, the Foreign Ministers of Russia and England. These two powers agreed "to settle by mutual agree- Partition of ment the different questions concerning the interests Persia of their states on the Continent of Asia."   Because of her fear of Germany, England was willing to come to terms with her old enemy, Russia.   Defeat by Japan convinced Russia that the best way of expanding in Asia was to coöperate with the power most interested in the region that she desired.   Persia was divided into three "spheres of influence": the north was to be Russian; the south, British; and the center, "neutral"; that is, open to the capitalists of both nations.   Tibet was to be a vassal state of China, as hitherto; both powers agreed neither to seek concessions in Tibet nor to influence her politically.   Afghanistan was organized as a buffer state under English influence; Russia promised to deal with the Ameer only through England.

The economic partition of their country roused the Persians to fury.   In 1909, the Shah was deposed, and his son placed on the throne.   Two years later, parliament selected an Shuster's American, W. Morgan Shuster, as financial adviser to efforts to the government.   Shuster was deeply interested in the free Persia welfare of the Persian people, and he saw clearly that financial reform was the first step to their political independence.   In his efforts to put the Persian finances on a sound basis, he encountered the determined opposition of Russia and England, who feared that if Persia put her house in order they would be deprived of a pretext for intervention.   Accordingly, Russia demanded that Shuster be dismissed and that a financial adviser be appointed who had her approval and that of England.   Too weak to resist, Persia was forced to yield.   Shuster was dismissed, the government fell into the hands of corrupt tools of the partitioning powers, and Persia virtually ceased to exist as an independent nation.

ASIA MINOR

European imperialism was also active in Asia Minor.   In ancient times that region had been the seat of mighty empires and flourish-

Favorable position of Asia Minor

ing civilizations; but now it was a backward region inhabited by poor peasants and wandering tribes. Geographically Asia Minor is very favorably situated; it is a bridge connecting Europe with central and southern Asia; and it is bordered by large bodies of water, the Caspian, the Black Sea, the Mediterranean, the Red Sea, and the Persian Gulf.   It was therefore coveted by the European powers.

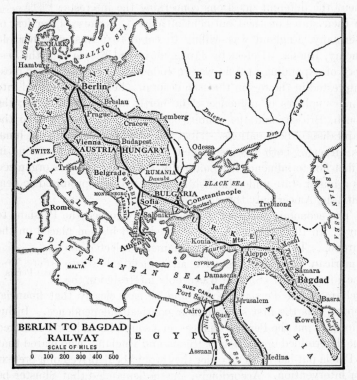

Here it was Germany that was first on the scene.   In Asiatic Turkey she beheld vast possibilities for business enterprise which would furnish an outlet for her trade and capital.   In modern times

the exploitation of an undeveloped region begins with the building of railways. As soon as rapid means of com- Germany
munication and transportation are established, con- ambitious in
necting isolated with civilized regions, the pulse of com- Asia Minor
merce begins to beat more rapidly; factories are built, cities grow,
and even agriculture is stimulated by the prospect of new and
better markets. Along the railway soon appear bustling towns
and well-cultivated fields. German financiers determined to link
progressive Europe and backward Asia by means of a great railway
from the Bosphorus to the Persian Gulf. This scheme was the
famous Bagdad Railway.

No sooner was the Kaiser "his own Chancellor" than Germany
became actively interested in the Near East. In order to gain
concessions from the Sultan, Germany had to gain The Bagdad
influence in Constantinople. The Kaiser paid several Railway
visits to Abdul Hamid, who was greatly honored to receive the most
powerful Christian monarch. In his speeches the Kaiser flattered
Turkey by a fervent declaration of friendship for her and for the
entire Mohammedan world. His visits were followed by concessions to German capitalists to build a railway through Asia Minor.
A German railway company was organized, backed by the Deutsche
Bank, the greatest financial institution in Germany, which built
a line connecting a point opposite Constantinople with Konia.
The most important concession was that of 1903 which permitted
the company to extend its line to Bagdad, and then to a point on
the Persian Gulf. Turkey also granted to the company mining
rights within a zone twenty kilometers on each side of the railway.

There was great enthusiasm in Germany over the masterly and
far-seeing policy inaugurated by her capitalists and statesmen.
The Bagdad Railway, together with the railways of Germany's
central Europe, would create a gigantic "corridor" economic
reaching from the North Sea to the Persian Gulf. empire
Should the project be realized, Germany would be "satiated"
once more; she would be mistress of an economic empire comprising middle Europe and western Asia. Her manufacturers would
have easy access to new markets; and she would tap the undeveloped resources of Asiatic Turkey, food, cotton, oil, and min-
erals.

In order to secure the successful financing of the railway its

German backers invited the aid of English and French capitalists,
some of whom responded.   But a powerful opposition
soon developed in England, which had both economic
and political motives.   The Bagdad Railway was
another short route to India, much shorter than the
all-water route through the Suez Canal; it would therefore compete
with English shipping to the Orient.   Moreover, the English had
a monopoly of the shipping in the Persian Gulf and the Tigris River,
which would also find a competitor in the railway and its branches.

England opposes the railway on economic grounds

The Bagdad Railway roused new fears regarding India.   Germany might fortify its proposed terminus on the Gulf by establishing a naval station which, in case of war, could become a base of operations against India.   Germany, too, would then have a "road to the East."   There was also danger to the Suez Canal, the vital link in the chain of communication with India.   The Bagdad Railway Company was planning to build a branch through Syria, Palestine, and the Hedjaz, that would run near the Canal.   Great alarm was felt in England, and the Bagdad Railway was denounced as a German wedge between India and Egypt in order to split the British Empire.   Through British pressure the Sheik of Koweit, on the Persian Gulf, which was to be the terminus of the railway, defied the Sultan and refused to allow the extension of the railway to his district.   In 1903, Lord Lansdowne, the British Foreign Minister, made the following declaration: "We should regard the establishment of a naval base or of a fortified port in the Persian Gulf by any other power as a very grave menace to British interests, and we should certainly resist it with all the means at our disposal." France joined England in her opposition, and excluded the bonds of the railway from the Paris stock exchange.   Russia, too, opposed the railway lest it would revive the "sick man of Europe" by making Turkey more prosperous.   The Bagdad Railway, in origin purely a commercial enterprise, became in time a great diplomatic issue and a serious cause of friction between England and Germany.

On political grounds

As a result of the expansion of Europe in Asia, that vast continent, including the islands in Australasia, was partitioned into colonial empires of the powers.   Russia had the largest, though the poorest share on the Continent: the vast stretch from the Urals and the Caspian to the Pacific; in addition she had a sphere of influence in northern Persia.

The colonial empires in Asia

England got the best share: India, large in extent and in population and rich in trade and natural resources; in addition, she governed the Malay States, the Straits Settlements, the great port of Hongkong; had spheres of influence in southern Persia and in the Yangtze valley in China. England also possessed immense islands, Australia, New Zealand, Tasmania, part of Borneo, part of New Guinea, and Ceylon. France's colonial empire in Asia was small but valuable: Indo-China, about as large as the mother country; and a sphere of influence in China. Holland possessed a great colonial empire in Australasia: the large islands of Java, Sumatra, and the Celebes, rich in coffee, sugar, spices, and tobacco; and parts of Borneo and New Guinea. There were two newcomers in the Asiatic field of colonial imperialism, Germany and the United States. The former got the port of Kiao-chau, a sphere of influence in Shantung, part of New Guinea, and small islands in the southern Pacific. The United States got the Philippines, rich in rice, tobacco, sugar, and hemp; Hawaii; and a few islands in the southern Pacific.

What parts of Asia remained to the Asiatics? In the west, there was the Ottoman Empire stretching from the Mediterranean to the Persian Gulf. In the east there was the island- Little of empire of Japan, with its possessions in Korea and Asia for Asiatics Formosa. There was also the small kingdom of Siam. China and Persia were virtually partitioned among the powers; nevertheless, they enjoyed a nominal independence. In proportion to the size of their continent the Asiatic peoples held little that they could call their own.

REFERENCES

THE FAR EASTERN QUESTION:

P. J. Treat, *The Far East* (1934), a study of the question by a recognized American authority, political and diplomatic; E. Driault, *La question d'extrême Orient* (1908), a study by a recognized French authority; N. D. Harris, *Europe and the East* (ed. 1926); H. M. Vinacke, *A History of the Far East in Modern Times* (1937), good for the Westernization of China and Japan; R. K. Douglas, *Europe and the Far East, 1506–1912* (ed. 1928), an excellent summary by one of the authorities in the field; H. B. Morse and H. F. MacNair, *Far Eastern International Relations* (1931), G. H. Blakeslee, *Conflicts of Policy in the Far East* (1934), G. N. Steiger, *A History of the Far East* (1936), and P. H. Clyde, *A History of the Modern and Contemporary Far East* (1937), by authoritative writers; H. L. Stimson, *The Far Eastern Crisis* (1936), an important contribution to the Manchurian question by the American Secretary of State; A. E. Hindmarsh, *The Basis of Japanese Foreign Policy* (1936), J. B. Condliffe (ed.), *Problems of the Pacific* (1927), Proceedings of the second Conference of the Institute of Pacific Relations.

CHINA:

H. A. Giles, *The Civilization of China* (1911), is the best introduction to the subject, written by a well-known student of Chinese civilization; by the same author, *China and the Chinese* (1902) and *China and the Manchus* (1912); other good studies of China: E. T. Williams, *China Yesterday and Today* (ed. 1929) and *A Short History of China* (1928); H. H. Gowen and J. W. Hall, *An Outline History of China* (1926), contains good bibliography; and K. S. Latourette, *The Chinese* (rev. ed. 1934); P. H. Kent, *The Passing of the Manchus* (1912); P. Monroe, *China: A Nation in Evolution* (1928), by an American educator, sympathetic and understanding, one of the latest and best books on China. On China's political and diplomatic relations with Europe the following are the standard authorities: H. B. Morse, *International Relations of the Chinese Empire*, 3 vols. (1910–18); Mingchien Joshua Bau, *Foreign Relations of China* (1921); by the same author, *The Open Door Doctrine in Relation to China* (1923); and W. W. Willoughby, *Foreign Rights and Interests in China*, 2 vols. (ed. 1927); P. Joseph, *Foreign Diplomacy in China 1894–1900* (1928) deals with aggressiveness of powers; economic aspects: H. F. Bain, *Ores and Industry in the Far East* (1933) and H. B. Morse, *The Trade and Administration of China* (ed. 1920); cultural aspects: T. C. Wang, *The Youth Movement in China* (1927), description of the student movement; and P. W. Kuo, *The Chinese System of Public Education* (1915).

JAPAN:

F. Brinkley and Baron Kikuchi, *A History of the Japanese People from the Earliest Times to the End of the Meiji Era* (ed. 1915), the standard work in English; J. Murdoch and I. Yamagata, *History of Japan*, 3 vols. (1903–26), goes to 1868; good brief studies: H. J. Gubbins, *The Making of Modern Japan* (1922); J. H. Longford, *Japan* (1923); and W. W. McLaren, *A Political History of Japan during the Meiji Era, 1867–1912* (1916); descriptive: K. S. Latourette, *The Development of Japan* (1920); W. M. McGovern, *Modern Japan: Its Political, Military and Industrial Organization* (1920); A. S. and S. W. Hershey, *Modern Japan* (1919). On the relations between Japan and the United States: P. J. Treat, *Japan and the United States 1853–1921*, a plea for cordial relations; and T. F. Millard, *Our Eastern Question* (1916), emphasizes the rivalry of Japan and the United States; T. Iyenaga, *The Constitutional Development of Japan, 1853–1881* (1891); *Japanese Government Documents, 1867–1889* (1914), illustrating the transition from feudal to parliamentary government; S. Uyehara, *The Industry and Trade of Japan* (1926), a résumé of economic conditions; K. K. Kawakami, *Japan in World Politics* (1917), a defense of Japan's expansion policies; K. Asakawa, *The Russo-Japanese Conflict* (1904); *The Secret Memoirs of Count Hayashi* (1915), source for the Anglo-Japanese alliance.

THE MIDDLE EAST AND TURKEY:

P. M. Sykes, *A History of Persia*, 2 vols. (1915), especially good for modern conditions; W. M. Shuster, *The Strangling of Persia; a Record of European Diplomacy and Oriental Intrigue* (1912), a severe indictment of Russia's and England's policies in Persia by the American financial adviser to the Persian Parliament; E. G. Browne, *The Persian Revolution of 1905–1909* (1910); A. Vámbéry, *Western Culture in Eastern Lands: A Comparison of the Methods adopted by England and Russia in the Middle East* (1906), by a traveler and Orientalist, favorable to England; E. M. Earle, *Turkey, the Great Powers and the Bagdad Railway* (1923), the authoritative work on the subject, indispensable to the study of the alliance between finance and diplomacy in Turkey.

ADDITIONAL REFERENCES

H. Kohn, *History of Nationalism in the East*, trans. from the German (1929); R. Gilbert, *The Unequal Treaties* (1929); G. E. Hubbard, *Eastern Industrialization and its Effects on the West* (ed. 1935); E. R. Hughes, *The Invasion of China by the Western World* (1938); J. E. Tyler, *The Struggle for Imperial Unity (1868–1895)* (1938).

CHAPTER XXXI

EXPANSION OF EUROPE IN AFRICA

PERIOD OF DISCOVERY AND EXPLORATION

UNTIL the nineteenth century, Africa was known to the world only as a series of coast lines. The vast interior of a continent, three times the size of Europe, was an unknown and mysterious region. It was inhabited by savage tribes living amid primitive conditions. Vast stretches were uninhabited deserts or impenetrable jungles wherein roamed ferocious beasts of all kinds.

The northern part, facing the Mediterranean, had a history totally different from the rest of the continent. In ancient times

The North   it had been the seat of great civilizations, Egyptian, Carthaginian, Greek, and Roman. During the latter part of the seventh century, the region was conquered by Arabs who converted the inhabitants to Mohammedanism. For a long time afterwards it was known as a semi-civilized land inhabited by marauding tribes, and as a haunt for corsairs that preyed upon the merchant vessels of the Mediterranean.

Why had Central and South Africa been so long sealed to civilization? The answer is given chiefly by geography. Separating the

Isolation of Central Africa   North from the rest of the continent is the Sahara Desert, which, until recently, was an impenetrable barrier. Facing the eastern coast are high mountains which bar the way to the interior. The western coast is largely unindented; hence, there are few harbors to invite communication. Southern Africa is an immense plateau that is difficult of access because it is fringed on the east by mountains and on the west by a desert. If Africa was difficult to enter, it was even more difficult to traverse. The huge rivers, the Congo, the Niger, and the Zambesi, were unnavigable because of the many falls and rapids. The deserts, the jungles, the swamps, the mountains, the forests, and the hot and insalubrious climate discouraged all but the most daring from undertaking voyages of exploration. It seemed as if Nature herself had doomed Africa to remain a primitive, barbarous land.

At the end of the fifteenth century, the Portuguese navigators, Diaz and Vasco da Gama, rounded the southern coast. The Portuguese established trading-centers at various *The slave* points along the western coast, where they did a *trade* profitable business in ivory, gold, slaves, gum, and rubber. Merchants of other nations, Dutch, British, and French, established similar stations. For several centuries Africa was regarded by Europeans mainly as a source of supply for the slave trade, and nearly every nation was engaged in this inhuman, though profitable, traffic. Expeditions were regularly organized to kidnap the Negro inhabitants, and thousands were annually seized by brutal men, packed into the holds of ships, and transported to America to be sold as slaves on the plantations. On the eastern coast the Arabs established trading stations which were engaged chiefly in supplying slaves for the Asiatic market.

PARTITION OF SOUTH AFRICA

The first European settlers in Africa were the Dutch, who came to Cape Colony during the seventeenth century. They were chiefly Calvinists, and, like the Puritans of New England, very strong upholders of their faith. Cape Colony remained under Dutch rule until it was ceded to England by the Congress of Vienna. England desired the Colony chiefly as a station on the way to India.

British immigration now began to South Africa, and before long, two races, the Dutch and the British, confronted each other, each with its own language, laws, and customs. The Boers, as the Dutch were known, regarded the British as intrud- *Boer and* ers, and the British government as alien. Boer dis- *Briton* content was aggravated by the friendly attitude of the government to the natives, whom the Boers had enslaved. The abolition of slavery, in 1833,[1] was denounced by the Boers as an unwarranted interference by the British with their domestic affairs. Most of the compensation, allowed to the Boer masters, went into the pockets of the English bankers through whom the financial transaction was conducted. So incensed were the Boers at British rule that, like the Children of Israel of old, they decided to wander forth into the wilderness to seek other homes.

During 1834–40 an exodus of Boers took place, known as the

[1] See page 131.

"Great Trek." About ten thousand men, women, and children
took their household possessions and migrated northward. Some settled in Natal, others in the Orange
River country; but the British army followed them and took possession of these places. In disgust many of the Boers "trekked"
still farther north, and finally settled in a place called the Transvaal, north of the river Vaal, where they established two republics,
the Transvaal and the Orange Free State. Their independence
was recognized by the British, in 1852, in a treaty known as the
"Sand River Convention." The Boers now lived in peaceful
isolation, gaining their livelihood by pastoral and agricultural
pursuits like the patriarchs in the Old Testament, whom they
greatly admired.

The "Great Trek"

But their dream of independence was rudely shattered in 1877,
when Great Britain announced the annexation of the Transvaal on
the ground that the harsh treatment of the natives by
the Boers was endangering the peace of South Africa.
The loss of their independence so infuriated the Boers
that, in 1881, they rose in revolt and defeated a detachment of British troops at Majuba Hill. Feeling in England
rose high, and Premier Gladstone was urged to send an army to
crush the Boers. But Gladstone had little sympathy with British
aggression in South Africa; and, in 1884, he signed a treaty with the
Boers, known as the "London Convention," which recognized the
independence of the Transvaal, henceforth to be known as the
South African Republic. The treaty contained an important
clause which guaranteed the right of all white men to reside and to
trade in the Republic, and which also guaranteed fair treatment
to all of its inhabitants. There was great elation among the Boers,
who felt that they had humbled the British Empire.

Independence of the South African Republic

North of Cape Colony was a large, sparsely inhabited region,
known as Bechuanaland, which was proclaimed a British protectorate in 1885. Farther north was a larger and
more fertile region which, it was believed, would
attract European settlers. In 1889, the British South African
Company, organized by Cecil Rhodes, the famous "Empire
builder," was given control of the territory, later known as "Rhodesia." It sent settlers and governed them much in the manner of
the chartered companies in colonial America. South Africa was

Rhodesia

now partitioned between the British and the Boers, but it was destined to become entirely British.

DISCOVERY OF CENTRAL AFRICA

In 1815, the situation in Africa was as follows: In the north, Egypt, Tripoli, Tunis, and Algeria were theoretically parts of the domains of the Sultan of Turkey; practically, however, Africa in they were independent, and ruled by native chiefs. 1815 Morocco was independent under her own Sultan. In the south, Cape Colony belonged to Britain. At various points along the coast, particularly at the mouths of rivers, there were European trading posts. The interior was unknown.

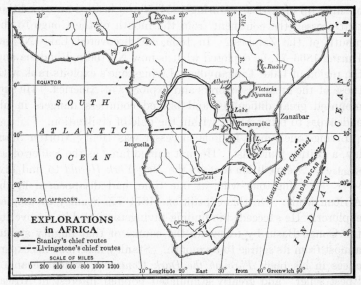

During the nineteenth century great interest was aroused by the wonderful tales that missionaries, traders, and adventurers brought back from Africa. They told of strange animals, Tales of giraffes and gorillas; of strange pygmy races; of African strange trees that produced rubber; and of strange wilds and wonderful flora of all kinds. They told of numerous heathen tribes with barbarous customs. The Christian imagination was aroused; millions of souls might be saved by fearless missionaries. At one time slavery had been justified by some Christians on the ground that if the Negro lost his body, he at any rate saved his soul by becoming a Christian.   The abolition of the slave trade during the first half of the nineteenth century acted as a stimulus to missionary effort; zealous missionaries now went to Africa to convert the heathen Negroes who now were no longer brought to Christian lands.

There began a movement for the exploration of "Darkest Africa." Among the many African explorers the most notable was Livingstone   the Scotsman, David Livingstone, who, in 1840, was (1813–73)   sent as a missionary to Africa by a Protestant missionary society.   But Livingstone became far more interested in exploring the country than in converting the heathen; he thereupon resigned his position as missionary, and devoted his life to the opening up of Africa.   During 1854–56, he headed an expedition that crossed the continent from the mouth of the Congo to the mouth of the Zambesi.   In 1859, he discovered Lake Nyasa. During 1866–71, he explored what is now Northern Rhodesia and the region of Lake Tanganyika.   Livingstone's exploits rank with those of the great discoverers and explorers of America.   He surmounted great difficulties and braved countless dangers in his endeavors to bring Africa within the pale of civilization.

Livingstone's most famous successor was Henry Morton Stanley, a British journalist.   He first gained fame as the leader of an Stanley   expedition sent by the *New York Herald* to find Liv-(1841–1904)   ingstone who, at one time, had disappeared in the African wilds.   On this expedition (1871–77) Stanley became an explorer.   He succeeded in finding Livingstone, and in discovering the Congo Basin by following the course of that mighty stream almost from its source to its mouth.   Stanley described his experiences in his book *Through the Dark Continent*, which became a "best seller" and greatly stimulated popular interest in African exploration.   Other explorers followed Livingstone and Stanley, and the map of central Africa, hitherto largely blank, began to show rivers, lakes, mountains, and plateaus.

PARTITION OF CENTRAL AFRICA

One of those who became greatly interested in Africa was King Leopold II of Belgium.   Although a monarch, he was interested chiefly in business, and he shrewdly surmised that the opening up of Africa would mean the opening up of new business enterprise. Hearing of Stanley's exploits, Leopold called an international conference, in 1876, at Brussels, where he formed an association for exploring and civilizing Central Africa. A corporation was organized by Leopold that had for its object the exploiting of Central Africa; this body later became known as the International Association of the Congo. King Leopold and the International Association As the representative of the Association, Stanley conducted an expedition to the Congo region (1879–82), where he made treaties with the native chiefs, who were induced to give their territories to the Association as "protectorates."

Leopold's activities attracted wide attention. A corporation with a "protectorate" over a large territory was of political significance. The East India Companies came to mind. A conference of the powers met in Berlin, in 1884–85, to discuss the Congo situation and to decide upon policies in Africa. The Conference declared that its purpose was "to protect the natives in their moral and material well-being." It recognized the rights of the Association, and organized its African territory as the Congo Free State with Leopold as "sovereign." Belgium had no control over the region. The "open door" policy was guaranteed; likewise, the free navigation of the Congo and Niger Rivers and their tributaries. To prevent conflicts over territory in Central Africa, the conference declared that no power could proclaim a protectorate without first notifying the other powers; and that a region must be "effectively" occupied before it can be recognized as a protectorate. The Berlin Conference

The Congo Free State proved to be rich in rubber and ivory. Concessions were granted to companies to exploit the region, which they proceeded to do by forcing the natives to bring rubber and ivory products as a "tax." Failure to do so was followed by cruel punishment, even by torture and death. The investors reaped a rich harvest; and Leopold carved out a rubber estate for himself from which he made a vast fortune. A philanthropic movement had become a lucrative business enterprise. But the cruel treatment of the natives, made known to the world by missionaries, created widespread indignation, and resulted in adoption of drastic reforms. In 1908, the Congo Free State went out of existence. The region was annexed to Belgium as a colony, and renamed Belgian Congo. Cruel treatment of the natives

Africa was now the center of Europe's colonial ambitions. Here

was a new continent, inhabited by weak, savage tribes who could
The powers   offer no effective resistance to conquest. In a very
divide   short time almost the whole of the continent was parti-
Africa   tioned among the powers. During the decade (1890–
1900) there began the "Great African Hunt," as the scramble for
African colonies was called. Each power did its best to "steal a
march on the other" by bribing Negro chieftains to sign treaties,
granting a protectorate over the lands which they ruled. Explorers, traders, agents, and soldiers would race for a certain district with presents in one hand and treaty blanks in the other.
Whether the district became British, French, or German depended
on who got there first. Claims would also be made for the "hinter-
land," or the region beyond that granted in a treaty.

England, as the great colonial power, naturally led in the
scramble. In western Africa she acquired Nigeria, the Gold Coast,
The share of Sierra Leone, and the mouth of the Gambia River;
England and   and in eastern Africa she acquired Uganda, Kenya,
of France   and part of Somaliland. France acquired, in western
Africa, French Congo, Dahomey, the Ivory Coast, French Guinea,
and Senegal; and in eastern Africa, a small part of Somaliland and
the large island of Madagascar. The latter is inhabited by tribes
of mixed Malay, Arab, and Negro origin, who were far higher in
civilization than the natives in Central Africa. French armies invaded the island in the eighties and conquered it, not, however,
without desperate fighting. In 1896, Madagascar was annexed to
France.

Germany made her début as a colonizing nation during the
partition of Africa. She was energetic in sending out explorers
Share of   and traders to lay claims to territory. In the west,
Germany   she acquired German South-West Africa, the Cam-
eroons, and Togo; and in the east, German East Africa. Although
large, the German colonies were not so desirable economically as
those acquired by her rivals. Moreover, Germany had serious
trouble with the natives who rose against their white masters.
The uprisings were suppressed with difficulty, and led the home
government to institute drastic colonial reforms.

Italy, too, made her début as a colonial power. She received
Share of   two coastal districts in eastern Africa, Eritrea and
Italy   Italian Somaliland. Between them was the "empire"
of Abyssinia, or "Ethiopia," a large and fairly fertile region. The

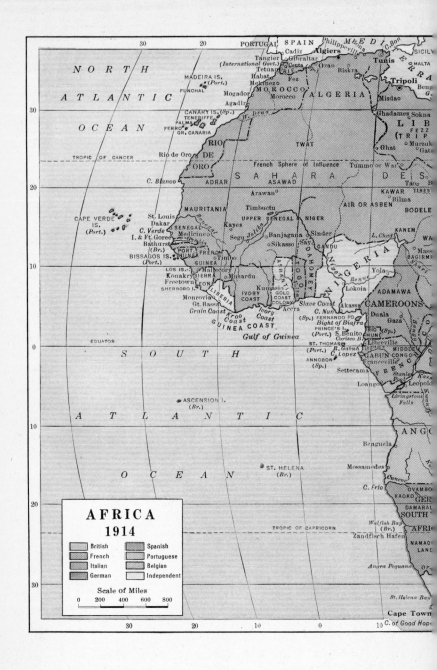

AFRICA
1914

British	Spanish
French	Portuguese
Italian	Belgian
German	Independent

Scale of Miles

0   200   400   600   800

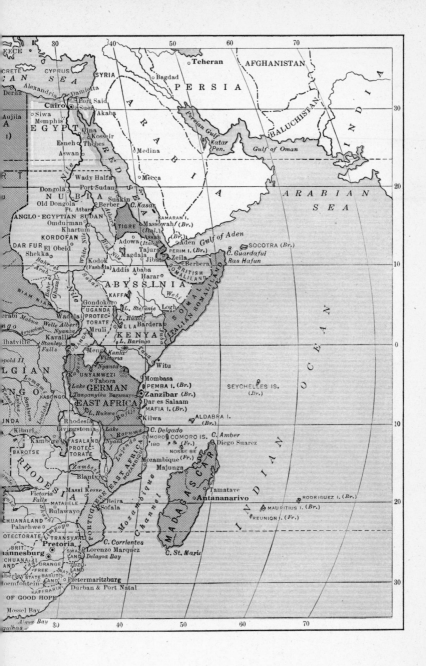

inhabitants, descendants of an ancient race and Christian in faith, were not helpless savages, but fairly civilized, with an organized government and a disciplined army.   In her designs upon Abyssinia, Italy fell foul of the rivalry of France and England in the Sudan, which will be described later.   France became friendly with Menelek, the Emperor of Abyssinia.   French officers drilled the Abyssinian soldiers, who were furnished with French arms.   England, on the other hand, encouraged Italy in her ambition to annex the region.   In 1896, Italian armies invaded Abyssinia.   At the battle of Adowa, Menelik inflicted a terrible defeat on the Italians, most of whom were killed or captured.   Italy promptly made peace, and recognized the independence of Abyssinia.   For once an African people successfully withstood the aggression of a European power.

Portugal, the pioneer in modern colonial expansion, acquired Angola, Portuguese Guinea, and Portuguese East Africa.   Being a small power, Portugal held the colonies on the suffer- Share of ance of the great powers.   In 1913, England and Portugal Germany made secret plans to acquire the Portuguese colonies, but the World War turned their attention from Africa to Europe.

PARTITION OF NORTH AFRICA

(a) ALGERIA AND TUNIS

North Africa differs so markedly from the rest of the continent that it might be regarded as a region entirely apart from it.   The indented shore with its many harbors, the mild and Keen rivalry salubrious climate, the many fertile valleys, and the of the powers easy accessibility from Europe are in striking contrast to the Dark Continent with its burning heat, savage jungles, and endless deserts.   When the spirit of the new imperialism seized the European nations, they naturally turned to North Africa as the most favorable region to colonize.   Being more desirable than Central Africa, it aroused larger ambitions and caused keener rivalries.   Unlike the partition of Central Africa, the partition of North Africa resulted in international crises that more than once threatened to plunge the world into war.   North Africa became a chessboard on which the powers played a desperate game, in the course of which old antagonisms were revived and new antagonisms arose.   The origins of the World War may be found as much in that region as in the Near East.

France became the leading power in North Africa, where she succeeded in establishing a colonial empire that rivaled the one France in   that she had lost in the eighteenth century. The Algeria   scene of her first intervention was Algeria, during the thirties of the nineteenth century. At that time Algeria was the chief haunt of the Barbary pirates, who were protected and encouraged by the local ruler, called the Dey. The pirates terrorized the Mediterranean, capturing ships, attacking European coast towns, kidnaping Europeans whom they enslaved or held for ransom. As the powers would not agree on taking measures against the evil, France, as the leading Mediterranean power, determined to act alone. However, there was another motive. Charles X desired to distract attention from his tyrannical rule at home to foreign conquest. By raising the prestige of France, which, since Waterloo, had fallen very low, he hoped to gain popularity for the Bourbon dynasty. An excuse for intervention was found in 1827, when, during a heated interview, the Dey struck the French consul with a fly-flapper. France demanded an apology, which was refused. Three years later, in 1830, a French expedition landed in Algeria to avenge the insult to French dignity. A desperate struggle began that lasted until the seventies, when the country was finally pacified. The Arabs and Berbers were splendid fighters, and fought with religious zeal in a Holy War against the Christian invaders. Once under full control, Algeria was given a unique status; she was made part of France and given representation in parliament. Algeria is France's most successful colony with many towns, fine roads, excellent agriculture, and a prosperous commerce.

Once firmly settled in Algeria, France cast longing eyes to the east, Tunis, and to the west, Morocco. Intervention in the former Rivalry of   was preceded by financial arrangements and diploFrance and   matic maneuvers. During the sixties the ruler of Italy for   Tunis, called the Bey, borrowed large sums of money Tunis   from European bankers which he was unable to pay. A commission was appointed, composed chiefly of Frenchmen and Italians, who took financial charge of the Bey's affairs. As it became evident that intervention would follow financial control, a rivalry began between France and Italy. The latter was ambitious to annex Tunis, which contained many Italian residents. But diplomacy came to the aid of France. After 1870, it was the rule among the powers that no colony could be acquired without some kind of international agreement. During the Congress of Berlin, a secret understanding took place between France, England, and Germany regarding Tunis. England agreed to the acquisition of Tunis by France in return for the agreement of France to England's acquisition of Cyprus. Bismarck lent his powerful aid in favor of France because he wished to distract her attention from Alsace-Lorraine.

It now remained to conquer Tunis. In 1881, on the pretext that border tribes were making raids into Algeria, a French army invaded Tunis on a "punitive expedition." It stayed there. The occupation of the country was chiefly the work of Ferry, the leading French champion of an aggressive colonial policy. To save the "dignity of the vanquished," the Bey was retained as nominal ruler, but the government was in the hands of French officials responsible to the French Foreign Office. The acquisition of Tunis by France infuriated Italy; it marked the beginning of unfriendly feeling between the two Latin nations who had been friends and allies during the Risorgimento.

France intervenes in Tunis

(b) EGYPT AND THE SUDAN

The next North African land to fall under European control was Egypt. Since the days of the Pharaohs, Egypt had been under the rule of foreigners; Persians, Macedonians, Romans, Arabs, Turks, French, and English have in turn ruled the country. In the beginning of the sixteenth century, it was organized as a province of the Ottoman Empire, and was ruled by a governor sent by the Sultan of Turkey. Egypt remained subject to the Sultan until the early part of the nineteenth century, when she gained virtual independence under Mehemet Ali, who agreed to recognize the Sultan as his suzerain.[1]

Egypt ruled by foreigners

When the construction of the Suez Canal was begun, in 1859, it was generally recognized that Egypt was the key to the control of the eastern Mediterranean because the Canal lay wholly within her borders; therefore the powers, especially England and France, became interested in her future. A process began of enmeshing Egypt in financial entanglements which proved so successful that she lost both her real and nominal

The Suez Canal

[1] See page 163.

independence. The process was aided by Ismail, the Khedive, or ruler (1863–79), who was very incompetent and recklessly extrava-

Misgovern-
ment by
Khedive
Ismail

gant. He spent enormous sums in lavish entertainments, money that was wrung from the toiling *fellaheen* (peasantry), who labored along the Nile that their ruler might enjoy himself on the boulevards of Paris. To raise money he raised taxes and floated loans. He could get little more taxes from his impoverished subjects, so he had recourse to borrowing money from European bankers by selling bonds much below par and at high rates of interest. But bankruptcy still pursued him; and, in 1875, he offered for sale his many shares of Suez Canal stock. Disraeli, realizing the great possibilities that lay in this offer, availed himself of the opportunity, and purchased the shares for the British government. England now had a controlling interest in the Canal, a vital point in her system of Imperial communications.

In spite of this deal, the financial condition of Egypt grew worse and worse. The bondholders became uneasy. An international

The Dual
Control

debt commission was appointed that consolidated all the loans and provided for revenues to meet the interest charges. But the revenues, in 1878, were so low that the interest due on the bonds could not be paid. The bondholders thereupon appealed to their governments to back their claims. France and England took prompt action. Through their influence, the Sultan of Turkey, as the suzerain of the Khedive, deposed Ismail. His successor recognized the right of France and England to supervise the finances of Egypt. The Dual Control, which lasted from 1879 to 1883, took charge of Egypt's financial situation; it reformed the system of taxation and guaranteed the rights of the bondholders. The country was really in the hands of a receiver.

There was great discontent in the land of Egypt. A nationalist movement arose that raised the cry, "Egypt for the Egyptians!"

Intervention
of England

and demanded the abolition of the Dual Control. So widespread was the movement that the bondholders became alarmed. Once more they appealed to their governments. England decided upon intervention, but France refused to join her. In 1882, a British fleet seized Alexandria and landed an army of occupation. Egypt was subdued, and England was now in sole control.

It was the anti-imperialist Gladstone who had sent the fleet. He had done so against his will, urged on by those who feared that the Egyptians would seize the Suez Canal. The British government, in 1883, made a declaration to the powers that it would withdraw from Egypt "as soon as the state of the country, and the organization of the proper means for the maintenance of the Khedive's authority will admit of it." To Gladstone this declaration was a "sacred pledge," but his successors showed no willingness to abide by it.

Promise of England to evacuate Egypt

British intervention in Egypt proved to be part of a comprehensive scheme of imperialism in Africa. As in the case of North America during the eighteenth century, England encountered, in France, a rival empire builder. England's ambition was to make eastern Africa, from Cape-to-Cairo, "all Red." France's ambition was equally grandiose; it was to establish a sea-to-sea colonial empire, from the Atlantic to the Red Sea. Their ambitions clashed in the Sudan.

Rivalry of England and France

That region was a tributary of Egypt. It was inhabited by warlike tribes of mixed Arab and Negro blood, many of whom belonged to a fanatical Mohammedan sect, called "dervishes." The Sudanese resented the rule of the Khedive, and all the more so when he fell under the control of the Christian Europeans. In the early eighties, an uprising took place under a warrior-prophet, known as the Mahdi (guide), who, like Mohammed, embarked on a religious-military career. He defeated an Egyptian army sent against him, which alarmed the British, who now became sensitive about the "rights of Egypt" and the "authority of the Khedive." Egyptian and British troops were stationed in Khartum, which enflamed the fanatical followers of the Mahdi. Dervish forces began massing toward Khartum. Gladstone was opposed to further intervention, and decided to evacuate the Sudan. He sent General Charles Gordon, a gallant soldier of fortune who had aided in suppressing the Taiping Rebellion in China, to negotiate with the Mahdi. Gordon's efforts to placate him were fruitless, and he and his Anglo-Egyptian army found themselves shut up in Khartum, besieged by the ferocious dervishes. England was greatly aroused. Appeals were made to Gladstone to send a British army to relieve Gordon, but Gladstone vacillated. The situation became very critical, and finally Glad-

Uprising of the Mahdi

stone did send a relief expedition. But it arrived too late. Khartum had been taken (1885), and all its defenders, including Gordon, had been put to the sword. For a time the Sudan was abandoned to the Mahdi.

A decade later the region again stirred the British. This time it was the scene of rivalry between French and English imperialism. In 1896, a French expedition, led by Major Marchand, undertook a great journey of exploration. Marchand started from the mouth of the Congo and proceeded through the heart of Africa. At the end of two years, having journeyed twenty-five hundred miles, he reached the town of Fashoda, in the Sudan. There he hoisted the French flag.

Expedition of Major Marchand

Meanwhile, another expedition was in progress. An army of Egyptian and British troops, led by General Herbert Kitchener, the British commander of the Khedive's forces, invaded the Egyptian Sudan. At the battle of Omdurman, in 1898, Kitchener routed the dervishes and entered Khartum in triumph. He then made haste to Fashoda, where he found Marchand, who "welcomed" him "in the name of France." A great crisis arose between England and France over the "mud flat," as Fashoda was called. War was imminent, but the crisis was safely passed. France hauled down the tricolor and left Egyptian Sudan to England. She was, however, compensated, being allowed to annex Wadai which connected her western and northern possessions.

The Fashoda affair

The Egyptian Sudan was now given a new status. In theory, it was a "condominium," under the joint sovereignty of England and Egypt; in fact, however, it was ruled by British officials. As in the case of Egypt, the rule of England greatly benefited the inhabitants, who were freed from the terrorism of slavers, marauders, and dervishes. The finest cotton in the world was grown there, which helped to make the region prosperous.

The "condominium"

(c) MOROCCO AND TRIPOLI

The peaceful settlement of the Fashoda affair was followed by a diplomatic revolution.[1] France and England were now friends after a quarrel that had brought them to the brink of war. With England at her side, France was encouraged to try another colonial

[1] See page 695.

venture in another direction. She turned her attention to Morocco, a large region sparsely inhabited by warlike Arab and Berber tribes who more often defied than obeyed their acknowledged ruler, the Sultan of Morocco. Her excellent climate, fine harbors, natural resources, and proximity to Europe made Morocco a choice morsel which the powers, especially France, were eager to seize.

The acquisition of Morocco by France was largely the outcome of diplomatic deals which gave "compensation" to her rivals. In 1902, France and Italy entered into a secret arrangement, according to which France promised not to oppose Italy's seizure of Tripoli, and Italy promised not to oppose France's seizure of Morocco. France then made an arrangement with Spain according to which the latter was promised several meager slices of Morocco. Far more important was the famous Treaty of 1904,[1] according to which England gave France a "free hand" in Morocco, and France gave England a "free hand" in Egypt. They agreed to support each other in these places.

France gets a "free hand" in Morocco

Diplomatic preparations having been made, France immediately began to intervene in Morocco. The disorganized state of the country, with its turbulent tribesmen and weak Sultan, gave the necessary opportunity. Attacks on foreigners brought demands for intervention. The Sultan was encouraged to borrow money from French bankers, which he could not pay. A rival sultan appeared who stirred up civil war. Revolts were constantly taking place. France, as Morocco's neighbor in Algeria, declared that she was most affected by the lawless situation. In 1905, she made demands of the Sultan, which, if granted, would have given Morocco the status of a protectorate.

France prepares to intervene

But France had reckoned without Germany, whom she had left out of account entirely. Germany felt infuriated at not even being consulted by France and England when they were partitioning North Africa. She emphatically objected to what was described as the "Tunification" of Morocco, and a critical diplomatic situation arose.[2] It was finally agreed to call an international congress at Algeciras, in Spain, to solve the problem. It met in 1906, and adopted the following measures: Morocco's independence was specifically recognized; her finances were to be managed by a bank under international control; the "Open Door" principle was adopted; order was

The Algeciras Conference

[1] See page 695.   [2] See page 701.

to be maintained by a police force chiefly under French control; and the regulation of the customs and of the traffic in arms was entrusted, on the Algerian front, chiefly to France.

France, however, was determined to acquire Morocco. She sent punitive expeditions, occupied towns, and, in other ways, prepared

France ac-   to seize the country. In 1911, a French army entered
quires   Fez against the protest of Germany. A German war-
Morocco   ship appeared at Agadir, and another international
crisis was precipitated.[1] Again there was a peaceful settlement. France was given special privileges in Morocco; and Germany received compensation by getting part of French Congo. In 1912, France proclaimed Morocco a protectorate, and adopted a system of government similar to that in Tunis. Again France got a choice morsel of North Africa.

There still remained one part of North Africa that was not yet under European control, the Turkish provinces of Tripoli and

Italy ac-   Cyrenaica. Disappointed at not getting Tunis, Italy
quires   determined to annex these lands. There was the
Tripoli   usual diplomatic preparation; the agreement of 1902
with France being especially important. In 1911, Italy suddenly declared war upon Turkey and invaded Tripoli and Cyrenaica. The Turco-Italian War (1911–12) consisted only of skirmishes with the Arab tribes. Turkey hastened to make peace because of the imminence of war with the Balkan States, and agreed to the annexation by Italy of Tripoli and Cyrenaica. The partition of the Turkish Empire in Africa was now complete, and its bene- ficiaries were England, France, and Italy. The acquisition of an African colony roused great enthusiasm among the Italians, who felt their imperial wings spreading.

Africa was now almost entirely partitioned; the only independent nations were Abyssinia and Liberia, the latter a protégée of the

Spread of   United States. The outcome of the European occu-
civilization   pation was the rapid spread of civilization over Africa.
in Africa   Jungles began to give way to cities and farm lands.
Wild beasts were exterminated. Savage tribes began to adopt the customs of civilization. Railways linked remote and inacces- sible places. Orderly government began to displace tribal wars. The rapid transformation of what was once the Dark Continent constitutes one of the striking pages in the history of modern times.

[1] See page 703.

REFERENCES

EXPLORATION:

D. Livingstone, *Missionary Travels and Researches in South Africa* (ed. 1860), and *Last Journals in Central Africa from 1865 to his Death*, edited by H. Waller (1875); Sir H. H. Johnston, *Livingstone and the Exploration of Central Africa* (1891), contains good maps of explorations; Sir H. M. Stanley, *How I Found Livingstone: Travels and Adventures in Central Africa* (1872), *Through the Dark Continent, or the Sources of the Nile*, 2 vols. (1878), *In Darkest Africa* (ed. 1897), and *Congo and the Founding of its Free State*, 2 vols. (1885); R. J. Campbell, *Livingstone* (1929).

PARTITION:

N. D. Harris, *Europe and Africa* (1927); Sir H. H. Johnston, *The Opening up of Africa* (1911), introductory volume by a famous authority on Africa; by the same author, *A History of Colonization of Africa by Alien Races* (ed. 1913); J. S. Keltie, *The Partition of Africa* (1895); Sir C. Lucas, *The Partition and Colonization of Africa* (1922); Sir E. Hertslet, *The Map of Africa by Treaty*, 3 vols. (ed. 1909), contains all important treaties relative to the partition; J. H. Rose, *The Development of European Nations, 1870–1900*, vol. II, chaps. IV–VIII, good on the diplomatic arrangements; E. Sanderson, *Great Britain in Modern Africa* (1906).

EGYPT:

Lord Cromer, *Modern Egypt*, 2 vols. (1908), a discussion of the problems of Egypt under British rule by the famous British administrator; W. S. Blunt, *Secret History of the English Occupation of Egypt* (1907), by a strong opponent of British imperialism; G. Young, *Egypt* (1927), history from the time of Napoleon's invasion.

SPECIAL TOPICS:

R. L. Buell, *The Native Problem in Africa*, 2 vols. (1928), the most important study of the subject, result of thorough research and of observation, contains reprints of important documents; L. Woolf, *Empire and Commerce in Africa* (1920), anti-imperialist.

For French Africa, consult bibliography at the end of Chapter XVIII; for German Africa, consult bibliography at the end of Chapter XX; for South Africa, consult bibliography at the end of Chapter XXXII.

ADDITIONAL REFERENCES

Lord Hailey, *An African Survey* (1938).

CHAPTER XXXII

THE BRITISH EMPIRE

IN all history there has never been a political organism so vast and so world-wide as the British Empire. "The sun in its daily course

Character-
istics: (1)
world-wide

never sets upon Englishmen" is no empty boast; about one quarter of the world's area and of its population is under British rule. Within its confines are to be found almost every race and every stage of civilization, from naked savages on the banks of the Niger to cultivated residents of Oxford, all bound together by the common tie of British allegiance. The influence of this world empire upon history has been profound. No great policy can be undertaken by any nation without reference to the British Empire, whose parts lie at all crossroads, and whose interests are everywhere. It is hardly an exaggeration to say that the policies of the British Empire have been the determining factors in world affairs.

It is predominantly non-European. Vast regions in Asia, Africa, the Americas, and Australasia, are subject to Britain, a country

(2) Chiefly
non-Euro-
pean

of about 43,000,000 inhabitants. In the main, the Empire is the outcome of an expansion of territory rather than of population; of its estimated population, in 1914, of 425,000,000 only fifteen per cent were of British stock. It is, therefore, a striking illustration of the sway of Europe over the rest of the world.

The British Empire lies scattered throughout the world, the parts varying from a fortified rock like Gibraltar to an island-

(3) Territory
not con-
tiguous

continent like Australia. To protect her far-flung dominions, England has developed the greatest sea power in modern times; in 1914, her fleet was as large as that of Germany and of France combined. In nearly every corner of every sea she holds a naval base or a convenient place where her warships may get fuel and other supplies. Especially important is the road to India: Portsmouth, Gibraltar, Malta, Cyprus, Suez, Aden, and Bombay mark the pathway of the British fleet to the East. Ceylon, Singapore, Hongkong, and Vancouver are the great stations in Pacific waters. To a limited degree,

Canada and the British possessions in the Caribbean accomplish a similar purpose in American waters. England's fleet is therefore in control of nearly every strategic water way, which has given her the proud position of "mistress of the seas."

Another distinctive feature is decentralization. Unlike Rome in ancient times, London does not give the law to all the lands of which it is the capital. Every variety of government (4) Variety is to be found in the Empire, from the most autocratic of government to the most democratic, from the most dependent to the most autonomous. The principle of nationalism is recognized by the grant of complete self-government to the Dominions, and even more by the recognition of the language and laws of non-British peoples such as the French in Quebec and the Boers in South Africa. Fully aware of the international character of the Empire, British statesmen have shown wisdom and tolerance in their attitude to the non-British elements, even those that they govern autocratically.

The foundations of the Empire were laid during the seventeenth century. Adventurous Englishmen left their country for other lands, some to seek homes in new continents, as in America; others, to seek fortune and adventure among ancient peoples, as in India. They planted the flag of their country wherever they went, little aided by the home government. For long the colonies were neglected by England who was chiefly interested in solving the problem of parliamentary government.

However, the challenge of France roused England to the importance of her colonies. During the eighteenth century a great struggle took place between these two powers for the The colonial mastery of North America and India, which ended in situation in the eighth the complete triumph of England. The latter realized eenth cen- that she was now mistress of a world-wide empire, and tury she set herself the task of binding the various colonies more closely to her. The methods that she adopted were: (1) by asserting the supreme control of Parliament over their affairs, especially in matters of taxation; and (2) by economic legislation, inspired by the Mercantilist System, which subordinated the interests of a colony to those of the mother country. These policies, as is well known, resulted in the American Revolution, and the consequent loss of the Thirteen Colonies.

A new period now began in the history of the Empire. It is

a period in which colonies were regarded as more of a burden
Reaction against colonies than an asset to the mother country. England no longer taxed them, and yet was obliged to maintain a large navy for their protection. "Are you attacked at home?" said Bentham. "Not a man can you ever get from them; not a sixpence. Are they attacked? They draw upon you for fleets and armies." During the first half of the nineteenth century the word "colony" brought to mind barbarous races that had to be kept down, or penal settlements for criminals shipped from home or, as in the case of India, a "gigantic system of outdoor relief for the aristocracy" who desired high salaried positions in the civil service.

After 1832, when the Liberals were in power, a decided anti-imperialist tendency set in. The Liberals were "Little Englanders," interested in domestic reform and in foreign trade, and they cared little for "Greater England" beyond the seas. "It would be far better for them [the colonies]," declared Bright, "and far cheaper for us, and less demoralizing for them, that they should become an independent state, and maintain their own fortresses, fight their own cause, and build up their own future without relying upon us." Gladstone believed that, as colonies developed, "separation from the mother country inevitably takes place," and that it should be the policy of the government so to arrange matters that when separation came, it "might be the result of a peaceful and friendly transaction." He was not, however, an anti-imperialist; what he preferred to separation was the extension of self-government to the colonies, who would then be in free and friendly relation with England. Curiously enough, the colonies were more eager than the mother country to keep up the connection. They feared that independence might lead to their being conquered by foreign nations who would force upon them an alien civilization. For a time, only the slender tie of sentiment held together the British Empire.

The American Revolution undoubtedly had a great influence in bringing about the reaction against imperialism. Another explanation was the breakdown of the Mercantilist System, due to the Industrial Revolution. As a manufacturing nation, England needed numerous customers for her surplus wares, and she therefore cared far more for the trade of Germany and France than for sparsely inhabited Canada and Australia. The Manchester School, whose influence was all-important in economic policies, was anti-colonial. It taught that a country should buy in the cheapest and sell in the dearest market, irrespective of political affiliations. To whom would the colonies send their raw material? From whom would they buy their manufactured articles? The answer, in both cases, was England, who then was the only industrialized nation. Many were convinced that a colony which became independent would prove a better customer than one that was tied to the mother country. "Turn to the United States," declared Bentham. "Before the separation Britain had a monopoly of their trade, upon the separation, of course, she lost it. How much less of their trade has Britain now than then? On the contrary, it is much greater. . . . Hear a paradox — it is a true one. Give up your colonies, they are yours."

A direct outcome of the reaction against the old imperialism was the establishment of Dominion government which will be described later. It recognized, for the first time, the right of a **Grant of** colony to complete self-rule, thereby giving it a na- **Dominion** tional status. Dominion government was granted **government** in the belief that it would be a halfway house to independence.

CANADA

Canada was originally a French settlement, and her white inhabitants were almost exclusively French when the provinces were ceded to England in 1763. On the eve of the **The French** American Revolution the British Parliament, in order **in Canada** to hold the loyalty of the French, passed the Quebec Act (1774), which recognized the French language, civil law, and customs, and which gave special privileges to the Catholic Church, to which the French inhabitants were devoted. As a consequence they remained loyal to the British during the American Revolution.

An English-speaking element was introduced into Canada from two sources: loyalists from the American colonies and emigrants from Great Britain. In 1791, the country was divided **Antagonism** into two parts, Upper and Lower Canada, the former **between gov-** inhabited by the English, and the latter, by both Eng- **ernors and** lish and French. In both provinces there was consider- **assemblies** able discontent with the system of government in which the governor and his council, appointed from England, predominated over the popular assemblies. The latter insisted on being supreme, and there arose serious quarrels between them and the governors. Moreover, there was intense racial antagonism between the French and English inhabitants. In 1837, an uprising took place which, though easily suppressed, alarmed the British government. A special commissioner, Lord Durham, was sent to Canada to examine into the Canadian grievances and to suggest reforms.

The Report of Lord Durham, issued in 1839, is the most famous document in colonial history. It has been called the Magna

Report of Lord Durham Charta of the colonies, for its liberal recommendations became the fundamental principles of England's new colonial policy. Lord Durham declared that he found "two nations warring in the bosom of a single state"; and he recommended that Upper and Lower Canada be united under a common legislature, which, he believed, would result in the predominance of the English. Conflicts between the royal governors and the popular assemblies, he maintained, were unavoidable because representative and irresponsible government could not be successfully combined. The British must therefore "submit to the necessary consequences of representative institutions" by granting to the Canadians a system of responsible government, or complete local autonomy. However, he made certain reservations which should be left in the hands of England, such as tariffs, foreign affairs, and the disposal of public lands. In the future, when conditions were more favorable, all the colonies in British North America should form a legislative union, which would make the connection with the mother country "more durable and advantageous, by having more of equality, of freedom, and of local independence."

The report was denounced as an attack on the integrity of the British Empire; nevertheless, its recommendations were acted

Responsible government upon, though not immediately. In 1840, Parliament passed a law uniting Upper and Lower Canada, but without any provision for ministerial responsibility. In 1848, Lord Elgin, Governor of Canada and the son-in-law of Lord Durham, established the principle of responsible government by choosing a cabinet having the confidence of the legislature.

The union of the French and English Canadians under a common government was not a happy one. Racial parties appeared which confused and embittered the political atmosphere. Could a

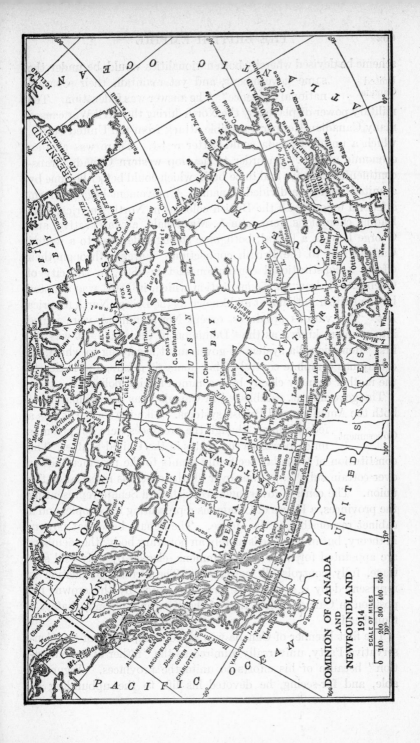

DOMINION OF CANADA
AND
NEWFOUNDLAND
1914

SCALE OF MILES
0 100 200 300 400 500

scheme be devised whereby both nationalities would be under the
United same government, and yet maintain their separate
Canada national existence? The answer was federation. The
military power displayed by the North during the Civil War caused
many Canadians to fear a possible attack from the United States,
which a united Canada could better resist. There was also an
economic motive. In order to develop western Canada, trans-
continental railways had to be built, which could better be done by
a united than by a divided Canada. A movement began to form
a federal union of all the British colonies in North America. Its
leading champions were John A. Macdonald, a conservative, and
George Brown, a liberal; both were strongly devoted to a united
Canada and to the British connection. Largely through their
efforts a constitutional convention met in 1864, in the city of
Quebec. It drew up a constitution which, in 1867, was adopted
by the British Parliament and known as the British North America
Act. The various provinces, except Newfoundland, were joined
into a union, known as the "Dominion of Canada." It was the
first "dominion," a system of government according to which the
colony has complete control of her domestic affairs, and is tied to
the mother country chiefly by a common foreign policy.

The government, established in Canada, was a combination of
both the American and British systems. Like the former it was a
Government federal union, though the provinces were not given as
much power as the States in the United States. The
constitution of Canada specifically grants to the provinces power
over certain subjects; power over all the others is reserved to the
union. The central government consists of a Senate representing
the provinces, a House of Commons representing the people, and a
cabinet responsible to the House. The Senate has great powers
in theory, but in practice is merely an honorary body; the members
are appointed for life. The Commons, elected by universal suffrage, fully controls all legislation. The British connection is
represented by a governor-general, appointed by the crown; his
position in Canada is like that of the King in England, that of a
figurehead.

The first Premier of Canada was Macdonald, leader of the Conservative Party, universally admired as the "father of confederation" because of his efforts to unite the provinces. Vigorous,
able, and far-seeing, he devoted his life to the upbuilding of

Canada. During the twenty-two years that he was in office, Macdonald pursued a "national policy" through railway building, protective tariffs, and centralization. It was during his premiership that the "Great Lone Land," the Canadian Middle West, was taken over by the government from the Hudson's Bay Company (1869). The Dominion now reached to the Pacific. An era of railway building began with the object of spanning the continent in order to develop the prairie region of mid-western Canada which corresponds to the Middle West of the United States. The Canadian Pacific, the first trans-continental railway in Canada, was built in the eighties. This enterprise was due, in great measure, to Macdonald and to a great capitalist, later known as Lord Strathcona. The opening up of western Canada brought many emigrants, from eastern Canada, from Europe, and from the United States.

Era of Conservative rule

The period of Conservative rule ended in 1896, when the Liberals came into power. Their leader was Sir Wilfrid Laurier, a French-Canadian, who proved to be as loyal a supporter of the British connection as Macdonald. As Premier, Laurier continued the policies of his predecessor, but less vigorously. The Liberals were inclined to favor low tariffs, and to stress the rights of the provinces as against those of the central government. They were driven from power by the elections of 1911 because they favored reciprocity with the United States, a policy strongly opposed by the Conservatives who feared that it would result in making the Dominion "an appanage of the United States."

Era of Liberal rule

Canada, although continental in size, is still sparsely inhabited. In 1927, it had a population of about 10,000,000, most of which was in Ontario and Quebec. A serious racial problem exists, due to the fact that the French and English Canadians live apart as separate nationalities. Most of the French, who number about one third of the population, and who have been very tenacious of their institutions, language and religion, live in the province of Quebec. Being very Catholic, they do not wish to be restored to France, which they regard as anti-Catholic and revolutionary; neither do they wish to secede, lest they expose themselves to annexation by the United States. Unlike the French Canadians, who are opposed to the participation of Canada in Imperial matters, the English Canadians

Relations between the French and English Canadians

are ready to coöperate with the mother country in matters affecting the Empire as a whole.

AUSTRALIA AND NEW ZEALAND

During the middle of the seventeenth century, a Dutchman, Tasman, made an extended exploration of the coasts of Australia and New Zealand. Later, at the end of the eighteenth century, an Englishman, Captain Cook, came to these islands and took possession of them in the name of England. In 1788, the English established a penal settlement at Botany Bay (now Sydney), in Australia, to which English convicts were sent. When, in time, free white settlers arrived from England, they objected to the convicts as an undesirable class of colonists; so, in 1840, the transportation of convicts was officially abolished. Population grew slowly; the island-continent, although about as large as the United States, afforded few economic opportunities besides sheep-raising. Immense regions were, and still are, arid wastes unfit for human habitation. In 1851, gold deposits were discovered, and the influx of settlers which followed caused the colony to grow more rapidly. The population of Australia is not large, and it is engaged mainly in grazing and mining.

In addition to the original colony of New South Wales, five others came into existence, Queensland, Victoria, South Australia, Western Australia, and the neighboring island of Tasmania. Common interests, as well as fear of the expansion of Germany and of Japan in the southern Pacific, gave birth to a movement for union. It found an energetic promoter in Henry Parkes who organized a number of conferences with the object of establishing a federation. A constitutional convention, held in 1897–98, drafted a constitution which was incorporated in an act passed by the British Parliament in 1900. It established the Commonwealth of Australia, a federal union of six "States," modeled on that of the United States. The central government consists of a popularly elected Senate, representing the States equally, and a House of Representatives representing the people. The government is carried on, as in England, by a ministry responsible to the lower house. To a supreme court is given the power to interpret the constitution.

Social reform occupied the attention of the government which, at one time, was under the control of a radical Labor Party, led by

William M. Hughes. Laws were enacted regulating the relations between capital and labor in the matter of hours, Social reform wages, and conditions of employment. Workman's compensation and old-age pension laws were passed in the interests of the laboring classes. In 1927, a new city was built, Canberra, which succeeded Melbourne as the capital of the Commonwealth. It was magnificently laid out as a model capital city with residences, office buildings, parks, and avenues.

New Zealand is the name of a group of islands, southeast of Australia, which were formally annexed to the British Empire in 1839. As early as 1852, local autonomy was granted New Zealand to the colony through the establishment of the cabinet system of government. In 1907, it was organized as a Dominion, and put in the same class with Canada and Australia. This far-off place, with few inhabitants, began to attract world-wide attention as a laboratory for experiments in political and social democracy. Parliament was made completely democratic through the popular election on the basis of Proportional Representation. As early as 1893, women were granted full parliamentary suffrage. Public ownership of railways, telephones, and telegraphs was established. The government also provided fire and life insurance, loaned money at reasonable rates, granted old-age pensions, and rented model homes to workingmen.

SOUTH AFRICA

It has already been described how South Africa had been divided between the Boers and the British. The latter really did not care to extend their sway over the Boer Republics which Discovery of they considered of doubtful value economically. But gold the situation suddenly changed when, in 1885, gold was discovered on the "Rand," a region in the South African Republic.

A large immigration began, chiefly of Englishmen, and in a few years the population of the Republic almost trebled. The town of Johannesburg became a bustling city inhabited Boer *versus* almost entirely by *Uitlanders* (Dutch: foreigners). Briton There were now two elements in the Republic that differed widely in racial origin and occupation. On one side were the Dutch Boers, engaged in agricultural and pastoral pursuits, whose chief desire was to live their lives in their own simple way. Their ideas and their patriarchal manner of living gave the impression of

Old Testament Hebrews who had strayed into the wilds of Africa. On the other side were the Uitlanders, chiefly Englishmen, adventurous gold-seekers, speculators, and business men who despised the Boers as a backward, old-fashioned folk who were unfit to rule a modern community. In the eyes of the Boers the discovery of gold was a great calamity, and they feared that it would lead to the disruption of their country.

The Boers were determined to maintain their control at all costs, and they, therefore, passed naturalization laws which made it difficult for a foreigner to become a citizen. Although practically disfranchised, the Uitlanders were compelled to bear all the burdens of citizenship, such as taxation and military service. The mining industry, mostly in the hands of Englishmen, was subject to heavy charges and restrictive legislation, which enraged powerful financial interests in South Africa and in England. The Boer government was denounced as incompetent and unprogressive, and unable to meet the needs of a rapidly increasing industrial population.

The position of the Uitlanders

The famous capitalist-statesman, Cecil Rhodes, became the leading protagonist of British interests. Rhodes was an Englishman who, early in life, had emigrated to South Africa, where he became immensely rich by getting control of the diamond mines in Kimberley. The history of South Africa is intimately connected with Rhodes whose influence in the region was so widespread that he controlled it both politically and economically. He was a new type of "empire builder," a financier-capitalist of great practical ability and foresight, whose plans were as bold and daring as the soldier "empire builders" of former days. Rhodes became an enthusiastic, almost fanatical believer in the British Empire as the supreme agency in civilizing the "lesser breeds." The Boers he regarded merely as an obstacle in the path of an all-British South Africa. Once out of the way, a new African empire would fall into the hands of England, South Africa, British East Africa, the Sudan, and Egypt, to be linked by a gigantic railway from the Cape to Cairo.

Rhodes (1853–1902)

Opposed to Rhodes in his scheme to obliterate the Boer Republics was Paul Kruger, the President of the South African Republic. As a child, Kruger had been in the "Great Trek," and he grew up to distrust the English, whom he suspected of constantly plotting against the Boers. To the petitions of the

Kruger (1825–1904)

Uitlanders for equal rights he replied, "This is my country, these are my laws. Those who do not like to obey my laws may leave my country." Kruger was like a character out of the Old Testament, patriarchal, simple in his ideas and in his manner of living, and a stern, unflinching Calvinist in religion. Although not a statesman in the accepted sense of the term, he proved himself to be no mean antagonist to the masterful Rhodes.

In Joseph Chamberlain, the Colonial Secretary in the Salisbury Ministry, Rhodes found a fellow spirit. Both men believed that the Boers were a danger to British supremacy in South Africa, and they determined to bring about the *The Jameson Raid* destruction of the Boer republics. A number of British adventurers, led by a Dr. Jameson, were encouraged by Rhodes to attack the Boers. In 1895, the Jameson raiders invaded the South African Republic, but they were captured by the Boers, who then handed them over to the British authorities for punishment. But the British treated the raiders leniently, and actually shielded Rhodes, the arch-conspirator against the independence of the Republic. The Boers were now convinced that the British cared little about the rights of the Uitlanders, and were merely using them as a pretext for aggression against the Republics.

A special commissioner, Sir Alfred Milner, arrived from England to investigate the grievances of the Uitlanders. His Report contained a severe denunciation of the Boer government *The Milner Report* which, he declared, was keeping British subjects in the position of helots. He also charged that the Boers were aiming at nothing less than the destruction of British influence in all of South Africa. Great Britain thereupon demanded of the Boer government that it extend the suffrage to the Uitlanders on more liberal terms, which was refused. An intense situation now arose. In 1899, Kruger sent an ultimatum demanding that the British cease military preparations, and when it was refused the South African Republic and the Orange Free State declared war against the British Empire.

It was generally believed that the conflict would be a short one, because of the overwhelming odds against the Boers; but it lasted three years, and seriously strained the resources of *The Boer War* Great Britain. Her armies suffered humiliating defeats inflicted on them by the Boer generals, De Wet and Botha, whose skillful strategy won the admiration of the world. In

England the government was denounced by many of the Liberals for making aggressive war against the inoffensive Boers in the interest of South African financiers. England sent large armies under the command of her ablest generals, Roberts and Kitchener, who finally succeeded in vanquishing the Boers. Peace was concluded in 1902; the two republics lost their independence and were annexed to the British Empire.

When the Liberals came into power, in 1906, they determined to spare no pains to bring about a reconciliation of the Boers to Boers British rule. Parliament promptly granted respon-granted au- sible government to the Transvaal and to the Orange tonomy Free State. Everything possible was done to make the Boers feel that the English did not regard them as a conquered people.

In 1909, the Cape of Good Hope, the Transvaal, Orange Free State, and Natal formed a union known as the "Union of South Union of Africa," to which the British government gave Do-South Africa minion status. A constitution was adopted which established a central government consisting of a parliament of two houses with a responsible ministry. Local autonomy was granted to the "provinces" as the colonies were now called. Both English and Dutch were recognized as official languages. The first Prime Minister of the Union was General Louis Botha, a Boer, who had fought valiantly in the Boer War, but who was now loyal to the British Empire. Although the Boers did not suddenly become enamored of their former enemies, they nevertheless were grateful to the British for their confidence and generosity in granting them self-government.

In spite of a century of immigration, the Negro natives in South Africa greatly outnumbered the whites, both Briton and Boer. A The Negro serious question arose in the convention that framed natives the constitution of the Union as to the status of the natives. The British were inclined to favor them, but the Boers, their former masters, strongly opposed giving them political recognition. Most of the natives in the Union were segregated in reservations, where they lived under tribal conditions. Those who lived among the whites were laborers, chiefly in the mines, where they were herded in "compounds," or barracks, under special supervision.

INDIA

Like China, India is continental in size and contains a population estimated at 300,000,000. During the Middle Ages there had been a flourishing trade between India and Europe, *The East India Companies* but as this trade was largely through intermediaries *India Companies* Europe knew little of the "Gorgeous East." It was not until the sixteenth century that European merchants settled in India with the object of trading with the inhabitants. East India Companies, French, English, and Dutch, were chartered by their governments and given a monopoly of the trade with India.

Politically India was a geographical expression. It was divided into many independent and semi-independent states whose princes waged war against one another. This situation gave *Rivalry between the English and the French* a new opportunity to the Companies. Originally they had come in search of wealth, not of empire, but the *English and the French* condition of anarchy gave them the idea of intervening in politics by aiding some rulers against others. The princes were eager to avail themselves of the superior arms and military tactics possessed by the Europeans. The Frenchman, Joseph Dupleix, greatly extended the influence of his Company by allying himself with powerful Indian rulers. This policy was also followed by Robert Clive of the English Company. A struggle for hegemony began between the French and English Companies, each supported by native princes. At the battle of Plassey (1757) the French and their allies were beaten by the English and their allies. The outcome was that the English Company became virtually master of Bengal.

There followed a period, lasting a century, of the expansion of Company rule until it embraced nearly all of India. A country as large as half of Europe, thickly populated and highly *Company rule* civilized, was governed by a corporation of business *rule* men. It established a civil administration, supported armies and navies, made war and peace, annexed territory, and, in all other ways, exercised the powers of a great state. Immense fortunes were made by the stockholders of the Company who now had a monopoly of all the foreign trade of India. Charges of corruption and oppression against its officials, especially in the famous case of Warren Hastings, brought the matter before the British Parliament. It led, in 1784, to the appointment of commissions in

England and in India with power to supervise the actions of the Company.

Not all of what is the present Empire of India was under its control at the beginning of the nineteenth century. A large region was ruled by the Mahratta Confederacy, a loosely organized union of Indian princes who disputed the Company's control of India. After years of intermittent warfare, the Confederacy was finally overthrown in 1818, and its territory annexed to that ruled by the Company. The warlike inhabitants of the mountainous regions of Punjab, on the northern frontier, gave trouble to the English and to the natives of the plains. In 1849, Punjab was conquered and annexed by Lord Dalhousie. The inhabitants, known as Sikhs, have since furnished the British army in India with excellent soldiers.

The Company extends its sway

The rapid growth of British authority in India aroused great dissatisfaction among the natives, who beheld a handful of Europeans in control of their country. The revolt, in 1857, of a regiment of Sepoys, as the native soldiers were called, was like a spark which set all India aflame. The famous Indian Mutiny followed which seriously threatened to overthrow the rule of the British. Fortunately for the latter, many of the Sepoys remained loyal, and the Mutiny was suppressed.

The Indian Mutiny

Although it failed, the Mutiny resulted in a great reform. In 1858, Parliament abolished the East India Company, and the government of India passed into the hands of the crown. A system of administration was inaugurated, which made India an integral part of the British Empire. At its head was a governor-general, called the Viceroy, the British equivalent of a Roman Pro-Consul, who was entrusted with the direction and control of civil and military matters. He exercised large powers, and was responsible only to the British government which appointed and dismissed him. The Viceroy was assisted by two councils, one executive, the other legislative, appointed by the crown. A new member of the British cabinet appeared, the Secretary of State for India, assisted by a council. He was the "crown" in matters pertaining to India; as he initiated all measures in Parliament affecting that country, he was consulted in the appointment of the Viceroy and of his councils, and was given direction of the revenues of India. Not all of India was under the direct

Government of India

rule of the British; about one fourth of the population lived in the Native States, which continued under the rule of their princes, who, however, were controlled by British officials. In no way did the new system recognize the principle of self-government; it was both autocratic and foreign.

Even during the anti-imperialistic period, England was determined to maintain her rule in India, as it was profitable to influential elements. The aristocrats were given civil and military positions at high salaries in the Indian administration. The manufacturers exported cheap articles, especially cottons, to supply the needs of an immense population whose native crafts were ousted by the products of the factory. At one time India had been a producer of famous textiles, especially muslins; she now became a producer of food and raw materials, wheat, tea, jute, and raw cotton which she sent to England in exchange for manufactures. Stringent regulations discouraged the establishment of native factories. India was in the position of being a customer without being a competitor, a situation very advantageous to the British manufacturers.

Economic dependence of India on England

Once firmly intrenched, the British began to consolidate their power. A policy of expansion was begun with the object of safeguarding the frontier. A number of wars in the east resulted in the conquest of Burmah, which was finally annexed. More serious was the northwestern frontier through which, in former times, invading tribes had poured into India. Early in the twentieth century Baluchistan was conquered and annexed; and Afghanistan and Tibet were neutralized by special agreements.[1] In 1912, the capital was moved from Calcutta to Delhi, the ancient seat of the Mogul Empire, whose successor was now the British.

Expansion of British rule

For about half a century after the Mutiny, India was untroubled by agitation. Its immense population submitted to the rule of about 100,000 British officials and soldiers. This situation can be explained chiefly by the fact that India is not a homogeneous nation; the population is divided into mutually hostile groups, racial, religious, and social, who are unwilling to unite against the British Raj, as the government is called.[2] The races vary from savage hill tribes to the

Religious divisions of India

[1] See page 632.

[2] It is estimated that there are in India as many as 40 distinctive races, speaking 150 different languages and dialects.

civilized inhabitants of ancient cities, renowned for their magnificence, their arts, and their learning. Between the Hindus [1] and Mohammedans bitter religious feuds have raged, often resulting in bloody riots. The Mohammedans were once the rulers of India, and the Hindus fear that, if the British were ousted, they would again fall under Mohammedan rule.

The Hindus are internally divided by a caste system so rigid that there is very little national sentiment. There are four main Caste divi- castes, the highest being the Brahmans, or priests; sions then follow, in order of dignity, warriors, merchants, and laborers. Each main caste is subdivided into many minor ones, according to occupations. A Hindu is born into a caste, and is obliged by his religion to marry within it, to follow its occupation, to wear its insignia, and to obey its rules. About a sixth of the population are considered so low as to be "outcasts," or "pariahs," whose very touch is defiling. These "untouchables" are segregated in certain districts and restricted to the lowest kind of labor. It is believed that they are of a race different from their social superiors, who had put the curse of untouchability upon them to prevent race mixture.

In spite of divisions, a nationalist agitation did manage to make its appearance. At the end of the nineteenth century, a move-
The nation- ment, known as "Young India," arose which pro-
alist move- claimed the doctrines of nationalism and democracy.
ment It was led by young men who had studied in Europe and America or in the Christian missionary schools in India, where they had imbibed Western ideas and had acquired Western customs. The educated young Indians were furious at being discriminated against in their own country, as they were not appointed to the higher offices in the government. Through societies, journals, and mass meetings they voiced the demand of "India for the Indians." British rule was denounced as the "Drain," whereby India was drained of her wealth for the benefit of England. India, the nationalists declared, was heavily taxed in order to maintain high-salaried officials and an army of occupation; the government, being alien, spent little for the benefit of the inhabitants, especially for their education. After the native crafts had

[1] The term "Hindu" is descriptive of a religion, sometimes called Brahmanism. The Hindus number 67 per cent of the population, and the Mohammedans, 22 per cent.

been destroyed by the importation of English manufactures, the development of home industry was hindered by restrictive excises. Some of the nationalists advocated a systematic boycotting of British goods and strikes of Indian workingmen against their British employers. The more violent began a campaign of terrorism by assassinating British officials.

The nationalists caused much concern in England. When the Liberals came into power, in 1906, John Morley was made Secretary of State for India. A lifelong champion of liberal ideas, Morley resolved to qualify the autocratic system *The Morley Reforms* by recognizing some of the demands of the Indians for a share in the government of their country. In 1909, the Morley Reforms were passed by Parliament. Indians were now appointed to the councils of the Viceroy and of the Secretary of State for India. Provincial bodies, already in existence, were made partly elective, and given larger powers. These reforms, moderate though they were, inaugurated a democratic policy in India which was later to find expression in more substantial concessions.[1]

From the viewpoint of the British imperialist, India derived great benefits from British rule. It brought internal peace to a land once distracted by tribal wars, established an enlightened civil and criminal code, and abolished barbarous practices. Irrigation works were constructed to the great benefit of agriculture; railways and factories were built; and India's commerce, both domestic and foreign, increased greatly. British rule unified India to an extent unknown in her history, by giving her a common government, a common official language, and a common legal code.

EGYPT

How England got control of Egypt has already been described. Once in the country, she determined to stay because of the vast importance of the Suez Canal as a safeguard of Imperial communications. The Canal was the principal station on the highway to India; and, moreover, much of England's foreign trade passed through it. It is, therefore, with reason that the region around Suez was called the "spinal cord" of the British Empire; if broken, India and Australasia would be beyond England's reach.

When the conquest of Egypt was completed, the British set about reorganizing the country. Nominally it was ruled by the

[1] See Chapter XXXIX.

Khedive, but the real government was in the hands of a British
high commissioner, appointed by the British government, who "advised" the puppet Khedive. Under
Lord Cromer, who was high commissioner from 1883 to 1907,
Egypt made notable progress. Taxes were fairly levied and
equitably collected, something very unusual in the long history
of that country. Life and property were made secure. The administration was able, honest, and economical. Forced labor, long
the curse of the country, was abolished. British engineers built
the famous Assuan Dam to conserve the waters of the Nile for
irrigation purposes. Under British control, Egypt was assured of
a tranquillity and prosperity that she had not known for centuries.

Rule of Lord Cromer

Nevertheless, there was much discontent. As with peoples
elsewhere, the Egyptians were more eager for self-government than
for good government. Once more the cry was raised,
"Egypt for the Egyptians!" A nationalist movement
appeared that began a vigorous agitation for political
independence. Riots broke out. British officials were assassinated. The British government made some concessions which,
however, failed to allay discontent. In 1914, when Turkey entered
the World War on the side of Germany, England openly proclaimed
Egypt a protectorate, which cut her slender tie with the Ottoman
Empire and bound her more tightly to the British Empire.

The nation-alist move-ment

SYSTEMS OF GOVERNMENT

As the British Empire has no written constitution, it is impossible to classify, except in a general way, the various types of
colonial government. Moreover, there has been a
constant "procession" of the colonies, moving in
stages from autocratic to democratic rule. The most important
type, Dominion government, obtains in Canada, Newfoundland,
Australia, New Zealand, South Africa, and the Irish Free State.
It was first initiated in Canada by the British North America Act,
and has become the goal of all the other British colonies. The control of their domestic affairs by the Dominions is "absolute, unfet-
tered, and free." In the words of Kipling, a Dominion is made to say:

Dominion government

> "Daughter am I in my mother's house,
> But mistress in my own."

Such matters as tariffs, coinage, immigration, and armament are entirely within their sphere; they may exclude even British goods and British emigrants. Foreign affairs, until the World War, were exclusively directed from London, but even in these matters the Dominions are now equal with the mother country.[1] The bonds of union, so far as they are legal, are so circumscribed that they are not effective. The people of the Dominions recognize the King of England as their "sovereign," but he wields no power over them. The governor-general, representing the British connection, has considerable authority which he, however, does not exercise. The British Parliament has the legal power to legislate for the Dominions, but it no longer has the "constitutional" right to do so. Fundamentally the ties that bind Greater Britain are racial and cultural, not political. As most of the inhabitants in the Dominions are of British stock, they feel an intense pride in their common heritage which they would loyally defend. To be severed from the mother country would leave them, at best, insignificant; at worst, a prey to foreign conquest.

The colonies inhabited by non-British races do not have Dominion government. They are known as "Crown Colonies," and their affairs are largely directed by the home government, especially by the Colonial Secretary. In all of them there is a governor appointed by the crown. In 1914, there were degrees of self-government in the Crown Colonies. Some, such as Bermuda and the Bahamas, had a legislature wholly elected by the people; others, such as Cyprus and British Guiana, had a majority of the legislature elected and a minority appointed; others, such as Jamaica and Malta, had a majority appointed and a minority elected; others, such as Honduras, Ceylon, Hongkong, and the Straits Settlements, had a legislature wholly appointed by the British government; and in others, such as Gibraltar and Uganda, the governor ruled without any legislature at all.

The "Crown Colonies" in 1914

British India, sometimes known as a "Dependency," was ruled autocratically by the home government. Egypt and the Native States in India were ruled ostensibly by their princes, but really by British officials who "advised" them. North Borneo and Rhodesia were ruled by chartered companies. The Sudan was a "condominium," governed jointly by British and Egyptian officials.

India and Egypt in 1914

[1] See Chapter XXXIX.

REVIVAL OF IMPERIALISM

England's attitude toward her colonies underwent a great change during the latter part of the nineteenth century. No longer was the dissolution of the Empire viewed with complacency; on the contrary, a powerful sentiment arose, both in England and in the colonies, which demanded closer bonds of union. The prophet of

Disraeli   the new imperialism was Disraeli, who appealed to the imagination of his fellow countrymen by picturing them as the rulers of many tribes and nations. His bold stroke in acquiring the Suez Canal thrilled all England. He occupied Cyprus, and annexed the Transvaal. When Parliament conferred upon Queen Victoria the additional title of "Empress of India," it effectively dramatized the pride of England in her Imperial possessions.

A book appeared in 1883 which had great influence in arousing Imperial sentiments. It was *Expansion of England,* by Sir John

Seeley   R. Seeley, dealing with the origin of the British Empire which, as the author declared, was acquired "in a fit of absent-mindedness."   Long neglected by British statesmen, the colonies were drifting farther and farther from the mother country. Seeley urged that England should now become conscious of her great position as the "world Venice with the sea for streets."

Even more influential was Rudyard Kipling. His poems and stories were inspired by an enthusiastic devotion to the Empire

Kipling   whose "dominion over palm and pine" fired his imagination. He urged his fellow countrymen to "take up the white man's burden" in order to bring civilization to the "lesser breeds."   Kipling's great mission was to sound the note of imperialism in English literature, and he was acclaimed as the "poet laureate of the Empire."

England witnessed an amazing growth of imperialist sentiment. At first only the Conservatives became its devotees; but so popular

All parties   was the movement that the Liberals, and even the
imperialist   Laborites, became upholders of the Empire. The only difference between the Conservatives, on the one hand, and the Liberals and Laborites, on the other, was that the latter were more ready than the former to extend self-government to the colonies.

The revival of British imperialism was part of the imperialist movement throughout the world,[1] but, in the case of England,

[1] See pages 601–09.

there were special causes of importance. As the economic rivalry of Germany became more threatening, England saw the possibility of maintaining her prosperity by developing her colonies. The latter offered an attractive field for investment: they had excellent natural resources, and their governments gave ample security to life and property. Commissions were appointed to study the natural resources and trade of the colonies with a view of developing them. There began a migration of British capital to the colonies which financed great enterprises: sheep ranches in Australia, gold and diamond mines in South Africa, cotton plantations in India, tea plantations in Ceylon, irrigation works in Egypt, lumber mills in Canada, rubber plantations in the Malay States, sugar plantations in the West Indies, and railways and factories everywhere.[1] Colonial trade increased rapidly, especially with India, which became England's best customer. From her colonies England received chiefly foodstuffs; to them she sent chiefly manufactured articles. The Empire is commerce, declared Chamberlain; "It was created by commerce, it is founded on commerce, and it could not exist a day without commerce. . . . For these reasons, among others, I would never lose the hold which we now have over our great Indian dependency — by far the greatest and most valuable of all the customers we have or ever shall have in this country. For the same reasons I approve of the continued occupation of Egypt; and for the same reasons I have urged . . . the necessity of using every legitimate opportunity to extend our influence and control in that great African continent which is now being opened up to civilization and to commerce." As political bonds of the British Empire were loosened by the extension of self-government the economic bonds were tightened by investment and trade.

Causes for revival of British imperialism: (1) economic

Another important cause for the revival of British imperialism was the change in the international situation that took place after the Franco-Prussian War. Every great power in Europe, except England, was in some combination, either of the Triple or of the Dual Alliance. England prided herself on her "splendid isolation" in international affairs, feeling sure that her insular position could be well defended by her powerful fleet. But the challenge of Germany to England's naval supremacy made the latter feel more and more uneasy, and she began to con-

(2) Military

[1] See footnote, page 292.

sider the help that the colonies might render in case of war. On
their part, the self-governing colonies had become all the more
loyal to the mother country because of the greater freedom granted
to them. They dreaded nothing so much as falling into the hands
of an alien power, and they therefore desired to be more closely
associated with the mother country than ever before.

THE NEW EMPIRE PARTNERSHIP

It was not, however, until the advent of the Salisbury Ministry,
in 1895, that imperialism became a leading interest in British
Chamber-   affairs. Its chief spokesman was Chamberlain, the
lain   Colonial Secretary, who showed great energy and
resourcefulness in planning ways and means to draw the colonies
and mother country into a closer and more perfect union. He,
more than any one else, was responsible for the new Empire partnership which marked a new stage in the history of the British Empire.

In 1897, the sixtieth anniversary of Queen Victoria's accession
to the throne, there took place a celebration known as the "Dia-
The Dia-   mond Jubilee." To London came representatives
mond Jubi-   from every corner of the world-wide Empire to do
lee   homage to their sovereign. The streets presented a
wonderful pageant of races, Malays from the Straits Settlements,
Chinese from Hongkong, Negroes from Africa, French and Indians
from Canada, Dutch from the Cape, Indians, Australians, Canadians, all happily mingling to show the unity as well as the diversity
of the British Empire.

Chamberlain seized the occasion to summon a conference of the
Dominion premiers over which he presided. Already, in 1887, a
The Confer-   colonial conference had been held, but it accomplished
ence of 1897 little. The Conference of 1897 created wide interest,
and brought about the adoption of the Imperial penny post, establishing uniform postal rates for all parts of the Empire. In 1900,
Parliament passed a law enabling colonial governments to float
loans in London at specially low rates of interest.

The test of the new unity came during the Boer War. To the
British, the war was one for the defense of the Empire; they feared
The Boer   that a Boer victory would encourage rebellions else-
War   where in the Empire. The colonies rallied loyally to
the mother country: Australians, Canadians, and New Zealanders
fought side by side with Englishmen, Scotsmen, Irishmen, and

Welshmen.   This was the first time that colonial troops fought the battles of the mother country.

The first conference after the Boer War was held in 1902, which adopted a resolution in favor of periodic meetings to be known as Imperial Conferences.   In 1907, a Conference formally organized the system of meetings, which were to con- sist of representatives of the governments of the Dominions and of Great Britain, each having only one vote; meetings were to be held at intervals of not more than four years; and the power of the Conference was limited to recom- mendations on Imperial matters to their governments, who were free to accept or reject them.

Establish- ment of periodic conferences

Two subjects were constantly debated at the Imperial Confer- ences: defense and preferential duties.   Should the colonies share the burden of maintaining the British navy in order to do their duty as active partners in the Empire? It was generally agreed that all colonial contributions to Imperial defense should be voluntary.   Some of the Dominions contributed warships to the British navy; others contributed money to the British naval budget.   Australia built a fleet which, in case of war, was to be at the disposal of the British admiralty.

Imperial defense

Even more important was "Imperial Preference."   Its champion was Chamberlain who devoted his energies and talents to further the idea which he made part of his general scheme of tariff reform.[1]   His plan called for a Zollverein to be formed between England and the Dominions, according to which there was to be, eventually, free trade among themselves with a protective tariff on all foreign goods; in the meantime, they were to establish preferential tariff rates, favoring British and colonial as against foreign goods.   Chamberlain believed that the Empire could be made self-sustaining, the colonies producing the food and raw materials; and England, the manufactures.   "We have an Empire," he declared, "which, with decent organization and con- solidation, might be absolutely self-sustaining.   There is no ar- ticle of your food, no raw material of your trade, no necessity of your lives, no luxury of your existence, which cannot be produced somewhere or other in the British Empire."   Imperial Preference found favor in the Dominions, who granted preferential rates to British goods, in some instances as high as half of the regular tariff.

Imperial Preference

[1] See page 293.

They demanded that England reciprocate, which she was unable to do as long as she maintained her free trade policy.

In the movement for Empire partnership there was a tendency on the part of England to favor as much as possible the desires of the colonies to be "mistress in their own house." Self-government, once granted as a step toward independence, was now granted as a step toward closer union. And well did this liberal policy justify itself! When the World War broke out the colonies responded to the call of the mother country with magnificent loyalty and devotion. They spared neither men nor money in aiding England in her desperate struggle with Germany.[1]

Loyalty of the colonies in the World War

REFERENCES

GENERAL:

Brief histories: J. A. Williamson, *A Short History of British Expansion*, 2 vols. (ed. 1930); and H. Robinson, *The Development of the British Empire* (1937); Sir J. R. Seeley, *The Expansion of England*, a famous work, see p. 676; W. P. Hall, *Empire to Commonwealth* (1928), political narrative of the last thirty years, special emphasis on growth of colonial nationalism; A. B. Keith, *Selected Speeches and Documents on British colonial policy, 1750–1921* (1922); Series: A. J. Herbertson and O. J. R. Howarth (editors), *The Oxford Survey of the British Empire*, 12 vols. (1914); K. N. Bell and W. P. Morell (eds.), *Select Documents in British Colonial Policy, 1830–1860* (1928); J. H. Rose (ed.), *The Cambridge History of the British Empire*.

SPECIAL TOPICS:

Economic: C. J. Fuchs, *The Trade Policy of Great Britain and her Colonies since 1860*, translated from the German (1905); L. C. A. Knowles, *The Economic Development of the Overseas Empire, 1763–1914* (ed. 1925); W. J. Ashley (ed.), *British Dominions: Their Present Commercial and Industrial Conditions* (1911); and G. von Schulze-Gaevernitz, *Britischer Imperialismus und Englischer Freihandel* (1906), a study of imperialism and economics, contains excellent historical introduction. On government: E. Jenks, *The Government of the British Empire* (1918), brief study; A. B. Keith, *Responsible Government in the Dominions*, 2 vols. (ed. 1927), best study of the subject, treats also special problems such as immigration, foreign affairs, and Imperial Conferences; R. Jebb, *Studies in Colonial Nationalism* (1905), and *The Colonial Conference*, 2 vols. (1911); H. E. Egerton, *Federations and Unions within the British Empire* (1911); G. W. Morris and L. S. Wood, *The English-Speaking Nations* (1924); P. and A. Hurd, *The New Empire Partnership* (1915); C. A. Bodelsen, *Studies in Mid-Victorian Imperialism* (1925), describes reaction and revival of im-

[1] For the history of the British Empire after the World War, see Chapter XXXIX.

perialism; A. Zimmern, *The Third British Empire* (1926), an interesting little volume on the evolution of the Empire from an autocratic to a democratic basis.

INDIA:

A good brief introduction is Sir T. W. Holderness, *Peoples and Problems of India* (1912); V. A. Smith, *Oxford History of India* (1919), from British Imperial standpoint; Sir S. Banerjea, *A Nation in the Making* (1926), memoirs by an Indian of pro-British sympathies.   Economic: Sir T. Morison, *The Economic Transition in India* (1911); and D. R. Gadgil, *The Industrial Evolution of India in Recent Times* (1924), has good bibliography.   On Indian nationalism: L. Rai, *Young India, an Interpretation and a History of the Nationalist Movement from within* (1916), and *England's Debt to India* (1917), severe indictments of British rule by an ardent Indian nationalist.

THE DOMINIONS:

On Canada: C. Wittke, *A History of Canada* (1941), a political and social history with special emphasis on American and Imperial relations; G. M. Wrong, *Canada* (1924); J. C. Bracq, *The Evolution of French Canada* (1924); R. G. Trotter, *Canadian Federation, its Origin and Achievement* (1924), the standard work on the subject; E. S. Montague and B. Herbert, *Canada and the Empire* (1904), deals with fiscal relations with England; Sir C. P. Lucas (ed.), *Lord Durham's Report on the Affairs of British North America*, 3 vols. (1912).   On South Africa: F. R. Cana, *South Africa from the Great Trek to the Union* (1909); G. M. Theal, *History of South Africa from 1795 to 1872*, 5 vols. (ed. 1920), detailed history of the British occupation; W. A. Cotton, *The Race Problem in South Africa* (1926), advocates segregation; and James (Viscount) Bryce, *Impressions of South Africa* (1897), a study of problems and conditions prior to the Boer War.   On the Boer War: Sir A. Conan Doyle, *The War in South Africa, its Cause and Conduct* (1902), pro-British; and J. A. Hobson, *War in South Africa, its Cause and its Effects* (1900), a severe criticism of the war by an English Liberal; *The Memoirs of Paul Kruger, Four Times President of the South African Republic, Told by Himself*, edited by A. Schowalter and translated by A. T. de Mattos (1902).   W. B. Worsfold, *The Union of South Africa* (1912). On Australasia: W. P. Reeves, *State Experiments in Australia and New Zealand*, 2 vols. (ed. 1923), and *New Zealand* (ed. 1925), by the authority on the subject; B. R. Wise, *The Making of the Australian Commonwealth, 1889–1900* (1913); H. G. Turner, *The First Decade of the Australian Commonwealth* (1911); G. Tregarthen and P. E. G. Bailey, *The Australian Commonwealth* (1924); V. S. Clark, *The Labor Movement in Australasia* (1906); A. Siegfried, *Democracy in New Zealand*, translated from the French (1914).

ADDITIONAL REFERENCES

R. L. Schuyler, *Parliament and the British Empire* (1929), scholarly and original study of imperial jurisdiction; L. Le M. Minty, *Constitutional Laws of the British Empire* (1928); J. B. Condliffe, *New Zealand in the Making* (1930); W. K. Hancock, *Australia* (1930); Jean-Jacques Chevallier, *L'Évolution de l'Empire Britannique*, 2 vols. (1931); *The Cambridge History of the British Empire*, Vol. V (1932); A. B. Keith, *The Governments of the British Empire* (1936); J. Stoye, *The British Empire*, trans. from the German (1936); G. T. Garratt (ed.), *The Legacy of India* (1937); E. Thompson and G. T. Garratt, *Rise and Fulfillment of British Rule in India* (1934); C. F. Mullett, *The British Empire* (1938); P. Knaplund, *The British Empire. 1815–1939* (1941).

PART V
THE WORLD WAR AND AFTER

PART V

THE WORLD WAR AND AFTER

THE World War was not a war in the ordinary sense, a conflict between two or more nations followed by a treaty of peace and the resumption of normal relations. It was rather a world upheaval which brought to ruin nations and empires, and repudiated old systems and ideas. In this sense the World War resembled the wars that resulted from the Protestant Revolution and from the French Revolution. Every continent and nearly all the nations were involved in the struggle; hence, it may fitly be named the "World War." Nothing like it had ever before happened in history.

A broken world issued from the conflict. The hatreds engendered by the most terrible of all wars were so bitter that, for a time, they foiled all attempts to make the world whole again. Neither side could forget its sufferings nor forgive those who had inflicted them. The losses of the victors were no less than those of the vanquished, and both sides realized that, unless efforts were made to reconstitute Europe, all would sink into a common ruin. Reconciliation began, but the problem of a permanently peaceful Europe remains one for future generations to solve.

CHAPTER XXXIII

THE DIPLOMATIC BACKGROUND OF THE WORLD WAR

1870–1914

THE TRIPLE ALLIANCE

THE system of international relations established by the Congress of Vienna was completely shattered by the events of 1870. Two great powers came into existence, Germany and Italy, The new which necessitated a rearrangement of the European balance of powers; and the new diplomatic structure that was power erected was based, like the old one, on the principle of the balance of power. Formerly it was France, now it was Germany, who was feared as a possible disturber of the peace of Europe.

For twenty years after 1870 the leading figure in international affairs was Bismarck, who dominated the policies of Europe as completely as Metternich had done during the first Bismarck's half of the nineteenth century. It was Bismarck's aim aim to organize a system of military alliances pledged to the maintenance of the *status quo* as fixed by the events of 1870. And that could be accomplished only through the isolation of France. Bismarck was "haunted by the nightmare of coalitions"; he regarded France as the prospective and willing ally of any power or combination of powers opposed to Germany. "As long as France has no alliances," he declared, "she is not dangerous to Germany."

At the Congress of Berlin, Bismarck began building his system of alliances. There, he supported France in her scheme to acquire Tunis, which somewhat mollified her *revanche*; at the Bismarck same time France's acquisition of Tunis infuriated supports Italy, which was exactly what Bismarck desired. He against also supported Austria against Russia, which resulted Russia in the first rift in a long historic friendship. Good relations with Russia had been a cardinal principle of Prussia's foreign policy since the time of Frederick the Great. Why, then, did Bismarck endanger this historic friendship? He feared that Russia might become an enemy of Germany in case of a collision between Slav and Teuton; and Russia could be held in check only with the aid of Austria. Moreover, Bismarck believed that Austria would be a more faithful ally than Russia because she was relatively weak and "under Germany's guns."

In 1879, Bismarck and Count Andrassy, the Hapsburg repre-sentative, negotiated a treaty of alliance between Germany and
The Triple Austria-Hungary which became the corner-stone of
Alliance Bismarck's diplomatic system. Each promised to assist the other in case of an attack by Russia. In 1882, Italy, through the influence of Crispi, joined the two powers, thus forming the famous Triple Alliance. It was renewed at regular intervals; and, at almost every renewal, new terms were added. By a secret clause in the treaty Italy had reserved the right to be neutral in a war that brought her into conflict with England.

The Triple Alliance pledged itself "to increase the guarantees of the general peace, to fortify the monarchical principle, and thereby
Objects of to assure the unimpaired maintenance of the social
the Alliance and political order in their respective states." In a sense, then, it was a revival of the Holy Alliance. The com-munards in France, the terrorists in Russia, the socialists in Ger-many, and the anarchists in Italy again roused fears of an interna-tional revolutionary movement. However, the Alliance had spe-cific objects. The members promised mutual assistance in case any of them was attacked by two or more great powers. Italy promised to aid Germany if attacked by France. Germany and Austria promised to aid Italy if attacked by France. In case one member was at war with a great power, the others were to maintain benevo-lent neutrality. Austria and Italy agreed to "reciprocal compensa-tions" in the Near East. Germany agreed to aid Italy in a war against France, should the latter extend her sway over Morocco and Tripoli. It was specifically stated that the Alliance was not directed against England. Therefore it could be directed only against France and Russia.

Once deadly enemies, Germany, Austria, and Italy were now friends and allies. What had drawn them together? In the case
Motives of of Germany it was to make France consider well before
Germany she engaged in a war of *revanche*; she would be faced
and of by a solid block of central European powers. Aus-
Austria tria's motive was security against an attack by Russia. Driven out of Italy and out of Germany she sought to find com-

pensation by expanding in the Balkans.   Austria's policy of *Drang nach Osten* began with her virtual acquisition of Bosnia-Herzegovina by the Treaty of Berlin.   This act was resented by the Serbs, who now regarded Austria as the enemy of their national aspirations.   She, therefore, needed Germany's backing to maintain herself against Slav nationalism within and without her borders. Moreover, both Germany and Austria had a common fear of Pan-Slavism.   Should the national movement among the Slavs in Austria receive the encouragement of Russia, the integrity of the Hapsburg monarchy would be seriously endangered; and Germany would find herself isolated.   "The existence of Austria as a strong and independent great power is for Germany a necessity," Bismarck declared.   To guarantee the integrity of the Dual Monarchy was, therefore, a matter of enlightened self-interest on the part of Germany, and she decided to support Austria in her struggle with the Slavs.

Italy had various motives in joining the Triple Alliance.   As she was weak she felt that her prestige would be heightened by being the ally of two great powers.   Moreover, the Alliance   Motives of was a protection against a possible attempt by France   Italy to restore the temporal power of the Pope.   But Italy's chief motive was to get the backing of the Alliance in her desire to found a colonial empire.   Unification had produced a great national spirit among the Italians who now thought of Italy as the heir and successor of Imperial Rome; and to convert the Mediterranean into an "Italian lake" was the dream of imperially minded Italian statesmen.   Italy's ambitions were centered in two regions, northern Africa and the Adriatic.   At first, she had designs on Tunis, but France got there before her.   Then she tried to conquer Abyssinia, but was defeated.   Now she looked to Tripoli.   The problem of the Adriatic was bound up with the movement, *Italia irredenta;*[1] her policies, therefore, clashed with the interests of her ally, Austria.   It soon became evident that Italy was the weak element in the Triple Alliance.   Should her differences with France be composed and her desire for expansion be appeased, Italy's adherence to the Alliance would become uncertain.

To Bismarck no diplomatic arrangement was complete which left out Russia, for he well knew Germany's strategic weakness in her exposed eastern frontier.   In 1872, he organized another com-

[1] See page 368.

bination, known as the *Dreikaiserbund* (Three Emperors' League),
The Re-   consisting of Germany, Austria, and Russia.   But the
insurance   League came to an end, in 1887, owing to the clash
Treaty   of Russian and Austrian interests in the Balkans.
However, Bismarck determined "to keep open the wires to St.
Petersburg."   Behind the back of Austria he negotiated the Reinsurance Treaty (1887) with Russia, in which Germany recognized
the predominance of Russian interests in the eastern Balkans.
Bismarck's masterful diplomatic feat of "keeping five balls in the
air at once" confused the diplomatic situation for every one except
himself.

Of the great powers, other than France, only England was not
in the orbit of German diplomacy.   England, Bismarck well knew,
Bismarck   would not intervene on the Continent unless the bal-
and England   ance of power was threatened by the ambitions of a
nation who also threatened her maritime and naval supremacy.
His opposition to colonial expansion and to a big navy was, in
part, due to his desire not to arouse the hostility of the British.
As long as Germany remained a land power, England had no cause
to be alarmed; in Bismarck's phrase there could be no war between
a "land rat" and a "water rat."   England's aloofness from Continental engagements was an important factor in the creation of
the Triple Alliance.   To make sure of England's friendship, Germany, in 1890, signed the Treaty of Helgoland in which she gave
extensive territory in Africa to England in return for the island
of Helgoland.   So friendly were the relations of Germany and
England that efforts were made to draw England into the Triple
Alliance.

Bismarck's attitude toward France was that of cynical friendli-
ness.   When France started on her career of expansion, she received
Bismarck   his encouragement and support.   He reasoned that, if
and France   she annexed large regions in northern Africa, her
attention would be distracted from the "hole in the Vosges Mountains," Alsace-Lorraine.   Moreover, she would come into conflict
with Italy over Tunis, and with England over Egypt, which would
abate her ardor for war with Germany.   "We have tried to conciliate France," he declared, "everywhere except in Alsace-
Lorraine.   We have no intention and no reason to attack her.   I
would never fight because I thought war was inevitable.   I cannot
see the cards held by Providence. . . . Do we want more French
territory?   I was not eager to take Metz."

THE DUAL ALLIANCE

Bismarck's astute diplomacy left France isolated for fully two decades following the Franco-Prussian War. Feelings of revenge and fear agitated the French: revenge for the humiliat- *Ascendancy* ing defeat and fear of Germany's power. Every year *of Germany* saw increases in her population and wealth, far greater *over France* than those in France. Single-handed, France was no match for Germany, and she therefore sought an alliance with Russia, whose teeming millions and geographical position on Germany's flank made her a most desirable ally.

After 1871, France made friendly advances to Russia. An alliance between them was then deemed impossible; they had fought each other during the wars of the two Napoleons, and *Rapproche-* they differed so widely in their political ideals, France *ment of* being a revolutionary republic, and Russia a reaction- *Russia and* ary autocracy. Nevertheless, friendly relations began *France* which became evident in 1875. In that year a crisis arose between Germany and France during which Russia showed a friendly attitude toward France. The anti-Russian attitude of Bismarck at the Congress of Berlin infuriated Russia; as she drifted farther from Germany, she drew nearer France. In 1887, Tsar Alexander III announced that Russia would "watch events on the Rhine" and would not permit a further weakening of France. In 1890, the Reinsurance Treaty between Germany and Russia expired. It was not renewed by the Kaiser, who was now at the helm, on the ground that it gave offense to Austria, and therefore threatened the existence of the Triple Alliance. Germany had to choose between Russia and Austria, and she chose the latter as likely to be a more faithful ally. Moreover, Germany was now becoming interested in the Near East, and she feared the hostility of Russia in that region.

Russia was now isolated as well as France, and almost immediately the two powers had an *entente cordiale.* What drew France to Russia has already been explained. But what drew Russia to France? It was chiefly money. Russia needed *Motives of* vast sums for the construction of the Trans-Siberian *Russia* Railway and for new military and naval armaments. Russia's credit was not of the best, and France agreed to float large loans which were subscribed to largely by French citizens. Later, during the Russian Revolution of 1905, more Russian loans were floated in Paris to keep the Tsar's government from toppling. Russia had another motive in joining France; she wished to establish an equilibrium in Europe by having a counterpoise to the Triple Alliance; she could then throw all her forces in the Far East where her ambitions were now centered.

Friendly relations between the two powers were signalized by visits exchanged between Tsar and President. A French fleet,
The Dual visiting Cronstadt in 1891, was welcomed with great
Alliance ceremony by Alexander III, who listened with bowed
head to the strains of the *Marseillaise*, a song forbidden in Russia. Later, a military convention was signed by Russia and France which provided that the former aid the latter if attacked by Germany, or by Italy and Germany; that France aid Russia if attacked by Germany or by Austria and Germany; and it specified the number of troops to be mobilized by both parties to the convention. The full terms of the agreement were not disclosed.

There was great joy in France when the "Dual Alliance" was officially confirmed in 1894. Her isolation was over, and she
France could now breathe more easily. Germany's diplomatic
emerges from hegemony was consequently seriously shaken, greatly
isolation to the chagrin of Bismarck, who, from his retirement,
made sarcastic comments on the diplomacy of the Kaiser.

THE TRIPLE ENTENTE

(a) ENGLAND AND GERMANY

During the reign of William II there came a profound change in Germany's foreign policies. Bismarck's cautious policy of "satia-
Weltpolitik tion" was abandoned in favor of an aggressive policy
of *Weltpolitik*, the object of which was to win for Germany a dominant position in world affairs. This change was emphatically expressed by the Kaiser when he said: "Without Germany and the German Emperor no important step in international matters should be taken, even beyond the seas."

After the advent of the Kaiser, an estrangement began between the Germans and the English who, for many centuries, had been
Estrange- on the most friendly terms. They had fought shoulder
ment be- to shoulder against Napoleon. During the wars for
tween Ger-
many and unification the Germans had the warm sympathy of
England the English. Friendly feeling continued during the
period of Bismarck's chancellorship, despite the fact that the

English had little liking for the semi-autocratic régime in the German Empire. Fundamentally, the estrangement was due to Germany's challenge of England's naval and commercial supremacy.[1]

The first sign of ill-feeling was the "Kruger telegram." When the Jameson raiders were captured by the Boers,[2] the Kaiser sent a telegram of congratulations to President Kruger. German sympathy for the Boers This incident caused a furor in England, where it was regarded as a sign of German hostility to the British Empire. During the Boer War German sympathy was on the side of the Boers, which greatly increased ill-feeling. In England, the pro-Boer attitude of Germany was interpreted to mean, not sympathy for the Boers, but hostility to the British.

But this unfriendliness might have passed away in time had it not been for the German naval laws which England regarded as a direct challenge to her position as mistress of the seas. The naval challenge to England A veritable panic reigned in England because of the rapid increase of the German navy, in spite of constant assurances that it was purely for defensive purposes. England felt that her very existence depended upon her control of the seas; and she therefore began to regard Germany as the successor to Spain, Holland, and France, her historic naval rivals.

(b) ENGLAND AND FRANCE

For centuries, England's foreign policy was based upon certain cardinal principles: (1) No great power must be permitted to control the mouth of the Scheldt, from which an invasion could be most easily launched against England. It was she who was primarily responsible for the treaty England's historic foreign policy guaranteeing the neutrality of Belgium. (2) Having no territorial ambitions on the Continent, England consistently refused to join any alliances unless the balance of power was disturbed by the ambitions of a Continental nation. As the "Mediator of Europe" she would then throw her weight against the disturber of the balance of power. (3) The safeguarding of the route to India was all-important in England's scheme of empire. It led her to acquire Gibraltar, Malta, Cyprus, and the Suez Canal, and it drew her to the side of Turkey in the Near Eastern Question.

After the Crimean War, England resumed her normal policy of

[1] See page 709.   [2] See page 667.

"splendid isolation." Toward the end of the nineteenth century,

however, this policy became perilous on account of the renewed hostility of France because of rivalry in North Africa, to the designs of Russia upon India, and to the rivalry of Germany. During the Boer War the sympathy of all the powers was with the Boers, and England keenly felt the disadvantages of isolation. With which of the powers should she come to terms in order to confront the others with an ally? In 1901, England began negotiating for an alliance with Germany, but her efforts came to naught chiefly because Germany feared that such an alliance would disturb her relations with Russia. When the German navy appeared, England became acutely aware of the grave danger that lay in a Germany, already supreme on land, energetically striving to be a great sea power. She thereupon decided to emerge from her isolation and enter into agreements with France and Russia who were urging her to come to their side. England's decision brought about so great a change in international relations that it might well be called a diplomatic revolution.

An extraordinary change took place in the relations between England and France. Always had they been enemies; their mutual

dislike and distrust had become proverbial. When France entered on her career of expansion in North Africa she encountered England as her rival. Memories of the colonial empire lost in the eighteenth century mingled with the memories of Waterloo, and the traditional hatred between the two nations flared forth. When the situation in Egypt and in the Sudan became aggravated, a powerful party appeared in the French government that favored a *rapprochement* with Germany in order better to pursue an anti-British policy.

A great crisis arose during the Fashoda affair [1] in 1898. when France and England were on the brink of war. However, peace

counsels prevailed, and the French Foreign Minister, Gabriel Hanotaux, was compelled to resign. His successor was Théophile Delcassé, one of the ablest diplomats of his day, who remained in office for seven years despite many ministerial changes. Delcassé was passionately anti-German, and favored friendly relations with England in order to bring her to the side of the Dual Alliance. Once the British Empire swung to the side

[1] See page 652.

of France and Russia, the Triple Alliance would be outmatched; Germany especially would find herself in the dangerous position, in the event of war, of being blockaded by the British fleet and of being encircled by Russian and French armies.

After much negotiation, an important treaty was concluded, in 1904, which liquidated the affairs of England and France in North Africa.[1] It was negotiated by Delcassé, Paul Cambon,   *The Entente* the French ambassador to England, and Lord Lans-   *cordiale* downe, the British Foreign Minister.   This treaty became the basis of the *Entente cordiale*, or a friendly understanding between the two powers to act together in foreign affairs.   Although no treaty of alliance was signed, as in the cases of the Dual and Triple Alliances, the *Entente cordiale* had the practical effect of one; in all the diplomatic crises that followed, France and England solidly supported each other.   Fear of Germany had ended the ancient feud between them.

(c) ENGLAND AND RUSSIA

As France was England's traditional enemy in western Europe, Russia was her traditional enemy in eastern Europe.   During the entire nineteenth century Russia and England met as   Enmity be- bitter opponents in the Near East.   Disappointed at   tween Eng- the outcome of the Russo-Turkish War, Russia had   land and sought to revenge herself on England by threatening   Russia India through Afghanistan and Tibet.   There was great indignation in England at Russia's machinations in the Middle East. Kipling denounced Russia as "a bear that walks like a man"; and Chamberlain warned England to beware of relations with Russia, as "he who sups with the devil must have a long spoon."

Fear of Germany had driven England to the side of France; it was now driving her to the side of Russia.   She no longer feared Russia's presence in Constantinople because the Suez   The Triple Canal made possible the safety of her Imperial com-   Entente munications.   She still feared Russian threats to India through Afghanistan.   English and Russian differences in the Middle East were settled by the Treaty of 1907 negotiated by Sir Edward Grey and Alexander Isvolsky.[2]   England was now joined to France and Russia in what was called the Triple Entente, which was based on the Dual Alliance, the Treaty of 1904 between England and

[1] See page 653.   [2] See page 633.

France, the *Entente cordiale*, and the Treaty of 1907 between England and Russia.

A wedge was driven into the Triple Alliance by Delcassé, who succeeded in virtually detaching Italy. According to the agree-

Italy drifts from Triple Alliance

ment of 1902, France granted to Italy a "free hand" in Tripoli, in return for a "free hand" by Italy to France in Morocco. Italy also promised not to join Germany and Austria in an attack on France. Friendly relations were now resumed between the two nations who had been estranged since the separate peace that Napoleon III had made with Austria. Italy's loyalty to the Triple Alliance was still more weakened, in 1909, by the Racconigi Agreement between herself and Russia according to which the latter agreed to the annexation of Tripoli in return for Italy's support of Russia in the question of the Straits. Italy was now in both camps, in case of a crisis she would have the advantage of being able to choose the side that offered her most.

Germany was furious at what she called the *Einkreisungspolitik* (encirclement policy) of her enemies, for the diplomatic revolution

Europe divided into two hostile groups

resulted in her being almost entirely surrounded by unfriendly powers. Europe was now divided into two great coalitions, the Triple Alliance and the Triple Entente, who faced each other threateningly; should a dispute arise which involved any member of either combination, a world conflagration might be precipitated.

MILITARY AND NAVAL PREPAREDNESS

Under such circumstances it behooved each nation to be well prepared for conflict; and an armament race began which trans-

Origin of conscription

formed Europe into an armed camp. A new military and naval system was adopted which was based upon conscription, scientific armament, and the dreadnaught. The idea of universal military service came with the *levée en masse* during the wars of the French Revolution, when all men were requisitioned to repel the invaders. Hitherto, armies in time of peace had been small, composed of professional soldiers and volunteers. In the event of war large armies were obtained through the application of the draft, generally to men of the lower classes. Conscription, or military service in time of peace, was originated by Prussia in preparation for the War of Liberation against Napoleon. Prussian armies, based on conscription, had proved their success on the battle fields of Sadowa and Sedan, and the new system was adopted in one form or another by nearly every nation in Europe. England, alone of the great powers, refused to adopt conscription; being an island, she could best defend herself by means of a navy. The conscript was "called to the colors" generally at the age of twenty; his active service lasted from one to three years, after which he was in the reserve until the age of forty-five.

Almost as important as conscription was the great change that took place in armament through the application of science to war. The simple rifle and cannon of former days gave place to highly complicated machinery of destruction, the handling of which required expert technical knowledge. A modern army is a highly scientific organism, demanding a great and varied knowledge of chemistry, physics, mathematics, sanitation, and other sciences for its efficient management. Generals are no longer the dashing figures of old, gallantly leading charges against the enemy, but highly trained technical experts in the science of modern war. The part of the common soldier is more simple now than it was in former days; he has become a cog in a great and complicated machine, the smooth running of which is essential to success. What the new military system demanded was a large number of men ready to spring into their places and a small number of highly trained officers to lead them. Hence, "preparedness" was necessary, as an army of raw volunteers, no matter how brave and patriotic, would be no match for troops trained scientifically. To maintain a large standing army and, particularly, to provide for its equipment, was enormously expensive. But the nations regarded the expense as an insurance against the greater evil of war, and bore the heavy burden of an "armed peace."

Application of science to war

Naval warfare also underwent a revolution. When the naval rivalry between England and Germany began, the English fleet was reorganized and completely remodeled. In 1906, a new type of warship was launched by England, the Dreadnought, an immense floating fortress made of steel and equipped with heavy guns. As Germany's army was the model for other nations so was England's navy; the number of dreadnoughts that a nation possessed was the measure of its naval strength. In order to remain "mistress of the seas," England's policy was the Two-Power standard; namely, to have a navy as large as that of any two other powers combined. A keen race in

Naval rivalry between England and Germany

naval armaments began between England and Germany which continued fast and furious. Many efforts were made to limit armaments by having both nations agree to a naval holiday; but these efforts were fruitless. England refused to accept any plan which took away from her the control of the seas, and Germany refused to reduce her naval armament unless England broke with the Entente.

THE PEACE MOVEMENT

The system of "armed peace" proved a staggering burden to all the powers.[1] More and more taxes were levied to maintain it,

Pacifism

which produced deep discontent among all classes. A widespread peace movement made its appearance with the object of substituting arbitration for war as a mode of settling disputes between nations. Alfred Nobel, the Swedish inventor of dynamite, left part of his large fortune to be awarded in annual prizes to those of any nation who rendered the greatest service to science, to idealistic literature, and to the cause of peace. The American ironmaster, Andrew Carnegie, spent large sums in furthering the peace propaganda. In 1898, there appeared a book, *The Future of War*, by Ivan Bloch, a Polish Jew, which created a deep impression. The author asserted that war, under modern conditions, was impossible; it was bound to lead to universal bankruptcy and to starvation. Another well-known peace book was *The Great Illusion*, by an Englishman, Norman Angell, who argued that modern social and economic conditions make military victories and defeats "illusions" because the essential economic life of a country remains undisturbed even though it might be conquered.

Support of the peace movement came from an unexpected quarter, from the Tsar of Russia. In 1898, Nicholas II issued a state-

The Hague Peace Conference

ment suggesting that an international convention be called to limit "the progressive development of existing armaments" which was ruinous to all countries. It resulted in the first Peace Conference at The Hague, at which twenty-six nations were represented. Hopes ran high when this parliament of man convened; to enthusiastic pacifists the dream of

---

[1] During the years 1872 to 1912, the military and naval expenditure of Germany increased 335 per cent; of Russia, 214 per cent; of Italy, 185 per cent; of England, 180 per cent; of Austria-Hungary, 155 per cent; and of France, 133 per cent.

universal peace was about to be realized.   It soon became evident, however, that the Conference would accomplish little because national rivalries did not abate even at this peace meeting.   Germany blocked every effort toward a reduction of military armament which would reduce her military power.   England opposed the giving of immunity to private property at sea which would reduce the effectiveness of her naval supremacy.   A second Peace Conference met in 1907, representing forty-four nations, but with no better results regarding the limitation of armament.

However, some things were accomplished by the Hague Conferences.   Humane rules for the conduct of warfare were adopted; the use of poison gas and the bombardment of cities The Hague from the air were forbidden; and the rules of the Court Geneva Convention [1] concerning the treatment of the wounded were adopted.   More important was the establishment of a Permanent Court of Arbitration at The Hague to which the nations might go, if they so wished, for the settlement of their disputes. The Hague Court was not really a judicial body with a definite jurisdiction and power to enforce its decisions; it was a panel of jurists, selected by the nations, from which disputants could choose a board of arbitrators.

The Hague Conferences failed of their chief purpose because the spirit of competitive nationalism was stronger than that of cooperative internationalism.   The Hague Court did Failure of settle a number of minor disputes; in important mat- the peace ters, the nations preferred war to arbitration.   The movement peace movement was followed by the outbreak of wars, the Russo-Japanese, the Turco-Italian, the Balkan Wars, and finally the World War.   It was plainly evident that the nations had no serious intentions to abolish war.

The leading characteristic of the system of international relations was the prevalence of secret diplomacy.   Democracy was the rule in domestic affairs where policies were openly discussed Secret and openly acted upon.   But in no country of Europe diplomacy did parliament control foreign affairs, which were conducted exclusively by the cabinet.   Not even all of the ministers had a part in diplomatic arrangements, generally only the Premier and the

[1] In 1864, an international convention, inspired by a Swiss, Jean Henri Dunant, met in Geneva which agreed to treat as neutral the hospital corps and equipment of every army.   It became known as the "Red Cross," and societies were organized in every country to carry out the rules of the Geneva Convention.

Foreign Minister. In some countries, notably in Germany and Russia, the monarch himself took a hand in the game, and sometimes committed the nation to serious responsibilities. Diplomatic officials were generally men of aristocratic birth and association, far removed from the democratic masses in ideals and sympathies. The fate of nations was in the hands of irresponsible diplomats who might be swayed by all sorts of motives in their conduct of foreign affairs.

All diplomacy was secret, but there were various degrees of secrecy. Some treaties were made in secret, but their terms were **Dishonest methods** published in full; others were published, but not in full, there being "secret annexes"; others were "secret treaties," that were not published at all and were known only to a few; and, finally, there was the *entente*, or "understanding" to act in common, but without definite agreements. Because of its secret methods diplomacy became a labyrinth of trickery. To tell the truth was not considered "diplomatic," and an ambassador was once defined as an honest man sent abroad to lie in the interests of his country. A sworn ally was not necessarily a loyal friend; not infrequently would a nation make secret agreements with the enemies of its ally.

International relations were based on the principle of complete national sovereignty. Each power had the right to do as it pleased **International anarchy** in all matters, to make war and peace, to make commercial agreements, to enter into alliances, and to accept or reject proposals made by international congresses or bodies. There existed no international authority that had the right to make decisions and the power to enforce them. International "law" existed, a body of rules and regulations governing international intercourse both in war and in peace; but the nations were answerable for any infraction of international law to the "judgment of mankind," not to the arm of the law. This system of "international anarchy" produced a sense of dread among the peoples of Europe over whom the clouds of war constantly hovered.

THE CRISES

The outbreak of the World War was preceded by a number of crises. Now they would arise in the Balkans, now in North Africa, the chief storm centers of European diplomacy; every time a crisis was tided over by means of diplomatic bargainings and "compensations," it was followed by an increase in armament.

In the beginning of the twentieth century France and Germany became bitter rivals in Morocco. When the Treaty of 1904[1] was signed by France and England, it looked as if the fate of Algeria and of Tunis would soon befall Morocco whose ruler, the Sultan, was unable to withstand foreign aggression. But he found a powerful supporter in Germany, who came out in favor of preserving the integrity of Morocco. The rivalry in North Africa became so intense that it strained to the breaking point the whole system of European diplomacy, though the issue was between France and Germany. Opposed to Delcassé, the chief actor on the scene, was Baron von Holstein, an official in the German Foreign Office who really directed the foreign policies of the Empire of which the Kaiser was only the mouthpiece. In 1905, Holstein determined that Germany should intervene in Morocco in order to weaken the *entente* between France and England. On his suggestion the Kaiser landed at Tangier, and paid a visit to the Sultan of Morocco whom he pointedly recognized as an independent sovereign. His act was an open challenge to France. Germany demanded that the Moroccan question be submitted to an international conference for settlement. The outcome of the crisis was a diplomatic triumph for Germany, as France backed down and agreed to Holstein's plan. The crisis led to the fall of the militant Delcassé, who was compelled to resign his position as Foreign Minister.

The Moroccan crisis of 1905

An international conference met at Algeciras, in 1906, to decide the fate of Morocco. There Germany found to her chagrin that France's claims were supported by Italy, England, Spain, and Russia; only Austria was on her side. It was now clear to Germany that the new trend in diplomatic affairs was decidedly against her. The Dual Alliance and the *Entente cordiale* proved stronger than the Triple Alliance. Holstein was driven from office, as he was blamed for Germany's diplomatic defeat because the Treaty of Algeciras[2] was regarded as a triumph for France. Germany was now convinced that her interests would suffer at the hands of international conferences which would be controlled by her opponents.

The Algeciras conference

The next crisis arose in the Balkans. At the beginning of the

[1] See page 653.   [2] See page 653.

twentieth century the diplomatic situation in the Balkans was
Serbia bars   favorable to the Triple Alliance. Turkey had fallen
the way   under German influence. Rumania, under King
Charles who was a Hohenzollern, was strongly pro-German.
Serbia, under King Alexander, was closely tied to Austria who
virtually dictated the foreign policy. All was well from the German-
Austrian point of view till the assassination of Alexander in 1903.
His successor, King Peter, showed a decided leaning toward
Russia. Great alarm was felt by the Teutonic powers at the growing friendship between Serbia and Russia; by Germany because
she feared a barrier across her "corridor" to Asiatic Turkey through
the Berlin–Bagdad Railway systems; and by Austria because she
feared a Pan-Slavic agitation which might disintegrate her empire
as it had disintegrated Turkey.

It was to the interest of both to crush any Balkan state that
played into the hands of Russia. They, therefore, determined to
The Balkan   deliver their first blow at Pan-Slavism before Russia
crisis of 1908 could recover from the effects of the Revolution of
1905 and from her defeat by Japan. In 1908, Baron von Aehren-
thal, the Austrian Foreign Minister, announced the annexation of
Bosnia-Herzegovina to Austria, thus violating the Treaty of Berlin.
Serbia strenuously protested against Austria's action; it meant the
permanent exclusion of Yugo-Slav territory from "Greater Serbia,"
the goal of her national ambitions. A crisis arose which involved
Russia and Germany. The Russian Foreign Minister, Isvolsky,
had tried to make a bargain with Austria promising the consent of
Russia to Austria's annexation of Bosnia-Herzegovina on condition
that Austria support Russia's demand for the opening of the
Straits to her warships. But the bargain fell through because of
the opposition of England and France. Russia then veered threateningly to the side of Serbia. Germany now came forward as a
mediator and induced Russia to yield to Austria. Later, the Kaiser
boasted that he had come to the support of Austria like a "knight
in shining armor." Russia was in no condition to fight; her
finances were badly involved and her army was in the process of
reorganization. Serbia, deprived of Russia's support, was obliged
to yield to Austria whom she now hated more bitterly than ever.
The crisis of 1908 ended in a diplomatic triumph for Germany and
Austria.

Morocco again became the scene of a crisis. France was determined to annex the country, and continued her "peaceful penetration" which provoked an uprising against the Sultan. The Moroccan crisis To aid the Sultan, a French army, in 1911, occupied of 1911 Fez; and it refused to leave "until order was restored." Germany denounced the action of France as a violation of the Treaty of Algeciras, and dispatched a warship to Agadir, ostensibly to defend German interests but really as a warning to France. Feeling rose high in both countries, and Europe was again trembling on the brink of war. Germany wanted to know the full extent of England's sympathy with France, and demanded that the matter be settled by France and herself exclusively. England now sprang to the side of France. Lloyd George, speaking for the British government, came out with a resounding statement in which he declared that if peace could be maintained only "by allowing Britain to be treated, where her interests were vitally affected, as if she were of no account in the Cabinet of nations, then I say emphatically that peace at that price would be a humiliation intolerable for a great country like ours to endure." The Entente was in perfect working order, and Germany was compelled to yield. The treaty that followed recognized France's hegemony in Morocco.[1] There was intense feeling in Germany against the Entente, which was denounced as a conspiracy of jealous powers bent upon hampering the growth of the Fatherland. Equally intense was the feeling in France, where the struggle over Morocco revived, in all its bitterness, the *revanche*. Secret naval conventions were signed, one by France and Russia providing for the coöperation of their naval forces in case of war; and another by France and England providing for a similar object. The Entente was now so greatly strengthened that it was virtually an alliance.

The prelude to the World War was the crisis that arose during the Balkan Wars (1912–13). It came as a result of a clash between Austria and Serbia, when the latter sought an outlet The Balkan to the Adriatic. Ports on the Albanian coast were crisis of occupied by Serbian and Montenegrin armies. Aus- 1912–13 tria demanded the evacuation of these ports, and a crisis arose that involved Russia and Germany. However, the matter was settled peacefully, due to the intervention of England and Germany. The ports were evacuated, and became part of a newly created state, Albania. Hatred between Slav and Teuton became more intense

[1] See page 654.

than ever.   In Austria, Serbia was regarded as another Piedmont that aimed to be the corner-stone of a great state at the expense of the Dual Monarchy.   In Serbia, Austria was regarded as the deadly enemy of Yugo-Slav nationalism.

Russia and Serbia were grimly determined to settle accounts with the Teutonic powers on some future day when conditions would be more favorable to them.   In the meantime they began a vigorous Pan-Slavic propaganda among the Yugo-Slavs in Austria with the object of weakening and even of disintegrating the Dual Monarchy.   The Triple Alliance was seriously weakened by the Turco-Italian War, as a result of which Italy gained Tripoli.   Her support of the Alliance became very doubtful, now that she had made territorial gains with the consent of the Triple Entente.   She was taking "extra dances" outside the circle of her legal partners.   Austria and Germany consequently drew more closely together.   Austria, fearful of disintegration, clung desperately to her mighty Teutonic sister; Germany, seeing in Austria her only friend, determined to support her to the utmost.

Hatred between Slav and Teuton

So tense was the diplomatic atmosphere in Europe that it needed but another incident to let loose a war of the nations.   Increased military and naval preparations were made during 1913.   France increased military service from two to three years.   Germany increased her army.   England concentrated almost her entire navy in home waters, and France concentrated hers in the Mediterranean.   Russia extended her strategic railways.   Austria reorganized her army.   The Triple Alliance and the Triple Entente were now face to face awaiting the next crisis. It was not long in coming.

Preparations for war

REFERENCES

SOURCES:

After the German Revolution of 1918 the newly established Republic began the publication of the secret documents in its diplomatic archives. During 1922–27 forty volumes appeared under the general title, *Die Grosse Politik der europäischen Kabinette, 1871–1914,* edited by J. Lepsius and others.

The British government also began the publication of secret diplomatic documents in the series, *British Documents on the Origins of the War, 1898–1914,* edited by G. P. Gooch and H. Temperley.

Secret Treaties of Austria-Hungary, 1879–1914, edited by A. F. Pribram,

English edition in 2 volumes by A. C. Coolidge (1920–21); *The Willy-Nicky Correspondence* (1918), consisting of telegrams exchanged between William II and Nicholas II during 1904–07, edited by H. Bernstein.

GENERAL:

The most authoritative studies of European diplomacy since 1870 are the works of W. L. Langer, *The Franco-Russian Alliance, 1890–1894* (1929), *European Alliances and Alignments, 1871–1890* (1931), and *The Diplomacy of Imperialism, 1890–1902*, 2 vols. (1935); S. B. Fay, *The Origins of the World War*, 2 vols. (1928), vol. I; A. Debidour, *Histoire diplomatique de l'Europe depuis le Congrès de Berlin jusq'à nos jours*, 2 vols. (1917); and G. P. Gooch, *History of Modern Europe, 1878–1919* (1923) and *Before the War*, 2 vols. (1938).

ENGLAND'S FOREIGN POLICIES:

Sir A. W. Ward and G. P. Gooch (editors), *The Cambridge History of British Foreign Policy 1783–1919* (1922–23), vol. I treats of periods 1783–1815, vol. II, 1815–1866, and vol. III, 1866–1919; H. David, *Englands Europäische Politik* (1924); G. P. Gooch and J. H. B. Masterman, *A Century of British Foreign Policy* (1917). On Anglo-German rivalry: C. Sarolea, *The Anglo-German Problem* (1912); and R. J. Sontag, *Germany and England* (1938).

GERMANY'S FOREIGN POLICY:

J. V. Fuller, *Bismarck's Diplomacy at its Zenith* (1922), covers period of formation of Triple Alliance; F. Rachfahl, *Deutschland und die Weltpolitik, 1871–1914* (1923), H. Plehn, *Bismarck's auswärtige Politik nach der Reichsgründung* (1920), E. Brandenburg, *From Bismarck to the World War*, translated from the German (1927) are the best general surveys by German authorities; Count Ernest zu Reventlow, *Deutschland's auswärtige Politik 1888–1913* (1914), biased view by a Pan-Germanist; P. Rohrbach, *German World Policies*, translated from the German (1915), a patriotic defense of Germany's policy from economic viewpoint; O. Hammann, *The World Policy of Germany, 1890–1912*, translated from the German (1927), by former chief of the press bureau in the German Foreign Office; A. C. Coolidge, *The Origins of the Triple Alliance* (ed. 1926); W. H. Dawson, *The German Empire 1867–1914*, 2 vols. (1919), vol. II deals largely with foreign affairs; E. T. S. Dugdale (ed.), *Bismarck's Relations with England* (1929), translations of diplomatic documents.

FRANCE'S FOREIGN POLICY:

G. Michon, *The Franco-Russian Alliance, 1891–1917*, trans. from the French (1929), the Dual Alliance, with respect to the World War; A. Tardieu, *France and the Alliances* (1908), trans. from the French; Baron S. A. Korff, *Russia's Foreign Relations during the Last Half Century* (1922), much about the Dual Alliance; G. H. Stuart, *French Foreign Policy, 1898–1914*

(1921), brief survey; W. L. Langer, *The Franco-Russian Alliance* (1929), latest and most authoritative study.

MILITARISM:

F. von Bernhardi, *Germany and the Next War*, translated from the German (1912), a plea for war as a "biological necessity" by a German military philosopher; J. A. Cramb, *The Origins and Destiny of Imperial Britain and Nineteenth-Century Europe* (ed. 1915), a chauvinistic plea for British imperialism; A. T. Mahan, *Armaments and Arbitration: or the Place of Force in the International Relations of States* (1912), a criticism of pacifism by the distinguished writer on naval affairs; E. F. Henderson, *Germany's Fighting Machine* (1914); A. S. Hurd and H. Castle, *German Sea Power, its Rise, Progress, and Economic Basis* (1913), a good account from the English point of view; J. Leyland, *The Royal Navy* (1914); A. J. Marder, *The Anatomy of British Sea Power* (1940).

PACIFISM:

Norman Angell, *The Great Illusion* (ed. 1914), a highly original study of the effects of war, see page 698; by the same author, *Foundations of International Polity* (1914); I. S. Bloch, *The Future of War in its Technical, Economic, and Political Relations*, translated from the Russian (ed. 1902), see page 698; E. B. Krehbiel, *Nationalism, War, and Society* (1916), a syllabus of international relations and of the peace movement; Nicholas Murray Butler, *International Mind: an Argument for the Judicial Settlement of International Disputes* (1913), a plea for international arbitration; Bertrand Russell, *Justice in War-Time* (1916), a criticism of diplomacy from the point of view of an English pacifist; on the Hague Peace Conferences: J. B. Scott, *The Hague Peace Conferences of 1899 and 1907*, 2 vols. (1909); W. I. Hull, *The Two Hague Peace Conferences and their Contributions to International Law* (1908); J. W. Foster, *Arbitration and The Hague Court* (1904); and G. G. Wilson (ed.), *The Hague Arbitration Cases* (1915).

INTERNATIONALISM:

On international organization: J. C. Faries, *The Rise of Internationalism* (1915); F. B. Sayre, *Experiments in International Administration* (1918); P. B. Potter, *An Introduction to the Study of International Organization* (1922); and Jessie W. Hughan, *A Study of International Government* (1923). On economic aspects: W. S. Culbertson, *International Economic Policies* (1925); A. Viallate, *Economic Imperialism and International Relations* (1923); and C. Hodges, *The Background of International Relations* (1926), a social interpretation, stresses economic and cultural aspects of internationalism. P. T. Moon, *Syllabus on International Relations* (1925), an invaluable guide to problems and methods, contains excellent bibliography.

SPECIAL TOPICS:

On the evils of secret diplomacy, E. D. Morel, *Ten Years of Secret Diplomacy* (ed. 1920) and P. S. Reinsch, *Secret Diplomacy* (1922); L

Dominian, *The Frontiers of Language and Nationality* (1917), one of the best studies of the problem of nationalities; A. J. Toynbee, *Nationality and the War* (1915); C. J. H. Hayes, *Essays on Nationalism* (1926), criticism of nationalism as a new universal religion that is hostile to Christianity, original and interesting volume.

ADDITIONAL REFERENCES

In 1929 the French government began the publication of diplomatic documents for the period 1871–1914 in *Documents Diplomatiques Français, 1871–1914, Publiés par la Commission de Publication relatifs aux Origines de la Guerre de 1914*; T. S. Dugdale (ed.), *The German Diplomatic Documents, 1871–1914*, selected and translated, 4 vols. (1928–31); *Oesterreich-Ungarns Aussenpolitik, von der bosnischen krise, 1908 bis zum Kriegesausbruch, 1914*, 9 vols. (1930); Sir J. W. Headlam-Morley, *Studies in Diplomatic History* (1930); H. Feis, *Europe, the World's Banker, 1870–1914* (1930); N. B. Giffen, *Fashoda: The Incident and its Diplomatic Setting* (1930); E. N. Anderson, *The First Moroccan Crisis, 1904–1906* (1930); R. B. Mowat, *The Concert of Europe* (1930); W. L. Langer, *European Alliances and Alignments, 1871–1890* (1931) and *The Diplomacy of Imperialism, 1890–1902*, 2 vols. (1935); F. L. Schuman, *War and Diplomacy in the French Republic* (1931); C. W. Porter, *The Career of Theophile Delcassé* (1936); A. F. Pribram, *England and the International Policy of the European Great Powers, 1871–1914* (1931); E. L. Woodward, *Great Britain and the German Navy* (1935); O. H. Wedel, *Austro-German Diplomatic Relations, 1908–1914* (1932); E. Staley, *Raw Materials in Peace and War* (1937); R. J. Sontag, *European Diplomatic History, 1871–1932* (1933); P. Knaplund, *Gladstone's Foreign Policy* (1935); J. A. Spender, *Fifty Years of Europe* (1933); R. W. Seton-Watson, *Britain in Europe 1789–1914* (1937); E. M. Carroll, *Germany and the Great Powers, 1866–1914* (1938).

Deutsches. The Founders of Modern Political Science (1917), one of the best studies of the problem of nationalism; A. E. Zimmern, Nationality and Government (1918); C. J. H. Hayes, Essays on Nationalism (1926), criticism of nationalism; H. A. Gibbons, Nationalism and Internationalism, theoretical and historical.

CHAPTER XXXIV

THE CAUSES OF THE WORLD WAR

FUNDAMENTAL CAUSES

THE roots of the World War lay deep in the history of the nineteenth century. Being largely the creation of the French and Industrial Revolutions, the Europe of that period struggled to solve the new political and economic problems that confronted it. A century of revolution and reform did not entirely solve these problems, and some of the most difficult ones became the heritage of the twentieth century. Only a brief summary can now be made of these unsolved problems.

Nationalism. The signal triumphs of nationalism during the nineteenth century were the unification of Germany and of Italy. Central as well as western Europe now consisted of nationalized states. But eastern Europe was still a region of heterogeneous empires, the Russian, the Austrian, and the Ottoman, in all of which "submerged" peoples were struggling to achieve nationhood. In Austria-Hungary and Turkey the violation of the principle of nationality was particularly flagrant; for in each of these empires the ruling race constituted a minority of the total population. The existence of the Austrian and Ottoman Empires, with their heterogeneous populations threatened the peace of Europe; sooner or later the various subject races were bound to rise in revolution or to appeal to their kinsmen in other lands to liberate them.

During the period 1870 to 1914, the spirit of nationalism rose to a greater height than at any other time in history. It may be truly said that nationalism was a new religion that roused the deepest emotions of mankind. Old nations such as England and France became more conscious than ever of their great place in the world. The new nations, Germany and Italy, inspired by their heroic unification movements, were convinced that they had a special "mission" in the world. The "submerged" peoples began creating legends of their one-time greatness, and asserted their superiority over those who ruled them. The spirit of fanatical nationalism boded ill for the peace of mankind.

Democracy. Popular government had made great strides during the nineteenth century. Feudalism had entirely disappeared, and nobles, peasants, bourgeois, and workingmen were citizens, all equal before the law. But the world was not "safe for democracy." Two powerful states, Russia and Germany, continued to adhere to the autocratic system, though they possessed constitutional forms. Tsarism in Russia had triumphed in the Revolution of 1905. Kaiserism in Germany was much more efficient than tsarism, and consequently much more dangerous to popular liberties. It had made Germany so powerful that all Europe stood in fear and admiration. At its head and profoundly influencing its policies was William II, unstable, irresponsible, whose egomania bordered on insanity. The autocrat of Russia, Nicholas II, was weak, ignorant, and feeble-minded to the point of imbecility. And the welfare not only of Germany and Russia but of all Europe might depend on decisions of these two monarchs. Truly a startling situation in the enlightened, progressive twentieth century!

Colonial imperialism. In spite of the rapid advance of modern industry, the economic life of the world at the beginning of the twentieth century was far from uniform. Industrially, England, Germany, and the United States were highly developed; France and Italy maintained an even balance between agriculture and manufacturing; much of eastern Europe was in the early stages of the Industrial Revolution; most of Asia was hardly touched by modern industry; and Africa was for the most part primitive. What was to be the relation between the advanced and the backward countries? Inevitably the hunger for territory and for profits, and the desire to make the backward regions an outlet for their surplus products and surplus capital, drove the advanced nations into a policy of annexation. There began a mad race for colonies, which revived old hostilities, intensified national hatreds, and roused new ambitions that, more than once, brought the world to the verge of war.

Rivalry of England and Germany. After 1890 there began a rivalry between England and Germany that caused an estrangement between these two nations. In England fear was expressed that German competition was driving English goods from the markets of the world. In Germany there was great concern as to England's plans for an Imperial customs union which, it was believed, would shut out German goods. In spite of the fact that both nations were progressing economically, and were each other's good customer, each believed that the ruin of the other would destroy a dangerous trade rival. An even greater source of discord was the appearance of a German navy. England believed that it was a direct challenge to her position of "mistress of the seas" and a threat to the very existence of her Empire. Jealousy bred suspicion, and suspicion hatred, with the result that the English and Germans, friends for centuries, became deadly enemies.

Disputed territory. There were certain regions in Europe whose status was not regarded as permanent. France would not forget Alsace-Lorraine and waited for her opportunity to regain the "lost provinces." *Italia irredenta* stirred the national spirit of Italy who hoped to complete her unification by annexing the Italian regions of Austria. Russia's ambition to acquire Constantinople was bound to draw her into any Balkan conflict. Serbia refused to give up hope of "redeeming" Bosnia-Herzegovina. And Bulgaria still dreamed of the "Greater Bulgaria," promised by the unfulfilled treaty of San Stefano.

"International anarchy." The nations of Europe did not succeed in establishing an effective system of international relations that promoted peace and guaranteed national safety. They all regarded war as an "instrument of national policy." The Congresses of Vienna, Paris, and Berlin, and the "Concert" of Europe, all had special purposes in view; hence, they did not function permanently and continuously. Each nation felt that it lived in a jungle-world, and likely to be attacked; therefore, it must be wary, or, better still, show its power by attacking its neighbors. Aggrandizement was the supreme test of national success; to conquer and annex territory brought respect and admiration. But none felt strong enough to be alone, either in defense or in attack; hence, the need for allies. Necessarily diplomatic arrangements had to be secret, otherwise plans would go awry. After 1870 the system of military alliances, inaugurated by Bismarck, resulted in dividing Europe into two coalitions, the Triple Alliance and the Triple Entente. Once a crisis arose the methods of "international anarchy" might tide it over by diplomatic negotiations. But they were entirely useless in the more important matter of preventing a crisis from arising.

IMMEDIATE CAUSES

On June 28, 1914, the world was startled by news from the obscure little capital of Bosnia, Sarajevo. The Archduke Francis

Ferdinand, heir to the Hapsburg throne, and his wife were assassinated in its streets. The motive for the murder was political; it was committed by two young Bosnian patriots as a protest against Austria's attitude toward the Yugo-Slavs.

Assassination of Francis Ferdinand

There was great indignation throughout Austria and Germany, where the assassination was regarded as a Slav challenge to the Teutonic world. Austria was convinced that the plot to murder the Archduke was aided and abetted, if not actually planned, by the Serbian government, and that it was the culmination of conspiracies organized by patriotic societies that were encouraged by Serbia in her campaign to destroy the Dual Monarchy. Investigations after the war revealed the fact that some high Serbian officials did know of the plot, but the complicity of the Serbian government was not established. Austria now determined to deal severely with Serbia, and she prepared to go to the length of suppressing her small but troublesome neighbor by force of arms. Realizing, however, that, as in 1908, Russia might intervene, she made sure to get the backing of Germany. On July 5 the Kaiser and Chancellor von Bethmann-Hollweg assured Count von Berchtold, the Austrian Foreign Minister, that Austria could "count on it with certainty that Germany would stand behind her as an ally and friend"; and that she would support her in whatever steps she (Austria) should take in her dealings with Serbia.

Austria determines to punish Serbia

The Austrian government, having what it regarded as a "blank check" from Germany, determined to push matters to the point of war. On July 23, Berchtold dispatched an ultimatum to Serbia the tone of which was so harsh and the terms so hard as to make it unacceptable to any nation jealous of its honor and independence. The ultimatum declared that Serbia had broken her promise "to live on good neighborly terms" by encouraging an unfriendly propaganda aimed against the Dual Monarchy, and it charged that Serbian officers had planned the Sarajevo crime in Belgrade and had provided the assassins with weapons for that purpose. The ultimatum then made several peremptory demands, the most important of which were: (1) that the government of Serbia officially condemn the anti-Austrian propaganda by her citizens; (2) that it suppress all publications and societies which incite hatred and contempt of the Dual Mon-

The ultimatum

archy; (3) that all anti-Austrian teachers and books be eliminated from the public schools; (4) that the public officials implicated in the anti-Austrian propaganda be dismissed; (5) that two Serbian officers, named in the ultimatum, be arrested at once; (6) that Serbia accept the "collaboration" of Austrian officials in the sup-. pression of the anti-Austrian propaganda within her borders; and (7) that Serbia accept the help of Austrian officials in the investiga- tion of the Sarajevo crime.   A reply was demanded within forty- eight hours.

Serbia's reply was conciliatory in tone.   It recalled her pacific attitude toward Austria during the Balkan Wars, and declared
Serbia's reply that, although not responsible for the activities of private individuals and societies against the Dual Monarchy, she was willing to condemn them officially.   Serbia was also willing to accept the demands of the ultimatum except those referring to the collaboration of Austrian officials which, she declared, was a violation of her sovereignty.   If Austria found her reply unsatisfactory, Serbia said that she was willing to refer the matter for arbitration to the Hague Court or to the powers. Germany as the backer of Austria and Russia as the backer of Serbia were naturally interested in the situation.   Germany considered the reply satisfactory.   The Kaiser declared that Serbia had capitulated in a humiliating manner, and therefore cause for war no longer existed.   He suggested that Austria occupy Belgrade as "hostage territory" until Serbia had fulfilled her promises.   The Russian Foreign Minister, Sazonov, also considered Serbia's reply satisfactory, and proposed to negotiate with Austria on that basis.

But the Austrian government refused to accept Serbia's reply. It was determined on war, and therefore would not be satisfied with
Problem of "localiza- tion" a diplomatic victory.   Even before the time limit of the ultimatum had expired, Austria began mobilizing on Serbia's frontier.   An intense feeling arose in the Tsar's dominions in favor of intervention on behalf of the "little Slav brother."   Russia threatened to mobilize against Austria the moment Austrian armies invaded Serbia.   Because of the system of alliances, Russia's intervention would create a great European crisis.   In order to prevent such a situation from arising, Sir Edward Grey, the British Foreign Minister, on July 26, proposed a conference of Germany, France, England, and Italy to mediate

in the Austro-Serb dispute. Germany refused to accept Grey's plan on the ground that the Austro-Serbian conflict concerned those two nations alone; it was therefore to be localized. Moreover, Germany believed that she would be outvoted in such a conference, as Italy was now in the orbit of the Triple Entente. Were Russia to make a move a rattle of the German sword would cause her to back down. "Localization" meant that Austria would crush Serbia, while Germany held back Russia.

The situation became more threatening as Russia prepared to mobilize. Germany began to fear that the Austro-Serbian conflict might not be localized. When, on July 27, Grey again proposed mediation, Bethmann-Hollweg wrote to Berchtold urging the consideration of Grey's proposal, saying that to refuse to consider it would cause a belief that Austria and Germany were instigating a general war. But Berchtold failed to reply promptly. On July 28, Austria declared war on Serbia. On the following day Berchtold finally replied to Bethmann-Hollweg saying that he could not consider Grey's proposal because it was "overtaken by events." The Austrian declaration of war was a crucial event in the great crisis. It was now plain that Austria was opposed to a peaceful solution of the problem. And behind Austria was Germany.

Austria declares war against Serbia

Sazonov had suggested a plan of direct negotiations between Austria and Russia. Bethmann-Hollweg advised Berchtold to agree to the plan, but the latter refused to take the advice. In the opinion of the Chancellor, Austria's refusal was a grave mistake. "We are indeed ready to fulfill our duty as an ally; we must, however, refuse to be drawn into a world conflagration through Austria-Hungary's not respecting our advice." In spite of her efforts, Germany did not succeed in convincing the Entente that she sincerely desired peace. Her "blank check" to Austria, her misleading statement that she had not been informed of the contents of the ultimatum to Serbia, and her rejection of Grey's first offer of mediation caused great uneasiness among the Entente powers regarding Germany's intentions.

Germany advises Austria to negotiate with Russia

Austria's declaration of war against Serbia brought on a far more dangerous situation. Hitherto the powers had either looked on or had tried to prevent a crisis. Now they prepared to intervene actively. On July 29, Tsar Nicholas

War parties in control

ordered a general mobilization.   There was no doubt now about Russia's determination to intervene, and consequently all hopes of "localization" were abandoned.   With the mobilization of Russia there arose the portentous danger of a war that would involve all Europe, and, for that matter, the whole world.   The war parties in Germany and Russia now gained the ascendancy. In Germany Bethmann-Hollweg, who did all in his power to bring about a peaceful settlement, continued to work for peace, but he gave ear to the army chiefs.   In Russia, the army chiefs got control of the weak-minded Nicholas, and were preparing for a general mobilization.

The Kaiser sent a telegram to the Tsar asking him to avoid taking military steps that would precipitate a calamity.   Nicholas promptly countermanded his order for general mobilization and decreed mobilization only on the Austrian frontier.   The Russian General Staff were in a quandary, since their plans were all for a general mobilization; a partial mobilization might disorganize the army.   Sazonov urged the Tsar to fall in with these plans.   Despite his disinclination, the weak Nicholas yielded.   On July 30 he ordered a general mobilization.   The situation was now critical.   The war between Austria and Serbia had drawn in Russia and Germany.   Once these two great powers were at war, a general European conflict was inevitable.   The local conflict between Austria and Serbia had, within a month, brought the many antagonisms of Europe to a head.

Russian mobilization

The Russian mobilization produced consternation in Germany. She was now in a serious situation, as, in case of war, France, Russia's ally and her own irreconcilable foe, would not remain neutral.   The long-dreaded war on two fronts was rapidly approaching.   All the more necessary for Germany to keep England neutral, for she appreciated the power of the British navy.   Both France and Germany made efforts to know England's attitude.   President Poincaré of France declared that war was inevitable if Germany believed that England would not intervene, and that the only way to prevent war was for England to declare her solidarity with France.   England's policy of refusing to ally herself definitely with France confused the Germans.   They were convinced that England would not intervene in case of war.   And they were strengthened in this conviction when Grey refused to give a statement of England's

Efforts of Germany to keep England neutral

solidarity with France. He declared that England's "hands were untied," there being no treaty of alliance, no "written bond," but only an "understanding"; hence, she was free to intervene or not to intervene. Germany endeavored in vain to induce Grey to formulate England's conditions of neutrality. He was asked by Prince Lichnowsky, the German Ambassador to England, whether England would intervene if Germany respected the neutrality of Belgium and if she guaranteed the integrity of France and her colonies. Grey's replies were vague and non-committal. His reasons for refusing to make a declaration of solidarity with France were that it would arouse opposition in the cabinet, and, especially, that it would precipitate a crisis by encouraging Russia, France's ally, to favor war rather than negotiation. Grey's persistent efforts for peace and his vague declarations regarding intervention convinced Germany that England would not fight; the threat of civil war in Ireland would distract England's attention from Continental matters.

On July 31, Germany sent a double ultimatum: one to Russia demanding that she demobilize, and another to France demanding to know her attitude in case of war with Russia. Russia did not reply, and, on August 1, Germany declared war against her. France replied that she would "act in accordance with her interests." Germany considered the reply unsatisfactory, and, on August 3, declared war against France. Germany's ultimatum to France caused great concern in England regarding Belgium, whose neutrality had been guaranteed since 1839.[1] Grey addressed notes to Germany and France inquiring whether they would respect Belgium's neutrality. France replied that she would respect it. Germany's answer was evasive; she was "not in a position to reply." On August 2, German troops occupied Luxemburg against the protest of her ruler.[2] On the same day Germany sent an ultimatum to Belgium demanding that she permit the passage of troops to invade France. Belgium's reply was a flat refusal. She declared that to permit the violation of her neutrality would be "to sacrifice her honor as a nation and at the same time betray her duty to Europe," and that she would "repel by all means in her power every attack upon her rights." On August 4, German troops entered Belgium.

Germany violates neutrality of Belgium

[1] See page 65. Germany, in 1871, inherited the obligations of Prussia.
[2] Luxemburg had been neutralized in 1867 by an agreement among the powers.

The world was profoundly shocked by Germany's open violation of international law and by her breach of faith. Bethmann-Hollweg acknowledged that his country had done wrong, but had done so in self-defense. "Necessity knows no law," he declared. "This is a breach of international law . . . but we shall try to make good the injustice as soon as our military goal has been reached." Germany's violation of Belgium's neutrality consolidated British opinion, and moved the hesitating government to decisive action. On the very day that German troops entered Belgium, England declared war against Germany. England's action greatly surprised Germany. Bethmann-Hollweg bitterly denounced England for going to war with a "kindred nation" because Germany, of necessity, violated the treaty guaranteeing the neutrality of Belgium.

Germany's defense

The great coalitions now lined up for battle. England, France, and Russia signed an agreement mutually pledging one another not to make a separate peace, and to accept a general peace only on terms agreeable to all. They were now the "Allies." A rift took place in the Triple Alliance. Italy declared her neutrality on the ground that Germany and Austria were engaged in an aggressive war; the terms of the treaty bound her to aid them only in defense. Rumania, a satellite of the Triple Alliance, was influenced by the action of Italy, and remained neutral. Montenegro and Turkey entered the war almost from the start. The former took common cause with Serbia, and declared war upon Austria. Turkey, fearful of Russia's designs upon Constantinople, joined the "Central Powers," as Germany and Austria were now called. In Greece a powerful party led by Venizelos favored the Allies, but King Constantine, who was pro-German, used his power to keep the country neutral. Bulgaria, as a Slav nation, might have been expected to join the Allies. But her hated enemy, Serbia, was on their side; hence, she decided to be neutral. All the Balkan States, however, were later drawn into the World War.

The Allies versus the Central Powers

The conflict in Europe cast its shadow over Asia. Japan, as the ally of England pledged to support her in Asiatic waters, demanded of Germany that she evacuate Kiao-chau. Germany refused, and Japan declared war against her on August 23. India, as a colony of England, was at war. Beginning as a conflict in the Balkans, the war had spread through Europe and

Japan joins the Allies

Asia. The New World was at peace, but it, too, was destined to be drawn into what was rapidly becoming a world conflict.

REFERENCES

SOURCES:

After the World War a great controversy arose as to Germany's responsibility for the war. On the outbreak of the war all the belligerents published official statements defending their position. Some of these statements were proved to be unreliable, as the governments made a selection of the documents that they wished to appear. Many editions and summaries of these official documents have appeared, the best known being J. B. Scott, *Diplomatic Documents Relating to the Outbreak of the European War*, 2 vols. (1916). After the war some of the governments issued fuller statements of the diplomatic crisis of 1914; in Germany was published K. Kautsky and others (editors), *Die deutschen Dokumente Zum Kriegsausbruch* (ed. 1927), translated into English under title "Outbreak of the World War," and published by the Carnegie Endowment for International Peace, the first reliable collection on the subject; in England, G. P. Gooch and H. Temperley (editors), *British Documents on the Origins of the War*, 1898–1914, vol. XI, "The Outbreak of the War" (1926). After the war many statesmen, diplomats, and soldiers published their memoirs relating to the outbreak and conduct of the war. The most important of these memoirs are those of Grey, Churchill, Asquith, von Bethmann-Hollweg, the ex-Kaiser (very unreliable), Lichnowsky, Poincaré, Andrássy, Isvolsky, and von Bülow, and Lloyd George.

SECONDARY WORKS:

The two best studies on the origins of the World War are S. B. Fay, *The Origins of the World War*, 2 vols. (1928), and B. E. Schmitt, *The Coming of the War: 1914* (1930). Both authors are scholarly to the last detail and fair in the presentation of their views. Fay's conclusions incline to favor the Central Powers, and Schmitt's conclusions, the Allies. P. Renouvin, *The Immediate Origins of the War*, translated from the French (1928), absolves Germany from charge of conspiring to bring on the war, yet believes that she was more guilty than the other belligerents; Count M. Montgelas, *The Case for the Central Powers*, translated from the German (1925), a moderate and fair presentation of Germany's case, view that war was caused by stubbornness of Austria and by the designs of Russia; Earl Loreburn, *How the War Came* (1919) and J. S. Ewart, *The Roots and Causes of the War* (1925), critical of all the belligerents; H. E. Barnes, *The Genesis of the World War* (1926), the best from extreme revisionist viewpoint, view that not Austria and Germany, but Russia and France were the guilty nations; partisan volumes: Sir C. Oman, *The Outbreak of the War* (1919), pro-British; R. Poincaré, *The Origins of the War* (1922), pro-French; G. von Jagow, *Ursachen und Ausbruch des Weltkrieges* (1919), pro-German. Very critical of all the belligerents are G. L. Dickinson, *International Anarchy* (1926) and A. Pevet, *Les responsables de la Guerre*

(1921); G. P. Gooch, *Recent Revelations of European Diplomacy* (1927), a discussion of the sources of the origin of the war, indispensable guide; H. Lutz, *Lord Grey and the World War*, translated from the German (1928), critical of Grey whom he regards as well-meaning but incompetent.

CHAPTER XXXV

THE WORLD WAR (1914–18)

ARMIES AND NAVIES

GERMANY's army was easily the first in organization and equipment. The best army on the side of the Allies was that of France which, as the war progressed, became the military backbone of the Allied cause. Russia had the largest standing army in the world, which, however, was badly organized and poorly equipped. In the last year of the war, when America joined the Allies, she threw into the scale her vast resources in men and supplies. At the outbreak of the war the small British army was increased rapidly by voluntary enlistments; in 1916, conscription raised it to a size comparable with that of France. But British strength was not only in Britain; it was also in the Empire with its enormous population and resources.[1]

The armies

England's navy easily led all the others. That of Germany was second, but only in tonnage; in equipment and organization it was equal to that of England. France's navy was fairly large, but far inferior to the navies of England and Germany. It was used chiefly in patrolling the Mediterranean. The American navy was small, but highly efficient; its chief work, however, was to insure the transportation of American troops across the Atlantic. Nearly all the naval battles were fought between the British and German fleets.[2]

The navies

[1] The following table gives the military forces of the leading combatants:

	STANDING ARMIES	WAR STRENGTH
Germany	791,000	5,000,000
Austria-Hungary	450,000	3,350,000
France	790,000	3,580,000
Russia	1,200,000	6,000,000

[2] The following gives the naval strength of the important combatants; only the large warships are listed:

	DREAD-NOUGHTS	PRE-DREAD-NOUGHTS	BATTLE CRUISERS	ARMORED CRUISERS	CRUISERS
Great Britain	20	40	9	34	74
Germany	13	20	4	9	41
United States	8	22	0	11	14
France	4	18	0	20	9
Japan	2	13	2	13	13
Russia	0	7	0	6	9
Italy	3	8	0	9	6
Austria-Hungary	3	6	0	2	5

THE GERMAN INVASION OF BELGIUM AND FRANCE

The German mobilization was marvelously efficient.   Millions of men fell into place and were transported to the frontiers, everything moving with the regularity of clock-work.   Germany's plan of campaign was to make a swift descent upon Paris, to reduce France to submission, and then to turn on Russia.   The quickest way of accomplishing it was through Belgium, as there were few French fortresses on the Belgian frontier.   The route taken by the German armies in 1870 was now so strongly fortified, all the way from Verdun to Belfort, as to make a rapid march in this direction well-nigh impossible.

German armies poured into Belgium.   On August 4, the first battle of the war took place at Liége, which, though splendidly fortified, surrendered to the Germans after a bombardment of only three days.   The small Belgian army could not hold back the German forces, and they retreated fighting stubbornly.   Two weeks later, the Germans entered Brussels, but the road to France was not yet open.   The Belgians were now joined by the French and by an expeditionary force of British under General Sir John French, who together opposed the German forces.   A number of battles took place in which the Allies were defeated by the Germans under General von Kluck and compelled to retreat to the main French line near the Belgian frontier.   The Germans pressed on, driving the French before them.   Nothing now seemed able to stop their march to Paris.   City after city was taken; and, at one time, they were within fifteen miles of the French capital.   Consternation reigned in France, and the government moved to Bordeaux.

When the situation was most serious, General Joffre, the commander of the French forces, suddenly launched an army at the German right flank.   By this time the Germans were across the Marne River.   When the Germans turned to meet the attack, another French army, under General Foch, attacked the center.   At this critical moment, von Kluck's army was weakened by the dispatch of some of his troops to eastern Germany, which was being invaded by the Russians.   A great battle took place at the Marne (September 6-10, 1914) in which the Germans were defeated and compelled to retreat.   They retired in orderly fashion to the Aisne River, where they entrenched themselves.   The battle of the Marne is one of the decisive battles of

The German plan of campaign

Von Kluck's drive

First battle of the Marne

UNCONQUERABLE

THE KAISER. "SO, YOU SEE—YOU'VE LOST EVERYTHING."
THE KING OF THE BELGIANS. "NOT MY SOUL."

The Challenge

—*From The Evening Sun, New York.*

UNCLE SAM: "You'll have to start it, William!"

history. Joffre's victory foiled the German plan of campaign of winning the war by a quick, decisive blow at Paris.

The position of the opposing armies, after the German retreat, left a gap of one hundred miles in the line from Arras to the sea; and both sides rushed toward it. In order to reach it, The Allies the Germans had first to take Antwerp, one of the best extend their line to the fortified cities in Europe; but their sixteen-inch guns sea compelled the Belgians to evacuate the city. However, the Allies reached the sea first, and extended their line to Nieuport, on the coast. Dunkirk, Calais, and Boulogne were now safe, and aid from England to France could come by the shortest route.

Belgium, now almost entirely in the hands of the Germans, was made to pay dearly for her refusal to allow her neutrality to be violated. Wherever the Belgians showed resistance Devastation to German occupation, they were severely punished. of Belgium Many Belgian towns were laid waste, and commerce and industry ruined. Famous buildings were burned, notably the Louvain Library. A once prosperous people was reduced to beggary, and had to rely on the charity of the Americans to keep from starvation. The military rule of the country was exceedingly harsh. An attack by snipers on German soldiers in a town would be followed by the destruction of the town and the execution or imprisonment of its leading citizens. Cardinal Mercier, the leading Belgian prelate, boldly denounced the Germans for their conduct and appealed to world opinion in behalf of his suffering fellow countrymen.

THE WAR IN THE EAST

At the outbreak of the war, one Russian army under General Rennennkampf invaded East Prussia, and another under General Brussilov invaded Galicia. German forces under Gen- The battle eral Paul von Hindenburg were sent to meet the Rus- of Tannen- sians in East Prussia. A great battle was fought in the berg last days of August, 1914, at Tannenberg, in which the Russians suffered a terrible defeat and were driven headlong out of Germany.

Hindenburg now invaded Russia and inflicted one defeat after another on the fleeing Russians, who retreated until they reached Riga. It is estimated that Hindenburg's drive cost Germans in- the Russians about 1,500,000 men and an enormous vade Russia amount of supplies. But the Russians were still in Galicia. A new drive of German and Austrian armies, under General von

THE EASTERN FRONT

☆   Forts
▬▬ January 1918
▬ ▬ ▬ Farthest advance of the Russians

Mackensen, was launched against the Russians. Again they suffered terrible defeats, and lost nearly all the territory that they had gained. The Russians re-formed their line leaving the Central Powers masters of much of their territory. After a year of invasions and counter-invasions, fighting on the Eastern Front came virtually to an end. So great were the losses of Russia that she was now powerless to render much aid to the Allies. The most that she could do was to compel Germany to maintain large forces to guard the Eastern Front.

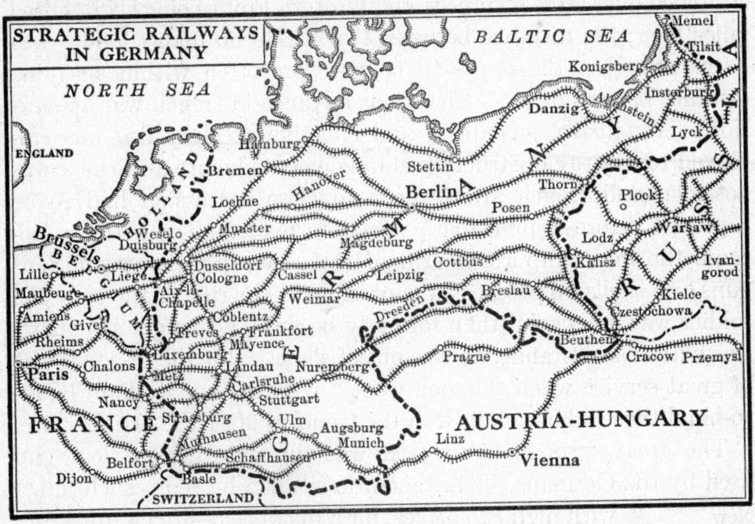

The Allies now determined to assume the offensive. A bold stroke was planned by the British to capture Constantinople. If successful, the campaign would have far-reaching consequences: it would put Turkey out of the war and compel the neutral Balkan States to join the Allies, which would open a possibility of an Allied drive against Austria; Russia, which had been "bottled up" by the closing of the Straits, would get much-needed munitions. The Dardanelles campaign began early in 1915. A powerful British fleet attempted to force the narrow strait, but was driven back with great losses by the Turkish batteries on each side. A land attack was then tried by British, Australians, and New Zealanders, who seized the peninsula of Gallipoli, but could make no advance despite many gallant efforts. By the end of 1915, the campaign was abandoned.

The Dardanelles campaign

NEW METHODS OF WARFARE

Methods of warfare were revolutionized during the World War. The strategic marches that had won victories in the past were superseded by strategic railways which transported troops rapidly to critical points over long distances. Trench fighting was as common as open battle. The combatants

Trench fighting

lay hidden in deep trenches protected by barbed-wire entanglements and by "nests" of machine guns. The lines of trenches
stretched over large distances, the Western Front being six hundred
miles long; the distance between the lines, "no man's land," was
so narrow that the opposing troops were often within speaking
distance of each other. Victorious advance in trench warfare was
slow. Extensive, sustained, and effective artillery fire was employed to destroy obstructing entanglements before an attack was
possible; and trench after trench in close succession had to be
captured before appreciable gains were made. The artillery became the most important arm of the service; without sufficient
guns and shells no progress was possible. The rifle of the common
soldier was less useful than formerly because, although the enemy
was within short range, he was out of sight. But the bayonet was
of great service when the men went "over the top" to fight hand-
to-hand those who remained in the trenches after the artillery fire.

The great surprise of the war was the sixteen-inch siege gun
used by the Germans. This gigantic weapon hurled a shell, filled
New   with high explosives, for a distance of fifteen miles and
weapons   more. Long-ranged cannon were improved to such an
extent that, in 1918, Paris was shelled by a German gun seventy
miles away. The machine gun, to a large extent, displaced the
rifle; the former discharged about five hundred bullets a minute,
"spraying" the enemy continuously. Poison gas in battle was
first used during the World War. It was wafted toward the enemy
when the wind was favorable, or shot from guns in explosive shells.
Armored motor trucks, armed with guns, often played an important part in battle. Immense rolling fortresses, called "tanks,"
spitting fire in every direction charged the enemy, brushing aside
barbed-wire fences and crushing those in their path. Airplanes
succeeded the cavalry as the "eyes" of the army. They hovered
over the enemy's lines and, by means of signals, reported his movements and directed the gun fire. The Germans used Zeppelins
that were effective in air raids on cities; nothing was more fearful
than the rain of death from the skies. In naval warfare the surprise
weapon was the submarine, which was perfected to such a degree
that it threatened the effectiveness even of the most powerful
battleship. In no other war in history did science play so great a
part. It might almost be said that the World War was fought by
machines directed by engineers.

There were no "battles" in the old sense of that word. The war was one long-drawn-out battle on each front. Fighting was going on all the time, more on some "sectors" and less on others. Now and then a "drive" occurred, a movement of large bodies of troops against a strategic point, which resulted in a battle lasting months.

The "drives"

For the first time in history whole populations were engaged in war activity. Hitherto, wars had been contests between armies only; hence, the distinction between combatants and non-combatants. During the World War this distinction tended to disappear, as the governments conscripted all men of military age, and directed the energies of the civil population toward aiding those in the field. It took over the railways, regulated the amount and nature of goods produced, the quantity of food raised, prices, hours, and wages of labor — in fact, all economic activity. Many were employed in the manufacture of munitions, of arms, of ships, and of supplies for the army. The soldiers in the trenches received continual aid from the civil population whose morale was as vital to success as their own; hence, the use of "propaganda" by the enemy. To undermine the morale of the nation, all sorts of methods were used by the enemy: rumors of defeat in battle, secretly subsidized newspapers advocating "defeatist" policies, appeals to revolution, and reports of discouraging conditions. It was a publicity campaign in which distinguished writers and scientists frequently took part.

War of populations as well as of armies

THE WESTERN FRONT

At the opening of the second year of the World War, the situation was favorable to the Central Powers. In the west, they held Belgium and the industrial section of France. In the east, they held a large part of Russia, which was defeated, "bottled up," and demoralized. The one element in the situation favorable to the Allies was the decision of Italy to join them. After negotiating for terms with both sides, Italy came to secret agreement with the Allies concerning her demands; and, in May, 1915, she declared war upon the Central Powers. An Italian army invaded Austria, and marched toward Trieste.

Favorable situation of the Central Powers

On the Western Front the repulse of the Germans at the Marne

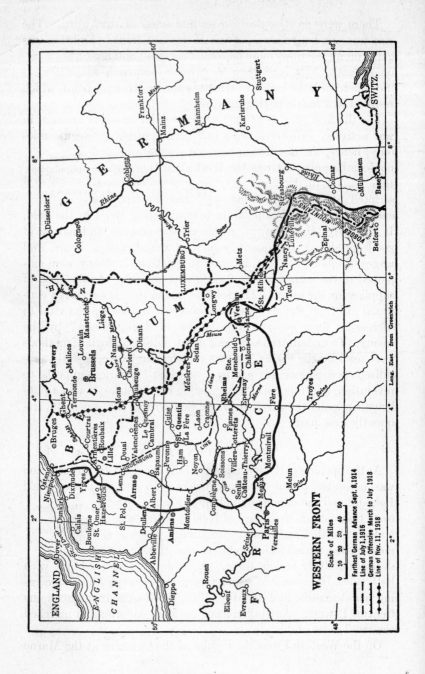

WESTERN FRONT

Scale of Miles

0   10   20   30   40   50

— · — · — Farthest German Advance Sept. 8, 1914
———————— Line of July 1, 1916
· · · · · · German Offensive March to July 1918
•—•—•—•—• Line of Nov. 11, 1918

was followed by a period of unremitting trench warfare. The enormous battle line, stretching from Nieuport to the Swiss frontier, ran through a corner of Belgium, the northeastern section of France, and along the frontier of Alsace. Early in 1916, the Germans decided upon a great effort to break the Allied line. Overlooking the Meuse Valley is Verdun, which was splendidly defended by rings of fortresses on the surrounding hills. It was a place of great strategic importance, threatening Lorraine, the chief iron region of Germany. Enormous German armies were massed in its vicinity. A battle began in February, which raged for over six months, during which about half a million men laid down their lives. The Germans were determined to take the city at any cost; and the French, to defend it at any cost. Fortifications were taken and retaken many times, and the whole region was blasted by shot and shell. The more desperate the German attack, the more determined the French defense. *Ils ne passeront pas!* (They shall not pass!) was the cry that rang throughout France. Reënforcements were poured in, and the Germans were compelled to give up their attack. Verdun marked the second great failure of Germany to conquer France.

The battle of Verdun

During the second half of 1916 there took place a great campaign along the Somme River. The British, under General Douglas Haig, their commander-in-chief, attacked the Germans under Hindenburg, now the commander-in-chief of the German armies. Desperate fighting took place lasting six months. The British advance was slow and costly, and was often halted by fierce German counter-attacks. Bad weather turned the fighting area into a sea of mud and blood. The loss of life on both sides was as great as that at Verdun. Directly, the battle of the Somme resulted in little gain for the Allies; indirectly, however, it had two important results: it relieved the German pressure on Verdun; and, in March, 1917, the Germans executed a general retirement to what was cal ed the Hindenburg Line. They retreated on a hundred-mile front, from Arras to east of Noyon, and evacuated about one thousand square miles of French territory, devastating the evacuated region.

The battle of the Somme

THE CAMPAIGN IN THE BALKANS

The invasion of the Austrians into Serbia, at the outbreak of the war, met with stubborn resistance. After the Serbs had succeeded

in driving out the Austrians, Bulgaria joined the Central Powers
Conquest of   (October, 1915). Serbia was invaded by Bulgarians
Serbia   on the east and by Austro-German armies on the
north, and was quickly conquered. Montenegro and Albania
shared her fate.

The remaining Balkan States now determined to be neutral if
possible. A year later, however, Rumania, influenced by the
Conquest of   French resistance at Verdun and by pressure from
Rumania   Russia, joined the Allies (August, 1916). Rumanian
armies invaded Transylvania, where they gained several successes.
But their triumph was short-lived. General Falkenhayn, at the
head of Austro-German forces, drove them out of Transylvania,
and proceeded to invade Rumania. At the end of three weeks,
Rumania was completely subdued. She signed the humiliating
Treaty of Bucharest, which took from her important strips of territory and gave important economic privileges to the Central Powers.

Greece was now the only Balkan State that was not under the
control of the Central Powers. The country was divided in its
Greece joins   sympathies. A pro-Ally party, led by Venizelos, was
the Allies   opposed by a pro-German party, led by King Constantine. In June, 1917, Constantine was deposed by an uprising
organized by the party of Venizelos. The pro-Ally element was
now in power, and Greece declared war against the Central Powers.

THE WAR IN ASIA AND AFRICA

When the European powers entered the war, their colonies and
their allies in Asia and Africa likewise did so. Japan, as the ally
Japan cap-   of England, represented the cause of the Allies in Asia.
tures Kiao-   At the outbreak of the war, Japanese forces attacked
chau   Kiao-chau, the great German stronghold in the Far
East. After a siege by land and sea, Kiao-chau capitulated and
was occupied by Japan. She now participated in the war only
to the extent of patrolling the Pacific to protect British merchantmen from German raiders.

In western Asia the Turks planned to seize the Suez Canal; and
the British planned to capture Bagdad. The campaign against
The war in   Suez ended in failure. In 1915, a British force from
Mesopo-   India invaded Mesopotamia and advanced as far as
tamia   Kut-el-Amara, where it was surrounded and captured
by the Turks. An invasion of Russians into Armenia, during the

same year, was repulsed by the Turks. It was followed by an Armenian massacre which was more terrible than any in the history of that unhappy race. Thousands of men, women, and children were "deported," driven into deserts, where they died of famine or were butchered by the Turks. Allied prestige in the Near East was at a low ebb as a result of the defeat of the British and Russians. But a change of fortune took place early in 1917. A British expedition invaded Mesopotamia, defeated the Turks, and entered Bagdad in triumph. Another British army, under General Allenby, invaded Palestine and, at the end of 1917, captured Jerusalem. After seven centuries the Holy City was once more in Christian hands.

A stubborn fight went on for the possession of the German colonies in Africa. Early in the war, British and French colonial armies seized Togo and Cameroon. South African armies, led by the Boer, General Jan Smuts, conquered German South-West Africa in 1915. In German East Africa, all the non-German colonial forces in the region coöperated, British, Portuguese, Boer, and Belgian, but a handful of Germans, leading native soldiers, held all at bay until almost the end of the war.

Conquest of Germany's colonies in Africa

NAVAL OPERATIONS

The mobilization of the British fleet was as wonderfully efficient as was that of the German army. Germany's coast was immediately blockaded, her commerce was swept from the seas, and most of her navy was reduced to impotence in Kiel Harbor. The British navy rendered incalculable service to the cause of the Allies by cutting off supplies to Germany from abroad, and by making safe the transportation of troops and supplies from one Allied country to another. To a large extent the victories gained by the German armies were nullified by the sea power of England.

England's sea power

When the war broke out, there were a number of German warships on the high seas which succeeded in inflicting serious losses on Allied commerce before their careers were cut short. The most famous of these raiders was the Emden, which sailed the seas, sinking many vessels and skillfully eluding her pursuers, until she was finally destroyed. Now and then German cruisers would slip through the blockade to prey upon

German raids

Allied commerce; some were bold enough to shell towns on the British coast.

There was only one important naval battle in the World War, and it was the greatest naval battle in all history, from the point of view of tonnage and armament. It took place in 1916, off the coast of Jutland. After careful preparation, the German High Seas Fleet, under Admiral von Scheer, slipped out of Kiel Harbor and was met by the British fleet under Admirals Jellicoe and Beatty. What followed was a gigantic conflict between the two greatest fleets in the world. Both sides claimed victory; the Germans, because they had inflicted greater losses than they suffered, and the British because the German fleet was forced to retire to Kiel. England remained mistress of the seas.

The battle of Jutland

England's blockade of Germany led to a situation similar to that in the Napoleonic Wars. Commanding every avenue of commerce in all the seas, she was able to divert the trade of neutrals away from Germany to herself; in fact, to make the neutrals her economic allies. She extended the list of contraband to include food and cotton. It was peculiarly difficult for England to maintain the blockade because of Germany's geographic position, with neutral states near her borders. England, therefore, "rationed" these neutrals, Holland and the Scandinavian states, on the ground that much of the goods that they imported was really destined for Germany.

The blockade

The position of the United States in this matter was of vital importance. As the only great neutral power, each of the combatants was eager to get supplies from her, and even more eager that the other should not get them. Germany appealed to America, as the historic champion of the rights of neutrals, to maintain the "freedom of the seas." President Wilson sent vigorous protests to England because of her interference with American trade.

America demands "freedom of the seas"

Germany soon realized that she must break the blockade which was slowly strangling her. Her food supply was large, but not sufficient to feed her population; and before long she would exhaust her supplies of oil, rubber, cotton, gasoline, materials vitally necessary for military purposes. Germany's answer to the British blockade was the submarine. Early in 1915, she announced a "war zone" of the waters around the British Isles in which enemy merchantmen would be sunk

Germany's submarine campaign

without warning. This policy was in violation of international law, which required that a ship must be warned before being sunk, and that the lives of the passengers and crew must be safeguarded in every way possible. Germany contended that the submarine, being small and frail, could be destroyed by a single shot from an armed merchantman; therefore, its effectiveness was in striking suddenly and secretly. As the submarine was a new weapon, not regulated by existing international law, Germany claimed that she was not restricted in its use.

Germany's submarine campaign was terribly effective. Allied ships were sunk almost daily; sometimes neutral vessels were also torpedoed. The English were deeply concerned at the loss of their shipping, as they depended so greatly on foreign food and raw materials. There was a great protest against Germany's submarine policy which was making war upon non-combatants and even upon neutrals who traveled in belligerent ships. Several American ships were torpedoed, and President Wilson sent a warning note to Germany that the United States would hold her to a strict accountability for the loss of American lives and ships. *Protest of America against the submarine campaign*

In 1915, there took place a tragedy that sent a thrill of horror throughout the entire world. The British liner, Lusitania, was torpedoed without warning near the coast of Ireland by a German submarine. She sank almost immediately with nearly all on board; about 1100 men, women, and children were drowned, among them many Americans. President Wilson sent a sharp protest to Germany, denouncing the sinking of the ship as a violation of international law and of the rights of humanity, and demanding that Germany disavow the act and make full reparation. He declared that the United States would not "omit any word or act" to maintain the right of neutrals to travel on their legitimate business anywhere on the high seas. Germany's reply was that the Lusitania carried munitions and that she was armed; hence, she was an auxiliary of the British navy. The liner did carry munitions, but it was not proved, either at the the time or since the war, that she was armed. The sinking of the Lusitania, like the violation of the neutrality of Belgium, solidified world opinion against Germany. *The Lusitania tragedy*

AMERICA JOINS THE ALLIES

At the outbreak of the war, America immediately declared her neutrality. This policy was in harmony with her traditional foreign policy which is based upon Washington's injunction to avoid alliances with the European powers, and upon the Monroe Doctrine in which America assumed the guardianship of the New World. The autocratic and military spirit of the government of Germany, her violation of Belgian neutrality, and her ruthless methods of warfare turned American public opinion in favor of the Allies.

American policy and Germany

As the war progressed and became world-wide in extent, it became increasingly difficult for America to maintain her neutrality. England's blockade seriously hampered her commerce, but Germany's submarine campaign endangered American lives. Whenever an American ship was torpedoed, and whenever American citizens were drowned, as in the Lusitania tragedy, anti-German feeling in the United States became exceedingly intense. It was evident that the submarine campaign, if continued, would result in bringing America into the war on the side of the Allies. In Germany a powerful group, headed by General von Ludendorff and Admiral von Tirpitz, insisted on ruthlessly maintaining the submarine campaign. The Germans were loath to give up the one weapon on which they relied to break the blockade. They reasoned that, if America did join the Allies, which they believed exceedingly doubtful, she was too far away and too unprepared to render them any effective service. England would be starving, and France exhausted by the time American forces in sufficient numbers would be on the battle-field.

Germany's dependence on the submarine

President Wilson made many efforts to convince the belligerents to agree on a "peace without victory." He sent Edward M. House, his most trusted adviser, to Europe to sound the belligerents on their peace terms. Early in 1917, the Allies made public their terms which, in effect, demanded the partition of Austria-Hungary into its constituent nationalities, the restitution of Alsace-Lorraine to France, and the cession of Constantinople to Russia. The German government refused to make known its terms, but the Reichstag passed a resolution which declared that it was in favor of "peace and a mutual understanding and lasting reconciliation among the nations. Forced acquisitions

Peace terms

of territory and political, economic, and financial violations are incompatible with such a peace." But neither side was willing to go into conference: the Germans, because the "war map" favored them; and the Allies, because they feared that peace terms would be dictated by Germany.

The success of the submarine emboldened Germany to take a step which was to have a decisive effect on the conduct of the war. In January, 1917, she announced a policy of unre- *America de-* stricted submarine warfare in the waters around the *clares war* British and French coasts; all ships found in this zone, *against Germany* neutral and belligerent, armed or unarmed, would be sunk. A few slight exceptions were allowed. No sooner was this policy in effect than America broke diplomatic relations with Germany. After a month of "armed neutrality," Wilson finally came to a decision in favor of intervention. He appeared before Congress and delivered an address that resounded throughout the world. It was a forceful indictment of the German government for its violations of international law and for its inhumane practices. He denounced it as autocratic, irresponsible, and untrustworthy, and as a menace to civilization. He appealed to the American people to fight for the ultimate peace of the world and for the liberation of its peoples, the German people included; for the rights of nations, great and small; and for the privilege of men everywhere to choose their way of life and of obedience. "The world must be made safe for democracy." On April 6, America declared war against Germany. Later, she declared war against Austria-Hungary, but not against Turkey and Bulgaria; with Turkey only diplomatic relations were broken.[1]

Wilson became the spokesman of the Allied cause. He declared that America wanted nothing for herself, but would fight to the limit of her resources in order to destroy German mili- *The Four-* tarism. On January 8, 1918, he announced the famous *teen Points* Fourteen Points, a detailed statement of America's war aims.

[1] The following is the complete list of the belligerents during the World War. On the side of the Allies: Serbia, Russia, France, Belgium, the British Empire, Montenegro, Japan, Italy, Portugal, Rumania, the United States, Cuba, Panama, Haiti, Honduras, Guatemala, Nicaragua, Costa Rica, Brazil, Greece, Siam, Liberia, and China. Virtually all Asia and Africa were on the side of the Allies. Several of the South American states broke diplomatic relations with Germany. On the side of the Central Powers: Austria-Hungary, Germany, Turkey, and Bulgaria.

The neutrals were: in Europe, Holland, Switzerland, Norway, Sweden, Denmark, and Spain; in the New World, all the Latin-American nations except those already named.

These were: (1) abolition of secret diplomacy; (2) freedom of the seas; (3) equality of trade conditions; (4) reduction of armaments; (5) adjustment of colonial claims in the interest of the nations; (6) evacuation of Russian territory; (7) restoration of Belgium; (8) restoration of Alsace-Lorraine to France; (9) rectification of Italy's frontier on the basis of nationality; (10) reëstablishment of the Polish nation; (11) evacuation of Serbia, Montenegro, and Rumania; (12) the right to self-determination of the races in Turkey; (13) of those in Austria-Hungary; and (14) the establishment of a league of nations.

Now that America was in the war, the question was, how could her vast resources in men and materials be mobilized in sufficient time to aid the Allies who had reached almost the limit of their resources? The answer to this question is one of the amazing chapters in the history of the World War. Congress passed a draft law which mobilized about 5,000,000 men, and armies were rapidly organized and transported to France. Fleets of American and British warships guarded the ocean lanes through which the transports passed. President Wilson appointed "dictators" and administration boards to organize the resources of the country for the prosecution of the war. Immense quantities of food, ships, munitions, and materials of all sorts were sent to the needy Allies. Money was mobilized as well as men and materials. "Liberty loans" were floated, aggregating over $21,000,000,000, that were widely subscribed to by the American public. This huge sum was used for prosecuting the war and for loans to the Allies. By the end of 1917, large American armies were in France, ready for action, under the command of General John Pershing. There was frantic rejoicing among the French as they beheld the Americans streaming in at the rate of 50,000 a month. "Life came to us in new waves," said a French writer, "bringing fresh strength to the almost bloodless body of France."

America mobilizes her men and resources

RUSSIA MAKES A SEPARATE PEACE

The crushing defeats of the Russian armies in the first year of the war aroused widespread discontent among the Russian people. It quickly led to a revolutionary mood which resulted in bitter attacks upon the government. Revolution was always near the surface in Russia. In March, 1917, the world

The Russian Revolution

WOODROW WILSON

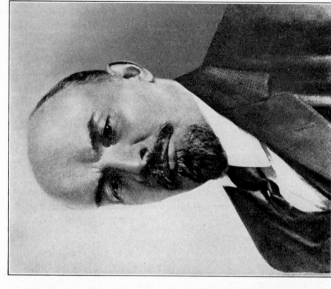

NICHOLAI LENIN

GEORGES CLEMENCEAU

was astounded at the news that the Duma had deposed Tsar Nicholas II, and had established a provisional government. The Russian Revolution was now begun, and the various revolutionary parties contended for supremacy. In November of the same year there took place an uprising led by the Bolshevists, the most extreme of the revolutionary parties. The provisional government was overthrown, and a new system was established called the "Soviet." At its head were the Bolshevist leaders, Nicholas Lenin and Leon Trotsky.[1]

What was to be the attitude of Soviet Russia to the war? The Bolshevists wanted immediate peace, and proposed a plan to end the war on the basis of "no annexations and no indemnities" and of "self-determination" of all subject nations. The Allies refused to agree, and the Bolshevists opened negotiations for a separate peace with Germany. A conference took place at Brest-Litovsk, to which came the delegates of the Central Powers and those of Russia. It soon became evident that there were to be no "negotiations"; the terms were dictated by the Germans to the Russians, who were compelled to accept them on pain of further invasion of Russia. The principal terms of the Treaty of Brest-Litovsk (March 3, 1918) were: Esthonia, Livonia, Courland, Lithuania, and Poland were taken from Russia and were to be reorganized by the Central Powers; Ukrainia and Finland were declared independent; Erivan, Kars, and Batum, in the Caucasus, were likewise taken from Russia; and (by a supplementary treaty) Russia agreed to pay an indemnity of $1,500,000,-000. By this treaty Russia lost nearly all the territory that she had won since Peter the Great. Brest-Litovsk aroused world indignation as much as the violation of the neutrality of Belgium.

Treaty of Brest-Litovsk

THE MARCH OFFENSIVE

Russia had collapsed, but the war was not over. Germany now realized that it would have to be won on the Western Front, as the Allies were determined to continue the fight. The battles of the Marne and Verdun convinced her that she needed every available man in order to break the Allied line. With the defeat of Serbia and Rumania, the Balkan front collapsed.

Battle of Caporetto

[1] For a detailed description of the Russian Revolution, see Chapter XXXVII.

With the Russian Revolution the Eastern Front was no more. German and Austrian armies now launched a drive at the Italian armies on the Isonzo, just across the Austrian frontier. At Caporetto (October, 1917) the Italians suffered a disastrous defeat, retiring precipitately into Italy until they reached the Piave River. The losses of the Italians were so great that, for the time, they were also virtually out of the war.

The situation at the beginning of 1918 was more favorable to the Central Powers than it had been since von Kluck's dash for Paris.

Favorable position of Germany at the beginning of 1918

They were impregnably entrenched on the Western Front; the Allies made desperate attempts to break the Hindenburg Line, all of which ended in costly failure. Russia, Italy, Serbia, and Rumania were eliminated as factors in the military situation. The submarine campaign was working havoc among Allied shipping, and England was facing starvation. There was now a solid block of states, "Middle Europe," from Berlin to Constantinople, organized and directed by the General Staff of the German army. Unity of command was the advantage that Germany enjoyed over the Allies, all of whose armies were under the independent direction of their national commanders. America was preparing feverishly, but was not yet ready to put troops in the field sufficiently trained and equipped to meet the German veterans. It looked dark for the cause of the Allies, and a feeling of discouragement spread in Allied countries where some sought a negotiated peace with Germany. "Defeatism," as it was called, was, however, opposed by a stronger will to fight to the bitter end. In France, Clemenceau, who was an uncompromising opponent of peace by negotiation, became Premier in November, 1917. He mercilessly suppressed the "defeatists," and prosecuted the war more vigorously than ever. In England, Lloyd George had succeeded Asquith as Prime Minister in December, 1916. His great energy put new heart in the British prosecution of the war.

On March 21, 1918, the Germans launched a great offensive from a point east of Arras to La Fère. The new plan was to end the war by a series of hammer strokes, and it was directed *The March offensive* by the ablest generals in the German army, Hindenburg and Ludendorff. The British and French defending the line felt the terrific shock of the drive, and were forced to retire, with great losses, to the Oise River. They lost fifteen hundred square miles which they had won after three years of bloody fighting. The immediate object of the Germans was to capture Amiens, a great military and railway center. So critical was the situation that, for the first time, the Allies agreed to something like unity of command, under General Ferdinand Foch, the French commander who had shown extraordinary ability on many a battle-field. He was given the power to coördinate the actions of the Allied armies on the Western Front, though the tactical direction was reserved to each commander-in-chief.

The next German blow was struck on April 4. It was against the British holding the line from La Basée to Ypres. The Germans captured many important places, among them being *Defeat of the British* Messines Ridge and Kemmel Hill, driving the British for a distance of ten miles. A break in their line would result in the capture of the Channel ports, so vitally important to the safety of England. In the words of General Haig, the British were now "with their backs to the wall."

Another German drive was directed against the French, from La Fère to Rheims. It was now the turn of the French to receive the hammer strokes of the Germans. They were *Defeat of the French* defeated, and retired as far as the Marne, yielding important places, Chemin des Dames and Château-Thierry. The Germans were halted for a time, but continued their drive and, by the middle of July, they succeeded in crossing the Marne. The immediate objective of the drive was Rheims, which, if taken, would seriously endanger the Allied line to Verdun.   Now it was the French who had their backs to the wall.

THE ALLIED COUNTER-OFFENSIVE

The fortunes of the Allies were now at the lowest ebb.   Whenever the German drive threatened to break the Allied line, re-enforcements were poured in to save the situation.   Always had the Germans been halted, but so great were the losses of the Allies that another great offensive might break through for lack of man power to prevent it.   Then it was that America "arrived."

America "arrives"

An American army, under Pershing, took over the sector from the Meuse River to the Argonne Forest.   American regiments strengthened the weakened armies of the Allies.   And American soldiers in large numbers were behind the line awaiting the call for reënforcements.   Foch was now prepared to retaliate on the Germans.   In July, 1918, he launched a great counter-offensive which spread all along the line.   The British resumed fighting on their old battle-field, the Somme, and drove the Germans out of nearly all the positions that they had gained in March.   In this campaign the Canadians particularly distinguished themselves by taking some of the most powerfully entrenched German positions.

Germans defeated by British

It was the determination of Foch to give the Germans no rest, to attack them now in this sector, now in that, thus maintaining the element of surprise.   The French, from Amiens to Rheims, delivered terrific blows at the Germans, and compelled them to retire from the positions that they had won at such cost.   By September they were back to the Hindenburg Line, having lost all the gains of their March offensive, on which they had staked all their hopes of winning the war.

by the French

The Allies now prepared to break the Hindenburg Line.   A force of Americans and French, under Pershing, attacked the Saint-Mihiel salient, one of the key positions of the Line.   It was taken after desperate fighting in which the raw American troops gave a good account of themselves alongside the seasoned veterans of France.   This victory was followed by the Meuse-Argonne campaign conducted by the Americans.   Some of the most desperate fighting of the war took place in the Argonne

by the Americans

Forest, where the Germans were defeated and compelled to retire.

The reverses suffered by the Germans revived the hopes of the Serbs, Greeks, Rumanians, and Italians, who realized that Austrian armies could no longer be "stiffened" by German reënforcements. Serb, Greek, and other Allied forces attacked the Bulgarians and won a decisive victory. Bulgaria collapsed and, at the end of September, sued for peace.

Bulgaria makes peace

Turkey was next to collapse. In September, the British, under General Allenby, marched victoriously through Mesopotamia, Palestine, and Syria, conquering city after city. By the end of October, Turkey, too, made a separate peace.

Turkey makes peace

Germany and Austria were now without allies, and open to attack in the rear through the Balkans. The Italians took the offensive on the Piave, and drove the Austrians out of Italy. Defeat of the Hapsburg forces acted as a signal to the subject races to rise and throw off their age-old yoke. Revolutions took place throughout Austria-Hungary. Republics were proclaimed in Bohemia and in Hungary. The Yugo-Slavs, Rumanians, and Italians joined their kindred across the frontier. Austria was rapidly disintegrating. Early in November, she surrendered and signed an armistice with the Allies.

Austria makes peace

During October, the Allies were delivering hammer strokes at the Hindenburg Line. Behind it were all the forces that Germany could muster. It was to be her last desperate stand. The French took Saint-Quentin, and the British, Lens, two pivotal points in the famous Line, which was now dented. Then Cambrai fell, and the Line was broken. The Germans retired on a wide front "according to plan," as it was stated. But the Allied offensive continued. Retreating slowly and fighting desperately all the way, the Germans evacuated nearly all of France and a part of Belgium. They were now almost to their own frontier, and the jubilant Allies prepared to invade Germany. Since Foch's successful counter-offensive, German morale had been badly shaken; now it was broken. The great military power that had almost conquered Europe surrendered to the Allies.

Germany sues for peace

On November 11, 1918, an armistice was signed between the Allies and Germany that terminated the greatest war in history. It provided for the evacuation by the Germans of France, Belgium, Luxemburg, and Alsace-Lorraine, the surrender of prisoners of war and refugees; the surrender of a

The Armistice

specified amount of war material and a number of warships; abandonment of all claims under the treaties of Brest-Litovsk and Bucharest; and the occupation of the Rhineland by Allied troops. All countries celebrated with fervent enthusiasm the coming of peace to a distracted world.

REFERENCES

MILITARY:

The best one-volume history of the World War in English is Liddell Hart, *A History of the World War* (1935); F. H. Simonds, *The Great War,* 5 vols. (1914–20), very vivid, combines military and political; J. Buchan, *A History of the Great War,* 4 vols. (1922), excellent for military matters, bad for diplomatic and political matters; D. W. Johnson, *Topography and Strategy in the War* (1917) and *Battlefields of the World War* (1921), technical studies of modern war methods; C. R. Gibson, *War Inventions and How they were Invented* (1917); A. Bidou (ed.), *La Grande Guerre* (1922), good for campaigns on the Western Front; G. A. B. Dewar and J. H. Boraston, *Sir Douglas Haig's Command, 1915–1918,* 2 vols. (1922); E. von Falkenhayn, *General Headquarters Decisions, 1914–1916* (1919); J. B. McMaster, *The United States in the World War,* 2 vols. (1918–20); M. Schwarte (ed.), *Der Grosse Krieg, 1914–1918,* 10 vols. (1921–25); Sir H. J. Newbolt, *A Naval History of the War, 1914–1918* (1920); memoirs of Hindenburg, Tirpitz, Ludendorff, Conrad von Hötzendorff, Moltke, and French.

NON-MILITARY:

J. T. Shotwell (ed.), *Economic and Social History of the World War,* a great series written by authorities in every country; J. W. Garner, *International Law and the World War,* 2 vols. (1920); C. Seymour, *Woodrow Wilson and the World War* (1921); C. Seymour (ed.), *The Intimate Papers of Colonel House,* 4 vols. (1926–28); L. Raemaeker, *Raemaeker's Cartoon History of the War,* 3 vols. (1918–19); H. Barbusse, *Under Fire,* translated from the French (1917), a vivid picture of life at the front; E. Bevan, *German Social Democracy during the War* (1919).

ADDITIONAL REFERENCES

L. Guichard, *The Naval Blockade,* trans. from the French (1930); P. Renouvin, *La crise européenne et la grande guerre (1904–1918)* (1934); C. R. M. F. Cruttwell, *A History of the Great War, 1914–1918* (1934).

CHAPTER XXXVI

THE CONFERENCE OF PARIS

THE DELEGATES AND THEIR PROBLEMS

THE greatest war in all history was now over. It is estimated that over 8,000,000 men were killed in battle and 21,000,000 wounded. How many died as a result of starvation, disease, and grief due to the war will never be known. Losses in the war The destruction of property was so enormous that it cannot be estimated. And the war expenses of all the belligerents were so great that most of them were on the brink of bankruptcy. Whole classes of people sank into ruin, and whole nations were impoverished.

A peace conference met in Paris, representing thirty-two nations.[1] Its task was stupendous: a torn and shattered world was to be made whole again; great empires were to be sundered and made harmless; new nations were to be delimited and given a place in the family of nations; and a new era was to be inaugurated that would guarantee peace and security to the world. To the Conference came statesmen and diplomats attended by hosts of experts of every description, financial, legal, diplomatic, military, and economic. It was clearly realized The leading delegates to the Conference that the importance of the decisions of the Conference required that they should be the outcome of the best knowledge available. The leading figures were Clemenceau, who was the chairman of the Conference, Lloyd George, and Wilson. Clemenceau's undeviating purpose was to obtain a treaty that would give security to France, whatever the cost to Germany. This cynical politician and witty journalist had been the soul of France in the darkest hour of the war. He now represented the mood of a nation embittered by the fearful sufferings of four and a half years of conflict waged on her soil. Before the war, Lloyd George had been the idol of the

[1] These were first, the Big Five, Great Britain, France, the United States, Italy, and Japan; second, the minor belligerents, Belgium, Brazil, China, Cuba, Czecho-Slovakia. Greece, Guatemala, Haiti, Hedjaz, Honduras, Yugo-Slavia, Liberia, Nicaragua, Panama, Poland, Portugal, Rumania, and Siam; third, the British possessions, Australia, Canada, India, New Zealand, and the Union of South Africa; fourth, those powers who had merely broken off diplomatic relations with Germany, Bolivia, Ecuador, Peru, and Uruguay.

British masses because of his social reforms.   As war Premier he
had won the entire nation by his redoubtable energy.   At the
Conference he, too, represented the war mood of his fellow countrymen; but, at the same time, without the desire of completely crushing the fallen foe.   The eyes of a war-torn world turned to the
American President as the one who represented a nation that
wanted nothing for herself, as the one statesman who had seen a
vision of a fraternity of nations that would unite mankind to
abolish war forever.   His Fourteen Points had made him the
spokesman of a peace without vengeance, which would be the
starting-point for a new and a better system of international relations.   At the Conference he ardently and consistently supported
the League of Nations; and to get the support of his colleagues for
the League, he was compelled to modify the Fourteen Points.

The Conference opened its sessions on January 18, 1919, the
forty-eighth anniversary of the founding of the German Empire,
Organiza-   now disrupted and ruined.   Being too large to deal
tion   effectively and expeditiously with all the questions
before it, a Supreme Council was organized, consisting of the representatives of the "Big Five," England, France, the United States,
Italy, and Japan, to formulate all important matters, which were
then to be passed upon by the Conference in plenary session.   Japan
was concerned only with matters affecting the Far East, and therefore paid little attention to the European problems before the
Conference.   Italy withdrew for a time because of her opposition
to the settlement of the Adriatic question.   Therefore, it devolved
chiefly on the "Big Three," Clemenceau, Lloyd George, and Wilson, to make the great decisions.   To the Council came the delegates of the minor powers to present their claims.   Assisting the
Council were numerous commissions, composed of representatives
from the various powers, that dealt with special problems, making
investigations and presenting their recommendations which often
had great weight with the Council.

After four months of deliberation, sometimes public, sometimes
secret, the treaty was ready.   On May 6, a German peace delega-
The Ger-   tion was admitted to the Conference and was informed
mans com-   of the terms.   They protested against the harshness
pelled to sign
the Treaty of of the treaty, claiming that Germany had surrendered
Versailles   on the basis of the Fourteen Points.   But no attention
was paid to their protest.   The formal signing of the treaty took

place, on June 28, in the famous Hall of Mirrors in the palace of Versailles. After the Treaty of Versailles was signed, the Conference was virtually at an end, as the leading delegates departed. A number of plenipotentiaries remained in Paris for another year to prepare treaties with the other enemy powers and to work out the numerous problems affecting the succession states that emerged from the empires of central and eastern Europe.

When the Conference met, it did not have a free hand to deal with the momentous problems that demanded solution. Its decisions were influenced by secret treaties, entered into *The secret* by the powers during the war, which were imperialistic *treaties* in character. These treaties were made public by the Bolshevists when they got control of the government of Russia. England and Russia had an agreement according to which the latter was to get Constantinople and the territory bordering on the Straits; and the former, most of the neutral zone in Persia, which contains valuable oil wells. For entering the war on the side of the Allies, Italy was promised Trieste, the Trentino, Gorizia, part of the Dalmatian coast, part of the Tyrol, and the Dodecanese Islands. Rumania was promised Transylvania, the Banat, and Bukovina. Russia, England, France, and Italy agreed to partition Asiatic Turkey, and to divide nearly all her territory among themselves. Russia and France had an agreement concerning Germany: France was to have Alsace-Lorraine and a special position in the Saar Valley; the left bank of the Rhine was to be organized as a buffer state under French protection; and Russia was to have a free hand in determining Germany's eastern boundary and in reorganizing Poland. Because of the withdrawal of Russia from the war, this treaty was not considered at Paris. Japan and the Allies had an agreement that the former was to become the heir of Germany in the Far East: to get Kiao-chau, and the economic privileges in Shantung.

ALLIED TERMS TO GERMANY

Although the Allies subscribed to Wilson's principles, they carried out their secret arrangements wherever they could. The following is a résumé of the chief provisions of the *Territorial* Treaty of Versailles: The neutralizations of Belgium *arrange-* and of Luxemburg were declared to be at an end; their *ments* future status was to be determined by the League of Nations. To Belgium was ceded Moresnet, Eupen, and Malmédy. Luxemburg was no longer to be included within Germany's tariff laws. The Saar district, rich in coal mines, was to be governed by a commission appointed by the League. At the end of fifteen years its inhabitants were to decide, by a plebiscite, whether they desired the existing system, union with France, or union with Germany. Alsace-Lorraine was restored unconditionally to France. Such districts in Schleswig as voted to join Denmark were to be permitted to do so.[1]

The problem of rectifying the eastern frontier of Germany caused much debate, due to the claims of the Poles and of the Germans.

German territory ceded to Poland
Those districts that were inhabited chiefly by Poles, such as Posen and most of West Prussia, were given outright to Poland. She failed to get districts in East Prussia due to adverse plebiscites. What Prussia had gained from the Partitions of Poland was now restored to the reborn nation. Danzig, overwhelmingly German, was organized as a Free City with an independent government under the protection of the League. In order to give Poland an outlet to the sea, Danzig was included in the Polish tariff system. East Prussia was now separated from the rest of Germany by the "Polish Corridor"; but Germany was permitted free transit of goods and of persons across this area. Upper Silesia, rich in coal mines, was to hold a plebiscite to determine whether it would be Polish or German.[2] Germany ceded to the Allies the city of Memel and its environs; its disposition was to be decided later.[3]

Germany surrendered all her overseas possessions. What was to be done with them? An interesting experiment in international

The German colonies given as "mandatories" to Allies
control of backward regions was attempted in the "mandatory" system. These regions were not distributed directly among the Allies; they were given the status of "mandatories," whose government was to be administered by those powers into whose care they were entrusted. To the League of Nations was given the power to organize the mandatories and to supervise the administra-

---

[1] The northern district of Schleswig was united with Denmark after a favorable plebiscite, held in 1920; the southern district voted to remain with Germany.

[2] The plebiscite was held in 1921, and the result was favorable to Germany. The matter was referred to the Council of the League of Nations, which awarded those districts in Upper Silesia which voted Polish to Poland, and those that voted German to Germany.

[3] A body of Lithuanians seized the city; in 1924, it was given to Lithuania by the League of Nations on the recommendation of a commission.

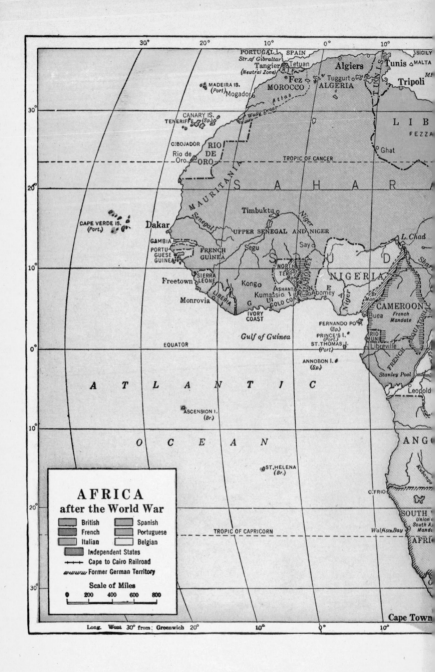

AFRICA
after the World War

British Spanish
French Portuguese
Italian Belgian
Independent States
Cape to Cairo Railroad
Former German Territory

Scale of Miles
0   200   400   600   800

Long. West 30° from Greenwich 20°   10°   0°   10°

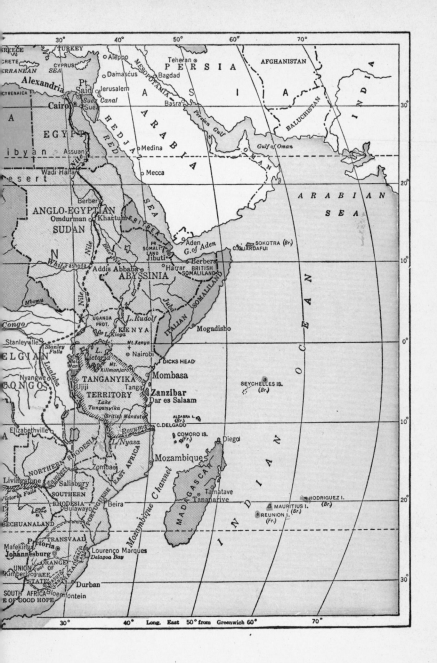

tion of the mandatory nation. Great Britain was given a mandatory over German East Africa, which was renamed Tanganyika Territory; the Union of South Africa, over German South-West Africa; New Zealand, over the German Samoan Islands; Japan, over the German Pacific islands north of the Equator; Australia, over German New Guinea and over the German Pacific islands south of the Equator; and Great Britain and France, over Togo and Cameroon. In apportioning the German colonies the Allies were confronted with the problem in the Far East. Japan demanded that the terms of her secret agreement with the Allies be fulfilled. But the Chinese delegates insisted that German possessions in China should be restored to the latter to whom they had originally belonged. But the Conference paid no heed to the Chinese protest, and awarded Germany's leasehold of Kiao-chau and her rights, concessions, and public property in Shantung to Japan.

Germany ceded to the Allies all her merchant ships over 1600 tons as compensation, "ton for ton," for her destruction of Allied shipping; and she was required to build ships for the Allies to make up any deficit. Germany renounced ^{Economic} property and treaty rights in Siam, Liberia, Morocco, Egypt, Turkey, and Bulgaria. All public property in Alsace-Lorraine went to France. The Allies reserved the right to liquidate all property rights and interests belonging to German nationals within their territory, including that ceded to them by Germany. All public property in the former German colonies passed to the new governments. Germany was required to deliver large quantities of coal, annually for ten years, to France, Belgium, and Italy. Most of these deliveries were to be to France as compensation for the destruction of French coal mines by German armies. Germany was also required to give to the Allies 5000 locomotives and 150,000 cars. The Allies were to be granted a "most favored nation" clause in German tariff arrangements. For a limited time German imports from Alsace-Lorraine, Luxemburg, and from the territory ceded to Poland were to be free of duty. The administration of the rivers Elbe, Oder, Danube, and Rhine was to be in the hands of an international commission under the supervision of the League of Nations.

The destruction of property caused by the German invasions, especially in the devastated regions of France, was so enormous

that it was impossible to compute an indemnity. Therefore,
Reparations Germany was required to make "reparations" to the Allies on the ground that she was solely responsible for the damage. The treaty declared that "Germany accepts the responsibility of herself and her allies for causing all the loss and damage to which the Allied and Associated Powers and their nationals have been subjected as a consequence of the war imposed upon them by the aggression of Germany and her allies." A Reparations Commission, representing the Allies, was established to supervise and to enforce the economic terms of the treaty. It was given oversight of Germany's system of taxation and of her economic organization in order to compel her to provide the means with which to fulfill the economic terms. The Reparations Commission was to draw up a bill of damages against Germany, to be presented on or before May 1, 1921. In computing the amount, it was agreed that Germany was to compensate the Allies for all damage done to their civilian population during the war, for military pensions to Allied soldiers, and for separation allowances made to the families of Allied soldiers; she was also to pay Belgium's war debt to the Allies; and the cost of carrying out the treaty, such as the expenses of the armies of occupation and of the Reparations Commission. The Commission had power to determine Germany's liability in accordance with her capacity to pay, as well as the method, time, and conditions of payment.

Conscription was abolished in Germany. Her maximum military strength was fixed at an army of 100,000, all volunteers for
Military a period of twelve consecutive years. Germany was
and naval required to surrender her stock of munitions and was greatly restricted in the manufacture and importation of munitions. There were to be no fortifications or troops on the left bank of the Rhine and in a zone fifty kilometers east of the river. The fortifications on Helgoland were to be dismantled as well as those on a zone bordering on the Baltic. German naval strength was limited to a specified number of warships. Germany surrendered her entire fleet to the Allies.[1] She was forbidden to maintain a force of military airplanes.

To guarantee the execution of the treaty, the left bank of the Rhine, together with the bridgeheads on the right bank, was to be

[1] The German fleet was interned by the British at Scapa Flow. In 1919, it was scuttled and sent to the bottom by the Germans themselves.

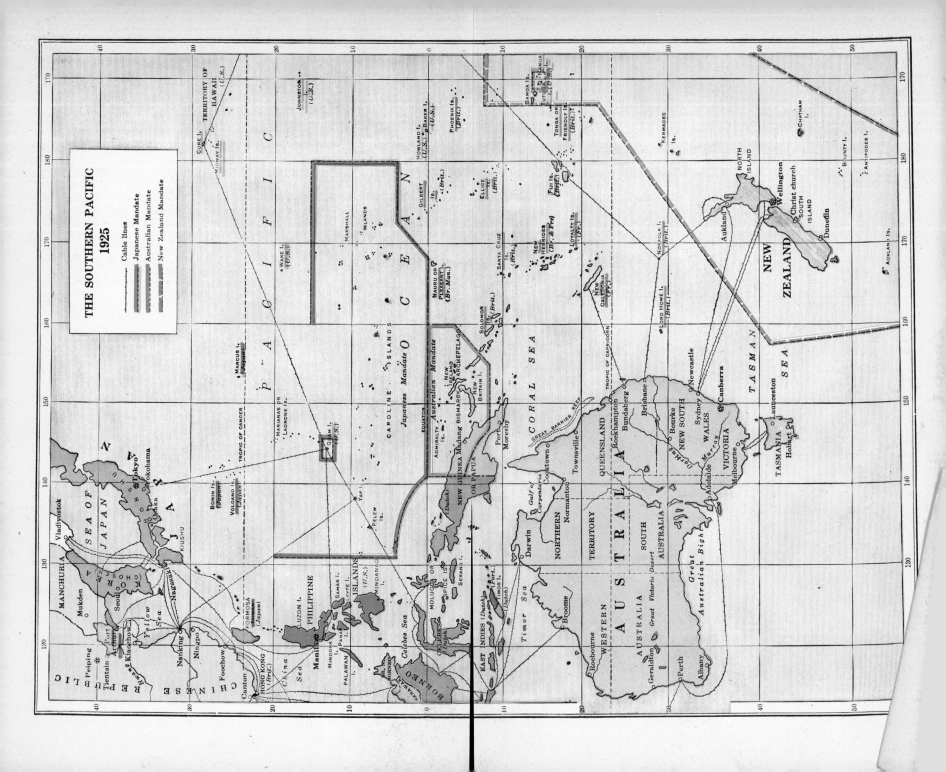

occupied by the Allies for fifteen years. Evacuation was to take place gradually, one part at the end of five years, another at the end of ten years, and the remainder at the end of fifteen years. If, in the opinion of the Reparations Commission, Germany did not fulfill her obligations in regard to Reparations, the whole or part of the left bank was to be reoccupied. **Occupation of the left bank of the Rhine**

The Germany that emerged from the war was a smaller, a poorer, a weaker, and a humbler Germany than the Empire of 1914. She lost about 27,000 square miles of territory in Europe, and all her possessions overseas. Her army was insignificant; and her navy at the bottom of the sea. Her foreign investments, including the Bagdad Railway, were gone. Her foreign trade and merchant marine were almost gone. Her natural resources were seriously diminished by the loss of Lorraine with its iron, and of the Saar with its coal. **Losses of Germany**

The terms of the Treaty of Versailles were severe. Four and a half years of truceless war had greatly embittered the Allies against Germany who, they believed, was responsible for the conflagration. Moreover, the exceedingly harsh Treaty of Brest-Litovsk that Germany had dictated to Russia, gave the Allies an idea of the terms they would have received from a triumphant Germany.

THE LEAGUE OF NATIONS

An integral part of the Treaty of Versailles is known as the "Covenant," providing for the organization of a League of Nations. The preamble to the Covenant states that the object of the League is "to promote international coöperation **Object** and to achieve international peace and security, by the acceptance of obligations not to resort to war, by the prescription of open, just, and honorable relations between nations, by the firm establishment of the understandings of international law as to actual rule of conduct among governments, and by the maintenance of justice and a scrupulous respect for all treaty obligations in the dealings of organized peoples with one another." Machinery for the working of the League was provided for in: (a) two representative bodies, the Assembly and the Council; (b) a secretariat; (c) executive commissions; and (d) a court.

The Assembly is a large body representative of all the member states, each having only one vote and not more than three delegates.

The Assembly — The powers vested in the Assembly are, on the whole, rather general; it may deal with matters "affecting the peace of the world." However, it does have some definite functions: (a) it can investigate disputes referred to it; (b) it can admit new members to the League; and (c) it can elect the non-permanent members to the Council, and by a two-thirds vote it can fix the rules of their election and of their term of office.

The chief functions of the League are exercised by a Council consisting of permanent and non-permanent members. Each of

The Council — the great powers in the League was given a permanent seat; the minor powers were to be represented by four members elected by a majority of the Assembly.[1] Unless otherwise provided for, decisions of both the Assembly and the Council require a unanimous vote.

A permanent Secretariat is located at the capital of the League, Geneva. The chief of this body, the Secretary-General, is ap-

The Secretariat, Commissions, and Court — pointed by the Council with the approval of the majority of the Assembly. The chief duty of the Secretariat is to conduct investigations concerning disputes and to register and publish treaties. Commissions perform much of the work of the League, although their character and jurisdiction are not clearly stated in the Covenant. All existing international bureaus were to be supervised and controlled by executive commissions of the League. A Permanent Court of International Justice was provided for to hear and determine disputes between nations. It was empowered also to give advisory opinions on disputes submitted to it by the Assembly or by the Council.

As the main object of the League was the prevention of war, the articles dealing with the methods to preserve peace are of special

Prevention of war: (1) compulsory arbitration — interest. The Covenant lays down the rule that all disputes between members must be submitted to compulsory arbitration, to judicial settlement, or to an inquiry by the Council. War is not to be declared until three months after the award by the arbitrators or the report by the

[1] The original permanent members were England, the United States, France, Japan, and Italy. But the United States refused to join the League. In 1926, Germany was elected to the League and given a permanent seat. In 1933, the number of non-permanent members was increased to ten.

Council; "the award of the arbitrators or the judicial decision shall be made within a reasonable time, and the report of the Council shall be made within six months after the submission of the dispute." The members agree not to resort to war against a member of the League which complies with any award or decision. "If a report by the Council is unanimously agreed to by the members thereof other than the representatives of one or more of the parties to the dispute, the members of the League agree that they will not go to war with any party to the dispute which complies with the recommendations of the report." The Council may refer the dispute to the Assembly; and in that case the "action and powers of the Council shall apply to the action and powers of the Assembly, provided that a report made by the Assembly, if concurred in by the representatives of those members of the League represented on the Council and of a majority of the other members of the League, exclusive in each case of the representatives of the parties to the dispute, shall have the same force as a report by the Council." If the dispute is found by the Council "to arise out of a matter which by international law is solely within the domestic jurisdiction" of one of the parties, the Council shall make no recommendations.

If a member resorts to war in disregard of the Covenant, "it shall *ipso facto* be deemed to have committed an act of war against all the other members of the League." The offending nation is to be subjected to an economic boycott; and the Council may recommend military action. Members agree to support one another in financial and economic measures against the breaker of the peace and to permit the passage of armies to protect the Covenant.

If a non-member is in dispute with a member, the former is to be asked to accept the obligations of membership for purposes of such dispute. If the non-member refuses and goes to war, the penalties are the same as if it were a member.

The Covenant declares that "the maintenance of peace will require the reduction of national armaments to the lowest point consistent with national safety and the enforcement by common action of international obligations." The Council is to propose plans for the reduction of armaments.

(2) limitation of armaments

Secret diplomacy is declared abolished. Treaties, to be binding, must be published and registered with the Secretariat. All treaties, present and future, that are inconsistent with the Covenant are declared null and void, except "treaties

(3) public diplomacy

of arbitration or regional understandings like the Monroe Doctrine."

What is considered by many as the most important provision in the Covenant is Article X. It declares that "the members of the (4) territorial League undertake to respect and preserve as against integrity external aggression the territorial integrity and existing political independence of all members of the League. In case of any such aggression, or in case of any threat or danger of such aggression, the Council shall advise upon the means by which this obligation shall be fulfilled."

Colonies and territories formerly under the control of Germany and her allies, that are "inhabited by peoples not yet able to stand by themselves," are to be a "sacred trust of Mandatories civilization." Such peoples are to be placed in the tutelage of advanced nations, who are to exercise a mandatory over them in the name of the League. The mandatory power is responsible for its administration to the Council.

An amendment to the Covenant is valid only when accepted Amend- by all the states represented on the Council and by ments a majority of all the members of the League.

The original membership of the League was made up chiefly of the Allied powers and neutrals. Any nation or self-governing colony could be elected by a two-thirds vote of the Membership Assembly. It was provided that a member could withdraw from the League after two years' notice, provided it had fulfilled all its existing obligations.

An interesting and novel feature of the Treaty of Versailles was the section dealing with labor legislation. The League was to Labor legis- establish a permanent organization to promote the lation international adjustment of labor conditions because universal peace "can be established only if it is based upon social justice," and "conditions of labor exist involving such injustice, hardship, and privation to large numbers of people as to produce unrest so great that the peace and harmony of the world are imperiled."

Annual international labor conferences are provided for, to which each member of the League is entitled to send delegates, representing capital, labor, and the government. These conferences are empowered to recommend measures affecting labor to the members of the League, but with "due regard to those countries in which climatic conditions, the imperfect development of industrial organization, or other special circumstances make the industrial conditions substantially different."

An international labor office was to be established at Geneva, the members of which were to be appointed by the states in the League, and by the labor conference. It was empowered to collect and to distribute information on labor conditions and to prepare programs for the conferences.

THE TREATIES WITH GERMANY'S ALLIES

Even before the Conference had met, the Dual Monarchy had entirely disintegrated. A number of new nations emerged from the ruins of the ancient empire, who sought recognition from the Conference of Paris. The Treaty of Saint-Germain (1919) with Austria, and that of Trianon (1920) with Hungary officially recognized the dismemberment of Austria-Hungary. Part was ceded to neighboring states; part became succession states; and what remained became two small states, Austria and Hungary. In economic and military matters, the treaties followed, in general, the provisions of the Treaty of Versailles.

Treaties with Austria and with Hungary

Great difficulty was experienced by the Conference in partitioning the Hapsburg dominions because of the claims and counterclaims of the nationalities who became its heirs. No compromise would satisfy the claimants, all of whom made demands which would have resulted in war but for the restraining hand of the Conference. To Czechoslovakia were given Bohemia, Moravia, and Slovakia; to Poland, Galicia; to Rumania part of the Banat, Transylvania, and Bukovina; to Yugoslavia, Bosnia-Herzegovina, Croatia, Slavonia, Carniola, part of the Banat, and part of Dalmatia; and to Italy, the Trentino, southern Tyrol containing the Brenner Pass through the Alps, Gorizia, Trieste, Istria, and part of Dalmatia.

Partition of the Dual Monarchy

In apportioning Austria's Adriatic coast, the Conference faced the conflicting demands of Italy and Yugoslavia. Both claimed it, the former because the cities were Italian, and the latter because the region as a whole was Yugoslav. The dispute focused on the city of Fiume, one of the important ports on the Adriatic. Wilson was opposed to the giving of Fiume to Italy on the ground that Yugoslavia would thereby be deprived

The Fiume dispute

of the only port to which it had any claim. Italian sentiment flared up at Wilson's decision, and Fiume became the symbol of an aroused nationalism throughout Italy. Gabriele D'Annunzio, the poet-novelist, led an expedition of Italian patriots that seized the city. In 1920, the matter was temporarily adjusted by a treaty between Italy and Yugoslavia which gave to the former the peninsula of Istria, the island of Cherso, and the port of Zara. Fiume was recognized as a Free City like Danzig. But Italy was bent on getting Fiume. A new treaty, in 1924, between Italy and Yugoslavia provided for the annexation of Fiume to Italy in return for a guarantee by Italy of Yugoslavia's frontier as established by the Conference of Paris.

The Treaty of Sèvres, in 1920, with Turkey partitioned the country, to which was left virtually only Anatolia. In its main Treaty of   outlines the treaty followed the secret agreements
Sèvres   made during the war, except that Russia was out, and Greece was in. The latter became the chief heir of the "Sick Man"; to her was given eastern Thrace and the region of Smyrna in Asia Minor. The treaty was signed by the Sultan, virtually a prisoner of the Allies who occupied Constantinople.

A Turkish nationalist party appeared that refused to accept the Treaty of Sèvres. The nationalists repudiated the Sultan and the
The Turkish treaty which he had signed, and they established a
nationalist new government at Angora, in Asia Minor. Fearing
movement   to lose her heritage under the treaty, Greece declared war (1921) against the Angora government, and invaded Asia Minor. But the Turks, under Mustapha Kemal, showed their old prowess by crushing the Greek armies, who, in 1922, were hurled out of Asia Minor. During the war Greece received unofficial aid from England, and Turkey, from France; the *Entente cordiale* had become very strained because of the different views of England and France on Reparations. A peace congress was called at Lausanne which adopted a new treaty, drastically revising the Treaty of Sèvres.

The chief terms of the Treaty of Lausanne were: (1) Constantinople, eastern Thrace, and Gallipoli in Europe, and Anatolia,
Treaty of   Cilicia, and Adalia in Asia were to remain under
Lausanne   Turkey; (2) the Capitulations were abolished; (3) there
(1923)   was to be an exchange of populations: the Greeks in Turkey were to leave for Greece, and the Turks in Greece were to

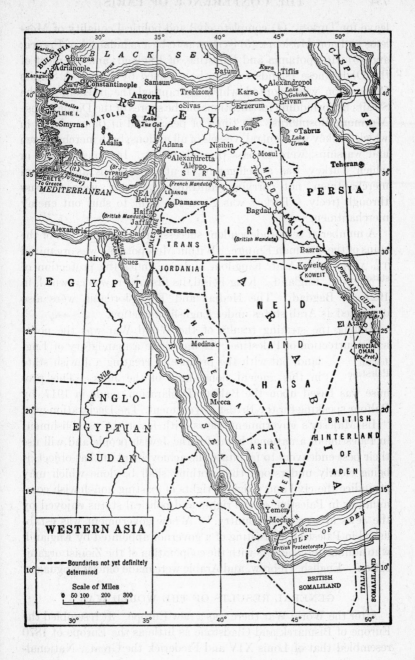

WESTERN ASIA

Boundaries not yet definitely
determined

Scale of Miles
0 50 100   200   300

leave for Turkey; (4) complete civil and political equality of Moslems and non-Moslems; (5) Syria was to be a mandatory of France; and (6) Mesopotamia and Palestine, of England; and (7) most of the Dodecanese Islands were to be retained by Italy.   A Straits Convention was adopted which guaranteed the freedom of the Straits by forbidding fortifications on the shores of the Dardanelles–Marmora–Bosphorus.   In times of peace, and in times of war in which Turkey was neutral, vessels of all nations, both merchantmen and warships, were to pass through freely.   In times of war in which Turkey was a belligerent, neutral warships and neutral merchantmen, not carrying contraband of war, were to pass through freely.   Turkey was given the right to shut out enemy merchantmen.

A number of semi-independent succession states arose out of the ruins of the Ottoman Empire.   Within Mesopotamia was organized The Arb states the Arab Kingdom of Iraq, under the protection of England.   King Feisal, its first ruler, was crowned, in 1921, at Bagdad.   The Hedjaz and Trans-Jordania were also organized as Arab states under English protection.

Among the striking results of the World War was the political resurrection of Palestine.   It was made a mandatory of England, but with the promise of creating a Jewish state Jewish Palestine in this ancient home land of the Jews.   This promise was based upon the Balfour Declaration, made in 1917, by Balfour speaking for the British government.   The Declaration was: "His Majesty's government views with favor the establishment in Palestine of a national home for the Jewish people and will use their best endeavors to facilitate the achievement of that object, it being clearly understood that nothing shall be done which may prejudice the civil and religious rights of existing non-Jewish communities in Palestine or the rights and political status enjoyed by the Jews in any other country."   A new government was established in Palestine, consisting of a governor appointed by England, who administered affairs with the coöperation of the Zionist organization.   English, Hebrew, and Arabic were made official languages.

GENERAL RESULTS OF THE WORLD WAR

After the World War there was a new Europe.   It resembled the Europe of Bismarck and Gladstone as little as the Europe of 1870 resembled that of Louis XIV and Frederick the Great.   Nationalism was the leading characteristic of the new political order.   Before 1914, Europe consisted of empires and large nations with small nations wedged in here and there. After the war it was a continent of small nations; in 1928, there were twenty-eight independent nations of which only six were large.   The long-buried peoples in eastern and central Europe at last had their resurrection, and they emerged strong, vigorous, and even aggressive.

Europe now composed of small nations

Not in every case was the principle of nationalism recognized by the Conference.   Sometimes geographic, sometimes political conditions dictated the inclusion of national minorities within states not of their choice.   To protect the rights of these minorities, special treaties were made by the Allies: with Poland who had Ruthenians, Jews, Russians, and Germans; with Rumania who had Hungarians and Russians; with Yugoslavia who had other Balkan races, also Hungarians; with Greece who had other Balkan races; and with Czechoslovakia who had Germans and Hungarians.   The minorities in Turkey, Bulgaria, Hungary, and Austria were protected by the general treaties; and those in the other central and eastern European states by special arrangements among themselves.   In general the "minorities of race, minorities of language, or minorities of religion" were guaranteed full and equal rights of citizenship and complete religious freedom.   In addition, they were given special cultural rights, such as freedom to use their language in the courts of law, in their system of privately established schools, and in the public schools wherever a considerable portion in a district demanded it; and a proportionate share of the subventions from the state to their schools and charitable institutions.   To the League of Nations was given the power to supervise the enforcement of these agreements, the purpose of which was to prevent the persecution of national minorities, so common before the World War and not the least among its causes.

Protection of minorities

Democracy also emerged triumphant.   All the new states were democratic republics; and the reorganized states, Germany, Austria, Hungary, Yugoslavia, Turkey, and Rumania, adopted democratic constitutions.   Four powerful dynasties went down to ruin, the Hohenzollern, Hapsburg, Romanov, and Osmanli; and republics were now the rule instead of the exception.[1]   Democracy was now understood to include women.

Advance of democracy

[1] Of the twenty states in 1914, only three were republics; of the twenty-eight in 1928, only thirteen were monarchies.

Nearly all the states adopted woman suffrage,[1] and gave women equal rights with men in many important matters. Many also adopted Proportional Representation and the Initiative and Referendum.

All the European nations now recognized the principle of state intervention in the affairs of capital and labor. Many of the new constitutions provided for social reforms, and laws

Social reform

were passed establishing systems of insurance against sickness, accident, and old age. France and Germany passed national eight-hour laws. There was a remarkable increase in trade-union membership, and organized labor was recognized as never before. An International Labor Bureau was established by the League of Nations to collect and disseminate information on labor conditions throughout the world and to supervise international agreements regarding labor. Annual conferences have been held by this body for the purpose of drafting labor laws which are submitted to the nations for adoption. At one of these conferences the following principles were adopted: (1) that labor should not be regarded as a commodity; (2) that it should have the right to organize for all lawful purposes; (3) that a living wage should be maintained; (4) that an eight-hour day should be established; (5) that child labor should be abolished; (6) that men and women should receive equal pay for equal work; and (7) that a system of factory laws be adopted.

The peasant, even more than the workingman, benefited greatly from post-war conditions. The cost of living rose rapidly, especially of foodstuffs, which enabled many peasants to

Peasant proprietorship

gain large profits. In those countries where peasant proprietorship was widespread, as in France, the peasants greatly increased their holdings. In eastern Europe a veritable agrarian revolution occurred. The vast estates in Russia were confiscated by the Soviet and turned over to the peasants. In the Baltic States, in Poland, in Czechoslovakia, and in Rumania, where landlordism had flourished in almost feudal grandeur, the large estates were expropriated and turned over to the tillers of the soil. Peasant proprietorship was now almost universal in Europe.

The great result of the war in the field of diplomacy was the abolition of the "balance of power" as the leading principle of European diplomacy. There could be no "balance" when Russia,

[1] France, Italy, and Spain were notable exceptions.

Germany, and Austria were no longer great powers. A new diplomatic structure was reared by the League of Nations   Disappear-
destined to bring about the coöperation of all the   ance of the
nations in an association for purposes of peace instead   "balance of
of a few great powers in alliances for purposes of war.   power"

America got no territory and but a small amount of reparations
in return for her efforts in behalf of the Allies. She repudiated
Wilson's efforts at the Conference by refusing to   The eco-
ratify the Treaties of Versailles and Saint-Germain.   nomic he-
In 1921, during President Harding's administration,   gemony of
the United
America made separate peace with Germany and Aus-   States
tria. But America emerged from the war as the economic dictator
of the world. She was the creditor of the Allies to the extent of
about $12,000,000,000 of war loans. Foreign loans, to be success-
ful, had to be floated in New York, and the dollar became the
financial standard of the world. The economic rehabilitation of
Europe depended upon America, who began to export capital on
a vast scale. In 1925, America's foreign investments, chiefly in
Latin-America, Canada, and Europe, were larger than those of
England, long the chief exporter of capital. There was also a
notable increase in America's foreign trade. Before the war she
had concentrated chiefly upon her domestic market; but now she
entered upon the conquest of foreign markets. From 1913 to
1924, her foreign trade almost doubled; as a result of the war
Germany disappeared as a commercial rival of England, but the
latter found a far more formidable rival in America whose resources were greater than those of any other country.

To the war also was due, though indirectly, the Russian Revolution. The overthrow of tsarism and the establishment of a socialist
state was an event of momentous importance in his-   The Russian
tory, as momentous as that of the French Revolution.   Revolution
It sent a new revolutionary current throughout the world which
disorganized the old socialist movement. At the outbreak of the
war the socialists in nearly all the belligerent countries supported
their governments, which resulted in the disruption of the Second
International.[1] As the war progressed, many socialists seceded
from their party, and agitated for a general peace. They formed
minority socialist parties which opposed the war; they even held
international conferences in order to revive the Second Inter-

[1] See page 592.

national.   When the Russian Revolution took place, there was another, and even deeper split in socialist ranks.   The majority were bitterly opposed to communist tactics and to the doctrine of the Dictatorship of the Proletariat, and they denounced the communist leaders as desperate and unprincipled.   The communists, on the other hand, denounced the socialists as "social traitors" and tools of the bourgeois, who, they declared, were using the socialists to suppress the revolutionary spirit of the working class. It was impossible to revive the Second International, so bitter was the feeling caused by the war and by the communists.   In 1919, at Moscow, there took place an international convention of communists who organized the Third International.   It adopted a platform of communist principles [1] to which every member had to subscribe.   This body, at whose head was a Russian, Gregory Zinoviev, began a world-wide agitation for the overthrow of bourgeois governments.   In every country a communist party was formed, sometimes openly, sometimes secretly, often both, which was under the direction of the Third International.   There was now bitter rivalry between the socialist and communist parties, both of whom appealed to the working class for support.

REFERENCES

The texts of the treaties are to be found in *The Treaties of Peace, 1919–23*, published by the Carnegie Endowment for International Peace; H. W. V. Temperley (ed.), *A History of the Peace Conference of Paris*, 6 vols. (1924), authoritative history of the Conference, written by experts, contains reprints of important documents, indispensable source of information; R. S. Baker, *Woodrow Wilson and World Settlement*, 3 vols. (1922), defense of American President, contains many original documents; R. Lansing, *The Peace Negotiations* (1921), a severe criticism of Wilson's activities by his Secretary of State; E. M. House and C. Seymour (eds.), *What Really Happened at Paris* (1921), articles by some of Wilson's advisers; C. Seymour (ed.), *The Intimate Papers of Colonel House*, 4 vols. (1926–28), Vol. IV, views of Wilson's confidential advisor; J. M. Keynes, *The Economic Consequences of the Peace* (1920), a severe criticism of the treaty and its makers, brilliantly written; by the same author, *A Revision of the Treaty* (1922), a plea for modification of the terms, gives history of Reparations question; A. Tardieu, *The Truth about the Treaty* (1921), translated from the French, a defense by a French nationalist; C. H. Haskins and R. H. Lord, *Some Problems of the Peace Conference* (1920), G. L. Beer, *African Questions at the Peace Conference* (1923), and D. H. Miller, *The Drafting of the Covenant*, 2 vols. (1928), by American experts at the Conference.

[1] See pages 581–84.

CHAPTER XXXVII

THE RUSSIAN REVOLUTION OF 1917

THE MARCH REVOLUTION

THE uprising in 1905 had familiarized the Russian masses with the idea of resistance to tsarism. Though savagely suppressed, the revolutionary movement had left the people sullen and ready to rise at the first favorable opportunity. Nicholas II made the error, characteristic of many other autocrats, of making no attempt to conciliate his subjects. He was serenely certain that his dynasty would continue to rule Russia by using the same repressive methods that had proved so successful in the past.

When the World War broke out, it was greeted with enthusiasm throughout the country. The Russians opposed the Teutonic powers as the oppressors of their race, and they rallied to the side of the government which was now fighting for the freedom of the "little Slav brother." Many of the revolutionaries supported the war in the belief that a war to destroy German militarism and autocracy in which Russia was allied with the democratic nations of the West might lead to a modification of the tsarist system.

Popular support of the war

The terrible defeats suffered by the Russian armies naturally discredited the government. Inefficiency and corruption were widespread in the management of military affairs; unarmed soldiers were sent into battle by drunken officers. Army contractors were so corrupt that the army often received half of the supplies contracted for, and that half of inferior quality. "Dark influences" at court endeavored to persuade the Tsar to sign a separate peace with Germany. Both Nicholas and his wife were under the spell of a religious fanatic, named Rasputin, who dominated their minds and influenced their policies. All elements in the nation were shocked at the scandalous state of affairs.

Inefficiency and corruption

As the war progressed, it became evident that the autocracy was incapable of leading Russia to victory. All the political parties in the Duma, even the most conservative, solidly opposed the government. Discontent spread rapidly among all classes. Rasputin was assassinated by a group of patriotic nobles who believed that the country would be well rid of such an evil

Spread of discontent

influence. Business suffered severely because of the closing of the
Straits, and foreign trade virtually disappeared. In the country
the peasants became restless, and raised their old demand for more
land. In the cities the workingmen needed but little encouragement to start revolutionary activity.

Early in March, 1917, great strikes broke out in Petrograd.
Starving workingmen rioted, and the military were called out to
Fall of the   restore order. But, unlike the situation in 1905, the
Romanov   soldiers refused to fire on the strikers; instead they
dynasty
fraternized with them. Hostility to the Tsar was so
widespread that delegations came to the Duma demanding the
abdication of Nicholas. Moderates as well as radicals now favored
decisive action against the government. Although controlled by a
conservative majority, the Duma voted to establish a provisional
government. The issue was now joined, and, to his great astonishment, the Tsar found himself without the support of any influential element. He could not rely upon the army which had gone
over to the side of the people. On March 15, Nicholas abdicated
his throne. In this unexpected way the Romanov dynasty, which
had withstood so many revolutionary assaults, came to a sudden
and inglorious end. The Revolution took place, declared one of
its leaders, Miliukóv, because "history does not know of another
government so stupid, so dishonest, so cowardly, so treacherous as
the government now overthrown."

THE PROVISIONAL GOVERNMENT

A provisional government was established headed by a liberal
noble, Prince Lvov. Its members were chiefly Octobrists and
Reforms of ·   Cadets,[1] and its leading figure was Miliukóv. A few
the provi-   radicals were included, the most prominent being
sional gov-   Alexander Kerensky. The political complexion of the
ernment
provisional government was liberal; it favored a constitutional monarchy under a liberal-minded member of the Romanov dynasty. In a proclamation to the people the provisional
government announced the following program: (1) a general amnesty to political offenders, including terrorists; (2) freedom of
speech, of the press, and of association; (3) abolition of social, racial,
and religious restrictions; and (4) the calling of a constitutional
convention. Disregarding the Duma and the Imperial administra-

[1] For a description of the Russian political parties see pages 455–62.

tion, the provisional government issued a number of decrees which carried out its proclamation. The constitution of Finland was restored; the anti-Jewish laws were repealed; and steps were taken to grant self-government to the Poles. Thousands of exiled revolutionaries from Siberia and from foreign lands returned to Russia, where they were now welcomed as heroes and martyrs.

The attitude that the new government would take toward the war was a matter of great concern to the Allies. In no uncertain terms it declared its loyalty to the Allies and to the agreements made by the ex-Tsar. Miliukóv came out strongly in favor of getting Constantinople, promised to Russia by the Allies. Russia's historic policy in the Near East did not change with revolution.

Government supports the war

The reforms of the provisional government did not allay discontent. Was the Revolution to be merely political, or was it to become also social? The provisional government desired to transform Russia into a modern democracy, but it had no intention of attacking the rights of property which it definitely and clearly promised to protect. A new revolutionary movement appeared that had for its object a social transformation of Russia. It arose in the extreme parties, the Menshevists, the Bolshevists, and the Social Revolutionists. The Menshevists and Social Revolutionists were willing to support the provisional government, provided its membership and policies were more radical. But the Bolshevists were totally opposed to it on the ground that its character and membership were bourgeois, and, therefore, hostile to the interests of the peasants and workingmen. New organizations appeared, "soviets" (councils), consisting of soldiers', workingmen's, and peasants' delegates. At first the soviets collaborated with the provisional government, but they soon fell under the control of the more radical elements and demanded recognition as the representatives of the people. There were now two rival organizations that claimed to rule Russia, the provisional government and the soviets.

The soviets

Two extraordinary men now appeared on the political scene, the Bolshevist leaders, Vladimir Ilyich Ulianov, known by the pseudonym "Lenin," and Leon Bronstein, known by the pseudonym "Trotsky." [1]   In the annals of revolution

Lenin (1870–1924)

[1] Russian revolutionists were accustomed to use pseudonyms in order to escape detection.

there is no more remarkable figure than Lenin.   Like many another Russian revolutionist he was of aristocratic origin.   Early in life Lenin became a devoted student of the writings of Marx whom he admired as the greatest of all social philosophers.   He entered the revolutionary movement, and, for many years, his life was typical of the professional revolutionists of Russia: Siberia, prison, foreign residence, "underground" agitation, conspiracy, and controversy.   Lenin lived many years in England and in Switzerland, where he was active among his fellow exiles in organizing socialist groups and in conspiring against the tsar.   Unlike the typical Russian revolutionists he was neither a speculative thinker nor a dreamy idealist, but a man of action, cool, practical, shrewd, and daring.   To Lenin revolution was a science to be studied and applied in the same spirit as an engineer studies and applies himself to a problem of building a bridge.[1]   He had scant sympathy for heroic efforts that ended in failure, and he opposed the idealistic tendencies of his fellow revolutionists as ardently as he opposed the tsaristic system.   His was the master mind that conceived the Bolshevist Revolution.

Trotsky was as different in temperament from Lenin as Danton was from Robespierre.   An eloquent and volcanic orator and a vivid and penetrating writer, he exerted great influence on popular opinion.   Trotsky came of a middle-class Jewish family, and, early in life, threw himself into the revolutionary movement.   He, too, lived the life of a professional revolutionist.   Trotsky was a socialist, at first belonging to the Menshevist faction; later, he joined the Bolshevists and became the most influential follower of Lenin.

Trotsky
(1877–1940)

THE RÉGIME OF KERENSKY

The soviets demanded of the provisional government that it repudiate Russia's war aims and declare itself in favor of "peace without annexation and indemnities on the basis of self-determination of peoples," which became the soviet peace formula.   In the lead was the Petrograd soviet around which rallied the opponents of the provisional government.   As mobs became more menacing, and the army more mutinous, the government was forced to take a more advanced position.   In May, Mīliukóv, whose support of the war

The provisional government becomes more radical

[1] See page 581 for description of Lenin's ideas.

had aroused the hostility of the extremists, was compelled to resign. Later the government was reorganized; more places were given to Menshevists and Social Revolutionists. The government was still headed by Prince Lvov, though its most prominent member was Kerensky, who had won great popularity as a radical orator. The reorganized government adopted the peace formula of the soviets, and favored the extension of state control over industry, the special protection of labor, and land reforms.

Again the question arose as to the attitude of the government toward the war. Kerensky came out firmly against a separate peace with Germany, but, at the same time, he favored a conference of the Allies to formulate their war aims. Demands for peace The war was becoming increasingly unpopular in Russia. The first All-Russian Congress of Soviets denounced the war as capitalistic in origin and imperialistic in aim, and favored a general peace by appealing to the democracies of the world. At the front discipline was seriously undermined. The soldiers fraternized with the Germans, and attacked their officers, who were denounced as tsarist and counter-revolutionary. They organized committees that took matters into their own hands, and, in some cases, chose officers. The army was disintegrating into rebellious mobs.

Kerensky's plan of a peace conference received no encouragement from the Allies. Instead, they urged him to fight the Germans more vigorously. To show his loyalty to the Allies, Kerensky himself led a drive of the Russian army in Galicia, which, for a time, made some headway. But mutinies among the soldiers encouraged the Germans, who began a counter-offensive and succeeded in recovering their lost ground. Kerensky's drive

The failure of the drive made the provisional government very unpopular. Again there was a shift to the left. Early in August, Kerensky succeeded Lvov as Prime Minister, and the cabinet now consisted almost entirely of Menshevists and Social Revolutionists. But the change did not satisfy the soviets, who raised the cry, "Peace, Land, Bread," and demanded "All Power to the Soviets." Kerensky Prime Minister

Kerensky's régime encountered the uncompromising hostility of the Bolshevists, who denounced it as a tool of the imperialist Allies. The country, defeated, starved, exhausted, disappointed, and embittered, lent a willing ear to the Bolshevist agitation for peace with Germany. **Disci-** Breakdown of discipline in the army pline at the front completely disappeared; so many deserted that the army was virtually demobilizing itself without waiting for peace to be declared. In the country, the peasants were seizing the estates without waiting for the land reforms promised by the government. In the cities, the workingmen were seizing the factories. Chaos reigned in Russia.

It soon became evident that there was as little force behind Kerensky as there had been behind his predecessors. Property owners became greatly alarmed; they feared that the rising tide of bolshevism, if not checked, would engulf all property interests. Kerensky they regarded as a man of words, and they wanted a man of action who would put down the Bolshevists with an iron hand. Such a man they found in General Kornilov, who became the leader of a counter-revolutionary movement. He restored discipline among his troops by wholesale execution of deserters and mutineers. Kornilov repudiated the government of Kerensky, and prepared to overthrow it by a *coup d'état*. At the head of an army he began a march on Petrograd. The Revolution was now in danger, and it was the soviets rather than the provisional government that made the most energetic efforts to defend it. A Red Guard appeared, organized by the soviets and composed of militant Bolshevists, which was the nucleus of a new army that was emerging to defend the Revolution against the counter-revolutionists. As Kornilov advanced, his forces began to melt away under the influence of Bolshevist propaganda, and the remnant of his army was easily defeated by the Red Guard. The failure of the counter-revolutionary movement completely discredited the liberals who had supported it. Kerensky was even more discredited, having shown himself too weak to defend his government against both revolution and counter-revolution. "All Power to the Soviets," cried the now exultant Bolshevists.

The Kornilov movement

THE NOVEMBER REVOLUTION

Of all the Bolshevist leaders, Lenin most clearly saw that the situation was favorable to the overthrow of the provisional government. Kerensky had neither popular opinion nor armed forces behind him. The only powerful organizations were the soviets, and the only armed force was the Red Guard, both under the control of the ex

Overthrow of the provisional government

tremists. The bourgeois and aristocrats were helpless, having no organized forces to protect them. "We regard the provisional government," declared Trotsky, "as nothing more than a pitiful, helpless half-government, which awaits the motion of a historical broom to sweep it away." The Bolshevists were splendidly organized, and they were aided by the left Social Revolutionists, a faction of the party that favored an uprising. What, then, could prevent the extremists from seizing power? Nevertheless, they hesitated, fearful of taking the step; and it was with great difficulty that Lenin managed to win over his associates in favor of an uprising. Suddenly, on November 7, 1917, the provisional government was overthrown by an insurrection in Petrograd, organized by the Bolshevists and left Social Revolutionists. Most of its members were seized, but Kerensky managed to escape. A new government was organized called the "Council of the Peoples' Commissars." It consisted of Bolshevists and left Social Revolutionists, headed by Lenin and Trotsky.

There was, however, another body that confronted the triumphant Bolshevists; and that was the constitutional convention which had been called by the provisional government. It met early in 1918, and contained an anti-Bolshevist majority. But the Bolshevists were opposed, both in theory and in practice, to any political system which would be established by a majority of the citizens irrespective of class; what they desired was the control of the government by the lower classes, or the Dictatorship of the Proletariat. "It is not general, national institutions," said Lenin, "but only class institutions such as the soviets which can overcome the resistance of the propertied classes and lay the foundations of a socialist society." The constitutional convention met the same fate as the provisional government; it was suppressed by a body of revolutionary soldiers. An All-Russian Congress of Soviets, in 1918, adopted a new constitution which established a soviet system of government. Russia was now completely in the grip of the Bolshevists.

The first problem to which Soviet Russia addressed herself was peace with the Central Powers. At the conference of Brest-Litovsk the Russian delegates insisted upon the formula of "no annexations and no indemnities." They also attempted to rouse the German masses to revolution by appeals against the annexationist terms

demanded by the German delegates. But they were brusquely told
to sign the treaty presented to them, which took from Russia over
thirty per cent of her European territory. The Bolshevists, especially Trotsky, wanted to reject the treaty and continue fighting.
But Lenin counseled peace on the ground that peace would give the
Soviet government "a breathing space" to consolidate the Revolution, which, he believed, would be the nucleus of a world revolutionary movement after the powers had exhausted themselves in
the war. Lenin's counsel prevailed, and Russia signed the Treaty
of Brest-Litovsk (1918).[1]

The signing of the treaty caused a break between the left Social
Revolutionists and the Bolshevists, and the former left the government. Prominent among the Social Revolutionists
was Maria Spiridonova, who denounced the Bolshevists as traitors to the Revolution because they made
peace with bourgeois Germany. A campaign of
terrorism was begun by the Social Revolutionists against the Bolshevists, but the terrorists were suppressed and more effectively
than in the days of the tsar.

*Social Revo-
lutionists
oppose
Bolshevists*

For three years after its establishment, the Soviet government
carried on a desperate fight for its existence. Civil War raged
between "Reds," or the Bolshevists, and "Whites,"
or the supporters of tsarism, in which the latter were
encouraged by the Allies. Although not at war with
Russia, Allied troops seized the Murman coast, and American troops
seized Archangel, where they encouraged a local government hostile
to the Soviet. Japanese and American troops seized Vladivostok.
Russia was blockaded by the Allies, which intensified the misery
caused by war and revolution. The Allies were infuriated with the
Soviet government for making a separate peace, and they openly
charged the Bolshevist leaders with being in the pay of Germany.
Moreover, the Soviet government declared its uncompromising
hostility to the capitalist world, and began a propaganda in favor
of world revolution. On assuming power it repudiated all foreign
debts, which especially aroused France who had made enormous
loans to the tsarist government. Naturally the Allies were bitterly
hostile to the new "firebrand" among the nations.

*Allies sup-
port counter-
revolution*

To fight its enemies the Soviet government established the Red
Army based upon conscription. It was organized by Trotsky and

[1] See p. 735.

commanded by former tsarist officers who, in many instances, were forced to accept their positions. Trusted civil officials, however, went along with the troops to watch the officers. In combating the enemy the "Reds" used propaganda as well as arms; they undermined the discipline and loyalty of the opposing troops by revolutionary appeals. The Red Army

To destroy their foes within, the Bolshevists, now called the Communists,[1] resorted to terroristic methods. Reactionaries, liberals, Menshevists, and Social Revolutionaries all felt the heavy hand of the Soviet government. Kerensky and Miliukóv barely escaped with their lives. Landlords, capitalists, and former tsarist officials were imprisoned, exiled, or executed by Soviet tribunals. Thousands fled the country, and became *émigrés* in foreign lands. To ferret out its enemies the government established a secret police, the *Cheka*, which excited as much terror as did, in former times, the Tsar's Third Section. Its director was Felix Djerzinsky, one of the sinister figures thrown up by the upheaval, whose ruthless efficiency was inspired by a fanatical devotion to his ideals. This "saintly executioner" labored incessantly to safeguard the Revolution, sparing himself as little as he did its opponents. So thoroughly did the *Cheka* do its work that it was abolished in 1922; there were no more counter-revolutionists to apprehend. However, some of its functions were exercised by a new political police, called the *Ogpu*. Terrorism

In 1918, a "White" government was established in Omsk, Siberia, headed by Admiral Kolchak. Civil war followed in which Kolchak gained many successes over the "Reds," pushing rapidly toward Moscow. But the tide turned. The peasants, fearful of losing the lands that they had gained by the Revolution, rallied to the side of the Soviet. Kolchak had openly declared that, if successful, he would restore most of the estates to the former landlords. Attacked by the Soviet forces in front and harassed by bands of peasants in the rear, he was forced to retreat, losing all that he had gained. By the end of 1919, Omsk was captured, and Kolchak, executed. The Kolchak campaign

During the Kolchak drive the ex-Tsar met a terrible fate. After his deposition, Nicholas and his family were confined under guard;

---

[1] When the Bolshevists were finally established, they called themselves "Communists," the name used by the first socialists in the days of the *Communist Manifesto*.

and, as the Revolution progressed, they were moved from place
Execution of to place. When the Communists came into power,
the Tsar   they determined to execute the imperial family. It
was reported much later that, in July, 1918, Nicholas and his
entire family were secretly shot by their jailers. Unlike Charles I
and Louis XVI, who suffered death in the glamour of public martyrdom, Nicholas II died, unseen and unheard, beside a prison
wall in a lonely town.

During the summer of 1919, another attempt was made to over-
              throw the Soviet. "White" forces under General
The   Denikin got control of the south, and marched rapidly
Denikin-
Judenitch   northward. At the same time another "White"
campaign   army under General Judenitch invaded Russia from
Esthonia. But the "Reds" under Trotsky turned furiously on the
counter-revolutionists, and compelled them to retreat. Early in
1920, this counter-revolutionary movement also collapsed.

During 1920 there took place the most formidable attempt to
              overthrow the Soviet. Poland declared war against
Soviet strug- Russia, and invaded the country. At the same time
gles against
the Poles   a powerful "White" army, under Baron Wrangel,
and Wrangel   marched toward Moscow from the Crimea. The
Soviet was now between two fires. It made haste to sign a treaty
with the Poles, surrendering considerable territory. Trotsky now
turned on Wrangel, and completely routed his army. All counter-
revolutionary movements thereupon came to an end, as the military triumph of the Soviet consolidated its political triumph.

In the war between the "Reds" and "Whites," the Allies liberally
              aided the latter with money and supplies. But the
Allies recog- triumph of the Soviet brought a change in their policy.
nize Soviet
Russia   They evacuated Archangel, the Murman coast, and
Vladivostok; lifted the blockade; and entered into treaty relations
with Russia.

THE SOVIET SYSTEM

Moscow became the capital of Soviet Russia, and the new national flag was the red flag of international socialism. Russia
Hierarchy of also adopted a new system of government, which was,
soviets   in essence, a pyramid of soviets from locality to the
nation. The unit of the structure of the Russian Socialist Feder-
ated Soviet Republic was the local soviet. It consisted of delegates

elected according to a franchise that was novel in principle and in application. All Russian men and women over eighteen and engaged in occupations that were "productive and useful to society" were permitted to vote. There were property and occupational disqualifications. The disfranchised were those who employed labor to increase their incomes; who engaged in private trade; who were clergymen and former police officials. Citizens were given the franchise on the basis of occupation, not on that of natural right. They voted as peasants, factory laborers, officials, housekeepers, professionals; hence, a representative of the local soviet represented primarily an occupational group, not a geographical division. In the country the village soviets sent delegates to district soviets, which in turn sent delegates to provincial soviets. The central body, the All-Russian Congress of Soviets, was made up of delegates from the provincial soviets and from the local city soviets, who sent delegates directly to the central body. A village soviet was generally made up of the peasant inhabitants; but a city soviet was made up of delegates from factories, workshops, and professional bodies.

Although it was the sovereign power in Soviet Russia, the chief function of the All-Russian Congress of Soviets was to elect a large Central Executive Committee; in turn the latter chose a sort of cabinet, called the Council of the People's Commissars, which was the official ruling body in Russia.

Hierarchy of executive bodies

There were several striking features in the soviet system. There was nothing corresponding to the separation of powers, either in the strict sense as in the American system, or even in the loose sense as in the parliamentary system. Both local and national soviets had full legislative and executive authority, which they delegated completely to small responsible groups. In general, laws were not passed by a legislature; instead, decrees were issued by a group responsible to the legislature. The chief purpose of the many representative bodies was to bring forth the strong, all-powerful Council of the People's Commissars. Although the local soviets had considerable power, yet their acts could be set aside, and even the election of delegates could be nullified. There were no general elections and no definite terms of office for representatives. Those elected remained in office until they were recalled. If there was one basic purpose in the

Control by the workingmen

soviet system, it was to secure the Dictatorship of the Proletariat. To the working classes was given an overwhelming proportion of power. In choosing the All-Russian Congress of Soviets the city delegates were elected in the proportion of 1 to 25,000 voters, and the provincial delegates of 1 to 125,000 inhabitants. The working-man was more directly represented than the peasant in the complicated pyramid of the soviet system; he also shared with the peasant the control of the provincial soviets, to which the city soviets sent delegates. As the pyramid of soviets rose, the power of the proletariat became more and more until it was in full control at the top. The Communists frankly stated that the proletarian originated the November Revolution and was the driving force in its success, therefore he must remain in power.

However, the Dictatorship of the Proletariat really meant the dictatorship of the Communist Party. Behind the elaborate framework of the soviet system there was a powerful political organization, the Communist Party, which dictated nominations and appointments, and formulated domestic and foreign policies. One could not be a power in the government without being a power in the Communist Party. Its members were those who had dedicated their lives to the cause, the "shock troops" of the Revolution. Only those who were above suspicion were accepted as party members; and constant purging of the rolls took place to keep up the morale. The members were instructed in communist doctrine, and were subjected to an iron discipline. In party conferences there was the freest discussion and the widest difference of opinion; but once a decision was made, the "party line," all had to bow to it unquestioningly.

Soviet Russia became the basis of a federal union that included the border states. The Union of Soviet Socialist Republics (U.S.S.R.) consisted of Russia, including Siberia, the Ukraine, White Russia, the Trans-Caucasian Federation (Armenia, Azerbazan, and Georgia), and a number of autonomous regions in Asia. Its constitution was based upon soviet principles and organization. The chief organs were a Council of the Union, representing the people of the Federation; and a Council of Nationalities, representing the states and autonomous regions. Both Councils chose a cabinet, called the "Presidium," to conduct their common affairs. The U.S.S.R. recognized the principle of nationality by permitting, under certain circumstances, the right of secession and by complete freedom in regard to language and to culture generally.

When the Communists came into power, they determined to destroy the "institutional apparatus of the bourgeois," the civil and religious as well as the political institutions of the country. Inheritance was limited so greatly that it was virtually abolished. Civil marriage was made compulsory. Divorce was granted at the request of either or both parties, but with safeguards for all concerned, husband, wife, and children. The administration of justice was completely reorganized; in 1923, a new system of people's courts was established that applied a code based upon socialist ideas. To eliminate lawyers as much as possible, public defenders were instituted. The hardest blow fell upon the Orthodox Church, which was regarded as one of the pillars of tsarism. Church and State were separated. The landed estates of the Church, likewise its treasures, were confiscated. Religious toleration was granted, but the government discouraged the spread of religious doctrines.

Social reforms

The most important acts of the Soviet government were in the field of economics. All land was declared to be national property; estates of the nobles and of the Church were confiscated and given to the peasants. Land was divided into holdings sufficiently large to be worked by a peasant family without hired labor. No addition could be made to the allotment given to each family; neither could it be sold, leased, or mortgaged. All industrial property, factories, mines, stores, were confiscated and turned over to the state. Not even during the French Revolution did confiscations take place on so gigantic a scale. Wealthy landowners and capitalists suddenly lost all their possessions and were compelled to flee for their lives. Banking and foreign trade were declared national monopolies to be conducted by the state. A Supreme Economic Council was established to link together all economic activity.

Economic reforms

The sudden transformation of Russia from a reactionary to a revolutionary nation was, perhaps, the most important event in the political history of Europe since the French Revolution. There are many striking similarities between the French and Russian Revolutions, but the contrasts are even more striking. The French Revolution reaffirmed the property basis of society by distributing property

Contrasts between the French and Russian revolutions

more widely and by making title deeds more definite and more complete than those under the Old Régime. Its great beneficiaries were the peasant and the bourgeois. The Russian Revolution repudiated private property altogether. The peasant and the workingman became partners, in theory at least, in the enterprises in which they worked. Politically the French Revolution proclaimed the doctrines of nationalism and democracy; the Russian Revolution, of internationalism and class dictatorship. In the course of events from 1789 to 1799 there was a continual struggle between the more and less radical elements, which led to factional struggles and finally to the suppression of all the revolutionists. Reaction came with the triumph of anti-revolutionary elements, Napoleon and the Bourbons. The story of the Russian Revolution is quite different. No counter-revolutionary forces triumphed in any way. The Lenin who let loose the November uprising was the Lenin who later modified it.

REFERENCES

The Russian Revolution of 1917 roused as much bitter hatred as did the World War. Nearly all the books on the subject are, therefore, bitterly partisan. L. Trotsky, *The History of the Russian Revolution*, 3 vols. (1932), by the famous associate of Lenin; V. Chernov, *The Great Russian Revolution* (1936), from its outbreak until the Bolsheviks came into power, by a follower of Kerensky; F. A. Golder (ed.), *Documents of Russian History, 1914–1917* (1927) and J. Bunyan and H. H. Fisher (eds.), *The Bolshevik Revolution, 1917–1918* (1934), documents; W. H. Chamberlin, *The Russian Revolution, 1917–1921*, 2 vols. (1935), excellent narrative, anti-Bolshevik; G. Vernadsky, *Lenin* (1931), reliable, though hostile; J. Stalin, *Leninism* (1928), by the successor of Lenin.

For additional titles consult bibliography at the end of Chapter XXIII.

CHAPTER XXXVIII

INTERNATIONAL CONDITIONS AFTER
THE WORLD WAR

THE LEAGUE OF NATIONS

THE appearance of the League of Nations was an event of great importance in history in that it marked the beginning of an organized and permanent system of international gov- Defeated ernment. And this, despite the fact that the League powers ad- was limited in its powers, and that its members were mitted to the League still jealous of their national sovereignty, hence, not too enthusiastic in their adherence to an international government. On November 15, 1920, at Geneva, there took place the first meeting of the Assembly of the League of Nations, consisting of delegations from forty-one nations who had been victorious or neutral during the war. But, at almost every session, new members were admitted, among them the defeated nations, Austria, Hungary, Bulgaria, Germany, and Turkey. In 1934 there were sixty members in the League; the United States was the only great power that had refused to join it. When Germany was admitted to membership, in 1926, she was given a permanent seat on the Council. The German delegates received an enthusiastic reception when they appeared in Geneva. "Is it not a moving spectacle," declared Briand, the representative of France, "and especially a noble and comforting one, when only a few years after the most frightful war which ever devastated the world . . . the same peoples, who were hurled against each other, are meeting in this peaceful assembly . . . to collaborate in the work of world peace."

The peaceful settlement of disputes being one of the objects of the League, the first Assembly organized the Permanent Court of International Justice, commonly known as the World Court. The statute organizing this body and defining its powers was drawn up by an international commission of jurists, appointed by the Council of the League. It was then submitted to all the nations of the world, whether members of the League or not, for adoption or rejection. A nation could be a member of the World Court with- The World out being a member of the League. Nearly all the Court nations of the world adopted the statute, and the World Court came into existence in 1921. Its members were elected, independent of nationality, for a term of nine years, by separate majority votes of the Assembly and Council of the League. The World Court was a permanent court of law with international jurisdiction, not a body of arbitrators, such as the Hague Tribunal, which continued to exist. It decided cases bearing on international affairs that were submitted to it, and rendered opinions on such affairs whenever requested by the League. Those nations that accepted the jurisdiction of the World Court had to abide by its decisions, as in the case of courts under national sovereignty.

The League now had the framework of an international government: a cabinet, the Council; a legislature, the Assembly; an ad-
Weakness of ministrative system, the Secretariat and the many
the League bureaus; and a judiciary, the World Court. However, it lacked a vital element in order to be truly a government; it had no international army to enforce its will. According to Article XVI of the Covenant, the League could request its members to order an economic and financial boycott and even to use their armies against a recalcitrant member. The willingness of the members to enforce League decisions was, however, bound to be an uncertain quantity, considering their rivalries and their continued insistence upon the supremacy of national aims. Perhaps the greatest source of weakness of the League was the refusal of the United States to become a member. (It likewise refused to join the World Court.) The United States, because of its vast economic resources, could nullify an economic boycott ordered by the League by trading with the offending nation.

The work of the League has been chiefly in investigating and administering matters of every sort affected with an international
Work of the interest. There is hardly a matter of interest to man-
League kind that has not its League bureau or commission. It has maintained an international labor office to collect information on labor conditions throughout the world, and to draft labor laws to be adopted by the various nations. Through its agency numerous refugees and prisoners of war were repatriated. It has held conferences on international waterways and railways, on traffic in opium, on international coöperation, on health conditions, on labor, and on the protection of children. It has floated international loans for Austria and Hungary, which enabled these bankrupt nations to rehabilitate themselves.

Its greatest service has been to act as an impartial agency to carry out many of the provisions of the treaties adopted by the Conference of Paris.   The League supervised plebiscites in disputed areas to insure fairness in bitterly fought national contests. In the Minorities Treaties, insuring fair treatment to national minorities in the Succession states, the League looked after the rights of some 30,000,000 people.   An infraction of minority rights could be taken up by the Council.   The League also supervised the government of the mandates, as each mandatory power was required to render an account of its administration to the League.   There were established three classes of mandates according to the stage of the development of the inhabitants: Class A consisted of those lands that were formerly part of the Turkish Empire which were to be given their independence as soon as they were considered fit to govern themselves; Class B included more backward regions, the former German colonies in central Africa; and Class C, the still more backward regions of the former German colonies in south-western Africa and in the Pacific islands.   The first mandate to achieve national independence was Iraq.   In 1932 England's mandatory control of the region ceased, and Iraq was elected a member of the League of Nations.   Directly, the League administered the government of the Saar and the Free City of Danzig.   In the former a League commission was to govern the region until the plebiscite in 1935, when the inhabitants were to determine their political future.   A commissioner, appointed by the League, exercised supreme authority in Danzig.

However, the chief object of the League of Nations was to establish a system of "collective security" which would preserve peace more effectively than had the system of alliances of the past, (1) by use of the collective power of the League against an aggressor, and (2) by the reduction of armaments.   The first real test of collective security would come when a great power committed an act of aggression.

It came in 1931 when Japanese armies seized the Chinese province of Manchuria, violating not only the Covenant but also the Nine Power Treaty and the Pact of Paris.   China *The League* appealed to the League and asked for economic sanc- *and* tions against Japan.   A commission was appointed by *Manchuria* the League, headed by an Englishman, Lord Lytton, to investigate the dispute between Japan and China.   The report of the commission, in 1932, recommended that Manchuria be restored to Chinese sovereignty. Although not a member of the League, America's interest in the Far East caused her to take a positive stand on the Manchurian question. Her policy was clearly stated by Secretary of State Henry L. Stimson, who declared that the United States would not "recognize any situation, treaty or agreement, which may be brought about by means contrary to the covenants and obligations of the Pact of Paris...." The "Stimson doctrine" was endorsed by the League.

In 1933 the League accepted the report of the Lytton Commission, whereupon Japan gave notice of her resignation from the League. The issue was now joined. Would the League vindicate collective security by ordering the application of economic sanctions against Japan, as provided by Article XVI of the Covenant? Guided chiefly by the attitude of Great Britain, it refused to take this step. The weakness of the League, when confronted by the defiance of a great power, was a blow to its prestige.

Japan resigns from the League

Until 1933 the only great powers who were not members of the League were Russia and the United States. In that year a movement away from the League began. Germany and Japan gave notice of their resignation. But in the following year, 1934, the League was strengthened by the admission of the Soviet Union with a permanent seat on the Council.

Russia joins the League

The next test of collective security came with the Ethiopian War. On October 3, 1935, Italian armies, with hardly a pretext, began the invasion of Ethiopia. Italy's action was clearly a case of aggression by one League member against another. There was great indignation throughout the world, especially in England, where popular opinion was strongly in favor of League action. This time the League acted promptly. The Council of the League designated Italy as the aggressor in the conflict with Ethiopia; and, on October 11, the Assembly, almost unanimously, voted to apply economic sanctions against Italy. Members agreed to refuse to ship arms and munitions of war; to refuse to send essential war materials; to refuse credit or financial relations; and to refuse all imports. These sanctions were applied by the League members with surprising fidelity. As a consequence of sanctions Italy gave notice of her resignation from the League of Nations.

League votes sanctions against Italy

The League's action against Italy was greeted throughout the world as a victory for collective security.   It was the first serious attempt by the League to resist a flagrant act of aggression.   A demand arose for an embargo on oil, which would have brought Italy to her knees in a few months, as she depended on imports of oil to move her motorized armies in Africa.   Mussolini declared that an embargo on oil would be cause for war against the nation applying it.   England and France began to waver, as a consequence of which the League refused to take this crucial step.

The sanctions were felt seriously in Italy, despite heroic efforts on the part of Italians to find ways of circumventing them.   But the early collapse of Ethiopia saved Italy, who _{Defeat of} emerged triumphant not only over her small victim _{the League} but also over the League of Nations.   In July, 1936, the League removed the sanctions against Italy.   Because of the half-heartedness of England and France, the unprecedented effort of the League to restrain an aggressive nation suffered a humiliating defeat.

There was now only the shadow of a League.   Three great powers — Japan, Germany, and Italy — had withdrawn their membership.   England, France, and Russia were in- _{Eclipse of} different.   And America was more than ever deter- _{the League} mined to keep out.   The organization was maintained at Geneva, but it was without authority or prestige.   When, in 1936, civil war broke out in Spain, the League did nothing to prevent Italy from openly intervening on the side of the Rebels.   When, in 1937, Japan invaded China, the League gave its "moral support" to the victim.   And when, in 1938, Germany openly threatened to attack Czechoslovakia, the League did not even take notice of the crisis.   With the collapse of the system of collective security established by the League of Nations, there reappeared the old Europe of military alliances, of armament races, and of secret diplomacy.

THE PROBLEM OF REPARATIONS

All the victorious Allies hoped to recoup at least part of their losses from German Reparations.   Especially so France, _{Division of} who was heavily in debt to both the United States and _{the Repara-} England, and who, in addition, had the immediate _{tions among} problem of rebuilding her devastated regions.   After _{the Allies} a number of conferences, the Allies finally agreed, in 1920, on the share of each of German Reparations: France was to get 52 per cent; the British Empire, 22 per cent; Italy, 10 per cent; Belgium, 8 per cent; and the rest was to be divided among the others. In the following year the Reparations Commission declared Germany's total liability to be 132,000,000,000 gold marks (about $33,000,000,000), which was accepted by the Allies, who then drew up a schedule of payments.

Against this bill of damages Germany protested most vigorously. She declared that the amount was so exorbitant that she could not Germany ac- pay it; to attempt to do so would bring ruin to her cepts Allied economic life and enslavement to her people. But the conditions Allies paid no attention to Germany's protest, and sent an ultimatum threatening the occupation of the Ruhr unless she acceded to the terms. Germany accepted the ultimatum unconditionally.

But the Reparations problem was not solved. Sharp differences arose between France and England which, at times, threatened to Differences break their good relations. France was unyielding in between her demand that Germany pay in full; an economically France and weak Germany, mortgaged to the Allies, would not England be in a position to wage a war of revenge. England was inclined to follow a moderate policy. Her foreign trade was seriously injured by the economic chaos following the war. If Germany, the most important industrial nation on the Continent, was rehabilitated, all Europe would soon resume a normal economic life, and a revival of English trade would follow. Unlike France, England had no fear of a rehabilitated Germany whose fleets were at the bottom of the sea.

In 1922 Germany was declared to have defaulted on her Reparations payments. Early in 1923, Premier Poincaré sent a French Occupation army into the Ruhr, where it assumed control over of the Ruhr political and industrial matters. The inhabitants of the Ruhr determined on a policy of passive resistance, in which they received the support of the German government. Both mine owners and miners coöperated in restricting the output of the coal mines, and the industrial system in the Ruhr was disorganized despite the coercive measures of the French. The situation became acute, and feeling between France and Germany was as intensely bitter as it had been during the war. Germany now ceased paying Reparations altogether.

Attempts had been made to solve the Reparations problem by negotiations, by conferences, and finally by force. All had failed, largely because they were influenced by political con- The Dawes siderations. A new method was then tried. In 1924 Plan the Reparations Commission appointed an international commission, headed by Americans, General Charles G. Dawes and Owen D. Young, to make a study of economic conditions in Germany and to suggest methods by which she could pay according to her capacity. The Dawes Commission issued a Plan, which was accepted by Germany and the Allies. Its leading features were: (1) that Germany stabilize her currency by the creation of a national bank, capitalized by gold marks and having the sole power to issue paper money; (2) that Reparations payments begin at $250,000,000 annually and increase gradually over a four-year period to a normal figure of $625,000,000; and (3) that future payments be based upon an "index of prosperity," the amounts to be increased or diminished depending upon business conditions. As Germany began paying under the Dawes Plan, the French began leaving the Ruhr; by 1925, the region was entirely free of French troops.

The purpose of the Dawes Plan was to give Germany a "breathing spell" financially. Therefore, the payments for the first four years were made reasonably low. During 1924–28 Germany promptly met her obligations under the Dawes Plan. But when the transitional period was over, the Reparations problem again came to the fore. Germany declared that she could not meet the heavy payments beginning with 1929. Early in that year a committee of experts, headed by Owen D. Young, was The Young appointed by the Reparations Commission to revise Plan the Dawes plan. In 1929 the committee presented a new plan of settling the Reparations problem, which was accepted by Germany and the Allies. It was known as the "Young Plan" in honor of its chairman, who was largely responsible for its provisions.

(1) *International Bank.* An international banking institution was to be established to act as trustee for the creditor countries and as a central agency for the receipt and distribution of Reparations. The Reparations Commission and the agencies of the Dawes Plan were to be abolished, and their functions taken over by the Bank.

(2) *Annuities.* A system of annuities was adopted for the period of 58½ years, from 1929 to 1988. For the first 37 years Germany was to pay an average annuity of $473,700,000 to be distributed

among the Allies and the United States. For the remainder of the period the annuities were considerably lower.

(3) *Postponable annuities*. The payments were divided into two categories, postponable and non-postponable. If, at any time, Germany's economic situation was bad, she could, by giving notice, delay for a maximum period of two years the "postponable" part of her Reparations.

By abolishing the Reparations Commission and other agencies of foreign control, the Young Plan gave financial autonomy to Germany. Moreover, the average annuity under the Young Plan was considerably less than that under the Dawes Plan.

The year 1929 was the beginning of a business depression of world-wide extent. Especially hard were the conditions for Germany, The Hoover who had to carry the extra burden of Reparations. Moratorium Business was stagnant, and unemployment was rising rapidly. Hitherto, Germany had paid Reparations by borrowing money abroad. Huge sums were invested in German industrial enterprises, chiefly by American and English investors, whose money was instrumental in rebuilding German industry. Largely as a result of these borrowings Germany was enabled to pay Reparations to the Allies, which enabled them, in turn, to pay their war debts to America. With the beginning of the depression, the flow of money from America began to slow down, and practically ceased in 1931. Germany now had to pay Reparations from her own resources. Government finances were in a bad way, and Chancellor Bruening made desperate efforts to remedy the situation by budget reforms, but his efforts were only moderately successful. On the suggestion of the American President, Herbert Hoover, a moratorium was declared of one year, beginning July 1, 1931; there was to be a postponement "of all payments on inter-governmental debts, reparations, and relief debts, both principal and interest."

Conditions in Germany did not improve, and it became evident that Reparations payments could not be resumed at the end of the End of moratorium. In 1932 a conference took place at Reparations Lausanne for the purpose of making a final and drastic settlement of Reparations. The Young Plan was put aside, and a financial scheme was adopted which, in effect, allowed Germany to pay $714,000,000 in final settlement of all Reparations.

WHAT GERMANY PAYS

WHAT EACH CREDITOR of GERMANY RECEIVES

Dominions
Britain
France
Italy
Belgium
Other Countries
America

WHAT EUROPEAN COUNTRIES DO WITH IT

A. Paid to Britain
B. · · America
C. Retained by Country concerned

A   B   C   France
A B C   Italy
A B C   Belgium   Others

WHAT BRITAIN PAYS AMERICA & WHERE SHE GETS IT FROM

From Germany   From France   From Italy   From Other Countries

WHAT AMERICA RECEIVES

From Britain   From France   From Italy   From Belgium   From Others   From Germany

WHAT FINALLY HAPPENS TO GERMANY'S PAYMENTS

Dominions   Italy   Others
France   Belgium   America

A CHART[1] OF THE *Young Plan* AS PRESENTED TO THE AUGUST, 1929
HAGUE CONFERENCE

[1] Reproduced by permission of the Academy of Political Science, New York City, and of the *New York Times*.

THE INTER-ALLIED DEBTS

During the war the Allies had aided one another by advancing loans, as well as by armies and navies. America and England had advanced enormous sums, especially to France and to Italy. All the nations were now debtors, except the United States, which emerged from the war as the creditor nation of the world. At the end of the war the Allied powers owed the United States the huge sum of over $10,000,-000,000.

America the creditor of the Allies

A movement began in Europe in favor of debt cancellation. The debtor nations argued that their debts were "political" not commercial, as the money, loaned during the war, was but one form of a contribution to a common cause. France argued that she, who had borne the brunt of the struggle, ought not to have the additional burden of paying her war debts. She was willing, however, to pay them, provided they were indissolubly bound up with Reparations; her payments to her creditors would depend upon the payments of Germany to her. England's position was made known by the Balfour note of 1922, in which she asserted that she would collect Reparations from Germany and debts from the Allies sufficient only to satisfy her debt to the United States.

France and England favor cancellation

America insisted that international good faith could be upheld only by the payment of the inter-Allied debts. From the very beginning of the controversy she has consistently maintained that the debts owed by the Allies were in no way related to or dependent upon Reparations from Germany, which was solely a European matter. Not all the money due her, America insisted, was spent for war purposes. Some of it was for food for the civil population; some was loaned to pay maturities of previous debts; some to maintain the value of the franc and the pound sterling; and some was loaned after the Armistice. Furthermore, America declared that she had paid cash for Allied goods and services used by the American armies in Europe, hence the Allies should pay their war debts to her because the loans were used chiefly for goods and services purchased by the Allies in the United States. To cancel the debts meant that the American taxpayers would be burdened with the European war debts. The Allies had borrowed and loaned, whereas the United States had only loaned, therefore a general cancellation of debts and Reparations would not be reciprocal.

America opposes cancellation

America, however, was not disposed to be a harsh creditor by insisting upon the full payment according to the terms of the contract. In 1922 America established a World War Foreign Debt Commission to negotiate for a settlement with each debtor nation separately. The Commission adopted the principle of "capacity to pay" as the basis of agreements to fund the Allied debts.

Debt funding agreements

Between 1922 and 1929 debt funding agreements were made, according to which interest charges were reduced and payments were to be made in sixty-two annual installments. England's funded debt of $4,715,310,000 was reduced by 19.7 per cent; Belgium's funded debt of $483,426,000 was reduced by 53.5 per cent; Italy's funded debt of $2,150,150,000 was reduced by 75.4 per cent; France's funded debt of $4,230,777,000 was reduced by 52.8 per cent.

The Hoover moratorium and the Lausanne Reparations settlement caused intense feeling in Europe, especially in France and in England. According to their funding agreements they had to pay interest charges to America, but Reparations from Germany were no longer forthcoming. When, in 1932, interest payment was due, England paid under protest. France, who was the chief loser by the Lausanne settlement, asserted that the scaling down of Reparations should be followed by the scaling down of war debts, and that in proposing the Hoover moratorium America had admitted the connection between Reparations and war debts. She "deferred" interest payments to the United States until the latter agreed to adjust all international obligations. When interest was again due, in 1933, France completely defaulted; and England gave a "token" payment, a small amount as an "acknowledgement of the debt." Five other debtors made merely "token" payments. Only Finland has continued to pay in full.

The Allies default on their interest payments

The inter-Allied debt problem has since remained unsettled. America was infuriated at having the great burden of the World War debts laid on her shoulders by the European powers. In 1934 Congress passed the "Johnson Act," which forbade defaulting nations to float loans in the United States.

The Johnson Act

THE NEW PEACE MOVEMENT

The "war to end war" found expression in Article VIII of the Covenant, which declared: "The Members of the League recognize that the maintenance of peace requires the reduction of national armaments to the lowest point consistent with national safety and the enforcement by common action of international obligations." The destructive powers of airplanes, submarines, and poison gas were being perfected, and another world conflict might result in the total destruction of civilization. The fear of new wars resulted in a world wide movement for the limitation of armaments.

"Arbitration, security, and disarmament" was the formula of the new peace movement. The first important step was taken by President Harding, who summoned a conference to consider ways and means to limit naval armaments, and to consider the Far Eastern Question, which was looming up as a menace to world peace. The conference met in Washington in 1921, and was composed of representatives from the United States, Great Britain, France, Italy, Japan, China, Holland, Belgium, and Portugal. The United States, Great Britain, Japan, France, and Italy agreed on a ten-year "naval holiday," during which no capital ships were to be built, and on a tonnage limitation of capital ships for each power, according to the ratio of 5:5:3:1.75:1.75 respectively. A Nine Power Pact of all the signatories guaranteed the territorial integrity and independence of China and proclaimed the policy of the Open Door. In a Four Power Pact the United States, Great Britain, France, and Japan agreed to respect one another's rights in the insular possessions in the Pacific, the islands of the Japanese homeland not being included; and to confer if outside aggression menaced these possessions. One result of the Washington Conference was the end of a rivalry in battleships that had begun between the United States and Great Britain. Another result was the abrogation of the Anglo-Japanese alliance, which was superseded by the Four Power Pact.

The Washington Conference (1921–22)

The next peace move came from Germany. Her Foreign Minister, Gustav Stresemann, declared that Germany was willing to renounce Alsace-Lorraine; and he proposed that a security pact be formed to bring permanent peace to Europe. In response to his suggestion a famous conference took place, in 1925, at Locarno, Switzerland, where a number of peace agreements were made.

The most important agreement was a security pact for western Europe. England, France, Germany, Italy, and Belgium guaranteed the frontier between Germany and France, and that between Germany and Belgium, as The Locarno treaties; (1925) fixed by the Treaty of Versailles; the treaties neutralizing Belgium were abrogated; the Rhine zone, as demilitarized by the Treaty of Versailles, was declared to be inviolable either by France or by Germany. In case Germany violated this zone, England and Italy were to go to the assistance of France; and in case France violated it, they were to go to the assistance of Germany. France, Germany, and Belgium agreed not to resort to war against each other except in support of action by the League of Nations; and to submit all disputes which might arise to peaceful settlement. Germany did not accept her eastern frontier as fixed by the Treaty of Versailles, with Danzig and part of Upper Silesia out of Germany and East Prussia cut off by the Polish Corridor; but she agreed not to wage war in order to rectify it.

Another important peace move came as a result of an agreement between Briand, the French Foreign Minister, and Frank B. Kellogg, the American Secretary of State. In 1928, at Paris, the representatives of fifteen nations met to Pact of Paris (1928) ratify the Pact of Paris, or the Briand-Kellogg Pact, as it was called. It declared that the contracting parties condemn "recourse to war for the solution of international controversies, and renounce it as an instrument of national policy in their relations with one another." They agreed that the settlement "of all disputes or conflicts of whatever nature or of whatever origin . . . shall never be sought except by pacific means." The Pact of Paris was accepted by nearly all the nations of the world, and it was hailed as a milestone in the movement for permanent peace. However, a fundamental weakness of the Pact was that it did not provide special machinery to enforce its provisions, relying upon the machinery already established by the League of Nations.

Germany's prompt payment of Reparations under the Dawes and Young Plans convinced the Allies that she was sincere in her "policy of fulfillment." Locarno and the Pact of Paris gave some feeling of security to the nations of Europe. Therefore, in 1930, about five years before the date Evacuation of the Rhineland fixed by the Treaty of Versailles, the Allies evacuated the Rhineland. The presence of an Allied army of occupation in Germany had kept alive war memories and war hatreds. Now that it was gone, many hoped that an era of reconciliation would begin between Germany and her former enemies.

After the steps toward security came steps toward disarmament. The Washington Conference had initiated the movement for limiting naval armaments by limiting competitive building in capital ships. A new conference, representing England, the United States, France, Italy, and Japan, met in London, in 1930, with the object of limiting armament in all classes of war vessels. At the outset the Conference encountered two serious obstacles: the rivalry between France and Italy, and the rivalry between England and the United States. Italy demanded naval parity with France. But France refused to accede to Italy's demand on the ground that parity would result in making France inferior to Italy in the Mediterranean. Italy was confined to that sea, whereas France had territories to defend, not only in the Mediterranean but also in other waters. The Conference was unequal to the task of solving this problem, and both France and Italy withdrew their delegations.

The London Conference (1930)

Another problem of parity arose between England and the United States. The United States, having few naval bases, demanded parity with England in fast-sailing cruisers, a type of warship that is effective as a protector of merchant vessels scattered in the various seas. England refused to accede to this demand, but a compromise was effected that was satisfactory to both nations.

The Treaty of London was signed by Great Britain, the United States, and Japan. Its chief provisions were: (1) The existing "naval holiday" in capital ships was extended to 1936. (2) Maximum tonnage levels were established for cruisers, destroyers, and submarines. The United States was granted substantial parity with England in these categories. Japan was assured seventy per cent of the American tonnage in small cruisers and destroyers. Parity was established in submarines between the three signatories. (3) An important provision, the "Escalator Clause," declared that any of the signatories, when its security was menaced by the increased armament of any power not a signatory, could exceed its tonnage by notifying the other two, who would then be free to increase their tonnage proportionately. This clause was inserted in the treaty at the instance of England,

Treaty of London

who feared that her two-power standard might be undermined by a naval race between France and Italy. Under no circumstances was she willing to grant parity to any European power.

However modest the limits of naval armaments set by the Washington and London Conferences, a naval race between the powers was, nevertheless, effectively prevented. Could not similar limits be set to land armaments? The Council of the League of Nations issued a call for a world Disarmament Conference, which met in Geneva in 1932.

The Geneva Disarmament Conference

For months plan after plan was presented, and the only result was deadlock after deadlock. The great problem before the Geneva Conference was how to reconcile the French demand for security with the German demand for equality. France was willing to reduce her armaments, provided she was guaranteed security by the other nations against an attack by Germany, which she constantly dreaded. Germany demanded that either the world disarm down to the level set for her by the Treaty of Versailles or that she be permitted to rearm to the level of her neighbors. The Conference passed a resolution recognizing Germany's right to arms equality in a system which would provide security for all nations.

While the Conference was in session there took place a great political upheaval in Germany. Adolf Hitler became Chancellor in January, 1933. Hitler represented the national spirit of Germany in its most militant mood, and he demanded the immediate fulfillment of Germany's

Germany leaves the League

recognized claim to equality of armaments. His demand produced consternation, and fears of a revival of German militarism. The Conference proposed plans for giving Germany eventual equality through trial periods, which did not at all suit Hitler. Suddenly Germany left the Conference and gave notice of her withdrawal from the League of Nations. This move of Germany resulted in the breakdown of the Conference. After two years of negotiations it ended, in 1934, without any accomplishment whatsoever.

The year 1935 witnessed the end of the era of armament reduction by means of treaties. A new armament race, far greater than that before the war, began. The League of Nations was in eclipse, and collective security a broken reed.

Rearmament of Germany

As before the war, the pace was set by Germany. During that year she re-established universal conscription in violation of the Treaty of Versailles. Every possible sacrifice was made by the

Nazi government to rearm on land, on water, and in the air as speedily and as effectively as possible in order to make Germany the dominant power in Europe.

England was alarmed at the rapid growth of the Germany navy. In 1935, in violation of the Treaty of Versailles, she made a naval agreement with Germany according to which the latter was to have a naval tonnage thirty-five per cent that of the English navy. But as England greatly increased her navy this limitation had the effect of increasing the naval armament of both powers.

Naval treaty between England and Germany

The armament race received another great impetus when, in 1936, German armies marched into the Rhineland in violation of the Treaty of Locarno. The region was quickly militarized despite the protests of the other signatories of that treaty.

Remilitarization of the Rhineland

When the Washington and London Naval Treaties expired, in 1936, Japan demanded naval equality with England and with the United States as a condition for participating in new naval agreements. Because of her aggressive designs in the Far East she needed a navy capable of meeting the challenge of any power that would try to balk her designs. England and the United States raised the issue of "equality in security" versus "equality in armaments." They refused to grant Japan's demand for "equality in armaments" on the ground that an inferior ratio in capital ships gave Japan "equality in security," with a fleet adequate for the defense of her territory.

Japan demands naval equality

All the great powers in the world were now in the armament race. Staggering sums were spent on armies, navies, and airplanes. It is estimated that world armament expenditure in 1938 was *four times* that in 1913, allowing for changes in price levels. The dictatorships — Russia, Italy, and Germany — armed in secret as well as in public. No one knew the extent of their expenditures. "Shadow" factories were built, equipped to produce goods useful in both peace and war, as for example airplanes and automobiles. In case of war these "shadow" factories could be quickly transformed into munitions works. A new world war was in preparation which, if it occurred, would be far more destructive than the great conflict of 1914.

The armament race

THE NEW SYSTEM OF ALLIANCES

The diplomatic history of post-war Europe may be divided into two periods: (1) from the Treaty of Versailles to the appearance of Nazi Germany in 1933; and (2) from 1933 to the present. The outstanding characteristics of the first period were: (1) the dominance of France on the Continent and her support of the "Versailles system"; (2) the attempt to establish a system of collective security through the League of Nations; and (3) the movement for the reduction and limitation of armaments.

France emerged from the World War victorious but frightened. All during the terrible years of the conflict her national life hung as if by a thread; she was under no illusion as to her fate at the hands of a victorious Germany. After the war she was haunted by the fear of a war of revenge *France fears German revenge* by a revived Germany, whose population was larger and whose economic resources were far superior to those of France. At the Peace Conference she proposed a triple alliance of England, the United States, and herself to give her the desired security. But the proposal fell through because the United States refused to become a party to the scheme. Thereupon, France looked elsewhere for security.

"Your neighbor is your enemy but your neighbor's neighbor is your friend." It was on this principle that France proceeded to organize a chain of alliances with the nations on Germany's borders. In 1920 she entered into an alliance with Belgium, which was no longer a neutralized state. *Security in the west* This alliance and the demilitarized Rhineland, as provided by the Treaty of Locarno, gave France security in the west.

For all her great military strength in 1914 Germany's weakness lay in having to fight on two fronts. To take Russia's place on Germany's eastern front France formed close alliances with a chain of small states, Poland, Czechoslovakia, Rumania, and Yugoslavia. The position of Poland was an important factor in post-war Europe; she was the largest of the Succession states whose territorial integrity depended on the *Alliance of France and Poland* existence of the "Versailles system." Poland had two powerful enemies, one on the left, Germany, and the other on the right, Russia. Germany refused to renounce the Polish Corridor, which isolated East Prussia from the rest of Germany. Communist Russia was a standing menace to Poland, where communist agitation was rife among the poverty-stricken Polish masses. Against these two powers Poland needed the aid of a powerful protector. In 1921 she formed a close alliance with France. French officers organized the Polish army, and French loans helped greatly to put Poland on her financial feet.

The Succession states that had profited from the dismemberment of Austria-Hungary feared the return of the Hapsburgs. To pre-
The Little vent the loss of their territories Czechoslovakia, Ru-
Entente mania, and Yugoslavia, in 1920–21, formed an alliance known as the Little Entente, whose moving spirit was Eduard Beneš, the Foreign Minister of Czechoslovakia. They promised to support one another to prevent a Hapsburg restoration or attempts by Hungary to regain her lost territory. The Little Entente was, in a sense, a great power, with 50,000,000 inhabitants pledged to maintain the status quo in central Europe. But what made the Little Entente even more powerful was that each member had a close alliance with France. In 1924 France entered into an alliance with Czechoslovakia; in 1926, with Rumania; and in 1927, with Yugoslavia. Through her treaties with Poland and with the Little Entente, France believed that she had firmly established her security system. In case Germany engaged in a war of revenge against France she would have to fight, as in 1914, on two fronts.

All these alliances were within the framework of the League of Nations. France was a consistent supporter of the League because
France its fundamental principle of "collective security"
upholds the could be invoked against any attempts, by war or by
League threats of war, to overthrow the "Versailles system," to the maintenance of which France was deeply committed. What the League did to maintain collective security has already been described.

Opposed to the "Versailles system" were of course the defeated nations: Germany, Austria, Hungary, and Bulgaria, who demanded a revision of the peace treaties. Though a victor in the war Italy could be classed with the "revisionist" group because she was
Italy favors discontented with her share of the fruits of victory.
revision It was Italy that made herself the champion of the nations that wished to revise the treaties. Like France, Italy became a center of alliances. When Mussolini came into power his policy was both shrewd and bold. It had two objectives: (1) the

control of the Adriatic; and (2) the organization of central Europe under Italy's leadership. In 1924 Italy acquired Fiume by a treaty with Yugoslavia. But the vital point in the mastery of the Adriatic was the control of the Strait of Otranto, on one side of which was Italy, and on the other side, Albania. In 1926 Italy signed a treaty with Albania which made the latter virtually a protectorate of the former. Italy, having control of the entrance to the Adriatic, could now bottle up Yugoslavia.

Mussolini's ambition in central Europe was to place Italy at the head of a coalition of Danubian states. In 1927 Italy allied herself with Hungary, and thereafter espoused Hungary's claim to territorial revision. Italy was deeply hostile to Germany's plan for an Anschluss with Austria, which would bring Germany to the Brenner Pass, and *Alliance of Italy with Austria and Hungary* thereby accentuate the problem of the German-speaking population in southern Tyrol, which Italy had received from Austria after the war. In 1934 Mussolini scored another diplomatic triumph. Italy, Austria, and Hungary entered into an agreement with the object of maintaining peace, and of bringing about the economic restoration of Europe "on the basis of respect for the independence and the rights of every state." They agreed to increase the facilities for their common trade and to develop the traffic through the Adriatic ports. It was Italy that now barred the way to the Anschluss by virtually guaranteeing the independence of Austria.

Italy's diplomatic triumphs alarmed the Balkan states and the Little Entente. To resist Italian aggression a new combination was formed in 1934, called the Balkan Pact, consisting of Greece, Turkey, Rumania, and Yugoslavia. They *The Balkan Pact* agreed to refrain from acting with any Balkan state not a member of the Pact, without consulting the others; and to guarantee one another's frontiers. Bulgaria, having territorial claims against her neighbors, refused to join the Pact. Yugoslavia and Rumania formed a junction between the Balkan Pact and the Little Entente, being members of both combinations.

The triumph of Hitler in Germany, in 1933, marked the beginning of a new period of European diplomacy. The outstanding characteristics of this period have been (1) the dominance of Nazi Germany on the Continent; (2) the disruption of the "Versailles system" and the eclipse *Hitler and German hegemony* of the League of Nations; and (3) an unprecedented armament race in which even the United States took part.

Germany realized, that, in order to attain her ambition to dominate Europe, her first step must be to remove the armament restrictions imposed on her by the Treaty of Versailles.

Germany abolishes armament restrictions

Soon after coming into power Hitler, by the use of various disguises such as "labor training" and "sport organizations," increased the armed forces of Germany beyond the limit of 100,000 set by the Treaty of Versailles. In March, 1935, Germany openly established universal conscription. A year later, in March, 1936, she violated the Treaty of Locarno by remilitarizing the Rhineland. Deserted by England and Italy, signatories of the treaty, France did nothing to prevent Germany's violation. These moves of Germany were well timed. France's internal dissensions and financial difficulties prevented any action by her against Germany. Moreover, Hitler, for a time after the war, had the sympathy of England, who, following her old policy of balance of power, favored Germany as a check to France's influence on the Continent.

The next objective of Hitler was to destroy France's security system by detaching her allies. The first move in this direction astonished the world. Despite the bitter hatred be-

Germany and Poland in a pact

tween the Germans and the Poles, Hitler, in 1934, made a non-aggression agreement with Poland for a period of ten years. Pilsudski, who negotiated this treaty, was convinced that France would not come to Poland's aid in case of an attack by Germany because she had refused to act when Hitler, the sworn enemy of France, came into power.

The Polish treaty ended Germany's isolation and was the first dent in France's security system. After Germany had militarized the Rhineland, France's allies in central Europe were

German influence in eastern Europe

skeptical of her ability to come to their aid in case of an attack by Germany. Confronting the famous Maginot line on the French side of the frontier was the Westwall that the Germans were rapidly building on their side of the frontier. An invasion of Germany by France was now doubtful. The Little Entente began to show signs of crumbling as German influence began to penetrate central and eastern Europe. Germany adopted a barter system in her economic relations with these countries that greatly advanced her political influence. She would take a large share of their exports, chiefly foodstuffs and raw materials, and in return give them manufactured articles. In this way they became economically dependent on Germany.

This economic penetration had decisive diplomatic results favorable to Germany. In Rumania, the pro-French Foreign Minister, Nicolas Titelescu, was dismissed, and a pro- France's German policy was inaugurated. Yugoslavia also allies favor shifted from France to Germany. Greece, under the Germany dictatorship of Metaxas, did likewise. Only Czechoslovakia remained loyal to France. Her grave danger from Nazi Germany, who was encouraging disaffection among her German minority, as well as her strong adherence to democracy, made impossible a Czech *rapprochement* with the Nazis.

The alliances of France with Poland and with the Little Entente continued, but their value to France in case of an emergency was doubtful. Therefore France sought to ally herself The Franco-with Soviet Russia, who was now also isolated. Dur- Russian ing the period of the Weimar Republic, Germany and Pact Russia had been on terms of intimate friendship. In 1922 they had signed a treaty at Rapallo, Italy, according to which all claims against each other were mutually cancelled. And in 1926 they signed another treaty in which each promised not to participate in any economic boycott directed against the other, and to remain neutral in case the other was attacked. But with the advent of Hitler the friendship between Russia and Germany became decidedly cool. To Hitler, communist Russia was the enemy which he was sworn to fight. A common fear of Germany drew France and Soviet Russia together. Early in 1935 they signed a pact according to which each promised to come to the aid of the other in case of an unprovoked attack.

To balance this combination Germany and Japan, in 1936, formed the Anti-Comintern Pact, to which, later, Italy, Hungary, and Spain gave their adherence. The members Anti-Comin-pledged themselves to combat communism "any- tern Pact where the world over." Like the Holy Alliance in the early nineteenth century, the Anti-Comintern Pact was really a combination of reactionary powers to fight the democracies.

Even in the west Germany managed to weaken France's security system. The alliance of France with Belgium was a vital point in this system. In 1936, after Germany had occupied the Rhineland, Belgium renounced all alliances, and declared that henceforth she would be neutral in disputes between her neighbors.

Belgium leaves France

England and France then released Belgium from her obligations under the Treaty of Locarno, but promised to go to her assistance in case she was invaded. Germany, in 1937, signed a non-aggression agreement with Belgium.

Nazi Germany's great success in central Europe was not only at the expense of France but also at the expense of Italy, whose influence waned before the Nazi advance. A conflict between the two Fascist powers could have but one outcome, the destruction of both and the triumph of the democracies. They had "to hang together or hang separately." How could they dissolve their antagonism? Only too often in the history of Europe have conflicts between great nations been avoided by sacrificing small neighbors. The bone of contention between Germany and Italy was little Austria, that Hitler had sworn to annex and that Mussolini had

The Rome–Berlin Axis

sworn to defend. A combination between the two dictators, known as the Rome–Berlin Axis, took place, in 1936, during the Ethiopian War. Italy needed German aid to fight the sanctions imposed on her by the League of Nations. Hitler and Mussolini agreed to support each other against the democracies, but on the condition that Germany was to have central Europe as her sphere of interest, and Italy, the Mediterranean as her sphere. No longer would Italy balk Germany's ambition to annex Austria.

For long Italy had dreamed of dominating the Mediterranean. Wholly a Mediterranean power, she felt herself a "prisoner" in the

Antagonism between Italy and England

sea that she called *Mare Nostrum*. By her control of Gibraltar and Suez, England could, in case of war, effectively blockade Italy, almost all of whose foreign trade was by sea. Italy's foreign policy, therefore,

generally had to follow England's lead, a fact which she bitterly resented. The latent antagonism to England broke out with virulence in Fascist Italy. Mussolini laid plans to cut England's "life line" through the Mediterranean by destroying the value of Gibraltar, Malta, and Palestine, the vital points in England's imperial "life line." When civil war broke out in Spain, in 1936, Mussolini came promptly to the aid of the Rebels. Spain has great strategic value in that she fronts both the Mediterranean and the Atlantic. A Fascist Spain, under Franco, would be an ally of

Italy, who then could find an exit to the Atlantic without passing by Gibraltar. Mussolini also fortified Sicily and a small island, Pantellaria, near Tunis, which seriously endangered Malta, and might cut England's Mediterranean route in the narrow neck between Tunis and Sicily. When a conflict over Palestine began between Arabs and Jews, Mussolini aided the former in order to oust England from her mandate over Palestine. Haifa in Palestine was fortified by England as a naval station to protect the Suez Canal. An oil pipe line from the oil fields of Iraq to Haifa had been built by England to supply her fleet in the eastern Mediterranean. The success of the Arab nationalists in Palestine would deprive England of this important base for the defense of the Suez Canal.

In his efforts to wrest control of the Mediterranean from England, Mussolini had the loyal support of Hitler. But, in turn, he promised to back Hitler's plans for aggression in central Europe. Once assured of Italy's support Hitler determined to upset the territorial status quo established by the "Versailles system." In 1938 he brought pressure to bear on Chancellor Schuschnigg of Austria, forcing him to resign. Austria was then occupied by a German army and annexed to Nazi Germany.[1] By the addition of Austria, Germany gained a population of 6,700,000, a strategic position which controlled railway communication between the Adriatic and the Baltic, and, most important of all, a direct road to Middle Europe. *Germany annexes Austria*

What now barred the road was the "bastion of Europe," Czechoslovakia. "Who holds Bohemia is master of Europe," Bismarck had once declared. In September, 1938, a great European crisis occurred when Germany prepared to attack Czechoslovakia. After much consultation a conference met in Munich, consisting of Hitler, Mussolini, the English Prime Minister, Neville Chamberlain, and the French Premier, Edouard Daladier. The Munich Conference agreed to the partition of Czechoslovakia as demanded by Hitler.[2] *Partition of Czechoslovakia*

The betrayal of Czechoslovakia by her "friend" England and by her "ally" France was explained by Chamberlain as a policy of "appeasement" of Germany. England, having few interests in eastern Europe, was willing to give Germany a "free hand" in order to have her leave *Eclipse of France's security system*

[1] See p. 870.   [2] See p. 873.

western Europe in peace. For France the Munich agreement marked a complete breakdown of the security system that she had so assiduously built up since the war. The Little Entente ceased to exist when Czechoslovakia disappeared as a powerful factor in central Europe.

Italy was doing her part in the Balkans to break up the French security system. In 1937 Italy and Yugoslavia signed a treaty guaranteeing their frontiers and the status quo in the Adriatic. But no treaty could create real friendship between the two nations that faced each other across the Adriatic. Mussolini evolved a plan to place Yugoslavia at his complete mercy. In April, 1939, an Italian army suddenly invaded Albania. King Zog fled, and the country was promptly annexed to Italy. As Italy now controlled both sides of the Strait of Otranto, Yugoslavia could be easily bottled up. Moreover, she was open to invasion by the Axis powers: Germany from the north, and Italy from the south. Before the conquest of Czechoslovakia and Albania, Yugoslavia was the most sheltered of the Balkan States; now she was the most vulnerable. She therefore made haste to extend the diplomatic orbit of the Axis powers.

Italy conquers Albania

Both England and France might be willing to "appease" Germany by giving her a free hand in central and eastern Europe, but they were not willing to give Italy a "free hand" in the Mediterranean, where they had great interests to protect. England's interest in the Mediterranean, as a short route to her colonies in Asia and in Australasia, was a vital one. France, too, had a "life line" in the Mediterranean, the short route from her southern ports, Marseilles and Toulon, to her North African ports, Bizerta and Algiers. On the man power of her African colonies France depended to balance the superior man power of Germany. In case of war, large colonial armies could be easily transported to France by this route. Franco's success in Spain, through Italian aid, might lead to the cession by Spain of the Balearic Islands to Italy. An Italian naval and air base in these islands would threaten France's "life line." Moreover, Italy made no secret of her desire to annex Tunis. Her constant demand for naval parity with France signified that if it were granted she would be stronger in the Mediterranean than France, and therefore in a position to seize the French colonies in North Africa.

Antagonism between France and Italy

It was clear that both England and France were threatened by Italian ambitions in *Mare Nostrum*. And Italy was tied to Germany by the Axis. As before the World War, England and France were driven into each other's arms by their common enemies. The rapid growth of the German air fleet greatly worried the English, as London was vulnerable to an air attack. In 1934 Prime Minister Stanley Baldwin, in a warning to Germany, declared: "When you think of the defense of England you no longer think of the chalk cliffs of Dover; you think of the Rhine."

Alliance of England and France

When Germany remilitarized the Rhineland, the security system established by the Treaty of Locarno in the west was at an end. As in 1914, England would have to come to the aid of France in case of an attack by Germany; her own safety, not love of France, dictated such action. Negotiations between England and France led finally to an agreement, in 1938, that was in effect a military alliance between them. This agreement was closer and more binding than the Entente Cordiale that had existed between the two powers before the war.

REFERENCES

GENERAL:
  F. L. Benns, *Europe Since 1914* (ed. 1936); W. C. Langsam, *The World Since 1914* (ed. 1936); J. H. Jackson, *The Postwar World* (ed. 1939).

LEAGUE OF NATIONS:
  J. S. Bassett, *The League of Nations: A Chapter in World Politics* (1928); W. E. Rappard, *International Relations as Viewed from Geneva* (1925); M. O. Hudson, *The World Court* (1931); A. S. de Bustamente, *The World Court* (1925); P. B. Potter, *An Introduction to the Study of International Organization* (ed. 1928); F. Morley, *The Society of Nations* (1932); Q. Wright, *Mandates under the League of Nations* (1930); O. I. Janowsky, *The Jews and Minority Rights* (1933); L. P. Mair, *The Protection of Minorities* (1928); O. Junghann, *National Minorities in Europe* (1932); J. Lestschinsky, *Das jüdische Volk im neuen Europa* (Prag, 1934); and H. M. Vinacke, *International Organization* (1934); *The League of Nations: Ten Years of World Cooperation* (1930); W. E. Rappard, *The Geneva Experiment* (1932); C. Eagleton, *International Government* (1932); Sir A. Zimmern, *The League of Nations and the Rule of Law* (1936); F. F. Andrews, *The Holy Land Under the Mandate*, 2 vols. (1931); C. Streit, *Union Now* (1938).

ARMAMENT:
  B. H. Liddell Hart, *Europe in Arms* (1937); R. E. Dupuy and G. F. Eliot, *If War Comes* (1937).

ECONOMIC CONDITIONS:

E. M. Friedman, *International Finance and its Reorganization* (1922); E. M. Patterson (ed.), *Europe in 1927* (1927); P. l'Espagnol de la Tramerye, *The World Struggle for Oil*, translated from the French (1924); P. Einzig, *World Finance, 1935–1937* (1937); E. Staley, *Raw Materials in War and Peace* (1937); G. Clark, *A Place in the Sun* (1936). On Reparations: H. G. Moulton and C. E. McGuire, *Germany's Capacity to Pay: A Study of the Reparations Problem* (1923); K. Bergmann, *The History of Reparations* (1927); and N. Mullen, *Schacht* (1939). On war debts: J. F. Bass and H. G. Moulton, *America and the Balance Sheet of Europe* (1921); H. G. Moulton and C. Lewis, *The French Debt Problem* (1925); H. G. Moulton and L. Pasvolsky, *Russian Debts and Russian Reconstruction* (1924); H. G. Moulton and L. Pasvolsky, *War Debts and World Prosperity* (1932); Sir A. Salter, *Recovery* (1932); E. Staley, *World Economy in Transition* (1939).

DIPLOMATIC RELATIONS — GENERAL:

A. J. Toynbee, *Survey of International Affairs, 1920–1923* (1925) and additional volumes for succeeding years; J. W. Wheeler-Bennett (ed.), *Documents on International Affairs, 1929* (1930 ff.); W. H. Cooke and E. P. Stickney (eds.), *Readings in European International Relations since 1879* (1931); F. L. Schuman, *International Politics* (1933); R. J. Sontag, *European Diplomatic History, 1871–1932* (1933); E. H. Carr, *International Affairs Since the Peace Treaties* (1937); F. H. Simonds and B. Emeny, *The Great Powers in World Politics* (1935); J. T. Shotwell, *On the Rim of the Abyss* (1936); Vera M. Dean, *Europe in Retreat* (1939); G. Hutton, *Survey After Munich* (1939); F. L. Schuman, *Europe on the Eve* (1939).

SPECIAL:

J. O. Crane, *The Little Entente* (1931); R. L. Buell, *The Washington Conference* (1922); J. W. Wheeler-Bennett, *Disarmament and Security After Locarno* (1932); R. J. Kerner and H. N. Howard, *The Balkan Conference and the Balkan Entente, 1930–1935* (1936); G. Schacher, *Central Europe and the Western World*, trans. from the German (1937); M. H. H. Macartney and P. Cremona, *Italy's Foreign and Colonial Policy, 1914–1937* (1938); Elizabeth Monroe, *The Mediterranean in Politics* (1938); A. Wolfers, *Britain and France Between Two Wars* (1940).

ADDITIONAL REFERENCES

H. Nicholson, *Peace Making* (1919); E. H. Carr, *The Twenty Years' Crisis, 1919–1939* (1940); P. Birdsall, *Versailles Twenty Years After* (1941).

CHAPTER XXXIX

GREAT BRITAIN AND FRANCE AFTER THE WORLD WAR

GREAT BRITAIN

(a) SETTLEMENT OF THE IRISH QUESTION

TRUE to her historic policy, England, at the end of the war, demanded no territory in Europe. What she received were colonies. Nearly all of Germany's African colonies passed under Gains of the control of the British Empire as mandates. Pales- England tine, Iraq, Trans-Jordania, and the Hedjaz became British mandates. The control of the Berlin-Bagdad Railway fell into British hands. The German fleet, which had threatened England's naval supremacy, was at the bottom of the sea. German commerce and industry, which had threatened England's economic supremacy, were ruined. Vast as was her expenditure in life and property during the war, England could yet boast of a great triumph over a mighty foe.

British political life underwent profound changes after the World War. The movement for woman suffrage, which had progressed before the war, was greatly accelerated by the new Reform Bill democratic forces that emerged from the great conflict. of 1918 In 1918 England passed another great Reform Bill which marked a notable triumph for woman suffrage. Its chief provisions were: (1) universal manhood suffrage; (2) women, over thirty, were granted the franchise provided they or their husbands were qualified to vote in local elections; (3) an election day was established for the entire country; and (4) plural voting was so greatly limited that it was virtually abolished. Later, in 1928, a new franchise law gave the vote to women on the same terms as men. At last, after a century of agitation and reform, England was a complete political democracy. However, she continued to maintain her traditional form of government by King, Lords, and Commons.

Parliament had, on account of the war, continued since the general elections of 1910. Now, in 1918, it was dis- The Coalisolved and women, for the first time in England, tion ministry participated in parliamentary elections. The Conservatives and Liberals united to advocate a peace based upon victory.   They won an overwhelming triumph over the Labor Party, which advocated a moderate peace.   A Coalition Ministry took office, headed by Lloyd George.

An old problem, that of Ireland, suddenly and sharply confronted the government.   During the war Britain's irreconcilable enemies

Proclama-
tion of an
Irish Re-
public

in Ireland had raised the old cry: "England's difficulties are Ireland's opportunities."   An uprising took place in Dublin, in 1916, known as the "Easter Rebellion," which was suppressed.   After the war the Irish were in a mood that boded ill for a peaceful settlement of their problem.   In the elections of 1918, Sinn Fein [1] appeared as a political party in opposition to both Nationalists and Unionists.   So overwhelming was the success of the Sinn Fein candidates that the party of Parnell was annihilated.   Instead of taking their seats in the British Parliament, the Sinn Fein members met in Dublin, where they organized themselves as the Dail (Gaelic, national assembly).   This body proclaimed Ireland an independent republic.

A guerilla war began between an Irish republican army and the British forces.   It was waged with the utmost ruthlessness: am-

Struggle be-
tween the
British and
Sinn Fein

buscades, kidnapings, bombings, burnings, and assassinations were committed by both sides.   The British administration was boycotted, and many Irishmen resigned or were coerced to resign their positions, which disorganized the public service.   There were now two governments in Ireland: the British, which had ceased to function, and the Sinn Fein, which was outlawed.

To end this intolerable situation, Parliament, in 1920, passed a law establishing home rule in Ireland.[2]   It provided for two par-

Northern
Ireland

liaments: one in Belfast with jurisdiction over Ulster, and the other in Dublin with jurisdiction over the rest of Ireland.   Ulster accepted the scheme, and a new political entity appeared, known as Northern Ireland.   It elected a Parliament with jurisdiction over local affairs; in addition, it elected representatives to the British Parliament.

But southern Ireland now rejected home rule as inadequate, and demanded independence.   The struggle between the Irish and the British resulted in a compromise which, in 1922, established southern

[1] See page 317.

[2] This law repealed the third Home Rule law, which had not been applied.   See page 319.

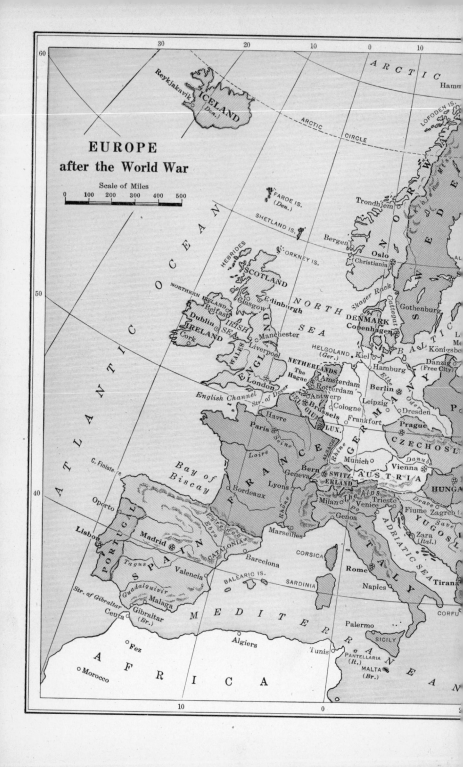

EUROPE
after the World War

Scale of Miles

0   100   200   300   400   500

ARCTIC

ARCTIC   CIRCLE

Reykjakavik
ICELAND
(Den.)

FAROE IS.
(Den.)

SHETLAND IS.

ORKNEY IS.

HEBRIDES

SCOTLAND

Glasgow Edinburgh

NORTHERN IRELAND
Belfast IRISH
Dublin SEA
IRELAND
Cork

WALES Manchester
Liverpool

ENGLAND
London

English Channel
Str. of Dover

Havre
Paris
Seine

Loire
FRANCE

C. Finisterre

Bay of
Biscay

Bordeaux

Oporto

Lisbon
PORTUGAL

Madrid
Tagus
SPAIN
Ebro

Valencia

CATALONIA

Barcelona

Guadalquivir
Malaga

Str. of Gibraltar
Gibraltar
(Br.)
Ceuta

Fez

Morocco

AFRICA

Algiers

BALEARIC IS.

CORSICA

SARDINIA

MEDITERRANEAN

Trondhjem

Bergen

Oslo
Christiania

NORWAY

SWEDEN

Gothenburg

Skager Rock
Cattegat

DENMARK
Copenhagen

BALTIC

HELGOLAND
(Ger.) Kiel

Hamburg

The
Hague Amsterdam
Rotterdam
NETHERLANDS
Antwerp
Brussels
BELGIUM
LUX.
Cologne
Frankfort

Berlin

Leipzig

Dresden

GERMANY

Elbe
Oder

Danzig
(Free City)

Königsberg

Prague

CZECHOSL

Rhine

Munich

Bern
SWITZ-
ERLAND
Geneva

Alps

Milan

Po

Genoa

Rhone

Marseilles

Lyons

AUSTRIA

Vienna

Drave

HUNGA

Trieste
Venice

Fiume Zagreb

ITALY

ADRIATIC SEA

Rome

Naples

Palermo

SICILY

Tunis

PANTELLARIA
(It.)

MALTA
(Br.)

Zara
(Ital.)

YUGOSL

Tirana

CORFU

NORTH
SEA

ATLANTIC OCEAN

LOFODEN IS.

Hamm

Me

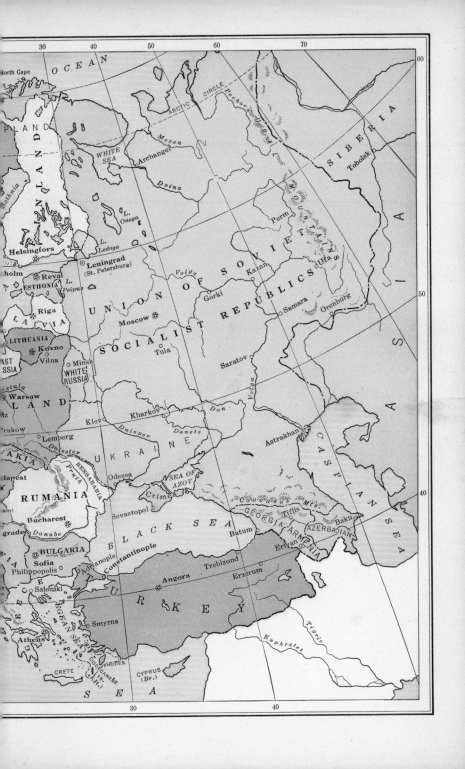

ARCTIC OCEAN

North Cape

FINLAND

WHITE SEA

Archangel

Mezen

Dvina

Pechora

Ural

SIBERIA

Tobolsk

ARCTIC CIRCLE

L. Onega

L. Lodoga

Helsingfors

Leningrad (St. Petersburg)

Reval

ESTHONIA

L. Peipus

Riga

LATVIA

LITHUANIA

Kovno

Vilna

Minsk

WHITE RUSSIA

EAST PRUSSIA

Warsaw

POLAND

Krakow

Lemberg

Kiev

Dnieper

UKRAINE

SLOVAKIA

Dniester

Pruth

BESSARABIA

Odessa

RUMANIA

Bucharest

Belgrade

Danube

BULGARIA

Sofia

Philippopolis

Adrianople

Constantinople

Salonika

AEGEAN SEA

Athens

CRETE

Dodecanese (Is.)

Smyrna

TURKEY

Angora

Trebizond

Erzerum

CYPRUS (Br.)

MEDITERRANEAN SEA

UNION OF SOVIET SOCIALIST REPUBLICS

Moscow

Tula

Gorki

Volga

Perm

Kazan

Ufa

Samara

Orenburg

Saratov

Don

Donetz

Kharkov

Astrakhan

SEA OF AZOV

Crimea

Sevastopol

BLACK SEA

Batum

Caucasus Mts.

GEORGIA

Tiflis

ARMENIA

Erivan

AZERBAIJAN

Baku

CASPIAN SEA

Euphrates

Tigris

Stockholm

Gothnia

30 40 50 60 70

60

50

40

30 40

Ireland as the "Irish Free State," having the status of a Dominion, like that of Canada. The Irish Question was solved by creating two Irelands: one in Ulster, with home rule that it had so long opposed; and the other in the south, with Dominion status. In 1922 the British army evacuated Ireland, after an occupation lasting over seven hundred years.

The Irish Free State

However, the conflict between Ireland and England was not entirely over. An independence party appeared in the Irish Free State, led by Eamon de Valera, that aimed to transform Ireland from a Dominion to an independent republic. In 1932 elections to the Dail, or lower house of the Irish Free State, gave control to de Valera, who became Prime Minister. His policy was to have the Irish Free State adopt a series of measures which would be so many steps to virtual independence. One law abolished the oath of allegiance to the British king. Another made approval by the Governor-General unnecessary for laws passed by the Irish Parliament. A more serious conflict arose over the payment of the land annuities. These were annual payments, due from Irish peasants, on loans that had been advanced to them by the British government to buy their farms. The Irish Free State had agreed to collect these annuities and to turn them over to the British government. In 1932 de Valera refused to turn over the annuities. In retaliation England laid a prohibitive tariff on imports from the Irish Free State. Thereupon the latter laid heavy duties on imports from England.

The Irish Free State cuts English ties

In 1937 Ireland took a long step toward virtual independence by adopting a new constitution. It was drawn up by the Dail and was accepted by a popular referendum. The Irish Free State, which according to the constitution of 1922 was a coequal member of the community of nations forming the British Commonwealth of Nations, went out of existence. In its place appeared "Eire," the ancient name of Ireland, which the new constitution declared to be a "sovereign independent democratic state." Its head was a President, elected by the people for a term of seven years. Executive power was exercised by the President and by a ministry appointed by him that was responsible to Parliament. Legislative power was vested chiefly in a chamber, the Dail, elected by universal suffrage according to proportional representation. The Senate represented occupational groups, such

Constitution of Eire

as agriculture, industry, labor, and the universities; its power over legislation was limited. Both Irish and English were declared official languages.

The constitution was followed, in 1938, by an Anglo-Irish agreement that settled most of the differences between them. Some of the Irish ports, important in coastal defense, which had been put under the control of the British Admiralty in 1922, were transferred to Eire. The quarrel concerning land annuities was settled by the payment of a lump sum of £10,000,000 by Eire to England. Each abolished the special tariff duties on the imports of the other in order to put an end to the tariff controversy. England and Eire then entered into trade agreements similar to those established by the Ottawa Conference between England and her colonies.

(b) LABORITES AND CONSERVATIVES

Party politics in England underwent great changes after the war as a result of the advent to power of the Labor Party. It succeeded the Liberal Party as one of the two governing parties, the other being the Conservative. The Liberals steadily and rapidly lost popular support, and the once great party of Gladstone and Bright degenerated into a small faction. As a result of its success the Labor Party ceased to be narrowly trade unionist in membership and policy. It now appealed for support to all who "live by working" against those who "live by owning." It adopted a general platform which was socialist in character, though it carefully avoided Marxian phraseology and doctrines. The declared purpose of the Party was "to secure for the producers by hand or by brain the full fruits of their industry and the most equitable distribution thereof that may be possible, upon the basis of the common ownership of the means of production and the best obtainable system of popular administration and control of each industry and service." Among its immediate demands were the nationalization of mines, land, railways, and electric power; a national minimum-wage law; and the adoption of the principle of the "right to work or maintenance."

The remarkable growth of the Labor Party from a small faction to a party in power had several causes. In the first place, it appealed to moderate sentiment by being opposed to class war, and by favoring changes through "parliamentary means and in progressive stages." There was to be no confiscation; as each industry was nationalized, compensation would be paid to the owners. The Labor Party's policy was well described as the "inevitability of gradualness," by which was meant that socialism would be established in England, step by step, through social reform measures. It repudiated communism as repugnant to English traditions and methods. In the second place, the Labor Party was in harmony with British national sentiment in that it was monarchist and imperialist. It accepted the English monarchy as a form behind which democracy could function as well as in a republic. It also favored the maintenance of the British Empire, and "its progressive development on the lines of local autonomy."

Reasons for growth of Labor Party

As a result of the elections in 1923 a Labor Ministry came into power in 1924, with J. Ramsay MacDonald as Prime Minister. His chief associates were Philip Snowden, Sidney Webb, and Arthur Henderson. For the first time in the history of Britain the government of the Empire was in the hands of men avowedly socialists.

The first Labor Ministry (1924)

But the Ministry did not have a majority in the Commons. It took office with the tacit consent of the Liberals, who held the balance of power. Therefore, MacDonald was cautious in his policies and urged only those measures that would meet with the approval of the Liberals. The government recognized Soviet Russia in order to facilitate commercial relations. But an increase of communist agitation in England caused much uneasiness, and, in 1924, the Labor Ministry was overthrown by a combined vote of Conservatives and Liberals. Parliament was dissolved, and the new elections resulted in a Conservative triumph. The Labor Party came in second, losing seats, but gaining votes.[1]

---

[1] The growth of the Labor Party has been phenomenal. The following table is a record of its progress:

YEAR	SEATS	VOTES (in round numbers)
1906	29	323,000
1910 (Jan.)	40	505,000
1910 (Dec.)	42	370,800
1918	63	2,245,000
1922	142	4,237,000
1923	191	4,348,000
1924	151	5,600,000
1929	289	8,300,000
1931	52	6,650,000
1936	154	8,325,000

The great problem that confronted the Conservative Ministry, headed by Stanley Baldwin, was unemployment. Since the war

The second Labor Ministry (1929–1931) England had been in a chronic state of business depression which defied all efforts to cure it. Unemployment rose as high as 2,000,000 at one time. There was consequently profound discontent with Conservative rule, and the elections, held in 1929, resulted in a second success for the Labor Party. It came out first, but, as in 1924, it did not have a majority in the Commons. Again MacDonald became Prime Minister with the tacit consent of the Liberals.

MacDonald's efforts were exerted chiefly in the direction of reducing armaments. A lifelong advocate of international peace, he was greatly alarmed over the new armament race that followed the World War. His peace efforts resulted in the limitation of naval armaments by the London Naval Conference, already described.

Economic conditions were becoming worse and worse. Exports continued to drop. Cotton manufacturing, a highly important *The financial crisis* industry in England, dropped to its lowest point in many years. Unemployment was rising. Tax receipts were decreasing, but the expenses of the government were increasing, because of heavy outlays for social legislation. The year 1929–30 closed with a deficit in the budget, and a still greater deficit loomed up for the following year. This situation affected the financial credit of England, which had always been of the very highest. There were three ways of meeting the emergency: (1) floating more loans; (2) increasing taxes; and (3) reducing expenses. The government experienced great difficulty in getting sufficiently large loans from foreign bankers. Higher taxation was opposed by the business interests on the ground that it would ruin England's industry, already in a serious condition. MacDonald was persuaded that the only way to balance the budget was to reduce the salaries of government employees and the allowances given to the unemployed. His policy was opposed by the Labor Party, which thereupon repudiated its veteran leader. A Cabinet crisis followed, and MacDonald resigned his premiership. A new ministry was organized, called the National Government, headed by MacDonald, consisting of Conservatives, Liberals, and a few Laborites who followed MacDonald.

This Ministry reduced government salaries and unemployment

benefits, but the budget was not balanced. Foreign bankers began to withdraw gold, which threatened the reserve of the Bank of England. In 1931 the situation became critical, and England went off the gold standard by suspending the law requiring the Bank of England to sell gold at a fixed price of $4.8665 to the pound sterling.

England goes off the gold standard

Parliament was dissolved in 1931. In the elections the National Government appealed to the country for a "doctor's mandate" to cure the financial ills of England. The outcome was a sweeping victory for the National Government, and MacDonald continued as Prime Minister. In opposition was the Labor Party, whose representation fell from 289 to 52 seats.

Defeat of the Labor Party

MacDonald was supported in the Commons by a Conservative majority. He had begun his career as a socialist, had been one of the founders of the Labor Party, had been a Labor Prime Minister twice by the sufferance of the Liberals, and was now a partyless Prime Minister by the sufferance of the Conservatives. By the Laborites he was regarded with bitter hatred as one who had betrayed his lifelong convictions. Old, sick, and disappointed, he retired as Prime Minister in 1935 and was succeeded by the Conservative, Stanley Baldwin.

Ministry of Baldwin

King George V died in 1936, and was succeeded by his son as Edward VIII. A curious situation arose when the new monarch expressed his desire to marry an American woman, Mrs. Wallis Simpson, who had been twice divorced. Baldwin insisted that an English king's marriage was not a private but a state matter, hence the King must act on the advice of his ministers, who were opposed to the marriage. But Edward insisted that his marriage was a private matter, and refused to take the advice of his ministers. The King broke the deadlock by abdicating. He then married Mrs. Simpson, and retired to private life as the Duke of Windsor. He was succeeded by his brother, who was crowned George VI.

Abdication of Edward VIII

Prime Minister Baldwin's retirement followed Edward's abdication. In 1937 he was succeeded by Neville Chamberlain, son of the famous Joseph Chamberlain. His premiership marked an epoch in England's foreign policies, described elsewhere. One great crisis followed another in European relations in which England's very existence was deemed at stake. Chamberlain put through a rearmament program that was unprecedented. An outlay for armaments of about £2,750,000,000 was made for 1939–40. The climax came in 1939 when Parliament passed a law establishing conscription. Never before in her history had England established conscription in time of peace. But so great was the fear of German and Italian aggression that the people accepted calmly this departure from the ancient and cherished tradition of voluntary military service.

Conscription

(c) LABOR PROBLEMS

The social reforms enacted before the war proved to be entirely inadequate in the situation after the war. The rise in the cost of living and the increasing unemployment demanded a radical revision of the social insurance laws by whatever ministry was in power. In 1925 the Conservatives enacted a new old-age pension law to supplement the one of 1908. All manual workers, and all non-manual workers earning less than a certain amount, were required, at the age of sixteen, to insure against old age. A fund was established, consisting of equal contributions by employer and employee, to which were added annual subsidies by the state. At the age of sixty-five the insured man and his wife each received a pension. In case of death of the insured, his widow and his children under fourteen received pensions. The sickness insurance law was revised to include all manual workers, and all non-manual workers earning less than a certain amount, between the ages of sixteen and sixty-five. A fund was established by equal contribution from employer and employee; the state paid the cost of administration. In case of sickness the insured was entitled to a weekly allowance for a maximum period of twenty-six weeks in any given year, medical services, and all necessary medicines. In case of disablement the insured received a similar allowance until the age of sixty-five, when the old age pension began. Maternity was included within the sickness insurance law; the wife of an insured man, or an insured woman worker, received a sum of money on the birth of a child.

Old age and sickness insurance

Of all the social legislation the most important was that on unemployment insurance. In 1927 a new law was passed which radically changed all previous legislation on the subject. All manual workers, and all non-manual workers earning less than a certain sum, between the ages of

Unemployment insurance

sixteen and sixty-five were compelled to be insured against unemployment. In 1936 the law was extended to agricultural laborers. A fund was created from equal contributions by employers, employees, and the state. All those capable and willing to work, but unemployed, were required to register in Labor Exchanges established by the government for the purpose of placing the unemployed. An unemployed worker received a weekly allowance for himself, and in addition an allowance for a dependent wife and dependent children under fourteen. Unemployment was so widespread in England that the maximum period of benefit constantly varied. Along with unemployment insurance there had been established a system called the "dole." It was an allowance paid entirely from government funds to those who had been unemployed so long that they were unable to make contributions to the unemployment insurance fund. In 1934 the "dole" was abolished as part of the insurance system.

After the war England experienced a great housing shortage. Moreover, many of the houses, both in the city and in the country, were unfit for human habitation. A series of laws was New passed with the object of encouraging the building of housing homes for the working class. Some were built by the municipalities, others by private builders, aided by government subsidies. England went vigorously to work in the campaign of slum clearance. Over 3,000,000 houses were built between 1919 and 1937.

During the war the trade unions had won many concessions in wages and hours which they were determined to maintain. But the depression in business after the war resulted Labor unin a demand by the employers for a decrease in rest wages and an increase in hours. As a consequence conflicts took place in almost every important industry. It was most aggravated in the coal industry, which had become demoralized by bad business conditions and poor management. In 1925 the mine owners proposed a reduction of wages and an increase of hours. The miners refused to accept. To avoid a strike, the government intervened by voting a subsidy for a definite period to the mine owners to enable them to maintain existing conditions. When the period expired, a critical situation arose. The mine owners demanded a reduction in wages and an increase in hours of work. The reply of the miners was "not a penny off the pay; not a second on the day." The trade unions, fearing that a reduction of the wages of the miners would be followed by similar attempts in other industries, determined to support the miners.

The strike of the miners was followed by a general strike that involved over 2,000,000 men in many industries, particularly in transportation. Although feeling was intense on both sides, there was almost no disorder; not a shot was fired. But the entire economic life of the nation was seriously affected, and Premier Baldwin denounced the general strike as an attack upon the power of Parliament and upon the rights of the nation. He declared that the government was bound to intervene in a situation which affected the whole people, though the issue was between private parties. It was feared that if the general strike was prolonged many British industries, already badly crippled because of the loss of trade, would be permanently ruined. Baldwin demanded that the strike be called off, and he promised to resume negotiations with the mine operators. The labor leaders realized that defiance of the government might precipitate revolution, which was not at all their intention. After nine days the general strike was called off.

The general strike, 1926

There was bitter feeling among the property-owning classes against the trade unions. In 1927 Parliament passed a law which had for its object the curbing of the trade unions. It declared illegal all strikes whose object was to coerce the government, either directly or by inflicting hardship on the community; and all strikes that had "any object other than or in addition to the furtherance of a trade dispute within the trade or industry in which the strikers are engaged." Trade unions were forbidden to punish any member who refused to participate in an illegal strike. It was made unlawful for pickets to persuade or induce any one from abstaining from work, if done in such a manner as to intimidate him or his dependents. An illegal strike rendered a union liable for damages, and the strikers liable to punishment. Trade-union members were not obliged to contribute to the political fund of their union unless they specifically contracted to do so; hitherto, they had been obliged to contribute unless they had specifically contracted not to do so.

New trade-union law

(d) ECONOMIC PROBLEMS

The war was followed by an economic dislocation throughout the world that was ruinous to England's foreign trade, the chief source of her prosperity. Silent factories and shipyards and closed mines were the "devastated regions" of England. The large numbers of the unemployed drained the national treasury through the social services paid for by heavy taxes. Only a business revival on a broad scale could cure England's industrial ills.

Until 1914 England had successfully maintained her lead as the great industrial nation of the world. After 1870, however, her lead had been maintained by a shift in markets. Loss of Hitherto, the Continent and America had been the foreign great markets for her manufactures; but with the markets progress of industry in these places, high tariff walls were erected to keep out English goods. England's great markets then shifted to China, India, and Africa. After the war, England faced an economic world that was no longer dependent upon her manufactures. Because of the exigencies of the war many nations had established industries which they sought to maintain by high tariffs; even backward China, India, and Russia succeeded in establishing large factories. As a consequence English manufactures had an ever decreasing market. Furthermore, England encountered sharp competition from Japan, the United States, and Germany.

To maintain her position in the new economic world England was compelled to modify radically her economic policies and methods. In her staple industries, such as cotton, The old coal, iron, and steel, England's methods were largely industries those of the old Industrial Revolution, with old machinery and small competing factories. A movement for "rationalization" began, by which was meant the introduction of American methods of mass production, automatic machinery, scientific management, and industrial consolidation.

In establishing new industries, it was easier and less costly to introduce new methods than to rationalize the old. A notable shift in manufacturing took place when electrical, The new chemical, motor, and rayon factories were built in the industries region around London. The old industrial centers in the north, with coal, cotton, and shipping, became known as the "depressed areas," where recovery was slow and unemployment high.

The coal industry, one of the pillars of British prosperity during the nineteenth century, underwent a serious decline after the war. English coal met serious competition. The cost of mining was

high in England because of the expense of extracting it from
seams far below the surface. Moreover, oil and hydro-electric power furnished new competition, lessening the demand for coal. Nevertheless, mining, though
an "ailing industry," was still important and demanded rehabilitation. Many of the English coal mines were unprofitable ventures. Their ownership was largely in the hands of aristocratic
landlords who leased them to operating companies on a "royalty"
for every ton mined. In 1938 the Conservative Ministry put
through a law nationalizing the coal mines, to take place gradually
during a period of four years. The plan was to combine public
ownership with private management, the advantage of the former
being the elimination of private profit, and of the latter the elimination of bureaucracy. The government purchased the royalties
for the sum of £66,450,000, which was to be distributed to the
various owners. The mines were leased by the government to
the operating companies on terms advantageous to the public. A
Coal Commission was given full power to reorganize the industry.

Nationalization of coal mines

Not only industry but agriculture underwent a great transformation. The German submarine campaign during the war had
reduced England almost to starvation, as she was dependent on foreign food supplies. After the war
England determined to raise her food production
through government regulation of agricultural production and
through tariffs on foodstuffs. In 1931 the Agricultural Marketing
Act was passed, giving to the producers of any foodstuff power to
organize an association which could control production, assign
markets, fix prices, and regulate conditions of marketing. On the
advice of these associations the government regulated the tariff or
fixed the quota on imports of certain foodstuffs.

Regulation of agriculture

The aristocratic system of landholding was modified. Large
estates which could no longer be maintained by their owners were
divided into small farms and sold to farmers. Laws
favorable to tenants and to agricultural laborers were
enacted. Especially important were the laws that
created wages boards in the rural districts with power to fix minimum wages and maximum hours for agricultural laborers.

Rise of peasant proprietorship

A far more important change in England's economic life came
with the abandonment of her historic policy of free trade. In the

new economic world that arose after the war there was no possibility for England to recover her former leadership in the world's markets. Could not her decline be arrested by developing her domestic and Imperial markets? The great victory of the Conservative Party

Protection and Imperial Preference

in the elections of 1931 plainly indicated that the English people had left their free trade moorings. In 1931 England definitely adopted the policy of protection by levying high duties on a long list of manufactured articles. On the free list were chiefly agricultural products and raw materials. To carry out fully the scheme of tariff reform, it was essential to include the Dominions. A conference was held in 1932 in Ottawa, Canada, by Great Britain, the Dominions, and India. The problem of the Ottawa Conference was to arrange a system of preferential duties among the members of the British Empire. A number of bilateral trade agreements were adopted giving preferential rates to British manufactures imported by the Dominions, and to Dominion agricultural products and raw materials imported by England. However, the preferential rates on English manufactures were given by the Dominions with due regard to the maintenance of their own domestic industry.

The year 1934 saw a marked change in England's economic condition. Prosperity began to return; exports rose, and the domestic market expanded. For the first time since the war an optimistic spirit pervaded the country.

(e) IMPERIAL PROBLEMS

When in 1914 England declared war against Germany the whole British Empire was at war. Whether or not the Dominions should participate actively, however, depended on their own governments. They rallied enthusiastically to the side of the mother country, and raised armies to fight the battles of the Empire in Europe, Asia, and Africa.

Colonies support England in the World War

England recognized the efforts of her colonies by establishing, in 1917, an Imperial War Cabinet, composed of representatives of Great Britain, the Dominions, and India, to direct war policies. A prominent member of this cabinet was the Boer statesman, Jan Smuts, once the foe of the Empire but now its loyal supporter.

Before the war the Dominions had gained control of their domestic affairs; after the war they sought equality with England in foreign affairs. Dominion nationalism was recognized by giv-

ing the Dominions (also India) separate representation at the
Conference of Paris, and by admitting them to the

Colonies
gain influ-
ence in for-
eign affairs

League of Nations. The Treaty of Locarno specifically declared that it was not binding upon the British
Dominions and India unless ratified by them. Foreign
policies were no longer exclusively directed by the British government; they were now formulated by Imperial Conferences.

The Imperial Conference of 1926 adopted an important definition of the new Dominion status in the "British Commonwealth
of Nations," as the Empire was now called. It de-

The new
Dominion
status

clared that Great Britain and the Dominions "are
autonomous communities within the British Empire,
equal in status, in no way subordinate one to another in any aspect
of their domestic or external affairs, though united by a common
allegiance to the crown and freely associated as members of the
British Commonwealth of Nations."

In 1931 the British Parliament passed the Statute of Westminster, which translated into law the resolution of the Imperial
Conference of 1926. The Statute declared that the Crown was

Statute of
Westminster

"the symbol of the free association of the members of
the British Commonwealth of Nations"; therefore,
any change in the succession of the throne would require the assent
of the Dominions as well as that of England. No law of the
Dominion was henceforth to be declared void on the ground that
it was repugnant to a law of England. No law passed by the British Parliament could apply to any Dominion without its consent.
The king, on the advice of his ministers, could no longer nullify
a law of a Dominion parliament. The Statute did not abolish the
right of the judicial committee of the Privy Council in Britain to
hear appeals from the courts in the Dominions, but it did give to the
Dominions the power to refuse permission for appeals to be taken
to Britain. The Dominions attained a degree of self-government
hardly distinguishable from independence. Ties of sentiment and
good will alone now bound the British Commonwealth of Nations
far more firmly than in the days when kings and parliaments had
sought to bind them by coercive laws and tyrannical officials.

What now remained of the old British Empire was chiefly India.

Concessions
to India

But after the World War India also took the road
toward self-government. Her loyalty to the Empire
during the war was rewarded by a law, enacted by Parlia-

ment in 1919, which established a new system of government for British India. A national Legislative Assembly, elected by a propertied suffrage, was created. But as its powers were greatly limited the Assembly was not truly a parliament. More important concessions were made to the Indians in local government. Popularly elected provincial legislatures shared power with the British officials; each element in the "dyarchy" had control of certain matters.

These concessions had the effect of stimulating, not allaying, Indian discontent. A revolutionary party demanded complete independence and was prepared to use every method Discontent to attain it. A more moderate party known as the in India "Swaraj" favored self-government under the British flag, to be achieved through popular agitation.

By far the most important leader that appeared in the Indian nationalist movement was the saintlike personality of Mahatma Gandhi, whose career and ideals attracted world-wide Gandhi attention. Gandhi believed that India should gain her freedom neither through revolutionary violence nor through political intrigue and obstruction, but through "non-coöperation" with the British government. Indians should refuse to hold public office, to attend public schools, to pay taxes, to buy British goods, or to appear in court. In Gandhi's opinion, this method of passive resistance would disorganize the British government and lead to freedom for India. In spite of his eloquent preaching against violence a number of riots took place which were severely suppressed.

Indian discontent became particularly prominent during the period of the Labor Ministry. Prime Minister MacDonald, who had championed self-government for India, resolved The Round to coöperate with the moderate Indian nationalists. Table In 1930 he called together a Round Table Conference Conferences consisting of representatives of India, among whom was Gandhi, and of the British political parties. In this conference, and others that followed, many acrimonious debates took place between the Indians, who wanted almost complete self-government, and the British, who wanted to safeguard their own interests. A constitution for India which went far beyond the concessions of 1919 was passed by the British Parliament in 1935.

A new political system was to be organized in India. It was to be a federal union consisting of the provinces of British India and

of the native states, should the latter accept the constitution.
Constitution A parliament was established consisting of an upper
of India   house, the Council of State, and a lower house, the
House of Assembly. The Council was to be composed in part of
representatives from the provinces elected by a highly restricted suffrage; in part of representatives from the native states to be elected
by methods of their own choosing; and of a few appointed by the
Governor-General. The Assembly was to be composed in part of
representatives from the provinces elected by the provincial legislatures; and in part of representatives from the native states.
Parliament was given the usual powers of a legislature subject to
the powers reserved to the local legislatures and to the British
Crown.

The "dyarchy" established in the provinces was abolished. In
its place local legislatures were to be elected by a fairly liberal
Power of   franchise with large powers over local matters. In
the Crown   both federal and local legislatures a designated number of seats were allocated to minorities such as the Mohammedans, Christians, and Europeans. British control was by no means
eliminated. As the representative of the Crown the Governor-
General, or Viceroy exercised considerable powers. National
defense and external relations lay wholly within his discretion.
Partly within his discretion were such matters as the preservation
of order and the protection of minorities.

The new constitution of India illustrated the liberal yet cautious
attitude of England to her colonies. Much was given but much
was retained. It did not bring universal satisfaction in India.
Especially did the extreme nationalists protest against the "reserved" powers of the Governor-General. However they finally
agreed to coöperate with the British in working the new system,
which was after all a long step in the direction of Dominion
status.

FRANCE

(a) RULE OF THE NATIONAL BLOC

France was almost "bled white" by the war. Her losses were
so great that, in 1925, the population was actually smaller than in
Losses   1914, despite the addition of Alsace-Lorraine. As
              the chief theater of the war, France suffered losses in
property impossible to estimate. The devastated regions pre-

sented an indescribable scene of ruin and horror. "A dreary waste with mile after mile of gaunt trees, shell holes, barbed-wire entanglements, deserted fields, demolished towns — with no cattle, no horses, no living beings anywhere except in an occasional oasis where a town had in some miraculous way escaped destruction." Remnants of the population huddled amidst the ruins of once prosperous towns. Industrial establishments, factories, shops, and stores were battered down, and their machinery and wares destroyed or taken away. Mines were flooded. Railways, bridges, and canals were wrecked. The earth itself suffered damage; constant bombardment and the many trenches tore up the soil, and poisonous gases destroyed vegetation.

If France suffered great losses, she also made considerable gains. Alsace-Lorraine was again French territory. In Africa, France was given a mandate for the German colonies, Togoland *Gains* and Cameroon. In western Asia, she got a mandate for Syria. By acquiring the iron of Lorraine, the potash of Alsace, and, for fifteen years, the coal of the Saar, France was in a position to be highly industrialized. With the defeat of Germany, the prestige of France rose high. Once more she became the great power on the Continent, guiding its diplomatic policies, especially those of the Succession states, which looked to her for protection against a restoration of the Hohenzollerns and the Hapsburgs.

In the elections of 1919, the parties that upheld the Treaty of Versailles united to form the National Union. Opposed to them were the Socialists, who demanded a revision of the *The National Union* Treaty. Patriotic feeling was so intense that the outcome was an overwhelming victory for the National *(1919–24)* Union. When the new Chamber assembled it witnessed a dramatic event: the reappearance of representatives from Alsace-Lorraine after an absence of forty-eight years.

Poincaré was the soul of the National Union. Intensely nationalistic, he feared and hated Germany as the mortal enemy of France. The recalcitrant attitude of Germany in the matter of Reparations roused Poincaré's ire, and, as has already been described, he sent a French army into the Ruhr.

But the results of the occupation of the Ruhr were disappointing. The German miners and mine owners refused to work the mines, and France received little benefit from the occupation. The expense added burdens to the already overburdened French

budget.   An opposition to Poincaré arose in the Chamber, known
The Left   as the Left Cartel, consisting chiefly of Radical
Cartel   Socialists and Socialists.   In the elections of 1924 the
(1924-26)
                 Left Cartel was successful.   A new ministry came
into power, and Edouard Herriot, a Radical Socialist, became
Premier.   The Herriot ministry took a more moderate attitude
toward Germany.   It collaborated with England in accepting the
Dawes Plan.   It agreed to evacuate the Ruhr.   It recognized
Soviet Russia, a step to which the Poincaré ministry had been consistently hostile.

(b) FINANCIAL PROBLEMS

Although France was victorious in the war, she was burdened
with an enormous debt.   Her public expenses were increasing rap-
France as   idly because of the higher cost of public services, the
debtor and   maintenance of a large army, the policing of a large
creditor
                  colonial empire, and especially the reconstruction of
the devastated regions.   Very pressing were her war debts to the
United States and to England, the financial dictators of the world,
who could destroy her credit and plunge her into financial ruin.
But she was a creditor for almost as much as she was a debtor.
Unfortunately her chief debtors were Germany, who was reluctant
to pay; Russia, who had repudiated her debt; and Belgium, who
was impoverished.   Heavy taxes were laid, but a large part of the
revenue from taxation went to pay the interest on the public debt.
France hoped to get out of her financial difficulties through Reparations payments; in the meanwhile, she staved off bankruptcy by
floating new loans to pay those due, a vicious financial circle that
might ruin her credit.

The financial situation became critical in 1926 after a succession
of ministries had failed in their attempts to cope with it.   As in
Poincaré   other critical situations in the history of the Third
solves the   Republic, factional differences vanished.   A cabinet
financial   of National Union was organized, headed by Poincaré.
problem
(1926-28)   It was supported by all the groups in the Chamber
                  except the extreme Left.   Poincaré was voted dic-
tatorial powers in financial matters by the Chamber, and his decisive character and remarkable financial ability proved equal to
the emergency.   He introduced drastic reforms in the system of
taxation, and reduced the expenses of the government.   In 1926

France funded her war debt to the United States, though the agreement was not ratified until 1929. The most notable accomplishment of Poincaré was the stabilization of the currency, with the franc at 3.93 cents. France resumed gold payments, and her credit rose. The stabilization of the franc at about one-fifth of its pre-war value brought great hardship to those who held government bonds; by this act France virtually repudiated about four-fifths of her internal debt.

Foreign policies during this period were directed by Briand, who was almost continuously in the cabinet from 1924 to 1931, mainly as Foreign Minister. Briand was dominated by the idea of a *rapprochement* between France and Germany. He loyally collaborated with the German Foreign Minister, Stresemann, in their common efforts to bring about friendly relations between France and Germany as the means of establishing lasting peace in Europe. Shrewd and persuasive, he succeeded in allaying, partially at least, the fears regarding Germany on the part of his fellow-countrymen. Briand, along with Stresemann, was instrumental in drawing up the Locarno Treaties; and along with the American Secretary of State, Kellogg, in drawing up the Pact of Paris.

Briand's foreign policy

(c) SOCIAL REFORM

After the war France became a predominantly industrial nation. She now had the iron deposits of Lorraine, the coal deposits of the Saar, and the extensive textile industry of Alsace. In 1928 France for the first time produced more steel than England. The factories that were rebuilt in the devastated regions were equipped with the latest machinery. France made rapid progress in the textiles, especially in cotton goods and in rayon. The small factories so common in pre-war France began to give way to large industrial plants.

Industrialization of France

As a result of industrialization a large working class appeared; hitherto, the bulk of the French population had consisted of peasants, artisans, and shopkeepers. A demand arose for social legislation of a more drastic character than that before the war. In 1930 a law was passed establishing a comprehensive, unified system of social insurance. All workingmen and workingwomen, including agricultural workers, whose earnings were below a certain amount, were compelled to enter the

Social insurance

system. A fund was set up from contributions from the employees, from the employers, and from state subventions. When unemployed, the insured were exempted from contributing. The following were the benefits:

Sickness. In case of illness the insured was given, for a maximum period of six months, medical care, medicines, and hospital service; an allowance of half the wages; and a smaller allowance for dependents.

Maternity. An insured woman or the wife of an insured man was entitled to medical care during pregnancy and for six months after childbirth; a cash benefit to an insured woman of about half her wages; and an extra allowance for nursing for a maximum period of nine months.

Invalidity. If the insured was incapacitated as a result of sickness or accident not covered by the workmen's compensation acts, he received an invalidity pension of about half his wages. An allowance was also given to his dependents.

Old age. At the age of sixty the insured could retire if he so desired; he was, however, permitted to defer his retirement to a later age. When he retired, he received a pension of about forty per cent of his average wage.

Death. In case of death the heirs of the insured received a benefit of twenty per cent of his annual wage. An allowance was also given to his dependents.

In 1932 a law was passed establishing family allowances for working-class families. This law required employers to establish funds from which employees were to receive allowances for their children under sixteen.

(d) THE POPULAR FRONT

France began to feel the great depression after 1932, three years later than the other nations. As she remained on the gold standard Depression her exports had to compete in the world market with in France the devalued currencies of England and America. As a consequence her foreign trade suffered; likewise her profitable tourist trade, since fewer francs for the dollar brought fewer American tourists to France. Unemployment rose, and discontent was widespread. Public finance was also in a parlous state. Increased expenditures and falling revenues caused mounting deficits in the national budget.

To add to France's difficulties came a scandal that threatened to assume the proportions of the Panama Affair. In 1934 France was startled by the revelations of the activities of a swindler named Stavisky, whose financial operations involved high officials in the government. There was a burst of fury throughout France, and the parliamentary system was held responsible for corruption in government, for weakness before Nazi Germany, and for inefficiency in financial matters. *The Stavisky Affair*

Old enemies of the Republic, the royalists, raised their heads. And new and far more powerful enemies, the Fascists, attacked the Republic. A number of Fascist organizations appeared, the most prominent being the *Croix de feu* (Cross of Fire), led by Colonel de la Rocque. Armed and uniformed, like the German Nazi Storm Troops, the French Fascists threatened the existence of the democratic order. The crisis came on February 6, 1934, when great riots took place in Paris. Fascist cohorts marched threateningly toward the Chamber of Deputies. Premier Edouard Daladier promptly met the situation by calling on the armed forces to protect the government. The rioters were dispersed amidst scenes of extreme disorder. *February 6*

"February 6" caused great uneasiness among the loyal upholders of the Republic. This uneasiness was increased by the distrust felt for Premier Doumergue, who succeeded Daladier. Disloyal ministers were suspected of plotting with the Fascists against the life of the Republic. This situation, as in the days of the Dreyfus Affair, created a movement for united action among all parties on the Left. A combination was formed, called the Popular Front, consisting of Radical Socialists, Socialists, and Communists. It adopted a common platform demanding the suppression of the Fascist leagues and drastic social and economic reforms. In the elections of 1936 the Popular Front gained a signal victory by winning 394 out of a total of 618 seats in the Chamber. The Socialists, led by Léon Blum, emerged as the leading party. *Victory of Popular Front*

A Popular Front ministry took office, consisting of Socialists and Radical Socialists. The Premier was Blum, who became the most prominent figure on the French political scene. A moderate Socialist, Blum was convinced that the salvation of France depended not on Marxian doctrines but on a "New Deal" which would raise the working class to a higher stand- *Léon Blum* ard of living by means of far-reaching social reforms. Blum's accomplishments during his Premiership (June, 1936–June, 1937) constitute a landmark in the history of the Third Republic.

Social security laws in favor of the working class were passed, the most important of which provided for a forty-hour week to Labor   be introduced gradually in all industrial and com- reforms   mercial establishments; paid vacations of two weeks after one year's continuous employment in any enterprise; collective agreements in commerce and industry between the trade unions and associations of employers that were to regulate wages, conditions, and "hiring and firing."

The Popular Front aided the peasant as well as the city worker. It established a national "Wheat Office," which set a standard Peasant   price for wheat and made arrangements for storing and reforms   exporting excess supplies. By this system speculation in wheat was curbed, and the profits of middlemen were controlled. Credit on easy terms was given to the peasants by the government.

The most powerful financial institution in France was the Bank of France, the fiscal agent of the government and the nerve center Reform of   of French economic life. It was ruled by a board the Bank of   elected by the two hundred largest stockholders, the France   "two hundred families" who were denounced as an economic oligarchy using its power for the benefit of the rich. The Blum Ministry put through a law that democratized the Bank by establishing a new board, representing finance, industry, commerce, labor, agriculture, and the state.

Because of the rearmament of Nazi Germany, France determined to strengthen her defenses. The largest military budget Nationaliza-   since the war was passed by Parliament with little tion of mu-   opposition. A powerful line of fortifications facing nition works   Germany, the famous Maginot line, had already been and railways   built; it was now extended along the Belgian frontier. An important step in the rearmament program was the nationalization of munitions and airplane factories. Laws and decrees, in 1937, nationalized airplane factories and the munitions factories in the famous Le Creusot steel works. Compensation, as agreed upon by the government and the companies, was paid to the expropriated owners. Another important step, taken in 1937 by the Popular Front government, was the nationalization of the railways. All the French railways were consolidated into one company in which the state owned fifty-one per cent of the stock. Compensation was paid to the expropriated owners.

To protect the Republic against Fascism the government dissolved the *Croix de feu* and other Fascist leagues. The followers of de la Rocque organized as a political party, but it attracted little popular support. Unlike the German Socialists, the French Socialists vigorously protected the Republic against its enemies.

Suppression of Fascism

Under the Popular Front, France had to bear the cost both of rearmament and of the new social security laws. The latter imposed a heavy burden on the small business men. Widespread complaints arose against the forty-hour law which, it was claimed, was responsible for a fall in industrial production. Prices rose to meet the increased costs. As government expenses increased, capital, fearing increased taxation, migrated from France. Unable to balance the budget, the government issued bonds and borrowed money from the Bank of France to cover expenses. These methods brought only a temporary respite, and the Blum Ministry asked Parliament for full power to deal with the financial situation. The Senate refused, causing Blum to resign in June, 1937. A new Popular Front ministry, under the Radical-Socialist, Camille Chautemps, failed to solve the problem, as did a second Blum Ministry. In April, 1938, Daladier formed a ministry in which the Socialists did not participate, thus marking definitely the end of the Popular Front.

Fall of the Popular Front

Reaction immediately set in. The Daladier Ministry issued a series of decrees which nullified the forty-hour-a-week law; increased direct taxes on low incomes, and laid higher indirect taxes on wine, tobacco, coffee, and transportation fares. These decrees aroused the bitter opposition of the working class. The General Confederation of Labor, led by Léon Jouhaux, ordered a general walkout of all labor in France on November 30, 1938, as a twenty-four-hour demonstration against the decrees. Daladier's reply was to requisition the public services, which were put under military rule. To obey the strike order meant court martial and dismissal, and few workers in the public services responded. But many engaged in private industry participated in the walkout. On the whole the labor demonstration of November 30 was regarded as a failure.

The general walkout of labor

Domestic problems were forgotten during the international crisis that followed Germany's seizure of Czechoslovakia.   On March 17, Daladier 1939, Parliament granted the Daladier Ministry full rules by power to rule by decree until November 30 in order decree to speed up war preparation.   A series of decrees turned France into a vast workshop for national defense.

REFERENCES

GENERAL:

I. Bowman, *The New World: Problems in Political Geography* (ed. 1928); H. L. McBain and L. Rogers, *The New Constitutions of Europe* (1922); M. W. Graham, *New Governments of Central Europe* (1924) and *New Governments of Eastern Europe* (1927); W. B. Munro, *The Governments of Europe* (ed. 1938); H. Finer, *The Theory and Practice of Modern Government*, 2 vols. (1932); P. O. Ray, *Major European Governments* (1931); L. L. Lorwin, *Labor and Internationalism* (1929); and J. Davis, *Contemporary Social Movements* (1930).

ENGLAND:

On economic conditions: A. Siegfried, *England's Crisis*, translated from the French (1931); *Britain's Industrial Future: Report of the Liberal Industrial Inquiry* (1928), important document by a committee of Liberal economists; I. Lubin and H. Everett, *The British Coal Dilemma* (1927); *Great Britain: Parliament Committee on Industry and Trade. A Survey of Industries*, 4 vols. (1927–28); G. C. Allen, *British Industries and Their Organization* (1933); Sir W. Beveridge (ed.) *Tariffs* (1931); G. D. H. Cole, *British Trade and Industry* (1933); L. W. White and E. W. Shanahan, *The Industrial Revolution and the Economic World of Today* (1932); J. H. Richardson, *Industrial Relations in Great Britain* (1938); A. Plummer, *New British Industries in the Twentieth Century* (1937); J. H. Richardson, *British Economic Foreign Policy* (1936).   On social conditions: D. Bloomfield (ed.), *Modern Industrial Movements* (ed. 1920), source book; W. B. Catlin, *The Labor Problem in the United States and Great Britain* (1926); M. B. Gilson, *Unemployment Insurance in Great Britain* (1931); H. F. Hohman, *The Development of Social Insurance and Minimum Wage Legislation in Great Britain* (1933); C. W. Pipkin, *Social Politics and Modern Democracies*, 2 vols. (1931); P. Cohen, *The British System of Social Insurance* (1932); *The New Survey of London Life and Labor*, 9 vols. (1930–35).   On Ireland: W. A. Phillips, *The Revolution in Ireland, 1906–23* (1923); D. Gwyn, *The Irish Free State, 1922–1927* (1928); and L. Paul-Dubois, *The Irish Struggle and its Results*, trans. from the French (1934).   On the British Empire: A. G. Dewey, *The Dominions and Diplomacy*, 2 vols. (1929); Sir John Simon (Chairman), *Report of the Indian Statutory Commission*, 2 vols. (1930); W. I. Hull, *India's Political Crisis* (1930); C. F. Andrews (ed.), *Mahatma Gandhi's Ideas* (1930); Sir J. Cumming (ed.), *Modern India* (1931);

W. K. Hancock, *Australia* (1931); A. Zimmern, *The Third British Empire* (1926); and W. Y. Elliott, *The New British Empire* (1932); J. A. Spender, *Great Britain, Empire and Commonwealth, 1886–1935* (1936); A. B. Keith, *The Dominions as Sovereign States* (1938).

FRANCE:

G. Welter, *La France d'aujourd'hui* (1927); M. Augé-Laribe, *Le Paysan Français après la Guerre* (1923); C. W. Pipkin, *Social Politics and Modern Democracies*, 2 vols. (1931); D. J. Saposs, *The Labor Movement in Post-War France* (1930); W. F. Ogburn and W. Jaffé, *The Economic Development of Post-War France* (1929); C. J. H. Hayes, *France, A Nation of Patriots* (1930); C. Gide et W. Oualid, *Le Bilan de la Guerre pour la France* (1932); W. L. Middleton, *The French Political System* (1932); A Werth, *Which Way France* (1937); H. G. Daniels, *The Framework of France* (1937); G. Peel, *The Economic Policy of France* (1937); W. R. Sharp, *The Government of the French Republic* (1938).

CHAPTER XL

THE RISE OF DICTATORSHIPS

SOVIET Russia created a system of government that became the model for the Fascist states, Italy and Germany. This system
Party may be described as "party dictatorship," which
dictatorship flourishes in essentially the same way, though under different appearances, in the three countries. It is in sharp contrast to the democratic state, which is "a government of laws not of men," wherein the civil rights of the individual are carefully protected and the government is responsible for its actions to the representatives of a sovereign people. It is also different from the old system of absolute monarchy, which was a government by an autocrat whose power, in practice if not in theory, was limited by the privileges of classes, churches, and regions. Party dictatorship repudiates responsibility to the people, and it equally repudiates class and religious privileges. It owes account to no one for its actions. It may inaugurate the most drastic changes without notice. No individual's life, liberty, or property is held sacred or inviolable; civil rights do not exist under a party dictatorship. A secret police, such as the Ogpu in Russia, the Ovra in Italy, and the Gestapo in Germany, may at any time arrest an individual and secretly punish him with death or imprisonment, without recourse to the regular courts. It is a silent terrorism, and its actions are shrouded in mystery and secrecy.

The party members are the governing group; only those who are deemed capable of being rulers irrespective of class are ad-
Party mitted to the ranks. Completely devoted to the doc-
membership trines of the party, ever ready to engage in hazardous tasks, disciplined like soldiers, unquestioningly obedient to their chief — the Duce in Italy, the Führer in Germany, and the Secretary-General in Russia — the members form a governing hierarchy that completely controls the nation. To make sure of their loyalty and devotion the members are subject to constant "purges"; those who are suspected of disloyalty or even of faint-heartedness are drastically eliminated from the party.

In order to govern effectively, party dictatorship creates the "totalitarian" state. In a "totalitarian" state there exists no such distinction between private and public life as exists in a democracy. All activities, political, economic, social, and cultural, are controlled and regulated by the state. What materials should go into the making of shoes, how much steel should be manufactured, what athletic contests should be held, and what lullabies a mother should sing to her child are all prescribed by the state. "Everything in the state, everything for the state, nothing against the state," proclaimed Mussolini. *The "totalitarian state"*

All the dictatorships have an official philosophy which every citizen must accept as a sort of established religion. In Russia the official philosophy is Marxism; in Germany, Nazism; and in Italy, Fascism. None but those who firmly adhere to the official philosophy are permitted to fill responsible positions, whether political or non-political. The official philosophy is dogmatic in ways similar to those of the established churches during the seventeenth century. Therefore heresy-hunting has become a normal function of the dictatorships. *Official philosophy*

To direct popular opinion in favor of the government and its policies, the dictatorships control all forms of intellectual activity through "propaganda." The schools, from the kindergarten to the university, are under government control, and teaching must conform to the tenets of the official philosophy and to the policies of the government. The radio, the newspapers, the theater, the movies are all directed by the government. Authors must submit their manuscripts to a board of censors. There is, strictly speaking, no censorship of the press, by which is meant that some matters only are forbidden publication. It is more correct to say that the press is completely suppressed; in its place there are journals that are used by the government as a means of communicating its wishes to the people and of creating popular approval of its policies. A newspaper in a dictatorship is an official mouthpiece, not an independent organ of opinion. *Propaganda*

There are important differences, however, between the Communist and the Fascist dictatorships. In the former, private enterprise is forbidden; in its place is government ownership of all means of production and distribution. In the latter, private enterprise is permitted though with many governmental restrictions and regulations. Another important difference is in the attitude toward national minorities. Communist Russia recognizes the principle *Differences between the Communist and the Fascist dictatorships*

of "cultural nationalism," and treats equally all nationalities and
all races within its borders.   On the other hand, Fascist Germany
and Italy recognize the principle of "racialism."   They persecute
to the point of extermination all national and racial minorities
that they consider outside the German or Italian "race."   Anti-
Semitism is a cardinal principle of Fascist policy.

COMMUNIST RUSSIA

(a) WAR COMMUNISM

After the November Revolution of 1917, the Communists found
themselves in complete control of Russia.   The situation that they
faced was one of great difficulty, even greater than that faced by
the French Jacobins in 1793.   The country was in a state of incredible disorder and disorganization.   War, revolution, counter-
revolution, famine, and drought had created a situation serious
enough to tax the abilities and courage of any revolutionary party.
The Communist aim was nothing less than to create a socialist
society from the Russian chaos.

The history of Soviet Russia may be divided into three stages,
the first of which was War Communism, lasting from 1917 to 1921.
War Com-   When the Communists came into power, they national-
munism   ized all land, industry, and commerce.   But the situa-
(1917–21)   tion which arose as a result of war and revolution
disorganized the economic life of Russia.   Production went down
to a low level because of the incompetence of the new managers and
the slackness of the workers.   Fuel and raw materials were scarce.
The railways were in a bad condition.   Worst of all was the agricultural situation.   The peasants refused to send food to the
cities because they could get few manufactures in exchange.   To
get food the government resorted to requisitions; troops raided
the farms and seized the supplies of the peasants.   As a consequence the peasants stopped raising food except for their own
needs.   A failure of the crops in the Volga region resulted in a
famine.   The Communists were in the seat of power, but communism was proving disastrous.

(b) THE NEW ECONOMIC POLICY

Lenin frankly admitted that the Soviet's economic policy was a
failure, and persuaded his associates to change their course.   In
1921, the New Economic Policy (NEP) was inaugurated, modify-

ing the socialist experiments of Russia by making concessions to capitalism. The peasants were made practically pro- The NEP prietors by being given an hereditary leasehold of their (1921–28) farms and the right to hire labor. They were to pay regular taxes instead of giving their surplus food to the government. Private business enterprise was permitted, under certain restrictions, in the retail trade and in small manufacturing. Concessions were given for definite periods to foreign capitalists to exploit the natural resources of the country; the profits of these enterprises were to be shared by the capitalists and the government. In the "restoration of the market," the government, however, continued its monopoly over foreign trade, banking, transportation, communication, and the heavy industries.

Under the spur of the New Economic Policy, Russia began to recover from her economic collapse. Production in agriculture and in industry increased; within five years it almost Rehabilita- reached the pre-war level for the same territory. A tion of new currency was established backed by a gold reserve. Russia Economic stability brought political recognition. For a time the Soviet government was not recognized by the great powers. The first to do so was the Republic of Germany in 1922. England, Italy, and France followed, and finally the United States in 1933.

In order to coördinate the economic activities of the people, the government established the State Planning Commission. Its duty was to plan the development of the economic life of the Economic entire nation. The work was carried on by a board of planning experts, who blocked out the future of agriculture, commerce, industry, and power by apportioning capital, regulating production, locating factories at most advantageous points, and developing power. Economic planning was established in order to avoid the waste that competitive capitalism engenders through duplication of plant, overproduction, and multiplication of services.

The great beneficiary of the Revolution of 1917 was the peasant. At last he got "more land," for which he had struggled so long; he had acquired about half of the land before the Revolu- The kulaks tion, and now his holding was much larger. The more prosperous peasants, the kulaks, became the controlling group in the villages. These peasants were not interested in communist theories; they had the land and wanted to hold it. And at first the government was inclined to take a conciliatory attitude toward them because it feared to disrupt the movement for reconstruction.

(c) THE FIVE-YEAR PLAN

The New Economic Policy created differences of opinion among the Communists. Some feared that it was a retreat to the capitalism which they had overthrown in the Revolution. With the death of Lenin, in 1924, these differences led to the formation of an opposition to the government led by Trotsky. A struggle for the leadership of the Communist Party took place between Trotsky and Joseph Stalin. The fundamental difference between them was that Trotsky believed in "permanent revolution," and Stalin in "socialism in one country." By "permanent revolution" Trotsky meant the encouragement by Soviet Russia of a world revolutionary movement in order to overthrow capitalism throughout the world. Then, and then only, he believed, could the world be made safe for socialism. Stalin contended that the government should concentrate its efforts to establish socialism in Russia. If successful, this object lesson would constitute the best propaganda for communism throughout the world. In the factional struggle that ensued, victory was won by Stalin, who became the leader of the Communist Party.

Trotsky versus Stalin

The Opposition, as Trotsky's faction was called, was suppressed, but its criticisms were heeded by the victorious Stalin. There was great uneasiness among the Communists at the growing power of the kulaks, who now formed a powerful class of peasant proprietors. There was even greater uneasiness regarding Russia's dependence upon foreign nations for manufactures. Stalin came to the conclusion that Russia must be freed from her industrial dependence upon foreign nations; and that the Russian industrial workers must be freed from their dependence upon the peasantry for food. In other words Russia should become industrialized very rapidly, and the kulaks should be eliminated as the chief providers of food for the population.

Stalin's views

Industrialization requires natural resources, labor, and capital. Russia had a sufficient supply of the first two, but she had no accumulated supply of capital; and she could not borrow abroad because her credit was bad, having repudiated the tsarist debts and having confiscated the property

The Five-Year Plan (1928–33)

of foreigners as well as that of Russians. Nevertheless, in 1928 Russia virtually abandoned the New Economic Policy and inaugurated the Five-Year Plan, an ambitious and far-reaching plan of economic reconstruction. By means of a planned economy the Soviet aimed to transform backward agricultural Russia into an advanced industrial country in the short period of five years without having recourse to the private enterprise of capitalists. Russia proposed to get capital from domestic loans, from profits of the new industries, and especially from the sale of foodstuffs abroad, from the proceeds of which she could purchase machinery.

Although Russia had a plentiful supply of unskilled labor she was woefully deficient in skilled labor, and especially in highly skilled technicians. Great inducements were offered to foreign engineers to come to Russia to aid in the accomplishment of the Five-Year Plan. Many American and German engineers entered the service of Russia.

The chief objects of the Five-Year Plan were as follows: the establishment of a power base consisting of a great network of central electric stations reaching out to every part of the Soviet Union; the creation of basic industries such as coal, oil, steel, chemical, and machine enterprises; automotive developments, railways, and roads; and large-scale scientific agriculture. Production was planned by rationing raw material and regulating output, and by the assignment of labor, both skilled and unskilled, to every industry. The greatest possible emphasis was laid on the production of heavy industries, and little on the production of consumers' goods. What Russia aimed *Industry under the Plan* to do in the Five-Year Plan was to create a gigantic modern factory system capable of large-scale production. Every industry was expected to show a profit, which, however, did not go into private hands, as in capitalistic countries, but went to the state to be used as future capital. Laborers were engaged and paid wages, differing in amount according to the nature of the industry and the skill of the workman.

The vital element in the Five-Year Plan was the production of a surplus supply of food for the city population, and for export in order to get machinery from foreign countries. Russian agriculture had been backward from time immemorial. The small farms, cut up into strips, were *Agriculture under the Plan* poorly cultivated by ignorant peasants; and the Revolution had not altered this situation. Increased production could come only by the consolidation of small farms into large units and by mechanization, or the application to farming of modern machinery such as tractors and combines.

The government entered on a campaign to establish "collectives" by consolidating small farms into large units that could greatly increase production through coöperative labor, the elimination of strips, and the use of machinery. When the peasants of a district formed a collective they pooled their land holdings and their draft animals. The collective was administered by the members, who regulated conditions of labor, wages, and other matters. The collective had to enter into a contract with the government, by which it agreed to deliver to the latter, at fixed prices, all the foodstuffs produced above the needs of the members and of the livestock. In return the government rented machinery, extended credit, and gave technical advice to the farmers. Each member of the collective had his individual garden patch, his homestead, his tools, and small animals as property that he could leave to his children. Whatever surplus he produced he had a right to sell directly to consumers.

Great opposition to this scheme arose among the kulaks, who were loath to give up their farms. The government, by dictatorial

Opposition
by the
kulaks

methods, endeavored to coerce them to enter the collectives. In retaliation the kulaks refused to sow more grain than their own needs required; they also slaughtered their livestock wholesale. Thereupon the government determined to "liquidate the kulaks as a class." Their lands were confiscated, and they were driven into exile or made to labor as convicts in public works. As a result of the war between the government and the kulaks, the harvest of 1932 was so bad that a widespread famine took place, in which many died of starvation.

How successful was the Five-Year Plan? Because of the complete control of information by the government and the strict cen-

Extent of
industriali-
zation

sorship of news sent from Russia, it is impossible to give an accurate estimate of the accomplishments of the Plan. The rapid march of the Industrial and Agricultural Revolutions in Russia, in the incredibly short period of five years, did succeed in establishing methods of large-scale production. What took western Europe over a century was telescoped in Russia into twenty years. There were now great industrial centers that did not exist before, such as the electrical power plant at Dnieperstroy, the automobile plant, on the Ford model, in Gorki, the tractor plant in Stalingrad, and the agricultural machinery plant in Rostov. However, the advance was accomplished at the expense of the standard of living of the people. The country was put on a strict rationing system; every person was given a card which allowed him a limited amount of bread, butter, meat, clothes, and other necessaries of life. The government did succeed in its plan of establishing collectives, as a consequence of which production of foodstuffs gradually increased. In 1935 the harvest was so good that the rationing of food was abolished.

(d) RUSSIA'S FOREIGN POLICY

Soviet Russia's foreign policy underwent changes that, in the main, corresponded with the changes in her domestic policy. In the period of War Communism, when she was inspired by the ideal of world revolution, Soviet Russia aided the communist parties in the various countries in their efforts to overthrow their governments. The defeat of the revolutionary movements in Hungary and in Italy caused her to change her tactics. She resolved to destroy capitalism in the West by rousing the natives in the East against western imperialism. This policy, known as the "Asia Detour," was for a time successful in China, where the Chinese revolutionary movement, the Kuomintang, fell under the influence of Russian advisers. But when Chiang Kai-shek came into power he ousted the Russians and eliminated communist influences from the Kuomintang. By 1932 the "Asia Detour" proved to be a failure.

Again Soviet Russia changed her tactics. She needed all her energies to carry out the scheme of industrialization inaugurated by the Five-Year Plan. She needed protection from Japan in the East and from Nazi Germany in the West; both of whom were determined to destroy her. It was Foreign Minister Litvinov who led in the reconciliation of Soviet Russia with her old enemies France and England. To coöperate with them she joined the League of Nations. To quiet their fears she virtually scrapped the Third International, known as the "Comintern," as an agency of world revolution. The communist parties in the democracies were advised to support their governments by organizing Popular

Front movements against Fascism. In 1936 Soviet Russia made a pact with France which marked the great success of Litvinov's diplomacy. Relations between England and Russia became friendly, and steps were taken to form an alliance between these two powers. Stalin's new policy of a common front with the democratic powers against Fascism was making rapid headway.

Suddenly, in May, 1939, Litvinov was dismissed as Foreign Minister. His successor, Molotov, gave evidence of hostility to England and France. There was uneasiness in these two countries; it was feared that Stalin might strike hands with his fellow-dictator, Hitler. However, diplomatic and military missions from England and France were invited to Moscow to negotiate the terms of an alliance with Russia. In August, 1939, as later described, the world was startled by the publication of a non-aggression pact between Germany and Russia. While he was negotiating with the English and French, Stalin came to a secret agreement with Hitler aimed against the democracies.

(e) DICTATORSHIP OF STALIN

The Bolshevist Revolution established the Communist Party in control of Soviet Russia. The Party was a small minority of the population, and like other ruling minorities it was thoroughly organized under an iron discipline. It used the power of the state to crush all opposition to its views and policies. The base of the Party machine was the "cell," a group organized in factories, offices, and villages. Above this "cell" was a hierarchy of local, provincial, and national bodies that culminated in the All-Union Party Congress, which exercised supreme authority in the Party. All policies were freely debated in the Congress, but once a decision was reached by a majority it became the Party "line" that all members had to obey. To refuse was counter-revolution, and the punishment was exile or death. Through this "monolithic unity" the Party was able to crush opposition in the bud. Between sessions of the Congress power was exercised by a Central Committee elected by the Congress. In turn it chose a number of "bureaus," the most important of which was the "Politbureau" of ten members; it also chose the Secretary-General, the highest official of the Party, the position greatly sought by ambitious leaders. It was the Politbureau, of which the Secretary-General was a member, that dominated the policies of the Party and therefore the policies of the Soviet Union. The highest officials in the government were members of the Polit-bureau, where important government policies like the Five-Year Plan were first formulated.

The issue that arose between Trotsky and Stalin was, in one sense, "socialism in one country" versus "permanent revolution." In another and even more important sense the issue was: who was to be the dictator of Russia. Demo-cratic methods within the Party prevailed; majority rule decided the Party "line." But democracy within the Party and dictatorship in the nation was a contradiction that could not be reconciled. As the Dictatorship of the Proletariat became the dictatorship of the Communist Party, so did the dictatorship of the Communist Party become the personal dictatorship of Stalin.

Issue of personal dictatorship

Stalin's triumph over Trotsky was complete when, as Secretary-General, he controlled Party machinery. He promptly proceeded to eliminate all who had opposed him. Trotsky, the most intimate associate of Lenin in the Bolshevist Revolution, was driven into exile. He was stigmatized as a "re-actionary," and the term "Trotskyism" was made synonymous with treason to the Soviet Union. Anyone not a whole-hearted follower of Stalin was suspected of "Trotskyism." A series of "purges" of the Party began which eliminated all opposition to Stalin. Sometimes men would be openly tried and convicted of Trotskyism, which meant death or long imprisonment. More often they disappeared as a result of the mysterious activities of the Ogpu. The terrorism exercised over the country was reflected in an aggravated form inside the Community Party.

Party "purges"

During 1936–38 the "purges" in Russia attracted world-wide attention. The "fathers" of the Bolshevist Revolution, among them Zinoviev, head of the Comintern (Third International), Radek, the chief Soviet publicist, Marshal Tukachevsky, the head of the Red Army, and Bukharin, the leading communist philoso-pher, were accused of Trotskyism. Their trials astonished the world by the unjudicial methods employed, and by the fact that the accused vied with one another in confessing their guilt and in accusing others. These trials were in fact "purges" staged in the courtroom. The prisoners were found guilty, and were executed or imprisoned.

As a result of the "purges" the Communist Party was terrorized

into becoming a personal machine of Stalin.   Congresses of the
Dictatorship Party were convoked irregularly and infrequently;
of Stalin   they met merely to register the will of Stalin, who
now made the Party "line."   To all practical purposes Stalin was
the dictator of Russia, ruling through an obedient bureaucracy
and through the activities of the Ogpu.

A new constitution for the Soviet Union was adopted in 1936
by the All-Union Congress of Soviets.   It abolished the system
The new   of government established by the constitution of 1922,
constitution and inaugurated a new one that provided for a federal
union of eleven states.   The central government was to consist
of a bicameral parliament, the Council of the Union and the Council
of Nationalities, having equal power over legislation; and of a
number of administrative bodies, the most important of which
was the Council of Commissars.   The Council of the Union was to
be elected by all citizens over eighteen, irrespective of sex, race, and
nationality, by a direct, secret ballot.   The Council of Nationalities was to be elected by the local legislatures in the eleven states
and by the Autonomous Provinces, the number of delegates being
in proportion to size and importance of the regions represented.
The Council of Commissars was to be chosen by a joint session of
both houses of parliament.

The constitution established civil rights and religious liberty and
equality for all citizens in all spheres of life.   Church and state
were made separate as in the previous constitution.   One new feature was the recognition of property rights in "houses, household
furnishings, articles of personal consumption and comfort, and savings accounts," and the right of inheritance of these things.   Another was the adoption of the principle, "From each according to
his ability, to each according to his work."

It soon became evident that the constitution did not abolish
the dictatorship.   The first elections for the Council of the Union
The dicta-   took place in 1937.   Only the Communist Party was
torship con- permitted to put up candidates; no opposition parties
tinues   of any sort, Communist or non-Communist, were permitted.   The outcome of the elections was naturally a unanimous
Council.   The guarantees of civil liberty did not protect Trotsky-
ists, as was seen in the wave of arbitrary arrests and disappear-
ances during the "purges."   It became only too evident that civil,
religious, and political liberty was to be enjoyed by the upholders
and not by the opponents of the dictatorship.

If new oppressions came to Russia with communism, old oppressions disappeared along with tsarism. The many non-Russians in the Soviet Union had been persecuted to a more or less *Equality of* degree under tsarism. The Soviet government, both *races and* in theory and in practice, treated all races and nation- *nationalities* alities with equality. It freely permitted and even aided the non-Russians to maintain their language and culture. Discrimination against non-Russians was made a criminal offense. Religion was "tolerated," but with many restrictions. As Marxism, with its belief in materialistic atheism, was the official philosophy, no official and no Party member could belong to any faith. Obstacles were put in the way of spreading religion. But the churches were permitted to hold services, and many devout people continued to practice their faith unmolested.

FASCIST ITALY

(a) POST-WAR CONDITIONS

Italy's territorial gains, though not considerable, were important. The Conference of Paris gave her the Trentino and southern Tyrol, containing the Brenner Pass which safeguarded her *Italy's war* from invasion from the north; and Gorizia, Trieste, *gains* Istria, and part of Dalmatia, which gave her a large share in the control of the Adriatic. Later she acquired Fiume from Yugoslavia and the Dodecanese Islands from Turkey. She also managed to extend somewhat the boundaries of her African colonies, Libya and Somaliland. But Italy's new boundaries were not drawn "along clearly recognizable lines of nationality," demanded by Wilson's Fourteen Points. Southern Tyrol contained a German-speaking population that wished to remain with Austria. The newly acquired Adriatic territory contained Yugoslavs who wished to remain with Yugoslavia.

The serious problems that had confronted Italy since unification were aggravated by the war. On the solution of these problems depended the very existence of the parliamentary system *Italy's* itself. Italy's losses in the war were great; and being a *"mutilated"* poor country, she could bear them far less easily than *victory* rich England and France could bear their greater losses. Before the war Italy's expansion had not been very successful. Blocked by France in Tunis, driven from Abyssinia, Italy had to be satisfied with a desert, Tripoli, which she got by the grace of France.

During the war Italy joined the Allies on the promise of large rewards in case of victory. Although *Italia irredenta* was now "redeemed," Italy was sorely disappointed with what she regarded as her "mutilated" victory. She had hoped to share in the distribution of the German colonies in Africa and in the partition of Turkey, but her "sacred egoism" was flouted by the Allies. There was widespread dissatisfaction with the government, which was blamed for the unsuccessful efforts at the Conference of Paris to satisfy national aspirations.

Economic conditions, always bad, were aggravated by the war. Unemployment was widespread, and masses of the poor reached

Revolutionary discontent
the starvation point. As a consequence a powerful revolutionary agitation, inspired by the success of the Bolshevists in Russia, was soon under way. Despite the fact that the Communists in Italy were few, their influence was considerable in the Socialist Party and in the trade unions because of their strategy of "boring from within." Violent strikes were of almost daily occurrence, and industry was on the verge of collapse. The peasants on the large estates in the south were drawn into the revolutionary current. They began seizing the land and dividing it into farms for themselves.

The government was weak in face of this critical situation. Parliament as it functioned in Italy was almost a caricature of its

Inefficiency of Parliament
English model. Elections were "managed" by the office-holders, often through coercion and bribery, so that in spite of the democratic suffrage, Parliament was not a truly representative body. The many political groups in the Chamber were engaged in constant strife and intrigue, and the needs of the nation were forgotten in the struggle for office. There did not take place, as was so often the case in France, a "concentration" of the parties on the Left that in times of crisis resolutely put through drastic reforms. As a result of the elections in 1919 the Socialists became the leading party. But they refused to collaborate with the other Left groups to form a ministry; instead, they hoped to come into power by fomenting revolutionary strikes to overturn the government.

Political ineptitude and governmental inefficiency and corruption were by-words among the people, and many Italians became skeptical of parliamentary government. Premier Giolitti typified the worst aspects of the system. Cunning, unscrupulous, and cynical, he always sought to manipulate situations either by secret deals with his opponents or by granting concessions that would not be fully applied. He feared to take resolute action against the revolutionary strikes that created widespread disorder. This situation caused great uneasiness among the propertied classes, who feared the possibility of a proletarian dictatorship as in Russia.

(b) THE FASCIST COUP D'ÉTAT

Among the revolutionary groups that appeared in post-war Italy was one founded in 1919 by Benito Mussolini, an ex-Socialist. Later the group became known as the "Fascists," from the Latin *fasces*, a Roman symbol of authority and discipline. Most of the Fascists were young ex-service men who advocated radical social and political reforms. Being ardent nationalists they bitterly resented the "defeatist" attitude of the Socialists. Organized as a private army with arms and uniforms, the most distinguishing part of which was a black shirt, the Fascists attacked the Socialists on every occasion. Socialist meetings were broken up, their headquarters wrecked, their journals burned, and their leaders maltreated or killed. A strike would precipitate a street battle between the strikers and the "Black Shirts." The police and magistrates were inclined to be lenient with the Fascists and severe with their opponents. In the face of this growing disorder and violence the government did little or nothing. Sometimes Giolitti secretly supplied arms to the Black Shirts instead of using forces of the government to suppress rioting.

This situation became acute in 1920 when a great strike took place in the steel industry throughout Italy. The workers, led by revolutionists who were in control of the union, occupied the factories. They organized a soviet and a Red guard on the Russian model. However, they were unable to run the factories, and negotiations began between them and Premier Giolitti, as a result of which the factories were evacuated. The revolutionists had failed in their attempt to establish the Dictatorship of the Proletariat, as a consequence of which revolutionary feeling in Italy was now at a low ebb. The danger of a social upheaval was past.

But there was alarm among the conservative elements in the nation. Property had been seized and the government had done nothing. Confidence in the authority of the parliamentary system received a shock from which it never recovered. Mussolini

Growth of the Fascist movement

saw that his opportunity was at hand; he could ride into power by playing on the fears of the middle class. He vehemently denounced the government as weak and cowardly, and urged that all who opposed the Socialists and the unions should support the Fascists as the only force that would mercilessly suppress all revolutionary activity. From small bands the Fascists grew rapidly into an army of over 100,000. Funds came from the great capitalists and landowners, and recruits from the lower middle class. Opposed to the government now were the Fascists, secretly supported by powerful elements in the government itself, such as the army, the King, and many officials. Mussolini insistently declared that real power in Italy lay with the Fascists, not with the government. Nevertheless the mass of the Italian people were opposed to any dictatorship, whether by Fascists or by Communists. In the elections for the Chamber in 1921, the last elections under the parliamentary régime, the Fascists won 35 and the Communists 16 out of a total of 535 seats.

All was prepared now for a seizure of the government by the Fascists. During October, 1922, Mussolini repeatedly demanded

"March on Rome"

of Premier Facta, who had succeeded Giolitti, that the government be turned over to him. Fascist bands all over Italy began a "March on Rome." The Premier prepared a decree proclaiming martial law, but the King refused to sign the decree. Instead, on October 30, he appointed a new cabinet with Mussolini as Premier. The "March on Rome" was a coup d'état executed by the Fascists with the connivance of those in power.

(c) FASCISTIZATION OF ITALY

A ministry was now in office unsupported by Parliament. Mussolini repudiated democracy frankly and ruthlessly and stood defiant

Mussolini repudiates democracy

"over the dead body of Liberty." Democracy, according to Mussolini, had utterly failed to meet the needs of a country which required a strong, determined government that would bring discipline and order to Italy. He openly advocated the suppression of the parliamentary régime and the establishment of a dictatorship by the Fascist Party. In the meanwhile he demanded and received from Parliament virtual dictatorial power until the end of 1923. Elections took place in

MUSSOLINI, HITLER, AND STALIN

1924; by terrorizing their opponents the Fascists succeeded in winning a large majority of the seats.

But it was the intention of Mussolini to establish a dictatorship, not to win elections even by terrorism. His Ministry was now the legal government backed by a majority in Parliament; the small minority of Liberals was helpless. Step by step the government proceeded to "Fascistize" Italian institutions. During 1925–26 local self-government in the villages and municipalities was abolished; in its place appeared officials named by the Ministry. In 1926 the trade unions were abolished, and new labor organizations were established according to Fascist principles. In 1928 a new electoral law Fascistized Parliament. The Chamber was to consist of 400 members elected by what was practically universal manhood suffrage. A list of 1000 names was to be submitted by trade and labor bodies; from this list the Fascist Grand Council was to choose 400 who were to be the candidates. This Fascist list, and no other, was to be submitted to the voters with the choice of voting "yes" or "no" on the entire list. The passing of this electoral law marked the end of liberalism in Italy — a liberalism that had put up a stubborn resistance for six years.

Fascistization of the government

In the new scheme, as in the old, the government of Italy consisted of the King, the Ministry, and Parliament. The Premier was appointed by the King and was responsible to him, not to Parliament. But the Premier was always to be the head of the Fascist Party. He then chose the ministers, who were responsible to him directly. Parliament consisted of two houses: the Senate, a purely honorary body, and the Chamber, already described. In 1938 the Chamber voted itself out of existence and was succeeded by a body called the Chamber of Fasces and Corporations, consisting of the high party officials and members of the National Council of Corporations, all of them appointed directly or indirectly by Mussolini and removable by him at his pleasure. Neither this Chamber nor its predecessor has had much to do with the making of laws. The really important body was the Fascist Grand Council, which was both a party and a government organ. It was this body that considered the important policies of the nation; once it reached a decision it was issued as a decree by the Ministry. Legislation by decree has been the essential characteristic of law-making in the dictatorships.

Dictatorship of the Fascist Party

The "efficient secret" of the Fascist system of government was the complete control exercised by the Fascist Party, a highly cen-

Organization of the Party tralized organization with an iron discipline over its members. Local "cells," grouped into federations, rose like a pyramid to a small group, the Fascist Grand Council, consisting of the leading members of the Party. It is this body that had supreme power in the Party, hence in the government. At the very apex of the pyramid was the *Duce*, or leader, who presided over the Council and appointed most of its members, and whose word was law in the Party and in the government. Hence the Duce-Premier was the dictator of Italy. The principle of organization in the Party was "leadership." From the Duce down there was a hierarchy of leaders; every part of the organization was controlled by a leader; those above appointed and dominated those below. Membership in the Party was limited to those who were completely in favor of its doctrines and militant in asserting them. To keep the ranks solid and united, "purges" constantly took place. It was a great privilege to be enrolled in the Party, the only door of political opportunity open to young Italians.

Fascism was as revolutionary in the economic as in the political sphere. In 1927 the government issued the Charter of Labor, which proclaimed Fascist economic principles. Later

Fascist economics a number of Corporations laws were enacted, the latest in 1934, which established organizations in harmony with these principles. One Fascist economic principle was class coöperation, in opposition to the class struggle preached by the socialists. Strikes and lockouts were declared illegal. Industrial disputes were to be settled by compulsory arbitration in industrial courts. Another principle was state intervention in economic life in opposition to the laissez faire preached by the liberals. Fascism insisted on the preservation of private property and private enterprise. But capital, like labor, was to be under the control and direction of the state, which could intervene in business matters whenever the interests of the nation demanded it. The state could take over industry, forbid the establishment of new enterprises, compel the merging of individual enterprises into one large corporation, and even confiscate property.

All occupied persons in any trade, business, profession, or handicraft were compelled to join a local syndicate, or union. There were to be separate syndicates for employers and for employees in each occupation. The local syndicate was made the basis of a hierarchy of federations reaching to two national confederations, one of employers and another of employees, for twenty-two specified groups of occupations. Wages, hours, and conditions of labor were to be settled through contracts by joint committees representing both confederations. Finally, there was the National Council of Corporations, consisting of representatives from both confederations and functioning as an economic general staff to plan and regulate the economic life of the nation. The "corpo-
rate state"

This system was devised to create self-government and industrial peace through the coöperation of representatives of capital and labor. However, the real work of the syndicates was done not by their members, but by Fascist Party politicians who guided them. It was plain that the Corporations law was a scheme devised "by a political party to serve its own purposes under color of promoting industrial peace." Party con-
trol of the
corporation

Fascism abolished the old political and social order and established a new one, hence it was a revolutionary movement. While its policies were constantly subject to change, its political and social "ideology," or philosophy has remained the same from the beginning. Its fundamental tenet is the supremacy of the state in the public and private life of the nation. All actions must be based on the principle of "the rights of the state, the pre-eminence of its authority, and the superiority of its end." Fascism was opposed to the democratic view that regarded the state as an instrument of the individual to protect and to develop his freedom, and to the socialistic view of the state as an instrument of the working class to establish its dominance. Under Fascism the state would control and direct the "economic and intellectual forces of the nation toward a common goal," and entrust the government to men "capable of rising above their private interests and of realizing the aspirations of the social collectivity." There was to be a "revolution in the national soul" through the introduction of discipline and efficiency among the easy-going Italians. Aggressive nationalism was the dominant note of Fascism, and the life of the nation was to be organized with the aim of preparing Italy to occupy a higher position in the world. All the energies of the nation were to be bent toward making Italy a great military power. According to Mussolini, Fascism Fascist
"ideology" "believes neither in the possibility nor the utility of perpetual peace.... War alone brings up to its highest tension all human energy and puts the stamp of nobility upon the peoples who have the courage to meet it."

Like Communist Russia, Fascist Italy was a "totalitarian state" under a party dictatorship. Only Fascist Party members were per-

Suppression of freedom of speech

mitted to hold office; all opposition parties were ruthlessly suppressed. All means of intellectual freedom, such as schools, books, and journals, were compelled to preach Fascism, the official philosophy of the Italian state. Those who refused to do so were compelled to flee for their lives. A net of secret police, called the Ovra, was thrown over the entire nation to ferret out the enemies of Fascism. As in the days of the Risorgimento, the capitals of western Europe harbored Italian exiles, chiefly liberals and socialists.

(d) FASCIST ACHIEVEMENTS

An outstanding achievement of the Fascist régime was the final settlement of the Roman Question that, since 1870, had created a deep antagonism between the papacy and the Italian state. In 1929 church and state in Italy signed a number of agreements, known as the Lateran Accord, which terminated their estrangement of fifty-eight years.

The Lateran Accord consisted of a political treaty, a religious concordat, and a financial arrangement. The treaty provided for

Lateran Accord

the recognition by Italy of the temporal power of the pope, who was to reign as an indisputably independent sovereign in the "State of the Vatican City," a district in Rome set aside as his territory. The Holy See recognized the House of Savoy as sovereign in Italy, with Rome as the capital. The State of the Vatican City, consisting of about a hundred acres, was now an independent state, the smallest in the world. As a consequence of this treaty the pope was no longer the "Prisoner of the Vatican."

According to the concordat Roman Catholicism was made "the sole religion of the state." Laws were later enacted which guaranteed religious toleration by permitting religions other than the Catholic. Bishops and archbishops had to swear loyalty to the Italian government before taking office. There were important clauses in the concordat concerning education and marriage. The teaching of the Catholic faith was declared to be "the basis and crown of public education." Religious instruction was made compulsory in the public elementary and secondary schools, under the direction and control of the clergy. Marriage was recognized as a sacrament by the state; no divorce was permitted. However, non-Catholics were not compelled to receive Catholic instruction in the schools.

The financial agreement consisted of a payment to the Holy See of about $95,000,000 "as a final settlement of its financial relations with Italy resulting from the events of 1870."

The Fascist régime was very active in promoting industry and agriculture. Italy was not self-supporting either agriculturally or industrially, and therefore was always in a serious economic situation. The government set to work energetically to increase the food supply by putting more land under cultivation through reclaiming marshy places The government also assisted industry by promoting the better organization of factories and by loans. A powerful merchant marine appeared. Public works, especially automobile highways, were built. As in the other dictatorships, it is difficult to get an accurate picture of the economic achievements of Fascism in Italy because of censorship of news as well as of official reports. The great expense of the rearmament program and the Ethiopian War seriously affected Italian finances. Taxes were many and onerous, and the revenues were not sufficient to meet the outlays. In 1936 the government had recourse to a capital levy of five per cent, laid on the value of all real estate. In 1937 a levy of about seven per cent was laid on the capital of joint stock corporations. Business men had expected that under Fascism they would be protected and favored. Instead they were harassed by many onerous taxes and by many restrictions that seriously hampered their enterprises.

In one respect Fascist Italy made great progress: war preparedness. The army, navy, and air services were enlarged and efficiently organized. A military spirit was instilled in the nation. The youth of the land especially were roused to great enthusiasm for a resurgent Italy through propaganda disseminated in the schools, in the youth organizations, and in the press. The distinction between civil and military life virtually disappeared; all Italians, both men and women, were in one way or another under military discipline from birth to death. Military training, according to the law, began at the age of eight and continued to the age of fifty-five, service in the army being now only a short period in the comprehensive scheme of militarizing the nation.

Italian national pride was greatly stimulated by the conquest of Ethiopia in 1936, which is described elsewhere. Ethiopia was Expansion annexed to Italy and the King was given the title of Italy "Emperor of Ethiopia." The Italian African colonies — Ethiopia, Eritrea, and Italian Somaliland — were united into a single unit called "Italian East Africa." Italy now had regions in Africa large enough to make her an important colonial power. Mussolini's intervention in Spain on the side of Franco was costly, but Franco's victories, in which the Italian armies participated, appealed to national pride. The conquest and annexation of Albania, in 1939, gave Italy complete mastery of the Adriatic.

Italy's diplomatic coöperation with Nazi Germany in the Rome–Berlin Axis led to the adoption of anti-Semitism as a domestic Anti- policy. In 1938 the government announced that the Semitism Italians were a "pure race," constituting a physical and psychological type to be preserved from intermixture with non-Aryan races. This new policy of "racialism" resulted in laws against the Jews modeled on those of Nazi Germany. Anti-Semitism had formerly been practically non-existent in Italy and had been denounced by Mussolini himself.

NAZI GERMANY

(a) ESTABLISHMENT OF A REPUBLIC

Toward the end of the World War, when the German armies were being driven out of France, popular discontent in Germany spread Flight of far and wide. In November, 1918, a mutiny broke the Kaiser out in the navy, and the sailors in Kiel Harbor raised the red flag over the fleet. Uprisings took place in the various states, where republics were proclaimed. The local dynasties abdicated and fled the country. The Kaiser and his family fled to Holland, where they were received as refugees. The inglorious flight of the last of the Hohenzollerns discredited the dynasty. Now, in the hour of defeat, the once popular Kaiser found himself a lonely refugee in a foreign land, deserted by his former supporters and despised by his former subjects.

The Social Democrats, under their leaders, Friedrich Ebert and Philipp Scheidemann, became the liquidators of the Empire. They were committed to Marxist doctrines, and had consistently opposed the government until the war. Would they now seize the opportunity to establish a socialist commonwealth? What determined their policy was the sudden appearance of a revolutionary movement, inspired by Bolshevism, which became known as "Spartacist," after Spartacus, the leader of a slave rebellion in ancient Rome. The Spartacists proclaimed the Dictatorship of the Proletariat, and established councils in imitation of the soviets in Russia. The Social Democrats were determined to put down the Spartacists, and they received the support of the conservative elements: army officers, aristocrats, and capitalists. In January, 1919, the Spartacists rose in rebellion, and desperate fighting took place in the streets of Berlin. The uprising was mercilessly suppressed by the government, which was determined to defend the Republic against violent revolutionists. Karl Leibknecht and Rosa Luxemburg, the leaders of the Spartacists, were killed during the uprising. A socialist republic had been established in Bavaria, under the leadership of Kurt Eisner. It was overthrown, and Eisner was slain. Confidence was now felt in the Ebert-Scheidemann régime by the conservative classes in Germany, to whom the defense of the existing social order was of paramount importance.

> Suppression of the Spartacists

There was need of a responsible government to sign a treaty with the Allies and to establish its authority among the people. Elections were held in 1919 for a National Assembly on the basis of universal suffrage. It resulted in an overwhelming victory for the republican parties — the Social Democrats, the Center, and the Democrats (formerly the Radicals). The monarchist parties — the Nationalists (formerly the Conservatives) and the People's Party (formerly the National Liberals) — were a small minority. The National Assembly, in order to be far from the madding crowds of Berlin, held its sessions in the quiet town of Weimar, famous as the literary center of Germany in the days of Goethe and Schiller. It proclaimed Germany a republic, and chose Ebert as provisional President. A constitution was finally adopted and promulgated by the Assembly.

> The Weimar Assembly

The Weimar constitution established Germany as a federal republic of eighteen states. Prussia continued as the largest state, but without the special privileges that she had enjoyed under the The Weimar Empire.   Suffrage, for both federal and state legisla-constitution tures, was to be universal, equal, direct, and secret. The federal government was to consist of a President, Ministry, and Parliament.   The President was to be chosen by popular vote for a term of seven years; his powers were limited except in times of emergency, when he was given power to rule the nation by decrees.   Executive power was to be exercised by a ministry appointed by the President and responsible to the Reichstag.   Parliament was to consist of two houses: the Reichstag, to be elected by the people according to proportional representation; and the Reichsrat, a federal senate, with limited powers, consisting of delegates to be appointed by the state governments.

The Weimar constitution contained provisions which made it the very model of progressive democracy.   It incorporated the old political, civil, and religious liberties through democratic elections and a Bill of Rights.   It also adopted the newer democratic proposals, such as woman suffrage, proportional representation, initiative, referendum, and recall.   Furthermore, it included social and economic provisions, new in the history of constitutions.   Education for children was made free and compulsory for eight years. Marriage was to be based on equality of husband and wife.   The government was given power "to transfer to public ownership private economic enterprises suitable for socialization" but with compensation to the owners.   Industrial councils were to be established to regulate working conditions.   Special protection to labor was guaranteed by social reform.   The "right to labor" was recognized by a provision requiring the public maintenance of the unemployed.

(b) RECONSTRUCTION

The problems that faced the young Republic were many and serious.   The war, the blockade, and the uprisings created a situa-The Kapp tion that was desperate.   Yet Germany set bravely Putsch to work to reorganize herself and once more take her place among the great nations of the world.   The government was supported by the Weimar combination, the Social Democrats, the Centrists, and the Democrats; in opposition were the Nationalists, the People's Party, and the Communists.   The bitterest opposition to the Republic came from the ex-army officers who had lost both their positions and their privileges as a result of the overthrow of the Empire. In 1920 the Republic was suddenly faced with a new danger, this time from reactionaries. A body of soldiers and officers, led by a reactionary named Kapp, prepared to overthrow the Republic by a *Putsch*, or coup d'état. They seized Berlin, and the government was compelled to flee. But the conspiracy was foiled as a result of a general strike by the workers and refusal by the financial interests to back Kapp. The *Putsch* quickly collapsed, and the Republic was safe once more.

After the war the finances were in a state of chaos because of Reparations payments, curtailed credits, and adverse trade balances. Germany sought to weather the storm by resorting to paper money inflation. The paper mark *Inflation* rapidly sank as more and more money was printed. Its value varied from week to week, from day to day, and even from hour to hour; in 1923, it was almost worthless. Business became impossible as no one knew what would be the future value of money. It was the middle class that suffered most from inflation; their incomes from investments, from savings, and from pensions became practically worthless. Some industrialists benefited from inflation because the cost of labor and of raw materials was greatly reduced; and they invested their profits in foreign securities. Some reaped a harvest by speculating in marks. The government, however, was able to repudiate its internal debts by paying almost worthless paper money. By 1923 the situation had become intolerable, and a new currency was issued, on a gold basis, with the mark at the same value as in 1914.

Germany's industrial system was untouched by the havoc of war, as she had not been subject to invasion. During the inflation her industrialists took advantage of the depreciated money *Industrial* to renovate their machinery and to build new plants. *revival* Germany's industrial production began to advance rapidly as a result of the introduction of the American system of mass production, called "rationalization." Once more German goods competed in the markets of the world. A new merchant marine appeared, consisting of oil burners and of motor ships, that rapidly approached the tonnage of pre-war days. Reparations payments were met from the great inflow of money that came, chiefly from America and England, as investments in German private industrial enterprises and in the bonds of municipalities and states.

The Republic had been established mainly through the efforts of

the Social Democrats, whose influence was seen in the radical provisions of the Weimar constitution. To carry out
these provisions a national eight-hour law was passed
in 1919. The sickness and accident insurance laws of the Empire
were revised to meet changed conditions. A new old-age pension
law was passed in 1923, which provided for a pension to the insured
at the age of 65; in case of death of the insured his widow and or-
phaned children received allowances. Before the war, Germany
had no unemployment insurance laws, but the trade depression
following the war created widespread unemployment. In 1927 an
unemployment insurance law was passed according to which unemployed workers received money benefits for a maximum period of
twenty-six weeks a year.

Social in-surance

The first election for President took place in 1925, when Ebert
died. The successful candidate was the war hero General Paul
von Hindenburg. Before the war he had been a
staunch upholder of the Hohenzollerns and a member
of the Junker class that then ruled Germany. When an old Prussian general became President of the Republic it was an ominous
sign that democratic sentiments among the German people were
not very strong, despite the progressive character of the Weimar
constitution.

Election of Hindenburg

In the new Republic, foreign relations were almost as important
as domestic relations. The first foreign minister to distinguish
himself was Walter Rathenau, who devoted himself
to the problem of rehabilitating Germany in international relations. In 1922 he signed the Treaty of Rapallo with
Russia, which established intimate relations between Germany
and Russia. These greatly benefited the former, enabling her to
export large quantities of manufactured goods into Russia. There
was prejudice against Rathenau because he was a Jew, and he
was assassinated by a group of fanatical nationalists.

Rathenau

Rathenau's most famous successor was Gustav Stresemann, who
was Foreign Minister from 1924 until his death in 1929. In the
movement to bridge the chasm in the life of Europe
caused by the war, no name stands higher than that
of Stresemann. Locarno, the admission of Germany to the League
of Nations, and the Dawes plan — the first steps in the "final liqui-
dation of the war" — were chiefly ascribable to Stresemann's
efforts, seconded by those of his intimate friend, the Frenchman,

Stresemann

Briand. Under his guidance Germany followed faithfully a "policy of fulfillment," which allayed the distrust of her felt by the Allies.

(c) THE NATIONAL SOCIALISTS

The widespread economic distress which began with the world depression in 1929 was felt acutely in Germany. Unemployment mounted high; in 1932, it rose to 6,000,000. Germany was seething with all kinds of discontent: Reparations, high taxes, the Republican régime, and even with the system of parliamentary government itself. Discontent found expression in the rapid growth of two revolutionary movements, the National Socialist and the Communist. *The Depression*

The National Socialists, or more popularly, the Nazis, were organized shortly after the war, and came under the leadership of Adolf Hitler, who was born in Austria in 1889. The Nazis, a new element in German political life, began to attract widespread attention as popular discontent grew apace. Their program was a strange mixture of racial intolerance, socialist policies, and communist tactics. They asserted that the German people were of a pure race, descendants from the ancient Teutonic tribes, and not the result of a mixture of races, as were the English, the French, and the Italians. Hence they were a superior people, with a racial culture and racial virtues superior to those of other nations. Because of this superiority the Germans were a people with a world mission, destined to create a new civilization for mankind. *Ideas and policies of the Nazis (1) Racialism*

To fulfill their mission the Germans should keep their race pure from non-German influences. Within Germany there were about 600,000 Germans of Jewish origin who, according to the Nazis, never could become real Germans because they were not of Teutonic stock. Racialism became the inspiration of a bitter and uncompromising anti-Semitism, which was the fundamental spiritual principle of Nazis. They advocated the complete elimination of the Jews from German life by any and all means. Jews were to be boycotted in business and in labor; driven from the public service and from the professions; and strictly limited in the schools and universities. Citizenship was to be denied all Jews, who were to live in Germany as perpetual aliens. Realizing that Christianity was largely the work of the Jews, the Nazis advocated *(2) Anti-Semitism* a remodeling of Christian teaching, according to the principles of "German Christianity," by eliminating the Old Testament, and by remodeling the New Testament in accordance with the German racial ideals. Some of the Nazis advocated the revival of ancient German paganism. As a sign of their pure Germanism they adopted the swastika 卐, a pagan symbol supposedly used by the ancient Teutons.

The Nazis demanded the abrogation of the Treaty of Versailles. They asserted that the German armies were not defeated in the (3) Abrogation of Treaty of Versailles field by the Allies, but were "stabbed in the back" by the Socialists and the Jews. Germany was to wipe out the "shame of Versailles" by striving to regain her lost territories, by refusing to pay Reparations, and by arming herself to fight those who might oppose her. War to the death was to be waged against France, Germany's chief enemy.

In political matters the Nazis were inspired by Italian Fascism. Like the Fascists the Nazis were bitterly hostile to parliamentary (4) The "totalitarian state" government and to democracy in general. They advocated the overthrow of the Weimar Republic, and the establishment of a "totalitarian state" that would coördinate and direct all the activities of the people, economic, social, political, cultural, and religious, in order to create a nation that would be completely united in thought and in deed. Like Communist Russia and Fascist Italy, Germany was to be under the rule of a party dictatorship. The National Socialist Party and the German state were to be one and inseparable, and both were to be based on the principle of "leadership." The leader of the Party was to be in supreme command of the state.

The Nazis preached unrelenting war against Marxism, the body of principles espoused by both the Social Democrats and the Communists. They claimed that they were National Socialists in that they favored the "social liberation of the worker" through the coöperation of capital and labor in promoting German national policies, not through the class struggle and the international action of the proletariat, as preached by the Marxists. The Nazis also made attacks upon "capitalism," demanding the aboli- (5) Anti-capitalism tion of "interest slavery," or the payment of interest on loans due the mortgage and bond holders. They also demanded the nationalization of trusts, the confiscation of war profits, and the distribution of the profits of large industries. To aid the independent retailer they demanded the suppression of department and chain stores; to aid the skilled worker they demanded the suppression of mechanized industry; and to aid the peasant they demanded the extension of peasant proprietorship through the expropriation of large estates.

The Nazis were organized as a political party under Hitler, their *Führer*, or leader. From their members was formed a political army, known as the Storm Troops, who drilled in military fashion clad in uniforms, the distinguishing part being a brown shirt with an armband bearing the swastika. It was the special duty of the Brown Shirts to attack their opponents and protect their supporters. Bitter warfare raged between the Nazis and the Communists. Street battles were of almost daily occurrence. As in Italy, the government was weak and irresolute; it did not have sufficient courage to uphold public order by suppressing the enemies of the Republic.

Conflicts between Nazis and Communists

(d) FALL OF THE WEIMAR REPUBLIC

During 1930–33 a critical situation arose in Germany that boded ill for the Republic. Economic conditions continually grew worse, and millions in despair began to look to revolution as the way out of their troubles. The elections of 1930 brought startling results. The Communists increased their delegation from 54 to 77 seats; and the Nazis, from 12 to 107. The great success of the Nazis made them the second largest party in the Reichstag, the first being the Social Democrats with 143 seats. Another encouragement to the Nazis came as a result of the Presidential election of 1931, when Hindenburg won over Hitler by a small majority. The gains of the extreme parties continued. In the elections held in July, 1932, the Communists won 90 seats and the Nazis 230. The gains of the former were at the expense of the Social Democrats; and of the latter, at the expense of the moderate and conservative parties.

Electoral gains of the Nazis and Communists

As the Communists grew so did the Nazis, and the latter at a faster pace. As in Italy, the advance of Communism frightened the middle class, which was far more powerful and more numerous in Germany than in Italy. Out of fear that Germany, in desperation, might go the way of Soviet Russia, the propertied classes turned to the Nazis as the only ele-

Fear of Communism

ment capable of preventing such a calamity. The big industrialists subsidized Hitler, who now had the means to organize his many recruits from the ruined middle class and from the unemployed.

The Chancellor during most of this critical period was Heinrich Bruening, the high-minded leader of the Centrists, who had difficulty in getting the support of the Reichstag. He had no solid majority behind him, as the Social Democrats refused to participate in his Ministry. Opposed to him were the Nazis and the Communists, both of whom were striving in all ways to bring about not only his downfall, but that of the Republic as well. So great was their hatred of the democratic Republic that the Communists frequently joined forces with their deadly enemies, the Nazis, rather than with their socialist brethren, the Social Democrats. They believed that, as in Russia, the overthrow of the Republic would result in the Dictatorship of the Proletariat. But their tactics resulted in a revolution that they little dreamed of — that of their bitterest opponents, the Nazis, who, like them, favored violent methods in order to establish a party dictatorship on the ruins of a democratic Republic.

Nazis and Communists oppose Republic

In order to prevent financial chaos and government disorganization, Bruening was compelled to resort to "emergency decrees," which President Hindenburg promulgated. Parliamentary government in Germany was now clearly breaking down. The President was distrusted as being secretly hostile to the Republic. The Chancellor was unable to get firm support for his measures. And the Reichstag was demoralized by the obstructionist tactics of the Nazis and the Communists. Those in power had neither the will nor the courage to suppress the deadly enemies of the Republic. In May, 1932, Bruening was dismissed by the President because he planned to relieve unemployment by settling the unemployed on the large estates. Bruening's proposal roused the ire of the President, who regarded it as an attack on the Junker class.

Dismissal of Bruening

The new Chancellor was Franz von Papen, a personal favorite of the President. A movement now began "to liquidate" the Weimar Republic. It had the support of the President and the Chancellor, and was backed by the Nazis and the Nationalists. Socialist officials were summarily ousted, and trusted men were put in their place. On January 30, 1933, Hindenburg appointed Hitler as Chancellor in a

Hitler appointed Chancellor

ministry composed of Nazis and Nationalists. The Reichstag was then dissolved in order to get a majority to back up the new ministry.

Elections took place in March, 1933, during which the police were active in suppressing the meetings and journals of the opponents of the Nazi-Nationalist combination. The results showed that the combination was supported by 52 per cent of the popular vote. Out of a total of 648 seats, the Nazis won 288 seats; the Social Democrats, 120; the Communists, 81; the Centrists, 74; the Nationalists, 52; and the minor groups, the rest. When the new Reichstag met, the Communist members were not permitted to take their seats. It passed a series of resolutions which, in effect, suspended the constitution and granted Hitler governmental dictatorial powers for four years. The Weimar Republic was now at an end. *Elections of 1933*

The fall of the Republic occasioned no demonstration in Germany; no popular uprising and no general strike took place against the newly established dictatorship. Millions of Liberals, Social Democrats, and Communists succumbed without raising a finger in defense. So rapid and so complete was the Nazi triumph that the entire world was astonished. The destruction of the Republic came as a result of coöperation between the heads of the government, the President and the Chancellor, and the Nazis. It was an overturn not unlike the Fascist overturn in Italy. *Fall of the Weimar Republic*

One of the causes for the downfall of the Republic was the Treaty of Versailles. Deep and bitter was the chagrin felt by the German people because of the humiliating terms that were dictated to them by the victorious Allies. Their national pride would not let them believe that their army could be defeated in the field. At first they blamed President Wilson, who, they said, had deceived them into surrender by promising a treaty based upon the Fourteen Points. Then they sought to put the blame on the Socialists and the Jews, despite the fact that these two elements loyally supported the government throughout the war. "The policy of fulfillment," followed by the Republic, did result in a modification of the Treaty of Versailles: the evacuation of the Rhineland region before the period fixed by the Treaty; the admission of Germany to the League of Nations on the basis of equality with the other powers; and the end of Repara- *Causes of the downfall of the Republic* tions. But these concessions did not at all satisfy the German people. The Nazis pledged themselves to wipe out the "shame of Versailles," and to give Germany a leading place among the powers of the world, which brought them the support of millions of patriotic Germans. In the second place, the Nazis received the support of the lower middle class: small merchants, clerks, craftsmen, civil servants, farmers, and professionals, who were ruined as a result of the inflation and the depression that followed the war, and who saw themselves sinking to the level of the lower classes, whom they despised. Especially did the Nazis appeal to the younger generation of the middle class, who could look forward to no future compatible with their education and their traditions, and who saw in National Socialism a hope for the future in that it promised them positions of influence and power in the government and in society. In the third place, the growth of communism in Germany caused many to feel that the only way to avoid the fate of Soviet Russia was to throw their influence on the side of the strongest opponents of the Communists, the Nazis. Finally, there was no deeply rooted adherence to parliamentary government in Germany, as there was in England and in France. The most energetic elements in the nation were anti-liberal, anti-democratic, and anti-parliamentary. Before the war the parliamentary system had existed, but in an emaciated form. The Bismarckian methods had prevented the growth of political education of the masses by a system of government in which parliament played a secondary rôle under the Empire. The Republic, which was established after the war, was backed by the least influential elements in the nation, the Social Democrats and the Center. Among the influential elements in the nation were the army officers, who now remained in the background awaiting their opportunity to throw their powerful support to the Nazis. The Kaiser departed but the generals remained. The experience of Germany under a full parliamentary system was not a happy one. In a sense the political parties were the spokesmen of various dogmatic philosophies rather than of political policies, and they showed themselves to be incapable of the compromises necessary to the success of party government. Parliamentary government, with its deadlocks, bickerings, and frequent elections, disgusted the German people, whose traditions were those of authority, efficiency, and discipline, not those of liberty and equality. In the last free elections, those in 1933, a large majority actually supported those parties — the Communists, the Nazis, and the Nationalists — that openly favored the overthrow of the democratic Republic in favor of a dictatorship.

(e) THE NAZI GOVERNMENT

The year 1933 witnessed events in Germany that attracted world-wide attention. The Nazis proceeded to carry out their program completely and ruthlessly. The first move was against the Jews. Suddenly, all over Germany, *Attacks on the Jews* Nazi Storm Troops made attacks on Jews in which many were killed and wounded. Jews holding public office and teaching positions were summarily ousted. A boycott was ordered against Jews engaged in business and in the professions, which was carried out ruthlessly. Laws were passed that deprived all Jews of citizenship; and not being citizens of other countries, they were in the position of outlaws. Marriage between Jews and non-Jews was forbidden. Jews were barred from the universities, public office, journalism, teaching, the arts, the professions, and from the manual trades. Those who were in business were required to make preparations to sell out at any price. In 1938 an organized attack on Jews took place that horrified the world. All over Germany bands of Nazis dynamited synagogues, destroyed Jewish homes and stores, and arrested and mauled the owners. The police, as ordered, remained passive during these terrible scenes. No news of this pogrom was permitted in the German press.

The inhuman treatment of the helpless Jews by the Nazis roused a storm of indignation throughout the world. Not even in tsarist Russia were Jews treated with such cruelty. It was clearly the object of the Nazis not merely to persecute the Jews, but to exterminate them. They put every obstacle in the way of the Jews leaving Germany, lest they find a haven in other lands.

Germany's treatment of the Jews was in harmony with the Nazi principle of "racialism," which is as distinctive of Fascism as the principle of nationalism is of democracy. In a national state all men have equal rights, irrespective of race, faith, or national origin. Anyone can become a member of a *Nationalism* national state by acquiring citizenship. Racialism, *versus* on the contrary, insists on "blood brotherhood," *racialism* according to which mankind is divided into distinct physical and psychological groups called "races," a grouping having little scientific validity. Racial states, such as Germany and Italy, give rights only to the dominant "race," and exterminate or persecute all those whom they designate as not belonging to it.

Germany proclaimed that it regarded every person of German blood, wherever he may live and wherever he may be naturalized,
The Nazi International tional
as its representative and agent. "Blood knows no state borders." In order to organize an "indissoluble community of blood and destiny" uniting the Germans all over the world, Nazi Germany established organizations at home and abroad to conduct propaganda for Germanism among those of German origin in Europe, in the United States, and in South America. By means of schools, journals, societies, clubs, and semi-military groups like the Storm Troops, the Nazis spread their influence in many lands.

Once in the seat of power, Hitler proceeded to "coördinate" all institutions in Germany under his dictatorship. The Social
Coördination tion
Democratic and Communist Parties were dissolved, their leaders arrested, and their property and offices confiscated. The Center, the Nationalists, and the other parties were compelled to order their own dissolution. The trade unions were taken over by the Nazis and reorganized as the German Labor Front, under the control and direction of Nazi leaders. The Nazis were particularly eager to get control of all organs of public opinion. A Ministry of Propaganda and of Public Enlightenment was organized, under the leadership of Doctor Paul Joseph Goebbels, who proceeded to coördinate the entire press in the Reich. Journalists were licensed and made members of a union pledged to spread Nazi principles. Famous journals in Germany went out of existence, and the entire press became merely the mouthpiece of the government, as in Italy and Russia. The schools and universities were likewise coördinated. The students in the universities were organized in one body to uphold Nazi policies and principles. Academic freedom was abolished, and both teachers and students had to teach their subjects in harmony with Nazi principles.

The government was likewise reorganized. The federal sys-
Centralization of government
tem was abolished, and the states became administrative divisions under the rule of governors appointed by the highly centralized government in Berlin. When President von Hindenburg died in 1934, the office of

President was abolished. Hitler simply added its powers to his own as Chancellor. The Reichstag was elected by universal suffrage, but only the Nazi Party could present candidates; all opposition parties were banned. The Reichstag met only to act as a sounding board for Hitler's speeches. Laws were enacted by ministerial decrees.

The all important element in Germany was the Nazi Party, of which Hitler was Führer. It completely dominated the life of the nation, like the Fascist Party in Italy and the Communist Party in Russia. In 1934 a left element in the Party, under Captain Roehm, threatened to depose Hitler from his leadership. Suddenly Hitler and his special bodyguard, the black-shirted Élite Guard, descended upon Roehm. A bloody "purge" followed, in which Roehm and many of his followers were shot down in cold blood. The triumph of Hitler over Roehm solidified the Nazi Party by eliminating all opposition to the Führer.

The "purge" of 1934

The Nazis determined to coördinate the churches. The many Protestant churches were unified into a single organization, the German Central Protestant Church, under the leadership of Bishop Ludwig Mueller. The new Bishop believed in the principles of "German Christianity," and proceeded to Nazify the Church by revising the Bible to harmonize with Germanism and by insisting on the "Aryan paragraph," a regulation which demanded the elimination from the ministry of anyone of Jewish origin. Many Lutheran ministers refused to accept these changes on the ground that they were contrary to the principles of Christianity. A struggle followed between the government and the ministers, as a result of which many were ousted from their positions and persecuted.

Nazification of the Protestant Church

The problem of coördinating the Catholic Church was far more difficult because the Nazis had to come to terms with the pope. A concordat was signed between Germany and the Vatican, according to which the Church was granted freedom in religious matters. However, conflicts arose between the Nazis and the Catholics because the former violated the concordat. Catholic priests were attacked by Storm Troops, Catholic newspapers suppressed, and Catholic schools were closed. In their ruthless policy of coördination the Nazis encountered only one opposition, that of the Protestant and Catholic clergymen who bravely upheld their principles despite persecution.

Attacks on Catholics

When it came to economic problems the Nazis were exceedingly cautious in making changes. They did not put into practice the radical demands of their program. But they did abolish free economy by a system of government intervention that minutely regimented commerce and industry in every aspect. The principle of leadership in industry was applied by establishing the employer as the "leader" and his employees as his followers. Strikes and lockouts were forbidden; industrial disputes were settled by shop councils appointed by the employers and directed by Nazi Party members. Workers were required to join the Labor Front, a Nazi-managed organization that superseded the trade unions. Wages and hours were regulated by the Labor Front. In agriculture, peasant proprietorship was established on the principle of "blood and soil." Only peasants of the Teutonic race were permitted to own land; and inheritance of land was to be on the principle of primogeniture. Small peasant properties were made inalienable; they were to be in the hands of the same family forever. Despite their promises the Nazis made no effort to divide the large estates of the Junkers into peasant farms.

Regimentation of industry

Nazi policies in regard to industry were far-reaching; they affected not only Germany's economy but that of the world as well. A Four-Year Plan was adopted in 1936, establishing a planned economy having for its aim "autarchy," or national self-sufficiency. Marshal Herman Goering, one of Hitler's closest associates, was made economic dictator. The aim of the Plan was to make Germany independent of foreign countries with respect to foodstuffs and those materials that could be produced by chemical processes or by more intensive development of Germany's resources. Germany would then be in a position to defy a blockade, which had proved so disastrous to her in the World War. The government put in force a system of agricultural planning by regulating production, prices, and methods. It greatly encouraged the production of artificial rubber and textiles, and the extraction of oil from coal.

Autarchy

Foreign trade was strictly regulated by a license system. The government, having little gold and no credit, sought to obtain food and necessary raw materials like iron, copper, oil, and cotton by a system of barter, according to which Germany entered into arrangements with

Barter displaces free economy

certain foreign countries who agreed to accept her manufactures in return for their raw materials or foodstuffs. Germany had great need of increasing her exports, which for a time languished because of a world-wide boycott against German goods by Jews and their sympathizers. Her exporters were induced, in some instances, to sell below cost because they received subsidies from the government. Germany's subsidized exports competed successfully, especially in South America, with exports of England and America, which roused considerable indignation in these countries. Despite all her efforts, however, Germany's exports, in 1938, showed a marked decline. As with Russia and Italy, it is difficult to give an accurate estimate of economic conditions in Nazi Germany because of the system of censorship, official propaganda, and secret budgets.

Great sums were devoted to armament, which became the all-absorbing industry of Nazi Germany. Heavier and heavier grew her debt burden. Taxes rose, and the standard of living of the masses fell. But the slogan of the Nazis was, "Guns, not butter!" At first Doctor Hjalmar Schacht was made head of the Reichsbank and given control of the nation's financial policies. He devised a system whereby foreign holders of the bonds of industrial corporations and of cities received only part of the interest due. The rest remained in Germany, and was used to subsidize German exports. In other words, Germany's creditors were made to aid German exports at their expense, and at the expense of their country. The chief sufferers were Americans and Englishmen, who had invested heavily in German industry.

But the Four-Year Plan demanded ever larger sums for export subsidies, rearmament, and public works. The cost of living rose, and real wages fell. Doctor Schacht opposed the rigid system of regimentation of business; and he favored the slowing up of the pace of rearmament because of the enormous increase of the public debt. His objections were brushed aside, and in 1938 he was dismissed as head of the Reichsbank.

Nazi Germany's success in diplomacy was so great that domestic troubles were put aside. Hitler determined to destroy the "Versailles system," (1) by breaking the restrictions on Germany's armaments, and (2) by territorial changes in defiance of Treaty provisions. He aimed not to restore but to enlarge Germany's frontiers of 1914. By the establishment of conscription and the remilitarization of the Rhineland, already described, he accomplished his first objective. He attained his second objective far beyond his original hopes without firing a shot by the annexation of Austria in 1938, and of Czechoslovakia and Memel in 1939. As in the case of Mussolini, Hitler's diplomatic successes gained him widespread popularity with his fellow-countrymen.

REFERENCES

COMMUNIST RUSSIA:

Descriptive are M. Dobb and C. H. Stevens, *Russian Economic Development since the Revolution* (1928); C. B. Hoover, *The Economic Life of Soviet Russia* (1931); S. N. Harper, *Making Bolsheviks* (1931); H. von Eckhardt, *Russia*, trans. from the German (1932); B. Brutskus, *Economic Planning in the Soviet Union* (1935); W. R. Batsell, *Soviet Rule in Russia* (1929); L. E. Hubbard, *Soviet Money and Finance* (1936); H. Kohn, *Nationalism in the Soviet Union* (1933); and M. T. Florinsky, *World Revolution and the U.S.S.R.* (1933) and *Toward an Understanding of the U.S.S.R.* (1939).

Favorable are G. F. Grinko, *The Five Year Plan of the Soviet Union* (1930); W. H. Chamberlin, *Soviet Russia* (ed. 1931); M. G. Hindus, *Humanity Uprooted* (ed. 1930); and S. and B. Webb, *Soviet Communism*, 2 vols. (1936).

Unfavorable are W. H. Chamberlin, *Russia's Iron Age* (1934); L. Trotsky, *The Revolution Betrayed* (1937); and E. Lyons, *Assignment in Utopia* (1937).

FASCIST ITALY:

Descriptive: C. McGuire, *Italy's Economic Position* (1926); H. W. Schneider, *Making the Fascist State* (1928); C. F. Schmidt, *The Corporate State in Action* (1939); H. A. Steiner, *Government in Fascist Italy* (1938); G. L. Field, *The Syndical and Corporative Institutions of Fascism* (1938); H. Finer, *Mussolini's Italy* (1935); L. Rosenstock-Frank, *L'Economie Corporative Fasciste* (1934); W. G. Welk, *Fascist Economic Policy* (1938).

Favorable are T. Sillani (ed.), *What is Fascism and Why* (1931), and F. Pitigliani, *The Italian Corporative State* (1934).

Unfavorable are G. Salvemini, *The Fascist Dictatorship in Italy* (1927) and *Under the Axe of Fascism* (1936); M. Rader, *No Compromise* (1939); G. Megaro, *Mussolini in the Making* (1938); M. Ascoli and A. Feiler, *Fascism for Whom?* (1938); and C. T. Schmidt, *The Plough and the Sword* (1938).

GERMANY:

R. H. Lutz, *The German Revolution, 1918–1919* (1922); R. H. Lutz (ed.), *The Fall of the German Empire*, 2 vols. (1932); L. Strobel, *The German Revolution and After*, trans. from the German (1923); J. Mattern, *Principles of the Constitutional Jurisprudence of the German National Republic* (1928); Sir

P. Dawson, *Germany's Industrial Revival* (1926); H. Quigley and R. T. Clark, *Republican Germany* (1928); C. W. Guillebaud, *The Works Council* (1928); N. Reich, *Labor Relations in Republican Germany* (1938); D. Warriner, *Combines and Rationalism in Germany* (1931); J. W. Angell, *The Recovery of Germany* (1929); P. Kosok, *Modern Germany* (1933); F. F. Blachly and M. E. Oatman, *The Government and Administration of Germany* (1928); J. W. Wheeler-Bennett, *Wooden Titan, Hindenburg in Twenty Years of German History, 1914–1934* (1936); A. Rosenberg, *The Birth of the German Republic*, trans. from the German (1931) and *History of the German Republic* (1937); H. Kraus, *The Crisis of German Democracy* (1932); R. T. Clark *The Fall of the German Republic* (1935).

On Nazi Germany: Adolf Hitler, *Mein Kampf*, trans. from the German. The Annotated Edition (1939); *The Nazi Primer*, trans. from the German with a Foreword by H. L. Childs (1938); "Nordicus" (L. L. Snyder), *Hitlerism* (1932); K. Heiden, *A History of National Socialism* (1934); F. L. Schumann, *The Nazi Dictatorship* (ed. 1936); R. A. Brady, *The Spirit and Structure of German Fascism* (1937); F. Ermath, *The New Germany* (1936); H. Lichtenberger, *The Third Reich*, trans. from the French by K. Pinson (1937); S. H. Roberts, *The House that Hitler Built* (1937); O. I. Janowsky and M. M. Fagen (eds.), *International Aspect of German Racial Policies* (1937); V. Trivanovitch, *Economic Development of Germany under National Socialism* (1937); A. Kolnai, *The War Against the West* (1938); and C. W. Guillebaud, *The Economic Recovery of Germany* (1939); H. Rauschnnig, *The Revolution of Nihilism*, trans. from the German (1939); G. Reimann, *The Vampire Economy* (1939); H. Rosinski, *The German Army* (1940).

CHAPTER XLI

THE OTHER NATIONS AFTER THE WORLD WAR

SPAIN

(a) THE SPANISH REVOLUTION

DURING the war Spain had been neutral. This policy had been to her great advantage: she profited by selling supplies to both sides; she did not face a collapse of her currency after the war; she was not entangled in post-war diplomacy; and she had no problems of territory lost or gained. Yet the country was seething with discontent, the old discontent that had troubled Spain all during the nineteenth century, stemming from political corruption, illiteracy, lawlessness, and revolutionary plotting.

Prosperity of Spain

Barcelona was the scene of the greatest disaffection. The working classes in that city waged desperate war against their employers. Violent strikes were frequent, paralyzing industrial life. In Catalonia a separatist movement was gaining rapid headway, which threatened the unity of the country. In Spanish Morocco the Riff tribesmen were attacking Spanish armies and driving them to the coast. Parliament proved unequal to the task of solving the serious problems confronting the country. It was denounced as a corrupt clique of politicians who were interested chiefly in army contracts and in office-holding.

General discontent

Between revolution on one side and defeat on the other, the government was in a precarious condition. A violent overturn was imminent which would destroy the monarchy and plunge the country into revolution. To avoid such a contingency a coup d'état was planned. In 1923 General Primo de Rivera seized control of the government with the consent of King Alphonso XIII. A "Directorate" was established, headed by the General, that governed the country by issuing decrees in the name of the King. Parliament was dissolved, and the constitution was suspended. All opposition to the dictatorship was relentlessly suppressed.

Dictatorship of General Primo de Rivera

The dictatorship lasted for seven years, and was maintained with difficulty against the rising tide of discontent. Widespread demonstrations and rioting by workingmen and students were constantly taking place. Even the army, the bulwark of the régime, was becoming rebellious, and mutinies took place which were suppressed with difficulty. King Alphonso, at one time very pop- Fall of the ular, was now bitterly denounced as the man behind monarchy the dictatorship. A secret revolutionary movement was spreading rapidly, especially in the large industrial cities. In 1931 the Spanish monarchy was suddenly overturned by an uprising in Madrid. Alphonso fled, and a republic was proclaimed by a provisional government.

The Spanish Revolution proved to be more than the overturn of the monarchy and the establishment of a republic. Like the French Revolution it proposed to transform Spain into an advanced democratic state. For long, Spain had continued to be a land of the Old Régime, with an almost feudal land system, a The Old powerful and intolerant church, a politically active Régime professional army, and a corrupt and inefficient government. The majority of the people consisted of poverty-stricken, illiterate peasants and underpaid industrial laborers. About three-quarters of the population was dependent, directly or indirectly, upon agriculture. The best lands consisted of huge estates, owned by aristocrats known as "grandees," that were badly cultivated by laborers on starvation wages. The poorer lands, divided into tiny farms that rarely produced enough to feed a family, were worked by peasants either as proprietors or tenants.

With the fall of the monarchy came a perfect avalanche of revolutionary sentiment that was bitterly hostile to the Old Régime. No monarchists were elected to the constitutional con- Parties in vention that met in 1931, pledged to establish a new the Republic order in Spain. On the extreme left were the Socialists, the largest party in the convention. Next were the Radical-Socialists, who were republicans with an advanced social program. In the center was the Republican Alliance, a large group of moderate republicans. On the right sat the Catalans, a regional party representing the special interests of Catalonia and the Right republicans. Outside of the convention were powerful labor organizations — the National Confederation of Labor, which was syndicalist, and the General Workers Union, which was socialist. These labor organizations conducted an active agitation, causing a ferment of strikes in many industrial centers.

(b) THE GOVERNMENT OF THE REPUBLIC

Spain was declared "a democratic republic of workers of all classes." The government was to consist of a single-chamber parliament, called the Cortes, elected by universal suffrage. Executive power was to be vested in a President elected by the Cortes and an equal number of electors, and in a cabinet appointed by the President and responsible to the Cortes. Radical as was the change politically, from a dictatorship to a democratic republic, it was even more radical in matters religious, cultural, and economic. The constitution provided for the separation of church and state; the dissolution of the Jesuit order and the confiscation of its property; the strict regulation of the other Catholic orders; and for civil marriage and divorce. Primary education was made compulsory, and the public schools were to be free and secular. The state was to have the right to expropriate, with compensation, any business enterprise. A declaration of war was to be "subject to conditions prescribed in the Covenant of the League of Nations." Provision was made for the establishment of "autonomous regions," such as Catalonia, which were to have large powers of local self-government.

The constitution of the Spanish Republic was the most advanced of all democratic constitutions. Spain could be described as a democratic republic with tendencies in the direction of socialism. After completing its prescribed work of adopting a constitution, the convention did not dissolve, but continued to sit as the first Cortes. The reason for this procedure was that the parties in control wished to complete the Revolution by drafting legislation supplementing the constitution. The pillars of the Old Régime — the monarchy, the church, the army, and the aristocracy — were shattered by the drastic laws that were enacted. This legislation was largely the work of Premier Manuel Azaña, backed by a compact majority of Socialists and advanced Republicans. Alphonso was declared guilty of high treason and was deprived of all his titles and possessions in Spain. The army was reduced in size and put under strict civil control. The anti-clerical provisions of the constitution were ruthlessly carried out by drastic laws against the Catholic Church. The attack on the landed aristocracy was even more severe, as agrarian reform was the prime need of the country. In 1932 the Cortes passed a law which radically transformed the land system in Spain. Some of the large estates were expropriated in a manner that amounted to virtual confiscation; others were expropriated with compensation. The lands were to be distributed to the peasants, either in small individual farms or in large units to be worked coöperatively.

There was bitter opposition to the revolutionary legislation, not by the reactionaries only but also by the moderate Republicans. The attack on property rights and the spread of syndi- Opposition calism and socialism caused many of the bourgeois to of the fear the confiscation of all property. Especially bitter Church was the opposition of the Church, which feared that the wave of anti-clericalism might lead to the abolition of Christianity. Riots against the Church broke out, instigated chiefly by anarchists and syndicalists. Many churches and monasteries were burned, and priests and monks, murdered.

In 1933 elections for the Cortes took place; the outcome of which was a victory for the Right. Feeling between Left and Right was so intense that compromise was impossible. The Victory of government, now controlled by the Right, disregarded the Right or suspended the anti-clerical and the land laws. The revolutionary elements — anarchists, syndicalists, and communists — were aroused to fury. Violent strikes, demonstrations, uprisings, burning of churches, and assassinations were almost daily occurrences. Violence by the Left bred violence by the Right. Fascist groups appeared that battled with the "Reds."

This situation made orderly government impossible. Parliament was dissolved in 1936, with the object of ascertaining more clearly the will of the Spanish people. Two coalitions ap- Victory of peared during the elections: the Popular Front, con- the Left sisting of Left elements, Radical Republicans, Socialists, and Communists; and the Right, consisting of Monarchists, Clericals, Fascists, and conservative Republicans. The Popular Front won a majority of the seats, though the popular vote was about equal. A Popular Front ministry came into power pledged to carry out the reforms of the Spanish Revolution.

Would the Right now accept the rule of the Left? No more than did the Left when the Right was in power. Fascist groups began a campaign of terrorism, which was met by violence Civil War from the Left groups. The government was as incap- (1936–39) able of restraining its supporters as it was of suppressing its opponents. In July, 1936, a mutiny of the army took place, led by General Francisco Franco. It was a signal for civil war, in which the supporters of Franco, called the "Rebels," fought the supporters of the government, called the "Loyalists." The Rebels had an immediate success in the south and west, and organized a government with Burgos as the capital. Madrid remained in the hands of the Loyalists, but the capital was shifted to Valencia. During the struggle the Ministry was reorganized to include all supporters of the government, Radical Republicans, Socialists, and Communists. The civil war in Spain raged with great fury. It was a conflict inspired not only by political differences but even more by class and religious hatreds. The stark cruelty of the conflict was consuming Spain.

Franco's government soon became frankly Fascist, and received the prompt support of Italy and Germany. As the Loyalist government shifted more to the Left, it received the support of Russia. Both the Fascists and the Communists were fishing in the troubled waters of Spain. Italy and Germany recognized the Burgos government and sent large armies into Spain to fight for Franco. Mussolini especially was intensely pro-Franco and openly proclaimed his intention to do all in his power to bring about a Franco victory. Many sympathizers from all over the world enlisted in the Loyalist armies.

The civil war in Spain soon became a matter of grave concern to the powers. There was fear that it might spread to all Europe. In order to confine the war to Spain, a Non-Intervention Agreement was made in 1936, according to which the powers agreed to refuse aid to both sides. But the Agreement was more honored in the breach than in the observance; Italy, Germany, and Russia, openly or secretly, aided one side or the other. And the conflict became what might be described as a European war on a small scale, waged in Spain at the expense of the Spanish people.

To the well-disciplined and well-armed soldiers of Franco the Loyalists at first opposed hastily organized volunteers. The latter, though enthusiastic and daring, were seldom a match for the Rebels, who steadily gained territory, reaching the outskirts of Madrid. At first it was expected that Franco would win the war in six months, but the conflict dragged on for almost three years. The Loyalists managed to organize large disciplined armies that succeeded in slowing up the pace of Franco's forces. At times the Loyalists would win important battles, notably over the Italian troops at Guadalajara in 1937. Franco's forces, however, made steady advances and gained a great victory in 1938 by reaching the Mediterranean. Loyalist Spain was now cut in two. Catalonia was separated from the rest of Spain, and now had to face Franco's forces without aid from Madrid. In January, 1939, Franco began a powerful drive to conquer Catalonia, and gained a great victory by the capture of Barcelona. The Rebels then quickly advanced to the Pyrenees, and Catalonia was entirely under Franco's control.

The position of the Loyalists in Madrid was now hopeless. Cut off from France by the fall of Barcelona and blockaded by Franco's fleet, they realized their desperate plight. On March 28, 1939, Madrid surrendered, after thirty-two months of bloody conflict. Franco was now master of all Spain. Surrender of Madrid

AUSTRIA

When Austria surrendered to the Allies the doom of the Hapsburgs was sounded. A republic was proclaimed in Vienna, and Emperor Charles, who had succeeded Francis Joseph in 1916, was obliged to flee the country. Fall of the Hapsburgs

A National Assembly met in 1920 to draw up a constitution for the new Republic. The leading parties were the Socialists, who controlled Vienna, and the clerical Christian Socialists, who controlled the provinces. In order not to give Vienna too much power, the Assembly established a federal republic. The new government consisted of a President and a bicameral legislature. The President was elected by a joint session of both houses; his powers were like those of the President of France. The lower house was elected by universal suffrage; and the upper house by the local diets in the provinces. Executive power was exercised by a cabinet responsible to Parliament. Government of the Republic

The boundaries of Austria, as fixed by the Treaty of St. Germain, reduced the once great empire to a small, landlocked state of about 6,500,000 inhabitants, one-third of whom lived in Vienna. A movement began for an Anschluss, or union, with Germany. It was fostered by the Germans, who would thereby make a considerable gain in territory; and by the Austrians, Anschluss who were German in sentiment and closely tied economically to the Reich. But an Anschluss was forbidden by the Treaty, unless the Council of the League of Nations consented.

Austria was an "economic vacuum." For some years after the war she was in a state of dire distress. Her currency was worthless; her trade ruined; her debts were enormous; and her people starving. Famine stalked in the streets of the beautiful, and once gay, Vienna. The League of Nations set about rehabilitating the country. It appointed a representative to supervise its finances, which, in fact, meant that Austria was bankrupt but in the hands of a friendly receiver. Through the League's efforts a loan was floated, which greatly revived her credit. The currency was stabilized, and conditions began to improve.

Post-war Austria

Internally Austria was the scene of a bitter strife between two parties, the Socialists, led by Otto Bauer, and the Christian Socialists, led by Ignaz Seipel and Engelbert Dollfuss. Supporting these parties were semi-military organizations, the socialist Schutzbund and the fascist Heimwehr, which paraded, demonstrated, and rioted against each other.

The Socialists and the Christian Socialists

The Socialist administration of Vienna attracted world-wide attention because of its reforms. It established a magnificent system of public housing by building apartment houses, equipped with modern improvements, to accommodate 60,000 families. These municipal apartments were rented to the workingmen at low rentals. Vienna also established municipal ownership, in some cases, of lighting, transportation, breweries, bakeries, and ice plants.

Socialist Vienna

Externally, Austria was the pawn of a great diplomatic game between Germany, Italy, and France. For long it had been Germany's dream to organize "Middle Europe" under her direction. An Anschluss with Austria would create a Greater Germany, which would make up for her territorial losses in Europe as a result of her defeat in the World War. Although inclined to favor Germany as against France, Mussolini was hostile to Germany's ambitions in central Europe. He feared that if the Anschluss were accomplished, Italy would have a powerful Germany as her neighbor, which would create a serious irredentist movement among the German-speaking inhabitants of southern Tyrol, annexed by Italy. The interest of

Austria, the pawn of Germany, Italy, and France

France in Austria was largely based on her relationship with the states of the Little Entente. She was opposed to an Anschluss because it would result: (1) in almost surrounding Czechoslovakia by a Greater Germany; and (2) in placing a block of German territory between Czechoslovakia and Yugoslavia. Hence, in case of war, the Little Entente would be seriously weakened. What France favored was a Danubian confederacy, consisting of the members of the Little Entente, Hungary, and Austria.

The great success of the Nazis in Germany in the elections of 1930 caused a rapid growth of a similar movement in Austria. The Austrian Nazis openly advocated an Anschluss and proclaimed their national solidarity with Germany. Austria was now the scene of a bitter struggle between the Nazis, supported by Germany; the Christian Socialists, supported by Italy; and the Social Democrats, suppported by France. The most powerful of the three were the Christian Socialists, whose leader, Dollfuss, became Premier in 1932. *Dictatorship of Dollfuss*

When Hitler came into power in Germany he was intensely eager to effect a union of Austria, his native land, with Germany. He greatly encouraged the Austrian Nazis in their attacks on the Dollfuss régime. Aided by their brethren in Germany, they inaugurated a campaign of terrorism by exploding bombs, attacking officials, and breaking up meetings. *Hitler's plan of a "cold Anschluss"*

The Nazi movement was making rapid progress, which caused great concern to both the Christian Socialists and the Socialists. The latter realized full well what their fate would be in case of a Nazi triumph, and they offered to coöperate with the Christian Socialists. But Dollfuss had other plans and refused to accept Socialist aid against the Nazis. Instead he determined to eliminate the Socialists from the political scene. In 1934 he ordered the dissolution of all political parties and the ousting of the Socialist officials of Vienna, preliminary to the establishment of a fascist state. A desperate struggle followed between the Heimwehr and the Socialists. The Heimwehr bombarded the Socialist headquarters and the municipal apartment houses, which were defended with magnificent bravery by the Socialists. Fighting took place in other Austrian cities. But the poorly armed Socialists were no match for the artillery and airplanes of the Heimwehr, and, after a desperate resistance, they *Fall of the Republic* were forced to surrender. The democratic Republic was abolished, and Austria was established as a fascist state on the Italian model.

Dollfuss had been persuaded by Mussolini that only a fascist Austria, supported by Italy, could withstand Germany's demand Dictatorship for an Anschluss. He was now virtually in the position of Dollfuss of a dictator. The powerful Socialist Party, which had a majority in Vienna, was suppressed. The Austrian Nazis, backed by Germany, could not be so easily eliminated. Their party was outlawed, but they carried on their activity despite government hostility. In suppressing the Socialists, Dollfuss had eliminated the element that would have contributed the strongest supporters against the Nazis.

The new order in Austria was in existence only six months when a Nazi uprising took place. Germany made ready to intervene, Assassination but Mussolini promptly mobilized his army on the of Dollfuss Austrian frontier, which caused Germany to halt. During the uprising Dollfuss was assassinated by the Nazis, but the uprising was suppressed.

The successor to Dollfuss was Kurt von Schuschnigg, a Christian Socialist, who was determined to continue the policies of his pred-Austria and ecessor. The Nazis were not discouraged by their the Axis failure, and continued their agitation. As Nazi Germany became stronger, and as the Rome–Berlin Axis drew Italy and Germany closer together, Schuschnigg became uneasy. He therefore sought a *rapprochement* with Germany. In 1936 Austria and Germany signed an agreement in which the former declared that she would coöperate with Germany, and the latter affirmed her recognition of Austria's independence.

But the international situation boded ill for Austria. Having little support among the people, Schuschnigg leaned more and more on Mussolini. But the Rome–Berlin Axis made Austria's position precarious. Mussolini was now dependent on Hitler for support of Italy's ambitions in the Mediterranean. Would he not, as a quid pro quo, give his support to German ambitions in central Europe?

In February, 1938, Hitler demanded of Schuschnigg that he Germany include Nazis in his cabinet, which was a serious threat annexes to Austria's independence. Schuschnigg discovered to Austria his dismay that Mussolini was behind Hitler, not behind him. He was compelled to yield. Now he sought the support of the Austrian people by announcing a plebiscite to determine whether or not the voters favored the independence of Austria. Hitler demanded that the plebiscite be postponed. Schuschnigg "yielded to force" and resigned his position as Chancellor. A German army promptly occupied Austria.

On March 13, 1938, the Austrian government, now fully under Nazi control, issued a decree declaring that "Austria is a state of the German Reich." Austria disappeared as an independent nation. She was now part of Nazi Germany, and her institutions and policies were rapidly coördinated with those of Germany. Neither the League of Nations, nor France, nor England, made a move to protect her. And Italy, her sworn ally and the guarantor of her independence, openly endorsed Germany's action.

CZECHOSLOVAKIA

The most important state to emerge from the ruins of the Dual Monarchy was Czechoslovakia. Her territory was made up of what was formerly Bohemia and Moravia in Austria, Masaryk and of Slovakia in Hungary. A constitution was and Beneš adopted, in 1920, which established the new nation as a democratic republic on the model of the French Republic. The first President was Thomas Garrigue Masaryk, a distinguished historian and publicist who for many years had been an ardent champion of his people against Austrian domination. Associated with him as Foreign Minister was his disciple, Eduard Beneš. In 1935, on the retirement of Masaryk, Beneš was chosen President. Of all the statesmen in post-war central Europe, Masaryk and Beneš were most admired for their liberal ideals and democratic policies.

Two serious problems faced the Republic: (1) the economic problem, and (2) the national minorities. Of all the Succession states Czechoslovakia was most fortunate in having fairly normal economic conditions. A highly developed industry was balanced by a fairly developed agriculture. The large estates, owned chiefly by Austrian and Hungarian aristocrats, were expropriated by the state, with compensation to the owners. Peasant pro- These estates were divided into small farms and sold prietorship by the state to peasants on easy terms. Peasant proprietorship was as characteristic of the Republic as aristocratic estates had been of the region under the Hapsburgs.

Czechoslovakia consisted of a number of nationalities that had been included in order to give strategic boundaries to the newly
National established Republic. Of the 15,000,000 inhabitants,
minorities fifty per cent were Czechs and sixteen per cent were Slovaks, who were closely related to the Czechs; twenty-two per cent were Germans, who lived chiefly in territory that bordered on Germany; five per cent were Hungarians; and about four per cent were Ruthenians, closely related to the Ukranians in Russia. The rights of the national minorities were protected by the Minorities Treaty that Czechoslovakia had signed with the Allies, which protected their special interest; and, even more, by the constitution, which guaranteed the rights of all citizens irrespective of race or nationality. Despite official favoritism often shown to the Czechs, the government, on the whole, respected the rights of the minorities, far more so than did the other governments in central Europe. Czechoslovakia planned eventually to establish a multi-national state on the model of Switzerland.

However, there was bitter feeling among the national minorities against the Czechs. For centuries there had been racial strife in
Discontent Bohemia between the Slavic Czechs and the Sudeten
of the Sude- Germans, as they were known in that region. The
ten Germans Germans, who had dominated Bohemia before the war, now resented being under the Czechs, and they ardently desired annexation to Germany. Less important, but no less bitter, was the attitude of the Hungarians, who desired annexation to Hungary. Even the Slovaks were discontented because Czech officials predominated in their region; what they desired was autonomy. The depression of 1929 aggravated the situation, especially among the Sudeten Germans, who lived chiefly in the industrialized sections. Discontent, originating in widespread unemployment, was directed against the government, which was charged with discriminating against the industrial areas.

Of all the new nations that had emerged from the war Czechoslovakia was in the most dangerous position. She was land-
Alliances of locked and almost entirely surrounded by potential
Czechoslo- enemies — Germany, Austria, Hungary, and Poland
vakia — who were ever ready to "redeem" their nationals. To protect herself against attack Czechoslovakia joined Rumania and Yugoslavia to form the Little Entente. She also formed close alliances with France and with Russia.

When the Nazis came into power in Germany the situation in Czechoslovakia became critical. She now lived in the shadow of a Nazi Germany sworn to annex all German-speaking Nazi lands in central Europe. A Nazi movement, aided agitation by Germany, captured an overwhelming majority of the Sudeten Germans, who flocked to the support of the Nazi Sudeten Party, led by Konrad Henlein. As a result of the elections of 1935, the Sudeten Party became the largest single political group in the Czechoslovak Parliament. The government was supported by a majority consisting of parties loyal to the existing régime. A furious Nazi agitation began that led to riots, demonstrations, and strikes. So serious was the situation that the government was ready to make large concessions, but no concessions would satisfy the Nazis.

If a conflict arose, Czechoslovakia could put a powerful army in the field; moreover, she had been promised aid by her allies, France and Russia. In case of war she would be a link of Czechoslo-Franco-Russian coöperation and a base for air attacks vakia looks on important German centers. France had repeat- to her allies edly assured Czechoslovakia, her one consistently for aid loyal ally in central Europe, of her readiness to fulfill her treaty obligations.

A great crisis arose in September, 1938, involving Germany and Czechoslovakia, that threatened to develop into a general war. The Sudeten Germans began rioting, and Czecho- Munich slovakia proclaimed martial law. Germany mobilized (1938) and openly threatened to invade Czechoslovakia. This crisis brought England and France on the scene. The English Prime Minister, Neville Chamberlain, went to Germany to consult with Hitler. At a conference which met in Munich on September 29, Hitler, Mussolini, Chamberlain, and the French Premier Daladier came to an agreement to partition Czechoslovakia. Russia proclaimed her willingness to come to the aid of Czechoslovakia if France was ready to do so. France refused. This left Czechoslovakia, who had calmly and bravely prepared to fight for her independence, alone before Nazi Germany. She could do nothing but yield.

What followed stunned and outraged the entire world. A peaceful, democratic nation was partitioned without a blow in her defense. Czechoslovakia first gave up the Sudeten districts, con-

To Germany, Sept. 1938
To Germany, March 1939
To Hungary, Sept. 1938
To Hungary, March 1939
To Poland, Sept. 1938

PARTITION OF CZECHOSLOVAKIA

taining a population of about 3,600,000, with a fairly large Czech minority. Then Poland threatened to attack, and was given the district of Teschen, bordering on Poland. Then Hungary threatened to attack, and was given lands bordering on Hungary. Then Slovakia demanded autonomy, which was granted. Czechoslovakia lost thirty per cent of her territory, rich sections containing coal and iron deposits, and textile, pottery, and glass manufactures. Under pressure from Hitler Czechoslovakia abolished her democratic system and instituted a fascist régime modeled on Nazi racial ideals and policies. President Beneš resigned and took the road to exile.

First Partition of Czechoslovakia

Germany gave a solemn pledge to respect the independence of what was left of Czechoslovakia, which was now almost wholly Slavic in population. But German pledges did not save hapless Czechoslovakia from annihilation as a nation. In March, 1939, a German army entered Prague, and Czechoslovakia disappeared from the map. The country was annexed to Germany; a small part of Slovakia, called Carpatho-Ukraine, was given to Hungary; the Czech and Slovak parts were each designated as "protectorates," to be ruled by German governors. As in the case of the Jews, citizenship was not granted to

Second Partition

the Slavic inhabitants; they were to be "subjects," with an inferior status to the "master race," the Germans. In her treatment of Czechoslovakia, Germany's ambition was made clear to the world: it was to conquer central and eastern Europe.

HUNGARY

During the dissolution of the Hapsburg Monarchy, Hungary emerged an independent nation. When Austria surrendered to the Allies, a revolution broke out in Hungary that over- Hungary, a threw the existing régime. A provisional government Republic was formed which proclaimed Hungary a republic, and chose Count Michael Karolyi as President. Karolyi was a member of an aristocratic family, but his views were exceedingly liberal. He proposed to reorganize Hungary as a federal republic with full rights to the non-Magyar races. But the latter were determined to secure their complete independence, and they received the support of the Allies, who were planning to dismember Hungary.

Karolyi faced two serious problems: the maintenance of Hungary's territorial integrity and a new revolutionary movement inspired by the communist ideals of Soviet Russia. Downfall of There was intense anger among patriotic Hungarians Karolyi when it became evident that their country would share the fate of Austria. Karolyi was blamed for weakness in dealing with the Allies, and his régime was utterly discredited. In March, 1919, he resigned in despair, and the government was seized by the Communists, headed by Bela Kun.

Communist Hungary greatly alarmed the Allies, who did not relish the idea of another communist nation in Europe. Russia had given them trouble enough. They encouraged a Communist hostile attitude toward Hungary among the neighbor- Hungary ing states who expected to receive Hungarian territory. A Rumanian army invaded Hungary and entered Budapest. In the meanwhile an anti-communist movement, under Admiral Horthy, was gaining headway. After several months, the Communist régime was overthrown.

A "White" terror followed which mercilessly suppressed all radical agitation. Many fled the country, among them Bela Kun and Count Karolyi. In order to establish a stable government, a National Assembly was convened in 1920, which proclaimed

Hungary a monarchy with Horthy as "Regent." Hungary was
Semi-dicta-   now in the anomalous position of being a monarchy
torship in   without a monarch.   Decrees issued by the Regent
Hungary   established a parliament, with limited suffrage and
open voting.   In practice Hungary was a dictatorship somewhat
modified by popular elections, in which moderate opposition was
permitted.

The Horthy régime, much against its will, was compelled to sign
the Treaty of Trianon, which left Hungary a petty state about one
Revisionism   quarter its former size.   Very bitter was the feeling
              among Hungarians against the Treaty, which put one
third of the Hungarian people under the rule of Rumania, Czechoslovakia, and Yugoslavia.   A demand from an almost unanimous
Hungary arose for the revision of the Treaty.   "No! No! Never!"
was the slogan of the revisionists, who refused to accept the new
frontiers.

War and revolution had left Hungary prostrate.   The economic
situation was desperate, and the League of Nations came to the
Economic   rescue by taking charge of Hungary's finances.   A
conditions   foreign loan was floated; the administration was reorganized; and the system of taxation was reformed.   At the end of
a year economic conditions became normal.

Fascism was rampant in Hungary, where fear of communism
was widespread.   It was to Fascist Italy that Hungary first turned
Gets part of for inspiration and for help in her efforts to regain her
Czechoslo-   lost territory.   In 1927 a treaty of friendship was
vakia   signed by Italy and Hungary.   And when Nazi
Germany appeared, Hungary promptly sought her aid.   During
the great crisis of 1938, when Czechoslovakia was being dismembered, Hungary asserted her claims to parts of Czechoslovakia.
Her claims were supported by Germany and Italy, and she received
a strip of territory from Czechoslovakia.   But her revisionist
demands remained unsatisfied.

POLAND

The national resurrection of Poland was one of the dramatic
results of the World War.   Poland was recognized, in 1919, by a
treaty with the Allies, but the great problem was to determine her
boundaries.   The Poles demanded the boundaries before the Par-

tition, which, if granted, would have included a population chiefly non-Polish. The first installment of territory was at the expense of Prussia (Germany) and Austria, who were compelled to give up the territory that they had seized during the Partition. Poland now had access to the sea through the "Corridor," and through her special privileges in Danzig. In 1921 she got additional territory from Germany in the part of Upper Silesia, assigned to her by the League of Nations.

Territory of Poland taken from Germany and Austria

The second installment was at the expense of Russia. The Peace Conference gave to Poland the solidly Polish region known as "Congress" Poland.[1] But the Poles were not content, and they prepared to extend their eastern frontier. In 1920 Poland declared war against Russia. At first the Soviet forces won a number of victories, and quickly advanced toward Warsaw. French generals took command of the Polish army, and forced the Russians to sue for peace. By the Treaty of Riga (1921) Poland gained considerable territory from Russia.

From Russia

The third installment of territory came from Lithuania. A volunteer force of Poles seized the city of Vilna, which, in 1923, was given to Poland by the Allies. The Allies gave generous treatment to Poland because they wished: (1) to establish a powerful state on the flank of Germany; (2) to erect a bulwark against the spread of communism from Russia; and (3) to keep Russia and Germany apart in order to prevent possible alliances.

From Lithuania

Within the boundaries of the new Republic of Poland there were large national minorities, chiefly Ruthenians, Jews, Germans, and Lithuanians. Although they had been a persecuted people, the Poles were not generous in their newly found independence. In spite of the protection afforded by the Minorities Treaties with the Allies, the minority races in Poland suffered discrimination at the hands of the now dominant Poles. In 1934 Poland declared that she would not coöperate with the League of Nations in enforcing the Minority Treaty.

Racial minorities

After the war a provisional government was established, headed by General Joseph Pilsudski, an ardent patriot who became the leading figure in the reborn Poland. Later, in 1921, a constitution was adopted which established a democratic republic on the

[1] See page 56.

model of that in France.   But parliamentary institutions did not
Poland, a   work well in Poland; moreover, Pilsudski was ambi-
semi-fascist   tious to be a dictator.   In 1926 he led a "March on
state   Warsaw" and compelled Parliament to bow to his authority.   For a time Pilsudski managed to be a quasi-dictator by
browbeating the opposition.   But a new constitution, adopted in
1935, definitely provided for a semi-fascist régime.   Parliament was
to be elected by a restricted suffrage and to exercise limited power
over legislation.   Real power was to be in the hands of a popularly
elected President, who was empowered to appoint and to dismiss
cabinets.   On Pilsudski's death in 1935, a group of generals became all powerful.   The government of Poland was now virtually
in the hands of a military oligarchy.

Poland was in a dangerous position strategically.   On her long
exposed frontiers were Russia and Germany, both enemies, ever on
Gdynia   the watch to attack her.   Her only link to the Baltic
                was the bottleneck Corridor, which could easily be
seized by Germany.   On its narrow coast Poland, at great expense, built the city of Gdynia, which was developed both as a port
and as a naval base.   A small merchant marine appeared, which
gave great satisfaction to the almost landlocked nation.

Poland realized the necessity of being allied to one of the great
powers.   In 1921 she formed an alliance with France, who aided
her financially and diplomatically.   But the advent of Hitler to
power in Germany caused great fear in Poland.   Hitler's policy
was to cultivate good relations with Poland in order to detach her
from France.   In 1934 Germany and Poland signed a ten-year
Non-   treaty, in which they agreed to settle peacefully all
aggression   disputes between them.   About the same time Poland
treaty with   signed a non-aggression pact with Russia.   Fearing
Germany   both Germany and Russia, the foreign policy of Poland
oscillated between them, sometimes favoring one, sometimes the
other.

After the annexation of Austria and Czechoslovakia it was plain
that Poland would be the next victim of Nazi Germany's ambitions
England   in central Europe.   Danzig and the Corridor were
guarantees   Hitler's objectives.   Realizing her danger Poland ap-
independence   pealed to her ally, France, and to England for protec-
of Poland   tion.   A threat of Germany, in 1939, to annex Danzig
brought a guarantee from England of Polish independence.   Whereupon Germany renounced her treaty with Poland.

THE BALTIC NATIONS

From tsarist Russia arose a number of democratic republics. In 1920 Finland was recognized as an independent nation. During the following year, Latvia, Esthonia, and Lithuania were also recognized. All these Succession states adopted democratic constitutions.

Finland, Latvia, Esthonia, and Lithuania

A serious difficulty arose over the disposition of the city of Memel, which had been taken from Germany and was being held by the Allies. Lithuania was eager to annex it in order to get an outlet to the sea. In 1924, through the agency of the League of Nations, a plan was adopted according to which Memel was given to Lithuania, but with a provision for local autonomy. As Memel was largely German, its racial sentiments were aroused when Hitler came into power. A Nazi party appeared which won control of the city. On the demand of Hitler, in 1939, Lithuania surrendered Memel, which was annexed to Germany.

Memel

By far the most serious problem confronting the Baltic nations concerned the large estates owned chiefly by aristocrats of German origin. In 1919 Esthonia passed a law virtually confiscating all large estates; and in 1922, Latvia did likewise. Lithuania, in 1922, expropriated the large estates with moderate compensation to the owners. In all these instances the estates were divided into small holdings and sold to the peasants on liberal terms.

Peasant proprietorship

THE NEAR EAST

(a) TURKEY

As a result of the World War, Turkey lost about half her territory, but she emerged from the struggle a modern nation. The Ottoman Empire, which had played so fateful a part in history, was abolished. In 1923 the Sultan was deposed, and Turkey was proclaimed a republic with Mustapha Kemal, the conqueror of Greece, as the first President. Ankara (formerly Angora) was made the capital. A constitution was adopted in 1924 which provided for a parliament of one house, elected by universal manhood suffrage. Executive power was to be exercised by a President and cabinet chosen by parliament. All citizens of the Republic were declared equal before the law, irrespective of race or religion.

Turkey, a democratic republic

Mustapha Kemal became the soul of the new Turkey.   Although virtually a dictator he used his power in a manner that won gen-

Modernization of Turkey

eral admiration.   His object was to transform Turkey into a strong, modern, national state.   With this object in view he prevailed upon Parliament to pass drastic laws, which violated cherished ideals, customs, and traditions.   Church and state were separated by the abolition of the Caliphate, which had been part of the Sultanate since the sixteenth century.   The system of courts and laws, based upon the Koran, was abolished; and new codes were adopted based upon modern ideas of jurisprudence.   Polygamy was abolished, and civil marriage was instituted.   The fez, as the distinctive headdress for men, and the veil, as the distinctive headdress for women, were abolished.   The Latin alphabet was introduced, and books printed in Arabic characters were forbidden.   These innovations shocked many conservative Turks, but they were vigorously applied by the government.

A comprehensive public works program was carried out that included railway and road construction, irrigation, and reclamation.   Manufactures were encouraged by tariffs and subsidies. Financial aid came from foreign countries, and it came not as formerly, without political control.

Though much reduced in size, Turkey was still a power to be courted because of her important strategic position in the eastern

Foreign policies

Mediterranean.   Friendly relations with Greece were established in 1933 by a non-aggression treaty.   In 1934 Turkey joined with her fellow-Balkan States, Yugoslavia, Greece, and Rumania, to form the Balkan Pact, which mutually guaranteed their frontiers.   In 1936 Turkey gained at the same time a great victory and the good opinion of the world.   She requested the League and the signatories of the Treaty of Lausanne for permission to fortify the Straits, which had been demilitarized by the Treaty.

A conference of the signatories took place in Montreux, Switzerland, where a new convention was signed that radically modified

The Montreux Convention

the Treaty of Lausanne.   Turkey was permitted to fortify the Straits on condition that in time of peace they were to be open equally to all merchant vessels and to a limited tonnage of foreign warships.   In time of war Turkey could close the Straits, but her action in this matter was to be regulated by the League of Nations. Russia was accorded exceptional treatment by Turkey. In time of peace she was permitted to send her entire Black Sea fleet into the Mediterranean; and in time of war she was assured the freedom of the Straits, in case the League decided that she was a victim of aggression. Fear of Italy in the eastern Mediterranean was chiefly responsible for these concessions to Russia. In 1939, as has already been described, Turkey formed close alliances with England and France.

(b) GREECE

Greece had lost heavily as a consequence of her disastrous war with Turkey. She was compelled to surrender nearly all her gains under the Treaty of Sèvres. The government was blamed for the defeat, and a number of officials, charged with incompetence, were executed. King Constantine was dethroned, and once more he was obliged to go into exile. But his son and successor, George II, did not succeed in reviving the popularity of the dynasty. In 1924 Parliament deposed the King, who thereupon followed his father into exile. As a result of a referendum, Greece was proclaimed a republic. *Greece, a republic*

But the Republic was fated to have a short and stormy life. For a decade it was busy defending itself against conspiracies and uprisings organized by both Left and Right. When Nazi Germany appeared, a fascist movement encouraged by the Germans began in Greece. In 1935 the Republic was abolished, and King George II was restored. But real power was in the hands of a fascist group, led by General John Metaxas, who became Premier. Suddenly, in 1936, Metaxas dissolved parliament, suspended the constitution, abolished all political parties, and proclaimed a military dictatorship. Greece was now essentially a fascist state. *Greece, a dictatorship*

For a time Metaxas favored Germany. But fear of Germany's partner, Italy, was stronger than admiration of fascist ideas. When Italy conquered Albania, Greece felt that her safety lay with the democratic powers. In 1939 she accepted a guarantee of her independence given to her by England. *Greek independence guaranteed*

(c) YUGOSLAVIA

As a result of the war, little Serbia expanded into a large state,

Yugoslavia. It was founded on the principles enunciated by the
Founding of   Declaration of Corfu, in 1917, by representatives of
Yugoslavia   the three main groups: the Serbs, the Croats, and the
Slovenes.   They had agreed to unite into a single nation under the
Serbian dynasty, to establish a democratic government, and to
treat equally the Greek Orthodox, the Roman Catholic, and the
Mohammedan faiths.   Yugoslavia came into existence in 1918,
when Peter of Serbia was chosen King of the new kingdom, which
consisted of Serbia, Montenegro, and parts of Austria-Hungary.
The constitution provided for a single-chamber parliament elected
by universal manhood suffrage and for a responsible ministry.

No sooner was the new government established than internal
strife began between the various elements in Yugoslavia.   Most of
Croats and   the Croats and Slovenes are Roman Catholic in faith
Serbs   and western European in culture; and most of the
Serbs are Greek Orthodox in faith and eastern European in culture.
The government was dominated by the Serbs, which caused much
dissatisfaction among the Croats and Slovenes, who opposed the
centralized monarchy under Serb auspices, and favored a federal
republic which would guarantee local self-government to each
element.

The issue of centralization versus federalism was in reality the
desire of the Croats to obtain equality with the dominant Serbs.
Dictatorship   Conspiracies, assassinations, and attempts at revolt
of King   by the Croats resulted in the establishment of a dicta-
Alexander   torship, in 1929, by King Alexander.   Two years later
a new constitution was proclaimed, which provided for a voting
system that favored the Serbs and the conservative elements in
Yugoslavia.   There was great discontent throughout the country,
and the elections were boycotted by many voters.   Alexander
was hated by the Croats as the chief obstacle to their nationalist
aims.   In 1934, while on a visit to France, he was assassinated by
a Croat terrorist.   Peter, his successor, was a boy.   A council of
regency was established, the chief member of which was Prince
Paul, a relative of the boy King.

Yugoslavia's international problems were as serious as her
domestic problems.   To secure her territorial gains at the expense
Foreign   of Hungary she joined the Little Entente.   A far
policies   more serious threat came from Italy, who was determined to dominate the Adriatic.   The annexation of Fiume and

the domination of Albania by Italy caused Yugoslavia to seek an alliance with a great power. In 1927 she signed a treaty of alliance with France. As a Balkan state, Yugoslavia in 1934 joined Greece, Turkey, and Rumania to form the Balkan Pact.

The death of King Alexander, who was a friend of France, brought a change in Yugoslav foreign policy. Prince Paul, the Regent, favored Nazi Germany because of the close economic ties that had developed between Germany and Yugoslavia. As Italy and Bulgaria were close to Germany, Yugoslavia had to establish friendly relations with these two nations. In 1937 she signed one treaty of friendship with her old enemy Bulgaria, and another with her post-war enemy, Italy, which had the effect of seriously weakening the Balkan Pact. When Albania was conquered by Italy, Yugoslavia's position became very serious. She was between Germany and Italy, and therefore was compelled to follow the policies of the fascist powers. *Pro-German policy*

(d) RUMANIA

Rumania emerged from the World War double in size. She acquired Bessarabia from Russia; and Transylvania, Bukovina, and part of the Banat from Austria-Hungary. In these territories there were national minorities, chiefly Hungarians, Jews, and Ukrainians, who did not wish to be under Rumanian rule. *Greater Rumania*

A radical reform transformed old Rumania, dominated by a landed aristocracy, into a peasant democracy. The agrarian law of 1920–21 expropriated most of the large estates, which were divided into farms and sold to the peasants on easy terms. *Land reform*

In 1923 a new constitution established a democratic system for Rumania. However, most of the voters were poor, illiterate peasants who could be terrorized or manipulated by the powerful interest around the crown. The most influential monarch in the post-war era of Rumania was King Carol II, who was actively engaged in manipulating parliament when it was on his side and dissolving it when it opposed him. *King Carol*

As in the other Balkan states, domestic politics in Rumania echoed the international situation. Rumania joined the Little Entente to protect herself against Hungary. In 1926 she formed a treaty of alliance with France. Friendly *Foreign relations*

relations with Russia were maintained by a non-aggression pact, signed in 1933, according to which Russia tacitly recognized Bessarabia as part of Rumania.

With the appearance of Nazi Germany, the situation in Rumania began to change. A strong fascist movement, the Iron Guard, appeared and agitated for a pro-German policy. As a result of the many shifts of Rumanian politics the fascist element succeeded, in 1936, in ousting the pro-French Foreign Minister Titelescu. Thereafter, French influence waned, and German influence waxed.

With the growth of fascist influence, Carol abandoned the democratic system established in 1923. A new constitution, which Political gave considerable authority to the King, was adopted reaction in 1938. He was given power to appoint and dismiss ministers and to veto bills. Parliament was to be elected by a restricted franchise, and its powers over legislation were greatly limited.

What Carol desired was his own and not Germany's brand of fascism. The success of the Iron Guard, which was aided by the Foreign Nazis, would mean the control of Rumania by Ger-policies many. Carol had no intention of becoming a vassal of Hitler. He therefore took strong measures against the Iron Guard. It was dissolved, and its leaders were imprisoned or assassinated.

As in the case of Greece, Rumania feared Italy, who backed Hungary's claims of Rumanian territory taken from her as a result of the war. And, like Greece, Rumania accepted in 1939 the offer of England to guarantee her independence.

(e) BULGARIA

By the terms of the Treaty of Neuilly, Bulgaria lost small but important strips of territory. To Rumania she ceded southern Losses of Dobrudja with its Black Sea coast; to Greece, the part Bulgaria which constituted her only outlet to the Aegean; and to Serbia, several strategic border towns. There was deep resentment against King Ferdinand, whose policy in aligning Bulgaria with Germany had brought disaster to the country. In 1919 he was compelled to abdicate, and was succeeded by his son, Boris.

One of the remarkable men who appeared in Bulgaria was Alexander Stamboulisky. As the leader of the Peasants' Party, he became Premier and inaugurated a policy of radical reconstruction, largely in the interests of the peasants. A compulsory labor law was passed which conscripted all citizens for industrial service. Crown and church lands were given to the peasants. These policies roused the bitter opposition of the wealthy elements, who were as hostile to the "green" socialism of the peasants as to the "red" socialism of the workingmen. In 1923 the government was overthrown by a coup d'état, and Stamboulisky was killed. *Stambou-lisky*

For about a decade Bulgarian politics is a record of plots and counter-plots, uprisings, and assassinations by both Left and Right elements. In 1934 a coup d'état was organized by a group of army officers who dissolved Parliament and established a dictatorship. But the dictatorship was unable to master the country, and in 1938 Parliament was reëstablished. *Political changes*

Bulgaria, being a defeated nation, kept outside the Balkan system of alliances, which had for their chief object the maintenance of their boundaries. She naturally favored the revision of the war treaties. When, in 1937, Yugoslavia signed a treaty with Bulgaria, the latter's isolation was broken. In 1938 the Balkan Pact removed the military restrictions imposed on Bulgaria by the Treaty of Neuilly. *Treaty with Yugoslavia*

THE NEW ORIENT

(a) INDEPENDENCE OF PERSIA

The war "to make the world safe for democracy" roused great hopes among the colonial peoples of Asia and Africa. They now demanded that they too be given the right of self-determination proclaimed by the Allies. A strong anti-European movement arose, reaching from China to Morocco, which led to important concessions to nationalism in the Orient. *Nationalism in the Orient*

The first Oriental nation to free herself from European domination was Persia. Soviet Russia renounced her rights in Persia under the partition treaty of 1907, which the tsarist government had signed with England. England was now alone in control. She compelled Persia to sign a new treaty which virtually made that country her protectorate. The Persian nationalists were infuriated, and waged a bitter struggle against British imperialism. In 1921, encouraged by Russia, Persia defiantly annulled her treaty with England, and asserted her *Persia ousts England* complete independence. England accepted the situation and evacuated the country. During the struggle the Persian dynasty was overthrown. In 1926 a popular general, named Reza Khan, ascended the throne as Shah.

Persia under Reza Khan, like Turkey under Kemal Pasha, was organized as a national state on Western models. Foreign political Persia, a na- and economic influences, so long powerful in Persia, tional state were largely eliminated. A national army, school system, and fiscal system appeared. Persia now embarked on a vigorous national life as a sovereign state.

(b) INDEPENDENCE OF EGYPT

In Egypt, too, nationalism triumphed over imperialism. Under the leadership of Zaghlul Pasha, the Egyptian nationalists de-Nationalism manded the evacuation of their country by England. in Egypt They resorted to riots, conspiracies, assassinations, and boycotts. So violent was the agitation that England was alarmed and prepared to make important concessions.

In 1922 England terminated her protectorate and recognized Egypt as an independent nation. But she reserved to her "dis-England's cretion" the following matters: (1) the security of "reserva- communications of the British Empire by stationing tions" troops along the Suez Canal and elsewhere in Egypt; (2) the defense of Egypt against foreign aggression and the direction of her foreign policy; (3) the protection of foreign interests and of foreigners in Egypt; and (4) the control of the Sudan.

A new government came into existence. It was a constitutional monarchy, with Fuad I as King. Parliament was elected by a Opposition propertied suffrage. England's concessions had not to the "res- caused the nationalist movement to subside. It now ervations" insisted that Egypt should be completely freed of English control, and that the Sudan be evacuated.

But a new situation arose as a result of the conquest of Ethiopia by Italy. Both the British and the Egyptians now feared that Treaty Italy's ambitions in North Africa would turn toward between Egypt. As a consequence they hastened to patch up England their quarrels. In 1936 England and Egypt signed and Egypt a treaty of alliance in which they agreed to mutual aid in case of war; to a joint rule of the Sudan; to the restriction of British troops to the zone of the Suez Canal; and to the right of the British to use Alexandria and Port Said as naval bases and to move troops through Egypt in case of war. The Treaty of 1936 gave Egypt, for the first time in many centuries, the status of an independent nation.

(c) THE CONQUEST OF CHINA

The establishment of the Chinese Republic in 1912 was followed by conflicts between the different sections, the different parties, and the rival military chieftains. Japan determined to exploit China's weakness, which came from these conflicts. For long Japan had been planning to be- come the "guardian of the peace of the Pacific," by which she meant the conquest of China and the elimination of all foreign influences and interests in the Far East. In order to further this great ambition, Japan's policy was to weaken China by encouraging conflicts and rivalries among the Chinese, and to wait "for the time of the confusion of Europe" in order to strike at China without fear of intervention by the Western powers. Her first opportunity to establish control over China came when Europe was distracted by the World War. In 1915 Japan presented to China the notorious Twenty-One Demands, the most important of which were: China was to consent to whatever agreement Germany and Japan might make regarding Shantung; she was to consult Japan before granting concessions to foreigners in southern Manchuria and in eastern Mongolia; her most important iron and steel works were to be a joint Sino-Japanese enterprise; she was not to lease any part of her coast to foreigners without Japan's consent; she was to employ Japanese civil and military advisers; she was to purchase half of her munitions from Japan; and she was to grant important economic concessions and privileges to Japan. To many of these demands China was compelled to yield, which placed Japan in a dominant position in China.

Japan plans to conquer China

To guarantee her control, Japan had need of the support of the powers. In 1916 she entered into a treaty of alliance with Russia, her recent enemy, to support each other's interests in the Far East. During the following year she signed a secret agreement with the Allies according to which Japan was to be the heir of Germany's holdings in China. The next step was to make sure of the United States. In the same year the Lansing-Ishii Agreement was signed, in which the United

China in the grip of Japan

States recognized that Japan had special interests in China. At the Peace Conference China tried to free herself from the chains in which she was bound by Japan. But in vain. The Treaty of Versailles carried out the secret agreement to the letter. Not since the Opium War had China been in so humiliating a position.

After the World War the country was in a state bordering upon chaos. The government at Peking was flouted; civil war raged be-

The Kuo-
mintang

tween the north and south; military adventurers seized provinces which they looted; and the powers made ready to intervene. It was Young China that jumped into the breach to save the country from partition and ruin. Largely through the efforts of the student movement, a Nationalist government was established in Canton, which was controlled by the Kuomintang (the People's Party), an outgrowth of the revolutionary groups organized by Sun Yat-sen. It preached the "Three Principles of the People": the people's nationalism, or freeing of China from foreign control; the people's sovereignty, or the establishment of democracy; and the people's livelihood, or the improvement of social and economic conditions. The Kuomintang demanded the abolition of all treaties not based upon equality of both contracting parties, universal suffrage, freedom of speech and of assembly, universal military service, abolition of *likin*, or tax on goods in transit inland, universal education, equality of the sexes, government ownership of natural monopolies, and land and labor reforms. Young China, like Young Italy in the days of Mazzini, began a political apostolate, preaching its ideas to the masses with religious fervor. Its success was amazing; within a short time almost the entire country was behind it.

The Nationalists faced two enemies: the foreign powers and the "tuchuns," or military chieftains, who held large provinces. A

Methods of
the Nation-
alists

strong anti-foreign sentiment developed which took many forms: patriotic agitation, riots, boycott of foreign goods, strikes against foreign employers, and denunciation of the unequal treaties. There were three stages in the development of China's attitude toward the West. The Boxers had been reactionary in that they aimed to preserve Old China from the ways of "foreign devils." The reformers of the first decade of the twentieth century had been extravagant admirers of everything foreign, and had derided Chinese ways and ideas. But the Nationalists had a critical attitude toward both China and the West.

They wished to establish a new China that would preserve the best features of Chinese life and ideals, to which would be added all that was best in Western civilization. They were anti-foreign only in the sense that they were opposed to the intervention of foreign powers and to the privileges enjoyed by foreigners in China.

The movement for "the recovery of national rights" made rapid progress. As a result of the World War, Germany and Austria lost their privileges in China. Soviet Russia relinquished the privileges and claims established by the tsarist government. The most important step taken by the powers in favor of China was at the Washington Conference, already described. By the *The Nine* Nine Power Treaty of 1922 the powers agreed "to *Power* respect the sovereignty, the independence, and the ter- *Treaty* ritorial and administrative integrity of China"; to oppose the creation of spheres of influence; and to favor "equal opportunity for the commerce and industry of all nations throughout the territory of China." The Nine Power Treaty, for a decade, "froze the Pacific" by fixing the status quo in the Far East according to the principles of the Open Door.

The Chinese Nationalists realized only too well that China herself must become united and strong in order to make the guarantees of the powers effective. Therefore the Nationalist *Advance of* government organized armies which, under General *Nationalism* Chiang Kai-shek, won notable victories over the war *in China* lords. The Nationalist forces advanced rapidly toward the north. In 1928 they entered Peking in triumph. The name of the city was then changed to Peiping.

The problem that now confronted the Nationalists was to reorganize China on a national basis. It was an immense task, and only beginnings were made. Nanking became the new capital. A constitution was adopted. As the unification of China made progress, the powers became more willing to yield their special privileges under the unequal treaties.

Japan, ever watchful of the situation in China, feared that a united, rejuvenated China would balk her great ambition to become the "lord of the Far East." Her first move was to consolidate her gains in Manchuria, a region which has both economic *Impor-* and strategic importance, and is, therefore, a valuable *tance of* prize over which three nations, Japan, China, and *Manchuria* Russia, have struggled. Manchuria is a very large, fertile region, mainly prairie land like the Middle West. What wheat is to the Middle West, the soya bean, rich in food values, is to Manchuria; in addition it contains large natural resources, coal, iron, gold, lumber. Strategically it has been described as the shaft of a spear aimed at Japan, the point of which is Korea. Concerning Russia, it cuts off direct communication with the great port, Vladivostok, which is the reason why Russia built the Chinese Eastern Railway through Manchuria. For China, Manchuria, being sparsely settled, was a great outlet for emigration. Almost its entire population of 35,000,000 is Chinese, chiefly immigrants. To Japan, Manchuria offered a fertile field for industrial expansion and a source for the raw materials that she lacked at home. Manchuria was the "life line" of Japan, which alone would maintain her as a great power.

For centuries Manchuria had been under the sovereignty of China. In 1910 it was partitioned into a Russian "sphere of influence" in the north, and a Japanese in the south. On account of the growth of nationalism, China began to assert her sovereign rights in Manchuria. Japan watched the advance of nationalism in China with considerable uneasiness. She had really never resigned herself to a "frozen Pacific" as was planned by the Washington Conference. Moreover, new developments began in the Far East which threatened to balk her ambition to dominate that region. Russia was strengthening her position in her Pacific provinces by concentrating large military forces and by developing local factories and farms to make the armies in the region independent of supplies across the Trans-Siberian Railway. In addition, Russia was building a branch of this railway from a point near Lake Baikal, going north, to the Pacific. England was rapidly strengthening her great naval base at Singapore, at the main crossroad of the routes from eastern Asia to the Mediterranean and from Suez to China and Australia. America was building a vast chain of naval and air bases in the Pacific, with its chief points in Alaska, Hawaii, Guam, and the Philippines. All these developments had for their ultimate object the curbing of Japanese aggressive designs.

Threats to Japan's ambitions in China

Japan determined to strike before it was too late. Taking advantage of the great depression which began in 1929, causing Europe and America to concentrate their attention on domestic problems, Japan took the first step in her long-matured plan to conquer China. In 1931 Japanese armies

Conquest of Manchuria

invaded Manchuria and drove the Chinese armies out of the province. Manchuria was then reorganized by Japan as a separate state, called "Manchukuo," under the rule of the exiled former Emperor of China. In fact, Manchukuo was a protectorate of Japan, with its government completely controlled by Japanese officials appointed "to advise" the ruler. Japan's control of all of what was formerly Manchuria became complete in 1935, when she bought Russia's half interest in the Chinese Eastern Railway.

Japan's seizure of Manchuria was in direct violation of the Covenant of the League of Nations and of the Nine Power Pact. It marked the beginning of what she called "the New Order in East Asia." Japan asserted for this region a "Monroe Doctrine" by which she proposed to eliminate European and American influences in China. Under Japanese pressure foreign business enterprises in Manchukuo were greatly restricted in their activity or entirely ousted for the benefit of Japanese business men. *The "New Order in East Asia"*

Japan's next step was to advance quickly into China proper; the Chinese were too disorganized to offer effective resistance. In 1933 Japanese armies moved south of the Great Wall and seized the Chinese province of Jehol; later, in 1935, they conquered two more provinces in northern China. *Japan seizes Chinese provinces*

Ever since the seizure of Manchuria, China was acutely aware of the grave danger of being conquered by Japan. Under the cautious and skillful leadership of her patriot leader, Chiang Kai-shek, the Chinese made remarkable progress toward national unity. The various parties united. The military chieftains were conquered. North and south joined together. A large national army was in process of organization. Munitions factories were established. *Union of Chinese factions*

These facts did not escape the notice of Japan. Another decade, and China would be a powerful, united nation, hence too strong to be conquered. Ever since the advent of Nazi Germany the situation in Europe favored Japan's designs in China. The powers that were likely to intervene, Russia, England, and France, were too busy strengthening their defenses against a re-militarized Germany to come to the aid of China. *Germany aids Japan*

On July 7, 1937, Japanese armies began a rapid invasion of northern China. An undeclared war, like that between Italy and Ethiopia, was waged over vast areas, now in the north, now in the

east, now in the south.   The Japanese quickly overran northern
China, thus blocking aid to the Chinese from Russia.
Next the Japanese captured Nanking, the capital.   In
1938 the Japanese got control of the south by capturing, first Suchow, a key railway junction; then Canton, the great
port from which supplies came; and finally Hankow.   The Chinese
armies, under Chiang Kai-shek, fought desperately but were constantly compelled to retreat before the large, well-disciplined, well-
armed Japanese armies.

War be-
tween Japan
and China

By the end of 1938 organized resistance to the Japanese virtually
came to an end.   But a new resistance began with guerrilla warfare.
The Japanese lines were thinly held over a vast territory, and were vulnerable to sudden attacks.   The
war proved to be a great drain on Japanese resources,
and by continuing it the Chinese hoped to bring about an economic
collapse of Japan.

Defeat of
the Chinese
armies

The undeclared war in the Far East aroused great feeling against
Japan in the democratic countries.   China urged the League of
Nations to take action against Japan as an aggressor,
but that body, now almost moribund, merely adopted
a resolution of sympathy for China.   The signatories
to the Nine Power Pact, which Japan had plainly
violated, as she had also violated the Pact of Paris, met but
took no action.

No action
taken
against
Japan

Japan was now emboldened to take a new step.   She openly
repudiated the Open Door and declared the treaty rights of foreigners null and void.   This step meant that the
"New Order in East Asia" to be established by
Japan would not tolerate Western business enterprise.
Already foreign interests in China, especially those of England,
had suffered heavily.   The United States and England sent notes
to Japan rejecting her scheme of a "New Order" and refusing to
consent to her unilateral repudiation of the Nine Power Pact.

Japan re-
pudiates
Open Door

But these protests did not halt the march of Japan.   In February,
1939, Japanese forces seized the Chinese island of Hainan, a
strategic point near French Indo-China.   This act
violated an agreement between France and Japan.   By
the possession of Hainan, which stands across the sea line between
the British possessions Singapore and Hong Kong, Japan has a
base from which to make an attack on French Indo-China.

Japan seizes
Hainan

The embodiment of vested foreign interests in China is to be found in the "Concessions," or privileged foreign settlements in the port cities, notably in Tientsin, Shanghai, and Amoy. For Japan to attack these settlements would be almost a direct attack on those Western powers that ruled them. In May, 1939, the Japanese blockaded the British settlement in Tientsin, which created a serious diplomatic strain between England and Japan.

Japan attacks British Concession

REFERENCES

SPAIN:
J. A. Brandt, *Toward the New Spain* (1933); G. Young, *The New Spain* (1933); J. T. Reid, *Modern Spain and Liberalism* (1937); A. Mendizabal, *The Martyrdom of Spain* (1938); F. Manuel, *The Politics of Modern Spain* (1938).

CENTRAL EUROPE:
M. W. Graham, *The New Governments of Central Europe* (1927); L. Pasvolsky, *Economic Nationalism of the Danubian States* (1929); T. G. Masaryk, *The Making of a State* (1927); P. Crabitès, *Beneš* (1934); M. W. Fodor, *Plot and Counter-Plot in Central Europe* (1938); Elizabeth Wiskemann, *Czechs and Germans* (1938); C. A. Macartney, *Hungary and Her Successors* (1938); R. Machray, *The Poland of Pilsudski, 1914–1936* (1937); R. L. Buell, *Poland* (1939).

THE BALTIC NATIONS:
M. W. Graham, *New Governments of Eastern Europe* (1927); T. W. Atchley, *Finland* (1931); J. H. Wuorinen, *Nationalism in Modern Finland* (1931); A. Bihlmans, *Latvia in the Making, 1918–1928* (1928); *The Baltic States: Estonia, Latvia, Lithuania,* prepared by the Information Department of the Royal Institute of International Affairs (1938).

THE NEAR EAST:
H. F. Armstrong, *The New Balkans* (1926); W. Miller, *Greece* (1928); C. U. Clark, *United Roumania* (1932); D. Metrany, *The Land and the Peasant in Rumania* (1930); G. Ellison, *Yugoslavia* (1935); L. Adamic, *The Native's Return* (1934); H. E. Allen, *The Turkish Transformation* (1935); H. N. Howard, *The Partition of Turkey* (1931); E. E. Webster, *The Turkey of Atatürk* (1939); G. Antonious, *The Arab Awakening* (1939); *Southeastern Europe: A Political and Economic Survey,* prepared by the Information Department of the Royal Institute of International Affairs (1939).

THE FAR EAST:

P. H. Clyde, *A History of the Modern and Contemporary Far East* (1937); H. B. Morse and H. F. MacNair, *Far Eastern International Relations* (1931); H. M. Vinacke, *A History of the Far East in Modern Times* (1933); G. F. Hudson, *The Far East in World Politics* (1937); L. S. Hsu (ed.), *Sun Yat-sen* (1933); L. Sharmon, *Sun Yat-sen* (1934); H. F. MacNair, *China in Revolution* (1931); N. Peffer, *China, the Collapse of a Civilization* (1930); J. E. Orchard, *Japan's Economic Position* (1930); F. Utley, *Japan's Feet of Clay* (1937); H. G. Moulton and J. Ko, *Japan: An Economic and Financial Appraisal* (1933); H. S. Quigley, *Japanese Government and Politics* (1932); T. A. Bisson, *Japan in China* (1938); and R. K. Reischauer, *Japan: Government and Politics* (1939).

CHAPTER XLII

THE SECOND WORLD WAR

INTRODUCTION

TWENTY-FIVE years after the beginning of the First World War another world conflict arose in Europe. That turbulent continent, for all its great contributions to civilization, had signally failed to establish a system of international relations in which the various nations could live in peace and harmony. A treaty of peace, following one war, has generally been the starting-point of another war. This was especially true of the Treaty of Versailles, which, by its harshness to the conquered and by its unwise provisions concerning national boundaries, was the starting-point of the Second World War.

For a time after the signing of the Treaty of Versailles there was peace in the world, the peace of exhaustion. But as recovery began, the dissatisfied powers, now established as power- Localized ful dictatorships, used their growing strength to pre- wars prepare for new conflicts, not only to satisfy their griev- pare for a world war ances but also to establish themselves as world powers by destroying the democracies and dividing their wealth and territories. A number of localized wars broke out, beginning with the invasion of China by Japan in 1931. It was followed by the invasion of Ethiopia by Italy, and by the Civil War in Spain, in which the Fascist powers openly aided Franco. "Bloodless" wars paralleled these sanguinary conflicts. Nazi Germany and Fascist Italy pounced upon small neighbors, who surrendered their independence in order to avoid a hopeless struggle against greatly superior forces. By this method of "bloodless" war Nazi Germany seized Austria and Czechoslovakia, and Italy seized Albania. Communist Russia was arming to the teeth presumably to defend herself against the rival dictatorships, Germany and Japan. In reality she, too, was preparing to seize the territory of her small neighbors and to assert herself as a world power. The Second World War was the culmination of almost a decade of brutal aggression by the dictatorships.

THE DANZIG DISPUTE

The immediate cause of the Second World War was the dispute over Danzig, established as a Free City under authority of the League of Nations. In March, 1939, Hitler compelled Lithuania to cede Memel to the Reich. This success was followed by the Nazi demand for the union of Danzig with the Reich on the ground that it was German in population. In addition Hitler demanded the cession to Germany of a road through the Polish Corridor to connect East Prussia with Germany. Poland was vitally concerned in this matter, as Danzig was situated at the mouth of the Vistula, Poland's most important river. Germany in possession of Danzig might put hindrances through tariffs and port dues in the way of Polish commerce reaching the sea. Moreover, as Danzig was included in Poland's tariff system, its cession to Germany would leave Gdynia as Poland's only access to the sea, thereby hindering her economic development. Poland also realized that to grant Germany right of way through the Corridor, which was predominantly Polish, would eventually lead to its return to Germany.

Importance of Danzig to Poland

The government of Danzig had fallen under the control of a local Nazi party. The authority of the League Commissioner was flouted. Nazi propaganda, both in Germany and in Danzig, became active in favor of annexation. All opposition was terrorized. German soldiers, disguised as tourists, moved into Danzig. All was made ready for a move by Danzig to join Germany in defiance of the treaty that gave her the status of a Free City.

Danzig under the Nazis

Like the Serajevo incident in 1914, the Danzig crisis in 1939 had vast international implications. The real issue was not Danzig but the aggressive designs and insatiable ambitions of Nazi Germany. After the seizure of Czechoslovakia it became evident that Hitler would not be content merely to annex contiguous German-speaking lands, such as Austria and the Sudetenland, but to make the Germans the "master race" of Europe. No non-German nation was safe once Nazi Germany dominated the Continent. And democratic ideals would be submerged by fascism once Germany and her ally, Italy, triumphed over England and France. Nazi Germany's policy was to conquer, one by one, the small nations of central Europe which would strengthen her in the final struggle with the democracies.

Ambitions of Germany

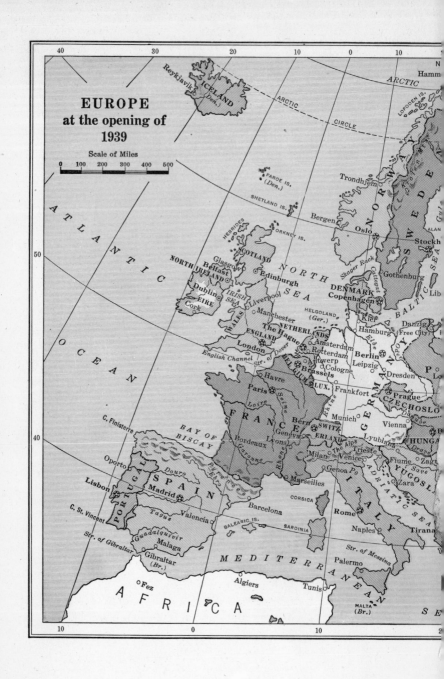

EUROPE
at the opening of
1939

Scale of Miles

0   100   200   300   400   500

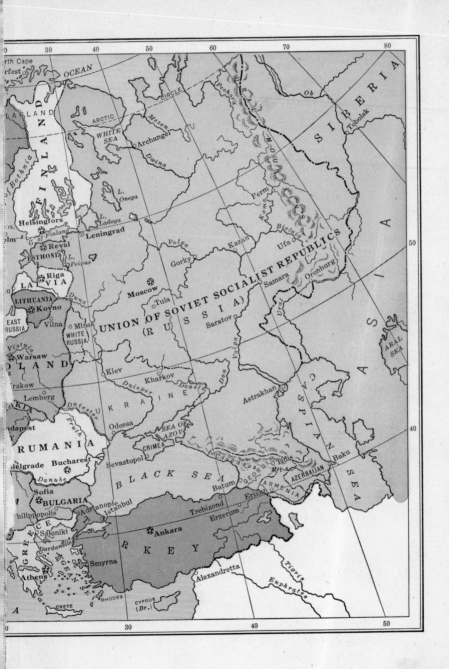

England and France realized their perilous situation. Prime Minister Chamberlain abandoned his "appeasement" policy and began building a new security system against fascist *England* aggression by alliances with those nations whose inde- *opposes the* pendence was threatened by the Axis powers. His *Axis* change of policy marked a diplomatic revolution as significant as that before the First World War, when England joined France and Russia to oppose Imperial Germany.

The Danzig crisis revealed that Poland was the next nation marked for destruction by Nazi Germany. England promptly came to the support of Poland by promising to aid *England* her "in the event of any action which clearly threat- *guarantees* ened Polish independence." This promise to Poland *Rumania,* was followed by similar guaranties to Rumania and to *and Greece* Greece on condition that they resist aggression with their national forces.

These commitments of England in eastern Europe, which were seconded by France, infuriated the fascist powers. In retaliation Hitler renounced two important treaties that he had *Hitler re-* signed: the ten-year non-aggression pact of 1934 with *nounces* Poland and the naval limitation agreement of 1935 *treaties* with England.

In order to have an effective "Stop Hitler Front," England and France had need of the support of Russia. They sent representatives to Moscow with the object of negotiating a mili- *Agreement* tary alliance with the Soviet that had been the chief *between* object of Nazi hatred. Hitler had more than once *Germany* openly proclaimed his bitter antagonism to Russia. *and Russia* He had come into power in Germany as the uncompromising enemy of communism. He had organized the Anti-Comintern pact to fight communism the world over. On August 23 a diplomatic bombshell burst that astounded the world and caused consternation in England and France. Vyacheslav M. Molotov, Foreign Minister of Soviet Russia, and Joachim von Ribbentrop, Foreign Minister of Nazi Germany, announced the signing of an agreement between the two powers in which each promised "to refrain from every act of force" against the other; and neither was to "associate itself with any other grouping of powers which directly or indirectly is aimed at the other party." Economic relations between Germany and Russia, "on the basis and in the spirit of the general political understanding," were to be greatly developed. The latter country promised to send raw materials to the former in exchange for industrial products. While he was negotiating with the English and French, Stalin, behind their backs, had come to an agreement with the Nazis. What was called the "Berlin–Moscow Axis" created bewilderment mingled with deep resentment throughout the world. Hitlerism had been welcomed by many conservatives as the force that had saved Europe from communism; and now Hitler gave Stalin a free hand to spread communism in large sections of central Europe. Communism had been tolerated by many liberals as the energetic force that was creating a "popular front" against fascism; and now Stalin gave the powerful support of Communist Russia to Fascist Germany against the Allied democracies.

Hitler's pact with Stalin, in effect, nullified the Anti-Comintern pact. Japan and Italy, who had signed it, found themselves deserted by Germany, much to their chagrin. Japan then made overtures to Russia, whose military power was now vastly increased by being relieved of the necessity of fighting on two fronts. The Rome–Berlin Axis now began to weaken, as Italy feared that the Russo-German combination would assert itself in the Balkans and eliminate her influence in that important region. Mussolini, while stoutly asserting his friendship for Hitler, began friendly "conversations" with France and England.

Eclipse of the Anti-Comintern pact

The Stalin-Hitler combination was fraught with danger for Poland, which was the object of their aggression. The Danzig situation became critical as Hitler, now assured of not having to fight on the eastern front in case of war, demanded that Poland yield to his wishes. Poland refused. Prime Minister Chamberlain issued a clear warning to Hitler saying that England would surely go to the aid of Poland in case of aggression against her. He suggested direct negotiations between Germany and Poland for a settlement which was to be guaranteed by the other powers. Poland agreed to the plan. Hitler, on August 29, stated that he also agreed to it, and requested the appearance of a special Polish envoy on August 30 to receive the German proposals. England declared that it was unreasonable to expect so quickly the arrival of a Polish envoy in Berlin where he would be required to accept at once proposals

Hitler pretends to negotiate with Poland

which neither he nor his government had seen. It was plain that Hitler merely pretended a willingness to negotiate. All day, August 30, no proposals were made to the English or to the Polish ambassadors. Suddenly the German radio broadcast to the world a set of proposals to settle the dispute between Germany and Poland. The Polish ambassador tried to communicate with Warsaw, but the German government had closed all communication between Germany and Poland. Hitler then denounced Poland for refusing Germany's proposals because no special Polish envoy had arrived in Berlin.

CAUSES OF THE WAR

On September 1 German armies invaded Poland without any declaration of war. On September 3, England and France, faithful to their pledge, declared war on Germany. The six years of continuous aggression on the part of Nazi Germany had created a situation in Europe that caused every nation to fear for its very existence. After every aggression Hitler had given promises of peace and then promptly broke them. Before annexing Austria he had declared that "Germany has neither the wish nor the intention to mix in internal Austrian affairs or annex or unite with Austria." Before annexing Czechoslovakia he had declared that the Sudetenland was Germany's "last territorial ambition in Europe." His demand for Danzig and the Corridor roused the democracies to a realization of the danger of a continuously expanding Nazi Germany dedicated to war and ambitious to dominate all Europe. They went to war less to defend Poland and far more to defend Europe from falling under the Nazi yoke. Our general purpose, declared Chamberlain, is "to redeem Europe from the perpetually recurring fear of German aggression and to enable the peoples of Europe to preserve their independence and their liberties. No threats will deter us or our French allies from this purpose."

England and France declare war

In contrast to the First World War, which was undertaken in a spirit of great emotionalism and was fought with crusading fervor, the Second World War was undertaken in a spirit of calm determination. England and France came to the conclusion that a conflict with Germany was unavoidable, since every effort toward "appeasement" had only led to further demands, which, they were convinced, would ultimately lead to the disruption of their empires.

War of calm determination

The war began between Germany on one side and England and France on the other. Promptly the British Dominions — Canada, Australia, New Zealand, and South Africa — rallied to the side of England; only Eire declared her neutrality. Italy remained neutral, either because Germany did not at first desire her help or because she was vulnerable to attacks by the Allied fleets. As a neutral she could assist Germany by sending her supplies and by immobilizing a French army on her French frontier. Russia, too, remained neutral, which was of immense service to Germany, who did not, as in 1914, have to fight on two fronts.

Belligerents and neutrals

THE WAR IN POLAND AND THE BALTIC

Germany unleashed against Poland a *blitzkrieg* (lightning war) whose pattern was later to make itself felt throughout the European continent. Four armies, supported by heavy tanks and fleets of bombers, invaded Poland from different directions. The country was swiftly overrun, German planes spreading havoc and destruction. Hampered by the lack of natural defenses, inferior equipment, and an inadequate air force, the Polish forces retreated steadily. No important battles were fought. The collapse of Polish resistance was hastened when, on September 17, Russian troops suddenly invaded eastern Poland. Ostensibly it was to protect the Ukrainian and White Russian minorities; actually it was to share in the spoils. Caught between two fires, Poland was doomed. After three weeks the war was virtually at an end, except for Warsaw's heroic defense against superior German forces until September 27. Two days later, Germany and Soviet Russia partitioned the hapless republic. About two fifths of Poland, the agricultural region in the east, went to Russia; the remainder, including the industrial areas, went to Germany. Danzig was annexed to the German Reich.

Partition of Poland

Following the partition of Poland, Russia quickly proceeded to strengthen her western frontiers by establishing control over the Baltic states. Yielding to threats of force, Esthonia, Latvia, and Lithuania concluded mutual assistance pacts with Russia, surrendered strategic naval and air bases, and permitted the stationing of Soviet garrisons. Similar demands on Finland for the cession of strategic islands in the Gulf of Finland and certain territories on the Finnish-Russian frontier met with refusal. After futile diplomatic conversations, Soviet forces invaded Finland on

November 30, 1939, and launched air attacks on Helsinki and other Finnish cities. The Allies sent supplies to Finland's aid, but the refusal of Norway and Sweden to permit passage prevented the dispatch of Allied troops. After a bitterly fought struggle, Finland was obliged to capitulate. The treaty, signed March, 1940, gave Russia the Karelian Isthmus and other strategic areas, as well as a naval base at Hangoe. Three months later, Russia occupied Lithuania, Latvia, and Esthonia, accusing them of having violated the mutual assistance pacts; and these states were formally incorporated into the Soviet Union. Germany, who had long dominated the Baltic Sea, was obliged to acquiesce in Russia's expansion in that area as the price for support in the Polish war. At the same time Russia sent an ultimatum to Rumania demanding the return of Bessarabia and surrender of northern Bukowina, which Rumania was obliged to yield.

Expansion of Russia in the Baltic and in the Balkans

THE WAR IN THE WEST

On the western front the situation during the first few months was less dramatic. Facing the Maginot Line in France was a similar system of fortifications in Germany, known as the Westwall. So formidable were these fortifications that a frontal attack was considered almost suicidal. French troops did capture a few advance posts on German territory, but were soon withdrawn. The British sent a large expeditionary force to France, as in 1914, and unity of command was established under General Maurice Gamelin. The Allies prepared for a long "war of attrition," relying on their superior resources for ultimate victory.

The Maginot Line

When the Polish campaign was over, Hitler turned to France and Great Britain with a "peace offer." His terms included the recognition of the Polish conquest, a free hand for Germany and Soviet Russia in eastern and central Europe, and the return to Germany of her former colonies. Unless his proposals were accepted, he threatened to let loose a "war of destruction." The Allies replied that no peace was possible with a government that had forfeited confidence by its record of broken promises, and expressed a determination to continue the war until Europe had a guaranty of lasting security.

Hitler's "peace drive"

The lull on the western front ended on April 9, 1940, when

German forces invaded Denmark and Norway on the pretext of
"protecting" them from Allied designs.   Denmark
offered practically no opposition.   In Norway, where
troops were landed both by planes and ships, general
resistance developed.   With the aid of "fifth col-
umnists" and the use of "Trojan horse" tactics, the Germans
completed their conquest of Norway within a month, despite the
efforts of an Allied expeditionary force to dislodge them.   The
occupation of Denmark and Norway gave the Nazis additional air
and naval bases on the North Sea.   In Great Britain, mounting
public criticism of the Chamberlain government's inept conduct
of the war led to the appointment of Winston Churchill as head of
a coalition government.

German oc-
cupation of
Denmark
and Norway

Without warning, on the morning of May 10, 1940, the Nazis
invaded Luxemburg, Belgium, and the Netherlands.   As in the
case of Norway, the justification given was that the
Allies themselves were planning to violate the neutrality of the Low Countries.   The invasion was by
land, sea, and air, German planes landing parachute
troops at strategic points.   Great Britain and France hurried large
bodies of troops in an effort to stem the fury of the onslaught.
But the Germans' overwhelming superiority in the air, the tremendous power of their mechanized units, and the treachery of
"fifth column" sympathizers combined to crush all resistance.
General Weygand, who replaced Gamelin as commander-in-chief,
found it impossible to organize a large-scale counter-offensive.
The Dutch command capitulated in four days "to prevent further
bloodshed and annihilation."   Queen Wilhelmina took refuge in
England.   King Leopold surrendered the Belgian army on May 28.
After piercing the Maginot Line at Sedan, the Germans swept to
the Channel ports and encircled an Allied army of approximately
a million and a half soldiers.   The British troops fought desperately to escape the trap.   The greater part succeeded in evacuat-
ing Dunkerque, though harassed continually by German bombing
planes.

German
conquest of
the Low
Countries

The débâcle in Flanders made the position of France precarious.
The Germans, who had early in the campaign forced a crossing of
the Meuse River, shattered French opposition in the
Battle of the Somme, and broke through the defenses
on the Marne.   With France almost prostrate, Italy declared war

The fall of
France

on the Allies (June 10, 1940) and Fascist troops crossed the Alpine frontier. Four days later, a Nazi army entered Paris unopposed. German tanks and motorized divisions, in the meantime, drove southward, completely outflanking the Maginot Line. With the military situation hopeless, Premier Reynaud (who had supplanted Daladier) resigned and was succeeded by the elderly Marshal Henri Philippe Pétain. On June 17, Pétain appealed to Germany for an end to hostilities, and five days later, the French delegates signed an armistice at Compiègne, in the same railway car where Germany had surrendered to the Allies in 1918. Under the terms of the armistice, France yielded to Germany military occupation of more than half her territory, including the entire west coast, the cost of occupation to be borne by France. The French army was demobilized and all military equipment and coast defenses were placed at the disposal of the Nazis; French prisoners were to be held until the signing of a formal peace; the French fleet was to be demobilized and interned by the victors. Two days later, a separate armistice was signed with Italy, which was now in a position to demand cession of French territory. In order to prevent the French navy from falling into Axis hands, the British seized or disabled the larger part of it in engagements at Oran, Algeria.

The military collapse of France marked the end of the Third Republic. The French Parliament, meeting at Vichy, the new seat of government, voted itself out of existence, and gave Pétain plenary powers as "Head of the French State." The new régime, totalitarian in character, embarked on a policy of "collaboration" with the conquerors. Frenchmen who favored continuance of the war organized a "Free French" government in London, under the leadership of General Charles de Gaulle. Several French colonies in West Africa proclaimed their allegiance to de Gaulle and joined Britain's campaign in Libya.

By the summer of 1940, all western Europe, from the Arctic to the Pyrenees, was under Nazi domination. Britain alone stood in the way of a complete totalitarian victory. And it was to crush Britain that Germany now directed her efforts. While making preparations along the Channel for an invasion attempt, the Germans sought to "soften" the British by systematic air raids. Waves of Nazi bombers swept over the British Isles, blasting industrial centers and naval bases, and devastating large parts of London with incendiary and explosive bombs. The Royal Air Force (R.A.F.) retaliated by pounding the "invasion ports" on the Continent and raiding vital industrial and military objectives in Germany and German-held territory. England converted herself into a virtual fortress, with a deep "defense zone" along the coast to guard against invasion. The British war effort was strengthened by the ever-increasing stream of American planes, guns, and tanks and by the receipt of fifty over-age destroyers from the United States in exchange for eight naval and air bases on British possessions in the Western Hemisphere.

The crucial battleground of the war, for Britain, was the Atlantic. With the opening of hostilities British sea power quickly demon-

Battle of the Atlantic — strated its strength. The Royal Navy swept German shipping from the high seas and established a blockade of the German coast. As in the First World War, Germany retaliated by declaring a counter-blockade of the British Isles to prevent the delivery of foodstuffs and war supplies. Once more the chief German weapon was unrestricted submarine warfare, accompanied by air attacks on shipping and harbor facilities. Axis U-boats and surface raiders took a serious toll of British and neutral merchant vessels. But the tonnage lost was gradually reduced with the organization of strong convoys and improved aircraft protection.

THE BALKANS AND THE WAR

The increased power and prestige won by German arms led the Balkan countries to orient their foreign policy toward the Rome-

Germany seizes the Balkans — Berlin Axis. Acting as arbiters, Germany and Italy "persuaded" Rumania to satisfy the revisionist claims of Hungary and Bulgaria by ceding half of Transylvania to the former and southern Dobruja to the latter. Hitler then proceeded to achieve complete control of southeastern Europe, with Soviet Russia apparently committed to a "hands off" policy. In the fall of 1940, Hungary became a puppet state under a diplomatic agreement permitting German troops to use Hungary as a corridor into the Balkan peninsula. Rumania, already torn by internal strife, was converted into an armed camp when large bodies of Nazi troops poured in, ostensibly "to protect" the oil wells against British sabotage. The occupation of Rumania gave

Hitler a base on the Black Sea and cleared the way for the penetration of Bulgaria.   In March, 1941, Bulgaria joined the Axis and allowed Nazi soldiers to enter her territory.   Germany then turned her attention to Yugoslavia and Greece.   Yugoslavia signed an agreement to join the Axis camp, but a *coup d'état* brought an anti-Axis government into power which repudiated the agreement.   Greece, who had been successfully fighting an Italian invasion since October, 1940, likewise resisted German pressure. In April, 1941, the Nazi war machine struck simultaneously at Yugoslavia and Greece in the familiar *blitzkrieg* manner.   Despite heroic resistance and British aid, they were conquered in three weeks.   With the fall of Greece, Germany seized most of the islands in the Aegean Sea and even occupied the British-defended island of Crete by an air-borne invasion.

Turkey's foreign policy changed with the changing fortunes of war.   In the early part of the conflict (November, 1939), she entered into a military alliance with Great Britain and France.   After the collapse of France, however, and the Nazi occupation of the Balkans, Turkey sought to insure her neutrality by signing a trade agreement and non-aggression pact with Germany (June, 1941).

Turkey's foreign policy

THE WAR IN EASTERN EUROPE

One of the most astounding events of the war was Germany's sudden attack on Soviet Russia.   The invasion began on June 22, 1941, along a 2000-mile front extending from the Baltic to the Black Sea.   The non-aggression pact was scrapped without warning, furnishing still further evidence of the perfidy of the Nazi régime.   As justification for the invasion, Hitler accused Russia of threatening the German frontiers and of carrying on anti-German propaganda.   He described his assault on the Soviet Union as a "crusade" against Bolshevism, hoping thereby to split public opinion abroad.   His real aims obviously were to smash the Red army, thus removing the only possible obstacle to complete German domination of the European continent; and to obtain sufficient grain, oil, and mineral supplies to carry on what now seemed certain to be a long war.   Italy, the Axis satellites — Rumania, Slovakia, and Hungary — as well as Finland joined in the attack on Russia.   Prime Minister Churchill promised British help for Russia, despite his aversion for com-

Germany wars on Russia

munism, declaring that any country defending itself against Hitlerism was entitled to support. This statement was followed by a formal military alliance between Great Britain and the Soviet Union. President Roosevelt pledged all possible aid from the United States.

During the first five months of the fighting, the German war machine made impressive gains. The Nazi legions overran eastern

Resistance of the Red Army
Poland and the buffer states of Lithuania, Latvia, and Esthonia. They besieged Leningrad, conquered the Ukraine, and threatened Moscow with encirclement. They smashed their way into the Crimea and the Donets industrial area, gateways to the Caucasian oil fields. Though suffering terrible losses, the Red armies offered surprisingly fierce resistance and, in accordance with their "scorched earth" policy, destroyed everything of value in their retreat. In November, 1941, they finally wrested the initiative from the enemy and began a steadily advancing counter-offensive which hurled the supposedly invincible Nazi troops back along the entire front. This extraordinary reversal was variously attributed to the inability of the Nazis to make full use of their mechanized equipment in the severe winter frost and snow, and the rising strength of the reinforced Soviet armies.

THE WAR IN AFRICA AND NEAR EAST

While Germany was consolidating her power in Europe, Italy carried the war to the Mediterranean and Africa. Striking from

Battle of Libya
Libya, Fascist troops invaded Egypt in September, 1940, in a drive toward the Suez Canal, and advanced about sixty miles within the Egyptian border. Two months later the British launched a counter-offensive in which they not only regained the entire Egyptian coast but also conquered eastern Libya, taking thousands of prisoners. However, reinforced by German planes and armored divisions, the Axis forces by April, 1941, recovered the Libyan territory. There the situation rested until November, 1941, when British Imperial troops, their strength augmented with American planes and tanks, began a new drive against the Axis which carried them once more into Cyrenaica. A considerable part of the British success was due to the efficiency with which the Royal Air Force and British fleet in the Mediterranean interfered with the lines of communication between Italy and North Africa. Another blow to Italian pride was the shatter-

ing of the Italian empire in East Africa. By May, 1941, the British conquered Eritrea, Italian Somaliland, and Ethiopia.

Having frustrated the Axis threat to Suez from Africa, the British proceeded to strengthen their Near-Eastern position. In June, 1941, after a short campaign, they ousted the British Advance in Near East pro-Axis government which had seized control of Iraq, site of valuable oil fields. The same month British and Free French troops entered Syria, accusing the Vichy government of permitting the Nazis to use Syrian air bases. After brief resistance, the British acquired full control of Syria, which was promised its independence after the war. In August, 1941, British and Russian forces occupied Iran, following the refusal of the native government to expel large numbers of Nazi "tourists."

THE UNITED STATES AND THE WAR

When the war in Europe began, the United States declared its neutrality. In compliance with existing neutrality legislation, President Roosevelt prohibited the export of war Neutrality legislation materials or extension of loans and credits to belligerent nations, and forbade the entry of American ships in "combat areas." Although the American people were determined to keep out of the European war, public opinion overwhelmingly favored the democracies. Accordingly, Congress repealed the arms embargo in November, 1939, and replaced it with a "cash-and-carry" provision. This permitted the sale of arms, munitions, and other implements of war to belligerents provided they paid cash and transported them in other than American ships. The lifting of the embargo was a great help to Britain and France, whose control of the seas and financial resources enabled them to purchase immense quantities of war supplies.

It soon became evident, however, that neutrality was unable to withstand the impact of an ever-widening war. As the Nazi legions overwhelmed country after country, there was Aid to Britain a crystallization of American opinion in favor of utmost aid to Britain. The expressed intention of the Axis powers to establish a "new world order" which would rid mankind of "decadent pluto-democracy" emphasized the serious threat to American security of an Axis victory. In March, 1941, therefore, Congress passed the Lease-Lend Act which authorized the President to "sell, transfer, lease, or lend" war supplies to nations fighting the Axis. This law virtually converted the United States into a great "arsenal of democracy." Shortly thereafter, American troops occupied Greenland, Iceland, and Dutch Guiana to forestall their possible use by Germany as air or naval bases. Following attacks on several American destroyers and merchantmen, the United States navy was instructed to "shoot on sight" Axis submarines and surface raiders found within American "defense waters." To insure the safe delivery of American goods to Britain, Congress further modified the neutrality act in November, 1941. The new law authorized the arming of United States merchant ships and permitted them to enter any belligerent ports. The United States could now throw the full weight of its material resources on the side of the nations fighting Hitlerism.

In August, 1941, President Roosevelt and Prime Minister Churchill held a historic meeting in the North Atlantic. Sub-
The "Atlantic Charter" sequently they announced an eight-point program setting forth Anglo-American war aims and peace objectives. These were: (1) no territorial aggrandizement for Great Britain or the United States; (2) no territorial changes, not in accord with "the freely expressed wishes of the peoples concerned"; (3) the right of all peoples to choose their own form of government; (4) free access for all nations, "victor or vanquished," to trade and raw materials needed for their economic prosperity; (5) "improved labor standards, economic adjustment, and social security" for all; (6) general peace "after the final destruction of the Nazi tyranny"; (7) freedom of the high seas; and (8) disarmament of aggressor nations.

WAR IN THE FAR EAST

American relations with Japan, in the meantime, showed signs of steady deterioration. The outbreak of war in Europe had
Strained relations between America and Japan encouraged Japanese militarists to pursue a more aggressive policy of territorial aggrandizement. Shortly after the fall of France, Japan obtained from the Vichy government economic control of Indo-China as well as the right to establish air and naval bases. The Japanese threat to move southward into the Netherlands East Indies, with their rich oil, rubber, and tin deposits, brought a sharp warning from the United States that any interference with the "status quo" of those islands would jeopardize the peace of the Pacific. Tokyo's reply

was to enter into a military alliance with the Axis powers in September, 1940. Under its terms Japan recognized the leadership of Germany and Italy in the establishment of "a new order" in Europe; the Axis partners, in turn, recognized Japan's hegemony in the Far East. This tripartite pact was evidently designed to keep the United States from becoming an active belligerent in the European war or from combatting Japan's expansionist program in Asia. In retaliation, the American government placed an embargo on the shipment of essential war materials to Japan, halted the purchase of Japanese products, and "froze" Japanese credits in the United States.

The Japanese government then sent a special envoy to Washington, with the professed desire of negotiating a peaceful settlement of its differences with the United States. Prolonged conversations failed to produce any agreement. The United States asked Japan to withdraw from China, reopen the "closed door," and break her tie with the Axis. The Japanese, on the other hand, insisted they would not deviate from their "immutable policy" of setting up a "New Order in East Asia" and demanded the immediate lifting of the economic blockade. Tension mounted as the Japanese gave no satisfactory explanation for the massing of additional troops in Indo-China.

While the peace discussions in Washington were still in progress, the Japanese launched a surprise air and sea attack on Pearl Harbor, the American naval base in Hawaii, on Pearl December 7, 1941. It was followed by a formal Harbor declaration of hostilities on both the United States and Great Britain. It was now apparent that the Japanese military leaders had been using the period of diplomatic conversations to prepare for this treacherous assault upon the American outposts in the Pacific. A wave of indignation swept the American people, firmly uniting them behind the administration. With virtual unanimity Congress, on December 8, declared war against Japan. On December 11, Japan's Axis partners announced themselves at war with the United States. Congress met the challenge the same day by unanimously declaring war against Germany and Italy. The unprovoked and infamous attack on American soil dispelled every illusion of security. In a world ruled by lawlessness and "gangsterism" there could be no security for any nation.

APPENDIX

RULERS OF THE EUROPEAN NATIONS SINCE THE FRENCH REVOLUTION

Albania
Prince William of Wied, 1913–1914.
Provisional Government, 1920–1925.
Republic, 1925–1928.
Kingdom, 1928–1939.
Annexed to Italy, 1939.

Austria
Part of Holy Roman Empire, until 1806.
Francis I, 1804–1835 (*Holy Roman Emperor, as Francis II,* 1792–1806).
Ferdinand I, 1835–1848.
Francis Joseph, 1848–1916.
Charles I, 1916–1918.
Republic in 1918.
Annexed to Germany, 1938.

Belgium
Part of Austrian Monarchy, 1713–1797.
Part of France, 1797–1815.
Part of Holland, 1815–1830.
Leopold I, 1831–1865.
Leopold II, 1865–1909.
Albert, 1909–1934.
Leopold III, 1934–

Bulgaria
Part of Turkey, 1393–1878.
Alexander, *Prince,* 1879–1886.
Ferdinand I, *Prince,* 1887–1908; *King,* 1908–1918.
Boris III, 1918–

Czechoslovakia
Part of Austrian Monarchy, 1526–1918.
Independent Republic, 1918.
Annexed to Germany, 1939.

Denmark
Christian VII, 1766–1808.
Frederick VI, 1808–1839.
Christian VIII, 1839–1848.
Frederick VII, 1848–1863.
Christian IX, 1863–1906.
Frederick VIII, 1906–1912.
Christian X, 1912–

Esthonia
Part of Swedish Monarchy, 1561–1721.
Part of Russian Empire, 1721–1918.
Independent Republic in 1918.

Finland
Part of Swedish Monarchy, 1290–1809.
Part of Russian Empire, 1809–1918.
Independent Republic in 1918.

France
Louis XVI, 1774–1792.
First Republic, 1792–1804.
Napoleon I, *Emperor,* 1804–1814.
Louis XVIII, 1814–1824.
Charles X, 1824–1830.
Louis Philippe, 1830–1848.
Second Republic, 1848–1852.

APPENDIX

Napoleon III, *Emperor*, 1852–1870.

Presidents of the Third Republic
Adolphe Thiers, 1871–1873.
Marshal MacMahon, 1873–1879.
Jules Grévy, 1879–1887.
F. Sadi Carnot, 1887–1894.
Casimir-Périer, 1894–1895.
Félix Faure, 1895–1899.
Émile Loubet, 1899–1906.
Armand Fallières, 1906–1913.
Raymond Poincaré, 1913–1920.
Paul Deschanel, 1920.
Alexandre Millerand, 1920–1924.
Gaston Doumergue, 1924–1931.
Paul Doumer, 1931–1932.
Albert Lebrun, 1932–

Germany
Part of Holy Roman Empire, until 1806.
Part of Germanic Confederation, 1815–1866.
German Empire, 1871–1918.
William I, 1871–1888 (*King of Prussia,* 1861–1888).
Frederick III, 1888.
William II, 1888–1918.
Republic, 1918.
Presidents of the Republic
Friedrich Ebert, 1919–1925.
Paul von Hindenburg, 1925–1934.
Nazi Dictatorship in 1933.
Hitler, 1933–
Chancellors of the German Empire, 1871–1918.
Prince Bismarck, 1871–1890.
Count von Caprivi, 1890–1894.
Prince Hohenlohe, 1894–1900.
Count von Bülow, 1900–1909.
T. von Bethmann-Hollweg, 1909–1917.
Georg Michaelis, 1917.
Count von Hertling, 1917–18.
Prince Maximilian, 1918.

Great Britain
George III, 1760–1820.
George IV, 1820–1830.
William IV, 1830–1837.
Victoria, 1837–1901.
Edward VII, 1901–1910.
George V, 1910–1936.
Edward VIII, 1936–
Abdicated, 1936.
George VI, 1936–
Prime Ministers since 1806.
Lord Grenville, 1806–1807.
Duke of Portland, 1807–1809.
Spencer Percival, 1809–1812.
Earl of Liverpool, 1812–1827.
George Canning, 1827.
Duke of Wellington, 1828–1830.
Earl Grey, 1830–1834.
Viscount Melbourne, 1834.
Sir Robert Peel, 1834–1835.
Viscount Melbourne, 1835–1841.
Sir Robert Peel, 1841–1846.
Lord John Russell, 1846–1852.
Earl of Derby, 1852.
Earl of Aberdeen, 1852–1855.
Viscount Palmerston, 1855–1858.
Earl of Derby, 1858–1859.
Viscount Palmerston, 1859–1865.
Lord John Russell (Earl Russell), 1865–1866.
Earl of Derby, 1866–1868.
Benjamin Disraeli, 1868.
William E. Gladstone, 1868–1874.
Benjamin Disraeli (Earl of Beaconsfield), 1874–1880.
William E. Gladstone, 1880–1885.
Marquess of Salisbury, 1885–1886.
William E. Gladstone, 1886.
Marquess of Salisbury, 1886–1892.

APPENDIX

William E. Gladstone, 1892–1894.

Earl of Rosebery, 1894–1895.

Marquess of Salisbury, 1895–1902.

Arthur James Balfour, 1902–1906.

Sir Henry Campbell-Bannerman, 1906–1908.

Herbert Henry Asquith, 1908–1916.

David Lloyd George, 1916–1922.

Andrew Bonar Law, 1922–1923.

Stanley Baldwin, 1923.

J. Ramsay MacDonald, 1923–1924.

Stanley Baldwin, 1924–1929.

J. Ramsay MacDonald, 1929–1935.

Stanley Baldwin, 1935–1937.

Neville Chamberlain, 1937–

Greece
Part of Turkey, 1453–1829.
Provisional Government, 1829–1832.
Otto I, 1832–1862.
George I, 1863–1913.
Constantine I, 1913–1917.
Alexander I, 1917–1920.
Constantine I (restored), 1920–1922.
George II, 1922–1924.
Republic, 1924–1935.
George II (restored), 1935–

Hungary
Part of Austrian Monarchy, 1526–1918.
Independent Kingdom, 1918.

Italy
Victor Emmanuel II, 1861–1878 (King of Sardinia, 1849–1861).
Humbert, 1878–1900.

Victor Emmanuel III, 1900–
The Popes
Pius VI, 1775–1799.
Pius VII, 1800–1823.
Leo XII, 1823–1829.
Pius VIII, 1829–1830.
Gregory XVI, 1831–1846.
Pius IX, 1846–1878.
Leo XIII, 1878–1903.
Pius X, 1903–1914.
Benedict XV, 1914–1922.
Pius XI, 1922–1939.
Pius XII, 1939–

Latvia
Part of Swedish Monarchy, 1629–1721.
Part of Russian Empire, 1721–1918.
Independent Republic in 1918.

Lithuania
Part of Polish Monarchy, 1501–1793.
Part of Russian Empire, 1793–1918.
Independent Republic in 1918.

Montenegro
Peter I, 1782–1830.
Peter II, 1830–1851.
Danilo I, Prince, 1851–1860.
Nicholas I, Prince, 1860–1910; King, 1910–1918.
Part of Yugoslavia in 1918.

Netherlands (Holland)
William V, Hereditary Stadholder, 1751–1795.
Republic, 1795–1806.
Louis Bonaparte, King, 1806–1810.
Part of France, 1810–1813.
William I, King, 1813–1840.
William II, 1840–1849.
William III, 1849–1890.
Wilhelmina, 1890–

APPENDIX

Norway
Part of Denmark, 1397–1814.
Part of Sweden, 1814–1905.
Independent Monarchy in 1905.
Haakon VII, 1905–

Poland
Stanislaus II Poniatowski, 1764–1795.
Partitioned among Russia, Prussia, and Austria, 1795–1918.
Independent Republic in 1918.
Partitioned between Germany and Russia in 1939.

Portugal
Maria I, 1786–1816.
John VI, 1816–1826.
Pedro IV, 1826.
Maria II, 1826–1828.
Miguel, 1828–1834.
Maria II, 1834–1853.
Pedro V, 1853–1861.
Louis I, 1861–1889.
Charles I, 1889–1908.
Manuel II, 1908–1910.
Republic in 1910.

Prussia
Frederick, William II, 1786–1797.
Frederick William III, 1797–1840.
Frederick William IV, 1840–1861.
William I, 1861–1888 (German Emperor, 1871–1888).
After 1871 part of German Empire.

Rumania
Part of Turkey, 1500–1856.
Alexander John Cuza, Prince, 1861–1866.
Carol I, Prince, 1866–1881; King, 1881–1914.
Ferdinand I, 1914–1927.
Michael, 1927–1930.
Carol II, 1930–1940.
Michael, 1940– .

Russia
Catherine II, 1762–1796.
Paul, 1796–1801.
Alexander I, 1801–1825.
Nicholas I, 1825–1855.
Alexander II, 1855–1881.
Alexander III, 1881–1894.
Nicholas II, 1894–1917.
Provisional Government, Mar.–Nov., 1917.
Communist Dictatorship in 1917.
Lenin, 1917–1924.
Stalin, 1924–

Serbia
Part of Turkey, 1459–1830.
Karageorge, Prince, 1804–1813.
Milosh, 1817–1839.
Milan, 1839.
Michael, 1839–1842.
Alexander, 1842–1858.
Milosh, 1858–1860.
Michael, 1860–1868.
Milan, Prince, 1868–1882; King, 1882–1889.
Alexander, 1889–1903.
Peter, 1903–1921.
Part of Yugoslavia in 1918.

Spain
Charles IV, 1788–1808.
Joseph Bonaparte, 1808–1813.
Ferdinand VII, 1813–1833.
Isabella II, 1833–1868.
Amadeo of Savoy, 1870–1873.
Republic, 1873–1875.
Alphonso XII, 1875–1885.
Alphonso XIII, 1886–1931.
Republic, 1931–1939.
Fascist Dictatorship in 1939.
Franco, 1939–

Sweden
Gustavus III, 1771–1792.
Gustavus IV, 1792–1809.
Charles XIII, 1809–1818.
Charles XIV, 1818–1844.
Oscar I, 1844–1859.

APPENDIX

Charles XV, 1859–1872.
Oscar II, 1872–1907.
Gustavus V, 1907–

Turkey
Selim III, 1789–1807.
Mustapha IV, 1807–1808.
Mahmud II, 1808–1839.
Abdul Medjid, 1839–1861.
Abdul Aziz, 1861–1876.
Murad V, 1876.
Abdul Hamid II, 1876–1909.

Mohammed V, 1909–1918.
Mohammed VI, 1918–1922.
Republic in 1923.
Presidents
Mustapha Kemal, 1923–1938.
Ismet Inonü, 1938–

Yugoslavia
Peter I, 1918–1921 (*King of Serbia*, 1903–1918).
Alexander I, 1921–1934.
Peter II, 1934–

INDEX